PANZER

A Revolution in Warfare, 1939–1945

PANZER

A Revolution in Warfare, 1939–1945

ROGER EDWARDS

ARMS AND
ARMOUR

Left: Tigers and Pz Kpfw IVs of
Panzer Group West roll forward
to face the invading Allies on
D-Day. Panzer action at
Villers-Bocage ended any
hopes of an early British
Second Army break-through to
the south.

First published in Great Britain in 1989 by Arms and Armour Press, Villiers House, 41-47 Strand, London WC2N 5JE.

This paperback edition 1993.

Distributed in the USA by Sterling Publishing Co. Inc., 387 Park Avenue South, New York, NY 10016-8810.

Distributed in Australia by Capricorn Link (Australia) Pty. Ltd, P.O. Box 665, Lane Cove, New South Wales 2066, Australia.

British Library Cataloguing in Publication Data
Edwards, Roger
Panzer.
1. Germany. Heer. Armoured combat vehicles: Panzer tanks, 1939–1941
I. Title
623.74'752
ISBN 1-85409-208-1

Designed and edited by DAG Publications Ltd. Designed by David Gibbons; edited by Michael Boxall; layout by Anthony A. Evans; typeset by Typesetters (Birmingham) Ltd; camerawork by M&E Reproductions, North Fambridge, Essex; printed and bound in Great Britain by Scotprint Ltd, Musselburgh, Scotland.

About this book

The thematic structure of *Panzer* is intended to advance the exploration of a radical military concept and its implementation in battle; an arrangement that I believe to be of greater benefit to the reader in saving time tracing specific aspects of the revolutionary ideas than that afforded by a more conservative and wholly chronological plan.

A preamble establishes Hitler's rise to power, noting the Führer's influence as a national leader fostering rearmament and in particular the armoured idea in Germany after 1933, giving rise to the Second World War. The military role of Hitler's subordinates and some anti-tank developments of significance are also introduced at this stage.

In reviewing the progress of the German Army restoring (or acquiring) the mobility denied it by the Versailles Treaty of 1919, Part 1 takes as its starting point the endeavours of British tank pioneers seized upon and expanded by German devotees; a formative phase in panzer force history succeeded by campaigning experience gathered in Europe and Asia over a period of five and a half years.

So broad a view of panzer force history as that required of Part 1 in furnishing a rounded picture of an Army exploiting exceptional mobility in early campaigns but falling apart in operations after spring 1943 is enlarged upon in Part 2 by a review of the structure of the panzer force and in particular by profiling the wartime movement of all panzer and panzer grenadier divisions.

Fighting the mobile battle in Part 3 is also a thematic exploration of the role and combat effectiveness of panzer force elements, while in Part 4 the decisive influence of the air force shaping the capability of ground forces is revealed for what it was – the key to panzer success or failure.

But it is in the war action of panzer armies, the supreme expression of panzer force organization and mobility, originating in pre-existing panzer corps and panzer groups, that true success or failure of the panzer revolution is to be sought. With this point in mind, Part 5 is constituted as a visual guide to panzer force operations: twenty maps, organizational tables and commentaries reveal the aims and scope of panzer leaders serving as force commanders.

Their progress in battle is elaborated in Part 6, a chronological review of all campaigns undertaken by Panzer armies and their predecessors the panzer corps and panzer groups of the early wartime era upon whose experience in Poland, France and, to a lesser degree, the Balkans these same commanders and their successors drew so deeply.

Hitler's influence on panzer operations and the problems encountered by panzer leaders, not the least of which was the Führer's inability as self-proclaimed warlord to leave operational matters to the judgement of those on the spot, is clearly apparent in these day-to-day chronicles of panzer battles on all fronts, but more especially during the Allied invasion of north-west Europe, Pz-AOK5 (Europe), June 1944.

The post-war history of armoured forces is not included in the scope of this book; I nevertheless believe that no modern army can escape indebtedness to the panzer revolution for leading the way to effective battlefield mobility. What this book makes clear is that the Wehrmacht failure to modernize its armed services in time for more protracted battles than those entailed in *Blitzkrieg* sounded the death knell of the panzer force before even the inplacable will of Hitler's enemies brought about the downfall of an inglorious Third Reich.

Acknowledgements

My gratitude is due to the following for their very kind help in the preparation of this book:

To Walther Nehring and Fritz Morzik, General Officers respectively of armoured troops and transport fliers whose helpful advice based upon events of the period enabled me to devise a suitable format for the project.

To Oberst a.D. Heinrich Nolte Ia 18th Panzer Grenadier Division July 1940 – February 1943; Oberst a.D. Friedrich von Hake CO, 4th Panzer Regiment September 1942 – June 1944; Major a.D. Hans Sittig CO, 16th Panzerjaeger Bn; Peter Strassner battalion adjutant S. S. Wiking and others whose comments on technical and other aspects of panzer force history broadened my concept of mobility.

To the librarians and archivists who guided me through their collections at the Bundesarchiv Coblenz; Imperial War Museum, Lambeth; Museum of Army Flying, Middle Wallop; Royal Corps of Signals, Blandford Forum; RAF Museum Hendon and Ministére de l'Armée, Paris.

My gratitude is also due to those professionals whose skills served me in turning ideas into print; translators Beryl Osmond and Petra Becker, cartographers Jane Pugh and Anne Duffy, photographer Malcolm Slater, secretaries Anne Cowlin and Wendy Newman. The AFV profiles were drawn by Mr Geoffrey Boxall and the project was advanced editorially by Chris Westhorp, David Gibbons and Michael Boxall of Arms & Armour Press. I must also place on record my appreciation of the help that I have received at various times from the historical institute of the Bundeswehr, the Militärgeschichtlichen Forschungsamt, Freiburg. I am especially grateful to Doctors Friedrich Forstmeir and Horst Rohde.

Lastly my thanks to those family members and friends who provided seemingly endless hospitality while writing, an area of support encouraged by a wife whose commitment to the project never wavered. Thank you then Patricia, Christopher and Margaret, Linda and Timothy, Peter and Janet, Sara, Jonathan, David and Marylyn and Timothy Walker. I am grateful to you all.

Roger Edwards

Contents

Key to Panzer Battles

Right: *Die Woche*, Berlin 1935, and the Führer is pictured sharing a friendly moment with Dr Joseph Goebbels. Appointed Minister for Propaganda in 1933, Goebbels performed his duties enthusiastically, dominating the media and ensuring absolute government control. Teams were attached to service headquarters to take front-line pictures, items which are now stored in official archives.

Prelude: the road to war

GERMANY UNDER HITLER

During the years 1933 to 1945 the political and military fortunes of the German Army, like that of the German people, became inextricably bound-up in the obsessions and aspirations motivating a single individual.

Adolf Hitler, leader of the National Socialist movement in Germany, came to power in January 1933 following moderate success at the polls. Winning popular support with

196 out of 584 parliamentary seats – 75 more than his nearest rival, the future dictator and commander-in-chief of the German armed services was accepted as Chancellor of the Third Reich by President Hindenburg. Using fresh elections to consolidate his position, Hitler suspended the constitution of the outgoing Weimar administration and in its place substituted government by personal decree. So unassailable did he proceed to make himself as a dictator that for the next twelve years (he died in April 1945) Hitler alone determined the political, economic and military future of Germany. Secret plans for German re-armament and economic advance, already in train when Hitler came to power, were speeded-up then followed by open steps to war, but not until 1939 did the Western powers resort to military action to stop Hitler's progress.

The Chancellor's approach to war was clear for all to see. Military conscription was introduced early in 1935 and the Rhineland re-occupied in 1936. This stretch of German territory adjoining France had been declared a demilitarized zone under the terms of the Treaty of Versailles and all German military presence excluded. Two years later, in March 1938, Hitler incorporated Austria into the Third Reich and in October of the same year ordered the occupation of Czech Sudeten (border) territories where German-speaking inhabitants predominated. In the same year Hitler ordered the re-occupation of Memel, another strip of former German territory, also forfeited under 'Versailles', this time adjoining East Prussia on the Baltic Coast and previously awarded to Lithuania. When Hitler decided that possession of more Czech territory, including the city of Prague and the western provinces of Bohemia and Moravia, was vital to the strategic interests of the Reich, they were annexed. Hitler's moves to rally the German people after their defeat in 1918, were foreshadowed in *Mein Kampf*, published in 1925. This was a personal programme to raise Germany to the level of supreme power in Europe. By restoring the nation's pride and extending its living-space or *Lebensraum* (Germany was the most populated country in Europe), Hitler proposed by his actions to unit all German-speaking people into a single Greater Germany – Gross Deutschland – knowing full well that war was a likely consequence.

Moving purposefully at a time of wide-spread unemployment, when Germany lay in the grip of economic recession, Hitler espoused many causes to increase his popularity. A road-building programme, partially inherited from the previous administration, created a motorway (*autobahn*)

Left: After Hitler's conscription decree and the unveiling of the Luftwaffe in March 1935, three panzer divisions were raised in October. In November *Die Woche* focused public attention upon a new, national war flag which was hoisted over Berlin on the 7th of that month.

network destined for the rapid transit of military personnel. Work organized by a National Labour Service (Reichs Arbeits Dienst or RAD) provided employment for 200–300,000 workers every year. More of the unemployed were absorbed into armament industries which, despite shortages of steel and other critically important materials, supplied countless, if inadequate numbers of weapons, vehicles and aircraft to the expanding armed services. Pursuing mobilization through sport, including Party flying and motoring clubs, physical education and sporting activities were widely promoted in Hitler's Germany. When the time came for full mobilization the armed forces would benefit substantially

from such pre-service training. As time progressed, the nation became increasingly and irreversibly regimented for war. Boys of upper school age, assisted by the Army in their training, were recruited into the Hitler Youth Organization. Their seniors were inducted into pre-service work schemes organized by RAD. Girls joined a separate society; juniors enrolled in the Jungvolk.

Above all, Hitler was determined to re-vitalize the armed services and in particular to re-establish the air force whose fledgling military presence within the Air Ministry (RLM: Reichsluftfarhtministerium), would remain an official secret until 1935. Thereafter the air force would receive a higher

Above: Printed propaganda published in Berlin in 1936 which instructed the German people to be grateful to the Führer for his outstanding leadership.

German Army, Hitler insisted, would possess a strength of thirty-six divisions. By September 1939 this had risen to one hundred and seven including fifteen tank and motorized formations of a type still undergoing development in foreign armies. Simultaneously the German air force, disbanded under 'Versailles' rules, but secretly re-organized and created for army support, would reach a strength of 4,000 front-line aircraft deployed in thirty-eight (incomplete) Geschwader (equivalent of RAF Group); this was double the strength of either the Royal Air Force or l'Armée de l'Air. Neither Army nor Air Force planned to reach optimum operational levels until 1942. When war did come in 1939 neither service was fully equipped for it. The German Navy, of which only a token 15,000 men remained in service after 1918, would before September 1939 under Admiral Raeder commission two battleships, *Scharnhorst* and *Gneisenau*, three 'pocket battleships', *Admiral Scheer, Deutschland* and *Graf Spee*, two heavy and six light cruisers, twenty-two destroyers and forty-nine U-boats with more on the stocks.

Hitler's massive reconstruction of German armed strength, coupled with his repudiation of the widely resented Treaty of Versailles and the steps taken to reduce unemployment became a significant part of Nazi appeal to the electorate, and plans for the future of Germany. When President Hindenburg died in 1934 the field marshal's death left Hitler undisputed Leader (Führer) of the German people. But, unsatisfied with supreme political office and unconvinced of the loyalty of the Army, he decided in 1938 to consolidate his hold on the armed services by establishing a supreme command – Oberkommando der Wehrmacht (OKW) – nominating himself as Commander-in-Chief. Taking advantage of a scandal involving senior army officers (War Minister, General von Blomberg and Army Commander-in-Chief, General von Fritsch), Hitler, whose military endeavours during the First World War were limited to the rank of corporal, proposed henceforth to direct the nation's military affairs in person. The war minister's office (Wehrmachtsamt) had until then been supervised by General Wilhelm Keitel whom Hitler promptly appointed professional head of OKW. But Keitel would discover all too soon that his advice, like that of other senior officers and staffs, would more often than not be ignored. OKW would serve Hitler as a personal staff; he alone would decide the action. In later years this situation would prove wholly disastrous as a means of initiating and directing a successful war strategy.

Certainly there were times when Hitler's military decisions would benefit the services, particularly those taken against advice from generals who for years before 1940 had been cautious about endorsing National Socialist expansionist plans – a caution that planted ineradicable seeds of distrust in Hitler's mind. The Führer's 'standfast' order in the winter of 1941 undoubtedly saved the army on the Eastern Front, yet more often than not Hitler as Commander-in-Chief interfered in local matters and destroyed service efficiency by forbidding and inhibiting initiative. In later years, with events in the field taking catastrophic turns, the 'gentlemen' of the general staff became a frequent target for Hitler's jibes and reproaches. Following the opening of a third front in the west in 1944, the general staff, appalled at the destruction threatening the Reich on all sides, plotted the assassination of the leader whose

proportion of re-armament finance and resources than the other two services. After 1938 its ranks would include all parachute troops of the Wehrmacht. On land, the Treaty of Versailles imposed on Germany by the victorious Allies, permitted the army no general staff, no tanks and no heavy artillery. Furthermore, the Reichsheer under General von Seeckt, the army of the Weimar administration, a force of seven infantry and three cavalry divisions, was limited to 100,000 men served by a handful of motor transport battalions. A 'state within a state', the German Army enjoyed a privileged and influential position in German society. Without its support no government could hope to survive. Hitler would eventually come to terms with it, but only after much anguish and the 'surrender' of the party's million-strong private army, the Sturmabteilung (SA).

SA leader Ernst Roehm and others, at the head of this force with its own general staff and training facilities, were opposed to Hitler's support for an Army High Command view that the basis of government power should lie solely with the Army. Hitler ordered Roehm's murder and that of a hundred others. The fateful event known as the 'Night of the Long Knives' took place on 30 June 1934. The new

amateurish military intutition was (mis)directing their campaigns. On 20 July a group of Generals all but succeeded in their attempt on Hitler's life. He was saved by chance when a briefcase bomb planted at his feet during a conference at Rastenburg was accidentally removed out of effective range. His retribution was swift and ruthless. Five thousand victims of his unrestrained vengeance – including eminent and popular army leaders – were condemned to death when their part in the plot was uncovered or suspected by the SS. With Hitler in full control, the war continued on a savage and fanatical course; an unbridgeable rift now divided Commander-in-Chief from general staff with the Führer's jibes degenerating into vilification.

HITLER'S SUBORDINATES

The first of several subordinates to be awarded high office after Hitler came to power, and directly concerned with the armed services, was Hermann Goering, a flying ace of the 1914–1918 war. Goering had served Hitler and the Party more or less from the outset. Appointed Special Commissioner for Aviation in February 1933, he was to continue as Air Minister in March of the same year when his commissariat was expanded into a ministry which started secretly to organize a German air force. When this was revealed by official announcement in March 1935 Goering, with the rank of general, assumed the title Commander-in-Chief of the Air Force. He was also to benefit in stature from important political and economic planning responsibilities including the 1936 four-year plan to make Germany self-sufficient in raw materials. Promoted Generalfeldmarschall in 1938, Hitler would again reward this staunch supporter in 1940 when, following a successful conclusion to the campaign in France, the Field Marshal was created Reichsmarschall.

Pre-eminent among Goering's advisers and responsible for air force policy (opting mostly in favour of concentrated offensive support for the army) were three former Flying Corps officers: General Erhard Milch, Goering's deputy, Secretary of State for Air and Chairman of Lufthansa, who was promoted Generaloberst in November 1938; General Walter Wever, first Chief of Air Staff, transferred in 1933 from a comparable post in the Heeresamt; and Colonel (later Generaloberst) Ernst Udet, appointed Director, Technical Department of the Air Ministry in 1936 and thereafter, in 1939, Director-General, Air Force Equipment. Wever's death by accident in 1936 robbed the fledgling Luftwaffe of an able organizer and policy-maker. His successor, Generaloberst Hans Jeschonnek, appointed in 1937 from Chief of Operations (Ia) to the Air Staff, succeeded to Wever's post in February 1939. In that year Generaloberst Milch became Inspector-General of the Air Force, an appointment that he retained until January 1945. These developments allied to the rise and fall of the Luftwaffe are elaborated in Part 4. The Air Force's failure to subdue the RAF during and after the Battle of Britain, or to keep pace with foreign technical development and prevent the destruction of German industries by Anglo-US air power, was to cost Goering his credibility and Udet and Jeschonnek their lives at their own hands; Udet in 1941, Jeschonnek in 1943. Goering, in 1945, was to make an unsuccessful bid to supplant Hitler as head of state, thus prompting an outraged Führer to order the Reichsmarschall's arrest. The

distinction of succeeding Hitler, albeit for as little as seven days, was instead accorded to Admiral Doenitz.

Surpassing Goering in power and influence was Reichsführer SS, Heinrich Himmler. He was appointed by Hitler in January 1929 to organize a dependable Party protection troop (SS or Schutzstaffel) responsible, above all, for the Leader's security. Hitler promoted Himmler in June 1936 to organize and preside over the centralized criminal and secret police forces. Himmler's powers were greatly extended in 1943 as Minister of the Interior. This allowed him to streamline control of the secret police (Gestapo), Party troops (SS) and the security services (Sicherheitsdienst or SD). The latter were inaugurated in 1931 by Reinhardt Heydrich (assassinated in Prague, May 1942). As a consequence of the generals' attempt on Hitler's life in July 1944, Himmler was immediately given control of military counter-intelligence, the Abwehr. With so vast an apparatus of surveillance at his command, few aspects of German life could escape the notice of Reichsführer SS. Wherever Himmler's jurisdiction held sway, at home or in the occupied

Below: An outing to Nuremberg on Party Day 193 Members of the League of German Girls (BDM), a quasi military organization which, like the Hitler Youth (HJ) movement, would prove a valuable source of recruitmen for the services in time of wa

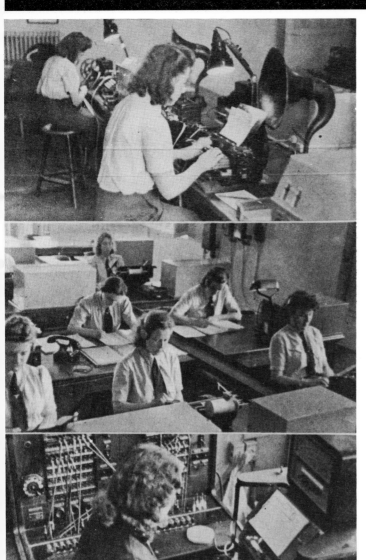

Above: Luftwaffe air defence teletype trainees and army signals personnel at work in 1941. Women served widely in flak commands, army headquarters and in industry.

arms, Himmler recruited from ideologically and physically qualified SS or others, an élite SS 'Verfügungstruppe'. The nucleus of this body (guard) was the Leibstandarte SS Adolf Hitler, established in Berlin in March 1933, with a strength of 120 men under the command of 'Sepp' Dietrich. An ex-Reichswehr general, Paul Hausser, was recruited to train and imbue the new corps with military confidence. By 1939 four motorized regiments, including the Leibstandarte, were ready to join in the invasion of Poland.

Other Reichswehr professionals joining the SS at this early stage included Majors Felix Steiner and Wilhelm Bittrich. The force expanded in later years to embody volunteer or drafted personnel from all over Europe including the eastern territories. Thus, legions of 'Germanic' Danes, Dutch, French, Flemish and east-European 'Volksdeutsche' entered into service with the SS to campaign ruthlessly alongside army formations. Swearing personal loyalty to Hitler and dedication to National Socialism, the SS Verfügungstruppe (SS-VT) was placed under operational control of the Army in 1938 and renamed Waffen SS in 1940. By June 1944, swelled by the influx of foreign recruits, it had risen in total to 21½ SS divisions serving with 257 Army divisions. SS numbers would continue to grow and ultimately reached close on a million. In the process of expansion, the Waffen SS raised fifteen exceptionally powerful armoured and motorized divisions; their military prowess and reputation as Hitler's élite guaranteed them a wide measure of respect on the battlefield. At times shouldering a disproportionately high share of the fighting, the finest of them were equal to the best of the Army formations, but SS loyalty to Hitler would prove small compensation for his military interference prompted by the, more often than not imagined, shortcomings of Prussian-German generals and the general staff.

After February 1942 armament production became the concern of Albert Speer, promoted to succeed Fritz Todt who was killed in an air crash. Speer proved a gifted organizer, advancing industrial and tank output to record levels. A former architect and town planner, he created grand city designs for Hitler, including the Chancellery. Speer was a war leader – there were others, including active army commanders – who, by disobeying orders in 1945 when Hitler was insisting that Germany be destroyed rather than surrender, were able to moderate the consequences of the Führer's increasingly fanatical directives. Other prominent leaders of the German war effort included Dr. Joseph Goebbels, Hitler's propaganda Chief, and Rudolf Hess, Hitler's deputy, who flew to Britain in 1941. Hoping to arrange a peace settlement, Hess achieved nothing. Instead he was interned and eventually sentenced to life imprisonment. Martin Bormann won distinction as the senior Party administrator, working in Berlin while the Führer spent his time at field headquarters. Bormann deputized as Party boss, organizing the civilian war effort through the work of Gauleiters whose territories or *Gaue* became Reich Defence Districts in 1942; their bosses were known as Reich Defence Commissioners. At the end of the war many of Hitler's immediate subordinates were committed for trial by an international military tribunal at Nuremberg; their minions being indicted at lesser courts elsewhere. Many of the twenty-one found guilty of war crimes at Nuremberg in September 1946 were sentenced to death, including OKW

territories, Jews and Slavs – Poles, Czechs and Russians – the main targets of a National Socialist obsession with racial purity, were ruthlessly repressed and annihilated. Fear and hatred of German domination spread throughout Europe. With the war in full swing, Himmler's powers continued to grow. Elevated to command of the Reserve Army in 1944 and responsible for army personnel and supplies, Himmler followed this new appointment with the active command of an army group on the Vistula – a post for which he proved totally unsuited and quickly relinquished.

Himmler's name is also linked with a 1935 development of considerable significance in subsequent German military success; the creation of an 'armed' or 'Waffen' SS. Pursuing instructions received from Hitler, and notwithstanding the Führer's 1933 pledge that the Army alone should bear

JB SONDERNUMMER

Preis: 40 Pfg.

VERLAG FRANZ
EHER NACHF,
G.M.B.H.
MÜNCHEN 22

So schlagen wir zu!

DER FELDZUG
DER 18 TAGE

Left: *JB*, Munich 1939, and
the special issue which mark
the defeat of Poland in a
campaign lasting eighteen
days.

chiefs Keitel and Jodl. Others received terms of imprisonment including life sentences. The SS, without exception,
was accused of unmitigated terror and criminal aggression
on and off the battlefield. It was condemned as a criminal
organization thereby tarnishing for all time the outstanding
combat achievements of the Waffen SS.

The end for Hitler came in May 1945, four months after
his return to Berlin, in mid-January, from field headquarters
in the west. Working from an underground bunker in the
shattered city, the Führer took his own life, thereby escaping
Allied retribution just hours before Russian armies closed in
on the Chancellery. Goebbels died with Hitler; Himmler and
Goering were taken into Allied captivity, but were also to
die at their own hands and thus avoid being hanged. After
more than forty years' incarceration in Spandau prison,
Berlin, Hess died there in 1987. Bormann, although
officially declared killed while escaping from Berlin in 1945,
continues to excite Press attention, as does the fate of other

missing Nazi officials whose whereabouts are unknown (mostly presumed dead but some still hunted by Israeli agents if thought to be living in exile).

Armoured fighting troops of the Third Reich, the tank and motorized formations raised by the Army (and later Waffen SS) were known collectively in 1938 as Schnelltruppen (fast troops), renamed in 1943 as Panzertruppen. These troops became the decisive force in the country's aggressive expansion, and its subsequent defence. Concentrated into

powerful spearheads with air force support, their moment came in September 1939 when Hitler called for the return of Danzig and transit rights across territories ceded to Poland; his demands were rejected outright. He invaded and conquered Poland, and Denmark, Norway, Holland, Belgium, France, Yugoslavia, Greece, the Baltic states and western tracts of the USSR. This run of victories fell in rapid succession, bringing much of Europe under the domination of the Third Reich, was, above all, the consequence of a new military doctrine. In daring to exploit the power and flexibility of fast armoured troops, deployed in conjunction with an equally powerful and flexible air force, Germany had created a decisive weapon out of the tank. This was due in no small measure to the persistent initiative of panzer generals, especially Heinz Guderian, who inspired a generation of gifted professional soldiers to combine traditional tactical skills with new armoured (and aviation) technology. German superiority on the battlefield was to prevail until such time as opponents with greater material resources could correct their mistakes and, by the narrowest of margins, reverse the situation.

The German Army of 1939 was otherwise not dissimilar to its traditional rivals in Europe, being largely infantry based and horse-drawn. Its overwhelming advantage, strengthened by a proficient general staff, lay in well-trained tank crews, gunners, signallers, engineers, motorized infantry and support services teamed for self-contained combat in co-operation with the air force. Early German victories which pioneered the flexible deployment of fast troops to conduct offensive operations were christened *Blitzkrieg* by the Press. In more analytical vein we might regard them as prime examples of co-ordinated action by land and air forces working to out-manoeuvre their opponents and defeat them by superior pace and power. Yet for all their apparent conclusiveness, as successive chapters will testify, these early victories would yield no lasting profit for the victors.

FACING UP TO THE OPPOSITION

German success with the panzer arm inevitably provoked countertactics and weapons. Pre-war anti-tank schemes, especially those of Anglo-French origin, relied for effect upon fixed installations; they thus erred in one vital respect: they failed to provide mobile forces to complement their static defences. By not possessing mobile forces capable of responding flexibly to the panzer threat – which was totally misjudged by Allied military commanders – the Allied armies were to suffer grievous consequences. Concrete bunkers and barricades shared defensive lines with impromptu devices such as flame-traps and flame-barrages. These were installed by the thousand in areas threatened by invasion – for instance the land frontier between France and Germany protected by The Maginot Line, or the south coast of England in the summer of 1940 when invasion was expected hourly. Such measures were intended to restrict panzer movement, allowing anti-tank squads to get to close quarters and artillery fire to destroy immobile targets. In the event the French defences were rapidly outflanked and the viability of British schemes went unchallenged after the German invasion plan 'Sea-lion' was abandoned late in 1940. In the east, the Red Army proposed the same solution as Britain and France. By siting minefields and earthworks, digging ditches and erecting barricades to create tank-proof localities, they hoped to channel panzer units into zones where the defence could concentrate against them. Such rudimentary measures would, it was hoped, win time in which more efficacious methods of combating the panzer menace could be developed. Anti-tank armouries in 1939 – and in this the German Army was no exception – were poorly served by small-calibre, 2pdr or equivalent 37mm weapons. Yet the inexhaustible energy of ordnance staffs,

searching for effective weapons with which to counter armoured assault, would be rewarded by noteworthy progress in Britain, the United States, Germany and the Soviet Union; all, however belatedly, producing outstanding contributions to anti-tank technology.

Significant trends in this sphere of design, upon which came to depend, if not the outcome of the war, then certainly a large measure of Allied (and German) success in defeating armoured attacks after 1942, are evident in several critical developments, one of the most significant being the self-propelled anti-tank gun. A German innovation, attributable directly to von Manstein, the mounting of direct-fire artillery weapons (7.5cm and later 8.8cm guns) on tank chassis, thereby improving rapid deployment against selected targets (*see* Part 2, Sturmgeschütze), would

Above: Service chiefs pictured in *Signal*, 1940, conferring over Hitler's map table. From left to right: Reichsmarschall Goering, Hitler and Keitel.

be matched by the Red Army who showed a remarkable capacity for employing even heavy-calibre guns up to 15.3cm in the role of tank destroyers; a weapons development programme in which Anglo-US ordnance teams would follow suit. Self-propelled anti-tank artillery would consequently evolve in a wide range of models and variants, entering service with all combatant forces.

Artillery improvements to strengthen the anti-tank protection of infantry would be marked by the introduction of British 6- and 17-pounder weapons which, combined with developments in armour-piercing technology, would halt panzer attacks at ever-increasing ranges, posing a threat even to the Tiger at 500 yards and notably hampering panzer operations in North Africa and subse-

Below: Berlin, 1945; a chilling reminder of the consequences of Hitler's warmongering. The victorious Red Army unfurls its banner over a ruined city. 'No bomb will ever fall here,' Goering had boasted in 1940.

quently in Italy and Europe. When fitted into Shermans and Valentines the 17-pdr would prove a formidable opponent as would the more powerful 9cm gun mounted by the US Ordnance Department on Sherman tank chassis and issued in 1944 as the M10 Tank Destroyer. No less potent in defeating panzer attacks would be an entirely new class of weapon modelled upon the 'Bazooka', a shoulder-fired 2.36in rocker-launcher introduced by the US Army in time for Operation 'Torch', the invasion of North Africa in November 1942. This extremely clever device, combining rocket propulsion with a new type of warhead to create a portable anti-tank weapon of undeniable power, would spawn a host of variants both Allied and German. Their distribution to forward companies would add immeasurably to the confidence of infantry expecting assault by armoured fighting vehicles. Easy to manufacture, like the *Panzerfaust* which would move significantly into this category in 1944, hand-launched rockets together with airborne systems were to prove indispensable in anti-tank combat.

Infantry defence would focus otherwise upon a variety of purpose-built and extemporary weapons including mines, grenades and projectiles, certain traditional forms of which could be extended in range by use in conjunction with projectors; the British projector infantry anti-tank (PIAT) was one such device.

But the greatest German respect for the opposition it was to encounter on an ever-increasing scale after 1942 was to be reserved for Allied air power. This weapon above all was to reverse the tide of panzer success, highlighting in the process an astonishing flaw in German planning – one no less deep-seated in its implications than the complacency exhibited by Allied commands in pre-1939 appreciations of German progress in armoured and airborne warfare. Hitler's inability as supreme commander to recognize the underlying strength of the opposition and his failure to appreciate the true potential of air power – matched by an equally evident failure of the high command when confronted by air force demands for more and better equipment to see further than army/air operations – was to bring these services to their knees. The army that had achieved outstanding success in applying new technology and tactical innovation in swift moving campaigns would discover all too late that its days were numbered by opponents purposefully and methodically exploiting more potent developments. Nevertheless, German progress in the design and construction of armoured fighting vehicles, in particular the Panther and its heavy counterpart the Tiger, both armed with high-velocity guns, is immediately traceable in the armoured establishment of every modern army. Equally influential in setting the trend of post-war armoured technology was panzer force success with armoured personnel carriers and, at a tactical level, the battle group integration of all arms into flexible, self-contained units.

This legacy, like that of the Luftwaffe's pioneering of ground attack, air reconnaissance and transportation methods to confer exceptional mobility on ground forces, is as relevant today in planning mobile operations in the harsh conditions of a nuclear age as in any previous era when the principles underlying the panzer revolution – decentralization of initiative, speed and flexibility in fire power and manoeuvre – proved indispensable to any would-be ruler of the battlefield.

Part 1. Restoring mobility to the German Army

1. 'Other things being equal, the most mobile side must win.' (J. F. C. Fuller, 1917)

The story of German involvement with armour leading to the creation of a panzer force, the armoured fighting troops of the Third Reich, can be said to have started during the First World War when the 'tank' idea was first formulated. A war of movement started by the German Army in August 1914 had brought the Kaiser's armies sweeping through Belgium and France to within fifty miles of Paris. Stalemated by September, both sides lay deadlocked. Lines of entrenched infantry seeking protection from the shattering effects of artillery fire, stretched from the Channel coast to Switzerland. Artillery and machine-gun dominated the battlefield. Sited in heavily protected fieldworks, so thickly secured with barbed wire entanglements that 'daylight could scarcely be seen', the machine-gun cut deep swathes in assaulting infantry. Offensives stumbled to a halt, casualties reached appalling levels.

A solution to the problem was put forward by a British Officer, Colonel E. D. Swinton, serving with the British Expeditionary Force. In a memorandum to the War Office during the closing months of the year, the Colonel recommended the construction and employment of a fighting vehicle; its purpose being to combat machine-gun nests and break the trench deadlock. Tracked for mobility, constructed of armour plating to withstand rifle or automatic fire, the revolutionary machine would open a path for the infantry by flattening the wire and crushing the machine-gun. Mobility would be restored – at infantry pace. Looking to the future, Colonel Swinton and later British tank enthusiasts envisaged the tank speeded-up, reinforced with infantry and artillery and deployed in mobile formations to the extent where armies, corps and divisions became the decisive weapon in land warfare. By April 1916, following an intensive period of trial and experiment in Britain, 150 28-ton machines, to be known in the interest of security as 'tanks', were ready for use or in production. Two companies each of twenty-five Mk I vehicles were sent to the Western Front. In mid-September they were used by British Fourth Army (Rawlinson) in action at Flers; of fifty machines on establishment, eighteen finally taking part in support of an infantry attack. Twelve months later three tank brigades each with two battalions had been formed.

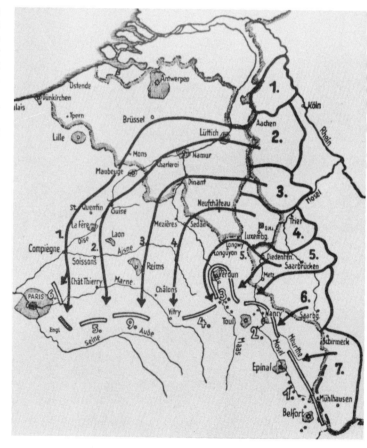

Disappointment attended the early efforts of the British pioneers when tank attacks in appalling conditions slewed to a halt. The lumbering steel giants working in two and threes impeded by shell craters, hampered by thick mud and heavy rain, quickly bogged down or otherwise failed to keep their schedules. At this early stage the tank idea might well have foundered, but a British success eighteen months later

Right: Cambrai, November 1917, was the first true tank offensive of the war. It was launched by the British Fourth Army led by Rawlinson and was intended to break the trench deadlock. After gaining ground the British discovered they lacked the means to exploit it and quickly forfeited much of it to German counter-attacks.

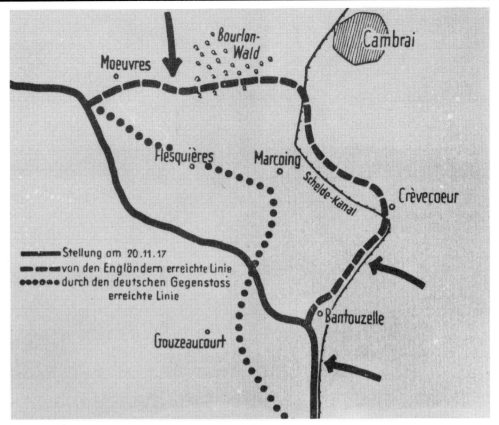

Right: This reconnaissance shot of the Cambrai battlefield reveals the British tank objectives. The Hindenburg Line was a stretch of concrete and steel shelters secured with barbed wire.

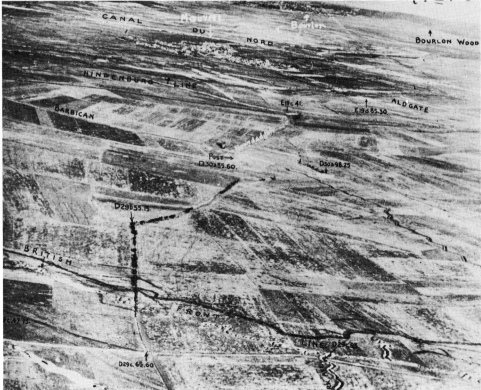

Left: Winter 1914 and Germany's railways transport the seven armies considered necessary by Count Alfred von Schlieffen for the decisive offensive against France. His plan envisaged the German Army investing Paris and trapping French forces against the Swiss frontier. The bold scheme failed when von Kluck, commanding First Army on the outer wing of the offensive, swung his troops off line and east of Paris in order to maintain contact with second army on his left. Soon the battle lines were drawn and the war became one of stalemated trench warfare.

Left: Amiens, August 1918; the tanks went in again. These tanks, visible next to uncompleted sections of the Hindenburg Line, breached the German lines in October.

Left: Lorry-borne infantry reinforcements for the shattered German front.

in a new tank offensive showed what could be achieved. Success in November 1917 lay to a great extent in the thorough preparations carried out by the newly appointed Chief of Staff of the Tank Corps, Lieutenant-Colonel J. F. C. Fuller. Using improved tanks *en masse* for the first time in history and fighting over ground specially chosen for the attack, objectives were clearly defined and accompanying infantry drilled in tactical support. In this way, on 20 November at Cambrai, four hundred or so Mk IVs of the British Army broke the German line in a surprise move. The planners' reward was a clear indication of the future role of armour.

German Second Army (Marwitz), defending this sector of the heavily protected Hindenburg Line, were stunned and demoralized by the appearance of tanks flattening their wire and, with infantry following in file close behind, thrusting towards their artillery positions. But the breach remained unexploited and the true fruits of the offensive, the paralysing effect of armoured troops driving deep into rearward areas, interrupting lines of communication, isolating and destroying headquarters and nerve-centres, was lost. Whereas future Allied tank offensives would employ modified Mk IVs as light pursuit tanks to move infantry and supplies forward in support of fighting tanks, no such vehicles were available in 1917. Instead, unprotected cavalry falling inevitably to the machine-guns, demonstrated their declining powers on the battlefield.

Allied plans for 1918 and 1919, however, were to develop on the basis of an all-mechanized force, initiated by Colonel (later Major-General) Fuller and elaborated by other creative British proponents of the new weapon, notably Captain (later General) Gifford le Q. Martel and Captain (Sir Basil) Liddell Hart. Fuller's proposals and his later writing would do much to influence post-war, particularly German, theories and practice of armoured warfare, but sadly for him and the defence of the west in general his ideas were to be largely disregarded by the British military hierarchy whose enthusiasm for the tank was to degenerate into complacency. Meanwhile, light tanks, a British-designed 14-ton Whippet and later the French 6-ton Renault FT – the first with a revolving turret – both intended for an exploitation role on the battlefield, were leaving the drawing-board for action in 1918. German counter-attacks starting on 30 November but without the benefit of armoured fighting vehicles, had recovered much of the ground lost to British initiative at Cambrai. During the counter-offensive a hundred or more tanks were retrieved by Second Army and, with some French machines taken later, prepared for German service.

In France, where the authorities were unaware of British progress in mobile technology, armoured fighting vehicles were evolving at two levels: a heavy trench-crossing vehicle, the 17-ton Schneider, fostered commercially by Colonel J. E. Estienne, and a competitor sponsored by the French General Staff, the 23-ton Saint-Chamond. The first of these French machines saw action at Berry-au-Bac on 16 April 1917, but neither design was a success. By agreement between the Allies, it was left to the Renault Company to build the first effective French tank, the Light FT, of which several variants would remain in service for more than two decades, some finding their way into both German and foreign service after the fall of France in 1940 (*see* Part 2,

satellite armour). The immediate reaction of the German High Command to the British and French tank attacks was to study and improve anti-tank measures. Trenches were widened and the first infantry anti-tank weapon, a 13mm Mauser (tank) rifle, was swiftly designed and produced. A light mortar designed to fire at low angles, and armour-piercing shells for use by the field artillery were also developed. Within the Imperial War Ministry the Allgemeine Kriegsabteilung 7, Verkehrswesen (A7V) was set up in 1916 to advise on the design and construction of tanks and armoured vehicles, and British and French machines captured at Cambrai and Berry were studied, repaired and pressed into service. Up to that time neither the Austrian nor German governments had displayed much interest in 'gun vehicles running on moving tracks' as proposed as early as 1911 by the Austrian, Leutnant Burstyn.

The first example of A7V departmental work was a 32-ton turretless machine, based on a Holt tractor, with a crew of eighteen, six machine-guns and a 5.7cm gun mounted forward. In December 1917 twenty of these were completed and formed into two companies. In March 1918 this all-German tank detachment, deployed in conjunction with four companies of captured vehicles, mainly British Mk IVs, went into action with air support at St-Quentin. The A7V design was unsatisfactory at trench crossing, and after these wartime operations the Germans had no further use for it, but their experience of army-air co-operation – no less progressive than that of the Allies' – proved timely in focusing General Staff attention on critical developments. It was left chiefly to British tank pioneers to demonstrate the true value of tanks in breakthrough and, to a lesser extent, exploitation battles with a great Allied offensive in August 1918. Encouraged by results with sixty Mk V tanks introduced against German Second Army at Hamel on 4 July, 500 mainly British tanks, including 96 Whippets, were concentrated at Amiens on 8 August for a renewed assault eastwards against the Hindenburg Line. The Allied plan of attack, based on a scheme of Colonel Fuller's, was to push improved fighting tanks, Mk VI infantry- (machine-gun) carrying tanks and lightly armoured exploitation Whippets deep into the German lines, disrupting communications and destroying headquarters. Specially designed Mk IX supply tanks, projected as early as 1916, remained factory bound, their place being taken by modified Mk IVs. An armoured car battalion was to be made available to maintain the tempo of the attack.

The great Allied tank offensive unrolled on 8 August 1918. Supported by bombing and strafing attacks – much as earlier in the year the Germans had supported their March offensive at St-Quentin – the Royal Flying Corps neutralizing the defence with machine-guns and bombs, the tank force ripped a ten-mile breach in the defenders' positions. In the words of General Ludendorff, 'August the 8th was a black day for the German Army.' Least satisfactory were the results achieved by the light tanks committed under command of the cavalry. Pushing forward after the breakthrough to a depth of eight miles, they were frequently pinned down and halted by heavy counter-fire. Nevertheless, a single Whippet handled with much verve achieved spectacular results, shooting up artillery batteries, cavalry patrols, barracks, motor transport and more. The armoured cars, four-wheeled Austins with twin machine-gun turrets, proved their worth in dashing sorties against rear headquarters. Ludendorff records the German plight. 'British Fourth Army broke deep into our front, divisional staffs were surprised in divisional headquarters by hostile tanks. Our divisions allowed themselves to be completely overrun, six or seven divisions of good fighting troops were completely smashed. At many points officers lost control.'

German morale now evinced signs of collapse. Within three months the war was at an end, the Allied offensive at Amiens having contributed significantly to German defeat. The Treaty of Versailles imposed harsh conditions on Germany. No tanks were permitted to the Reichsheer, the army of a new (Weimar) administration, no General Staff and no heavy artillery. All German research in the important field of tank development was brought to a halt. The Imperial Air Force was ordered to disband. Britain and France, on the other hand, and indeed the United States too, in the person of Lieutenant-Colonel George Patton who, from January to September 1918 (with British and French equipment), had formed and operated an independent tank force on British lines, renewed their research into the capabilities of the new weapon. All had gained a wealth of experience in wartime operations, not only in the construction of tanks and their tactical employment with air support, but also in wireless control of tank formations introduced by the British Army with mixed results as early as 1916. Plans for mechanized infantry were continuously formulated.

Ground-attack bombers and fighters, including forward-firing and lightly armoured models, had demonstrated their merits in action on both sides and if, as was the case with wireless, considerably short of perfection, had progressed to a point of departure for the future. The antecedents of *Blitzkrieg* and developments associated in the post-war years with new weapons and technology – culminating in an irresistibly powerful German fusion of armoured fighting vehicles and ground-attack aircraft – are all too evident in the great confrontations of March and August 1918. In amalgamating foreign innovation with tactical tradition and creative power, turning the resulting weapons system to sound operative account, the German Army of 1939 would be first to capitalize on 1914–18 experience.

In Britain the tank idea continued to be fostered by Major-General Fuller and those who succeeded him in command of the Tank Corps or at the War Office; British state of the art advancing in 1927, 1931 and 1934 with experiments at brigade level on Salisbury Plain – the learning process promoted by tank and motorized infantry exercises and radio control of tank formations. New British contributions to the theory of armoured warfare appeared in works published by Captain (Sir Basil) Liddell Hart and Major-General Fuller. The views of these gifted British theorists concerning the viability of long-range operations helped immeasurably in shaping post-war thinking; but nowhere would their ideas make more impression or gain wider acceptance than in Germany, albeit at first limited to a narrow circle of professional officers prominent among whom was the young Captain Heinz Guderian, generously acknowledged by colleagues as creator of the panzer force.

British endeavours during the post-war period would lead to no more than the creation of two incomplete armoured divisions – light all-tank formations intended for the dual purpose of strategic reconnaissance and exploitation; one at

home, the other in Egypt. A brigade of 24-ton 'I' tanks, 'Matildas', was also raised, for infantry support at walking pace. Professional circles in Britain no less than in France and the United States, and by no means excluding Germany, where conservative General Staff views on the primacy of infantry held sway, allowed infantry tanks and the infantry-support idea to dominate strategic and tactical thinking. Although presaged by Allied wartime experience and post-war experiments, opportunities for infantry-bound armies to create mobile forces capable of independent, that is to say self-contained, action through the inclusion of all arms in a fighting formation were neglected. Not only was this so in Britain and France, but also in Russia where embryonic tank and air forces were under development. The Russian General Staff, disposed towards new ideas under its chief of staff, Mikhail Tukhachevsky, later Deputy Commisar for War, was quick to recognize the growing importance of aircraft as a means of combating tanks. But Tukhachevsky, with other marshals, generals and brigadiers 'disappeared' in the Stalinist purges of the Red Army. Not before 1942 and the Battle of Stalingrad would the Red Army prove itself theoretically and materially ready to contend with high-powered aggression of the kind that it faced in 1941.

Above: Ground-attack aircraft from both sides caused havoc among troop concentrations and trench systems.

Above: An infantryman writing of his experiences of trench warfare on the Somme in 1917 spoke of German positions so thickly protected by barbed wire that daylight was scarcely to be seen.

Right: German ground-attack squadrons (Schlachtgruppen), flying the Halberstadt two-seater, played a significant role in assisting tank and infantry attacks.

Left: By March 1918 the German A7V tank, mounting a 5.7cm gun and manned by a crew of eighteen, was to be seen in action at St. Quentin alongside captured British and French machines.

2. 'If the tanks succeed, then victory follows.' (Guderian, 1937)

Only in Germany, encouraged by Hitler's arrival on the scene in 1933, were revolutionary military ideas to germinate into a strike force of exceptional power. Forbidden all but the most limited of resources in the aftermath of defeat, the German Army's Truppenamt, a substitute for the forbidden General Staff (responsible to the Commander-in-Chief of the Reichsheer, General Hans von Seeckt) was determined to circumvent by every possible means, Allied intentions of destroying German capacity for military resurgence. Concealing armament stocks and production centres from Versailles 'observers', von Seeckt and his colleagues resolved secretly to build a new German Army in which motorization would play a crucial part and foreign ideas particularly in the employment of tanks would be most enthusiastically reviewed and adopted.

Captain Heinz Guderian, encouraged in 1922 by the Inspector of Motor Transport Troops, General von Tschischwitz, to study motor repair and workshop practice in the Motorized Transport Department of the Inspectorate of Transport Troops (In 6) to which Guderian was seconded, was one of many pioneering spirits who in the next decade would evolve plans for creating a new German armoured force, despite hostility of the kind expressed by Tschischwitz's successor as Inspector, Colonel von Natzmer – 'To hell with fighting, you're supposed to carry flour.' Guderian moved out of the department in 1924 transferring to Stettin where he instructed staff candidates in military history. From practical understanding of motorization, through lecturing on tactics and in due course leading armoured formations in the field, Guderian's enthusiasm more than any other would motivate a generation of panzer leaders. Promoted major in 1927, Guderian's work as a staff instructor was followed by employment in the troop transport department of the Truppenamt until 1931. Meanwhile, in a notable change of emphasis inaugurated by von Vollard-Bockelburg, appointed (third) Inspector of Kraftfahrtruppen in 1926, succeeding von Natzmer, no time was lost in broadening Kraftfahrtruppen into Kraftfahr(kampf)truppen.

Extending the scope of his duties to lecture on tank tactics, Guderian studied and reported on progress in foreign armies; made visits abroad, digested published works including British training manuals and worked out new ideas. It was during this period of the late 1920s that the structure and handling of a panzer division firmly crystallized in Guderian's mind. From teaching military history for three years (especially Napoleon's campaign of 1806 – the one in which Berlin was occupied) to staff candidates and then as tactical instructor on courses organized for the Army by the Fahrlehrstab (motor transport instruction staff) at Döberitz, forty miles west of Berlin, Guderian progressed to practical application.

Commanding No. 3 Motor Transport Battalion at Berlin in 1931 – one of the seven allowed to Germany under 'Versailles' – Major Guderian used dummy tanks and wooden artillery to represent fighting vehicles and anti-tank guns, experimenting with various tactical configurations. Similar work was undertaken in other 'transport' battalions doubling as combat units; No. 6 at Münster, for instance,

Left: Dummy tanks taking part in secret training sessions in Germany, 1929. Made of wood and steel, these 'vehicles' drew their motive power from Austin Seven-type runabouts formed into Motor Transport Battalions. Such events gave rise to Polish worries as to the true nature of the panzer threat.

where Captain Walther Nehring commanded No. 1 (motor infantry) Company. During 1931 command and staff changes instituted by von Hammerstein, one of von Seeckt's successors, laid the foundations of a tank force that would enjoy outstanding success in the conflict to come. In April of that year Guderian was promoted colonel and posted as chief of staff to a new Inspector of Kraftfahr(kampf)truppen, General Oswald Lutz. Lutz had succeeded yet another incumbent at the head of In 6, General Otto von Stülpnagel; Vollard-Bockelburg having moved up to promote army motorization. Major Walther Nehring, drafted to the staff of In 6 to serve as Guderian's deputy, arrived soon afterwards, replacing vehicle design pioneer, Major Werner Kempf. Kempf was posted to Munich as OC, No. 7 Motor Transport Battalion. These three officers – Lutz, Guderian and Nehring – were to prove zealous proponents of the tank idea, ably supported by like-minded staff; Captains Hermann Breith, Chales de Beaulieu, Ritter von Hauenschild and Walter Hünersdorff all energetically promoted German involvement in armoured technology – creating step by step a panzer force as yet little in evidence, untried and unbloodied, but destined in the space of ten years to dominate Europe.

In November 1933 training courses originating in 1925 and progressively expanded were established at a new school in the garrison area of Wünsdorf-Zossen, thirty miles south of the capital. This Panzer School 1 was the first of many to be established over the next fourteen years. Tank-gunnery was taught separately at Putlos, a training facility in Holstein on the Baltic coast north of Hamburg. Ironically, by encouraging the German High Command to collaborate in establishing secret experimental stations at Kazan and Lipetsk deep in the Russian hinterland, the technical development of German tanks and aircraft was promoted by the Soviet Union as early as 1926. Both stations were surrounded by ample space for training and development and the arrangement was to prove advantageous to officers of both countries, but it was brought to an end by Hitler in 1933. At Kazan, otherwise known as 'Kama' from its proximity to the river of that name, General Lutz, one of the key figures, founded a programme for evolving and testing a new generation of German (and Russian) tanks and aircraft. Among future panzer army commanders to benefit from training at Kazan were Ritter von Thoma and Josef Harpe; von Thoma rising to lead the Condor Legion's tank component in Spain in 1936 before promotion to Waffen general (Schnelletruppen) 1940, command of DAK and briefly GOC, Panzer Army Afrika in 1942. Generaloberst Harpe was to become GOC, Fourth Panzer Army in 1944. Wilhelm Bittrich, another student at Kama, was destined for command of an SS panzer korps. The crucial aircraft and aviation technology upon which a future Luftwaffe would find strength and direction was pursued equally enthusiastically at Lipetsk where many of the Luftwaffe's future leaders contributed to the process of founding a new air force. Aviation developments are elaborated in Part 4.

In Berlin during the 1920s, when Captain Heinz Guderian (major, 1927), destined for the highest office as a panzer leader, was going about his instructional duties with the

Kraftfahrlehrstab, the Heereswaffenamt had placed contracts with private firms not only for new tanks, but for half-track vehicles to move artillery and assist the mobility of other panzer support arms. When the projected tanks – Panzerkampfwagen (Pz Kpfw), intended for trial at Kazan, a 23-ton medium machine armed with a 7.5cm gun and a lighter model fitted with a 3.7cm gun proved slow to evolve, a Carden-Loyd chassis was indirectly purchased from Britain and taken as the basis for a new 6-ton training tank, the Pz Kpfw I built by Krupp. A second 10-ton vehicle, Pz Kpfw II, equipped with a 2cm gun and coaxial machine-gun was developed and manufactured by MAN. In 1934 these new armoured fighting vehicles, the first of their kind, would go to equip panzer regiments forming at Zossen and Ohrdruf, but when establishments failed, tanks were supplemented by tractors used for training. Within the year, six panzer regiments (four battalions of four companies, 32 Pz Kpfw each) – paired in panzer brigades – were raised and incorporated into three panzer divisions.

Recruits were provided initially by the cavalry, an arm of service with its own ideas on the role of army motorization and one that would raise partially armoured 'light' divisions for cavalry tasks. Contrary to expectation, the production of halftracks, in 1-, 6-, 12- and 18-ton models, crucial to the mobility of the supporting arms of the panzer force, soon lagged behind schedule. Shortages in this and other vital areas of motorization, particularly in the provision of cross-country transport for the infantry, would weigh heavily against future success in trackless terrain – such as might be expected in Russia. Better progress was recorded in the important sphere of training. At Wünsdorf-Zossen instructional courses pioneered by the Kraftfahrlehrstab were expanded by General Lutz and the first 'research and technical exercises', commencing as early as 1932, continued to be held annually. Theoretical knowledge benefited from publication of *Der Kampfwagenkrieg*, an Austrian study of tank tactics. The author of this work, General Ludwig Ritter von Eimannsberger, recommended the massing of tank wedges at the decisive point (*Schwerpunkt*) of the battle. A more significant contribution, to warfare in general, *Command of the Air*, by Italian air force General Giulio Douhet, pointed the way to the strike role of the bomber. Douhet also argued the case for the air force being used as a weapon to break civilian morale by intensive raids against population centres.

With Hitler installed as Chancellor in 1933 and taking a special interest in tank development, the year to come would record a milestone in the progress of armoured troops. Visiting the army depot at Kummersdorf where new equipment, including tanks, was displayed and exercised in conjunction with infantry and aircraft, the future C-in-C of the Army was impressed to the point of declaring. 'That is what I want – and that is what I will have.' Twelve months later, on 15 October 1935, the vital step taking Hitler on the high road to power followed the conclusion of annual exercises – the first in which an embryo panzer division (von Weichs) was put through its paces – a panzertruppen command was established. The date is regarded in the German Army as the armoured troops' birthday; the new panzer command (Lutz) absorbing the old Kraftfahrlehrstab, cavalry and motorized infantry (Schützen) – the future panzer grenadiers. The event was significant not only in

Above: General Heinz Guderian was responsible more than any other individual for the training and subsequent success of the panzer force. He served in Signals from 1914 to 1918, and lectured on mobility from 1924 to 1929; in 1931 he was appointed Chief of Staff, Kraftfahrkampftruppen. He followed theory with practice and commanded XIV Panzer Corps in February 1938. In November 1938 he became Chief of Mobile Troops, then led XIX Panzer Corps in 1939 before Pz-Gruppe Guderian was formed in 1940. In 1941, until Hitler placed him on the reserve list, he was GOC, Second Panzer Army. Recalled in February 1943, Guderian was made Inspector-General of Armoured Troops; his last appointment was Chief of the General Staff in July 1944.

creating a nucleus of armoured forces for future offensive tasks, but also in affirming recognition at the highest political level of strategic potential in mechanization – a potency by no means universally accepted among the upper echelons of the German military establishment. The Army Chief of Staff, General Ludwig Beck, a former cavalry officer, was only one of many senior and influential officers not wholly in tune with Lutz and Guderian's ideas on the independent role of armoured divisions in battle; a situation not unknown abroad where horse and army were to prove inseparable.

For example, the position of tank development and employment in the French Army, the largest and potentially most powerful army in Europe (4.4 million, 1939), is revealed in the French General Staff's handbook on tank warfare published in 1930. In this work, tank formations

Above: Colonel (later General) Walther Nehring served Guderian as his deputy on the staff of the Kraftfahrkampftruppen in 1931, a partnership which continued into the war. Pictured here serving with Panzer Gruppe Guderian in 1940 (Guderian on the right and C-in-C von Brauchitsch on the left), he went on to command 18th Panzer Division that year. In 1942, serving with DAK, he was promoted to General after the fall of Tobruk. He subsequently served in the east as GOC, XXIV Panzer Corps (1943), GOC, Fourth Panzer Army (1944) and finally, in March 1945, as GOC, First Panzer Army.

B, at the core of French armoured formations in which the 11-ton Hotchkiss and 20-ton Somua predominated, would nevertheless prove superior in construction to German types while at the same time, the Somua was better armed (4.7cm) and more numerous than the Pz Kpfw III (3.7cm) deployed in the panzer divisions. A fourth, incomplete, *division cuirassée*, raised under de Gaulle after the commencement of hostilities, would serve with equally little influence on the course of events.

German armoured progress in the thirties, in contrast to developments abroad where, in Britain for instance, General Staff orthodoxy coupled with financial constraints continued to inhibit evolution of the tank idea, was rapid, and in emphasizing the need for balance in structuring armoured formations, distinctively different. Guderian only hints at this in his preface to the most important and frequently reprinted German work on the subject, Fritz Heigl's 1938 *Handbook of the Tank*: 'The difference of opinion concerning the value of tanks and their employment in battle is greater than ever,' he writes. 'Memories of the battles of the First World War [a reference to the origination of the tank in support of infantry] are now fading. The most recent fighting in Spain so far as this concerns tanks, was carried out on a relatively limited field and on too small a scale to allow accurate assessments to be made.' In referring to Spain (map 1), where companies of German and Italian tanks assisted General Franco's Nationalist army to defeat Soviet-supported Republican forces, Guderian is deceptively indifferent to opportunities for the collective training of tanks, infantry and aircraft.

The Spanish civil war in fact provided a German expeditionary force, the Condor Legion, with immensely beneficial training facilities. Flying old and new machines, improving ground-attack methods and equipment, Luftwaffe tactics and technology in later European campaigns would owe much to the unhappy Spanish conflict; air force action in particular illuminating a terrifying trend towards area bombing and the unconstrained use of air-power. Fulfilling its first major engagement in support of a Nationalist offensive against Bilbao on the northern front in April 1937, the Condor Legion laid waste the town of Guernica five miles behind the front and midway to Bilbao. Co-operating with White brigades seeking to breach and outflank a determined Republican defence, the Legion set out to inhibit rearward movement. Waves of Ju 52 transports, doubling as bombers until such time as the He 111 would arrive in squadron service, co-ordinated their attacks with Italian formations supporting the offensive with Savoia Marchetti S 81s flying under Legion command.

Guernica's importance to both sides lay in its road and rail connections to and from the front and its position on a river crossing at a point where Republican troops threatened with envelopment might be expected to slip the net and regroup. For two hours or more, led by He 111s of the Legion's bombing trials squadron, thermite incendiary and high-explosive missiles rained down upon the town, reducing historic timbered buildings to smoking ruins, destroying the railway station and blocking all movement for 24 hours – but leaving the vital river crossing in the suburbs undamaged. The devastation revealed to journalists was exploited to outstanding propaganda effect by Republicans alleging terror bombing as the prime motive for the

are relegated to an infantry support role. A contrary stand was taken by Colonel Charles de Gaulle. Far-sighted like Lutz, Guderian and Fuller, De Gaulle realized that independent tank divisions would become a decisive weapon of the future, but not until the autumn of 1939 did the French Army actively set about establishing *divisions cuirassées* with tank brigades of 174 tanks, motorized infantry, artillery, armoured cars and motor cycles organized on German lines. Until then the French Army of the 1930s placed its faith in three 'armoured' divisions of a different kind; motorized cavalry formations (*divisions légères mécaniques*), each with a strength of about 170 tanks. In the forthcoming Battle of France, three *divisions cuirassées*, three *divisions légères mécaniques* and a handful of independent tank brigades dispersed over a wide front would be divided in support of infantry. The 31-ton Char

attack. The incident provoked world-wide comment and diplomatic intervention by the British and French governments. Responsibility for the Luftwaffe-directed attack lay with Legion commanders, General-Major Sperrle and Chief of Staff Oberst Wolfram Freiherr von Richthofen. Von Richthofen had previously served at home and in Spain, leading air force technical research projects – and would eventually continue as the Legion's commanding officer. Both they and their accusers would be familiar with Douhet-inspired philosophy that wars could be won by inducing terror in the enemy's civilian population. Whatever the truth of the incident, the plight of Guernica's civilian population would be repeated a thousand-fold as bombing of this description, elevated into a strategy distinct from that of *Blitzkrieg*, spread across Europe giving rise to multi-national research and development programmes seeking ever new and efficient means of delivering incendiary and high-explosive material against area targets.

In attacking Guernica so ruthlessly, and it was not the only Spanish town to suffer uncompromising bombing attacks on this scale, the Luftwaffe gave notice that in exploiting military opportunities civilian centres could no longer expect exclusion; henceforth all cities could expect to become front-line cities. The Luftwaffe's challenge did not go unheeded in Britain where counter-measures undergoing development included radar, a novel radio wave transmitting and echo-recording system for detecting approaching aircraft, and the Supermarine Spitfire which the RAF would introduce into combat service in time for the 1940 Battle of Britain. In this future conflict, Field Marshals Kesselring and Sperrle (2nd and 3rd Air Fleets) would face Air Vice-Marshal Sir Hugh Dowding, creator of Fighter Command. The consequences for the Luftwaffe are noted in Part 4. In fact, so effective in attack would the RAF and its ally the USAAF become that by 1942 it would prove capable of neutralizing the power of the panzer divisions in North Africa and by 1944 in Normandy of destroying every threat by the German Army to concentrate panzer forces for a counter-offensive. In France, on the other hand, the Armée de l'Air would neglect either to develop the dive-bomber, to advance army-air co-operation or to organize an adequate system of air defence.

German advantage in the experimental use of new weapons in Spain was further demonstrated when the fighting spread east of Teruel in February 1938. In these battles the Legion introduced the hitherto secret Ju 87A (Stuka) in support of ground troops. Designed to deliver a 250kg, or when flown as a single-seater, a 500kg high-explosive bomb in a near vertical dive, the Stuka would prove capable of pin-point accuracy with devastating effect. Focusing on fixed targets, generally bridges and road-crossings or redoubts and resistance points, the Luftwaffe hammered home its superiority; a novel system whereby forward observers were linked to their ground-attack headquarters by wireless strengthening contact between ground forces and dive-bombing (Stuka) squadrons contributed notably to forward progress. From its experience in Spain, the Luftwaffe was to nurture developments of profound importance to mobile warfare, improving wireless range and performance in particular. For the future of a shock force intended for deep penetration, closing around the enemy in swift co-ordinated manoeuvres, like that

taking shape in Germany where the momentum of fast troops would be dubbed *Blitzkrieg*, such developments were crucial.

Meanwhile in German workshops new vehicles for infantry cross-country work, wireless command and signal trucks, repair, artillery and engineer vehicles were undergoing development and, like the new ground-attack and reconnaissance aircraft coming into service were progressively reaching the formations for which they were intended; but never in adequate numbers and far from ideal in form. A greater obstacle to the creation of a panzer force than either design or supply deficiencies was the General Staff's strongly conservative attitude. Guderian's deeply rooted views on the need for a panzer command to control the development and

Above: A dive-bombing squadron of the Condor Legio tests the Ju 87 on active service. Later versions of this aircraft were assigned to tank busting roles while more advanced ground-attack aircraft such as the Fw 190 replaced them in service with Schlachtgruppen.

Above: Ju 52s over Burgos, their base at the time of the infamous bombing of Guernica. The Ju 52 served as a temporary bomber with a 1,200kg load while the purpose-built He 111B was being prepared for service.

Below: The work-horse of the Kampfgruppen, the He 111B could carry a bomb-load of 1,500kg. It flew in Spain in 1937 and remained on active service on other war fronts until 1945.

training of all armoured and motorized units, including the mobile units that the cavalry and infantry would raise between 1935 and 1938, were not universally shared. Traditionalists lead by General Beck, the Army Chief of Staff, considered infantry and cavalry as the main battlefield arms. Guderian's concept of centralized development for mobile forces – placing them on equal footing with infantry and cavalry – would consequently remain unfulfilled until late 1938 and only then at Hitler's insistence would a token gesture be made in this direction. Yet despite equipment and material shortages, motorization of the German Army in the middle thirties continued to gain momentum – encouraged by Hitler, whose enthusiasm for the idea dated from the time that he had witnessed the new force in embryo at Kummersdorf shortly after taking office.

Panzer divisions, light divisions (a cavalry concept) and motorized infantry divisions – the nucleus of a panzer force requiring substantial numbers and types of vehicles – had been progressively raised and trained since 1935. Vehicle production, however limited by production resources, was to benefit from rationalization into a manageable programme, but at the expense of quality. In the absence of Army-designed trucks, many commercial trucks proved all too flimsy for sustained military use. During this late period in the development of the panzer force Guderian, whose bluff approach was not always helpful in promoting the panzer cause, served in command of 2nd Panzer Division at Würzburg and also as chief of staff to XVI Corps – formerly the panzertruppen command still lead by General Lutz. Comprising three panzer divisions: 1st, von Weichs; 2nd, Guderian and 3rd, Fessman, XVI Corps represented the fullest expression to date of German armoured progress. Promoted Generalleutnant in February 1938, Guderian's next challenge was in succeeding Lutz as corps commander; both Lutz and Army Chief of Staff Beck – equally critical of

Left: Reconnaissance flying between the wars assumed critical importance for the future of the panzer force. This Hs 126 observer doubled as a photographer; when not in use his cameras were stored behind the gun-mounting.

Hitler's war aims – were among many seniors about to be retired or transferred when the Führer took command of the armed services (4 February 1938) following the resignation of the Army Commander-in-Chief, von Fritsch, and the dismissal of the State Defence Minister, von Blomberg; events that were engineered by Hitler's supporters within the supreme leadership and turned by him to advantage.

In March 1938, within days of this radical change in the high command (Beck was a strong critic of 'independent' panzer development), Hitler fostered the 'Union' of Austria with the Third Reich and in October ordered the occupation of Czech Sudetenland. The uncontested, 400-mile advance of XVI Corps into Austria, in which the Leibstandarte Adolf Hitler (the Führer's bodyguard from Berlin) took part, helped the panzer training process and valuable lessons were learned; not the least of which, given that numerous vehicles broke down on the road to Linz, was the importance of repair and maintenance.

Guderian's philosophy on the employment of tanks – shaped in no small measure by the widely disseminated

Left: Colonel (later Generalfeldmarschall) Wolfram Freiherr von Richthofen, looking relaxed while observing the effects of a ground attack by a Legion squadron. He became the Luftwaffe's leading exponent of this type of warfare and in 1938 succeeded General Helmuth Volkmann as Legion commander. During the war he was GOC, Flieger Division zbv in Poland and then commander of VIII Air Corps in France, the Balkans and Russia before becoming GOC, 2nd Air Fleet Italy in 1943.

Right: The key to mobility: wireless equipment for transmitting orders and information between panzer leaders, subordinates and rear headquarters. The picture shows Guderian in his command vehicle; also visible is the famous 'Enigma' machine which encoded classified messages. The breaking of these codes at Bletchley Park in England compromised many German actions.

views of British tank theorists, Martel, Fuller and Liddell Hart, and by British Army training manuals – had crystallized in the late twenties before his promotion as Chief of Staff to General Lutz. Out had gone the notion that the tank was a secondary weapon intended solely for infantry support. Now he believed that the tank should be regarded as the key component of a panzer force possessing the capacity for independent action, proceeding at its own rate of advance; pace and power, and intimidation of the enemy by fear of encirclement, being relied upon to carry the day. In his book *Achtung! Panzer!*, outlining the composition and employment of armoured forces, published in 1938, Guderian expanded his philosophy – the kernel of *Blitzkrieg*. If armoured potential is to translate into dynamic and effective power on the battlefield, runs his argument, all arms of the service must unite to form a carefully composed, balanced and versatile, fighting machine – the panzer division; a formation of all arms in which tanks, infantry, engineers, anti-tank, signals, motor-cyclists, artillery and other troops with logistical support, are trained for self-contained action and employment *en masse*. In the war to come, Guderian's was the decisive formula for German success. Impeded by higher authority and reactionary arms of the service at every stage in translating ideas into practice, the indomitable general provided the army and consequently the nation with a touchstone of unparalleled military power. By the end of 1938 the number of panzer divisions had increased to five with a sixth still forming. Nearly 500 armoured fighting vehicles mostly 35(t) tanks acquired when Hitler annexed Bohemia and Moravia in March 1939, were followed by improved 38(t) models armed with a reliable 3.7cm gun. The tank production capacity of Czech armament and vehicle industries would prove immensely beneficial to new panzer divisions raised in time for action in France in May 1940.

More significantly, in October Hitler issued a vital instruction in the interests of armoured progress. Guderian would be promoted general of panzer troops on 20 November; his brief – to supervise all mobile troops, designated Schnelltruppen. The Light divisions, hitherto raised and trained by the cavalry, and motorized infantry divisions formed by the infantry, were henceforth his nominal responsibility as Chief. Yet despite the clear logic of Hitler's intentions there was to be no *carte blanche* for Guderian to train and organize all mobile forces. Not in fact until 1943, in the aftermath of two disastrous campaigns in Russia, would this far-sighted and creatively inspired professional achieve a position from which to co-ordinate and unify the development of panzer forces. Instead, with an allotment of two staff officers, an adjutant and the assistance of a working-party representing anti-tank, motorized infantry and cavalry interests, Guderian, who theoretically was answerable for all questions of army mechanization, prepared training manuals and disputed endlessly with the cavalry and High Command over his proposals to re-organize the former. Even this limited success was short-lived. Within the year, on the outbreak of war, Guderian's 'command' was dissolved and he was transferred, not without 'difficulty', to head XIX Motorized Corps; in his place, but as an Inspector comparable to those of other arms of the service supported by an appropriate department in the General Army Office, came General Friedrich Kühn,

hitherto Wünsdorf school commandant (Schnelltruppen-schule, June 1941). Kühn's successor, appointed from command of 5th Light Division in the summer of 1942, was to be General-Major Johannes Streich, once Guderian's colleague, teaching tactics in the early days of the Fahrlehrstab. At a higher level, serving panzer interests at OKH, General Ritter von Thoma, the veteran of panzer action in the Spanish Civil War, was appointed Waffen General in March 1940.

When the Führer celebrated his 50th birthday with a grand parade in Berlin on 20 April 1939, the event was described in the German Press as the 'greatest display in the world'. Members of the new panzer force joining in the march-past sported distinctive black berets and uniforms. But as the war progressed, the beret would be replaced by more practical headgear, the peaked fieldcap – once reserved for mountain troops, soon to become general issue. In the same four-and-a-half-hour parade, paratroops, united under Luftwaffe control since December 1938, when the Army gave up its experimental battalion, made their first public appearance. Meanwhile, Army Group IV Headquarters, established in Leipzig in 1937 under von Brauchitsch (Army

Below: *Die Wehrmacht*, 193 This was the issue in which Guderian and Nehring publicized their concept of t panzer division: 'A formatio all arms teamed and trained for mobile warfare.' Foreign military Intelligence took litt notice of these comprehensi plans offered by *Blitzkrieg*'s leading exponents. The cove shows a tank crashing a bar wire obstacle, drawn by Theo Matjek.

3. Victory without profit, 1939–41

The earliest opportunity for the panzer force to show its paces in action five years after the setting-up of the first tank regiments and their incorporation into panzer divisions or independent panzer brigades though not equipped to the scales laid down, came in September 1939. Many divisions still lacked a variety of equipment – medium tanks, 20mm Flak and more; certain panzer regiments made do with the Pz Kpfw 38(t). A tabulated growth of the panzer force is included in Part 2. For Operation 'White', the campaign against Poland (map 2) fifteen mobile divisions – six panzer, four light, four motorized (infantry) and an impromptu panzer division (Kempf) apportioned between two army groups were allotted air support of two Air Fleets (Kesselring and Löhr) with 1,900 aircraft. The German Army assembled some 3,000 armoured fighting vehicles, mostly Pz Kpfw I and II series. These light tanks, little better than training machines, were supported by a small number of Pz Kpfw IIIs and IVs, and armoured cars, principally of the Type Sd Kfz 222. The Commander-in-Chief of the German Army in 1939 was von Brauchitsch who from his early days as a colonel in the Truppenamt had encouraged motorization developments, first by organizing army–air co-operation exercises and later, as group (IV) commander in Leipzig, supervising the tactical co-ordination of tank and motorized divisions in corps exercises – to which Guderian's XIV Corps had been subordinate.

Against the panzer divisions of two army groups, the Poles could bring only two tank brigades with some five hundred armoured fighting vehicles and an air force of fewer than five hundred serviceable machines. Not only did the country possess fewer tanks and aircraft than the Germans, but many of the tanks were British-inspired designs, light Carden-Loyds and Vickers Armstrongs built under licence. They were too few in number and under-armoured. They were also ineffectually commanded. Polish propaganda, misleading its forces into believing that the mass of German armour consisted of runabouts built for training purposes, was no help in the situation. The result, a military disaster for the Poles. German armies in a double encirclement strategy lead by powerful tank thrusts were supported by the Luftwaffe which, striking hard at the opposing air force and destroying much of it on the ground, also greatly hampered Polish reserve movement by all-out assault on communications. In no time, panzer divisions penetrated the Polish lines, breaking through into open country. Large number of Polish infantry, with their supporting tanks, were cut-off, trapped and destroyed in ever-tightening rings.

When Brest-Litovsk, east of Warsaw and deep in the Polish rear, was reached by Guderian's XIX Corps leading the northern wing of the offensive fifteen days after the start of the campaign, the issue was virtually decided. Two days later, on 17 September, when von Kleist, striking from Czechoslovakia, made contact with Guderian east of Warsaw, the encirclement of Polish forces was complete. In the capital itself, armoured action by 4th Panzer Division fighting in built-up areas proved less effective. Warsaw held out to capitulate on the 27th day of the campaign. The

Above: Field Marshal Gerd von Rundstedt GOC (Generaloberst), Army Group South, Poland 1939; Army Group 'A', France 1940; Army Group South, 1941 and OB West 1944 (*See maps 2, 3, 7 and 16*).

C-in-C, 1939 in succession to von Fritsch) followed by von Reichenau, exercised training and operational command over motorized units organized into mobile corps: XVI (Panzer) Lutz–Guderian; XV (Light) Hoth; XIV (motorized infantry) von Wietersheim. Equipment for the panzer divisions – the 20-ton Pz Kpfw III and 25-ton Pz Kpfw IV in particular – was nevertheless slow in reaching panzer regiments, fourteen of which, comprising mainly light battalions, were formed and, with few exceptions (7th, 8th, 11th and 25th Panzer Regiments) organized by OKH into panzer brigades of four battalions – the organic tank component of five panzer divisions raised by April 1939. A sixth panzer division (10th Panzer) incorporating 8th Panzer Regiment, taken from 4 Panzer Brigade, one of only two brigades serving at the time as Army troops, followed in time for action in September 1939.

contribution of the panzer force working in conjunction with Luftwaffe close-support groups proved decisive. SS participation in the thrust from East Prussia involved a motorized regiment, SS Standarte Deutschland, in action with Army Group North. The regiment formed part of a mixed Army and SS 'Panzer Division Kempf'. At the same time 'Adolf Hitler' moved from Lodz (Eighth Army) to Warsaw (Tenth Army) and 'Germania' (both in Army Group South), joined in the advance to Lemberg.

The Polish campaign vindicated a strategy of grand manoeuvre unique in the annals of military history. Exceeding in pace and power any offensive yet seen, the Wehrmacht took the military establishments of the world by surprise. Panzer divisions leading the infantry in concentrated thrusts while working in fast-moving battle groups supported by air force ground-attack formations – von Richthofen's Stukagruppen in particular – isolated resistance, demoralized the defence and created alarming envelopments on a battlefield extending across several thousand square miles. *Blitzkrieg* had triumphed, not exactly in accordance with Guderian's precepts, by independent free-ranging formations, but by motorized (panzer) corps allotted to infantry armies; their spearhead role coordinated by superior infantry army headquarters. Nevertheless these same tactics when repeated in the west against armies unable to adjust to the pace of a renewed German offensive would produce correspondingly successful results.

Using the knowledge which it had gained as a result of the fighting in Spain and Poland, the Army High Command (OKH) started to remould its panzer force. The light divisions, consisting principally of motorized infantry with a single tank battalion, were reformed as panzer divisions. Panzer regiments were strengthened with a greater number of better-armed tanks, the Pz Kpfw III and IV and supported by an increase in motorized infantry. But there was little time to introduce much new equipment before the forthcoming campaign in France. The Pz Kpfw I and II series were of necessity retained as the main types, while some of the Pz Kpfw III series were to be upgunned by rearming them with a 5cm weapon. The Pz Kpfw IV series too, when fitted with a new (long) 7.5cm gun, would prove even more of an asset; but production of these 'specials' was to be delayed until early 1942. More of the infantry units accompanying the tanks, the future panzer grenadiers, would be mounted in armoured personnel carriers, Schützenpanzerwagen (SPWs). The first of these vehicles, issued only in small numbers to 1st Panzer Division, had proved their effectiveness; less well-provided formations retained standard trucks to lift their motorized infantry as far forward as possible. Heavier armour was incorporated into new SPWs and weapon shields fitted to their on-board machine-gun. Henceforth, in numerous variants, these vehicles would become an indispensible part of the panzer force, conferring exceptional power and mobility on its motorized infantry. Panzer regiments would benefit increasingly from this partnership. In battle groups operating in close or wooded country, the escorting infantry would often fight ahead of the armour or on its flanks. Overcoming river barriers, clearing villages and so on, motorized infantry would prove their merits in countless situations where tanks alone would prove highly vulnerable to counter-measures by infantry and anti-tank detachments.

The first assault guns – Sturmgeschütze – turretless tracked vehicles fitted with a powerful low-velocity gun and intended for use in an infantry support role also made their appearance in the Polish campaign. They too were retained and expanded in numbers. In later operations they would often be used as substitutes for tanks. The white cross emblem painted on all German armoured vehicles as an identification mark was replaced by the straight-edged black cross.

At 0535 hours on 10 May 1940, Hitler launched Operation 'Yellow', (panzer order of battle and map (3)) with a force of more than 2,000 tanks formed into ten panzer divisions. Deployed as hitherto, in battle groups, the divisions advanced through Belgium and Luxemburg to lead the attack on France. Holland was also invaded. The ratio of opposing forces was 120 German divisions including ten panzer divisions with 2,574 tanks opposed by 83 French, nine British, 22 Belgian and ten Dutch divisions with a total of 3,600 tanks; a marked difference in armoured strength.

Above: Field Marshal Fedor von Bock, GOC (General-oberst), Army Group North, Poland 1939; Army Group 'ᴮ' France 1940; Army Group Centre, 1941 and Army Grou[ ]'B', 1942 (*See* maps 2, 3, 7 and 10).

in the impregnability of the Maginot Line, but more significantly clinging to the notion that the role of the tank was first and foremost to provide support for non-motorized infantry, was outmanoeuvred and brought to defeat, its tanks ineffectually spread in small numbers across a wide front.

In marked contrast to Allied dispositions, powerful concentrations of German armour with Luftwaffe support – especially Panzer Group von Kleist at the point of main effort – forced crossings of the River Meuse notably at Sedan and Monthermé, pausing only to consolidate before striking west through France and rupturing the defence on a narrow front. Wheeling north to isolate demoralized and outmanoeuvred Allied armies, the panzer divisions were followed by motorized and marching infantry; their task being to maintain the tempo of the attack, and line the shoulders of the 'corridor' created by the panzer divisions, freeing them for further operations. In secondary action upstream across the Meuse at Dinant, less powerful armoured spearheads with varying degrees of air force support reinforced the offensive (map 3).

Allied staffs expecting a repeat of Schlieffen's 1914 manoeuvre when the German Army swept through Belgium towards Paris, had moved the bulk of their forces north into Belgium to oppose von Bock's Army Group 'B' deceptively threatening invasion. But it was Army Group 'A' that struck the decisive blow, moving against France through Luxemburg; von Bock's infantry divisions pressing forward at an appropriate moment to complete the encirclement of the Allies armies.

The principal phase of Operation 'Yellow' lasted no more than eleven days following von Kleist's storming of the Meuse on the 13th. The greater part of Belgium and much of northern France was occupied by the 24th and the British Expeditionary Force was penned into a pocket totally cut off from its Atlantic coast bases at Cherbourg and Brest. With no mobile counter-attack force in reserve and unable to comprehend the magnitude of the defeat facing them, the armies of Britain, Belgium and France proved incapable of effective resistance and were shattered in the process. Holland had already fallen to an assault in which parachute and glider troops lead the way. Salvation for the BEF and a fraction of the French Army lay in escape through the Channel port and beaches of Dunkirk to England.

British and French forces that succeeded in crossing the Channel from Dunkirk owed their deliverance to Hitler's order halting the panzer divisions fifteen miles away. On 24 May, fearing that British or French counter-attacks might succeed in cutting the Flanders (panzer) 'corridor' (map 4) and thereby separate oncoming infantry divisions from the panzer spearheads, Hitler supported by von Runstedt, called a halt. The Royal Navy, with the support of hundreds of small boats, was quick to seize the opportunity of evacuating what it could of the defeated Allied armies. When Dunkirk was closed by air action, men were taken from the beaches.

At Goering's suggestion, the Luftwaffe attempted to finish off the embattled defenders. The plan was unrealistic; an overstretched air force, unable to meet the commitment, failed to prevent the escape of 3,300 mostly British troops. Total victory eluded the panzer force and Hitler's hopes of putting a swift end to the war faded, for good. Daring in concept, swift, precise and economical in

Above: Field Marshal Erich von Manstein, when chief of staff (Generalleutnant) to von Runstedt in Poland and France. He was credited with Plan 'Yellow' which employed the panzer divisions on the opposite axis to the von Schlieffen Plan which Hitler and OKH originally intended to repeat. Thereafter as Corps, Army and finally Army Group Commander, he reaffirmed his reputation as the Wehrmacht's leading strategist (see maps 3, 7, 10, 13 and 14).

Superior German leadership, tactics and inter-service co-operation, particularly between army and air force, would more than offset the disparity in numbers. Once again, a key feature of the German plan would be to win immediate air supremacy, destroying the enemy air force on the ground and over the battlefield. This the Luftwaffe would do with notable success, hindering in the process every attempt by Allied land forces to concentrate for counter-attacks against the invading Army Groups.

As hitherto, the Commander-in-Chief of the German Army was von Brauchitsch. His forces, Army Group 'B' (von Bock) with three panzer divisions would attack Holland and Belgium, Army Group 'A' (von Runstedt) strongest in armour with seven panzer divisions and the bulk of the German forces would strike at France through Luxemburg. Army Group 'C' (Leeb) would take up defensive positions in front of the Maginot Line. Applying the tactics successfully demonstrated in Poland, panzer spearheads raced to lightning victory while the French General Staff, believing

Above: Paratroops of 7th Air Division leading the way into Holland to secure key points the western axis of von Bock Army Group 'B' (see map 3).

execution, the German plan of attack carried the day. The decisive stroke delivered by von Kleist's Panzer Group, a phalanx of three panzer corps with 1,260 tanks concentrated into a powerful spearhead, had smashed through French Second Army on the Meuse and then bypassed or outflanked all other opposition. With Guderian's XIX Corps in the lead, the panzer group exceeded all but executant expectations. On 20 May Guderian's 2nd Panzer Division (Veiel) was first to reach the Channel at Abbeville.

The panzer divisions created such alarm and confusion by their surprise deployment in deeply echeloned attacks out of the Ardennes, a ravined and forest-bound area, considered impassable to tanks, that the opportunity for mounting a determined counter-offensive was never seized and the panzer columns with their powerful air support rolled to an astounding victory – prostrating the armies of four nations.

The success of Blitzkrieg in the west was virtually decided in its first phase when the German forces covered 160 miles in seven days to reach Abbeville, splitting the Allies and sealing the fate of the British Expeditionary Force. Prompt support by the Luftwaffe in impeding British and French counter-attacks on the flanks of German columns strung along the panzer 'corridor' contributed substantially to Allied defeat. Although French troops went on to offer resistance

during the second phase of the fighting, when regrouped German armies in Operation 'Red', once again spearheaded by armoured troops, wheeled south to encircle Paris, they were no match for the panzer divisions and failed to halt the advance. On 14 June 1940 Paris surrendered. On the 22nd an armistice was signed and on the 25th, the guns fell silent.

Despite Hitler's misgivings over the safety of flanks, the deft handling of the panzer divisions combined with the maximum possible air support proved decisive in German victory. Panzer commanders and staffs at all levels contributed to the success. Many would capitalize their experience in senior command or staff appointments in later campaigns: Colonels Eberbach, von Manteuffel and Breith leading the offensive across the Meuse at Maastricht (map 3), Major Rothenburg, Rommel's panzer commander at Dinant (killed in action, 1941), Colonel Balck, whose motorized infantry paved the way for Guderian at Sedan; Generals von Kleist, Guderian, Hoepner, Reinhardt and Hoth, foremost in command at crucial stages in the battle.

Elsewhere at the time, Generalleutnant Walter Model served as Chief of Staff, Sixteenth Army, Colonel Walther Nehring was Chief of Staff to Panzer Group Guderian, while Major Fritz Bayerlein served in the same Group as 1a (Ops). Colonel Erhard Raus, the future GOC Fourth, First and Third

Panzer Armies, held a staff appointment outside the panzer force until 19 July. All served vital apprenticeships leading to high-ranking careers in Africa or Russia. Major-General Erwin Rommel, in command of 7th Panzer Division, crossed the Meuse at Dinant before sweeping on through Flanders leading his formation (like Heinz Guderian at Sedan) from the front. Given command of Deutsches Afrika Korps and

subsequently Panzerarmee Afrika, Rommel would prove a wily and resourceful adversary in the Western desert.

The Waffen SS played a small but busy role in this campaign. The motorized regiments (excluding the Leibstandarte) that had fought in Poland and now formed part of an SS Verfügungs Division (SS-V) were lead by Paul Hausser. All joined in the attack on Holland (Eighteenth

Right: Motor-cycle troops preceding the main body of Army Group South *en route* through Poland. This is a typical early picture of a panzer division vanguard.

Army) advancing to Rotterdam, Amsterdam and beyond. Thereafter in Flanders, particularly around Arras and Dunkirk, they and a new motorized division, SS Totenkopf (Theodor Eicke) raised from state security personnel, supported the panzer groups, driving the BEF back to the Channel.

In the 'Red' phase of the battle for France, a partly motorized SS Polizei Division (Pfeffer von Wildenbruck) came into action across the Aisne; building bridgeheads to assist Guderian's southward advance while SS-V and SS Totenkopf served Panzer Group von Kleist.

The successful outcome of the battle for France, concluded on 25 June, found the German High Command with no contingency plans for continuing the land war against Britain; the BEF had escaped from Dunkirk by the narrowest of margins – thanks to tireless efforts by the Royal Navy and Royal Air Force – and returned home in a much depleted state. However, a German plan to pursue the BEF and thereby complete the humiliation of the British army quickly materialized. On 30 June 1940, in a war aims memorandum submitted to Hitler by General Jodl (OKW chief of staff), the idea of invading Britain was established at the highest level. By 12 July, Jodl's notes were being shaped into Operation 'Sea-lion' and plans to involve all three services in summer assault operations across the English Channel were initiated; Army Group 'A' (von Runstedt) consolidating on the Channel coast was directed by OKH to develop the Army side of the operation. Von Runstedt was to be responsible for two armies disembarking simultaneously in three waves between Worthing (Ninth Army) and Hythe (Sixteenth Army).

Assault infantry in the first wave, landing on open beaches from improvised landing craft, were to be followed in the second (principal) wave of the invasion by four panzer and two motorized divisions divided between Hoth (XV) Ninth Army and Reinhardt (XXXXI) Sixteenth Army. They too practised open coast landings in case no suitable harbour was available (see Third Panzer Army, July–October 1940). Armoured support for first wave infantry would be provided additionally by three panzer battalions equipped mainly with Pz Kpfw III (Tauchpanzer) submersible battle tanks, and a fourth equipped with flame-throwers. Primary operations would focus upon Brighton, Folkestone and, above all, Dover where parachute landings to secure the flanks of the invasion force might equally be expected to accelerate the capture of port facilities needed for handling heavy equipment and follow-up waves.

Despite prodigious efforts by the Luftwaffe to win air superiority as a pre-requisite for success, Blitzkrieg against England was never to achieve reality. Goering failed and the German Navy under Admiral Raeder, ill prepared for such an eventuality,* baulked at transporting and re-supplying in safety an invasion force opposed by a much superior Royal Navy and an undefeated Royal Air Force. These and degenerating weather in the Channel prompted Hitler in October to postpone and early in 1941 to cancel the projected operation. 'Sea-lion' divisions were instead re-deployed and in common with others required to give up one of their two panzer regiments as cadres for new formations (Panzer Divisions 11–21), re-organizing for action against Russia. The next Blitzkrieg commitment for the panzer force, Operation 'Marita' (map 6) came in 1941

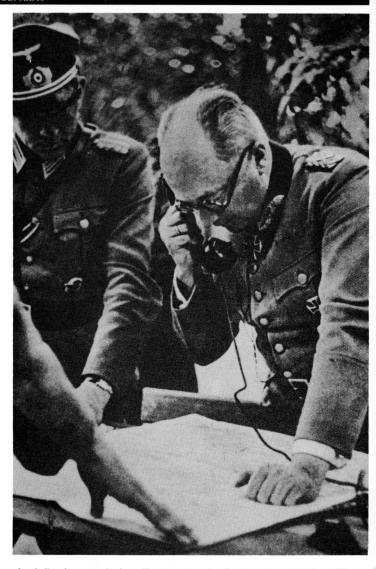

after Italian Army attacks from Albania against the Greek Army had failed to produce results. German forces were then drawn into a Balkans campaign to rescue an ally. Once again panzer divisions headed a German offensive. When the friendly state of Yugoslavia unexpectedly turned against the Axis that country too was included in a hastily inaugurated German plan of attack. On 6 April 1941 Luftwaffe raids against Yugoslav Army headquarters and transport installations in Belgrade signalled the simultan-eous invasion of both Greece and Yugoslavia. Roumania, Bulgaria and Hungary all provided jumping-off points for the attacking force. Nevertheless, one-third of the panzer divisions intended for the operation, the responsibility of Field Marshal List's Twelfth Army and at the last moment von Weichs' Second Army, were not needed. Air opposition

Above: Field Marshal Hans von Kluge, GOC (Generaloberst), Fourth Army in the battle of France, led the strongest of von Runstedt's armies – at the crucial assault stage. Thereafter in 1941 he commanded Army Group Centre, in 'Barbarossa' and in August 1944 he replaced Rommel at Army Group 'B' before committing suicide (see maps 3 and 7).

*German capital ships out of commission: Scharnhorst, Gneisenau, Lützow (formerly Deutschland) torpedoed. Graf Spee scuttled. Bismarck, Prinz Eugen and Tirpitz not expected in service before spring or autumn 1941.

was negligible. Twelfth Army's Panzer Group von Kleist supported by von Richthofen's VIII Air Corps thrusting via Nish to the Yugoslav capital brought swift surrender.

A southwards advance by Twelfth Army into Greece where a British expeditionary force from Egypt had arrived at Piraeus and Volos on 7 March, made equally rapid progress. The panzer divisions aided by mountain troops, the first of many collaborations, turned the Metaxas Line – fortified frontier heights protecting Salonika. 2nd Panzer Division, striking out on a daring and successful 130-kilometre thrust into the city and unnerving the defence, contributed notably to success. Further west a turning movement southwards through Skopje giving List control of strategic north–south rail connections and access to mountain routes leading into the heart of the country further

imperilled the defence. On 21 April the largely immobile Greek Army capitulated; disaster threatened the British expeditionary force. But the German advance through Greece in the direction of Athens faltered at Thermopylae when British and Empire troops with Matildas diverted from Egypt held the advance at bay. Taking to the road and retreating via the Peloponnese, 45,000 troops reached Crete where a further reverse at the hands of General Student's (XI) Parachute (and glider) Corps was waiting. A British seaborne evacuation followed and the German campaign in the Balkans was over.

The war in the Mediterranean (map 5) was nevertheless far from finished. Other German forces in the shape of Rommel's DAK, had been committed to North Africa, once again bolstering Italian forces. Mobile operations over vast

Right: Rommel inspecting units of 7th Panzer Division. It was during the Battle of France that both commander and division won a reputation for thrustfulness.

Above: The ubiquitous Ju 87, employed against ground targets, opened the way for advancing panzer divisions, notably at Maastricht and Sedan (*see* map 3).

Left: The Me 110 was deployed in 1939 as a long-range fighter and issued to certain Jagdgeschwader following successful outings in Spain. In Poland and France it flew ground-attack missions; later version flew as night fighters.

Opposite page, top: The results of dive-bombing and artillery fire on a fixed installation, the Namur fort on the Belgian–German frontier, is all too evident.

Opposite page, bottom left: Colonel Georg Rothenburg, CO, 25th Panzer Regiment, 7th Panzer Division, leading Rommel's armour across Meuse at Dinant (*see* map 4).

Opposite page, bottom right: Colonel Eugene Meindl who became CO, Assault Regiment of XI A Corps. In May 1940 constituent glider units served Captain Koch (Sturmabteilung) and Oberleutnant Witzig (Pionierzug) in their seizure of Fort Eben Emael which opened the way for Fourth Panzer Div Sixth Army. Meindl later played a distinguished pa in defending St-Lô in Normandy.

distances would take on new and greater dimensions stretching the panzer force to its limit and diverting men and equipment needed for operations against Russia. German armour committed in support of the Italian adventure into Albania and Greece had triumphed over admittedly inferior opponents. Superior skills and mobility prevailed in taking panzer divisions the length of the peninsular through rugged terrain under gruelling conditions. When units were obliged to replan operations resulting from the high wastage rate of their equipment, panzer troops learned valuable lessons in improvisation. The Luftwaffe, by delaying the movement of enemy reserves and reinforcements and combating active opposition, supported the Army as it had earlier in the west, assisting the forward progress of panzer divisions and corps directly and indirectly through VIII Air Corps attacks against resistance centres and road and rail communications.

The Leibstandarte SS Adolf Hitler raised to brigade strength and SS Das Reich Division, both motorized, also supported Army panzer divisions in the Balkans offensive. Das Reich, under the leadership of Paul Hausser, future GOC, German Seventh Army in Normandy in 1944, strengthened Panzer Corps Reinhard, the northern arm of Panzer Group von Kleist thrusting to Belgrade. A battle group from Hausser's division ceremoniously accepted the surrender of the city on 13 April. The Leibstandarte, reinforced with an assault gun battery and commanded by 'Sepp' Dietrich, future commander of Sixth SS Panzer Army in the Ardennes in 1944, waged a bitter campaign through Greece, assisting 9th Panzer Division in the drive south outflanking the British forces. On 9 April Dietrich's brigade stormed the Klidi Pass, winning a gateway for the continuation of the offensive, then quickly secured the Klissura Pass, another key defile, and Yanina, a communications centre in the rear of Greek armies fighting in Albania. Pushing on south, Dietrich followed these successes with a crossing of the Corinth Canal in Hussar style while paratroops of 2nd Paratroop Regiment (Sturm) seized the Corinth bridge on the 25th, but failed by 24 hours to trap retreating British, Australian and New Zealand units. List pushed his divisions further into the Peloponnese; 5th Panzer reached Kalamata on the 28th. Protected by rearguards, the Allied troops embarked at Nauplion and other ports for Crete. But however successful and daring the small panzer force had proved, thrusting the length of the peninsula against more or less immobile opponents, the largely unforeseen Balkans Campaign – considered essential to the security of oil-fields in Roumania and Hungary by putting them out of range of the RAF, and the bolstering of the Italian Army struggling in Albania to defeat the Greeks – was to effect delay in the opening of Operation 'Barbarossa', the invasion of Russia, for which plans had been made since July 1940. 'Barbarossa' would be fatally compromised by the delay. When the panzer divisions were eventually re-deployed for their new task, only one month separated the two campaigns.

Starting at 0300 hours on 22 June 1941, 'Barbarossa' (map 7) would rank as one of the great military misadventures of the Second World War, a trial of strength for German and Russian forces; the death-knell of the panzer force. Estimates put Russian opposition at 150 infantry divisions (15 motorized) 32 cavalry divisions and 36 motorized brigades; with 10,000–20,000 tanks supported by 10,000 aircraft. On the German side the forces deployed in three army groups, North, Centre and South, totalled some 153 divisions of which 140 were actually German, with 3,417 tanks. Each army group was supported by an air fleet. The German armoured force consisted basically of nineteen panzer divisions, ten motorized infantry divisions, three motorized SS divisions and one motorized SS brigade. A reinforced Gross Deutschland motorized infantry regiment and a small number of independent (Army) assault-gun batteries, heavy artillery, anti-aircraft and anti-tank units supported the deployment. The SS contribution would rise to fifteen panzer or motorized divisions; about one-third of the panzer force.

Whatever the precise tally of the Russian land and air forces, their gross underestimation by Hitler and the General Staff was to prove disastrous to German hopes of quick victory. General Franz Halder, Chief of Staff to the Army High Command, would record in his diary at the end of November: 'No fewer than 360 Russian divisions have so far been identified.'

The Red Army, erroneously concluding from its experience in the Spanish Civil War, where several hundred light tanks had been committed by both sides, that large armoured units could not carry out independent tasks, had consequently based its pre-war tank organization on the French infantry-support model. Not until the battle for France did the Russian General Staff make belated attempts to reorganize on German lines. Thereafter Russian armoured forces would improve out of all recognition in armament, tactics and above all, in heavy armour. The later preponderance of tracked heavy weapons – tanks and tank destroyers – would prove a decisive element in defeating the panzer force. Tank production would also prove markedly superior. Marshal Sokolovsky records: 'At the beginning of 1945, the Red Army had eight times as many

Below: General (later Generaloberst) Kurt Student conferring with General Ring OC, 5th Mountain Division. T[ ] was the first strategic deploy ment (Operation 'Mercury') [ ] paratroops and glider-borne troops (*see* map 6).

Above: A 3.7cm anti-tank gun deployed on the road to Leningrad. When faced with the T34 and KWII only larger calibres, generally 7.5cm, could provide effective protection.

while in the south, First Panzer Group led by von Kleist was given to von Runstedt. The two panzer groups of Army Group Centre had the largest combined strength in tanks – about 1,800 in all. The strategic objectives of the army groups were set out in Hitler directives giving the army groups Leningrad, Moscow (direction), Kiev and subsequently Rostov as their targets. The panzer groups would be committed on widely divergent courses, their objectives lying hundreds of miles distant and hundreds of miles apart. Despite the distances involved, the panzer force would come close to success; a startled world taking little comfort in the extent to which the Wehrmacht was so evidently over-stretched. Planned to end in weeks (but in the event destined to last close upon four years), the unusually harsh winter of 1941–2 would take a savage toll of increasingly worn-down and exhausted panzer divisions. Within months of the start of the campaign, battle losses were severely depleting the panzer force. Frostbite and a hostile winter climate paralyzed its operations. Evidence of defects in equipment and the unsuitability of panzer force vehicles for operations in exceptionally roadless conditions soon became apparent. The toll inflicted by stubborn Russian resistance, the aggravation of excessive demands by the Army High Command for advances to Leningrad and Moscow, taking the panzer force well out of reach of its railheads, jeopardized its future.

In the offensive against Leningrad, Hoepner's panzer group, beating off counter-attacks at Rossieny where the heavy Russian KV–1 made an unexpected appearance, swiftly overcame the River Duna, a major obstacle in its path, and within a week reached the shores of Lake Peipus. By mid-July von Leeb, developing plans to encircle the city, had captured the Schlusselberg, a fortress guarding the eastern approaches to the city. The position was taken on 8 September by which time the slower infantry units had caught up with the leading panzer divisions. But Hitler postponed the capture of Leningrad, instead ordering the transfer of much of the investing panzer force to the centre, leaving the infantry armies around the city to pursue only partial investment. A desperate but unsuccessful attempt to snap the ring tight would be made later with Hitler ordering a link with the Finns. In the centre, where Panzer Groups 2 and 3 lead by Guderian and Hoth fought their way towards Moscow, German double encirclement tactics resulted several times in the capture of large Russian forces, near Bialystok, Bryansk and Smolensk. Smolensk fell on 15 July. But in August Hitler announced a new plan. Instead of Moscow the emphasis of the assault would be on the wings of the offensive. The advance towards the Soviet capital by Army Group Centre was postponed in favour of supporting Army Group North attacking Leningrad and Army Group South aiming to capture Kiev and the Donetz industrial basin. Guderian's panzer group, forging east in the centre, was swung south and west behind Kiev, joining with a northward-circling von Kleist; Hoth Group was partially diverted to assist von Leeb's Leningrad offensive.

With 13th Panzer Division leading Panzer Group von Kleist to the outskirts of Kiev by mid-July, the invasion of the south had made steady if unspectacular progress. But in consequence of Hitler's change of plan and a fruitful collaboration between Panzer Groups von Kleist and Guderian, creating an envelopment of major Russian forces

tanks as it had possessed in December 1941.' Soviet emphasis on heavy tanks had started as early as 1939 with the manufacture of the 44-ton KV–1 and 53-ton KV–2A running parallel with the medium 26-ton T34. From the time that they were first encountered all proved superior to German models. As early as mid-1940 these unknown new Russian tanks including 1,000 T34s were arriving in border defence zones. The planned output for 1941 was 5,500 a year!

At the start of the campaign four panzer groups, including all the available motorized SS formations, were deployed to lead the armoured thrusts of Army Groups North, Centre and South. Their commanders were, respectively: von Leeb, von Bock and von Runstedt. None of the panzer groups handling a burgeoning number of panzer divisions and corps were allowed total operational freedom. In the north, Hoepner's Fourth Panzer Group was allotted to von Leeb. Von Bock was provided with Second and Third Panzer Groups commanded by Guderian and Hoth respectively,

Below: The 7.5cm long-barrelled Pz Kpfw IV, introduced in 1942 (seen h in Tunisia), was a match fo most early opposition encountered by the panzer force.

in the Kiev region, the occupation of the city by Army Group South on 18 September brought an end to the greatest of all German encirclement battles; enormous booty being taken from annihilated Russian armies. Renamed First Panzer Army, von Kleist's group, then struck out across the Dnieper towards the Sea of Azov and on 20 November captured Rostov, von Kleist's gateway to the Caucasus and Russian oil. But Russian flank attacks in the north, forcing the army group into untimely retreat to the River Mius, was to bring Rostov-on-Don once more into Russian hands.

Meanwhile, launching Operation 'Typhoon' (map 8), in the centre of the eastern front, Hitler resumed the advance to Moscow. Redeploying Panzer Groups 3 and 4 (the latter withdrawn from Leningrad) and pushing hard for the Soviet capital while Panzer Group 2 (Guderian) joined the action from the south-west, the great advance was re-started. But all too late. The momentum of the sweeping advances was lost. Autumn mud slowed the offensive; snow with 30° of frost, blizzards, undernourishment, decrepit vehicles and unserviceable equipment including tank turrets that failed to traverse, rendered operations well-nigh impossible. Winter clothing and supplies failed. Frost-bite and counter-attacks took a deadly toll. Exhaustion brought the offensive to a halt. All movement north and south of Moscow intended to bring about the fall of the city failed utterly.

With winter conditions, snow especially, restricting German mobility to the few serviceable roads, fresh Russian armies transported from the east, equipped and experienced in winter warfare, their presence only vaguely suspected by the General Staff, pressed home their advantage. For the

German Army the situation deteriorated daily in mid-winter. Panzer divisions thrusting to within twenty miles of Moscow, were unable to find the power required to fight their way forward; even to extricate themselves required a super-human effort. *Blitzkrieg* strategy had failed and on this front would never restart. Moscow would not again experience a threat to its security. A Russian counter-offensive, starting on 5 December, swung purposefully into action. Cutting deep swathes into the central front, the German armies facing Moscow under von Bock and his successor, von Kluge, were brought within an ace of collapse. Hitler's response on 16 December was a stand fast order – the first of many. Bitter disputes over unscheduled withdrawals consumed Guderian and von Kluge, the army group Commander. Stalled in exposed positions north of Tula on the south-west approaches to Moscow, Guderian had been unable to find the strength to advance further. Seeing that Red Army attacks were a constant menace the prudent general pulled back to better positions. On Hitler's orders he was relieved of his command and transferred to OKW's officers' pool on 26 December. Other generals disobeying Hitler's instructions to stand fast were similarly dismissed.

For the Luftwaffe, no less than for the Army, its airfields blanketed in deep snow and barely a machine flying in leaden skies, supplies of all kinds dried-up. So traumatic became the onset of deep winter that for both services the period was one of agonizing adjustment to defensive operations and a new strategy. Towns and villages were organized for all-round defence in a 'hedgehog' system. Tanks, what few remained, were formed into counter-attack detachments. Tankless crews found themselves employed as infantry. The home front had meanwhile been active, but tank production showed little sign of upward movement and would remain virtually static for a further twelve months. Technical development had nevertheless resulted in the long-barrelled tank gun. New tank designs, a Pz Kpfw V Panther weighing 43 tons and a 56-ton Pz Kpfw VI Tiger were developed to counter the T34 and its heavy partners. The contribution of these new machines to the battlefield fighting alongside increasing numbers of Pz Kpfw IVs would prove effective by the middle of 1943. Hitler, eager as always to promote technical progress in tank design, ordered the construction of a new super-heavy tank (Mouse) weighing 170 tons.

Assault-gun production was increased and armour skirting introduced to improve the protection of vehicles such as the Pz Kpfw IV. Of equally far-reaching importance to the panzer force was a decision to mount the 8.8cm gun, hitherto employed in anti-aircraft and ground defence roles, in the Tiger. The first half-company of this new tank would be introduced into trial service on the Leningrad front within a year (September 1942). It was there and also on Guderian's sector in the early days of the invasion that the panzer groups discovered to their consternation that not only were their opponent's T34s and KV-1s heavily armoured and dangerous, but largely impervious to German 3.7cm and 5cm anti-tank guns. The need for improvements in anti-tank defence was self-evident. More 7.5cm and 8.8cm guns were essential. Until such time as they were available, preferably mounted in self-propelled form as Panzerjaeger (tank destroyers), captured Russian 7.62cm guns would be improvised to serve on Czech 38(t) mountings. One

advantage of Russian weapons, and this included the T34, was simplicity of construction. Most needed little servicing, but were vulnerable to the Stuka dive-bomber. By contrast many of the German weapons, and in this the tanks were no exception, were liable to break down because of their complicated design. Then too there was the problem of their high petrol consumption; for example, the Panzer IV, with a fuel tank holding 470 litres, had a maximum range of only 150 kilometres.

Steadily mounting air attacks by the Red Air Force making good its disastrous losses at the start of the invasion, emphasized the need for motorized anti-aircraft detachments to escort armoured formations. The experience lead to the inclusion of an additional AA company in the motorized infantry and panzer regiments. Negligence in the provision of adequate anti-aircraft protection for panzer columns would prove a significant factor in later reverses. As more and increasingly powerful air forces out-matched the Luftwaffe east and west, the panzer force would discover all too late that it possessed too few effective means with which to combat the menace. Panzer engineers engaged in lifting mines, demolishing tank-traps, bridging rivers and laying roads in the trackless eastern hinterland, proved themselves indispensable in early operations, although the speed of the German advance frequently gave the defenders no time to destroy bridges. For engineers in the forefront of the action, improved protection became a matter of priority. Special armoured vehicles for engineer use or captured ones

Above: The famous '88', an anti-aircraft gun deployed b**y** Flakkampfgruppen which co**u** also protect against tanks a**nd** other ground targets.

Above: In Russia manhandling anti-tank guns was a problem for both armoured troops and infantry. The heavier calibres were naturally the most cumbersome, requiring self-propelled mountings.

until such times as purpose-built machines could be produced were a necessity. During the first year of the campaign submersible tanks, originally intended for invasion of Britain, were used by the panzer force to cross the River Bug.

The setbacks and severe losses suffered by the German Army in the winter of 1941–2 emphasized a clear need for new and improved equipment of all types. The Army's order of battle for the period shows that of twenty-one panzer divisions on establishment, only eight were then fully operational and with production running at a low ebb, not all could be rebuilt. Moreover, instead of renewing the

advance on Moscow, as soon as the Russian counter-offensive had spent itself at the end of spring 1942, Hitler decided that the axis of the 1942 attack should be switched from Moscow to oil-fields in the Caucasus. For these reasons, panzer divisions allotted to First and Fourth Panzer Armies (expanded panzer group headquarters) spearheading Army Groups 'A' (List) and 'B' (von Bock) in Operation 'Blue', the new offensive, were given priority in supplies and equipment. The Pz Kpfw IIIs and IVs, although no match for the heavier T34s now appearing in masses on the front, had been upgunned in an effort to restore the balance.

4. Outrunning resources, 1942

With no hint of the disaster soon to befall it at Stalingrad, Hoth's Fourth Panzer Army, re-enacting the tactics that had won the battle for France, raced into Voronezh (map 10). Renewed German attacks also brought success for von Kleist whose First Panzer Army recaptured Rostov-on-Don. The industrial basin of the Donetz also succumbed and a tank drive by von Kleist in the direction of Maikop and Mozdok threatened oil towns of the eastern Caucasus. The panzer army's main objectives, Soviet oil centres at Tiflis, Grozny and Baku, lay 400 miles across the Kalmuck Steppe. Within weeks the German drive into the Caucasus, seizing outlying

towns and pressing forward into the foothills of the range, reached Malgobek (SS Wiking) and the outskirts of Ordzhonikidze (23rd Panzer). There German progress ended – the panzer force once again at the end of its resources. Maikop destroyed by retreating Russians, would never contribute oil to the German war effort and the thrust would never be resumed. A Red Army counter-offensive encircling Stalingrad in the North and threatening von Kleist's rearward services would finally seal the fate of Operation 'Blue/Brunswick'. The great advance had been enormously hampered; trucks standing idle for want of fuel, supplies drying-up and putting a brake on progress. Von Kleist's strength was either dissipated in drawn-out engagements or creamed off for action at Stalingrad and elsewhere. The offensive in the south slowly stalled. Persia and its oil-fields, long coveted by Hitler as a contributor to the nation's economy, would remain an unattainable dream. And then, too, the Russians had learned to evade the encircling panzer thrusts and no great losses had been inflicted by von Kleist or Hoth on Russian forces deployed in the land corridor between the Donetz and the Don.

Faced with vehicle shortages in operations across the Europe/Asia frontier, the panzer force turned to the camel as a pack-animal. Cossacks and other martial races of the regions were recruited as allies; a Cossack cavalry regiment serving with an over-extended First Panzer Army. The

Cossacks screened the panzer army's open flank on the Kalmuck Steppe. But events on the Volga where Fourth Panzer Army was supporting Sixth Army (Paulus), attacking Stalingrad in the course of Hitler's eccentric offensive, pursued simultaneously with von Kleist's advance into the Caucasus, would turn all too soon into unmitigated disaster, forcing both panzer armies into retreat.

The battle for Stalingrad had begun well enough (maps 10 and 11). Army Group 'B' had crossed the Don and panzer divisions leading Sixth Army (Paulus) forward on 23 August had reached suburbs on the Volga immediately north of the city. A concentric attack by Fourth Panzer Army approaching from the south-west also had eventually carried through bitterly contested suburbs to the centre. Yet by late October, hampered by a lack of fuel and unrelenting Soviet

Below: Panzer grenadiers assisting the tanks in their fighting tasks as the platoon commander observes a river crossing operation. The vehicle is an Sd Kfz 251 mounting a 3.7cm anti-tank gun.

Right: September 1941; Stuka crews wait on the northern front for orders to attack. Their machines were to prove progressively obsolete against Russian air opposition and by 1943 they were outclassed.

resistance, only two-thirds of Stalingrad city was in German hands. Heavy fighting to reduce the town continued with slow German progress. A strong Russian counter-offensive launched with the benefit of a snowstorm at dawn on 19 November enveloped the city. Sixth Army and much of Fourth Panzer Army were isolated. A Luftwaffe promise of resupply, despite prodigious efforts by aircrews and ground staff operating at a great disadvantage in a second winter of appalling conditions, would go unfulfilled. Within weeks Paulus, forbidden by Hitler to break out, was surrendering his entire army conscious of an even greater disaster threatening Army Group 'A' as the Red Army lunged west to endanger Rostov and von Kleist's lifeline into the Caucasus. Immediate withdrawal of First Panzer Army from the jaws of a gigantic trap was vital if a greater catastrophe were to be avoided.

Weakened by battle losses and diversions – Gross Deutschland transferred to the west and 23rd Panzer and Wiking sent north to assist Hoth in an Army Group plan to relieve Stalingrad and stiffen the outer defences of Rostov – the depleted panzer army (which had also given up much of its air cover) started the long return trek to Rostov, hoping to negotiate the 'gateway' before the Red Army could seize it. In this endeavour von Kleist was successful, but an attempt by Fourth Panzer Army to relieve Stalingrad was to end in failure (map 12). On 2 February 1943 Stalingrad and Paulus's entire force totalling 250,000 men of 22 divisions, six of them mobile, fell to the investing Russians. Panzer General Hube, succeeding von Wietersheim as Corps Commander of the first panzer contingent to reach the Don at Kalatsch and help in the fighting for the northern suburbs of the city, was flown out before the collapse. Three panzer and three motorized divisions were lost in the capitulation – the worst in German history, a turning-point in Wehrmacht military fortune.

Viewed in retrospect, the summer battles leading to disaster at Stalingrad had seen German fighting spirit and leadership in battle as strong as ever. In seizing Voronezh, *Blitzkrieg* renewed had taken the opposition in its stride.

Left: Terrain factors increasingly entered into the operational planning of panze leaders; in this picture Guderian has halted for a progress report.

Left: Whenever marshland threatened to delay the advance, panzer engineers were called forward to lay temporary roads. Guderian's staff car can be seen displayir the identifying 'G' of his Gruppe and a corps headquarters tactical sign.

Left: During summer, the movement of heavy weapons was not a problem. Here a 15cm howitzer SFH18 is draw by an 8-ton purpose-built machine, the Sd Kfz 7. Artiller was generally moved well forward to play a crucial role i defeating enemy attacks, usually before they could reac the main battle line.

Above: The autumn and spring rains turned the ground to mud which led to a loss of mobility for even the light Volkswagen 82.

First and Fourth Panzer Armies, leading the summer offensive, pressed home their attacks in conjunction with powerful air support, working tirelessly, yet to no real advantage. For the Russians, preliminary battles at Issyum had resulted in a repetition of large-scale losses. Tank actions of rare ferocity had been fought out on the Ukranian Steppe; in the Don bend in particular. Fourth Panzer Army in action with VIII Air Corps, the best-equipped of the available Luftwaffe ground-attack forces, had been constantly engaged; first in the eastwards thrust to Voronezh and then southwards in the Don corridor to Stalingrad, while simultaneously First Panzer Army pressed into the Caucasus. Such victories as these proved worthless. The 250,000-strong German Sixth Army, including six mobile divisions, had been lost at Stalingrad and no significant envelopment achieved. Nothing could hide the fact that 1942 had not produced the expected decisive victory.

No review of the changing fortunes of the panzer force can ignore the fighting in North Africa (map 5). In Libya, as hitherto in the Balkans, German forces were deployed in the role of 'fire brigade', assisting the Italian Army which was facing disastrous military setbacks.

At first only two panzer divisions served to create the Deutsches Afrika Korps progressively organized into Panzer-armee Afrika under General Rommel; 5th Light, converted to 21st Panzer and shortly afterwards 15th Panzer. Two light divisions, 90th and 164th, fighting alongside Italian infantry and armour substantially improved the offensive capacity of Rommel's desert force. German strength in North

Africa was also to benefit from the timely deployment of 2nd Air Fleet in Sicily and finally the arrival of a third, 10th Panzer Division in Tunisia. Rommel's armoured divisions, 15th and 21st, were basically equipped to the same scale as divisions fighting on the eastern front. Three Italian armoured divisions: Ariete, Littorio and eventually Centauro, contributed more in numbers than power to the panzer army. But the African theatre was never considered more than a side-show by OKW. Consequently Rommel, who might have linked-up with von Kleist pushing through the Caucasus and on through Persia, was starved of the resources that could have taken him to Suez and beyond.

The tanks used in the earliest days of desert fighting were standard Pz Kpfw I, II and III series. Later came the much respected Pz Kpfw III and IV 'specials' with long-barrelled 5cm or 7.5cm guns respectively. These and other armoured fighting vehicles, including 8-wheeled armoured cars, unlike Italian armour serving with Ariete and Littorio, were on a par with if not superior to those in service with the British Army, the Matilda and 'Cruiser' tanks. But an influx of new American equipment into the theatre, Honeys, Grants and, above all, the formidable, 30-ton Sherman, armed and armoured to match the panzer 'specials', would go far towards tipping the armoured balance in favour of Eighth Army.

Broadly speaking, the 'African' panzer divisions – according to reports released by Wünsdorf technical centre and Panzer School I – were reasonably satisfied with the performance of their armoured vehicles. Motor cycles and 'soft' transport were less well regarded. All suffered the scouring effect of sand on engine performance. In respect of numbers, regimental strengths, like supplies in general, gave much less cause for optimism. War establishments were rarely fulfilled; reinforcement and supplies mostly ended up at the bottom of the Mediterranean – intercepted as a result of outstanding British Intelligence successes with 'Ultra' (*see* Part 2, Panzer signals and 'Ultra'). Yet despite such unfavourable circumstances, Rommel's more often than not inspired handling of armour, demanding and mostly receiving the highest level of support from subordinate commanders and staffs, would force British opponents to the brink of collapse. But Axis air power in North Africa was never able more than fleetingly to challenge the supremacy of the RAF or later the combined RAF and US air forces in Tunisia. Rommel's supreme disadvantage in the air was also fatally matched by Italian inability to guarantee the security of a long and constantly interrupted German supply line stretching back through the desert across the Mediterranean to Naples, or alternatively through Greece into Germany itself, the source of replacement engines and new vehicles. After twice outmanoeuvring British Eighth Army, inflicting savage defeats and reducing Tobruk in June 1942 (map 9), Rommel reigned supreme, forcing British commanders back upon Cairo and a battle of attrition. At El Alamein the Desert Fox was beaten; a tenacious British defence and an overwhelming counter-stroke tearing the heart out of Panzerarmee Afrika.

The Luftwaffe, eclipsed in air battles and unable to push its ground organization forward at the same rapid pace as the Panzerarmee, left Rommel particularly short on air reconnaissance and at the mercy of Allied air power. Lacking air support of his own, and resources with which to fight a mobile battle, Rommel could do no more and, after conflict with Hitler over intentions, turned about. The British counter-stroke 'Lightfoot' followed by 'Supercharge', starting on 23 October 1942 and directed by General Bernard Montgomery, had been a set-piece armour and infantry assault supported by massive air force and artillery concentrations. Montgomery had 'crumbled' Rommel's infantry. Starting with a superiority of more than four to one in (German) armour – a preponderance of Grants and Shermans tipping the balance in Eighth Army's favour and easily outnumbering Rommel's few Pz Kpfw IV 'specials' and lesser support – all that remained for the Panzerarmee after 4 November, when Montgomery's offensive had reduced the combined German-Italian tank strength to fewer than twenty machines, was a long fighting withdrawal to Tunisia. There, more than 1,500 miles away under Fifth Panzer Army, a newcomer to the German order of battle, a fresh German build-up was bringing new divisions to Africa – Hermann Goering, 10th Panzer, a Tiger battalion and more – which, had they been made available earlier, would have totally changed the picture for Rommel's panzer army.

But more unrewarding battles, command changes and conflict with higher authority leading Rommel into short-lived command of Army Group Africa before departing the desert for higher employment in the Balkans and Italy signalled an end to the Field Marshal's African career. Thereafter as inspector of coastal defences western Europe and C-in-C, Army Group 'B', Rommel would plan the defence of the west-European seaboard including Normandy where his experience of Allied air power pinning the panzer force to the ground before and after Alamein would all too strongly shape his views on the vulnerability of armoured formations to air attack. In consequence Rommel was to stress to Hitler the need to subject the defensive movement

Left: Wehrmacht supply columns, transferring from the eastern to the western theatres, frequently broke down as a result of water-logging; the provision of half-tracks helped to ease this problem.

of panzer divisions to the least possible degree of intervention; a warning destined to fall upon deaf ears. With operational control in North Africa passing to Army Group Tunis (von Arnim), the combined German and Italian force in North Africa enduring concentric pressure in consequence of the Anglo-US invasion of Morocco and Algeria (Operation 'Torch') proved unable to stave off disaster and collapsed. By the middle of May 1943 the war in Africa was over. DAK, three panzer, four motorized divisions, and 230,000 infantry went into Allied prisoner-of-war camps. Before the collapse, some personnel did manage to escape to Sicily or Italy. Of those that did, elements of Herman Goering and 15th Panzer without heavy weapons, many were to rejoin rear echelons to be reconstituted; HG was to be rebuilt, 15th Panzer converted to a panzer grenadier division and, like HG, deployed in support of Italian infantry divisions in Sicily. Both divisions would strengthen the defence of mainland Europe.

Right: The T34, which Second Panzer Army first encountered at Mzensk on the road to Moscow, came as an unpleasant surprise to Guderian who demanded increased firepower to counter it.

Right: Rail-borne supplies were no safer from attack, this time by partisans, and local defence units had to be raised to protect them.

5. Decline and fall of the panzer force, 1943–5

The disastrous consequences for the German Army of overwhelming Allied victories absorbing and destroying panzer divisions piecemeal in Africa and southern Russia during the winter of 1942–3 had been compounded by an unsuccessful Fourth Panzer Army attempt to raise the siege of Sixth Army which, together with a substantial part of Fourth Panzer Army, had been locked into Stalingrad since 19 November 1942 (map 12). Hoth's urgently assembled relief force of three panzer divisions – 23rd taken from von Kleist in the Caucasus, a refitted 6th railed from France to join 17th brought down from Army Group Centre – in the hands of experienced LVII Panzer Corps commander, Friedrich Kirchner, struggled forward despite midwinter conditions; Sixth Panzer (Raus) leading.

Opposed by a Red Army equally determined to halt the relief attempt, Kirchner thrust to within 48 kilometres of the city at which point, on 19 December, a new threat emerged close by, giving von Manstein, GOC, Army Group Don, cause for grave concern. Crumbling Italian resistance to renewed Russian attacks launched on an adjoining front along the River Chir started the rot. Faced with danger to Stalingrad's resupply points, von Manstein called off the relief operation and the exhausted panzer divisions were redeployed to cope with the new crisis which, should it result in the loss of Tazinskaya and Morovskaya, would destroy all continuity in air transport operations sustaining Sixth Army. Despite a successful intervention by panzer divisions sealing off the Russian spearheads on the very outskirts of the resupply points, von Manstein's worst fears were realized; the crucial airfields were lost and Paulus, deprived of supplies and unable to offer further resistance, surrendered an entire army.

So great a reverse shamed Hitler into action. He dismissed the Chief of the Army General Staff, Franz Halder, and replaced him with Kurt Zeitzler, a current favourite. He also shunned his generals and, distrustful of Prussian-German leadership of the Army, agreed with Himmler on expansion and strengthening of the Waffen SS with panzer divisions; quarrels developed between Zeitzler and Jodl over resource allocations and a general air of despondency seized the supreme military leadership. Strategically, the thrusting emphasis of *Blitzkrieg*, notwithstanding plans to break the Red Army at Kursk in July, would change to aggressive counter-action in self-defence; the Army, contending with counter-offensives, benefiting from arms and equipment deliveries from the west. Panzer divisions instead of sweeping forward in tightly co-ordinated mass would re-learn their tactics, turning individual mobility to account – sealing-off break-through offensives, organizing relief columns and adopting new measures to contain the progress of massive Russian motorized penetrations. At Hitler's senseless insistence, panzer divisions would succumb time and again defending ground unnecessarily.

The sacrifice of so many troops in coming months as Red Army Fronts deployed tanks and motorized forces in manoeuvres surpassing even the best of *Blitzkrieg* operations, would rarely win benefits for the defence. In passing from years of sweeping victory in Poland and France, where the panzer force had swept all before it, future action would degenerate into desperate battles for survival. German belief in victory, despite the menacing power of the Red Army and its increasingly sophisticated methods of warfare, no less so than that of the Red Air Force, revitalized and secure in new production localities in the Urals, would remain unshaken.

Left and right: Russian resistance necessitated close contact between the advancing German armour and fighting troops; panzer grenadiers were lifted into combat in semi-tracked armoured carriers (SPW) which assumed increasing importance on the battlefield. The work-horse in this area was the Sd Kfz 251 which was produced in a variety of forms with the needs of commanders, mortar crews, medical teams, etc., all provided for.

But of gave concern to the General Staff was a host of new Russian equipment, including aircraft deliveries from the Western Allies, legions of tanks and armoured fighting vehicles, not the least of which were powerful assault guns copied from the German model and soon to take effect on the battlefield. In another Russian development, increased fire-support from the 'Stalin organ' – a fearsome multi-barrelled rocket-launcher which the Army would counter with its own projector, the six-barrelled *Nebelwerfer* – would raise artillery concentrations to new levels.

In response to challenging conditions at the front, a new generation of German armoured fighting vehicles and transport machines bred in the harsh conditions of Eastern Front operations were shortly to enter service. Yet mounting evidence of Hitler's failure to provide effective war direction was to surface in unending retreat, vehicle, weapon and equipment shortages, declining fuel supplies and in crisis situations a general disregard for the views of commanders on the spot. Reporting divisional tank strength in December 1942 during the attempt to relieve Stalingrad, 17th Panzer Division listed fewer than thirty armoured vehicles on establishment. Above all, the absence of the Luftwaffe, drawn-off

for action to defend the Reich from increasingly effective Anglo-US bombing or cleared from the skies by the Red Air Force, would accelerate the demise of the Wehrmacht. But all was not yet lost and the German Army was to demonstrate in future battles its remarkable resilience. Following the catastrophe at Stalingrad, von Manstein in particular would succeed with First and Fourth Panzer Armies in restoring the southern front (map 13). The spring of 1943, moreover, would witness a new milestone in the history of the panzer force.

On the unemployed list since December 1941, General Guderian was recalled by Hitler in February 1943 and appointed to a new post – that of Inspector-General of Armoured Troops; Panzertruppen – hitherto Schnelltruppen. The Inspector-General's responsibilities covered technical development of weapons and vehicle production planning, training and replacement programming for the Army, Waffen SS and Luftwaffe. Motorized infantry, renamed panzer grenadiers, were also included in the shake-up. With characteristic zeal Guderian set about the crucial task of revitalizing the worn-down panzer force. With combat efficiency at a low ebb, following years of action and

Below: Rail routes were also defended by well-sited anti-aircraft and anti-tank guns, often mounted on platforms on the trains themselves.

Above: An improvised ferry carrying a motor-cycle unit across the Dnieper. The motive power comes from a 20-man engineer assault boat lashed to a pneumatic infantry model driven by an outboard motor. Rafts were constructed to carry heavier items; these were made from assault boats and pontoon decking.

vehicles mounting a 7.5cm gun to combat the menacing power of Russian armour. An increase in heavy (turretless) self-propelled weapons to assist in attack or defence, and easier to produce than tanks, was decided upon as an urgent requirement. Production of these weapons, the Pz Kpfw III/IV assault gun (Sturmgeschütz) in particular, consequently increased elevenfold. From 788 vehicles produced in 1942, numbers rose to 3,406 in 1943 and would continue to expand at a faster rate than tank production – a true measure of change in store for the panzer force. In the aftermath of German failure at Stalingrad, Russian exploitation had continued for 300 miles between the Don and the Dnieper across the Donetz until von Manstein's (Army Group Don) counter-stroke had brought the offensive to a halt (map 13); the re-capture of Kharkov by SS Panzer Corps Hausser under command of Fourth Panzer Army proving the culminating point of von Manstein's achievement. During the course of the action, planned and executed in high *Blitzkrieg* fashion (*see* Part 4, Stukagruppen – Schlactgruppen), skillfully combined army-air operations inflicted grievous damage on Russian armour. When von Manstein had disposed of the Russian winter threat, the focus of OKW attention in the east swung to plans for a great summer offensive Operation 'Citadel' – the battle for Kursk. The German armoured build-up to 'pinch out' this threatening Russian bulge was prodigious (map 14).

Concentrating panzer and panzer grenadier divisions on abnormally narrow sectors and in greater numbers than at any time since the invasion began, the point of main effort would lie with Hausser's SS Panzer Corps deployed north of Bjelgorod in the centre of the southern build-up. North of the bulge, Ninth Army (Model) disposed of a near equivalent number of armoured formations. Forty-three divisions, including eight panzer divisions, Gross Deutschland and supporting units with 2,700 tanks and assault guns, were drawn up to face 100 Russian divisions (five tank armies with 3,306 tanks and assault guns). The most violent and decisive tank battle in history, Operation 'Citadel', opened on 5 July 1943 with considerable success attending the early efforts of the panzer force despite bad weather. New tanks and self-propelled guns, Panthers, Tigers, Ferdinands and Hornets, the product of hard-won Eastern Front experience were brought into service – not all with Guderian's approval. Some, such as the Panthers and Ferdinands were committed prematurely with disappointing results. Shortcomings in most cases were made good, but the SP 'Ferdinand', renamed 'Elefant', failed totally and the surviving vehicles found future employment in defensive battles either in Italy (Anzio) or in the east where operations would increasingly favour delaying action involving tanks and SP guns in ambush-like situations.

The battle for Kursk, coinciding with Operation 'Husky', the Allied invasion of Sicily on 12 July, ended in total German disaster. After losing more than a thousand tanks and three hundred assault guns in the attempt to force six successive lines of defence, and counter a new Russian offensive ploughing into Second Panzer Army (which had long since given up most of its armour), Hitler called it off. The power of the panzer force, into which everything had been committed at Kursk, faded in a welter of engagements. Soviet tanks and aircraft striking against the flank of Hoth's Panzer Corps at Prochorowka on 12 July finally put an end

crippling losses in men and material, both in Africa and Russia, Guderian's neglected expertise was a dire necessity. Inaugurating a new training command with programmes at Wünsdorf and Krampnitz (the Schnelltruppen School's re-designated Panzertruppenschule I and II) and collaborating with Albert Speer, the Armaments Minister, Guderian proposed to reduce the number of tank models to a minimum. Speer and Guderian were to prove remarkably successful in rationalizing tank design and raising production – increasing Pz Kpfw output by 30 per cent in 1943 and more than doubling it from the 1942 level of 4,278 vehicles to a high peak of 9,161 in 1944. Losses, on the other hand, continued to increase faster than production so that by the end of 1944 the actual surplus would amount to a disappointing 15 per cent.

Reviewing equipment tables and personnel strengths of panzer and panzer grenadier divisions, the new Inspector-General paid special attention to the need for better self-propelled artillery and anti-tank weapons – Panzerjaeger and Jagdpanzer – predominantly turretless Pz Kpfw III/IV

to panzer progress – despite the intervention of Luftwaffe ground-attack squadrons flying the newest Hs 129 and breaking up concentrations of enemy armour (a significant development, discussed in Part 4, Stukagruppen – Schlactgruppen), German offensive power was never to recover from the setback at Kursk although in the following year a dozen or so SS and Army panzer divisions would be deployed in the west contesting Operation 'Overlord', the Allied invasion of Normandy; the losses in trained crews and fighting machines at Kursk and its aftermath would never be made good.

At the conclusion of 'Citadel' with the strategic initiative swinging irretrievably in favour of the Red Army, the forward progress of the panzer divisions was finally halted. In the air, Luftwaffe resources were increasingly diverted to defend the Reich and no great Army reliance could be placed upon an air force mainly dependent upon obsolete and inadequate machines; the Ju 87s of Spanish Civil War days proving unable to cope with modern Russian types – their successors, the Fw 190 and Hs 129 in short supply. Russian air power on the other hand, gaining strength from new manufacturing locations hidden deep in the Urals and well out of reach of a Luftwaffe lacking a four-engined bomber, imposed its authority with much improved fighter and ground-attack types including tank-busting Stormovicks. Pursuing summer and autumn offensives to encircle Manstein (with four armies deployed west of the Donetz and south of Pripet), the Red Army struck powerful blows at Kharkov and Kiev; Fourth Panzer Army holding grimly on to Kharkov for a time while to the south First Panzer Army fought without success to retain Krivoi Rog and Nikopol. Despite local successes in counter-attacks, the retrograde movement of the panzer divisions continued unchecked.

Carrying the war into 1944, the Red Army would strike again with concentrated force at Army Group South before turning its attention to Army Groups Centre and North, trapping the panzer force time and again and exhausting its energies. A timely operation by II SS Panzer Corps in the spring of 1944 (map 15) rescued First Panzer Army, reduced to thirty tanks and encircled with a Leibstandarte divisional battle group at Kamenets Podolsk in North Ukraine. Disaster on the scale of Stalingrad was narrowly averted. Only weeks earlier First Panzer Army in the relief of Cherkassy, fifty miles to the east, had organized the escape of SS Wiking surrounded on the Dnieper. One of the most formidable German divisions on the Eastern Front, Wiking lost all its equipment in the débâcle; the Luftwaffe played a vital role in transporting supplies to encircled formations. (*See* Part 4, New Horizons in Transport.)

In the Mediterranean, where collapse of Axis resistance in Tunisia was followed by the Allied invasion of Sicily on 12 July 1943, panzer divisions were to fight tough delaying battles. The action in Italy is summarized in Part 6. In France, the Western Allies compounded German problems by opening a third front in Normandy, bringing Fifth Panzer Army (Europe) into action. Demands on the panzer force were now set to increase out of all proportion to available resources. Despite Guderian's efforts to rebuild divisions for limited offensive roles there would be too little equipment and, given the overwhelming presence of Allied air power, too few opportunities for their concentrated use in counter-attacks.

In a year of destiny for Hitler and the Wehrmacht, June 1944 marked the beginning of the end for the panzer force. Starting on 22 June, the third anniversary of Hitler's invasion of Russia, four Russian army groups (Fronts) deploying 5,000 tanks and 6,000 aircraft would henceforth allow no respite for Army Group Centre which collapsed almost at once under the hammer blows of tank and infantry attacks; defensive actions such as that forced upon Third Panzer Army holding the line at Vitebsk, demanded great sacrifice in the flux of disaster. Understrength panzer divisions lacking even the most basic of vehicles and weapons, as the year progressed, were switched between sectors and fronts, from west to east and back again. Schools were combed out by OKH, and truly impoverished formations, with grandiose names, Clausewitz, Muncheberg and others, were raised for action in daunting circumstances. All would serve to the best of their limited abilities.

On the Russian side, tank armies bolstered by masses of transport delivered by the Western Allies and benefiting from tank production soaring to new levels made sweeping

Above: The great turning-point of Stalingrad as seen from a Stuka, with burnt-out fuel tanks visible on the right bank of the Volga. The devastation for the Wehrmacht was total with some 200,000 troops taken prisoner (*see* map 11).

Right: A panzer battle group passes a burning T34.

Right: The '88' on a Pz Kpfw IV chassis (Hornet) provided much needed support for those divisions expected to cope with a new breed of Russian tanks and assault guns.

advances through German fronts stretched between Baltic and Danube. Leningrad was prised free of Army Group North by Russian Fronts clearing a way through Estonia and Lithuania, while at Jassy and Debrecen panzer battles flared as other Fronts driving through Roumania and Hungary closed on Budapest (map 19). Operation 'Bagration', the Red Army's June offensive against Army Group Centre, carried to Warsaw and the Vistula, progressing a distance of 200 miles in four weeks, culminating in battles for the Polish capital. Reorganizing its tank and motorized forces on German lines, the Red Army, although lacking sophisticated infantry personnel carriers of the German type, exploited heavy fire power and manoeuvrability to remarkable effect.

In this fifth year of war, with Berlin itself threatened east and west, there would be a marked change of emphasis in German armament production – switched from the all-out manufacture of tanks to the production of defensive armoured fighting vehicles, notably Jagdpanzer. In tabling strengths for 1945 panzer divisions, Guderian's concept

would be wholly defensive; the tank complement of a future panzer regiment amounting to no more than 54 vehicles, a far cry from pre-war tank strengths when in 1935 a panzer brigade comprised 561 tanks. Suffering the consequences of Hitler's war direction, with its maladroit insistence on rigid defence, tying the Army to first one string of 'fortress' towns – Vitebsk, Kowel, Tarnopol, Bobruisk, Minsk – and then another, panzer battles to shield or relieve immobile infantry sapped every sinew of the once formidable panzer force – mortally weakening the defensive capacity of the Wehrmacht. During the summer of 1944, Army Group Centre alone suffered the loss of 28 infantry divisions. And not only in the east was the army saddled with Hitler's mismanagement leading to the wasteful employment of panzer divisions in unsuitable defensive tasks.

The return of vast new Allied armies to the continent, in Operation 'Overlord' on 6 June had heralded a renewal of panzer operations in the west (map 16). In month-long battles of attrition the panzer force was bled white. The Führer's uncompromising attitude towards winning the war

(which he directed from East Prussia), allowing no respite for the armed services, accelerated the destruction of two complete armies, Seventh and Fifth Panzer including eleven Army and SS panzer divisions. Contending with land, sea and air opposition arrayed against them in overwhelming strength, the panzer divisions fought the Battle of Normandy to the point of extinction.

Jagdpanzers, a new category of self-propelled defensive vehicles — including the formidable King Tiger making an appearance on the battlefield in Normandy — were too few to do more than fleetingly sustain the powers of resistance needed by panzer divisions enduring day and night assault by US, British, French and Polish armour sweeping forward to the Seine and beyond. Allied air power, destroying German tanks and transport in vast numbers while sealing the Normandy battlefield against reinforcement, robbed the panzer force of its vitality. Rommel's views on the need to avoid unnecessary movement by deploying panzer divisions close to the beaches and thereby counter constant air surveillance and attack were ignored by Hitler and the High Command — with grievous consequences. Panzer divisions were decimated by air power. Anti-aircraft tanks, Whirlwind and Ostwind, that might have protected the panzer divisions, were only belatedly entering service. Without them and in the absence of air cover, Fifth Panzer Army under General Eberbach, was rendered impotent. Aided by a brilliant deception plan focusing Hitler's attention on the wrong (Pas-de-Calais) invasion area, Field Marshal Montgomery's strategy of attrition followed by the sweeping advance of US armour led by General Patton proved decisive. In this situation, verging once more on total disaster, the Army leadership in Normandy was obliged to defer its professional responses in favour of instructions coming direct from Führer Headquarters in East Prussia; none of the senior commanders on the spot, von Runstedt, Rommel or von Kluge, being allowed to make even the slightest alteration to counter-offensive plans conceived over

a map table in Rastenburg. The predictable result was a disaster greater even than Stalingrad. Forty-three German divisions were sacrificed in a strategy of unyielding defence; none of the mainly SS panzer divisions escaping across the Seine with more than ten tanks! (Model).

At the height of the battle on 20 July 1944, a number of disaffected Generals made an unsuccessful attempt on Hitler's life. In its aftermath General Guderian, enjoying Hitler's grudging respect, was promoted Chief of the General Staff in succession to General Zeitzler, and Field Marshal Model arrived in the west to take command of the theatre. Opting to continue the evacuation of Normandy, Model withdrew the broken Wehrmacht across the Seine to the western frontiers of Germany. Dramatic battles such as the defence of Arnhem (II SS Panzer Corps) and fighting around Aachen, would steal newspaper headlines bolstering German morale, but a panzer force equipped and organized for swift, effective, retaliatory action no longer existed. All attempts by the new Chief of the Army General Staff Guderian to assembles such a force on the Eastern Front were to end in frustration. In the west Hitler was planning a counter-strike to recapture Antwerp so as to isolate Allied armies in Holland and north-west Germany. Allowing little respite for the panzer divisions, Hitler's new offensive, 'Autumn Mist' starting on 15 December, would destroy much of what was being committed within 5th Panzer and a new Sixth SS Panzer Army (map 17).

Despite protests from von Runstedt, C-in-C, West, recalled from retirement to direct the offensive, Hitler gambled with nine re-equipped panzer divisions to restore the Army's fortunes. Lead by Generals von Manteuffel and Dietrich, the panzer armies were to be launched against US forces, surprising them in rest sectors of the Ardennes and catching them off-balance. But 'Autumn Mist', materializing west of the Rhine in the short daylight hours of December and benefiting from the bad weather which grounded British and US air forces, was thwarted by American troops holding

Above: A graveyard of wrecked Russian armour of passing interest to the inquisitive.

Right: Equipment became heavier and more powerful after Stalingrad with steel skirts, as seen here, fitted to protect assault guns and medium tanks.

Right: A towed 7.5cm Pak. This gun allowed German crews to engage marauding Russian armour at longer ranges and with increased effectiveness.

out in Bastogne and turning other towns into strong points. Five or six hundred priceless tanks and assault guns, Germany's last reserve diverted from hard-pressed armies in the east, were sacrificed in the attempt. The armies involved were extricated with difficulty. In the east, where Soviet progress had brough the Red Army to the Vistula opposite Berlin and through Roumania to the Danube, Hitler decided upon a new move. In January 1945 Sixth SS Panzer Army was transferred across Europe not to defend Berlin but western Hungary where the Red Army, having encircled Budapest, was threatening the Wehrmacht's oil-producing centre at Nagykanizsa – more important than ever to the

economy after the loss of Roumanian capacity at Ploesti (map 19). Nevertheless the vital oilfields were soon lost with dire consequences (*see* Part 4).

Unable to halt the Red Army driving for Berlin and Vienna in January 1945, the heartlands of Germany were exposed to attack from offensives launched on all sides. On the Eastern Front, 12½ panzer divisions were all that remained to serve two army groups deployed between the Carpathians and the Baltic. Fourth Panzer Army, holding the line south of Warsaw, collapsed leaving Panzer Corps Nehring and others to survive in a moving pocket before contacting Gross Deutschland Corps, sent from Lodz to relieve them (map 18). Protracted and ferocious battles for Berlin and Vienna absorbed panzer divisions, independent panzerjaeger battalions, assault-gun brigades and a new but ineffectual Eleventh (SS) Panzer Army, also the rumps of First and Fourth Panzer Armies and, fighting for Budapest, a re-deployed Sixth SS Panzer Army (map 19). All confronted the enemy in suicidally small numbers on fronts crumbling into nothing. In north-west Europe, powerful Anglo-US armies lead by armoured and motorized divisions at full strength, extended their drive to encircle the Ruhr, the heart of German industrial power in the west. In the process, Fifth Panzer Army was trapped and destroyed. The Red Army sweeping through Hungary, overruning Poland and isolating East Prussia, surged uncontainably through Pomerania and Silesia, closing up to the Oder less than a hundred miles from Berlin (map 20).

Panzer divisions in continuous action on all fronts were reduced to battalion and company battle groups with handfuls of vehicles and men, contesting step by step every new Russian or Allied advance. Third Panzer Army on the Oder defending Stettin, make-shift armoured units serving Ninth Army at Küstrin and Frankfurt, and Fourth Panzer Army deployed along the Neisse at Cottbus, Spremberg and Bautzen, recorded local successes, all dearly bought. Depleted battle groups standing four-square in the path of the Red Army's ruthlessly conceived offensive against Berlin, survived through grim determination, closing on enemy armour with the deadly *Panzerfaust* – a hand-held, anti-tank rocket-launcher modelled on the American Bazooka and, like anti-tank mines in determined hands, used to crippling effect. Reporting on a week's fighting during march 1945, OKW recorded 300 Russian tanks destroyed in eight days, 135 of them in close combat. The armoured fighting troops that had once so triumphantly sown the seeds of

victory for Hitler and the Third Reich, finally reaped a whirlwind of annihilation. When tanks and transport were stranded for want of fuel, their crews destroyed them before joining mixed formations of all kinds to fight on foot until they too were swept into defeat; the Luftwaffe, stretched in all directions, would occasionally find the strength to re-supply encircled formations, at the same time supporting 'fortress' cities such as Breslau, holding out for three months and counting the days to capitulation.

In this desperate hour panzer divisions, gravely weakened by years of action taking a heavy toll of experienced commanders and units, counted for no more than symbols on enemy situation maps. When the Red Army broke into Pomerania, Third Panzer Army possessed fourteen tanks and 164 assault guns with which to oppose six Russian armies. In the ruined shell of Berlin, no more of a safe haven for Hitler than any other of Germany's shattered towns and cities, where battle raged before fuel supplies dried up completely, single-vehicle combat by SS and Army battle groups was the order of the day. Sharing the defence with Volkssturm veterans of the First World War, Hitler Youth and refugees from the eastern provinces – many of them women and girls – with swastikered armbands declaring allegiance to a state on the verge of collapse – battle groups continued the fight; bicycles serving as transport for anti-tank auxiliaries. The life expectancy of junior leaders in those grim days was forty-eight hours. For the defenders of the city, isolated from all landward connection with the interior of Germany after 27 April, the situation was hopeless. The efforts of Muncheberg and surviving battle groups, including those of SS Nordland and SS Charlemagne fighting in the Tiergarten only blocks away from Führer HQ, were doomed to failure. Yet Hitler, wrecked in mind and body, following years of treatment for health disorders and never properly

Below: Emulating Germany's success with self-propelled weapons, the Red Army introduced a similar range of heavily armoured vehicles using the T34 chassis. The 3[ ]ton SU-85, pictured here, required a crew of four, carri[ ]an 8.5cm gun and had a roa[ ]speed of 34mph.

Below: An upgunned version of the same vehicle carrying a 12.2cm howitzer.

Bottom: The 45-ton Josef Stalin JSU-152 required a crew of five. It carried a 15.2cm gun howitzer and could travel at 23mph.

recovered from the attempt on his life in July 1944, was determined to fight on – obsessed with map flags and disputing with Guderian (who had wanted to re-deploy Sixth SS Panzer Army in defence of Berlin but had been overruled) how best to make use of meagre and failing resources. Bitter recrimination followed. Guderian fell from favour and was sent on indefinite leave to be replaced by General Krebs. Directing operations from a command bunker sited beneath a garden of the Chancellery, Hitler took his own life in Berlin on 30 April.

For the Panzer troops and others of the German armed services bolstering armies and army groups of indifferent size and power, fighting in defence of Courland, East Prussia, Berlin and Alpine Germany, the end came officially nine days later on 9 May 1945. Campaigning the length and breadth of Europe, von Seeckt's Kraftfahrtruppen, the motor supply troops of the twenties, Guderian's Schnell-truppen of the thirties – Hitler's Panzertruppen – had witnessed triumph wither into defeat. In *Blitzkrieg* against unprepared and incompetent opponents the panzer divisions

Left: Rocket weapons raised the power of artillery fire to new levels and were used to good effect by both sides on the Eastern Front. The multi-barrelled 'Stalin organ' was matched by a six-barrelled 15cm Nebelwerfer towed into action and a ten-barrelled self-propelled version.

Left: A later version Pz Kpfw assault gun with rounded gun mantlet and close-defence machine-gun. Production gradually overtook tank output and in 1945 it had equal importance in the panzer divisions.

had reigned supreme, principally in the battle for France. But in later campaigns, bolstering infantry with no adequate anti-tank or anti-aircraft protection of their own and thus easy prey to the *Blitzkrieg* tactics of their opponents, the panzer and panzer grenadier divisions suffered the consequences of Hitler's maladroit war direction (self-appointed Army C-in-C, December 1941). Seldom willing to accept professional advice on the need for concentrating panzer divisions in a counter-attack role – exploiting their potential for rapid intervention in a crisis – Hitler instead allowed that power to be frittered away in generally wasteful defensive tasks; a doctrinaire insistence on 'not one step back' proving no substitute for a strategy of flexible defence.

Von Manstein's recovery of Kharkov in 1943 and less spectacular success by other army group commanders, counter-attacking the Red Army as it smashed a way through Roumania, Poland and Hungary at Jassy, Wilomin and Debrecen in 1944, all demonstrated effective mobile intervention. Nevertheless, in conceiving air power as a strike weapon more potent than the tank, Hitler's implacable enemies broke the Wehrmacht and its panzer force to pieces. With an advantage in high-grade Intelligence pinpointing targets in 'Ultra' detail, Allied air power secured the defeat of the panzer divisions, nailing them to the ground and sealing their fate. The Third Reich assailed from all sides collapsed in the process.

Part 2.
The grand design

1. Panzer and panzer grenadier

Starting with three panzer divisions raised in October 1935, the German Army put into the field in the space of ten years, 86 panzer and panzer grenadier divisions, thirty or more panzer corps and eight panzer armies of which, one – Fifth Panzer Army following its destruction in North Africa in 1943 – was reformed for action in Normandy 1944. Subordinate armoured units including panzer regiments and battalions were raised in varying numbers to serve these formations or to fight independently as Army and Corps troops at the disposal of relevant headquarters. At the highest operational level stood the Panzer Army (abbreviated to PzAOK=Panzer Armee Oberkommando) which according to the German system was essentially a command body of specialist officers controlling combatant units and formations allotted in accordance with changing operational needs. Panzer armies were identified by number or name, and made their first appearance in action against the Red Army on the Central Front in 1941 – their role being to control increasingly complex mobile operations and a burgeoning number of panzer divisions in the battle for Moscow. Raised in a separate series from the normal type of army (AOK), their numbers, First, Second, Third and Fourth, were expanded to include Panzer Army Afrika (PzAOK 5) (Tunisia 1943, reformed Normandy 1944), Sixth (SS) in action on main fronts east and west, and Eleventh (SS) mostly engaged by the Red Army in Pomerania and the battle for Berlin in 1945. A war chronology of these formations, featuring subordinate panzer corps and divisions, also panzer action in Italy where the highest regular armoured formation to take the field was the panzer corps – two of which serving regular armies were deployed in defence of the peninsular – is provided in Part 6.

At each panzer army headquarters, evolving with (SS) exceptions out of *ad hoc* panzer groups whose origins lay in pre-existing panzer corps, permanently appointed personnel were supervised by a chief of staff whose main branches – Operations (1A), Supply and Rear Services (1B) Intelligence (1C) – were supplemented by Army supply, signals, field security, legal, cartographic and other ancillary personnel. An army artillery commander (Arko) and air liaison officer (Koluft), also with subordinates, worked alongside permanent headquarters staff. Executive assis-

tants (ordnance officers, e.g., 01 Ops, 03 Intelligence) and additional technical and administrative officers, including anti-tank specialists and translators, might also be seconded to a headquarters when operations so required. Upwards of 600 officers and men served at a panzer army headquarters. A panzer group (Panzergruppe) like any other group (or gruppe) whether Armeegruppe, Korpsgruppe or Battalion Kampfgruppe was essentially an impromptu battle formation whose 'standing' was indicated by the rank of its commanding, commissioned or non-commissioned, officer. Generals(Obersten) von Kleist, Hoth and Guderian, in France in 1940 and afterwards in Russia together with Generaloberst Hoepner, all operated panzer groups (controlling armoured, motorized and regular infantry corps) within the framework of higher (Army) operations until their own commands were upgraded to panzer army. Panzer and panzer grenadier divisions organized into regiments and battalions all created Kampfgruppen (battle groups) within their permanent structure. The composition and strength of these *tactical* units depended upon whatever operational tasks were required of them; numbers if deficient being made up by 'outside' units.

The battle group system employed by tank (and infantry) formations was a means of concentrating and balancing a formation's powers where it was most needed. In so far as the panzer division was concerned, this more often than not entailed the creation of Kampfgruppen around the division's three principal combat units: the panzer regiment, with divisional armour concentrated into a powerful strike force; the panzer grenadier regiment, organized for action in a less demanding, usually supportive role; and the panzer reconnaissance battalion, equipped and organized for skirmishing and, like other units, reinforced when necessary with extra weapons from support companies. A prime early example of the battle group system in Africa during Operation 'Scorpion' is provided in Part 6 by Panzer Army Africa, 21 May 1941. A later example of battle groups in action (at Falaise in the closing stages of the war in Europe) is provided by 12th SS Hitler Jugend deployed in defence of Normandy (*see* Fifth Panzer Army, 8 August 1944 (D+ 63)). Battle groups, incidentally, posed considerable problems for Allied Intelligence staffs. With units of mixed kinds finding their way into battle groups, particularly in the

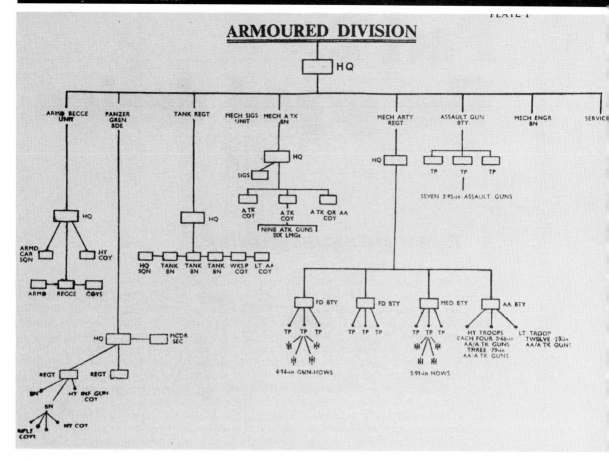

ARMOURED DIVISION

confusion of battle, the Intelligence officers' task of building a picture of a German order of battle could prove both difficult and time-consuming.

Panzer corps (Pz-Korps abbreviated to PzK) originated in the motorized armee-korps serving regular armies in the 1939/early 1940 campaigns. Throughout the war, divisions of any type, not only panzer and panzer grenadier, but also infantry divisions, might be allocated to a panzer corps in the light of changing operational needs; numbers varying usually from two to four, often daily. At times in later campaigns panzer corps consisted solely of infantry divisions. The number of panzer corps in the German Army, no more than four (motorized corps) at the start of the campaign in Poland and twelve at the outset in Russia, grew ultimately to about thirty, not all of which were in action at the same time (twelve on 1 January 1943, fifteen on 10 December 1944, including four Waffen SS), some having been lost in action. As the war progressed, these corps, particularly those of the Waffen SS, were favoured with extra heavy weapons; by mid-summer 1944, Tiger or King Tiger and Werfer (mortar) battalions were notably strengthening corps establishments and firepower. If required, additional engineers (Pioniere), medical (Sanitäts) and observation (Beobachtung) units would be available to corps commanders 'on loan' from Army (OKH) reserve. Other Army troops (Heerestruppen) at OKH disposal, included heavy bridging columns, road construction, railway artillery, heavy anti-tank and tank destroyer (Panzerjaeger and

Jagdpanzer) battalions and companies. Gross Deutschland (two battalions) the Leibstandarte SS Adolf Hitler and three other SS regiments, all motorized, plus two independent panzer brigades were included in this category in 1939. Support units of this kind could expect to operate with any formation, working alongside its 'organic' units.

The panzer division – the German Army's most powerful regular combat formation with a permanent establishment of weapons, vehicles and personnel – whose individual roles are elaborated in Part 3 – varied substantially in strength and composition over the years depending upon war organization tables in use or simply material availability. Identified by number or name, starting with three formations in 1935 (numbers 1 to 3), the panzer division was initially founded upon two (brigaded) panzer regiments – reduced to a single regiment by June 1941 in order to create additional divisions – one Schützen (panzer grenadier) brigade of two motorized infantry regiments (each of two Schutzen battalions with motor cycle companies), one reconnaissance battalion of three companies (one motor cycle), one anti-tank battalion, one artillery regiment, signals, engineers and supporting services.

The first three panzer divisions undergoing training in 1938 with XVI (mot) Corps, forerunner of Panzergruppe 4 in1941 (later Fourth Panzer Army) were followed over the years by divisions numbered 4–27, 116, Gross Deutschland, Panzer Lehr, Feldherrnhalle and, in 1944/45, divisions of lesser stature – FBD, FGD, Clausewitz, Holstein, Munche-

Above: Layout of an armoured (panzer) division comprising two panzer grenadier regiments and three tank battalions. In practice, by the end of 1943, most divisions were fighting with only a single panzer grenadier regiment and only one or two tank (or assault gun) battalions.

berg and others, none more powerful than brigade or regimental battle groups. Following no regular pattern of expansion, but raised in expectation of operational needs, the original 1935 panzer divisions were joined by three more in September 1939. This total of six panzer divisions plus a mixed (Division Kempf) joined in the campaign against Poland (map 2). By May 1940 in time for the Battle of France, the total stood at ten (map 3). In June 1941 at the start of the campaign against Russia (map 7), by the over-simple expedient of halving divisional tank strengths, the total was more than doubled to twenty-one; subsequent progress was less dramatic and after June 1941 the number of regular Army panzer divisions as distinct from the seven contributed from 1943 onwards by the Waffen SS, and to which an increasingly high proportion of new equipment was diverted, would not rise above twenty-nine. Impromptu panzer divisions raised in 1945 increased the total by ten. Certain divisions destroyed in action like those that had served Sixth Army at Stalingrad in 1942 (14th, 16th and 24th) or in the same year lost with Fifth Panzer Army in Tunisia (15th and 21st) were subsequently reformed. A handful of reserve Panzer Divisions, 155th, 178th, 179th, 233rd and 273rd, ended by providing personnel for the refitting of front-line divisions. None of the late 1944/45 divisions raised from panzer schools or war remnants with the outstanding exception of Panzer Lehr, formed basically from Panzer School 2 cadres at Krampnitz, exceeded battle group status. But it must be said that in times of crisis on the Eastern Front, following the collapse of Army Group Centre in June 1944, culminating in the battle for Berlin in 1945, these and other 'scratch' panzer formations of indifferent size and power, made a much needed contribution to the over-strained and rapidly diminishing resources of the panzer force.

Panzer grenadier divisions raised by the Army and Waffen SS, no more than twenty-one in the 1943 order of battle and rarely exceeding fifteen in action at any one time, were originally termed motorized (mot) infantry divisions. Unlike their more powerful panzer division counterparts, panzer grenadier divisions were neither designated nor numbered in a separate series, but their establishments varied similarly in accordance with changing organization tables and availability of equipment and personnel. Several, mostly SS, panzer grenadier divisions, were converted to SS panzer divisions. Independent panzer brigades, consisting basically of two battalions (one panzer, one panzer grenadier) were a 1944 emergency measure to create new defensive formations in the wake of catastrophes on both main fronts. Numbered 101–113 and of limited strength (35 tanks, twelve assault guns), they were mostly too weak and were incorporated into panzer or other divisions. In contrast to the declining number and power of Army panzer divisions as they were exhausted or destroyed in action was the growing contribution of the Waffen SS. Providing OKW with seven SS panzer, eleven SS panzer grenadier divisions, four SS panzer corps and two SS panzer army headquarters, the Waffen SS shouldered a burden of heavy and continuous fighting in later years. SS panzer divisions, notably those with Tiger companies on establishment, were exceptionally powerful formations. At their head, elevated from panzer grenadier status in 1943, were 1st Leibstandarte SS Adolf Hitler, 2nd SS Das Reich, 3rd SS Totenkopf and 5th SS

Wiking. Prior to their up-grading, all were superior even to Army panzer divisions. With the advent of 9th SS Hohenstaufen, 10th SS Frundsberg and 12th SS Hitler Jugend in 1944, the number of SS panzer divisions increased to seven. All were regularly kept up to strength, but as the quality of recruits declined and establishments were reduced, differences between SS and Army panzer divisions in strength and composition became less pronounced.

SS panzer grenadier divisions other than those converted to panzer status and mostly expanded from motorized infantry regiments serving on the Eastern Front included 4th SS 'Polizei', 11th SS 'Nordland', 16th 'Reichsführer'-SS and 17th SS 'Goetz von Berlichingen'. Less prominent formations by virtue of late or incomplete establishments were 18th SS 'Horst Wessel', 23rd SS 'Nederland', 27th SS 'Langemarck' and 28th SS 'Wallonien'. SS panzer corps (I–IV) served east, west and briefly in northern Italy (II) but never entered North Africa. The first SS panzer corps formed under Paul Hausser, designated II SS Panzer Corps, took control of the Leibstandarte, Reich and Totenkopf in the battle for Kharkov in 1943 (map 13). In Normandy in 1944 (map 16), 'Sepp' Dietrich lead I SS Panzer Corps until his promotion to GOC, Fifth Panzer Army; Felix Steiner commanded III (Germanisches) SS Panzer Corps in Courland and Pomerania before a new appointment brought him command of Eleventh (SS) Panzer Army. Herbert Gille also served only in the east, bringing IV SS Panzer Corps through 1944–5 campaigns east of Warsaw and west of Budapest (map 19). Two SS panzer armies were raised and deployed late in the war. Sixth SS Panzer Army (Dietrich), spearheading 'Autumn Mist', Hitler's 1944 Ardennes offensive (map 17), was – on Hitler's instructions and contrary to the general situation at the time – fully equipped with heavy weapons, tracked and wheeled vehicles; it controlled I and II SS Panzer Corps, and more, in battles for Brussels and Antwerp. The other, Eleventh SS Panzer Army (Steiner), a hybrid Army SS Headquarters, defended Pomerania and outer Berlin before redeployment in the Hartz Mountains took the Army briefly to the west in 1945.

The Luftwaffe created an air-mobile intervention force for OKW in 1943, by rebuilding its premier (1st and 2nd) Fallschirm Divisions and concentrating them at Istres in Provence, later raising by stages the powerful Hermann Goering (Fallschirm) Panzer Division – intended partly for commitment by air – a scheme that never materialized. The Panzer Division demonstrated sterling worth in Italy. The Luftwaffe's ultimate contribution to the panzer force, Fallschirm Panzer Corps HG, comprising HG 1st (Panzer) and HG 2nd (Panzer Grenadier) Divisions, campaigned vigorously in both East Prussia and Silesia, counter-attacking Russian spearheads at crisis points in battles for Königsberg and Berlin.

Panzer and panzer grenadier divisions raised by the Army, Waffen SS and even the Luftwaffe in 1943, spearheaded all critical German attacks and counter-attacks from 1939 to 1945. Concentrating heavy fire-power in their panzer regiments, the panzer divisions constituted the core of the German Army's offensive capacity – despite battle attrition, production shortages, terrain factors and changing tactical requirements frequently giving rise to modifications in equipment and organization. In later years these formations, instead of exploiting their flexibility and striking power to the degree apparent in *Blitzkrieg* campaigns 1939–41, were more often than not unable to break free from a day-to-day commitment to Hitler's linear 'no step back' strategy. They were, in any event, too few to win more than temporary respite from retreat. Ironically, as the war progressed and the number of panzer and panzer grenadier divisions increased, tank strengths declined. From four (brigaded) battalions with 324 tanks per panzer division in 1939, by 1944 the level had fallen to two battalions of 159 tanks per division. The 1944 panzer division then consisted of a single panzer regiment, a panzer grenadier (motorized infantry) brigade of two regiments and supporting reconnaissance, artillery, engineer, signals, anti-tank and workshop personnel – 13,833 officers and men. A further reduction of tank strength by two-thirds was planned for 1945 panzer divisions.

For the 1945 panzer division, establishment changes increasing the number of self-propelled (SP) weapons, would reduce the number of tanks to 54 plus 22 Jagdpanzer – shrinking the offensive power of a panzer division and reducing personnel strength to 11,500 effectives – the equivalent of a panzer grenadier division. Account should nevertheless be taken of powerful reinforcement available to divisions from higher formations. Tiger and flame-throwing tanks (Flammpanzer), multiple rocket-projectors (Flammen Werfer) supported by heavy SP anti-tank guns (Panzerjaeger and Jagdpanzer) being re-allotted by divisional commanders to battle groups in accordance with the latter's tactical needs. Motorized infantry (Panzerschützen) in regimental strength intended for the new German tank arm were raised from the cavalry or infantry as early as 1935. Their role was to serve as assault infantry alongside tank battalions. A Schützen regiment in the 1935 panzer

division consisted basically of two lorry-borne battalions and a motor cycle battalion. By the end of 1943, 47 such regiments were serving with Army panzer divisions.

The motorized division, forerunner of the panzer grenadier division, evolved in stages out of motorized infantry regiments raised by the infantry and trained independently of panzer divisions. By 1939, four such divisions supplemented by four light divisions – motorized infantry with a single tank battalion (88 tanks) intended for strategic reconnaissance and raised by the cavalry, stood ready for action either alongside panzer divisions in mixed panzer/motorized infantry corps or in separate army corps (mot). Responsibility for forming and training motorized divisions lay initially with XIV Corps at Magdeburg. Light divisions were raised and trained at Jena by XV Corps, expanded in 1940 into Panzer Gruppe 3, the 1941 Third Panzer Army. By October 1943, thirty-one light or motorized divisions had been raised by the Army and Waffen SS, some converted to full panzer status, others lost in action. Following General Guderian's appointment as Inspector-General of Armoured Troops in February 1943, and the consequent reorganization of Panzertruppen to which these troops would henceforth belong, two motorized divisions reverted to the infantry arm. At this time twenty-eight motorized infantry regiments, served twelve Army motorized infantry divisions; twenty-two served the Waffen SS. Sixteen more were to follow in 1944.

Renamed panzer grenadiers (the High Command's intention being to confer an élite infantry status upon such troops with a name derived from the original grenadier who threw his grenades and had to fight in advance of his unit armed only with the rifle), the motorized divisions would be re-equipped and re-organized to include tank or assault gun

Below: Layout of a panzer grenadier division of normal type. Certain 'ideal' divisions Gross Deutschland and Leibstandarte for instance – were the equal of panzer divisions in strength and capability, but by 1945 a common organizational table had united them into a single formation equipped with self propelled anti-tank guns equal in importance to tanks.

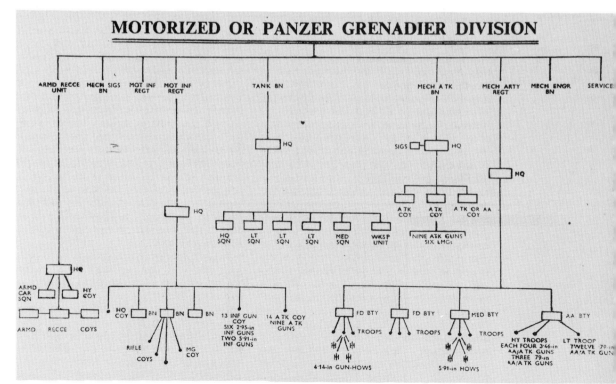

battalions. Armoured infantry carriers (SPWs) already in service would be scaled-up in numbers and provided in sufficient strength for one of the motorized infantry regiment's two battalions. The specially designed personnel carrier (Schützenpanzerwagen = SPW) was designed to improve fighting on the move. Until the advent of SPW companies, motorized infantry moved less effectively to the attack in standard trucks. Panzer grenadier companies benefited immensely from these specialized combat vehicles – a largely German innovation. Panzer grenadier divisions, including Gross Deutschland and Feldherrnhalle – 3rd, 10th, 15th, 16th, 18th, 20th, 25th, 29th, 90th, also Brandenburg and, after 1943, seven Waffen SS divisions – would constitute an integral part of the panzer force. The Brandenburg Division, after retraining and conversion to this mobile category, was OKW's special-purpose unit (800) of the early years, once entrusted with covert operations in Europe and North Africa – responsible to Abwehr Director, Admiral Canaris. The planned role of the panzer grenadier division was to work in conjunction with the panzer division, remedying the special weakness of the tank in its inability to hold the ground that it had won. More often than not the panzer grenadier division by virtue of its tank component would serve as a substitute for the panzer division. The 1944 panzer grenadier division, with a strength of 14,267 men, consisting of either one or two panzer grenadier regiments plus a tank or assault gun battalion of 42 vehicles and supporting arms, was completely motorized. Army commanders, in rearguard situations, relied greatly upon these mobile divisions to screen and support less well-endowed infantry. Panzer divisions were in theory retained for concentrated counter-strokes. After 1943, the planned war organization of panzer and panzer grenadier divisions was rarely fulfilled; divisions usually fought well below strength, in some cases little more than a brigade of one or perhaps two 'panzer' battalions supported by an equivalent number of trucked infantry battalions.

Mobility was restricted by petrol and other shortages, equipment was frequently lost in action and manpower deficiencies never made good. Regimental tank strengths declined and the once irresistible power of the panzer division waned in the face of opponents fielding more and overwhelming strength in ground and air forces. The distinction between panzer and panzer grenadier divisions became increasingly blurred, confusing their roles, resulting often in the misuse of the weaker division in mobile action.

2. Satellite contributions for the panzer force

Satellite support for the panzer force was in general limited, by out-of-date equipment and inexperience, to subordinate operations on secondary fronts; foreign contributions being particularly sought after by Hitler in the winter of 1941 when the Wehrmacht was pre-occupied with plans for 'Blue'/'Brunswick' (map 10) – the demand for numbers surpassing the need for proficiency. Germany's principal ally fighting in North Africa from September 1940 onwards – when Italian Tenth Army (Berti), comprising eight divisions and eight tank battalions (six light, two medium), crossed out of Libya into Egypt – contributed two armoured (Ariete, Littorio) and two motorized (Trento, Trieste) divisions to Rommel's 1942 offensive against British Eighth Army (map 5). The mobile divisions were supported by four–five non-motorized infantry divisions. At this time the Italian Army consisted of 61 infantry, four armoured (Centauro, Ariete, Littorio – one in embryo), two motorized (Trento, Trieste) and seventeen other divisions; a strength of 84 divisions. This order of battle was to remain broadly unchanged for the rest of the war; in Italy's case ending in September 1943. Before June 1940 when Italy entered the war, Ariete and Littorio Armoured Divisions had been grouped with two existing motorized divisions – Trento and Trieste – into an armoured corps. This, with a mobile (cavalry) and truck-borne corps formed Italian Sixth Army known as the Army of the Po; the main component of Ariete and Littorio being 'light' tank regiments consisting of 3½-ton (CV33) or experimental 6-ton (CR30) – eventually 6.8-ton (L6/40) vehicles.

By 1940, 11-ton medium tanks (M11/39) were in production, marginally enhancing the assault power of the armoured division. Centauro, deployed in Albania against the Greeks, had three light and one medium tank battalion; all fared badly, Centauro's place in the armoured corps being taken by Littorio converting to armour after fighting in Spain (map 1). In the 15-day Italian campaign against France – 10–25 June 1940, coinciding with the final stages of Operation 'Red' (map 3), when Italian Fourth and First Armies (north to south) crossed into France between Mount Blanc and Ventimiglia – Littorio and Ariete remained in reserve ready to exploit a break-through to Marseille. That break-through never came. Thereafter Littorio moved to Yugoslavia, eventually linking-up with Centauro, while Ariete moved to Libya in January 1941. Comando Supremo (Cavallero) still in the process of rebuilding its armour in 1941, after reverses in Europe and North Africa, then determined upon a new establishment for the tank regiments of armoured divisions – henceforth three medium and one heavy tank battalion; improved mediums (M14/40 and M14/41) making their appearance in North Africa with both Ariete and Littorio after the latter's redeployment from Yugoslavia. Captured Renault T35s of about 10 tons and Somuas of 18- or 21-tons also entered service with certain Italian tank battalions. But even with these improved mediums, the Italian armoured division as constituted in North Africa, with three medium battalions (165 tanks), was incapable of more than light assault. Trento and Trieste, it should be noted, were distinguished at times from other North African truck-borne infantry divisions by the inclusion – in common with the armoured division – of a Bersaglieri regiment; such formations normally consisting of two semi-motorized formations only.

Campaigning against Wavell before Ariete and Rommel arrived on the North African desert scene in February 1941 (map 5), Italian Tenth Army was obliterated, losing more than 100 M 11s in action at Beda Fomm. In this engagement an Italian army of ten divisions reinforced by an armoured brigade (Babini) withdrawing west from

Benghazi was finally intercepted by mobile forces under O'Connor and overwhelmed; 7th Armoured (Hobart) and 4th Indian Division (Tuker) leading the way. Twelve months later, defending Cyrenaica against 'Crusader' (see Panzer Army Africa, 18 November 1941) much the same could be said of Italian forces supporting DAK. Deploying obsolete artillery (half the range of British equivalents), fielding uncompetitive armour and failing with much other military equipment, the outcome of Italian failure in the desert was a predictable dependence on German support. On the advice of Wünsdorf specialists, the Italian armoured division was strengthened; SP guns, improved medium tanks, heavier supporting weapons and a Bersaglieri regiment being added to establishment. In the run-up to Alamein (map 5) these developments taken in conjunction with German support were to prove advantageous, but in southern Russia where Italian Eighth Army (Gariboldi) was barring the progress of SW Front in the concluding phase of 'Blue'/'Brunswick', the absence of German support was to prove catastrophic (map 12). Deployed in defensive positions on the Don north of Stalingrad, Eighth Army included the Italian expeditionary force in Russia – Corpo di Spedizione Italiano (CSIR) – which, under General Messe since the July days of 'Barbarossa', had campaigned vigorously with Army Group South on its Voronezh–Stalino axis.

Comprising 'Pasubio' and 'Torino' – neither more than semi-motorized and one other infantry division, the CSIR serving Eighth Army on the Don as XXXV Corps, was lost together with an Alpini and II Corps, ten divisions in total, when German reinforcement for Eighth Army was sucked into the battle for Stalingrad. By May 1943, reporting 130,000 dead, wounded and missing and 90 per cent of its equipment abandoned on the battlefield, the remnant of Italian Eighth Army was withdrawn from the front. This débâcle was immediately followed by another in Tunisia where Italian forces serving First Italian Army (Messe) were equipped and deployed to approximately the same scale as those in Libya; seven Italian and ten German divisions capitulating in the theatre on 12 May 1943. In the autumn of 1943, there occurred a 'peaceful' sequel to the catastrophes overtaking Italian arms in Russia and Tunisia, when in consequence of Italy's defection from the Axis, broadcast on 8 September, Centauro (Count Calvi) was disarmed in Rome. Re-equipped, at Mussolini's request, with new Pz Kpfw IIIs and IVs Centauro was one of seven Italian divisions including Ariete and Piave that were concentrated by Comando Supremo in the neighbourhood of the capital; their presence threatening German communications with the panzer and other divisions deployed in the south. A 'ceasefire' brought the crisis to an end without bloodshed. The Pz Kpfw IIIs and IVs were re-possessed (see Part 5, Panzer Action in Italy, page 202).

Much the same story of lamentably weak allies creating unforeseen, and ultimately irreconcilable difficulties for the Wehrmacht when these same allies defected from the German cause, unfolds in the case of Finnish, Roumanian, Hungarian and Slovak contingents; obsolete ground and air forces limiting their employment to secondary fronts and their eventual defection tearing gaps in German strength and dispositions that were impossible to make good. Equipped in pre-war days with AFVs purchased abroad or manufactured at home under licence (Skoda-Roumania, Ansaldo-Hungary, etc.) or fortuitously supplied by the Wehrmacht with captured Czech and French vehicles – satellite armies deployed in the east were to prove no match for the power of the Red Army. As the war progressed new German equipment came their way, albeit in small quantities; assault guns for the Finns supplementing either captured Soviet T34s and towing machines taken in Karelia, or imported foreign types, and heavier AFVs for the Roumanians, Czechs and others. In the Roumanian case, captured Renaults (T35s) and Hotchkiss H35s taken by the Germans from French and Belgian stocks in 1940 following the Battle of France found their way on to the strength of a Roumanian armoured division. This, and two cavalry divisions eventually converting to 'armour', were also allotted a small percentage of new German equipment. From the outset of 'Barbarossa' the Roumanians contributed two armies – Third (Dumitrescu) and Fourth (Ciuperva) – to Army Group South; neither were strong on motorization, anti-tank weaponry, artillery or signals equipment.

These same armies, in a strength of 25 divisions (one armoured) with their own air support, participated in 'Blue'/ 'Brunswick'. Arriving on the Don in October 1942, Roumanian Third Army reached the river north of Stalingrad deployed between the Italians (Gariboldi) left, and German Sixth Army (Paulus) right; Fourth Army (Constantin-Claps) traversed the Kalmuck Steppe to arrive south of the city on Fourth Panzer Army's right flank. The consequences of this deployment, despite the presence in reserve of German XXXXVIII Panzer Corps (Heim) – 22nd Panzer, 1st Roumanian Armoured – was to prove an unmitigated disaster (map 11).

The nucleus of Hungarian support for 'Barbarossa' was concentrated in a motorized corps (Szombathelyi) of three divisions (one cavalry). Equipped with 65 Italian 3½-tonners and 95 8½-ton Swedish-Hungarian Toldis, the corps served Seventeenth Army, Army Group South, advancing via Nikolaev to the Donez at Issyum. A subsequent Hungarian contribution to 'Blue'/'Brunswick' was provided by Hungarian Second Army (Jány) alone. In that fateful winter of 1942-3, when the Roumanians collapsed on the Don, the Army was deployed between Italian Eighth Army right and German Second Army (von Salmuth) left. Woefully short of anti-tank guns and with only a single panzer battalion (38ts) on hand to counter Voronezh Front (map 12), the Hungarians were overrun. The survivors, excluding 105,000 dead, wounded and missing, were withdrawn from the front on 24 January. The army returned home in March 1943. In September 1944, with the Red Army driving into Hungary, three Hungarian armies – First, Second (re-activated) and Third – were deployed under Army Group South Ukraine (Friessner) – from 24 September Army Group South – defending a Hungarian national redoubt. Heading the Hungarian order of battle were two 'armoured' divisions mostly equipped with German material (Pz Kpfw IIIs and IVs). Both divisions participated in battles for Budapest (map 19).

As regards a Bulgarian contribution to the panzer force, Guderian records that 138 Pz Kpfw IIIs and assault guns (intended for a Bulgarian armoured division?) were lost when that country changed sides at the end of August 1944.

Finally, in this summary of satellite support for the panzer

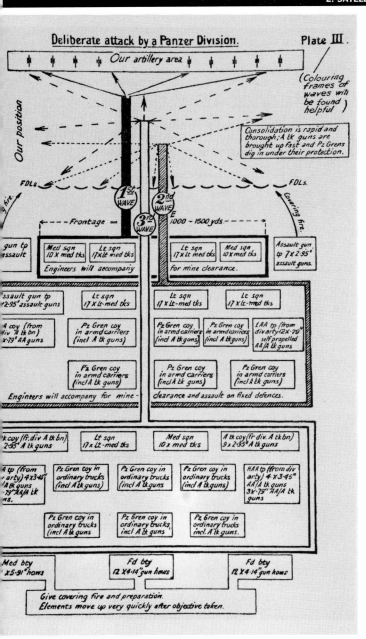

Deliberate attack by a Panzer Division.   Plate III.

Our artillery area

(Colouring frames of waves will be found helpful)

Our position

Consolidation is rapid and thorough; A tk guns are brought up fast and Pz Grens dig in under their protection.

FDLs.   FDLs.

1st WAVE   2nd WAVE
3rd WAVE
Frontage   1000 - 1500 yds

Covering fire.

gun tp assault | Med sqn 10 X med tks | Lt sqn 17 X lt med tks | Lt sqn 17 X lt-med tks | Med sqn 10 X med tks | Assault gun tp 7 X 2·95" assault guns
Engineers will accompany | for mine clearance.

ssault gun tp 2·95" assault guns | Lt sqn 17 X lt-med tks | Lt sqn 17 X lt-med tks | Lt sqn 17 X lt-med tks
4 coy (from div A tk bn) x·79" AA guns | Pz Gren coy in armd carriers (incl A tk guns) | Pz Gren coy in armd carriers (incl A tk guns) | Pz Gren coy in armd carriers (incl A tk guns) | LAA tp (from div arty) 2 X·79 self propelled AA/A tk guns
| Pz Gren coy in armd carriers (incl A tk guns) | Pz Gren coy in armd carriers (incl A tk guns) | Pz Gren coy in armd carriers (incl A tk guns)
Engineers will accompany for mine - | clearance and assault on fixed defences.

tk coy (fr. div A tk bn) 2·95" A tk guns | Lt sqn 17 X lt-med tks | Med sqn 10 x med tks | A tk coy (fr div A tk bn) 9 x 2·95" A tk guns
4 tp (from arty) 4 X 3·45" A tk guns ·79" AA/A tk ns. | Pz Gren coy in ordinary trucks (incl A tk guns) | Pz Gren coy in ordinary trucks (incl A tk guns) | Pz Gren coy in ordinary trucks (incl A tk guns) | HAA tp (from div arty) 4 X 3·45" AA/A tk guns 3x ·79" AA/A tk guns
| Pz Gren coy in ordinary trucks (incl A tk guns) | Pz Gren coy in ordinary trucks incl A tk guns. | Pz Gren coy in ordinary trucks incl. A tk guns.

Med bty x 5·91" hows | Fd bty 12 X 4·14" gun hows | Fd bty 12 X 4·14" gun hows

Give covering fire and preparation. Elements move up very quickly after objective taken.

Above: Schematic plan for a 'deliberate attack by a Panzer Division'.

force, a short note on the Slovak 'Schnelle' Division (Turanec). Following Fourth Panzer Army into the Caucasus in 1942 (map 10), the division enjoyed a proportion of new German equipment replacing the division's – formerly Schnelle Brigade's – antiquated Pz Kpfw 38ts and 'Tatra' 4-wheeled armoured cars. By February 1943, however, the Slovak Schnelle Division had practically ceased to exist, having lost most of its equipment retreating from the Kuban across the Sea of Azov to the Crimea (map 11).

With action at Rostov, Maikop and Tuapse behind it, the Schnelle Division's 4,000–5,000 survivors were reformed into Slovak 1st Infantry Division (Jurech), continuing a presence in the area until October 1943 when at Kachovka, west of the Dnieper, the division again experienced the full

weight of the Red Army, this time removing it from the German order of battle.

Spanish and French contingents consisted solely of infantry sent to the Eastern Front. The Spanish Blue Division (Munoz-Grandes), German-equipped when deployed under Eighteenth Army, Army Group North, in the Battle of Leningrad, served at first on the Volkhov, where the action was brisk, before returning home to Spain in October 1943; a Spanish Legion of 2,000 effectives being left in action on the Narwa until April 1944. That too was then withdrawn to Spain. 'Charlemagne' (Puaud), a French infantry contingent elevated in the autumn of 1944, to the status of an SS Waffen grenadier division, originated in a pre-existing volunteer regiment known as the Légion Volontaires Françaises (LVF). Incorporated into the German Army as 638th Regiment (7th Infantry Division), the LVF served Fourth Army in the battle for Moscow (map 8) before seeing action against partisans on the same Central Front in 1942–3. Re-constituted in 1944 as an SS division, some 7,000 French volunteers served briefly in two battle groups – one under Army Group Weichsel, surrounded in Pomerania and virtually destroyed there, the other including survivors from Pomerania defended Hitler in the Reichs Chancellery until forced to capitulate on 2 May 1945 (see Third Panzer Army, 16 April 1945).

Other foreign troops serving the panzer force included Osttruppen recruited in Russia as 'Hiwis' – (see Part 3, Panzer Supply) and those recruited and formed into certain SS panzer or panzer grenadier divisions (see Part 3, Divisional Profiles). Italy's defection from the Axis in September 1943, was matched by the exit of Hitler's other partners in the war on the Eastern Front. In August 1944 the Roumanians had changed sides to support the Red Army with 22 divisions in the advance through Hungary. Within days Bulgaria followed suit; nine divisions joining in the advance through the Balkans. Finland left Germany's side in September, turning from 'Waffenbrudder' to active hindrance of Twentieth Mountain Army (Rendulic) withdrawing south by road from the far north of the country, while in October an unsuccessful attempt by the Horthy government to negotiate a ceasefire with the Soviets lead to Hungarian desertions, a German take-over of Hungarian military forces and, in December, a declaration of war against Germany by a counter-regime established in Debrecen under Soviet auspices. By the end of the year, foreign support for the Wehrmacht outside the framework of regular Waffen SS divisions still being raised by Himmler as late as March 1945 and 'Hiwis', had faded into insignificance. In Italy just two or three non-motorized divisions continued in action with Tenth Army (OB, South West), while in Yugoslavia (OB, South East) a comparable number of German-Croat divisions served in two German mountain corps, supporting twelve national Croat divisions clustering in defence of Zagreb, Sarajevo and key Croatian localities. Only in Hungary, where twelve Hungarian divisions including the two panzer 'divisions' serving Army Group South (Wöhler in succession to Friessner), was there any significant concentration of Axis divisions deployed in support of the Wehrmacht, and much of this was of dubious value, some 'divisions' consisting of no more than 1,500 men; Hitler's grip on events in the theatre had long since faded into history.

3. Panzer force growth, 1939–45

1. GERMAN MOTORIZED INFANTRY AND PANZER GRENADIER DIVISIONS

1939	1940	1941	1942	1943	1944	1945
2 MotDiv*	2 MotDiv	[12]				
13 MotDiv*	13 MotDiv	[13]				
20 PzGrDiv*	20 PzGrDiv	20 PzGrDiv	20 PzGrDiv	20 PzGrDiv	20 PzGrDiv	20 PzGrDiv
29 PzGrDiv*	29 PzGrDiv	29 PzGrDiv	29 PzGrDiv[2]	29 PzGrDiv	29 PzGrDiv	29 PzGrDiv
1SS PzDiv A Hitler	1SS PzDiv A Hitler	1SS PzDiv A Hitler	1SS PzDiv A Hitler[2]	1SS PzDiv A Hitler[4]	[1SS PzDiv A Hitler]	
2SS PzDiv	2SS PzDiv Das Reich[1]	2SS PzDiv Das Reich[1]	2SS PzDiv Das Reich[1]	2SS PzDiv Das Reich[4]	[2SS PzDiv Das Reich]	
	3SS PzDiv Totenkopf[1]	3SS PzDiv Totenkopf[1]	3SS PzDiv Totenkopf[1]	3SS PzDiv Totenkopf[4]	[3SS PzDiv Totenkopf]	
	4SS PzDiv Polizei[1]	4SS PzDiv Polizei[1]	4SS PzDiv Polizei[1]	4SS PzDiv Polizei	4SS PzDiv Polizei	4SS PzDiv Polizei
		5SS PzDiv Wiking[1]	5SS PzDiv Wiking[1,2]	5SS PzDiv Wiking	[5SS PzDiv Wiking]	
	Gross Deutschland	Gross Deutschland	Gross Deutschland[2]	Gross Deutschland[4]	Gross Deutschland[5]	Gross Deutschland
		3 PzGrDiv	3 PzGrDiv[2]	3 PzGrDiv	3 PzGrDiv	3 PzGrDiv
		10 PzGrDiv	10 PzGrDiv	10 PzGrDiv	10 PzGrDiv	10 PzGrDiv
		14 MotDiv	14 MotDiv	(14 MotDiv)		
		16 PzGrDiv	16 PzGrDiv[2]	16 PzGrDiv	[116]	
		18 PzGrDiv	18 PzGrDiv	18 PzGrDiv	18 PzGrDiv	18 PzGrDiv
		25 PzGrDiv	25 PzGrDiv	25 PzGrDiv	25 PzGrDiv	25 PzGrDiv
		36 MotDiv	36 MotDiv	(36 MotDiv)		
		60 MotDiv	60 MotDiv[2]	60 MotDiv	[FH1]	
				90 PzGrDiv	90 PzGrDiv	90 PzGrDiv
				386 MotDiv		
				999 MotDiv		
				15 PzGrDiv	15 PzGrDiv	15 PzGrDiv
				Brandenburg	Brandenburg	Brandenburg
H Goering Div	H Goering Div	H Goering Div[3]	H Goering Div	(H Goering Div)	H Goering Div 2	H Goering Div 2
				9SS PzDiv HOH	[9SS PzDiv HOH]	
				10SS PzDiv FRU	[10SS PzDiv FRU]	
				11SS PzGr Div NDL	11SS PzGr Div NDL	11SS PzGr Div NDL
				16SS PzGr Div RSS	16SS PzGr Div RSS	16SS PzGr Div RSS
					17SS PzGr Div GvB	17SS PzGr Div GvB
					18SS PzGr Div HW	18SS PzGr Div HW
				23SS PzGr Div NED	23SS PzGr Div NED	23SS PzGr Div NED
				28SS PzGr Div WAL	28SS PzGr Div WAL	28SS PzGr Div WAL
					27SS PzGr Div LMK	27SS PzGr Div LMK
						PzGrDiv Kurmark
						+

[Heavier type indicates SS division.]
See also satellite contributions to the panzer force, page 66.

Key

[ ] Motorized infantry or panzer grenadier division converted to a panzer division.
( ) Motorized infantry division reverting to former infantry status.
+ 1944–5: impromptu panzer grenadier divisions raised from schools, training or other units; 31SS Bohmen-Maren, 33SS 30 Januar and 38SS Nibelungen.
____ Motorized regiment expanded into a brigade or division.
_____ Brigade expanded into a division.

* 1939 motorized infantry division deploying *three* motorized infantry regiments, each of *three* battalions (I Bn, Companies 1–4; II Bn, Companies 5–8; III Bn, Companies 9–12; plus Company 13, infantry gun; and Company 14, anti-tank) together with reconnaissance, artillery, anti-tank, engineer, signals, supply, administrative and medical services. In 1940 the motorized infantry division was reduced to *two* motorized infantry regiments of *three* battalions each; but see also the following notes.

[1] 1940–1/2 SS motorized infantry division retaining *three* motorized infantry regiments, usually with extra companies (e.g., 2SS in May 1941 deployed 16 companies in each regiment). After September 1943, SS motorized infantry divisions were reduced to two panzer grenadier regiments.

[2] 1942 motorized infantry division favoured with a panzer battalion (88 tanks in three companies) for the summer offensive (map 10). In September 1943 a panzer or assault gun battalion was provided for all motorized divisions plus an Army AA (Flak) battalion for the majority.

[3] Air Force motorized anti-aircraft regiment reinforced with an Air Force jaeger battalion.

[4] 1943 divisional panzer battalion or 1SS, 2SS, 3SS panzer regiment reinforced with a Tiger company for the summer offensive (map 14). Note that Gross Deutschland had a Tiger battalion.

[5] Gross Deutschland, the Army's most powerful panzer grenadier division, with an exceptional weapon establishment.

2. GERMAN PANZER AND LIGHT DIVISIONS

1939	1940	1941	1942	1943	1944	1945
1 PzDiv*	1 PzDiv*	1 PzDiv	1 PzDiv	1 PzDiv	1 PzDiv	1 PzDiv
2 PzDiv*	2 PzDiv*	2 PzDiv	2 PzDiv	2 PzDiv	2 PzDiv	2 PzDiv
3 PzDiv*	3 PzDiv*	3 PzDiv	3 PzDiv[1]	3 PzDiv	3 PzDiv	3 PzDiv
4 PzDiv*	4 PzDiv*	4 PzDiv	4 PzDiv	4 PzDiv	4 PzDiv	4 PzDiv .
5 PzDiv*	5 PzDiv*	5 PzDiv	5 PzDiv	5 PzDiv	5 PzDiv	5 PzDiv
1 LtDiv[3]	[6 PzDiv]	6 PzDiv	6 PzDiv	6 PzDiv	6 PzDiv	6 PzDiv
2 LtDiv[3]	[7 PzDiv]	7 PzDiv	7 PzDiv	7 PzDiv	7 PzDiv	7 PzDiv
3 LtDiv[3]	[8 PzDiv]	8 PzDiv	8 PzDiv	8 PzDiv	8 PzDiv	8 PzDiv
4 LtDiv[3]	[9 PzDiv]	9 PzDiv	9 PzDiv[1]	9 PzDiv	9 PzDiv	9 PzDiv
10 PzDiv	10 PzDiv*	10 PzDiv	10 PzDiv	10 PzDiv		
Kempf		11 PzDiv	11 PzDiv[1]	11 PzDiv	11 PzDiv	11 PzDiv
		12 PzDiv	12 PzDiv	12 PzDiv	12 PzDiv	12 PzDiv
		13 PzDiv	13 PzDiv[1]	13 PzDiv	13 PzDiv	FH2
		14 PzDiv	14 PzDiv[1]	14 PzDiv	14 PzDiv	14 PzDiv
		15 PzDiv	15 PzDiv	[15 PzDiv]		
		16 PzDiv	16 PzDiv[1]	16 PzDiv	16 PzDiv	16 PzDiv
		17 PzDiv	17 PzDiv	17 PzDiv	17 PzDiv	17 PzDiv
		18 PzDiv	18 PzDiv	18 PzDiv	(18 PzDiv)	
		19 PzDiv	19 PzDiv	19 PzDiv	19 PzDiv	19 PzDiv
		20 PzDiv	20 PzDiv	20 PzDiv	20 PzDiv	20 PzDiv
	5 LtDiv[3]	[21 PzDiv]	21 PzDiv	21 PzDiv	21 PzDiv	21 PzDiv
			22 PzDiv[1]			
			23 PzDiv[1]	23 PzDiv	23 PzDiv	23 PzDiv
			24 PzDiv[1]	24 PzDiv	24 PzDiv	24 PzDiv
				25 PzDiv	25 PzDiv	25 PzDiv
				26 PzDiv	26 PzDiv	26 PzDiv
				27 PzDiv		
		90 LtDiv[3]	90 LtDiv[3]	[90 LtDiv]		
			164 LtDiv[4]	164 LtDiv[4]		
				H Goering	H Goering 1[2]	H Goering 1[2]
					FHH1	FHH1
					Norwegen	Norwegen
					116 PzDiv	116 PzDiv
					Pz Lehr[2]	Pz Lehr
					1SS PzDiv A Hitler[2]	**1SS PzDiv A Hitler**
					2SS PzDiv Das Reich[2]	**2SS PzDiv Das Reich**
					3SS PzDiv Totenkopf[2]	**3SS PzDiv Totenkopf**
					5SS PzDiv Wiking[2]	**5SS PzDiv Wiking**
					9SS PzDiv HOH	**9SS PzDiv HOH**
					10SS PzDiv FRU	**10SS PzDiv FRU**
					12SS PzDiv HJ	**12SS PzDiv HJ**
					Führer Begleit	Führer Begleit
					Führer PzGr	Führer PzGr
						+

[Heavier type indicates SS division.]
See also satellite contributions to the panzer force, pate 66.

Key
[ ] Converted from light to panzer division.
(__) Converted from panzer or light division to panzer grenadier division.
(__) Reorganized as an artillery division.
+ 1944–5: Impromptu panzer divisions raised from schools, reserve units, etc.; 232, 233, Clausewitz, Donau, Holstein, Jüterbog, Muncheberg, Schlesien, Thuringien, Westfalen.

* 1939–40 panzer division deploying a brigade of *two* panzer regiments of 324 tanks in four panzer battalions (3 companies). 6, 7 and 8 Panzer Divisions deployed *one* panzer regiment of three battalions (9 Panzer Division two panzer battalions only) plus one motorized infantry (Schützen) regiment of *two* battalions (5 companies each), one motorcycle battalion (5 companies), reconnaissance, artillery, anti-tank, engineer, signals, supply, administration and medical services. In 1941 the panzer division was reduced to *one* panzer regiment of 196 tanks in two panzer battalions, but an increase in motorized infantry to *two*

regiments of *two* battalions each. Many minor variations existed between divisions.
[1] Certain 1942 panzer divisions had the panzer regiment strengthened to *three* battalions for the summer offensive (map 10). Beginning in mid-1942, an Army anti-aircraft (Flak) battalion was proposed for all panzer and certain motorized infantry divisions, limited at first to those taking part in the summer offensive.
[2] 1944 panzer divisions favoured with abnormal complements of weapons, vehicles and personnel. 1SS, 2SS, 3SS and 5SS had *two* panzer grenadier regiments

with *three* battalions and extra weapons; Hermann Goering, Panzer Lehr and Gross Deutschland (nominally a panzer grenadier division but, like SS panzer grenadier divisions, originally superior to an Army panzer division).
[3] Light division deploying a single panzer battalion of 88 tanks otherwise organized as a motorized infantry division (two regiments).
[4] Light division with *no* integral panzer battalion.

4. Divisional profiles

1. Motorized infantry and panzer grenadier divisions, 1934–45

2ND MOTORIZED DIVISION

Raised **Oct 1934** at Stettin as 2nd Inf Div; 1937 motorized; Sept 1939 Poland (map 2); May 1940 France (map 3); July 1940 Germany; Jan 1941 reorg as 12th Pz Div (q.v.).

3RD PANZER GRENADIER DIVISION

Raised **Oct 1934** at Frankfurt/Oder as 3rd Inf Div; Sept 1939 Poland; Jan to Sept 1940 France; Oct 1940 Germany, reorg as 3rd Mot Inf Div; **June 1941** Eastern Front, Ostrov, Luga, Demjansk (map 7); Oct to Dec 1941 Moscow (map 8); Jan to April 1942 Gshatsk, Vyasma; May 1942 refit; July 1942 Voronezh (map 10), Don corridor; **Feb 1943** destroyed at Stalingrad; Mar to June 1943 at Lyon reform as Pz Gren Div incl. 386th Mot Div and 103rd Pz Bn; July 1943 to July 1944 Italy (Rome occup. 9 Sept 1943); Aug 1944 Mosel, Metz; Dec 1944 to Feb 1945 Ardennes (map 17); **Mar 1945** Cologne; April 1945 destroyed in Ruhr pocket.

10TH PANZER GRENADIER DIVISION

Raised **Oct 1934** at Regensburg as 10th Inf Div; Sept 1939 Poland; June 1940 France; Oct 1940 Germany, reorg as 10th Mot Inf Div; **June 1941** Eastern Front, Bobruisk, Smolensk (map 7); Oct to Dec 1941 Gomel, Kiev, Bryansk, Tula (map 8); Jan to Dec 1942 Mozaisk, Juchnow, Demjansk; **Jan to Mar 1943** Demjansk, Orel; April 1943 renamed 10th Pz Gren Div; July 1943 N. Kursk (map 14); Aug 1943 Bryansk inc. 239th Assault Bn; Oct to Dec 1943 Dnieper; Kanev (Bukrin) bridgehead, Kremenchug, Kirovograd inc. 7th Pz Bn; Jan to July 1944 Dnieper/Bessarabia; Aug 1944 practically destroyed serving Sixth Army at Husi; Sept to Oct 1944 reform as battle group at Krakow; **Jan 1945** destroyed at Radom; Feb 1945 reform as battle group at Gorlitz; Mar 1945 Silesia; April 1945 Moravia; May 1945 surrendered to Russians at Olmutz/Deutsche Brod.

13TH MOTORIZED DIVISION

Raised **Oct 1934** at Magdeburg as 13th Inf Div; 1937 motorized; Sept 1939 Poland (map 2); May 1940 France (map 3); July 1940 Germany; Oct 1940 reorg as 13th Pz Div (q.v.); Nov 1940 Roumania.

14TH MOTORIZED DIVISION

Raised **Oct 1934** as 14th Inf Div; Sept 1939 Poland (map 2); Jan to Sept 1940 France; Oct 1940 Germany reorg as 14th Inf Div(mot); **July 1941** Eastern Front (map 7), Minsk, Smolensk; Oct to Dec 1941 Vyasma, Klin (map 8); Jan 1942 Velish; **Feb to Mar 1943** Rshev; April 1943 Neva; May 1943 revert inf status, retained East Front; 1945 E. Prussia, surrendered to Russians Stathof/Frisches Nehrung.

15TH PANZER GRENADIER DIVISION

Formed **May 1943** as Sicily Div from remnant 15th Pz Div (destroyed Tunisia), Army 215th Pz Bn and other troops in Italy; July 1943 renamed 15th Pz Gren Div, served in Sicily until June/July 1943, thereafter Tenth Army Salerno, Cassino, Anzio; Aug 1944 E. France; Sept 1944 incl. 111th Pz Bde; Dec 1944 Ardennes (map 17); **Feb 1945** lower Rhine Gennep–Reichswald; April 1945 Ems, Weser; May 1945 surrendered to British.

Popular Guide to the **German Army No. 1** *(This pamphlet supersedes Nos. 1 and 5 of 1941)*

The German Armoured Division (Panzer Division) **and The German Motorized Division** (Panzer Grenadier Division)

RESTRICTED
The information given in this document is not to be communicated, either directly or indirectly, to the Press or to any person not authorized to receive it.

Prepared under the direction of the Chief of the Imperial General Staff

THE WAR OFFICE   NOVEMBER 1943

16TH PANZER GRENADIER DIVISION

Raised **Aug 1940** at Sennelager as 16th Inf Div(mot) from 16th and 228th Inf Divs; Dec 1940 France; **April 1941** Yugoslavia (map 6), Hungary; June 1941 Germany; July 1941 Eastern Front (map 7), Dubno, Nikolayev; Oct 1941 Kiev; Jan 1942 Kursk; July 1942 Voronezh (map 10); Aug 1942 Caucasus (map 10), Armavir, Maikop, Elista; **Jan 1943** Don, Rostov; Mar 1943 Stalino, Mius; June 1943 incl. 116th Pz Bn and renamed Pz Gren Div; Sept to Dec 1943 Zaporoshe/Krivoi Rog; Jan to Mar 1944 S. Ukraine, destroyed Uman serving Sixth Army, remnant to 116th Pz Div (q.v.).

18TH PANZER GRENADIER DIVISION

Raised **Oct 1934** at Leignitz, as 18th Inf Div; Sept 1939 Poland; June 1940 France; Oct 1940 Germany reorg as

Above: By November 1943 much of the mystique surrounding the panzer force had been dissipated and its invincible reputation broken. The diagram is one of a series of British and American Intelligence appreciations depicting panzer and panzer grenadier division layouts.

18th Inf Div(mot); **June 1941** Eastern Front (map 7), Minsk; Aug 1941 Novgorod; Nov to Dec 1942 Volkhov, Tikhvin; **Jan to April 1943** Staraya Russa/L. Ilman; May 1943 incl. 18th Pz Bn and renamed 18th Pz Gren Div; Aug 1943 Yelnya; Oct to Dec 1943 Orscha; Feb to June 1944 Bobruisk, destroyed serving Fourth Army; Sept to Oct 1944 Silesia, reform as battle group; Dec 1944 to Feb 1945 practically destroyed E. Prussia; **April 1945** reform from Pz 'Div' Schlesien and Holstein (A Gp Weichsel); late April 1945 Berlin; May 1945 encircled and practically destroyed; break-out group to Twelfth Army, Tangermünde.

20TH PANZER GRENADIER DIVISION

Raised **Oct 1934** at Hamburg as 20th Inf Div; 1937 motorized; Sept 1939 Poland (map 2); May 1940 France (map 3); July to Oct 1940 preparing for 'Sea-lion'; Dec 1940 Magdeburg; **June 1941** Eastern Front (map 7), Bialystok, Minsk; Sept to Dec 1941 Tikhvin, Volkhov, Velish until May 1943; **June 1943** incl. 8th Pz Bn and renamed 20th Pz Gren Div; July to Dec 1943 Orel, Bryansk, Dnieper, Zhitomir; Jan to Feb 1944 Winniza; Mar to April 1944 Hube pocket (map 15); May to July 1944 Brody; Aug 1944 Baranov/Weichsel until Dec 1944; **Jan to April 1945** Weichsel (map 18), Silesia, Oder (Küstrin Seelow), late April 1945 Berlin; May 1945 Potsdam, break-out group to Twelfth Army, Tangermünde.

25TH PANZER GRENADIER DIVISION

Raised **April 1936** at Ludwigsburg as 25th Inf Div; Sept 1939 Saar; Jan 1940 France; Oct 1940 Germany reorg as 25th Inf Div(mot); **July 1941** Eastern Front (map 7), Zhitomir, Uman, Kiev; Oct to Dec 1941 Bryansk, Tula, Venev; Jan 1942 to May 1943 Mzensk, Orel; **June 1943** incl. 5th Pz Bn (delayed until Oct 1943) and renamed 25th Pz Gren Div; July 1943 to July 1944 Bryansk, Orel, Smolensk, Orscha, destroyed serving Fourth Army, remnant to 107 Pz Bde; Oct/Nov 1944 reform Grafenwöhr/ Baumholder inc. 107th Pz Bde; Dec 1943 Saar; Jan 1945 Saar; Feb to April 1945 East Front, Oder (Küstrin) then west to Oranienburg (27 April); May 1945 Mecklenburg, surrendered to US at Radelübbe.

29TH PANZER GRENADIER DIVISION

Raised **Oct 1936** at Erfurt as 29th Inf Div; 1937 motorized; Oct 1938 Sudetenland (8–15 Oct); **Mar 1939** Prague (15 Mar); Sept 1939 Poland, Radom, Modlin, Bug (map 2); May 1940 France (map 3); Nov 1940 to Feb 1941 Antwerp preparing for 'Sea-lion'; **Feb 1941** Germany; June 1941 Eastern Front (map 7), Minsk, Smolensk, Bryansk (Oct), Dec 1941 Tula; Jan to June 1942 Orel, Kharkov; July to Sept 1942 Don corridor to Stalingrad (map 10); **Feb 1943** destroyed at Stalingrad serving Sixth Army; May 1943 SW France reform, June 1943 renamed 29th Pz Gren Div incl. 345th Inf Div(mot); June 1943 Italy; Sicily (10 July), Salerno (10 Sept), Cassino (6 Nov); Feb 1944 Anzio (10–19 Feb), refit Florence, Rimini (4–28 Sept), Bologna, Po, Veneto until May 1945 surrendered to British Piave (Feltre).

36TH MOTORIZED DIVISION

Raised **Oct 1936** at Kaiserlautern as 36th Inf Div; Sept 1939 Saar; May 1940 Lux/France until Sept 1940; Oct 1940 Germany; Nov 1940 reorg as 36th Inf Div(mot); **July 1941** Eastern Front (map 7), Pleskau, Leningrad; Oct to Dec 1941 Moscow, Kalinin, Klin; Jan 1942 to Feb 1943

Rshev; **May 1943** practically destroyed serving Ninth Army at Dorogbusch; April–June 1943 rebuild for 'Citadel' (reserve); July 1943 committed N. Kursk and Orel sustaining heavy losses; Oct 1943 revert to inf status on Central Front; June 1944 destroyed at Bobruisk.

60TH MOTORIZED DIVISION

Raised **Oct 1939** at Danzig as 60th Inf Div; July to Oct 1940 Germany reorg at Grossborn as 60th Inf Div(mot); Nov 1940 Poland; Dec 1940 Vienna; **Jan 1941** Roumania; April 1941 Yugoslavia (map 6); July 1941 Eastern Front (map 7), Zhitomir, Uman, Rostov; Jan 1942 Mius, Stalino; Mar 1942 Kharkov; June 1942 incl. 160th Pz Bn; July 1942 Issyum; Aug 1942 to Jan 1943 Don corridor, Stalingrad (map 10); **Feb 1943** destroyed at Stalingrad serving Sixth Army; Mar 1943 reform SW France; June 1943 renamed Pz Gren Div Feldherrnhalle; Dec 1943 East Front, Orscha; Jan 1944 Vitebsk; July 1944 practically destroyed serving Fourth Army; Aug 1944 reform; Oct 1944 Hungary, Debrecen; Nov 1944 reorg as Pz Div Feldherrnhalle (q.v.).

90TH PANZER GRENADIER DIVISION

Raised **July 1943**, *see* 90th Light Africa Division.

386TH MOTORIZED DIVISION

Raised **Nov 1942** at Frankfurt/Oder; **Mar 1943** Lyon inc. into 3rd Pz Gren Div reform after Stalingrad.

999TH MOTORIZED DIVISION

Raised **Feb 1943** at Bizerta–Tunis from penal units; May 1943 destroyed Tunisia.

PANZER GRENADIER DIVISION BRANDENBURG (BR)

Raised **Oct 1939** at Brandenburg/Havel as Bau-Lehr-Kompanie zbv 800, responsible to OKH/Abwehr for covert ops; autumn of 1940 increased to three bns: Brandenburg, Düren, Vienna; Nov 1942 expanded to Div Brandenburg; **Oct 1943** NW Belgrade reorg as Pz Gren Div Brandenburg inc. Gross Deutschland cadre and part Festungs Div Rhodos; Nov 1944 inc. Pz Battle Group von Wietersheim (GD) bracketed with GD (E. Prussia) into Pz Corps Gross Deutschland; **Jan 1945** redeployed, with GD corps staff but not GD Div, from Rastenburg to Lodz and with HG1 committed to relief of XXIV Pz Corps Nehring at Petrikau (map 18); Feb 1945 rearguard action with HG1 to the Neisse (Görlitz); Mar/April 1945 retired Görlitz/Dresden; May 1945 encircled at Olmütz (Olomouc), remnant surrendered to US/Russians via Deutsch-Brod.

PANZER GRENADIER DIVISION FELDHERRNHALLE (FH), *see* 60th Motorized Division.

GROSS DEUTSCHLAND DIVISION (GD)

A panzer Grenadier division in name only, *see* Profiles 2. Expanded from mot regt (1939) to pz corps (1944), GD was unrivalled in stature among Army formations, surpassed in strength only by premier SS and HG divisions. In action at crisis points on Eastern Front only. Assoc formations raised with help of cadres from GD: Brandenburg; Führer Begleit; Führer Grenadier; Pz Gren Kurmark (all entitled to GD cuffbands).

HERMANN GOERING DIVISION (HG: HG1, HG2)

Mot div N Africa – Italy 1942-3; July 1943 Sicily, upgraded to pz div; Oct 1944 reorg as HG1 and HG2, eventually with weapons and personnel estab superior to any in Wehrmacht.

Raised **Feb 1933** at Berlin as mot police detach (Wecke) from Prussian police volunteers; from July 1933 responsible to Ministerpräsident Hermann Goering; Sept 1935 inc. into Goering's Luftwaffe, renamed Regiment General Goering and expanded to two bns one of which, Brauer, later became first Fallschirm (paratroop) bn, plus support and guard coys; 1936–8 reorg at Reinickendorf into three flak bns and a guard bn for Luftwaffe and Führer HQ protection; Mar 1938 Austria; **Mar 1939** Bohemia; Sept 1939 Berlin protection; May to June 1940 Belgium, France (map 3) reinforcing XVI Pz Corps (Hoepner) as Flak Regt 103 under II Flak Corps; **April 1941** inc. Jaeger bn, Balkans (map 6); June 1941 Eastern Front under Kleistgruppe Dubno, Zhitomer; July 1941 Uman; Aug 1941 Nikopol; Nov 1941 Orel; May 1942 Brittany, reorg as Bde HG; July 1942 Bordeaux reform as mot div; Nov 1942 to May 1943 Tunisia, Regtl Battle Group Koch, arty regt, flak regt, et al; **May 1943** practically destroyed serving Fifth Panzer Army, Tunisia; May to June 1943 reform S. France and Naples; July 1943 Sicily, renamed HG Pz Div (q.v.).

PANZER GRENADIER DIVISION KURMARK (KMK)
Raised **Jan 1945** at Cottbus from GD replacement personnel with one pz(v) and one pz Jaeger (Hetzer) bn; Feb 1945 Frankfurt/Oder; April 1945 narrowly escaped encirclement at Halbe, remnant retired Elbe, surrendering to US at Tangermünde.

2. Panzer and light divisions, 1935–45
LIGHT DIVISIONS 1–4 reorganized as panzer divisions after participating in Polish campaign (map 2): **1st Light Division** raised April 1938 became 6th Panzer Division Oct 1939 at Wuppertal. **2nd Light Division** raised Nov 1938 became 7th Panzer Division Oct 1939 at Gera. **3rd Light Division** raised Nov 1938 became 8th Panzer Division Oct 1939 at Cottbus. **4th Light Division** raised April 1938 became 9th Panzer Division Oct 1940 at Vienna.

5TH LIGHT AFRICA DIVISION
Raised **Feb 1941** Wünsdorf/Tripoli from 3rd Pz Div(Staff 3 Pz Bde, 5th Pz Regt; two pz bns only, recce, anti-tank and arty bn) also Army troops incl. 2nd, 8th, MG bns(mot) hvy anti-tank and flak bn; Mar 1941 'Sunflower' (map 5) Rommel's advance El Agheila – Sollum (May 1941); July 1941 reorg and renamed 21st Pz Div (q.v.), 2nd MG Bn transf to 15th Pz Div.

90TH LIGHT AFRICA DIVISION
Raised **Nov 1941** N. Africa as Afrika Div zbv with inf units flown from Germany, incl. 361st Afrika Mot Regt (former Fr Foreign Legion personnel) and Army troops; Jan 1942 'Theseus' (map 5); April 1942 renamed 90th Light Div; May to Oct 1942 Gazala, Tobruk (21 June) to El Alamein (23 Oct) (map 9); Nov to April 1943 in retreat west; **May 1943** destroyed in Tunisia; July 1943 Italy, reform Sardinia as 90th Pz Gren Div (q.v.); Oct 1943 reorg Tuscany, thereafter in action mainland Italy; **1945** surrendered to US N. Italy.

164TH LIGHT AFRICA DIVISION
Aug 1942 N. Africa inc. two pz gren regts of Festungs Div Kreta (formerly 164th Inf Div) redeployed by air from Crete, also Army troops but no pz bn; Oct 1942 practically destroyed at El Alamein (23 Oct) (map 9), thereafter in

retreat west (map 5); **Feb 1943** reorg; May 1943 destroyed in Tunisia.

1ST PANZER DIVISION
Raised **Oct 1935** at Weimar from 3rd Cav Div; Sept 1939 Poland (map 2); May 1940 France (map 3); Sept 1940 E. Prussia, Soviet border; **June 1941** Eastern Front (Map 7), Dunaburg, Leningrad; Oct to Dec 1941 Moscow (map 7); Mar to Dec 1942 Rshev; **Jan to June 1943** refit France; July to Oct 1943 Greece; Nov 1943 East Front: N. Ukraine, Zhitomir (17 Nov); Feb 1944 Cherkassy relief; Mar 1944 Brody, 'Hube' pocket (map 15); Sept 1944 Carpathians; Oct 1944 Hungary: Debrecen, Nyiregyhaza; **Jan 1945** Budapest relief (map 19); May 1945 surrendered to US at Enns.

2ND PANZER DIVISION
Raised **Oct 1935** at Würtzburg; 1938 Vienna; Sept 1939 Poland (map 2); May 1940 France (map 3); July to Aug 1940 Germany; **Jan 1941** Poland; Mar 1941 Roumania; April 1941 Greece (map 6); June 1941 Germany; Aug to Sept 1941 France; Oct 1941 Eastern Front (map 8), Vyasma; Nov 1941 Klin, Krasnaya Polyana (31 Nov–5 Dec); Feb to Dec 1942 Rshev; **Jan to Mar 1943** Rshev; April 1943 Smolensk; July 1943 N. Kursk (map 14); Oct 1943 Kiev; Nov 1943 Gomel; Jan 1944 France (Amiens); June 1944 (D+6) Normandy (map 16); Aug 1944 practically destroyed in Falaise pocket (20 Aug); Sept 1944 refit Bitburg; Dec 1944 Ardennes (map 17); **early 1945** middle Mosel, Hunsrück/Rhine; April 1945 Karlsbad-Pilsen; surrendered to US at Kötzing.

3RD PANZER DIVISION
Raised **Oct 1935** at Berlin; Sept 1939 Poland (map 2); May to June 1940 Belgium/France (map 3); July 1940 Germany; **June 1941** Eastern Front (map 7); Smolensk, Kiev, Tula (map 8); Feb 1942 transf south to Kharkov; July to Dec 1942 Caucasus (map 10); **Jan to Mar 1943** Donets/Stalino (map 13); July 1943 S. Kursk (map 14); Aug 1943 Kharkov; Sept 1943 Kiev; Dec 1943 Cherkassy relief (map 15); April to July 1944 S. Ukraine; Aug to Nov 1944 Poland, Baranov; Dec 1944 Hungary; **Jan to April 1945** Hungary: Budapest relief (map 19); May 1945 Steirmark, Warsaw, reserve; surrendered to US at Enns.

4TH PANZER DIVISION
Raised **Nov 1938** at Würzburg; Sept 1939 Poland (map 2); May to June 1940 Belgium/France (map 3); July to Nov 1940 preparing for 'Sea-lion'; Dec 1940 Germany; **Feb 1941** W. France; April 1941 Balkans, reserve; June 1941 Eastern Front (map 7): Gomel, Kiev, Tula (map 8); Jan to Dec 1942 Orel (Severssk 7 Mar); **Jan to June 1943** Orel/Kursk; July 1943 N. Kursk (map 14); winter 1943–4 A Gr Centre: Bobruisk, Kowel; summer 1944 Latvia, Courland; **Jan to May 1945** refit Danzig for ops E. and W. Prussia, surrendered to Russians at Frisches Nehrung.

5TH PANZER DIVISION
Raised **Nov 1938** at Oppeln; Sept 1939 Poland (map 2); May to June 1940 Belgium/France (map 3); **Jan 1941** Roumania; Mar 1941 Bulgaria; April 1941 Yugoslavia/Greece (map 6); July 1941 Germany (Berlin OKH reserve); Oct 1941 Eastern Front (map 8): Vyasma; Nov 1941 Istra; Dec 1941 Moscow; Jan to Dec 1942 Gshatsk, Rshev; **Jan**

to Mar 1943 Gshatsk; April 1943 refit Orel; July 1943 Kursk (reserve); Sept 1943 Dnieper; early 1944 Dnieper: Bobruisk, Kowel, Minsk; Aug 1944 Lithuania, Courland; Nov 1944 E. Prussia; **Jan to April 1945** Königsberg, Pillau, surrendered to Russians Hela Peninsular.

6TH PANZER DIVISION

Raised **Oct 1939** at Wuppertal from 1st Lt Div(Poland) (map 2) (three pz bns only, with Czech 35(t) equip); May 1940 France (map 3); July 1940 Germany; Sept 1940 E. Prussia, Soviet border; **June 1941** Eastern Front (map 7), Ostrov, Leningrad; Oct 1941 Vyasma (map 8); Nov 1941 Klin; Dec 1941 Moscow; May 1942 Brittany; Dec 1942 Stalingrad relief (map 12); **Jan to Mar 1943** Donets/Kharkov (map 13); July 1943 S. Kursk (map 14); Mar 1944 Hube pocket (map 15); June 1944 refit with German equip Bergen; Dec 1944 Hungary, Danube (map 19); **Jan 1945** Budapest relief; April 1945 Vienna; May 1945 Moravia, surrendered to Rusians at Brno.

7TH PANZER DIVISION (THE 'GHOST' DIVISION)

Raised **Oct 1939** at Gera from 2nd Lt Div(Poland) (map 2) (three pz bns only, with Czech 38(t) equip); May to June 1940 Belgium/France (map 3); July 1940 preparing for 'Sea-lion' until Jan 1941; **Feb 1941** Bonn; June 1941 Eastern Front (map 7), Smolensk; Oct to Dec 1941 Kalinin, Dimitrov (map 8); Jan 1942 Rshev; June 1942 NW France, Niort, refit with German equip; Nov 1942 Vichy, Toulon (occup. 27 Nov); **Jan 1943** Donets (map 12); Feb 1943 inc. remnant 27th Pz Div; Mar 1943 Kharkov (map 13); July 1943 S. Kursk (map 14); Nov to Dec 1943 Kiev, Zhitomir; Mar 1944 Tarnopol, Hube pocket (map 15); Aug 1944 Lithuania, Courland; Oct to Nov 1944 Doblen, Memel; Dec 1944 evac to Danzig, Arys (E. Prussia) for refit; **Jan 1945** Vistula; Feb to Mar 1945 E./W. Prussia, Danzig, Hela; April 1945 evac to Swinemünde; May 1945 after refit Krampnitz remnant surrendered to British Schwerin/Hangow.

8TH PANZER DIVISION

Raised **Oct 1939** at Cottbus from 3rd Lt Div(Poland) (map 2) (three pz bns only, with Czech 38(t) equip); May to June 1940 Belgium/France (map 3); July to Dec 1940 preparing for 'Sea-lion'; **Jan 1941** Germany; April 1941 Yugoslavia (map 6); June 1941 Eastern Front (map 7), Luga, Leningrad; Nov 1941 Tikhvin; 1942 Leningrad, Cholm, Smolensk, Velish; **Feb 1943** Vitebsk; April 1943 Orel; Oct 1943 Tarnopol, Kiev; Jan to Sept 1944 Winnitza, Brody, Lemberg, Carpathians (Dukla Pass); Oct to Nov 1944 refit in Slovakia; Dec 1944 Hungary/Budapest (map 19); **Feb 1945** Silesia (Lauban); Mar 1945 Moravia; May 1945 surrendered to Russians at Brno

9TH PANZER DIVISION

Raised **Jan 1940** at Vienna and lower Austria from 4th Lt Div(Poland) (map 2); May to June 1940 Holland/France (map 3); July to Sept 1940 refit at Vienna; Dec 1940 Poland; **Jan to Feb 1941** Roumania; Mar 1941 Bulgaria; April 1941 Yugoslavia/Greece (map 6); May 1941 Germany; July 1941 Eastern Front (map 7), Uman, Kiev; May 1942 Bryansk, Kursk; June 1942 Voronezh (map 10); Dec 1942 Rshev; **Mar 1943** Orel; April 1943 refit; July 1943 N. Kursk (map 14); late summer 1943 Dnieper, Stalino; Nov 1943 Krivoi Rog; Jan 1944 Nikopol; April

1943 S. France (Nîmes) reform by inc. 155th Res Pz Div; Aug 1944 (D+51) Normandy (map 16) Alençon, practically destroyed in Falaise pocket (20 Aug), then to Metz; Sept 1944 Aachen/Geilenkirchen; Nov 1944 refit Zanten inc. 105 Pz Bde; Dec 1944 Ardennes (map 17); **Jan 1945** Eifel; Mar 1945 Cologne, Remagen; April 1945 encircled Ruhr pocket, with remnant in Harz surrendered to US.

10TH PANZER DIVISION

Raised **April 1939** at Prague; Sept 1939 Poland (map 2); Oct 1939 to April 1940 Lower Silesia; May 1940 France (map 3); July 1940 to Feb 1941 preparing for 'Sea-lion'; **Mar 1941** Lower Silesia; June 1941 Eastern Front (map 7), Minsk, Smolensk, Moscow (map 8), Juchnow until April 1942; May 1942 NW France refit; Aug 1942 Dieppe; Nov 1942 Marseille (occup.); Dec 1942 N. Africa, W. Tunis (map 5); **Feb 1943** Kasserine; Mar 1943 Medenine; May 1943 destroyed defending Tunis.

11TH PANZER DIVISION

Raised **Aug 1940** at Neuhammer from 11 Schützen Bde, 5th Pz and other cadres; **Feb 1941** Roumania; Mar 1941 Bulgaria; April 1941 Yugoslavia, Belgrade (map 6); June 1941 Eastern Front (map 7), Uman; Oct 1941 Vyasma (map 8); Dec 1941 Moscow; Jan 1942 Gshatsk; June 1942 Voronezh (map 10); Aug 1942 to Jan 1943 Don/Donets (map 12); **Feb to Mar 1943** Donets/Kharkov; July 1943 S. Kursk (map 14); Sept 1943 Kremenchug; Jan 1944 Cherkassy relief (failed); Mar 1944 Hube pocket (map 15); April 1944 Jassy; May 1944 S. France refit inc. 273rd Res Pz Div; July 1944 Toulouse/Carcassonne; Aug 1944 Rhône valley; Sept 1944 Belfort refit inc. 113 Pz Bde; Dec 1944 Saar, Ardennes (map 17); **Jan 1945** Trier; Mar 1945 Remagen; May 1945 surrendered to US in Bavaria.

12TH PANZER DIVISION

Raised **Oct 1940** at Stettin from 2nd Inf Div(mot); **July 1941** Eastern Front (map 7), Minsk, Smolensk; Sept 1941 Leningrad, Tikhvin, Volkhov; Jan 1942 refit Pleskau/Estonia; Feb 1942 to Feb 1943 Volkhov, Leningrad, Beliya, Vitebsk; **Mar 1943** to A Gr Centre: Gomel, Orel, Pripet until Jan 1944; Feb 1944 Leningrad, Luga, Pleskau; April 1944 refit Ostrov; July 1944 Bobruisk; Aug 1944 E. Prussia/Courland, **April 1945** surrendered to Russians in Courland.

13TH PANZER DIVISION

Raised **Oct 1940** at Magdeburg and Vienna from 13th Inf Div(mot) thereafter 'instructional' duties Roumania; **June 1941** Eastern Front (map 7), Uman, Kiev, Rostov; Aug 1942 Caucasus: Armavir, Mozdok until Dec 1942 (map 10); Jan 1943 Kuban; July 1943 refit Crimea; Oct 1943 to Jan 1944 Krivoi Rog; Feb 1944 Cherkassy relief (failed); April 1944 transf to Moldavia; May 1944 Kishinev, inc. Pz Gren Regt Feldhermhalle; Aug 1944 practically destroyed serving Sixth Army at Husi (Roumania); Sept 1944 reform SE Vienna; Oct 1944 Hungary: Debrecen, Nyiregyhaza; Dec 1944 to Jan 1945 Budapest (map 19), encircled and again practically destroyed; **Jan 1945** reform as Pz Div Feldhernhalle 2 (q.v.).

14TH PANZER DIVISION

Raised **Aug 1940** at Köningsbrück/Milowitz by reorg of 4th Inf Div; Nov 1940 to Feb 1941 Germany; **Mar 1941** Hungary; April 1941 Yugoslavia (map 6); June 1941

Germany; July 1941 to Nov 1942 Eastern Front (map 7), Don, Rostov, Mius, Stalingrad (map 10); **Feb 1943** destroyed at Stalingrad; Mar 1943 reform France (Angers); Nov 1943 Krivoi Rog; Dec 1943 Kirovograd pocket; Jan to Feb 1944 SW Cherkassy; Mar to April 1944 Bug/Dniester; May to June 1944 Moldavia: Jassy; July 1944 refit; Aug 1944 Lithuania: Tilsit, Schaulen; Sept 1944 Latvia: E. of Riga, Baldone (20 Sept); Oct 1944 Courland (Lithuania) 1st–3rd battles; **Jan to May 1945** Courland, 4th and 5th battles, surrendered to Russians at Libau.

15TH PANZER DIVISION
Raised **Nov 1940** at Darmstadt/Landau by reorg of 33rd Inf Div; **May to Aug 1941** North Africa (map 5), Tripoli, Derna, Libya/Egypt frontier; Nov 1941 to Jan 1942 in retreat ('Crusader' counter-action 24–27 Nov) to El Agheila; Jan 1942 renewed offensive 'Theseus'; May 1942 Gazala/Tobruk (21 June) to El Alamein (23 Oct) (map 9); Nov 1942 again in retreat to Tunisia; **Feb 1943** Mareth Line; Mar 1943 8th Pz Regt (Irkens) reinf by 5th Pz Regt (21st Pz Div) responsible to Pz Führer Afrika Irkens, later weak Pz Gr Irkens; May 1943 destroyed at Tunis serving Fifth Pz Army; July 1943 Sicily, remnant used to raise 15th Pz Gren Div (q.v.).

16TH PANZER DIVISION
Raised **Aug 1940** at Münster by reorg of 16th Inf Div; Dec 1940 Roumania 'training'; **April 1941** Balkans (map 6); June to Dec 1942 Eastern Front (map 7), Uman, Kiev, Kharkov, Stalingrad (map 10); **Feb 1943** destroyed at Stalingrad; Mar 1943 reform Brittany; June 1943 Taranto; Sept 1943 Salerno, Naples; Oct 1943 Sangro; Nov 1943 Bobruisk, Kiev; Feb 1944 Cherkassy relief; Mar 1944 Hube pocket (map 15), Vistula; Dec 1944 Kielce, reorg with 17th Pz Div into XXIV Pz Corps Nehring (map 18); **Jan 1945** Baranov (Kielce); Feb 1945 Glogau, Lauban; Mar 1945 refit inc. Pz Div Jüterbog; May 1945 Moravia, Tropau, surrendered part Russians/part US.

17TH PANZER DIVISION
Raised **Nov 1940** at Augsburg by reorg of 27th Inf Div; **June 1941** Eastern Front (map 7), Smolensk, Kiev; Oct to Dec 1941 Tula, Kashira (map 8); Jan to Nov 1942 Orel, then transf south; Dec 1942 Stalingrad relief (map 12); **Jan to Mar 1943** Donets/Kharkov; April to Sept 1943 Issyum (map 13); Oct 1943 to Jan 1944 Cherson, Winnitza; Feb 1944 Cherkassy relief; Mar 1944 Hube pocket (map 15); April to Aug 1944 E. Poland; Sept 1944 Baranov; Dec 1944 Kielce, reorg with 16th Pz Div into XXIV Pz Corps Nehring (map 18); **Jan 1945** Baranov (Kielce); Feb 1945 Oder, Glogau, remnant surrendered to Russians in Moravia.

18TH PANZER DIVISION
Raised **Oct 1940** at Leisnig from elements of 4th and 14th Inf Divs; in Germany until **June 1941** Eastern Front (map 7), Smolensk; Sept 1941 Bryansk; Dec 1941 Jefremov (map 8); Jan 1942 Suschinitschi relief; Feb to Dec 1942 Orel; **Jan to June 1943** Orel; July 1943 N. Kursk (map 14); Aug 1943 Bryansk, Orscha; Oct 1943 Vitebsk, virtually destroyed; reorg in Lithuania as 18th Arty Div; April 1944 destroyed there.

19TH PANZER DIVISION
Raised **Nov 1940** at Hanover by reorg of 19th Inf Div; **June 1941** Eastern Front (map 7), Minsk, Smolensk: Veliki Luki (20 July), Velish (22 July); Oct to Dec 1941 Moscow, Naro-Forminsk (map 8); Jan to Dec 1942 Juchnow, Orel, Beliya (8 Dec); Dec 1942 transf south to Kupjansk; **Jan 1943** Starobjelsk, Millerovo; Feb to Mar 1943 Donets, Kharkov; July 1943 S. Kursk (map 14); late summer escaped encirclement Graivoron (9 Aug) before joining GD in action at Achtyryka, Kiev, Kanev (Bukrin) bridgehead (25 Sept), Zhitomir, Kaments-Podolsk; Mar 1944 Hube pocket (map 15); June 1944 refit Holland; July 1944 Poland: Grodno, Bialystok; Aug 1944 to Jan 1945 Warsaw region SE and SW Warka/Magnuschev bridgehead (2–17 Aug); **Jan 1945** Radom; Feb to Mar 1945 Silesia: Breslau SW (9 Mar); April 1945 upper Oder: Rogau; May 1945 Slovakia, SW Olmütz (Olomouc), surrendered to Russians in Bohemia.

20TH PANZER DIVISION
Raised **Oct 1940** at Erfurt from elements of 19th Inf Div; **June 1941** Eastern Front (map 7), Minsk, Smolensk; Oct to Dec 1941 Moscow (map 8); Jan 1942 to June 1943 Gzhatsk, Orel, Beliya, Toropez; **July 1943** N. Kursk (map 14); Oct 1943 to Feb 1944 Vitebsk; Mar to July 1944 Bobruisk, practically destroyed serving Ninth Army; Aug 1944 Roumania; Oct 1944 to Jan 1945 refit Arys (E. Prussia); **Jan 1945** Hungary (map 19), Silesia; May 1945 surrendered to Russians at Görlitz.

21ST PANZER DIVISION
Raised **Aug 1941** in N. Africa by reorg and renaming 5th Light Africa Div (q.v.); Nov 1941 to Jan 1942 retreat and 'Crusader' counter-action (20–27 Nov) between Sollum and El Agheila; Jan 1942 renewed offensive 'Theseus'; May 1942 Gazala/Tobruk (21 June) to El Alamein (23 Oct) (map 9); Nov 1942 in retreat west to Tunisia; **Feb 1943** Kasserine (map 5); Mar 1943 reorg. Contributed Pz Kampfgruppe 5 to Pz Führer Afrika (see 15th Pz Div Mar 1943); May 1943 destroyed at Tunis serving Fifth Pz Army; July 1943 France, reform at Rennes from Schnelle Bde 931 and other units inc. Pz Regt 100, with French equip; June 1944 (D-Day) Normandy; Aug 1944 practically destroyed Falaise pocket (20 Aug); Sept 1944 Lothringa refit inc. 112 Pz Bde; Dec 1944 Saarpfalz; **Jan 1945** N. Strasbourg; Feb 1945 Oder, Lauban; April 1945 Görlitz, Halbe, surrendered to Russians at Cottbus.

22ND PANZER DIVISION
Raised **Sept 1941** in SW France, inc. Pz Regt 204, three pz bns with Fr, later Czech 38(t) and Ger (Pz Kpfw III and IV) equip; Mar 1942 Crimea, Feodosia; May 1942 Kertsch, Sevastopol; June 1942 Donets/Slavjansk; July 1942 Rostov except detached Kampfgruppe Michalik (reinf Pz Gren Regt 140) at Voronezh (used Sept as kernel 27th Pz Div (q.v.)); Aug to Sept 1942 Don crossing Kalatsch; Nov to Dec 1942 Chir, surrounded and practically destroyed serving Roum Third Army (map 12), thereafter Pz Kampf Gr Oppeln/Burgsthaler in action Donets/Dnieper; **Jan to April 1943** weak battle groups absorbed into 6th and 23rd Pz Divs (Burgsthaler).

23RD PANZER DIVISION
Raised **Oct 1941** in Paris region inc. Pz Regt 201 with Fr equip; April 1942 Eastern Front: Kharkov; Aug to Nov 1942

Caucasus (map 10); Dec 1942 Stalingrad relief (map 12); **April 1943** refit Stalino inc. elements 22nd Pz Div; summer to winter 1943 Dnieper; Jan 1944 Krivoi Rog; Feb 1944 Pz Bn to First Pz Army; April to July 1944 Jassy; Aug 1944 Vistula/Baranov; Oct 1944 Hungary: Debrecen, Nyireghyaza; Jan 1945 Budapest (map 19); Feb to May 1945 Hungary/Austria, surrendered to British in Steiermark.

24TH PANZER DIVISION (THE 'LEAPING RIDER' DIVISION)
Raised **Nov 1941** at Stablack E. Prussia by reorg of 1st Cav Div; June 1942 Eastern Front, Kursk; June 1942 Voronezh (map 10); Sept 1942 Don corridor to Stalingrad; Oct 1942 to Feb 1943 Stalingrad; **Feb 1943** destroyed at Stalingrad; Mar to Aug 1943 reform France; Aug to Sept 1943 N. Italy security; Oct 1943 East: Ingulez/Dnieper: Nikopol, Krivoi Rog; Mar 1944 Nikolayev, airlifted to Kishinev 22 Mar; April to July 1944 Jassy; Aug to Sept 1944 Poland: Dukla Pass (18 Sept); Oct 1944 Hungary: Debrecen (Szolnok); Dec 1944 Slovakia; **Feb to April 1945** E. Prussia: Allenstein, Heiligenbeil Balga (26 Mar) reduced to weak battle group transp by sea to Schleswig Holstein; May 1945 surrendered to British at Eckenford.

25TH PANZER DIVISION
Raised **Feb 1942** in Norway as Mot Kampf Gp, Oslo (146th Mot Inf Regt, Pz Jaeg Coy, etc.), later Pz Bn 214; Mar to Oct 1942 additional cadres to full strength; **Aug 1943** France, training at Mailly-le-Camp; Nov 1943 Eastern Front: Fastov (7 Nov); Dec 1943 to April 1944 Zhitomir, N. Ukraine Hube pocket (map 15), practically destroyed except Lemberg, Kampf Gp Treuhaupt (inf, arty, two pz coys); May 1944 reform Varde (Esbjerg), Denmark, inc. Pz 'Div' Norwegen (q.v.); Sept 1944 Warsaw, Radom; Nov 1944 inc. 104 Pz Bde; **Feb 1945** Oder; April 1945 lower Danube; May 1945 surrendered to US at Passau.

26TH PANZER DIVISION
Raised **Sept 1942** at Amiens by reorg of 23rd Inf Div, occup. France until July 1943; **July 1943 to Aug 1945** Italy: Calabria, Salerno, Anzio, Cassino, Rimini, Bologna; **April 1945** surrendered at Imola.

27TH PANZER DIVISION
Raised **Oct 1942** at Voronezh from detach 22nd Pz Kampf Gp Michalik (Pz Gren Bn 140 and a pz bn) and Army troops (Pz Verband 700); Nov to Dec 1942 Rossoch (NE Millerovo) in rear It Eighth Army on Don. Practically destroyed there opposing Russian winter offensive; **Jan to Feb 1943** weak battle groups Oskol/Donets; Mar 1943 disband: units to 7th, 19th and 24th Pz Divs (France).

116TH PANZER DIVISION (THE 'GREYHOUND' DIVISION)
Raised **Mar 1944** in NW France by Fifteenth Army from reorg 179th Res Pz Div inc. remnant 16th Pz Gren Div; mid-July 1944 Normandy (map 16), released to Fifth Pz Army (Caen); Aug 1944 Mortain (7 Aug) and action with 9th Pz Div to halt US drive on Alençon (map 16), practically destroyed in Falaise pocket (20 Aug); Sept 1944 Aachen; Oct 1944 refit inc. 108 Pz Bde; **Dec 1944 to Jan 1945** Ardennes (map 17); Feb to Mar 1945 lower Rhine/Kleve, Wesel; April 1945 encircled in Ruhr pocket serving Fifth Pz Army. With elements in the Harz, surrendered to US.

232ND PANZER DIVISION
Raised **Feb 1945** in Slovakia from Pz Feldausbildungs Div Tatra: two pz gren regts only; Mar 1945 destroyed at Raab.

233RD PANZER DIVISION
Raised **April 1945** at Aarhus/Viborg, Denmark by renaming 233rd Res Pz Div (reconstituted prev Feb after having provided cadres for Pz Div Holstein (q.v.)); security Denmark until capitulation; Battle group to 'Clausewitz' at Lübeck.

1ST FELDHERRNHALLE PANZER DIVISION (FHH1)
Raised **Sept 1944** in Hungary by reorg of Pz Gren Div Feldherrnhalle (60th Mot) (q.v.); Oct 1944 Debrecen, inc. 109 Pz Bde, and renamed Pz Div FHH; Dec 1944 Danube, serving Pz Kampf Gp Pape; **Jan 1945** Komorn, Budapest (map 19), practically destroyed; **Jan 1945** joined Pz Div Feldherrnhalle 2 (13th Pz Div) (q.v.) in Feldherrnhalle Pz Corps (formerly IV Pz Corps); Mar to April 1945 E. Hungary, Gran, lower Austria; May 1945 surrendered to US in upper Austria.

2ND FELDHERRNHALLE PANZER DIVISION (FHH2)
Raised **Feb 1945** by renaming 13th Pz Div elements outside Budapest, plus elements of FHH1 (q.v.), both divs otherwise destroyed defending Budapest (map 19); Feb 1945 Komorn; May 1945 surrendered to US in upper Austria.

FÜHRER BEGLEIT PANZER BRIGADE (FBB), LATER FÜHRER BEGLEIT PANZER DIVISION (FB-D)
Originally Führer Begleit (mot escort) Bn **(Oct 39)**; Regt (June 1944); Brigade Nov 1944 E. Prussia/Cottbus, two pz (or assault gun) bns, three pz gren bns with GD personnel; Dec 1944 Ardennes (map 17); **Jan 1945** Division: Feb 1945 Stargard offensive; Mar 1945 Troppau/Ratibor; April 1945 encircled and practically destroyed at Spremberg, remnant surrendered to US.

FÜHRER PANZER GRENADIER BRIGADE (FGB), LATER FÜHRER PANZER GRENADIER DIVISION (FGD)
Brigade: raised **July 1944** at Cottbus from GD replacement bde, two pz (or assault gun) bns, three pz gren bns; Oct 1944 E. Prussia; Dec 1944 Ardennes offensive (map 17); **Jan 1945** Division: Feb 1945 Stargard offensive; Mar 1945 Stettin, Küstrin relief (failed); April 1945 Vienna; May 1945 surrendered to US/Russians.

GROSS DEUTSCHLAND PANZER GRENADIER DIVISION (GD), LATER GROSS DEUTSCHLAND PANZER CORPS
A pz gren div in name only, GD developed as the army's premier armoured formation, comparable to 1SSLAH and HG. Progressively expanded from Regt to Division and finally Corps, by July 1944 the weapons estab incl. a pz regt (Aug 1943) with a third (Tiger) bn, six pz gren bns (two regts of 16 coys), an assault gun bde (three battys) and an arty regt (I–IV Bns). Oct 1939 raised at Grafenwöhr as Inf Regt (mot) GD by expand and reorg Wacht (guard) Regt (formerly Wachttruppe Berlin (1933)) inc. part Inf Demo Bn Döberitz; Aug 1939 provided cadre for Führer Begleit Bn; May 1940 France, Sedan (map 3); **April 1941** Balkans (map 6); June 1941 Eastern Front (map 7), Minsk, Smolensk, Jelnya, Konotop, Romny (Kiev); Oct 1941 Bryansk (map 8), Orel, Tula; Jan 1942 Oka; April 1942 expand to inf div mot; May 1942 Orel; June to July 1942

Voronezh/Don corridor (map 10); Aug to Dec 1942 Rshev; **Jan 1943** Bjelgorod; Mar 1943 Kharkov, recapt Bjelgorod (map 13); June 1943 renamed Pz Gren Div GD; July 1943 S. Kursk (map 14); Aug 1943 transf to A Gp South, Achtyrka; Sept 1943 Kremenchug bridgehead; Oct 1943 Krivoi Rog, Kirovograd; Jan to end April 1944 in retreat S. Ukraine to Carpathians, Jassy, Targul Frumos; July 1944 refit; Aug 1944 E. Prussia: Gumbinnen for counter-offensive E. and then N. to restore contact between Army Gps Centre and North at Tukkum (failed at Doblen); Oct 1944 Schaulen, Memel bridgehead (evac 26 Nov); Dec 1944 Rastenburg reorg with Brandenburg Div (q.v.) into Pz Corps GD (never in action together); **Jan to April 1945** practically destroyed with HG2 defending Königsberg, evac Balga (29 Mar) to Pillau, remnant transp by Baltic to Schleswig-Holstein; May 1945 surrendered to British.

HERMANN GOERING FALLSCHIRM (PARATROOP) PANZER DIVISION (HG: HG1 (ARMOURED), HG2 (MOTORIZED), LATER HERMANN GOERING FALLSCHIRM PANZER CORPS

Raised **July 1943** in Sicily as Pz Div HG from replacement personnel, staff and cadres from HG Div (practically destroyed in Tunisia). Reform S. France and Naples (*see* Div Profiles 1). Sept 1943 Salerno; Oct to Nov 1943 rearguard action Volturno, Garigliano; Nov 1943 refit Frosinone to exceptional estab (21,0000 field effectives, Pz Regt two bns plus assault gun bn, two pz gren regts with four bns, recce and support units). Guard Regt Berlin, Replacement Regt Holland, battle school, etc. Battle group action Monte Maggiore, Monte Troccio.
Jan 1944 renamed Fallschirm Pz Div HG; Anzio (22 Jan) until early Mar; refit Lucca/Pisa; May 1944 Valmonte (US Anzio breakout); June to July 1944 Chiusi, Arno; 15 July redeployed to Warsaw; Aug 1944 Volomin (NE) Magnuschev (SE); Sept 1944 Bugmunde (NW); Oct 1944 Modlin reorg as HG1 (two pz bns, five pz gren bns) and bracketed with new HG2 Pz Gren Div and corps troops (pzjaeg bn, Sturm bn, eng bn, flak regt) into Fallsc Pz Corps HG; until mid-Jan 1945 redeployed E. Prussia defending Königsberg E. At Nemmersdorf; **Jan 1945** HG1 redeployed south to Army Gp Centre. In action Lodz-Petrikau with Brandenburg (Pz Corps GD) to relieve encircled Pz Corps Nehring (map 18); rearguard action Oder/Neisse to Muskau; Mar 1945 upper Silesia, Neisse, Gorlitz; April 1945 Bautzen/N. Dresden. In action with Fallsc Pz Corps HG survivors (HG2); evac Heiligenbeil by Baltic after abortive defence E. Prussia; May 1945 most remnant surrendered to Russians, others to US.

HOLSTEIN/CLAUSEWITZ* PANZER DIVISION

Raised **Feb 1945** as Kampfgruppe Holstein from principal combat units 233rd Res Pz Div; East: Pomerania, Stargard Baltic coast; Mar 1945 encircled with Korpsgruppe Tettau at Horst before leading breakout (10 Mar) to west at Stettin; redeployed Oder near Küstrin inc. with Schlesien (Döberitz) into 18th Pz Gren Div; April 1945 Berlin, Potsdam, surrendered to US at Tangermünde.
April 1945 Holstein HQ personnel posted Lüneburg, S of Hamburg as kernel Pz Div Clausewitz (pz bn ex-Putlos, two coys eleven Pz Kpfws each plus mot inf bns and support units); 12–21 May in action S. of Lüneburg against flank

of Allied drive to Elbe; May 1945 surrendered to US at Lauenburg.

KEMPF PANZER DIVISION (K)

Raised in **Sept 1939** in Poland, improvised from Staff 4 Pz Bde, 7th Pz Regt, SS Deutschland Regt, SS arty regt, recce, anti-tank and support units (map 2).

NORWEGEN PANZER DIVISION (NWN)

Raised in **Sept 1943** at Oslo after departure of 25th Pz Div (q.v.) to France; June 1944 transf to Varde (Esbjerg) Denmark and absorbed into 25th Pz Div.

PANZER LEHR DIVISION (PL)

Raised in **winter of 1943** at Bergen, Germany from Pz Schools 1 (Bergen) and 2 (Krampnitz); an exceptionally well-equipped formation, both pz gren regts in SPWs, a Tiger bn and Goliath coys; Feb 1944 France; Mar 1944 Hungary; June 1944 (D+2) Normandy (map 16); Aug 1944 practically destroyed in path of US breakout ('Cobra'); Sept 1944 Germany (Swabia) refit; Dec 1944 Ardennes (map 17); **Jan 1945** Eifel; Feb 1945 Wesel; Mar 1945 Remagen, Siegen; April 1945 Ruhr pocket serving Fifth Pz Army, surrendered to US.

TATRA PANZER DIVISION

Raised **Oct 1944** *see* 232nd Panzer Division.

CLAUSEWITZ[1]*, COURLAND[2], DONAU[1], JÜTERBOG[1], MÜNCHEBERG[1], NIBELUNGEN[3], SCHLESIEN[4], THURINGIEN[1], WESTFALEN PANZER DIVISIONS

In Feb, Mar and April 1945, impromptu pz divs (Kampfgruppen of one/two pz coys, one/two pz gren bns and support units) raised mostly for action in the east.

3. SS panzer and panzer grenadier divisions, 1933–45
1ST SS PANZER GRENADIER/PANZER DIVISION LEIBSTANDARTE ADOLF HITLER (AH, LSSAH)

Raised **Mar 1933** in Berlin as SS Stabswache (Führer mot escort coy); Sept 1933 designated Leibstandarte SSAH; 1938 expanded into mot regt; Mar 1938 Austria; Oct 1938 Sudetenland; **Sept 1939** Poland (map 2); May 1940 Holland, France (map 3), Dunkirk; Aug–Dec 1940 expanded into bde inc. heavy (assault gun) coy; **Mar 1941** Balkans; April 1941 Greece (map 6); June 1941 expanded into inf div (mot); June 1941 Eastern Front (map 7): Uman, Perekop, Rostov, Mius; Aug to Dec 1942 France, reorg as pz gren div; Toulon occup. (21 Nov); **Feb 1943** Donets, Kharkov (map 13); April 1943 refit Bjelgorod; July 1943 S. Kursk (map 14); Aug 1943 N. Italy; Oct 1943 Milan occup. and reorg as pz div; Nov 1943 Zhitomir (Brusilov); Feb 1944 Cherkassy relief; Mar 1944 Hube pocket (Skala) (map 15), Tarnopol; April 1944 Belgium refit; June 1944 (D+19) Normandy (map 16), Caen; Aug 1944 Mortain (7 Aug), practically destroyed in Falaise pocket (20 Aug); Sept 1944 refit Siegburg; Dec 1944 Ardennes (map 17); **Feb 1945** Hungary: Gran (Estergom) bridgehead; Mar 1945 Stuhl-

---

[1]Inc. schools, training and replacement personnel. *See* *Holstein.
[2]Remnant 14th Pz Div and others.
[3]Inc. SS Junker School Bad Tolz: *see* 38th Pz Gren Div (Divisional Profiles 3).
[4]*See* Holstein.

weissenburg (Szekesfehervar) (map 19); April 1945 St Polten; May 1945 surrendered to US at Linz.

2ND SS PANZER GRENADIER/PANZER DIVISION 'DAS REICH' (R, V)

Raised **Oct 1939** at Pilsen as Verfügungs (mot) Division inc. SS Standarte (regiment) Deutschland (Poland), Germania (Poland) and Der Führer; May 1940 Holland (map 3), Flanders; June 1940 Soissons, Orléans, Bordeaux/SW France; July to Dec 1940 Holland; Dec 1940 renamed 'Reich'; **Mar 1941** Balkans (map 6): Belgrade (12 April); June 1941 Eastern Front (map 7), Brest-Litovsk; Sept 1941 Romny; Oct 1941 Borodino; Nov to Dec 1941 Istra/Moscow (Der Führer destroyed W. of Rshev); July to Dec 1942 refit NW France inc. new Regt Langemark; **Feb 1943** Donets/Kharkov (map 13); June 1943 refit; July 1943 S. Kursk (map 14), Mius; Oct 1943 reorg as pz div; Nov 1943 Fastov/Zhitomir (R. Teterev); Jan 1944 Shepetovka; Feb 1944 France, refit Montauban leaving Battle Group (Weidinger) Hube pocket Proskurov (map 15), Tarnopol; June 1944 (D+9) Normandy (map 16) via Oradour-sur-Glane; Aug 1944 Mortain (7 Aug), practically destroyed in Falaise pocket (20 Aug); Nov 1944 refit; Dec 1944 Ardennes (map 17); **Feb 1945** Hungary: SE Komorn (map 19); Mar 1945 Stuhlweissenburg (Szekesfehervar), Raab; April 1945 Vienna, St Polten; May 1945 surrendered to US at Pilsen.

3RD SS PANZER GRENADIER/PANZER DIVISION 'TOTENKOPF' (T)

Raised **Nov 1939** at Dachau as SS Totenkopf (part mot) Div from 'Totenkopf' personnel; May 1940 Cambrai, Arras, Dunkirk (map 3); June 1940 Loire, Lyon; July 1940 to April 1941 occup. SW France, full motorization; **May 1941** Germany; June 1941 Eastern Front (map 7), Kaunus, Dunaburg; Aug 1941 Luga/Leningrad; Jan 1942 L Ilmen; Feb 1942 Denmjansk; Oct 1942 France, refit; Nov 1942 S. France occup.; **Feb 1943** Kharkov/Donets (map 13); July 1943 S. Kursk (map 14); Sept 1943 Mius; Oct 1943 reorg as pz div, Krivoi Rog/Dnieper; Jan to April 1944 in retreat Roum border; June 1944 Poland (Grodno); Aug 1944 Warsaw; Dec 1944 Modlin/W. Hungary (Komorn); **Jan 1945** Budapest relief (failed) (map 19); Feb 1945 Stuhlweissenburg; April 1945 Vienna; May 1945 surrendered to US/Russians at Linz.

4TH SS 'POLIZEI' PANZER GRENADIER DIVISION (P)

Raised **Sept 1939** at Wandern as SS Polizei Inf Div from police and specialist army personnel; May 1940 (part mot) Belgium, Flanders; June 1940 Aisne, Champagne; **June 1941** Eastern Front (map 7); Dunaburg, Luga, Leningrad, Volkhov; Jan 1942 to June 1943 Volkhov/Leningrad; **July 1943** onwards Bohemia reorg as pz gren div leaving battle group in action Leningrad; Mar 1944 Greece counter partisan; Sept 1944 Serbia, Belgrade; Oct 1944 Hungary, Debrecen (Szolnok); **Jan 1945** Stettin; Feb 1945 Stargard, Danzig; April 1945 Hela by sea to Swinemünde for refit Mecklenburg; May 1945 surrendered to US at Wittenberge.

5TH SS PANZER GRENADIER/PANZER DIVISION 'WIKING' (W)

Raised **Dec 1940** at Munich/Vienna as SS inf div (mot) from Dutch/Flemish volunteers for SS Standarte (regt)

'Westland' and Danish/Norwegian volunteers for SS Standarte 'Nordland', with 'Germania' as third regt; **June 1941** Eastern Front (map 7), Tarnopol, Zhitomir, Azov, Rostov, Mius; May 1942 inc. 5th Pz Bn (later Regt); July 1942 Rostov/Bataisk (map 10); Aug 1942 Maikop; Nov 1942 Terek/Malgobek S. of Mozdok; Dec 1942 Kotelnikovo (SW); **Feb 1943** Donets/Krasnoarmeyskoye (Kharkov) (map 13); April 1943 Don; July 1943 Kharkov; Sept 1943 Kiev; Oct 1943 reorg as SS pz div; Dec 1943 to Feb 1944 encircled and practically destroyed at Cherkassy (breakout 17 Feb); Mar 1944 remnant reform Debica; Mar to April 1944 Kowel (Battle Group Mühlenkamp); July 1944 Maciejov; Aug 1944 Warsaw; Oct 1944 Modlin; Dec 1944 Hungary; **Jan 1945** Budapest relief (failed) (map 19); Feb 1945 Stuhlweissenburg; Mar 1945 partly encircled SW of town; May surrendered to British at Furstenfeld.

9TH SS PANZER GRENADIER/PANZER DIVISION 'HOHENSTAUFEN' (HOH)

Raised **Mar 1943** at Mailly-le-Camp as pz gren div; June to Oct 1943 Amiens reorg as Pz Div; Feb 1944 Nîmes; March 1944 Poland; April 1944 Buczacz relief ops to save First Pz Army (map 15), Tarnopol ops to relieve garrison; June 1944 (D+19) Normandy (map 16), Caen; Aug 1944 practically destroyed in Falaise pocket (20 Aug); Sept 1944 Arnhem refit and counter-attack Br 1st Airborne Div ('Market Garden'); Siegen; Dec 1944 Ardennes (map 17); **Jan 1945** Hungary; Mar 1945 Stuhlweissenburg (map 19); May 1945 surrendered to US at Linz.

10TH SS PANZER GRENADIER/PANZER DIVISION 'FRUNDSBERG' (FRU)

Raised **Feb 1943** in the Charente (SW France); Oct 1943 reorg as pz div inc. 10th SS Pz Regt; Mar 1944 Poland; April 1944 Tarnopol/Buczacz relief ops to save First Pz Army (map 15); June 1944 (D+19) Normandy (map 16), Caen; Aug 1944 practically destroyed in Falaise pocket (20 Aug); Sept 1944 Arnhem refit and counter-attack Br 1st Airborne Div ('Market Garden'); Nov 1944 Aachen; Dec 1944 reserve Ardennes (map 17); **Jan 1945** upper Rhine: Haguenau forest, Strasbourg; Feb 1945 Stargard; Mar 1945 Stettin, Cottbus; April 1945 encircled and practically destroyed at Spremberg; May 1945 remnant surrendered to Russians at Shonau.

11TH SS FREIWILLIGE PANZER GRENADIER DIVISION 'NORDLAND' (NDL)

Raised **May 1943** at Grafenwöhr from German, Dutch, Norwegian, Danish and other volunteers (Freiwilliger) inc. 11th SS Pz Bn; Sept 1943 Croatia (Zagreb), counter-partisan; December 1943 Eastern Front: Orianenbaum (Leningrad); Jan to April 1944 Narwa bridgehead; Sept 1944 Courland; Tukkum; Dec 1944 transp. Baltic to Libau/Stettin after 3rd Battle of Courland; **Feb to Mar 1945** Stargard, Stettin, Altdamm bridgehead; end Mar 1945 refit Schwedt-Angermünde; April 1945 Berlin, Reichskanzlei, encircled and practically destroyed; May 1945 break-out group to Twelfth Army, surrendered to US Elbe.

12TH SS PANZER GRENADIER/PANZER DIVISION 'HITLERJUGEND' (HJ)

Raised **July 1943** at Beverloo (Belgium) as pz gren div from Hitler Youth members and cadres from ISSLAH; Oct 1943 reorg as pz div inc. 12th SS Pz Regt, again with help from ISSLAH; April 1944 Normandy (map 16): Evereux; June 1944 (D+2) Caen; Aug 1944 practically destroyed in Falaise pocket (20 Aug), Beauvais, Kaiserlautern; Sept 1944 Hirson, Meuse (Houx); Oct 1944 refit Oldenburg; Dec 1944 Ardennes (map 17); **Feb 1945** Hungary (map 19): Gran (Estergom) bridgehead; Mar 1945 Stuhlweissenburg; April 1945 Wienerwald; May 1945 surrendered to US at Enns.

16TH SS PANZER GRENADIER DIVISION 'REICHSFÜHRER SS' (RSS)
Raised **May 1941** in Berlin as Reichsführer SS Escort Bn; **Feb 1943** Debica, expand to RSS Sturm-Brigade with a gren regt, assault gun, flak and other detachments; July to Oct 1943 Corsica; Nov 1943 Lubljana reorg as pz gren div inc. assault gun bn; Feb to April 1944 Anzio battle group; Mar 1944 Debrecen; May to Dec 1944 Italy inc. SS Pz Lehr Bde: Grosseto, Pisa, Carrara, Bologna; **Feb to Mar 1945** Hungary (map 19): Nagykanizsa oilfield protection; Mar to April 1945 lower Steiermark and Yugoslav mountain pass security (battle group); May 1945 Klagenfurt, Villach, surrendered to US/British Steiermark.

17TH SS PANZER GRENADIER DIVISION 'GOETZ VON BERLICHINGEN' (GvB)
Raised **Oct 1943** at Tours; June 1944 (D+5) Normandy (map 16) US sector Carentan/Tribehou; July 1944 Savigny; Aug 1944 Mortain battle group (7 Aug), practically destroyed in Falaise pocket (20 Aug); Sept to Nov 1944 Metz inc. SS Pz Gren Bdes 49, 51 (raised Denmark) and SS Signals School Metz; Dec 1944 West Wall, Rheinheim/Habkirchen, refit Zweibrücken; **Jan to Mar 1945** N. Alsace, Lothringia, Rimlingen (11 Jan), Rhine bridgehead, Germersheim (25 Mar); in retreat SE to Nuremberg, Munich, Bad Tolz; April 1945 Donauwörth; May 1945 surrendered to US at Achenthal.

18TH SS FREIWILLIGE PANZER GRENADIER DIVISION 'HORST WESSEL' (HW)
Raised **Feb 1944** at Zagreb (Agram/Cilli), Croatia from 1 SS Inf Bde (mot) and Bashka Volksdeutsch volunteers inc. SS assault gun bn; Mar 1944 W. Hungary, counter-partisan; July to Nov 1944 Lemberg (battle group); Aug to Oct 1944 Slovakia/Hungary, then redeploy and refit SE of Budapest; **Jan to Mar 1945** upper Silesia, practically destroyed Ratibor, Leobschütz; May 1945 Silesia, surrendered to Russians at Hirschberg.

23RD SS FREIWILLIGE PANZER GRENADIER DIVISION 'NEDERLAND' (NED)
Raised **July 1943** as pz gren bde (two regts) from 'Germanic' Dutch volunteers 48 Gen Seyfard, 49 de Ruiter; Dec 1943 SE Hungary: Agram (Zagreb), counter-partisan; Jan to Dec 1944 Oranienbaum (Leningrad), Narwa bridgehead, Estonia, Riga, Doblen, Courland; transp Baltic to Libau/Stettin (Pomerania), some units sunk *en route*, after 3rd Battle of Courland; Feb 1945 Stettin, Altdamm reorg as weak pz gren div; deployed Staargard, Furstenwalde; Mar 1945 Schwedt; April 1945 encircled at Halbe, practically destroyed. Some escapees crossed Elbe, surrendered to US.

27TH SS FREIWILLIGE PANZER GRENADIER DIVISION 'LANGEMARCK' (LMK)
Raised **May 1943** at Debica (Poland) as SS Sturm-Brigade Langemarck, from Flemish volunteers; July 1943 Prague inc. Flemish bn and further Flemish volunteers (Freiwilliger); Dec 1943 completed training; Jan 1944 Zhitomir, encircled with 'Das Reich', loosing 60% strength; April 1943 refit Bohemia; July 1943 Narwa bridgehead (Courland) battle group (decimated); Nov 1943 reorg Lüneburg as incomplete Pz Gren Div Langemarck from Flemish, Todt, Luftwaffe, naval and other personnel; Dec 1943 Eifel battle group; **Jan to Mar 1945** Arnswalde, Zachan, Stargard, Stettin, Altdamm bridgehead; April 1945 Oder, Prenzlau; May 1945 Mecklenburg, Neustrelitz/Lübeck, surrendered to British.

28TH SS FREIWILLIGE PANZER GRENADIER DIVISION 'WALLONIEN' (WAL)
Raised **July 1943** at Wildflecken as SS Sturm-Brigade 'Wallonien'; Nov 1943 Dnieper bend under command SS Wiking; Jan to Feb 1944 encircled with Wiking at Cherkassy losing heavy weapons and transport during breakout (17 Feb); spring of 1944 refit at Wildflecken, interrupt by posting east: Narwa bridgehead, practically destroyed; summer 1944 Hanover/Hildesheim; Oct 1944 reorg from Walloons, Belgians, French and others as incomplete pz gren div; Dec 1944 Cologne; **Jan to Feb 1945** Stargard/Altdamm bridgehead battle group; Mar 1945 Stettin; April 1945 Prenzlau; May 1945 Lübeck, surrendered to British at Schwerin.

31ST SS FREIWILLIGE GRENADIER DIVISION 'BOHMEN-MAREN'
Raised **Oct 1944** in south-east: Hungary inc. Volksdeutsch units of 23rd SS Div 'Kama'; Nov 1944 Pecs, practically destroyed; Dec 1944 refit Steiermark S. of Marburg inc. schools personnel; **Feb 1945** Silesia: Striegau, Strehlen; May 1945 decimated units disbanded Königgratz.

32ND SS FREIWILLIGE GRENADIER DIVISION '30 JANUAR'
Raised **Jan 1945** at Grunow/Briesen (Kurmark) from SS arty, anti-tank and eng schools replacement units and Battle Group Schill; 25 Jan 1945 Frankfurt/Oder; Feb to April 1945 practically destroyed defending outer Berlin, encircled at Halbe, remnant Beelitz; May 1945 surrendered to US at Tangermünde.

38TH SS PANZER GRENADIER DIVISION 'NIBELUNGEN'
Raised **Mar 1945** at Freiburg/Schwarzwald then Grafenwöhr (Franconia) from Junkers School Bad Tolz, RAD and other personnel – six/seven part mot bns; April 1945 Neustadt/Kehlheim, Ingolstadt, Landshut; May 1945 surrendered to US at Reit-im-Winkel, upper Bavaria.

Part 3. Fighting the mobile battle

1. The panzer battle group

The thrusting tactics leading to encirclement of the enemy, a tradition taught to all combat arms of the German Army but for which panzer divisions in the early campaigns became particularly notorious, were put into effect by divisional battle groups (Kampfgruppen) varying in size and composition. The driving force in all such manoeuvres, as in any tank offensive, was provided by the panzer regiment employing tank battalions in close formation; a proportion of divisional and, if necessary, corps supporting arms assisted the tanks in their fighting task. Panzer artillery engaged fixed defences, engineers cleared obstacles, anti-aircraft troops protected bridges or other defiles on the axis of advance. The role of these specialists is explained in later sections. A regimental or supporting Kampfgruppe like those created around panzer grenadier and panzer reconnaissance battalions were organized by divisional commanders determined to exploit boldness and initiative, operating more or less independently along roads or across open country; battle group objectives, either enemy positions or terrain features, being dependent upon intentions and orders of higher commanders. But whatever the intended objective of a battle group, speed and surprise were vital considerations in every operational plan – fewer than twenty-five minutes being the time expected for a panzer regiment to shake-out from march order into attack formation; light tank companies in the lead.

The tank battalion of a regimental battle group advancing in waves, deployed its companies in wedge-shaped formation (Panzerkeil); at other times panzer battle groups adopted a bell-shaped formation (Panzerglocke), attacking with heavy tanks screened by medium or light vehicles. Liaison officers from ground attack, engineer and artillery units supporting the armoured movement, operated close to forward headquarters moving behind the leading tank wave

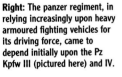

Right: The panzer regiment, in relying increasingly upon heavy armoured fighting vehicles for its driving force, came to depend initially upon the Pz Kpfw III (pictured here) and IV.

ready to summon immediate help as resistance developed. Divisional attacks, launched in waves of up to fifty tanks abreast on a 2,000–3,000-yard front, were carried out by regimental battle groups with two tank battalions forward. If the regiment had three battalions, the third battalion was held in reserve. Accompanied by engineer and other specialists, the first wave would drive deep into the enemy's artillery positions accompanied or followed by a second wave of panzer grenadiers mopping-up surviving resistance. A third wave of tanks and supporting infantry followed if necessary. The tank company, one of three or four in a battalion, moving with platoons in wedge formation, would have as its immediate objective enemy infantry, anti-tank and artillery positions which it would attack with high-explosives and machine-gun fire. Tank guns served equally as a major offensive weapon and as anti-tank protection. Flame-throwing tanks cleared positions immune to tank fire. Panzer engineers, assault artillery or other units reinforcing the attack, would be allotted to the leading tank wave or positioned close behind. In built-up or wooded areas panzer grenadiers fighting either from their vehicles or in dismounted action would lead the way. In operations to encircle the enemy when a breakthrough had been achieved, tank battalions changing to an appropriate formation would advance directly forward before bearing back in a wide circle to the original point of penetration; or two battalions starting on a narrow front would diverge after penetrating the enemy position and bear round in opposite arcs. Encirclement was complete when the forward tanks of either battalion met at a point approximately opposite the original breach. On a given wireless signal, the destruction of the enveloped forces would begin by simultaneous thrusts from

four points 90° apart. The following dramatic account of Panzer action in 1942 is taken from the diary of an artillery officer in 33rd Artillery Regiment, 15th Panzer Division, attacking Tobruk in Rommel's second and successful attempt to capture the port (map 9).

'The attack began at 0520 hours with a few minutes of intense artillery fire from every type of gun. This was followed by a Stuka attack [numbers not stated]. At 0600 hours infantry and engineers advanced and after three-quarters of an hour had crossed the anti-tank ditch. This was bridged over and first one then two lanes were made in the minefield. The tanks advanced closely followed by artillery. At 0930 hours 15th Panzer Division reported to DAK that Ariete was lagging behind.'

'Ariete was offered the use of the way-in which had been established by 15th Panzer Division, but managed to get on with the help of Stukas. At 1630 hours 15th Panzer Division reached the Tobruk–Acroma road and turned left.' At 1815 hours the officer records that his troop opened fire on Solaro, a defended locality astride the road three miles from their objective. By nightfall it was considered that the battle was won. The diary then records: 'The English destroyed all arms and vehicles, but some "fanatics" were still resisting the next morning.'

Rommel, in the forefront of battle, epitomized the practice of trained panzer commanders leading from the front. The need to set a personal example was instilled into all ranks – leading to staggering losses in officers and NCOs. In only five weeks of fighting, from 22 June to 26 July 1941, one panzer division recorded the loss of 147 officers (35 per cent) and 367 NCOs (19 per cent). Even greater casualties were experienced by another panzer division whose losses

Above: The Pz Kpfw III and IV only featured during the earlier campaigns in limited numbers; here a Pz Kpfw III prepares to move into action (*see* map 3).

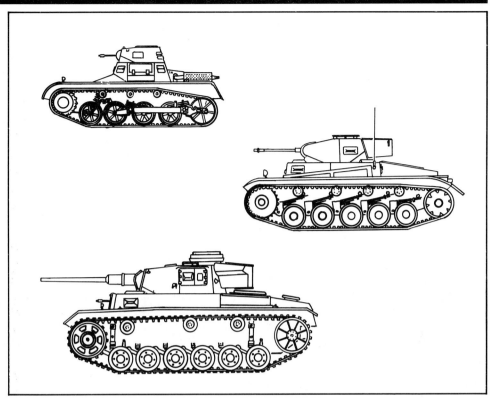

Right: The Pz Kpfw I, Sd Kfz 101, was armed with two machine-guns and crewed by two; it weighed six tons and could reach a speed of 32mph with a range of 95 miles.

Right: The Pz Kpfw II, Sd Kfz 121, carried a 2cm gun and a crew of two. The vehicle weighed ten tons, had a speed of 32mph, and a range of 112 miles.

Right: The Pz Kpfw III, Sd Kfz 141, had a 5cm gun and weighed 22 tons; it carried a crew of five and could manage a speed of 28mph over a range of 100 miles.

in dead or wounded during the period 22 June to 5 December 1941 reached a level of 351 officers (64 per cent) and 1,122 NCOs (47 per cent). Other divisions were to experience losses on a similar scale. Whenever a division was strong in assault guns (Sturmgeschütze) or other self-propelled artillery, the commander would move them well forward within battle groups. There they would engage likely targets over open sights at ranges of 1,000 yards or below. Anti-tank guns played an important role in tank battles. At first towed into action, later self-propelled (Jagdpanzer), they were intended to perform the same functions as destroyers in relation to battleships, to screen and protect the main body. Used at first in a static role countering advances by the opposing tank force, their employment in the Western Desert and eastern theatres developed into offensive action leap-frogging with tanks in the attack. Such tactics lead to heavy losses in British and Russian armour.

Heavy weapons of the Jagdpanzer and Sturmgeschütz type, able to attack and destroy their heavy opponents with 7.5cm or 8.8cm guns, equalled tanks in importance in the final (1945), establishment of the panzer division. The evolution of these weapons symbolized a distinct change in German strategic and tactical thinking, a measure of which can be read into the planned production of the new weapons, which in 1945 would have exceeded tank production by 350 per cent. During the closing stages of the war, Sturmgeschütz and panzer divisional battle groups were employed in direct support of infantry formations lacking basic tank protection. The practice served to increase the fragmentation of the panzer force, destroying its potential for swift and concentrated mobile intervention.

2. The panzer regiment

The strength of a panzer regiment, concentrated in battalions organized into three or four companies varied widely over the years and between formations; three was an average number of companies, but an SS panzer regiment in 1944 would contain up to five companies. Foreign vehicles, Czech (t) 35 and (t) 38 models in particular, served several regiments during the early years, constituting the core of 6th, 7th and 8th Panzer Divisions. At other times Sturmgeschütze were substituted for Panzer-kampfwagen.

In 1935 a panzer regiment of two battalions would consist of four, light companies each of 32 vehicles. By 1939 this had changed to three light and one medium company, each of 22 vehicles. But by 1944 a panzer regiment at the peak of wartime development consisted theoretically of two tank battalions each with four companies of seventeen vehicles (reduced from 22 in 1943). Half of these companies, were Panthers and half Pz Kpfw IVs. Together with headquarter company vehicles, the tank strength of a regiment then totalled 159. A 1945 panzer regiment, reflecting the change to a defensive strategy in its establishment, was intended to have only 54 tanks supported by 22 Jagdpanzers.

Starting in 1935, panzer regiments were equipped with vehicles weighing between 6 and 25 tons – the Pz Kpfw I to IV series of which after 1943 only the Pz Kpfw IV remained in production. Although intended to be replaced by the Pz Kpfw V Panther, the Pz Kpfw IV would nevertheless remain to serve out the war – overshadowed

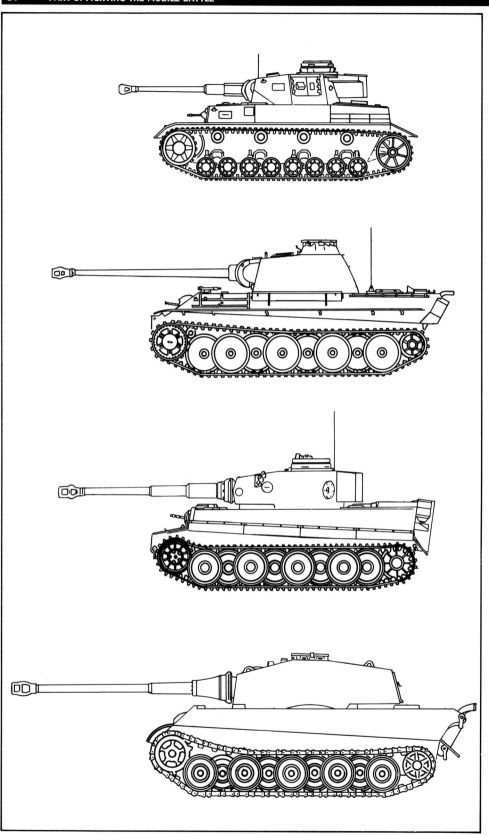

Left: The Pz Kpfw IV, Sd Kfz 161, was crewed by five men and armed with a 7.5cm gun. It weighed some 26 tons, but could still manage a speed of 30mph with a range of 100 miles.

Left: A Panther (Pz Kpfw V) Sd Kfz 171 armed with a 7.5cm 42 L/70 gun and manned by a crew of five. This mighty machine weighed 50 tons, had a speed of 35mph and a range of 60–120 miles.

Left: A Tiger (Pz Kpfw VI) Sd Kfz 181 armed with an 8.8cm 36 L/56 main armament and two 7.92mm MG 34s as secondary. It carried a crew of five, weighed 62 tons and could manage a speed of 25mph with a range of 50–80 miles.

Left: The King Tiger (Pz Kpfw VI IIB) Sd Kfz 182 had a crew five. Its firepower was provided by an 8.8cm 43 L/71 gun; it weighed 70 tons and travelled at 15–24mph.

by more illustrious counterparts. Introduced into service in 1934, the Pz Kpfw I at 6 tons was the lightest German tank model. Like its contemporary, the 10-ton Pz Kpfw II, it was phased-out after 1943 – other than for command or training purposes.

The Pz Kpfw III, a 20-ton medium tank, and the Pz Kpfw IV, a 25-ton vehicle, served as the main battle tanks in early campaigns. Main armament was improved by substituting the long-barrelled 5cm gun for the 3.7cm in the Pz Kpfw III and a 7.5cm gun replaced the 5cm weapon in the Pz Kpfw IV. Both vehicles were adapted to commanders' use

and as ammunition-carriers. Other roles included flame-throwing and armoured observation for panzer artillery. In Poland, France and in Russia until 1943, when mediums predominated in the panzer regiments, the ratio of medium to light tanks changed only slowly.

Regarded by many who knew it as the best tank of its generation, the greatly feared Panther, intended in 1942 as a replacement for the ageing Pz Kpfw IV, was introduced on to the battlefield at Kursk by Panzer Brigade Decker in mid-1943 (map 15). Teething troubles reduced the brigade's combat-ready vehicles from 200 to 40, but when

Right: This picture shows the Pz Kpfw IV.

Right: The increasing power of anti-tank weaponry inevitably led to heavier armour in an attempt to afford crews greater protection. After 1942 the panzer force was receiving tanks of up to 70 tons; pictured here is a 50-ton Panther which has halted at the roadside – note the protective skirt.

overcome, the Panther served notably with tank regiments on all fronts. The Panther's powerful 7.5cm gun, high speed, heavy (122mm) sloping armour and easy manoeuvrability commended it highly to its crew of five. The Jagdpanther, a noteworthy variant of the Panther incorporating an 8.8cm gun, was issued to panzer divisions and independent SP anti-tank battalions. The Bergepanther was employed in the recovery sections of regimental workshop companies.

The Tiger, an early German answer to the T34, planned as early as 1940, was introduced prematurely in August 1942 along an unsuitable, forested axis near Leningrad. The units concerned, 1/502, in action at Mga east of the city lost all four of its vehicles. The Western Allies first encountered the Tiger in North Africa at Tebourba where in December 1943 British First Army's drive to Tunis was halted. Engagements between Tigers and T34s with disastrous results for the latter, started at Kharkov in 1943 when II SS Panzer Corps recovered the city. A redoubtable armoured fighting vehicle, the Tiger was issued to heavy (schwere) tank battalions in the Army series 501–510 and SS series 501–503 (formerly 101–103). In company and eventually battalion strength, Tigers were also issued as standard equipment to selected panzer divisions: Gross Deutschland, Leibstandarte SS Adolf Hitler, Das Reich and Totenkopf. Delivering a severe jolt whenever it appeared on the battlefield, the Tiger went on to become the most famous tank of the war, winning a fearful but undeserved reputation for invincibility. Designed on familiar squat German lines with heavy frontal armour (144mm) and equipped with a high-velocity 8.8cm gun, the Tiger required skilful driving and maintenance from well-trained crews.

Tigers in panzer regiments or independent battalions served alongside Panthers or Pz Kpfw IVs on all war fronts. Slightly fewer than 1,500 vehicles were delivered to field and training units.

The King Tiger (Tiger II), a late development of Tiger I with heavier, sloped, armour and improved 8.8cm gun, made its first appearance on the battlefield in Normandy during August 1944 (a company from SS schwere Panzerabteilung 503) followed by action in the Ardennes and the Ruhr. By virtue of its great weight and low speed, the King Tiger was essentially a defensive weapon and in that capacity made its greatest impression. Fewer than five hundred were built during and after 1944 replacing Tiger Is in declining numbers mostly in Army and SS panzer corps heavy tank battalions. In company or lesser strength, on the Eastern Front, King Tigers reinforced the defence at crisis points in Hungary, Pomerania and in the final battle for Berlin (Panzerabteilung 503) Sturmtiger, *see p 105*.

	1 Sept 1939	10 May 1940	22 June 1941
Pz Bns	33[1]	35[2]	57[3]
Pz Kpfw I	1,445	523	180
Pz Kpfw II	1,223	955	746
Pz Kpfw III	98	349	965
Pz Kpfw IV	211	218	439
Others	218	469	1,187[4]
Total	3,195	2,574	3,417

[1]20 in five pz divs. [2]35 in ten pz divs. [3]47 in nineteen pz divs. [4]Includes 772 Pz Kpfw 38(t). The difference between pz bn total and numbers deployed in pz divs is accounted for by OKH allocations to light divisions (1939) and/or Army troops and pz divs in Africa (1941).

3. The panzer grenadier regiment

Fighting on the move from armoured personnel carriers, termed Schützenpanzerwagen (SPW) or, when the situation so required, fighting dismounted – clearing woods and villages or effecting river crossings – armoured (gepanzert) panzer grenadiers were organized into battalions of three or four (armoured) panzer grenadier companies. Deployed alongside panzer regiments and to complement tanks in action, panzer grenadier regiments were broadly comparable in mobility, but the second of the two panzer grenadier regiments in the establishment of a panzer division was usually motorized; élite SS panzer grenadier regiments and Panzerlehr excepted.

The medium weight, 3-ton Schützenpanzerwagen Sd Kfz 251, a lightly armoured and semi-tracked combat vehicle – not to be confused with the 1-ton machine used by panzer reconnaissance battalions – soon proved its value in action. In October 1943, following General Guderian's review of combat efficiency, no fewer than twenty-one variants of the Sd Kfz 251 were planned to meet differing needs of regimental units or support teams. Heavy weapon, engineer, signals, medical and other companies with specialized equipment were all provided for, but adequate numbers of SPWs were rarely available and although 16,000 were produced in numerous versions up to 1944, only a small proportion of the units for which they were intended actually received them. When SPWs were unavailable wheeled

vehicles were substituted and the norm more often than not became a mixture of both types of transport.

Evolved in 1937 from artillery tractors undergoing trials for the army, the basic 3-ton SPW was issued from 1939 onwards, at first on a limited scale to 1st Panzer Division. Lifting twelve men including a driver and commander, 23 such vehicles were required to transport a panzer grenadier company of 190 officers and men. Deploying two 8.1cm mortars, seven 20mm AA guns, two 7.5cm guns, 30 light and three heavy MGs, the 1944 armoured panzer grenadier company, with or without the support of tanks, became a powerful influence on any battlefield.

The six (armoured) panzer grenadier companies of a 1944 panzer division, organized into *two* panzer grenadier battalions each incorporating a battalion heavy weapons company and supported by regimental infantry gun, flak and engineer companies, provided a panzer grenadier regiment at full strength with outstanding firepower and independence. More powerful SS panzer grenadier regiments, found in élite formations, were sometimes – like Army panzer grenadier divisions (three regiments) – composed of *three* battalions each of four companies numbered 1 to 12, possessing extra (i.e., SP anti-tank) companies numbered 13 to 16. A panzer grenadier regiment would operate by forming battle groups around battalions or companies and allotting individual objectives to them.

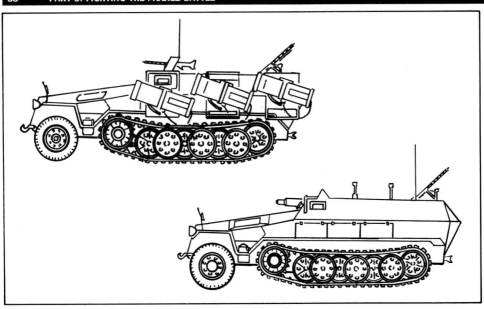

Left: Another SPW variant issued to panzer grenadiers was the 251/1 equipped with launching plates for 6.28cm rockets carried on frames inside the vehicle.

Left: A 251/9 SPW armed with a 7.5cm assault gun.

Below: Panzer grenadier regiments which fought on the move were served by numerous types of personnel carriers; pictured here is a medium-weight Hanomag 3-ton 251/10, armed with a 3.7cm anti-tank gun. This vehicle was issued to platoon commanders and this particular one was captured by the British in Libya.

Right: A rear view of a '251'
deployed in the Balkans; it
could carry twelve men
including driver.

Medium SPW:
Schützenpanzerwagen Sd Kfz
251 Variants
251/1: Standard vehicle
251/2: 8cm Mortar carrier
251/3: Radio vehicle
251/4: Ammunition carrier
   (for light infantry gun)
251/5: Assault engineer
   vehicle
251/6: Command vehicle
251/7: Engineer equipment
   carrier
251/8: Armoured ambulance
251/9: SP 7.5cm L/24 gun
251/10: SP 3.7cm A/T gun
251/11: Telephone/line laying
   vehicle
251/12: Survey section
   instrument carrier
251/13: Sound recording
   vehicle
251/14: Sound ranging vehicle
251/15: Artillery spotting
   vehicle
251/16: Flamethrower vehicle
251/17: SP AA vehicle, 2cm
   gun
251/18: Mobile observation
   post
251/19: Telephone exchange
   vehicle
251/20: Infra-red searchlight
   vehicle
251/21: SP AA vehicle with
   triple 1.5 or 2cm cannon
251/22: SP 7.5cm A/T gun

4. Panzer reconnaissance

Armoured reconnaissance battle groups leading a division
or protecting vulnerable flanks flushed out and overcame
light opposition. Advancing to contact, their role in addition
to seeking Intelligence about the enemy was to smooth the
way for oncoming armour. Such panzer Aufklärungsabtei-
lungen (alternatively termed Vorausabteilungen, forward
units) consisted of motor-cycle troops (Kradschützen), and
infantry in wheeled or semi-tracked armoured vehicles
accompanied by air, artillery and engineer liaison officers.
But the all too familiar image of motor-cycle troops
swarming along the roads ahead of an armoured division
was relevant only to summer campaigns in the west and
the early months of the war against Russia. Motor-cycle
combinations, at first civilian machines of all types, sprayed
uniformly dark-grey when employed in motor-cycle battalions, proved exceptionally manoeuvrable and capable of

making 'U' turns within the width of a road. They were also
exceptionally vulnerable to small-arms fire. Not until 1941
was a specially designed cross-country motor-cycle combination, with engine geared to both rear and side-car wheels
introduced into military service with motor-cycle battalions.
The BMW R75 and Zundapp KS750, both fitted with 2-
cylinder, 4-stroke engines, were built in the same factory.
Characteristic features included road and cross-country
gearing, reversing gear, exceptionally strong frames, high
positioning of engine and exhaust and large-profile tyres.
Solo machines were only issued to dispatch riders. Their
uses included traffic duty and road escort work.

Kradschützen armament included light machine-guns
mounted on combination side-cars and mortars to provide
covering fire whenever the two non-driving members of the
3-man crew were obliged to dismount. Dismounted riflemen
in turn provided covering fire while the driver moved his
machine out of hostile range. Kradschützen battalions were

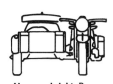

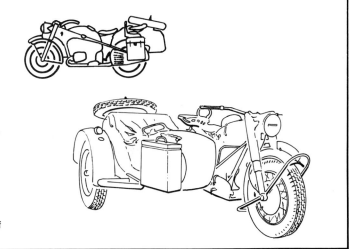

Above and right: Panzer
reconnaissance battalions
required fast and light vehicles
with which to advance, to
contact or protect the flanks of
their division. The motor cycle
served this purpose and
depicted here is a Zundapp KS
750 with sidecar which was
issued to motor cycle (m/c)
recon' battalions during the
early years of the war. It had a
speed of 60mph and a range of
175–200 miles.

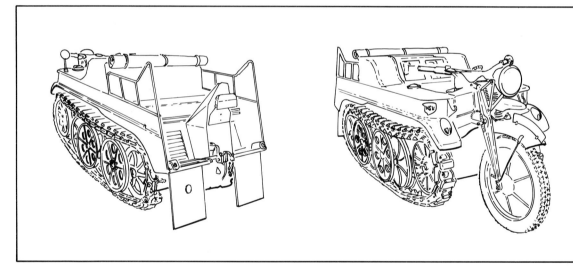

kept up to strength with captured and newly manufactured stocks of French and Belgian machines, but quite early on in Russia, where mud and snow predominated during autumn and winter, conditions proved radically different from those prevailing in the west and it soon became evident that motor-cycles were not suited for work in such terrain. Neither did they prove of more than temporary value in the Balkans or Africa where their performance was badly affected by dust.

In order to offset the limitations of the motor-cycle, new types of vehicle were introduced into panzer service and the armed forces generally. They were, the easy to maintain VW Kubel (bucket) and its variant the VW

Schwimmwagen (amphibian), both of which could be produced economically and in large numbers; also the Kettenkrad. Although less manoeuvrable than any of the motor-cycle combinations, the VWs had the advantage of being able to transport four or five men with extra weapons, ammunition and equipment. The Schwimmwagen, with its amphibious characteristics, certain of which detracted from its cross-country performance, was a great advantage in river crossings. So useful was the vehicle that it won the unofficial title of Kradschützenwagen.

The Kettenkrad, a small tractor with motor-cycle front, was equally versatile. Development commenced in July 1940, issues to reconnaissance companies beginning soon

Above: Front and rear views of the NSU Kettenkrad Sd Kfz 2. It had a speed of 70mph, weighed 1.2 tons, and had a range of 120–150 miles.

Top left: Motor cycle troops waiting for orders to move off on a reconnaissance exercise. The symbols (lower left) identify the unit as No. 1 m/c Coy of Schützen Regiment 69, 10th Panzer Division.

Top right: The Russian countryside, and changing battle conditions, soon revealed the motor cycles' limitations, especially in mud and snow. The VW 82 Kubelwagen and its schwimm-wagen variant, VW 166, although not immune to the motor cycles' problems, improved the mobility and tactical resources of panzer grenadiers and recce units. The vehicle in this 1943 picture carries a Gross Deutschland emblem and a tactical sign which identifies it as that of the panzer grenadier regimental CO.

Right: Kettenkrads demonstrated excellent mobility and performed widely varying duties for all services on all fronts.

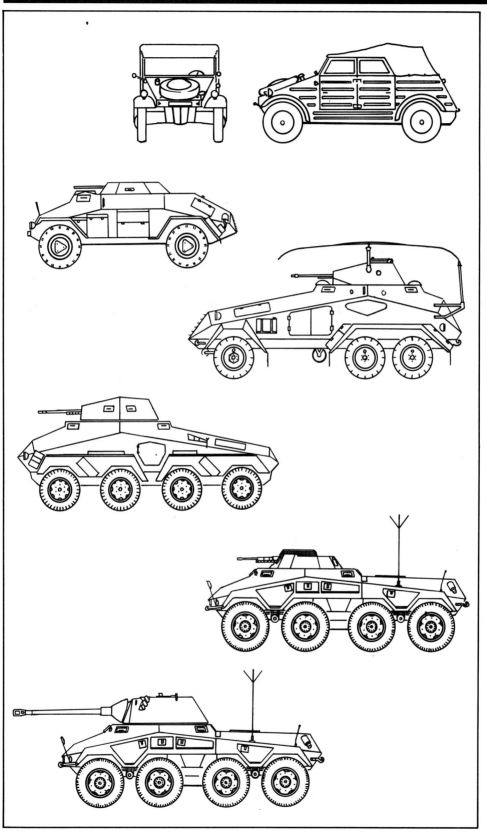

Left: A VW 82 Kubelwagen transporter could carry four t five men with weapons and equipment at a speed of 50mph. Some 37 variants existed for the use of army a Luftwaffe units on all fronts.

Left and right: Armoured ca serving reconnaissance companies varied in weight a battle-fitness. Both the light, four-wheeled Sd Kfz 221/2 a the heavy, eight-wheeled Sd 231 were retained in service for most of the war in one fo or another, while the six-wheeled Sd Kfz 232 was not. Shown right is the Sd Kfz 22 four-wheeled armoured car which could mount a single machine-gun or 2cm gun an coaxial MG (222), weighed 5 tons and had a speed of 50mph.

Left: This Sd Kfz 232 eight-wheeled armoured car (command model) had a 20mm armament, weighed 8 tons and had a speed of 50mph. It was a replacement for the six-wheeler.

Right: A Sd Kfz 232.

Left: Sd Kfz 234/1 mounting 2cm KWK L/55 cannon.

Left: Sd Kfz 234/2 eight-wheeled armoured car mounting a 5cm KWK L/60 gun. Known as Puma, it was crewed by three, weighed 11 tons, and had a speed of 50mph.

Left: Some eight-wheeled armoured car variants mounting a single 20mm gun and a coaxial machine-gun.

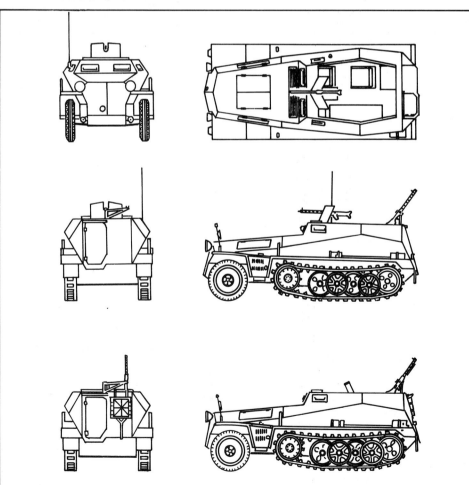

Left: Measures to improve reconnaissance mobility resulted in the production of small armoured semi-track. The Sd Kfz 251 had fourteen variants which served special needs; this particular one is Demag Sd Kfz 250/1 Light SPW. It weighed 1 ton, and transported six men at 37mph with a range of 200 miles.

Left: An Sd Kfz 250/7 armed with an 8cm mortar.

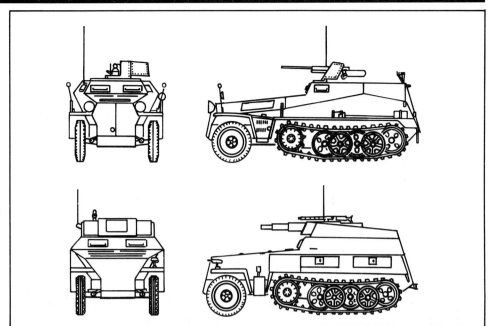

Right: An Sd Kfz 250/10 armed with a 3.7cm Pak.

Right: An Sd Kfz 250/8 armed with a 7.5cm assault gun.

Right: The Sd Kfz 250 light reconnaissance half-track, would have superseded road-bound armoured cars.

Light SPW:
Schützenpanzerwagen Sd Kfz 250 Variants
250/1: Standard vehicle
250/2: Telephone/line laying vehicle
250/3: Radio vehicle
250/4: Air support (Flivo) vehicle
250/5: Mobile observation post
250/6: Ammunition carrier
250/7: 8cm Mortar carrier
250/8: SP 7.5cm gun
250/9: Armoured reconnaissance vehicle
250/10: SP 3.7cm A/T gun
250/11: SP 2.8cm Panzerbüchse
250/12: Light survey instrument vehicle
252: Armoured ammunition carrier
253: Armoured mobile observation post

afterwards. The Kettenkrad was employed in many and varied roles, towing weapons, laying cables and transporting supplies. From Karelia to the Caucasus this diminutive workhorse served panzer troops, paratroops and most other arms of the services; 8,000 were produced up to the end of 1944.

Kradschützen were eventually absorbed into panzer grenadier or infantry reconnaissance battalions. By 1944 armoured reconnaissance companies replacing motor-cycle companies were transported either in 1-ton Sd Kfz 250 armoured troop-carriers or Volkswagens, leaving only a small proportion on motor-cycles. Battalion organization comprised one armoured car (Panzerspähwagen) company and three armoured reconnaissance companies. Issued to reconnaissance battalions in 1942, the '250' was to become the principal combat vehicle of the recce companies. Lightweight, fast across country, the basic '250' lifted a complement of six men; variants using the same semi-tracked chassis-mounted anti-tank and close-support guns.

By no means perfect, the '250', evolved in 1939 out of earlier light unarmoured vehicles designed for anti-tank or

other weapon-towing duties, restored the prestige and fitness for purpose of the Auflkärungsabteilungen. by 1944 some 7,599 machines had been built for use in twelve versions. Armoured cars serving the recce companies included a light 4-wheeler, a 6-wheeler (quickly phased out) and a heavy 8-wheeler. All entered service before 1939; two remained largely unchanged, but in the trackless conditions of European Russia and opposed by increasingly effective anti-tank weapons, they too were superseded by semi-tracks, notably the 250/9 with a superior cross-country performance and a turreted 20mm gun.

The original Sd Kfz 222 4-wheeler mounted a 20mm automatic gun; other versions were armed with a single MG or were fitted our as radio vehicles (Sd Kfz 223) equipped with folding, overhead frame aerial.

The Sd Kfz 231 8-wheeler was developed in a limited number of variants: the Puma with a 5cm gun mounted in a turret (Sd Kfz 233) and a turretless version (Sd Kfz 234) armed with a 7.5cm gun. These and a signals variant equipped with the familiar overhead frame aerial became the principal types in service.

5. Panzer engineers

Panzer engineers (Panzerpioniere) working in support of panzer or panzer grenadier battle groups were carried into action either in armoured semi-tracked SPWs or wheeled vehicles. They were usually positioned well to the fore in assault formations, demolishing tank obstacles, clearing lanes through minefields or in defensive situations creating strong points. More often than not panzer engineers worked under heavy fire using specially developed assault equipment including armoured (SPW) flame-throwers, remote-controlled Goliath demolition tanks and, at times, a radio-controlled, explosives-filled Pz Kpfw IV. In the poorly drained countryside in Russia where streams and rivers with marshy banks frequently needed permanent crossings, engineer bridging responsibilities proved highly demanding. In the experience of 6th Panzer Division's engineer battalion, 153 bridges were required in 150 days of fighting during the division's advance to Leningrad in the summer of 1941.

Heavy bridging operations were supervised by a Commander, Armoured Engineers (Panzerarmee Pionierefuhrer) at Army Headquarters, at whose disposal were heavy bridging columns supplemented if necessary by columns from OKH Reserve. Panzer commanders deploying heavy armoured fighting vehicles frequently taxed the load-carrying capacity of bridging columns; the mobility of their heavy panzer companies being greatly impaired by bridging limitations only gradually increased from 40 tonnes to 60 tonnes and later to 90 tonnes. Panzer engineer battalions were reorganized several times during the course of their existence. Their work under fire as early as 1939 made the introduction of armoured troop carriers essential. Yet by 1943, when a panzer engineer battalion was organized into three companies, only one-third was lifted in armoured SPWs; the remainder being motorized.

Within days of the attack on Russia, a true 'mine-war' started for the panzer force – requiring an exhausting effort by engineers to push through seemingly endless minefields.

LVII Panzer Corps recording progress on 12 July 1941 did so in the following terms: 'At the moment the advance can only proceed step by step because the enemy has blockaded all streets and roads with entanglements of trees and mines.' Similarly at the end of September, XXXXVII Panzer Corps, responsible to Second Panzer Army, reported: 'All streets in the advance area are mined. All bridges blown . . . six hundred mines lifted at one stream crossing.' In November, according to a report issuing from 3rd Panzer Division, mines were located in one town, '. . . in the main street, at the approaches to all bridges, on all access roads, at the railway station, in the town park, at the waterworks and water tanks, in all food stores and bakeries, around all public and corner buildings'. Anti-tank ditches arranged row upon row across their line of advance further slowed the progress of the panzer divisions. Between the ditches additional hazards such as buried heavy aerial bombs created long delays. Observers following the progress of panzer divisions in their lightning campaigns in Poland and the west might well have been forgiven for believing that nothing could halt them, but in Russia skilfully sited obstacles and minefields, often concealed under a thick layer of snow and only discovered when the foremost vehicle ran on to them, effectively stopped tanks for long periods. Quotations from the war diary of another panzer corps demonstrate the extent to which panzer tactics were affected by minefields and the need of panzer engineers to neutralize them. 'Intensively mined areas are forcing us to attack, as if in an infantry action.' And, 'The tanks of 4th Panzer Division have not advanced but lie trapped in a minefield.' 'In three days' fighting from 1st–3rd December 1941, 21 Panzer Regiment lost no fewer than 10 tanks due to damage caused by mines.' Panzer engineers, in their efforts to reduce mine losses, performed a crucial service to panzer divisions often in the most hazardous of circumstances. In demolishing tank obstacles of all descriptions, neutralizing fortified positions, bridging water obstacles or anti-tank ditches, and helping the division through defiles, the engineers earned a reputation as the hardest of the hard men in the German Army.

Right: A prefabricated box girder bridge of 40-ton capacity, bolted together in sections and capable of spanning 64 feet, carried th[e] Pz Kpfw IV to safety if need[ed] Fascine bundles were nevertheless essential in see[ing] the vehicles through swamp[s] and over soft river banks.

Right: Recovering ditched vehicles was work for the ta[nk] recovery sections of the workshop companies.

Left: Panzer engineers were called upon to solve many assault and engineering problems in order to keep panzer divisions moving; bridging and ferrying were [the] two of the most frequent tas[ks] undertaken by engineers in [the] trackless Russian interior.

6. Panzer artillery

Artillery that could advance with panzer divisions and provide equally mobile fire support was no less vital a part of Guderian's formula for a balanced force of all arms breaking through and operating in the rear of enemy positions than tanks or motorized infantry. The first tracked weapon of this kind was a 15cm heavy infantry gun sIG 33, mounted on a light tank (Pz Kpfw I) chassis. In 1942 a more stable version using Pz Kpfw II chassis was issued to the heavy infantry gun companies of panzer grenadier regiments and panzer artillery battalions.

A heavy (15cm) field howitzer SfH 18/1 known as Hummel (bumble-bee) increased the power of panzer artillery. Produced from 1943 onwards, the Hummel remained in service until the end of the war, by which time more than 600 had been built. Equally effective, serving at first with DAK (Deutsches Afrika Korps), was the SfH 13/1, an older heavy howitzer mounted on a French Lorraine chassis. But most popular of all panzer artillery weapons was the Wespe (wasp), a light, 10.5cm field howitzer mounted on the Pz Kpfw II chassis introduced in 1942 (Pz Kpfw II's principal use after February 1943). When production ceased in 1944 due to deteriorating economic and military conditions, more than 600 of these exceptionally useful support weapons had been produced for panzer service.

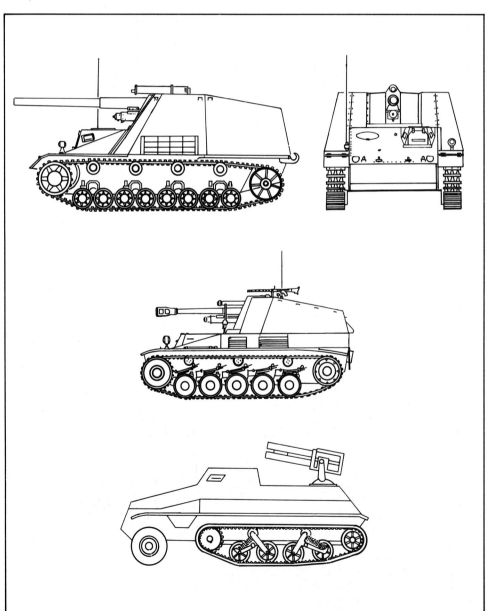

Left: A Hummel Sd Kfz 165 in profile. The 15cm field howitzer had a range of 14,000 yards, a crew of 6 and a weight of 26 tons.

Left: Wespe Sd Kfz 124 in profile. This 10.5cm field howitzer had a range of 14,000 yards, a crew of 5, and a weight of 12.5 tons.

Left: A Panzerwerfer 42, Sd 34/1, in profile. The ten-barrelled 15cm rocket projector was mounted on an Opel 'Maultier' (mule). It weighed 7 tons and had a speed of 25mph.

Right: Panzer artillery, deployed in mobile support of the panzer regiments, was a vital part of Guderian's concept of a mechanized force of all arms. Two of the most effective and widely used self-propelled artillery weapons were the Hummel and Wespe. Here a battery of Hummels (bumble bees) is in a firing position waiting for orders.

Right: A rear view of the Panzerwerfer 42, one of a growing family of rocket-launchers which matched the 'Stalin organ' in mobility and firepower. Its successor, the Nebelwerfer 42, could traverse through 360 degrees with a range of 7,000 yards, but its accuracy was less than that of conventional artillery weapons.

Left: A Wespe (wasp) negotiating rough ground to change its position.

7. Panzerjaeger and Jagdpanzer

The tracked anti-tank weapons of the panzer force, broadly classed as Panzerjaeger, started with anti-tank guns on improvised mountings, mostly tank chassis; crews were protected by an open armour-plated superstructure. More satisfactory were the fully enclosed, purpose-designed and produced weapons, Jagdpanzer, resembling tanks in appearance and at times in performance. In the first category, rushed into service in 1940 during the Battle of France, was the makeshift Marder series initially featuring a Czech 4.7cm anti-tank gun mounted on a German Pz Kpfw I chassis – Marder I. This was followed by Marder II mounting a (captured) Russian 7.62cm anti-tank gun on the Pz Kpfw II chassis. In turn, Marder II was succeeded in 1942 by Marder III employing first the Czech 38(t) mounting, but later substituting the French Lorraine chassis and armed with the German 7.5cm PaK, anti-tank gun, 40/3.

Of greater significance was the Nashorn (rhinoceros) formerly Hornisse (hornet) armed with the powerful 8.8cm PaK. 43 introduced during the Battle of Kursk, 1943. Other anti-tank weapons, either improvised armoured car chassis or mounted in SPWs, afforded basic protection for panzer grenadier companies. These same companies were also issued with the Panzerfaust, a hand-held rocket-launcher. A second and more elaborate category of weapons – Jagdpanzer (tank destroyer) – was a natural outcome of the first. Excluding a Sturmgeschütz III adaptation armed with a 7.5cm gun, the first true Jagdpanzer, Ferdinand, introduced in 1943 at Kursk, was a re-designed Porsche Tiger (Henschel being responsible for the production Tiger). Although armed with a powerful, long-barrelled 8.8cm gun,

the vehicle's poor vision, mechanical unrealiability and lack of a machine-gun for close protection disappointed designer and user alike.

A turretless Jagdpanzer IV using Pz Kpfw IV chassis, Sd Kfz 162 followed in late 1943 and in two variants both armed with the 7.5cm PaK served out the war with the anti-tank battalions of panzer divisions. But not until the arrival of the Jagdpanther, armed with the 8.8cm PaK 43, was the panzer force provided with a truly successful tank destroyer design. Production of this fast, well-armoured, low-profile vehicle, carrying a crew of five, started in February 1944 and by April 1945 some three hundred had been delivered to anti-tank battalions.

Equally successful and produced in sizeable numbers (more than 15,000 by the end of the war) was a light Jagdpanzer, the Hetzer (baiter) using the Czech 38(t) chassis. Introduced in May 1944, for the use of infantry anti-tank battalions, the Hetzer was armed with the 7.5cm PaK 39. A variant entered service as a flame-thrower.

Finally, the Jagdtiger, Jgd Pz VI, a hunting version of the Tiger (B) armed with the formidable 12.8cm PaK 44, earned distinction as the biggest and most powerful fighting vehicle of the war. This distinction failed to translate into success on the battlefield and the few vehicles that entered service in 1945, notably with two companies of 512th Schwere Panzerjaeger Battalion during March against the US bridgehead at Remagen and, until capitulation, in the Ruhr pocket at Iserlohn (*see* Fifth Panzer Army, 14 April 1945), proved sluggish in manoeuvre and subject to unremedied mechanical faults.

Right: Panzerjaeger and Jagdpanzer tracked anti-tank weapons and assault guns came to equal tanks in importance in the 1945 establishment of a panzer division. The principal types discussed in the text are illustrated here in profile.

Right: Marder I, 4.7cm Pak, weighed 6.4 tons and was crewed by three.

Right: Marder III, 7.5cm Pak 40/3 Sd Kfz 138, weighed 10 tons and was crewed by four. It had a speed of 26mph and a range of 115 miles.

Right: The Nashorn (rhinoceros) was an 8.8cm Pak 43, Sd Kfz 164, which weighed 27 tons and required a crew of five. It could manage speeds of 25mph with a range of 160 miles.

Right: Jagdpanzer IV 7.5cm Pak, Sd Kfz 162, had a crew of four, a speed of 24mph and a range of 160 miles; quite impressive for its weight of 28 tons.

Right: The Elefant (Ferdinand) 8.8cm Pak, Sd Kfz 184, weighed 68 tons and had a crew of six. It could reach speeds of 25mph with a range of 100 miles.

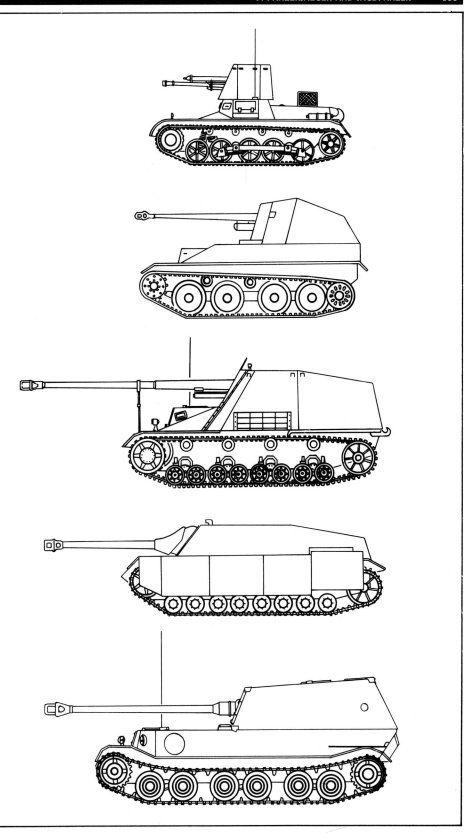

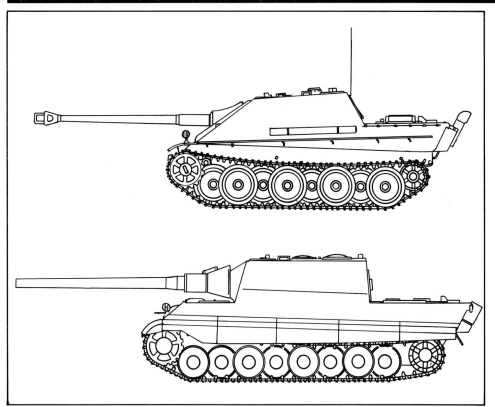

Left: The Jagdpanther 8.8cm Pak 43/3, Sd Kfz 173, was crewed by five and weighed 5 tons. It had a speed of 29mph and a range of 85 miles.

Left: The Jagdtiger 12.8cm P 44, Sd Kfz 186, weighed 77 tons and had a crew of six. It had a speed of 25mph, a range of 105 miles, and was the heaviest vehicle in panzer force service.

8. Flakpanzer

When enemy air opposition expanded to the point of sweeping the weak and overstrained Luftwaffe from the skies after 1943, anti-aircraft protection for panzer divisions at rest or on the move demanded urgent reassessment. In Russia, Italy and France enemy air forces hammered panzer columns unmercifully reducing them more often than not to blackened wrecks – destroying all efforts at swift concentration and counter-attack. Flakpanzer, tracked anti-aircraft weapons with power-driven turrets, to protect panzer formations against harassing low-flying attack were devised all too late. Of the types planned, few entered service. The first of an early generation of tracked anti-aircraft weapons to serve the panzer force was the Sd Kfz 140, a 20mm FlaK 30 mounted on a Czech 38 chassis. This was followed by two- (zwilling) and four- (vierling) barrelled versions of the gun on Pz Kpfw IV chassis. A more powerful 3.7cm gun belatedly entered service at Guderian's insistence in 1943. Nicknamed Mobelwagen (furniture van), this too was mounted on a Pz Kpfw IV chassis.

Anti-aircraft protection for panzer divisions had been part of German thinking from the earliest days but never to the extent necessary. Pre-war and early wartime production shortages delayed the introduction of 20mm dual-purpose weapons (into the anti-*tank* battalions) to all but a few of the panzer, motorized infantry, light as well as infantry divisions for which it was intended. When available the gun was employed against both air and ground targets; twelve to a flak company. Steps to improve matters brought Army flak battalions into panzer divisions re-equipped for the 1942 summer offensive (map 10). By 1943, flak battalions equipped with eight 88s and fifteen 20mm weapons were intended for all panzer and certain panzer grenadier divisions. At the same time a 20mm weapons company was introduced into panzer grenadier regiments serving both panzer and panzer grenadier divisions. But when SPWs similarly armed were distributed throughout the regiment, seven guns each to individual panzer grenadier companies, the need for this company became less pronounced.

Not until mid-1944 did the establishment of a panzer division provide for a panzer regiment with a flak section of eight Wirbelwind (whirlwind) or later (3.7cm) Ostwind (east wind) incorporating powered revolving turrets to deal with high-speed, low-flying attack.

Until the advent of Army flak battalions in 1942, reliance was placed largely upon anti-aircraft units allotted to panzer formations by the Luftwaffe; these, while tactically under Army control, remained Luftwaffe property (*see* Part 4). Luftwaffe units of this type equipped either with the 20mm Flak 30 standard light anti-aircraft gun, or the heavy 8.8cm gun first produced in 1934 to become the standard (mobile) anti-aircraft gun, accompanied the Condor Legion to Spain. Both guns quickly proved their effectiveness – in the role for which they were intended and in action against ground targets. The 8.8cm gun in particular produced devastating effects against tanks and fortified positions and was exploited to the maximum by crews firing over open sights. The '88' evolved as probably the most versatile weapon of the war, playing a crucial role in defeating tank attacks.

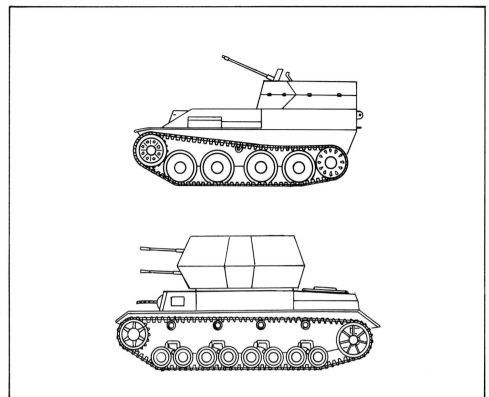

Right: The 2cm Flakpanzer (38t) Sd Kfz 140, had an open turret, weighted 10 tons, and had a crew of five.

Right: The 2cm × 4 'Wirbelwind' (whirlwind) was built on a Pz Kpfw IV chassis with an enclosed power turret. It weighed 22 tons, had a crew of five, and was introduced into panzer service in 1944.

Right: Flakpanzer, starting with the 2cm Flak, became an increasingly important class of self-propelled weapons. Used against both air and ground targets, the 2cm Flak seen here is deployed in a static role with its SS crew preparing their defence against low-flying attack. It was towed into action and had an effective ceiling of 3,500 feet.

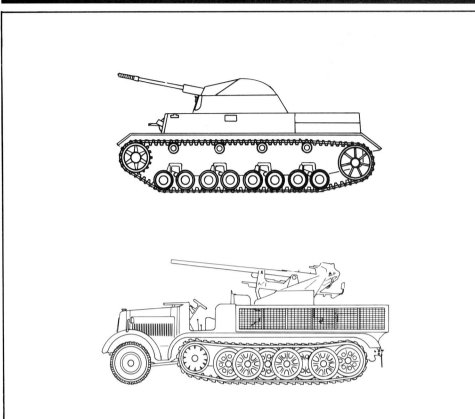

Left: The 3cm × 2 'Kugelblitz' was built on a Pz Kpfw IV chassis. This experimental Daimler-Benz model, with high-speed, enclosed power turret, weighed 24 tons and had a crew of five.

Left: The 3.7cm Flak mounted on a 5-ton half-track was replaced with an armoured model needing an 8-ton half-track which gave better protection to the crew of seven. It had an effective ceiling of 5,000 feet.

Above: An 8cm Flak in its travelling position. This weapon had an effective ceiling of 20,000–30,000 ft and together with two hundred or more types of tanks, assault guns, Sturmpanzer and other FVs, made a notable contribution while serving the panzer force.

Left: The 2cm × 2 Flak mounted on a 5-ton halftrack provided poor protection for its crew of five, but was a useful mobile weapon.

9. Sturmgeschütze, Sturmpanzer and miscellaneous vehicle types

Considerably more than two hundred types of armoured vehicle were designed or planned to serve the panzer force during the period 1929 to 1945: 94 tanks, 42 SPWs, 19 armoured cars, thirteen Panzerjaeger, ten Jagdpanzer and twelve Flakpanzer. Among miscellaneous vehicle types introduced into panzer service during the course of the war the following were most prominent.

Sturmgeschütz, turretless, self-propelled assault guns not intended for panzer divisions but soon in widespread use were designed for infantry support; their role in the attack being to provide close assistance for assaulting infantry. In defence, especially against tank attacks, assault gun manoeuvrability and fire power greatly strengthened divisional capacity to resist. Organized as army/corps troops into assault gun battalions (Sturmgeschütze Abteilungen) (renamed brigades in 1943) with 21 guns in three batteries each of seven weapons, their numbers increased at the expense of tank production. By the spring of 1944, 45 assault gun brigades were serving in the east. A German innovation attributed to von Manstein during his service with the Truppenamt in 1935, the Sturmgeschütz, equivalent to a turretless tank with heavy frontal armour, introduced into service in 1939, required a crew of four and initially mounted a low-velocity weapon in the front hull. But as the war progressed other higher performance guns were substituted. Several variants using Panzer III chassis (no longer required for tank production after 1943) entered service; one, the Sd Kpfz 162 armed with a 7.5cm anti-tank gun, becoming the forerunner of the Jagdpanzer.

Sturmpanzer IV, Brummbär, 15cm Stu. Howitzer produced in small numbers and a handful of Sturmtigers armed with a massive rocket-projector were intended for street fighting. Introduced in 1944 the howitzer contributed to the fire power of panzer artillery and heavy weapons companies of panzer grenadier regiments. The Sturmtiger, of which no more than ten were built early in 1944 and divided between two companies, 1000 and 1001, served as Army troops to break Polish resistance in Warsaw 1944, before their transfer to the Ardennes (Fifteenth Army) followed by action in the Ruhr pocket in 1945.

Miscellaneous types of unarmoured vehicles developed in other categories included experimental weapon carriers (Waffenträger), ammunition carriers (Munitionsschlepper), armoured rocket-launchers (Panzerwerfer) and observation vehicles (Beobachtungspanzerwagen). Fuel delivery trucks and armoured recovery vehicles (Bergepanzerwagen) together with supply transport raised the wheeled and tracked complement of a 1944 panzer division to more than 3,000 vehicles, excluding tanks and SP artillery.

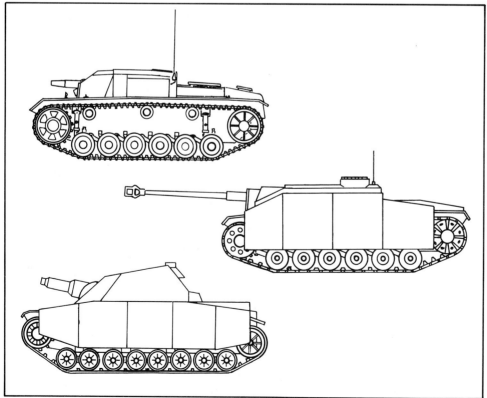

Left: The Sturmgeschütz III, 7.5cm L/24 Sd Kfz 142, tu[r] less AFV. Intended as infant[ry] support, the assault gun nevertheless served in panz[er] regiments and independent brigades. It weighed 22 ton[s], had a crew of four and a sp[eed] of 20mph. Higher performa[nce] guns were substituted in lat[er] models.

Left: Sturmgeschütz III, Sd [Kfz] 142/1, assault gun armed w[ith] the 7.5cm StuK 40 L/48 w[hich] remained in use until 1945.

Left: The five-man Brumbä[r] (grizzly bear) 15cm howitze[r] Sd Kfz 166, was based on t[he] Pz Kpfw IV chassis and weig[hed] 28 tons. A late developmen[t in] the 'sturm' or close-support category, together with the more limited Sturmtiger, it [was] issued to panzer-grenadier heavy-companies and Army panzer battalions.

Left: Sturmgeschütz III, Sd Kfz 142/1, assault gun armed with the 7.5cm StuK 40 L/48.

10. Panzer signals (and 'Ultra')

The signals system of a panzer division was the responsibility of a divisional signals officer (Nachrichtenführer) with both line (telephone) and wireless companies at his disposal. The purpose of the system was to transmit instructions and information between commander, staffs and subordinate or attached units; the mobility of signal detachments particularly those on the move with a commander at battle headquarters being assured by transportation in wheeled or half-tracked vehicles. At rear headquarters the Nachrichtenführer co-ordinated all communications of the division, whether at rest or on the move, supervising links to rearward and neighbouring formations, and liaising continuously within units; a generous distribution of divisional wireless and telecommunications equipment achieving the desired results. At corps and army level the signals equipment included facilities for wireless Intelligence; panzer commanders, Rommel in particular, setting great store by the work of signals specialists who deduced enemy strengths, dispositions and intentions from radio intercepts. The importance of wireless communication directing and controlling mobility and firepower on the battlefield, had been recognized by those in authority from the earliest days of the panzer force.

During the early thirties a key figure guiding Army signals technology and organization was General Erich Fellgiebel, a 1914–18 veteran appointed Inspector of Signal Troops (In 7) in October 1934. Fellgiebel's experience of wartime communications began when he was a signals officer with 4th Cavalry Division. In charge of a signals detachment working with a reconnaissance troop, his duty was to advise headquarters of enemy movement through the use of rudimentary wireless equipment transported in a 6-horse wagon.

The fundamental step in the process of linking panzer commands to subordinates as required by Guderian, who was intent upon welding panzer divisions into ever larger battle formations, was the introduction into military service

of ultra-short-wave radio – the brainchild of Colonel Gimmler, head of signals section 7 of the Heereswaffenamt. In 1938, when Guderian's XVI Corps epitomized panzer progress, the signals officer of that formation, Colonel (later General) Albert Praun, promoted from command of 2nd Panzer Signals Battalion, played a leading role in the development of wireless communication at command level. Following the attempt on Hitler's life in July 1944, Praun was to replace General Erich Fellgiebel as the Army's senior signals officer. Guderian, although inheriting a family tradition of infantry (Hannoverjaeger) service had, at his own wish, acquired a thorough understanding of wireless procedures and potential both prior to and during the course of the First World War, serving with a telegraph company in Coblenz (1912), a cavalry unit at the Battle of the Marne (1915), and in Fourth Army signal staff appointments (1915–17).

Spurred by foreign (notably British in 1931) experiments in the tactical control of armoured formations, Guderian's interest in wireless technology continued undiminished during the inter-war years. By 1940 thanks to Fellgiebel, Praun and Gimmler, progress in mobile communications had been so swift that, working from a suitably equipped armoured command vehicle, Guderian was able to keep pace with his units on the battlefield, ordering changes in deployment by wireless immediately such action became necessary – an advantage denied to his opponents until much later.

From a mobile battle headquarters, Guderian extended communications forward so that orders travelling via intermediate levels reached advance units and individual tanks whose wireless operators, with ultra-short-wave sets ranging up to six miles, worked under orders of the tank commander. During the course of battle, radio operators when not actually transmitting, would keep sets on 'receive'; in a crisis they were also expected to man the hull machine-gun. In addition to wireless equipment German tanks had an

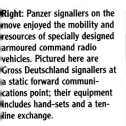

Right: Panzer signallers on the move enjoyed the mobility and resources of specially designed armoured command radio vehicles. Pictured here are Gross Deutschland signallers at a static forward communications point; their equipment includes hand-sets and a ten-line exchange.

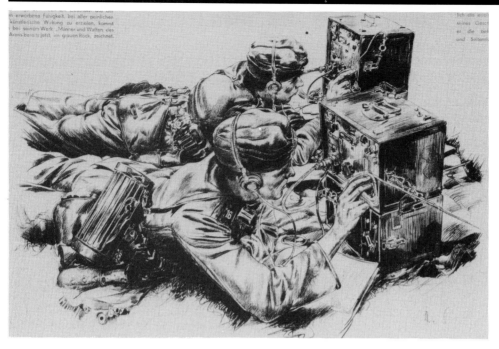

Left: Wireless communication between dismounted panzer grenadiers, their headquarters and mobile units was facilitated by portable W/T equipment (used in the illustration by men of 16th Infantry Regiment). More than thirty different types of transmitter and fifteen types of receiver were in use by signallers in 1941.

internal telephone system allowing tank commanders access to both driver and wireless operator and, by speaking-tube, to the gunlayer and loader. Individual tanks in wireless contact with platoon (and upwards through company) benefited from battalion links to other units and to supporting units such as artillery and engineers. During static periods, as an alternative to wireless, the telephone companies were expected to lay land-lines between units and thereby reduce wireless traffic to a minimum rendering communications 'silent'. When at such times, units were not actively mobile, a very complete telephone network was built up; dispatch riders or couriers supplementing land-lines proved essential when communications were interrupted by enemy action. The network of lines established by a formation such as DAK in North Africa, would typically comprise connections to individual staff officers, headquarter units, corps troops and main divisional formations. Lines were also laid to fixed exchanges at rearward points where further connection could be made to formations or units not directly under DAK control. The work of signals personnel at higher headquarters, for example that of an army signals regiment – two battalions each of three companies – included wireless interception analysis and direction-finding. In consequence the monitoring of enemy call-signs and the systematic logging of their orientation provided Intelligence staffs with invaluable information.

For a time, when Eighth Army, with a notable exception that was to prove Rommel's undoing (see Panzer Army Africa, 18 November 1941), was lagging behind German efficiency in this important sphere of Intelligence, the British order of battle, tank strength, equipment levels and tactical progress were as well known to the German commander as to his opponents; Rommel came to rely heavily upon signal Intelligence to supplement meagre photographic reconnaissance and laid plans accordingly, particularly at times when the air situation was not in his favour. Unfortunately for

Rommel, total British awareness of Mediterranean transport movement – individual cargoes even – intended for Panzer Group Africa would contribute directly to defeat. At the heart of this success lay one of the Second World War's best kept secrets – the breaking of German Enigma ciphers. In early and widespread use by all three services, including the panzer force at appropriate levels, the Enigma cipher machine fell into British hands early in the war. Thereafter much of what was 'Ultra' secret being transmitted by Enigma link between Berlin, Rome and North Africa, more especially Flivo's requesting air support in Normandy (see Part 4), was read by the Government Code and Cipher School at Bletchley and passed to field commands. The consequence of this German security failure was a major factor in Allied victory.

A distinctive feature of a panzer division's wireless plan, 16th Panzer's, for instance, during the advance to Uman in 1941, was the allocation of a fixed call-sign for the exclusive use of formation commanders at division and above, enabling them to interrupt wireless traffic on any link and be immediately recognized.

In the important sphere of defensive planning, signals security required call-sign and frequency changes to be made at irregular intervals – often daily; the highest frequencies with least chance of interruption being reserved for tank regiments and air to ground traffic. Other defensive measures included long wireless 'silences' and jamming action. German army group information bulletins covering weather or the military situation in general, were regularly broadcast; programmes going on the air at set times. Lower formations were expected to listen-in two or three times daily. Air co-operation broadcasts served to transmit important reports quickly, and could be expected at any time. Such broadcasts, provided with serial numbers, helped recipients to check that none had been missed.

Right: Panzer repair and recovery teams operating within regimental workshop companies provided round the clock service to the panzer regiment. Here an armoured command vehicle is receiving replacement engine at the hands of regimental personnel in Libya.

Far right, top: More elaborate workshop repairs necessitating heavy lifting gear were carried out in base workshops operating within panzer army transport/maintenance parks. In this photograph a Panther has come in for repair.

Far right, bottom: Recovery platoons collecting damaged vehicles, like this 'Marder' I anti-tank gun, would use the 22-ton low-loader; the towing machine is a 12-ton Sd Kfz 8. The restoration of armour to battle-fit condition was a crucial function.

11. Panzer recovery and repair

Tank repair and maintenance troops (Panzerinstandsetzungs-struppen), not withstanding their limited distribution within a panzer division, provided services vital to maintaining the tempo of an attack. When replacement tanks were in short supply, as was generally the case, prompt action by repair and recovery units proved decisive. Damaged tanks were swiftly recovered and defective ones rehabilitated by repair and recovery sections of regimental workshop companies. Recovering battle-damaged tanks or other vehicles of a panzer regiment by collecting on low-loaders, or alternatively bringing them in behind suitable towing machines, was nominally the responsibility of regimental workshop tank recovery sections. But so great was the need at times of stress for armoured fighting vehicles to be returned into action with the least possible delay that *ad hoc* recovery teams were organized at short notice by fighting units on instructions from divisional commanders. Facing hazards of enemy air attack, working through undetected minefields or under constant shellfire, recovery teams laboured round the clock to maintain panzer strengths at the highest possible level. In Africa, where a tremendous toll of armour was taken by enemy ground and air action, twenty minutes was regarded as a good time for loading a damaged tank on to

a low-loading transporter. At other times suitable vehicles were sent out to bring tanks in with hawsers.

Salvaged machines, including captured ones, were returned by day or night to assembly points at the rear where repair units could deal with them; captured vehicles constituting a high proportion of panzer division establishments. But the use of transporters became less and less frequent in all theatres until they were eventually confined to roads where they could maintain comparatively high speeds. Instead, tanks were regularly towed by standard towing machines of either 6- or 18-tons. For recovering heavy tanks like the Tiger, recovery sections were theoretically issued with a variant of the Tiger itself, the Bergpanzer Tiger equipped with spade and winch. In practice, two 18-ton towing machines were usually coupled and damaged Tigers hauled off in this way.

Bergepanthers and Pz Kpfw IIIs adapted to recovery roles were also employed in salvage operations. Tank repair, as distinct from tank recovery, sections were included in panzer establishments at company, battalion and regimental level. Tank crews were nevertheless expected to make their own running repairs – only heavy work being undertaken in regimental workshops. Equipped with mobile cranes and

recovery vehicles, regimental workshops were a crucial part of the German concept of an independent mobile force. Workshop companies at panzer army level undertook more difficult and time-consuming work; their equipment including heavy lifting gear. Ranged alongside panzer army heavy workshop companies were army motor transport parks and other specialist units allotted to panzer formations by OKH

– including tank spares and motor tyre depots. Separate transport columns were sometimes allotted to panzer formations for transporting these essential stores. The repair and maintenance of wheeled vehicles belonging to a panzer division was the responsibility of a divisional workshop company; only in a crisis would this unit undertake tank repairs.

12. **Panzer supply and transport**

The supply and transport services of a panzer division were the responsibility of a Kommandeur der Divisions Nach-schubtruppen, abbreviated to Kodina. At panzer army headquarters a 'Nachschubführer' with wider organizing and co-ordinating powers was ultimately responsible for all questions relating to supply and transport within the formation. Divisional supplies were usually brought forward by attached motor transport columns, each of standardized capacity, working between army railheads and divisional supply points. A light column, twelve or more vehicles, had a capacity of 90 tonnes and a heavy column, 22 or more vehicles, 120 tonnes. Although numbers of columns and vehicles varied considerably between divisions, four to six such columns were usual in a 1944 panzer division establishment. A keynote of the system was flexibility enabling army and divisional supply commanders to switch columns and concentrate them wherever they were tactically required.

Under army control, road tankers or more often 4–5-ton standard trucks supplemented Kodina's resources. Organized into columns of either 5,500 or 11,000 gallons capacity, they transported petrol in 200-litre steel drums filled from rail tankers at army railheads, bringing them to issue points in forward areas. In a crisis, standard supply arrangements were frequently varied; the movement of petrol, ammunition or rations then being undertaken by improvised columns or transport groups of the Luftwaffe. This later likelihood was catered for as early as April 1940 when panzer divisions in the west were advised of air supply procedures (see Part 4, New Horizons in Transport); crisis facilities becoming increasingly necessary in later years as divisions and entire panzer armies outran or were cut off from landward re-supply.

In 1943 a radical step was taken towards centralizing divisional supply services following Guderian's appointment as Inspector-General of Panzertruppen. Supply facilities were then concentrated in battalion supply companies attached to panzer, panzer grenadier and reconnaissance battalions – thereby gathering into a single unit the former rear echelon transport vehicles of fighting companies leaving company commanders with only their battle transport. Fighting company commanders, hitherto responsible for the movement of their own supplies, were consequently relieved of this administrative duty and freed to concentrate more upon tactical problems. The work of loading and unloading divisional supply columns was the responsibility of a divisional supply company. Theirs' was the primary duty of establishing supply points from which the new battalion supply companies using their own vehicles provisioned the combat companies for which they were responsible. A

volunteer labour force of east Europeans and Russian prisoners-of-war, 'Hiwis' (Hilfeswilliges), many of whom were Georgians or Ukrainians, were used to augment supply company personnel. Hiwis accompanying transport drivers also assisted in handling supplies and setting up supply points.

Panzer corps were largely bypassed in the chain of supply until 'organic' panzer corps such as Gross Deutschland – consisting of a panzer and a panzer grenadier division – were being established in 1944–5. Only then, when a corps supply company became responsible for both organic divisions, did this intermediate level between division and army assume real importance in the chain of supply. Notwithstanding attempts by OKW to standardize transport and fighting vehicle production, a characteristic of all supply columns was the varied number and types of vehicles on establishments; multifarious German and foreign vehicles creating an exceptional problem for the workshop companies responsible for repair and maintenance. In 1944 upwards of 96 different types of vehicle could still be found in the wheeled complement of a panzer division; Panzer Lehr, for instance, in Normandy recorded 60 per cent of its transport as being of foreign origin. When autumn and spring rains turned the Eastern Front into a morass rendering vehicle movement impossible, peasant transport was commandeered and pressed into service. Horse-drawn *Panje* wagons, troikas, and sledges were gathered into panzer supply columns. Camel-trains served First Panzer Army in the south. In the west, where summer conditions prevailed during the early campaigns, panzer supply arrangements although not altogether satisfactory gave no great cause for concern. In Poland (map 2) supplies for Guderian's XIX Motorized Corps travelled barely more than 350 kilometres from East Prussia. Rail networks remained largely intact and compatible with the German gauge. Shortages that did occur were of a minor kind, and the mobile troops, although occasionally requiring air assistance, were never seriously hampered in their sweeping advance to Brest-Litovsk.

In France, on the other hand, supply lines were stretched considerably. Guderian's motorized corps pushing west from Sedan needed its supply columns to travel about 160 kilometres daily – clocking up 6,000 kilometres by the end of the campaign. First Panzer Division, advancing over good metalled roads south of the Aisne with Panzer Group Guderian in phase two of the battle for France (map 3), reported fuel shortages, but the deficiency was made good from captured stocks. Reporting ammunition shortages after a tank engagement, Panzer Group von Kleist also in the drive south with the equivalent of eight mobile divisions,

Right: The Bussing NAG
5-ton semi-track entered
transport service during the
autumn of 1943.

once recorded '. . . no sign of resupply . . .'. After this campaign OKH emphasized in training manuals the need for proper logistical administration, stressing that every movement and action of a panzer division required thorough preparation and servicing; a clear-sighted theoretical approach soon at variance with the realities of Operation 'Barbarossa'. In the view of many commanders the offensive started with hopelessly inadequate stocks of petrol, tyres, replacement engines, gearboxes and a host of other crucial war materials without which the panzer divisions would grind to a halt. Thrusting deep into Russia, panzer divisions rapidly out-stripped their supplies. OKH Chief of Staff Halder recorded in his diary, 'The number of supply trains is insufficient for a widespread attack. Because of a difference in railway gauges, only a limited volume of supplies can be moved forward until such time as the Russian wide gauge can be converted to the German standard.'

Manhandling supplies between gauges, until conversion work (moving one of the Russian rails 9cm inwards) was completed, despite the prodigious efforts of railway engineers and labour battalions, was only the start of the problem. When winter gripped the front in sub-zero temperatures, '. . . there were days when as many as a hundred locomotives broke down and water-tanking stations were totally unsuitable for the unusually cold spell'. So fundamental was this problem in occupied Russia that Hitler charged the German State Railways with responsibility for the entire railway system leaving General Gercke, chief of military transport, to concentrate on arrangements for road supply. With panzer divisions, follow-up infantry and other services, vying for the few available routes, the supply situation in the east degenerated to near collapse. Transport columns moving over vast distances struggled mightily to overcome their difficulties. Consequently, as panzer and other formations moved east their supplies were carried by transport columns using roads of deteriorating condition; roads becoming increasingly congested. In later stages of the advance to Moscow and Lenningrad, passing through remote hinterlands, roads were totally absent. Maps for service use frequently proved useless in this situation; Russian road classifications bearing little resemblance to Western standards.

A measure of the problem facing panzer supply staffs is recorded in the diary of 9th Panzer Division advancing with Second Panzer Army south-west of Moscow. Over a period of eight weeks the division required petrol for nearly 200,000 kilometres. Desperately trying to beat a harsh winter and reach the Soviet capital in December 1941, panzer armies were reporting: 'Troops could go no further from railheads than could be reached by horses and sledges.' Second Panzer Army, reduced to living from hand to mouth on local supplies, was defeated by the inability of transport columns either to negotiate seas of mud into which vehicles at first sank up to their axles, or snow-drifts into which both they and tanks with narrow tracks floundered uselessly. The result, by the end of 1941, was to bring panzer operations to a standstill; halted as much by climatic conditions and munitions shortages as exhaustion of men and materials. The vast quantities of petrol, oil and lubricants needed to ensure operational mobility of panzer divisions became overnight as important to the plans of panzer commanders as terrain or enemy strengths and dispositions. Success in battle came to depend as much upon considerations of supply as fighting capacity. And not only petrol, but oil consumption too proved much higher than expected. In trackless terrain vehicles were driven for long periods in first gear; LVII Panzer Corps reported as early as 6 August 1941 that vehicles required 20–30 litres of oil per 100 kilometres instead of the planned half-litre. The same division reported 50 per cent of its armoured vehicles engaged in the attack on Kiev falling out because of shortage of oil. Second Panzer Army recorded in late November that it was receiving 300,000 litres of fuel, whereas one million litres were required to sustain operational efficiency. From 22 June 1941 when Guderian's tanks crossed the Polish demarcation line until mid-November when Second Panzer Army approached Tula in a final bid to reach Moscow, many vehicles had travelled 4,000 kilometres and had served for weeks without maintenance.

Typical of panzer division states at the time was 4th Panzer Division reporting on 5 December: tanks down to 15 per cent of establishment, personnel reduced to 30 per cent, transports to 34 per cent and motor cycles no more than 10 per cent. Partisans directing their attacks against road and rail routes with increasing boldness and effectiveness aggravated the supply position. Endless stoppages were recorded in the rear of advancing panzer armies where territories were unoccupied or lightly held. The diary of Field Marshall Keitel confirms the experience of the field formations: '. . . more than a hundred stretches of railway line blown up in one night'. In mid-winter 1941 the entire German front opposite Moscow might have collapsed had it not been for Hitler's stand fast order of 16 December. During the following months panzer formations were rehabilitated and supply arrangements gradually improved. At key road and rail junctions supply bases were established and lines of communication, wherever they were exposed to guerrilla attack, wired-in and protected by local security groups, but never to the extent required. Tank tracks were widened, wheeled transport, especially motor cycles, were partially replaced. Tracked or semi-tracked machines were introduced into supply service – the diminutive Kettenkrad and the light Raupenschlepper-Ost. Heavier vehicles introduced in 1943 for transport duty in the east included a semi-tracked transport and towing machine, the Wehr-

machtschlepper, and another semi-track, the Maultier (mule).

In occupied territories, especially in Russia, railway engineers, army personnel, prisoner-of-war construction battalions and locally impressed labour, worked continuously to maintain the railway system. Armour-protected locomotives with improvised ground and anti-aircraft protection using captured weapons or the ubiquitous 20mm AA guns were introduced in small numbers. But the menacing problem of supply shortages was never wholly eradicated; ammunition, food, fuel and a thousand other stocks continued in short supply. On any war front in the east, west, south-east, Italy or Africa, the total collapse of supply arrangements was never far from the thoughts of panzer commanders. Improvised air transport programmes played a vital role at times in supplying panzer formations and many of the problems facing supply staffs might have been resolved in this way but, as is made clear in Part 4, there were never sufficient transports available and an infrastructure for aircraft servicing and dispatch with a centralized command was instituted too late to become more than a qualified success.

Left: Early in the war Army divisional transport columns placed their faith in commercial vehicles, but bad weather led to more robust vehicles being brought into service. The mobility of supply columns and divisional units was essential. The Opel 'Blitz' 3-ton general-purpose truck improved with a 4-wheel drive was suitable for the task.

Far left: The Mercedes-Benz 'Maultier' 4.5-ton halftrack adopted the Panzer II chassis and was introduced in 1943. Other halftrack transports were built by Ford, Opel, Magirus and French factories, while Raupenschlepper Ost (light halftrack) served the infantry.

Near left: The Wehrmacht Schlepper sWS entered transport service during the autumn of 1943.

Left: A Bussing NAG 4.5-ton truck. This vehicle was the standard Wehrmacht heavy duty transport, and a forerunner of the sWS. Mercedes also produced a 4.5-ton, 4-wheel drive model for service with transport columns.

Part 4. Air support: the decisive factor

1. Key to victory

The shock tactics used by the German Army to extraordinary effect in eliminating opposition in Poland, France and the Balkans, or again in Russia until the Red Air Force gained supremacy, depended to a great extent upon co-operation with the Luftwaffe. Without this crucial component of mobile operations characteristic notably of the Wehrmacht, the rapid advance of the panzer divisions would have been unlikely to succeed.

Consider the plan for zero hour in the battle for France, when the mass of German armour was poised to strike across the Meuse on 13 May 1940. The level of support afforded by 3rd Air Fleet[1] to Panzer Group von Kleist leading Operation 'Yellow' (map 3) at this critical time can be gauged from orders issued to 1st Panzer Division by General Guderian, commanding XIX Panzer Corps. Concentrated with other attacking divisions in the neighbourhood of Sedan, 1st Panzer Division was deployed in battle groups ready to strike west.

'The point of main effort of our western offensive', reads Guderian's order, 'lies in the Sector von Kleist. Almost the whole of the German Air Force will support this operation. By means of uninterrupted attacks lasting for eight hours, the French defenders along the Meuse will be smashed. This will be followed by an assault across the river by Gruppe von Kleist at 1600 hours and the establishment of bridgeheads.'

Army High Command (OKH) orders rationalizing joint action by Army Group 'A' and 3rd Air Fleet into Operation 'Yellow', a 'Sichelschnitt' plan aimed at rupturing the Meuse defences on a narrow front, had been issued three months earlier and derived from an updated OKW (Hitler) directive of October 1939; von Kleist's orders came to him directly from the army group ('A') to which his group was initially subordinate. Lead by Panzer Group von Kleist the panzer divisions would exploit their break-through in a deep enveloping thrust to the west, isolating Allied armies from rearward support in France and Belgium and rendering them ineffective. Indirect support by 3rd Air Fleet restraining opposition air forces while at the same time dislocating command centres and communications over a wide area was an essential pre-requisite. Initiated by von Runstedt's chief of staff, Erich von Manstein, looking to exploit the surprise effect of an armoured offensive out of the Ardennes forest – a direction from which the Allies least expected attack – the sweeping manoeuvre was to succeed beyond the expectations of all but a few involved in its planning and execution. The role played by the Luftwaffe was decisive. Attacking on sectors of the Meuse where opposition by French Second and Ninth Armies was thinly concentrated, Sperrle's fighter and bomber groups lead by Stukas assailed the defenders in terrifying force, smashing artillery positions, scattering opposition and creating favourable conditions for the armoured columns to force the river and race 240 miles to the Channel at Dunkirk. Eleven days after the crucial break-through the campaign in France was virtually at an end. By 24 June, joint action by Army Group 'A' and 3rd Air Fleet with the advantage of surprise had provided the key to German victory; success, foreshadowed by similar events in Poland, had been swift and conclusive.

German experience of ground-attack operations as entailed in the Battle of France was rooted in war experience and secret trials stretching back more than twenty years via Poland and Spain to the First World War. Then, as early as November 1917, armour protected aircraft strafing Allied artillery and infantry with forward-firing – and in later models synchronized machine-guns, notably the Junkers CL-1 (1918) – supported German infantry in the attack. By March 1918 the number of battle squadrons supporting ground operations on the Western Front had risen to thirty-eight. On the British side the Sopwith Salamander (1918), another expressly designed ground-attack machine but less prominent in support of Allied military operations by virtue of fewer numbers, served the Royal Flying Corps in much the same role as the Junkers. Indirect support for land forces in the shape of bombing attacks to delay the movement of enemy counter-attack reserves, contributed to offensive success by both sides. By 1923 the German Army, in common with western counterparts, was once more experimenting with tactical schemes to advance army air

[1]At the start of Operation 'Yellow' (map 3), 3rd Air Fleet (Sperrle) was composed of two air corps (Fliegerkorps): II (Lörzer) deployed in support of Army Group 'A' (von Kleist) at Sedan, and V (Greim) supporting Army Group 'C' (von Leeb); 2nd Air Fleet (Kesselring) comprising XI Air Corps Landing, I, IV and VIII Air Corps supported Army Group 'B' (von Bock). From 13 May onwards, VIII Air Corps (von Richthofen) was co-operating with II Air Corps at Sedan – flying in support of Army Group 'A'.

co-operation; in the German case by secretly developing ground-attack machines – the Hs 51, and (modelled on the American Curtiss Helldiver), the Hs 123 – culminating in the notorious Ju 87 dive-bomber (Stuka) making an appearance on active service in Spain and winning early wartime victories for the Luftwaffe.

Dive-bombing in fact was to come as a very unpleasant shock to early German opponents none of whom had effectively developed this type of attack and, short of winning air supremacy for protection, were unable to deploy immediately effective counter-measures. Much of the credit for generating Luftwaffe enthusiasm for the dive-bomber lay with Germany's First World War ace, Ernst Udet. Early in 1931 this champion aerobatics pilot flew the American Curtiss Helldiver privately in the United States and thereafter tested the Hs 123 in trials in 1935. But the Hs machine handled uncomfortably and Udet expressed his dislike of it. Von Richthofen, director of research at the Technical Office of the Air Ministry, was unenthusiastic about dive-bombing and in consequence no real progress in design and development of Stukas leading to production of the Ju 87 was possible. But fortunately for Udet the situation changed when Goering persuaded him to take charge of the Office in 1936 – which he did; von Richthofen departing for Spain to promote operational research before becoming Chief-of-Staff to Hugo Sperrle (map 1).

The Luftwaffe's first dive-bombing unit was raised at Schwerin in 1936 (1-StukaGeschwader 162) equipped with the Hs 123. But it is to Spain following von Richthofen's career that we must turn for developments in dive-bombing. For three years, from July 1936 onwards, the Condor Legion under Hugo Sperrle and Chief of Staff Wolfram Freiherr von Richthofen, the Legion's last commander (29 November 1938), introduced wireless for transmitting target information from forward Luftwaffe observers to squadron headquarters, improved the machines and evolved the tactics that the Luftwaffe would use in Poland and France on a grand scale. The experience of these officers' pioneering army/air operations in Spain, including the notorious incident at Guernica (page 25) followed by action along the Ebro eastwards in the direction of Valencia and Barcelona, contributed notably to Luftwaffe progress in tactical flying. Von Richthofen was to emerge from these operations as the leading exponent of the new style of battlefield support for the Army – a lustrous career taking him from command of the Condor Legion (Generalmajor, November 1938) to command of 4th Air Fleet in Russia (Generaloberst, June 1942) and 2nd Air Fleet in Italy where he was promoted Field Marshal in October 1944.

Directing action against ground targets in Poland, the General gathered Stuka groups into an Air Division 'for special purposes' – the kernel of VIII Air Corps detailed to assist Panzer Group von Kleist in its sweeping advance through France. In these campaigns, forward observers were provided with wheeled (and eventually tracked) transport, facilitating mobility in the company of fast troops; ground-control systems were further refined and air force tactics for reducing or eliminating ground opposition greatly improved by massed concentration of dive-bombers. The technical accomplishments of *Blitzkrieg* – joint army-air operations, deciding in the space of short campaigns, the fate of powerful yet confused opposition, was most persuasively

demonstrated during the Battle of France in 1940; but not to the full – communication between tank and air force commanders remained imperfect and not until 1941, when 'Barbarossa' burst upon Russia, would the technology reach an effective level of clear speech contact for the exchange of information and orders.

In the meantime mobile operations, including the campaigns in the Balkans and North Africa, would owe much of their effectiveness to wireless technology promoted by Guderian and von Richthofen's development of close-support techniques and communications without which *Blitzkrieg* would have been stillborn. Later proof of German success in uniting ground and air forces into powerful and flexible shock formations is evident in von Manstein's recovery of Kharkov in 1943 (map 13). By 1939, the Luftwaffe's dive-bombing strength had grown to a total of 219 aircraft deployed in nine groups; a group consisting theoretically of three squadrons, each of twelve Stukas. But the Hs 123 having proved unsatisfactory as a dive-bomber in Spain was scheduled for replacement by the Ju 87A. Deployed instead in a single ground-attack Schlachtgruppe (11/LG2, formerly Schlactgeschwader 100), the type was phased out of production in 1942. On the other hand, approximately 5,000 Ju 87s were to be produced for wartime service with the Luftwaffe. But Luftwaffe ground-attack units, subordinate to von Richthofen in his Air Division for special purposes (eventually VIII Air Corps) and deployed in support of the panzer divisions in *Blitzkrieg* campaigns, whether organized initially into Schlacht or Stuka squadrons – the difference is elaborated later – were not the sole representation of Luftwaffe presence on the battlefield. Air reconnaissance units working with the panzer force gathered crucial Intelligence. Observing and photographing troop movements and more, their contribution to panzer operations was to prove indispensable.

As early as 1915 cameras were being carried in aircraft over the Western Front by both sides. Oscar Messter, a German film pioneer, experimented with semi and later fully automatic cameras. His apparatus, the prototype of much subsequent service equipment, produced overlapping aerial views easily adapted into maps, while a growing band of specialists, organized into (Army) photographic units (Stabs-bildabteilungen) attached to air reconnaissance battalions for photo interpretation purposes, employed the stereoscope to reveal detail in overlapping prints. Defeat in 1918 might theoretically have been expected seriously to impede German progress in this important field of technology. Yet by 1935, following secret experiments at Lipetsk and the establishment of training schools at Brunswick and Hildesheim, the Luftwaffe's first air reconnaissance schools (Fliegerbildschule) were re-established at Cottbus, Münster and Göppingen, with five reconnaissance squadrons flying either Heinkel He 45 or He 46. A succession of reconnaissance aircraft types was developed beginning in 1912 with the primitive, low-wing Rumpler-Taube which served the army in a two-seater observation and ultimately photographic role. In 1913 the Albatross B11 arrived in service; the Rumpler C1 followed in 1916; the DFW CV in 1917; Heinkel He 45 and He 46, 1932–5 and Henschel Hs 126, 1935–41. The Focke-Wulf Fw 189 (Owl) also arrived in service in 1941. Fast single-seaters, basically fighter types, also provided reconnaissance data for the Army from 1917

Above: Ground-attack flying played a key role in eliminatin opposition to the panzer divisions. The Ju 87B Stuka was a principal ground-attack aircraft of the early war years and was capable of delivering 1,000lb of high-explosives wit pin-point accuracy. It is seen here being prepared for active service.

onwards. This practice, matched by foreign air forces, would continue with the Me 109 flying photographic missions in 1940; the Fw 190 in 1942 and briefly in 1944–5 the jet-propelled Me 262.

A key figure in the promotion of photographic Intelligence during the inter-war years was Oberst Theodor Rowehl. His enthusiasm for reconnaissance flying motivated much of the Luftwaffe's pre-war progress in photographic work. The success of his organization, methods, and training given to aircrews and ground staff demonstrated a remarkably innovative approach to all questions of Intelligence during the Luftwaffe's formative years. Starting in reconnaissance as early as 1917, when he flew Rhombergs over England, a demobilized Rowehl exchanged a service career for private flying from Kiel. Using chartered aircraft for the purpose of nefarious Intelligence-gathering, Rowehl snapped Polish border fortifications for the Abwehr. In 'experimental' flying on subsequent missions he piloted a Ju 34 to heights approaching the world altitude record of 41,800 feet set by Walter Neuenhofen in May 1929. More flying for the Abwehr was followed by a return to air force service and in 1936 a move from Kiel to Staaken (Berlin West) where Rowehl's squadron (Fliegerstaffel zbV) was expanded three-fold and its name in the Luftwaffe order of battle changed to Aufklarungsgruppe OKW. A fourth squadron was added to establishment at the outbreak of war when Aufklarungs-gruppe OKW was re-designated Aufklarungsgruppe (F) OKL.

Extending German Intelligence cover over Russia in the late thirties, Kronstadt, Leningrad, Pskov and Minsk were reconnoitred under guise of high-altitude research. Border defences, military and other installations located deep within Russia, France, Czechoslovakia and Poland were photo-graphed, analysed and sorted into target files for the later use of bomber crews.

Intelligence flying continued in the late thirties with long-distance flights over Great Britain under the pretext of route-proving for Lufthansa. In 1937 Rowehl moved headquarters to Potsdam (Oranienburg). There a joint army/air force photographic centre (Hauptamt für Lichtbild) adjoining Luftwaffe headquarters and within easy reach of Berlin's Intelligence agencies, was placed under his control. These were the years in which Intelligence agencies flourished in Germany: Abwehr, OKW, OKL and OKH all demanding Intelligence of Rowehl who turned such oppor-tunities to marked advantage. Co-opting commercial firms, leading Europe in optical technology, among whom Carl Zeiss was pre-eminent, or companies developing ideas in the air survey business, Rowehl created a Luftwaffe technical service in the forefront of Intelligence agencies – collecting, sorting and analysing a wide range of espionage data. Foremost of his colleagues whose progress was to influence the wartime performance of the Luftwaffe were those engaged in the business of Intelligence planning and liaison.

Dating from the era when von Seeckt as head of the Reichswehr established a desk for air Intelligence in the Truppenampt (T3), Major Hilmer Freiherr von Bülow directed Foreign Air Forces (5th Branch) over a period of ten years from the spring of 1927 to the autumn of 1937. Fifth Branch responsibilities extended not only to target evaluation, filed for the future briefing of bomber crews – for which purpose Rowehl's imagery was a prime source – but also appreciations of foreign military resources, notably in connection with air-war command. Von Bülow's successor, Oberst Hans Jeschonnek, held the post for little more than a year from the autumn of 1937 until February 1939 when promotion to Chief of Air Staff removed him to the High Command. Jeschonnek was followed by Oberstleutnant 'Beppo' Schmid. As head of Foreign Air Forces, Schmid held this key Intelligence post until October 1942 when reorganization drafted him to field command. That Luftwaffe Intelligence, notwithstanding its pre-war lead in reconnaissance technology, would prove unable to match the supreme challenge of wartime action after 1940 – failing time and again when information about enemy capabilities and intentions was vitally important to army and Luftwaffe alike – would soon become all too apparent. For example, during Schmid's tenure of office a faulty appreciation of RAF strength probably contributed to Luftwaffe failure in the Battle of Britain. In fostering OKW belief that the RAF was outstripping its resources, which it certainly was not, the Luftwaffe prelude to 'Sea-lion' (page 36) may have been prematurely suspended. Neither was the Luftwaffe aware at the time of the crucial role played by radar in controlling RAF fighter defence. Reconnaissance/Intelligence failures of

this magnitude were soon to become commonplace.

A significant development in inter-service co-operation upon which the success of mobile operations depended and dating from the inter-war years was the installation of a senior Luftwaffe representative at OKH. General Paul Bögatsch was the candidate selected for this High Command appointment and it was he who in 1937 took the post of Luftwaffe General to the Commander-in-Chief of the Army von Brauchitsch (Fritsch having been replaced in February 1938 when Hitler promoted himself C-in-C). The General's title, Kommandeur der Luftwaffe, was abbreviated to Koluft. This liaison link between Army and Luftwaffe involving control of air reconnaissance units was further developed by appointing Koluft personnel downwards – officers and staff varying in numbers according to command level. Koluft personnel attached to army group and subordinate commands, including panzer and motorized corps when needed, were an important link in the chain of photographic reconnaissance support for the army. Flak detachments were also theoretically under Koluft control, but not ground-attack units. The Koluft arrangement was to continue unchanged until the winter of 1941–2. This was the critical phase of 'Barbarossa' when aircraft shortages and the overlapping dictates of army and Luftwaffe commanders frequently competing for the same Intelligence led to a wide-ranging review of reconnaissance procedures – to the advantage of both services. The change is summarized in The Army's Eye in the Sky, page 130.

By 1939 the Luftwaffe's photographic Intelligence effort was proceeding at two levels: 'H' (Heer = army) units served the tactical support needs of the army, mostly

Above: A Stukaleiter (controller) in close proximity to panzer headquarters briefs pilots temporarily under his command. Targets, weather information, the position of friendly and enemy troops were typical of the data communicated direct by radio.

attached to mobile formations; 'F' (fern = distant) long-range units were deployed for strategic work with higher army and Luftwaffe commands. 'H' units comprising 29 squadrons served nine wings (provided also with eight F units), while three 'F' wings controlled an additional thirteen F squadrons. Rowehl's wing comprised four 'F' squadrons; leaving one other independent. Total: 29 'H' and 26 'F' squadrons, 342 'H' and 260 'F' aircraft respectively – 7 per cent of Luftwaffe strength. The aircraft selected pre-war for re-equipping 'H' units was the Hs 126, an open, two-seater biplane; other types dating from before the Spanish Civil War continuing to serve 'H' squadrons in small numbers. Long-distance reconnaissance units, flew the Do 17F, He 111, Ju 86P and later the K high-altitude series, also the Ju 88D an adaptation for photo-reconnaissance of the standard Ju 88 bomber. War production of reconnaissance aircraft included in the 113,515 all-types total of aircraft delivered to the Luftwaffe or satellite air forces from 1939 to 1945 amounted to 6,299 aircraft.

Pre-war German progress in optics and aircraft was matched by significant developments in radio equipment. By 1935 radio had moved from the 1914–18 era of Morse code to speech transmission and reception. Two-way contact between ground and air force units linking the two into flexible working teams was to prove the decisive step in mobile operations. Major von Richthofen, before taking up his Legion appointment in Spain, was one of the key figures promoting technical development in this field of technology.

As the Second World War progressed, robbing *Blitzkrieg* of momentum, air transportation emerged as a new and demanding form of military aviation. At the core of Luftwaffe transport operations from 1939 to 1945 stood the Ju 52 'Judula'. This work-horse of 1936 vintage was to play a key role – not only in refuelling and provisioning fast troops by providing air-landed and parachuted supplies – but also in sustaining encircled panzer formations. The transporting of infantry from North Africa to Andalusia during the Spanish Civil War (map 1) provided the renascent Luftwaffe with highly realistic training opportunities; testing aircrews, equipment and ground organization. The military début of the Ju 52 was followed in 1938 by experience in Austria when transport units flew infantry into Vienna at the time of the Anschluss. Hitler's annexation of Czechoslovakia proved another opportunity for rehearsing transport aircrews and ground organization. So too did Operation 'Green', a plan to seize Prague and the Sudetenland – by war action – carried out instead as an elaborate training exercise; political agreement at Munich having achieved Hitler's aims 'peacefully'. The taxing realism and complexity of 'Green' exercised the Luftwaffe in assembling, loading and operating a fleet of 250 Ju 52/3m under command of 7th Air Division (Student). The event marked a significant stage in air transport operations. Infantry Parachute Battalions I and II, two battalions of 1R16 and SA Regiment Feldhermhalle organized into two regiments (six battalions) also participated in the action. Dispatched on a one-battalion to one-transport group basis, the modestly equipped infantry supported by mountain artillery were lifted over Czech border defences and landed – not dropped for security reasons – in the vicinity of Freudenthal. Here, reminiscent of action in Holland 1940 and the relief of First Panzer Army in the spring of 1944 (map 15), open-country landing

arrangements played a significant part in success.

Also participating in the action under Student's command (Chief of Staff Oberst Jeschonnek) was Schlachtgeschwader 100 equipped with ground-attack Hs 123s and Ju 87s. Their protection was ensured by the inclusion of a fighter Group in Student's command. Such opportunities as 'Green' enabled transport groups to perform in war situations, advancing their planning, organization and procedures to an exceptional degree – especially in relation to parachute and air landing troops. (At the conclusion of 'Green', Student was nominated Inspector of Parachute and Air-Landing Troops (L In XI); a post held simultaneously with command of 7th Air Division – later XI Air Corps). The deployment of parachute and air-landing troops (Fallschirmjaeger and Luftlandetruppen) in campaigns against Denmark, Norway (Operation 'Weserübung'), Holland (Operation 'Yellow') (map 3) and Crete (Operation 'Mercury') (map 6) is outside the scope of this inquiry except to note them in passing as prime examples of transport enterprise and initiative.

Of greater relevance to mobile operations is transport action at a later date when, for instance, in the spring of 1944 First Panzer Army, encircled in the Ukraine, survived only through the efforts of air transport groups to resupply and maintain them; enterprise and resourcefulness being no less characteristic of transport flying at this late stage in the war than at earlier and more dramatic times in the first flush of airborne innovation in the west (*see* New Horizons in Transport). A common denominator in all air transport operations carried out by the Luftwaffe from 1936 to 1945 was the Ju 52/3m developed from a civil prototype. First flown by Junkers in 1932, the Ju 52 right from the start proved an exceptionally robust transport with a reputation for safe and reliable flying. Three engines and an all-metal construction commended it highly, not only to Lufthansa the state carrier with whom it entered service in 1933, but also to numerous foreign airlines, early versions carrying 15–17 passengers. When the Spanish Civil war erupted in 1936 and the Condor Legion required bombers, the Ju was converted to serve as a temporary (*behelfs*) bomber until purpose-built He 111s under test there at the time were declared operational. In its improvised role the Ju 52/3m could carry a maximum bomb-load of 2,300lb (1,500kg). As regards transport numbers and organization at the outbreak of war, twenty Ju 52/3m squadrons were deployed in five transport groups, each of *four* squadrons divided between two battle groups: KG zbV 1 (Morzik) at Stendal (three Wings, one detached at Gardelegen) and KG zbV 172 at Berlin Tempelhof (two Wings and a DFS 230 glider HQ). Contingency planning in 1938 also provided for Group staff, KG zbv 2 (Conrad), and a heavy weapons group to be found from flying schools' personnel and aircraft engaged on pilot and blind-flying training. At the disposal of these early transport groups stood upwards of 250 Ju 52/3ms including 145 of the improved radio version (gbe). Another 250 or so machines deployed in training schools or on courier service brought the 1939 service total of Ju 52/3ms to 552. Production continued until June 1944 by which time almost 3,000 'Judulas' had been delivered to Luftwaffe or satellite air forces.

Organized for Army support and committing 75 per cent of its strength to this activity during the Second World War, the Luftwaffe improvised methods and equipment to meet many and varied contingencies in air reconnaissance, ground attack and re-supply. But in furthering the effectiveness of panzer operations extending the length and breadth of Europe, Luftwaffe resources were rarely if ever adequate for such a high-priority task. Neither in the early days of the war, nor later, were there sufficient transports or adequate numbers of reconnaissance and ground-attack units. The deplorable shortages evident soon after the start of 'Barbarossa' were soon to become apparent on all other fronts. Disparities in equipment and organization, distinguishing Luftwaffe from RAF in 1940, were rooted in conflicting views and strategies determining the growth and uses of air power. Foreign air forces generally tended towards the German notion of maximizing close support for the army. Not so the RAF, pursuing a policy of 'independence'.

Formed in 1918 by merging the RNAS and RFC, the aviation agencies in Britain responsible for naval and military flying, the Royal Air Force (Trenchard) – itself a response to 'strategic' bombing of London by Gothas in 1917 – resisted every attack intended to deprive it of integrity and independence. Much of the opposition to current British policy of centralizing air power after 1918 was fostered by War Office and Admiralty critics who were greatly concerned over the loss of highly prized air-support arms. Many also doubted the value of 'strategic' bombing. Despite vitriolic differences of opinion, the RAF emerged from pre-war debate intact and while neglectful of army co-operation to an alarming degree, free to explore air war possibilities untrammelled by inward-looking army and navy close-support considerations. After 1938, fighter resources assumed a high priority in air staff deliberations – radar control of air formations in particular.

Independent status in the German case was conditioned by General Staff planning in the aftermath of 'Versailles'. These were the years from 1920 to 1933 when von Seeckt, or those who followed at the head of the Heeresleitung – Haye, 1926–30 or Hammerstein, 1930–4, controlled expansion of the army and military flying by allocating executive responsibilities mainly to army officers; those with General Staff training in particular. The key expansion project of the late twenties and early thirties, before Hitler arrived on the scene to take control, was a Russo-German training and research scheme operated secretly, 200 miles south-east of Moscow. This was the Lipetsk project started in 1925 and officially known as Fliegerschule Stahr; Major (aD) Stahr being the school commandant. By 1929 Stahr's command included more than 60 aircraft stationed at Lipetsk – predominantly Fokker D XIII single-seat fighters acquired from Holland plus a two-seater aircraft establishment that included a small number of Heinkel He 17 or even more venerable types. Aircraft and equipment intended for proving also passed through the hands of trials units at Rechlin and Staaken. Naval flying was pursued on the Baltic coast at Strahlsund and north of Hamburg at Travemünde. A command link uniting Lipetsk with the Heeresleitung (Seeckt, Haye, Hammerstein) lay with Fliegerstab Wilberg, a command staff set up within the Truppenamt and lead by Oberstleutnant Helmut Wilberg.

Wilberg's activities, illegal under the Treaty of Versailles, were progressively concealed in Truppenamt Sections T 2 IV and T 2 V (2) followed by a merger with the inspectorate of flying schools (von Mittelberger); the In 1 designation of this branch of the Heeresleitung, concealing the covert presence of a Luftwaffe executive – the inspectorate's chief of staff, Oberstleutnant Helmut Felmy.

Leading the development of von Seeckt's aviation programme at this time and founding future wartime careers for themselves mostly as distinguished field commanders, were Oberst Albert Kesselring, C-in-C, South 1944 (Field Marshal) Oberst Wolfram von Richthofen, C-in-C, 4th Air Fleet 1944 (Field Marshal) and Major Kurt Student, C-in-C, First Parachute Army (Generaloberst). But this step towards establishing an air force command within the Reischwehr was almost immediately overtaken by Hitler's decree of 15 May 1933; merging military (Luftschutzamt) and civil (Lufthansa founded in 1926) agencies into an Air Ministry – Reichsluftfarhtministerium (RLM) – under the control of Hermann Goering, hitherto Reichskommissar for air traffic. And not only did Hitler's decree centralizing air power remove aviation from the army's grip, but anti-aircraft units too were taken away and placed under Goering's control; the army's flak units would henceforth serve as Luftwaffe units leaving the army with a meagre tally of heavy machine-gun units with which to effect local anti-aircraft protection. At this critical stage in an accelerating programme of rearmament taking the fledgling Luftwaffe from a strength of sixteen squadrons in 1933 to 302 in September 1939, many more army officers arrived in service of the RLM – either posted by the Reichswehr or recruited from the reserve list. Setting aside conflict at the outset, military and civil sides of the RLM settled into a harmonious relationship; key posts would nevertheless remain in the hands of army or civilian heads of branches. Below Goering, Minister of State for Aviation and C-in-C, Luftwaffe, stood his deputy Milch, Secretary of State for Air and a former director of Lufthansa. A new Air Command Office (Luftkommandoamt) supervised inspectorates governing planning, and setting standards in all areas of equipment and training. Oberst Wever headed this important office. Oberst Kesselring took over administration; Oberst Wimmer, technical development, Oberst Stumpff, air personnel. Oberst Felmy continued in RLM service and so too did Oberst Wilberg, subsequently first commandant of the Air War Academy. Majors Student, von Richthofen and Hauptmann Jeschonnek were joined by others taking important posts and set to rise in the Luftwaffe. Their ranks included Josef Kammhuber, Josef Schmid and Hugo Sperrle, the Condor Legion commander, later GOC, 3rd Air Fleet.

In the aftermath of this and more open stages of expansion, when its existence was announced by the Führer in March 1935, there was to emerge an air force created in the image of an army and substantially dependent upon military tradition. Lead by a General (air) Staff incorporating the now defunct Luftkommandoamt and organized on military lines, i.e., air fleet – army group, air corps – army corps, and downwards even to include ground forces in the form of parachute infantry (Fallschirmjaeger), the Luftwaffe, like the army an offensive concept, was to be prematurely locked into a pattern of land warfare determined by Hitler's expansionist designs. But another important event was to shape Luftwaffe policy before war became inevitable in 1939 – the loss to the air force of its prime mover in 'strategic' bombing. General Wever's death by misadventure in June 1936 was to prove a most damaging blow to Luftwaffe prospects in later years. Coinciding with air-war developments in Spain, this resulted in strategic bombing being relegated to the background of air force policy, enabling army-support circles including von Richthofen to gain ascendancy in matters affecting equipment and employment of the air force.

A glance at the organizational difference between the Luftwaffe and the RAF in 1940 underlines the conflicting approach of opponents to air power. Whereas the RAF was split between functional commands, Fighter Command, Bomber Command, etc., and subsequently a Tactical Airforce Command, the Luftwaffe was divided territorially into operational commands headed by air fleets (Luftflotten). By 1938 three air fleets were spread across Germany: 1, Berlin; 2, Brunswick; 3, Munich; while a fourth with headquarters in Vienna following the incorporation of the Sudetenland and Austria into the Third Reich was added in March 1939. Three more air fleets appeared in the Luftwaffe's order of battle as the war spread across Europe: 5, Christiansand embracing Scandinavia; 6, Brest-Litovsk Eastern Front (Centre); and Luftflotte Reich, Germany after December 1943. Operational areas and headquarter locations of these air fleets varied with time and in accordance with military needs. Air formations (Fliegertruppen) allotted to air fleets were organized into air corps (Flieger Korps) by expansion of air divisions, Geschwader (Groups), Gruppen (Wings) and Staffeln (squadrons). The building-block of Luftwaffe strength – three to a Group – was the wing of three squadrons; each consisting of 9–12 similar types of aircraft. An air corps, on the other hand, was a composite command, allocated a geographical area within which it would support the army for specific operations, or for the whole or part of a campaign, with a varying number of bomber, dive-bomber, ground-attack, fighter and reconnaissance wings.

Battle groups (Gefechtsverbandes) organized for limited operations were also formed by air corps and others. Such short-term groupings of fighter or ground-attack units appeared during the Battle of France, in North Africa and subsequently in Russia, notably at Bryansk and Orel (*see* page 153). This was the organizational basis upon which the Luftwaffe founded its strike force. Excluded from the common framework until 1942 were air force 'H' and 'F' reconnaissance units supervised by Koluft. Flak too, when placed under army control, was nominally responsible to Koluft, but in practice mobile anti-aircraft units were left to determine their own course of action in conjunction with superior army formation headquarters. Motorized flak units – corps, divisions and regiments accompanying the army proved formidable adversaries. In action against ground and air targets in the course of mobile battles, for example, I Flak Corps/Panzer Group Guderian or II Flak Corps/Panzer Group von Kleist, June 1941, destroyed aircraft, concrete bunkers and armoured vehicles alike; all falling easy prey to 8.8cm mobile (towed) Flak. The tally of enemy tanks destroyed by such versatile units frequently exceeded the number of aircraft shot down. During the advance to Voronezh by Fourth Panzer Army (map 10) starting on 28 June 1942, 10th Flak Division reported 50 Russian aircraft and 66 tanks destroyed.

Another area of co-operation serving the army to advantage in 1939–40 was that of fire-support. The shortage of divisional artillery in the panzer division – 36 field and medium guns compared with 48 in an infantry division – and the relatively limited use expected to be made of it in the spearhead of the attack, could only be made good by the Luftwaffe; Stukagruppen in particular.

Luftwaffe inability to withstand long and ruinous campaigns, evident on all fronts by 1944, originated not only in the unprecedented capacity of Anglo-American air forces after 1942 to dominate air battles in general and eradicate key German industries – aircraft manufacture and oil production in particular – but also in the Luftwaffe High Command's (OKL) own shortcomings. Failures in aircraft replacement programmes by way of mishandled procurement, poor Intelligence about Allied (especially Russian) strength and production resources, but above all an Air Staff failure to convince the Supreme Command (OKW) – an army dominated directorate – of the need to allocate to the Luftwaffe resources consistent with the demands of air supremacy were root causes of defeat, leading in turn to the

Below: With the Ju 87 proving slow and vulnerable in battle by 1940, Stukagruppen demanded new equipment and the Fw 190 was eventually settled upon as a replacement. Fast and efficient though they were, the new attack machines nevertheless failed to materialize in the numbers that panzer divisions had expected.

army's failure. Add to this catalogue of misdemeanours Hitler's scorn for Reichsmarschall Goering as Commander-in-Chief of the Luftwaffe when 'Barbarossa' failed in December 1941, and his wavering control of Wehrmacht priorities – depressing Luftwaffe material and labour requirements into fifth place in September 1940 and second place to the army in January 1942 – and there emerges the formula for a catastrophic prosecution of the war. A formula for self-destruction was compounded by the narrowness of the nation's industrial base – one wholly incapable of sustaining growth in overlapping rearmament programmes upon which three competing services were totally dependent. For air staffs contemplating re-equipment programmes at any time in the war, the outlook was indeed bleak, but, given the prodigious efforts of a new armaments minister (Albert Speer), not entirely without high spots.

2. Stukagruppen-Schlachtgruppen

Swift action by ground and air forces acting jointly against centres of resistance was crucial to the success of panzer operations when tank thrusts were halted or in danger of delay. Yet despite appearances to the contrary fostered by swift and obviously successful military campaigns in Poland and France, Luftwaffe ground-attack responsibilities were surprisingly divided. Whereas Ju 87s entering service with dive-bomber Wings (Stukagruppen) from 1936 onwards were responsible to the bombing arm of the Luftwaffe, other types, particularly the Hs 123 and successors such as the Me 109, Me 110 and Hs 129, were formed into ground-attack Wings (Schlachtgruppen) answerable to the fighter arm. The result of this dichotomy was Luftwaffe failure to meet the challenge of expanding commitments. Training went unco-ordinated and technical developments upon which future potency depended remained at a low ebb. Not until 1943 – and then too late – did Air Staff appreciate the overriding importance of uniting Stukagruppen and Schlachtgruppen into a single ground-attack arm under a General of Ground Attack Flying. The mainstay of ground-attack operations in the early campaigns was the Ju 87 – organized into nine Wings (Gruppen). In Poland these Wings were more frequently engaged on Luftwaffe than army business. That is to say, Stuka targets were mostly short-range and 'strategic', aimed at winning air superiority for the Luftwaffe – by destroying opposition on the ground – leaving only a single Schlachtgruppe II/LG2 flying Hs 123s and performing more or less exclusive army tasks under Fliegerführer zbV (von Richthofen). Theoretically the Stuka-gruppen were answerable to von Richthofen for both army and Luftwaffe work, but in practice the prior needs of the Luftwaffe were answered before assistance was given to panzer divisions.

Introduced in 1936 as a dive-bomber, the elderly but robust Hs 123.A-1 biplane used for ground-strafing was armed with two 7.92mm machine-guns positioned ahead of the pilot. The Hs 123 could also deliver a single 500lb bomb from a centre-line rack beneath the fuselage. A more useful B variant was introduced in 1941 intended for action against enemy armour. Armed with two 20mm cannon, this version flew with a modified bomb-load. The Ju 87B, on the other hand, was capable of delivering twice the high-explosive load of the Henschel – one 1,102 pounder on centre-line and four small 50-pounders on wing racks. In addition to its bomb-load, the early Ju 87 (Stuka) was armed with two 7.9mm machine-guns located in the wing roots. Another (MG15) for defence was operated by the observer/radio operator in the rear cockpit. The D-1 version introduced in 1940 demonstrated a much improved performance with a new engine, better armour protection for the pilot and a greater bomb-load – 3,968lb. This version flew most of the Luftwaffe's ground-attack missions after 1940. A Ju 87 G variant, flying in 1943 with two 3.7cm cannon, was to win fame as a tank-buster, but this development explored later was limited by obsolescence to Eastern Front operations (*see* anti-tank operations, page 124).

In so far as the future of the dive-bomber was concerned, the Luftwaffe's early model, the Henschel Hs 123, relegated to ground-attack duties after a disappointing performance in the role in Spain, would remain in production until 1942. The Ju 87, by contrast, would maintain a continuous if at times precarious level of production until 1944, by which time some 5,000 various marks would have entered service with Stukagruppen and Schlachtgruppen.

In conditions of air supremacy achieved by the Luftwaffe at no great cost in Poland, France, the Balkans and, at first, in Russia, the Luftwaffe's machines and its highly trained personnel and organization performed well enough. Enjoying the benefits of pre-war planning and progress, particularly in army co-operation, the Luftwaffe created a strike force of immense power demonstrating its prowess in a spectacular run of victories. Opponents in Poland and France were surprised and overwhelmed by the combined efforts of army groups and air fleets. After the fall of France the Luftwaffe reigned supreme on the continent in 1940, but in the high summer of that year as the air war developed over Britain the fortunes of the Luftwaffe suffered a dramatic change. In operations clearing the way for 'Sea-lion' – bringing Stukas and their fighter escorts into conflict with the RAF – the Luftwaffe was outclassed, driven from the sky by resolutely handled Spitfires and Hurricanes.

Despite dedicated flying by experienced crews determined to press home pin-point attacks against RAF ground targets, the Stukagruppen concentrated under von Richtho-fen – VIII Air Corps/3rd Air Fleet (Sperrle); or Lörzer – II Air Corps/2nd Air Fleet (Kesselring) were outmanoeuvred and after suffering unacceptable losses withdrew from the conflict.

When VIII Air Corps entered the Balkans supporting von Kleist, von Richthofen's Stukagruppen and Schlachtgruppen were in no way stretched. Little or no interference being suffered from Greek or Yugoslav air forces chased off by the Luftwaffe (map 6). But when the Stukas joined in new offensives launched by Hitler in Africa and on the Eastern Front (maps 5 and 7) the situation again changed dramatically for the worse. So inadequate was the Luftwaffe in the face of its old adversary the RAF and in due course new opponents like the Red Air Force – struggling to win time and recover from invasion – or the USAF that it was

Right: The Ju 87B-2 was a two-seat dive-bomber armed with two 7.92mm MG17 machine-guns in the wings and one 7.92mm MG in the rear cockpit. It carried a bomb-load of one 1,102lb (500kg) bomb on the centreline and four 110lb (50kg) bombs on the wing racks. It had a speed of 242mph and a range of 373 miles.

Right: The Ju 87B D-1 improvement on the B-2 had twin 7.92mm MG81 machine-guns in the rear cockpit. The bomb-load increased to 3,968lb (1,800kg), speed to 252mph and range to 620 miles. Later versions were armed with two 20mm MG151/20 wing cannon.

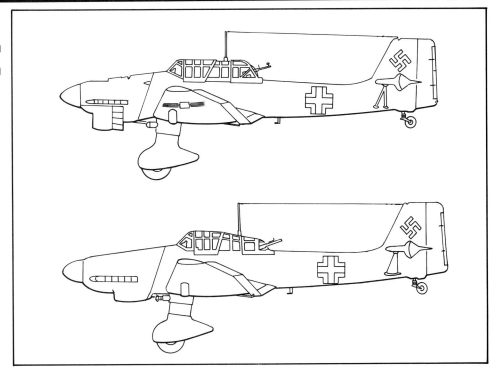

to meet in action in North Africa, the Ju 87s could operate only with a strong fighter escort. In Tunisia in 1942–3, for instance, a squadron of 8–12 Ju 87s needed the protection of up to 30 Me 109s if it were to perform effectively. In Russia, at a time when the Red Air Force was relatively unprepared for invasion, the Stukas recorded better results; but the days of overwhelming support for the army in conditions of Luftwaffe superiority were drawing to a close. Few suitable replacements were on hand to assist the rebuilding of depleted Stukagruppen. The Fw 189 (Owl), having failed to measure up to Luftwaffe ground-attack requirements, had been diverted to air reconnaissance work (*see page 134*), other projects were late (Ju 87 D-G), abandoned (Me 210) or still on the drawing-board (Me 410). In this situation the Air Staff turned to ideas of employing fighters as fighter-bombers ('Jabos').

During the Battle of Britain and afterwards in the Balkans and North Africa, before the war turned east, the Me 109E flying with fighter Wings (Jagdgruppen) attacked RAF ground installations with 500lb high-explosive bombs.

The Me 110C, a 'heavy' twin-engined fighter flying in support of the Me 109 and deployed in destroyer Wings (Zerstörergruppen), could deliver twice that explosive load, while the much superior Fw 190, a fighter by design, but developed in G and F series as a ground-attack fighter-bomber, could unleash a devastating 3,968lb of high-explosives. Capable of speeds up to 400 miles per hour, the Fw 190 was eventually decided upoon as the ground-attack successor for the Luftwaffe's ageing fleet of Ju 87Bs – limited by engine performance to 255mph. Notwithstanding the remarkable capacity of one Fw 190 variant to obliterate any target with a massive weight of high explosives, the standard bomb-load of this, the Luftwaffe's best all-round tactical aircraft of the war, was to settle into a combination

of one 500lb and four small 100lb, SC 50 bombs. Alternatively, the Fw 190 could operate with two 3cm anti-tank cannon (BK103) modifying a bomb-load supplemented by two 7.9mm machine-guns (MG17). In fact, no fewer than forty bomb, cannon and machine-gun alternatives were devised for the Fw 190 in close-support work. Production, including a late F9 variant armed with 8.8cm rocket-projectiles, continued until May 1945. The rockets were used to better effect against air targets than in operations against tanks where their effectiveness was much less a matter of note.

Somewhat less commendable than the Air Staff decision to replace its Ju 87s with new Fw 190s was a lack of motivation in developing tank-busting aircraft of the kind entering service with foreign air forces. In 1942, when the Red Air Force introduced the Bell P-39 Airacobra into its operations on the Eastern Front, and the new Ilyushin Il-2m3 Shturmovik appeared over the battlefield in droves, much to the consternation of the German Army, the Luftwaffe faced another unwelcome challenge to its authority. Received under a lend-lease arrangement with the USA, the P-39's principal armament was a reasonably powerful but low-velocity – later improved – 3.7cm cannon firing through the hub of the propeller. In its improved version, the Airacobra was to prove effective against all but the most heavily armoured ground targets; its speed of 360–376mph placing it in the fighter class. The Bell's Soviet-designed companion was a heavily armoured ground-attack (Shturmovik) Ilyushin (Il-2m3) equipped with two high-velocity 23mm cannon or any of several weapon packages. In the role of tank-buster, the Shturmovik proved superior to both the P-39 and Hs 123. In action against panzer columns, P-39s and Shturmoviks quickly made their mark. Flown by pilots whose skill and

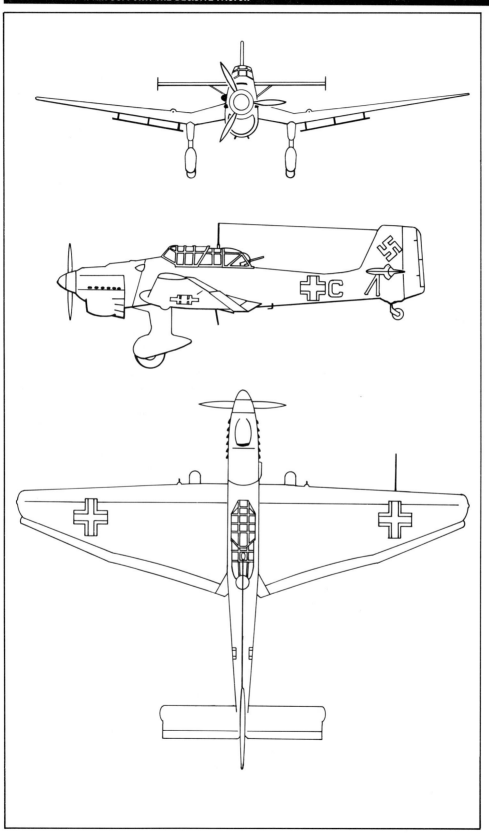

Left: A Ju 87-B1 three-view
arrangement of the Luftwaff[e]
most famous and distinctive
gull-winged dive-bomber. Th[e]
term Stuka was dropped in
1943 in favour of Schlacht,
meaning battle or ground-
attack aircraft.

Right: The Ju 87-G tank-busting version of the Stuka was introduced into limited service in 1943. It was armed with two 3.7cm BK (Flak 18 or 36) cannon, or later six MG81 machine-guns, in underwing pods. The speed and range were significantly reduced by drag, but Hauptmann Rudel of Schlachtgeschwader 2 flew the Ju 87-G with enormous anti-tank success.

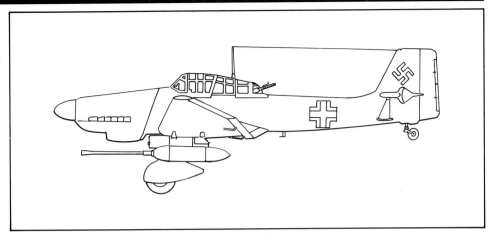

resolve matched their German opponents, the Bells and Ilyushins supported by one or two other close-support types raised the stakes in the air war. Luftwaffe response was to hinge on the new, heavily armoured twin-engined Henschel Hs 129B2 whose main armament consisted of one 3cm (ultimately 3.7cm) Mk 103 anti-tank cannon with two 7.9mm machine-guns; 841 Henschels of this type were built for service with the Luftwaffe. Experiments were also set in train to adapt the ubiquitous Ju 87 to a tank-busting role – armed with two 3.7cm Flak mounted in underwing fairings. When flown by Hauptmann Rudel, whose exploits in ground-attack are touched upon later, the G variant of the Stuka – despite a lack of aerodynamic finesse – was to become a renowned but largely illusory symbol of Luftwaffe power.

In the spring of 1942 with the Luftwaffe expanding its ground attack forces, in anticipation of Operation 'Blue/ Brunswick' (map 10), II/LG2, the veteran army support wing of operations in Poland, France and the Balkans, was incorporated as II Gruppe in Shlachtgeschwader I. A second Schlachtgeschwader, SchG 2, was formed out of Stukageschwader 2 later in the year; neither formation being more than two Wings strong.

These Schlachtgeschwader supported by twelve to fifteen Stukagruppen equipped with the surviving Ju 87Bs and Ds, and various marks of Me 109, Fw 190 and Hs 129, were eventually to stage a qualified return to effective Luftwaffe

ground-attack flying on the Eastern Front. The flare-up followed a period of Luftwaffe eclipse during which time the Red Air Force, drastically improved in numbers and equipment, dominated the Eastern Front. On the German side the ground-attack units that had accompanied the army into Belorussia, serving in offensives against Leningrad and Moscow and before supporting Eleventh Army in the Crimea, were more often than not concentrated at the point of attack under VIII Air Corps (von Richthofen). Progress, however, was rarely spectacular and when VIII Air Corps reached Stalingrad (map 12) the fiasco there was somewhat less than a triumph. But in two subsequent operations during and after 'Citadel' at Bjelgorod and Bryansk in 1943, the ground-attack Wings performed in worthy fashion; operations in which VIII Air Corps, subordinated to von Richthofen's 4th Air Fleet, played a key role. However, far from heralding a return to power of a pre-eminent Luftwaffe enjoying much improved equipment – welcome as this was to Stukagruppen and Schlachtgruppen starved of equipment and resources in 1941–2 – the new aircraft at the centre of operations served more to swell Luftwaffe pride than generate power at the heart of a reinvigorated air force. In this respect, army expectations of Luftwaffe battlefield support matching its own expanding commitments were to prove unfounded. In action against tank forces of much superior strength on at least two of its many fronts in 1944–5, but unprotected from opponents enjoying infinite

Right: The Hs 129 single-seat ground-attack fighter was usually armed with a 3cm MK101 canon, but other versions carried four MG17s, 551lb of bombs or a BK 3.7cm gun. An experimental model was provided with a 7.5cm gun, the muzzle of which projected eight feet in front of the aircraft! The versions depicted here and overleaf had a maximum speed of approximately 250mph. Hauptmann Bruno Meyer earned distinction with the Hs 129 in action with IV/SG9 against Russian armour at Kursk.

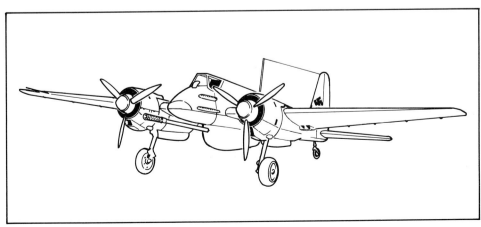

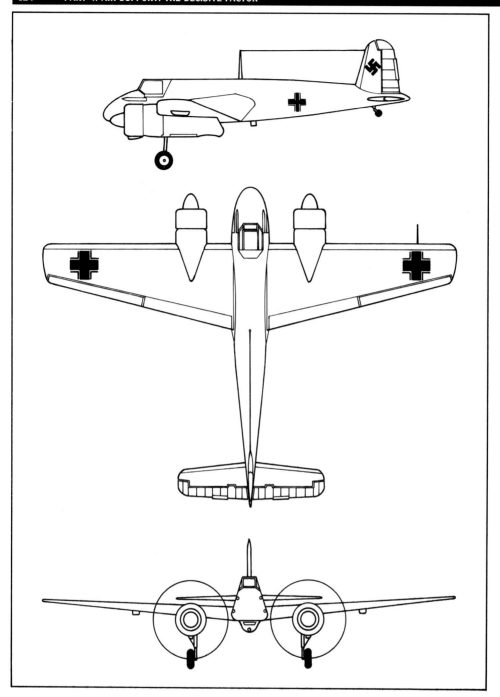

Left: The Hs 129 ground-attack fighter.

resources, the German Army would collapse; the panzer divisions unable to contend with modern air power simply melting away.

Consider the Luftwaffe's unexceptional progress in anti-tank warfare. Until September 1943, when close-support operations were completely reorganized under a General of Ground Attack Flying, Hs 129s served only in (panzer) squadrons numbered 4 and 8 in Schlachtgeschwadern SG1 and SG2. Each of these under-strength Geschwader, equivalent to an RAF Group (USAF Wing), comprised two instead of the normal three Wings (gruppen) although each consisted of four staffeln (squadrons). A fifth Panzerjaeger squadron operated with JG51. The first of these Panzer-jaeger panzer squadrons – 4 and 8 SG1 – made their début on the central front in the summer of 1942, flying with VIII Air Corps/4th Air Fleet in operations against Voronezh (map 10). On this front they demonstrated a marked advantage over other types when attacking Soviet armour.

On the other hand, 4 (Pz) SG2, operating in North Africa during November 1942, served unremarkably with engine trouble plaguing operations. Thereafter ground-attack operations in Tunisia, where Fifth Panzer Army Africa faced the prospect of early defeat, was left to 8 (Pz) SG2, the Jabos of two Zerstörergruppen and Stukas of two other depleted units assembled under Stukageschwader 3.

At this point, in the spring of 1943, service trials at Rechlin and Bryansk under the supervision of Oberst Otto Weiss were devoted to testing the effectiveness of a variety of aircraft and weapons paired in anti-tank combinations. The Sonderkommando für Panzerbekâmpfung (Stepp) formed specially for the purpose by the air staff, was responsible for the field trials and, when a crisis developed in the Kuban during February and March 1943, a certain amount of operational flying. Air battles in this region of Russia, where 4th Air Fleet was engaged, brought test units and all five Hs 129 squadrons into action, before Stepp rejoined SG2. The best of the aircraft/weapon pairings tried out by the Sonderkommando were the Ju 87G, fitted with two 3.7cm anti-aircraft guns, and the Hs 129, tried out with a similar heavy-calibre weapon. Both Junkers and Henschel types were favoured as 'standard issue' to future panzer-jaeger squadrons, but the production capacity of the Luftwaffe being what it was in 1943, despite prodigious efforts by Armaments Minister Speer too few entered service. Other aircraft/weapon pairings included the Ju 88 (P-1) fitted with a 7.5cm anti-tank gun (PaK 40) which proved impracticable, and the Me 110, also fitted beneath the fuselage with a 3.7cm PaK, but which could not be spared from fighter production.

The saga of Luftwaffe anti-tank operations continued in 1943 with preparations for 'Citadel' (map 14), the battle in which Panzerjaeger were to make a distinguished contribution to an otherwise disastrous undertaking. Thereafter in a reorganizational sequel to 'Citadel', panzerjaeger would be re-grouped and all five panzer squadrons concentrated in IV/SG9 (Meyer). Only one other Wing was raised for inclusion in this formation. Furthermore, the few Ju 87Gs becoming available for service were distributed as a 10th squadron to four of the six Schlachtgeschwader created during the course of reorganization; the selected Gesch-wader being SG1, 2, 3 and 77; those not so fortunate, SG4 and SG10. This was the organizational tally of Luftwaffe progress in anti-tank operations.

After the spring of 1943 when the war against the Soviet Union resumed in earnest after the fall of Stalingrad (map 12) – a period of operations during the winter of 1942 in which any number of reserve and training aircraft had to be brought forward to sustain Luftwaffe front-line strength – ground-attack operations were to reveal a more revolutionary dimension of battlefield support. Equipped with new and improved aircraft types – the Fw 190, Ju 87D and Hs 129 – yet still requiring the veteran Hs 123 to make good their strength, Schlachtgruppen and Stukagruppen gave new tactical meaning to the notion of flexible response in a crisis. The recovery of Kharkov by 4th Air Fleet and Army Group South in March 1943 (map 13) illustrates the point to advantage; in this action the all-important air support arrangements leading to a re-enactment of Blitz-krieg were the responsbility of von Richthofen. No Luftwaffe commander possessed his experience in directing ground-attack operations. From the time of the Spanish Civil War onwards, von Richthofen's service career had been devoted

almost exclusively to this area of flying. Under his tutelage, VIII Air Corps had been deployed at the point of attack in Poland, France, the Balkans, at Leningrad, Moscow, Voronezh and Stalingrad, evolving as the prime command for this form of warfare. However, the exigencies of the military situation being what they were at Stalingrad and then in the Kuban, VIII Air Corps was temporarily employed there as a transport command; notwithstanding which von Richthofen initiated a series of judicious moves to provide the best possible support for von Manstein preparing a counter-stroke against an over-extended Red Army pressing west from Stalingrad.

Re-grouping 4th Air Fleet, but excluding VIII Air Corps (IV Air Corps was used instead), von Richthofen created anew the condition for success that had eluded the Wehrmacht since the Battle of France (map 4). Concentrat-ing close-support units in the shape of two air corps: I (Korten) at Poltava; IV (Pflugbeil) at Dnepropetrovsk; and an ad hoc Fliegerdivision Donets (Mahnke) at Stalino for the benefit of von Manstein's armies and Armeeabteilung Kempf (map 13), von Richthofen retained the air fleet's long-range bombers under personal command. On hand at headquarters with advice for von Richthofen if required was Oberst Weiss, the Panzerjaegerführer guiding trials of the anti-tank units assembled at Bryansk. The (proto)types available for action included the Ju 88-C (P) armed with a 7.5cm cannon. This unsatisfactory fighter-bomber was eventually discarded, but not before making something of a name for itself as a railway (Eisenbahn)-buster. The key to von Richthofen's close-support success is to be seen in its most advanced form in the recovery of Kharkov. Two aspects invite comment: concentration and flexibility. In the first place concentration was achieved by making disposi-tions that embraced every available aircraft; all being pressed into tactical service including his own long-range bombers. Secondly, flexibility was achieved by a policy of switching the main effort from one air corps to another in accordance with von Richthofen and von Manstein's reading of the tactical situation. The creation of ad hoc battlefield support groups, remarkably effective at Bjelgorod and Bryansk during 'Citadel' – the sequel to von Richthofen's battles for Kharkov, was to prove a significant factor in local success. With von Richthofen's full support for von Manstein, Kharkov was recovered and Russian spearheads destroyed.

One other praiseworthy contribution that von Richthofen made to the consolidation of army-air operations was the Panzerverbindungsoffizier or Stukaleiter (Stuka controller). By using a two-way (R/T) link making contact with battle groups flying temporarily under his control, the Stukaleiter allotted to a panzer regiment was able to direct or redirect Stukas to opportunity targets, theoretically ensuring their profitable employment. This concept of creating radio links between tanks and aircraft evolved out of von Richthofen's experience in the Spanish Civil War when he allocated forward observers to ground troops, linking them by wireless to their air force headquarters. By 1940 the arrangements had changed; a panzer commander needing air support notified an air liaison officer (Fliegerverbindungsoffizier – Flivo) serving divisional headquarters. Flivo in turn con-tacted the division's appointed close-support group com-mander who arranged the required sortie. In 1941 a more effective method of consolidating ground and air forces was developed within VIII Air Corps (von Richthofen) when an experienced Stuka pilot was appointed regimental tank liaison officer (Panzerverbindungsoffizier). He was allocated a Pz Kpfw III tank in which was installed Luftwaffe radio equipment (Fluggerate VII) capable of communicating directly with the Stukas. When they appeared overhead the controller took complete charge of the sortie, giving advice on approach, method of attack and confirming the target, which, more often than not, he was able to observe at close range; at times uncomfortably close. The Stukaleiter was not a Flivo and rarely usurped that officer's function at division or higher headquarters; liaison between army and Luftwaffe at these levels continuing unchanged.

British Intelligence, reporting the interrogation of a Stukaleiter from 7th Panzer Regiment, 10th Panzer Division, appointed by 5/StukaGeschwader 3 in Tunis, does so in the following terms:

'Medjez el Bab, 10th December 1942. On this the first day of the liaison officer's appointment, there was no activity on account of the unsuitable weather but on 11th December a conference was held in Tunis at the HQ of Generalmajor Harlinghausen (Fliegerführer Tunisia), attended by the panzer commander and commanders of the air formations.'

'It was decided to attack Medjez el Bab and the Stukas were given three targets which they were to destroy; one a battery, another an Allied tank concentration on the road, and a third a bridge at or near Medjez.'

'The liaison officer joined the tanks early morning and commenced by transmitting a weather report to the Fliegerführer. There was 5/10th cloud at 800 metres which was considered favourable for a Stuka attack.'

'When the attack was due to commence it was found that the battery had already moved, and the liaison officer therefore directed the Stukas to the Allied tank formations. He took up a point of vantage on a hill nearby where he could view the whole operation and sat on top of the tank to obtain a better view.'

'The Stukas arrived on the scene and were duly directed to their target, but dropped their bombs some 300 yards ahead of the tanks.'

Before considering developments in close-support at Bjelgorod and Bryansk during and after 'Citadel' in August 1943 – where Schlachtgruppen demonstrated a remarkable propensity for breaking up dangerous Russian counter-offensives – this change of emphasis in ground-attack operations is worth noting as a new and powerful contribution to the defensive resources of the Wehrmacht.

Launching Stuka and panzerjaeger attacks at short notice against Russian armour, the Luftwaffe would strike effective, if somewhat limited, blows – substituting for non-existent army group reserves. Successful actions of the kind to be witnessed at Bjelgorod and Bryansk, where von Manstein and Model faced grave problems with no reserves, were to become all too necessary as the war entered a critical phase and air corps at danger points were required to execute ground-attack operations – albeit on a diminishing scale – to protect armies facing crises on widely separated fronts. Consider the itinerary of Schlachtgeschwader 2 (Rudel) over a period of twenty months from September 1943 to May 1945. During this time, SG 2 flew ground-attack missions in the Ukraine, Roumania, Poland, East Prussia and

Courland. After returning to Roumania, SG 2 moved to Hungary, Silesia and Pomerania, subsequently defending Berlin itself on the Oder at Küstrin. Only the American bombing of Czech airfields in support of the Red Army, brought the odyssey of SG 2 to a close, destroying most of III/SG2, the Geschwader's best equipped and most celebrated unit at Kletzen. From this secondary airfield north of Prague the 'Immelmanner' (as the personnel of this Geschwader were known in tribute to the 1914–18 air ace) flew their last Ju 87G and Fw 190 missions in aid of Army Group Schörner.

Close-support provided by the Luftwaffe for the armies at Bjelgorod and Bryansk during 'Citadel' (map 14) marked a significant development in ground-attack operations. From aircraft operating in small numbers against tanks, more or less at random during early campaigns, their employment developed to the stage where they were used *en masse* as a decisive weapon with which to counter superior enemy ground forces. In the first instance, at Bjelgorod, the panzerjaeger element of various geschwader subordinate to VIII Air Corps (Siedeman) flying with 1st Fleet/Army Group South, were committed in a powerful and remarkably effective *ad hoc* battle formation to destroy an opportunity target. Panzerjagdverband Meyer (so named after Hauptman Bruno Meyer) under whose command were 4 (Pz), 8 (Pz) SG1 and 4 (Pz), 8 (Pz) SG2, represented the most powerful concentration of anti-tank aircraft available to the Luftwaffe on the Eastern Front. The situation that Meyer turned to advantage arose out of the failure of III Panzer Corps to close up and protect the open flank of II SS Panzer Corps leading the Kursk offensive north of Bjelgorod; (Fourth Panzer Army, July 1943). Patrolling ahead of SS Liebstandarte, Meyer detected the presence of a Russian armoured brigade, raised the alarm and in an hour long engagement left fifty Russian tanks crippled or destroyed on the battlefield; the SS divisions were able to regroup and, under intensive pressure from Shturmoviks newly provided with 3.7cm cannon, eventually withdrew to their start-line. The subsequent retreat from Kursk was to lead within days to the second notable example of this form of anti-tank support for the army; this time, on 19 July, when at a point on Second Panzer Army's front a Russian penetration of the main battle line north of Bryansk threatened to split Army Group Centre. The German response was to assemble all available panzerjaeger and Schlacht units into Gefechtsverband Kupfer, a battle group responsible to the commanding officer of SG2 (Kupfer), comprising his own Ju 87G/Fw 190s and Meyer's Hs 129s. Co-operating with bomber and fighter units stripped from other sectors to reinforce 6th Air Fleet (Greim) in what is now recognized as the last significant concentration of Luftwaffe strength in the east, Kupfer's anti-tank group launched blistering attacks against Russian tank thrusts. Targeting T34s and KVs (I and II) with 3cm and 3.7cm cannon-fire, or dispersing supporting infantry with fragmentation clusters and high-explosives, Kupfer's combined force of Stukas, panzer-knackers and protective fighters played the key role in eliminating a dangerous and unexpected threat to Army Group Centre.

But these Panzerjagd and Schlacht units operating under Meyer and Kupfer, whatever their success in defeating Russian intentions at Bjelgorod and Bryansk, represented a waning fraction of declining Luftwaffe effort. In the wider

Anglo–Canadian forces and US 9th Air Force divided between IX TAC (US First Army) and XIX TAC (US Third Army). In excess of 100 ground-attack squadrons (57 US, 51 RAF) equipped with Mustangs, Thunderbolts and rocket-firing Typhoons, also Mosquitoes and Spitfires supplemented by bombers in the Fortress class, shattered all German hopes of halting the Allied drive to the Seine and beyond. German armies in the west, reduced to a pitiful level of Luftwaffe support, were grossly under-resourced.

Generals Eberbach and Hausser, in common with panzer commanders on other fronts, lacked the vital air component needed to win battles – none more so than Panzer Group Eberbach, Fifth Panzer Army (Europe) seeking to counter Patton [D+62] or retreating without air cover [D+72]. At times like these panzer divisions deprived of support at Mortain and Falaise suffered unprecedented reverses. Six months later much the same can be said of operations by von Manteuffel, Fifth Panzer Army (Europe) and Dietrich, Sixth SS Panzer Army in the Ardennes. As soon as weather conditions permitted Anglo-American Air Forces their customary freedom of action the fate of these armies was sealed.

In 'Autumn Mist' (map 17), a single Schlachtgeschwader, SG4, on loan to Luftwaffenkommando West from Greim's 6th Air Fleet, Army Group Centre, deployed on the Vistula in critical battles for Berlin, contributed fewer than one hundred Fw 190s to the offensive. Sharing ground-attack duties with Jagdgruppen diverted from home defence, SG4 made little impression in the battle for the Meuse crossings. And neither were a handful each of Kampf and Nachtschlachtgruppen of much use. The outcome was all too predictable and after participating in 'Bodenplatte', the Luftwaffe's New Year's Day offensive against Anglo-US close support airfields in north-west Europe, SG4 and the Jagdgruppen were hurriedly redeployed east. Serving 6th Air Fleet SG4, like other depleted ground-attack units faced by the Red Air Force, enjoying a superiority of 6:1 in aircraft, contemplated the impossible task of delaying the disintegration of eastern army groups (map 20).

Most at risk was Schörner's Army Group Centre (First and Fourth Panzer Armies, 12 January–May 1945) and Rendulic's Army Group South (Second Panzer and SS Sixth Armies). But it was painfully clear that the Luftwaffe no longer possessed the omnipotence of early campaigns supporting the army while winning the air war. For allowing so deplorable a state of affairs to develop this self-appointed Commander-in-Chief could blame no one but himself. He had raged at Goering, Goering had been reduced to tears, and officials at the highest levels of procurement and operations had committed suicide. Udet in November 1941, Jeschonnek in August 1943. Operational losses had continued to plague the Luftwaffe – even in fighters which enjoyed the highest of the armaments minister's priorities. Speer's dispersal policy, distributing aircraft production to more than three hundred sites either at home or in occupied zones most certainly helped to put off the day when aircraft manufacture would cease completely, either through enemy occupation or destruction in air raids. Nevertheless, the most crippling factor in the history of army/air operations – beyond any help that Speer could give – was the total destruction of Germany's oil industry. Other than promoting the manufacture of jet aircraft using the lowest grade fuel,

for instance, the Hs 162 fighter, Speer was powerless. By December 1944, following an interval in which stocks improved to the advantage of 'Autumn Mist', home production had been ravaged almost beyond repair and fuel stocks reduced to emergency levels.

Operational flying was consequently proscribed by OKL for all but 'decisive situations' – bringing Luftwaffe bombing operations to an end and imposing severe constraints on ground-attack flying. Schlachtgruppen still operational and capable of offensive action (like SG2, driven into Bohemia) were henceforth committed if and when the fuel situation permitted. Thus grounded for want of fuel, Luftwaffe units were of no more use to the Wehrmacht than panzer battalions halted with dry tanks. Ironically, the type of fuel required to keep the Ju 87 flying was available in substantially greater quantities than that required for the Fw 190; an argument used by Air Staff to retain the Ju 87 in service. But with or without improved versions of the Ju 87 to expand re-equipment schedules, any presumption on the part of the Air Staff of raising Schlacht units equipped with new Fw 190 variants, the Panzerblitz, Me 410 or later types including the Do 335 and Ar 334 were, to say the least, unreal. The fuel facts were stark. Eighteen months earlier an Anglo-American air offensive against synthetic (coal-related) fuel production plants in north Germany – Leuna in particular – had by September 1944 reduced the output of this region from 195,000 tons in May 1943 to less than 7,000 tons. No less catastrophic than the virtual destruction of the synthetic oil plants was the loss of crude oil output from eastern Europe; Ploesti, the most important centre in Roumania falling to 2nd Ukrainian Front on 31 August. Other centres were immediately threatened, especially Nagykaniska in western Hungary with related refineries at Komorn and Vienna. 'Spring Awakening', Hitler's last offensive in the east (map 19), was intended to forestall this loss of capacity, but the final nail in the coffin of Luftwaffe tactical and general flying was a resurgence of Anglo-American air attacks against production centres in Silesia followed by a return to Leuna and associated plants in January 1945; by April the industry was wrecked.

The effect of dwindling fuel stocks on Luftwaffe operations when aircraft were being lost at an irreplaceable rate and production resources were increasingly curtailed was to inhibit a successful prosecution of the war. Tactical flying faded for days a time. Replacement aircraft failed to arrive on schedule – abandoned in assembly plants east and west as they fell into enemy hands, and transport arrangements degenerated alarmingly. Command arrangements too suffered dislocation when headquarters moved uncertainly from one threatened locality to another. Reduced to impotence by the air war being waged against military and economic targets, battlefield support for the army ended in failure eclipsed by Allied air forces in all but a few significant aspects of research and development. A true reflection of the Luftwaffe's inability to meet the army's demands for close-support on the battlefield after 1941 can be read in an official German report, compiled by the Luftwaffe's own historical branch, in December 1944. 'In Italy fighter escorts could be provided for an average of only one ground-attack sortie per day . . . early hopes that the Fw 190 could operate without fighter protection were never realized.'

3. The Army's eye in the sky

Light aircraft organized into army close-reconnaissance squadrons (Heeres 'H' Staffeln) and at the request of panzer commanders making regular sorties to the limit of their range, observing and photographing hostile tank and infantry movements, would also spot for artillery or report the position of their own and neighbouring units. Other tasks included the gathering of topographical Intelligence to augment out of date or otherwise unsatisfactory official maps. Two types of aircraft flew this kind of operation, the Hs 126 and, after 1941, the Fw 189 (Owl). At higher army and Luftwaffe headquarters the work of the close-reconnaissance squadrons was supplemented by long-distance reconnaissance units (Fernaufklärungstaffeln) flying Dornier Do 17s and Ju 88s. The arrival of a photographic mission at (mobile) squadron headquarters was usually the signal for intense activity; roll film being taken from the aircraft's cameras, swiftly processed and wet negatives studied. Results were then compiled into Air Photo Interpretation reports and forwarded to Koluft or, following changes instituted in 1942, to Luftwaffe/panzer Intelligence staffs (Ic). For more elaborate second-phase viewing, prints were made in stereoscopic pairs; reports and prints being distributed to interested parties including Berlin Intelligence agencies for third-phase analysis and long-term storage. The practised ease with which in the early campaigns API reports were prepared by the Luftwaffe and acted upon by panzer commanders is indicative of the high standards achieved in pre-war training, equipment and liaison. Equally commendable was the trend towards clear speech contact between air and ground forces, developed through wireless technology in the shape of the VHF radio telephone (RT). An observer witnessing the progress of German Twelfth Army (List) through Yugoslavia in April 1941, most probably SS Liebstandarte Adolf Hitler, recorded a typical example of army/air co-operation in the early days of the war. '. . . the radio outfit and observer in the advanced unit was housed in a fairly heavy closed truck. I noticed that it contained both receiving and broadcasting equipment . . . Two German planes had previously been seen scouting westwards for the road unit at low altitude . . . A closed car, preceded by a motor-cyclist came back towards us from the west, it was travelling fast along the road and had apparently been doing reconnaissance co-operation with the planes. Shortly afterwards the main body was moved up.' The observer then describes the deployment of four heavy guns positioned on each side of the road facing west, and the subsequent leap-frogging of motor-cycle units after which the planes were again noticed scouting over the road in the direction of a mountain pass.

These tactics were those most frequently encountered by British and Allied troops in the Balkans. British Intelligence, reporting the incident, noted the presence of a radio vehicle well forward in the column; commenting too that the radio sets employed were of very high frequency (42100–47800 kc/s) which limited their range and made interception difficult. Other units would also have been in radio contact with the scouting aircraft especially the artillery waiting to be given opportunity targets; all diligently displaying their own identity to the air-arm by using white or yellow strips

and swastika flags spread out on vehicles. Air sentries too would have been posted to warn of the approach of enemy aircraft. In the words of a training memorandum issued at the time by Koluft at OKH (Bogatsch), the crux of army-air co-operation lay in '. . . the need to obtain the most complete possible picture of the enemy by the extremely close working of motorized ground and air co-operation squadrons. Commanders are advised to agree starting times for aircraft, reconnaissance limits and action in case of forced landing, also call-signs and the line of march of ground troops.' A reconnaissance sortie such as this would have been at the centre of a wireless 'star' disseminating information to both reconnaissance units and dependent headquarters. In addition to R/T speech, bringing air and ground units into contact, messages were often conveyed to the foremost tank or tactical headquarters in the form of marked maps or written messages. During a single day in France 1940, von Kleist Gruppe received no fewer than 22 dropped messages, all reporting the enemy situation on 19 June. A yellow smoker marker fixed to the message cylinder helped ground troops in its recovery. Other means of air-to-ground signalling followed a prearranged code involving the use of coloured flares or smoke signals. A green flare fired by an observer/pilot usually preceded a dropped message; red signified enemy anti-tank activity and blue/violet a warning – beware enemy tanks! For signalling their own presence or needs to the air force, ground troops were provided with national flags and white cloth strips. Displaying the strips in code would bring a resupply of weapons, ammunition and equipment – not always into the right hands.

Army/Luftwaffe success with reconnaissance sorties was short-lived however. The inability of the Luftwaffe to penetrate hostile air space in later years – a consequence of obsolete aircraft equipment and a loss of air superiority on all fronts – was to lead to a marked deterioration in the army's performance. Panzer commanders and staffs denied photographic Intelligence at critical times were all too often incapable of reading enemy intentions and thereby develop an effective counter-strategy or maximize tactical opportunities. In Normandy in 1944, Panzer Group West, facing the prospect of invasion, was gravely disadvantaged by the failure of Luftwaffe long-range reconnaissance missions to observe and photograph the build-up to 'Overlord' (map 16). Equally unsatisfactory was the subsequent dearth of battle reconnaissance which hampered effective counter-action. Defective surveillance – partially offset by an increase in wireless Intelligence (see Panzer Signals) – was nothing new to panzer commanders brought up on the Eastern Front. On a significant number of occasions there commanders were surprised by the scale of Russian counter-offensives. In the closing stages of 'Typhoon' for example (Second Panzer Army, 5 December 1941), the undetected build-up of Red Army Fronts concentrating for action against Panzergruppen attacking Moscow was a consequence of air reconnaissance failures. The lack of such information compounded, to a disastrous degree, the tactical and supply problems facing exhausted panzer troops. Intelligence of this kind was normally to be read in an increase of traffic densities on lines of communication, on support air fields and in burgeoning supply and storage installations. Denied such Intelligence (assisted by Russian deception) and at the end of its resources, von Bock's Moscow offensive collapsed. (Hitler's obscurantism also contributed to the army's defeat in the battle for Moscow. In refusing to countenance any suggestion of Russian superiority – dismissing unfavourable appreciations of enemy strength as 'rubbish' – the Führer was to prove, as on many subsequent occasions, a potent factor in the army's downfall).

As regards aircraft, the mainstay of the 'H' squadrons accompanying the panzer force in Poland and France in 1939–40, thereafter in the Balkans and in Russia in 1941, was the Hs 126 supported to a lesser degree by the Fieseler Fi 156 Storch. Tested in Spain and selected for squadron service in 1938, the Hs 126 was to become standard aircraft equipment for army air co-operation, displacing an older He 46 and a small number of He 45s considered unfit for front-line service. But the high-wing Henschel, seating pilot and observer in a semi-enclosed cockpit, was soon to fail, being too slow and ill-adapted to a crucial role in mobile operations even in 1940. Production ceased early in 1941.

Surviving machines served in glider squadrons as towing machines for the DFS 230 and GO 240; others found employment in action against partisans where speed limitations were less of a handicap. Standard German cameras, as installed in the Henschel, included both hand and automatic models; a Reihenbild (serial picture) 50×30 apparatus being accommodated in the fuselage behind the observer, and a hand camera when not in use stowed beside the observer. Despite inter-war progress in wireless technology, early Henschels arrived in service without the all-important R/T speech facility (FuG VII) of later models. Nevertheless, by 1939 most of the thirty-eight 'H' squadrons – mustering 342 reconnaissance types – were flying the VII radio-improved Hs 126B. Until the Owl arrived in service (summer of 1941) or improvised types like the Me 109E or Me 110G served reconnaissance needs during the Battle of Britain, the usual mix of aircraft in 'H' squadrons allotted to headquarters of army, corps and divisions was six or seven Hs 126s and two or three Storche. These aircraft would be further deployed, for example to the divisional artillery when required for battery ranging or target identification work.

In the campaign against Poland (map 2) twenty-two 'H' squadrons, almost all of which were equipped with the Hs 126, were committed to army corps and divisions, leaving no more than a handful of squadrons in the west where the slower He 45s and He 46s were less of a liability. In May 1940, when army/air forces were regrouped for Operation 'Yellow' (map 3), the number of close-reconnaissance squadrons in army service increased to 34; deployment by squadrons following the pattern established in Poland. Similarly in the Balkans (map 6), although in that offensive fewer than twelve 'H' squadrons participated in the action against Yugoslavia and Greece. These early campaigns were marked by few losses or surprises to disturb reconnaissance routines. Not in fact before the Battle of Britain was the Luftwaffe seriously challenged. In that conflict with the RAF, reconnaissance flying over the Channel and south-east England revealed the extreme vulnerability of the Hs 126 to fighter attack and in consequence the need for better aircraft equipment in 'H' squadrons. Unfortunately the planned replacement, the Fw 189A-1 (Owl), intended in 1938 as a dive-bomber, but when revealed as inadequate during trials, decided upon as a substitute for the ageing Hs 126, was still unavailable; the reconnaissance squadrons on the Channel coast receiving instead a handful of Me 109E fighters adapted for photographic service. This stop-gap measure in the face of RAF superiority was helpful in reviving effective reconnaissance, but prospects for the 'H' squadrons, condemned by procurement failures to flying inferior aircraft in 1940, were to prove no better at the work twelve months later in North Africa and Russia. In fact, by the end of 1941, only nineteen of the original 56 'H' air reconnaissance squadrons accompanying the army into Russia were still intact.

The consequent decline in the army's ability to acquire tactical and topographical Intelligence, more necessary than ever in Russia, was sorely felt – in particular the photographic resources of attached squadrons with facilities for map-making at scales of 1:20,000. Their contribution to official mapping by way of providing amendments to out-of-date Russian reprints was irreplaceable. In a slightly

Below: The Luftwaffe High Command, January 1943. From right to left: Reichsmarschall Hermann Göring, General Feldmarschall Erhard Milch, and Generaloberst Hans Jeschonnek. The occasion for this unflattering group portrait was a visit to the Eastern Front for the Reichsmarshall's 50th birthday.

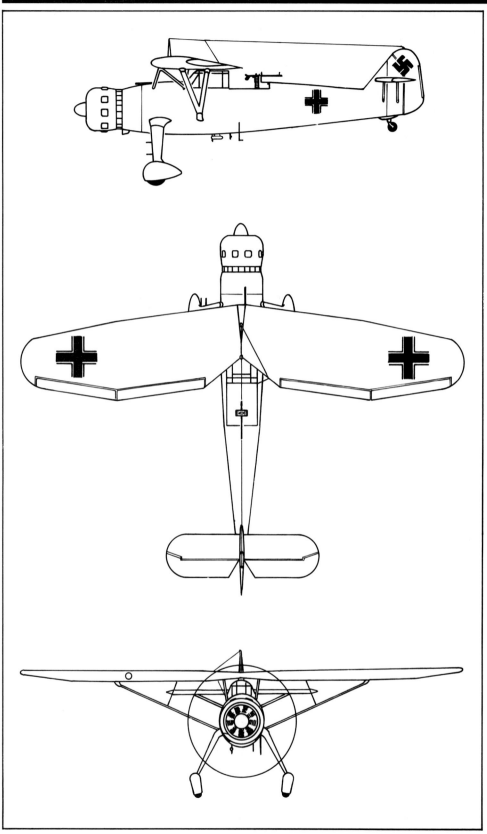

Left: When successfully undertaken, reconnaissance flights provided panzer commanders with details of enemy dispositions and movement. Their role was vital in terms of Intelligence. The Hs 126 (seen here in 3 view) was a two-seater observation and photograph machine which served close reconnaissance wings on all fronts until air superiority w lost to the opposition. After 1941 their role was ceded mainly to the Fw 189 Owl which had superior speed — 326mph compared to 221m

different category to the ubiquitous Hs 126 work-horse of the 'H' squadrons was the slow-flying Fiesler Fi 156 Storch introduced to army service in 1937. This diminutive cabin monoplane with folding wings and capable of a remarkably short take-off and landing run, earned a well-deserved reputation for outstanding design; much admired – prized even – by opponents. An ideal performer in many battlefield situations, the Storch was especially welcome in liaison and communications work – exploiting its characteristic ability to operate in all weathers from improvised airstrips adjacent to operational headquarters. And although it was never intended that the Storch should serve photographic recon-naissance, it did in fact share such missions especially in later years with the purpose-built Henschels and the Fw 189 (Owl). The Storch's most attractive feature appreciated by those working aloft – normally a crew of two and passenger – were the sweeping views afforded by wrap-around

plexiglass windows. In fact, so effective was the Fieseler Storch in surveillance roles, patrolling the battlefield or working forward with panzer reconnaissance detachments, that General Hasso von Manteuffel, later GOC, Fifth Panzer Army and one of Germany's leading panzer tacticians, expressed the view that the commander of a tank division should command in this way from the air.

Rommel in Africa was to spend much of his time aloft, assessing battle situations before arriving unexpectedly to liven up subordinates. Panzer headquarters to which a flight of one or two of the versatile Storche were allotted for command and staff use were generally encouraged to make full use of them. This they did, attending other headquarters and staff conferences or visiting forward positions, at times with disastrous results; the slow and easily recognizable Storch being frequently shot down. Generaloberst Model, GOC, Ninth Army, visiting Second Panzer Army in action at

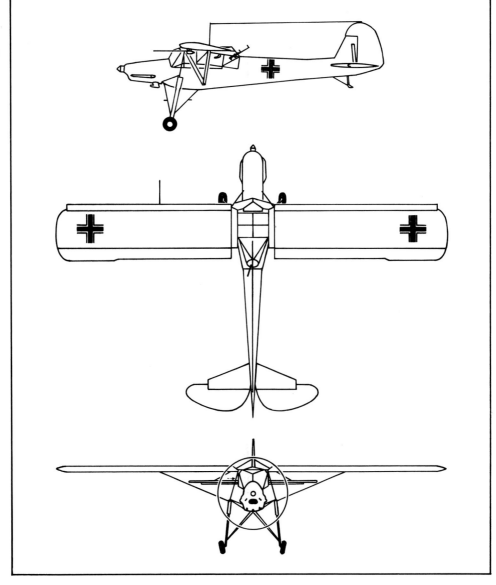

Right: Liaison flying enabled panzer commanders to maintain visual contact with forward troops, visit higher headquarters and personally reconnoitre the battlefield. The Fieseler Fi 156c Storch, seen here in 3-view, was ideal for such work with its low speed (32mph), short take-off run (213ft), its long range (600 miles) and its good all-round observation facilities.

Rshev opposite Moscow during May 1942, sustained leg injuries in this way. In a notorious incident a few weeks later, OKH plans for Operation 'Blue' were to fall like manna into the hands of Russian commanders when the Storch carrying Ia (Reichel) 23rd Panzer Division crashed in enemy territory when hit from the ground following a corps conference. In the western desert, too, accidents happened. In May 1942 General Crüwell was taken prisoner when his Storch was brought down by ground fire. Kesselring, von Richthofen and their senior army and air force colleagues all used Storches on liaison visits to outlying headquarters, and when the British Eighth Army commander, General Bernard Montgomery, was flown in a captured Storch he too admired the machine's versatile qualities. Storch production, including C1 and C2 variants produced for communications and reconnaissance work, reached a total of 2,549 peaking in 1943. Other roles for the Storch included that of medical transport courier, observation, and towing.

When the Fw189 (Owl), a twin-boom cabin monoplane with a built-in photographic facility, finally arrived in service during the late summer of 1941, the panzer force possessed a seemingly fast modern aircraft designed and produced especially for mobile operations. The Owl's camera position(s) were located in a fully enclosed and partially glazed cabin designed for a crew of three. Frontal areas were armour plated. Four machine-guns provided defence, but the extra weight told against performance and Soviet fighters would soon outclass the army's 'Flying Eye', the total production of which by 1945 reached fewer than 900 machines. Unlike the practice of British and American reconnaissance teams, committing Spitires (IV, X, XI) and Mustangs to high-speed and very often unarmed high-altitude reconnaissance work, the Luftwaffe's use of the fighter in a reconnaissance role was less than notable. The cumbersome Rb 50/30 camera at 160lb proving difficult to install in a narrow fighter fuselage. Fighter types were nevertheless employed increasingly on photographic work and the Messerschmit Me 190E introduced in 1940, followed by F and G variants into which small wing cameras were fitted, all flew Mediterranean or Eastern Front sorties in support of panzer armies; sluggish Henschels, easy prey for the RAF in North Africa, were instead redeployed to work with panzer formations in the east. But life for the Henschels

Top left: Flying in contact with ground reconnaissance units, the Storch extended a commander's ability to see and to plan ahead; two-way radio maintained a link between units while headquarters listened in.

Left: Many versions of the Storch were produced for specialized duties; here a medical Storch is evacuating casualties above a northern morass. The inhospitable terrain would have inhibited any other form of transport.

Above: Storchs frequently served on reconnaissance although this was not their intended role. A panzer detachment is pictured standing-by for information which it expects to be dropped in a metal tube if radio contact has not been established.

was to prove no more certain in the long term than their uneasy life left behind in Africa; newer types – Me 109Gs, Me 110Gs and 'Owls' – were consequently brought in during 1943 to replace them.

In the early campaigns, reconnaissance flights attached to panzer formations performed a variety of photographic, observation or communications duties, and to all intents and purposes were a formation's own. Following the invasion of Russia, however, the system of army/air co-operation was reviewed and instead of direct army control, reconnaissance flying was brought under Luftwaffe supervision. In place of Koluft staffs, air fleets appointed their own liaison officers and in the same shake-up air Intelligence personnel (Luftwaffe Ic) were posted to higher headquarters where their work entailed photo interpretation and air analysis. The Koluft system, supervised by General Paul Bogatsch since 1937, had removed reconnaissance flying from the framework of regular air fleet operations – necessitating the attachment of air force staff and signals personnel, to Army Group, Army and certain lower headquarters. Thereby Koluft could *order* photographic missions as and when required by the army commander to whom he was responsible. But such were the losses depleting 'H' squadrons in six months of operations in Russia that a policy review was inevitable and changes followed in March 1942. Koluft was consequently abolished and in a plan to rationalize army and air force reconnaissance all such activity was brought under control of General Günther Lohmann, nominated General of Reconnaissance Flying. Henceforth reconnaissance was to become a wholly Luftwaffe-controlled activity available to the army only *on request.*

In line with this development 'H' and 'F' squadrons were regrouped into Nahauflkärungsgruppen (NAG) for close-range and Fernaufklärungsgruppen (FAG) for long-range reconnaissance. In place of Koluft, Air Liaison Officers (Fliegerverbindungsoffiziere – Flivos) would forge new links between army and Luftwaffe, working in contact with locally deployed reconnaissance group commanders (Grufl). Under their new Chief of Reconnaissance Flying 'H' groups would continue tactical support for the army, making increasing use of fighters, while the long-distance groups, whose performance is reviewed in a concluding paragraph, served both army and Luftwaffe strategic requirements – flying improved Ju 88s. Despite a modest improvement in aircraft strength in time for Operation 'Blue' (map 10), reconnaissance numbers continued to dwindle at an alarming rate. During the Battle of Stalingrad alone, fourteen squadrons were destroyed or reduced to a nucleus; 150 aircraft being totally written-off together with 400 aircrew and ground staff. Despite General Lohmann's preference for the new, fast fighter types, Me 109G-8s, Me 110Gs and 'Owls', as replacements for the Hs 126, the situation was never to improve to the extent of matching the Luftwaffe's deployment for 'Barbarossa' in 1941. With operations expanding into the farthest corners of Europe, new tasks came the way of reconnaissance units; traffic observation control and searching for evidence of partisans in particular.

On the central front especially, forest belts provided much needed sanctuary for guerrilla bands. Their tell-tale tracks, carelessly felled trees, removed to widen a field of fire, or smoke escaping from carefully camouflaged bunkers, revealing their clandestine presence. Fieselers or Henschels patrolling at low speeds were particularly suitable for this kind of observation work. In the forest regions around Minsk, bypassed in the drive to the east in 1941, partisans were especially active; their presence in large numbers requiring joint panzer army action to reduce or eliminate the threat to supplies and communications (see Second Panzer Army, March 1942 and Third Panzer Army, spring of 1943). Elsewhere in western Europe, in the Balkans, Italy and France, panzer detachments suffered damaging attacks aimed at carelessly guarded headquarters or beleaguered units, despite motor-cycle patrols designed to guard against such eventualities.

Most frequent were attacks by guerrilla bands, some armed with heavy weapons, seeking by day and night to disrupt supply traffic and requiring air surveillance patrols to warn of their presence.

The performance of the long-range reconnaissance groups (Fernaufklärungsgruppen) whose work at the centre of Luftwaffe Intelligence was initiated by Rowehl in the early thirties (see page 115) is an appropriate note on which to conclude this section. The 1939 establishment of a long-range reconnaissance group consisted basically of three squadrons of twelve aircraft in which the Do 17F and Ju 88D predominated. Converted from bombing to recon-naissance, the Dorniers and Junkers carried their heavy cameras installed for vertical photography in empty bomb-bays. Most operated close to their service ceiling, which in the case of the Do 17 approached 20,000 feet, and that of the Ju 88, 27,000 feet. German cameras although technically sound and easy to operate were mostly cumbersome and difficult to manipulate – the standard Rb 50/30 producing a 12in×12in negative weighing 160lb – and although not impossible to install in high-flying fighters, created a significant drag on performance. Camera develop-ment too, failed to match the technology evident in the best Allied equipment, particularly for high-altitude work; little or no use being made of colour or infra-red film. The Do 17 introduced into squadron service in 1937 performed well enough in Poland and France, but in reconnaissance over Britain in 1940 performance defects signalled an early end to an unremarkable career. Typical Do 17 activity at this time included port watching and the monitoring of shipping lane movement, also high-level surveillance of RAF installations to obtain evidence of target destruction by Kampfgruppen. But in carrying out these tasks the 'Flying Pencil' fell easy prey to Dowding's Fighter Command.

Despite improvements in Dornier Z and 215 variants taking the 'Flying Pencil' higher and faster than hitherto, none was to prove effective at avoiding interception. Neither was a follow-on type, the Do 217E, introduced in 1941 and capable of flying fast or high enough to escape the RAF's radar-directed fighters. More successful at avoiding inter-ception on battle fronts east and west, was the versatile Ju 88. Pressed into Luftwaffe service in a variety of fighter, bomber and reconnaissance roles, production of variants for the latter purpose during the war reached 1,915 or 24 per cent of all Ju 88 production, totalling 8,000 machines. A better aircraft, designed for high-altitude Intelligence-gathering, was the Ju 86 (P and R series) developed from a pre-war civil prototype. Capable of carrying three cameras without difficulty and constructed around a pressurized cabin, facilitating operations up to 40,000 feet, the Ju 86

was introduced over Britain in 1940, frustrating RAF interception until August 1942 when it was countered by the high-flying Spitfire. In consequence of this development constraining Ju 86 P and R variants, operations in the Mediterranean and thereafter in the west, Luftwaffe intelligence was to fail in penetrating 'Overlord' security – arguably the gravest of all German Intelligence defeats during the Second World War.

This is not to say that the Luftwaffe was the sole cause of German failure to wake up to 'Overlord' in June 1944. Their inability to provide the High Command with positive evidence of 'Overlord' intentions and timing – the raw material of OKW defence planning – was matched by the equally unproductive efforts of every other German Intelli-gence agency. Nevertheless, in one vital area of its operations, namely signals security, the Luftwaffe was to make a notable contribution to its own defeat in battles for control of air space over Normandy, a defeat that – as Field Marshal Model was later to complain – robbed the land forces and Luftwaffe alike of a crucial element of power (however unwittingly effected); all at root cause down to 'Ultra'. When the code-breakers at Bletchley Park broke into Flivo cipher communications throughout the battle in Normandy – one of fifteen Luftwaffe 'keys' to succumb to

Below: The Fw 189 Owl was robust, three-seat twin-engined, twin-tail aircraft. Intended as a dive-bomber, the Owl instead entered service with close reconnaissance 'H' squadrons in the summer of 1941. It remained in service until 1945, but reconnaissance had by then degenerated into fiasco, leaving panzer commanders without 'eyes'.

Bletchley expertise – and continued to do so throughout the battle, the result was a devastating volume of highly rewarding Intelligence delivered, often currently, into the hands of Allied commanders. By decrypting Flivo transmissions, British Intelligence garnered every worthwhile detail of Luftwaffe deployment in Normandy, its order of battle, strength and intentions, particularly in respect of panzer operations. This vital data was most often obtained from Flivo traffic requesting reconnaissance coverage at critical stages in the battle. The consequence of security lapses such as these were without precedent (see Fifth Panzer Army Europe [D+62], 7 August 1944).

As German war performance degenerated in ever more disconcerting phases, leadership changes in directorates responsible for Luftwaffe reconnaissance and Intelligence became inevitable. After only nine months' service, Günther Lohmann, General of Reconnaissance Flying, appointed March 1942, was replaced by General Karl-Henning von Barsewisch, left to continue in office until the end of the

war. By December 1943 Rowehl had retired from active service; his Aufklärungsgruppe ObdL having lost its identity in KG200 deployed on covert missions as well as pure reconnaissance. At 5th Branch, where Schmid had supervised air Intelligence operations since 1939, Oberst Josef Kögl, Schmid's successor for a year, was eventually followed by Oberst Walter Kienitz. Kienitz was succeeded as head of Foreign Air Forces, West by Major Hubert Owe, promoted from a sub-section; control of that section falling to Hauptmann Zetzschka who was to observe candidly, 'The German Ic service has in fact failed from 1939 to the end of the war.' Allied air forces proceeded to wreck the power of the Wehrmacht in Normandy, ending German domination of France and precipitating the retreat of burned-out and harassed divisions to the Rhine. Battles for the Reich itself were soon to begin, but with defeat of the Luftwaffe east and west, spelling an end to all but the most slender chances of a Wehrmacht revival, air reconnaissance missions sank to meaningless proportions.

4. New horizons in transport

By the spring of 1944, when 300,000 men of First Panzer Army (Hube) were trapped in the Ukraine (map 15), threatened with annihilation by Ukrainian Fronts, the years of aggressive panzer force action were clearly at an end. The armies that had once advanced powerfully as far as the Caucasus had been checked and forced into headlong retreat. In Hube's case, First Panzer Army was totally isolated and bereft of all landward means of resupply. In such catastrophic circumstances air transports alone could provide a life-line to keep supplies flowing; Hube's panzer divisions, if they were to survive, could rely only upon the efforts of the Luftwaffe to provision them. The process had been introduced into panzer operations on a very small scale as early as 1939 in Poland (map 2), when armoured troops of von Kleist Corps, outrunning supplies, were provisioned by Ju 52s landing with ammunition and fuel at forward airfields. By April 1940 the movement of supplies by air was recognized in panzer divisional orders. For instance, 10th Panzer Division making ready for the Battle of France: 'Aircraft can, to a certain degree, assure the transmission of supplies in small quantities partially by parachute, partially by landing. This method of supply must only be used in cases of emergency. Application must be made to division either by telephone or wireless. In the case of supplying by parachute, a Ju 52 can carry, in addition to 1,500kg of supplies, four containers to drop. The contents of a container can consist of fuel or ammunition to the following scale: 100 litres of fuel or 250kg of ammunition. Example – 6,000 rounds of SAA or 500 rounds for the 2cm tank gun or 150 rounds for the 3.7cm anti-tank gun, 20 rounds for the 7.5cm tank gun, 55 rounds for the 8cm mortar.' Divisional orders continued with instructions to save both parachutes and containers for return to army ordnance depots. During the campaign in France which followed, Panzertruppen made no exceptional demands for this facility.

Not, in fact, until much later did air transport operations expand to the point of provisioning encircled troops. Starting in mid-winter 1941 with the German Army at the end of its first eastern offensive and struggling to retain 'hedgehog'

positions at Demjansk and elsewhere in the north, the Russian 1941 counter-offensive surrounded many infantry and ancillary units. Air supplies landed in the Demjansk pocket kept the force of 90,000 men intact, but the loss of more than 250 transports here and elsewhere on the front, so soon after sustaining equally high losses in Holland and Crete, was a blow from which the air transport groups would never recover. These operations also established a precedent that the Luftwaffe, when called upon to repeat it was soon to regret. Within the year, Sixth Army (Paulus), encircled at Stalingrad in December 1942, was for a time maintained and kept partly mobile by air transports. But the tonnage delivered proved much less than promised, failing utterly to sustain the needs of 250,000 men – a force of 22 divisions including three panzer and three motorized divisions (map 12). When dispatching airfields, notably 'Moro' (sovskaya) and 'Tazi' (nskaya), feeding supplies into Gumrak and Pitomnik under the supervision of VIII Air Corps, were finally overrun, Sixth Army surrendered unconditionally. Epidemics and intense winter conditions compounded the German problem. The panzer and motorized divisions were lost.

Similarly in the Mediterranean (map 5), so great was the loss of supply tonnage in sea transports attempting the crossing to Africa, that air transports were increasingly committed to the maintenance of DAK and Panzerarmee Afrika. When the battle moved into Tunisia the desert panzer divisions – 10th, 15th, 21st and 90th Light – if they were to retain even partial mobility, needed even more transport groups as a substitute for freighters and tankers that mostly went to the bottom, their fuel and ammunition lost to both air and ground operations in North Africa. At the root of Axis Mediterranean difficulties, compounded by 'Ultra' revelations to British intelligence of cargo manifests and timings, were British naval and air forces operating mostly from Malta in defiance of 2nd Air Fleet (Kesselring). Redeployed with II Air Corps from the Moscow Front to Sicily in December 1941 (twelve months after the arrival of X Air Corps), Kesselring was expected to eliminate all island-based opposition. Responsibility for subsequent air-bridge

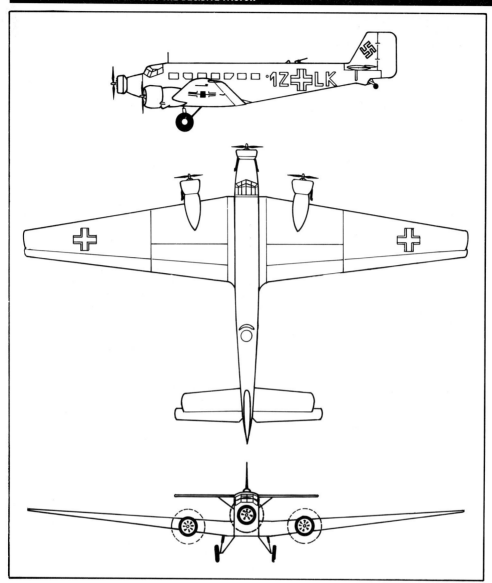

Left: This 3-view shows th Ju 52 three-engined transp (and temporary bomber if required) aircraft. It had a speed of 190mph, a range 800 miles and a useful car capacity. It could carry seventeen fully armed men addition to a crew of three a maximum bomb load of 3,300lb (1,500kg).

Right: The Luftwaffe under air transport operations in support of the army throug the war, although after 19 they still relied upon vetera aircraft of the pre-war era. Ju 52 and Heinkel III were initially deployed in Kampfgeschwader zbv; the Ju 52, apart from its use as assault transport in attacks Norway, Holland and Crete, served ground troops in a variety of roles: transportir fuel, munitions and weapor beleaguered garrisons such Cholm, Demjansk and Stali grad; evacuating casualties all theatres; and maintainin the mobility of encircled panzertruppen (*see* maps 1 and 18).

operations linking North Africa and Europe (Catania-Tripoli) lay initially with III/KGzbvl whose commander, Oberst Starke, under X Air Corps, served also as Transport Commander, Mediterranean. Starke's Wing had been operating in the Mediterranean since December 1940 when Hitler answered an Italian request for air transport assistance; III/KGzbvl operating transport missions from Foggia to Albania.

As the Mediterranean war intensified and sea transport services for Rommel between Naples and Tripoli suffered mounting disruption by the Royal Navy and Air Force, more transport units were brought in from training schools in Germany and the Eastern Front. By the end of July 1942, following Rommel's success in capturing Tobruk, six transport Wings centred on Brindisi, Calabria or Heraklion (Crete) were ferrying supplies and reinforcements to Panzerarmee Afrika via Benghazi, Derna and Tobruk (HQ III/KGzbvl). The air-lift supplemented sea transports docking

at Tripoli and Benghazi. But however valuable these contributions to panzer army strength and mobility were, so precarious was Rommel's supply situation, manifest in chronic fuel and food shortages, that all his attempts to outmanoeuvre and defeat British Eighth Army were gravely compromised, despite help from an unlikely source. In the summer of 1942 Panzerarmee Afrika, advancing from Gazala to Alamein, was refuelled by immense British stocks captured in the neighbourhood of Tobruk (map 9). British vehicles were also pressed into service, some with fighting units others in panzer supply columns; Rommel's transport strength then being 85 per cent British in origin. Largely on account of this windfall, a Luftwaffe plan ('Hercules') to invade Malta and eliminate the threat posed by the island to Mediterranean supply routes was cancelled.

But Rommel's advantage in captured petrol and transport was to prove short-lived with formations outrunning supplies as the advance continued to Mersa Matruh and beyond to Alamein. Tanks and transports with empty tanks were forced to a standstill. Panzer engagements were curtailed and battle refused or broken off. Rommel's diary records the panzer army's plight before and after the battle in October 1942 (map 9): 'The supply situation remained as wretched as ever, although petrol showed a slight improvement as a result of increased supplies brought across by air to Tobruk. The ammunition situation was as bad as it could be. Only 40 tons has reached Africa since the launching of the British offensive and we were being forced to the strictest economy.' On 15 November (three weeks after Alamein) the petrol crisis took an even more acute turn when several ships on their way to Benghazi were turned back. Added to this the Luftwaffe was still getting only very small quantities across. Rommel continues: 'Lack of petrol prevented the Afrika Korps from getting under way until midday and by evening it was halted again without a drop in its tanks. In motorized forces we were hopelessly inferior . . . quite apart from the fact that our petrol would not possibly run to a mobile battle.' Coinciding with Rommel's problems in the aftermath of the Battle of El Alamein, a new German build-up to counter Anglo-US landings in Algeria and Morocco in November 1942 were succeeding 1500 miles to the west in the neighbourhood of Tunis – thanks to rigorous efforts by air transport groups deployed in a new air-bridge operation.

The very fact that this could, or even should, be done was of immense concern to Rommel whose depleted panzer divisions withdrawing from Libya were in urgent need of assistance. After Alamein the Panzer Army possessed fewer than twenty tanks and was appealing for help, even to Hitler. Instead reinforcement ten times that number would soon be *en route* for Tunisia – the kernel of a new (Fifth)

Panzer Army under command of General von Arnim. From the outset, the new air-bridge was gravely compromised by Luftwaffe inferiority in numbers. Organized by a new Transport Commander, Mediterranean, Generalmajor Bucholz, the hazardous work of moving men and materials from Europe to Africa was divided between transport groups based in Sicily and Naples. But the 200 or so Ju 52s and other types remaining in action (after withdrawals were taken to fly supplies into Stalingrad) suffered grievously working between Trapani in south-west Sicily and Tunis (or Bizerta) on the African coast – a much shorter distance than hitherto flown across the Mediterranean in support of DAK. The desperate shortage of Ju 52 transports in the Mediterranean theatre could only be made good as on other fronts by Heinkel He 111s and freight gliders. Those deployed for the operation included a new tail-loading Go 240 and the Me 323. A cavernous, 6-engined transport, developed from the glider of the same name, the Me 323 'Gigant' joined the transport force for the first time, to ferry weapons, equipment, troops and vehicles to the African battle zone. Twelve-ton towing machines and 8.8cm Flak were not unusual in Me 323 loads. Casualties, up to 130 at a time, were evacuated on return flights.

Defying exceptionally strong opposition put up by US and British fighters, the Luftwaffe pursued its Mediterranean transport operations with horrendous losses; transports flying with little if any fighter cover were written off in dozens. On 5 April 1943 no fewer than fourteen Me 323s were lost on a single supply sortie. Despite the sacrifice of so many transport and crews, a German collapse in Africa was inevitable and in May 1943 Army Group Tunis (von Arnim) capitulated to the Allies. Field Marshal Alexander's 'bag' included 230,000 German and Italian troops, three

Left and right: Resupply by parachute container was one means of delivering basic needs to encircled troops. A container would consist of three or four fitted compartments; each filled according to requirements. Alternatively, supplies were released from transports in drums and bundles.

Left: Freight gliders were introduced into Luftwaffe service in 1942 to supplement the resources of transport wings. A Go 242 tail-loader would lift 23 fully armed men or their equivalent; the Ju 52s were used as tugs.

panzer and four motorized divisions. Some panzer personnel were saved by sea and air for new assignments in Europe, and certain formations, notably Hermann Goering and 15th Panzer Division (reformed as a panzer grenadier division) redeployed in Sicily. For the transport groups fortunate enough to survive the rigours of Mediterranean action or at Stalingrad where some 500 transports of all types (266 Ju 52s) were sacrificed in a vain attempt to save Sixth Army (Paulus) there followed a period of rationalization under XIV Air Corps (Coeler). Coeler's headquarters at Tutow – until air raids forced it out to Rügen on the Baltic north of Berlin – enjoyed the status of a 'Transport Command' promoting air transport interests and guiding development in this specialized area of army-support flying. Under the new transport chief Coeler, simultaneously appointed Waffen-general Transportflieger in October 1943, stood two air transport commanders: (1) Mediterranean, Bucholz and (2) East, Morzik. Theirs was the responsibility for conducting large-scale operations of the kind required in building the Tunisian bridgehead and maintaining Sixth Army at Stalingrad.

Henceforth, the Kampfgruppen zbV at the heart of Luftwaffe air transport operations would be referred to as Transportgruppen and incorporated into Transport Geschwader (Groups) 1 to 4, each of three Ju 52 wings and TG5 comprising two Me 323 or mixed units. In the spring of 1944, when heavy demands were being made on transport units – evacuating the Crimea and maintaining encircled divisions at Cherkassy and Kaments-Podolsk (map 15), the Luftwaffe's air transport strength comprised the same two transport commanders, six transport groups, 24 transport

Wings (each with fourteen Ju 52s) and a number of independent squadrons flying the He 111, Me 323 or the Italian SM 81 and SM 82. The catastrophes during the winter of 1942–3 in Africa and Europe, had cast warning shadows over the campaign in South Russia where, in a third winter campaign, in January 1944, 5th SS Panzer Division Wiking, cut off from Eighth Army and trapped with other divisions on the Dnieper at Cherkassy–Korsun, was defying all Russian attempts to annihilate them (map 15). Starting on 31 January 1944 and continuing for twenty days, transport groups would brave appalling weather in search of improvised landing strips necessary for provisioning the Cherkassy–Korsun garrison of 54,000 men and a relief column driving towards them under III Panzer Corps (Breith). In this timely operation, air transport groups risked exceptionally precarious operations using frost-hardened landing strips prepared inside the pocket or adjoining the relief column's snowbound approach route. Notwithstanding the flying difficulties involved, the garrison's crucial supplies – originally consigned to the relief column in wheeled vehicles but failing to arrive – were successfully brought in by air. Whereas only the weather could hamper transports flying out of Uman, land transport floundering in thick snow or locked axle deep in morasses of mud and sleet failed totally. Three transport Wings, II, III/TG3 and I/TG1 – each 30 to 40 strong in Ju 52s – served VIII Air Corps (Seidemann) in the Cherkassy–Korsun action, flying an average outward distance of 75 miles. Their resolute flying was rewarded on 17 February when 30,000 of the troops besieged in Cherkassy–Korsun and lead by SS Wiking escaped the encircling Russians to join with III Panzer Corps at Lissjanka; none would have survived without air transports to provision them.

But German air transport problems in South Russia were by no means at an end. Within six weeks of Wiking's narrow escape, First Panzer Army withdrawing west was itself overtaken by the Russian 1944 spring offensive and trapped against the River Dniester at Kaments-Podolsk. Lead by Air Transport Commander, East (Morzik), organizer of the Demjansk and Stalingrad air lifts, transport units redeployed with him from the Crimea came to the rescue, preserving the strength and mobility of 300,000 men and saving them from extinction (map 15). Separated on 24 March 1944 by a distance of 180 miles from the main body of Army Group South/North Ukraine withdrawing into eastern Galicia, First Panzer Army would eventually fight its way into contact with II SS Panzer Corps thrusting from Lodz. Until that time, fourteen days after the panzer army's breakdown in supplies, a mixed force of transports and gliders (before the latter were diverted to relief work of greater urgency at Tarnopol) ferried ammunition, fuel, spares, weapons and medical equipment daily to the beleaguered army. Responsibility for provisioning the panzer army's 19 (nine panzer) divisions' 300,000 men – an exceptional problem by any reckoning – lay with Generalmajor Fritz Morzik, Transport Fliegerführer 2. When the call for air transports went out from GOC, 4th Air Fleet (Desloch), Morzik was in Odessa directing another air transport operation relieving the supply problems of Seventeenth Army (Jaenecke) cut off in the Crimea. Acting promptly on orders received on 25 March, Morzik moved headquarters to Krosno and established the signals and

ground-support facilities required for handling the new situation.

For this unprecedented task he was allotted four Ju 52 Wings: a He 111 Wing, a Wing of towed gliders (Schleppengruppe) (He 111s and DFS 230 gliders) and additional He 111 capacity; total 150 Ju 52s and 100 He 111s.

Despite wintery conditions inhibiting operations on the Eastern Front at the time, Ju 52s, mostly from Lemberg, transported more than 2,000 tonnes of supplies into the moving panzer army pocket. On return flights they evacuated 2,500 sick and wounded; seven hundred severe cases. Thirty-two Ju 52s were lost in the action, some defying a three-day blizzard, others attempting to evade interception. A small proportion of the losses fell to anti-aircraft fire; 113 more were withdrawn for extensive repair. In good conditions the air transports flew direct to serviceable airfields or improvised landing strips inside the pocket. Aircraft loads were picked up and distributed internally by unit transport. But when conditions deteriorated, making landing impossible, loads were parachuted in by container or dropped in free-fall from low altitudes; the cushioning effect of mud or deep snow being relied upon to absorb ground shock to cases, bundles and even 200-litre drums of fuel released a few feet above ground.

Morzik's air-bridge operation had started on 26 March, with He 111s from Krosno dropping container supplies to the panzer army while Ju 52s from Lemberg were landing at Proskurov – the only serviceable airfield remaining to the troops in the pocket. The operation continued until 10 April, two days after the army reached Buczac. At dispatching airfields around Lemberg the weather was often greatly different from that prevailing at bridgeheads in the pocket 180 miles away, so that even experienced flyers found difficulty in locating dropping zones. They frequently overshot and watched containers fall into Russian hands. When prevailing conditions over the pocket were at their best, anti-aircraft fire became intense and Russian fighters were drawn into the conflict. Morzik then resorted to night operations, with aircraft departing at 50-minute intervals on and after 28 March. Weather permitting, three or four flights were made in a single night. Despite the fixing of flight paths with radio beacons set up by 4-man teams sent in by the Fliegerführer, aircrews had great difficulty in locating the constantly moving pocket. Ground troops also joined in the reception activity, firing signal lights and arranging fires in agreed patterns of circles and crosses. Landing zones, indicated to incoming flights by radio at the last minute, were also helpful in guiding the transports in. But such tactics were soon detected by the Russians and, with their own fires and signals, they quickly replicated German communications to confuse the approaching transports.

By 2 April 1944 Proskurov airfield was lost, and supply containers, 11,000 in total – however uncertain their delivery by parachute – became the principal means of resupply. Night landings on strips less than 400 × 30 metres, laid out in the snow and illuminated by headlights, were attempted but soon abandoned. Only to the west of Kaments-Podolsk, were landing conditions marginally suitable for experienced pilots actually to set down their loads at a make-shift strip. The operation was concluded on 8 April 1944 by which time the panzer army was safe. Caught up in a deteriorating military situation, panzer formations east and west came to depend increasingly for survival upon the rapidly shrinking numbers of air transport Wings which by January 1945 totalled fewer than ten, of which only seven still possessed Ju 52s. On the Vistula (Weichsel) south of Warsaw during January 1945, when the Red Army aiming for Berlin broke out of its Baranov bridgehead, XXIV Panzer Corps (Nehring) deployed west of the river as a mobile reserve and threatened with annihilation, fought desperately to stave off disaster. Opposed on all sides by Russian armour, Nehring's weak 17th and 18th Panzer Divisions narrowly escaped the tightening ring (map 18). Isolated from connection with Fourth Panzer Army (the Corps's parent formation), the harassed divisions, hardly stronger than regimental battle groups, started a fighting withdrawal via Petrikau to the main battle line fast receding in the direction of the Oder.

Air transport groups, already facing an exhausting future conforming to Hitler's insistence on rigid defence and thereby obliged to contend with the resupply problems of beleaguered 'fortress' cities – Breslau, Posen and Schneidermühl, later Arnswalde, Glogau and Berlin itself, rose unstintingly to the occasion. Containers of petrol and ammunition were parachuted to the corps on the night of 21 January; eighty-two desperately needed canisters being dropped by eleven He 111s at Petrikau; the panzer divisions narrowly remained mobile. On 31 January, after nineteen days of bruising battle with 1st Ukrainian Front, Nehring brought his decimated divisions – swelled by units collected *en route* – into contact with Gross Deutschland Panzer Corps (von Saucken), a relief force first railed from East Prussia to Lodz and then pushed forward to find Nehring, despite Guderian's protests (as Chief-of-Staff) over the dire consequences of weakening Army Group Centre. Driving south-east from war-torn Lodz, von Saucken too received air transport assistance.

Two squadrons of He 111s were initially deployed on Gross Deutschland resupplying missions, 163 containers of ammunition being dropped to the Corps on 25 January; 91 containers of fuel and 25 containers of ammunition on the 26th. A day later fourteen Ju 52s supplied fuel and diesel oil in a direct landing operation; 114 wounded were flown out on the return flight. With the further help of a mixed fleet of 27 Ju 52s and 40 He 111s, Nehring and von Saucken regained the main battle line at Glogau, but with little power remaining for further action. In later weeks pursuing panzer operations in Silesia, Panzer Group Nehring (Fourth Panzer Army), like those of other war-weary panzer corps fighting in Pomerania, Courland and East Prussia, owed something of their mobility and battle-fitness to fuel and munitions flown to them by the few remaining air transports. In the east at the conclusion of hostilities these machines were for the most part concentrated under VIII Air Corps (HQ Prague). In the west, transport wings reduced to squadron strengths flew no less demanding missions provisioning Hitler's Atlantic coast 'fortresses'. Consequently few Ju 52s were left for the relief of Army Group 'B' encircled in the Ruhr. Supplies were nevertheless flown into the pocket by a Ju 52 squadron until 18 April when Model's capitulation ended all further need for air transport to provision them.

Left and right: The Me 232 'Gigant' originated in 1942 out of the freight glider of the same name. A six-engined transport of surprising capacity, the Gigant was nevertheless slow and vulnerable. The ponderous five-man machines flew transport missions on main fronts, most notably in support of the panzer armies in north Africa where, in action between Sicily and Tunisia, Gigant squadrons suffered grievous casualties carrying 130 fully armed men, or complete with towing-machines or munitions to von Arnim.

Part 5. Panzer action in maps

Explanatory note.

Maps 1–20 with their supporting text and data concerning panzer order of battle and comparative military strengths, require little further elucidation except to note that taken as a whole they illustrate not only the operative involvement of panzer divisions at crucial stages in the great campaigns and battles of the Second World War, but they also serve as a visual index of the ensuing panzer army histories (Part 6). And although not every action in which panzer divisions

participated is mapped and tabulated in this way, most are included in Part 6 where the Chronology includes tank battles by armies on adjoining fronts, e.g., Pz-AOK4, 2 August 1944 *[Ninth Army defending Warsaw]* or Pz-AOK5 (Europe), 25 July 1944 *[Seventh Army shattered by 'Cobra']*. When a panzer army included in the map text is named in brackets and followed by a date, e.g., map 3: Hoth (Third Panzer Army), 13 May 1940, it is to the history of that panzer army at that date in Part 6 that the reader

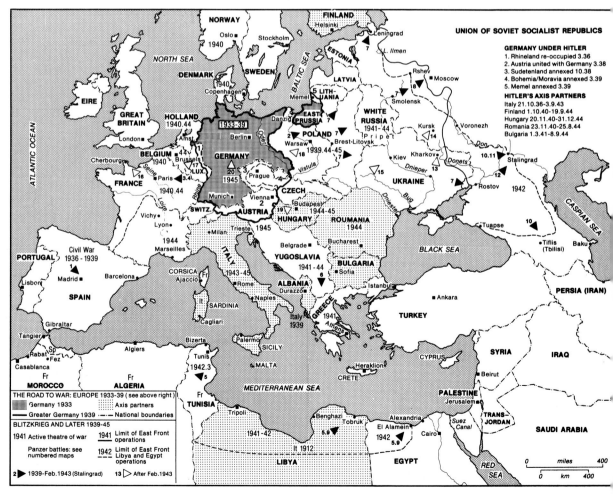

should turn for elaboration; the panzer corps or panzer group serving the commander (Hoth) at the time having been upgraded at a later date. Transliteration of map place names conforms, in general, with English practice. Minor place names, e.g., Narwa, reflect German map traditions and, like the symbols used for army corps, army and group, are consistent with the official Wehrmacht usage.

1. Testing Time in Spain, 1936–9

The Spanish Civil War is seen by certain foreign governments as a unique opportunity to test and develop new military equipment under active service conditions: Germany and Italy support General Franco's Nationalists, Soviet Russia the Republicans; motorized forces and tanks are committed in small numbers on both sides.

A German armoured contingent – Panzer Bn 88 (Colonel von Thoma) – is deployed in conjunction with a Luftwaffe expeditionary force – the Condor Legion. Consisting of three light mainly Pz Kpfw I companies, transport, anti-tank (3.7cm) and signal units, the battalion serves basically as a Nationalist training cadre.

Italian involvement in the civil war north-east of Madrid is headed by 'Littorio' a motorized division serving General Gervasio Bitossi. The division is accompanied by 60 light tanks (see Part 2, Satellite contributions for the panzer force).

A lightly equipped Russian contingent fighting on the Republican side is equipped with 500–600 BT and T26 type tanks led by General Dimitri Pavlov. Italian and Russian national contingents are both accompanied by air force detachments. Action is generally limited to company schemes planned in conjunction with infantry attacks.

Hitler 1 July 1936, approves the use of Ju 52 transports to move 13,000 Franco troops from Tetuan to Seville. Four months later the Condor Legion (Major-General Hugo Sperrle) arrives from Germany. Chief of Staff and eventually Sperrle's successor (29 November 1938) is Colonel Wolfram Freiherr von Richthofen. Initially 4,500 strong, the Legion remains on active service for three years. By rotation of personnel 18,000 officers and men gain war experience in Spain.

Sperrle, Richthofen ❶ After capturing Bilbao and Malaga with Legion support, Nationalist armies link up north and south. *See* Guernica 26 April 1937 page 000. In April 1937 Madrid is partially invested but 'Littorio', assisting a Nationalist attack from the north-east, is repulsed at Guadalajara.

Volkmann, von Richthofen ❷ Action towards Valencia east of Teruel and along the Ebro east of Belchite is marked by an increase in dive-bombing and ground-attack missions flown here and elsewhere in the north-east by the Legion.

Von Richthofen ❸ The Nationalist offensive continues in the direction of Barcelona.

19 May 1939, the Condor Legion stages a victory parade through Madrid. The Condor Legion, constituted principally from Luftwaffe aircrews and ground staff, comprises three squadrons of Ju 52 transports, three of He 51 fighters, a dive-bombing (Hs 123), reconnaissance (He 45/70) and a bombing research (HE 111) squadron. The Legion is eventually re-equipped with improved aircraft types, notably the He 111, Ju 87 A (Stuka) and Me 109 fighter.

Three heavy and two light anti-aircraft batteries support the Legion with (towed) 8.8cm and 20mm flak. The guns engage both ground and air targets.

2. Panzer action in Poland, 1939

In Operation 'White', Hitler commits the German Army and Luftwaffe to the invasion of Poland. When two Army Groups, North and South, strike concentrically at a weak opponent – mostly infantry divisions deployed within fifty miles of the frontier, Polish forces are encircled and within seventeen days the campaign is virtually at an end. Warsaw, unsuited to armoured attack, continues to resist until 27 September. German double encirclement strategy and previous experience gained from Condor Legion operations in Spain prove decisive.

Hoth and Hoepner (Third and Fourth Panzer Armies) 1 September 1939. The main weight of Panzer assault lies

[Map]

0   miles   150

0   km   150

Lyon

FRANCE

Bordeaux

Gijón

Guernica

Bilbao

N A T I O N A L I S T ❷

❶

❸

Barcelona

Belchite

G

Teruel

MADRID

Toledo

Balearic Islands

Valencia

PORTUGAL

Lisbon

Alicante

Seville ❶

MEDITERRANEAN

Cadiz

Malaga

Tangier   Tetuan

July 1936 Airlift Franco Troops

NATIONALIST OCCUPIED AREAS

1936-37

1938

Condor

Guadalajara G   1939

Spanish Morocco

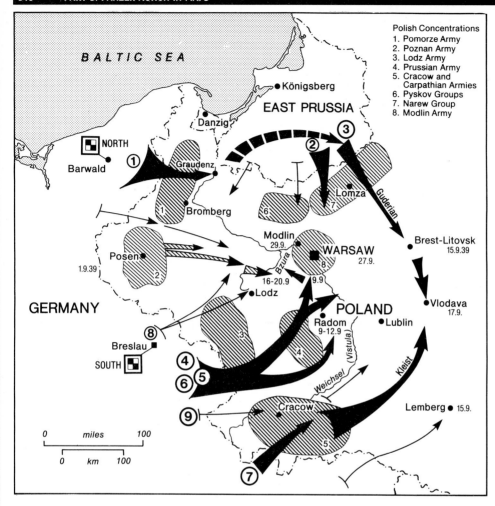

Polish Concentrations
1. Pomorze Army
2. Poznan Army
3. Lodz Army
4. Prussian Army
5. Cracow and
   Carpathian Armies
6. Pyskov Groups
7. Narew Group
8. Modlin Army

with the three motorized corps, XIV, XV and XVI, spear-heading German Tenth Army (von Reichenau).

Von Kleist and Guderian (First and Second Panzer Armies) 1 September 1939, also deployed in conjunction with infantry armies, operate on the wings of the offensive.

Operations are led by six panzer divisions, including a 'mixed' division (Kempf), four light divisions, and four motorized divisions. Included in the invasion force are SS Regiments: Adolf Hitler (SSLAH), Deutschland and Germania.

Guderian ❶ XIX MotK: 2nd, 20th MotDivs; 3rd PzDiv

Kempf ❷ PzDiv Kempf: 7th PzRegt, SS Regt Deutschland, etc.

Guderian ❸ Redeployed XIX MotK: After 7 September includes 10th PzDiv

Von Wietersheim ❹ XIV MotK: 1st LtDiv, 13th, 29th MotDivs; and later 5th Pz Div

Hoepner ❺ XVI MotK: 1st, 4th PzDivs; two InfDivs

Hoth ❻ XV MotK: 2nd, 3rd LtDivs; 25th PzRegt

Von Kleist ❼ XXII MotK: 2nd PzDiv; 4th LtDiv

❽ (Eighth Army) XIII AK includes SS Regt Leibstandarte Adolf Hitler before transfer to Tenth Army

❾ (Fourteenth Army) VIII AK includes SS Regt Germania

A Gr North/South von Bock/von Runstedt; 37 infantry, three mountain, fifteen mobile divs, 3,195 tanks

Polish Army 38 infantry divisions, eleven cavalry, two motorized brigades, 600–700 light tanks (500 battle-fit)

Luftwaffe Kesselring 1st Air Fleet-A Gr North; Löhr 4th Air Fleet-A Gr South, 1,550 aircraft

Polish Air Force 750 aircraft (500 battle-fit)

3. Victory in the West, 1940

In Operation 'Yellow', Army Groups 'A' and 'B' with Luftwaffe support, smash across the Meuse and in ten days outmanoeuvre the Western Allies whose armies, including a British Expeditionary Force of nine divisions, serve a French commander-in-chief – General Gamelin, replaced 19 May 1940 by General Weygand.

Schmidt and Hoepner (Fourth Panzer Army) 10 May with two panzer corps ❶ and ❷ allotted to Army Group 'B', lead a decoy offensive into Holland and Belgium where airborne operations under General Kurt Student aim to reduce key defences astride the Army Group axis of advance.

Von Kleist and subordinate Guderian (First and Second Panzer Armies) 13 May attack west across the Meuse at Sedan–Monthermé **4, 5, 6** initiating the main armoured movement of Operation 'Yellow' – a westward thrust by two panzer and one motorized infantry corps under Panzer Group von Kleist (K) – the vanguard of Army Group 'A'. See also Panzer break-through, France (map 4).

Von Kleist leads German Twelfth Army (List), but under pressure from superior headquarters, limits subordinates to a narrow range of action. Despite this, the panzer group pushes ahead until Hitler's nervousness at the danger to the resulting panzer 'corridor' and technical considerations finally halts the armour.

Hoth (Third Panzer Army) 13 May starting from a Meuse crossing at Dinant – **3** – also strikes west, reinforcing von Kleist.

A total of ten panzer divisions, six and two-thirds motorized infantry divisions support Army Groups 'A' and 'B'. The panzer force is swiftly regrouped for phase two of the battle – Operation 'Red'* commencing 5 June 1940.

Schmidt 1 XXXIX PzK: 9th PzDiv; SS Verfügungs Div; After 13 May LSSAH

Hoepner 2 XVI PzK: 3rd, 4th PzDivs; 20th InfDivMot; SS Totenkopf

Hoth 3 XV PzK: 5th PzDiv; 7th PzDiv

(K) Reinhardt 4 XXXXI PzK: 6th PzDiv; 8th PzDiv

(K) Guderian 5 XIX PzK: 1st PzDiv; 2nd PzDiv; 10th PzDiv; Inf Regt Mot-Gross Deutschland

(K) Von Wietersheim 6 XIV MotK: 2nd, 13th, 29th InfDivs Mot

*Hoth 7 XV PzK: 5th, 7th PzDivs; 2nd InfDiv Mot

*Von Kleist Gr 8 XIV PzK von Wietersheim: 9th, 10th PzDivs; 13th Inf Div Mot, SS Verfügungs Div, InfReg Mot-Gross Deutschland. After 12 June SS Totenkopf Div XVI PzK Hoepner: 3rd, 4th PzDivs; Reserve LSSAH

*Guderian Gr 9 XXXIX PzK Schmidt: 1st, 2nd PzDivs; 29th InfDiv Mot XXXXI PzK Reinhardt: 6th, 8th PzDivs; 20th InfDiv Mot

German Army Von Brauchitsch: 120 infantry divs, 16⅔ mobile divs, 2,574 tanks

A Grs 'A', 'B' Von Runstedt 45⅓ divisions; von Bock 29⅓ divisions

Luftwaffe Kesselring 2nd Air Fleet-A Gr 'B'; Sperrle 3rd Air Fleet-A Gr 'A': 2,750 aircraft

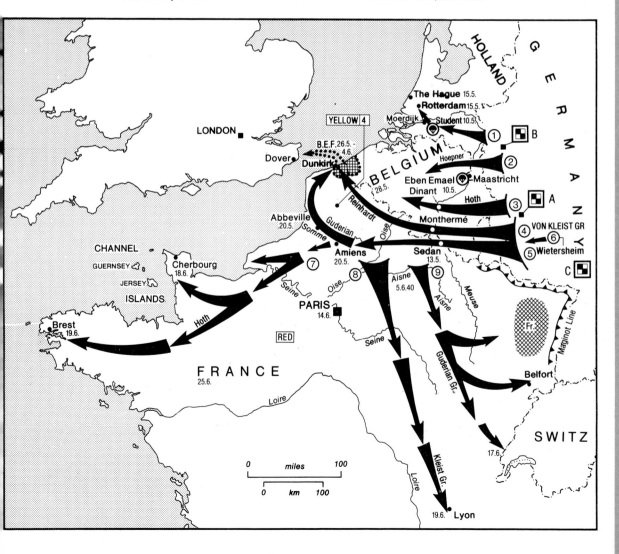

Western Allies Gamelin; 10 Dutch, 22 Belgian, 9 British (plus 1 Inf Tank Bde), 77 French infantry divs, 6 (Fr) mobile divs, 3,600 tanks
Allied Air Forces 2,372 aircraft incl 1,151 fighters.

4. Panzer break-through: France, 1940

Striking west across the Meuse at Sedan and Monthermé, Panzer Group von Kleist (K) – two panzer and a motorized corps – is responsible for the main armoured movement of Operation 'Yellow' (map 3). Weak opposition is concentrated in French Second and Ninth Armies deployed along the west bank of the river.

Orders issued to the leading divisions, especially 1st Panzer Division at Sedan, illustrate the high level of air support required to give effect to *Blitzkrieg; see* Part 4.

Panzer Group von Kleist (First Panzer Army) leads the offensive commencing 0530 hours 10 May 1940, when five panzer, three and a half motorized divisions strike through the Ardennes to the east bank of the Meuse, ready to smash all opposition and establish a west bank bridgehead.

Guderian (Second Panzer Army) 13 May 1940. Arriving at Sedan with *three panzer divisions* XIX Panzer Corps leads von Kleist across the Meuse in mid-afternoon; timed for 1600 hours, the assault is initiated by panzer grenadier/engineer battle groups of 1st Panzer Division. Simultaneously downstream at Monthermé, Reinhardt's XXXXI

Panzer Corps, attacking westwards with *two panzer divisions,* also secured a foothold on the west bank, while von Wietersheim's XIV Motorized Corps waits in reserve to follow through when called.

Hoth (Third Panzer Army) 13 May precedes the main effort by von Kleist at Sedan with XV Panzer Corps providing flank protection at Dinant. Hoth wins a Meuse crossing with *two panzer divisions* on the morning of the same day and prepares to drive west; Rommel (7th Panzer Division) in the lead.

Hoepner (Fourth Panzer Army) 19 May. XVI Panzer Corps redeployed from Army Group 'B' with *two panzer divisions* joins Hoth to form a Gruppe reinforcing the main armoured effort. N.B. On 24 May, *9th Panzer Division* joins Kleistgruppe from Rotterdam.

Allied counter-attacks – 17 May. A French armoured contingent under General de Gaulle pushes north-east from Laon. On the 21st, a scratch British armoured force led by General le Q. Martel strikes south around Arras. These attacks create concern in higher German headquarters, but

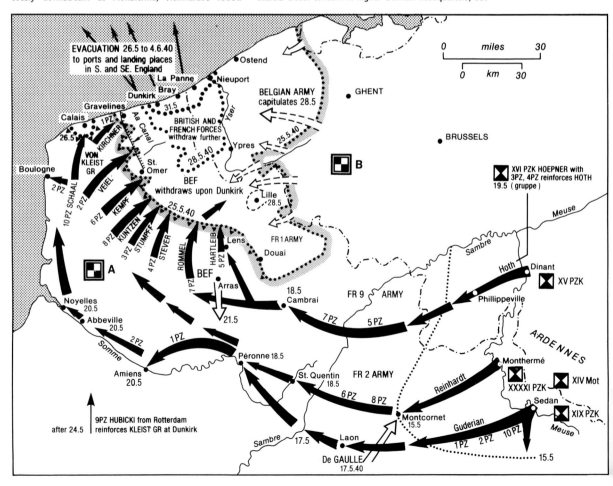

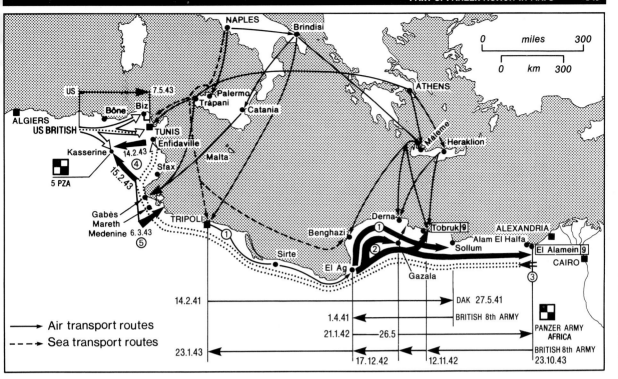

do little to stem the tide of armour which on reaching the coast at Abbeville 20 May, swings north-west and by the 24th, co-operating with Army Group 'B' closing on Ypres, is shepherding the BEF and other Allied troops into a coastal pocket around Dunkirk.

But Hitler's nervousness puts a brake on operations; the thought of danger to an over-extended panzer force operating in unsuitable terrain and the need to conserve armour for the next phase of the offensive – Operation 'Red' – is enough to halt armoured progress at the Aa canal. Slow-moving infantry catch up in forced marches while the Luftwaffe unsuccessfully attempts to finish off defenders besieged in Dunkirk. 330,000 British and French troops evacuated from Dunkirk port and beaches by an armada of small ships, escape to England in Operation 'Dynamo'.

5. Desert side-show: North Africa, 1941–3

Rommel (Panzer Army Africa) 14 February 1941 arrives in North Africa with Deutsches Afrika Korps, abbreviated DAK, to oppose a British desert force (later British Eighth Army) under Field Marshal Wavell threatening Tripoli. Military operations extending over two years involve DAK and Italian units in heavy fighting, developing into a confrontation between Army Groups; Afrika – First Italian Army (formerly Panzer Army Africa) plus Fifth Panzer Army versus British 18th Army Group – First and Eighth Armies plus US (II) and a French Corps.

Despite a nominal military balance, the key to successful panzer action lies in supply facilities, but German-Italian sea and air transports running a Mediterranean gauntlet, rarely escape the punishing attention of naval and air attacks mounted from Malta or Alexandria – notwithstanding the aggressive presence of German 2nd Air Fleet based in Sicily. Hitler's shortsightedness over reinforcements for Rommel, coinciding with an OKW view that the theatre is a side-show, invites disaster and his decision to cancel 'Hercules', a Luftwaffe plan for eliminating Malta by airborne invasion, will prove fatal.

Rommel ❶ (Panzer Army Africa) 31 March 1941. 'Sunflower' slowly increasing in power is Rommel's first offensive with DAK, but instead of 'blocking' Wavell, Rommel outmanoeuvres Eighth Army to reach Sollum on the Egyptian border but is thrown back to El Agheila.

DAK 5 Lt Div vanguard/Ariete, two It inf divs; by 20 November 1941 DAK = 21st, 15th Pz, part 90th Lt Div, 178 Pz Kpfw III-IVs
X AirCorps, 50 Stukas plus fighters.

Rommel ❷ (Pz-Army Africa) 21 January 1942. Rommel's second offensive 'Theseus', as a Gruppe with more Italian units, develops into 'Venezia' capturing Tobruk (map 9) before pushing on to Alam Halfa/El Alamein. A shortage of supplies, offsetting Rommel's often brilliant tactics, cripples panzer operations.

Pz-Gr Africa DAK as hitherto. 'Ariete', 'Trieste', 'Littorio' (arriving) four other It. divs inc. Trento, 560 tanks (320 Pz Kpfws) (see map 9). II Air Corps, 530 aircraft inc. 80 Stukas.

Rommel ❸ Pz-Army Africa 23 October 1942. The 'Desert Fox', promoted Field Marshal after a triumph at Tobruk (map 9), is defeated at El Alamein – and turns about.

Pz-Army Africa at Alamein; DAK plus 164th Lt Div, Para Bde (Ramcke), It. deployment as hitherto plus Folgore

(Para) Div. 285 Pz Kpfws – reduced to twenty by 4 November 1942; 150 German aircraft.

A hazardous withdrawal, almost 2,000 miles via Tripoli into Tunisia, is followed by 'Springwind' an offensive involving both PzAOK5 and DAK in counter-attacks against US forces at Kasserine. PzArmy Africa (Messe) meanwhile faces Montgomery at Mareth; Rommel is now GOC, Army Group Africa – promoted 23 February 1943.

Von Arnim ❹ 'Springwind', Fifth Panzer Army 14 February 1943, involves 10th, 21st Panzer and a DAK battle group in attacks against US II Corps at Kasserine, but suffers from poor co-ordination. After early success against an inexperienced US defence, the attack is called off. A new plan follows.

Fifth Pz-Army At Kasserine (Gruppe Zeigler) 15th, 21st Pz; DAK Battle Group (Liebenstein), 164th Lt, Centauro.

Rommel, Messe ❺ 'Capri', Pz-Army Africa 6 March 1943. At Medenine with Rommel's help Messe's Pz-Army Africa strikes at Eighth Army forming up to assault Axis positions at Mareth. Rommel expects to prevent a British First and Eighth Army link-up, but the attack fails and 'Supercharge II', a British armoured counter-strike turns the defence, forcing Pz-Army Africa into retreat.

At Medenine 15th, 21st, 10th Pz, 90th Lt – 141 Pz Kpfws.

Messe Thereafter Pz-Army Africa renamed Italian First Army withdraws to Enfidaville fighting rearguard battles. All German and Italian forces in North Africa capitulate on 13 May 1943.

Army Gr Africa Rommel, after 9 March 1943 von Arnim; Fifth Pz-Army, and It. First Army: ten German divs (three pz), six It. divs.

Western Desert Force/Eighth Army ❶ Wavell, elements one armd div, three inf divs; by 20 November 1941 (Eighth Army), 6 divs (one armd) plus ind bdes, 577 tanks.

Br Eighth Army ❷ Ritchie six divs (four mot, two armd) plus ind bdes 800–1,000 tanks, see (map 9) 530 aircraft.
❸ Montgomery ten divs (three armd) 1,200 tanks (see map 9) 1,200–1,500 aircraft.

Br First Army ❹ Anderson: II US Corps (Fredendall) part 1st US Armd Div, Fr inf, later Br 6th Armd.

Br Eighth Army ❺ Montgomery three divs (one armd), 300 tanks.

Br 18th Army Gr Alexander; Br First and Eighth Armies, 24 divs inc five US (two armd), four Fr, fifteen Br (four armd).

6. Conflict in the Balkans, 1941

In the aftermath of victory over Western Allies in May 1940 (map 3), a prime German concern is to safeguard Roumanian oil supplies and deter Turkish intervention in the Balkans. The German Army and Luftwaffe are consequently filtered as 'training' units into friendly Roumania and Bulgaria. But Hitler is faced with an unexpected military situation when Axis partner Mussolini, invading Greece from Albania (28 October 1940), fails against the Greek Army and a British expeditionary force lands in Greece in November.

Instructing German Twelfth Army (List) to invade Greece ('Marita') and eliminate opposition to the Italians in Albania ('Alpine Violet'), Hitler also thereby expects to counter British intervention in the region. But anti-German moves in Yugoslavia complicate the issue and Hitler deploys German Second Army (von Weichs) in Austria and Hungary for Operation '25' – the subjugation of Yugoslavia – in which Twelfth Army, invading the southern part of the country, will also participate.

Kleistgruppe (First Pz-Army) 8 April 1941 joins the German offensive. Striking at largely immobile opponents, military operations are concluded in twenty days. The British Expeditionary Force, including a tank brigade deployed in northern Greece, is outmanoeuvred by XXXX PzKorps and withdraws south – escaping mainly to Crete; 5th Panzer reaches Kalamata 28 April 1941.

The Luftwaffe then takes control of the offensive, improvising Operation 'Mercury' at short notice. Enlarging upon the paratroop and glider assault tactics that had taken the west by surprise in May 1940, XI Air Corps (Student) with the assistance of 5th Mountain Division (Ringel) and a panzer detachment, landed late in the campaign, captures the island in twelve days; VIII Air Corps (von Richthofen) in support.

Six panzer divisions, three and two-thirds motorized divisions including SS Das Reich and LSSAH lead the Balkans offensive.

Kuebler ❶ XXXXIX Mtn K; LI AK six infantry inc. 1st MtnDiv

Vietinghoff ❷ XXXXVI PzK: 8th, 14th PzDivs; 16th InfDiv Mot

Von Kleistgruppe ❸ Von Wietersheim XIV PzK: 5th, 11th PzDivs; 60th InfDiv Mot; Reinhardt XXXXI PzK: SS Das Reich Div, Regt Gross Deutschland, Regt General Goering XI AK: 294th InfDiv, 4th MtnDiv

Stumme ❹ XXXX PzK: 9th PzDiv; SS InfBde Mot Leibstandarte AH and after 12 April, 5th PzDiv

Boehme ❺ XVIII AK: 2nd PzDiv; 5th MtnDiv; 6th MtnDiv; XXX AK: three InfDivs

OKH uncommitted Reserve; 4th, 12th, 19th PzDivs, three InfDivs. Twelfth Army reserve, 16th PzDiv (frontier security Bulgaria-Turkey)

German Second, Twelfth Army von Brauchitsch; 23 Infantry, 9⅔ mobile divisions, 1,200 tanks

Luftwaffe Löhr 4th Air Fleet, 800 Aircraft (400 Stukas, 210 fighters)

Yugoslav Army/YAF 28 inf divs, three cav divs, 400 aircraft
Greek Army/GAF 20 inf divs, one motorized division. 80 aircraft

Brit.Exp. Force Greece: 1 Tank Bde, 2–3 inf (Brit. NZ, Aust) divisions, Crete: 2–3 inf (Brit. NZ, Aust, Greek) divisions. No air support

Italian Ninth, Eleventh Armies in Albania: 38 divs (two armd) 320 aircraft.

'Mercury' Student XI Air Corps: 1st Para Div, 1st Assault (glider) Regt, 5th Mtn Div; part 5/31st Pz Regt landed 29 March 1941. 530 Ju 52 transports. Von Richthofen VIII Air Corps 150 Stukas, 180 fighters, 320 other aircraft.

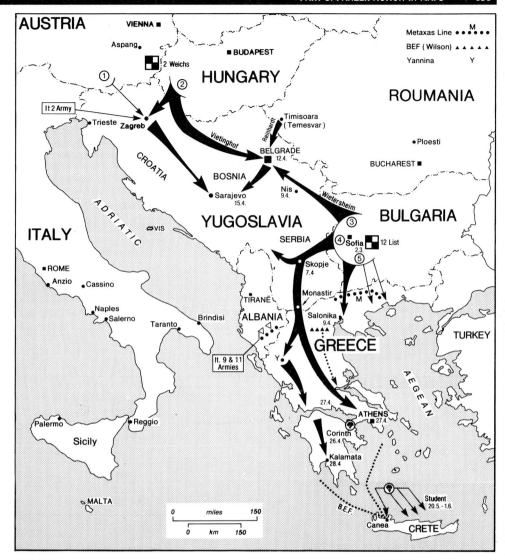

7. The war moves east, 1941

In Operation 'Barbarossa', Army Groups North, Centre and South with powerful Luftwaffe support strike in three directions: Leningrad, Moscow and Kiev–Rostov.

Encirclements of the Red Army are a triumphant feature of the early days, but military operations fanning out over a vast and often trackless interior are soon brought to a standstill. Halted by difficult terrain, bad weather, inadequate supplies and exhausted by an unyielding defence, the panzer divisions after capturing Kiev are driven to unrewarding battles for Leningrad and Moscow.

Hoepner (Fourth Pz-Army) 22 June leads Army Group North (von Leeb) to Leningrad. Guderian and Hoth (Second and Third Pz-Armies) 22 June responsible for the main German effort, lead Army Group Centre (von Bock) in the Moscow direction. Von Kleist (First Pz Army) 22 June leads Army Group South (von Runstedt) to Kiev and Rostov.

The outstanding panzer success of the early weeks is an envelopment of five Russian armies east of Kiev resulting in

600,000 prisoners for which von Kleist and Guderian are responsible. In the course of a subsequent operation, 'Typhoon' (map 8) 2 October 1941, convergent action by Guderian, Reinhardt and Hoepner encircling Bryansk and Vyasma proves equally rewarding.

Seventeen panzer divisions, thirteen and a half motorized divisions lead 'Barbarossa' – but despite optimistic predictions of a three-week campaign, operations are destined to last four years. Expanded and re-equipped, in later campaigns the panzer force will nevertheless fail to match Russian numbers or strategy. Divisions are switched between theatres, fronts, and controlling corps. Four years later on the Central Front in January 1945, when the Red Army pushes across the Vistula (map 18), only four panzer divisions supporting indifferently equipped infantry divisions face 163 Russian divisions. At the conclusion of hostilities the panzer force is totally burned out and only weak battle groups remain at the Army's disposal.

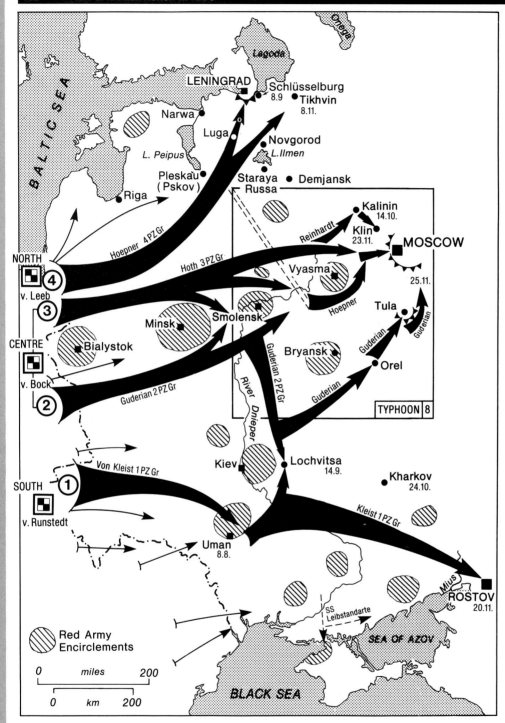

Red Army Encirclements

0   miles   200

0   km   200

Hoepner ❹ PzGr 4: XXXXI PzK Reinhardt, LVI von Manstein: three PzDivs 1st, 6th, 8th: three MotDivs 3rd, 36th and SS Totenkopf (later trapped with SS 'Polizei', 'Danemark' and others at Demjansk).
Hoth ❸ PzGr3: XXXIX PzK Schmidt, LVII PzK Küntzen: four PzDivs 7th, 12th, 19th, 20th: three MotDivs 14th, 18th, 20th: No SS formations

Guderian ❷ PzGr 2: XXIV PzK Geyr, XXXXVI PzK Vietinghoff XXXXVII PzK Lemelsen, five PzDivs 3rd, 4th, 10th, 17th, 18th: 3½ Mot Divs 10th, 29th, SS Das Reich (later switched to Hoepner for attack on Moscow) and Regiment 'Gross Deutschland'
Von Kleist ❶ PzGr 1: III PzK von Mackensen; XIV PzK von Wietersheim; XXXXVIII PzK Kempf; five PzDivs 9th, 11th,

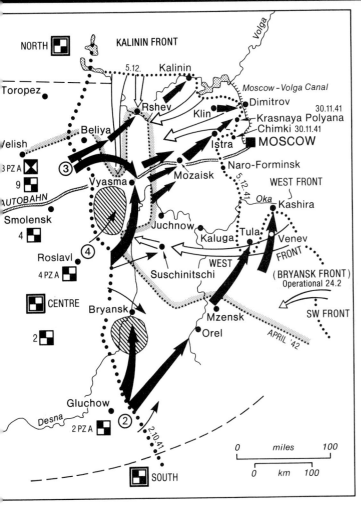

Leningrad, create delay and all thoughts of a short campaign are ruled out by October when the panzer groups are redeployed for Operation 'Typhoon' – a three-point Army Group Centre (von Bock) offensive to encircle the Soviet capital. Autumn mud slows 'Typhoon' starting early October. Efforts are re-doubled when frost hardens the ground, and the final phase of the attack begins 15–17 November. Attacks in sub-zero temperatures continue until 5 December, but with no winter clothing, short of supplies and air support diverted to the Mediterranean, the advance to Moscow is paralysed.

❸ Hoth/Reinhardt (Third Pz-Army) 2 October 1941. 3rd Panzer Group: – three panzer, two motorized divisions fight north-east to Kalinin before being re-directed on Klin to co-operate with Hoepner in a final attempt to seize Moscow from the north. 1–5 December, 7th Panzer Division forces the Moscow–Volga canal near Dimitrov but is repulsed by fresh Siberian divisions; 1st Panzer in support reaches Belyi-Rast 25 miles from the Soviet capital.
XXXXI Pz Corps (Reinhardt); LVI Pz Corps (Schaal); PzDivs 1st, 6th, 7th; 14th, 36th Inf Divs Mot plus infantry.

❹ Hoepner (Fourth Pz-Army) 2 October 1941. 4th Panzer Group: – six panzer, two motorized divisions responsible to Fourth Army (von Kluge, who replaces von Bock as Army Group Commander 19 December 1944) encircles the Red Army at Vyasma before pushing on to Mozaisk and Istra – assisting Third Pz-Group in a revised plan of operations to assault Moscow from the north. By 5 December 1941, 2nd Panzer Division at Krasnaya Polyana, eighteen miles from the Soviet capital and Army Pz Engineer Bn 62 in Chimki is within sight of the Kremlin. XXXX Pz Corps (Stumme); XXXXVI (Vietinghoff); LVII Pz Corps (Kuntzen); PzDivs 2nd, 10th, 5th, 11th, 19th, 20th; 3rd Inf Div Mot, Das Reich, plus infantry.

❷ Guderian Second Pz-Army 30 September 1941: Five panzer, four and a half motorized divisions strike for Moscow via Bryansk and Orel, but fail to seize Tula, a tightly defended road and rail junction *en route*. The town is bypassed. Counter-attacks by fresh Red Army divisions starting 25 November finally bring Guderian to halt at Kashira, 80 miles south of Moscow. XXIV Pz Corps (Geyr); XXXXVII Pz Corps (Lemelsen); XXXXVIII Pz Corps (Kempf); PzDivs: 3rd, 4th, 9th, 17th, 18th; Inf Divs Mot: 10th, 16th, 25th, 29th IR(Mot)Gross Deutschland, plus infantry.

A Russian counter-offensive under Zhukov with divisions fresh from the interior and far east, all but succeeds in collapsing the German Army on this front – but Rshev in the north and Vyasma in the centre remain bulwarks against the Red Army tide.

Nehring Second Pz-Army 16 January 1942. Infantry units surrounded in December 1941 at Suschinitschi hold out until relieved by 18th Panzer Division (Nehring).
German Army Von Brauchitsch: 46 Inf Divs; fourteen panzer, eight mot, two Ind Pz Bds, 1,700 tanks and assault guns.
Luftwaffe Kesselring: 2nd Air Fleet, II, VIII, Air Corps 1,320 aircraft, by 5 December, reduced to 600–700
Red Army, Air Force Zhukov 92 divs, thirteen tank bdes 700–800 tanks, 1,170 aircraft. By 5 December, 1,200 aircraft.

13th, 14th, 16th; four MotDivs 16th, 25th, SS 'Wiking', SS (Brigade) 'Leibstandarte' AH, Regt Gen Goering.
OKH Reserve 2nd, 5th PzDivs: 60th MotDiv
German Army von Brauchitsch 153 divisions (seventeen Pz, + two reserve, 134 mot divs) 3,417 tanks
Luftwaffe Keller, 1st Air Fleet; I Air Corps/A Gr North; Kesselring 2 Air Fleet, II, VIII Air Corps/A Gr Centre; Löhr 4th Air Fleet, IV, V Air Corps/A Gr South; – 3,800 aircraft
Red Army/Air Force 150–180 divs, 20,000 tanks, but only 1,000 T34s and 500 KVs, 10,000 aircraft (2,750 modern types).

8. Paralysis before Moscow, 1941

Operation 'Typhoon'. Despite spectacular gains in territory and *matériel*, the German Army's 'Barbarossa' offensive (map 7) has failed to destroy the Red Army or reach Moscow before the onset of winter 1941. Panzer diversions to the flanks either to assist Army Group South encircling the Red Army at Kiev or assist Army Group North stalled before

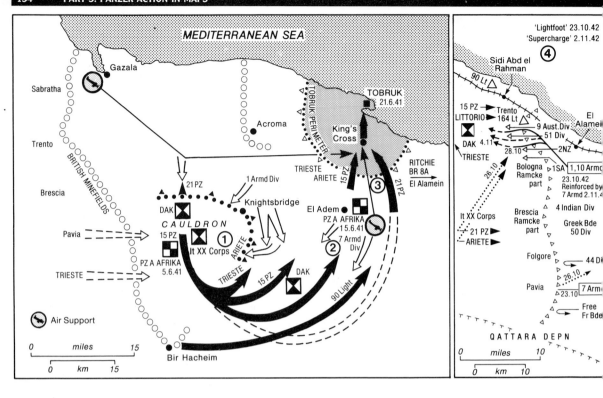

9. 'Victory or Death': Rommel in North Africa, 1942

Developing Operation 'Theseus' (map 5) into Operation 'Venezia' Rommel succeeds at the second attempt in capturing Tobruk on 21 June 1942. This highpoint in the General's career earns him promotion to Generalfeldmarschall and 'Venezia' opens the way for a renewed offensive into Egypt.

Rommel (Pz-Army Africa) within a fortnight, starting 21 January 1942, 'Theseus' carries DAK (Nehring) and three Italian corps – organized into Panzergruppe Afrika – to Gazala – Bir Hacheim.

Rommel Pz-Army Africa 26 May 1942 then develops offensive operations eastwards against Tobruk. 'Venezia' renews the clash of armour.

Nehring ❶ DAK (15th, 21st Panzer and 90th PzGr Divisions with Italian motorized infantry support) fights in the 'Cauldron' with its back to British minefields north of Bir Hacheim. For several days following Rommel's attempt to overcome the defence from the rear, this strong point held by Free French battalions denies every attempt to reduce it. The position is bypassed when a new route is opened through the minefield.

Rommel ❷ Swinging DAK in a right hook towards El Adem, and beating off ineffectual counter-attacks, the panzer divisions prepare for Rommel's second assault on Tobruk from the south-east.

Rommel ❸ Supported by Italian XX Corps including 'Ariete' and 'Trieste', and the Luftwaffe flying from airfields near Gazala and El Adem (80 Stukas), Rommel personally conducts operations to smash the defence. Tobruk, held by 32,000 British and Empire troops, falls 21 June 1942.

On 22 June 1942 Panzer Army Africa captures British fuel and motor transport in unexpected quantities so Rommel decides to pursue British Eighth Army eastwards in the direction of El Alamein and Suez.

Stumme/Rommel ❹ Pz-Army Africa 23 October 1942. Opposed at El Alamein by a reinforced British Eighth Army deployed in conjunction with powerful air support, Pz Army Africa once more short of supplies and outclassed in the air is decisively beaten in a setpiece battle conducted by a newcomer to the desert; General Bernard Montgomery.

Despite a 'victory or death' call from Hitler to the Field Marshal, Montgomery's victory over Rommel at El Alamein precipitates retreat via Tripoli into Tunisia. Panzer battles follow at Kasserine (see Pz-AOK5 Africa) 14–19 February, and Medenine, 6 March, before Rommel departs the theatre for Europe on 9 March 1943.

Pz Army Africa ❶–❸ Rommel; DAK (Nehring) – 15th, 21st Pz, 90th Lt. It. XX Corps (Baldassare) Ariete, Trieste. It. X Corps (Gioda) Brescia, Parvia. It. XXI Corps (Navarrini) Trento, Sabratha: Littorio arriving, 320 Pz Kpfws (560 total), II Air Corps 400–500 aircraft inc. 80 Stukas.

Eighth Army ❶–❸ Ritchie; XIII Corps (Gott) 50th, Ist SA, 5th Indian Divs. XXX Corps (Norrie) 1st, 7th Armd, 4th Indian Divs. plus ind. tank bdes 800–1,000 tanks (170 Grants) 530 aircraft.

Pz Army Africa ❹ Rommel at Alamein; DAK (Thoma) as hitherto plus 164th Lt Div Para Bde (Ramcke). It. strength as hitherto plus Folgore (Para) Div. 285 Pz Kpfws – reduced to twenty by 4 November 1942. 150 Ger. aircraft.

Eighth Army ❹ Montgomery at Alamein; XXX Corps

(Leese) 9th Aust, 51st, 2nd NZ, 1st SA Divs. X Corps (Lumsden) 1st, 10th Armd Divs. XIII Corps (Horrocks) 4th Indian, Greek Bde, 50th, 44th, 7th Armd Divs: plus indp.

tank bdes. 1,200 tanks (205 Grants, 267 Shermans), 1,200–1,500 aircraft.

10. New Objectives in the East, 1942

Operation 'Blue' ('Brunswick'). Failing with 'Barbarossa' and 'Typhoon' to achieve anything more in 1941 than astronomical numbers of prisoners-of-war and jumping-off points from which to continue the campaign in the east, Hitler assigns new objectives to the Army Groups.

A shortage of armour restricts offensive operations to Army Group South (later divided 'A' and 'B') whose re-equipped panzer force in consecutive stages of Operation 'Blue' renamed 'Brunswick' 30 June, will be expected to trap the Red Army west of the River Don – seize Stalingrad in Operation 'Siegfried' (Army Group 'B') – and in Operation 'Mouse' (Army Group 'A') advance into the Caucasus to occupy Russian oil-producing centres at Grosny, Tiflis and Baku. None of the objectives is attained.

The inclusion of more than thirty non-German formations – sixteen Roumanian, ten Hungarian, nine Italian in the August total of one hundred divisions committed to 'Blue'/ 'Brunswick' will further undermine Hitler's flawed strategy of widely diverging offensives. Deployed north and south of Stalingrad, the relative inability of satellite divisions to withstand attack will be ruthlessly exploited by the Red Army. *See* Part 2, Satellite contributions for the panzer force.

Hoth Fourth Pz-Army 28 June 1942 succeeds in capturing Voronezh on 6 July for Army Group 'B', but disaster follows in action supporting Sixth Army at Stalingrad (map 11).

Von Kleist First Pz-Army 9 July 1942 joins operations that will take the Pz-Army into the Caucasus, but the strenuously resisted offensive is abandoned after supplies and air support are curtailed.

Nine panzer and seven motorized divisions lead the offensive.

Hoth ❶ Fourth Pz Army: XXIV PzK; XXXXVIII PzK; three PzDivs, 9th, 11th, 24th; three mot divs, 3rd, 16th, Gross Deutschland.

Von Weichs Second Army; Hungarian Second Army

Geyr ❷ XXXX PzK: 3rd, 23rd PzDivs, 29th InfDivMot; Paulus Sixth Army

Von Kleist ❸ First Pz Army: XIV PzK; 14th, 22nd PzDivs; 60th InfDivMot, III PzK, LSSAH, 16th Pz; Roumanian Third Army

Kirchner ❹ (von Wietersheim) LVII PzK; 13th PzDiv, SS Wiking; Ruoff, Seventeenth Army: Part Italian Eighth Army

Von Kleist ❺ First Pz Army; Armeegruppe Ruoff, Seventeenth Army and Roumanian Third Army; XXXX, III, LVII Pz Corps, 23rd, 3rd, 13th Pz Divs, 16th Mot, SS Wiking, and GD until August 1942

Army Gr 'B' ❶ von Bock/von Weichs 27 divs inc. three Pz, three PzGr, ten Hungarian, 400 tanks ❷ nineteen divs inc. two Pz, one PzGr

Army Group 'A' ❸ List 16 divs inc. three Pz, two mot, four Roum. ❹ eighteen divs inc one Pz, one PzGr, four Roum., six It. ❺ twenty divs inc. three Pz, three Mot, four Roum. one Slovak (Schnelle), 400 tanks (total Army Grps 'A' and 'B' 1,500 tanks)

4th Air Fleet Von Richthofen: I, Fiebig VIII Air Corps. 2 Pflugbeil IV Air Corps (until 26 July, then 5), 3, 4, 5 = 1,500 aircraft

Red Army, Air Force ❶ ❷ Golikov Voronezh/Bryansk Fr; five armies (one tank) 1,000 tanks. ❸ ❹ Timoshenko SW/ Stalingrad Fr seven armies (two tank forming) by 20 July, 38 divs, one air army 400 aircraft. ❺ Budenny N. Caucasus Fr; four armies, one air army 120 tanks, 130 aircraft.

11. Battles for Stalingrad, battles for oil, 1942

Operation 'Blue'/'Brunswick', had made a promising start for Army Gr 'B' by securing Voronezh on 6 July. Operations 'Siegfried' and 'Mouse' were unfolding in reasonably good time (map 10) and by mid-November more than 90 per cent of Stalingrad is in the hands of von Weichs. In the Caucasus, List's Army Group 'A' stands within striking distance of prime Soviet oil-producing centres until a Red Army counter-stroke reverses the double offensive.

Hoth ❶ Fourth Pz-Army/Sixth Army (Paulus) 19 November 1942 is immediately incapacitated by a Red Army pincer movement breaking through Roumanian positions north and south of the city and uniting at Kalatsch.

Hube, Heim German Sixth Army, XIV Panzer Corps (Hube) and much of Fourth Pz Army is isolated. A mobile reserve – 22nd Panzer bracketed with Roumanian 1st Armd Div in XLVIII Pz Corps (Heim) – supporting the Roumanians is destroyed in abortive counter-attacks.

Trapped in the pocket are 14th, 16th, 24th Pz and 3rd, 29th, 60th Mot Divs.

Hoth, Kirchner ❷ Fourth Pz-Army 12 December 1942 launches 'Winter Storm', a relief operation improvised by A Gr Don with panzer divisions brought great distances; 6th Pz from France, 17th Pz from A Gr Centre, and 23rd Pz from First Pz-Army. The panzer divisions under LVII PzK (Kirchner) brought from Seventeenth Army in the Caucasus, fight to within 30 miles of the city. Relief operations are called off as a new Russian offensive west across the Chir threatening Millerovo exacerbates the situation. *See* (map 12) LVII Pz-Corps action at Stalingrad.

Von Kleist, Von Mackensen ❸ First Pz-Army 22 November 1942 to 1 January 1943 is obliged to release 23rd Pz, SS Wiking and air support to assist Hoth and Paulus at Stalingrad. Von Kleist is further threatened with the loss of Rostov-on-Don – the Pz Army's principal supply and communications centre, 400 miles behind the front. But under von Mackensen, (von Kleist's successor) – First Pz-Army will fight its way to safety.

Von Mackensen, Hoth ❹ Army Group Don (von Manstein) regroups First and Fourth Pz Armies and launches counter-attacks against Red Army spearheads crossing the Donets and exploiting success westwards. But Kharkov is lost and Zaporoshe (Army Group headquarters) threatened.

Hoth Fourth Pz-Army 22 February 1943 leads the recapture of Kharkov (map 13).

Army Gr 'B' ❶ Von Weichs in Stalingrad; 22 divs (three Pz, three Mot, two Roum.) 100 tanks.

Army Gr Don ❷ Von Manstein; thee Pz divs, six Roum. inf divs, 170–200 tanks.

First Pz-Army ❸ Von Kleist (von Mackensen after 1 January 1943) six divs (two Pz).

First, Fourth Pz-Armies ❹ Von Mackensen, Hoth; 17–18 divs (nine Pz) *see* (map 13).

4th Air Fleet Von Richthofen; I Fiebig, VIII Air Corps. 2, 3, 4, Pflugbeil IV Air Corps.

Red Army, Air Force ❶ Stalingrad counter-offensive 19– 20 November; nine armies, forty divs, 979 tanks and SP guns, four air armies, 1,350 aircraft. ❷ Kotelnikovo axis; three armies, 19½ divs, 635 tanks. ❸ N. Caucasus; four armies, 24 divs, one air army, 232 aircraft. ❹ Kharkov *see* (map 13).

12. The agony of Stalingrad, 1942

Hitler's fatally flawed summer offensive continuing into winter 1942 (map 11) is a turning-point in the fortunes of the German Army and its panzer force. 'Citadel' (map 14) and 'Autumn Mist' (map 17) excepted, panzer divisions will

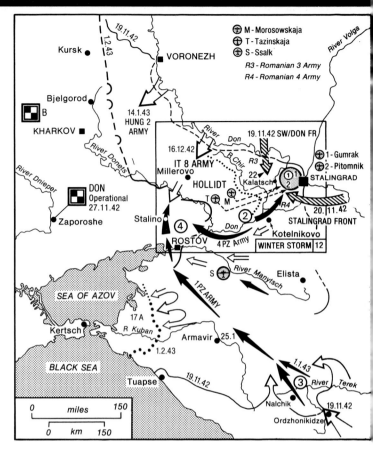

henceforth exploit mobility and fire power in a 'fire brigade' role, relieving encircled formations, delaying or containing Russian offensives and generally bolstering unprotected and immobile infantry. This change of emphasis is reflected in the relief of Stalingrad, December 1942.

Hoth, Hube ❶ Fourth Pz-Army/Sixth Army (Paulus) 19 November 1942. 22 divisions including three Panzer (14th, 16th, 24th), three motorized (3rd, 29th, 60th) and XIV Panzer Corps (Hube), more than 220,000 men, are besieged in Stalingrad by seven Russian armies.

Hoth, Kirchner ❷ Fourth Pz-Army 12 December 1942 launches relief Operation 'Winter Storm', spearheaded by 6th Panzer. Urgently railed from France the division leads LVII Panzer Corps (Kirchner) 6th, 17th and 23rd Panzer to within 30 miles of the Stalingrad perimeter. Provisioned by VIII Air Corps from 'Moro' (sovskya), 'Tazi' (nskya) and other airfields, the defenders of Stalingrad offer bitter resistance, but the tonnage received, on average 150 tons daily, is much less than the minimum 550 tons needed to sustain them.

Hoth ❸ Fourth Pz-Army 17 December 1942 faces further difficulty when a new Red army offensive on the upper Chir smashing through Italian Eighth Army threatens to engulf the airfields. The panzer divisions are diverted to the new crisis point. The relief attempt is called off and efforts to stabilize the situation bring another (7th Panzer) division from France. Panzer action is dissipated over a wide area.

North and south of Rostov, panzer divisions are switched between sectors to delay the Red Army's drive on von

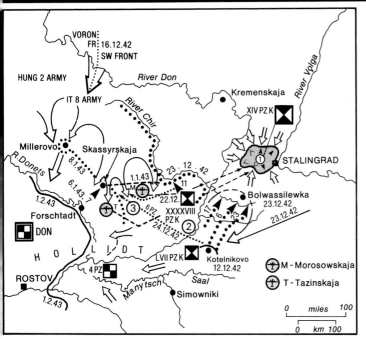

The Army Group commander will regroup much-depleted armour and launch a counter-offensive (map 13), to seal off Red Army spearheads exploiting success westwards. Von Manstein's offensive against an over-extended Red Army is to prove remarkably successful and the situation is 'miraculously' turned to German advantage.

Army Gr 'B' ❶ Von Weichs in Stalingrad; 22 divs (three Pz, three Mot, two Roum inf), 100 tanks.

Army Gr Don ❷ Von Manstein/Armeegruppe Hoth (4 PzA, 4 RomA); three Pz divs, six Roum inf divs. 175–200 tanks (6th and 23rd Pz=141 Pz Kpfw III-IVs).

Army Gr 'B' ❸ Von Weichs; Garibaldi It. Eighth Army, 9–12 It. inf divs; Jány, Hung Second Army, ten inf divs, one Hung Pz div, von Salmuth, German Second Army, etc.

A Gr Don Von Manstein/Armeeabteilung Hollidt; six Roum. inf divs, one Roum. Pz Div, three Ger. inf divs.

4th Air Fleet Von Richthofen; ❶❷ Fiebig VIII Air Corps, ❸ Pflugbeil IV Air Corps.

Red Army, Air Force ❶ Investing Stalingrad 47 divs; ❷ Kotelnikovo axis 19½ divs, 635 tanks; ❸ Stalingrad counter offensive 36 divs, 1,030 tanks.

13. Von Manstein's miracle, 1943

In a bid to outmanoeuvre and complete the destruction of German and satellite armies surviving the onslaught at Stalingrad, the Red Army (Voronezh and South West Fronts) flushed with victory, exploits success across the Donets, thrusting towards Zaporoshe and the Sea of Azov. The offensive is brought to a standstill by First and Fourth Panzer Armies – regrouped and launched into a well-timed

Mackensen's Rostov 'gateway'. A successful panzer defence of Rostov allows First Panzer Army 1 January 1943 to fight its way back from Caucasus – but at catastrophic cost to German Sixth Army and surviving Fourth Panzer Army units in Stalingrad.

Von Manstein By 1 February 1943 both Panzer Armies under control of Army Group Don are relatively safe between the Donets and the Dnieper.

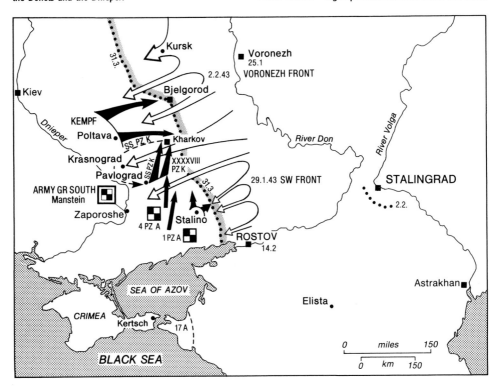

counter-stroke devised by von Manstein C-in-C, Army Group South (formerly Don).

Von Mackensen First Pz-Army 27 January 1943 concludes an arduous retreat from the Caucasus with the task of holding Stalino and, with two Pz-Corps striking north on 22 February, biting into the flank of Russian Sixth Army and its armoured spearheads (Popov) leading SW Front in the drive to the Dnieper at Zaporoshe.

Hoth Fourth Pz-Army 22 February 1943 is allotted the principal role in von Manstein's counter-offensive. Supported by 4th Air Fleet, Hoth pushes two Pz-Corps northwards and on the 22nd is reinforced by a newly created SS Pz-Corps (Hausser) – released by Armeeabteilung Kempf (previously Lanz) after defying Hitler's orders and evacuating Kharkov on the 16th. Hoth aims to slice through Voronezh Front's extended left wing and re-occupy Kharkov, previously lost to Russian 69th Army and Third Tank Army spearheads. The offensive is a success, cutting-off Russian Sixth Army (and Popov) spearheads, recapturing Kharkov on 12 March and continuing on to Bjelgorod, an equally important railway junction falling to Gross Deutschland on the 18th. Bjelgorod, like Kharkov, becomes a

spring-board for Hitler's projected summer offensive 'Citadel' (map 14).

Von Mackensen First Pz-Army: XXXX PzK Henrici; 11th Pz, SS PzGrenDiv Wiking, 333rd InfDiv; III PzK Breith: 3rd, 7th PzDivs.

Hoth Fourth Pz-Army: LVII PzK Kirchner; XXXXVIII PzK von Knobelsdorff; 6th, 17th, 19th PzDivs.

Kempf Army Abteilung: II SS PzK Hausser; 1st SS PzDiv Leibstandarte Adolf Hitler, 2nd SS PzDiv Das Reich, 3rd SS PzDiv Totenkopf; PzGrenDiv Gross Deutschland.

Army Gr South Von Manstein Kharkov offensive; nine pz divs (3SS), two mot divs, 6–7 inf divs, 350–450 tanks, mostly deployed in the SS divisions.

4th Air Fleet Von Richthofen; Korten I Air Corps-Kempf, Pflugbeil IV AirCorps-Hoth, Mahnke Air Div Donets-von Mackensen/Hoth.

Red Army, Air Force Vatutin, SW Front 29 January; 29 rifle divs, four armies, 137 tanks (Front Mobile Group Popov) – one air army, 300 aircraft.

Golikov, Voronezh Fr 2 February; three armies (one tank) 120 tanks.

14. Break-point: 'Citadel', 1943

After suffering two disastrous winters in the east, a revitalized panzer force enjoying new weapons and equipment – Tigers, Panthers and Ferdinands – is assembled on sectors north and south of a huge and strongly defended Red Army salient centred on Kursk. Operation 'Citadel' involving Army Groups Centre and South will strike concentrically to eliminate the salient.

Hoth Fourth Pz-Army 5 July 1943 responsible to Army Group South will carry the main weight of the offensive; SS PzKorps (Hausser) providing the cutting edge; Army Abteilung (AA) Kempf in support.

Model Ninth Army responsible to Army Group Centre will co-operate in attacks from the north. But 'Citadel' is not a success.

Losing more than half its armoured strength, 'Citadel' fails to break the deeply echeloned Russian defence and after seven days' fighting when the offensive coincides with 'Husky', the Allied invasion of Sicily, Hitler calls it off. (Panzer Action in Italy, page 201.)

Critically drained of resources, the German Army will never recover the strategic initiative. Fourth Pz-Army, failing to reach Kursk and link up with Ninth Army, is shattered in the attempt; the decimated panzer divisions lose their power and German domination of European Russia is permanently broken.

Twenty panzer/panzer grenadier divisions (including OKH reserve) plus infantry and Army troops assemble for 'Citadel' led by Hoth and Kempf (Army Group South) and Model (Army Group Centre).

Hoth ❶ Fourth Pz-Army, II SS PzK Hausser: 1st SS PzDiv, 2nd SS PzDiv, 3 SS PzDiv: XXXXVIII PzK von Knobelsdorff; 3rd, 11th PzDivs, Gross Deutschland, 167th Inf Div, 10 Pz (Panther) Bde Decker, LII AK Ott, two Inf divs.

Kempf ❷ Army Abteilung, III PzK Breith: 6th, 7th, 19th PzDivs, 168 Inf Div, 503 (Tiger) Bn; XI AK Raus, three Inf

divs: XXXXII AK three Inf divs.

Model ❸ Ninth Army, XXXXVII PzK Lemelsen: 2nd, 4th, 9th, 20th PzDivs, 505 Hvy (Tiger) PzBn, 6th Inf Div, XXXXI PzK Harpe: 18th PzDiv, 10th PzGrDiv, 653, 654 Pzjaeger (Ferdinand) Bns; XXXXVI PzK Zorn: Five infantry divisions and Gruppe von Manteuffel: XX and XXIII AK with seven infantry divs.

A Gr South Reserve (uncommitted) XXIV PzK Nehring: 5th SS 'Wiking', 17th PzDiv.

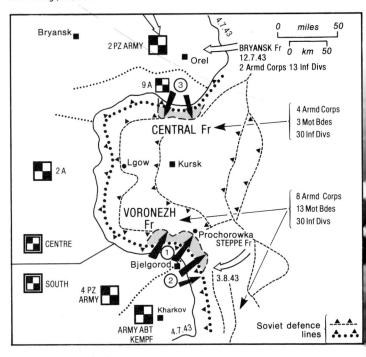

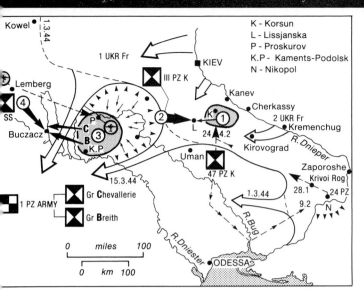

K - Korsun
L - Lissjanska
P - Proskurov
K.P - Kaments-Podolsk
N - Nikopol

OKH/A Gr Centre Reserve 5th PzDiv (OKH) switched to Second Pz-Army, 12th PzDiv, 36th I.D. Mot.

A Gr Centre Von Kluge; 21 divs inc 6 PzDivs, 2 Pzgr, 700–800 tanks (45 Tigers), 350 assault guns.

A Gr South Von Manstein; 22 divs inc 11 PzDivs, 1 Pz bde, 1,300 tanks (101 Tigers), 250 assault guns. (Total 2,700 tanks/assault guns, inc. 146 Tigers).

Luftwaffe ❶ ❷ Dessloch, 4th Air Fleet, Seidemann VIII Air Corps – 1st, 4th Air Divs. 1,100 airc. ❸ Greim, 6th Air Fleet, Deichmann 1 Air Corps – 700 aircraft (Total 1,800 aircraft).

Red Army/Air Force Rokossovsky Central Fr; Vatutin Voronezh Fr; Konev Steppe Fr (from 18 July). 100 divs inc five tank armies, 3,306 tanks and assault guns, 2,650 aircraft.

15. A moving pocket in the Ukraine, 1944

Following a disastrous German outcome to 'Citadel' (map 14) the Eastern Front lacks armoured reserves with which to counter powerful Russian offensives aimed principally at enveloping von Manstein's Army Group South. Bjelgorod and Kharkov are lost; disaster threatens on the scale of Stalingrad. Hitler reluctantly sanctions retreat.

Consequently, in September 1943, panzer action focuses upon the Dnieper between Kiev and the Black Sea, where a million German troops struggle to evade encirclement. Success depends on von Manstein's ability to evacuate a 200-mile wide zone east of the river, using crossings at Kiev, Kanev, Cherkassy, Dniepropetrovsk and Zaporoshe.

Von Mackensen, Hoth First and Fourth Pz-Armies August–December 1943 stand with Eighth Army at the centre of the fighting.

Thirteen panzer divisions: 3rd, 6th, 9th, 11th, 13th, 14th, 17th, 19th, 23rd, 24th, SST, SSW, GD and three PzGr divisions: 10th, 16th, 20th, serve at crisis points.

Vormann, Breith ❶ On 28 January 1944 the threat to

von Manstein is significantly heightened when 54,000 men of two Army Corps including SS Wiking, are trapped in a pocket at Cherkassy–Korsun on the Dnieper. A relief attempt by Eighth Army devolves upon 24th Panzer – transferred from Nikopol, 150 miles south and temporarily under command of XXXXVII Panzer Corps (Vormann). But even before the attempt is defeated by 2nd Ukr Front, 24th Panzer is ordered to return to Nikopol and counter a renewal of Red Army attacks on the bridgehead there. A fresh attempt to relieve Cherkassy from the west, organized by First Pz-Army (III Pz Corps Breith) will succeed by a narrow margin.

Hube ❷ First Pz-Army 17 February 1944. Reinforced by 503rd Tiger Bn (Pz Regt Bäcke) III Panzer Corps (Breith) approaches within reach of the Cherkassy defence, allowing 30,000 men trapped for twenty days and supplied by air, to break out and join Breith at Lissjanska. SS Wiking, one of the most redoubtable panzer divisions on the Eastern Front, leading the breakout, loses all its heavy weapons and equipment. But von Manstein's problems are far from over.

Hube ❸ First Pz-Army 24 March 1944 with 300,000 men is encircled at Kaments-Podolsk. Air transports from Lemberg resupply the divisions in a constantly moving pocket. Organized into corps-groups and fighting north-west to make contact with an SS relief force (II SS Pz Corps), the Pz-Army is reduced to a handful of tanks in 1st, 6th, 7th, 11th, 16th, 17th, 19th Pz, 20th Pz Gr and battlegroups 1SSLAH, 2SS Reich. Supplies, at first flown into Proskurov, are subsequently delivered by parachute. Transport action continues until 10 April 1944 (*see* Part 4, page 141).

Hube, Bittrich ❹ First Pz-Army and II SS Panzer Corps (Bittrich) unite at Buczacz on 8 April 1944.

Army Gr South ❶ Von Manstein; in Korsun–Cherkassy pocket, (Gruppe Stemmermann) SS Wiking, SS Bde Wallonien, seven inf divs. ❷ Breith relief corps; 16th, 17th Pz Divs, Tiger Bn 503. ❸ Hube in First Pz-Army pocket 22 divs (seven Pz, one pz gren div), Tiger Bns 503, 509.

II SS Pz Corps ❹ Bittrich, 9th SS, 10th SS PzDivs.

4th Air Fleet Dessloch: South of Kiev; August 1943, 1,150 aircraft by March 1944, 165 aircraft.

Red Army ❶–❹ Vatutin 1st UKr Fr; 63 rifle divs, six tank, two mech corps; Konev 2nd Ukr Fr; six armies in action to reduce Korsun, 135 tanks, thirteen rifle divs.

16. The West springs a trap: Normandy, 1944

On 6 June 1944, when 21st Army Group (Montgomery) invades Normandy in Operation 'Overlord', six panzer divisions and a panzer grenadier division stationed in northern France are mostly deployed too far away for immediate intervention. The opportunity for a concerted panzer offensive that might throw 21st Army Group back into the sea is lost. Divided command, faulty Intelligence, an almost total lack of air support and a faulty appreciation of Allied intentions contribute to German failure.

After a weak start the panzer divisions, rising to ten in number also a Pz Gr division, are deployed piecemeal mainly in defence of Caen. They are SS Panzer Divisions: 1st, 2nd, 9th, 10th, 12th and 17th (PzGr); Army panzer

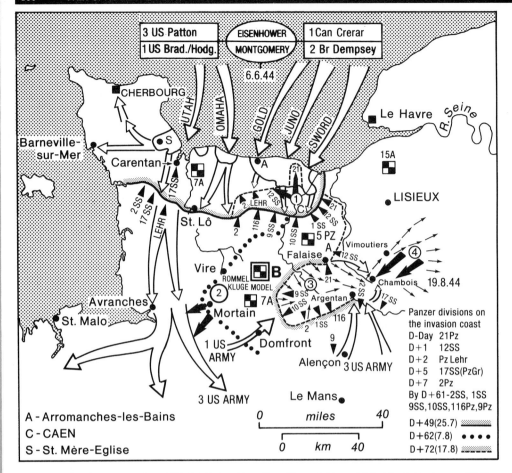

3 US Patton	EISENHOWER	1 Can Crerar
1 US Brad./Hodg.	MONTGOMERY	2 Br Dempsey

A - Arromanches-les-Bains
C - CAEN
S - St. Mère-Eglise

Panzer divisions on
the invasion coast
D-Day 21Pz
D+1   12SS
D+2   Pz Lehr
D+5   17SS(PzGr)
D+7   2Pz
By D+61-2SS, 1SS
9SS,10SS,116Pz,9Pz

D+49(25.7)
D+62(7.8)
D+72(17.8)

0   miles   40
0   km   40

divisions: 2nd, 9th, 21st, 116th and PzLehr. During this time 11th Panzer at Bordeaux is committed in the south against 'Anvil', later renamed 'Dragoon': *see* Fifth Pz Army Europe, 15 August (D+70).

Geyr, Eberbach ❶ Pz-Group West (Fifth Pz-Army) 6 June 1944. 21st Panzer Division counter-attacking the beach-head thrusts to the coast at Lion-sur-Mer. Reinforcements – 12th SS (Hitler Youth), Panzer Lehr and 2nd Panzer Division – are slow in arriving. Hitler is deceived into concentrating most of the available panzer divisions on the German right around Caen to counter continuous British/Canadian offensives, 'Epsom', 'Charnwood', 'Goodwood', 'Totalise' and more. Von Kluge, the German Army Group Commander (after Rommel is wounded 17 July 1944), sees his weak left wing driven in and enveloped by a US armoured thrust lead by General George Patton – Operation 'Cobra', Fifth Panzer Army, Europe [25 July].

Hausser, von Funck ❷ Fifth Panzer Army Europe [7 August] Starting from Mortain with two Panzer Corps, XXXVIII – 2nd and 116th PzDivs; 1st SS PzK – 1st and 2nd SS PzDivs, a German Seventh Army counter-attack 'Lüttich', is shattered by Allied air power and aborted: 9th Panzer, north-west of Alençon, momentarily slows the US advance.

Dietrich, Hausser, Eberbach ❸ Fifth Pz-Army, Europe 19–21 August 1944 is one of two German armies, Seventh and Fifth Pz, also Pz-Group Eberbach, trapped south of Caen. The pocket is resolutely defended by Army and Waffen SS; 12th SS follows a tenacious defence of key points with a notable role in holding open an escape route for both Armies and Panzergruppe.

Bittrich ❹ Battle groups from 2nd and 9th SS Pz Divisions counter-attacking under II SS Pz-Corps previously evacuated from the pocket, assist in extricating the trapped divisions. None, according to Model, escape across the Seine 'with more than ten tanks'.

C-in-C West Von Runstedt; 59 divs (nine Pz, one Pz Gr including four SS) two SS Pz arriving.

Western Allies Eisenhower; 86 divs (39 for 'Overlord' 17 in first wave inc. two armd).

Army Gr 'B' ❶ Rommel 41 divs. Pz dispositions D-Day 21 Pz Divs. south of the Seine, 2nd, 116th Pz Divs north of the Seine. By D+7 also includes 12th SS, Pz Lehr, 17th SS from OKW reserve (Pz Gr West). By D+61 (6 August 1944) ten Pz divs, one Pz Gr Division (six SS including 9th SS, 10th SS from A Gr N. Ukraine.

Seventh Army ❷ Hausser; four Pz Divs (two SS), two Pz Div battle groups.

Fifth Pz Army, Seventh Army ❸ Dietrich, Hausser; twelve-thirteen div. battle groups (six-seven Pz).

II SS Pz Corps ❹ Bittrich; 2/9 SS Pz Div battle groups.

3rd Air Fleet Sperrle; 800–1,000 aircraft rising to 1,300 by D+10. Invasion front II Jagd Korps (Junck) 496 aircraft all types – battle-fit 319 inc. II Flieger Korps (Bülowius) with 75 ground-attack types.

Allied Forces ❶–❹ Montgomery, Br 21 A Gr; Bradley, US 12 A Gr. By 25 August 1944, 39 divs (thirteen armd– four Br, six US, one Fr, one Can, one Pol).

US Third Army Patton seven divs (three armd).

Allied Exp. Air Forces Leigh Mallory; in Britain 12,837 aircraft, 7,774 battle-fit.

17. 'Autumn Mist', autumn disaster: Belgium, 1944

Operation 'Autumn Mist', formerly 'Watch on the Rhine', is Hitler's last offensive in the west. After weeks of secret preparation, two panzer armies are launched west through the Ardennes attacking US First Army resting on the River Meuse. Hitler intends to recapture Antwerp and Brussels, encircle Allied armies deployed between the Ardennes and the German front in Holland and, wishfully, force an Allied evacuation of the continent.

Dietrich and von Manteuffel Sixth SS and Fifth Pz-Army (Europe) 16 December 1944 report early gains when the Allies are once again taken off-guard by an armoured stroke delivered out of the Ardennes. But progress is unspectacular, even less so in the north where, hampered by a staunch American defence squeezing attacking SS divisions into a narrow operational area from which they are unable to break-out, the offensive loses momentum.

Von Manteuffel Fifth Pz-Army (Europe) 24 December 1944 records better progress in the south. But Bastogne, a vital communications centre *en route* to the west, has steadfastly refused to surrender. The SS divisions are redeployed. German efforts are redoubled – absorbing effort

intended for the westwards thrust. Bastogne nevertheless remains a thorn in the German side, refusing to surrender. Petrol and ammunition shortages curtail panzer operations and the German offensive is hamstrung. On 26 December 1944 Bastogne is relieved by US III Corps.

Von Manteuffel Fifth Pz-Army (Europe) 3 January 1945. When good flying weather allows Anglo-US air forces to strike at extended panzer supply columns, and Allied armies re-grouped under temporary command of Field Marshal Montgomery are launched into powerful counter-attacks, 'Autumn Mist' has run its course and Hitler calls it off.

Von Manteuffel Fifth Panzer Army 4 January 1945 orders a final effort by I SS Pz Corps (Priess) to capture Bastogne. The action ends in failure.

Sixth SS Pz-Army Dietrich; I SS PzK Priess: 1st SSLAH, 12th SS HJ, two VGDs and 3rd Para Div: II SS PzK, Bittrich: 2nd SS Reich, 9th SS Hohenstaufen LXVII AK two VGDs.

Fifth Pz-Army von Manteuffel; XLVII PzK von Lüttwitz; 2nd Pz, PzLehr, 26th VGD; LVIII PzK, Krüger: 116th Pz, 560th VGD, later FBB: LXVI AK two VGDs, XXXIX PzK Decker arriving 27 December co-ordinates offensive against

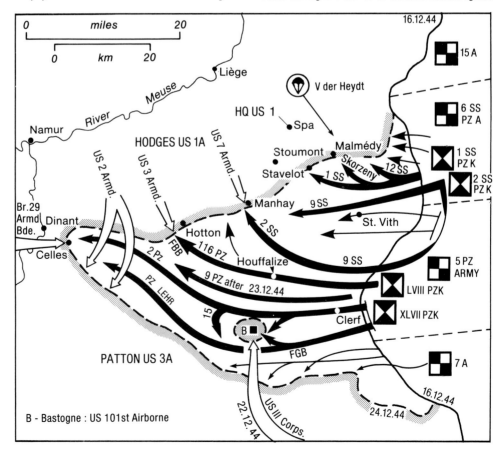

B - Bastogne : US 101st Airborne

Bastogne with 11th Pz, 3rd, 15th PzGrDivs: thereafter joins *ad hoc* Armeegruppe von Lüttwitz 30–31 December before transferring south to Alsace for 'North Wind'.

Fifteenth Army von Zangen; Four Army Corps including 15th PzGrDiv and 9th PzDiv.

Seventh Army Brandenburger; Three Army Corps with three VGD and 5th Para Div.

OKW Reserve; 10th SS Frundsberg, 11th Pz, 3rd PzGr, 6th SS Mtn Div.

Führer Grenadier Bde FGB – reinforces Seventh Army on 22 December.

Führer Begleit Bde FBB – reinforces Fifth Pz Army on 23 December.

Army Group 'B' Model; nine panzer divisions (inc two reserve), two pz-grenadier divs, fourteen inf divs (inc two para) 1,750 tanks and SP guns inc. 30 King Tigers.

Luftwaffen Kdo West Schmid; II Fighter Corps (Pelz) 1,800 aircraft inc. 91 ground-attack types (Schlacht Geschwader 4) Pickert, III Flak Corps.

US First Army Hodges, six Inf divs, 82nd Airborne, three armd divs.*

US Third Army Patton, six Inf divs, 101st Airborne, two armd divs.*

British XXX Corps Horrocks, 6th Airborne Div, two inf divs, three armd bdes.

*Together rising to 29 divs.

18. Retreat through Poland, 1945

When the Red Army returns to the offensive in eastern Poland, striking west across the Vistula to threaten Berlin, 1st Ukranian Front at Baranov crushes German infantry in Fourth Pz-Army's first line of defence. XXIV Pz corps (Nehring), a mobile reserve comprising two panzer divisions (16th, 17th) and a panzer grenadier division (20th), also a Tiger Bn (424), is deployed to attack the flank of any penetration west of the river, but is instead engulfed in fighting around Kielce and forced to retreat.

Nehring (Fourth Pz-Army) 12 January 1945 fights north-west to Petrikau, seeking contact with Panzer Corps Gross Deutschland (von Saucken).

Von Saucken, Pz Corps Gross Deutschland comprises the powerful Hermann Goering (Fallschirm) Panzer Division (HG1) and the new Panzer Grenadier Division Brandenburg (BR), both diverted from East Prussia for the relief attempt. The move is contrary to Guderian's advice to Hitler and to the detriment of the defence there.

Nehring and von Saucken retain their mobility only with the help of air transports operating from the area north-west of Breslau. Neither Pz Corps will survive without container supplies of fuel and ammunition. *See* Part 4, New Horizons in Transport, page 137.

Two other panzer divisions (19th, 25th) and a 10th Pz-Grenadier battle group deployed in reserve west of Warsaw, none more capable than a regimental Kampfgruppe, face equally devastating Red Army attacks.

These panzer divisions: 16th, 17th, 19th, 25th and the Pz-Gr battle groups deployed in reserve behind infantry of

Army Group 'A' are all that can be spared of a burned-out panzer force to oppose the Red Army's direct drive on Berlin (163 divisions, 6,500 tanks and assault guns). Powerless to restore the situation, the depleted formations withdraw fighting to the west.

Army Group 'A' Harpe; 26 inf divs, four Pz divs, two Pz Gr divs includes Kampfgruppe 10th PzGr.

East Front excl. Courland, 145 Inf divs, eighteen Pz divs, ten Pz Gr divs.

6th Air Fleet Greim, 1,060 aircraft all types (300 ground-attack) rising to 1,500 aircraft (450 ground-attack).

Red Army/Air Force Zhukov 1st BeloRuss Fr, Konev 1st UKR Fr; ten armies (two tank), 163 rifle divs.

Russian superiority(:) 6,500 tanks and SP guns (5:1), 4,772 aircraft (17:1).

19. Last cauldron: Army and SS in Hungary, 1945

Following an unsuccessful conclusion to 'Autumn Mist' (map 17) Sixth SS Panzer Army (Dietrich) is switched across Europe to reinforce Army Group South (Wöhler) defending western Hungary. There on 26 December 1944 Budapest, the capital city of 800,000 inhabitants housing numerous military agencies and defended by upwards of 70,000 men including 13th Pz Division and Feldhermhalle responsible to SS General Pfeffer von Wildenbruck (IX SS Mtn Corps), is encircled by two Ukrainian fronts.

Balck, Gille ❶ (Sixth SS Pz-Army) 13 February 1945. Operation 'Konrad' is the first of three attempts by Armeegruppe Balck (Sixth Army) to relieve Budapest. Starting on 1 January with IV SS Panzer Corps (Gille) transferred with Totenkopf and Wiking from Ninth Army/Army Group Centre, 'Konrad' is a failure; despite heavy fighting by SS Wiking to within fifteen miles of the perimeter. Budapest remains besieged. 'Konrad 2' a second

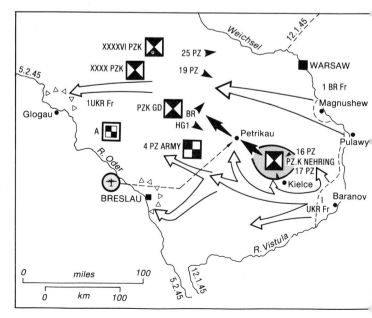

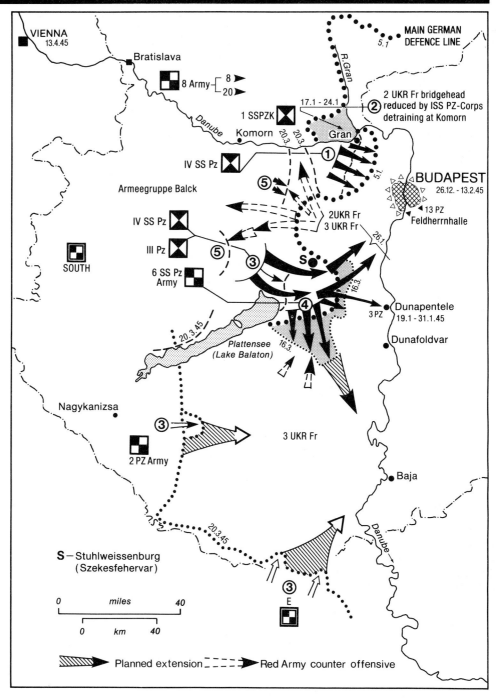

VIENNA
13.4.45

Bratislava

8 Army ⌈ 8 ▶
        ⌊ 20 ▶

MAIN GERMAN
DEFENCE LINE
5.1

R.Gran

Danube

1 SSPZK

Komorn   20.3   20.3

17.1 - 24.1   ②

2 UKR Fr bridgehead
reduced by ISS PZ-Corps
detraining at Komorn

Gran   ①

IV SS Pz

Armeegruppe Balck

⑤

5.1

BUDAPEST
26.12. - 13.2.45

◀ 13 PZ
Feldherrnhalle

IV SS Pz

III Pz   ⑤

2UKR Fr
3 UKR Fr

⑤

SOUTH

6 SS Pz
Army

③

S   26.1.

16.3.   ④

Dunapentele
19.1 - 31.1.45

3 PZ

20.3.45

Plattensee
(Lake Balaton)

16.3.

Dunafoldvar

Nagykanizsa

③

2 PZ Army

3 UKR Fr

Baja

20.3.45

Danube

S — Stuhlweissenburg
(Szekesfehervar)

③

E

0   miles   40

0   km   40

▨▨▶ Planned extension - - - -▶ Red Army counter offensive

---

attempt by III PzK (Breith) 9–12 January fares no better.
Priess ❷ Panzer battles next develop east of Komorn
where an unexpectedly powerful Operation 'South Wind'
lead by I SS Pz Corps – LSSAH and 12 SS HJ – reduces
2nd UKR Front's bridgehead on the River Gran. Pz Corps
Feldhermhalle with remnants of units isolated in Budapest
provides mainly infantry support.
Balck, Gille, Breith ❸ Meanwhile Sixth Army's third relief
attempt 'Konrad 3' follows on 18 January 1945, from a new
direction. But the reinforced SS Panzer Corps (Gille)

attacking south around Stuhlweissenburg with 1st and 3rd
Panzer Divisions, SS Totenkopf and SS Wiking while flank
protection to the north is provided by Breith's III Panzer
Corps – 6th and 23rd Panzer Divisions and south by Pz
Recce Bns 1st, 3rd, 23rd again fails to relieve the city. A
break-out attempt by the defenders on 11 February is
equally unsuccessful; Budapest surrenders on 13 February
1945. Hitler's arbitrary diversion of panzer divisions to this
secondary front is nevertheless set to continue.
Dietrich, Balck, de Angelis ❹ Sixth SS Pz-Army 6 March

1945 opens a new offensive 'Spring Awakening' in which Sixth Army (Balck), Second Panzer Army (de Angelis) – four infantry divisions and a weak 16th Reichsführer SS Panzer Grenadier Division (Baum) – are also involved in Hitler's plan to encircle the Red Army west of the Danube, recapture Budapest and retain oil-production centres at Nagykaniscza south-west of Lake Balaton. But 'Spring Awakening' falters in waterlogged terrain and when counter-attacked in strength by 3rd UKr Front fails to recover momentum. ❺ A renewal of Russian attacks aiming at Vienna and the Danube valley threatening German communications precipitates a general retreat; by 20 March, panzer rearguards are fighting desperately to defend positions west of their original start-line.

6th Armeegruppe Balck; Sixth Army, Hung Third Army, Gille, IV SS Pz Corps; Breith III Pz-Corps, Harteneck I Cav Corps, SS Wiking, SS Totenkopf, Pz Divs 1st, 3rd, 6th, 23rd,

three cav divs, Hungarian tanks, infantry, Army troops. After 14 January, 503, 509 Tiger Bns. By 20 January, 274 Pz Kpfw IV–VIs, Jag Pz and SPs. By 6 March, 138 mixed tanks. **Eighth Army** Kreysing (north of Danube) 8th, 20th Pz Divs, remnant battle groups Feldherrnhalle, 13th Pz.
Sixth SS Pz-Army Dietrich; Priess I SS Pz Corps, Bittrich II SS Pz Corps, SS Pz-Divs 1st, 2nd, 9th, 12th. Reinforced 6 March, 23rd Pz and two cav divs. By 6 March, 540 tanks and SP guns (320 battle-fit).
Second Pz-Army de Angelis; Lanz XXII Mtn Corps, Konrad LXVIII Corps, 16th SS PzGren Div, four Inf divs (two Mtn).
4th Air Fleet Dessloch; Deichmann, I Air Corps, by 6 March 850 aircraft.
Red Army/Air Force 1 January 1945, Malinovsky 2nd UKr Front; Tolbuchin 3rd UK Front; 54 Inf divs; five mech corps; three armd corps, two cav corps. By 6 March, 407 tanks, 965 aircraft.

20. Germany in defeat, 1945

Armageddon 1945. Panzer divisions starved of petrol at times to the point of immobility, with few if any towing machines, lacking in ammunition and air support, record local successes against overwhelming odds. All are swept into defeat. The Red Army advancing in overwhelming strength in the east employs tank and motorized forces patterned on the German model and much of its transport supplied by Western Allies. Equally powerful US and British armies close in from the West.

East: First and Fourth Pz-Armies 12 January 1945, face the eastern threat to Berlin, but with only four panzer divisions between them to support an infantry defence of the Vistula and Carpathians south of Warsaw (map 18) collapse under massive attacks. Second Pz-Army March 1945 deployed south of Budapest with no armour at all also gives way under Russian pressure. Third Pz Army 8 February 1945 after failing to protect Königsberg and East Prussia, withdraws to Pomerania and the Oder north of Berlin under command of Army Group Vistula; Sixth SS Pz-Army 6 March 1945, the best-equipped formation, defeated in western Hungary (map 19) withdraws to Vienna. The city falls on 13 April.

North-east: Army Group Courland possesses only two panzer divisions in its order of battle.

South-west: Only a single panzer division opposing Anglo-US armies is left in northern Italy.

West: Fifth Pz-Army, Europe 16 December 1944 follows an abortive joint offensive Fifth/Sixth SS Pz-Army in the Ardennes (map 17), with encirclement and surrender in the Ruhr. Reduced to forty tanks, Fifty Panzer Army capitulates on 18 April.

Berlin is encircled by the Red Army on 25 April 1945 (*see* Third Panzer Army, 16 April). Hitler takes his own life on the 30th. Keitel signs the Wehrmacht's capitulation to the Russians in Berlin on 9 May 1945.

With the last of the panzer divisions contained in East Prussia surrendering to 2nd BR Front on 14 May, the remnant of a once omnipotent panzer force count for little more than flags on Red Army and Allied Intelligence maps. Dispersed far and wide, surviving units serve mostly in the east with Army Groups Centre and South.

Berlin LVI Pz K Weidling; 18th, 20th, 11th SS PzGrDivs. Pz Division Muncheberg.
A Gr Centre Schörner; First PzA Nehring, Fourth PzA Gräser: 6th, 8th, 16th, 17th, 19th, 20th, 21st, HG1, FBD, 2nd SS, 10th SS PzDivs; Brandenburg; 10th PzGrDiv.
A Gr South Rendulic; Second PzA de Angelis, Sixth SS PzA Dietrich: 1st, 3rd, 23rd, 25th, FGD PzDivs; 1st, 3rd, 5th, 9th, 12th SS PzDivs, Feldherrnhalle.
A Gr Vistula Student; Third PzA Raus: 4th SS, 25th PzGr Div.
East Prussia Von Saucken, formerly German Second Army: 4th, 5th, 7th PzDivs: Gross Deutschland.
North-east. A Gr Courland Hilpert, formerly A Gr North: 12th, 14th PzDivs.
West: A Grs 'B', 'G'. 'B', Model: Fifth PzA Harpe, 9th Pz Div, Fifteenth Army; PzLehr, 116th Pz. Seventh Army; 2nd, 11th Pz. 'G', Schulz: First Army, 17th SS.
South west: A Gr 'C' Vietinghoff, Tenth Army; 26th PzDiv. 29th, 90th PzGrDivs.

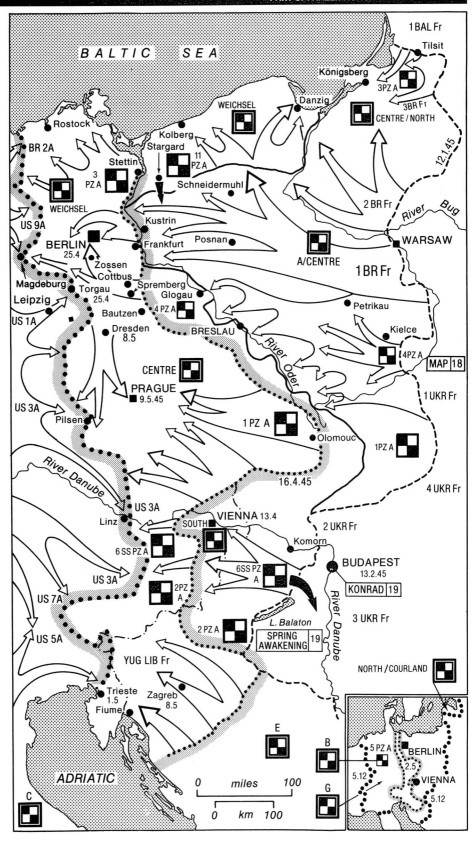

BALTIC SEA

1 BAL Fr

Tilsit

Königsberg

3PZ A

3BR Fr

CENTRE / NORTH

Rostock

WEICHSEL

Danzig

BR 2A

Kolberg
Stargard

WEICHSEL

Stettin

3
PZ A

11
PZ A

Schneidermuhl

2 BR Fr

River Bug

12.1.45

US 9A

Kustrin

Posnan

A/CENTRE

WARSAW

BERLIN
25.4

Frankfurt

1 BR Fr

Zossen
Cottbus

Spremberg
Glogau

Petrikau

Magdeburg
Leipzig

Torgau
25.4

4 PZ A

BRESLAU

Kielce

US 1A

Bautzen

Dresden
8.5

River Oder

4PZ A

MAP 18

US 3A

CENTRE

PRAGUE
9.5.45

1 PZ A

1 UKR Fr

Pilsen

Olomouc

1PZ A

16.4.45

4 UKR Fr

River Danube

US 3A

VIENNA 13.4

2 UKR Fr

Linz

SOUTH

Komorn

6 SS PZ A

6SS PZ
A

BUDAPEST
13.2.45

KONRAD 19

US 3A

2PZ
A

3 UKR Fr

US 7A

2 PZ A

L. Balaton

River Danube

SPRING
AWAKENING 19

US 5A

YUG LIB Fr

NORTH / COURLAND

Trieste
1.5

Zagreb
8.5

Fiume

E

B

5 PZ A

BERLIN
2.5

ADRIATIC

C

0   miles   100

0   km   100

G

5.12

VIENNA

5.12

Part 6. Campaigns and battles, 1939-45

1. First Panzer Army (PzAOK 1)

Originally XXII motorized Infantry Corps, raised near Hamburg in August 1939. Corps Commander General der Kavallerie Ewald von Kleist (Generaloberst 19 July 1940).
Poland, 1939 (map 2) 1–16 September. Spearheading Fourteenth Army (List), concentrated in eastern Czechoslovakia for Operation 'White', von Kleist developed panzer operations on the outer wing of Army Group South. The Corps consisted basically of 2nd Panzer Division (Veiel) and 4th Light Division (Hubicki). On 17 September von Kleist Corps thrusting north-east through Poland to the Bug via Tarnow completed a double encirclement of the Polish Army by joining up with Guderian at Vlodava east of Warsaw (*see* Second Panzer Army, 17 September 1939). 5 March 1940 redesignated Panzer Group von Kleist.
France: Operation 'Yellow', 1940 (map 3). On 10 May at the start of the operation Panzer Group von Kleist, consisting of three motorized corps, XIX, XXXI and XIV, was concentrated east of Luxemburg on the German side of the Ardennes. Initially responsible to Army Group 'A' (von Runstedt), von Kleist's Group would lead the main armoured movement against the Allies, subsequently answering to German Tenth Army (List) and ultimately Fourth Army (von Kluge). Allotted five of the ten panzer divisions committed to the western offensive, von Kleist's leading panzer corps, XIX (Guderian) and XXXXI (Reinhardt), followed by XIV Motorized Corps (von Wietersheim), pushed west through the Ardennes forest towards the Meuse. Brushing aside a weak cavalry screen, von Kleist confronted 1st French Army Group (Billotte) with two of its four armies, Ninth (Corap) and Second (Huntziger), deployed on the west bank of the river north and south of Sedan.
France: Panzer Corridor, 1940 (map 4). On the afternoon of 13 May, von Kleist stormed the Meuse supported by II Air Corps (Lörzer) and Stuka Wings of VIII Air Corps (von Richthofen), the latter having been diverted from Hoepner's decoy offensive under Army Group 'B' at Maastricht (Fourth Panzer Army, 10 May). Overcoming mainly weak infantry opposition, von Kleist built west bank bridgeheads at Sedan (Guderian) and Monthermé (Reinhardt). Guderian was immediately successful (Second Panzer Army, 13 May), but Reinhardt was delayed by spirited opposition and was not ready to move west until the 15th. Starting on that date, von Kleist's Group lead

Twelfth Army thrusts to the Channel via St-Quentin and Péronne. Secondary action by Hoth's XV Corps (mot) crossing the Meuse downstream at Dinant and driving in the direction of Arras secured the right flank and reinforced the offensive. In concerted panzer operations, joined by Hoepner on the 19th (*see* Fourth Panzer Army), von Kleist and Hoth Groups thrust west to the Channel coast and created a panzer 'corridor', splitting the Allied front and forcing French armies apart. The British Expeditionary Force was pinned to the coast at Dunkirk (*see also* Second and Third Panzer Armies, 13 May). On 23 May, with von Kleist and Hoth sharing all the panzer divisions between them, and subordinate to Fourth Army (von Kluge), Army Group 'B' prepared for a final offensive. Events turned out differently. On 24 May, in accordance with Hitler's instructions, panzer operations were halted outside Dunkirk. At Goering's prompting the Luftwaffe was left to complete the work of destruction, but failed and allowed the BEF to escape to England in Operation 'Dynamo', ending 4 June.
France: Operation 'Red', 1940. In the 'Red' phase of the Battle for France (map 3), with the panzer force redeployed in three attacking groups facing south along the Somme and Aisne, von Kleist at Amiens, co-operating with XVI Corps (Hoepner) at Péronne, was given the central role leading Sixth Army – Army Group 'B' (von Bock) in the drive to envelop Paris from the west. Lined up with Hoth (Fourth Army) on the Seine to the west at Abbeville, and Guderian (Twelfth Army) – Army Group 'A' (von Runstedt) on the Aisne to the east at Rethel, the Group prepared for action. On 5 June von Kleist's corps, consisting basically of XIV Panzer Corps with two panzer and one SS motorized division, attacked south-west from Amiens with the intention of bypassing Paris to the west and, in conjunction with Guderian, encircling Paris Army and French forces concentrated about the capital. Supportive action devolved upon XVI Panzer Corps attacking south at Péronne, but determined opposition by French 3rd Army Group brought Sixth Army's offensive to a halt. Instead, on the 9th, OKH switched von Kleist eastwards to join Ninth Army close by Guderian serving Army Group 'A' (von Rundstedt).
[*Hoth, meanwhile, working south across the Seine from Abbeville, bypassed Paris to the west before sweeping into Normandy and Brittany.*]

Arriving in south-east Europe for action against the Greek Army [*von Kleist's redeployment followed the arrival of a British Expeditionary Force at Volos and Piraeus on the 7th*], von Kleist's Group with two panzer corps was concentrated in Bulgaria north of Sofia. But in a change of plan following anti-German moves in Belgrade, von Kleist was committed instead against Yugoslavia. On 8 April, two days after the start of Operation '25' (von Weichs), with XXXXVI Panzer Corps (von Vietinghoff) pushing towards Zagreb (14th Panzer Division), von Kleist lead the offensive against Belgrade, entering Nish on the 9th and Belgrade (11th Panzer Division, Crüwell) on the 12th – making contact there with XXXXI Panzer Corps (Reinhardt) from the north-east. Thereafter, subordinate to Second Army less 5th Panzer Division, transferred to Stumme, von Kleist's group linked up with 16th Motorized Division (Henrici) following the capture of Sarajevo (15 April). The panzer group was then allotted to Army Group South (von Runstedt) for the invasion of Russia, a hazardous undertaking in which von Kleist's task was to lead the attacking forces in the direction of Kiev.

Russia: Operation 'Barbarossa', South 1941 (map 7). On 22 June, consisting initially of three panzer corps von Kleist's Group, with a total of eight divisions and the motorized SS Leibstandarte Brigade (Dietrich), overcame determined opposition, breaking the Stalin line (16th Panzer Division) and taking Zhitomir on 19 July (19th Panzer Division) and encircling Russian Sixth, Twelfth and Eighteenth Armies at Uman, before crossing the Dnieper at Kremenchug on 11–12 September. The Kremenchug crossing was followed within days by the most rewarding of all 'Barbarossa' encirclement battles. On 14 September 1941, von Kleist's XLVIII Panzer Corps (Kempf), acting in conjunction with Guderian's arrival east of Kiev, pushed 16th Panzer Division (Hube) northwards to meet 3rd Panzer Division (Model) and co-operate in Hitler's plan to envelope five Russian armies (*see* Second Panzer Army, 14 September). Von Kleist followed this move by capturing Stalino (1st Mountain Division, XIV Panzer Corps) and subsequently Taganrog on the Sea of Azov. Thereafter proceeding to the Mius, von Kleist won a bridgehead on the 20th. On 25 October 1941, up-graded and renamed First Panzer Army, von Kleist pressed on to Rostov; III Panzer Corps (von Mackensen) reached the town on 20 November. But weakened by the absence of XXXXVIII Panzer Corps (9th Panzer Division and two motorized infantry divisions), transferred to Guderian for 'Typhoon' (*see* Second Panzer Army, 30 September 1941), von Kleist was unable to retain Rostov and its vital Don crossings won by the Leibstandarte. Therefore, losing Rostov to the Red Army, von Kleist retired behind the Mius for the winter. On 17 May 1942, preceding von Kleist's commitment to a summer offensive leading Army Group 'A' into the Caucasus, two preparatory undertakings yielded profitable results. 'Fridericus I' centred on III Panzer Corps (von Mackensen) – two panzer, one motorized and eight supporting infantry divisions – routing two Russian armies south-east of Kharkov, recapturing Issyum and claiming 214,000 prisoners. 'Fridericus II', taking more prisoners winning Kupjansk, gained a bridgehead on a tributary of the Donets, crucial to the forthcoming summer offensive – Operation 'Blue' (*see* Fourth Panzer Army, 28 June).

Above: Field Marshal Ewald von Kleist served with distinction in Poland, France and Russia. He was GOC, Army Group South, Ukraine, in March 1943 and died a prisoner in Russia in 1956.

On 11 June in a revised plan of operations von Kleist bypassed Paris to the east after crossing the Marne south of Laon. Incorporating XVI Panzer Corps (Hoepner) Kleistgruppe negotiated Château-Thierry to reach Troyes on 14 June – the day on which 87th Infantry division (German Eighteenth Army) entered Paris. Général Wegand, the French C-in-C, authorized an armistice on 22 June and Hitler followed the army into Paris on the 23rd. Von Kleist reached Angoulême on the 25th – the day on which the armistice became effective. At the conclusion of the battle, the French Government accepted the partitioning of France into occupied (German) and unoccupied (Vichy Government) zones, broadly north and south of Lyon, with an Atlantic coast extension to the Spanish frontier. Lyon itself remained unoccupied until Operation 'Anton' brought II SS Panzer Corps into action (*see* Fifth Panzer Army Africa, 11 November 1942).

Diversion in the Balkans, March 1941 (map 6).

Russia: Operation 'Blue', 1942 (map 10) renamed
'Brunswick' on 30 July 1942 (map 10). Operation 'Blue'
and its successor 'Mouse' would take von Kleist (from July
1942 to 1 January 1943) from the area south-east of
Kharkov to the foothills of the eastern Caucasus. Advancing
from Rostov to the Terek in the final stage of the offensive,
First Panzer Army extended its communications by more
than 400 miles. In the battle for Rostov on 23–25 July, III
Panzer Corps (von Mackensen), co-operating with LVII
Panzer Corps (Kirchner) – Seventeenth Army made heavy
demands on 13th, 14th, 22nd Panzer and SS Wiking
Divisions. On 26 July, First Panzer Army/4th Air Fleet (von
Richthofen) forced the River Don east of Rostov. The operation was lead by III and LVII Panzer Corps with three panzer
and two motorized divisions assisted by four infantry and a
Slovak (Schnelle) division. On 2 August von Kleist was reinforced by XXXX Panzer Corps (Geyr) making good the loss
of LVII Panzer Corps transferred to Seventeenth Army. The
Panzer Group then bypassed Armavir on 6 August, pushing
south-east to Maikop (13th Panzer Division) reached three
days later. Mozdok (3rd Panzer Division) fell on the 25th
and Malgobek (SS Wiking Division) north-west of Grosny
on 5 October, but supply shortages halting movement for
weeks at a time, relentless opposition by the Red Army and
the onset of winter forced von Kleist on to the defensive.
Starting on 25 October von Kleist renewed the offensive
with immediate success at Nalchik and by 2 November had
pushed III Panzer Corps (von Mackensen) to the outskirts of
Ordzhonikidze – furthermost point in First Panzer Army's
drive to the Caucasus (map 11). But armour attacks lead
by 13th Panzer Division (Herr) failed to capture the town,
a key road and rail junction at the head of the Georgian
Military Highway, giving access to oil-producing regions in
the south, and Ordzhonikidze remained firmly in Russian
hands. Despite intensive action by 13th, 23rd Panzer and
SS Wiking Divisions in the vanguard of the offensive, von
Kleist's bid to capture Russian oil-producing centres at
Baku, Grosny and Tiflis came to a standstill.

Meanwhile, Hitler had dismissed Field Marshal List, C-
in-C, Army Group 'A', on grounds of incompetence, and
decided to direct operations in the Caucasus himself, from
Führer HQ, Rastenburg. But after fourteen days as GOC
Army Group 'A', Hitler nominated von Kleist as his
successor. Consequently, on 22 November command of First
Panzer Army passed to General von Mackensen, but the
panzer army's future was soon to be compromised by the
loss of major ground and air formations diverted to assist
'Winter Storm' operations at Stalingrad (map 12). (See
Fourth Panzer Army, 12 December 1942.)

Starting on 1 January 1943, First Panzer Army,
abandoning the Terek for Rostov, began a fighting
withdrawal to the north-east, firm contact being established
with Fourth Panzer Army on the 20th. Armavir was
evacuated on the 25th. On 27 January after releasing 13th
Panzer Division to reinforce Seventeenth Army defending
the Kuban bridgehead, von Mackensen was taken under
command of Army Group Don (Field Marshal von Manstein);
the panzer army's remaining four divisions continuing north
through Rostov or immediately west across the frozen Sea
of Azov under pressure from North Caucasus Front.

By 4 February First Panzer Army was safely behind the
Don, regrouping in the Don-Donetz triangle. [On 14

February Rostov, defended by LVII Panzer Corps (Fourth
Panzer Army) was evacuated and von Manstein's Army
Group Don was renamed Army Group South.]

Von Manstein's Miracle (map 13). By 22 February,
First Panzer Army was regrouped north of Stalino, co-
ordinating operations with Fourth Panzer Army in a battle
to recover Kharkov. In a series of deftly contrived
manoeuvres the Panzer Army first intercepted and then
struck back at Popov's armoured group leading South West
Front, exploiting Russian success westwards after the
victorious siege of Stalingrad; battles in which SS Viking,
7th and 11th Panzer Divisions (XXXX Panzer Corps),
outflanking Popov, forced a Russian retreat to the Donets.
On 28 February von Mackensen reached the Donets south
of Issyum, sealing the fate of Popov's armoured group and
destroying South West Front units still south of the river and
mostly unable to re-cross to safety.

During the spring and early summer of 1943,
Generaloberst von Mackensen and First Panzer Army played
no direct part in von Manstein's Operation 'Citadel', the
battle for Kursk, unfolding on the army's left flank in the
summer of 1943 (see Fourth Panzer Army, 5 July 1943).
But from August to December 1943, the collapse of
'Citadel', followed by thrusting Russian exploitation westwards greatly endangered First Panzer Army, obliging von
Mackensen to retire from the Donets. On 15 September he
retreated to the Dnieper, defending Zaporoshe, Dniepropetrovsk and Nikopol, the manganese-producing centre,
south of the city. Together with German Sixth Army (reconstituted) and Seventeenth Army, First Panzer Army held
an east bank Zaporoshe bridgehead with XXXX Panzer
Corps (Henrici), protecting essential electrical power installations. Von Manstein's deployment on the Dnieper blocked
a Red Army approach to the Crimea from the Ukraine. On
14 October 1943 von Mackensen evacuated Zaporoshe, a
move following months of heavy defensive fighting with only
two panzer divisions, 17th and 23rd, on a strength of
twenty-one formations. From mid-October until 20 November First Panzer Army struggled to contain Malinovsky's 3rd
Ukrainian Front striking south across the Dnieper between
Nikopol and Krivoi Rog. The front made deep inroads into
the defence, forcing costly action upon the panzer army –
now under command of General Hube (appointed 29
October). Bloody November battles defending Nikopol and
Krivoi Rog in conjunction with Sixth Army sapped the power
of 9th, 13th, 17th, 23rd SS Totenkopf and Gross
Deutschland Divisions.

On 29 December 1943, GOC, Army Group South (von
Manstein) switched First Panzer Army northwards from the
lower Dnieper bend to partner Fourth Panzer Army, creating
a strong defensive block north (Fourth Panzer Army) and
south (First Panzer Army) of Kiev. Reading Red Army
intentions in this area, the Field Marshal anticipated thrusts
breaking south-west across the Dnieper into the rear of the
Army Group. [*Meanwhile at Nikopol* (map 15) where the
defence of the city and its manganese installations had been
entrusted to Army Group Schörner, 24th Panzer Division
(Edelsheim) returning from an abortive journey northwards
to lead a XXXXVII Panzer Corps attempt to relieve
Cherkassy, arrived too late to save the situation and Nikopol
was lost. **At Kirovograd** on First Army's right flank in
January 1944 (map 15), where 2nd Ukrainian Front (Konev)

advancing west of the Dnieper after breaching the river north of Krivoi Rog had trapped part of Eighth Army's XXXXVII Panzer Corps (Vormann) – 3rd and 14th Panzer Divisions, 10th Panzer Grenadier Division and 376th Infantry Division – 3rd Panzer Division (Bayerlein) defied Hitler's stand-fast order by breaking out of encirclement and linking up with 11th Panzer Division, Gross Deutschland and SS Totenkopf to mount a successful relief action from the south-west.] The Russian offensive west of the Dnieper nevertheless gained ground, enveloping more of Army Group South.

Russia: The Relief of Cherkassy, North Ukraine

(map 15). On 17 February 1944 Hube overcame opposition by 1st Ukrainian Front (Vatutin) and, with a reinforced III Panzer Corps (Breith), succeeded in driving a relief corridor eastwards through Russian forces investing Cherkassy to reach Lissjanska enabling 54,000 men of XI Army Corps (Stemmerman) and XXXXII Army Corps (Lieb) – Eighth Army – to escape encirclement; 1st and 2nd Ukrainian Fronts having trapped the hapless corps at the junction with Eighth Army (Wöhler) since 28 January when their converging thrusts united 30 miles south-west of Cherkassy at Swenigorodka. But a greater shock was in store for Hube than seeing ten flanking divisions encircled. On 4 March 1944, an unexpected Russian spring offensive split First and Fourth Panzer Armies, forcing Hube into giving ground to Ukrainian Fronts under Zhukov and Konev. These Red Army Groups, in powerful westward drives, forced a wedge between Hube and Raus (Fourth Panzer Army) encircling Hube's divisions between the Dnieper and the Bug, cutting them off from all landward communication with Army Group South. Subsequent operations introduced a new dimension into armoured warfare.

Russia: A moving panzer pocket, North Ukraine

(map 15). Hube's panzer army of 300,000 men, including elements of Fourth Panzer Army, mainly Leibstandarte Adolf Hitler and 7th Panzer Division, 22 divisions in total, eight panzer – 1st, 6th, 7th, 11th, 16th, 17th, 19th, Leibstandarte – Kampfgruppe SS Reich and 20th Panzer Grenadier Division, but none with more than eleven tanks (16th Panzer Division) became totally enveloped for fourteen days while continuing to fight north-westwards supplied by air transport groups under Major-General Morzik. (Transport action in support of the panzer force is elaborated in Part 4, page 141.) On 24 March, Hube (air-lifted out of Stalingrad before the surrender in 1942 and a key figure in early battles for Sicily and Calabria) organized his much weakened divisions into three separate corps groups two of which, Chevallerie and Breith incorporating III Panzer Corps (Breith), XXIV Panzer Corps (Nehring) and XXXXVI Panzer Corps (Schultz), divided the panzer divisions between them. Expected by the Red Army to turn south the Panzer Army, sustained by air-transported and local supplies, instead moved north-west on von Manstein's orders, fighting off all attempts by Zhukov to destroy the encircled divisions. On 8 April 1944, First Panzer Army made contact with II SS Panzer Corps (Bittrich), a relief force sent from the west via Lodz with SS Panzer Divisions Frundsberg, Hohenstaufen and a Jaeger division in support. All eventually reached the security of the main battle line in eastern Galicia (Army Group North Ukraine).

On 20 April 1944, Hube was promoted Generaloberst for

his success in extricating First Panzer Army, but a flying accident immediately afterwards brought about his death, robbing the panzer force of a most able commander – one of the few in whom Hitler evinced much confidence. From the time of the Army's escape from encirclement in the North Ukraine in April 1944 until its surrender on 8 May 1945, defensive operations continued in southern Poland protecting the region west of Tarnopol against encroaching 1st and 4th Ukrainian Fronts. The Panzer Army's run-down order of battle in July 1944 included 1st and 8th Panzer Divisions and 20th Panzer Grenadier Division. Deployed on the southern wing of Army Group Centre (First Panzer Army, Seventeenth Army, Fourth Panzer Army, Ninth Army), First Panzer Army served new commanders: General Raus (22 April 1944), Generaloberst Heinrici (16 August 1944) and finally General Nehring (21 March 1945).

In Roumania during the summer of 1944, Russian progress south of the Carpathians against First Panzer Army's right-flanking neighbour, Army Group South Ukraine (Friessner), threatened catastrophe when German Sixth Army (Fretter-Pico) was encircled by 2nd and 3rd Ukrainian Fronts striking from Jassy and Kishinev (Tiraspol) and uniting on 29 August at Husi.

[The destruction of Sixth Army at Husi in August 1944, from which GOC Fretter-Pico, command staff, 13th Panzer Division, 10th Panzer Grenadier Division and elements of Eighth Army escaped, opened the way for 2nd Ukrainian Front (Malinovsky) to strike via Ploesti into western Roumania north of the Danube, penetrating Hungary in the direction of Debrecen and threatening to turn First Panzer Army's southern flank. Panzer intervention by Sixth Army (Fretter-Pico) at Nyireghyaza in October 1944, involving panzer divisions in running battles with Russian armour, deferred the impending collapse of Army Group South Ukraine. Starting on 2 October at Grosswardein 40 miles south of Debrecen and culminating 25 miles to the north at Nyireghyaza, LVII Panzer Corps (Kirchner) and then III Panzer Corps (Breith) struck back at 6th Guards Tank Army spearheads, cutting them off from rearward support and destroying the substance of three mechanized corps. By 29 October the efforts of three under-strength panzer divisions (20–30 tanks each), 1st (Thunert), 13th (Schmidhuber) and 23rd (von Radowitz) allotted to Breith (III Panzer Corps) for action against 6th Guards Tank Army rear communications at Nagy-Kallo (22 October 1944) – supported by Feldherrnhalle (Pape) – while 24th Panzer Division (von Nostitz-Wallwitz) and 4th SS Polizei Division (Schmedes) assisted with diversionary attacks elsewhere, successfully concluded three weeks of mobile operations, removing the threat of envelopment from Army Group South Ukraine (re-named South 24 September 1944) and relieving First Panzer Army of much anxiety.] Army Group South meanwhile claimed 632 Russian tanks and assault guns destroyed and a similar number of anti-tank guns destroyed or captured.

Germany in defeat

(map 20) October 1944–April 1945. After a period of respite from major operations, with only 8th Panzer Division serving briefly in reserve during October, First Panzer Army was bypassed on both flanks by Soviet Fronts – North, thrusting to Berlin across the Weichsel on 12 January 1945, and South along the Danube to Budapest (13 February 1945) and Vienna (13 April 1945) – leaving the Army exposed and semi-isolated at the eastern end of a defensive Carpathian wedge. When threatened front and rear by Russian and US Armies converging on Czechoslovakia, First Panzer Army (Nehring), lying east of Olomouc, withdrew into Moravia taking up positions east of Prague. By 5 May a renewal of panzer strength – 6th, 8th, 19th Panzer Divisions and two panzer grenadier divisions (Feldhernhalle, Brandenburg), none more powerful than a regimental battle group was intended as the eastern shield for an Alpine redoubt. Hopes were short-lived. On 6 May concentric Ukrainian Front operations leading to the capture of Prague brought about the collapse of Army Group Schörner. On 9 May 1945, First Panzer Army joined the general surrender.

Career note. After being relieved of his command (Army Group 'A') in March 1944, at the same time that Field Marshal von Manstein was dismissed as GOC, Army Group South, von Kleist surrendered to the Americans in 1945 who handed him over to the Yugoslavs in 1946. They delivered von Kleist into Russian hands in 1948. He died at Vladimirovk in October 1954 during imprisonment in Russia.

Other commanders of First Panzer Army: von Mackensen died on 19 April 1969, Raus at Bad Gastein in 1956, Heinrici on 13 December 1971, Nehring lives in West Germany.

2. Second Panzer Army (PzAOK 2)

Originally XIX Motorized Infantry Corps, raised near Vienna in July 1939, controlling 2nd Panzer Division and 4th Light Division. Corps Commander General Heinz Guderian (Generaloberst 19 July 1940).

Poland, 1939 (map 2). At the start of Operation 'White' on 1 September Guderian's corps, comprising 3rd Panzer Division (Geyr von Schweppenburg) and two motorized divisions, concentrated in Pomerania, spearheaded German Fourth Army (von Kluge) – Army Group North. The Corps faced Pomorze Army deployed in defence of the Danzig corridor. On 5 September pushing east to Graudenz with Geyr von Schweppenburg's 3rd Panzer Division in the lead, Guderian cut the Danzig corridor, encircling and destroying the greater part of Pomorze Army. Guderian's troops included panzer and reconnaissance demonstration (Lehr) battalions from army training schools. On 7 September OKH switched XIX Panzer Corps to the outer wing of the Army Group offensive, instructing Guderian, directly under Army Group control and reinforced by 10th Panzer Division (Stumpff), to push south behind Warsaw in a bid to frustrate possible Polish plans for a withdrawal east of the city. Brest-Litovsk was reached on 15 September. Two days' journey to the south on 17 September, 3rd Panzer Division (Geyr von Schweppenburg), leading the Corps into Vlodava, joined up with von Kleist pushing north from eastern Czechoslovakia. This manoeuvre completed the outer ring of a double encirclement of the Polish Army, bring mobile operations to a successful conclusion.

France: Operation 'Yellow', 1940 (map 3). By 10 May Guderian's XIX Motorized Corps was concentrated east of Luxemburg (Bitburg) on the German side of the Ardennes, in readiness for the battle for France. The Corps was subordinate to von Kleist spearheading the German offensive in the west. (*See* First Panzer Army, 10 May 1940.)

France: Panzer Corridor, 1940 (map 4). On 13 May, deploying three of von Kleist's five panzer divisions, 1st (Kirchner), 2nd (Veiel) and 10th (Schaal), Guderian lead Army Group 'A' across the Meuse at Sedan. Reinforcing 1st Panzer Division (Kirchner) with Infantry Regiment Gross Deutschland (Graf von Schwerin) and heavily supported by corps artillery and air attacks (see Part 2, page 113), Guderian shattered the front of French Second Army

(Huntziger), securing a 12-mile deep bridgehead preparatory to pushing west – and disputing with von Kleist over restraining orders received on the evening of the 15th, again on the 17th and finally on the 24th. By 15 May all three of Guderian's panzer divisions were across the Meuse ready to push west. For a short time 10th Panzer Division served behind as left flank guard at Stonne. On 16–17 May at Montcornet Guderian brushed aside an armoured counter-attack by 4ème Division Cuirassée, recently formed under General de Gaulle, and directed against the corps left flank. On the 19th, 1st Panzer Division secured a bridgehead across the Somme at Péronne. On the 20th 2nd Panzer Division reached Abbeville and the Channel. The Corps then directed its divisions northwards against Boulogne, Calais and Dunkirk. (*See* First Panzer Army, 24 May 1940.)

France: Operation 'Red', 1940 (map 3). On 8 June German forces in the west, having been regrouped for the 'Red' phase of the battle for France, faced south along the Rivers Somme and Aisne. Guderian's command, broadened into a Group, was in control of armoured forces concentrated behind Rethel on the upper Aisne north of Reims. Responsible to German Twelfth Army (List) – Army Group 'A', for the task of breaching French 4th Army Group defences, Guderian was allotted four panzer and two motorized divisions which he organized into two motorized (panzer) corps. On 10 June, 1st Panzer Division leading XXXIX Corps pushed out of an infantry bridgehead at Château-Porcien, west of Rethel, bypassed Reims to the east and spearheaded the advance of the Army Group to the south-east; 3rd Air Fleet in support. Von Kleist's Group, also with two panzer corps, redeployed alongside after failing to exploit Somme bridgeheads westwards at Amiens and Péronne, thrust south, bypassing Reims to the west, towards Vichy and Lyon. On 17 June, transferred with Sixteenth Army under command of Army Group 'C', Guderian's push carried to Belfort and the Swiss border south-east of Dijon; 1st Panzer Division making contact with German Seventh Army fighting on the west bank of the Rhine. The arrival of panzer divisions in the Franche-Comté isolated the bulk of the French Army holding the Maginot Line and brought about the surrender of some 500,000 men of French Second, Third, Fifth and Eighth Armies in the Nancy–Belfort area; 250,000 attributed to panzer group

Above: Generaloberst Heinz Guderian, born in 1888, entered the Army Cadet School at Colmar in 1901. He rose through various commands and by 1931 was Chief of Staff, Inspectorate Motor Troops (Kraftfahrkampftruppen). In 1934 he was Chief of Staff at Armoured Troops Command: then GOC, XVI Motorized Corps (1938) where he was promoted to General der Panzertruppen. He served from 1939 to 1940 as GOC, XIX Motorized Corps and then Guderian Gruppe, becoming Generaloberst in July 1940.

corps was to destroy enemy forces immediately opposite and prevent their regrouping or forming a new front further east. The action started briskly. At Minsk 17th Panzer Division, Guderian's leading division at the time, made contact with 3rd Panzer Group, turning aside from its parallel course to complete the encirclement of the city on 27 June. Inside the Bialystok–Minsk pocket 32 Russian infantry and eight tank divisions, 324,000 men, were encircled and destroyed. Smolensk fell to 29th Motorized Division on 16 July. On 20 July, the Group followed this success, with the capture of Elnya and Roslawl (4th Panzer Division), 1 August, bringing in large numbers of prisoners from Russian Thirteenth and Twenty-eighth Armies. For all intents and purposes the road to Moscow was open. Yet instead of regrouping to renew the drive eastwards, the panzer groups were directed north and south [one of Hoth's panzer corps being taken to assist in the drive to Leningrad (Army Group North) see Fourth Panzer Army, 15 August 1941]. Guderian was instructed to turn south. Accordingly, on 25 August, Guderian changed direction and with only two panzer corps, XXIV and XLVII, swung south through 90 degrees, thrusting in the direction of Kiev where von Kleist's Group would co-operate in a bid to trap South West Front. Guderian's first objective was Konotop; Gross Deutschland and SS Reich arrived on 2 and 3 September as reinforcements for the drive.

On 14 September Guderian's thrust to link up with von Kleist was successfully completed and the two Groups led by 3rd Panzer (Model) and 16th Panzer (Hube) met at Lochvitsa. The subsequent destruction of South West Front was accomplished with 600,000 prisoners being taken from trapped Russian armies. (*See* First Panzer Army, 14 September 1941.)

Russia: Operation 'Typhoon', 1941 (map 8). On 30 September, 2nd Panzer Group briefly rested and regrouped 360 miles south-west of Moscow in readiness for Operation 'Typhoon' – to be pursued in conjunction with 3rd and 4th Panzer Groups (2 October) – was ready to strike north-east for the Soviet capital. For this task Guderian's command was reconstituted as Second Panzer Army, directly subordinate to Army Group Centre (von Bock). Guderian started his push on Moscow two days earlier than other groups, pursuing a north-easterly route via Orel to Tula – a key road and rail junction south-west of the capital. Despite autumn rains turning the 'going' to mud, 3rd Panzer Division (Breith) entered Orel on 3 October. On 6 October Bryansk fell to 17th Panzer Division (von Arnim). By breaking into the rear of Bryansk Front, Guderian completed the encirclement of three Russian armies, which together with the envelopment of a further four at Vyasma (*see* Fourth Panzer Army, 7 October) yielded 657,000 prisoners. But supply deficiencies and appalling autumn and winter conditions at the front hampered further progress, in particular at Mzensk on the 10th where, for the first time, the superior T34 was encountered, sending a shock wave of consternation through the German military establishment. Immobilized divisions were resupplied by air transports arriving at forward airfields. On 15 November, coinciding with the beginning of winter frost (17 November in the north) the final assault on Moscow was ordered by Army Group Centre. But at the distant end of a long supply line, the offensive stalled in exceptionally severe conditions; 40 degrees of frost being recorded on some sectors. Guderian's

action. Von Kleist's arrival at Lyon and Vichy on the 20th completed the isolation of Paris in conjunction with Hoth's advance from the west. The move signalled an end to the campaign in France. On 22 June the French Government signed an armistice at Compiègne. On 16 November, Guderian's command was redesignated Panzer Group 2 (Panzergruppe Kdo 2) followed by training and redeployment for 'Barbarossa'. Subordinate to German Fourth Army (von Kluge), Army Group Centre (von Bock) and with three panzer corps on the Bug at Brest-Litovsk, Guderian lined up with Hoth – 3rd Panzer Group (Ninth Army) – to the north. The panzer groups would spearhead operations in the direction of Moscow. (*See* Third Panzer Army, 22 June 1941.)

Russia: Operation 'Barbarossa', Centre, 1941 (map 7). On 22 June 1941, thrusting to Bialystok, Minsk and Smolensk, 2nd and 3rd Panzer Groups pushed towards Moscow – restricted in radius by OKW fears of over-extended flanks. Guderian's objective with his three panzer

objective, taking Tula *en route*, and outflanking Moscow in a wide sweep through hostile and unrewarding country, now looked decidedly ambitious.

On 20 November, after tightening the ring at Bryansk, XXXXVII Panzer Corps thrust eastwards, with 18th Panzer Division (Nehring) protecting the Panzer Army's right flank at Jefremov, the most easterly point in the Moscow offensive. From 25 November until 5 December, with the battle for Tula at its height, Guderian's worn out, inadequately supplied and equipped combat units reduced at times to *panje* (sledge) transport met Russian resistance everywhere determined to exploit winter terrain and harsh campaigning conditions to a maximum. Failing to seize Tula in an outflanking move from the north-east (3rd and 4th Panzer Divisions XXIV Panzer Corps), Guderian's best effort was to secure Venev (17th Panzer Division) and, in deteriorating circumstances, with the same division reach Kashira, 37 kilometres further on the road to Moscow. On 5 December, lacking the necessary power to break the Red Army's defence of Tula or extend his offensive eastwards, Guderian's drive to Moscow ended in mid-winter. *Blitzkrieg* on this front was over and within weeks its prime exponent, General der Panzertruppe Guderian, would be sacked. On 20 December, winter withdrawals to ease the plight of advanced units exposed to the mounting pressure of counter-attacks by new, Siberian divisions brought General-oberst Guderian into conflict with von Kluge, the new Army Group Commander appointed on 19 December. The result; on 25 December Guderian was dismissed by Hitler, and General Rudolf 'Panzer' Schmidt was appointed in his place.

In opposing the Red Army's Moscow counter-offensive lead by Zhukov, which broke the German defence into 'island' fragments varying from Army-sized areas down to companies and battalions, locked into 'hedgehog' positions, the remnants of panzer divisions would be committed to local action. On 16 January, 1942, on Second Panzer Army's 'front', two battle groups organized by General Walther Nehring around 18th Panzer Division – reduced to twelve tanks – pushed 80 kilometres to relieve Suschi-nitschi. The town was a communications centre vital to the German defence of the front at a point where Russian Sixteenth Army threatened to turn the Army Group's southern flank. Defended all-round for thirty days by 206th Infantry Division, Nehring's efforts were rewarded with success; the defenders were relieved but the town was evacuated. By the end of February 1942 German tank strength in the east had sunk to 140 battle-fit machines and Second Panzer Army was to remain in Army Group Centre's order of battle only for the next twenty-one months until September 1943. Controlling mainly infantry corps in defensive action south-east of Rshev, where German Ninth Army's bastion opposite Moscow anchored the front, this period in the Panzer Army's declining fortunes was marked by local commitments north and east of Orel and between Belew and Shisdra.

Russian partisans in February–March 1942 and thereafter were a new factor in panzer operations in the east, especially in rear areas north and south of Bryansk where the need to control them brought action from Schmidt. Operations 'Grunspecht', 'Klette' and 'Vogelsang' during the spring of 1942 – and again in April 1943 with 'Ferkel', 'Hamburg', 'Zigeunerbaron' and 'Freischütz', indicate the scale of Moscow-directed guerrilla action – the menace of which, involving more and more active troops in combating the threat to supply lines and dumps, can be gauged from an OKW memoir dated 8 June 1943: '3,000 Russian dead, 2 aircraft and 3 tanks captured, 2,900 bunkers destroyed'; 18th Panzer Division was closely involved in these clearing-up tasks. Despite local successes, the problem of losing supplies to widespread guerrilla action and consequent operational disruption would never be totally eradicated, reaching a peak in June 1944 with more than 10,000 acts of sabotage – two days before the Red Army's 22 June offensive resulted in the total collapse of Army Group Centre. In August 1942 the Army's panzer strength was temporarily renewed for Operation 'Wirbelwind' (whirlwind), a determined attempt at improving Army positions south-west of Moscow, involving 4th, 9th, 11th, 17th, 18th and 20th Panzer Divisions in action around Suschinitschi. But operations failed within days; minefields and heavily defended localities bringing the offensive to a stand-still. Panzer action before Moscow was nevertheless set to continue.

[*At **Rshev** in August 1942, Stavka was as intent upon capturing the cornerstone of Ninth Army defences west of the capital as Hitler was of holding on to it. Coinciding with the German 'Blue' summer offensive in the south, Red Army attacks tied down 1st, 2nd, 5th Panzer and Gross Deutschland Divisions struggling to prevent a breakthrough; their presence on this front kept them out of the offensive in the south. Averting a crisis at Systchewka, midway between Rshev and Vyasma, 1st and 6th Panzer Divisions parried particularly dangerous attacks disrupting the Army Group front, but Rshev remained German – until the spring of the following year.*

*In **Operation 'Buffalo'**, starting on 1 March 1943, Ninth Army (Model) evacuated the Rshev salient, involving the withdrawal of 29 divisions including 23rd and 5th Panzer, in action at key points along a 300-mile front. The operation was completed on 25 March, shortening the line and releasing the panzer divisions and Ninth Army for Operation 'Citadel'. (See Fourth Panzer Army, 5 July 1943.)*]

On 15 August 1943, General 'Panzer' Schmidt was replaced by General der Infantry Lothar Rendulic. This change of command followed a critical week in which General Walter Model (Ninth Army) while engaged in the 'Citadel' offensive, was also directing the deployment of Second Panzer Army. Under fierce attack by the Red Army developing offensive operations during and after 'Citadel', and suffering heavy losses in men and material, Rendulic withdrew to the west, seeing Vyasma, Bryansk and Smolensk change hands as the Red Army surged forward. Second Panzer Army was now retained in Army Group Centre reserve until 21 August 1943, when it was transferred to Army Group 'F' (von Weichs) in the Balkans.

The Balkans. After 22 August 1943, the redeployment of Second Panzer Army south of Belgrade would significantly strengthen German presence in a region of south-eastern Europe where Hitler and OKW expected imminent Allied invasion. General Rendulic continued in command until 24 June 1944 when Franz Bohme, a temporary successor, was followed by General der Artillerie Maximilian de Angelis – the Army's last commander, serving from 18 July 1944 until the end in May 1945. Rendulic's first action, coinciding with

Operation 'Axe' across the Adriatic (*see* panzer action in Italy, 9 September 1943) was to disarm Italian troops in Yugoslavia. Then, in a country dominated by partisans, operating in extensive tracts of remote and mountainous country, Rendulic, with no panzer divisions on his strength, engaged Tito's partisans at Brod. From 9 to 18 October 1944, Second Panzer Army moved to hold Belgrade – delaying Red Army and Tito groups converging on the capital long enough to ensure safe passage for German units evacuating Greece and other occupied regions in the Balkan peninsula. Henceforth, until 27 November 1944, the Army was continuously in action against partisans – organized under Russian auspices into four armies – initially in the Danube-Drave area and then on the Dalmatian coast before withdrawing north into Hungary and eventual collaboration

with Sixth SS Panzer Army (Dietrich). In **Hungary**, 1945 (map 19) on 6 March, the 'panzer army' deployed south of Budapest and Lake Balaton, co-ordinated offensive action with the Waffen SS (Operation 'Spring Awakening'). But drained of resources and powerless to protect oil-production centres in western Hungary (*see* Sixth SS Panzer Army, 6 March 1945) de Angelis failed to resist Russian pressure exerted in the Vienna direction, and with no forces except infantry, withdrew into Austria.

Germany in defeat (map 20). On 8 May 1945 Second Panzer Army (de Angelis) capitulated in Steiermark (map 20).

Career Note: Generaloberst Guderian died at Schwangau in 1953, 'Panzer' Schmidt at Krefeld in 1957 and General-oberst Rendulic at Seewalchen in 1971.

3. Third Panzer Army (PzAOK 3)

Originally XV Corps (motorized), raised at Jena on 10 October 1938, in control of 1st and 3rd Light Divisions. Corps Commander General Herman Hoth (Generaloberst 19 July 1940).

Poland, 1939 (map 2). In the battle for Warsaw starting on 1 September, Hoth Corps, basically two light divisions reinforced by 25th Panzer Regiment was deployed in upper Silesia facing the junction between Lodz and Cracow Armies. Under German Tenth Army – Army Group South – the Corps was to play a leading role in the advance to Warsaw, sharing the vanguard with XVI Corps (motorized). (*See* Fourth Panzer Army, September 1939.)

From 9 to 12 September Hoth completed the first encirclement of Polish forces on this front, taking 60,000 prisoners at Radom. The operation was developed in conjunction with XIV Panzer Korps (von Wietersheim). Transferred to the west for Operation 'Yellow', Hoth's Corps, with two panzer divisions under German Fourth Army – Army group 'A' – was accorded a secondary role in the western offensive. From an assembly area east of the Meuse opposite Dinant, Hoth would provide flank protection for von Kleist, the spearhead commander at the point of main effort, 40 miles upstream at Sedan (*see* First Panzer Army, 10 May 1940).

France: Operation 'Yellow', 1940 (map 3). On 13–14 May, supporting von Kleist Group in the advance to the Channel, Hoth Corps in control of 5th (von Vietinghoff) and 7th (Rommel) Panzer Divisions, forced the Meuse at Dinant and consolidated there before pushing west in the direction of Cambrai. Rommel's division, first across the Meuse on the morning of 13 May, exploited a reconnaissance success at Houx by securing the west bank with 7th Infantry Regiment (motorized) lead by Colonel Balck – the first assault formation to breach the barrier. The division's 25th Panzer Regiment (Rothenburg) followed on the 14th. On the 15th, a few miles to the west of the crossing at Dinant, Rommel encountered and brushed aside 1ère Division Cuirassée (Bruneau), counter-attacking at Philippeville.

France: Panzer Corridor, 1940 (map 4). On 19 May, Hoth Corps, temporarily expanded as a Group and responsible to Fourth Army, was deployed on von Kleist's right in the race to the Channel. The combined panzer groups created a panzer 'corridor' with Hoth pushing

powerfully to Cambrai in control of 3rd and 4th Panzer Divisions, SS Totenkopf (XVI Panzer Corps) reinforcing his own 5th and 7th Panzer Divisions (XXXIX Panzer Corps). Three days later at Arras, Hoth Group engaged the British Expeditionary Force – making a belated and unrewarding armoured counter-attack south, striking at 7th Panzer Division.

BEF action by Frank Force on 21 May, with two infantry battalions supported by 58 Mk I and sixteen Mk II tanks under General le Q. Martel, was poorly co-ordinated with a French intention to drive south, thereby cutting the panzer corridor. Failing in this intention, the BEF withdrew to the west. The action nevertheless gave rise to OKW fears for the safety of von Kleist's armour at the western end of the corridor, and still pushing north-west along the coast from Abbeville, partly resulting in Hitler's famous stand still order. Outmanoeuvred by the armour of two groups the BEF, penned into Dunkirk, nevertheless escaped to England (*see* First Panzer Army, 24 May 1940).

France: Operation 'Red', 1940. On 5 June, at the start of the Red phase of the German offensive against France (map 3), Hoth, with 5th and 7th Panzer Divisions, was concentrated opposite French Tenth Army (Altmayer) on the Channel wing of the panzer line-up, facing south towards Paris. Crossing the lower Somme east of Abbeville, Hoth drove from Hangest to the Seine at Elbeuf reached on the 9th, diverting Rommel to the channel coast at St-Valéry – entered on the 11th. Rommel was instrumental in taking 46,000 British and French prisoners. Encountering only light opposition at Elbeuf, Hoth crossed the Seine on the 10th (followed by Rommel on the 17th) to push through Normandy and Brittany with his two panzer divisions, overrunning the Headquarters of French Tenth Army at Rennes in the process. On 19 June Rommel reached Cherbourg, and Brest fell to the Corps. Nantes was reached on the 20th. [*On the opposite flank south-east of Paris, von Kleist's simultaneous arrival at Lyon signalled an end to panzer operations in France.*] Général Weygand, the French C-in-C, authorized an armistice on the 22nd and after further easy corps progress to Royan on 25 June, the 'front' stabilized along the line Royan–Angoulême–Grenoble.

Operation 'Sea-lion', July–October 1940. Co-operating with ground-attack units of 3rd Air Fleet, Hoth's

XV Panzer Corps – 4th, 7th Panzer, 20th Motorized Division – prepared to spearhead Ninth Army/Army Group 'A' in Operation 'Sea-lion', OKW's impromptu plan to invade the South of England (*see* page 173). Intended for embarkation at Boulogne in the second (principal) wave of the invasion, D+2, Hoth's Corps, following in the wake of assault infantry and paratroops, would consolidate in the Brighton area shielding the main effort by Sixteenth Army seizing harbours at Folkestone and Dover to the east. Thereafter the corps would swing out northwards in the first phase of an army plan to isolate London and occupy south-east England between the Thames estuary and Portsmouth. [*The main effort of 'Sea-lion' was the responsibility of Sixteenth Army/ 2nd Air Fleet (VIII Air Corps especially) with XXXI Panzer Corps (Reinhardt) – 8th, 10th Panzer, 20th Motorized, Gross Deutschland and the Leibstandarte SS Adolf Hitler – embarking at Rotterdam/Antwerp in second-wave operations. After assisting in the Army task of securing Folkestone and Dover (from the west and north), Reinhardt too would break out northwards in accordance with von Runstedt's plans.*] Because of the failure of the Luftwaffe and the inability of the navy to guarantee a successful crossing of the Channel, 'Sea-lion' was postponed in October, and cancelled early in 1941. Luftwaffe 'difficulties' are elaborated in Part 4, page 120. On 16 November, officially designated 3rd Panzer Group and still under Hoth's command, the Group remained for a time in the west before moving to Germany in December and further training until June 1941, when the corps was allotted to Ninth Army (Strauss) Army Group Centre (von Bock) for the 'Barbarossa' offensive against Russia. (*See* also First, Second and Fourth Panzer Armies, 22 June 1941.)

Russia: Operation 'Barbarossa', Centre (map 7). Serving Ninth Army on 22 June 1941 with two panzer and two infantry corps supported by ground-attack wings of VIII Air Corps, and co-operating with Guderian's 2nd Panzer Group (Fourth Army) to the south, Hoth spearheaded Army Group Centre's northern axis of advance, enveloping three Russian armies to the east of Minsk. Striking for Smolensk on 5 July, 3rd Panzer Group reached Vitebsk (7th Panzer Division), entered five days later by 20th Panzer Division. On 5 August, Hoth and Guderian's combined Panzer Groups pursuing the destruction of opposing Russian armies with undiminished energy, trapped fifteen Russian divisions at Smolensk (XXXIX Panzer Corps), 7th Panzer Division in the lead. On the outer northern flank of Hoth's offensive, 19th Panzer Division reached Veliki Luki on the evening of the same day. The city fell on the 18th. There for a time, while Hoth gave up XXXIX Panzer Corps (Schmidt) for the offensive against Leningrad (*see* Fourth Panzer Army, 16 August) and Guderian was diverted south to Kiev (*see* Second Panzer Army, 25 August), the offensive towards Moscow was at a standstill.

Russia: Operation 'Typhoon' (map 8). By 2 October 1941, Hitler had decided after all to attack Moscow and Army Group Centre (von Bock) was instructed to mount a full-scale offensive – Operation 'Typhoon' lead by three panzer groups. Still serving Ninth Army, but with a change of panzer corps, Hoth was subsequently concentrated north of the Smolensk/Moscow highway, deployed as the northern arm of a three-point – north, centre and south – offensive; 4th Panzer Group (Hoepner) redeployed by OKH from Army

Group North being accorded the decisive central role. 2nd Panzer Group (Guderian) was to join the attack from the south-west. Hoth with two panzer corps, XXXI (Reinhardt) diverted from Leningrad, and LVI (Schaal), would launch into the attack against Moscow co-operating with Hoepner (Fourth Panzer Army, 2 October) and Guderian (Second Panzer Army, 30 September). OKW's new plan of offensive was intended to take the Panzer Group far to the north-east and into the rear of Moscow in a wide sweeping movement. Hoth was in command of the Group until 5 October when he was replaced by General Reinhardt; a new appointment taking Hoth to command of Seventeenth Army, South Ukraine. Reinhardt pressed forward against determined opposition by the Red Army. On 7 October snow fell on the Eastern Front. Supply difficulties and over-long routes necessitated air transport assistance for the leading panzer divisions. Nevertheless, in a successful envelopment of Vyasma lead by 7th Panzer Division (LVI Panzer Corps),

Above: Generaloberst Herman Hoth entered the army as a cadet in 1904 and served with the infantry until 1934. He was GOC, XV Motorized Corps in November 1938; serving in Poland and France before promotion to Generaloberst in July 1940. In 1941 he became GOC, Seventeenth Army and during 1942–3 he was GOC, Fourth Panzer Army.

Reinhardt collaborated with Hoepner on his right swinging north, to take more than 600,000 prisoners from four encircled Russian armies; LVI Panzer Corps (6th and 7th Panzer Divisions) tightened the ring. In the weeks following the occupation of Vyasma, 'Typhoon' slackened in mud and adverse terrain, but on 14 October, despite poor campaigning conditions, Kalinin, north-west of Moscow, a strong point in the outer defences of the capital, fell to 1st Panzer division, XXXXI Panzer Corps (Model). Despite problems with supplies the advance continued broadly in the direction of Moscow.

On 23 November, in deteriorating winter conditions and suffering increasingly from fuel and ammunition shortages, Reinhardt received instructions from von Bock to change direction and move south on Klin (7th Panzer Division) LVI Panzer Corps. Instead of continuing with the enveloping thrust, taking the panzer group far to the north and east behind Moscow, Hitler planned to capture the city by turning them south – despite increasing opposition from Russian Thirtieth Army. The new manoeuvre co-ordinated by von Bock and involving Guderian and Hoepner was intended by Hitler as the final phase in the battle for the Soviet capital. Leading the Army Group's northern arm of the offensive, Reinhardt's LVI Panzer Corps (Schaal) with 6th and 7th Panzer Divisions and 14th Motorized Infantry Division, struck south, beating down determined opposition. On 27 November a 7th Panzer Division battle group (von Manteuffel) won a bridgehead at Yakhroma, crossing the Volga–Moscow canal at Dimitrov. But within hours, and in the absence of follow-through forces, Reinhardt was obliged by fresh Siberian reserves under Russian Twentieth Army to relinquish the vital foothold. LVI Panzer Corps remained on the defensive, alert for signs of a counter offensive. From 1 until 5 December, Model's XXXXI Panzer Corps – 1st and 6th Panzer, 23rd Infantry Division – lead the Panzer Group, pushing on south to reach Belyi-Rast, a suburban settlement within 25 miles of the Soviet capital. But corps progress was blocked by superior forces and in an exhausted state the panzer group offensive ground to a halt.

[On Reinhardt's inner flank, Hoepner's 4th Panzer Group achieved marginally better results (see Fourth Panzer Army, 17 November 1941), but von Kluge's Fourth Army facing Moscow at Naro – Forminsk remained inexplicably inactive – despite the urging of colleagues to press forward.]

For the German Army, at the limit of its resources and likely to face vigorous (but unexpectedly ferocious) counter-measures, retreat in mid-winter was decidedly in prospect.

The turning-point in the battle for Moscow came on 5 December 1941 with Kalinin Front (Konev), counter-attacking boldly in a Stavka three-Front plan to sweep forward against both flanks and centre of von Bock's Army Group, regaining the initiative west of the capital. Reinhardt's spearheads, like Guderian's on the southern wing, were forced to withdraw in hazardous conditions as the Red Army almost succeeded in trapping Army Group Centre in a vast encirclement manoeuvre. Pulling back to less exposed positions the way it had come – via Klin – the Panzer Group was obliged to traverse a single snowbound axis upon which it and its supporting corps relied wholly for supplies and communication. Moves to protect this vital artery in wintry conditions involved 1st Panzer Division and others in exhausting action. Locked waist-deep into snow-drifts and

often fighting on foot (Raus's 6th Panzer Division engaged the enemy with its last two tanks), Reinhardt's exhausted formations fought hard at this critical point on the Army Group flank – countering relentless pressure with totally inadequate resources. Frostbite claimed more casualties than battle. In a very short time an ailing von Bock would be replaced as GOC, Army Group Centre by von Kluge. On the Russian side, General Georgi Zhukov, appointed 10 October to direct West Front, continued with responsibility for the Moscow counter-offensive in general. Also on 5 December, Hitler ordered the transfer of the Army Group's supporting 2nd Air Fleet (Kesselring) to the Mediterranean. [Second Panzer Army advancing to Moscow from the south-west via Tula was simultaneously halted. There too in bleak mid-winter and at the limit of its resources, the German offensive against Moscow was at an end.]

On 3 January 1942, Hitler reaffirmed a 16 December order ('Not one step back!') and von Kluge's Army Group held on, defying the winter and the worst of the Red Army's counter-attacks. Redesignated Third Panzer Army, and for a while after 8 January subordinate to Fourth Panzer Army, Reinhardt's forces continued defensive action on the northern wing of the Army Group, strenuously contesting possession of important railway centres – Velish and Veliki Luki – turned into 'hedgehogs'. Further south, around Rshev and Vyasma, German winter positions west of Moscow remained threateningly within 80 miles of the city. When the spring mud dried-out, compaigning conditions improved. On 1 May 1942, Reinhardt's Third Panzer Army was redeployed forward of Vitebsk, replacing Fourth Panzer Army, transferred South for 'Blue' – the 1942 German summer offensive. (See Fourth Panzer Army, 28 June 1942.) Henceforth the action opposite Moscow, where four armies: Third Panzer Army, Ninth Army, Fourth and Second Panzer Armies were deployed (from north to south in Army Group Centre), would become increasingly bitter and the panzer divisions' task of countering local break-ins correspondingly harsh. On this front the Red Army, maintaining a constant pressure to eliminate the German threat to Moscow, was intent upon re-possessing Rshev, the eastward-pointing cornerstone of German Ninth Army defences at the eastern end of a deep salient. Consisting mainly of infantry corps, Reinhardt's panzer strength, diminished by the demands of other sectors, would only occasionally be renewed. Like Model's Ninth Army, the principal formation holding on to Rshev itself, Third Panzer Army would become indistinguishable from others pre-occupied with defensive operations west of Moscow. Panzer divisions employed in sealing dangerous gaps in the front around Moscow would later assist Ninth Army to evacuate the Rshev salient. (See Operation 'Buffalo', Second Panzer Army, 1 March 1943.)

During the spring of 1943, anti-partisan sweeps co-ordinated with Second Panzer Army in Operation 'Maige-witter' proved only moderately successful. While in the forthcoming July offensive against Kursk (Operation 'Citadel') (see Fourth Panzer Army, 5 July 1943) the Panzer Army would play no part.

In the aftermath of 'Citadel', with the Red Army surging powerfully forward to the west, August battles involved Reinhardt in defence of Vitebsk – a railway junction vital to the supply and communications of the central front, and a town which the Panzer Army fought desperately to retain – continuing in action until February 1944 and claiming 40,000 Russian dead and 1,200 tanks destroyed. From 3 to 17 February, the battle for Vitebsk developed into further bitter confrontation with Russian Fronts and a withdrawal to new positions west of the city; but no respite.

Russia: The collapse of Army Group Centre. On 22 June 1944, at the start of the Red Army's decisive 'Bagration' offensive, planned to destroy Army Group Centre (Busch), Third Panzer Army, composed solely of infantry formations, lost an entire infantry corps, cut-off and destroyed in the city. Engulfed in the Army Group collapse and, like other formations, powerless to halt the Russian offensive which was driving a deep wedge through its northern wing, splitting it off with Army Group North while simultaneously exploiting the Army Group's exposed southern flank, Third Panzer Army retreated westwards to the Baltic in the direction of Königsberg and East Prussia.

[*At Bobruisk, situated in the far south of the Army Group 'front', at the time of the June catastrophe, only a single division (20th Panzer) (von Kessel) in Army Group reserve was available for immediate counter-attack. Despite brisk action under Ninth Army XXXXI Panzer Corps (Hoffmeister then von Kessel), securing a vital bridgehead for trapped divisions to escape across the Beresina, the lone panzer division could achieve nothing to affect the general situation. But in a remarkably swift redeployment of armour, ordered or requested by Field Marshal Model, Army Group Centre's new commander, appointed 28 June 1944, and successor to Busch (von Kluge's replacement), 4th, 5th, 7th and 12th Panzer Divisions from flanking army groups rushed to the assistance of the defence north and south of Minsk. Divisional tasks, for example under XXXIX Panzer Corps (von Saucken) defending Borisov on the Beresina, north-east of the city, were to secure exit routes, hold bridgeheads and by judicious counter-attacks assist the Army Group's stricken infantry divisions – 28 of which, 350,000 men and 47 general officers, were trapped and lost between the Beresina and the Niemen following the fall of Minsk on 3 July. Without the crisis redeployment of armour and associated heavy anti-tank support to secure escape routes for the Army Group across the Beresina and Niemen, especially at Baranovitchi where 4th and 12th Panzer Divisions were deployed, even greater numbers of German troops would have perished in the east.*]

On 6 August 1944, following the loss of Vitebsk, a new commander was appointed to Third Panzer Army – Generaloberst Erhard Raus. Holding the Red Army's drive to Königsberg in check with Gross Deutschland (Hasso von Manteuffel) – the army's most powerful panzer grenadier division, re-deployed from Roumania (where in May under its same commander at Jassy the division had destroyed Red Army spearheads driving for the oil-fields at Ploesti), Raus was required by Hitler to lead counter-attacks designed to restore cohesion between the shattered Army Group Centre and the ever more tightly besieged Army Group North forced away from Leningrad and pocketed against the Baltic north of Riga.

Lithuania: Two Heads. On 16 August Raus launched Operation 'Doppelkopf', with Gross Deutschland, 4th, 5th, 12th Panzer Divisions and Panzerverband Graf Strachwitz (two panzer brigades) subordinate to XXXIX Panzer Corps

(von Saucken). In support, XXXX Panzer Corps (von Knobelsdorff) assisted the progress of 'Doppelkopf' with 7th and 14th Panzer Divisions. In a daring operation Raus succeeded notably in driving north from Tilsit via Schaulen to establish short-lived contact between Army Groups, a junction being effected east of Riga by Graf Strachwitz's arrival at Tukkum. Despite this momentary set-back to its Baltic offensive, the Red Army continued heavy attacks with autumn and winter offensives in massive strength, overwhelming the Panzer Army and penning Gross Deutschland, 7th Panzer Division and others into Memel from which they were fortunate to escape by sea – to be reinserted into the German defence under Fourth Army forward of Königsberg. In the course of the subsequent Red Army drive encircling Königsberg east of the city, Panzer Army Headquarters, sited near the coast, avoided capture by the narrowest of margins. On 8 February 1945, Hitler ordered Raus and his staff to move out of East Prussia and prepare the emergency defence of Pomerania – 2nd BR Front's prime objective. Königsberg, assailed by 3rd BR Front, was left to German Fourth Army and held out until 12 April 1945.

Germany in defeat (map 20). On 25 February 1945, following Steiner's abortive Staargard offensive, Third Panzer Army subordinate to Army Group Weichsel, assumed responsibility for Eleventh Panzer Army's commitments in Pomerania (see Eleventh Panzer Army, 15 February 1945). Raus nevertheless failed to make a lasting defensive impression and with other defeated elements of the Army Group retreated east to Stettin. Anchoring the northern wing of the Army Group on the Oder, with an east-bank bridgehead near the mouth of the river at Altdamm, which Hitler intended as a base for future operations, Raus held on grimly; the kernel of the Panzer Army's defence being provided by III SS (Germanisches) Panzer Corps (Steiner), controlling Nordland, Nederland, Wallonien and Langemarck Divisions. With these SS divisions and miscellaneous infantry deployed in the Altdamm bridgehead, Steiner fended off relentless Russian assault. But Third Panzer Army's last commander, General Hasso von Manteuffel, appointed 15 March 1945, relinquished the army's vigorously defended east-bank (Altdamm) bridgehead, and the much diminished III SS (Germanisches) Panzer Corps, formerly at the heart of the defence, was redeployed north of Berlin – where at Eberswalde the Corps was reconstituted as Armee Abteilung (or Gruppe) Steiner.

[*The Battle of Berlin, 16 April 1945. Drained by battle losses and the transfer of divisions to other fronts (Wallonien destroyed, Nordland allotted to Ninth Army), Steiner's weak and understrength 'Army', consisting of little more than a burned-out 4th SS Polizei Division (Harzer) as its principal formation, a Marine division and later for a time 25th Panzer Grenadier Division, was powerless to contain a massive Red Army offensive crossing the Oder at Küstrin. Reduced to impotency, Steiner watched helplessly as Zhukov, encroaching on the capital, separated von Manteuffel and himself from south flanking German Ninth Army (Busse) blocking direct access to Berlin from the east. Hitler then accorded Steiner the impossible task of relieving Berlin from the north. Nothing came of the plan. No less likely to succeed in conditions of total Russian superiority (6,250 tanks and SP guns, 2,500,000 men) was a relief offensive by a new German Twelfth Army (Wenck), which Hitler*] ordered to approach Berlin from the west at Tangermünde. Progress was slow and the intended link-up was never achieved. The army's only motorized formation, 'Clausewitz', constituted from parts of the Panzer School at Putlos, 233rd Reserve Panzer Division, Feldherrnhalle and others, had been transferred early on to counter US progress in the Ruhr. After 16 April 1945 Berlin was rapidly encircled; 1st BR (Zhukov) and 1st UKR (Konev) Fronts uniting on 25 April west of the city at Ketzin. LVI Panzer Corps (Weidling) comprising Nordland, 20th and 25th Panzer Grenadier Divisions and Muncheberg, defending Ninth Army's front immediately east of Berlin, was instructed to take over the city's defence. Additional battle groups were contributed by 18th Panzer Grenadier Division, 9th Paratroop Division and ad hoc units including detachments from SS 'Charlemagne'. The Berlin garrison in the meantime was increased by miscellaneous units to 300,000 men.

Retreating through the outer suburbs to the city centre, LVI Panzer Corps was reduced to individual vehicles of Nordland and Muncheberg, defying the Red Army until 15.00 hours on 2 May. In the last resort, SS battle groups

from Nordland, Charlemagne, Polizei, Hitler Youth and Volksturm units defended the zoo, the Air Ministry and the Chancellery block where, until his suicide on the 30th, Hitler's HQ was located. Here and there around the perimeter desperate battle groups broke out of the city hoping to reach safety. On the southern outskirts in the Potsdam sector local counter-attack groups from 18th and 20th Panzer Grenadier Divisions, after a futile defence of Tempelhof, broke out with others to join the survivors of Ninth and Fourth Panzer Armies seeking contact with Twelfth Army (Wenck) approaching Berlin from the Elbe.]

On 8 May 1945, after retreating through Mecklenburg north of Berlin, Third Panzer Army (von Manteuffel), largely bypassed in the battle for Berlin and including Steiner's Group with barely more than Polizei and 25th Panzer Grenadier Division by way of regular 'divisions' with which to fight rearguard actions, surrendered mainly to the US Army.

Career Note: Raus died on 3 April 1956, Reinhardt on 22 November 1963 and Hoth at Goslar on 25 January 1971.

4. Fourth Panzer Army (PzAOK 4)

Originally XVI motorized Infantry Corps, formed in February 1938 from the Berlin panzertruppe command. The Corps' purpose under General Oswald Lutz and subsequently General Heinz Guderian, was to supervise the raising and training of 1st to 5th Panzer Divisions. On 24 November 1938, after Guderian had been appointed chief of Mobile Troops, command of the corps changed to General der Kavallerie Erich Hoepner (Generaloberst 19 July 1940).

Poland, 1939 (map 2). At the start of Operation 'White' on 1 September, Hoepner's corps, consisting of 1st (Reinhardt) and 4th (Schmidt) Panzer Divisions was concentrated in upper Silesia facing Polish Lodz Army deployed south-west of Warsaw. Pushing north-east in conjunction with XV Corps (Hoth), Hoepner lead German Tenth Army (von Reichenau) through Poland via Petrikau to Warsaw, reached on 9 September by 4th Panzer Division. From 16 to 20 September panzer action by Hoepner's two divisions, fighting on a reverse front, destroyed a determined Polish counter-attack directed from north-west of the city against the River Bzura (northern) flank of German Eighth Army. The Polish threat by twelve or more divisions of regrouped Poznan (Bortnowski) and Pomorze (Kutrzeba) Armies was swiftly disposed of; 170,000 prisoners being taken at Kutno.

France: Operation 'Yellow' (map 3). By 10 May 1940, XVI Panzer Corps was redeployed in Germany serving Sixth Army (von Reichenau) west of the Rhine and opposite Maastricht in readiness for Operation 'Yellow'. In control of 3rd (Stumpff) and 4th (Stever) Panzer Divisions, Hoepner's role in the forefront of Army Group 'B', opposite Allied armies in Belgium and Holland, was to draw the defence forward to the Dyle Line diverting attention from the focal point of panzer action by Army Group 'A' at Sedan. (See First Panzer Army, 13 May 1940.) Starting punctually at 0400 hours, preliminary operations by 2nd Air Fleet (Kesselring) and, later in the day, ground-attack wings of

VIII Air Corps (von Richthofen) immediately south and west of Maastricht aimed to neutralize key objectives in front of Sixth Army moving against Brussels. Most of the preliminary skirmishing proved remarkably successful, especially the commando use of parachute and glider detachments by 7th Air Division (Student). Committed in surprise action at dawn, the Fallschirmjaeger (85 men carried in eleven gliders) neutralized the fortress at Eben Emael while also capturing intact two of the three bridges spanning Sixth Army's major obstacle – the Albert Canal. Hoepner's Maas crossing-point in Maastrict itself was demolished by Dutch army engineers. The obstacle was swiftly overcome by IV Corps engineer bridging columns. With Stever's 4th Panzer Division temporarily under command, IV Corps was initially responsible for the Maastricht bridgehead, but movement was exceptionally cramped by Allied air attacks, and development was hampered by limited bridging capacity.

[*Airborne attacks across the Maas* were launched simultaneously against Rotterdam and The Hague by 7th Air Division detailing other detachments to seize bridges at Moerdijk, Dordrecht and the airport at Waalhaven (Rotterdam). Airborne operations here were part of Student's tactical plan to seize key objectives in surprise action. They were carried into effect in conjunction with the air transported 47th and 65th Infantry Regiments from 22nd Air Landing Division (Graf von Sponeck). Bracketed into Airlanding Corps, Student, the attacking divisions were dependent for survival upon the prompt arrival of ground support in the shape of 9th Panzer Division (Hubicki) XXXIX Panzer Corps (motorized) detailed by Eighteenth Army for the relief task – a crucial element in the general plan of operations. Few of Student's attacks were an outright success, but surprise and confusion, assisting the invasion process, enabled air-transported and paratroops to mount a serious attack on Rotterdam while threatening to capture The Hague.]

On 11 May at 0430 hours, 5 Panzer Brigade (Breith), initiating Hoepner's deceptive curtain-raiser to Operation 'Yellow' with the full support of VIII Air Corps (von Richthofen), lead Fourth Panzer Army into action while 3rd Panzer Division, preceded by its motorized infantry regiment (von Manteuffel), followed on. Moving out of the Army Group bridgehead on the west bank of the Maas, the panzer divisions were to thrust south-west through Belgium via Hannut and Tirlemont to Gembloux where Hoepner's corps would confront French First Army (Blanchard) and the BEF (Gort) drawn forward to the Dyle Line in anticipation of a major German offensive in this direction. On 12 May at Hannut, Hoepner brushed aside a French counter-attack lead by General Prioux's cavalry corps. The French force, equipped with Hotchkiss and heavy Somua tanks, consisted of two light mechanized divisions; 2nd DCM (Langlois) and 3rd DCM (Bougrain). The engagement brought Stever's 35th Panzer Regiment (Eberbach) into action – the first of the western offensive. Battle was joined next day by 5th, 6th and 36th Panzer Regiments (560 tanks).

[*Victory in Holland where confusing airborne attacks unnerved the defence, drew appreciably closer on 12 May when 9th Panzer Division (Hubicki), pushing towards Rotterdam and The Hague under command of XXXIX Pz Corps (motorized) made contact with Fallschirmjaeger holding the Moerdijk bridge. Thereafter, with 9th Panzer Division proceeding via Dordrecht to Rotterdam, the offensive continued with devastating air attacks on the city, breaking Dutch resistance and concluding with the surrender of the Dutch Army on 14 May.*]

On 14–15 May at Gembloux, where French and Belgian forces under General Blanchard held fortified positions covering Brussels and Flanders, renewed opposition by Prioux's two French light mechanized divisions and the resistance of infantry supported by artillery in fixed defences was swiftly overcome by 3rd and 4th Panzer Divisions clearing the way to Brussels. But in accordance with OKW intentions to reinforce the main armoured movement of Operation 'Yellow' successfully initiated by Panzer Group von Kleist at Sedan on the 13th, a change of direction was imminent. Brussels was instead entered by 14th Infantry Division on the 17th, the day after Allied forces evacuated the Dyle Line and started their retrograde movement in the direction of the Channel.

France: Panzer Corridor (map 4). On 19 May, Hoepner's corps was switched from Belgium to Flanders, joining XV Corps in Hoth Group (Fourth Army) (*see* Third Panzer Army, 19 May 1940). Co-operating with Panzer Group von Kleist at the point of main effort, now moving east of Lille, panzer battles developed in expectation of trapping the BEF and its supporters retreating to the Channel. By the end of May, with Dunkirk falling to 18th Infantry Division (Cranz) on 4 June, Hoepner's corps was redeployed with other attacking formations for phase two of the Battle of France.

France: Operation 'Red' (map 3). On 5 June, at the start of 'Red' operations, Hoepner was directly responsible to Sixth Army at Péronne. But when the attack south from the Army's Somme bridgehead at Péronne failed against determined opposition, the corps was redeployed eastwards, reinforcing von Kleist Group (10 June) and preparing for a Marne crossing on the 12th in the direction of Montmirail

and Château-Thierry. On 12 June, serving Panzer Group von Kleist – re-directed east from Sixth Army at Amiens to Ninth Army South of Laon (*see* First Panzer Army, 5 June 1940) – Hoepner crossed the Marne south of Soissons, driving south-east via Montmirail and Château-Thierry to negotiate the Seine at Nogent and Romilly before pressing on to Dijon and Lyon, entered by 4th Panzer Division on the 21st. Thereafter, detached from von Kleist and serving Twelfth Army, Hoepner thrust to Grenoble, threatening the rear of French Army of the Alps, which was opposing Italian forces deployed aggressively between Menton and Mont Blanc. Hoepner was promoted Generaloberst on 19 July. His Corps, responsible to Second Army until the end of October, remained at Orléans until returned to Berlin. On 15 February 1941, redesignated 4th Panzer Group and subordinate to Army Group North, Hoepner's command was redeployed east in preparation for a new undertaking; the spearheading of Hitler's 'Barbarossa' offensive in the

Above: Generaloberst Erich Hoepner entered the army as a cadet in 1905 and from 1906 to 1938 served in the cavalry. He was GOC, XVI Motorized Corps in 1938, then promoted to General der Kavallerie in 1939. He served in Poland, France and Russia. He was implicated in the Generals' plot to assassinate Hitler and was hanged for treason.

direction of Leningrad. In the forthcoming thrust of 500 miles to Leningrad via Pleskau, Luga and Novgorod, Hoepner's group would encounter some of the most difficult tank terrain on the Eastern Front; marsh, forest and swamp, hampering panzer movement at critical times.

Russia: Operation 'Barbarossa', North, 1941

(map 7). Initially, the weakest of the four panzer groups leading the invasion on 22 June 1941, Hoepner's two panzer corps, XXXXI (Reinhardt) and LVI (von Manstein), with three panzer, three motorized divisions, including SS Totenkopf, and two infantry divisions, were concentrated on the East Prussia/Lithuanian border in the neighbourhood of Tilsit. On 25 June, thrusting north-east across the Lithuanian border to Leningrad, Hoepner defeated a determined Russian counter-attack launched against his XXXXI Panzer Corps (Reinhardt) by North West Front at Rossieny where heavy Russian KVI tanks, making their first appearance of the campaign, created considerable alarm. Kovno was entered a day later; 8th Panzer division, LVI Panzer Corps (von Manstein) crossed the Duna on the 27th. On 2 July, Hoepner breached an incomplete line of fortifications protecting the former Lithuanian/Russian border. During August battles flared at Staraya Russa and Novgorod on the outer flank of the Army Group offensive, where von Manstein's LVI Panzer Corps repulsed further determined Red Army counter-attacks. On 16 August, 4th Panzer Group was reinforced; XXXIX Panzer Corps (Schmidt) bringing 12th Panzer Division and two motorized divisions from Hoth's 3rd Panzer Group/Army Group Centre. By the 25th the new panzer corps was ready to assist in attacks on Leningrad directed towards Schlüsselburg on the east side of the city. On 8 September, lead by XXXXI Panzer Corps (Reinhardt), Hoepner renewed the Leningrad offensive, involving 1st Panzer Division in heavy fighting to break Russian resistance on the Duderhof hills fifteen miles from the city centre; Schlüsselburg fell and by the end of the month investing forces of Eighteenth Army had closed in from the suburbs, reaching Lake Ladoga in the east. The landward blockade of Leningrad appeared to be complete, but siege proved ineffective, the defenders continuing to receive supplies across frozen Lake Lagoda.

On 17 September Hoepner's attacks were brought to a standstill by unbreakable Russian resistance. Although persistent attacks had carried the panzer group to within an ace of its objective, the Red Army's steadfast defence of the inner city defeated further intentions and 4th Panzer Group was instead transferred to Army Group Centre/Fourth Army to spearhead 'Typhoon', a new German offensive against Moscow. Schmidt's XXXIX Panzer Corps then tightened the blockade by extending operations eastwards and cutting Leningrad's rail connection with the hinterland at Tikhvin on 8 November (12th Panzer Division).

Russia: Operation 'Typhoon' (map 8). On 2 October

1941, Hoepner spearheaded Operation 'Typhoon' striking east for Moscow in conjunction with 2nd and 3rd Panzer Groups (*see* Second and Third Panzer Armies, 30 September and 2 October respectively). Departing from a concentration area east of Roslawl and in control of four Army corps, six panzer divisions, SS Reich and five infantry divisions, Hoepner forced the Desna with infantry before directing XXXX Panzer Corps (Stumme) on Vyasma; 10th Panzer Division (Fischer) in the lead. On 7 October 10th Panzer

Division reached the vicinity of Vyasma, uniting with 7th Panzer Division from 3rd Panzer Group to the north. The move sealed the fate of four Russian armies (400,000 prisoners). Notwithstanding this, and Guderian's success at Bryansk which raised the total of prisoners captured by the Army Group to 600,000 officers and men (*see* Second Panzer Army, 6 October 1941), mud, poor 'going' and supply difficulties took the pace out of the German offensive. On 17 November, von Bock's Army Group Centre renewed the attack on Moscow (starting on the 15th in the south where Guderian initiated the winter phase of the offensive). Hoepner's divisions – 10th Panzer and Das Reich (XXXX Panzer Corps Stumme), 5th and 11th Panzer Divisions (XXXXVI Panzer Corps von Vietinghoff) struck hard for the Soviet capital, taking advantage of frost-hardened ground. But with no better clothing and equipment than other groups committed to the offensive, and equally short of supplies in midwinter, the offensive slowly lost momentum. Nevertheless, by 5 December, two important outposts in the central defensive arc around Moscow: Istra, 26 November (Das Reich and 10th Panzer Division), and Chimki, 30 November (62nd Panzer Pioneer Battalion) were in German hands. Hoepner's drive continued with 2nd Panzer Division (V Corps) closing on Krasnaya Polyana and there, within 20 miles of the Kremlin, the German Army's offensive against Moscow in mid-winter failed on this sector as elsewhere along the Front – baulked by the Red Army's unyielding resistance, beset by frostbite, unserviceable equipment and every kind of shortage.

On 1 January 1942, 4th Panzer Group was redesignated Fourth Panzer Army and on the 8th Hoepner was dismissed; never to be re-employed. In his place, General Richard Ruoff was appointed GOC, Fourth Panzer Army. Defensive operations involving the panzer divisions in much hard fighting continued in the area west of Moscow. During May 1942, Ruoff's panzer army headquarters was transferred to Army Group South (von Bock) to serve with German and Hungarian Second Armies under Army Group von Weichs. The Panzer Army under a new commander, Generaloberst Hoth (appointed 31 May) would spearhead Operation 'Blue', a summer offensive taking the panzer divisions on the fatal road to Stalingrad.

Russia: Operation 'Blue', 1942 (map 10). On 28

June 1942, Fourth Panzer Army under its new commander, Generaloberst Hoth, comprising XIV and XXXXVIII Panzer Corps with refreshed and refurbished divisions, concentrated at Kharkov before advancing powerfully to Voronezh with the support of VIII Air Corps (Fiebig). Kempf's Panzer Corps – 24th Panzer, Gross Deutschland and 16th Motorized Infantry Division – provided the spearhead. Russian Thirteenth (Pukov) and Fortieth (Parsegov) Armies of Bryansk Front bore the brunt of violent fighting.

[*Sixth Army joined the 1942 summer offensive, starting 30 June 1942, with Paulus thrusting east lead by XXXX Panzer Corps and co-operating with Second Panzer Army in an Army Group plan to trap Russian forces west of the Don; an expectation destined to go unfulfilled.*]

On 6 July 1942, the ninth day of Operation 'Blue', 24th Panzer Division (Hauenschild) in a renewal of *Blitzkrieg*, driving powerfully across rolling steppe at the head of Kempf's XXXXVIII Panzer Corps entered Voronezh. In conjunction with Gross Deutschland, 24th Panzer Division secured the left flank of an Army Group South claiming 28,000 prisoners, 1,000 tanks and 500 guns destroyed or captured at the conclusion of the first phase of the offensive. Nevertheless, the bulk of Russian defenders succeeded in escaping eastwards in good order. Army Group South was then divided into new Army Groups 'A' (List) and 'B' (von Bock); 'A' would lead the offensive into the Caucasus while 'B' protected the east flank at Stalingrad. On 9 July when Army Group 'A' (List) – First Panzer Army (von Kleist) and Seventeenth Army (Ruoff) – also joined in the summer offensive, panzer operations between the Donetz and the Don were set for expansion. Ordering Fourth Panzer Army to change direction and, together with Sixth Army (General Paulus), thrust broadly south-east following the river Don in the direction of Stalingrad, Hitler planned to trap the Red Army deployed west of the river. On 13 July, Fourth Panzer Army was transferred from von Bock to List and subsequently directed south alongside von Kleist in another effort to trap Russian forces between the Donets and the Don, north of Rostov. Nothing came of the plan except an adverse concentration of panzer divisions mostly removed from the main axis of advance. On 21 July Fourth Panzer Army, on the Don facing south with First Panzer Army to the west, won a bridgehead across the river at Nikolayevskaya. XL Panzer Corps (Geyr von Schweppenburg), controlling 3rd and 23rd Panzer Divisions, led the way south to the River Manych; 3rd Panzer Division (Breith) being first into Asia. [*Sixth Army continued alone in the direction of Stalingrad.*] On 23 July 1942 [*with First Panzer Army entering Rostov, the 'gateway' to the Caucasus*], Hitler directives named Grozny and Baku as List's primary objectives; List's Army Group 'A' (less Fourth Panzer Army) implemented the directive on 25 July. [***Sixth Army progressing** towards Stalingrad from the north-west, and protecting a long open flank on the Don, was assisted by the arrival of XIV Panzer Corps, but suffered protracted delay. Operational plans were again revised.*]

On 30 July, Hoth was instructed to release Geyr von Schweppenburg's XL Panzer Corps to von Kleist (Army Group 'A') and return under command of Army Group 'B' which, with XXXXVIII Panzer Corps comprising 14th and 16th Panzer Divisions and 29th Infantry Division (motorized), followed a new line of march toward Stalingrad along the south bank of the Don. Striking powerfully for the city, a Russian arms-manufacturing and river freight trans-shipment centre, stretching thirteen miles along the west bank of the Volga, the panzer army encountered strong opposition from 64th (Schumilov) and 57th (Tolbuchin) Armies. General Georgi Zhukov, the master co-ordinator of Moscow West Front defensive operations 1941, and future Stalingrad defence co-ordinator, had yet to be appointed.

[*First Panzer Army meanwhile continued south into the Caucasus, extending divergent operations in the direction of Mozdok – a useful but minor oil-producing centre in the western foothills.*]

[***Sixth Army was beset by problems.** Approaching Stalingrad from the north and west in late July–August 1942, operations were curtailed for eighteen days – XIV Panzer Corps suffering in particular as fuel supplies were diverted to von Kleist whose First Panzer Army's more distant objectives demanded and received a greater (none the less inadequate) measure of support.*]

On 7 August, Sixth Army operations against Stalingrad were renewed from the north (XIV Panzer Corps) and west (XXIV Panzer Corps) enveloping Russian First Tank Army (Moskalenko) and 62nd Army (Lopatin), blocking access to Kalatsch – the traditional Don crossing-place leading 70 kilometres east to the city.

On 19 August Paulus ordered a start to the final phase of the attack on Stalingrad. On the 22nd, XIV Panzer Corps (von Wietersheim) supported by VIII Air Corps (Fiebig) crossed the Don north of Kalatsch and pushed 16th Panzer Division (Hube) on to Rynok – a riverside settlement immediately north of the city. On 23 August 1942, 2nd Panzer Regiment (Graf Strachwitz) reached the Volga. Kalatsch fell to LVI Army Corps (von Seydlitz) on the 25th. But Hube's panzer division on the Volga was practically surrounded for a week and obliged to rely upon air-transported supplies.]

Meanwhile, approaching Stalingrad from the south-west, Hoth was delayed by Russian 64th Army at Abganerovo and not until 19 August, co-ordinating operations with Sixth Army, did he move simultaneously to attack Stalingrad from this direction; 24th Panzer Division (Hauenschild) leading XXXVIII Panzer Corps (Kempf). But not without difficulty. Suffering the bitter resistance of Schumilov's 64th and other Russian armies defending Stalingrad, Hoth like Paulus, would be obliged for more than three months to fight for every inch of the city 'mouseholing' residential districts, clearing barricades and assaulting the defence factory by factory and block by block. But German resources would prove totally inadequate for the task. Pushed to the brink of the Volga, six Russian armies, responsible to Zhukov for the defence of Stalingrad since 26 August, retained a slender grip on the city.

Russia: The battle for Stalingrad (map 11) entered a new phase on 19 November when a well-judged Russian counter-offensive, Operation 'Uranus', launched north and south of the city with 1,500,000 men, almost 1,000 tanks and strong air and artillery support, enveloped Sixth and Fourth Panzer Armies– 22 divisions, three panzer and three motorized, Army engineers, Panzerjaeger, signals, flak, bridging columns, supply staffs, corps troops, army troops and administrators, totalling 220,000 officers and men. Fourth Panzer Army, fighting in the southern half of the city, was struck in the flank and split apart. Hoth at Panzer Army Headquarters outside the encirclement was left with little more than Roumanian infantry with which to combat the onslaught. But relief for the defenders of Stalingrad was in prospect.

Russia: Operation 'Winter Storm' (map 12), starting on 12 December, was initiated by LVII Panzer Corps (Kirchner) hurriedly transferred north from Seventeenth Army in the west Caucasus. Conceived by Army Group Don (von Manstein), a new headquarters established on 24 November at Novo Cherkassy north-east of Rostov, the operation was carried out by three panzer divisions, notably 6th (Raus) brought at full strength and in quick time by rail from France to join 23rd (von Senger und Etterlin) and subsequently 17th Panzer Division (Lengsfeld) east of Kotelnikovo. With 6th Panzer Division leading, the relief attempt drove forward supported by Roumanian infantry and IV Air Corps. But to no avail.

After twelve days of bitter mid-winter action, 11th Panzer

Regiment (Hünersdorff), at the centre of operations, was brough to a standstill by Second Guards Army and three armoured brigades, when fewer than 30 miles (48 kilometres) separated 6th Panzer Division from German Sixth Army perimeter. Meanwhile on the Panzer Army's left flank, between the Don and Donets, a new crisis was developing. [*Catastrophe on the Chir materialized on 17 December 1942 when Italian Eighth Army, deployed on the upper Chir, collapsed under pressure from Southwest Front; 22nd Panzer Division, grievously weakened in earlier battles staving off a Roumanian (Third Army) break-up, was virtually eliminated in counter-attacks.*]

Von Manstein's Plan (map 12) for coping with the emergency would require 6th Panzer Division (Raus) to discontinue attacks in the Stalingrad direction (24 December 1942) and instead swing north to join 11th Panzer Division (Balck) in XXXXVIII Panzer Corps (von Knobelsdorff)/Army Detachment Hollidt. Hollidt was charged with the defence of the vital Army Group Don area west of Stalingrad where transport wings of VIII Air Corps, flying mostly from Tazinskaya and Morosovska, linked beleaguered Sixth Army with its only supplies – now under threat from SW Front (Malinovsky) thrusting to the airfields' perimeter. Assisted by 7th Panzer Division (von Funck), dispatched by rail from France, on the heels of 6th Panzer and detraining at Forstadt, von Manstein reinforced Hollidt on the Donets at a point where the division would combat any hostile move across the Donets likely to prejudice plans for shielding Stalingrad air-supply centres and restoring cohesion to the German Army's shattered right wing. In destroying Malinovsky's Second Guards Army spearhead invading the vital airfields and subsequently in holding off the northern arm of a Russian pincer reaching out for Rostov, von knobelsdorff was dramatically successful. Fighting for Ordzhonikidze, 400 miles away, in the eastern Caucasus, von Mackensen was wholly dependent upon Rostov for supplies. South of Rostov, where Fourth Panzer Army was defending the outer approaches to the city, panzer operations between the Don and the Manych would eventually repay the effort involved, but with fewer than sixty serviceable tanks available in 17th and 23rd Panzer Divisions (LVII Panzer Corps), reinforcements for Fourth Panzer Army were an urgent necessity. Consequently, in late December SS Wiking Division (Steiner) was taken from von Mackensen, 11th Panzer Division (Raus) was switched from XXXXVIII Panzer Corps north of the Don, and 16th Motorized Division came in from outpost duty at Elista. With these divisions in aggressive action south-west of Kotelnikovo, Hoth held Rostov against Russian 51st and Second Guards Armies long enough for the fugitive First Panzer Army to slip through to safety.

'Winter Storm' had proved a failure and Sixth Army at Stalingrad was lost, but in subsequent battles across the Donetz between the Don and the Dnieper, where Kharkov fell to Voronezh Front on 16 February, panzer action within the framework of von Manstein's counter-strategy would do much to restore the power and confidence of the German Army. By 17 February 1943, First and Fourth Panzer Armies were regrouped behind the Donets in the triangle north of Rostov, and following a Führer conference at Zaporoshe, counter-attacks to recover Kharkov would soon start in earnest.

Russia: Return to Kharkov (map 13). On 22 February 1943, Fourth Panzer Army, striking north for Pavlograd with the support of VIII Air Corps (Fiebig) and First Panzer Army (q.v.), launched attacks sealing off Voronezh and South West Front spearheads (Popov) exploiting the Red Army's momentum in the Don bend following victory at Stalingrad. In thrusting south-west to the Sea of Azov, in the process of isolating and destroying Army Group Don, the Russian Fronts were dangerously extended. On 7 March, after regrouping north of Pavlograd, Hoth's offensive entered a new phase, aiming directly for Kharkov from Krasnograd. By 12 March 1943, Hoth had destroyed large parts of Russian Sixth Army, re-entered Kharkov with II SS Panzer Corps (Hausser), while Kempf prepared to recover Bjelgorod (Gross Deutschland Division) on the 18th.

Russia: Requiem for a Panzer Army (map 14). After consolidating in spring thaw conditions which inhibited mobile operations, Fourth Army was redeployed north of Bjelgorod for Operation 'Citadel' – the German 1943 summer offensive against the Red Army. The objective of Army Groups South (formerly Don) and Centre was to emasculate the Red Army on the Eastern Front by eliminating an enormous concentration of troops and weapons north and south of Kursk. Fourth Panzer Army/ Army Group South, with two panzer corps north of Bjelgorod and supported by Army Detachment Kempf, would strike the main blow from the south. Simultaneous action by Ninth Army (Field Marshal Model) striking concentrically from the north was planned to bring spearheads together in the centre of the bulge at Kursk. Seventeen panzer divisions were committed to the offensive. **Citadel** opened on 5 July with the divisions involved reporting minimal gains north and south. Violent artillery exchanges and a marked increase in air activity by both sides heralded the start of panzer operations on an unprecedented scale. But in attempting to overcome Russian opposition 'Citadel' was doomed to failure. Coinciding on 10 July with Operation 'Husky', the Allied invasion of Sicily, Hitler reviewed progress on the 12th in the wake of ferocious losses and – as the Red Army judged the time right for its own counter-offensive against Second Panzer Army, holding the adjoining Orel sector to the north – halted the offensive next day. From 5 to 16 July 1943, the day on which the attacking panzer divisions finally broke-off the action, 'Citadel' proved a death ride for Fourth Panzer Army. More than 1,200 tanks, more than half the strength of the seventeen panzer divisions committed to the offensive, were lost; individual divisions at the point of main effort being reduced to 20 per cent of their armoured strength.

At **Prochorowka** on Sunday the 11th and Monday 12 July, the heaviest tank fighting of the war developed on the SS front, 25 miles from the start-line and a further 25 miles from Oboyan, Fourth Panzer Army's objective half-way to Kursk. The battle developed at crisis level after the SS Panzer Grenadier Divisions Leibstandarte Adolf Hitler (Wisch), Das Reich (Krüger) and Totenkopf (Priess), had regrouped and side-stepped opposition by Katukov's First Tank Army. Three days earlier, on 8 July, at Teteravino, the SS Panzer Corps had been helped out of a potential crisis by ground-attack wings of VIII Air Corps, breaking-up a threatening flank attack by Russian II Guards Armoured Corps. This VIII Air Corps action is elaborated in Part 4, page 55. At the height of the battle for Prochorowka, Hausser's SS Panzer Corps was engaged by Fifth Guards Tank Army (Rotmistrov) released from Stavka reserve; some 900 Pz Kpfw III/IVs, Tigers, Panthers, Ferdinands and other German armour, clashing head-on with a roughly equivalent number of T34s, KVIs, IIs and SU76 (15.2cm) assault guns. With so great a concentration of armour fighting for supremacy, the Prochorowka battlefield turned overnight into a ferocious malestrom of German and Russian tanks and supporting vehicles swirling in combat while Stormovicks, Henschels and JU 87 tank-busters added weight to the engagement. On the SS right, III Panzer Corps (Breith) – 6th Panzer Division (Hünersdorff) especially – attacking northwards in support of the SS by taking Rotmistrov in the left flank, pushed hard against determined opposition; an 11th Panzer Regimental (Oppeln) battle group winning a Donets crossing at Rschavetz, pointing the way to Prochorowka and contact with the SS armour. But there 6th Panzer Division was stopped. On the opposite flank, supporting action by Gross Deutschland, 3rd and 11th Panzer Divisions, biting into the opposition, helped XXXXVIII Panzer Corps forward. But by nightfall on the 12th, hundreds of wrecked vehicles, 70 Tigers among them, testified to a terrifying defeat for Fourth Panzer Army. [Ninth Army, battling to reach Olchowtka and Ponyre, less than twelve miles from the northern start-line south of Orel, was even less successful; the progress of 2nd, 4th and 9th Panzer Divisions being delayed by extensive minefields, gun-pits, massed artillery fire and vicious counter-attacks all taking deadly toll of Model's armour.]

The Luftwaffe's loss of superiority and fruitless efforts by the panzer force to fight through defences organized in depth by a thoroughly prepared opponent were at the root of defeat; skill and courage of those involved, notwithstanding. So, with the Red Army passing to the offensive, attacking first the eastern face of the main battle line held by Second Panzer Army north of the bulge, and then focusing south upon Kharkov where Fourth Panzer Army was deployed, German positions north and south of Kursk would soon prove untenable. The initiative seized by the Red Army would never again be recovered and panzer diaries would henceforth record successes only in retrograde steps as German armies retreated along the entire length of the front; Hitler's plans to halt the Red Army involving the panzer divisions in vigorous, yet more often than not, fruitless counter-action.

From August to December 1943, neither Fourth nor First Panzer Armies (joining Hoth alongside in the New Year) could find the strength to withstand Russian motorized offensives trapping the German Army at all levels. Lacking armoured reserves with which to cope with overwhelming attacks in a rapidly deteriorating situation, Fourth Panzer Army, suffering under remorseless pressure from Voronezh Front (Vatutin), abandoned first Kharkov, complete with depots and war material, and then other key communications centres. On 7 August 1943, at Graivoron west of Kharkov where Hoth was resisting renewed Russian pressure, only the intervention of Gross Deutschland holding firm at Achtyrka saved 11th and 19th Panzer Divisions from encirclement. By 22 August, following the fourth Battle of Kharkov, the city was abandoned despite energetic counter-attacks by 3rd and 6th Panzer Divisions supported by II SS

Panzer Corps. Hitler, whose avowed intention it was to hold the city, nevertheless refused to countenance a phased Army Group withdrawal to the Dnieper. On 14 September 1943, with Army Group South's panzer strength amounting to no more than 250 tanks, Central Front broke through the northern wing defended by Fourth Panzer Army east of the Dnieper. The break-through endangered Kiev, Kanev (Bukrin) and Cherkassy. At other Dnieper crossings to the south, pressure mounted at Dniepropetrovsk and Zaporoshe (see First Panzer Army, August–December 1943). The Russian thrust aimed at Kiev immediately threatened von Manstein with encirclement. Hitler recanted over withdrawal and the Army Group (from north to south: Fourth Panzer, Eighth, First (Panzer) and Sixth Armies, was belatedly allowed to find sanctuary behind the Dnieper. Russian pressure increased in a race to win crossing-places.

[At **Kanev/Bukrin**, 22–24 September 1943, XXIV Panzer Corps (Nehring), separated from Hoth during Fourth Panzer Army's retreat from Kharkov to Kiev and attached to Eighth Army (Wöhler), was overtaken fifty miles away, east of the Dnieper, but promptly retired to counter-attack a west-bank bridgehead won by Third Guards Tank Army (Rybalko) at Bukrin on the 22nd. Committing his only regular mobile division (10th Panzer Grenadier) supported by impromptu motorized infantry groups organized from corps infantry divisions and launched into concentric attacks with 19th Panzer Division dispatched from Kiev, Nehring inhibited Voronezh Front's consolidation across the Dnieper. In the ensuing action, XXIV Panzer Group destroyed the greater part of three Russian paratroop brigades landed behind the front on 26 September with orders to widen the bridgehead into a sally-port for Rybalko's armoured brigades. But Nehring's success and the subsequent containment of the bridgehead by XXXXVIII Panzer Corps (Eberbach) proved short-lived with Vatutin redirecting Rybalko northwards on Kiev.]

During October 1943, Fourth Panzer Army continued its resistance to 1st Ukrainian Front (Vatutin) concentrating on Kiev. But unsuccessful in defending the city, Hoth abandoned it on 6 November and Vatutin pushed 100 miles further west to seize Zhitomir. On 15 November 1943, Hitler replaced Hoth with General Erhard Raus. The new commander would win respite from retreat by mounting energetic counter-attacks. On 19 November, launching powerful Army and SS formations under XXXXVIII Panzer Corps (Balck) north from Fastov, Raus sliced deeply into Vatutin's extended flank; 1st, 7th, 19th, 25th and 2nd SS Panzer Divisions recapturing Zhitomir and shortly afterwards recovering Korosten. The action continued with the Leibstandarte attacking 1st Ukrainian Front at Brusilov and along the River Teterev, destroying sizeable Russian formations. But uncontainable pressure (1,100 tanks, 6,000 guns and 452,000 men) building-up to smash the panzer army forced Raus and south-flanking First Panzer Army (redeployed on 29 December from Krivoi Rog on the lower Dneiper) to yield ground. Retreat was imperative. In January 1944, 7th Panzer Division was roughly handled losing its Co (Schultz) blocking 1st Ukrainian Front moving into Shepetowka. A crucial road and rail centre affording Army communications to the west, the town was for a time resolutely defended by this veteran of campaigns in France in 1940, before giving way to overwhelming pressure.

From 16 to 26 March 1944, a Red Army spring offensive forced Fourth and First Panzer Armies apart, splitting von Manstein's Army Group front wide open; Raus, left with only Balck's XXXXVIII Panzer Corps and sundry infantry defended Tarnopol. Enveloped since 11 March, in the yawning gap between panzer armies, this communications centre, a 'fortress' according to Hitler, and not to be yielded at any price, was one of many lost or threatened at the time. Kowel was another, besieged by 1st Ukrainian Front on the Army Group's northern boundary, and a 'fortress' to be held at all cost.

[*The relief of Kowel* on 5 April 1944, was accomplished by 4th (von Saucken) and 5th (Decker) Panzer Divisions, driving south under Second Army/Army Group Centre; heavy losses being reported by investing Russian formations. From 16 March the defence of Kowel had been entrusted to SS General Herbert Gille, GOC, SS Wiking, refitting at Debica after a catastrophic experience at Cherkassy (see First Panzer Army, 17 February 1944). Gille was expressly flown into Kowel as commander of the 'fortress' garrison while an SS panzer battle group (Mühlenkamp) incorporated into the relief force was subordinated to 4th Panzer Division.]

The relief of Tarnopol, at the second attempt, starting on 11 April 1944, was carried out by XXXXVIII Panzer Corps (Balck) fourth Panzer Army. On the 16th, an *ad hoc* panzer battle group (Friebe) with 24 Pz Kpfw Vs, nine Tigers (507th Panzer Battalion) and a 9th SS Panzer Division Hohenstaufen battle group with 30 Pz Kpfw IVs and 30 assault guns got to within seven miles of the town. Their proximity prompted 2,500 of the defenders to break out, but only 55 men, mainly from 357th and 359th Infantry Divisions, survived the attempt. There for a time the front stabilized. On 18 May 1944, when Raus was transferred to First Panzer Army, command of Fourth Panzer Army passed to Generaloberst Josef Harpe. The new GOC would serve until 28 June 1944, after which General Walther Nehring (DAK and XC Corps Tunisia) (see Fifth Panzer Army, December 1942) would deputise until 5 August. During this time Harpe was deputising for Model as commander of Army Group North Ukraine – formerly Army Group South. In June 1944, the Red Army's 'Bagration' offensive, overwhelming Army Group Centre (see Third Panzer Army, 22 June 1944), forced costly withdrawals upon an increasingly exposed and run-down Fourth Panzer Army. Retreating across southern Poland in July 1944, Fourth Panzer Army withdrew in the direction of Sandomierz (Baranov) and the Weichsel (Vistula); undergoing another change of command on 5 August – to General Herman Balck, a former GOC, 11th Panzer Division, now promoted from XXXXVIII Panzer Corps. Rearguard action in southern Poland was continued by a diminishing and overcommitted number of panzer divisions deployed without respite here as elsewhere east and west, especially in Normandy where 'Overlord' was draining much needed panzer strength, and in Italy.

[*Defending Warsaw* on 2 August 1944, Ninth Army launched counter-attacks against a 1st BR Front spearhead moving north-east around the city. The offensive was ordered by Field Marshal Model, commanding both Army Groups Centre and North Ukraine (to which latter headquarters First and Fourth Panzer Armies were now responsible). At the centre of operations XXXIX Panzer Corps

(von Saucken) shattered the Front's III Corps vanguard, driving to outflank the defence at Volomin. **Panzer intervention by Ninth Army at Volomin** involved four panzer divisions – 4th, 19th, 5th SS Wiking and Hermann Goering – in concentric action bringing temporary relief to a weak Army Group front forming east of the Polish capital. The involvement of SS Wiking in the defence of Warsaw presaged action by a new (IV) SS Panzer Corps (Gille); corps composition – 3rd SS Panzer Division 'Totenkopf' (Becker) redeployed from Roumania and 5th SS Panzer Division 'Wiking' (Mühlenkamp), refitted and re-employed after its disastrous experience at Cherkassy. At **Magnuschew**, south of Warsaw (map 18) on 8 August 1944, Hermann Goering and 19th Panzer were instrumental in containing a potentially explosive Red Army bridgehead established west of the Vistula by 1st Belorussian (1 BR) Front, threatening Berlin; Panzer action at this point reduced that threat.]

And there on the Vistula south of Warsaw, as at Baranov (Sandomierz) where Fourth Army was containing a 1st Ukranian (1 UKR) bridgehead, calm reigned for five months before the storm broke and the Red Army swept on to Berlin. During the autumn of 1944, Fourth Army/Army Group 'A' (Harpe) consolidated on the Vistula, building defences against a future Red Army assault. But with barely twelve panzer divisions out of a current total of about twenty armoured or motorized divisions (four for Harpe) to defend the entire Eastern Front against 61 Russian armies (six tank armies with 15,000 armoured fighting vehicles) this was unlikely. The cards, as Guderian would say, were stacked in favour of the Red Army. [In January 1945, IV SS Panzer Corps (Gille), the mainstay of Army Group Centre's defence of Warsaw, was transferred to Army Group South (Sixth Army). The SS Panzer Corps would drive east along the Danube to relieve Budapest in Operation 'Konrad' (map 19) (see Sixth SS Panzer Army, 13 February 1945.)] On the Vistula the long-awaited Red Army offensive was about to break.

A moving panzer pocket in Poland (map 18). On 12 January 1945, the Red Army opened the way to Berlin with a massive 1st Ukrainian Front (Konev) offensive erupting out of the Baranov bridgehead, shattering Fourth Panzer Army's front, held solely by infantry divisions. Pushing north-west to Kielce in conjunction with 1st Belorussian (1 BR) Front (Zhukov) breaking out from the Vistula at Magnuschew and Pulavy, and in so doing destroying Ninth Army's southern wing, Konev's offensive threatened the Army Group with total disaster. Outclassed in numbers and firepower, Fourth Panzer Army, with more infantry than armour, was scattered in the Red Army offensive. With Ukranian and White Russian Fronts thrusting to the Oder at Glogau and Breslau, more than halfway and less than 150 miles from the capital, the battle for Berlin assumed a grim reality. Within hours of Konev's break-out, Fourth Panzer Army's only mobile reserve, 16th and 17th Panzer Divisions (XXIV Panzer Corps Nehring) retained by the Army's last GOC, General Gräser, for action against the flank of any Russian penetration was encircled at Kielce. Nehring would nevertheless force a way into contact with a Gross Deutschland relief force of two divisions striking south-west from Lodz under von Saucken. The mobility of both formations would be narrowly assured by Luftwaffe re-supply wings (see Part 4, Transport action, page 143).

During the subsequent defence of Western Silesia by Army Group Centre, called into question on 25 January when the Red Army renewed its Berlin offensive across the Oder north and south of Breslau, Fourth Panzer Army retained Glogau until Gräser abandoned it on 31 March. Unrewarding Fourth Panzer Army counter-attacks then marked Red Army progress westwards to the Neisse, reducing what remained of industrial Silesia.

[The last panzer offensive of the war, by Seventeenth Army on 5 March 1945, involved Panzer Group Nehring – XXXIX Panzer Corps (Decker) and LVII Panzer Corps (Kirchner) deployed in defence of Silesia. Re-occupying Lauban, Decker's 19th Panzer Division and FGD joining Kirchner's 8th Panzer Division and FBD inflicted notable losses on a Russian mechanized corps.]

Germany in defeat (map 20). On 16 April 1945, when the Red Army struck for Berlin across the Oder-Neisse line, sizeable elements of both Fourth Panzer Army (Gräser) and Ninth Army (Busch) were encircled in a Frankfurt–Guben pocket. The battle for Berlin, from which Fourth Panzer Army was thereby effectively eliminated, can best be followed by referring to Third Panzer Army, 16 April 1945. On 6 May 1945, in Bohemia north of Prague, Fourth Panzer Army pulled surviving units together and with a semblance of 'panzer' divisions – Bohemia, Brandenburg (Grenadier), 2nd SS, 10th SS and 20th Panzer Division, reinforcing Volksturm and *ad hoc* units of all kinds, defied a final Russian offensive employing three Tank and seventeen Infantry Armies directed into the rear of Army Group Centre (Schörner). On 8 May 1945, Fourth Panzer Army, a shadow of its former self, and like other formations in the east lacking basic stores and vehicles, surrendered to the Red Army.

Career Note: Implicated in the Hitler assassination plot of 20 July 1944, Generaloberst Hoepner was one of many conspirators hanged for treason.

5. Panzer Army Africa (PzAOK Afrika)

In common with OKH practice in Europe this Panzer Army HQ, one of two raised in North Africa, the other being Fifth Panzer Army (Africa), evolved by stages to control increasingly complex mobile operations and a burgeoning number of panzer divisions and support units. Yet at the time of the Panzer Army's confrontation with General Bernard Montgomery on 23 October 1942 at El Alamein, the decisive battle of the African campaign, so determined was the High Command to regard Africa as a side-show that Field Marshal Erwin Rommel the army commander disposed of only two panzer divisions (and two Italian armoured formations equipped with much inferior machines), three motorized (one Italian), five unmotorized Italian infantry divisions, one Falschirmjaeger brigade (Ramcke) and support units. Montgomery's strength comprised three armoured and seven motorized divisions plus supporting brigades – with four or more times the number of German tanks. On 10 October 1940, four months prior to the arrival of Deutsches Afrika Korps (DAK), the veteran of Spain, von Thoma, currently Panzer Waffengeneral (5 March 1940), in a report to OKW on the employment of armour in the desert, recommended the employment of four panzer divisions in Africa taking into account the likely supply situation and operational needs.

On 14 February 1941, the first panzer units for DAK arrived at Tripoli. Taken mainly from 3rd Panzer Division to create a new 5th Light Division (Streich) for service in the desert came reconnaissance (AA3) and 39th Anti-tank Battalion (PzJaegAbt 39); a vanguard quickly followed to Africa by 5th Panzer Regiment, 8th Machine-gun Battalion, 605th Anti-tank Battalion, 606th Anti-aircraft Battalion, 75th Divisional Artillery Regiment, and signals – all to be incorporated within weeks into a new, 21st Panzer Division. Following on for DAK from May to August 1941 came 15th Panzer Division (von Prittwitz); tanks and vehicles – the heavy equipment of 8th Panzer Regiment – being shipped to Tripoli while grenadiers of 104th and 115th Infantry Regiments accompanied by light units were ferried forward to Derna in Ju 52s flying from Brindisi. Despite battle losses and frequent changes in their order of battle, these 'African' Panzer divisions were destined to remain in North Africa as core units of DAK until general capitulation two years later in Tunisia. There in May 1943 10th Panzer Division, after serving briefly in conjunction with the Corps, also surrendered to the Allies. The two 'African' divisions were reformed shortly afterwards; 15th Panzer in Sicily as a panzer grenadier division, 21st Panzer in France, March 1944.

Panzer command in Africa. DAK's first and most famous commander was General Erwin Rommel. Regarded by all who knew him as a forceful, highly professional soldier, an infantryman by training but panzer commander by ambition, Rommel won early distinction in action against the Italians on the Isonzo in October 1917. Leading an assault on positions considered by both sides to be impregnable, Captain Rommel's thrusting tactics resulted in the retreat of Italian Second and Third Armies resulting in 60,000 prisoners being taken by German XIV Army. Rommel's ambition to lead a panzer division was fulfilled by Hitler in February 1940 when the Führer, whose escort battalion he had commanded since 1938, gave him command of 7th Panzer Division at Bad Godesberg. Nominally subordinate to Comando Supremo in Rome, via Marshal Bastico, C-in-C, Africa to whom all African armed services were subordinate, Rommel was in practice responsible to OKW and Hitler via Field Marshal Albert Kesselring. [*Transferred from the Eastern Front to Rome on 28 November 1941, Kesselring was followed a week later by 2nd Air Fleet Headquarters under orders to move from Moscow to the Mediterranean. Kesselring's move, coinciding with Rommel's first retreat to El Agheila, was a timely one. In addition to commanding 2nd Air Fleet, co-ordinating Mediterranean air and sea operations with the Italians, Kesselring, as C-in-C, South (Europe) with additional staff, was destined to shoulder an increasing burden of German responsibilities in the theatre until 10 March 1945, his career then changing direction as OB West in succession to von Runstedt.*]

Right: In November 1917 Oberleutnant Rommel led six companies of Württembergers in a heroic action. After 50 hours of fighting, with a battle group that at the outset consisted of barely more than two companies, Rommel, at considerable risk from artillery fire, infiltrated Italian lines along the Isonzo to reach the summit of Monte Matajur and take 9,000 prisoners. For his achievement he was decorated with the 'Pour le Mérite' and promoted to Captain.

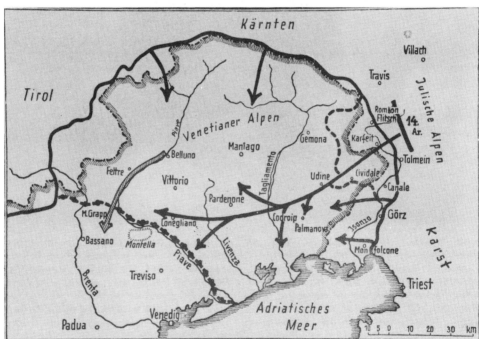

Rommel's career in Africa and his command of DAK started on 15 February 1941 – three days after arriving in Tripoli – when DAK became operational. Thereafter Generalleutnant Rommel, former commander 7th Panzer Division, promoted General der Panzertruppen on 1 July 1941, would serve in Africa for two years with few breaks in service until 9 March 1943 when as Field Marshal he returned to Germany to consult with Hitler. On 15 August 1941, following his promotion to General, Rommel assumed command of both German (DAK) and Italian (XXI) Corps with an expanded HQ – Panzer Group Africa – leaving DAK to General Ludwig Crüwell who, until his capture eight months later on 29 May 1942, when he crashed in his Fieseler Storch, would see the

Corps through its first major reverse – British Eighth Army's 'Crusader' offensive to relieve Tobruk, starting on 18 November 1941 (q.v.). Crüwell's successor in command of DAK, General Walther Nehring (18th Panzer Division), appointed 9 March 1942, would follow in time for Gazala battles leading to the capture of Tobruk. But before Nehring could cap this success by participating in the battle of Alamein, circumstances dictated otherwise and he returned wounded to Germany on 31 August 1942; a new appointment following in Tunisia (see Fifth Panzer Army, 8 December 1942). Command of DAK then passed briefly to von Vaerst and, during the battle of El Alamein, except for a day as GOC, Panzer Army, to von Thoma. Thereafter for varying

Left: Field Marshal Erwin Rommel entered the army a cadet in 1910. He served in the west from 1914 to 191 (Marne, Argonne, Vosges) a the east in 1917 (Austro/ Italian front). In 1929 he became an Instructor at the School of Infantry, Dresden, where he wrote the book *Infantry Attacks*. In 1935, a Hitler's instigation, he was posted to the War Academy Potsdam, and in 1937 was promoted to Colonel. He subsequently served in seve theatres although not in the east. He is best remembere for his leadership of Panzer Army Africa.

Right: Field Marshal Albert Kesselring served in artillery during the 1914–18 war. B 1936 he was Chief of the Luftwaffe General Staff in succession to General Weve In 1937 he became GOC, A District 3 (Dresden): then G Luftwaffe Group/1st Air Fle (Berlin) in 1938. He commanded 1st Air Fleet in Poland and 2nd Air Fleet in France, where he was promoted to Field Marshal. was on the Central Front in Russia in 1941, and then in southern Italy from 1942. I March 1945 he was chosen the replacement for von Runstedt.

spells, Bayerlein, Fehn, von Liebenstein, Ziegler and finally Hans Cramer served as DAK commanders.

Meanwhile Rommel's career continued upwards. Promoted Generaloberst on 21 January 1942, with a Panzer Group Headquarters expanded and redesignated Panzer Army Africa – the highest level of mobile command in the desert – Rommel controlled both DAK and three Italian corps (X, XX and XXI). Promotion to Field Marshal was Rommel's reward for capturing Tobruk on 21 June 1942. On 2 September, following eighteen months' service in the inhospitable North African climate, Rommel took sick leave in Europe. But when a heart attack at the start of the battle of El Alamein removed his successor, General der Kavallerie Georg Stumme, introducing Generalleutnant von Thoma to Panzer Army command – for the exceptionally short period of 24 hours – Rommel returned to Africa on 25 October, resumed his Panzer Army command and carried on the battle; von Thoma, reverting to his DAK command, was captured on 4 November 1942. The Field Marshal's last appointment in Africa commencing 23 February 1943, bringing him command of Army Group Africa, continued until 9 March when he visited Hitler – never to return. Thereafter Rommel's future as an army group commander

was to lie in Europe (*see* career note). Rommel's energy in opposing British desert commanders, Wavell, O'Connor, Cunningham, Ritchie, Auchinleck and eventually Montgomery in two years of mobile operations in the Western Desert, was characterized by thrustful and opportunist tactics, often brilliantly successful – like those of 7th Panzer Division under his command during the Battle of France (*see* Third Panzer Army, 13 May 1940). Briefed solely to block a British threat to Tripoli, the 'Desert Fox', as Rommel was nicknamed by British opponents, would instead lead his Africa Corps to legendary fame – in protracted battles with British Eighth Army.

The need for a German military presence in Africa arose out of successful action by General Wavell starting at Sidi Barrani in December 1940. In sweeping Italian forces five hundred miles out of Egypt to threaten Tripoli, Wavell's Western Desert Force (O'Connor) re-named Eighth Army 26 September 1941, including 7th Armoured Division 'Desert Rats' and Royal Tank Regiments with 50 Matildas taking 130,000 prisoners destroyed ten Italian divisions at Beda Fomm. Mussolini appealed to Hitler. A German 'blocking' force was raised. Subsequent Italian experience in Africa and on the Eastern Front can be followed in Part

the port. An interesting sidelight on Rommel's failure to reduce Tobruk, Eighth Army's forward supply and communications base, for which he blamed the divisional commander (Streich) and had him transferred out of the theatre, is contained in the following (edited) account of panzer action 10 April–1 May 1941, by a junior officer captured from 2nd Battalion, 5th Panzer Regiment. In this engagement the panzer battle groups suffered heavily, von Ponath's 8th Machine-gun battalion in particular; a staunch defence of Tobruk by a British and Empire garrison (Klopper) thwarting any intention Rommel might have had of extending offensive operations into Egypt.

Readers preferring to follow the course of events eastwards should turn on to 15 August 1941 or alternatively, for a British Eighth Army report illustrating 15th Panzer Division's battle group organization and tactics in the course of 'Scorpion', turn to Halfaya, 21–27 May 1941.

Tobruk, 10 April–1 May 1941. A first-hand account of panzer action in the first battle by 5th Light Division (Streich); this is a junior commander's view of desert warfare on 10–14, 23, 30 April, and again on 1 May 1941.

'Tobruk. 10 April 1941. Towards evening we reached our advanced positions 17½ miles in front of Tobruk. We have covered 100 miles . . . wearily we pitch camp. Vehicles are checked over. I have to force the louvres open with a hammer, the sand having jammed them.'

'Tobruk. 11 April 1941. At 0900 hours we move off into the desert again to the S.E. in order to cut off Tobruk from the south. With us are anti-tank, machine-gun and anti-aircraft units . . . Ten miles south of Tobruk and already the enemy's artillery is giving us an H. E. welcome. . . . As soon as they get the range we withdraw 100–200 yards. Their fire follows us – their observation must be good. At 1630 hours we attack with two half-squadrons. The artillery puts down a barrage, but can make little impression on us. Through! We career on for 1,000 yards and turn carefully through a minefield. As the smoke lifts I see barbed wire and anti-tank trenches. "Halt!" Gun-flashes. "Gun, 9 o'clock. A.P. shell, light-coloured mound, fire!" A hit. Again – 10 yards to the right . . . with six shots we have finished off the anti-tank position. We move along the wire looking for a gap and the leading tank finds one, and in doing so runs on to a mine, of course. Another goes to its rescue, while I give covering fire.'

'Tobruk. 14 April 1941. At 0010 I am called, and ordered to report with the company commander at 0100 hours. Situation: Machine-gunners and engineers have worked a gap through the anti-tank defences; 5 Tank Regiment, 8 Machine-Gun Battalion, anti-tank and anti-aircraft artillery will cross the gap under the cover of darkness and overwhelm the position. Stuka attack at 0645 hours. 0715 hours. Storming of Tobruk. With least possible noise 2 Battalion, Regimental H.Q. Company and 1 Battalion move off completely blacked-out. Bitterly cold. Of course, the enemy recognizes us by the noise and as ill luck will have it, a defective spot-light on one of the cars in front goes on and off.'

'Soon artillery fire starts up on us, getting the range. The shells explode like fireworks. We travel six miles, every nerve on edge. From time to time isolated groups of soldiers

raden
r einer
lfeldmar-
g, nach
ing mit
abes der
hrmacht,
avallero,

ibeichler
s)

2, Satellite contributions for the panzer force. On 31 March 1941, Rommel disregarded his 'blocking' directive, organizing cross-desert battle groups and launching his first offensive, 'Sonenblume' taking the Africa Corps 400 miles from El Agheila to the Italian/Egyptian frontier at Sollum. After a minor setback ('Brevity') DAK consolidated there on 27 May. But having failed to break Wavell's Eighth Army or capture the crucial supply port of Tobruk – the best-developed harbour on the coast midway between Tripoli and Alexandria – Rommel could do no more than sit on the frontier and, in the wake of Operation 'Scorpion', defend Sollum/Halfaya 21–27 May, while simultaneously investing

appear – men of 8 Machine-Gun Battalion – and then suddenly we are in a gap. Already the tank is nose-down in the first trench. The motor whines: I catch a glimpse of the stars through the shutter, then for the second time the tank goes down, extricating itself backwards with a dull thud, the engines grinding. We are through and immediately take up file in battle order. In front of us 8 Company, then 2 Battalion H.Q. Company, then 5 Company. With my troop I travel left of the (6) company commander. With 2 Battalion H.Q. Company about 60 men of 8 Machine-Gun Battalion with Oberst Ponath are marching in scattered groups. Tanks and infantry? – against all rules! Behind us follow the Regimental H.Q. Company and 1 Battalion plus the other arms. Slowly, much too slowly, the column moves forward. We must, of course, regulate our speed by the marching troops, and so the enemy has time to prepare resistance. The more the darkness lifts, the harder the enemy strikes. Destructive fire starts up in front of us now – 1 – 2 – 3 – 10 – 12 – 16 bursts and more. Five batteries of 25-pounders rain hail on us. 8 Company presses forward to get at them. Our heavy tanks, it is true, fire for all they are worth, so do we all, but the enemy with his superior force and all the tactical advantages of his own territory makes heavy gaps in our ranks.'

'Wireless; "9 o'clock anti-tank gun, 5 o'clock tank!" We are right in the middle of it with no prospects of getting out. From both flanks A.P. shells whizz by. Wireless "Right turn, Left turn, Retire." Now we come slap into 1 Battalion, which is following us. Some of our tanks are already on fire. The crews call for doctors, who alight to help in this witches' cauldron. English anti-tank units fall upon us, with their machine-guns firing into our midst; but we have no time. My driver, in the thick of it, says "The engines are no longer running properly, brakes not acting, transmission working only with great difficulty." We bear off to the right. Anti-tank guns 900 metres distant in the hollow behind, and a tank. Behind that in the next dip 1,000 yards away another tank. How many? I see only the effect of the fire on the terrace-like dispositions of the enemy . . . Above us Italian fighter planes come into the fray. Two of them crash in our midst. The optical instruments covered with dust. Nevertheless, I register several unmistakeable hits. A few anti-tank guns are silenced, some enemy tanks are burning. Just then we are hit, and the wireless is smashed to bits. Now our communications are cut off. What is more, our ammunition is giving out. I follow the battalion commander. Our attack is fading out. From every side the superior forces of the enemy shoot at us.'

' "Retire" There is a crash just behind us. The engine and petrol tank are in the rear. The tank must be on fire. I turn round and look through the slit. It is not burning. Our luck is holding. Poor 8th Machine Gunners! We take a wounded man and two others aboard, and the other tanks do the same. Most of the men have bullet wounds. At its last gasp my tank follows the others, whom we lose from time to time in the clouds of dust. But we have to press on towards the south, as that is the only way through. Good God! Supposing we don't find it? And the engines won't do any more! Close to our right and left flanks the English tanks shoot into our midst. We are hit in the tracks of our tank, and they creak and groan. The minefield lane is in sight. Everyone hurries towards it. English anti-tank guns shoot

into the mass. Our own anti-tank and 8.8 cm. guns are almost deserted, the crews lying silent beside them. The Italian artillery, which was to have protected our left flank, is equally deserted! We go on. Now comes the gap and the ditch! The driver cannot see a thing for dust, nor I. We drive by instinct. The tank almost gets stuck in the two ditches blocking the road, but manages to extricate itself with great difficulty. Examine damage to tank. My men extract an A.P. shell from the right-hand auxiliary petrol tank . . . The petrol tank was shot away, and the petrol ran out without igniting!'

'Tobruk. 14 April 1941. At 1200 hours we retire into the wadi south of us . . . We cover up. Heavy cumulus clouds cover the sky. Every 10–30 minutes 2 or 3 English bombers swoop out of them amongst the tanks. Every bomber drops 4 to 8 bombs. Explosions all round. It goes on like this until 1900 hours without a pause. . . . Casualties in 2 Battalion of 5 Tank Regiment, 10 tanks, apart from 5 7.5 cm. guns of 8 Coy.! A few dead, several wounded, more missing. The anti-tank units and the light and heavy A.A. were badly shot up and the 8th Machine Gunners were cut to pieces. The regiment has lost all its doctors – presumably captured. The regiment is practically wiped out.'

'Tobruk. 15 April. Artillery fire from 0700 hours. The bombers repeat yesterday's game. My troop has two heavy tanks again. Tank No. 625 isn't running any more. however. It only serves as a pilbox. According to orders, I report at the brigade commander's office at 1200 hours. Once more the principal subject discussed is the action in front of Tobruk on 14th April. We simply cannot understand how we ever managed to get out again. It is the general opinion that it was the most severely fought battle of the whole war. But what can the English think of us! A weak battalion, only two squadrons strong, bursts through the complex defence systems until it is just on a mile from the town, shoots everything to bits, engages the enemy on all sides, and then gets away again. . . . The war in Africa is quite different from the war in Europe. That is to say, it is absolutely individual. Here there are not the masses of men and material. Nobody and nothing can be concealed. It doesn't matter whether it is a battle between opposing land-forces, or between air-forces, or both; it is the same sort of fighting, face to face, each side thrusting and counter-thrusting. If the struggle was not so brutal, so entirely without rules, you might compare it with the joustings of knights. And now before Tobruk. . . .'

'Tobruk. 20 April. In the afternoon tank No. 623 rolls up with a new engine. Now I have the strongest squadron in the regiment: 4 Pz Kpfw II tanks, 4 Pz Kpfw III. Gradually, however, the job of squadron commander is becoming difficult. I have absolutely nothing to go by, everything is in the desert. Where are the tanks, where are the H.Q. cars and squadron office? And I have no command tank and no motor-cycle – and then the reports and the paper-war which begins as soon as the last shot has been fired!'

'Tobruk. 23 April 1941. The journey I planned has been postponed owing to the arrival of Lieut. Grim with 6 tanks. The engines of the tanks are partly new, partly overhauled in the factory. They have new gears, transmission, brakes, etc. The British do not miss the chance of sharing in the welcome with some well-aimed fire. The faithful 625, which is the only heavy tank of the squadron remaining with us,

Above: Tripoli 1941 and the unloading of Pz Kpfw IIIs for Rommel as part of 8th Panzer Regiment, 15th Panzer Division. They were soon in action with DAK at Tobruk and then throughout the campaign in North Africa (*see* maps 5 and 9).

will now be sent back to have its 6 shell-wounds cured. Whilst in the workshop it will have its engines changed.'

'Tobruk. 29 April. 50 dive-bombers circling over Tobruk. Tank 622 turns up. They tell us about the desert – of hunger and thirst, of Benghazi and of Derna. Since tank No 625 is still in the workshops, I am getting No. 634 as my 5th tank, with Serjeant Schäfer, my driving instructor from Wünsdorf.'

'Tobruk. 30 April. Finishing touches to our preparations for battle. 1745 hours. March to assembly place. Strong Stuka attacks. 2000 hours: our own strong artillery bombards the enemy heavily, 8 Machine Gunners in front. 1 Engineer Battalion and 1 Battalion of Assault Engineers break through and demolish the barriers on either side. The light signals show that the attack has begun. At 2200 hours sleep under the tank.'

'Tobruk. 1 May 1941. We intend to take Tobruk. My 4th attack on the town. Up at 0330 hours, leave at 0430 hours. We lose touch in the darkness and dust – and join up again. We file through the gap where many of our comrades have already fallen. Then we deploy at once, 6 Sqn. on the left, 5 Sqn. on the right, behind H.Q., 8 and 7 Sqns. The regiment is now Hohmann's Mobile Battalion and consists altogether of 80 tanks. The English artillery fires on us at once. We attack. No German patrol goes in front to reconnoitre. Tier upon tier of guns boom out from the triangular fortification before us. The two light troops of the company and my left section are detailed off to make a flanking movement. I attack. Wireless message: "Commander of 6 Coy. hit on track." Then things happen

suddenly. . . . A frightful crash in front and to the right. Direct hit by artillery shell. No! It must be a mine. Immediately send wireless message: "Commander Schorm on a mine, will try to get old direction." 5 metres back – new detonation. Mine underneath to the left. Now it's all up – with driving. Wireless message: "Getting back went on mine again." Now mount tank 623. Back through the artillery fire for 100 yards and got in. Wireless: "Tanks active behind ridge. The men of the mined tank all right." '

'Back carefully. Then with the last tank in Company H.Q. and Lieut. Roskoll I give cover to the north. 9 heavy and 3 light tanks of the squadron have had to give up owing to mines. Of my troop, the commander's tank and both of the section leaders' tanks are damaged. Of course the enemy went on shooting at us for some time. A slight change of position: forward – right – backwards – left! With the commander's approval I am to go up in front to salvage tanks. Whilst we are on the way we are fired at by M.G.s and anti-tank guns from about 500 yards. I silence them with H.E. and drive in the tracks of 624. I bring up the rear, and then the laborious work of salvaging begins. The anti-tank gunfire starts up again and has to be kept in check by constant fire. . . . At last I move off slowly with 624 in tow, through the gap and on 800 yards. 250,000 Marks saved. The crew is really delighted to have its tank back. It is now late afternoon. Dive-bombers and twin-engined fighters have been attacking the enemy constantly. In spite of this, the British repeatedly make counter-thrusts with tanks. As soon as the planes have gone the artillery starts up furiously.

It is beginning to grow dark. Which is friend, which is foe? Shots are being fired all over the place, often on your own troops and on tanks in front on their way back. Suddenly a wireless message: "British attacking gap with infantry." It is actually true. Two companies get off their motor lorries and extend in battle order. All sorts of light signals go up – green, red, white. The flares hiss down near our M.G.s. It is already too dark to take aim. Well, the attack is a failure. The little Fiat-Ansaldos go up in front with flame-throwers in order to clean up the triangle. Long streaks of flame, thick smoke, filthy stink. We provide cover until 2345 hours, then retire through the gap. It is a mad drive through the dust. At 0300 hours have snack beside the tank. 24 hours shut up in the tank, with frightful cramp as a result – and a thirst! Tobruk. 2 May 1941. Recovering tanks.' The panzer officer was subsequently captured.

The tactics of desert battle group commanders, reflecting training and experience in early campaigns, are dramatically illustrated in an Eighth Army report discussing Operation 'Scorpion' – the German re-occupation of Halfaya Pass by 15th Panzer Division (von Esebeck) on 27 May 1941. After a setback for DAK – opposing 'Brevity', Eighth Army's first counter-attack seeking to restore contact with Tobruk, and involving the loss and recovery of Sollum and other frontier positions on the 15th – the panzer division organized battle groups to accomplish the task required of it; the re-occupation of the pass (see Halfaya, 1–5).

'Halfaya. 1. 21 May 1941. General. Early in the day the division received orders by radio telephone to carry out a surprise attack on the Sollum front coinciding with the attack on Crete by XI Air Corps (Student) starting 20 May.'

'Major-General von Esebeck, GOC 15th Panzer at the time was away wounded and Colonel von Herff was responsible for the German forces in the frontier area. Believing the balance of strength to be sufficiently in his favour, the latter decided to widen the scope of the operation as ordered and, instead of merely keeping the British forces busy in the frontier area, to take Halfaya, the frontier pass giving access to the coastal plain. Von Herff hoped at the same time to force a tank engagement.'

'Halfaya. 2. 24 May 1941. Plan of attack. The actual orders for the operation were issued by the divisional commander; zero day – 26 May. Broadly speaking, the intention was to make a feint attack in the Capuzzo area and cause the British to reinforce their position there, while at the same time giving the impression that German reinforcements of about the strength of one division were moving from the Tobruk area to outflank the British Desert Force from the south (causing them to withdraw from the escarpment to the coastal area without fighting). The method adopted to implement this plan comprised a strong advance south-eastwards by three groups (two lorried infantry and one armoured), while the fourth group made a wide sweep from Sidi Azeiz – first moving south to the area north of Maddalena, and then eastwards to Deir el Hamra. This latter move was to be made in several columns in order to confuse Eighth Army as to the actual axis of advance.'

'Halfaya. 3. Composition of the German attacking force – 15th Panzer Division is divided into four battle groups. The Panzer or Cramer Group (commanded by Oberst Cramer, OC, 8th Panzer Regiment) consisted of:

8th Panzer Regiment less one troop.
Detachments from 5th Panzer Regiment and 33rd Reconnaissance Unit.
Two batteries and a half-troop of 33rd Artillery Regiment.
One battery from the Grati (Italian) Artillery Regiment (which failed to arrive on time).

Of the two lorried infantry groups one was commanded by Major Bach, OC, 1st Battalion, 104th Lorried Infantry Regiment.

The Bach Group consisted of:

1st Battalion, 104th Lorried Infantry Regiment.
The pioneer platoons of 3rd and 33rd Reconnaissance Units.
A mixed platoon from 33rd Anti-Tank Battalion.
One section of 33rd Artillery Regiment.
One troop of 8th Panzer Regiment.

The other lorried infantry group was commanded by Oberst Knabe, OC, 15th Motor-Cycle Battalion. The Knabe Group consisted of:

15th Motor-Cycle Battalion less one company.
The M/C companies of 3rd and 33rd Reconnaissance Units.
One reinforced rifle company of 14th Lorried Infantry Regiment.
One company (less one mixed platoon) of 33rd Anti-Tank Battalion.
Detachments of 33rd Artillery Regiment.

The Wechmar Group under the command of Oberst Freiherr von Wechmar, OC, 3rd Reconnaissance Unit, had

Below: A Pz Kpfw III 'special' with a long, 5cm gun and heavier armour (50mm instead of 30mm) which supplemented DAK's other 'special', the Pz Kpfw IV with a long-barrelled 7.5cm gun. These, together with a 7.5cm short-barrelled Pz Kpfw III, formed the mainstay of Rommel's armour.

sufficient heavy weapons to fight as an independent unit, combining striking force with speed. This group consisted of:

    3rd and 33rd Recce. Units (less elements allotted to other groups).

    One company of 605th Anti-Tank Battalion.

    One troop and two sections of 33rd Artillery Regiment.

    One troop of captured field guns manned by personnel of 33rd Artillery Regiment.'

'Halfaya. 4. Individual tasks of the four groups:

i. Panzer Group – The armoured or Cramer Group was to take up a position on the track Capuzzo–Bir Hafid–Sidi Omar. The general direction of advance was to be Bir Ghirba–Qaret el Ruweibit, i.e., south-eastwards. After confusing the British by frequently changing direction, the tanks were to cross the frontier in battle formation at 1600 hours and under cover of artillery fire to make for the first objective, Point 203 (Qaret abu Sayid) and Point 204 (two and a half miles south-east of Sidi Suleiman). This line is at right angles to the general line of advance. Further advance, either in the same direction or north-east towards the rear of the British forces at Halfaya, was to be held back pending the arrival of artillery and orders from divisional battle H.Q. which was to move with the Cramer Group.'

'ii. Bach Group – As the Bach Group was expected to meet strong counter-attacks it was given artillery support to the strength of one half-troop from 33rd Artillery Regiment and one battery from the Grati (Italian) Artillery Regiment. The task of the Bach Group was to follow up the Cramer Group and occupy Halfaya Pass. It was to advance on zero morning through the wadis of the escarpment as far as Qalah and, from noon on, to reconnoitre in the direction of the pass. The British forces at the pass and in the plain were to be pinned down by artillery fire. After 1545 hours fire was to be concentrated on the pass, and from 1600 hours the Bach Group was to be ready to capture Halfaya on foot and to thrust forward as far as Minqar el Shaba as British resistance weakened. Both roads at the pass were immediately to be consolidated by mining the forward slopes. The troop attached from 8th Panzer Regiment was to be used in the attack on the pass until the engineers had removed the mines from the south-western slope. Sollum was to be held by a reinforced troop, and reconnaissance of the coastal plain was to be carried out during the attack on the pass.'

'iii. Knabe Group – The Knabe Group was to form the mobile reserve of the division. It was to be ready from 1500 hours on zero day (26th May) in the neighbourhood of Capuzzo, and was either to follow the Cramer Group in its advance, or to go to the support of the Bach Group at Minqar el Shaba.'

'iv. Wechmar Group – The Wechmar Group was to assemble at Sidi Azeiz the evening before zero day, and to start at dawn on zero day for the frontier, north of Maddalena via Gabr Saleh. After crossing the frontier between Frontier Posts 68 and 71 at 1500 hours on 26 May, the group was then to split up into several columns, in order to confuse the British, and to advance on Deir el Hamra feinting in other directions to add to the confusion.

Above: An '88' in desert action. British tank attacks were often defeated by the aggressive presence of the '...' in the forefront of DAK batt... lines. Firing over open sight... and at ranges reducing to 5... yards, the '88' was more th... a match for the Cruisers iss... to Royal Tank Regiments.

Once over the frontier speed was to be the first consideration. The group was to avoid major engagements, and to restrict offensive action to attacking numerically weaker forces. If enemy opposition was not encountered, or was only weak, the Wechmar Group was to push on to Bir Sofafi, and lie up there. Contact with the British forces was to be maintained.'

'Halfaya. 5. German Intelligence – According to an Intelligence appreciation the British Eighth Army had withdrawn some of its forces still disposed in two groups, viz. a desert force and a coastal force. The former was believed to consist of a reinforced reconnaissance unit, about one battalion of tanks, four or five troops of artillery, and anti-aircraft and anti-tank detachments.'

'The British forward patrol line, held strongly by tanks and armoured cars, was thought to run from Halfaya Pass via Points 207 and 205 to Point 204 (Tumuls) whence it ran southwards parallel to the frontier wire. The forward defended locality was believed to have been strengthened by anti-tank guns and a few Mark II tanks.'

'The British artillery was believed to be concentrated in the Sidi Suleiman area, while strong reserves, probably including tanks, were suspected in the Bir Habata district.'

'It was expected that the Desert Force would attempt to hold up the German advance by laying down an artillery barrage. The Germans had little hope of destroying our mobile patrols, but it was considered possible that we might throw in our reserve tanks which would then be destroyed by the joint action of the Cramer and Wechmar Groups.'

'The British Coastal Force defending Halfaya Pass and the coastal plain was believed to consist – approximately – of one infantry battalion, with two or three troops of artillery, and at least one squadron of tanks.'

'Halfaya. 26 May 1941. i. Execution of the attack – The tank attack itself was timed for 1500 hours, and preparations were in full swing in the early morning of the 26 May when the British made two sorties, towards Point 206 and

Anza el Qalala respectively, and drove back the German patrols. Further advance was stopped by the Bach Group, which had moved forward during the night to the Wadi Agrab area. The Bach Group, reinforced by a company of lorried infantry and half an anti-tank company, then passed to the attack, and proceeded to carry out its task in the tank-proof country of the escarpment wadis. Elsewhere the German advance was proceeding according to plan. Shortly after 1500 hours the Cramer Group, together with Force H.Q., crossed the frontier, advancing south-east on a broad front, with two tank battalions forward and one echelonned in rear to the right flank. The battalion from 5th Panzer Regiment was sent off to attack in rear the British artillery harassing the German flank from the direction of Sidi Suleiman. The main body of the group continued its advance without pause and reached its first objective at 1700 hours, when the artillery attached to the Cramer Group was ordered up.'

'Command in this sector of the attack was rendered difficult by the lack of armoured fighting vehicles and the breakdown of wireless apparatus, with the result that headquarters received very few, or no, reports from the other attacking columns up to 1700 hours. It was, however, clear from intercepted enemy R/T and aerial observation that the enemy had been completely taken by surprise, though there appeared little likelihood that the enemy's tanks would be brought to battle in co-operation with the Wechmar Group. On the other hand the Bach Group reported by radio telephone that strong enemy tank formations were attacking their right wing.'

'Von Herff decided, therefore, to attack the enemy opposing the Bach Group at 1715 hours; the Knabe Group was accordingly ordered by radio telephone to advance south-east in the direction of Abar Abu Telaq. Verbal orders were given to the Cramer Group to turn north-eastwards in the direction of the escarpment south-east of Minqar el Shaba, and then attack the rear of the British opposing the

Bach column in conjunction with the Bach and Knabe Groups.'

'In execution of this order Cramer called in 1 and 2 Battalions of 5th Panzer Regiment, and wheeled the regiment north-eastwards at 1845 hours, with one battalion forward and two echelonned in rear to either flank. After a short time heavy gun fire was heard from a northerly direction, presumably from the direction of the Bach Group, which reported further heavy enemy attacks by British Mark II tanks against their right wing. The Cramer Group was therefore ordered, in spite of the arrival of darkness, to advance at full speed to Halfaya Pass in order to destroy the enemy opposing the Bach Group, which was given information to this effect by R/T. The Knabe Group was halted north of Abar el Silqiya in order not to leave it exposed to enemy tank attacks without anti-tank and artillery support.'

'The night was moonless, thus increasing the difficulties of keeping direction, and the Cramer Group was held up in the difficult sandy country north-east of Sidi Suleiman. Cramer decided to halt his tanks shortly after 2020 hours, about five miles south of Halfaya Pass.'

'The impression gained by Von Herff from reconnaissance reports and intercepts was that the British had not observed the left wheel of the Cramer Group. It was moreover established that the Wechmar Group had reached its objective for the day in the Deir el Hamra area, and that the British were completely ignorant of its whereabouts. It was also clear from intercepted enemy R/T that the British must have been completely bewildered by the German surprise attack, and had obviously received no reports from its units.'

'ii. 26 May 1941. Orders for 27th – Von Herff decided to make a surprise attack on the enemy opposing the Bach Group using the Cramer, Knabe and Bach Groups in conjunction. In accordance with the orders issued at 2200 hours the Cramer Group was to attack the escarpment at 0430 hours on the morning of 27th May on both sides of Minqar el Shaba, and to open fire from there with all arms on the enemy concentrations in the coastal plain. It was also to hold part of its troops ready for an attack on the Halfaya Pass positions from the rear.'

'The Knabe Group's orders were, first, to take up position by 0430 hours in the area a quarter of a mile north of Abar Abu Telaq and to move forward, with the Halfaya Pass road as its axis of advance, while the Bach Group, which had reached by dusk the height a quarter of a mile north of Halfaya Pass, was to attack Halfaya itself, at the foot of the pass. Lastly, the Wechmar Group was to move off before dawn in a north-westerly direction to reach the area east of Sidi Suleiman and then to cover the main body of the division from the south-east.'

'iii. 27 May 1941. Execution of the attack. The night of the 26th/27th May passed quietly, though the tanks' petrol columns failed to get through during the night. Had they got through, the Germans consider they could have carried the pursuit, after the next day's engagement, as far as Sidi Barrani. In the face of the shortage of petrol a decision had in fact to be taken whether to postpone the dawn attack on the 27th May, and so to lose the element of surprise, or to limit the scope of the tank advance. The latter alternative was chosen.'

'At about 0430 hours the Knabe Group, followed shortly afterwards by the Cramer Group, advanced as ordered, the armoured (Cramer) group moving, as on the previous day, with one battalion forward and one in rear on either flank. In spite of heavy enemy artillery fire the Cramer Group reached the escarpment at about 0530 hours, and brought concentrated fire to bear on enemy movements, gun positions, and tanks in the coastal plain, creating great disorder. The Knabe Group reached Halfaya Pass at 0540 hours, where elements of this group and of 5th Panzer Regiment (Cramer Group) forced their way, in the face of artillery, anti-tank and machine-gun fire, into the British positions. By 0615 hours Halfaya Pass was in German hands.'

'The Bach Group, whose advance was hampered throughout by British tank attacks, reached the foot of the pass at 0630 hours. Under concentric attack by the Cramer, Knabe, and Bach Groups, and suffering violent action by German artillery, Eighth Army withdrew, pursuit being immediately (0630 hours) undertaken by the Knabe and Bach Groups, whose orders were not to proceed with recconaissance beyond a reasonable distance. Subsequently, the Bach Group fell back on Halfaya Pass and later, with a high proportion of the 8.8 cm. guns available to the Panzer Group, took up defensive positions there. The other battle groups alert for counter attack also withdrew to their previous positions along the escarpment.'

Operation 'Battleaxe'. On 15 June 1941, British attacks aimed at restoring contact with Tobruk brought 5th Light and 15th Panzer battle groups back into action. Inflicting a severe defeat on underpowered British forces, Rommel retained control of the strategically important Halfaya Pass. On 15 August, Rommel's command was reconstituted as Panzergruppe Afrika controlling DAK (15th, 21st Panzer Divisions) and two, eventually three, Italian Corps: XX, X and XXI (Ariete, Trieste, Pavia, Brescia, Trento and Sabrata Divisions), 90th Light (incomplete) in reserve; Rommel's Corps appointment was taken over by General Ludwig Crüwell. Regrouping to assault Tobruk, Rommel prepared for action, but to no purpose. Forewarned by signal Intelligence, Rommel's action was pre-empted.

Operation 'Crusader'. Starting on 18 November, a British Eighth Army counter-offensive, under General Sir Alan Cunningham surprised Rommel, driving his Panzer Group back to El Agheila with heavy losses. In the blow and counter-blow following the British initiative, tank battles on Sunday, 23 November ended marginally in Rommel's favour, but on the 28th DAK's HQ was partly overrun, losing cipher and wireless equipment with disastrous consequences. Eighth Army's capture of cipher settings (see Part 2, Panzer Signals and 'Ultra') was to enable GC and CS Bletchley soon to listen almost permanently into wireless traffic between panzer groups, corps and divisions which, together with other ciphers being read, would place Rommel at a distinct disadvantage for the rest of the campaign in Africa. General von Ravenstein, GOC, 21st Panzer Division, and Major Bach, resisting the British onslaught at Halfaya until 17 January, were both taken prisoner along with many others. The Panzer Group suffered 38,000 casualties.

Operation 'Theseus' (map 9). On 21 January 1942, Rommel launched 'Theseus', his second desert offensive –

progressively reinforced by 90th Light Division brought up to strength. Rommel's order of battle in addition to DAK included three Italian corps; XX, X and XXI with two Italian armoured (Ariete and Littorio) and two motorized (Trieste and Trento) divisions plus infantry. Benefiting from improved air support and supplies – thanks to Kesselring's endeavours – 'Theseus' recovered some of the ground previously lost; Benghazi and Derna included. By 4 February the offensive had driven Eighth Army back to a line Gazala–Bir Hacheim.

Second Battle of Tobruk (map 9). On 26 May 1942, with a panzer group command broadened into Panzer Army Africa, Rommel initiated 'Venezia', an extension of his second offensive, planned to culminate in the seizure of Tobruk. The port with its coveted supply facilities would fall within three and a half weeks on 21 June. Facing odds of two to one in armour, Rommel more than justified his

famous nickname – outmanoeuvring and all but destroying Eighth Army in preliminary battles at Gazala. Panzer army strength consisted in the main of 400 Pz Kpfw IIIs fewer than twenty of which were the up-gunned version, mounting a long, 5cm gun and improved frontal armour. Cunningham's successor, Ritchie, faced Rommel with 843 tanks, slightly fewer than 250 of which, were the formidable new Grants with a 7.5cm gun. In the first round of operations at the end of May with but few of his Pz Kpfw IIIs and IVs re-equipped with long 5cm or 7.5cm guns respectively, Rommel tried by tank v. tank actions to obtain supremacy over British armour. When these actions became expensive German armour was conserved by refusing to engage in tank v. tank combat.

Instead, strong screens of anti-tank guns, including a high proportion of 8.8cm and Russian 7.62cm (Marder III) self-propelled guns positioned to cover the panzer force,

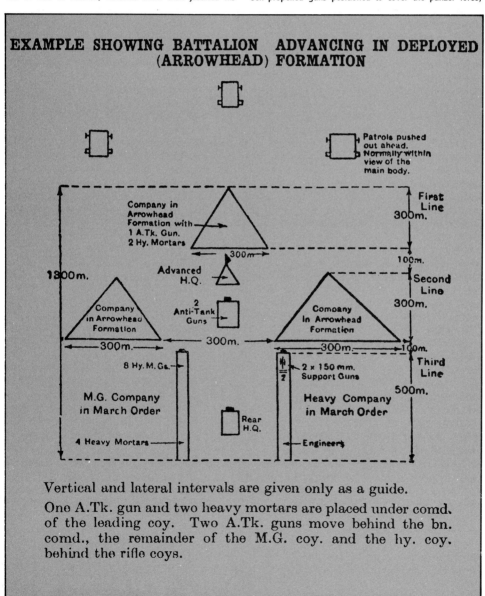

EXAMPLE SHOWING BATTALION ADVANCING IN DEPLOYED (ARROWHEAD) FORMATION

Vertical and lateral intervals are given only as a guide.

One A.Tk. gun and two heavy mortars are placed under comd. of the leading coy. Two A.Tk. guns move behind the bn. comd., the remainder of the M.G. coy. and the hy. coy. behind the rifle coys.

Left: A diagram illustrating the theoretical deployment of tanks and anti-tank guns (2cm, 3.7cm and 8.8cm) by a panzer battalion in Libya, 1941–2; the anti-tank guns following close behind the battalion commander.

prevented the enemy getting tanks into close-range conflict. If they were too heavily engaged by Ritchie's tanks or artillery the panzer companies were withdrawn. The panzer army had a very high proportion of anti-tank guns and could consequently cover its flanks very widely, making outflanking movements extremely difficult. When British tanks attacked, the panzer army subjected them to heavy artillery fire and worked their anti-tank guns forward, using every available bit of ground for cover to get within striking distance. The result was either to force Ritchie to attack at a disadvantage or to withdraw to avoid loss of tanks. The knocking-out of the anti-tank screen by 7.5cm and other artillery fire proved difficult when British tanks and guns had been considerably outnumbered, as they often were.

Eighth Army, caught off balance, out-gunned and out-manoeuvred by Rommel's handling of armour, suffered the loss of Tobruk and considerable stocks of fuel and vehicles. Reporting on its withdrawal after the débâcle at Gazala, the Army commented on its defeat in the following terms:

'Gazala 26 May–15 June 1942. The majority of our actions were of a counter-attack nature and were nearly always held up by anti-tank gun screens, which, because of their numbers and very clever concealment, were difficult to neutralize with the amount of artillery at our disposal.'

'The use of the 8.8 cm gun in the boldest possible manner had a considerable effect on these operations. This gun was often moved into position, particularly on the flanks of armoured formations, to within 1,500 yds of our tanks. German casualties must have been very high amongst crews and many of these guns were knocked out, but the damage they did, even to our Grant tanks, was considerable. The Russian 7.62 cm self-propelled gun was also used in the same way. Another feature of German tactics was continu-ous shelling of our tanks in their battle positions from Pz Kpfw IVs and guns on self-propelled mountings. This fire had little effect and did minor damage only, but it did cause a certain amount of exhaustion to our crews, who, of course, to avoid unnecessary casualties, could not be allowed to dismount for rest or any other purpose. 'The German tank attacks were usually heralded by very heavy artillery concentrations in order to inflict casualties both on the tanks and supporting artillery, after which the tank attack was pressed home.'

The Free French defence under General Koenig of Bir Hacheim, a strong point at the southern end of the Gazala Line, outflanked by Rommel, was broken by Stuka action after several days and withdrawn sustaining heavy losses. Among the many ruses devised by Rommel's staff to convey an impression of panzer strength being greater than actually was the case – during attacks on Benghazi for instance ('Sonenblume', 31 March 1941) was the trailing of cables behind infantry advancing to the attack in trucks. The resulting dust clouds gave the immediate impression that a tank attack was being launched. At other times captured British trucks, were fitted with concealed anti-tank guns, to the disconcertment of approaching British forces. Telegraph poles were used as dummy 8.8cm guns.

On 22 June 1942, after his success in capturing Tobruk – the high-water mark of a remarkable career – Rommel was rewarded with promotion to Field Marshal. The offensive continued eastwards with the benefit of fuel and transport obtained from vast British stores dumped in the neighbourhood of Tobruk, but against the advice of Kesselring and colleagues who wanted a safer and more dependable build-up. On 1 July Rommel reached Alam Halfa and El Alamein. Panzer army intentions: to renew the confrontation with British Eighth Army, complete its destruction and enter Cairo – an event for which, in addition to urgent military preparations, elaborate processional arrangements were being made to enable Mussolini to ride in triumph through the city. But things turned out differently. Strongly entrenched, progressively strengthened and enjoying swift access to resupply bases in the vicinity of Cairo and Alexandria, British Eighth Army immensely heartened under a new commander, turned at bay, enjoying the protection of an air umbrella that the Luftwaffe, trailing in ground organization and strength, was totally unable to match.

Rommel's (re-named) German–Italian Panzer Army, reinforced by 164th Light Division (von Liebenstein), but suffering endlessly from air attack was, by contrast, progressively weakened as supply arrangements betrayed to Eighth Army and the Desert Air Force in detail by Signal Intelligence faltered and air force support waned. When petrol supplies dried up, at times almost completely, operations were severely curtailed. This aspect of Rommel's desert war is elaborated in Part 4, page 137. On 30 August the panzer army failed to dislodge Eighth Army at Alam Halfa. In steadfastly refusing to expose his armour to Rommel's temporarily ascendent Pz Kpfw IVs equipped with the long 7.5cm gun, a new British commander, General Bernard Montgomery, called Rommel's future into question.

The turning-point for Rommel (map 9) came on 23 October 1942, at El Alamein, a railway halt, 60 miles west of Alexandria. At this unremarkable location, Eighth Army under Montgomery, striking back at Rommel after a massive built-up in artillery support and a four or more to one advantage in armour (1,200 British tanks facing 285 German and 278 Italian tanks) broke the weak German–Italian panzer army into pieces, precipitating a general retreat in the direction of Tripoli. On 3 November, just as the movement was getting underway, Hitler instructed Rommel to stand fast – despite the threat of encirclement. By the 4th, the panzer divisions deployed in the north were down to twenty tanks and DAK's commander von Thoma had been captured. In the south, surviving Italian formations with parachute Brigade Ramcke, found themselves stranded; Littorio and Trieste (XX Corps) fighting hard, were practically wiped-out. For the next three months, starved of supplies, transport and equipment of all kinds, fighting rearguard actions over more than 1,500 miles, desperate German and Italian formations receiving minor injections of strength *en route*, were fortunate indeed to ward-off pursuit. Rain and an unaccountably cautious follow-up saved the panzer army from extinction. On 15 February 1943, the panzer army reached the illusory protection of Fifth Panzer Army outposts in Tunisia. At Mareth the apparent strength of prepared fieldworks – a line of reinforced old French block-houses stretching twenty miles inland from the sea to rest on 'impassable' terrain, backed by Wadi Akarit in the coastal corridor south of Gabes, held promise of sanctuary, but Rommel was not impressed.

A re-organization of Axis forces in North Africa was now due. The presence of Fifth Panzer Army in Africa (q.v.) and a need to satisfy Italian claims to command were primary considerations. But a supreme headquarters – Army Group Africa – to be established in Tunis would fail to stifle strong German–Italian differences of opinion; whether for instance Tripoli, the Italian Army's prinicipal base and a prestigious colonial capital in Africa, with extensive military and stores-handling facilites, should have been evacuated by Rommel in defiance of Comando Supremo instructions. And, worried the Italians, did Rommel deliberately strand their units at El Alamein? Adding to the Field Marshal's problems (and Kesselring's, too) were other impediments to operational efficiency – rivalry between panzer army commanders. Unco-ordinated counter-attacks following Allied landings in Morocco and Algeria (see Fifth Panzer Army in Africa, 8 November 1942) led to missed opportunities when the Allies were gathering strength and at their most vulnerable in January and February 1943. This would be followed by Rommel's departure from Africa on 9 March after only fifteen days as Army Group Commander. Despite disaffection between Axis partners and commanders, the war in Africa continued unabated.

Operation 'Spring Wind'. On 14 February 1943, joint action by Rommel and von Arnim, was intended to drive off mainly US forces threatening Sfax and Gabes – crucial to the security of Rommel's communications. Attacks led by von Arnim's deputy, General Ziegler, from El Faid and later by Rommel himself at Kasserine employing a strong part of 10th Panzer Division (Hildebrandt) and a reassigned veteran 21st Panzer Division (Broich, after Fischer was killed in action 5 February 1943), and working briskly in support of a DAK battle group (von Liebenstein), scattered inexperienced US forces. But exploitation failed when command weaknesses surfaced (see also Fifth Panzer Army, 14 February 1943). Meanwhile 15th Panzer Division (Borowietz) deployed forward of the Mareth Line, acted vigorously in defensive action there. 'Spring Wind', although a failure, gained time for Axis armies to consolidate in Tunisia and Rommel's appointment to Army Group Command followed on 23 February 1943. Italian First Army, Rommel's former headquarters, reconstituted in the hands of General Messe, then intended a determined stand in the modest fieldworks at Mareth – an intention that, despite the arrival of a new Italian armoured division, Centauro (Calvi) and more infantry, would remain unfulfilled as Eighth Army closed in for the kill. Rommel planned to strike first, upsetting Eighth Army's timetable.

Operation 'Capri' was undertaken on 6 March 1943 by DAK (Cramer), employing 10th (Broich), 15th and 21st (Hildebrandt) Panzer Divisions with 150 tanks between them. But the offensive failed to disrupt Eighth Army forming up at Medenine to attack the German–Italian line. Forewarned of Rommel's intentions by SIGINT and deploying 600 carefully sited 6pdr anti-tank guns (destroying fifty tanks in this costly spoiling attack) helped Montgomery substantially in putting paid to Rommel's plan – his last in Africa. Devised but not directed by Rommel, this abortive panzer action caused little delay to the Allied counter-offensive that was building-up. On 9 March, before British and US Forces could lever the panzer army out of the Mareth Line, and final battles for Bizerta and Tunis would destroy both panzer armies in Africa, Rommel, who was about to benefit (unexpectedly) from a senior appointment

in Italy, departed for Europe and a meeting with Hitler.

On 20 March, Montgomery's Eighth Army (XXX corps with heavy artillery support) opened a breach in the Mareth defences. Simultaneous moves to outflank the line via the Tebaga gap to the west were started by the New Zealand Corps which brought 164th Light and 21st Panzer Divisions back into action; A US II Corps (Patton) move behind Messe also drew 10th Panzer Division into counter-attacks.

Blitzkrieg in reverse. On 26 March 1943, employing tactics reminiscent of the best German combined army/air operations, Operation 'Supercharge II' – executed in conjunction with the Desert Air Force (Broadhurst) – turned the Mareth Line, nullifying German–Italian plans for a protracted stand in the former French defensive system. The Mareth Line was consequently abandoned, despite 10th Panzer's success in stalling an American break-through to Gabes on the coast behind Axis defences. On 30 March, when US II Corps renewed its threat to First Italian Army communications (but not in time to prevent the panzer army's escape), Messe and von Arnim parried the drive with 10th and 21st Panzer Division battle groups. But within days US and British reconnaissance units were uniting to forge a ring securing the panzer armies. On 7 April, following fourteen days of heavy fighting, Messe's Army abandoned 'last ditch' defences at Wadi Akarit, falling back along coastal routes to Enfidaville. Under constant threat from Anglo-US air forces and increasingly short of supplies, Messe was unlikely to stay the course.

The **capitulation** of Rommel's former desert army, which Messe had taken over three months earlier, was accepted by the Allies on 13 May 1943, following four weeks of resistance that Eighth Army twice failed to break. Stripped of armour (transferred west of Tunis where the Allied Commander-in-Chief (Alexander) was directing 'Vulcan' 18th Army Group's main effort at breaking von Arnim's defence of the capital (see Fifth Panzer Army Africa, 22 April 1943), Messe was left powerless.

Career note: Field Marshal Erwin Rommel, 1943–4. Rommel left Africa for Europe on 9 March to press with Hitler his case for withdrawing into a mountain sanctuary, Enfidaville–Tunis–Bizerta. Hitler declined the proposal and Rommel was forbidden to return. Instead, Hitler offered Rommel a command in the invasion sensitive Balkans theatre. But on 15 August, in the aftermath of 'Husky' (see Panzer Action in Italy, 10 July 1943) Rommel was instead appointed to command Army Group 'B' with headquarters in Munich. Rommel's brief was to plan an Axis defence of the Alps and northern Italy. On 12 September Rommel moved HQ to Lake Garda. On 21 November Hitler resolved the question of who should defend Italy in favour of Kesselring who advised him to stand firm in the south. Rommel, with partly the same staff, was consequently appointed Inspector of Coastal Defences in the west.

In north-west Europe. On 15 January 1944, Rommel's status was changed to C-in-C, Army Group 'B' with an operational command stretching from the Zuider Zee to the mouth of the Loire, but one that was limited to twelve miles inland. By May 1944, with HQ at La Roche-Guyon west of Paris, the Field Marshal shared responsibility for the deployment of armour in Normandy with Geyr von Schweppenburg, GOC, Panzer Group West (see Fifth Panzer Army, Europe). Following his adverse experience of the effect of air power on mobile operations in Africa, Rommel planned to dispose the panzer divisions close to the beaches, alert for immediate counter-attack. But, with three divisions only – 2nd, 116th and 21st Panzer at his disposal, and overruled by C-in-C, West (von Runstedt) supported by Hitler – Rommel was instructed not to concentrate them. Instead, at Geyr von Schweppenburg's instigation, these and the other available panzer divisions held in OKW reserve in northern France – Panzerlehr, 1st SS, 12th SS, 17th SS (Panzer Grenadier) were deployed inland. A visit from Guderian on 28 April failed to resolve the problem in Rommel's favour.

On 6 June 1944 when the invasion of Normandy did come and Geyr von Schweppenburg was placed under Rommel on the 7th, the mobile divisions moving to support infantry divisions surviving on the coast were forced under furious air assault into time-consuming detours, delaying them beyond all expectation. Sizeable fighting elements were destroyed by air action before they could come completely into action and those that did, suffered equally from the destructive effect of air and naval gunfire. Disaster threatened and a personal tragedy was in the offing.

Rommel was injured on 17 July, barely five weeks before the Allies would destroy his Army Group. The incident occurred as he was returning from a front-line visit to I SS Panzer Corps on the eve of 'Goodwood' D+42; a low-flying air attack on the Field Marshal's car by 605 Squadron RAF at Ste-Foy-de-Montgommery immediately north of Vimoutiers, causing him severe head injuries and removing him from active service. Von Kluge succeeded him in command of the Army Group which, on 19 August, after losing most of its equipment and armour was encircled and practically destroyed in the Falaise pocket (*see* Fifth Panzer Army, 19 August 1944).

Thereafter, gravely concerned by developments in Normandy and the war in general, Field Marshal Rommel, a popular figure with subordinates and the public in Germany (but less endeared to the Italians who continued to believe that he had deliberately stranded them at El Alamein), was implicated in the Hitler assassination plot of 20 July 1944. Recriminations followed.

Rommel's death by suicide. Taken under escort from Herrlingen, his home town in Würtemburg, Rommel ended his own life on 14 October 1944; an ignominious death by poisoning belieing the trappings of a state funeral attended by Keitel among others in Ulm on 18 October 1944. Thus closed the career of a brilliant and respected panzer tactician, one of the ablest of the war. Rommel's talent for mobile operations – culminating in the capture of Tobruk, a shattering defeat for British Eighth Army – was at times more than offset by the knowledge that his British opponents learned of his intentions and difficulties from Sigint. Despite so unenviable a handicap, Rommel's ability to read the battle moves of his opponents and to counter them with superior tactics until battles of attrition and supply robbed his Panzer Army of vitality proved of the highest order.

6. Fifth Panzer Army Afrika (PzAOK 5, 1943)

Raised in Tunisia in December 1942, by upgrading XC Army Corps. The Corps Commander, appointed on 16 November, was General Walther Nehring. A former DAK commander, wounded and flown home from North Africa in August 1942, Nehring was not retained as GOC Fifth Panzer Army when the Army Corps was upgraded; the post instead being taken by Generaloberst Hans-Jurgen von Arnim, appointed on 8 December. Both commanders were responsible to C-in-C (Oberbefehlshaber, OB), South, Field Marshal Albert Kesselring, whose HQ was located at Frascati twelve miles southeast of Rome. In a command reshuffle on 9 March 1943, von Arnim moved up in the Axis military hierarchy, succeeding Rommel as GOC, Army Group Africa; command of Fifth Panzer Army then passing to General Gustav von Vaerst (15th Panzer Division) who would retain the appointment until Fifth Panzer Army – and all other German and Italian troops in Africa – capitulated during the second week in May. General Walther Nehring would meanwhile lead the Tunis build-up, promoting OKW intentions to establish a strong military presence in Tunisia, a province of Vichy France since June 1940, at a time when Anglo-American forces, after disembarking in North Africa 400 miles west of Tunis, were driving east along the Mediterranean coast, and threatening Sicily.

Allied presence west of Tunis arose out of Operation 'Torch', launched on 8 November 1942, when 107,000 British and American troops unexpectedly pouring ashore in Morocco and Algeria, seized Casablanca, Oran and Algiers before consolidating partially into British First Army (Anderson) and turning east to threaten Tunis and Sicily. At the time of 'Torch', in November 1942, following Rommel's defeat at El Alamein (*see* Panzer Army Africa, 23 October 1942), German–Italian military resources in North Africa were totally exhausted; the value of Rommel's Panzer Army, facing annihilation in Cyrenaica, being negligible. But no less important than helping to save Rommel's forces by establishing a sanctuary in Tunisia, was the overriding need to win time for the defence of Europe with a new, mainly German, build-up in the south. From 8 to 27 November 1942, Hitler's reaction to 'Torch' concentrated upon military and diplomatic action, not only in metropolitan France but also in North Africa where plans to protect this strategically important corner of the Mediterranean with its sea approaches to Italy, would rest upon a strong German led force occupying key points in Tunisia.

The race for Tunis and Bizerta. This started on 9 November 1942, with a build-up of German activity, codenamed 'Braun'. Directed by OB South it evolved with great alacrity and proved a remarkably effective counter to the Allied invasion. Disembarking on the North African coast 24 hours earlier, the Allied centre (Oran) and eastern (Algiers) task forces comprising seven divisions, including US 1st Armored Division (Fredendall), consolidated into British First Army (Anderson), were unfortunately slow in getting under way to Tunis.

[Operations 'Anton' and 'Lila' *starting on 11*

November, meanwhile inaugurated a German take-over of Vichy France; OKW's interest focusing in particular upon the maritime regions of the south including Corsica. 'Anton' would be followed on 27 November by 'Lila', a security operation in which 7th and 10th Panzer Divisions serving II SS Panzer Corps (Hausser) seized Toulon harbour, but failed to prevent the scuttling of the French fleet.] The German race for Tunis, starting within hours of the invasion, progressed daily, pulled together after 16 November by XC Corps Commander, General Walther Nehring. Nehring's brief, developed by his successor von Arnim, was to direct the deployment and action of all German/Italian armoured, motorized and support units arriving in Tunisia, to confront the Allies whose post-invasion lodgements at Bougie (11 November) and Bône (12 November) increased the threat to Tunis and compounded the Germans' problem. Notwithstanding the Allies' advantage in disembarking large numbers of troops in comparative safety, Allied planners were to be surprised at OB South's unexpected speed and adroitness in building a bridgehead, securing a strategic prize and keeping the Allies at arm's length from Europe. By midday on 9 November, the first of several Stuka and fighter groups dispatched from II Air Corps, Sicily subordinate to Luftwaffe Colonel Martin Harlinghausen, newly appointed Fliegerführer, Tunis (soon to succeed von Waldau similarly serving Rommel – but whose command would be abolished in favour of unified air force support directed from Tunis) were arriving at Tunis and nearby Djedeida. Over the next five days brisk air-trooping operations between Sicily and Tunis, accelerating the build-up, would involve giant Me 323 transports in hazardous and ultimately suicidal transport operations (see Part 4, page 139), combat troops of 5th Parachute Regiment (Koch) and Kesselring's escort battalion flown from Rome landing on the 11th; anti-aircraft and anti-tank detachments following on. So that by the time Walther Nehring arrived from Germany on the 14th, reported back to Kesselring on the 15th and then settled into his appointment on the 16th, after recuperating from wounds suffered at Alam Halfa in August, Tunis and its crucial transport facilities were firmly in German hands.

The build-up continued to gather momentum. From late November panzer units including Tiger detachments from 501st Heavy Tank Battalion, intended for Rommel, would be followed by 10th Panzer Division and Hermann Goering Division (minus its panzer regiment). These came mainly from France where 10th Panzer had been released from occupational duties in Marseille at the conclusion of 'Anton' and Hermann Goering Division at Cognac was interrupted in the early stages of converting to a panzer division. Motorized and infantry support, diverted from Rommel, especially 47th Infantry Regiment, the veterans of air-landing operations in Holland in 1940, joined in the race for Tunis together with both German and Italian artillery, heavy anti-tank, anti-aircraft and infantry units.

On 27 November the first panzer unit – a company of six Pz Kpfw IIIs and three Tigers from 501st Heavy Tank Battalion slipped into Bizerta harbour. Four hundred vehicles and more weapons arrived on the 28th.

Tigers (Pz Kpfw V), eventually no more than nineteen in number, were first used in action on 29 November west of Tunis, securing Nehring's grip on Djedeida; but fared badly. Lacking spares in subsequent operations, they were more

often out of action than in. Only the dedicated work of tank crews kept the massive vehicles operational. On 8 December, when XC Corps (or Stab Nehring) was upgraded in Tunisia to become Fifth Panzer Army the army commander appointed from the Eastern Front (XXXIX Panzer Corps) to replace Nehring – whose unpalatable but wholly realistic forecast that Tunisia could not be defended in the supply circumstances branded him defeatist – was Generaloberst Hans-Jurgen von Arnim.

By the end of December von Arnim's tank strength was reported to OKW as 350 – mainly Px Kpfw IIIs, but costly battles by both Nehring and von Arnim, securing key points and blocking Allied thrusts out of the mountains around Tunis, reduced their numbers. Soon only half would be fit for battle. Personnel strength in the theatre amounted to 66,000 by mid December with numbers continuing to rise.

Expanding the bridgehead. January 1943. At Kesselring's prompting von Arnim struck out of the confines of the bridgehead which Nehring had created. The early capture of road junctions Djedeida, Tebourba and Medjez el Bab, west of Tunis, also Mateur covering Bizerta, had

Above: General Walther Nehring served with distinct in North Africa, commanding DAK from March to August 1942 (second Battle of Tobr map 9) and XC Corps in Tur from November to Decembe 1942 before departing the theatre for the Eastern Fron and eventual command of Fi Panzer Army in March 1945

secured key sectors for OB South, although Medjez was later abandoned. New moves were intended to extend the bridgehead west and south-west.

Operation 'Courier'. On 18 January 1943, von Arnim struck out with 10th Panzer Division (Fischer) and the mixed Tiger-grenadier battle group (Weber), aiming to win time and space in Tunisia with offensive operations 'Courier I and II', executed in conjunction with the Italian Division Superga (Lorenzelli). Von Arnim's battle groups reinforced by paratroops and mountain infantry, supported by flak troops and engineers, pushed outwards, blocking Anglo-US forces advancing against Tunis from Pont du Fahrs, 50 kilometres to the south-west. The stalling effect of 'Courier' on British First Army and the presence of 21st Panzer Division sent back to Sfax by Rommel, whose rear was so obviously threatened by events in Tunisia, enabled Panzer Army Africa to withdraw safely out of Tripolitania and during February 1943 reach prepared positions at Mareth. This revitalized chain of old French block-houses, stretching twenty miles inland from the coast, had been constructed in the 1930s to deter Italian attacks from Tripoli. Now it was hoped by the High Command that the Mareth 'Line' with additional fieldworks would stand up to Eighth Army. Neither Rommel nor Messe, his successor in command of Panzer Army Africa, shared the view.

In February 1943, aggressive panzer action to deter Allied progress all around the 400-mile bridgehead, was undertaken by an incomplete 10th Panzer Division in conjunction with veteran 15th and (refurbished) 21st Panzer Divisions. Operations that were supported by *ad hoc* German and Italian battle groups including an impromptu motorized 'Division' von Broich (later von Manteuffel) – composed of any number of different units as they arrived in North Africa.

Operation 'Spring Wind', starting on 14 February 1943, was launched to counter US forces pushing deeper into central Tunisia. At Sbeitla the Americans threatened to extend their drive eastwards slicing across the Tunisian bridgehead between Mareth and Enfidaville to Sfax on the east coast; a move that would close the escape route of

Panzer Army Africa. Should Rommel decide to retire northwards via the coastal defile at Gabes, German retention of Sfax was essential; counter-action was imperative. Deploying battle groups from 10th and 21st Panzer Divisions under the direction of General Ziegler (von Arnim's deputy), operations against US II Corps (Fredendall) east of Sbeitla were pursued in conjunction with a DAK battle group led by Colonel von Liebenstein pushing north from El Guettar – bringing immediate results. On the first day, Zeigler won a resounding success, scattering green US troops. On the 19th, following a regrouping under Rommel, 'Spring Wind' culminated in the capture of the Kasserine Pass – a crucial sally-port for extending 'Spring Wind' into an encirclement manoeuvre reaching to the north coast behind British and US forces facing Tunis. Yet after further limited success the idea of wider action was abandoned and the pass was given up. In Kesselring's view, neither of the two commanders demonstrated much faith in exploiting 'Spring Wind' or evinced confidence in the other.

Rivalry between commands had quickly surfaced. Rommel favoured a deep thrust to capture Tebessa, the Allied supply base well behind the front and a significant staging-point *en route* to the coast at Bône. Comando Supremo and von Arnim preferred more limited action directed on Le Kef immediately to the Allied rear. Opportunities were lost through indecision; Tiger support promised by von Arnim was withheld for action in the north, fuel and ammunition continued in short supply. Rommel, disillusioned over the course of events in general, would anyway have preferred to withdraw into defensible mountain territory north of Enfidaville, but continued towards Le Kef as instructed. On 22 February, Kesselring called a halt. The result was to lose forever the greatest opportunity the Germans would have to defeat First and Eighth Armies in turn, and achieve a stalemate – however short-lived – in North Africa. Rommel, appointed Army Group Commander on the 23rd, planned instead to strike in the south at British Eighth Army, forming-up to attack the Mareth Line.

Operation 'Oxhead'. On 26 February 1943, panzer action was renewed in northern Tunisia with Fifth Panzer

Right: Generaloberst Hans-Jurgen von Arnim (left) with Generalmajor Wolfgang Fischer of 10th Panzer Division. Von Arnim served in Poland and France as GOC, 52nd Infantry Division. He was GOC 17th Panzer Division in 1940; GOC XXXIX Panzer Corps in 1941; GOC, Fifth Panzer Army in 1942; and in 1943 he became GOC, Army Group Tunis.

Army launching Operation 'Oxhead'. Lead by Corps Group Weber comprising 501st Battalion (Tigers) and three mixed infantry battle groups of regimental size, helped forward by strong air support, 'Oxhead' was intended to improve army positions around Medjez el Bab. The town controlled access to Tunis by the direct route from the east and was securely held by the Allies. Reinforced by an impromptu motorized 'division' under the battle-experienced Colonel von Manteuffel – the future Commander, Fifth Panzer Army in Europe 10 September 1944, and with the Italian Division Superga also participating, but all suffering heavy losses in vehicles and men, the offensive made only limited gains and was called off within two days. Unrelenting Allied pressure in March and early April, directed by Field Marshal Alexander, the new 18th Army Group commander who took up his appointment immediately after the US débâcle at Kasserine, drove the panzer armies relentlessly back upon their main areas Enfidaville, Bizerta and Tunis – there to conduct a tenacious but abortive defence. Attempting the best possible use of inadequate resources skilfully deployed to take advant-age of difficult mountainous country, in much the same way that the panzer divisions would operate in the forthcoming campaign in Italy, Fifth Panzer Army and Messe's First Italian Army – formerly Panzer Army Africa – suffered endless supply deficiencies; their petrol, ammuni-tion and supplies tightly rationed as one supply-ship after another, identified by British Sigint and attacked by the Royal Navy and Air Force were sent to the bottom of the Mediterranean.

Operation 'Vulcan'. By 22 April 1943, when Alex-ander's 18th Army Group launched Operation 'Vulcan' aiming directly at Tunis from the west, 10th, 15th, 21st and Hermann Goering Panzer Divisions were ready to defend the front, but suffering like all others from a shortage of crucial stores, disposed of fewer than 150 tanks against an estimated 1,400 possessed by 18th Army Group.

From 22 April to 6 May 1943, the burned-out divisions of Army Group Africa, ceaselessly attacked from the air, especially on the Central Sector west of Tunis between Medjez el Bab and Goubellat where DAK was now concentrated, were penned into an ever-shrinking bridge-head and reduced to impotence; in the case of 15th Panzer Division making a last-ditch stand in the path of British First Army's main effort – IX Corps (Horrocks) with 6th and 7th Armoured Divisions driving straight for Tunis on 6 May – to the point of destruction. By nightfall on 6 May 1943, the collapse of both German and Italian armies – subordinate to Army Group Tunis, successor to Army Group Africa – was imminent. Unable to resist Alexander's overwhelming pressure and desperate for ammunition (had it arrived it could not have been distributed because of lack of fuel), von Arnim lost control of the situation. The panzer divisions fought to the last round, but Tunis and Bizerta were yielded on the 7th.

Capitulation of Fifth Panzer Army in Africa followed on 13 May 1943 when the seniormost German commanders in the theatre, von Arnim and von Vaerst, were both taken prisoner. German military operations in North Africa

Below: Ju 52 wings from Sic **crossing the Mediterranean a** **wave height in airbridge** **operations to supply Rommel** **and von Arnim in North Afric**

concluded with the surrender of 230,000 German and Italian effectives; fewer than 700 officers and men escaped the Allied sea and air blockade to reach Europe. Three Army divisions, 10th, 15th and 21st Panzer, four motorized divisions and most of the Hermann Goering (Fallschirm Panzer) Division, minus its panzer regiment, were lost. Some, like HG and 15th Panzer were reformed, the latter as a panzer grenadier division (see Panzer Action in Italy, 10 July 1943). 21st Panzer Division, rehabilitated by Panzer Group West in March 1944, would have an important role to play in the defence of Normandy (see Fifth Panzer Army in Europe, 6 June 1944). The war in Africa was over, but new battles in Sicily were about to exact a further toll of the panzer force.

7. Panzer action in Italy, 1943–5

German reaction to the Allied invasion of Sicily, Operation 'Husky', in July 1943 – followed for almost two years by the demands of a gruelling campaign on the mainland of Italy, would absorb the energies of Hermann Goering, 16th and 26th Panzer Divisions and five panzer grenadier divisions. Until their numbers were reduced by transfers to other fronts, these powerful mobile divisions with supporting arms and services would provide a core of German resistance in Italy continuing until capitulation on 2 May 1945. Two panzer corps, but no panzer army headquarters served in the theatre. Responsibility for providing ground attack support for the panzer divisions and the air defence of Sicily lay with the fighter and Stuka Wings of II Air Corps (Bülowius).

The Panzer division commonly associated with the defence of Sicily and mainland Italy after suffering heavy losses in Tunisia (see Fifth Panzer Army, Africa, 13 May 1943) was the Hermann Goering Fallschirm Panzer Division. Reforming at the time of 'Husky' in the neighbourhood of Taormina, the division would operate in Sicily by forming two battle groups for mobile operations; basically the panzer regiment under the divisional commander General Conrath, and the other comprising divisional panzer grenadier units lead by Oberst Schmalz, the Brigade Commander. Later, on the mainland, two more panzer divisions, 16th (Sieckenius) and 26th Panzer (von Lüttwitz), redeployed from France, would join Hermann Goering in defending Calabria, Italy's southern-most province, separated from Sicily by the Straits of Messina. The five panzer grenadier divisions deployed in the theatre defending Sicily or mainland Italy, comprised 15th (Rodt), reforming on the island between Marsala and Trapani from remnants of 15th Panzer destroyed in Africa; 90th (Lungershausen), rebuilding in Sardinia after a similarly disastrous experience; 16th Reichsführer SS (Gesele), a new formation raised to brigade strength from a regimental nucleus stationed in Corsica; and two other first line divisions, 3rd (Gräser) and 29th (Friess), which, like the two panzer divisions, would be brought south from France. In northern Italy for a time during August 1943, following Mussolini's downfall, and prior to the exit of Italy from the war on 8 September, two other panzer divisions would be involved in security duties including sweeps against partisans. They were the Leibstandarte (Adolf Hitler) and 24th Panzer. The presence of these and other valuable divisions so far from main fronts would become a blight on German resources. Most would have been better employed in critical situations elsewhere, and with pressure mounting east and west the 'Italian' divisions were inevitably drawn off for action there. Eventually fewer than half of the panzer or panzer grenadier divisions committed in Italy against superior Allied land, sea and air forces would remain in support of a growing number of infantry divisions.

Defending Sicily, 10 July 1943. When General Patton's US Seventh and General Montgomery's British Eighth Armies, lead by airborne troops, initiated Operation 'Husky' at Gela and Pacino in the south-east corner of Sicily, nothing but incomplete German armoured formations were on hand to stiffen Italian Sixth Army (Guzzoni) resistance. The German divisions, Hermann Goering Division and 15th Panzer Grenadier, were divided in support of Italian formations; Italian Sixth Army consisting of four divisions of immobile infantry and miscellaneous coastal protection units with a German liaison officer, General von Senger und Etterlin serving at Army Headquarters at Enna. But on 14 July 1943, the picture changed rapidly with the arrival of German reinforcements in the shape of 1st Paratroop (Fallschirmjaeger) Division (Heidrich) followed soon afterwards by 29th Panzer Grenadier Division (Rodt) and, on 17 July, to take control of all German troops in Sicily, XIV Panzer Corps Headquarters (Hube). 2nd Parachute Regiment (Heilmann), the advance guard of 1st Paratroop Division, airlifted via Rome out of OKW reserve at Avignon, was parachuted into Catania airfield then transported into action by road. Under Hermann Goering command, these battle-seasoned paratroops formed by HG units into mixed battle groups, incorporating Tiger detachments of 504th Heavy Tank Battalion, fought aggressively in defence of key points. So unexpected was this development that Anglo-US planners were obliged to revise their strategies and reconsider formerly optimistic views on the chances of a swift and easy passage northwards through Sicily. Allied pressure on German ground and air forces defending the island nevertheless continued to mount unrestrainedly.

On 25 July, with the battle for Sicily approaching its height, Benito Mussolini, Il Duce, was dismissed by the Grand Council. As a result of this development Hitler issued orders to accelerate a German build-up in Italy; 16th and 26th Panzer Divisions followed by 3rd and 29th Panzer Grenadier Divisions moved swiftly into northern Italy from France, pushing down to Rome or to Calabria. On 26 July, also in response to developments in Italy, Hitler ordered 2nd Paratroop Division (Ramcke) with General Student's I Parachute Corps HQ, to be flown from the OKW reserve at Avignon to the neighbourhood of Rome; the order being executed next day. On 31 July, Italian Sixth Army, responsible for defending Sicily, was formerly subordinated to XIV Corps (Hube), and the German liaison staff under von Senger und Etterlin was disbanded. On 17 August, the evacuation of Sicily, in Operation 'Lehrgang' under Hube's direction, resulting in 40,000 German troops with 10,000 vehicles (47 tanks) evading encirclement, was concluded with all involved crossing the Straits of Messina to Calabria in good order; the bulk of their equipment being trans-shipped intact and Luftwaffe anti-aircraft protection playing a key role in the operation.

In **northern Italy** during August 1943, where a new Army Group, 'B', under Field Marshal Rommel, established on the 17th with headquarters in Munich, was expecting to take command of mainland operations, six infantry and two panzer divisions – Leibstandarte Adolf Hitler and 24th Panzer, responsible to II SS Panzer Corps Headquarters (Hausser), redeployed from the Mius to Reggio after failing with 'Citadel' – were involved in security sweeps; Operation 'Feurstein' especially. Rommel's first move as GOC, Army Group 'B' was to review the security of transalpine routes affording German access to central and southern Italy. In this respect the situation improved immediately with General Feurstein, a mountain warfare specialist from the Bavarian mountain training school at Mittenwald and a former commander of 2nd Mountain Division, leading mixed Tiger and infantry battle groups to gain control of vital arteries, the Brenner Pass in particular. Feurstein's com-mand was subsequently expanded into LI Mountain Corps and played an important role in the defence of Cassino early in 1944. These and subsequent moves to safeguard the German position in Italy, code-named 'Axe', were executed with small loss and by the time the Allies carried the war to the mainland on 3 September and the Italian Govern-ment, following a secret armistice, openly surrendered to the Allies on 8 September, the German order of battle in Italy totalled eighteen divisions; ten of which were responsible to Field Marshal Kesselring OB (C-in-C), South, where a new Tenth Army was created under General de Panzertruppen von Vietinghoff, and eight in the north serving another new, Fourteenth Army (von Mackensen), answerable to Rommel.

In **Calabria** on 3 September 1943, military operations on the mainland of Italy began to take firm shape. A British landing under Montgomery at Reggio was contested by 29th Panzer Grenadier and 26th Panzer Divisions although the latter's armour was retained in Rome for contingency action. German reaction to the British landing at Reggio was followed six days later by Tenth Army concentrating Hermann Goering, 16th Panzer, 3rd and 29th Panzer Grenadier Divisions against a fresh incursion into Calabria lead by US General Mark Clark at Salerno 150 miles to the north. On the same day German reaction to Italy's break with the 'Axis' (broadcast the previous day) set in train Operation 'Axe', the occupation of Rome and the disarming of Italian forces.

The occupation of **Rome** on 9 September 1943 was initiated by General Student who garrisoned the city with 2nd Parachute Division brought from Ostia and 3rd Panzer Grenadier Division redeployed south from Bolsena. Securing Rome against Regular Italian forces, Student disarmed Centauro, Ariete and other divisions of General Carboni's Motorized Corps; a move that he followed by organizing the capture of Italian Army HQ at Monte Rotondo (by airborne assault), and on the 12th released Mussolini from detention at the Campo Imperatore Hotel, a resort residence in the

mountains south of Rome. The operation was carried out by Obersturmbannführer Otto Skorzeny. In northern Italy, corresponding security moves by Army Group 'B' would take the Leibstandarte from Milan via Turin to Mont Cenis where divisional battle groups were deployed to break the resistance of Alpini and partisan units threatening German communications. At the conclusion of 'Axe' resulting in the seizure by Army Group 'B' of at least 230 tanks, 24th Panzer Division was stationed in Verona while the Leibstandarte stood guard over alpine communications. In the South two panzer corps headquarters, Hube's XIV evacuated from Sicily to Calabria and in Hube's leave of absence led by General Hermann Balck, and a new LXXVI Panzer Corps commanded by General Herr, both responsible to von Vietinghoff's Tenth Army, were on hand to direct operations against Anglo-US landings at Reggio and Salerno.

At **Salerno** on 13 September 1943, the US lodgement 30 miles south of Naples was counter-attacked by 16th and 26th Panzer Divisions supported by 29th Panzer Grenadier Division. Not withstanding vigorous action by the troops involved, the offensive was a failure and although renewed on the 14th panzer attacks were again defeated with the help of naval firepower. Baulked in this endeavour, Kesselring ordered Tenth Army back to the Volturno; the last 16th Panzer Division rearguards leaving the city on 30 September. Despite losing Naples to the Allies, OKW's determination to protect the southern flank of Europe by opposing every mile of Anglo-US progress through Italy was to be amply demonstrated in the months to come. During October 1943 on the Adriatic coast, LXXVI Panzer Corps (Herr) retreating from Foggia (abandoned 27 September) opposed British Eighth Army advancing northwards to Termoli and the Sangro; 29th Panzer Grenadier, 1st Paratroop and 16th Panzer Divisions bearing the brunt of heavy fighting. In November 1943, a new Army Group 'C' under Field Marshal Kesselring, changing his title from OB, South to OB, South West and pursuing a rewarding defensive strategy, was encouraged by Hitler at Rommel's expense. Accompanied by the staff of Army Group 'B', Rommel was consequently transferred to the west (see career note, Romel, concluding Panzer Army Africa). Not-withstanding the defection of the Italian Government from the German cause, and the relatively short distance from Salerno to the Reich's frontier north of the Po, there would be no easy push by Allied C-in-C, Field Marshal Alexander, through alpine passes to Vienna. By exploiting the natural strength of mountains extending almost from coast to coast and the delaying effect of swift-flowing rivers south of Rome, like the Sangro (LXXVI Panzer Corps) and Garigliano (XIV Panzer Corps), Kesselring converted Italy to a bastion that would require all the power the Allies could muster to dispose of it; the Sangro – Cassino – Garigliano (Gustav Line) defences especially.

Fighting for twenty months at a cost of 300,000 casualties, and not without the greatest of determination, would the Allies thread their way forward, every route barred by a steadfast defence. Deployed first on one sector and then another, panzer and panzer grenadier battalions proved their worth time and again in responding to Anglo-US pressure by conducting prolonged rearguard actions – holding off the enemy until the last possible moment and

Above: Italy, September 1943, and Tigers supporting the 'Leibstandarte' are guarding the alpine routes visible in the background. Deployed on security duties from head-quarters in Milan, SS armour (here of II SS Panzer Corps) helped Rommel to contain partisan attacks intended to disrupt the flow of supplies and reinforcements to the south.

then slipping away to new positions from which to dominate the battlefield. Panzer grenadiers employing these tactics in SPWs, supported by mountain troops or paratroops committed in ground roles, imposed frustrating delays from commanding ridges and strong points. With little or no Luftwaffe support to offset the air power ranged against the ground forces, German casualties soared; 500,000 by the close of hostilities. But an orderly front was always maintained – nothwithstanding a surprise Mediterranean coast offensive by US VI Corps (Lucas) landing at Anzio – Nettuno, 70 miles behind the main German battleline centred on Cassino.

Panzer action at Anzio–Cassino began on 22 January 1944 when the US-British lodgement (US VI Corps), 25 miles south of Rome and 70 miles to the rear of the main German battle line, was seen to threaten disaster to Tenth Army anchored at Cassino.

A cornerstone of the defence stretched across Italy since December 1943, Monte Cassino dominated the Liri valley, a north-south branch of the Garigliano, through which passed primary routes to Rome. Defended initially by 15th Panzer Grenadier Division (Rodt) and units of 5th Mountain Division (Schrank), battles for possession of this strong point would continue for four months with Tenth Army throwing back all attempts at its capture. Kesselring's reaction to the new threat to Cassino posed by the Anzio landing – anticipated by a contingency plan 'Richard' – would be as effective as it was swift.

All exits from the beachhead were sealed off by alarm units rushed from Rome. These emergency battle groups of motley character were followed into action by paratroops and panzer grenadier units under Paratroop General

Schlemm (I Fallschirm Korps); Schlemm being responsible for the Roman hinterland into which US VI Corps was intruding. In a supporting move, Fourteenth Army HQ (von Mackensen) was brought from the north to handle a concentration of Kesselring's best divisions – Hermann Goering (Schmalz), 26th Panzer (von Lüttwitz), 3rd (Gräser) and 29th (Rodt) Panzer Grenadier Divisions.

On the Garigliano/Cassino front, where US Fifth Army (Clark) was exerting maximum pressure, a reinforced 90th Panzer Grenadier Division (Baade) supported by Fallschirmjaeger units was moved to the centre of operations defending Cassino (XIV Panzer Corps), while to the north 5th Mountain Division (LI Mountain Corps) held on to the flanking massive, dominating the Rapido, an inland tributary of the Garigliano.

Operation 'Sunrise'. Starting on 16 February 1944, two experienced corps commanders – Schlemm, I Fallschirm Korps and Herr, LXXVI Panzer Corps (switched from the Sangro) – would lead the Anzio–Nettuno counter-offensive 'Sunrise' devised by Hitler. Yet despite powerful support provided by assault units issued with Tigers, heavy assault guns and a new weapon, Goliath – a radio-controlled demolition tank filled with high-explosives for use against fixed defences 'Sunrise' failed to make the expected progress. Notwithstanding the élan of battle groups mounting attacks against a strongly entrenched enemy while enduring violent assault by naval and air bombardment, all attempts to eliminate the Allied invasion force failed – although attacks were pressed home on the 16th, 18th and again on 22 February, then continued intermittently for four months. Von Mackensen's efforts came to nothing. Against a staunch defence 'Sunrise' proved fruitless. None of the

Goliaths reached their objectives; and the defenders shrugging off weeks of siege warfare made preparations to resume the offensive.

Last Battle for Cassino. Starting on 11 May 1944, XIV Panzer Corps (von Senger und Etterlin), holding the main German battle line at this point with 1st Paratroop Division (Heidrich), was heavily engaged in repulsing, powerful and repeated Allied ground and air assaults. Bombing attacks during February aimed at dislodging the paratroops around Cassino had resulted instead in the destruction of the Benedictine Abbey which, in crowning Monte Cassino, commanded strategic views of the Liri valley. Despite Tenth Army's profoundly admired powers of resistance (1st Paratroop Division in particular) Allied forces pushing north – French Moroccan troops in the lead – finally turned the defence. On 17 May 1944, Tenth Army engulfed in a new wave of attacks (Operation 'Diadem') instructed battleweary panzer crews, panzer grenadiers, mountain, paratroop and infantry battle groups to disengage from the fourth and final battle of Casino.

On the 22nd, the Anzio bridgehead too erupted with a US Division threatening Tenth Army communications at Valmonte. Hermann Goering Division, released by Kesselring from reserve on the 23rd to meet the threat of encirclement, suffered grievously in air attacks while moving up in daylight. In the retreat from Cassino, XIV Panzer Corps was redeployed to the rear of Tenth Army, leap-frogging most of the available panzer grenadier divisions in flank protection moves north. On 25 May, US Fifth Army units striking from the bridgehead at Anzio united in the coastal area at Terracina with those from the front at Cassino, while Alexander's other troops continued their efforts to destroy the retreating German Army.

In the **US race for Rome,** entered by Fifth Army on 4–5 June 1944, General Mark Clark, breaking free of Fourteenth Army constraints at Anzio, pushed into an empty

city; a move that allowed Tenth Army, retreating from Cassino, to bypass the town and, together with Fourteenth Army, occupy new defences north of Florence. Stalemate ensued and following Kesselring's evacuation of Rome and retreat north to the Green Line, Hermann Goering Division was ordered out of the theatre; 26th Panzer Division being left alone to work with three remaining panzer grenadier divisions, 29th, 90th and 16th SS, also 1st and 4th Paratroop Divisions (the latter raised in action at Anzio) and 23 other formations bringing German fighting strength in Italy up to 29 divisions by October 1944. These, and nineteen other divisions deployed in the Balkans, were left to delay British, US, Russian and satellite forces advancing towards Germany until Army Groups South West and South East capitulated officially on 2 May (Tenth and Fourteenth Armies having surrendered to Alexander on 29 April 1944). Panzer action in Italy never aspired to the dramatic scale of movement and deep penetration characterizing panzer-armee operations in North Africa and in the east. Instead, hull-down tanks revetted into reverse slopes exploited terrain opportunities to a maximum or, when lying concealed in maize fields and the masonry ruins of provincial Italian towns and villages, worked with panzer grenadiers in devising ambush tactics. Perhaps for a week or so in the retreat from Cassino (17 May 1944), when the mainly panzer grenadier divisions subordinate to XIV Panzer Corps played a key role in the escape of Tenth Army, was there a semblance of manoeuvre providing a basis for tactical success. Thereafter, when fighting vehicles were lost in action or abandoned for want of fuel, panzer crews and panzer grenadiers would fight long and hard on foot – exacting a heavy toll of advancing Allied armies, much as they would do elsewhere in Europe as the tide of military operations edged remorselessly towards Germany and Berlin itself. (see Third Panzer Army, 16 April 1945).

Right: Oberstgruppenführer and General der Waffen SS Paul Hausser served the army as a career officer from 1914 to 1918 and the Reichswehr until 1932. In 1933 he joined the SA (Sturmabteilung) and subsequently became Director of the SS Junkerschule at Braunschweig. In 1936 he was Inspector Verfügungstruppen and in May 1939, GOC, SS Verfügungs Division (Das Reich). From June 1942 to June 1944 he served as GOC, SS Panzer Corps, fighting at Kharkov and Buczac (see map 13 and 15). Late in the war he was GOC, Seventh Army in Normandy where he was wounded escaping from the Falaise pocket. In January 1945 he was appointed GOC, Army Group Upper Rhine in succession to Himmler, followed by Army Group 'G' in succession to Balck.

8. Fifth Panzer Army Europe (PzAOK 5, 1944–5)

Originally Panzer Group West, raised in December 1943 from the staff of Panzer General, West, Leo Geyr von Schweppenburg; Headquarters at Paris Auteuil. Geyr's appointment to OB West Headquarters, Paris (St-Germain-en-Laye), serving von Runstedt as panzer adviser, began in July 1943.

Command in the west. On 3 July 1944 (D+27), Geyr was succeeded as GOC Panzer Group West by General Heinrich Eberbach. On 5 August (D+58), after two days as Armeegruppe or Panzerarmee West, Eberbach's Headquarters, was upgraded and redesignated Fifth Panzer Army with Eberbach ccontinuing as GOC until Hitler required him to undertake more pressing employment on the invasion front, leading a new formation (Panzer Group Eberbach) against US Third Army [D+66]; SS Obergruppenführer Sepp Dietrich (I SS Panzer Corps) meanwhile assuming Eberbach's responsibilities as GOC, Fifth Panzer Army. But in a subsequent change of command on 12 September 1944, General Hasso von Manteuffel was appointed GOC to lead the army in the battle of the Ardennes, starting on 16 December. The change was not permanent, however,

and in March 1945 with new employment taking Manteuffel to Third Panzer Army, General Josef Harpe assumed the role of Panzer Army Commander, continuing until capitulation on 18 April 1945. *Bracketed dates starting [D+34] refer to Seventh Army which on D-Day, and subordinate to Army Group 'B' (Rommel), was the command body responsible for the coasts of Brittany and Normandy between the Loire at Nantes and the Orne north of Caen; HQ, Le Mans. After conceding Cherbourg to US First Army (Bradley) on D+23, Seventh Army continued in action at St-Lô south-east of the city, opposing a new US offensive leading to 'Cobra', the decisive break-out in Normandy [D+49]. On 2 July (D+26) following GOC Dollmann's death by suicide, command of Seventh Army passed to SS Oberstgruppenführer Paul Hausser – the first General of the Waffen SS to hold Army command; Dietrich and Steiner, Sixth and 11th SS Panzer Armies, reaching equivalent rank in due course.*

Panzer operations in Normandy are consequently split between Panzer Group West or its successor Fifth Panzer Army, and Seventh Army; distinctive phases being marked by block-dates in the following sequence with a D-Day

equivalent provided until D+85 (30 August 1944) when the last substantial bodies of German troops were crossing the Seine in flight.

PANZER CONTROVERSY AND 'OVERLORD'

The invasion of north-west Europe, Operation 'Overlord' on 6 June (D-Day) 1944, was undertaken by an Allied expeditionary force under the supreme command of General Dwight D. Eisenhower. The plan of assault and subsequent development was, however, the responsibility of 21st Army Group; Army Group Commander, General Bernard Montgomery. Eight weeks later on the invasion front, 'Overlord' was to give rise to a new Fifth Panzer Army; Army Commander, General Heinrich Eberbach. Following two months of intensive tank–infantry operations in a bitter struggle for supremacy in Normandy, the long overdue move by OKW was intended to correct a fatal flaw in command arrangements for panzer divisions in the west. Not in fact until 5 August (D+60) would Panzer Group West (Geyr/Eberbach) in control of panzer divisions since D+1 and responsible to Army Group 'B' (Seventh Army, Panzer Group West, Fifteenth Army) be up-graded and re-designated Fifth Panzer Army. During this crucial period Allied operations had reached their peak, with US forces operating in the western half of the invasion zone, initiating break-out operations on 25 July 1944 (D+49), breaching Seventh Army defences and moving into exploitation. Unfortunately for von Kluge, the Army Group commander who succeeded Rommel when he was injured on D+41, the headquarters and divisions best suited to handle the crisis – Panzer Group West with most of the available armour – was at the time deployed at the opposite end of the battle zone defending Caen; a consequence of 21st Army Group's skilfully applied strategy of attracting German resources away from the critical US break-out sector.

OKW's belated tightening of control of panzer action in Normandy – characterized by a frequent and calamitous loss of initiative – four weeks earlier when Eberbach was brought in to replace Geyr. A cavalry officer with a long history of professional appointments – Geyr was military attaché, London 1933; GOC, 3rd Panzer Division, 1937–40; GOC, XXIV Panzer Corps, 1940–2 – and the General who in July 1943, prior to inaugurating Panzer Group West (December 1943), created a rehabilitation and training command for panzer divisions re-fitting under OB, West von Runstedt. Geyr's training programme was noted for paying special attention to the role of mobile divisions in action against large enemy airborne formations, expected in the hinterland of the invasion front in conjunction with a seaborne assault. Concurrently with its training role, Panzer Group West was intended by OKW to serve as a panzer reserve controlling I SS Panzer Corps (and an incomplete XXXXVII Panzer Corps) with four panzer divisions, 1st SS, 12th SS, 17th SS and Panzer Lehr – the intended hammer in an OKW counter-invasion strategy. But Geyr's views on the operational employment of panzer divisions in the west, a subject upon which he tendered much advice to OB West, differed considerably from those of Field Marshal Rommel, GOC, Army Group 'B'. In Rommel's opinion, based upon personal experience of Allied air power in the Western Desert (see Panzer Army Africa, 1 July 1942), if panzer divisions were to retain their mobility serving in a counter-attack role, undue exposure to Allied air supremacy, such as might be encountered in a lengthy approach march to the invasion front, must be avoided at all costs; the crux of Geyr's argument being that the panzer divisions should be retained well clear of the coast and consequently outside the range of naval artillery, in central, well-camouflaged locations where they would be on hand to counter either sea or airborne invasion. The issue was never resolved to the satisfaction of the parties involved in the controversy. There were in any case too few under-strength panzer divisions deployed in the west, too little equipment and not much of an air force flying in support.

A compromise solution, in which three of the ten panzer divisions currently deployed in the west were allotted to Army Group 'B' (2nd, 21st, 116th), three to Army Group 'G', on the Mediterranean coast (9th, 11th, 2nd SS) and the remaining four to Panzer Group West (1st SS, 12th SS,

17th SS Panzer-Grenadier and Panzer Lehr) failed to provide adequately for any one of the options. In the event Rommel gained limited control of only three panzer divisions with which to support a front stretching from the Loire into Belgium and Holland. Geyr was denied the full orthodox deployment of a powerful mobile reserve considered essential by von Runstedt to his 'hammer' policy, and he himself needed permission from OKW to commit any of the (strategic) reserve panzer divisions allotted to Panzer Group West – the strongest of which was Panzer Lehr. Geyr's eventual replacement by Eberbach, nine years his junior with an equally impressive record of panzer service – CO, 35th Panzer Regiment, 1937; GOC, 4th Panzer Division, 1942; Commander, XXXXVIII Panzer Corps, 1942 and thereafter important professional appointments including a spell with the Inspector-General of Armoured Troops (Guderian), was expected to promote vigorous action halting the slide of Army Group 'B' into disaster. But all too late.

The Allies spring a trap (map 16). By 5 August 1944 (D+60), when Fifth Panzer Army (Eberbach) was inaugurated by up-grading Panzer Group West, ten first class divisions, most of which were superior Waffen SS panzer or panzer grenadier divisions, had been committed to the invasion front piecemeal and burned-out in local action generally contesting Anglo-Canadian (British Second Army) initiatives devised by 21st Army Group holding the panzer divisions around Caen. The ten panzer/panzer grenadier divisions committed in Normandy by D+60 included two (9th SS, 10th SS) withdrawn from the Eastern Front where the majority were deployed in action against the Red Army. Those involved in Normandy were the Army's 2nd, 21st, 116th and Panzer-Lehr, and those of the Waffen SS, 1st, 2nd, 9th, 10th, 12th Panzer and 17th SS Panzer Grenadier Divisions. Of two other Army panzer divisions in the west, as yet uncommitted and re-fitting in the south under Army Group 'G' (Blaskowitz) – 9th Panzer Division (Jollasse) at Nîmes and 11th Panzer Division at Toulouse – 9th Panzer would arrive at the front within hours to re-inforce Seventh Army (Hausser) resisting US First Army at Domfront, while 11th Panzer remained at Toulouse before moving into the Rhône valley and opposing Operation 'Dragoon', a second Allied invasion of France on 15 August 1944 (D+70). Despite so impressive an assembly of panzer divisions in Normandy, including a rare concentration of the best SS panzer divisions, their commitment under unified command to hammer the Allied expeditionary force and push it back into the sea – although this, as the following account illustrates, was intended by Hitler and OKW from the outset – never materialized. Indeed by D+60, Fifth Panzer Army, sharing the invasion front with Seventh Army, was already outmanoeuvred and committed in desperate counter-attacks trying vainly to hold together a rapidly disintegrating front as US forces, exploiting their opportunity for mobile operations after (D+49), swept south and then east, jeopardizing the future of von Kluge's Army Group.

In fact, such was the Army Group's plight following the US break-out (D+62–D+71) that Eberbach's command, by this time a 'Gruppe' acting independently of Fifth Panzer Army and counter-attacking US Third Army closing the ring on a Seventh Army and Fifth Panzer Army pocket forming south-west of Caen, was in imminent danger of annihilation; fortunate battle groups, looking to escape in the direction of the Seine, being sent scrambling for safety under horrendous conditions. The vexed question of how best to integrate the deployment of ten panzer divisions with that of fifty or so infantry and static divisions to form an effective defence against cross-Channel invasion of France, had generated deep-seated controversy in German command circles. Arising largely out of Geyr's limited eastern experience, the problem had been compounded by Hitler's equally paranoid refusal to allow either flexibility or responsibility to any single individual in handling the panzer divisions; a 'difficulty' that was resolved all too late in the day when Geyr was subordinated to Rommel on 7 June (D+1). But Hitler's dissatisfaction over developments in Normandy would lead not only to his replacing Geyr with Eberbach as noted, but on that same day, 3 July, retiring OB West, von Runstedt and substituting von Kluge. Two weeks later in consequence of an injury to Rommel on 17 July (D+41), von Kluge would assume the added responsibility of Rommel's Army Group 'B', an unsatisfactory arrangement soon to give way to another change of command in Normandy. Suspected of disloyalty to Hitler, von Kluge was recalled by OKW on 16 August (17th in practice, D+72); command in the west then passing to Field Marshal Walter Model, former GOC, 3rd Panzer Division in 1941, XXXXI Panzer Corps Commander in the battle for Moscow, 1941–2, and thereafter, still on the Eastern Front, GOC, Ninth Army in 1942. Model's subsequent commands, carrying promotion to Field Marshal

(1 March 1944), were as GOC, Army Group North Ukraine and finally Army Group Centre. But not even Model, the 'Führer's fireman', could save the situation.

By 20 August 1944 (D+75), the shattered remnants of more than forty of the divisions committed by OKW to the defence of the west, including eleven panzer and panzer grenadier divisions, six of them SS – escaping from the battle zone with fewer than 45,000 effectives – were of little military consequence. Senior commanders such as Model, Hausser and Eberbach, would evade capture by the narrowest of margins – only temporarily so in Eberbach's case, taken prisoner by British Second Army on 31 August 1944. Half a million casualties in the west, including 200,000 effectives abandoned in coastal 'fortresses' and the Channel Islands by the end of August, testified to the scale of destruction consuming the Wehrmacht. Evidence of the failure of Hitler's military direction and its consequences for the panzer force is nowhere better exemplified than in the mis-management of panzer divisions in France, particularly those of Panzer Group west in control of I SS, II SS and eventually XXXXVII Panzer Corps (or that Group's successor, Fifth Panzer Army) which from the earliest days of 'Overlord' was committed piecemeal against 21st Army Group lodgements 'Gold', 'Juno' and 'Sword' on the Calvados coast north of Caen.

Panzer Group West and Seventh Army facing invasion 6 June–10 July (D-Day–D+34). At 0330 hours on D-Day, 6 June, British airborne landings (commencing

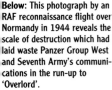
Below: This photograph by an RAF reconnaissance flight over Normandy in 1944 reveals the scale of destruction which had laid waste Panzer Group West and Seventh Army's communications in the run-up to 'Overlord'.

at 0015) to secure Ranville and other key localities on the east bank of the Orne – sealing the outer flank of a seaborne lodgement – were subjected to preliminary assault by II/192 Panzer Grenadier battle group found from 21st Panzer Division (Feuchtinger) which the divisional commander on his own initiative deployed against the airborne troops consolidating east across the river. Feuchtinger's division, stationed south of Falaise (HQ St-Pierre-sur-Dives) and nearest of all to the Calvados beaches, was not however released by Seventh Army (Dollmann) to LXXXIV Corps (Marks) for action against British 6th Airborne until 0700 hours, by which time Army Group headquarters (Speidel, deputising for Rommel, absent on 48 hours' leave) was receiving reports of amphibious assault craft supported by massive naval and air strikes disembarking tanks and infantry on the Calvados coast north of Bayeux. The reaction of OB West (von Runstedt) to 'invasion' in the early hours of D-Day was to alert Panzer Group West (1st SS, 12th SS, Panzer Lehr, 17th SS Divisions) and on his own initiative move 12th SS Division (OKW reserve) from Evreux towards the coast at Lisieux, while at the same time urging OKW (Jodl and Keitel) to release these panzer divisions for offensive action. By 1000 hours the full extent of the Normandy landings, but not their true significance as the main effort of 'Overlord', was being recognized at Army Group HQ; Speidel then moving 116th Panzer Division (von Schwerin) forward to the coast north of the Seine where, in common with 2nd Panzer Division at Abbeville, it was retained in expectation of further assault. But not until 1440 hours on D-Day was Seventh Army (Dollmann) advised by Army Group 'B' that OKW was at last releasing 12th SS Division (Witt) and Panzer Lehr Division (Bayerlein) for offensive action in the Normandy battle zone. Shortly afterwards OKW decided that I SS Panzer Corps (Dietrich) would assume control of these formations.

Meanwhile, on the invasion front two Allied armies – First US (Bradley) and Second British (Dempsey) – were disembarking assault formations along a 50-mile stretch of the Calvados coast between the Orne at Ouistreham and Quinéville ten miles south of Barfleur. 21st Panzer Division (Feuchtinger), regrouping during the day north of Caen with the revised intention of engaging the seaborne lodgement immediately west of the Orne, (Sword), recalled units *en route* to attack the British airborne troops east of the river – a move that attracted the attention of Allied fighter-bombers; a bad augury for the future of panzer operations in Normandy. Nevertheless, by 1600 hours 21st Panzer had assembled two strong battle groups ready to strike to the coast north of Caen. The most successful of these was a reinforced panzer grenadier battalion I/192 (Rauch) which reached the sea north of Caen at 1900 hours and luckily split 'Juno' and 'Sword' between Luc- and Lion-sur-Mer, but despite Rauch's good fortune in finding a gap between beach-heads the attack failed either to disrupt or deter Montgomery's eastern build-up. Stronger action by a more powerful concentration of tanks and infantry – both panzer battalions of 22nd Panzer Regiment (Oppeln-Bronikowski) and 1/125 Panzer Grenadier Battalion, intended to assist Rauch in the push north – resulted instead in the first armoured clash of the campaign in Normandy, at Biéville where armoured squadrons of the Staffordshire Yeomanry deployed in support of British 3rd Division drew 21st Panzer

on to a north-easterly axis leaving Rauch's panzer grenadiers on the coast without heavy support and thereby unable to make further progress. (The Luftwaffe was nowhere to be seen, having flown fewer than 320 sorties against an estimated Allied 14,000 D-Day missions.)

Panzer action to reduce the airborne lodgement on the east bank of the Orne, where Feuchtinger deployed 125th Panzer Grenadier Regiment (Luck) re-inforced by the 21st Divisional Reconnaissance Unit and 200th Assault Gun Battalion continued purposefully with attacks against strongly defended positions. At 2100 hours when a fresh wave of airborne landings – 6th Airborne's remaining parachute battalions, armoured reconnaissance and light artillery units – threatened the safety of his division, Feuchtinger recalled the panzer grenadiers on the coast and regrouped with the panzer regiment north of Caen, preparing for action next day in conjunction with 12th SS Hitler Jugend Panzer Division (Witt) arriving from Lisieux and taking up positions on the division's left flank north of Carpiquet where a usable airfield two miles west of the city had recently been evacuated by the Luftwaffe. At about the same time on the evening of D-Day, Rommel was returning to his headquarters on the Seine at La Roche-Guyon west of Paris, following 48 hours' leave of absence celebrating his wife's birthday at Herrlingen, near Stuttgart. Panzer action on D-Day – 21st Panzer Division striking in regimental strength at invasion forces east and west of the Orne with no advantage in Luftwaffe support and a lack of unified direction – suffered the additional handicap of OKW fears in releasing crucial reserves too early in the battle.

Such inhibition was above all the consequence of a brilliant Allied deception plan, Operation 'Fortitude', which even before the invasion began was successful in focusing OKW attention on the Pas-de-Calais, 150 miles to the north-east, where the main assault by a phantom force of forty divisions was expected hourly by Fifteenth Army (von Salmuth) and continued to be expected until late July, inhibiting the movement of 2nd and 116th Panzer Divisions that would otherwise have certainly intervened more quickly and powerfully in the Normandy battle-zone (2nd Panzer, D+7; 116th Panzer, D+43). The D-Day intentions of 21st Army Group (Montgomery) passing responsibility for action on the eastern flank of the invasion coast to British Second Army (Dempsey) – 6th Airborne Division (Gale) three assault divisions (50th, Canadian 3rd, British 3rd) and three armoured brigades – required spearheads from 'Gold', 'Juno' and 'Sword' to drive eight miles inland on the first day, seize Caen, a strategic communications centre with Carpiquet airport adjoining to the west, and then push on south in a bid to win good 'going' for armour and suitable terrain for airfield construction – an essential pre-requisite for future offensive support. Thirty miles to the west of the Anglo-Canadian (British Second Army) effort, US forces in simultaneously phased operations would pursue broadly comparable objectives. Deploying two US airborne divisions, 82nd (Ridgway) and 101st (Taylor) for the capture of Ste-Mère-Eglise and beach exit defiles, US First Army (Bradley) was struggling with reduced armoured support to establish 4th and 1st Infantry Divisions on 'Utah' and 'Omaha' Beaches north and east of Carentan.

On the US flank of the invasion coast, Montgomery's intentions were focused principally upon the port of

Cherbourg – which like Caen at the time was defended by German Seventh Army (Dollmann). Prompt US capture of the stores-handling facilities of Cherbourg was considered top priority by the Allies in order to link the US invasion force direct to the United States by sea. On the German side, Field Marshal Rommel's plan to counter invasion on this stretch of the Normandy coast was initially to eliminate the US threat by panzer intervention; a proposal vetoed by Hitler who instead directed that all available resources be concentrated in the east against British Second Army.

On **7 June (D+1)**, 12th SS Panzer Division Hitler Jugend (Witt), the first of four OKW reserve panzer divisions to reach the invasion battle zone – the others being Panzer Lehr (D+2), 17th SS (D+5) and SS Leibstandarte Adolf Hitler (D+22) – arrived west of Caen, secured Carpiquet and prepared to assist 21st Panzer concentrating for a renewed attack northwards to the coast. Moving to the attack in bounds via Lisieux, to reduce the danger of air attack between Evreux west of Paris and the division's assembly area, initially south-east of Caen, Hitler Jugend's 25th Panzer Grenadier Regiment (Meyer) and II Panzer Battalion/12th SS Panzer Regiment (Wunsche) would be followed into action by 26th Panzer Grenadier Regiment (Mohnke) and the Panzer Regiment's I Panther Battalion delayed at the Orne by a fuel shortage. But pre-emptive pressure exerted by Anglo-Canadian forces renewing offensive operations against Carpiquet and Caen was to rob the panzer divisions of their first opportunity to launch a co-ordinated counter-attack. The planned offensive evolved instead as independent action by Hitler Jugend's reinforced 25th Panzer Grenadier Regiment (Meyer) ambushing Canadian (3rd Division) spearheads at Authie a mile or so north of Carpiquet, while 21st Panzer (Feuchtinger) resisted British (3rd Division) attacks threatening Caen south of Biéville.

On **8 June (D+2)**, Panzer Lehr (Bayerlein), filtering into the battle zone from Le Mans 100 miles to the south, arrived on the left of Hitler Jugend at Norrey–Brouay twelve miles west of Caen, under orders from I SS Panzer Corps (Dietrich) to prepare for an offensive to the coast – in conjunction with HJ. Bayerlein's exceptionally well-equipped panzer division included 901st Panzer Grenadier Regiment (Scholtz) and 902nd (Gutmann), all four battalions riding in armoured personnel carriers; the division's panzer complement, however, lacked the Panther Battalion of 130th Panzer Lehr Regiment (Gerhardt) which at the time of OKW's order releasing the division to Seventh Army (Dollmann) was entrained for the east. During the night of D+2 Rommel shifted Panzer Lehr into positions opposite British XXX Corps (Horrocks). A war-experienced formation, XXX Corps comprised the veteran 7th Armoured Division (Erskine) and 50th Highland Division (Graham) consolidating Bayeux and preparing to outflank Caen in a powerful drive south. Moving in broad daylight from Le Mans to the invasion front on orders from Seventh Army, Panzer Lehr had been obliged to negotiate rubble and crater obstacles deliberately created by Allied bombers attacking key road and rail routes and centres. Like Hitler Jugend and other units arriving in the battle zone, Panzer Lehr suffered continuous air attacks resulting in unacceptable delays and casualties. Rommel at La Roche-Guyon on the same day – following his return there on D-Day evening – was meanwhile regrouping surviving infantry and the new

panzer divisions, entrusting the defence of Caen, currently in the hands of 21st Panzer and 716th Infantry Division with Carpiquet firmly secured by 12th SS HJ, to Geyr von Schweppenburg's Panzer Group West. But Geyr's Group, with I SS and eventually II SS and XXXXVII Panzer Corps, would all too soon suffer in battles of attrition with British and Canadian armies implementing Montgomery's plan to seize Caen and drive south.

On **9 June (D+3)**, Panzer Lehr, instead of participating with HJ in a I SS Panzer Corps offensive to the coast – for which available forces were inadequate – deployed two regimental-size battle groups (901st and 902nd Panzer Grenadier Regiments) astride the Tilly–Bayeux road, launching attacks to recover Bayeux held by 50th Infantry and a 7th Armoured support group. Conducted with orthodox precision, Bayerlein's attack failed under intensive artillery fire and air strikes. When an exposed flank was threatened attacks were halted and the division recalled; a setback followed next day by an altogether more shattering blow for Rommel preparing for decisive action against the Allied invasion force.

On **10 June (D+4)**, Panzergruppe West HQ at la Cain, four miles north of Thury-Harcourt (revealed by 'Ultra' intercepts), was destroyed in air attacks and Rommel's planned counter-offensive with Panzer Lehr, HJ and 21st Panzer Division was temporarily, and as it turned out fatefully, postponed. Thirteen staff officers died in the attack and Geyr was wounded. The crisis was resolved in part by substituting 'Sepp' Dietrich's I SS Panzer Corps HQ and making it responsible to Seventh Army; Geyr's own HQ would remain out of action until 26 June when a new staff was assembled.

On **11 June (D+5)**, 17th SS Panzer Grenadier Division (Ostendorff), arriving from Poitiers on the western (US) flank of the invasion coast, assembled defensively south of Carentan.

Deployed in conjunction with a Fallschirmjaeger battle group (FJR 6), the divisional commander was instructed to disrupt US First Army's build-up around Carentan, but with no assault guns – the division's only armour delayed by harassing air attacks – 17th SS Division (GvB) made little headway in splitting 'Utah' and 'Omaha' which undisturbed proceeded to join up eastwards with 'Gold', 'Juno' and 'Sword' to form a strongly held and continuous Allied front.

On **13 June (D+7)**, Panzer Lehr, the westernmost of three panzer divisions (Pz Lehr, HJ, 21st Panzer) deployed opposite British Second Army in defence of Caen, was subjected to an outflanking move by 7th Armoured Division seeking to bypass Caen as a result of which occurred one of the most celebrated panzer actions of the war. Unable to reach Caen via Tilly where Bayerlein's division, firmly in control of the locality since D+2, was fighting off heavy attacks, British XXX Corps (Bucknall) was instructed to change direction and, instead of confronting Panzer Lehr from this direction, swing south-west and as part of a pincer movement involving British I Corps in attacks north-east of the city, approach Caen from the west via Villers-Bocage; the vanguard of XXX Corps being provided by 22 Armoured Brigade/7th Armoured Division (Erskine). Unfortunately for XXX Corps the British offensive was brought to an abrupt conclusion by the action of a single section of four Tigers (No. 2 Company) lead by Obersturmführer Wittmann from

101st heavy SS Panzer Battalion. Deployed on Height 213 north-east of Villers, Wittmann's Tigers covered the same high ground that 7th Armoured had been given at its objective. The SS Tigers, corps troops of I SS Panzer Corps, had suffered both technical and tactical losses from air attacks, arriving behind the left wing of Panzer Lehr with only thirteen fit Tigers, brought from Beauvais, 40 miles north-east of Paris. The weakness of Panzer Lehr's left flank connecting with 352nd Infantry Division, a much depleted survivor of gruelling battles with the invasion forces, was clear to both sides and it was here that British Second Army planned to break through to Caen – until Wittmann and advance elements of 2nd Panzer Division (von Lüttwitz), brought unknown to 21st Army Group from Fifteenth Army north of the Seine to reinforce the threatened sector, forestalled the move.

Alerted to the approach of 22 Armoured Brigade – a powerful battle group of tanks, motorized infantry and support weapons – Wittmann moved into action at 0800 hours. Directing the fire of his own Tiger's powerful 8.8cm gun, the 55-ton vehicle's main armament, Wittmann destroyed the rear and leading vehicles of the British column caught napping at Montbroque effectively blocking the Villers–Caen road and preventing British withdrawal or reinforcement. Stalking the remaining vehicles in the space of a few minutes Wittmann and his section picked off twenty Cromwells, four Fireflies (SP 17pdrs) six light armoured cars and most of the infantry halftracks, leaving a trail of smoking wrecks and burning vehicles that a few minutes earlier had constituted the vanguard of 22 Armoured Brigade. Reinforced by a Panzer Lehr battle group (including Tigers from No. 1 Coy) and, during the afternoon, 2nd Panzer Division's reconnaissance battalion, Wittmann's aggregated battle group continued the action for a further three days; abandoning Villers-Bocage, 7th Armoured Division (Erskine) withdrew north-east to regroup. This unexpected check to British progress south around Caen was to leave Panzer Lehr at least temporarily in possession of the hotly contested Tilly-Villers sector, and 2nd Panzer Division (with no panzer regiment until D+12) in posses-sion of Caumont. Diversionary British attacks north-east of Caen faring no better against a 21st Panzer Battle Group (Lucke) were discontinued.

During the course of seven days' heavy fighting, 21st Army Group brought ashore 326,000 men, 54,186 vehicles and 104,428 tons of supplies. Rommel, disadvantaged by Anglo-US air forces destroying road and rail bridges across the Seine and Loire, received next to no replacement *matériel* or personnel. For whereas Allied armies continued to receive stores at an accelerating rate across open beaches or at temporary ports (Mulberries) towed 60 miles across the Channel and then anchored at Arromanches and St-Laurent – unhindered by the German Navy or Luftwaffe – the battlefield was largely sealed aganst increment for the panzer divisions. Suffering relentless assault by fighter-bombers picking off vehicles in daylight while heavy bombers of US 8th Air Force shattered road and rail centres by night, Rommel's transport communications were enorm-ously hampered; reinforcements and supplies were forced into ever-widening detours and time-consuming night marches. Yet despite the theatre-wide strain imposed by Allied air attack – which full-scale offensive was com-

pounded by the Maquis interfering with operational traffic at every possible opportunity – troop movements were soon recovering to the point where new divisions were reaching the invasion zone – 2nd Panzer Division (Lüttwitz) from Fifteenth Army at Amiens on D+7, SS Das Reich (Lammerding) from First Army at Toulouse on D+9 and various Army or SS heavy panzer battalions/Werfer brigades from home stations in Germany or occupied territories in the west. Although these improved the German order of battle in Normandy, Rommel's power to sweep the Allied invasion force back into the sea would remain inadequate; Hitler's aspirations were to go unfulfilled and the 'Overlord' armies unchallenged by any serious attempt to evict them from beach-heads consolidating into a continuous line between the Orne estuary in the east and Montebourg, fifteen miles short of Cherbourg in the west.

On **15 June (D+9)**, panzer reinforcements arriving for Rommel from Army Group 'G' included SS Panzer Grenadier Regiment Der Führer (Weidinger) bringing I/Der Führer and

Above: Hauptsturmführer Michael Wittmann, leader of a Tiger company from 101st SS Heavy Panzer Battalion, led his forces in the ambush on 13 June 1944 D+7 of 7th Armoured Division who were spearheading an attempt to outflank Panzer Lehr.

I/Deutschland while leading 2nd SS Panzer Division Das Reich from Toulouse to the battle zone south-east of St-Lô. Placed on stand-by for action at Caumont supporting 2nd Panzer Division (Luttwitz) opposite the junction of British Second and US First Armies, Der Führer prepared for action. Unhappily for those involved in transferring Das Reich from Army Group 'G' to the battle zone in Normandy, the move was surrounded by much notoriety; shameful reprisals taken by the division against civilians and Maquis at Tulle and Oradour-sur-Glane in the Dordogne north-west of Limoges during a four-day SS security operation (D+2–D+6) defaming the combat reputation of the Waffen SS from that day onwards. [*And not for the first or last time. During 'Autumn Mist' (see Sixth Panzer Army) Kampfgruppe Peiper's execution of American prisoners at Malmédy was a massacre no less criminal*]. At the centre of events in the Dordogne was the disappearance of Major Helmut Kämpfe, Der Führer's Panzer Grenadier (III) Battalion commander, ambushed by Maquis and at first believed imprisoned at Maquis headquarters in Oradour. It was this loss of a trusted leader and the discovery of German corpses at Tulle that provoked the infamous killing of local French men, women and children by the Waffen SS.

The involvement of Das Reich in internal security duties at a time when every available panzer division was needed in action at the front – whatever the short-term benefit to the Wehrmacht of inhibiting Resistance action in the Dordogne and perhaps beyond – was to exemplify the unsatisfactory and disjointed use of Das Reich in Normandy. Forced by events into providing battle groups for other divisions on widely separate sectors of the front, Das Reich more than any other panzer divisions was to fall victim to the piecemeal commitment of armour in Normandy forced upon the High Command by the unrelenting pressure of 21st Army Group operations. [*Not in fact until 27 July (D+51), in the aftermath of the US break-out west of St-Lô would Das Reich serve under united command, by which time it was too late for the division to influence events in Normandy by more than the slightest degree.*]

On and after **16 June (D+10)**, more of Das Reich was reaching the front. Moving in separate tracked and wheeled vehicle march columns, Der Führer (under a new commander, Weidinger, appointed on D+8 when Stadler was promoted GOC, 9th SS Panzer Division) was followed by 2nd SS Panzer Regiment (Tychsen) arriving 20 June (D+14) and assembling south of St-Lô opposite US First Army (Bradley). Nevertheless, a substantial part of Das Reich – two battalions of Deutschland (II and III), the division's second Panzer Grenadier Regiment – would remain for the time being incomplete and refitting in Toulouse–Montauban. During the period 17–24 June (D+11–D+18), following a Führer conference at Margival (D+11), Army Group 'B' (Rommel) initiated the planning phase of a boldly conceived counter-offensive against 21st Army Group. Employing three panzer corps, I SS (Dietrich), II SS (Hausser-Bittrich) and XXXXVII (Funck) to be concentrated in the area of Caumont, the offensive would be lead by Panzer Group West (Geyr). Panzer divisions already in the line, 2nd, 21st and Panzer Lehr, were to be replaced by infantry divisions from Britanny and the South of France. Two new SS Panzer divisions, 9th Hohenstaufen and 10th Frundsberg (II SS Panzer Corps) were confirmed *en route* from the east, and

1st SS Leibstandarte Adolf Hitler was confirmed moving from OKW reserve in Belgium. Convened in former 'Sealion' headquarters at Margival (Soissons), the Führer conference there had ended with no clear-cut decision on the future conduct of the battle. But within days of the meeting attended by Rommel, von Runstedt, Jodl and chiefs of staff, an Army Group plan was being shaped over a Seventh Army study envisaging an offensive northwards at the junction of US (First) and British (Second) Armies in the centre of the front at Caumont. The Army Group's intention was to strike for the coast at Bayeux and then according to circumstances expand into a single or double encirclement manoeuvre rolling up the exposed flanks of, it was to be hoped, a surprised and outwitted defence.

The shock formation in Rommel's projected offensive was to be II SS Panzer Corps (Hausser-Bittrich) switched from the east front to the west with two SS Panzer divisions after effecting the relief of First Panzer Army in the Ukraine (*see* First Panzer Army, 8 April 1944). Having entrained for Normandy on 12 June (D+6), the SS Panzer Corps was bringing two fairly strong panzer divisions, 9th SS Hohenstaufen (Bittrich) and 10th SS Frundsberg (Harmel). By nightfall on 24 June (D+18) GOC, Panzer Group West Geyr and Corps commanders Dietrich, Funck and Hausser were in agreement over inter-corps boundaries, start-lines, ammunition, stores and fuel replenishment programmes; the minutiae of a panzer offensive confidently expected to start early in July, following the arrival of replacement infantry and new assault divisions to join those released from the line. A night start was intended as the surprise element in the plan of attack. But OKW arrangements for concentrating armour under Panzer Group West and striking a decisive blow at the invasion force were then betrayed to 21st Army Group by 'Ultra'. Warned of the movement to Normandy of II SS Panzer Corps and others including the Leibstandarte *en route* from OKW reserve in Belgium, Montgomery accelerated plans for a new offensive.

On **25 June (D+19)**, British Second Army (Dempsey) launched Operation 'Epsom' – referred to in German military literature as the third battle of Caen. Overcoming delays by storms of rare violence raging through the English Channel and wreaking havoc on Mulberry harbours, the new British offensive was intended to isolate Caen from its hinterland by hooking around the city from north-west to south-east and securing a bridgehead astride the Orne at a point where the river approached the city from the south. Attacking on a two-corps front between Tilly and Carpiquet where Panzer Lehr (Bayerlein) and 12th SS HJ (Meyer) were still in the line under I SS Panzer Corps (Dietrich), Dempsey would be assisted by I Corps distracting 21st Panzer northeast of Caen.

In its principal phase timed for day two, **26 June (D+20)**, 'Epsom' intended slicing through 12th SS Panzer Division (Meyer) in the line north of Cheux, breach the Odon close by Gavrus and Baron-sur-Odon, and then exploit to the Orne via Hill 112, a prominent feature dominating routes between rivers. In order to provide a strike force for actions against 12th SS Panzer Division, Dempsey deployed the newly landed British VIII Corps (O'Connor) controlling 11th Armoured Division (Roberts), 15th Scottish, 43rd Wessex Infantry Divisions, and 4 Armoured Brigade. British XXX Corps (Bucknall) cast in a supporting role opposite

Panzer Lehr, west of HJ, would open the proceedings on D+19 by committing 49th Infantry Division and supporting armour in the direction of Rauray – HJ's connecting locality with Panzer Lehr. British tank strength, including 7th Armoured Division (Erskine) waiting in reserve behind XXX Corps, stood at 600 against an estimated 102 of 12th SS and 150 of Panzer Lehr (plus Panzerjaeger). Maximizing air and artillery support, including offshore 16in batteries of HMS *Rodney* and the monitors *Roberts* and *Erebus*, the British offensive recorded early success but then stalled in the face of determined resistance; that of 12th SS HJ Panzer Division (Meyer) in particular. Tearing a 3-mile gap in the front of I SS Panzer Corps (Dietrich) where HJ battle groups of 25th (Müller) and 26th (Mohnke) SS Panzer Grenadier Regiments defended the outermost localities of the main German battle line, Dempsey pushed hard with 11th Armoured Division exploiting to the Odon and Hill 112, but failing to break the defence.

Concealing half of his panzer strength (II/12th SS Panzer Regiment) in company localities, hull-down behind the forward panzer grenadier battle groups – as an immediate counter-attack reserve and anti-tank screen – while deploying I/12th SS Panzer Regiment and III/26th Panzer Grenadier Regiment (Olboeter) as a regimental panzer battle group (Wunsche) on the left wing at Rauray – Meyer soon dashed British hopes of a decisive breakthrough. Over the next few days until 28 June (D+22), confrontation on the Odon between two British corps and two much depleted panzer divisions of I SS Panzer Corps, HJ and Panzer Lehr (reinforced on D+21 and again on D+22) would develop into the costliest armour-infantry battle in the short history of Panzer Group West; HJ's defence of Rauray, Cheux and Hill 112 against British XVIII Corps attacks meriting well-deserted acclaim in the military histories of both sides.

On **27 June (D+21)**, a reinforced Das Reich regimental battle group, Der Führer, consisting of two SS panzer grenadier battalions and an Army panzer company under Otto Weidinger joined the action south of Rauray. Redeployed from the division's assembly area south of St-Lô, Weidinger's objective was to close a gap between HJ and Panzer Lehr, the result of British pressure splitting the defence. Next day on the other side of the British break-in, at Verson, two more SS panzer grenadier battalions – 1st SS Panzer-Grenadier Regiment (Frey) leading 1st SS LAH Panzer Division (Wisch), risking the journey through France from Belgium, also a 22nd Panzer Regiment panzer battle group, transferred to the crisis point from 21st Panzer Division, still guarding north-east Caen – joined in operations to constrict the British penetration which by the third day of the battle (D+21) had won through to the summit of Hill 112. At this point 'Epsom' failed; counter-attacks by 12th SS Panzer Regiment (Wunsche) redeployed from the defence of Rauray holding the offensive in check. Meanwhile on 27 June (D+21) II SS Panzer Corps (Hausser) with SS Panzer Divisions Hohenstaufen (Bittrich) and Frundsberg (Harmel), intended for Rommel's Caumont offensive, was assembling north-west of Alençon on urgent recall from the east; a three-weeks' journey from Lemberg spent mostly *en route* through France via Nancy or Epinal where the corps detrained at the conclusion of a four-day rail journey starting 12 June (D+6). When committed on the Odon (D+23) by a despairing Seventh Army com-

mander (Dollmann), anxious to relieve the pressure on German divisions suffering heavy losses in continuous action since D-Day, II SS Panzer Corps would succeed in taking the remaining momentum out of 'Epsom', changing the tactical picture temporarily to Panzer Group West advantage.

On **28 June (D+22)**, Panzer Group West, controlling four army corps, three of them panzer – I SS Panzer Corps (Dietrich), II SS Panzer Corps (Hausser) and XXXXVII Panzer Corps (Funck) – twelve divisions in all, became directly subordinate to Army Group 'B' (Rommel); Panzer Group responsibilities between the Seine and the Drôme (Caumont) focusing upon the defence of Caen. On this sector of the invasion front, no fewer than eight panzer divisions or significant elements of the Leibstandarte (1st SS LAH, 2nd SS (Der Führer only), 9th SS, 10th SS, 12th SS, 2nd, 21st and Panzer Lehr, subordinate to Panzer Group West (Geyr), were now drawn into battle on Montgomery's east flank. Only 17th SS Panzer Grenadier Division, reinforcing weak infantry formations deployed south of Carentan, opposed US First Army in the west, although the mass of 2nd SS Panzer Division retained in Army Group reserve south of St-Lô was soon to become involved (D+29), contributing battle groups to threatened sectors, e.g., Der Führer subordinated to 353rd Inf Division (Mahlmann) at La Haye-du-Puits.

[*This imbalance in the deployment of panzer divisions in Normandy was to continue mostly unchanged even after the fall of Cherbourg on 29 June (D+23); the release of US forces after gaining control of the base then causing Rommel to redeploy Panzer Lehr (Bayerlein) west to assist 17th SS Division at Pont-Hébert on 9 July (D+33) by which time 2nd SS Panzer Division would be strengthening GvB and Seventh Army at Sainteny (Périers). Thereafter, one or other of these panzer divisions, serving Seventh Army with the support of regular parachute and infantry battle groups responsible to LXXXIV Corps (von Choltitz) would be committed in counter-attacks opposing US First Army (Bradley) expanding south of Carentan; Bradley's aim thrusting south via St-Jean-de-Daye to St-Lô being to gain a start-line (St-Lô–Périers) from which to commence a future if somewhat delayed break-out on 25 July (D+49).*]

On **29 June (D+23)**, four days after the start of British Second Army's 'Epsom' offensive, counter-attacks by II SS Panzer Corps serving Wilhelm Bittrich – a new corps commander replacing Hausser promoted GOC, Seventh Army (Dollmann's suicide being reported at the time as a heart attack) – finally frustrated 21st Army Group's plan for isolating Caen by thrusting around the city from the north-west. Co-operating with I SS Panzer Corps (Dietrich) assaulting the eastern flank of the British penetration at Verson, II SS Panzer Corps (Bittrich), converging on nearby Cheux from the west and south-west, sealed the fate of 'Epsom' forcing Dempsey on to the defensive and leaving Panzer Group West (Geyr) temporarily in control of the battlefield. But whatever hopes OB West or Rommel entertained of extending the II SS Panzer Corps offensive into a strike northwards, splitting the Allied front around Caumont as Rommel originally intended – until 21st Army Group pressure had forced Seventh Army (Dollmann) into asking Rommel for the immediate and unscheduled use of II SS Panzer Corps in the Odon battle – were dashed by the crushing weight of Allied artillery and air power brought

Right: Hedgerow fighting in Normandy intensified as 'tank-hunters' armed with the Panzerschreck lay in wait to ambush Allied armour. Firing an 88mm hollow-charge missile, this Bazooka-type rocket-launcher proved to be devastating weapon. Here, a Fallschirmjaeger of II Paratroc Corps (Meindl) demonstrates its handling.

to bear on the attacking divisions. Notwithstanding HJ's check to 'Epsom' occasioned by a staunch defence of Rauray and Cheux, the deep penetration achieved by 11th Armoured Division (eventually withdrawn from Hill 112 through fear of encirclement by the converging SS panzer corps) created deep German concern for the safety of the sector, consequently involving 12th SS Panzer Division, the Corps Werfer Regiment, 101st SS Tiger Battalion and 8.8cm Flak from III Flak Corps in heavy fighting to retain a grip on the key features of the Odon battlefield; notably Hill 112.

However, such were the losses sustained by the panzer divisions in the Odon battles – particularly from 16in naval guns offshore – that the commander of Panzer Group West (Geyr) and subsequently von Runstedt himself proposed withdrawing out of naval artillery range and evacuating parts of the front north of the Orne including Caen where the river divided the city north and south. Following their replacement by infantry as earlier planned, Geyr would have redeployed the panzer divisions as a strong mobile reserve on the east flank of the front, ready to take advantage of any Allied thrusts eastwards in the direction of Paris.

Rommel disagreed; stressing the danger of exposing armoured concentrations to air attack.

On 3 July (D+27), Hitler's predictable reaction to Geyr's suggestion of surrendering ground in Normandy, freely supported by von Runstedt – who also advised making peace with the Allies – quickly surfaced; both men were dismissed. In Geyr's place Hitler appointed Eberbach and in von Runstedt's, von Kluge. For the panzer divisions fighting in Normandy the outlook was one of increasing bleakness; Hitler's obstinate refusal to countenance reality condemning them to operate at a disadvantage within range of naval artillery while also enduring day and night attacks by Allied air forces. There was also little chance of reinforcement or improvement in a deteriorating supply situation, sapping panzer confidence in a successful outcome to the struggle in Normandy – even more so when on 17 July (D+41) (q.v.) a low-flying air attack would remove Rommel from the scene of battle. From **4 July (D+28)** to **20 July (D+44)**, during which time Rommel was wounded, Panzer Group West (Eberbach) was to face 21st Army Group offensives growing in power and momentum. Operations

'Windsor' (D+25), 'Charnwood' (D+32), 'Jupiter' (D+34), 'Green-line' (D+39) and above all 'Goodwood' (D+42), were all designed by General Montgomery to fix the panzer divisions in the east, destroying their material basis, allowing neither rest nor respite to panzer grenadiers, crews or personnel of any kind – frustrating all Rommel's hopes of effectively strengthening the western flank of the invasion front where US First Army (Bradley) after celebrating the capture of Cherbourg on D+23 was pressing forward with renewed vigour south of Carentan, posing a serious threat to St-Lô, the western anchor of the German battle line. In this sector west of St-Lô, before Panzer Lehr joined Seventh Army (D+33), a handful of infantry formations reinforced by 17th SS Panzer Grenadier Division (Ostendorf) served LXXXIV Corps (von Choltitz) or, directly responsible for the town and the battlezone to the east, II Parachute Corps (Meindl).

In the meantime British initiatives west of Caen: Operation 'Windsor' **4 July (D+28)** extended on **8 July (D+32)** into Operation 'Charnwood', was bringing 12th SS HJ Panzer Division (Meyer) under renewed pressure defending Carpiquet and adjoining localities at Rots, Buron and Authie. Directed by British Second Army (Dempsey), Operation 'Charnwood' was preceded by a bombing offensive in which 2,000 tons of bombs were dropped on German positions in the northern half of the city – the built-up area containing Anglo-Canadian assault objectives defended by HJ or, when 21st Panzer Division was withdrawn a short distance into rest, 16th Luftwaffe Division (Sievers).

By **10 July (D+34)** 12th SS Panzer Division's resistance to 'Charnwood' had been broken by bombing and a ground assault led by 3rd Canadian Division. The same offensive crippled the neighbouring Luftwaffe Field Division. Threatened with encirclement, Meyer relinquished control of Carpiquet (I/25th Panzer Grenadier Regiment), evacuating the battle zone north-west of Caen and retiring through the city and across the Orne into Vaucelles. On the same day Hill 112 was lost to 43rd Infantry Division. In new positions south of the river, HJ would exploit the defensive potential of war-wasted streets until 11 July (D+35), when the division was relieved by 1st SS LAH (Wisch) and, in turn, 272nd Infantry Division which continued to deny Caen to Canadian II Corps (Simmonds) until D+42 when the city fell to Montgomery in the course of Operations 'Goodwood' and 'Atlantic'. Meanwhile, leaving Vaucelles and its other Orne sectors south of the river to Wisch, HJ was redeployed south of Caen to Potigny, five miles north of Falaise. Meyer then formed emergency battle groups around 25th and 26th Panzer Grenadier Regiments, and 12th SS Panzer Regiment (Wunsche). HJ's battle-fit tank strength stood at nineteen Pz Kpfw IVs and 25 Panthers with four Pak 7.5cm guns in support.

Seventh Army taking the strain 10 July [D+34] to 24 July [D+48]. The reaction of Army Group 'B' to US First Army (Bradley) attacks savaging Seventh Army (Hausser) south of Carentan, had necessitated the urgent redeployment of Panzer Lehr (Bayerlein), released from Tilly on 5 July (D+29) to reinforce 17th SS Panzer Grenadier Division (Baum), the mainstay of a sagging Seventh Army infantry defence north-west of St-Lô. Despite the pressures of 'Epsom' during which time it was replaced in the line at

Tilly by 276th Infantry Division, Bayerlein's division had served from 26 June to 5 July as XXXXVII Panzer Corps reserve. In its new location, right of the much weakened 17th SS Panzer Grenadier Division struggling north and west of St-Lô to contain US First Army spearheads probing south from St-Jean-de-Daye and threatening Pont-Hébert, Bayerlein was instructed to launch an immediate spoiling attack and then prepare a strong divisional offensive northwards. Following the collapse of Seventh Army resistance in Cherbourg on 29 June (D+23), eliminating a 20,000-strong mixed infantry battle group von Schlieben (709th Infantry Division), an intensification of US pressure southwards had long been expected by Army Group 'B', but effective counter-measures to reinforce surviving Infantry Divisions 77th, 91st, 243rd and 353rd (from Brittany) fighting south of the town had failed for want of resources to progress beyond the arrival on D+5 of 17th SS Panzer Grenadier Division (Ostendorf, Baum after 18 June) and starting on 5 July (D+29) Das Reich battle groups of varying size and power, including Der Führer (Weidinger) returning to the division from employment west of Caen since D+21.

Us First Army intentions in this the preparatory phase, of the break-out battle 'Cobra' scheduled by Bradley for 20 July (D+44), but deferred by Channel conditions delaying crucial supplies and reserves until 25 July (D+49), focused upon the capture of St-Lô and its associated network of roads. Possession of St-Lô, currently Seventh Army's forward communications and supply base, and in particular the St-Lô–Périers highway crossing the Vire to the west, with subsidiary routes (from Pont-Hébert) running south, was a pre-requisite for mobile operations by US Third Army (Patton) planning to attack out of the high hedgerow bocage country of Normandy and into Brittany. But for the arrival of Panzer Lehr, ejecting US spearheads from Pont-Hébert on 8 July (D+32), this Allied objective would have been realized. The defence of Seventh Army's battle line east and west of St-Lô was shared by two German army corps; LXXXIV (von Choltitz, former panzer corps commander, Anzio) covering the area west of St-Lô to the sea at Bretteville, and II Parachute Corps (Meindl, veteran assault regiment commander, Crete) responsible for the town itself and the line east to Caumont.

Panzer Lehr, 17th SS Goetz von Berlichingen and eventually 2nd SS Das Reich, deployed between St-Lô and Périers, were subordinated to LXXXIV Corps, whereas II Parachute Corps relied principally upon 3rd Parachute Division (Schimpf) and Infantry Battle Group 352 reinforced by the panzer reconnaissance battalion of 17th SS Panzer Grenadier Division. The first counter-attack of any significance developing after D-Day against US First Army in the western sector of the invasion front, and lead by 17th SS Division (Ostendorf) with the help of FJR6 (von der Heydte) had penetrated into the centre of Carentan but failed to adhere there. US 82nd Airborne and 2nd Armored Division, benefiting from heavy air cover, remained firmly in control while further counter-attacks, sapping the strength of 17th SS Panzer Grenadier Division, required the support of a Das Reich panzer battle group – II/2nd SS Panzer Regiment (Kesten) – to restore temporary stability to the line at Bois Grimot on 9 July (D+33), but failing to deter US progress southwards.

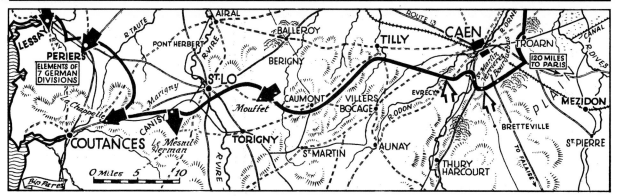

Above: 20 July 1944 was D+ 44. The main German battle line, following the Allied offensives code-named 'Epsom'. 'Charnwood' and 'Goodwood', was broken and the strong points of Carpiquet, Caen and Bourguébus had fallen to the Allies at a time when most of the panzer divisions were concentrated in their defence.

Heavy casualties on both sides (40,000 Americans) testified to the extreme bitterness of fighting in the close bocage country where armour was disadvantaged by limited vision, narrow lanes and high-banked hedgerows. On the German side too, casualties soared; 28 General officers and more than 90,000 other dead, wounded or missing to date. Supply deficiencies, particularly in petrol, oil and lubricants hampered the movement of even individual vehicles while ammunition shortages curtailing artillery barrages reduced the effectiveness of artillery support and ceaseless American air interdiction delaying unit assembly times destroyed operational groupings.

On 11 July [D+35], Panzer Lehr's (Bayerlein) offensive under LXXXIV Corps (von Choltitz), striking northwards from an assembly area between Pont-Hébert and le Hommet, followed preliminary action by a Das Reich battle group (Wisliceny) attacking towards le Dézert, also Panzer Lehr ejecting spearhead units of US 3rd Armored Division from Pont-Hébert; the recovery of this Vire crossing west of St-Lô thereby improving the security of the Corps sector. Bayerlein's instructions were to strike north, thrusting for St-Jean-de-Daye south of Carentan, recover Airel and similar key points facilitating US access to St-Lô, and then establish blocking positions on high ground overlooking the Taute–Vire Canal. Regimental panzer grenadier Battle Groups 901 (Scholtze) and 902 (Welsch), deployed two-up in the style of a panzer division attack in close country, opened the way forward. Neither battle group was equivalent (in SPWs) to more than five or six panzer grenadier companies, a panzer battalion of twenty – thirty Pz Kpfw IVs or Panthers, and an engineer company. The Das Reich battle group (Wisliceny), formed from a reinforced III Battalion Deutschland previously deployed like II/2nd SS Panzer Regiment (Tychsen) supporting 17th SS Panzer Grenadier Division, an FJR 14 battle group and other reinforcements assisted Panzer Lehr in the offensive. All in vain. After recording limited success against US infantry surprised at le Dézert and Bahois, less than halfway to St-Jean-de-Daye the offensive stalled. Subsequent US counter-attacks were immediately effective in eliminating an over-extended subordinate battle group – I/901st (Philipps) with ten Panthers encircled north of le Dézert.

[D+35–D+48]. For the next thirteen days the best that Panzer Lehr could do as US First Army (Bradley) preparing for 'Cobra' squared-up to the St-Lô–Périers highway, was to conceal its armour hull-down in twos and threes, fighting off powerful US armour and infantry attacks – culminating

on 25 July in Operation 'Cobra' (see Seventh Army, [D+ 49]). During this period of intensive operations by Seventh Army in the west, the panzer divisions suffered the loss of irreplaceable material and manpower including the commanders of 17th SS – Ostendorff, succeeded on 18 June by Baum (ex-38th SS Panzer Grenadier Regiment) and 2nd SS – Lammerding replaced on 24 July by Tychsen (ex-2nd SS Panzer Regiment). With divisional strengths declining to 40 per cent or less effectiveness, 17th SS Panzer Grenadier battalions were reduced to 120 men. 130th Panzer Lehr Regiment (Gerhardt), by the time that St-Lô fell to US First Army (after pushing through II Para Corps) on 18 July (D+ 37), had declined to 30 per cent of its D-Day establishment of 103 Panthers and 79 Pz Kpfw IVs. The divisional panzer grenadier battalions returned equally reduced strengths. But perhaps the greatest loss to Seventh Army lay in the unexpected way in which 2nd SS Das Reich was rendered impotent through seconding battle groups to other divisions at crisis points – Weidinger (Der Führer) to reinforce 353rd Infantry Division (Mahlmann) at La Haye de Puits, Wisliceny (Deutschland) to 17th SS and later Panzer Lehr at Pont-Hébert, also I/2nd SS Panzer Regiment with artillery support deployed east of St-Lô as a II Parachute Corps reserve (uncommitted). Consequently in Das Reich's own sector around Sainteny on 7 July there had remained only 2nd SS Panzer Regiment (Tychsen) with a single (II) Panzer Battalion; artillery support being provided by IV Battery/AR Das Reich assisted by II SS Werfer Battalion. Heavy anti-tank support for two weak panzer, one panzer grenadier and five infantry divisions deployed in the Sainteny sector was provided by Army 657th Panzer Jaeger Battalion equipped with Jagdpanzer IVs.

Meanwhile, in the South of France, desperately needed panzer grenadiers – II (Deutschland) and II (Der Führer) also III Panzer Artillery Regiment were still undergoing training. Other support units brought in to lace Seventh Army defences included Army Engineer Battalion 'Angers', 8 Werfer Brigade and various Army artillery battalions. The Luftwaffe was little in evidence. More powerful support for the critical St-Lô wing of Seventh Army facing Bradley's pre-'Cobra' build-up to fourteen US divisions (one motorized, two armoured) was in the offing, but Montgomery's strategy of attracting the panzer divisions to the Caen sector claimed 2nd Panzer (von Lüttwitz) withdrawn from the line at Caumont and 116th Panzer (von Schwerin) redeployed south of Caen from Fifteenth Army north of the Seine. Both panzer divisions under XXXXVII Panzer Corps (von Funck)

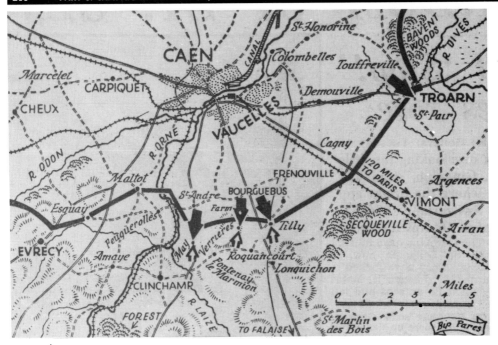

were intended for action west of the Vire, but with action flaring around Caen on D+42 found themselves instead opposing Montgomery's Operation 'Goodwood'.

Panzer Group West Defending Caen 10 July (D+34) to 24 July (D+48). In the aftermath of 'Charnwood' driving 12th SS Panzer Division (Meyer) out of Carpiquet across Caen and into the suburbs south of the Orne at Vaucelles – followed by redeployment north of Falaise – the focus of panzer action on the invasion front returned initially to the battlefield west of Caen where II SS Panzer Corps (Bittrich) blocked British Second Army (Dempsey) working south of the Odon.

10 July (D+34) to 16 July (D+40). Countering British VIII Corps (O'Connor) offensives 'Jupiter' (D+34) and 'Greenline' (D+39) striking south at Evrecy and Maltot or other points of tactical importance along the Odon, especially Hills 112 and 113, was to make heavy demands on 9th SS Hohenstaufen (Stadler) and 10th SS Frundsberg (Harmel). Other units drawn into the bitter second phase of conflict on the Odon included SS Corps' 102nd Tiger Battalion in action with a panzer battle group (I/12th SS Panzer Regiment) and advance elements of 277th Infantry Division relieving Hohenstaufen. But in a future and more vigorous clash of armour involving I SS Panzer Corps (Dietrich) in action on the battlefield east of Caen starting on 18 July (D+42), no fewer than six of the seven panzer divisions deployed around Caen – 1st SS LAH, 12th SS (HJ), 21st, 9th SS (switched from the Odon), 2nd (redeployed from Caumont), 116th (uncommitted at Creil) – were to face their greatest challenge yet, engaging Anglo-Canadian armour and infantry implementing Montgomery's grand slam Operation 'Goodwood'. Montgomery's strategy of fixing the panzer divisions in the east at a time when US First Army (Bradley) was preparing break-out operations opposite Seventh Army (Hausser) in the west was unfolding in heavily orchestrated actions around Caen inflicting

maximum damage on Panzer Group West and its subordinate SS Panzer Corps – I SS (Dietrich) and II SS (Bittrich). These SS panzer corps deployed east and west of the city – with SS Corps Tiger Battalions (101 and 102), Werfer and Army troops in support – constituted the mainstay of the panzer defence of Caen. Montgomery's intention was to engage them in the strongest possible way, bringing them to action defending sensitive localities on the axes of Anglo-Canadian thrusts wrongly interpreted at all levels of German command as 21st Army Group's attempt at breaking free of the Caen cauldron and, in conjunction with fresh landings in the Pas-de-Calais, heading for Paris.

Farther west, XXXVII Panzer Corps (von Funck), less troubled by British Second Army operations in the immediate vicinity of Caen diverting pressure from US First Army west of St-Lô, held the connecting Panzer Group/Seventh Army sector at Caumont. The relative inactivity of the Allies at this point was to persuade Rommel into withdrawing 2nd Panzer Division (von Lüttwitz) into reserve, replacing it with 326th Infantry Division (Drabich-Waechter) taken from Fifteenth Army north of the Seine. Together with 116th Panzer Division (von Schwerin), also on the move from Fifteenth Army, Rommel now proposed to reinforce the Seventh Army front west of St-Lô (see Seventh Army [D+34–D+48]. In the event, neither panzer division would be moving west in support of Seventh Army, their presence being considered essential in the east reinforcing Panzer Group West against a renewal of Anglo-Canadian operations expected any day ('Goodwood').

On 17 July (D+41) the day before 'Goodwood' – with Panzer Group West (Eberbach) poised to meet the challenge of a new offensive out of the British airborne bridgehead east of the Orne – Field Marshal Rommel was seriously wounded in a low-flying air attack. The incident followed Rommel's visit to I SS Panzer Corps headquarters at Urville. Returning by road to La Roche-Guyon the Field Marshal's staff car was overturned by Spitfires of 602 Squadron RAF patrolling at Ste-Foy-de-Montgommery. From the neigh-bourhood of the attack between Livarot and Vimoutiers, Rommel was evacuated to the Luftwaffe hospital at Bernay north-east of Paris. But so serious were his head injuries and so extraordinary the circumstances of his subsequent death by suicide (three months later) that Rommel was to play no further part in the war (*see* career note at the conclusion of Panzer Army Africa).

With Rommel in hospital, another Field Marshal, von Kluge (OB West) would assume the extra duties of GOC, Army Group 'B' – continuing in the dual role until 17 August (D+72) when, on Hitler's instructions, Walter Model arrived to take command in the west.

On **18 July (D+42)**, Panzer Group West (Eberbach) faced 'Goodwood' a British Second Army (Dempsey) offensive directed south around Caen from the outer north-east quarter of the city where Montgomery had chosen to concentrate three armoured divisions: 11th (Roberts), Guards (Adair) and 7th (Erskine) in the 6 Airborne bridge-head east of the Orne. Lead by VIII Corps (O'Connor) redeployed from the Odon, the British armoured divisions with 750 tanks and more than 7,000 other fighting and support vehicles, were given as their main objective the Bourguébus Ridge; a plateau of high ground some eight miles to the south. Whether Montgomery intended to convert a break-through at Bourguébus into an exploitation battle south across the Caen–Falaise plain – as declared to SHAEF and others beforehand – is questionable. The Bourguébus Ridge, a commanding feature on the way to Falaise and the tank-country beyond, held obvious attrac-tions for any south-bound expeditionary force, and its significance as an operational objective was not lost upon Panzer Group West (Eberbach) or other senior German commanders who were quick to incorporate it in defensive arrangements. Rommel's ill-fated visit to I SS Panzer Corps on D+41, the headquarters in control of the critical sector east of the Orne, was a consequence of Bourguébus-related planning. Panzer Group West's dispositions to meet the new offensive are considered later.

Canadian II Corps (Simmonds) would co-operate with the British 'armoured corps' by launching armour-supported infantry attacks on the inner (city) wing of the offensive; code-name for the Canadian operation – 'Atlantic'. On the other side of Caen, British I Corps was also preparing to co-operate in 'Goodwood' by launching armour-supported infantry attacks southwards. Canadian objectives were the industrialized eastern sectors of Caen and the south Orne suburb of Vaucelles from which 1st SS LAH Panzer Division had meanwhile withdrawn – relieved by 272nd Infantry Division – to be relocated in reserve west of Bourguébus. The success of 'Goodwood' was to be 'guaranteed' by Allied air forces unloading an unprecedented 7,000 tons of high-explosives on key targets throughout the battle zone – timed to commence less than two hours before the armoured start-time at 0745 hours. Yet despite the initial shock to the defence of 'the greatest bombing offensive ever undertaken in support of ground operations', 'Goodwood' was destined for a premature conclusion. When the British armoured divisions faltered in deeply echeloned defences established by Panzer Group West, Montgomery would call a halt. Panzer Group West dispositions to meet the long-

awaited attack – known to be in preparation at least four days previously – started in the forward line with the two infantry divisions, 16th Luftwaffe and 272nd holding well-defended localities. 16th Luftwaffe (Sievers), already reduced to a regimental-size battle group by bombing in support of 'Charnwood' (D+32) was to suffer the brunt of British Second Army's offensive – reinforced by 192nd Panzer Grenadier Regiment detached from 21st Panzer Division.

Behind the two infantry divisions stood the armour of 21st Panzer Division (von Lüttwitz) – less 192nd Panzer Grenadier Regiment supporting the Luftwaffe division – while I SS LAH (Wisch) in I SS Panzer Corps reserve stood behind 272nd Infantry Division. 21st Panzer Division's battle groups, especially von Luck's 125th Panzer Grenadier Regiment with both panzer grenadier battalions – rein-forced by thirty SP Jagdpanzer IVs (7.5cm), SP artillery (10.5cm) and the divisional Panzer (IV) Battalion plus 503rd (Tiger) Battalion, were allotted strong points in the depth of the battlefield, creating numerous defended localities while providing a mobile reserve to deal with break-ins. Further south, more units of 21st Panzer Division, the reconnaissance and engineer battalions, were protecting divisional and corps artillery deployed on the Bourguébus Ridge. Still further to the rear stood an (8.8cm) panzer-jaeger battalion and (8.8cm) flak. Other flak units, under Luftwaffe command (III Flak Regiment) and amounting to ninety (8.8cm) guns sited at tactically important points in the battlefield, at Cagny in particular, protected the Caen–Lisieux road. They were to present Allied armour with a formidable challenge. Werfer and Army artillery units too were brought in to reinforce divisional firepower. In Panzer Group reserve at Potigny, south of Caen, stood the much depleted 12th SS Panzer Division Hitler Jugend (Meyer) ready to intervene if required. Much to the surprise of HJ's commander, 'Panzer' Meyer, orders arriving on the 16th had given the division a new assembly area north-west of Lisieux requiring 12th SS Panzer Regiment (Wunsche), comprising I Mixed Panzer Battalion, II/26th Panzer Grenadier Regiment (Krause) and III/26th Panzer Grenadier Regiment in SPWs (Olboeter) to move out immediately. Others prepared to follow.

Promptly at 0745 hours on **18 July (D+42)** in the wake of a bombing offensive led by 1,500 heavy bombers of US 8th, 9th Air Forces, and RAF Bomber Command, 11th Armoured Division rolled forward against negligible opposi-tion. Pushing through German infantry and supporting panzer grenadiers shocked and disarrayed by the bombing, 11th Armoured pressed on towards Bourguébus, bypassing the 125th Panzer Grenadier battle group (Luck) surviving in Cagny, a key mid-battlefield position, gateway to Lisieux and the east. This strong point organized by von Luck incorporating Luftwaffe 88s employed in an anti-tank role, a Tiger detachment and others, defied 11th Armoured Division and follow-up waves of 7th Armoured Division until late afternoon. By mid-evening, Roberts's division was brought to a standstill in action against a powerful I SS LAH battle group (Peiper) comprising I (Panther) Battalion and I SPW Panzer Grenadier Battalion – counter-attacking in defence of Bourguébus; 126 tank wrecks, more than half of 11th Armoured Division's Sherman establishment being left to litter the sector. Supporting Guards and 7th Armoured Divisions fared no better against 21st Panzer and HJ defending Cagny and the communications point leading east at Vimont. It was the undeniable tenacity of panzer battle groups echeloned in depth with powerful anti-tank support protecting a battle front stretching from the Orne south of Caen (272nd Infantry Division) to Bourguébus (I SS LAH) and on to Cagny and Vimont (12th SS reinforced by Battle Group Wunsche recalled from Lisieux) to Troarn (21st Panzer) that denied the British offensive all chance of a dramatic break-through.

18 July (D+42) to 20 July (D+44). During the course of battle over the next few days Erskine's 7th Armoured Division, following Roberts's and then coming into action alongside at Bourguébus, gained a foothold on the disputed ridge while Guards Armoured secured the outer flank of the penetration opposite 12th SS but short of Vimont turned by HJ into a formidable strong point. In Operation 'Atlantic' the Canadians cleared Vaucelles and advancing south attacked

272nd Infantry Division – eventually bringing 9th SS Panzer Division across the Orne in support while 2nd and 116th Panzer Division moving up behind I SS LAH remained there until their redeployment in consequence of crisis developments in the west (*see Seventh Army [D+51]*). From the German point of view Panzer Group West's apparent success in containing the British offensive and limiting progress to Bourguébus, while also denying exploitation in the direction of Falaise masked the real success of Montgomery's initiative evident in the violent reaction of OKW and Panzer Group West. By aiming in massive strength at the high ground south of Bourguébus, threatening rupture to the main German battle line along the Caen–Falaise or Caen–Cagny–Lisieux axis, Montgomery deliberately fostered erroneous German appreciations predicting the new offensive as a prelude to a second landing north of the Seine. Even at this late stage OKW, deceived by Operation

Below: Casualties in the clas of armour at Villers. On the a knocked-out Pz Kpfw IV ar to the right, a Tiger bear witness to the ferocity of the fighting.

'Fortitude' (p. 58), was convinced that forty Allied divisions waited in Britain to carry out invasion tasks. In consequence of Montgomery's action OKW had moved 12th SS Division to Lisieux, *east* of Caen (and back again), diverted 2nd Panzer Division to the Caen battlefield (behind 272nd Infantry Division) therefore away from its intended course in support of Panzer Lehr at St-Lô, retained 116th Panzer Division after the 19th in the same general locality, while Panzer Group West transferred 9th SS Panzer Division across the Orne on D+46 reinforcing I SS Panzer Corps while also committing I SS LAH and 21st Panzer to frontline action.

21 July (D+45)–25 July (D+49). For the next five days II SS Panzer Corps was obliged to retain 10th SS Panzer Division on the Odon west of Caen implementing plans to contain the pressure of British XII Corps' subsidiary attacks at Maltot.

Seventh Army shattered by 'Cobra', 25 July [D+49] to 6 August [D+61]. At 1100 hours on 25 July, US First Army (Bradley) initiated the ground assault phase of Operation 'Cobra'. The new American offensive boasted powerful resources; three army corps (VII, VIII, XIX), fourteen divisions (one motorized, two armoured with a third arriving) and the unfettered use of US 8th and 9th Air Forces. 'Cobra' aimed once and for all to break the cordon of Seventh Army (Hausser) infantry and panzer divisions barring US progress out of the bocage. Lead by US VII Corps (Collins), three infantry divisions formed up on a narrow front to open the way west of St-Lô; US 2nd and 3rd armored divisions supported by motorized infantry (US 1st) waited to exploit the expected breach. The panzer and panzer grenadier divisions forming the backbone of the defence remained unchanged; Panzer Lehr (Bayerlein) deployed opposite US VII Corps blocked all approaches to

the network of roads immediately west of St-Lô; 17th SS (GvB) Panzer Grenadier Division (Baum) stood firm around Marchésieux and, next in line to the west, 2nd SS Panzer Division Das Reich (Tychsen) maintained an unshakeable grip on Périers. As has been noted [D+34–D+48] none of these divisions were at anything like full strength; their depressed state being reflected in correspondingly weak infantry support – 353rd Infantry Division, 1,500 effectives; 243rd Infantry Division no more than a 700-strong battle group; FJR 6 reduced to a half-company of 60 men, etc. Moreover, the 2nd and 116th Panzer Divisions, intended to reinforce Seventh Army, were instead fixed south of Caen by OKW fears of a renewed British Second Army offensive aimed at Falaise (see Panzer Group West (D+49)).

German LXXXIV Corps (von Choltitz), responsible to Seventh Army for the area west of St-Lô between the town's western outskirts and the coast at Lessay, controlled all three panzer/panzer grenadier divisions and their supporting infantry. This was the sector where the full weight of 'Cobra' was to be unleashed – preceded by a massive air bombardment with US 8th and 9th Air Forces unloading 4,000–5,000 tons of high-explosives and Napalm, mostly upon Panzer Lehr. The result of the US bombing offensive and the follow-up assault by US VII Corps was to destroy all cohesion of Panzer Lehr, reducing Bayerlein's division to a 'restgruppe' symbol on LXXXIV Corps' situation map. Of the 188 Pz Kpfw IVs and Panthers with which Panzer Lehr entered the Normandy battle zone on D+2, fewer than fifteen Pz Kpfw IVs (II Panzer Lehr Regiment 130) of the forty remaining to 130th Panzer Lehr Regt (Gerhardt) at the start of 'Cobra' had constituted Bayerlein's sole counter-attack reserve opposing US armour and infantry striking south. Bayerlein's other panzer battalion, I/6th Panzer

Regiment, with a broadly equivalent number of Panthers, was divided in support of 902nd Panzer-Grenadier Regiment (Welsch) split into battle groups holding forward defended localities about Hébécrevon – the division's principal defensive position west of St-Lô. On the Division's left flank around La Chapelle the divisional Panzerjaeger Battalion (7.5cm SP anti-tank guns) served 901st Panzer Grenadier Regiment (Hauser) in much the same support capacity as the panzer battalion on the right. Divisional flak (8.8cm towed and SP weapons) lay farthest back, well concealed and, like the divisional artillery, ready to meet the challenge of Shermans, Honeys or other US armour penetrating the main battle line. All to no avail.

Horrendous concentrations of high-explosives and Napalm hurled down upon Panzer Lehr by the US Air Force, reinforcing the destructive effect of VII Corps artillery fire, destroyed 50 per cent of Panzer Lehr units standing west of St-Lô; reducing Bayerlein's 'division' to 2,500 officers and men with only handfuls of tanks and guns. Despite this débâcle, Panzer Lehr faced US First Army with unexpected opposition, but with no reserves to call upon, Seventh Army was about to collapse, Collins's VII Corps achieving remarkable results over the next forty-eight hours driving through Panzer Lehr. Pushing south through Hébécrevon, Marigny and St-Gilles towards Coutances, US armour and motorized infantry – enjoying full tactical air support directed by forward air controllers – shattered all remaining opposition. At other points along the front – east and west of St-Lô where fewer than seventy Pz Kpfw IVs and Panthers faced subsidiary attacks by US VIII and XIX Corps, Das Reich, Goetz von Berlichingen and supporting infantry stood their ground; new orders followed.

On **27 July [D+51]**, obeying orders from von Choltitz,

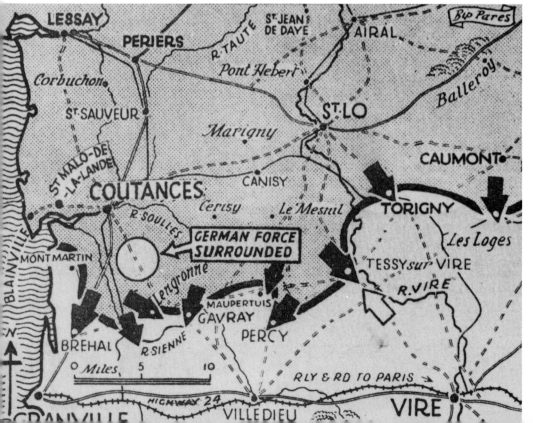

Left: Operation 'Cobra' swept onward from D+51 to D+53 creating the first of the Normandy pockets. In Roncey, 5–10 miles south of Coutances, elements of seven German divisions – including Panzer Lehr, Das Reich and Goetz von Berlichingen are trapped. The resultant break-out battles were very costly.

the defending divisions serving LXXXIV Corps west of St-Lô evacuated their positions and in phased operations degenerating into confused fighting as US armour sweeping towards Coutances threatened the retreating columns from the rear, sought to rally at Roncey, ten miles south-east of Coutances. Many panzer and infantry units caught up in the Seventh Army withdrawal were cut-off from parent formations, others engaged by marauding US armour were destroyed in bitter fighting. Acting upon their own initiative as communications failed, panzer battle groups varying in size and ability rallied as instructed in the neighbourhood of Roncey; Panzer Lehr to the east of the town, Das Reich, GvB and mixed infantry battle groups – the survivors of 275th, 353rd, 243rd and 91st Infantry Divisions also smaller combat and administrative units – were swept along in the crisis. OKW moves to restore the situation would come to depend upon panzer divisions transferred from the Caen wing of Panzer Group West (Eberbach) to the crisis sector south of St-Lô. In this area, between Tessy and Percy, 2nd Panzer Division (von Lüttwitz) and, twenty-four hours later, 116th Panzer Division (von Schwerin) bracketed into XXXXVII Panzer Corps (von Funck), were to launch heavy but unrewarding counter-attacks westwards. None of these attacks directed against US XIX Corps (Corlett) would translate into anything more than a local defensive success; the flow of US armour to the south continuing without interruption.

On the same day OKW ordered Army Group 'G' (Blaskowitz) to release 9th Panzer Division (Jollasse) reforming at Nîmes and dispatch it north to Alençon. Once there 9th Panzer could expect to join LXXXI Corps (Küntzen) moving in from Rouen. In control of 708th Infantry Division, taken from the Atlantic coast at Royan, local security battalions and 9th Panzer (elements), LXXXI Corps would form an offensive 'truppe' for the protection of Seventh Army's soon dangerously at risk southern flank [D+62–D+71]. Alençon's value to Seventh Army lay in its position at the centre of the Army's Normandy communications. Service installations of all descriptions packed the area; supply, engineer, workshop and signals units in particular. As a further measure in strengthening crisis command arrangements south-east of Mortain, a reserve Panzer Corps LVII (Krüger) was ordered north from Toulouse.

On **28 July [D+52]**, 2nd Panzer Division (von Luttwitz), redeployed by Panzer Group West from the Caen battlefield at Bretteville, arrived west of Tessy. After establishing blocking positions forward of Tessy, 2nd Panzer prepared to counter-attack XIX US Corps (Corlett) by striking west in the direction of Villebaudon and Coutances. On the same day Das Reich, retreating south of Coutances, lost its Commander (Tychsen); the divisional HQ battle group being overrun by US 4th Armored Division at Trelly. Das Reich was then taken over by Otto Baum commanding GvB 17th SS Panzer Grenadier Division. Baum was also given command of all LXXXIV Corps units rallying between Coutances (lost during the day) and Roncey ten miles to the south-east – a superficially small area fast assuming the character of a pocket as US armour (2nd, 3rd and 4th Armored Divisions) sealed every escape route.

On **29 July [D+53]** GOC LXXXIV Corps (von Choltitz) ordered the defenders of the Roncey pocket to break out south-east. Forming ad hoc battle groups at the expense of

many heavy weapons, particularly artillery, the encircled infantry and panzer/panzer grenadiers, seeking to bypass US blocking forces, struggled to comparative safety around Percy. Not all were to succeed in reaching XXXXVII Panzer Corps facing west with 2nd and (arriving) 116th Panzer Divisions; von Funck incorporated survivors of Panzer Lehr in defence of Percy. At St-Denis-le-Gast a particularly violent clash occurred when break-out units of Das Reich and GvB encountered 2nd US Armored Division. Casualties mounted. All too soon 2,500 German dead and 5,000 prisoners were testifying to the bitterness of the break-out battle while renewed attacks by II/116th Panzer Division west of Villebaudon failed against XIX US Corps (Corlett).

On **30 July [D+54]**, armoured columns of Patton's US Third Army, officially activated on 1 August (when Bradley stepped-up to command US 12th Army Group and Hodges assumed command of First Army), seized Avranches at the base of the Cotentin Peninsular. Next day Patton's armour would cross the Sélune to Pontaubault. The US break-through, which started six days earlier west of St-Lô, was complete; and while US First Army (Hodges) continued to press German Seventh Army battle groups further away from the Cherbourg–Avranches corridor, US Third Army (Patton) VII, XV and XX US Army Corps prepared for unrestricted mobile operations. The American's scheduled goal was Britanny, where the Atlantic coast ports (still strongly defended) were needed to supplement the limited stores-handling capacity of Cherbourg; but US Third Army's dynamic commander relished the prospect of breaking-out to the east. Driving for the Seine towards Le Mans (entered 10 August) through Seventh Army's open flank south of Mortain, Patton's hussar performance would precipitate the disastrous collapse of Army Group 'B' much feared by German commanders at the front. At this stage in the battle Montgomery devised a new plan for hastening the process of German disintegration.

Starting on **30 July [D+54]** and continuing until 6 August [D+61], whilst the panzer divisions south of St-Lô, 2nd, 116th, Battle Group Panzer Lehr, 2nd SS and 17th SS subordinate to XXXXVII Panzer Corps (von Funck) were striving to contain US First Army seeking to widen its corridor eastwards in the direction of Tessy, Vire and Mortain – British Second Army's 'Bluecoat' offensive (D+54) would threaten Vire from the north, creating fresh problems. Launched south-west of Caumont on an axis converging with US V Corps approaching Vire from the north-west Montgomery's new offensive struck 326th Infantry Division threatening to unhinge German defences at the junction of Seventh Army (Hausser) and Panzer Group West (Eberbach). Von Kluge's response to the dangers of 'Bluecoat' was immediate – Panzer Group West must further reduce its panzer commitment south of Caen concentrating instead for counter-action on the opposite flank south of Caumont – for which purpose Bittrich's II SS Panzer Corps headquarters was to quit the Odon, moving immediately to the area (see also Panzer Group West.)

31 July [D+55] to 1 August [D+56]. On 31 July, 21st Panzer (Feuchtinger) reinforced by 503rd (Tiger) Battalion, arrived south-east of Caumont, reinforcing 326th Infantry Division, unsettled by 'Bluecoat'; 10th SS Division Frundsberg (Harmel) meanwhile joined the action south-west of Villers-Bocage. They then launched counter attacks.

On **2 August [D+57]**, 9th SS Panzer Division Hohen-staufen (Stadler), the kernel of the counter-attack forces assembling under II SS Panzer Corps to oppose 'Bluecoat' south-east of Caumont, came into action east of Vire reinforced by 102nd SS (Tiger) Battalion. More transfers and a panzer battle group (Olboeter) raised by 12th SS Panzer Division Hitler Jugend joined the battle for Vire, striking at Chênedollé east of the town. Aiming concentric blows at British armoured and infantry divisions (11th Guards Armoured and 15th Scottish) driving south-west from Caumont under VIII Corps (O'Connor), II SS Panzer Corps would win the race for Vire, averting the threat to Seventh Army's rearward communications. But despite the success of the SS Panzer Corps in stalling the British offensive north of Vire and slowing subsidiary operations by XXX Corps immediately to the east, Vire would be lost to US V Corps (Gerow) on 6 August. Mortain would also fall, with US VII Corps (Collins) entering the town on D+58.

Simultaneously on **2 August [D+57]** OKW was com-municating Hitler's own counter-attack proposals to OB West. The proposals required von Kluge to mount a major offensive westwards across the Cotentin Peninsular, starting east of Mortain and aiming for Avranches; at least four panzer divisions would be needed for the twenty or so miles thrust to the coast and these, OKW argued, could be found by reducing Seventh Army/Panzer Group West commitments to a shorter line in general. Operation 'Lüttich' was intended once and for all to sever US Third Army's communications, bringing to an end the supplies and reinforcements flowing south to Patton. In the course of 72 hours this resourceful General had succeeded in passing no fewer than seven divisions across the Sélune bridge at Pontaubault. Sweeping aside a battle group rushed from St-Malo and ignoring attacks by the Luftwaffe, Patton turned XV Corps (Haislip) east into the practically undefended Seventh Army flank south of Mortain threatening Laval (7 August) and Le Mans (10 August). Other US (Third Army) Corps entering Britanny by way of Rennes (3 August) and St-Malo (18 August) pushed for the Atlantic ports – encountering determined resistance from 'fortress' garrisons. Hitler's counter-attack proposals, meanwhile developed by von Kluge, demanded the concerted effort of all the available panzer divisions under the command of a specially qualified panzer opera-tions staff (Eberbach). Such proposals were not only unrealistic in the circumstances of total Anglo-US air supremacy – but suicidal.

Hitler's map-table plans for an all out panzer offensive east of Mortain, redressing the strategic picture in the west came too late. There was no spare panzer capacity for operations on the grand scale envisaged by 'Luttich' – Montgomery's new offensive on the Vire had seen to that; for whatever panzer divisions von Kluge might have freed for a strategic offensive in the west in hope of destroying American chances of a rapid break-out, were (once again) absorbed in local fighting on the northern front. Further-more, Eberbach's commitment to panzer group operations on the Vire, reacting to 'Bluecoat' and rumbles east of the Orne where I SS Panzer Corps (1st SS, 12th SS Panzer Divisions) was facing renewed Canadian interest in driving for Falaise, was clearly an overriding consideration. In the circumstances von Kluge decided that XXXXVII Panzer Corps (von Funck) alone should lead Hitler's offensive against US

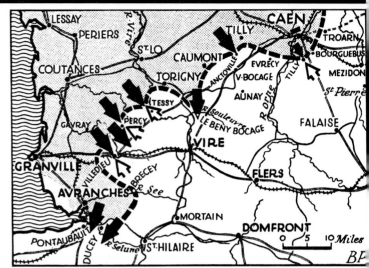

First Army, employing whatever panzer divisions could be assembled in quick time east of Mortain, and not as Hitler proposed in a comprehensive build-up waiting for relieving infantry and suitable (unsuitable for US air operations) weather.

3 August [D+58] to 5 August [D+60]. Patton's drive east in the direction of Paris and the Seine continued unopposed.

6 August [D+61]. By late evening of 6 August, 1st SS Pz Division en route from the Orne south of Caen (relieved by 89th Infantry Division) and 2nd SS Panzer Division disengaging from Seventh Army's front at Courson were assembling with 2nd and 116th Panzer Divisions east of Mortain. Supporting the projected panzer offensive were additional panzer battle groups – 17th SS (Fick) allotted to Das Reich, the assault formation at the centre of the counter-attack line-up east of Mortain, and 130th Panzer Reconnaissance Battalion taken from Panzer Lehr to protect the southern flank. Bayerlein's decimated division mean-while contributed a small but effective battle group (Hauser) to the western defence of Vire where II Parachute Corps (Meindl), finally prised out of St-Lô, was fighting to ward-off converging US and British attacks.

The effective panzer strength of 'Lüttich' was probably no more than 150 battle tanks; Pz Kpfw IVs and Panthers serving the panzer regiments involved, i.e., 3rd Panzer Regiment (2nd Panzer Division), 16th Panzer Regiment (116th Panzer Division), 1st and 2nd SS Panzer Regiments. The responsible Luftwaffe command (II Jagd Corps) had promised air cover and ground-attack support for the panzer divisions, with three hundred Me 109 and Fw 190 fighters flying from airfields around Paris. Other preparatory arrangements for 'Lüttich' involved the transfer of reserve infantry divisions, 363rd (Dettling) and 84th (Menny) from Fifteenth Army north of the Seine to LXXXIV Corps immediately north of the 'Lüttich' area. Under a new commander (von Elfeldt) LXXXIV Corps was to protect the right flank of the offensive. Zero hour was set for 0100 hours, 7 August [D+62]. But to the totally unexpected disadvantage of 'Luttich', the operation was fatefully compromised by another 'Ultra' coup. Forewarned on the eve of operations by 'Ultra' reporting tank concentrations

Above: On 31 July 1944 (D+ 55), General George Patton the break-through to Pontaubalt; the panzer divisions escaping from Ronc retreated south-east. When Patton traversed the Sélune with seven divisions the enem opposition was minimal. A week later Hitler ordered a suicidal counter-offensive to cut US lines of communicatic but it ended in failure having been betrayed by 'Ultra' and brought to a standstill by superior Allied air power.

north of Mortain, and air-support requests by the Leibstandarte (I SS) naming possible targets in the same locality. Allied Army and Air Force chiefs were given ample time in which to initiate counter-measures. The crucial element of surprise that might have carried the day for von Kluge was irretrievably lost and 'Lüttich', by which Hitler set much store would, by thrusting west away from the focal point of action by US Third Army driving east towards Le Mans, be turned instead to Allied advantage. The Mortain counter-offensive and von Kluge's crisis continued [D+62–D+71]. At this point we return to the northern front and action by Panzer Group West.

Too little, too late for Eberbach. 25 July (D+49) to 16 August [D+71]. Known as Panzer Group West until 2 August (D+57), Eberbach's HQ was redesignated, Panzer Army West 3–4 August (D+58–59), thereafter (D+60) Fifth Panzer Army. With Seventh Army in disarray as US First and Third Armies punched south, exploiting the breach west of St-Lô [D+49–D+61], British Second and Canadian First Armies were maintaining pressure to hold the panzer divisions in the east by bringing them into action south of Caen or, after D+54, south of Caumont. Montgomery's strategy of drawing the panzer divisions away from the American sector, enabling Bradley and Patton to break out of the Cotentin Peninsular and, with the least possible opposition, drive into Brittany, was to prove the positive factor in Allied success. At the time of the US break-out, with events at their most critical, there were more panzer divisions retained by Panzer Group West opposing the Anglo-Canadian armies on the Caen–St-Lô sector than facing US First/Third Armies on Seventh Army's sector between St-Lô and Lessay. A measure of the crisis gripping OKW and Army Group 'B' (von Kluge) as US armies developed 'Cobra' is evident in the changing ratio of panzer divisions deployed on the three main fronts; west and south opposing US First/Third Armies or north and east resisting British Second and eventually Canadian First Armies.

[D+49] Day one of the US break-out; west 3 : east 7

[D+52] Day four (Tessy attack); west 4 (excluding Panzer Lehr 'destroyed') : east 5

[D+61] Day thirteen (Mortain counter-attack); west 5 (excluding Panzer Lehr 'destroyed') : east 4

[D+69] Day twenty (Alençon counter-attack); south 8 (excluding Panzer Lehr 'destroyed') : north 2

Tank deployment on [D+49] confirms the imbalance of panzer strength east and west; west facing US First Army, 110 tanks east facing British Second Army, 600 tanks. Thus seven of the ten panzer/panzer grenadier divisions deployed by OKW in Normandy on D+49 – 1st SS, 12th SS, 21st, 9th SS, 10th SS, 2nd and 116th – were in action with Panzer Group West, opposing British Second or Canadian First Armies or, in the case of 116th Panzer, in OKW reserve at Creil. Three other panzer divisions – Panzer Lehr (destroyed day one), 2nd SS and 17th SS (Panzer Grenadier) – opposed US First Army in the west, while the last of the panzer divisions to be committed in Normandy, 9th Panzer arriving Alençon [D+61] was at the time still en route from Nîmes. Of the seven panzer divisions detained in the east by Montgomery around Caen, where Panzer Group West was preparing for a renewal of Anglo-Canadian pressure following 'Goodwood' D+42–D+44 and OKW was expecting the main threat in Normandy, 1st SS, 12th

SS, 2nd, 21st and 9th SS were serving I SS Panzer Corps (Dietrich) south of the town, leaving 10th SS on the Odon under II SS Panzer Corps (Bittrich) and 116th in OKW reserve.

The need for additional infantry divisions to free panzer divisions from front-line service had been recognized by Rommel and OKW soon after D-day, but Hitler's insistence upon maintaining the strongest possible force in the Pas-de-Calais, protecting V-1/V-2 sites or available to repulse an expected second landing, would deprive Army Group 'B' of its best source of reinforcement – Fifteenth Army, north of the Seine. When all too late at the end of July Hitler perceived the true threat to Seventh Army/Panzer Group West in the weight and direction of Allied attacks, OKW speeded the release of infantry divisions from Fifteenth Army to Normandy. Incoming infantry divisions – no fewer than eleven by 12 August (D+67) – were to be deployed along the northern front serving Panzer Group West or its successor, Fifth Panzer Army (D+60) on the Caen–Caumont sector especially. The panzer divisions freed by relieving infantry would then be expected to regroup for action under Eberbach at Mortain, but in practice failing to assemble in time would achieve success neither there [D+62] nor subsequently at Alençon [D+66].

25 July (D+49)–26 July (D+50). On 25 July with 'Cobra' west of St-Lô destroying Panzer Lehr [D+49], 1 SS Panzer Corps (Dietrich) in the east was subjected to renewed pressure by Canadian First Army (Crerar) pushing south towards Falaise.

Operation 'Spring' launched by the Canadians south of Caen from positions gained at the conclusion of 'Atlantic' – the Canadian counterpart to 'Goodwood' (D+42) – continued for 24 hours until the power of the defence, particularly by battle groups from 1st SS Panzer Division, proved unbreakable. But Allied pressure exerted simultaneously to the east by British XII Corps (Ritchie) on the Odon in Operation 'Express' D+46 and thereafter would result in bitter fighting for Maltot, a strong point eventually wrested from II SS Panzer Corps (Bittrich).

27 July (D+51) to 29 July (D+53). By 27 July, US success with 'Cobra' [D+49] was prompting Montgomery to re-assess Anglo-Canadian options for expediting the collapse of German Seventh Army (Hausser). Swinging VIII Corps west across the battlefield from Caen, where the Corps had stood at the conclusion of 'Goodwood', to Caumont where Panzer Group West linked up with Seventh Army, Montgomery proposed in Operation 'Bluecoat' to launch two armoured and three infantry divisions across the rear of German Seventh Army; Vire being selected as VIII Corps' objective. Subsidiary attacks by XXX Corps (Bucknall) would focus upon tactically important ground to the south-east. In the meantime, von Kluge's reaction to 'Cobra' was resulting in rapid panzer redeployment; 2nd and 116th Panzer Divisions being switched from Caen to a new concentration area south of St-Lô. 2nd Panzer (von Lüttwitz) leading the way west over the River Vire south of Vire itself on the night of the 27th made preparations for an immediate counter-attack westwards from Tessy; XXXXVII Panzer Corps (von Funck) in control (see [D+52]).

30 July (D+54). Operation 'Bluecoat', commencing on 30 July, with the intention of getting VIII Corps (O'Connor) into Vire, a point in the main battle line where Panzer Group

West (Eberbach) connected with Seventh Army (Hausser) – while XXX Corps (Bucknall) was making for Montpinçon the tactically important high ground to the east – provoked immediate response from von Kluge.

On **31 July (D+55)** II SS Panzer Corps (Bittrich) with Hohenstaufen (Stadler) and Frundsberg (Harmel) was ordered west from the Odon to Caumont; 21st Panzer Division (Feuchtinger), already under orders to move west from Caen where it had held the line in near continuous action since D-Day, leading the way. Feuchtinger's task was to restore the situation to von Kluge's advantage north of Vire where 11th Armoured Division (Roberts) driving for le Bény-Bocage had penetrated the defences of 326th Infantry Division. Hohenstaufen (Stadler) and Frunsberg (Harmel), trailing 21st Panzer Division in the race for Vire, where II Parachute Corps (Meindl), prised out of St-Lô by XIX Corps (Corlett), was holding the town with 3rd Parachute Division (Schimpf) and a Panzer Lehr battle group, were soon on the move. Other reinforcements for the defence of the threatened sector including a recce unit battle group (Olboeter) from 12th SS Panzer Division Hitler Jugend were also on the way. For the panzer divisions charged with neutralizing 'Bluecoat', speed was the order of the day. For von Kluge the 'Bluecoat' threat posed a grave dilemma. Coming as it did at a crucial moment, when the battle to contain the damage caused by the US break-out at Coutances [D+54] would require the commitment of at least four panzer divisions in counter-attacks expected of him by Hitler [D+57], Montgomery's powerful blow by three armoured and three infantry divisions striking at the hinge of Seventh Army and Panzer Group West while US Third Army punched east seemed likely to precipitate the kind of disaster predicted by Rommel.

31 July (D+55) to 2 August (D+57). Much to von Kluge's relief the counter-action started by 21st Panzer (Feuchtinger) and developed by II SS Panzer Corps (Bittrich) defending Vire – best viewed in the context of Seventh Army operations south of St-Lô [D+55–D+61] lifted the immediate threat to that Army's rear communications running eastwards south of the town. Despite this success by II SS Panzer Corps at a time of mounting tension occasioned by US success with 'Cobra', events on the northern front were moving towards no less a traumatic phase in the fortunes of Panzer Group West. Hitler's destructive influence on events in Normandy at this point is reflected in new orders from OKW reacting to 'Cobra' and its consequences – a Führerbefehl (directive) to von Kluge requiring him to mount a (suicidal) counter-attack east of Mortain (*see* Seventh Army [D+62]).

3 August (D+58)–4 August (D+59). Although Hitler intended that Eberbach should lead the action at Mortain, code-named 'Lüttich', von Kluge dissented, insisting instead that Eberbach should continue directing critical operations in defence of Vire and equally sensitive positions to the south-east of Caen. A renewal of British/Canadian pressure at these danger points could but not fail to snap an over-taut Army Group battle line, but as a first step towards improving command arrangements Panzer Group West was upgraded and redesignated Panzer Army West.

On **5 August (D+60)**, however, a further change of name converted Panzer Army West into Fifth Panzer Army. But stripped within days by the Führerbefehl for 'Lüttich'

[D+62] of all but two panzer divisions, 21st and 12th SS HJ, the Army would then consist of fewer than ten–eleven infantry divisions with which to defend a battle line stretching from the Channel coast at Cabourg south around Caen and on to Caumont 70 miles inland.

6 August (D+61)–7 August (D+62). British Second Army, exerting pressure north and east of Vire on 6 and 7 August, continued the task of holding II SS Panzer Corps (Bittrich) in action, closing a gap driven into II Parachute Corps lines at le-Bény-Bocage. In this sector 11th Armoured Division had breached the main battle line while other forces were assaulting Montpinçon, the tactically important high ground to the east. There, more British armour and infantry divisions including Guards and 7th Armoured Division supported the operation; II SS Panzer Corps, reacting to the threat, involved 9th SS, 10th SS, 21st Panzer and a HJ battle group in heavy defensive fighting. When a renewal of Allied pressure shifted the action once more to Caen, Canadian First Army offensives 'Totalise' (D+62) and 'Tractable' (D+67) would bring 12th SS Panzer Division Hitler Jugend back into the line with the support of 21st Panzer redeployed from Vire. This sequence of Allied attacks was to be largely successful in denying von Kluge an opportunity for massing all but four panzer divisions for the Mortain counter-offensive [D+61–D+62]. *While Fifth Panzer Army was juggling with panzer units in a bid to prevent a decisive break-through in the north, Seventh Army was launching Operation 'Lüttich', first mooted [D+57] and finally unfolding [D+62] under XXXXVII Panzer Corps (von Funck). In control of 2nd, 116th, 1st SS, 2nd SS Panzer Divisions and supporting battle groups, von Funck's offensive was not a success; Allied air attacks, 'Ultra' and a staunch US defence bringing the offensive to a standstill (see [D+57–D+62].)*

New orders were soon forthcoming from Rastenburg. On 9 August Hitler would demand that Eberbach renew 'Lüttich' with the additional power of II SS Panzer Corps and panzer divisions taken from Caumont (21st, 9th SS and 10th SS) and Caen (1st SS, 12th SS). *But in a rapidly deteriorating situation, with US Third Army racing east to Le Mans and threatening to isolate both Normandy armies, OKW was to re-shape its plans, directing Eberbach eastwards instead to counter Patton swinging an armoured corps (XV, Haislip) north from Le Mans [D+65] and threatening Alençon [D+66]. Situated 50 miles behind Seventh Army's front at Mortain and protected only by an emergency defence force, the Army Group's supply and communications centre at Alençon was directly in line with Patton's advance. Retention of the base was crucial to the maintenance and supply resources of the German Army in the west. More significantly, Patton's radical change of direction northwards at a time when 'Totalise' D+63 was threatening to break up Fifth Panzer Army's holding positions south of Caen, thereby threatening Falaise, engendered well-founded High Command fears of encirclement – the gap between Allies converging on Falaise and Alençon being no more than 55 miles. Faced with this prospect OKW would soon be demanding the release of panzer divisions from Caen, Caumont and Mortain, all to be regrouped under a new command, Panzer Group Eberbach. The force so assembled was to be launched against US Third Army spearheads striking north from Le Mans. Alençon*

7 August (D+62). Operation 'Totalise' launched by Canadian II Corps (Simmonds) south of Caen, coinciding with German Seventh Army's Mortain offensive [D+62] faced I SS Panzer Corps (Dietrich) with unexpectedly powerful opposition. The Canadian force included in its order of battle two armoured divisions landed mostly within the previous fortnight, three infantry divisions and two independent armoured brigades.

Starting shortly before midnight on 7 August, in the wake of a powerful bombing offensive (3,500 tons of high-explosives on key targets), two assault infantry divisions breached the Panzer Army front at a point where 89th Infantry Division (Heinrichs) held the Caen–Falaise road south of Bourguébus, more or less where 'Goodwood' had left off on 20 July 1944 (D+44). Heinrichs' forward infantry and flanking units of 271st and 272nd Infantry Divisions were unable to resist Allied ground and air offensives tearing a five-mile gap in the German front and were overwhelmed. Nothing more than the nub of 12th SS HJ Panzer Division (Meyer), resting with emergency battle groups in reserve north of Falaise, stood between the Canadians and their objective – Falaise; the Leibstandarte (I SS LAH), hitherto the main stay of Fifth Panzer Army's defence south of Caen – now in the hands of 89th Infantry Division – having meanwhile been transferred (5–6 August) to Mortain for Seventh Army's 'Lüttich' offensive.

8 August (D+63). At midday on 8 August, main force 'Totalise', including 4th Canadian (Kitching) and 1st Polish (Maczek) Armoured Divisions with 400–500 tanks, formed up in columns facing south on each side of the Caen–Falaise road waiting to exploit any breach won by the infantry. Despite support from yet another wave of bombers unloading high-explosives on the defence, the Canadian drive, opposed at this point by 12th SS HJ Panzer Division, fell apart. Although further attacks south would continue spasmodically over the next 48 hours, by evening the tempo of the offensive had been lost. By D+66 'Totalise' had been abandoned. This unexpected check to the Anglo-Canadian offensive is attributable to the handling and élan of HJ battle groups co-ordinating defensive action with the firepower of 101st SS (Tiger) Battalion; the German Army's battle skills, always a positive factor in the Normandy campaign, being seen here at their best despite the handicap of total air inferiority and the absence on other fronts of two sizeable battle groups; a Schnellgruppe (Olboeter) – one SPW and one pz coy with Wasp and Recce units at Vire, and one Panzer Regiment (Wünsche) with three panzer companies, a Tiger Company and two panzer grenadier battalions on a neighbouring front at Grimbosq. Grossly outnumbered in tanks and infantry, Meyer assembled HJ's remaining divisional and support units into a battle group (Waldmüller) comprising II Panzer Battalion (39 Pz Kpfw IVs), an anti-tank battalion (Jagdpanzer VIs), a Tiger Company (10 Pz Kpfw VIs), a panzer grenadier battalion (I/25), two other companies, ancillary flak (8.8cm) and Werfer troops.

The SS corps/divisional plan of defence was simple. Instructing Battle Group Wünsche to return immediately from Grimbosq where it was reinforcing 271st Infantry Division opposing a dangerous British incursion on HJ's left flank, Wünsche on arrival later in the day was deployed as a mobile reserve and second line of defence on high ground overlooking the Caen–Falaise road north of the River Laison

Above: SS Standartenführer Kurt 'Panzer' Meyer, GOC, 12th Panzer Division HJ. A career SS officer, Meyer entered the Leibstandarte in 1932, served in Poland, France, the Balkans and Russia. He was transferred to Hitler Jugend in 1944 as CO, 25th Panzer Grenadier Regiment. In June of that year he succeeded Brigadeführer Fritz Witt, HJ's commander, who was killed in action. Meyer was subsequently taken prisoner at Amiens that September and command of HJ passed to Hugo Krass who was GOC at the time of operations in the Ardennes ('Autumn Mist', *see* map 17) and Hungary ('Spring Awakening', *see* map 19).

would be saved and conditions restored for a renewal of 'Lüttich' westwards.

Such were Hitler's intentions. The actual course of events, culminating in the total defeat of the panzer divisions in Normandy, is best followed in the context of Seventh Army operations on the southern front [D+62–D+71]. On the northern front at this critical juncture Fifth Panzer Army continued in control of the main battle line stretching from the Channel coast at Cabourg to the Seventh Army boundary south of Caumont and on to Vire, but battle lines generally were being shortened to allow panzer divisions to disengage and provide the necessary strength for Panzer Group Eberbach. With Fifth Panzer Army confirmed in a static role (under Dietrich after D+64), Panzer Group Eberbach would prevail as the principal armoured formation in Normandy – responsible to Seventh Army until 18 August (D+73) and thereafter directly to Army Group 'B'. Notwithstanding Fifth Panzer Army's almost total dependence upon infantry with which to combat Allied armour continually probing for brittle points along a 70–80-mile front, future action by the Army's sole remaining reserve, 12th SS HJ Panzer Division (Meyer) opposing Canadian First Army between Caen and Falaise would rank as a major episode in the Normandy history of the panzer force.

– the last defensible Fifth Panzer Army position between Caen and Falaise. In a blocking move closer to the enemy, a detachment of Tigers under Michael Wittman, commanding 101st SS Tiger Battalion, with 138 tank destructions to his credit (see D+7), also panzerjaeger and flak troops – used in a ground role – would advance to Cintheaux blocking the Caen–Falaise road directly in the teeth of the expected Canadian armoured attack. HJ's main counter-attack battle group Waldmüller, with the remaining armour and support units, would be committed right flanking against Polish armoured spearheads rolling south in support of the Canadians. The resulting clash of armour, putting an end to Canadian hopes of a swift and decisive break-through to Falaise, was marked by the death of Michael Wittman – in action against a superior force of Shermans seeking to force a way through Cintheaux. The Canadians were nevertheless denied their objective until early evening. At other points along the sector Waldmüller halted Polish progress, later breaking free of encirclement. Regrouping after dark in new positions north of the Laison, the division prepared for yet another Canadian offensive.

On 9 August (D+64) with the battle for Falaise reaching new heights of violence, Canadian and Polish armoured divisions struggled to push south against HJ battle groups including panzer Kampfgruppe Wünsche now firmly established in blocking positions north of the Laison. At Fifth Panzer Army headquarters during the afternoon, orders arrived to the effect that Hitler required Eberbach to lead a renewal of 'Lüttich' [D+62]. Intending to take panzer divisions from Caumont and Caen – resisted in the case of HJ, totally unable to disengage – 'Lüttich' was now an unalterable Führerbefehl; Eberbach being Hitler's chosen executive. Bittrich's II SS Panzer Corps with 9th and 10th SS was to move immediately from Caumont to Mortain, joining 2nd, 116th, 1st SS and 2nd SS in a counter-

offensive aimed at Avranches across the rear communications of US Third Army (Patton) stretching back to Cherbourg. But to the concern of OKW and von Kluge, US Third Army spearheads identified north of Le Mans driving in the direction of Alençon 40 miles south of Falaise changed the picture completely and within days Eberbach would be preparing instead to save Alençon by counter-attacks against US Third Army (Patton) pushing north from Le Mans [D+65].

10 August (D+65)–11 August (D+66). On the Falaise front more heavy fighting was developing as Hitler Jugend inflicted severe losses on Polish/Canadian armour attempting to work south; HJ battle groups reinforced by 102nd SS Tiger Battalion (released by II SS Panzer Corps moving to Mortain where the Corps' heavy weapons would be less effective in the attack) and a bicycle battalion from 85th Infantry Division finally breaking the Canadian offensive. Counter-attacking a Canadian battle group (Worthington) occupying Hill 140, a key feature north of the Laison – HJ's last line of defence – a concentric attack by Panthers, IVs and Tigers destroyed 47 Shermans or other Canadian tanks. By the end of the day in the battle for Falaise with the advantage going to the defence, German tank strength opposing Canadian First Army stood at seventeen Panzer IVs, seven Panthers, eleven Tigers and perhaps ten Jagdpanzer IVs. When replaced in the line north of the Laison by 85th Infantry Division, HJ in its weakened state was withdrawn into corps reserve and at the end of D+66 prepared for the next Canadian onslaught.

12 August (D+67) to 16 August (D+71). Starting on 12 August, Operation 'Tractable' culminating on the 16th (D+71) in the capture of Falaise, renewed Canadian First Army's (Crerar) efforts to win the objective that had so long escaped its grasp. Assisted by air attacks launched against the defence in massive strength and the co-ordinated

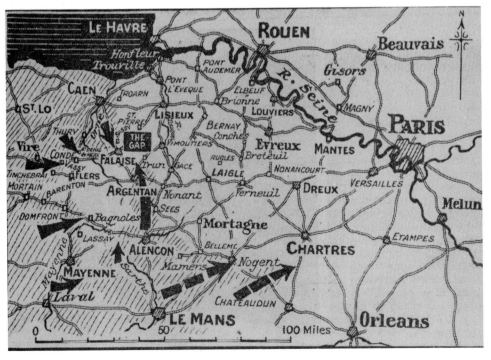

Left: 15 August 1944. D+70 Patton's Third Army swung north from Le Mans to threaten von Kluge with encirclement. When contact was established between the Anglo-Canadian and US Forces at Chambois (1st Polish Armed Division, US 90th Infantry Division) the 'gap' was closed until a relief attack by II SS Pz Corps, previously evacuated from the pocket, re-opened the escape route.

Above: 17 August 1944 D+ 72. Pictured here is a battle group of the Hitler Jugend (Hitler Youth) Division changing positions after defending the northern shoulder of 'the gap'; through this gateway Model evacuated the Falaise pocket, leaving behind 10,000 dead and 40,000 prisoners-of-war. Hitler Jugend was largely responsible for the Allied failure to push quickly into Carpiquet, Caen and Falaise.

pressure of British Second Army pushing from the north-west, 'Tractable' would bring HJ and the only other panzer division available to Fifth Panzer Army, 21st Panzer, back into action, holding off the northern arm of an Allied pincer closing inexorably behind two German armies and a Panzer Group. The gap between Allied armies was now less than 40 miles separating Canadians at Falaise from Americans north of Alençon. Neither HJ nor 21st Panzer Division in battles to ward off encirclement were to escape increasingly bitter fighting in defence of Falaise and eventually the northern shoulder of the pocket when Allied pincers closed on (D+74). In this critical situation HJ Panzer Division reduced to three panzer grenadier battalions of two companies (two in SPWs), 24 Pz Kpfw IVs a handful of Jagdpanzers, flak and ancillary troops – the equivalent of no more than a single regiment – yet the mainstay of I SS Panzer Corps on the Laison, resumed defensive operations against Canadian First Army. The German infantry divisions holding the Panzer Army line north of Falaise, 85th, 89th, 270th, 271st, notably under-provided with anti-tank weapons, were swamped in the Canadian attack; HJ battle groups reduced to fifteen Pz Kpfw IVs could no longer restore the situation for Fifth Panzer Army.

By **15 August (D+70)**, HJ battle groups supported by 21st Panzer Division were fighting either in the ruins of Falaise or defending tactically important ground to the east.

21st Panzer (Feuchtinger), forming two battle groups (Luck) and (Rausch) but no better equipped than HJ to stem the Canadian offensive, was to be set against 1st Polish Armoured Division redirected eastwards on Trun, a key communications point on the Panzer Army's main east-west route and still open to the defence in an increasingly constricted pocket. But for OKW the impending loss of Falaise was only one of several issues exercising staff minds. The southern arm of the pincer was closing fast. Alençon was lost, Argentan, hitherto regarded as a firm base for the defence of the southern front, going the same way; the entire Normandy campaign was a disaster with Seventh Army, Fifth Panzer Army and Panzer Group Eberbach virtually a write-off. And, to Hitler's consternation, von Kluge was missing. After setting out on a visit to Hausser and Eberbach at Nécy nothing more had been heard of him.

But the most pressing of problems besetting OKW in the west at this time of crisis was the landing of US and French forces in the area of Army Group 'G' (Blaskowitz) on the Mediterranean coast between Cannes and Toulon. In Operation 'Dragoon', aimed at the Rhône valley, the Allies were pouring ashore 86,000 men, 12,250 vehicles and 46,000 tons of stores – the *matériel* strength of US Seventh Army (Patch) with which French 1st Armoured Division (Vigier) was included. An Allied thrust north along the Rhône valley was clearly intended to bypass German First and Nineteenth Armies deployed in the south and still protecting Mediterranean or Atlantic coasts and hinterlands. At Toulon and Marseilles, 244th and 242nd Infantry Divisions stood firm as ordered; other garrisons were similarly expected to defend key Atlantic ports. For the rest, retreat was in prospect with 11th Panzer Division (von Buttlar) acting as rear and flank guard for Nineteenth Army departing from the Mediterranean coast and First Army making its way north-east from the Atlantic to the Rhine as best it might.

On **16 August (D+71)**, with the battle for Normandy degenerating beyond recovery, Hitler sanctioned the withdrawal of Army Group 'B' while simultaneously ordering the withdrawal of Army Group 'G' from the Mediterranean. Von Kluge – despite his belated reappearance at Fifth Panzer Army Headquarters, now operating outside the pocket at Meulles, was to be 'recalled' for consultation with Hitler.

In von Kluge's place Hitler appointed Field Marshal Walter Model, a panzer general whose loyalty and adroitness in defence of the Eastern Front had greatly impressed him.

Walter Model – 3rd Panzer Division; XXXXI Panzer Corps; Ninth Army and latterly Army Group North Ukraine – would arrive at La Roche-Guyon the following day, too late to change the course of events in Normandy, but in time to conduct the escape of ruined divisions in phased withdrawal. Retreating from encirclement in the Argentan–Falaise pocket before crossing the Seine and withdrawing through France and Belgium was to become a horrendous undertaking, one that would bring the German Army back to the frontiers of the Third Reich. This traumatic development of the war in Normandy, obliging II SS Panzer Corps to launch relief attacks from outside the pocket (D+75), would be followed by the capture of Eberbach on 31 August (see D+74–D+76). Here, panzer action in Normandy returns to Seventh Army's critical southern front [D+62–D+71], tracing the failure of Hitler's counter-attack at Mortain where 'Lüttich' proving ill-conceived would culminate in the encirclement of Army Group 'B' on 19 August (D+74) – the German Army's least glorious day in France.

Crisis in Normandy *7 August [D+62] to 16 August [D+71]. 7 August [D+62].* Hitler's intelligently conceived but in the circumstances suicidal plan to halt the flow of US armour and infantry pouring into Brittany and penetrating east behind Seventh Army, code-named 'Lüttich', was about to trigger an Army Group crisis of the first magnitude. Intended as a 20–25-mile thrust west from Mortain to the coast at Avranches to sever American First Army communications, but compromised from the outset by another 'Ultra' coup alerting the defence and allowing counter-measures to be initiated before midnight on [D+61], even as the first spearheads of XXXXVII Panzer Corps were crossing the start-line, 'Lüttich' was doomed to failure. With skies clearing and giving access to the battlefield on the morning of D+62, Allied air forces were soon inflicting serious delay on the panzer divisions: right, 116th and 2nd Panzer; left, 1st SS and 2nd SS Panzer. Launching round the clock air attacks against exposed panzer columns, US Air Forces brought 'Lüttich' to a standstill – the first time that a panzer offensive had been rendered wholly ineffective by the concentrated use of air power. Elsewhere, in ground action, US units moving into blocking positions prepared the

defence of strong points. But the crisis factor in 'Lüttich' was its timing and direction. Thrusting west with the best available panzer divisions at a time when US Third Army was driving powerfully and virtually unhampered in the opposite direction, 'Lüttich' was actively encouraging envelopment. And in the mean time at Mortain, where prolonged resistance by US 102nd Infantry Regiment (30th Division) was blocking Das Reich and delaying the movement of subordinate battle groups assaulting from the east (Battle Group Fick, 17th SS Panzer Grenadier Division), the offensive was fast losing momentum. At the same time other factors were giving rise to von Kluge's concern over slow progress – the late arrival of 1st SS Panzer Division from Caen (delayed when a crashed fighter aircraft forced the division to find a new and time-consuming route to the battlefield); a panzer battalion from 116th Panzer Division 'otherwise engaged', but above all the total absence of the Luftwaffe. Kept away from the battlefield by Allied air forces striking at II Jagd Corps (Pelz) on support airfields in the vicinity of Paris, the Luftwaffe was incapable of mounting a single sortie in support of the panzer divisions.

During the afternoon, the arrival at von Kluge's headquarters of a special courier (General Buhle, OKH chief of staff at OKW) bearing a Führerbefehl would require the Field Marshal to release panzer divisions immediately from other fronts and renew the offensive under General Eberbach (Fifth Panzer Army). The Führerbefehl raised more difficulties for von Kluge. Facing intense pressure at Caumont and Caen where the panzer divisions under Fifth Panzer Army (Eberbach) were fully committed – 9th SS, 10th SS and 21st Panzer at Caumont, 12th SS at Caen – the best that he could do for the moment was to get 10th SS moving from Caumont to Mortain and plan a follow-up with II SS Panzer Corps (Bittrich) bringing 9th SS and 21st Panzer south; 12th SS was also put on notice to move. Both II SS and XXXXVII Panzer Corps were then to be responsible to Eberbach. Most worrying to von Kluge was the openness of Seventh Army's southern flank, penetrated by US Third Army (Patton) as far as Le Mans – 50 miles to Seventh Army's rear. The arrival of 9th Panzer Division (Sperling) 24 hours earlier at Alençon, reinforcing 708th Infantry Division and security battalions contriving a south-facing front under LXXXXI Corps (Küntzen), gave rise to minor satisfaction, but immediately on arrival 9th Panzer Division's Panther battalion was redirected north, strengthening I SS Panzer Corps left with only 12th SS Panzer Division at Caen. The battalion was later returned uncommitted to cope with the mounting crisis in the south. By the end of the day von Kluge was advising OKW of his intention of renewing 'Lüttich' with the addition of II SS Panzer Corps. Subordinate to Eberbach as required by Hitler, a new start was planned for 10 August [D+65].

8 August [D+63]–9 August [D+64]. 'Lüttich' was meanwhile less than halfway to its Avranches objective, held in check by US ground and air forces and virtually at a standstill. At the centre of operations defending Hill 307 were four companies of US 102nd Infantry Regiment enveloped by Das Reich but denying the tactically important high ground east of Mortain to the SS and persistently inhibiting the westward movement of attacking units through the town. On other sectors too attacking divisions, for example 2nd Panzer Division (von Lüttwitz), farthest ahead at le Mesnil-Tôve, was failing against mounting opposition while being constantly hammered in low-flying attacks which robbed the offensive of energy and strength. Later in the week, with the tide of battle receding, US observers were to count more than a hundred panzer wrecks on the battlefield. For the Allies in Normandy D+63 was to prove a day of momentous decision. The beckoning opportunity for encircling Seventh Army and Fifth Panzer Army presented by Patton's unstoppable thrust to the east was not to be missed. Bradley proposed the motion; Montgomery concurred. Allied plans to envelop Army Group 'B' by uniting an Anglo/Canadian/US pincer movement on a north/south Falaise–Argentan–Alençon axis were agreed; Patton would swing north from Le Mans.

On 10 August [D+65], Intelligence reports reaching von Kluge confirmed US Third Army's change of direction; Haislip's XV Corps was identified swinging north from Le Mans threatening Alençon and the Army Group's vital east–west supply route Alençon–Flers. The move was correctly interpreted for what it was – the southern arm of an Allied pincer closing on Army Group 'B'. The Mortain offensive was called off. The panzer divisions were to be redirected. Panzer Group Eberbach [D+66] would instead launch a counter-attack into the flank of US Third Army threatening Alençon. On the outcome of Eberbach's action was to depend the future of the Army Group.

11 August [D+66]. The crisis gripping Army Group 'B', suffering pressure on three fronts, north, east and south, was a trial of strength for the Normandy High Command and its front-line leadership. Unable to find a strategy to match the situation, Hitler's orders were to stand firm here, shorten a line there, move panzer divisions and bring in the infantry, but served more to confuse than clarify the issue. The Luftwaffe's absence from the battlefield; petrol and ammunition stocks dwindling to the point of exhaustion because the area was largely sealed against replenishment by Allied air forces compounded the problem. The panzer divisions now faced tasks well beyond their powers. 9th SS Panzer Division, for instance, reported its strength as ten Pz Kpfw IVs, thirteen Panthers, fifteen assault guns and ten Pak 7.5cm. Inside the pocket, slowly closing but not yet sealed, motorized movement of troops and transport in daylight on roads swept by artillery and air strikes was time-consuming and hazardous; infantry supply columns choking the roads with horse-drawn vehicles added to the trauma. Night moves presented traffic control and transport staffs with endless problems deciding priorities, sorting traffic and handling units of all descriptions vying for the use of a decreasing number of roads in a slowly constricting pocket.

11 August [D+66] to 14 August [D+69]. Building Panzer Group Eberbach by redeploying panzer divisions from the north and north-west to meet the crisis at Alençon in the south was Army Group priority. But Alençon fell on 12 August [D+67] before Eberbach had gathered the strength necessary to choke-off American progress. The defence of Alençon, Seventh Army's supply base, enveloped by US XV Corps (Haislip) had been entrusted to LXXXI Corps (Küntzen), deploying 9th Panzer (Spurling) since 6 August [D+61], 708th Infantry Division, four security battalions and the rump of Panzer Lehr (Bayerlein). Much too weak to withstand the relentless pressure of US armour and infantry enjoying continuous air support in their drive toward

Falaise and a junction with Montgomery, the defence collapsed and fighting moved forward in the direction of Argentan where 116th Panzer Division, switched from Mortain and at first deployed south of the town, would reinforce the defence. Provoked by the loss of Alençon and the danger threatening Argentan, next in line and no more than twelve miles short of Falaise, Hitler issued fresh orders. Panzer Group Eberbach (LVIII Panzer Corps, XXXXVII Panzer Corps) was to be reinforced and US XV Corps was to be counter-attacked from the west. Starting from the area of Carrouges north-west of Alençon (where 2nd and 116th Panzer Divisions, redeployed from Mortain, stood their ground with the help of units from 9th Panzer), the offensive was to be supported by attacks from the opposite flank delivered by II SS Panzer Corps; the resulting pincer closing at Sées, midway between Alençon and Argentan, cutting off Haislip's XV Corps from US Third Army. Reinforcements for Eberbach, 9th SS, 10th SS and 21st Panzer Divisions were to move immediately.

In the event, demands for reinforcements elsewhere by I SS Panzer Corps defending Falaise against 'Tractable' [D+67–D+71] was to claim 21st Panzer; 10th SS, unable to break free of commitments under LVIII Panzer Corps (Krüger) arriving east of Mortain from Toulouse (originally a reserve Panzer Corps HQ) eliminated Frundsberg; 9th SS Hohenstaufen, on the other hand, was able to disengage from battle south-east of Vire, proceeding on 13 August [D+68] to join 2nd SS Das Reich, assembling for Eberbach's offensive in the Forêt de Petite Gouffern east of Argentan. But air attacks, delaying the movement of panzer divisions to assembly areas flanking US XV Corps driving north on its Alençon–Argentan axis, west (2nd, 9th, 116th) or east (2nd SS, 9th SS), and short-falls in ammunition and petrol supplies forced Eberbach on to the defensive. The unremitting efforts of US 12th Army Group (Bradley) to narrow the Falaise–Argentan gap by exerting pressure all along the front, compounded German problems. And, unknown to OKW or those in command at the front, US and British forces were warned by 'Ultra' of the dangers threatening US XV Corps on its crucial north-bound axis. Their reaction was to halt progress north of Argentan and shift the axis of envelopment eastwards from Argentan–Falaise to Chambois–Trun. This change of emphasis in OKW strategy departing from cordoning to belated armoured riposte, engaging US Third Army (Patton) on the Alençon–Argentan–Falaise axis, is illustrated in Panzer deployment.

14 August [D+69]. Day twenty of the US break-out.
Seventh Army and Panzer Group Eberbach.
10th SS (LVIII Panzer Corps), 2nd, 9th, 116th (XXXXVII Panzer Corps) 1st SS, 2nd SS, 9th SS (II SS Panzer Corps) plus Panzer Battle Groups Lehr and 17th SS.
Fifth Panzer Army: 21st, 12th SS (I SS Panzer Corps).

On 15 August [D+70], Hausser contracted Seventh Army battle lines in the west and north-west, allowing the panzer divisions to disengage for action at Alençon. US First Army (Hodges), extending its grip on operations at the conclusion of 'Lüttich', pushed east reinforcing the pressure of US Third Army probing north-east around Argentan (without Patton). On the opposite side of the pocket, attacking from north and north-west, British Second and Canadian First Armies stepped up the drive to enter Falaise. At this critical time for von Kluge and the panzer divisions in Normandy, *a fresh problem was creating anxiety for Army Group 'G' in the South of France where Operation 'Dragoon' involving a second Allied expeditionary force was disembarking men, vehicles and stores on beaches between Cannes and Toulon (see Fifth Panzer Army [D+70]). On this day of crisis von Kluge went missing. Travelling to Nécy, Eberbach's headquarters between Falaise and Argentan, contact was broken and although the Field Marshal reappeared early the next day at Fifth Panzer Army Headquarters, Meulles, outside the pocket, Hitler appointed a new OB West/GOC Army Group 'B' – Walter Model [D+71].*

16 August [D+71]. At this point, much to the surprise of his subordinates, Hitler ordered Army Group 'G' (Blaskowitz) to evacuate the South of France while also agreeing to the evacuation of the Falaise (Morteaux–Chambois) pocket by Army Group 'B' where command still rested with von Kluge who pulled II SS Panzer Corps (Bittrich), Das Reich and Hohenstaufen out of the pocket and into Army Group reserve east of Vimoutiers, a communications centre twelve miles to the east. On the same day, at Führer Headquarters in East Prussia, Hitler briefed Walter Model, OB West designate, on the situation in Normandy. Too late to change the course of events there, Model would preside over the escape of ruined divisions and a phased withdrawal of Army Group 'B', now perilously close to finding itself sealed into a pocket east of the Dives.

Model takes over. 17 August (D+72)–18 August (D+73). By **17 August (D+72)**, the plight of Army Group 'B', defending a pocket on the Dives extending seventeen miles west to Briouze and 12–15 miles deep between Morteaux and Chambois, was so desperate that nothing the new OB West, Field Marshal Walter Model could do was likely to turn the situation to German advantage – despite Model's distinguished record of defensive operations in the east. An evening conference with von Kluge and staff at Army Group 'B' Headquarters (La Roche-Guyon) followed a morning briefing by chief of staff von Blumentritt at OB West Headquarters (St-Germain-en-Laye) putting Model in the picture. Next day (D+73) for a close-up of operations in Normandy, the Field Marshal proposed to visit Fifth Panzer Army Headquarters at Fontaine-l'Abbé. There Hausser, Dietrich and Eberbach stated their views on the chances of survival for whatever remained of eleven panzer divisions, a comparable number of infantry and two parachute divisions facing an uncertain future in or about the Falaise pocket. Now closed to escape on three sides, there remained on the Dives to the east a gap of 12–15 miles between Morteaux and Chambois where exhausted divisions with their last vestige of strength held the Allies apart. Through this corridor, dominated by heavy artillery and tactical air forces operating at full power in support of American, British and Canadian armies re-directed to converge on Chambois, the remnants of two German armies and a Panzer Group would seek escape from envelopment on the scale of Stalingrad. But the state of the panzer divisions – key to any successful break-out operation – whose deterioration was daily more evident in strength returns to higher headquarters, and fuel and ammunition stocks diminishing to the lowest ever level following the loss of Alençon [D+67] allowed Model little optimism for believing that the 80,000–100,000 men

still inside the pocket could be evacuated to safety behind the Seine as initiated by von Kluge on [D+71].

For the troops at the front, artillery fire and air strikes launched by the besieging ground and air forces against every vehicle movement, troop concentration, bridge and cross-roads within the pocket were a constant danger. By inhibiting the use of traffic centres and forcing motorized columns into competing with infantry on back roads, sharing the protection of forest and woodland, assembly times and operational grouping were at all times significantly compromised. Nevertheless, the redeployment of panzer divisions in the crisis inherited by Model, starting with the pattern established by von Kluge [D+71], was set to continue. Hohenstaufen and Das Reich, already on the move out of the pocket into Army Group reserve at Lisieux, were halted by Model at Vimoutiers. Accompanying II SS Panzer Corps (Bittrich) eastwards the move was not without incident. When Hohenstaufen unexpectedly encountered Polish armour on the Trun–Vimoutiers road, the SS division was lucky to force a break-through, collecting evacuated units in a new assembly area west of Vimoutiers. At the same time, 12th SS HJ and 21st Panzer serving Fifth Panzer Army (Dietrich) defended the northern shoulder of the pocket. Standing their ground south and east of Falaise, 12th SS (Meyer) and 21st Panzer (Feuchtinger) battle groups persisted in bitter action, delaying Canadian 4th

(Kitchner) and Polish 1st (Maczek) Armoured Divisions directed south of Morteaux on a Trun–Chambois axis. The defence of this critical sector was the responsibility of I SS Panzer Corps (Krämer); other Fifth Panzer Army sectors between the coast and Condé being left to infantry divisions. Away to the south, separated from Dietrich by a 12–15-mile gap in which the hamlets of Trun, St-Lambert, Moissy and Chambois collected escape routes taking retreating columns nose to tail out of the pocket, Panzer Group Eberbach retained the strongest concentration of panzer 'divisions'.

Forced on to the defensive by the rapid advance of US Third Army pushing north from Alençon (on routes leading to Chambois) Eberbach sought to block American progress north of Carrouges and also at Argentan where 116th Panzer Division was turning the town centre into a strong point to be held until the last day of the break-out [D+76]. Weakened by failure at Carrouges [D+66–D+69], Panzer Group Eberbach comprised 2nd, 9th, 116th (plus 9th Panzer's Panther Battalion), Panzer Lehr remnants split and waiting release for refitting, 17th SS (mostly outside the pocket, forming battle groups for the defence of Dreux and St-Germain) and I SS LAH. The controlling head-quarters was that of von Funck's XXXXVII Panzer Corps. In resisting the pressure of US Third Army intensified by air attacks and 2ème Division Blindee (Leclerc) thrusting north-

west of Alençon through the Forêt d'Ecouves, 9th Panzer Division (Sperling) was practically destroyed. The American drive north from Le Mans, seeking contact with British and Canadians south of Caen had been led by French 2nd (Leclerc) and US 5th Armored Divisions, responsible to XV Corps (Haislip); but this situation was about to change following standstill instructions issued by Bradley to Patton on 13 August [D+68]. A new plan for closing the 'gap' would require a specially constituted US 'provisional' infantry corps (Gerow) to lead the operation.

Freed from the Argentan sector, Haislip's XV Corps would instead lead Patton on a 'long' envelopment of Army Group 'B', reaching the Seine at Mantes–Gassicourt [D+74].

At the western end of the pocket, where Seventh Army was retreating step by step under immense pressure, 10th SS Panzer Division – reduced to eight tanks and one-third of its normal strength, but reinforced by a 9th Panzer battle group – resisted all attempts by British and American divisions to collapse the Army's rearguard. Withdrawing north-east from Domfront, 10th SS imposed frustrating delays on both US First Army (Hodges) striking for Briouze, and British Second Army (Dempsey) squeezing a way east around Flers; control of the panzer divisions in the extreme western sectors rested with LXXXIV Corps (Elfeldt) and LVIII Panzer Corps (Krüger). Altogether some seventeen Allied armoured and infantry divisions were directly engaged in

the task of sealing the Falaise pocket – delayed for a while by a bomb-line controversy and minor confusions – but in the circumstances, a foregone conclusion.

On **18 August (D+73)**, at Model's morning conference with senior commanders outside the pocket at Fifth Panzer Army Headquarters (Fontaine–l'Abbé), crucial decisions were taken in respect of a relief operation by II SS Panzer Corps (Bittrich). The meeting was attended by von Gersdof, deputising for Hausser who at his own request remained behind at Panzer Army HQ (Villedieu); Dietrich and Eberbach both being present. Instructing Eberbach to supervise the operation using for the purpose Bittrich's HQ at Vimoutiers, Model proposed to block the jaws of the powerful Allied pincer closing on Chambois. Success would depend upon the speed with which Bittrich's two SS panzer divisions could collect sufficient strength west of Vimoutiers for the three–five-mile push to Trun–Chambois on fuel to be delivered by air transports to forward airfields. Within 48 hours, Seventh Army, Fifth Panzer Army and Panzer Group Eberbach would be across the Dives, regrouping behind the Toucques ten miles to the rear. Divisions fighting inside the pocket including Eberbach's Group (while he remained outside at Vimoutiers) were placed under the orders of Seventh Army (Hausser). For the relief thrust, Eberbach was allotted II SS Panzer Corps (Bittrich) comprising 2nd SS and 9th SS Panzer Divisions pushing to Trun (the northern shoulder of the pocket) and XXXXVII Panzer Corps (von Funck) deploying 2nd and 116th Panzer Divisions around Argentan (the southern shoulder of the pocket). But by mid-afternoon despite selfless action by HJ and 21st Panzer battle groups, Trun had fallen to Canadian 4th Armoured Division assisting the Poles of 1st Armoured Division pushing south to Height 262 above Coudehard and then on to Mont Ormel dominating the vital Vimoutiers-Trun relief/escape route. An alternative passage Chambois-Vimoutiers four miles south was not so threatened.

By late evening, Army Group 'B's escape corridor was at best no more than a 4–5 mile enfiladed gap separating encircling Allied armies. US progress with 90th Infantry Division striking north for Chambois with flank protection provided by 2nd French DB (Battle Group Langlade) had now carried to the southern outskirts of the village, leaving only St-Lambert and Moissy in the centre of the corridor to offer the best chance of escape. The pocket was all but closed. The disgraced OB West, von Kluge – recalled by Hitler 'for the sake of his health' – had started earlier that morning from La Roche-Guyon for Germany. News of his death by self-administered poisoning *en route* from Verdun to Metz arrived at La Roche-Guyon late in the day.

Break-out from the Falaise pocket 19 August (D+74) to 21 August (D+76). On **19 August (D+74)**, Allied armies closed the Falaise pocket. In the event this set-back to Model's plans for an orderly evacuation of Army Group 'B' as agreed with the Army Commanders (D+73) was not the outright disaster that might have been expected. Break-out groups, encouraged by the relief operation mounted next morning by II SS Panzer Corps (Bittrich), would succeed in escaping until D+76 when the relieving SS panzer divisions (2nd SS/9th SS) started their own phased withdrawal to the Seine. Previously withdrawn into Army Group reserve, Das Reich and Hohenstaufen pushing forward to the Dives from the east and north-east would

establish a corridor in the space of a morning, making contact with escape columns fighting their way out across the river between St-Lambert and Chambois. By the time of the break-out the Falaise pocket had assumed the character of an embattled bridgehead, box-shaped and with an area of less than 25 square miles; its escape side on the Dives to the east. Bounded by the river meandering four miles between Trun and Chambois, but nowhere more than five feet deep although in parts steeply banked and wooded, the Falaise pocket included the forested acres of Gouffern sheltering a mass of exhausted units: wheeled transport, horse transport, armoured fighting vehicles, ancillary services and headquarters constituting the embattled remnant of Army Group 'B'. At 1700 hours, when closure was effected by US 90th Division (Maclain) uniting with 1st Polish Armoured Division (Maczek) in Chambois, the area contained the headquarters of two armies (Fifth Panzer Army, Seventh Army) a Panzer Group (Eberbach, who personally remained outside the pocket at II SS Panzer Corps Headquarters Vimoutiers–Meulles, directing the relief operation), four army corps (LXXIV, LXXXIV, II Para, XXXXVII Panzer) six infantry divisions, six or seven panzer divisions and 3rd Parachute Division.

Certain panzer units and higher headquarters were already on their way out of the pocket, released by Model

Above: Obergruppenführer Wilhelm Bittrich served in the 1914–18 war as a pilot and from 1932 to 1933 as an air force officer. He then transferred, in 1934, to the S Verfügungstruppe and by 193 he was Battalion CO II/SS Deutschland. In 1939–40 he was a Standartenführer in Poland and France; then he served on the Moscow sector the Eastern Front in 1941 before leading 'Hohenstaufen' at Tarnopol in 1944, and the at Caen. He succeeded Hauss as GOC, II SS Panzer Corps a led the Falaise relief attack o D+75. He was subsequently prominent at Arnhem, the Ardennes, and Hungary.

for refitting (Panzer Lehr) or re-employment in defensive positions between the Dives and the Seine (17th SS, 21st Panzer, I SS Panzer Corps, LVIII Panzer Corps) where Patton's 'long' thrust – to the Seine at Mantes via Dreux – was threatening a second envelopment. Negotiating the chaos in the pocket due to a totally inadequate road system and artillery fire pouring in from all sides, evacuating units crossed the Dives between St-Lambert and Chambois; retreating transport, individual vehicles even, suffering the unavoidable hazard of marauding rocket-firing Typhoons and fighter-bombers. The Luftwaffe, long since vanquished and rarely appearing in its close-support role for the Army, occasionally provided some Ju 88s to assist the ground forces in difficult situations, but air-transported supplies of fuel brought to forward airfields for the panzer divisions (Eberbach) was the principal evidence of Luftwaffe battle-field activity. Timed for 2230 hours and phased to coincide with the relief operation by II SS Panzer Corps (0500 hours (D+75)), two break-out columns: left, II Para Corps (Meindl) moving via St-Lambert; right, XXXXVII Panzer Corps (von Funck) moving via Chambois, were to strike east in the direction of Vimoutiers. Meindl's column, mostly on foot, was to cross the Dives at St-Lambert protected by a vigorous rearguard defence of Magny delaying Canadian progress south of Trun. The column was to be lead by 3rd Parachute Division (Schimpf) and a small HJ detachment.

Von Funck's column, allotted the superior bridge and road facilities leading east via Chambois, incorporated panzer elements still mobile in the pocket; the Leibstandarte (1st SS LAH, 116th and HJ (tracked units)) leading. A key objective for both relief and break-out columns was Hill 262. (Overlooking Coudehard straddling the escape route five miles east of the pocket, this tactical feature, like Mont-Ormel east of Chambois, was already dominated by Maczek's armour.) A rearguard, basically 12th SS HJ (Meyer) and a 21st Panzer battle group (Rauch), would be responsible to LXXXIV Corps (Elfeldt). Such were the Army Group plans for breaking free of encirclement.

In the event, with communications failing, units whose movements were dictated by hostile artillery, tank and anti-tank fire, followed at dawn by air-attacks destroying the cohesion of most break-out groups, direction was often lost and units reduced to diminishing numbers. Many units planning to join 'organized' columns or making their own arrangements when communication with superior head-quarters was lost, failed to make good their escape. Hausser, the Seventh Army Commander, escorted by II Para Corps, was wounded; Elfeldt, the rearguard commander, with his HQ was captured. Wisch, the Leibstandarte's CO was among the severely wounded and Wünsche, the commander of 12th SS Panzer Regiment taken prisoner. Many others were killed, wounded or captured in break-out battles. Meindl's column was pinned down by fire from the Poles on Hill 262 and holed-up for much of D+75. Contact with the relieving panzer divisions pushing to Coudehard via Champosoult and Hill 262, where the Polish Armoured Division was taken under fire from all sides, was established at midday but not until dusk was the corridor properly secured. The mobile escape column directed on Chambois, including units of 1st SS, 12th SS, 2nd, 9th, 116th and 10th SS Panzer Divisions, found Chambois unshakeably held by Polish/US units. Break-out groups searching for

alternative ways across the Dives resorted to Moissy and St-Lambert, bringing out little more than battalion handfuls of men and vehicles; most heavy weapons, tractors and towing-machines being destroyed or abandoned before-hand.

The Dives was a killing-ground. Enfiladed by Canadian armour and artillery, the river banks, particularly in the key escape area of St-Lambert, proved a strong disorganizing factor for break-out groups; smashed transport and war matériel encumbering every possible crossing-point turned a comparatively minor obstacle into a hazardous hindrance.

The relief attack by II SS Panzer Corps had started on schedule at 0500 D+75, twelve miles east of the Dives. From positions south-west of Vimoutiers, where Bittrich had collected units of 2nd SS Das Reich and 9th SS Hohenstaufen, the relief attack would rely mostly upon surprise and stamina pushing with minimum support (Corps Werfer and Tiger detachments) into contact with the break-out columns. But Bittrich's attack in the direction of Trun and St-Lambert triggered a major confrontation between Das Reich and Polish armour; controlling Hill 262, the Poles dominated the break-out/relief route at this point. With panzer grenadiers of III SS Panzer Grenadier Battalion (Werner) mounted in SPWs, a handful of Pz Kpfw IVs and a Panther leading Der Führer (Weidinger) west, the SS isolated Polish strong points before making contact with Meindl's column at midday.

In the ensuing tank/anti-tank action around Boisjos, a defended helmet blocking the use of the Trun–Chambois road to escape groups, Polish and German casualties were particularly heavy. Hohenstaufen, in action north of Das Reich and attacking the Polish flank in the direction of Les Champeaux, was least successful and shortly after midday D+75 the offensive was discontinued.

Notwithstanding this check to the northern attack, Bittrich's escape corridor, won at heavy cost to both break-out and relief groups, was held overnight and well into next day. At 1600 hours on 21 August, D+76, orders for Der Führer to retire were received and acknowledged by the regimental commander (Weidinger); the battle of Normandy was entering its final phase – retreat to the Seine. Estimates of the numbers breaking-out and crossing Der Führer's lines vary from 8,000 to 10,000 of an estimated 20,000 'freed' by Das Reich; leaving 10,000 dead and 40,000 prisoners in the pocket. A lesser cause for satisfaction was the pitifully small number of armoured fighting vehicles brought out by the panzer divisions – fewer than seventy Pz Kpfw IVs and Panthers, a handful of SP flak and some personnel carriers (SPWs). The last panzer division to leave the pocket was 2nd Panzer Division (von Lüttwitz), defending St-Lambert where undestroyed bridges helped escape groups searching for east-west escape routes. At 2100 hours on D+76, calling in his west bank units, von Lüttwitz retired east across the Dives moving in the direction of Coudehard. Less fortunate was a 116/9th Panzer battle group blocking US progress through the town centre at Argentan. Unable to disengage in time to prevent encirclement, the battle group surrendered. In the subsequent and final phase of the Battle of Normandy, with fighting in the neighbourhood of the Dives subsiding as fewer escape groups filtered east or ended their resistance in isolated rearguard pockets, panzer divisions would be organized into heterogeneous battle

Above: Self-propelled anti-ta[nk] guns continued their domina[nt] role in tank battles, serving heavy Army anti-tank battalions east and west. Among the latest and best examples serving in Norman[dy] was the Jagdpanther Sdkfz 1[73] mounting an 8.8cm Pak 43 which was effective at 1,000 yards.

groups defending a Seine bridgehead at Elbeuf–Rouen. At the highest level of command, OB West's difficulties were multiplying, Paris was threatened and the chances of an orderly Army Group withdrawal west of the Seine diminishing. Equally at risk were joint OKW/OB West plans for the defence of northern France. The underlying cause of these problems was the unstoppable progress of Patton's US Third Army developing a 'long' envelopment to the Seine – sixty miles east of the Dives.

Escape across the Seine. 22 August (D+77) to 30 August (D+85).

Starting on 22 August (D+77) and continuing until 30 August (D+85), panzer operations in Normandy constrained by the loss of equipment in the Falaise pocket were restricted to defensive measures protecting Army Group 'B' withdrawing from the Dives to the Seine. Local counter-attacks culminating in defence of Rouen were all that panzer divisions could manage in the aftermath of the disaster at Falaise. Driven into a bridgehead of 200–300 square miles west of the Seine, protected on the north side by the Channel coast, in the west by the Toucques but with an inland flank stretching back 70 miles from Gacé via Dreux and Evreux to the Seine at Mantes, the future of Army Group 'B' was only marginally less precarious than at the time of its recent encirclement. In the fighting already described, the Western Allies had destroyed in less than three months the power of two German armies (Fifth Panzer Army and Seventh Army) and a Panzer Group (Eberbach),

eliminating in the process three times more panzer divisions than were lost at Stalingrad – three (plus three motorized infantry divisions). A new danger also threatened the retreating Army Group – the 'long' envelopment by US Third Army (Patton) thrusting to the Seine at Mantes–Gassicourt, a crossing-place giving access to north-west Paris. At this point on the river, Patton had already crossed to the north (east) bank, posing a threat to Paris while re-directing two army corps including XV (Haislip) north along the west bank of the river towards Elbeuf and Rouen – which if successfully concluded would finally choke-off all escape routes for Army Group 'B'. Outmanoeuvred yet again by the speed of Patton's advance, Fifth Panzer Army was forced into defending bridgeheads north and south of Rouen where inclusive of Duclair and Elbeuf sixty ferries were evacuating escape groups with their vehicles and equipment to the north (east) bank.

Only the presence of emergency battle groups formed from rear or reconstituted units of burned-out divisions – like that of 12th SS (Battle Groups Wahl and Mohnke) and 17th SS (Battle Group Fick) prevented the threatened US break through to Elbeuf. Defending bridgehead approaches at Vernon and Louviers (where Battle Group Fick was overrun), improvised battle groups incorporating replacement transport and artillery personnel held back the enveloping wing of US Third Army until I SS Panzer Corps could bring a contribution to reinforce the threatened flank. Much of this burdensome rearguard action, the key to

Model's programme of phased withdrawal to the Seine, exploiting natural obstacles in the west such as the Toucques 4–5 miles east of Vimoutiers, lay with II SS Panzer Corps (Bittrich). Collecting units that by filtering or fighting their way around Polish, Canadian, US and French armour, had run the gauntlet of escape routes leading out of the Falaise pocket, II SS Panzer Corps added 21st and 10th SS Panzer to 2nd SS and 9th SS Panzer Divisions previously employed in the relief attack (D+75). As other divisions – reduced to material levels equivalent to depleted panzer companies – were collected in viable numbers, notably 1st SS, 2nd and 116th Panzer, they too were employed in defence of important centres en route to the Seine where ferries, pontoon bridges, assault boats and local river craft transported all they could to the safety of the north (east) bank. With pressure increasing on the Elbeuf flank, II SS Panzer Corps was moved back in defence, bringing 2nd SS with twelve Pz Kpfw IVs and little more than two panzer grenadier battalions; Battle Groups 21st Panzer and 9th SS, remaining in the west would protect Orbec, Bernay and Lisieux (LXXXVI Corps) for as long as circumstances permitted.

Defending a contracting bridgehead until the night of 29/30 August (D+84/85) when 9th SS in Rouen crossed to the north bank, Army Group 'B' succeeded in transferring totally unexpected numbers of men and material across the river. Ignoring day and night attacks by Allied air forces, 25,000 vehicles were saved for the next phase of operations taking Fifth Panzer Army (Dietrich) and Seventh Army (Eberbach) over the Somme and Maas to the German frontier – but at the cost of more transport, tanks and heavy weapons (mainly flak) saved during the retreat from the Falaise pocket but now abandoned on the south bank. OB West was later to report that 'None of the panzer divisions crossing the Seine could muster more than ten tanks.' A total of eleven panzer divisions: 2nd, 9th, 21st, 116th, Panzer Lehr, 1st SS, 2nd SS, 9th SS, 10th SS, 12th SS and 17th SS (Panzer Grenadier) – (about one-third of the panzer force) caught in successive envelopments or near envelopments had been virtually eliminated from the German order of battle, and whereas they would nominally reappear in the west, notably in the Ardennes (Fifth Panzer Army, Sixth SS Panzer Army) on 16 December, their élan and fighting power had ended in Normandy.

Retreat through France and Belgium 31 August to 16 September. The consequences to Army Group 'B' of its loss of eleven panzer divisions in Normandy was an enforced retreat from the Seine north and east of Paris (entered 24 August by US 4th Infantry Division and 2DB Française, Leclerc) to the western borders of Germany; a movement simultaneously matched by Army Group 'G' retiring from Atlantic and Mediterranean coasts to the Rhine. With no panzer reserves to speak of and lacking the battlefield support expected of the Luftwaffe, Model was deprived of any of the crucial resources for turning retreat into victory – in the way that Manstein had shown possible in the Ukraine (Fourth Panzer Army) in February 1943. Such a telling riposte as Manstein's would have required no less than the total rehabilitation of the panzer divisions eliminated in all but name from OKW's order of battle – a re-equipment programme entrusted in fact to a new General der Panzertruppen West, General Horst Stumpff. Not sur-

prisingly a counter-offensive on this scale, involving Fifth Panzer Army (von Manteuffel) and a new Sixth SS Panzer Army (Dietrich) was already taking shape in Hitler's mind. Code-named 'Autumn Mist', Hitler's last offensive in the west would start shortly before Christmas (see Fifth Panzer Army and Sixth SS Panzer Army, 16 December). Meanwhile, whatever the state of battle groups recovering from defeat west of the Seine, panzer operations in the first week of September would continue in desultory fashion north and east of Paris, but without General Eberbach, taken prisoner (31 August) in circumstances described later. Battle groups brought together under temporary command, like those of Mohnke and Fick west of the Seine before evacuation, included Gruppe von Schwerin built out of 1st, 2nd, 12th SS and 116th Panzer, while other Battle Group 'divisions' – 9th SS, 10th SS and 21st Panzer provided I and II Panzer Corps with a modicum of strength, counter-attacking at crisis points as they developed on the line of retreat through France and Belgium.

Fifth Panzer Army (Dietrich) and Seventh Army (Eberbach in succession to Hausser, wounded escaping across the Dives with 3rd Paratroop Division) retreated across northern France and Belgium to Aachen, Germany's gateway to the Ruhr, closely pursued by 21st Army Group implementing a broad front strategy devised by General Eisenhower. North of Aachen a new headquarters, First Paratroop Army (Student) close by Tilburg, extemporized defences between the city and the coast north of Antwerp whilst First Army (Chevallerie von Knobelsdorff), redeployed from south of the Loire to south of Trier, established a grip on the Rhineland, separated by a short gap from Nineteenth Army (Wiese) arriving from the Mediterranean on the upper Rhine north of Basle. On the Channel coast, Fifteenth Army (von Zangen) filtering its remaining infantry divisions northwards across the Scheldt into Holland was bypassed by 21st Army Group thrusting to Antwerp. The Army was fortunate in escaping disaster on the Normandy scale. Meanwhile, on 31 August General Eberbach's Seventh Army Headquarters, temporarily located at Albert north of the Somme, was surprised by British Second Army (Dempsey) and overrun. Eberbach was taken into captivity. Other commanders and staffs had narrow escapes. Model (OB West) and Dietrich (Fifth Panzer Army and Seventh Army in succession to Eberbach), also threatened by the pace of the Allied advance, moved swiftly out of the area.

On the Allied side three Army Groups implementing Eisenhower's 'broad front' strategy while fanning out north and east of Paris, captured Antwerp (4 September) with its port installations undamaged (British Second Army, 21st Army Group) but unusable on account of Fifteenth Army's defiant retention of the Scheldt estuary – and a week later thrusting for the Ruhr, threatened Aachen (US First Army, 6th Army Group, Devers) and Metz (US Third Army, 12th Army Group, Bradley). By 12 September, when command changes and new dispositions were taking effect in the west, the majority of the 'Normandy' panzer divisions were deployed under Seventh Army (Brandenburger) aligned north to south: 9th, 1st SS, 12th SS, 2nd SS, 2nd and 116th – between Aachen and Luxemburg.

Seventh Army's primary role was the defence of Aachen (116th and 9th Panzer) where arterial routes via Jülich and Düren allowed access to Cologne, gateway to the Ruhr and a major concentration of German defence industries. Protected by the Siegfried Line (Westwall) – constructed before 1939 and now undergoing emergency rehabilitation – Aachen was rightly considered a vital post in the German scheme of defence in the west. Fifth Panzer Army also serving a new commander General der Panzer Truppe Hasso von Manteuffel (Seventh Panzer and GD) responsible to Army Group 'G' (Blaskowitz) was directed by OKW to prepare a new Hitler-inspired offensive. Manteuffel's task would be to assault the right flank of US Third Army (Patton) moving against Metz, jeopardizing production in the Saarland and indirectly threatening the Ruhr. These tasks thrust upon Fifth Panzer Army and Seventh Army by Hitler and OKW, were wholly inconsistent with their disastrously depleted strengths. With fewer than 100 tanks, 600 aircraft and no reserves in the west, OKW scraped together training units – whatever their state of readiness – drafted naval ratings, police units, Luftwaffe and SS personnel into *ad hoc* battalions of all kinds to reinforce depleted formations such as Fifth Panzer Army with 17,000 effectives (less than the strength of a single division), infantry formations reduced to company strength – about to face 2,000 Allied tanks backed by 14,000 aircraft.

RAD construction battalions and army engineers acting under the supervision of western Gauleiters with instructions to slave in restoring 'Siegfried' defences – linked with

stretches of the Maginot line into a somewhat illusory Westwall – discovered that vital maintenance equipment and artillery had been extracted for installation on the Atlantic coast. New panzer brigades, heavy (Army) anti-tank and assault gun battalions, Volksgrenadier infantry divisions (VGD) and VG support units – raised by Himmler in his capacity as OC, Replacement Army, would do little to regenerate the western Army Groups commanded once again by von Runstedt, recalled to serve as OB West (effective 5 September 1944). Troop transfers from other fronts, notably two panzer grenadier divisions, 3rd (Denkert) and 15th (Rodt) from Italy, deployed (26 August) west of Metz, were reinforcing First Army (von Knobelsdorff), Army Group 'G' (Blaskowitz), while certain of the panzer divisions, mostly burnt-out in Normandy, Panzer Lehr, 11th, 21st Panzer and 17th SS Panzer Grenadier Divisions, were falling back through Lorraine defending the Saar. In addition to these reinforcements, First Army would also receive 25th Panzer Grenadier Division (battle group) rebuilding in the west after returning in June from Army Group Centre.

Among other measures taken by OKW to rehabilitate the panzer force in the west (22 August) was the appointment already noted of a General der Panzertruppen West (Stumpff), supervising the refitting of the Normandy panzer divisions – especially those deployed along the German frontier Aachen–Trier where Army Group 'B' (Model) held

Left and right: Tank-hunting at close quarters was greatly assisted by a new generation of hand-held recoilless anti-tank weapons. The Panzerfaust could penetrate six or more inches of Allied armour at 50 yards with its hollow-charge grenade, whilst the Panzerschreck was used to strengthen the protective power of infantry and panzer grenadiers.

the line. A later OKW directive (11 September) would name 'Sepp' Dietrich as the general responsible for refitting the (six) SS Panzer divisions west of the Rhine (*see* Sixth Panzer Army). These developments, assisting Hitler's plans for continuing military operations for the next eight months, would frustrate all Allied hopes of putting an early end to hostilities entering their sixth year. Despite chronic short-comings in the Army's stocks of motor transport, armoured fighting vehicles, weapons, munitions, vehicle fuels and spares – compounded by massive Allied air attacks against targets deep in Germany – there was to be no collapse in the fighting spirit or command apparatus of the Wehrmacht. Nowhere was German refusal to countenance defeat more apparent than in Holland, north of the Albert Canal, where First Paratroop Army (Student) blocked a British Second Army thrust into north Germany. Reinforced with a single battalion of 25 Jagdpanzers and a company or two of mixed flak, Generaloberst Student's 'Army' with HQ south of Tilburg (Goirle), consisted of Luftwaffe recruits organized into five parachute regiments, reserve (convalescing) infan-try regiments, local defence militia and a martial miscellany of all kinds with a handful of regular paratroop battalions (FJR 6, 1/FJR 2) deployed in support.

Forming mixed battle groups with these and two low-grade infantry divisions, Student proceeded to establish a remarkably effective defence of a hitherto unprotected

northern flank and, in a later Command move, was given Army Group 'H' (18 November) with responsibility for defending Holland between the North Sea coast and Venlo. The Army Group comprised First Paratroop Army (Schlemm) and Fifteenth Army (von Zangen) withdrawn from Belgium across the Scheldt into South Beveland. But a greater surprise in store for Allied planners than Student's improvised defence of Holland was the presence there of panzer divisions redeployed from Normandy. Lying north and east of Arnhem in Army Group 'B' reserve behind First Paratroop Army were the northernmost of the panzer divisions refitting under II SS Panzer Corps (Bittrich) – 9th SS Panzer Division (Harzer) and 10th SS Panzer division (Harmel). It was to be the unconfirmed presence of these SS divisions in Holland and their reaction to airborne invasion that would compromise the forthcoming British offensive 'Market Garden'.

Panzer reaction at Arnhem 17 to 26 September. The remarkably swift reaction of II SS Panzer Corps (Bittrich), deploying emergency battle groups against British 1st Airborne Division (Urquhart) striking for the more distant of five bridges needed to provide a passage for British Guards armour thrusting for the Ruhr was to result in the destruction of all Montgomery's hopes of shortening the war by an imaginative although mishandled airborne operation 'Market Garden'. First Airborne's objective in Montgomery's

basically five bridge plan to pass Anglo-Canadian forces (21st Army Group) through Holland, and north Germany into the Ruhr, was the capture of Arnhem road bridge intact while simultaneously two US airborne divisions 101st (Taylor) and 82nd (Gavin), dropping south between Eindhoven and Nijmegen, seized others. The resulting Grave–Arnhem corridor was to have given British XXX Corps (Horrocks) an easy ride to the north and relief contact with 1st Airborne. But whereas the US paratroops, benefiting from collaboration with British armour at Nijmegen and twice fighting off 107 Panzer Brigade attacking from the west and cutting the corridor, secured their objectives, General Urquhart's men struggling to reach the bridge from a dropping zone located (in Student's view) too far west, and by a twist of fate close to Model's HQ in Oosterbeek – failed to win through in strength. And, once Model's appreciation of Montgomery's intentions was confirmed by orders recovered from a crash glider, their relief was to prove beyond the resources of British Generals. The consequences are well known. In ten days of violent battle, emergency action groups formed by 9th and 10th SS Panzer Divisions, bringing depleted units up to strength with local contingents and then progressively reinforced with Werfer, flak, MG and King Tiger (SS) battalions, destroyed the prospects of Urquhart's men (9th SS) and XXX Corps advancing north of Nijmegen (10th SS).

Notwithstanding the success of 2nd Paratroop Battalion (Frost) in reaching the northern end of Arnhem road bridge,

the firepower and battle-craft of reinforced SS battle groups deployed at speed against 1st Airborne, was to prove decisive. Frost's men, isolated from Division at Arnhem, while holding the northern end of the great bridge against assault by Battle Group Brinkmann (10th SS Reconnaissance Battalion) and Knaust (SS Panzer Grenadier School) were overrun (20 September); further British resistance by 1st Airborne elements cordoned off by Harzer at Oosterbeek ended six days later with 6,000 prisoners and 17,000 Allied casualties (3,300 German casualties). Co-ordinated action in the south by XXXXVII Panzer Corps (von Lüttwitz) – 9th Panzer, 15th Panzer Grenadier Division, attacking British XXX Corps' corridor from the east at Meijel, but bringing little success was soon abandoned. Thereafter 116th Panzer arriving in the Arnhem area released the SS panzer divisions for refitting under Sixth Panzer Army (Dietrich) q.v.

Panzer battles on the upper Rhine 18 September to 13 October. In contrast with the success won by SS panzer battle groups deployed against 21st Army Group's airborne spearheads at Arnhem – shortlived once Montgomery reasserted his grip on Allied operations clearing the Scheldt estuary and opening Antwerp – were German failures on the upper Rhine where Fifth Panzer Army (von Manteuffel) was concentrating divisions in the Vosges for an offensive against US 12th Army Group thrusting to Metz and threatening the Saar. The weight and direction of von Manteuffel's offensive, Hitler decided, should lie primarily

Above: North-west Europe 1944. The Allies had broken out of Normandy that August and were pursuing a broad front strategy which led to battles for the Ruhr, north of Brussels in September, Aachen in October, and Saarbrucken the same month – all with Fifth Panzer Army. In December Hitler's Ardennes counter-offensive 'Autumn Mist' proved a costly failure and the Siegfried Line an illusory barrier. Fifth Panzer Army was driven back across the Rhine and encircled in the Ruhr area north-west of Cologne, where surrendered on 18 April 1945.

with new panzer brigades (106, 108, 111 and 112), 3rd and 15th Panzer Grenadier Divisions, 11th and 21st Panzer striking northwards from the neighbourhood of Epinal into the flank of US Third Army driving east at Lunéville. From 18 to 25 September, when Fifth Panzer Army's Vosges offensive finally got underway, with much less than Hitler's intended strength and later by far than he originally proposed (3 September), scant progress was recorded by XXXXVII Panzer Corps (von Lüttwitz) committing 11th Battle Group (von Wietersheim) and 21st Panzer Division (Luk) reinforced by 111, 112 and 113 Panzer Brigades. Von Manteuffel's under-powered offensive was soon in trouble, petering out with little to show for the gruelling effort involved. The panzer brigades for the most part were subsequently incorporated into the panzer divisions and the Army Group Commander, General Blaskowitz, relieved of his command. In his place as GOC, Army Group 'G', OKH posted General der Panzertruppen Hermann Balck (11th Panzer, XXXXVIII Panzer Corps). Balck's tenure of command over Fifth Panzer Army, First and Nineteenth Armies (regrouped 29 November in favour of creating an SS Upper Rhine command out of Nineteenth Army) and two SS Corps would continue until 23 December when a new appointment on the Danube involving the relief of Budapest (map 19) (see Sixth Panzer Army) took him out of the theatre. Expected to conduct a vigorous defence of Alsace-Lorraine with woefully inadequate resources, the new GOC was to recall that at this critical time following defeat in Normandy, 30–70 German tanks were faced daily by more than 700 US tanks in action on key sectors.

For Balck's impoverished Grade IV infantry defending Metz (Saarburg) and Strasbourg against a rising flood of US armour, panzer support for the time being would rest with depleted battle groups of 17th SS Panzer Grenadier (Müller), 11th Panzer (von Wietersheim), 21st Panzer (Luk), 3rd (Denkert) and 15th (Rodt) Panzer Grenadier Divisions. Only the presence of Panzer Lehr (Bayerlein) reforming but as yet incomplete in OKW reserve and released for action in Lorraine south of Saar Union, prevented a premature collapse of the defence and a breach in the Westwall as US Third and Seventh Armies clearing Alsace-Lorraine closed up to the west bank of the Rhine.

The eventual loss of west bank Rhineland including Strasbourg (22 November), entered by 2nd French Armoured Division (Leclerc), working with US Seventh Army pushing north along the Rhine from Belfort, reflected not only the feebleness of OB West's order of battle arising out of defeat in Normandy, but marked a significant decline in critically important munitions-producing facilities which, in the case of Strasbourg, meant the loss of much of the Army's anti-tank ammunition.

Defending Aachen 14 October to 15 December. On 14 October, before further disasters on the upper Rhine could rebound to the discredit of Fifth Panzer Army or its commander, Hasso von Manteuffel, the panzer army was relieved of responsibility there and returned under command of Army Group 'B' (Model). OKW's intention in switching Fifth Panzer Army close to Aachen where US First and Ninth Armies were exerting heavy pressure in thrusts via Cologne to the Ruhr, was to prepare for a new Hitler offensive 'Watch on the Rhine' to be launched west out of the Ardennes against US First Army. But on 22 October, following a

renewal of American attacks culminating in the capture of Aachen – threatening to breach the Westwall uncovering the defence of Cologne – Fifth Panzer Army was returned to the line between Jülich and Düren controlling 9th Panzer (von Elverfeldt) and six or more infantry divisions subordinate to XII SS, LXXXI and, with more armour on the 29th, XXXXVII Panzer Corps (von Lüttwitz). Von Manteuffel's responsibilities at the heart of the defence included the key Hurtgenwald and Roer river sectors where over the next seven weeks gruelling operations by Fifth Panzer Army would pull 9th, 116th, 10th SS Panzer, and 3rd and 15th Panzer Grenadier Divisions into action against US Ninth Army pushing forward with massive air support and determined to improve its positions, around Düren especially. Fighting in the panzer army's sector continued until 16 December when more important events taking taking place in the Ardennes, 60 miles south, brought relief, but not to Fifth Panzer Army.

Von Manteuffel's part in 'Autumn Mist' 16 December 1944 to 2 January 1945. Formerly 'Watch on the Rhine' (see also Sixth SS Panzer Army) was at first concealed in a series of OKW measures planned to deceive Allied Intelligence. Fifteenth Army HQ was brought out of Holland on 14 November, replacing Fifth Panzer Army and designated Gruppe von Manteuffel; Fifteenth Army's place being taken by Wehrmachtsbefehlshaber Niederlande while similar measures were taken to disguise the true nature of Sixth Panzer Army, the SS Panzer Army (q.v.) with which von Manteuffel would share the operative employment of the panzer divisions allotted for the offensive (map 17).

At 0530 hours 16 December, the first phase of 'Autumn Mist' unrolled with Fifth Panzer Army in control of seven divisions (three panzer) concentrated east of the Ardennes between Bitburg and Prum. Von Maneuffel's three panzer divisions were divided unequally between panzer corps; XXXXVII (von Lüttwitz) with 2nd (Lauchert) and Panzer Lehr (Bayerlein), while LVIII (Krüger) controlled only 116th Panzer (von Waldenburg). Infantry support for the panzer divisions, in addition to one VG division allotted to each panzer corps, was provided by two VG divisions subordinate to LXVI Corps (Lucht). Army troops allotted to von Manteuffel included eight heavy artillery units, three Volkswerfer brigades, two Volks artillery corps, an artillery observation battalion, thirteen engineer and bridging units and four OT (construction) regiments. Two anti-tank support units, Panzerjaeger Abteilung 653 and Assault Gun Brigade 244 were released by OKH to serve as reinforcements for the panzer divisions, while air support (II Jagd Corps) and anti-aircraft protection (III Flak Corps) despite limitations on flying imposed at the time by fuel and equipment shortages would be provided by Luftwaffe OB West (Schmid) (see also Part 4, page 129).

Launching bold attacks from this quarter of the Ardennes four years earlier (map 3) (First Panzer Army, 10 May) the German Army had surprised and then defeated Allied commanders, but in December 1944 the new offensive constrained by a system of narrow and easily congested roads threading snowbound uplands would succeed by the barest of margins in advancing fewer than 60 miles to the river Meuse at Dinant. Directed by OB West, von Runstedt, returning to active duty on 5 September 1944, and OB Army Group 'B' Walter Model – both of whom had tried unsuccessfully to persuade Hitler into adopting more limited objectives than Antwerp and Brussels 120 miles across the rear of two powerful Allied Army Groups (21st, Montgomery and 12th US, Bradley) – the offensive was destined to fail as in Normandy on [7 August] in the face of a steadfast US defence and Allied airpower. Profiting from the absence of Anglo-US air forces held at bay by poor flying weather, von Manteuffel's panzer divisions pushed over the Our at Gemund and Dasburg, closing on the distant Meuse where a crossing between Fermoy and Namur would it was hoped, lead 60 miles on to Brussels, the Army's objective. Unfortunately for 'Autumn Mist', any such hopes of a breakthrough to Brussels were soon dashed by American resistance prolonged at St-Vith (106th Infantry/7th Armored) until 21 December, requiring the intervention of 9th SS Panzer Division re-deployed from Sixth Panzer Army and the release of Führer Begleit Brigade from OKW reserve; opposition followed by an even greater set-back at Bastogne, where the US Army would thwart not only von Manteuffel but Dietrich and German intentions in general. Bypassed north and south by 2nd Panzer and Panzer Lehr driving west, Bastogne, in the hands of US 101st Airborne Division (Mcauliffe – 'Nuts!' to a truce offer), would in consequence absorb much of the energy that should have taken the offensive forward, but was instead committed to futile operations intended to mask or reduce it.

On the 24 December 'Autumn Mist' reached its zenith at Foy-Notre-Dame (2nd Panzer, Lauchert) – three miles short of Dinant; the hitherto dismal weather clearing from the west allowing Allied air forces to sweep into action. Equally disastrous for chances of success was the arrival of a relief

column (US 4th Armored Division) from US Third Army striking from the south through Seventh Army and raising the siege of Bastogne on the 26th. Counter-attacks by FGB and subsequently 1st SS failed to disrupt the relief movement. On 27 December XXXIX Panzer Corps (Decker) arrived from Army Group Centre (Fourth Army) in a redeployment plan to tighten control at Bastogne. On the 29th, the Corps was bracketed with XXXXVII Panzer Corps (von Lüttwitz) into Armeegruppe von Lüttwitz, setting action in train to resolve the problem of Bastogne by concentric attack (east 1st SS, 167th VG, and west FBB, 3rd, 15th Panzer Grenadier). But to no avail. On 30 December, following a day's postponement, von Manteuffel's offensive to reduce Bastogne, unlocking communications to the west, failed completely; the panzer corps involved then reverted to Fifth Panzer Army followed in the case of XXXIX Panzer Corps by a transfer to Alsace. Redeployed north of Strasbourg, Decker was to reinforce a slackening diversionary offensive 'North Wind' (see below, 1 January 1945). On this front by 2 January, problems of road congestion, fuel and ammunition resupply compounded by devastating Anglo-US air attacks were delaying by hours if not days the movement of attacking battle groups and reserves. Despite a belated switch of the main effort from Dietrich and the release of OKW reserves, including 9th Panzer, 15th Panzer Grenadier Division and the 'Führer' Brigades (FBB) and (FGB), 'Autumn Mist' was all but dead.

1 January 1945. 'North Wind', a diversionary First Army (Obstfelder) offensive in Alsace, south of Pirmasens with seven divisions (three corps) attacking US Seventh Army deployed north of Strasbourg, relied principally upon

Left: General Hasso von Manteuffel entered the army in 1916 with the 3rd Hussar Regiment at Rathenow. He served in the Reichswehr as an instructor at the Panzertruppen school, Wünsdorf, and saw action in France as CO of 3rd Motor cycle Battalion and 3rd Schützen Regiment. In 1941 he was CO of 6th Schützen Regiment of 7th Panzer Division on the Moscow sector at Dimitrov. In 1943 he went to Tunisia as GOC, Division von Manteuffel, then east as GOC, 7th Panzer Division. He was transferred to Gross Deutschland in 1944 and was GOC, Fifth Panzer Army in the Ardennes; his final war action was with Third Panzer Army in Mecklenburg in 1945 (see maps 8, 17 and 20).

XIII SS Corps (Simon) led by 17th SS Panzer Grenadier Division (Lingner). Infantry battle groups were contributed by 36th Infantry Division. Spearheaded by 17th SS Panzer Grenadier Division, 'North Wind' made local gains north of Strasbourg between Rimlingen and Achern, but after running into heavy opposition, soon faded out. Renewed on 6 January by XXXXIX Panzer Corps (Decker, released from 'Autumn Mist' dying in the Ardennes), the new attack thrusting to Hagenau and creating momentary panic in Strasbourg also ended with nothing to show for it. The Seventh Army offensive north of Strasbourg where 21st Panzer and 25th Panzer Grenadier Divisions were involved under Decker, was supported by Nineteenth Army (Rasp) assaulting the defence concentrically from positions south of Strasbourg where Armeegruppe Oberrhein (Himmler), directly responsible to Hitler, was holding a west bank bridgehead at Colmar–Guebwiller. The efforts of those involved were in vain. At the conclusion of these abortive operations, draining panzer strength and manpower, Himmler's Armeegruppe (OB and Headquarters) was transferred to Pomerania (see Eleventh SS Panzer Army), leaving the upper Rhine and future operations under Ninth Army to Army Group 'G' (Hausser). In the north, where Fifth Panzer Army was fighting a rearguard action, events were moving to a similarly dismal conclusion.

'Autumn Mist' fade-out 3–31 January 1945. On 3 January Anglo-US forces subordinate to Field Marshal Montgomery – British XXX Corps and US First Army (north), US Third Army (south) – started concentric operations to squeeze the panzer armies out of their Ardennes bulge. When the converging armies united at Houffalize on the 16th, 'Autumn Mist' had run its course, but not before making one last attempt at reducing Bastogne. On 4 January a final attempt at breaking the US hold on Bastogne by I SS Panzer Corps (Priess) controlling 9th and 12th SS Panzer Divisions – reduced to 25 per cent tank strength – and panzer grenadier battalions less than 150 strong, also a weak 340 VGD, failed totally in its purpose. On 8 January when Hitler begrudgingly authorized limited withdrawals, the depleted panzer divisions 2nd, 9th, 116th (reduced to the effectiveness of a panzer grenadier regiment), Panzer Lehr, 3rd and 15th Panzer Grenadier Divisions, rallied to rearguard duties in circumstances made doubly difficult by the absence of Sixth Panzer Army (Dietrich) progressively withdrawn (8–24 January) and under movement orders to transfer east. Brisk action on 10 January by the Führer Grenadier Brigade (Kahler) subordinated to Seventh Army (Brandenburger) at Wiltz south-east of Bastogne, helped a shaky defence in resisting US Third Army pressure which was destroying 5th Paratroop Division (Heilmann). The action helped in preventing the collapse of an all too weak southern flank. By 31 January, after three weeks of hard fighting, von Manteuffel's divisions had reached the temporary security of the Westwall (Prum–Schleiden); retaining bridgeheads over the Our at Vianden and Dasburg, the divisions of Army Group 'B' were otherwise back at their start-line.

Crisis Point Rhine February to March 1945. In the aftermath of 'Autumn Mist' incurring 70,000 German casualties and the loss of 500 tanks and assault guns, defensive prospects for the German Army west of the Rhine looked distinctly bleak, with eighty British, Canadian, US

and French divisions, including 24 armoured (fifteen US, six British/Canadian, three French) deploying 6,000 tanks in three Army Groups – 21st (Montgomery), 12th US (Bradley) and 6th US (Devers) – resuming operations to clear the Rhineland, encircle the Ruhr and drive into Germany beyond. The strength of the Wehrmacht in the west – sixty much depleted divisions (nine panzer/panzer grenadier) organized into three Army Groups standing west of the Rhine: 'H' (Student) lower Rhine, 'B' (Model) middle Rhine and 'G' (Blaskowitz) upper Rhine – was spread 500 miles from the North Sea south of Rotterdam to the Swiss frontier at Basle. Fewer than 450 tanks and assault guns, supported by Jagdpanzers (Heerestruppen) deployed in company strengths stood at their disposal. Model's Army Group 'B', in action on the middle Rhine between Roermund and Trier, was appreciably weakened by panzer transfers to the east – Sixth Panzer Army (Dietrich), two SS panzer corps, four SS panzer divisions switched to Western Hungary, and the Führer Brigades, FBB and FBG, sent to Cotbus for expansion and then posting to Army Group Weichsel – retaining fewer than 170 battle-fit tanks and approximately the same number of heavy anti-tank guns serving 29 divisions (five panzer/panzer grenadier) holding left bank positions. Army Group 'G' was to be similarly weakened, losing panzer divisions to the east (see 24 March–1 April 1945).

A resumption of Allied pressure in the west brought panzer divisions into action at crisis points – in the case of Army Group 'H' (Student) defending the Reichswald between the Rhine and the Maas, in counter-attacks to delay 21st Army Group (First Canadian, Second British, Ninth US Armies) clearing the left bank south-east of Nijmegen where First Paratroop Army (Schlemm) held the line.

[*8 February 1945. Reinforcing First Paratroop Army in the Reichswald. On 8 February, XXXXVII Panzer Corps (von Luttwitz), withdrawn into OB West reserve at the conclusion of 'Autumn Mist' with 116th Panzer (von Waldenburg) and 15th Panzer Grenadier Division (Rodt), counter-attacked the Anglo-Canadian advance at Kleve in a sector where II Paratroop Corps (Meindl) called for assistance in containing overwhelming attacks. When XXXXVII Corps (von Lüttwitz) failed to restore the situation in the Reichswald, Geldern was lost on 3 March and Canadian First Army was able to link up with US Ninth Army (Simpson) converging from the south. By 12 March the left (west) bank of the Rhine south of the Reichswald, including a substantial First Paratroop Army bridgehead at Wesel, had been surrendered – notwithstanding the intervention of Panzer Lehr (Niemack) drawn into battle at various stages in the Allied offensive. And in the battle for Cologne on the adjoining sector to the south the panzer divisions were equally powerless.*

23 February 1945 [Reinforcing Fifteenth Army on the Rhine. On 23 February, when US First Army (Hodges) aiming for Cologne secured a bridgehead over the River Roer (Linnich–Jülich–Düren) the Westwall was decisively breached at a crucial point, affording access to the Ruhr. Neither 9th Panzer (von Elverfeldt) nor 3rd Panzer Grenadier Division, deployed under LVIII Panzer Corps (Krüger), challenging American progress could halt the offensive. Reinforcements drawn into the battle from south flanking Army Group 'G', 11th Panzer (von Brandenfels) failed equally in stemming the American onrush while 9th Panzer would soon be reporting the loss of its commander, von Elverfeldt. By 7 March Cologne city centre was in the hands of US First Army, and the great Hohenzollern bridge destroyed by retreating battle groups.]

At **Remagen** in Fifth Panzer Army's sector, where LXVII Corps held the line, an undamaged (Ludendorff) bridge fell unexpectedly into the hands of US First Army/9th Armored Division (Leonard); the Army commander (Hodges) seizing his chance promptly, developed a right (east) bank bridgehead. The corps adjutant, Major Scheller, arriving only hours before to organize the defence of the Ludendorff bridge was, with others, judged neglectful of his proper responsibility and on Hitler's orders he and they paid with their lives for the mishap. More positive measures to combat the threat to trans-Rhine defences posed by Hodges's expanding bridgehead at Remagen were initiated by Model, GOC, Army Group 'B' and (von Zangen) GOC, Fifteen Army; the defensive measures set in train involved panzer divisions in more abortive counter-attacks. Vigorous action over the next few days by 3rd Panzer Grenadier, Panzer Lehr, 9th and 11th Panzer Divisions serving LIII Panzer Corps (Bayerlein) and LXXIV Corps (Puchler) would all fail in eliminating the danger. The US bridgehead remained a thorn in German flesh. Fifth Panzer Army's strength on the right bank of the Rhine between Bonn and Duisberg, with an extension eastwards along the Ruhr north of Cologne, lay in nothing more than five VG and 3rd and 5th Paratroop Divisions deployed north and south of Cologne. On 10 March OB West, von Runstedt was relieved of his post for the last time and Field Marshal Kesselring, hitherto OB South West (succeeded by von Vietinghoff from Tenth Army), was installed in his place. On 12 March GOC, Fifth Panzer Army, von Manteuffel, was succeeded by General der Panzertruppe Harpe. Transferred to the Oder north of Berlin, von Manteuffel replaced Raus at Third Panzer Army (q.v.).

17–31 March. During the last fortnight in March, Allied armies were consolidating their hold on the west bank of the Rhine before mounting new offensives in reasonably quick time and winning Rhine crossings in strength: north, 21st Army Group at Wesel (23–24 March); centre, US 12th Army Group at Oppenheim (22 March); south, US 6th Army Group at Darmstadt (25 March) and Speyer (French First Army 31 March).

[17 March. Seventh Army on the Middle Rhine faced preliminary US tidying-up operations east of Trier (4 March) as US Third Army (Patton) thrusting along the Moselle engaged 2nd Panzer (Lauchert) and 11th Panzer (von Brandenfels) before reaching Coblenz on the 17th and swinging south into contact with US Seventh Army (Patch).

19 March. First Army defending the Saarland where US Seventh Army (Patch) was clearing the west bank and, penetrating the Westwall between Zweibrucken and Pirmasens, watched the Army's only remaining motorized formation, 17th SS Panzer Grenadier Division (Bochmann) flushed out of strong points on the River Blies and into Germesheim, the last German bridgehead standing west of the Rhine. Bochmann's division, reduced to 800 effectives, would then hold Germesheim until the bridgehead, swollen with retreating troops and civilians, was evacuated on the 25th].

24–31 March. A decisive factor in the collapse of

German resistance in the Saar, as elsewhere along the Rhine, was the absence of mobile divisions (drawn off for action on the Eastern Front) and the relative weakness of the remainder. Panzer divisions surrendered to the Eastern Front by Army Group 'B' (Model) at the conclusion of 'Autumn Mist' (SS 1st, 2nd, 9th, 12th) were followed soon afterwards by 21st, 10th SS and 25th Panzer Grenadier, withdrawn from Army Group 'G' (Blaskowitz) principally for the benefit of Army Group Weichsel (Himmler) preparing a new offensive in the east. All that remained on the upper Rhine was 17th SS Goetz von Berlichingen. On the middle Rhine serving Army Group 'B' stood Panzer Lehr, 11th Panzer, 3rd Panzer Grenadier, 2nd and 9th Panzer Divisions; and on the lower Rhine (Army Group 'H') 116th Panzer and 15th Panzer grenadier Divisions. On 24 March, when 21st Army Group (Montgomery) incorporating two airborne divisions, launched a powerful three Army offensive (Canadian First, British Second, US Ninth) across the lower Rhine at Wesel, destroying First Paratroop Army in the process, only a single panzer division battle group (von Waldenburg), 15th Panzer Grenadier Division (Rodt) and 106 Panzer Brigade, were on hand to bolster infantry and paratroop divisions scattered in overwhelming attacks. By the time these battles were concluded, with the loss of 10,000 men a day, surviving panzer divisions were reduced to regimental-size battle groups with few if any tanks, their mobility impaired by shortages of fuel, spares and vehicles, and their firepower severely curtailed by a lack of heavy weapons and dwindling ammunition supplies. Most would, nevertheless, continue in action at one crisis point after another as the Western Allies, thrusting into the heart of Germany, encircled the Ruhr and fanning out north, centre and south threatened Hamburg, Magdeburg and Munich. Eventually (24 April) on the Elbe south of Magdeburg, US First Army (Hodges), pushing hard for Leipzig, made contact with Russian Fifth Guards Army (Schadov) 30 miles north-east at Torgau. The move divided Germany into two battle zones (map 20).

Encirclement in the Ruhr By 1 April, with US Ninth Army (Simpson) and US First Army (Hodges) uniting 60 miles north-east of Cologne at Lippstadt, Harpe's Fifth Panzer Army and von Zangen's Fifteenth Army were encircled in the Ruhr with the remaining nineteen divisions of Model's Army Group 'B'. The Ruhr pocket created east of the Rhine by fast-moving US spearheads and at first broadly rectangular in shape, embraced within its northern limits the Ruhr-side industrial districts of Duisberg, Essen (Krupp), Bochum, Dortmund and Hamm – all for the most part located north of the river. Over to the south lay Düsseldorf and Wuppertal with their satellite industrial suburbs, but the greater part of the encircled area consisted of Sauerland countryside open to the east but limited in the south by the River Sieg. In the centre of the southern front stood Siegen, a communications centre affording good road and rail links northwards to Dortmund via Olpe, HQ Army Group 'B' (Model) and Witten. An Army Group in better shape than Model's 80 per cent Grade III formations, reinforced by urban defence volunteers raised by neighbourhood defence chiefs, might have been expected if adequately supplied and equipped to stage a protracted resistance. But despite the presence of four panzer/panzer grenadier divisions – 9th (Zollenkopf), 116th (von Waldenburg), Panzer Lehr (Hauser) and 3rd Panzer Grenadier (Dankert) – this did not happen. The formidable task of countering pressure from all sides of the pocket, especially north and south at Witten and Siegen, was to prove too much for an Army Group imperilled by shortages of every kind and fatally weakened by counter-attacks at Remagen (7–25 March) and Wesel (24 March).

8 April 1945. By 8 April, Fifth Panzer Army's dispositions in the Ruhr pocket fronting the Rhine lay north and south of Cologne (XII SS Corps, 3rd Paratroop Division and Volksturm) and eastwards along the Sieg via Siegburg to Siegen where LVIII Panzer Corps (Botsch) (Battle Group 9th Panzer and five infantry divisions) constituted the best of Harpe's meagre resources.

[*Fifteenth Army, encircled with Fifth Panzer Army and meanwhile reduced to three infantry divisions, held the country east of Siegen, driven into the pocket by US First Army thrusting from the Remagen bridgehead (25 March). The Army Group Commander then released Panzer Lehr (Hauser) and his only other reserve motorized formation, 3rd Panzer Grenadier Division (Dankert), for counter-attacks east of Winterberg. Supported by infantry of LIII Panzer Corps (Bayerlein), Model's intention was to use the mobile divisions at Madebach for breaking through US First Army, preventing Fifteenth Army from uniting with Lucht's new Eleventh Army (q.v.) forming to the east. But the rigorous opposition of US armour to any attempt at breaking through the daily widening corridor, pushing German Eleventh and Fifteenth Armies farther apart, defeated Panzer Lehr's purpose and those of supporting formations, executed from 30 March to 5 April. Forbidden by Hitler to make further break-out attempts, operations were closed down and there for a day or so the front stabilized – Bayerlein transferring to the north where another crisis was developing.*]

Armeegruppe von Lüttwitz, in the Ruhr and responsible to Army Group 'B' for the defence of war industries established since 1850 along the River Ruhr between Duisberg and the Mohne Dam, was an impromptu formation supervising XXXXVII Panzer Corps (von Lüttwitz) and LXIII Corps (Abrahams). Separated from First Paratroop Army (Schlemm) at the time of 21st Army Group's thrust east of Wesel, von Luttwitz retained 116th Panzer (von Walden-burg), some worn-out infantry, paratroop, Volksturm, flak and artillery units with which to assist neighbourhood forces defending industrial production crucial to the prosecution of the war. Despite the welcome arrival of Bayerlein's LIII Panzer Corps, taking over 116th Panzer and infantry support in the critical Castrop/Witten sector of the front, where US (Ninth Army) pressure to split the Ruhr pocket north and south was at its maximum, the outcome of this unequal struggle was never in question. Nothing that Bayerlein – or anyone else – could do, was to affect American progress. By 12 April 1945, Ruhrland industrial districts north of the river, including the giant Krupp works at Essen and the military complex at Sennelager, had been lost – many districts, including Essen, Duisberg and Bochum, going undefended for lack of resources, others like Castrop being bitterly fought over. On 14 April, the Ruhr pocket was split by US armour, driving south from Witten and north from Olpe. The result of this American action on Army Group 'B' was to create a western enclave surrounding Düsseldorf and Wuppertal (HQ Army Group 'B' transferred

from Olpe) enclosing Fifth Panzer Army (Harpe), 9th Panzer (Zollenkopf) and the mass of Armeegruppe von Lüttwitz.

Isolated eastwards around Iserlohn was a small pocket containing Fifteenth Army (von Zangen) with Panzer Lehr (Hauser), 3rd Panzer Grenadier (Denkert), 116th Panzer (von Waldenburg) and depleted Jagdtiger companies (Ernst and Carius). The battle state of Ruhr panzer/panzer grenadier divisions at the time of capitulation is typified by the strength returns of Denkert's 3rd Panzer Grenadier Divisions: 0 per cent panzerjaeger, 0 per cent panzer/ sturmgeschützen, 0 per cent pioneers, 10 per cent panzer grenadiers. By 18 April 1945 Army Group 'B' had officially surrendered 325,000 effectives, but not its GOC, Field Marshal Walter Model; his suicide followed three days later at Wedau on the southern outskirts of Duisberg.

Panzer Battle Group Divisions in the west. 19 April to 9 May 1945. With surrender in the Ruhr pocket claiming Fifth Panzer Army (Harpe), LIII Panzer Corps (Bayerlein), 9th, 116th, Panzer Lehr and 3rd Panzer Grenadier Divisions, fewer than a handful of regular – but severely depleted – panzer battle groups, 2nd Panzer, 11th Panzer, 15th and 17th SS Panzer Grenadier Divisions, survived in the west, pursuing near purposeless operations. The profitless employment of the four battle group divisions and impromptu formations such as 'Clausewitz', incorporating depleted Panzerjaeger battalions and *ad hoc* Panzer Verbande, created out of local resouces, would continue until 9 May when the unconditional surrender of the German Army in the east brought hostilities officially to an end (map 20). Facing west in the weeks prior to capitulation, battle groups were deployed in widely separated engagements between the North Sea and the Swiss frontier.

[*First Paratroop Army south of Bremen (Student, – Straube) committed Panzer Grenadier Division (Rodt) and Panzer Verband GD in counter-attacks to slow Second Army (Dempsey) thrusting to Hamburg.*]

[*Eleventh Army (Lucht) encircled in the Harz Mountains (see page 247), surrendered 9th/116th Panzer Division remnants and SS Panzer Verband Westfalen.*

A new Twelfth Army (Wenck) raised on the Elbe in early April, south-east of Magdeburg with HQ at Dessau, assembled Kampfgruppe Panzer Division Clausewitz (Unrein) from many and divers units collected south-east of Hamburg. The division was subordinated to XXXIX Panzer Corps (Decker), switched to the Elbe from the Oder (Ninth Army east of Berlin), and seconded to OB North West. Decker's task with Unrein's 'Clausewitz' and Heun's 'Schlageter' (motorized infantry division) was to drive a corridor south from Uelzen through British Second and US Ninth Armies investing Eleventh Army encircled in the Harz.

By 21 April, the relief attempt that had begun in fine style five days earlier on the 16th, south of Uelzen, failed short of Brunswick. Overwhelmed by Allied superiority, notably in the air, destroying the attacking formations, neither Clausewitz nor XXXIX Panzer Corps survived the engagement as viable military entities; the depleted corps staff being amalgamated for a time with other staffs to form XXXXI Panzer Corps (Holste).

On 22 April, Twelfth Army (Wenck) was directed by OKW to relieve Berlin from the south-east (see also Third Panzer Army, 16 April). Possessing no more than a handful of RAD units, infantry teaching cadres, one or two panzer school] units, HJ and Volksturm organized into impromptu divisions like Schlageter, Scharnhorst, Ulrich von Hutten and Theodor Korner, the attempt was unlikely to succeed although contact was affected with Ninth Army/Fourth Panzer Army elements retreating from Frankfurt (Oder) on the opposite (east) front. See also Pz AOK 3, 16 April 1945.

Seventh Army (Obstfelder) **east of the Rhine,** shattered in battles for the Saar and retiring south-east through Hesse and Thuringia, retained Kampfgruppe 2nd Panzer (von Berg) and 11th Panzer (von Bradenfels) at the centre of an otherwise feeble order of battle – mostly local infantry, flak and Wehrkreis emergency formations. Flank attacks by these 'divisions', directed south from Eisenach against US Third Army (Patton) advancing powerfully via Erfurth towards Chemnitz and the Tyrol during April, would do nothing to deflect Patton from his objectives.

First Army (Fortsch) **in Bavaria,** retreating from the upper Rhine through Wurtemburg and Bavaria, carried along 17th SS Panzer Grenadier Division (Bochmann) for action north

of Heilbron (3–12 April), around Nuremberg (17–20 April) and Munich (24–28 April) and finally with few if any heavy weapons remaining to it in the area south of Bad Tolz. The Army's order of battle, inclusive of 17th SS, 2nd Mountain, six other infantry divisions and local defence units – only marginally superior to Obstfelder's east flanking Seventh Army or Brandenburger's west flanking Nineteenth Army devoid of all regular motorized formations with which to hold Stuttgart (surrendered 22 April) or the Black Forest against French First Army (Tassigny) – precluded all but the most local of offensive operations in southern Germany. By 9 May 1945, Franco-US forces driving into southern redoubts – French First Army (Tassigny), US Seventh Army (Patch) and US Third Army (Patton) – were occupying the Tyrol and alpine foreland including Innsbruck, Salzburg and Linz, uniting with US Fifth Army (Truscott) from Italy at the Brenner Pass (Patch) and 3rd Ukrainina Front (Tolbuchin) from Hungary at Linz (Patton).]

9. Sixth SS Panzer Army (SS PzAOK 6)

Raised in September 1944 to lead a Hitler-inspired Ardennes counter-offensive – 'Autumn Mist' (formerly 'Watch on the Rhine') – ordered by OKW on 10 November 1944. Army Commander SS Oberstgruppenführer and Generaloberst der Waffen SS 'Sepp' Dietrich. Panzer Headquarters, Münstereifel. In control of I SS Panzer Corps (Priess), II SS Panzer Corps (Bittrich) and 150 Panzer Brigade (cover-name for a 2,000-strong SS sabotage commando led by Obersturmbannführer Otto Skorzeny), the Panzer Army was concentrated west of the Rhine on the German side of the Ardennes only three days prior to the offensive planned for 16 December 1944.

In **Operation 'Griffon',** Hitler required Skorzeny by means of infiltration with American-looking vehicles and personnel to create alarm and confusion among US forces deployed on the battle front opposite the SS Leibstandarte spearhead. Skorzeny was further charged with assisting the spearhead (Peiper) to secure bridges at Huy and Liège on the axis of advance to Antwerp. Two assault gun brigades (394) and (667) a Panzerjaeger battalion (653) and an assault panzer battalion (217) were allotted to Dietrich as Army troops in addition to three Werfer brigades and three Volks artillery corps. LXVII Army Corps (Hitzfeld) with two VG divisions (272nd) and (326th) would provide infantry support for the offensive.

The Panzer Army's objective, under the supervision of Field Marshal von Runstedt, called out of retirement on 5 September and reinstated as OB West, was to recapture the recently opened Allied supply port of Antwerp while Fifth Panzer Army (von Manteuffel), also on 16 December, secured Brussels, the Belgian capital. Both Armies were subordinate to Model's Army Group 'B'. Neither von Runstedt, Model nor von Manteuffel were optimistic about Hitler's plans which they received in 'do not alter' form. Once across the Meuse, the two attacking panzer armies were expected to swing 125 miles north-west, enveloping and destroying four US, British and Canadian armies trapped between them and Army Group 'H' (Student) in

Holland. The role of Seventh Army (Brandenburger) to the south and Fifteenth Army (von Zangen) to the north was to provide flank protection, but as events were to prove, Seventh Army operating within striking distance of Patton's US Third Army was much too weak for its role.

Operation 'Autumn Mist' (map 17). 'Autumn Mist' started on 16 December 1944 at 0535 hours, with bad weather keeping Allied air forces at bay. Of the four newly equipped SS panzer divisions, two, 1st SS Leibstandarte Adolf Hitler (Mohnke) and 12th SS Hitler Youth (Kraas) would lead I SS Panzer Corps (Priess), while two other SS panzer divisions in II SS Panzer Corps (Bittrich), 2nd SS Das Reich (Lammerding) and 9th SS Hohenstaufen (Stadler) prepared to follow on. Air support for the attacking divisions by II Jagd Corps was negligible.

Operation 'Stosser', a supporting parachute drop by 800 Fallschirmjaeger (von der Heydte) on the northern flank of the offensive was planned to confuse the defence and, by securing traffic points on the Hoher-Venn, block the advance of US reinforcements from this direction; but the operation was delayed for want of transports. Results on the first day were far less than expected with only limited gains being reported. US First Army, standing fast on the northern shoulder of the offensive, hemmed the attacking divisions into a narrow operational area from which they were unable to break out. The offensive consequently failled at a critical time and at critical points; defeated as much by a steadfast US defence of key communication centres as the constricting effect of ravines and forest terrain inhibiting off the road movement particularly at Butgenbach (12th SS, 12th VGD), Elsenborn and Monschau (326 VGD). At these points on the SS front and also in the south where Fifth Panzer Army was blocked at St-Vith and Bastogne, the offensive stalled never to recover momentum.

The spearhead of 'Autumn Mist', Kampffgruppe Peiper, a 4,000-strong Leibstandarte armoured battle group (I SS Panzer Regiment, Jochen Pieper with 72 Pz Kpfw IV/Vs and 30 Pz Kpfw VIs) pushing for the Meuse at Huy in

Right: SS Oberstgruppenführer and Panzer Generaloberst der Waffen SS, 'Sepp' Dietrich. A Bavarian, he entered the army in 1911, serving from 1914 to 1918 in the 42nd Infantry Regiment and the 5th Bavarian Panzer Detachment. In 1928 he joined the SS and rose rapidly through the ranks to become the OC Hitler's bodyguard in 1932, which was officially renamed Leibstandarte Adolf Hitler in 1933. From 1939 to 1943 he commanded an expanded Leibstandarte in Poland, France, the Balkans and Russia before moving, in July 1943, to head I SS Panzer Corps. In June 1944 he fought in Normandy and from September he was GOC, Sixth SS Panzer Army (*see* maps 16, 17 and 19).

conjunction with 40–50 Skorzeny commandos, four to a jeep, was rendered totally ineffective when trapped at La Gleize in the Ambleve valley east of Stourmont. Fitfully re-supplied by air, Peiper's battle group abandoned much of its equipment including 28 Pz Kpfw IVs and Panthers after all relief attempts had ended in failure. Reduced to 800 men by 24 December, the Kampfgruppe withdrew to the east. On 17 December, von der Heydte's scratch force of 800 paratroops was finally dropped a day late and mostly off-course. Fewer than 200 of the Fallschirmjaeger, descending ahead of the supposedly advancing 326th VG

Division, reached the neighbourhood of their objective – a cross-roads on the Hoher-Venn giving enemy access to the area from the north. Instead, rallying under von der Heydte, the group moved east in a bid to escape, but within seven days most were in captivity at Monschau. On 20 December OB West decided to switch the main effort of 'Autumn Mist' from Sixth SS to Fifth Panzer Army while a second and equally futile attempt by the SS divisions of II SS Panzer Corps to break through to the Meuse in the centre of the front at Vielsalm (9th SS) was rebutted. Here, as elsewhere to the north, a staunch American defence of the sector denied the SS the use of roads and bridges essential to progress.

[Fifth Panzer Army pushing forward in the south on 21 December, also suffered an unwelcome reverse with US resistance at Bastogne and St-Vith delaying or halting the leading Panzer divisions.]

On 24 December, eight days after the start of 'Autumn Mist', skies cleared above the battle-field allowing Allied air forces to operate at full power. The offensive was then swiftly brought to an end. By this time too, Skorzeny's mission ('Griffon') using mocked-up Panthers and personnel disguised as American troops to spread confusion in disruptive commando type operations, had proved largely ineffective and after a spell of more regular employment assisting Peiper with attacks on Malmédy, on 21 December, was withdrawn.

[On 26 December US Third Army (III Corps) drove a corridor through German Seventh Army, raising the siege of Bastogne (see Fifth Panzer Army.)]

On 3 January, Anglo-US counter-action was directed by Field Marshal Montgomery starting with operations against the northern flank of Sixth SS Panzer Army. On 4 January, following a last-minute switch of 1st, 9th and 12th SS Panzer Divisions (I SS Panzer Corps) to von Manteuffel, a new offensive failed to eliminate resistance at Bastogne. Consequently the town, reinforced from the south by US Third Army, continued to tie-down offensive capacity needed by Fifth Panzer Army for the drive to the Meuse. On 8 January, while obstinately refusing to acknowledge defeat, Hitler authorized limited withdrawals. The attacking panzer divisions, whose progress had fallen well short of major objectives – on fuel so limited that operations were at times brought to a standstill – withdrew under punishing air attack to the relative security of the Westwall. A new directive followed. On 21 January Hitler instructed OKW to switch Sixth SS Panzer Army to western Hungary, a sector of the Eastern Front where on 26 December Budapest had been encircled by Russian 2nd and 3rd Ukranian Fronts. Two days later, Hungary changed sides, joining Bulgaria and Roumania in declaring war on Germany. Into this dangerous military vacuum in an economically sensitive area the Wehrmacht's last significant panzer reserve was sent by Hitler to join Army Group South (Wöhler) – ignoring Guderian's view that panzer reinforcement was most desperately needed on the Oder (see Fourth Panzer Army, 12 January 1945).

[On the Danube (map 19) until 2 January 1944, when the transfer of IV SS Panzer Corps (Gille) from Army Group centre brought 3rd SS Totenkopf (Becker) and 5th SS Wiking (Ullrich) to Komorn, only LVII Panzer Corps (Kirchner) deployed north of Budapest and III Panzer Corps (Breith) to the south served Army Group South.

Despite the success of panzer divisions eliminating Russian spearheads at Nyireghyaza (see First Panzer Army, October 1944), Army Group South's seven divisions, 1st, 3rd, 6th, 8th, 13th, 23rd, 24th and Panzer Grenadier Division Feldhermhalle supported by 109 and 110 Panzer Brigades with a handful of infantry divisions, fighting south of the Carpathians had proved too weak and too few to stem the tide of Russian armour and infantry sweeping west and enveloping Budapest.

Defending Budapest. By 13 February 1945, when Buda

fell to 2nd Ukrainian Front, the defence of Budapest lead by Pfeffer von Wildenbruck (IX SS Mountain Corps) had swallowed up five German divisions including 13th Panzer and Panzer Grenadier Division Feldherrenhalle (60th Motorized). In an attempt to relieve Budapest on 1 January with IV SS Panzer Corps (Gille) using 3rd and 5th SS Panzer Divisions to assault the defence on the Danube east of Komorn, and again from the south-west cn 18 January when reinforced by 1st (Thunert) and 3rd (Phillips) Panzer Divisions, Sixth Army (Balck) approached to within fifteen miles of the Hungarian capital, but there the attempt failed. On 11 February a break-out led by 13th Panzer Division ended in disaster. On the 13th, Budapest surrendered 70,000 military effectives; Hitler at once devised a new scheme for re-occupying the town.]

Operation 'Spring Awakening' (map 19) on 6 March 1945 required Dietrich with his two SS panzer corps – I SS (1st SS Leibstandarte AH and 12th SS HJ), also II SS (2nd and 9th SS), to co-operate with Sixth Army (Balck) – III Panzer Corps (Breith), 1st, 3rd, 6th and 23rd Panzer Divisions plus IV SS Panzer Corps (Gille) – in a powerful thrust east. Starting east of Stuhlweissenburg (Szekesfeharvar), 'Spring Awakening' aimed to blunt Ukranain Front spearheads threatening Hungarian oil production at Nagy-Kanisza, also related refineries and essential war industries in Vienna. But no less crucial in Hitler's view was the need for Dietrich to re-take Budapest, and, in conjuction with Second Panzer Army to the south, establish bridgeheads across the Danube for future operations. Involving thirty divisions, eight of them panzer, 'Spring Awakening' secured early gains in the face of determined 3rd Ukranian Front opposition. But hampered by adverse terrain bogging armoured vehicles and restricting movement, the offensive slackened and failed; no more than local advantage accruing from the operation leaving the panzer army with only 185 battle-fit tanks and assault guns. Giving 'Spring Awakening' no more than a moment's consideration, Stavka could see few strategic problems arising out of Hitler's counter-attack conducted so far from its own primary objective – Berlin.

Germany in defeat (map 20). Gravely weakened by its abortive action at Stuhlweissenburg, reducing the Army's meagre tank strength to even less meaningful proportions, Dietrich ('Sixth Panzer Army means six tanks') in control of I and II SS Panzer Corps, was forced back on Bratislavia in mid-April giving more ground before fighting rearguard battles in Austria yet failing to hold Vienna. At the beginning of May 1945, prior to Sixth SS Panzer Army's surrender to US or Russian forces, Hitler's rage over SS 'failures' resulted in orders that the SS divisions under Dietrich's command, Leibstandarte, Totenkopf and HJ, the pride of the Waffen SS, should be stripped of their cuff titles. In refusing to comply with the Führer's directive, Dietrich told his divisional commanders, 'There's your reward for all that you've done these past five years.' No words are more suited than Dietrich's to express the futility of Hitler's war direction, or to summarize more succinctly a barren political ideology which, in aspiring to a thousand-year Reich, betrayed the faith of the German Army and people.

Right: SS Oberstgruppenführer and General der Waffen SS, Felix Steiner. A Prussian, he entered the army in 1914, serving with the 5th Infantry Regiment at Tilsit before seeing action in the east at Tannenberg and the west in Flanders. From 1921 to 1934 he was a member of the Reichswehr Infantry, undertaking staff and police training duties, becoming Training Director. In 1935 he moved to SS-Verfügungstruppe as battalion commander, serving in Poland and France as OC, Deutschland. In December 1940 he was appointed GOC, SS Wiking Division and in 1941–2, during the Russian campaign, he led it at Malgobek (see map 10). In May 1943 he raised III Germanisches Panzer Corps which comprised Nordland and Nederland. He was posted to Leningrad that December where he later fought at Narwa. In 1945 he was GOC, Eleventh Panzer Army but, with no divisions left to speak of, Steiner only theoreticaly pariticipated in the battle for Berlin (see map 20).

10. Eleventh SS Panzer Army (SS PzAOK 11)

Raised in Pomerania in January 1945, from the staff of SS Headquarters Upper Rhine. Army Commander appointed on 28 January 1945 from command of III SS (Germanisches) Panzer Corps was General der Waffen SS Felix Steiner. Prior to Steiner's appointment, at the conclusion of the third Battle of Courland, OKH had withdrawn III SS Panzer Corps Headquarters from Eighteenth Army by sea across the Baltic, followed by SS Brigades Nordland and Nederland. The SS Brigades would be refitted as panzer grenadier divisions. Steiner's (Germanisches) SS Corps was swiftly relocated south-east of Stettin, responsible to Himmler's Army Group Weichsel and in control of mainly SS divisions committed to the emergency defence of Pomerania.

[Defending the Narwa bridgehead. In July 1944, six months prior to Corps battles in Courland, Steiner had conducted a vigorous defence of Eighteenth Army's Narwa bridgehead. A land corridor strategically situated south-west of Leningrad between the Baltic and Lake Peipus, this neck of land with Narwa at its head connected the city's hinterland with Estonia and Baltic regions to the south. In blocking Lenningrad Front (Govorov) attempts to crash through the corridor, Steiner gained time for Army Group North (Schörner) – Sixteenth and Eighteenth Armies, to withdraw to the south-west in safety and consolidate in the Baltic peninsular (Courland) west of Riga.]

The battle for Arnswalde. On 15 February 1945, Eleventh SS Panzer Army/Army Group Weichsel launched Operation 'Sonewende' southwards from Stargard to Arnswalde. Although strategically unrewarding, Steiner's counter-offensive into the northern flank of the Red Army Fronts driving for Berlin nevertheless liberated Arnswalde for four days before pressure from 2nd BR Front forced the Army into retreat. At Guderian's insistence General Wenck, until a motor accident on the 17th prevented him from continuing, assisted Eleventh Army staff in the preparation of the offensive. At the centre of the Stargard attack stood III SS Panzer Corps lead by General Martin Unrein, promoted from command of 14th Panzer Division (retained by Eighteenth Army in Courland). The attacking formations included SS Panzer Grenadier Divisions Nordland, Nederland, Langemarck and the Army's Führer Begleit Division. Two other corps participated in 'Sonewende'; XXXIX Panzer Corps (Decker) and Corps Munzel with Holstein, SS Polizei, SS Wallonien and the Führer Grenadier Division shared between them. With these worn down and incomplete formations organized into weak battle groups, the 'Panzer Army' won local success and, as noted, recaptured Arnswalde, but there the offensive petered out. On 25 February 1945 – General der Panzertruppen Erhard Raus with Third Panzer Army (HQ) arrived in Pomerania from East Prussia, assuming responsibility for Eleventh Panzer Army operations – leaving the defence of Königsberg and East Prussia to Fourth Army (Hossbach).

In the **general retreat** to the Oder following Russian attacks which split the defence in Pomerania into isolated fragments, Steiner returned to his (Germanisches) Panzer Corps, withdrawing with it into the Altdamm bridgehead on the Oder east of Stettin. Thereafter the Corps was redeployed north of Berlin (*see* Third Panzer Army, 25 February 1945). With responsibility for the defence of Pomerania handed over to Raus, OKH posted Eleventh Army (HQ) to Mecklenburg north of Berlin – to be rebuilt there for operations in the west.

A **new Eleventh Army** under General Walther Lucht, responsible to C-in-C, West (von Runstedt), would subsequently resist British progress on the Weser and in the Hartz Mountains. On 4 May 1945, when operations in north-west Europe concluded with German surrender to Field Marshal Montgomery, 9th and 116th Panzer Division battle groups were serving Eleventh Army as a mobile reserve.

Source Notes and Bibliography

In the process of tracing armoured facts and philosophies for discussion in the present work I have extracted a certain amount of material from previous publications thereby incurring a debt of assistance to the following authors (and publishers):

1. To Rudolf Steiger (Rombach Verlag) for kind permission to quote from *Panzertaktik*; Dr Gerhard Hümmelchen (Bernard and Graef) whose work of joint authorship with Fritz Morzik – *Die Deutschen Transport Flieger in Zweiten Weltkrieges* provided me with the basis for New Horizons in Transport, Part 4, also the late editor B. H. Liddell Hart (Collins) whose Rommel Papers in translation by Paul Findlay with the assistance of Lucie-Maria Rommel, Manfred Rommel and General Fritz Bayerlein provides a valuable insight into Rommel's problems in North Africa; to Dr David Kahn (Hodder and Stoughton) for permission to quote from *Hitler's Spies* and to incorporate extracts into Part 4, The Army's Eye in the Sky.

2. Intelligence publications (used with caution) summarizing the organization and methods of the German Army and Air Force:
Current Reports from overseas, War Office 1944–5.
Brief Notes on the German Army in War, War Office 1940–3.
Periodical Notes on the German Army, War Office 1941–2.
Pocket Book on the German Army, War Office 1943–4.
War Information Circular, GHQ India, 1941–4.

3. British post-war Intelligence publications:
Hinsley F. *British Intelligence in World War II*, vols I–III, HMSO, 1979–88.
March, C. (ed) *Rise and Fall of the German Air Force 1933–45*. Arms & Armour Press, 1983.

4. Publishers in the Bundesrepublic of Germany whose military lists include many unit and campaign histories:
Bernardt and Graefe, Frankfurt (Main): Studien und Documente zur Gesichte des Zweiten Weltkrieges.
DVA Stuttgart: Schriftenreihe des Militärgeschichtlichen Forschumgsamt.
Motorbuch Verlag, Stuttgart.
Musterschmidt Verlag, Gottingen, Frankfurt (Main).
Munin Verlag, Osnabrück.
Podzun-Pallas Verlag, Bad Nauheim: notably the works of Dr Werner Haupt.

Verlag Rombach, Freiburg (Breisgau): Einzelschriften zur Militärischen Gesichte des Zweiten Weltkrieges.
Kurt Vowinckel, Osnabrück: Die Wehrmacht in Kampf.

5. Works consulted to advantage but excluding those of authors named above; the list is by no means a definitive one and is limited by considerations of space to fifty-two authors:

Barnett, Correlli. *The Desert Generals*. George Allen & Unwin, London, 1983
Belchem, David. *Victory in Normandy*. London, 1981
Bennett, Ralph. *Ultra in the West*. London, 1979.
Bond, Brian. *Liddell Hart: A Study of his Military Thought*. London, 1976
Carell, Paul. *Invasion. They're Coming!* London, 1962
Carver, Michael. *The Apostles of Mobility*. London, 1979
Cooper, Matthew. *The German Army: Its Political and Military Failure*. London, 1978
— *The German Air Force: An Anatomy of Failure*. London, 1981
D'Este, Carlo. *Decision in Normandy*. Collins, 1984
Diest, Wilhelm. *The Wehrmacht and German Rearmament*. London, 1981
Erickson, John. *The Road to Stalingrad*. London, 1975
— *The Road to Berlin*. London, 1983
Fleming, Peter. *Invasion 1940*. London, 1957
Fulgate, Brian, I. *Operation 'Barbarossa', 1941*. Presidio Novato, USA, 1984
Fuller, J. F. C. *Armoured Warfare: An annotated edition of FSR III (1932)*. Harrisburg, 1943
— *The Second World War: 1939–45*. London, 1948
Forty, George. *German Tanks of World War II 'In Action'*. London, 1987
Grandais, Albert. *La Bataille du Calvados*. Paris, 1973
Guderian, Heinz, *Die Grundlagen des Panzerangriffs*. Berlin, 1938
— *Die Panzerwaffe (Achtung! Panzer)*, 1943
– Panzer Leader. London, 1952
De'Guingand, Francis. *Operation Victory*. Hodder & Stoughton, London, 1947
Hamilton, Nigel. *Montgomery: The Making of a General*. London, 1981
Hastings, Max. *Overlord*. Joseph/Guild Publishing, London, 1984
Irving, David. *The Rise and Fall of the Luftwaffe*. Boston, 1973

Keegan, John. *Six Armies in Normandy.* London, 1982

Keitel, Wilhelm. *Memoirs.* Kimber, 1965.

Kesselring, Albert. *Memoirs.* Kimber, 1953

Lewin, Ronald. *Rommel as Military Commander.* London, 1971

— *The Life and Death of the Afrika Korps.* Batsford, 1977

Liddell Hart, Basil H. *The Remaking of Modern Armies.* London, 1927

— *The Other Side of the Hill.* London, 1948

Macksey, Kenneth. *Kesselring: The Making of the Luftwaffe.* Batsford, 1978

— *The Tank Pioneers.* London, 1981

Manstein, Erich von. *Verlorene Siege.* Bonn, 1955, published as *Lost Victories.* London, 1958

Martel, Giffard, le Q. *Our Armoured Forces.* London, 1945

Mellenthin, F. W. von. *Panzer Battles.* Cassell, 1956

Montgomery, Bernard L. *Memoirs.* London, 1958

Mueller-Hillebrand, Burkhart. *Das Heer 1933–45.* E. S. Mittler, Frankfurt, 1956

Munzel, Oscar. *Gepanzerte Truppen.* Herford, 1965

Nehring, Walther. *Die Geschichte der Deutschen Panzerwaffe 1916–45.* Stuttgart, 1974

Ogorkiewicz, Richard M. *Armoured Forces.* Arms & Armour Press, London, 1960

Piekalkiewicz, Janusz. *Unternehmen Zitadelle* and other works. Lübbe, 1983, onwards.

Pipet, Albert. *La Trouée de Normandie.* Paris, 1966

— *Mourir à Caen.* Paris, 1974

Rosinski, Herbert. *The German Army.* London, 1939

Ruge, Frederick. *Rommel in Normandy.* London, 1979

Schramm, Percy, E. (ed). *Kriegstagebuch des Oberkommandos der Wehrmacht 1940–41.* Bernardt and Graef Pawlak, 1982

Seaton, Albert. *The German Army.* London, 1982

— *The Russo-German War, 1941–45.* Praeger, 1971

Senger und Etterlin, Frido von. *Neither Hope nor Fear.* Macdonald, 1963 Technical works, 1957 onwards.

Shirer, William, L. *The Rise and Fall of the Third Reich.* London, 1964

Speidel, Hans. *We Defended Normandy.* London, 1951

Stanley, Roy M. *World War II Photo Intelligence.* Charles Scribner's Sons, 1979.

Stoves, Rolf. *Die Gepanzerten und Motorisierten Deutschen Grossverbände 1935–45.* Bad Nauheim, 1986

Strawson, John. *The Battle for North Africa.*

— *Hitler as Military Commander.*

— *The Battle for Berlin.* London, 1969–74

Tessin, Georg. *Verbände und Truppen der Deutschen Wehrmacht und Waffen S.S. 1939–45.* Biblio Verlag, Osnabrück, 1974

Trevor Roper, H. R. *The Last Days of Hitler: Hitler's War Directives 1939–45.* London, 1947, 1964

Warlimont, Walter. *Inside Hitler's Headquarters.* London, 1962

Westphal, Siegfried. *The German Army in the West.* London, 1951

Wheatley, Ronald. *Operation Sea Lion.* London, 1958

Young, Desmond. *Rommel: The Desert Fox.* London, 1950

Photographs and reproduction maps, unless otherwise stated, are from private archives. The author acknowledges the assistance received in this way from Rolf Guttermann and Oswald Finzel; other photographic sources to which credit is due are the Bundesarchiv Coblenz, Daily Express Newspapers, London and the Imperial War Museum, London.

Index

1. Index of German military formations and units

2. Index of German personalities

3. Index of places

1,001 Ingenious gardening Ideas

1,001 Ingenious gardening Ideas

New, Fun, and Fabulous Tips That Will Change
the Way You Garden—Forever!

Deborah L. Martin, editor

Contributing Writers: Sally Jean Cunningham, George DeVault,
Melanie DeVault, Erin Hynes, Tina James, Susan McClure,
Sally Roth, Jo Ellen Meyers Sharp, and Sara Jane von Trapp

Rodale Press, Inc.
Emmaus, Pennsyvania

We're always happy to hear from you. For questions or comments concerning the editorial content of this book, please write to:

Rodale Press, Inc.
Book Readers' Service
33 East Minor Street
Emmaus, PA 18098

Look for other Rodale books wherever books are sold. Or call us at (800) 848-4735.

For more information about Rodale Press and the books and magazines we publish, visit our World Wide Web site at:

http://www.rodalepress.com

Editor: Deborah L. Martin

Contributing Editors: Karen Bolesta, Christine Bucks, and Karen Costello Soltys

Researcher: Heidi A. Stonehill

Cover and Interior Book Designer: Nancy Smola Biltcliff

Layout Designer: Susan P. Eugster

Cover and Interior Illustrator: Elayne Sears

Copy Editors: Christine Bucher, Erana Bumbardatore, and Stacey Ann Follin

Manufacturing Coordinator: Mark Krahforst

Indexer: Lina Burton

Editorial Assistance: Sarah S. Dunn, Susan L. Nickol, and Pamela R. Ruch

RODALE GARDEN BOOKS

Executive Editor: Ellen Phillips

Managing Editor: Fern Marshall Bradley

Associate Art Director: Patricia Field

Associate Copy Manager: Jennifer Hornsby

Studio Manager: Leslie M. Keefe

Production Manager: Robert V. Anderson Jr.

Manufacturing Manager: Mark Krahforst

Library of Congress Cataloging-in-Publication Data

    1,001 ingenious gardening ideas : new, fun, and fabulous tips that will change the way you garden—forever! / Deborah L. Martin, editor; contributing writers, Sally Jean Cunningham...[et al.].

        p.   cm.

    Includes bibliographical references and index.

    ISBN 978-1-60529-814-6

    1. Gardening—Miscellanea.   2. Organic gardening—Miscellanea. I. Martin, Deborah L.   II. Cunningham, Sally Jean.   III. Title: One thousand one ingenious gardening ideas   IV. Title: One thousand and one ingenious gardening ideas

SB453 .A125 1999

635—dc21

                                    99–6038

Distributed in the book trade by St. Martin's Press

2 4 6 8 10 9 7 5 3 1   hardcover

Organic Gardening Starts Here!

Here at Rodale Press, we've been gardening organically for over 50 years—ever since my grandfather J. I. Rodale learned about composting and decided that healthy living starts with healthy soil. In 1940, J. I. started the Rodale Organic Farm to test his theories, and today, the nonprofit Rodale Institute Experimental Farm is still at the forefront of organic gardening and farming research. In 1942, J. I. founded *Organic Gardening* magazine to share his discoveries with gardeners everywhere. His son, my father, Robert Rodale, headed *Organic Gardening* until 1990, and today, the fourth generation of Rodales is growing up with the magazine. Over the years, we've shown millions of readers how to grow bountiful crops and beautiful flowers using nature's own techniques.

In this book, you'll find the latest organic methods and the best gardening advice. We know—because all our authors and editors are passionate about gardening! We feel strongly that our gardens should be safe for our children, pets, and the birds and butterflies that add beauty and delight to our lives and landscapes. Our gardens should provide us with fresh, flavorful vegetables, delightful herbs, and gorgeous flowers. And they should be a pleasure to work in as well as to view.

Sharing the secrets of safe, successful gardening is why we publish books. So come visit us at the Rodale Institute Experimental Farm, where you can tour the gardens every day—we're open year-round. And use this book to create your best garden ever.

Happy gardening!

Maria Rodale

Maria Rodale
Rodale Garden Books

Over the years, we've shown millions of readers how to grow bountiful crops and beautiful flowers using nature's own techniques.

Contents

Out in the Garden

How to Be an Ingenious Gardener

Gardening is about taking chances. Planting a garden is a gamble that the small, dry seeds and tiny plants you place in the soil will grow into something beautiful and productive. Being an *ingenious* gardener means doing things to improve your odds.

In this book, we've gathered more than 1,000 ingenious ideas from gardeners across the country and around the world who have found ways to tip the scales in favor of gardening success. Some of the ideas are remarkably simple, such as using the moistened tip of a toothpick to sow very small seeds. Others are full-scale systems that will let you garden year-round, no

matter where your garden grows. But large or small, complex or simple, every tip in this book has passed this test: A real gardener has used it to make gardening easier, more successful, more productive, and more fun.

Browse for Inspiration

If you're already feeling ingenious, use this book as a springboard to reach new heights of gardening creativity. Browsing through the best ideas from hundreds of other clever gardeners and growers is a great way to cultivate your own gardening know-how. Check out the many "Homegrown Hints" for ideas that have spelled success for "regular" gardeners like Nancy Sutton of Washington State, who aerates her compost with recycled ski poles. You'll also see lots of great tips from commercial growers— people whose livelihoods depend on their gardening skills. Not surprisingly, the tricks that large-scale growers use often make sense in the home garden, too.

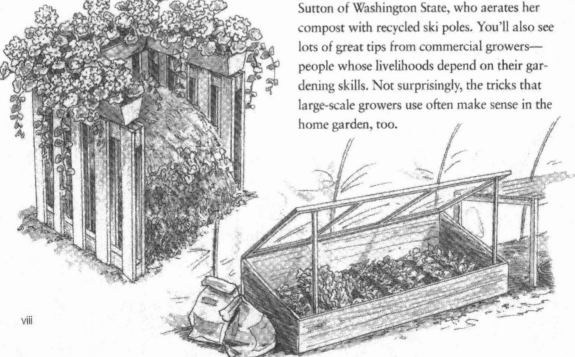

Go Straight to Solutions

You can also use this book to solve problems in your garden. We've arranged the ideas by subject so you can turn to the chapter that interests you and find tips that match your garden's needs. The book is divided into two parts: "Getting Ready to Garden," where you'll find chapters on such topics as soil care, composting, tools, and season extension, and "Out in the Garden," which includes chapters on specific kinds of gardening—vegetable, flower, herb, and more. If you're looking for ingenious ideas for a particular crop, turn to the chapter that covers that type of crop (for example, "Great Vegetable Gardens" or "Helpful Herb Gardening Hints"). Or, if you want ideas for a particular tool, technique, or plant, you can start with the index, where you're sure to pinpoint just the tips you need.

Within each chapter, we've called out certain kinds of ideas that we think you'll find especially useful. Watch for items with the "Problem Solver" logo—these are surefire solutions that other gardeners have proven effective. For example, container plants that dry out too quickly are a thing of the past when you add some compost to the soilless mix in each pot. "Timely Tips" are extra tidbits and twists that add to the great ideas you'll find on every page.

Most of all, have fun with all these ideas, from the amazing array of homegrown tools in Chapter 1 to the many ways to attract birds and butterflies in Chapter 12. Try them in your own gardens and landscapes, and use them as a way to stimulate your own ingenuity. A tip that you pass up on first glance may turn out—with a bit of tweaking—to be just what your garden needs. Gardening is an act of creativity, and every garden you grow will yield its own crop of ingenious ideas.

ingenious \in-'jēn-yəs\ *adj* **1 :** showing originality, resourcefulness, and brilliance of ideas or performance **2 :** distinguished by especial talent at inventing, discovering, or contriving

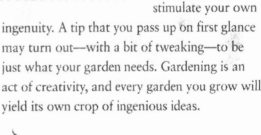

getting ready to
Gard

BEFORE YOU VENTURE into your garden, take a little time to plan your strategy: What will you do differently this year to get bigger yields, brighter flowers, and more fun from your garden? And how can you avoid any problems that have plagued your garden in the past? How will you stop weeds before they even start? What are some quick ways to boost soil fertility? How can you begin gardening earlier and make the growing season longer? What systems can you use to guarantee seed-starting success? Whether you're looking for a nifty tool to make planting a breeze, a simple technique to stretch the gardening season, or the latest ways to outsmart pests, in these chapters you'll find hundreds of garden-tested tips to help give your garden a great beginning.

chapter 1

terrific

Tools & Gadgets

What gardener isn't on the lookout for gizmos and gadgets that can make life in the garden easier? You'll find ideas in this chapter for tools you can make yourself and tools that can be improvised, scrounged, or recycled. You'll also discover new uses for traditional tools. There's no need to ever throw away a plastic soda bottle, bald tire, milk jug, or broken tool again! Breathe new life into these castoffs and others—turn them into handy implements that will make gardening a breeze.

2

Roll Out
the Barrel

Big planters don't have to cost a fortune. "I use the rugged, dense plastic barrels you find at recycling centers," reveals Pennsylvania garden writer Duane Campbell. "They run about $20 and come in blue, black, and dark green."

Duane says the barrels are about 38 inches high and easy to cut with a jigsaw. "Just drill a small hole in the middle, stick the blade in, and roll the barrel as you cut."

Duane recommends 12-inch-tall planters, so after he cuts the barrel into two 19-inch-tall halves, he cuts a 7-inch band from the top of each to make his foot-tall planters.

He then uses the two 7-inch-tall hoops to create small raised beds in his perennial garden. Duane has discovered that if he fills the hoops with very loose soil mix, he can create the perfect drainage conditions that many rock garden and alpine plants require.

So for $20, Duane creates two handsome, durable plant containers plus the borders for two miniature raised beds. What a bargain!

Plants in Your **Drawers**

"When we remodeled our kitchen, I saved several of the old wooden drawers that were about 3 × 3 feet," recalls free-lance garden writer Veronica Lorson Fowler of Ames, Iowa. "I drilled drainage holes in the bottoms and used them to start cuttings of 'Hicksii' Anglo-japanese yew (*Taxus × media* 'Hicksii')." Veronica adds that you can use drawers for rooting cuttings of just about anything, and she has even used them as indoor planters to grow lettuces in winter.

Mini-greenhouses

"I have discovered that the translucent, under-the-bed, plastic storage containers—the kind with snap-on lids—make excellent miniature green-houses when turned upside down over seedling trays," says horticulturist Paul B. Barden of Corvallis, Oregon. "You can easily remove the plastic tray cover to allow air circulation on warm days, or leave it on when you have the seedling tray outdoors and need to keep your plants safe from marauding birds."

problem SOLVer — MOBILE PLASTIC PLANT HOSPITAL

Use a plastic soda bottle to aid ailing plants. With a sharp knife, cut a 2-liter plastic soda bottle in half horizontally. The top half becomes a movable plant hospital for newly planted seedlings or plants that are suffering a bit. Just put the top over them to create a miniterrarium for them until they recover. As for the bottom half, cut drainage holes in it, then use it to raise seedlings. The bottoms of soda bottles also work well as flowerpots. Young children especially appreciate these, since the containers are clear and they can see the plant roots and can check that the soil is damp.

Anchored Milk Jugs

Covering cold-sensitive trans-plants with plastic milk jugs is a popular way of encouraging growth and preventing frost damage early in the season. New York home gardener Herb Mason offers this clever method for keeping those jugs in place. "I cut around the bottom of a jug on three sides, leaving a hinged flap. After I put the mini-greenhouse over young plants, I hold it in place by weighing down the flap with a mound of soil or a rock." Herb finds he can use these miniature greenhouses for two years before the plastic breaks down.

Herb says he sometimes cuts 1 to 1½ inches off the top of the jugs to make watering easier and allow more light to reach the transplants.

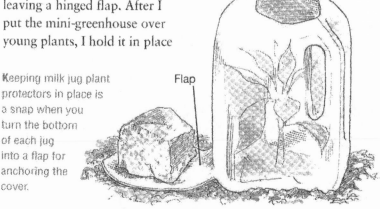

Keeping milk jug plant protectors in place is a snap when you turn the bottom of each jug into a flap for anchoring the cover.

Flap

Soda Bottle *Seedling* Nursery

Plastic 2-liter soda bottles make a good nursery for seedlings and transplants. Cut a 3-inch-wide flap in one side, starting at the bottleneck end and ending about 2 inches from the bottom. The flap gives you access for planting and watering and lets you adjust the humidity as your seedlings grow.

Then punch some drainage holes in the other side, and lay the bottle on its side with the flap facing up. Fill it about halfway with soil, then sow seeds in it. Try not to bend the flap back too much, so that it will stay closed and hold moisture in while the seeds germinate. When the plants get too big, you can either cut off the flap or move the plants to another container.

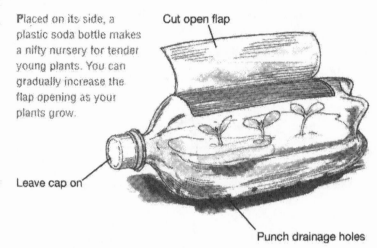

Placed on its side, a plastic soda bottle makes a nifty nursery for tender young plants. You can gradually increase the flap opening as your plants grow.

Cut open flap

Leave cap on

Punch drainage holes

Slick Mower *Trick* I

Moist grass clippings tend to clump and stick to the underside of lawn mowers. To keep them from clogging your mower, try this slick trick.

"Last fall, I noticed the paint on the underside of the mulching mower deck was peeling, and the roughness was letting the grass clippings build up badly," recalls botanist Kay Lancaster of the Northern Willamette Valley in Oregon.

"I wire-brushed the bottom of the mower and repainted it with slip plate, a graphite-based paint that farmers use to help grain slide out of a grain wagon easily. The clippings wash off the bottom of the mower easily now, and the buildup during mowing has been minimal."

According to Kay, slip plate is available at most farm stores and comes either as brush-on or spray paint. "It only comes in an ugly gray color, and it is electrically conductive. It sure seems to work for keeping gunk from building up on the mower deck."

Slick Mower *Trick* II

Here's another way to prevent grass clipping buildup on the underside of your lawn mower. Karen Bolesta, of Allentown, Pennsylvania, learned this trick from her father.

Periodically wax the underside of your lawn mower with automotive paste wax. If you begin to notice a bit of clumping or buildup, you'll know it's time to clean under the mower deck and apply a new coating of wax.

Heavy Crop? No Flop!

If you're tired of plant cages that flop under a heavy crop, here's the answer. "Concrete reinforcing wire makes the very best tomato cages," insists garden writer Duane Campbell of Towanda, Pennsylvania. "Those cages also work well for small vining veggies like malabar, spinach, minimelons, and cukes. They're especially nice for container-grown vining crops. And when stretched straight between two poles, a length of concrete reinforcing wire will support a major melon crop."

Duane adds that the wire cages are also great for tall but floppy flowers like delphiniums and dahlias. Cut a cage in half to make two shorter cages for peonies and other shorter perennials.

To cut the wire, Duane recommends using light bolt cutters, very heavy wire cutters, or "for the tool-impaired," a hacksaw. Take the same precautions you would when cutting any kind of fencing: Weigh it down so that it doesn't roll back up as you work with it (cinder blocks work well as weights), wear eye protection in case tiny clipped pieces go flying, and wear heavy work gloves so that you don't poke yourself with newly cut ends.

Timely tip

And what about maintaining the cages? Duane says, "After ten years or so, when the prongs break off the bottom, cut off the bottom circle of wire and you'll have all new prongs—although your cage will now be 6 inches shorter."

Reinforcing Wire Cages— *A Real Plus*

Pennsylvania garden writer Duane Campbell has another plant support solution made of concrete reinforcing wire.

"For totally floppy plants, like euphorbia, you can cut the wire into a fat plus-sign shape, and bend it into a cube with one open side," Duane explains. Set the cage over the plant, poking the open wire ends into the ground, and the cage will support both the sides and top of the plant.

Bend sides up to form a cage

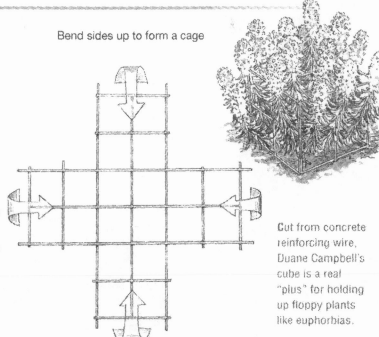

Cut from concrete reinforcing wire, Duane Campbell's cube is a real "plus" for holding up floppy plants like euphorbias.

Water *New Trees* with Ease

Watering new trees can be time-consuming, but with this submerged PVC pipe trick, you can save time and direct the water flow right where you want it—at the roots.

"Even though we get a fair amount of rain, getting trees established in our clay soil can be a challenge," admits Beverly Earls, Master Gardener from Memphis. "I've had success with using an 18-inch length of PVC pipe, in which we drilled ½-inch holes spaced about 1 inch apart. My husband then uses an auger attached to an electric drill to dig holes near the outer edge of the rootball of newly planted trees and shrubs (to avoid damaging the trunk or stem), and I push the pipe down into the soil beside the new tree."

Beverly notes that the top of the pipe should be level with the ground so you don't hit it with the lawnmower. Also, "If the ground is not level, put the pipe on the higher side so water runs toward the tree as you pour water into the pipe. This watering pipe method gets water to the roots of the tree slowly and works especially well on high ground where water runs off before it soaks into the soil."

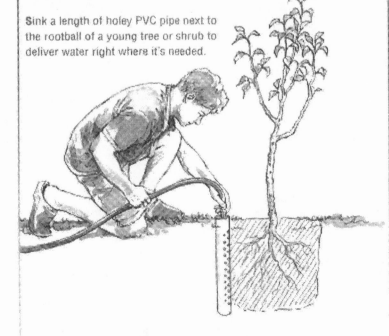

Sink a length of holey PVC pipe next to the rootball of a young tree or shrub to deliver water right where it's needed.

Garden *Groomer*

Combine two broken tools into one great homemade garden groomer.

"This is a bit prosaic, but handier than it sounds," insists Pennsylvania garden writer Duane Campbell. "When we moved into our home, there was a broken garden rake head in the garage. I fitted it with an 18-inch piece from the broken handle of another out-of-commission tool. It's perfect for grooming raised beds."

See Your *Dentist* Twice a Year

Put old toothbrushes to work when you sow seeds.

"Use the handle end of an old toothbrush as a dibble for making planting holes for medium-size and large seeds," suggests Sharon Gordon, of Ohio. "If you have several old toothbrushes, you can mark a different planting depth on each handle."

Timely tip

Once Sharon's seeds are sown, she uses the other end of the toothbrush to pull the soil over the seed, making this a double-duty tool.

Recycled Tire **Strawberry** Pot

For strawberries, Colin Wilson of Hull, England, suggests placing three tires on the ground to form a triangle. "Fill the center of each tire with potting soil. Then place three more tires on top of the others, but rotate them slightly away from the triangle below, so that pockets of soil show on the outside of the stack. Fill that layer with soil. Repeat with two or three more layers, then put strawberry plants in the pockets." Don't worry about the soil falling out of the tires that aren't in the first layer—the sidewalls are strong enough to hold the soil in place.

Stacking pattern

The next time you replace your tires, rotate them into a tiered strawberry planter. Or ask your local garage if they have tires to spare.

Clean *Protection* for Bulbs

An old washing machine drum offers perfect protection for your bulbs so burrowing animals can't devour them. "Our appliance repair technician gave me two old noncorroding, ceramic-coated, galvanized steel washing machine baskets— the agitator drums," recalls Nancy Lewis of Saint Helens, Oregon. Nancy sank one into the flowerbed, with the top flush with the ground, filled it with soil, then planted tulip bulbs in it. "No more rodent feasts!" Nancy says. "The washer drum prevents animals that use mole runs from digging into the bed from the sides."

Nancy uses the other basket as a planter in the greenhouse. It's filled with potting soil and planted with basil and 'Sun Gold' tomatoes. "The hole in the center of the drum, where the agitator used to be, makes an excellent support for the pole I tie the tomato plants to," Nancy says. "And the holes in the sides of the drum keep

Turn the drum from a washed-up washing machine into a below-ground planter to keep burrowing animals away from your bulbs.

the potting soil inside from getting too soggy."

Hold the Soap

Vickie Perrine of Curtice, Ohio, found this creative use for a broken hoe. "I hung the blade end of a broken hoe next to my hose, handle end up. It's a handy shelf for a bar of soap."

Depending on the length of the broken handle pieces, you can recycle them, too. A long section makes a sturdy stake. Or try George DeVault's tip below and sharpen one end to turn it into a dibble for making holes while standing.

When a tool breaks, there's bound to be another good use for it. Without its handle, a hoe blade makes a nifty outdoor soap holder.

Cast-Off Tools Become Handy Dibbles

When it comes to turning cast-off tools into handy dibbles, ingenious gardeners find that almost anything goes.

"I had one of those three-pronged cultivators that you hold in your hand for loosening the soil," recalls Audrey Bowman, a home gardener in Citrus Heights, California. "The weld on my cultivator broke, leaving only one prong, so now I use it to poke holes in the ground for seeds. It makes a nice round hole a bit larger than a pencil hole."

You could also convert an old set of screwdrivers, such as you might find at a garage sale, into dibbles for different seed sizes and planting depths.

problem solver

BROKEN-HANDLE DIBBLE

"You can pay $10 or more for a dibble from any of the garden catalogs, or you can make your own for free," observes garden writer George DeVault of Emmaus, Pennsylvania. "The dibble we use at Pheasant Hill Farm is simply a broken hoe handle. The handle broke at an angle, so it was easy to sharpen the broken end into a good point. Our dibble is about 20 inches long, so we can push it straight down into the soil while standing. It's just the ticket for making those nice, deep holes."

George suggests that a tool with a T-grip on top would make an even better dibble. "If you poke lots of holes all at once, remember that holding the rounded end of a dibble tends to cause blisters on the palm of your hand, so wear gloves."

Tired Potatoes
Grow Up

Even if your garden space is limited, you can still have an abundant harvest of potatoes. The secret is to grow up, not out, by recycling used tires to make space-saving raised beds.

To grow potatoes in a small space, advises Colin Wilson of Hull, England, place a tire on the ground, fill it with good, loose potting soil, and plant a few seed potatoes. "When they begin to sprout," Colin instructs, "place another tire on top of the first one and fill it with soil. Each time you see potato sprouts pushing through, add another tire to the stack and fill it with soil. Continue until you run out of tires or the stack gets too high to be stable." When it's time to harvest, unstack the tires. Your yield depends on how tall your tire stack is, but Colin estimates that you should get five to six times more potatoes than you would if you planted them in the ground.

A stack of used tires filled with soil yields spud-growing success in a small space.

More Pointers for Tired Potatoes

Marg Millard of Nova Scotia adds these pointers for growing potatoes in tires:

~ Set up the tires in full sun.

~ Check the soil daily to see if you need to water. The black tires hold a lot of heat, so the soil dries out very quickly.

~ Add soil gradually, up to about the top two sets of leaves on the sprouts. The buried portion of the stem will produce the potato tubers, and the stem above the soil line will produce more stem and leaves.

~ If you cut off the smooth sidewalls—leaving just the tread part—the tires are lighter and easier to stack. Tear-down and harvest are a lot easier, as well.

Stop the Rust

Trying to keep rust and dirt off your clean tools? "Just give them a shot of nonstick cooking spray, such as Pam," recommends freelance garden writer Veronica Lorson Fowler of Ames, Iowa.

homegrown HINTS

THE PERFECT PLANTING GRID

If your efforts to eyeball the right spacing at planting time leave your garden looking lopsided, head to the garden with a section of concrete reinforcing wire. "Each square of the wire is 6 inches on a side," notes garden writer Duane Campbell of Towanda, Pennsylvania. "Four squares of wire make 1 square foot. So, for example, if you want to plant peppers at one plant per square foot, put one transplant at the intersection of four squares. Beans can be planted one seed per 6-inch square. Onions can go two per 6-inch square, in opposite corners."

The squares also provide a frame of reference that helps you broadcast seeds more easily. For instance, instead of scattering carrot seeds over a large garden bed, you'll get more evenly spaced results if you broadcast them over the smaller, 6-inch areas one at a time. You'll still have to thin the seedlings, but you're less likely to have clumps of carrots in some spots and bare patches in others.

There's no reason to leave your grid in place once your garden has been planted. You can simply lift this spacing tool off the garden plot and store it in your shed, garage, or basement until next year.

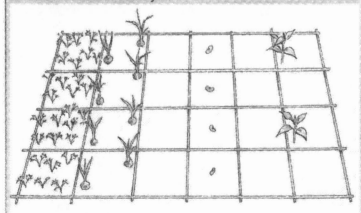

When you use a planting grid made from concrete reinforcing wire, it's easy to space seeds and transplants evenly.

Nimble Fingers and Clean Nails

If you can't stand garden gloves but don't like grubby fingernails either, take a tip from Mary Weaver of Knoxville, Tennessee.

"My favorite garden tool of late is a pair of disposable latex gloves, which I use as weeding gloves," says Mary. "It's nearly impossible for me to hand-weed in fabric or leather gloves (I can't feel the weeds), but these things are as good as bare hands—with the added advantage of preventing the perennial mud under the nails."

According to Mary, the most economical place to find these gloves is in the paint section of home-improvement centers. "And, if you don't puncture them while you're weeding," she adds, "you can even wash and reuse them, to really get your money's worth."

Timely tip

Mary adds that once a latex glove is shot, you can still get some use out of it. She cuts off the fingers and uses them to tie vines to trellises.

problem SOLVer

POISON IVY PATROL

Here's another great use for latex gloves—the heavy-duty dishwashing kind—from gardener Deb Martin of Allentown, Pennsylvania. The next time you spy a bit of poison ivy growing in your yard or garden, slip on an extra-large pair of dishwashing gloves (the longer they are, the more protection they give to your arms), and pull the poison ivy, roots and all, out of the ground. Place the plants in a plastic grocery bag, tie the handles closed, and toss them in the trash can. Toss the gloves out, too, so that you don't get the oil on anything else. Avoiding a bad case of poison ivy is well worth the price of the disposable gloves.

"To get the most out of a pair of gloves, I wait for a cool, cloudy day in early summer, then I patrol the whole yard, pulling out every piece of poison ivy I see," Deb says.

Tidy Tote

"I keep a 1-gallon plastic container in my garden cart to hold bits of broken glass, old plant labels, and other trash that shows up in the garden," says gardener and freelance garden writer Veronica Lorson Fowler of Ames, Iowa.

"I keep another container by my compost heap to collect old plant labels, plant ties, Legos, and other non-decomposing surprises."

Flat Shade for *Baby* Plants

Here's an easy way to keep young transplants from wilting while they adapt to the outdoors. "I use an ordinary, empty plastic plant flat with drainage holes, turned upside down, as temporary shade when I'm putting out new transplants," explains California home gardener Karen Winters. "I just prop the flat up on a few upside-down pots. It provides filtered light while the little plants are adjusting to the sunlight."

Besides clay or plastic pots, you can also use bricks, large yogurt containers filled with soil, or anything else that is heavy enough to stay put and high enough to elevate the flat over the plants. To keep the flat from blowing off, weigh it down with a small rock on each end.

A propped-up seed flat makes a great awning to shade young transplants on sunny days.

homegrown HINTS

TRÉS TRAY

If you like to bottom-water seedlings that you start indoors, you'll need a supply of sturdy, waterproof containers with low sides to set the pots or soil blocks in. Lee Lawton, of Over the Rainbow Farm in Junction City, Oregon, offers two inexpensive alternatives to specialized plant trays—Styrofoam meat trays and cafeteria trays.

"The butcher at your favorite grocery store is usually willing to give you a good deal on meat trays. You can wash and reuse them if you're careful with them. An even better choice is cafeteria trays, which are available, new or used, at many restaurant supply stores." Lee says, "I've purchased them for as little as three for $2. They last forever and are just perfect for the job!"

Diapers for Baby Plants

Tired of constantly watering young plants? Diaper them instead. "I want to water my seedlings only every four days, because the growing shed is not in the house, and in winter I don't care to run out back every day," explains Amy O'Donnell of Alexandria, Virginia. "So I 'borrowed' a newborn-size diaper from my neighbor. I laid it in the bottom of the tray liner under my 12 × 24-inch flats, with the plastic side down. I placed the seed pots on top. Twice a week, I pull one pot out and pour water in. The diaper soaks up the water and spreads it through the tray to all the pots."

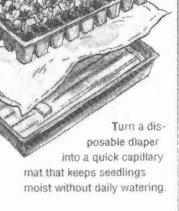

Turn a disposable diaper into a quick capillary mat that keeps seedlings moist without daily watering.

Measuring Tools

Here's a way to keep a measuring device handy when you work in the garden. "Use a permanent marker to calibrate the handles of your commonly used garden tools, such as a hoe or spade, in feet and inches," says Ada Davis of West Fork, Arkansas. Then, instead of running for a tape measure, you can easily measure the length of a bed, the distance between rows or plants, or the width you want your garden path to be.

Strawberry Basket Cover-Ups

Strawberry baskets can provide a bit of shade for tender new transplants. "If the weather is quite warm in late spring and early summer," says Sue Murphy, greenhouse manager of the Utah State University/Utah Botanical Garden in Ogden, Utah. "I use up-ended plastic mesh strawberry containers over some of the new plants to give them a bit of shade for a few days."

Sue adds that she pushes twigs through the sides of the baskets and into the ground to keep them from blowing away.

Jug-Handle Cultivator

A cut-up plastic milk jug works as a shallow cultivator. "Cut a triangular shape from the handle side of the jug, leaving enough plastic to provide a good stiff edge," says Annetta Green of Longwood, Florida. "Make it long enough to get a little of the bottom curve. With the handle still attached, it works as a small hoe for those little weeds that get in between plants." In a pinch, it also doubles as a funnel or as a small shovel or scraper for planting.

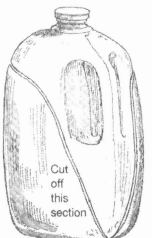

Cut off this section

Cut a triangular chunk that includes the handle from a sturdy plastic jug, and you'll have one handy—and free—cultivator.

Timely tip

Since you're cutting so much of the milk jug away when you use Annetta's cultivator idea, don't let the scraps go to waste. Use the remaining portion of the jug as a cloche to protect young transplants while letting in light and keeping plants moist.

homegrown HINTS

JUG INSULATORS FOR PLANTS

Opaque plastic jugs filled with water can help protect your plants from an ill-timed hard freeze.

"Use a dark-colored jug, like those for laundry detergent or antifreeze," advises Phil Uecker, a certified organic producer in Covington, Texas. "Dark jugs work better than clear milk jugs because they absorb heat. I put three filled jugs around a seedling or small transplant and four around a larger plant. Throw a blanket over them and you're good down to 24°F or so."

Phil says this method of frost protection lets him get tomatoes and peppers out a full month before the last frost date.

Army-Issue Digger

When a spade is too big and a trowel is too small, try an entrenching tool. Garden writer Duane Campbell says, "This infantry tool is a small folding shovel available at Army surplus stores or sporting goods stores that sell camping supplies. It's larger than a trowel and smaller than a spade—perfect for raised beds or crowded perennial borders."

homegrown HINTS

GARDEN ART DOES DOUBLE DUTY

Your old dishes can find a new life as useful garden art. "My daughter begged slightly imperfect pieces of glazed pottery from a neighborhood potter who was going to throw them out," recalls garden writer Erin Hynes of Chapel Hill, North Carolina. "She brought home teapots, mugs, and a pitcher that look fine, with just a chip or crack here and there."

When Erin's daughter got tired of her pottery treasures, Erin snatched them up to use in the garden, where she arranged them to look like a hastily abandoned Mad Hatter's tea party.

You can do the same thing with old chipped dishes, ceramic ware, and other treasures gathered from garage sales and flea markets.

Bricks Prevent Plant *Heaving*

To keep iris rhizomes and the roots of other perennials from heaving out of the soil during the winter's freeze-thaw cycles, try this heavy idea from Ginny Prins of British Columbia.

"I put a rock or brick on top of each newly planted iris before freeze-up," says Ginny. "Then I remove the bricks after the spring thaw, since iris rhizomes need to bake in the sun. It really works!"

Hanger Pins

Clothes hangers make inexpensive—or free—garden pins. "Use wire clippers to cut the curved tips and the corners off wire hangers," suggests Ada Davis of West Fork, Arkansas. "Use the sections as earth staples to hold down the bottom of temporary fencing or to secure soaker hoses."

If you run out of curves, you can use other parts of hangers to make more staples, but you'll have to bend them into shape yourself.

Cut corners and curved tips off wire hangers, and use the resulting pins to hold down hoses or row covers.

Protect Your Pants from Your *Pruners*

That old eyeglasses case can save you from poking holes in your pants. "Protect your pruners and your pants by using an eyeglasses case— the style where you slip the glasses in from one end— as a holder for the pruners," recommends Terry Klokeid of Amblewood Farm on SaltSpring Island, British Columbia. The padded eyeglasses case can protect your pants pocket from a folding pruning saw, too.

The *Tootsie* Temperature Test, Part I

Put your best foot forward when checking the temperature of your soil. If you can't wait to get out in the garden each spring and you're anxious to walk barefoot and feel the soil between your toes, this tootsie temperature test may be great for you to try.

"I tend to use my feet to see if the soil is warm enough for planting, because I can never find my thermometer," explains Natalie McNair-Huff, an organic gardener in Tacoma, Washington.

"I walk barefoot on the edge of my garden plot to test the soil temperature. If my feet start to hurt from the cold, I know the soil is 40°F or colder, and it's too early to plant anything. If I can walk a short distance without my feet hurting, but it's still not really comfortable, I know the soil is close to 50°F. If the soil feels 'mud-between-your-toes' great, I know it's nearing 60°F, and it's warm enough for transplants."

Your feet may be more or less sensitive than Natalie's, so you may want to "calibrate" your feet the first time by comparing your "feet" reading with one taken with a soil thermometer.

And, of course, you'll want to walk just along the edge, like Natalie does, so you don't compact your garden soil too much.

The *Tootsie* Temperature Test, Part II

Amy LeBlanc of Whitehill Farm in East Wilton, Maine, is another gardener who likes to use her bare feet to determine when it's time to plant her vegetables.

"I wait until I feel it's 'no pain,' but still chilly, to plant the peas and spinach," says Amy. "The no-chill point is safe for most transplants, like onions, cabbages, and broccoli."

Amy adds that, "The 'warm-as-toast' feeling is a requirement for planting beans and pole beans and transplanting tender seedlings like tomatoes, peppers, and eggplants."

problem solver — BLADE PROTECTOR

If you or your neighbor are having vinyl siding installed, save any scraps of the finishing strip. "The finishing strip is a long, narrow piece of siding material that is folded over so that the last sheet of siding can be slipped in and held tightly," explains Terry Klokeid of Amblewood Farm on SaltSpring Island, British Columbia.

"The finishing strip will grip any narrow blade that is slid into it, and it's easy to pull the blade out again. I use finishing strip to protect blades on garden tools, such as pruning saws, knives, and hoes, and other tools such as drywall saws and drawknives. Just cut the strip to the appropriate length for your tool," says Terry.

If you're cutting a small amount of the siding, you can get away with using a pair of craft scissors. If you happen to own tin snips, they'll work even better.

Mini *blinds* Make Mini *markers*

"I use an old miniblind, cut up into little pieces, to mark plants," says Pat Kolb of Phoenix, Arizona. "Write on it with a permanent marker, or with a pencil if you want to reuse it. You can even poke a hole in the miniblind and tie it to a larger plant."

Stirring Plant Labels

Veronica Lorson Fowler, of Ames, Iowa, advises, "Those paint stirrers that they give you at the hardware store make good plant labels. I always grab a handful!"

Depressing Plant Markers

"Use tongue depressors as plant markers," says Cyndi Lauderdale, horticulture agent with the North Carolina Cooperative Extension Service. "Depending on how many you need, they are cheap, or free from your doctor. You can also get them at craft stores." To identify a plant, write on the depressors with an indelible marker.

homegrown HINTS

MEAT TRAYS MARK THE SPOT

"I put those wimpy Styrofoam meat trays to use in my greenhouse," says Amy LeBlanc of Whitehill Farm, East Wilton, Maine. "I use a paper cutter to nip off the curved edges and cut the trays into strips. I cut the strips into slim triangles for plant markers. A medium-point ballpoint pen will write on them just fine and leave an impression in the foam, as well. I sell 3,000 to 4,000 heirloom tomato and pepper seedlings every spring, all with meat tray tags."

Laminated *Labels*

Home gardener Karen Helfert of Rockville, Maryland, offers some advice on an easy, inexpensive way to make long-lasting, waterproof plant labels.

"To make long-lived plant tags, buy plastic laminating sheets, not adhesive shelf paper. Print the plant information on squares of paper. Remove the protective layer from one laminating sheet, lay it sticky side up, and arrange the paper squares so that you leave approximately ½ to ¾ inch of space on the sides and bottom and at least 1 inch on the top. Generous spacing is better than too close."

Karen says to then apply a second laminating sheet, sticky side down, sandwiching the paper squares between the two sheets.

"Cut out the individual labels and use a paper hole puncher to make a hole about ½ inch from the top of each label," says Karen.

Use a twist tie to hang the label from the plant. Or fasten the label to a metal stake that you stick in the pot or into the ground.

Timely tip

Since the laminated labels are coated on both sides, you can make the labels double-sided by writing information on both sides of the paper. Make your labels more useful by including the plant name on one side and the care information on the other.

Clay Pot
Plant Pokes

Here's another clever idea for do-it-yourself plant labels. "I use broken clay pot shards as plant markers," says Candy Sheagley, a gardener in Brookston, Indiana.

"I write the plant name in indelible marker. For a personalized tuck-in gift tag, I paint the shards with fancy flowers or another garden theme."

problem
solver

RECYCLED CANS CAN'T MISS

Nancy Sutton, a home gardener from Federal Way, Washington, recycles soda cans to label her plants. To make long-lasting, nonfading plant tags, use craft scissors to cut the sides out of aluminum soda pop cans, then cut them to the desired size, says Nancy.

"Fold over one corner to make it double thick for strength, then punch a hole through the doubled corner with a paper hole puncher. Write on the tags firmly with a ballpoint pen to engrave the name. Then use thin wire to loosely attach the tag to a branch, or use 16- to 18-gauge wire to stick the tag into the ground. The labels should stay put and be readable forever," Nancy says.

Bucket Seats

If you tire of crouching and stooping while working in the garden, try this tip from Floridian Annetta Green, a home gardener. "In our garden, we use old 5-gallon buckets to sit on while weeding. We use outdoor materials glue to attach a small cushion or foam padding to the lid to make the seat comfy. If the work needs a closer look, you can lie across the cushioned lid and have two hands free.

"What's more, you can keep tools in the bucket—small scissors, a plastic sieve from a beach set, and more conventional garden tools—so they're handy as you walk through the garden and see a plant or weed that needs attention."

Annetta adds that you can also attach the cushion with Velcro, which makes the cushion easy to remove and launder. "Use some self-stick Velcro for the plastic lid and the sew-on type for the cushion."

Lots of gardeners use 5-gallon buckets in the garden—for carrying compost, weeding, and more. Make yours more useful—and more comfy—by adding a cushion and turning it into a portable weeding seat.

Funnel-*to*-Furrow Pipeline

Make a handy seed-planting tube so you won't have to stoop or bend to sow your seeds. "Use duct tape to attach a funnel to a 1-inch-wide length of PVC pipe," says Sharon Gordon of Ohio. (Choose a length of pipe that is comfortable for your height.)

"Then, open a furrow with a hoe, position the pipe over the furrow, and drop in the seed. Cover the furrow with a hoe after planting all the seeds in the row."

Planting Hole **Plunger**

Here's another back-saving device to use at planting time from Yvonne Savio, gardening education coordinator for the Los Angeles County Cooperative Extension Service.

"To punch planting holes for seeds like corn and beans without bending, place a rubber washer around a length of dowel at the correct planting depth," says Yvonne. "Move the washer up or down the dowel to adjust for different seed depths."

No-Turn *Compost* Tools, Part **I**

"The best and cheapest all-purpose compost tool is a 3- to 4-foot length of ½- or ⅜-inch rebar, the metal rod used in reinforced concrete," recommends Don Boekelheide, who coordinates and teaches community composting classes in Charlotte, North Carolina.

Don says that rebar cut to this length is usually available at large home-improvement centers, hardware stores, or lumberyards, and it generally costs less than a dollar.

"Rebar is perfect for poking through your compost to improve aeration. It's strong enough to open a passage—even in a new heap full of tough leaves or straw—creating a hole for adding kitchen scraps deep in the pile. By putting scraps in the center of the compost, you'll avoid any insect and critter problems."

Don adds that rebar offers another plus for composters. "As a bonus, the rod heats up, providing a low-cost 'thermometer' to show whether your pile is heating in the middle."

problem **SOLVer**

FREE PLANTING TUBES ARE HIDING IN YOUR HOME

Kay Lancaster, an Oregon gardener, recommends planting seeds through a tube, especially if you suffer from arthritis. Here are some of her suggestions for back-saving items you may find around the house or shed that will work great for planting larger seeds.

"Rummage around in the scrap pile to see if you can find a 3- or 4-foot piece of PVC pipe, electrical conduit, or skinny, lightweight pipe of some sort. Those of you with golfers in the family, see if your golfer uses the plastic tubes that keep the handles of the clubs from banging together in the bag." Kay also recommends the cardboard roll from gift-wrap tubes or a plastic shower curtain rod cover as planting tube ideas.

"Trace the planting line with a hoe or dibble, then walk along the line, dropping your seeds down the tube. Cover with a hoe or your foot after you're done planting."

homegrown HINTS

SKI POLE COMPOST POKER

Nancy Sutton, of Washington State, has her own method for making lightweight compost pokers. "I use old ski poles. They're usually aluminum, lightweight, smooth, and sharply pointed," says Nancy. "I remove the basket, and now I have an invaluable tool to aerate my compost, which is in a recycled plastic, perforated bin. I don't have to turn the bin because I can easily plunge the pole to the bottom and then rotate the top, make a circle as large as I can manage, and repeat this at various locations in the pile."

To remove the basket from the ski pole, you may need a hacksaw or a pair of pliers, depending on whether the basket is made of metal or plastic.

No-Turn Compost Tools, Part II

To go along with his rebar poker, Don Boekelheide also uses a tool he calls a hole enlarger and scraps poker.

1. Cut off one end of a 4-foot length of 2 × 4 at a 45-degree angle.

2. Drill a 1-inch hole 6 inches from the other end.

3. Put a 12-inch length of ¾-inch pipe through the hole as a handle.

"I open a hole in the compost with the rebar, then use the 2 × 4 tool to enlarge the hole," Don explains. "The pipe handle gives great leverage." Don adds kitchen scraps deep in the center of the pile, where hot microbial activity makes short work of everything, even citrus peels. "The 2 × 4 is great for ramrodding the scraps into the pile and covering them with material to avoid pests and smells."

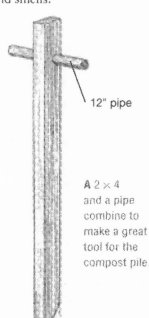

12" pipe

A 2 × 4 and a pipe combine to make a great tool for the compost pile.

Totally Tubular Seed Planting

If bending to plant seeds bothers your back, try this tidy tip from Donna Warren of Tennessee. "Because of a back condition, I try to garden without crouching," Donna says. "So I plant with a vacuum cleaner tube."

Donna drops the seeds through the vacuum cleaner tube into prepared soil, spacing the seeds according to the directions printed on the seed packet.

"I use the handle of a rake to push the seed to the right depth. If it's a new bed where soil still crusts, I funnel some compost on top of the seed, again using the vacuum cleaner tube. Then I tamp the soil in place with the business end of the rake to firm it."

homegrown HINTS

NO BIRDS ALLOWED!

Birds enjoy the vegetable garden just as much as humans do. But birds don't always wait for the veggies to mature. They just help themselves the minute they spy those tender seedlings. "Use plastic mesh baskets that cherry tomatoes or strawberries are sold in to protect newly sprouted seedlings such as corn, cucumbers, melons, and squash from birds," recommends Yvonne Savio, gardening education coordinator for the Los Angeles County Cooperative Extension Service.

"By the time the seedlings are tall enough to reach through the tops of the baskets, it's safe to remove them because the plants are no longer as tender and delectable as the birds prefer." The baskets also provide a temporary barrier against nibbling rabbits and voles.

Handle Pads Pad Hands

If the wooden handles on your rakes, wheelbarrow, and other garden implements are giving you blisters, head to the bike shop. "I've discovered that the thick, spongy, tube-shaped cushions bicycle shops sell for handlebars protect my hands from the wear and tear of wooden handles," reports garden writer Erin Hynes of Chapel Hill, North Carolina. "They can be a bit tricky to slip on. I find it helps to lubricate the handle and the inside of the tube with petroleum jelly or liquid dish soap."

Durable Plant Ties

Many people who suffer from respiratory problems use canisters of supplemental oxygen to aid in breathing. The tubing that connects to the oxygen canisters can also help in the garden. Susan Sam, a home gardener in El Reno, Oklahoma, has found that oxygen tubing—which must be changed fairly often—makes wonderful plant ties. "I have used it for everything from small trees to tomatoes to tall flowers, to even an emergency gate latch. It's soft and has never damaged anything that I have used it on."

Umbrella Cloche

Broken umbrella? "Take off the fabric, cover the metal frame with floating row cover—or the cover of your choice—and you have a cloche," points out Stephanie Ferguson of Indianapolis, Indiana. "When you don't need it for your plants, you can call it into duty as a handy gadget for keeping flies off food at a picnic."

Tomato Cages That Won't Blow Away

"In my part of West Texas, it isn't uncommon to experience wind gusts of 70 to 80 miles per hour during thunderstorms," says Debi Stewart of Abilene, Texas.

To keep her tomato cages from becoming airborne, Debi uses scraps of PVC pipe to anchor them. She hammers three pipes into the ground around the tomato cages, which are 6 feet tall, about 4 feet in diameter, and made of concrete reinforcing wire or other heavy fencing material. Then she lashes the cages, near the bottom, to the poles, using twine or wire.

Pick *This*, Part I

Create a lightweight fruit picker with PVC pipe. "Choose pipe wide enough for the fruit you want to harvest to fit through," suggests Pat Kolb of Phoenix. "Cut a notch in one end of the pipe to hook the fruit. When you snag the fruit from the tree, it rolls through the pipe into your basket. PVC by its nature is pretty lightweight, especially when compared to many commercial fruit pickers."

You can make your own lightweight fruit-picking tool with notched PVC piping.

Pick *This*, Part II

"To make a citrus fruit picker," says Michelle Doll, an organic home gardener in Tampa, Florida, "use long handles left over from brooms and other old or broken tools. Put a couple of nails, fairly close together, sideways through one end."

To harvest the fruit, simply put the nails on each side of the stem, and twist the handle to pick the fruit without damaging the skin, allowing it to drop into your basket.

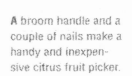

A broom handle and a couple of nails make a handy and inexpensive citrus fruit picker.

Electric *Currants*

The right tool for the job of harvesting berries comes from an unlikely source. "As an electronics constructor, I have a small pair of wire cutters that comes with a gadget that holds the cut piece of wire so that it doesn't fall into the equipment or fly into your eye," explains Alan Pemberton of Sheffield, England. "I have found them invaluable for harvesting my black currants. I can snip off strings of currants one-handed and then transfer the fruit, still clinging to the cutter, to my collecting vessel, leaving my other hand free to manipulate branches or hold the vessel."

Check your local hardware store for wire-grabbing wire cutters, and try them on anything with a small stem, such as grapes or currant tomatoes. They're even handy for cutting hard-to-reach flowers.

Sunflower Seed **Scraper**

"To separate sunflower seeds from the flower head," suggests Pat Kolb of Phoenix, "scrape the head across an old washboard."

Reinforced Recycled *Harvest* Basket

Recycle your leftover grocery bags into a durable, leak-proof harvest basket. "Simply start with three paper grocery bags and two plastic grocery bags that fit

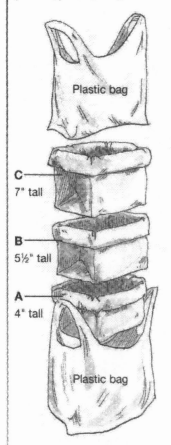

If you have a stack of grocery bags waiting to be recycled, put them to work in the garden instead as a durable harvest basket.

the paper bags," says Sharon Gordon of Ohio.

1. Fold a 1½-inch cuff in the top of one of the paper bags (Bag A).

2. Continue making 1½-inch folds until the bag is about 4 inches high.

3. Repeat for the second bag (Bag B), but make one less fold so that it's about 1½ inches taller than Bag A.

4. Repeat for Bag C, making one less fold than for Bag B.

5. Place Bag B into Bag A so that the top of Bag A's cuff is just touching the bottom of Bag B's cuff. Staple the bags together through Bag A's cuff.

6. Place Bag C into Bag B, and staple the bags together through Bag B's cuff.

7. Line Bag C with a plastic grocery bag.

8. Place the four-bag unit inside a plastic grocery bag with handles.

"The paper bags give the basket shape and stability, and the plastic bags keep it dry," Sharon explains.

Water Tube Makes Posting *Easier*

Now you don't have to mangle the tops of posts when you hammer them into the ground. "I soldered a female hose connection on the end of a 6-foot piece of ½-inch hard-wall copper tubing," says Jim Oberschelp of Minden, Nevada. "I attach the hose, turn on the water, and push the tubing into the ground where I want to place my pole. The pole then goes into the ground very easily."

Jim notes that this works for other projects, such as deep root watering of trees. He's even used it to blow debris out of his shop vacuum hose.

Quick Tool *Cleanup*

"I keep a bucket of gravel and coarse sand soaked with linseed oil near my tools," says Sally Anne Sadler of the Cooperative Extension Service in Seattle. "I dunk my tools, shovel, spade, and forks in it to scrape off rust and to oil them." Sally Anne also uses the linseed oil to season or protect her tools' handles.

Nifty Sifter

"Remove the seat from an old, metal, straight-legged kitchen chair to make a compost sifter," says Bonnie Knesek of Sparks, Oklahoma. "Make a sturdy wire mesh box, or a box from old boards with a wire mesh bottom. Attach the box where you would normally screw in the seat. Dump compost into the box and work it through the sifter."

Transform an old dinette chair or stool into a compost sifter with legs. You don't have to hold the sifter as you work, and it's easily moved to wherever you want to use the finished compost.

A *Soffit* Touch

Use scraps of vinyl soffit covering to make durable plant collars. "Because vinyl soffit material is perforated with many small holes, it lets air circulate around plants," says Terry Klokeid of Amblewood Farm on SaltSpring Island, British Columbia. "You can easily bend a scrap of soffit material into a circle about 4 to 6 inches around, and one side clips into the other, making a nice cylindrical plant collar."

Use plant collars on seedlings to keep birds, rabbits, and other critters away. As with vinyl siding, vinyl soffit material is extremely durable. And you can usually get scraps from a builder for free.

Garden *Forks* and *Knives*

Think twice before selling those old fondue forks at your next garage sale. "They come in handy for grilling or roasting marshmallows, but mainly I use them as digging forks out in the yard," says Laura McKenzie of Springville, Alabama. "Since they are skinny and small, they can reach the weeds right next to your plants. They also prick out lettuce seedlings when thinning.

"Another tool I couldn't do without is an old paring knife. I sharpened it and use it to dig out clumps of grass and other weeds that are really rooty."

Polish Up Those Handles

To keep from losing or misplacing your hand weeder, paint the handle bright orange or red. And, rather than buy paint when you only need a small amount for this purpose, use some old red nail polish. This is a job children really love. Let them mix all your old bright colors together, do their nails—however messily—and color the tool handles at the same time. Materials needed: one or more children, old red nail polish, and one bottle of nail polish remover for the remainder of their hands, your yard furniture, and your deck.

problem SOLVer

SELF-SUPPORTING WHEELBARROW

"Make your wheelbarrow support its own load by adding wheels to the rear legs," says Yvonne Savio, gardening education coordinator for the Los Angeles County Cooperative Extension Service.

Yvonne anchors a bar to each leg with a U-bolt. Then she attaches two small wheels to the ends of the bar with a bolt and washer on both the outside and inside of the wheel. The smaller the wheels, the less the rear of the wheelbarrow is raised.

"The wheels enable you to push without lifting the wheelbarrow, making heavy loads much easier to move with less strain."

"Waterfall" Planter

"We took an old wheelbarrow and tossed it on its side. Then we mounded up soil in it and let some spill out in front of the wheelbarrow," says C. J. England of Jonjea Acres Family Farm in Hope, Idaho. "We planted flowers in it that are low to the ground and will bloom blue, such as petunias and ageratum, to make it look like it's spilling out 'water'!"

Anything Goes

Wondering what to do with an old wheelbarrow? "If it's deep enough, use it as a planter. If it's not, it's a birdbath. Upside down, it can be a home for a toad," says Stephanie Ferguson of Indianapolis.

Flat Transporter

Anne Warren of Sudoa Farm, Notch Hill, British Columbia, recycles old wheelbarrows. "I pick up broken wheelbarrows at the dump to fix and rebuild. Last year I was able to make a flat-decked wheelbarrow from bits I'd scrounged," says Anne. "It is excellent for transporting flats from the greenhouse to the garden."

Salad to Go

"Plant a salad garden in a wheelbarrow. Lettuces and radishes look quaint, and they can be conveniently located near the door. Be sure to drill holes in the bottom for drainage," suggests Vera Smith of Rusk, Texas.

Vinyl Siding Scraps

Terry Klokeid of Amblewood Farm, SaltSpring Island, British Columbia, has lots of uses for light-colored vinyl siding scraps. Cut them into a variety of dimensions to make:

- plant markers for the garden
- seedling markers for flats
- large signs to install on posts in larger plots
- plant labels for the sides of homemade wooden planters
- relatively tall markers to place in the ground when laying out spacing for larger plants and perennials
- small labels that travel with small batches of seeds as they move from harvest to drying to storage
- dividers in flats, to keep seedling roots from becoming intertwined

"The best tool for cutting vinyl is aviation snips, which are widely sold in hardware stores," says Terry.

Timely tip

Empty plastic diaper-wipe containers are just the right size for storing seed packets.

Garden *Glove* Trap

"Create a glove trap by attaching a mousetrap to the door of your potting shed or wall near an entrance to the garden," suggests Yvonne Savio, gardening education coordinator for the Los Angeles County Cooperative Extension Service. "The gloves are accessible and will dry quickly."

Cardboard Box Raised **Beds**

A cardboard box can serve as a one-season raised bed. "To make a potato planter, fold both top and bottom flaps of a large box to the inside so that they are flush against the inner walls of the box," suggests Ada Davis of West Fork, Arkansas. "Bury the bottom edge of the box about 6 inches below ground level so that it won't blow away, then plant potatoes as usual." At the end of the season, toss the box on your compost pile to decompose.

Ada also suggests using small cardboard boxes as biodegradable planters. "But make sure the soil goes up to the top edges so that the box won't wick away moisture."

Garden Tool **Hang** Ups

Trying to organize all those tools cluttering the garage? "Hang an old garden rake and use the tines to hang smaller garden tools," suggests Sally Anne Sadler of Washington State University Cooperative Extension, King County.

More Garden Tool *Hang Ups*

If you have an old dish draining rack, you have an instant shed organizer. "Cut the drainer in half lengthwise with wire cutters," instructs Stephanie Ferguson of Indianapolis. "Form the newly cut wires into hooks. Then mount the drainer on the garage or shed wall and hang tools from it." If you hang the drainer with the cut side up, it forms a basket that will hold gloves, seed packets, and other nonhanging items.

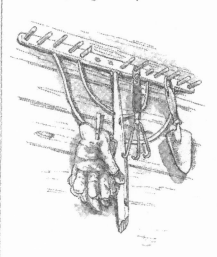

A garden rake with a broken handle (*left*), or a discarded wire dish rack cut in half (*right*) can both gain new life as hangers for tools. Two nails tapped into the shed or garage wall is all you need to hang these items—then you have space to hang gloves, trowels, cultivators, pruners, and more.

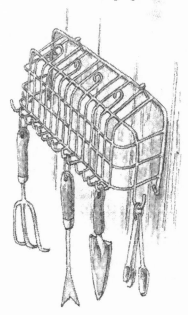

Tissue Box Seed Organizer

Organize your seed packets with empty tissue boxes. "Cut four diagonal slits in the top of an empty cardboard tissue box from the opening to each corner," explains Sharon Gordon of Ohio. "Fold each of the four wings to the inside, and staple each wing twice to the body of the box, near the ends of each flap. File seed packages in alphabetical order by type and variety. If you have a lot of seeds, use a different box for each type of plant, such as vegetables, herbs, and flowers."

To keep seeds moisture-free, Sharon recommends placing several of these cardboard seed boxes in a large, sealed plastic container.

Cut a slit diagonally to each corner.

Cut

Fold the flaps in, staple in place, and you're ready to store seed packets.

Catnip Protector

Cats destroying your catnip patch? "Set an old dish drainer over the planting of catnip to keep the cats from pulling the snack out of the ground by the roots," advises Natalie McNair-Huff of Tacoma, Washington. "They can still rub on it and prune it as it grows through the wires, but they won't be able to kill it." And don't worry about appearances—the bushy catnip will quickly grow large enough to hide the drainer.

Kitty can still enjoy the catnip as it grows through a dish drainer, but she won't be able to yank it out of the ground.

Seed Storage Units

If photography is one of your hobbies, it can benefit your gardening habit, too. "Most good gardeners take pictures and have plenty of 35-mm film containers laying around," says Bill Stockman, owner of Spider Web Gardens in Center Tuftonboro, New Hampshire. "These containers make excellent units to store seed." They're airtight and opaque, so seeds won't lose their freshness.

"Use peel-off stickers to label the containers so that you'll remember what's in them," suggests Bill.

Built-In *Hand* Cushions

"I wrap the handles of some of my tools with moleskin," says gardener Bambi Cantrell of Jacksonville, North Carolina. "It makes them more comfortable to hold and makes the wooden handle less likely to cause a blister."

Just make sure that you don't let the tools get wet, because moleskin will absorb the water and can even come unstuck, so you'd have to replace it.

Sheer Substitute for Row Covers

Sheer curtains can go from window covers to row covers to extend your growing season. "It's quite easy to buy secondhand, gauzy sheer curtains at garage sales. I've bought them for as little as a dime!" reveals gardener Eileen Anderson of Little Rock, Arkansas.

"Plenty of light seems to go through, and all sorts of plants profit from them. I use them over lettuce to moderate the temperature. The sheer curtains keep them warmer in the winter and cooler when it starts to get warm. And I couldn't grow tomatoes without using the curtains as protection from the birds. I imagine they would be good protection from cabbage moths, too."

To support the sheer row covers over summer crops, Eileen uses tomato cages that she makes herself from fencing material.

"I make tomato cages out of 4-foot fencing that I buy in a roll at a farmer's supply store. I simply trim the fencing in pieces to make cylinders that are about 18 inches in diameter, and fasten them together with wire. I use these cages for tomatoes and beans in the summer, and a group of them will support the sheers beautifully."

Eileen uses the same cages in the winter, but she lays them on their sides to protect her lettuce crop. "I can lay two or three cages in my lettuce patch and cover them with the sheers. The sheers let water through, and they'll even support snow with no sagging."

Eileen's secret to achieving no-sag sheers is to anchor the cages to the ground with clothes hanger garden pins (see page 14 for directions on making these). Then she attaches the sheers to the cages with clothespins.

Timely tip

Eileen has devised a way to use her sheer covers in raised beds, too. She stacks four bricks on the timbers and then lays a 4 × 6-foot chain-link fence gate on top of them. Eileen then covers the whole thing with a sheer curtain.

"I use this row cover system for spring lettuce, and the lettuce seems to love it. I even had a bunny living under there for a while—the lettuce was so prolific that there was plenty for both of us!"

homegrown HINTS

THE ALMIGHTY STICK

"I call my favorite—and darn near only—gardening tool the almighty stick," says Lee Flier of Atlanta, Georgia. "It's just a branch from a tree, about 1¼ inches thick, waist to chest high, forked at one end, and sharpened to a very blunt point on the other."

Lee uses the sharpened end as a digging stick for planting. "Assuming you have good soil and are doing no-till and deep mulch, all you need is the almighty stick to twist into the soil. Then mulch a little and make a hole, drop the seed in, and use the stick to brush a bit of soil back over the seed. The stick is also useful if you mulch with newspaper layers. Just make sure the newspaper is wet, and the stick will poke right through."

Lee has other uses for her almighty stick, too. She uses the forked end to move squash vines out of the way in order to harvest the beans off a "three sisters" bed of corn, beans, and squash so that she doesn't step on them. Other uses? How about harvesting fruit off of trees and aerating the compost pile? As Lee sums it up, "It's a great little invention!"

Bookcase Bed

Don't throw out that old bookcase, even if it is a little wobbly. "Take the back off and use it as a frame for a small raised bed," suggests home gardener Ada Davis of West Fork, Arkansas.

You can leave the shelves in as row dividers—or you can take them out, leaving just the outer frame to enclose your bed.

Kid's Stuff

Here are two garden-related recycling ideas for parents. "Diaper-wipe containers work as drainage trays. Each one holds two small pots really well," says Deborah Turton, a gardening columnist in Gaithersburg, Maryland.

"And save empty formula cans for scooping or storing dry stuff like birdseed or bonemeal."

Shocking Stop

When you use an electrical tool or lighting in the garden, you often need to use an extension cord. But you could be setting yourself up for a shock if you don't take a few precautions.

"Use a coffee can and two plastic lids to protect the connection of two outdoor extension cords from the weather," recommends Yvonne Savio, gardening education coordinator for the Los Angeles County Cooperative Extension Service. Here's Yvonne's method:

1. Remove the metal bottom from the can.

2. Slit each plastic lid from one edge to the center, and enlarge a center hole in each lid to be slightly smaller in diameter than the cord.

3. Slide the can over the end of one cord, connect the cords, center the connection in the can, and slip on the plastic lids.

Yvonne advises, "Keep the slits pointed downward to allow drainage, in case of condensation."

problem solver

PRYING ROOTBOUND PLANTS FREE

Have you ever tried to get a large rootbound plant out of an 18-inch pot? "The pressure of the roots makes it almost impossible without breaking the pot," says garden writer Duane Campbell of Towanda, Pennsylvania.

"I use a soil auger—the $5 kind designed to fit a ⅜-inch drill—to drill several holes through the soil right up against the side of the pot," says Duane. The result is a double benefit. "It relieves the pressure and root prunes the plant at the same time."

By using Duane's method, you spare the pot and give the plant a better start once it's planted in the ground. Be sure to wear eye protection while you're working with the drill.

Claw Your Way through Clay

If you have hard clay soil and just the thought of planting bulbs gives you blisters, try this idea from Edie Carlson of Saint Thomas, Ontario.

"I use a garden claw to dig holes for bulbs," says Edie. "Even in hard clay, I can dig a hole that is big enough for some bonemeal, good soil, and the bulb."

Spare Hands

Here's a helping hand for gardeners who have arthritis or who have lost strength in their hands or fingers. "Try to find hand tools with longer handles, or replace short handles with longer ones," recommends Nancy Anderson of the North Carolina Cooperative Extension Service in Fayetteville. "You may have to purchase a longer handle than you need and cut it to size. (I cut mine 8 to 10 inches long.) Then use Velcro to make a strap to attach the tool to your forearm. The idea is for the arm to do the work and not the hand."

Follow these steps to add a strap to your hand tools.

1. Cut a 12-inch strip of both the hook and loop sections of the Velcro.

2. Lay the smooth side of the hook section against the loops of the other piece of Velcro. Sew them together with a ¼-inch seam across one short end.

3. Sew another seam about an inch or so from the first seam. This will form a loop that you can slip over your tool handle. So make sure you leave enough room to fit the tool into the loop.

4. Slip the handle of the tool through the loop and wrap the Velcro around your arm, adjusting the straps so that they fit snugly.

Stitch

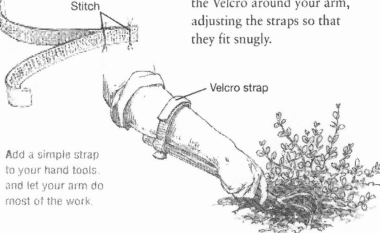

Velcro strap

Add a simple strap to your hand tools, and let your arm do most of the work.

Yo-Hoe Tool Grabs Weeds

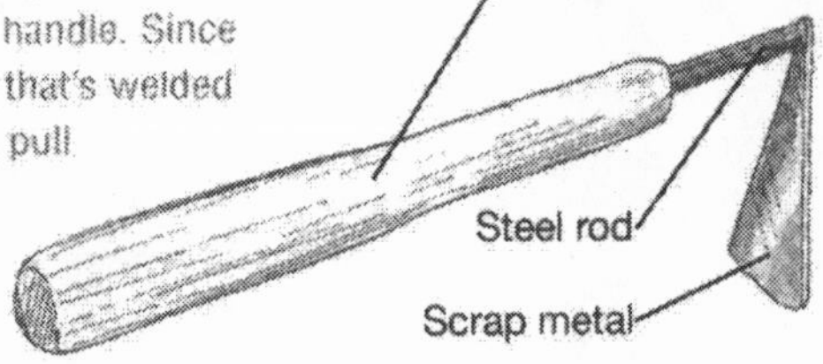

Here's a creative homemade gadget for up-close weeding. "My husband made me a tool we call a yo-hoe," reports Kim Cook of Prince Edward Island. "He cut a piece of scrap metal to form a triangle that's about 3 inches long and 1½ inches wide at the widest. He welded the end to a steel rod a little thinner than a pencil and attached the rod to an old hammer handle. The steel rod sticks out of the handle about 4 inches. The tool is shaped like a 7, and the inside edge of the blade is sharpened. I drag it toward

This homemade weeding tool makes use of an old hammer handle. Since the inside of the blade that's welded to the handle is sharp, pull it toward you to grab and slice weeds.

Old hammer handle
Steel rod
Scrap metal

me, and since the inside blade edge and the rod part of the handle form an angle, they trap the weeds, making it easier for the blade to slice through them."

homegrown HINTS

COMPUTER COVER DOUBLES AS COLD FRAME

"The ancient IBM Display Writers and similar machines from the early days of office computers had huge hoods to muffle the sound of the printers," says John Boston of Tulsa, Oklahoma. "They're natural cold frames! These covers are about 3 feet square, taller in the back than front, with a hinged Plexiglas cover and a layer of foam insulation inside. IBM was even so kind as to include an electric fan on one side for ventilating your plants on warm days. You can plug in the fan when needed, or do as I did and hook up an inexpensive thermostat to regulate the ventilation."

If you can find a company that still has these old clunkers around in storage, you can probably have one for free. Who knows—they may even pay you to haul the unused hood away!

By turning one of these old printer covers into a cold frame, you not only save money but you also recycle obsolete computer equipment that would otherwise have ended up in a landfill.

That Phone Wire Is Busy

Old telephone wire need not head to the landfill, according to master scrounger Terry Klokeid of Amblewood Farm on Salt-Spring Island, British Columbia. "If new telephone lines are being installed or upgraded in your neighborhood, you have an excellent source of wire for tying plants up and repairing stuff.

"If you get your mitts on the old wire, you can re-purpose it. Use it instead of string or anything else you may have to buy to tie up plants or to bundle wooden stakes together for storage."

Kindling
Splitting Support

"To make the job of splitting kindling for firewood easier, I have built a stabilizing gadget," explains Terry Klokeid of Amblewood Farm on SaltSpring Island, British Columbia. "It looks vaguely like a football goal post with a wooden base under it. The plywood base is about 24 × 9 inches. I attached two 2 × 4 posts near one edge of the base, using two screws per post through the underside of the plywood. Then I stretched a deflated bicycle inner tube taut between the posts."

Before attaching the inner tube to the posts, you can slip one or two metal rings over the tubing, to slide along the tubing to tighten it around the firewood and hold the wood secure. Any kind of ring large enough to slip over the tubing and strong enough to hold against pressure will do. Split rings, like those on key chains, are a good choice.

Then place the tube at a height that's about two-thirds the length of kindling you want. Finally, attach the tubing to the upright posts by screwing small pieces of plywood to the posts.

How do you use this contraption? Terry replies, "I insert a small piece of firewood between the two bands, rest it solidly on the plywood base, and split it into the desired thin bits of kindling. It's much safer than holding the wood in one hand and whaling away on the wood with an ax in your other hand. I find I can set two, three, or sometimes four pieces of wood in the stabilizer and process them all at once. This is a real timesaving gadget, not to mention a finger-saving one as well."

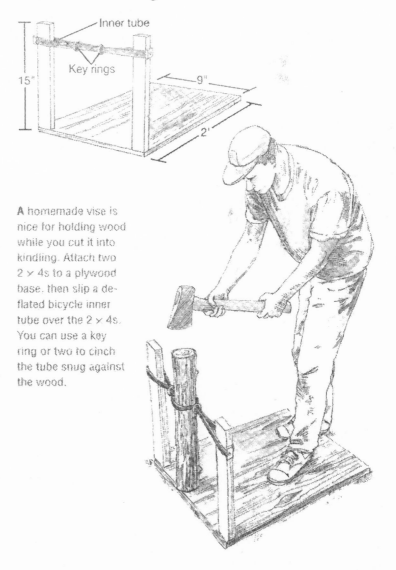

A homemade vise is nice for holding wood while you cut it into kindling. Attach two 2 × 4s to a plywood base, then slip a deflated bicycle inner tube over the 2 × 4s. You can use a key ring or two to cinch the tube snug against the wood.

chapter 2

clever

Compost Tips

It's been said before, but it really is true—
it all starts with the soil. From scrounging
on trash day to using up what you have on
hand, learn how to enhance your soil
and your yields with these ingenious
composting tips. Gardeners from around
the country share their best secrets, shortcuts, and solutions for improving the soil
you have. You'll also find clever ways and
places to compost—right down to how
to disguise that active compost heap in
the backyard!

Trash-Day *Sleuths* and Sunday **Night** Scouts

Almost everybody knows that adding organic matter is the way to improve any kind of soil, but *finding* enough organic matter isn't always easy. Here's an easy solution—use everybody else's throwaways! Trash or garbage day often yields bundled-up brush, piled leaves, newspapers, and even pots full of "used" soil. You'll also see lots of unwanted grass clippings set out after the weekend's mowing is done. Collect these, too, as long as you're sure they haven't been coated with pesticides and weed killers.

Post-Halloween *Treasures*

Another excellent time to scour your town for free compost and soil-building material is the week after Halloween. Lots of people decorate with bales of straw and corn stalks, and many of them gather leaves in those bright orange pumpkin-face bags. So be prepared to hit the brakes when you see curbside orange!

How to Become a **Rake**

Sally Cunningham, author of *Great Garden Companions,* needs lots of organic material, so she uses this ingenious technique to gather free leaves: "When I'm driving around in fall or spring, I often see wonderful piles of pine needles or leaves. The problem is, my rake is at home." But Sally always has garbage bags under the seat, so she developed her "human rake" technique.

Place a large trash bag facing a pile of leaves. If there's a curb, the bag goes beneath the edge of the curb. Facing the leaf pile yourself, put one foot on each side of the bag to hold the mouth of the bag open. Wait until no cars are coming by, since this looks ridiculous—or worse—from behind. Then bend from the hips and scoop with your arms, pushing all the leaves between your feet right into the bag. Sally adds, "It's one great waist exercise, too!"

Always carry trash bags in your car, and you'll be ready to gather up a wealth of curbside lawn waste for composting

Under-the-Sheets **Composting**

This tip earned writer Sally Cunningham some teasing over her years of teaching organic soil building. It's not about sleeping late or dreaming of compost. But it *is* an easy way to improve soil.

Whenever you cover the soil with black plastic sheets— a really good mulching and weed-killing material—use the opportunity to get lots of coarse organic material under it. Just stuff shredded news-paper, chopped leaves, grass clippings, weeds, and unfin-ished compost *right under the sheets!* The stuffing can be 4 to 6 inches thick, and it will be well decomposed by the end of the season.

This technique even protects the soil when you step on the plastic. "It feels spongy, and if you peek under it, you will be amazed at the earthworms enjoying it, too!" says Sally.

Timely tip

Gathering grass? Be sure to keep layers of grass clippings less than 4 inches deep when mulching or composting with it. Grass is mostly water, so a deep pile becomes oxygen-deprived, or anaerobic, very quickly—and when that hap-pens, it really smells!

homegrown HINTS

HELP OTHERS HELP YOU

Believe it or not, many homeowners rake up leaves or grass without a thought of composting or mulching, and they work hard to pick up the piles and put them into open containers or trash bags to go out to the curb.

So why wouldn't they gladly put the stuff into your containers? Just watch for a raking-gathering project in progress, stop by, and offer to leave your garbage bags, cans, or baskets for them to fill. People are glad to have the "trash" gone so quickly and especially appreciate it if you do the hauling. In addition, you'll be saving them the cost of all those trash bags and teaching them a lesson about recycling right on the spot. Maybe next year they will be composting their own yard waste.

Chicken Wire *Keeps* Critters at **Bay**

If you're trench composting, you shouldn't have a problem with animals digging up what you've buried if you avoid meat, bones, and fats. Even the most fragrant fruit and vegetable scraps will not attract scavengers when buried under 8 inches of soil!

However, if dogs do like to dig in your trenches, use a roll of chicken wire to cover your buried treasure, rolling it out over one hole at a time. The roll moves along gradually, so it also marks where you buried something last.

Trench composting is easy and trouble-free when you protect your trench with chicken wire.

Can't Compost? Use Trenches

If you have a small yard and no place to compost, you may find that trench composting is the best way to use your food scraps to add nutrients to your soil. How do you do trench composting? Just dig a hole in your garden every day, about 8 inches deep, and bury the kitchen scraps. If you start along one side of a garden row, you'll actually be side-dressing or fertilizing nearby vegetables as well as boosting soil texture and fertility for next season.

Wet Soil? Plant in *Compost*

Paul Kranz, a Master Gardener and environmental engineer in Amherst, New York, has heavy clay soil, which never dries out in time to plant spring peas and onions. He recommends, "Overlay the untilled soil with a 6-inch raised bed of compost." Paul gets his compost from the town compost facility. "Plant peas, lettuce seeds, or onion sets right in the compost for an early start. They grow great!"

The *Acid* Test

If you don't have time for a soil pH test, which is always a wise idea before starting a garden, nature may give you clues to the acidity or alkalinity of your soil. Check the weeds that sprout up in your gardens. If you find many of one type of the weeds or wild plants below, or a mix of several species from one of the lists, you'll have a a good indication of the general soil pH.

Plants that indicate acid (low pH) soil: Canada mayflower (*Maianthemum canadense*), star grass (*Hypoxis hirsuta*), wood anemones (*Anemone quinquefolia*), frost weed (*Helianthemum canadense*), rhododendrons, blackberries, or blueberries.

Plants that indicate alkaline (high pH) soil: Lady fern (*Athyrium filix-femina*) and most other ferns, Jack-in-the-pulpit, bloodroot (*Sanguinaria canadensis*), wild geranium (*Geranium maculatum*), poison ivy, enchanter's nightshade (*Circaea quadrisulcata*), figwort (*Scrophularia marilandica*), sweet cicely (*Myrrhis odorata*), goosegrass or catchweed bedstraw (*Gallium aparine*), and goldenrod.

Do the *Soil Ribbon* Test

Joanne Gruttadaurio, soil professor *extraordinaire*, has taught thousands of Master Gardeners and Cornell University students this down and dirty way to determine whether soil is clay or sand. Grab a lump of your soil and form it into a patty. Start flattening it out by pressing with your thumb against the soil, pressing toward your fingers. Squeeze a ribbon of soil out over your index finger, easing it along with your thumb. If you can form a ribbon that holds together for an inch or two, you have clay soil. If it fails to hold together in a ribbon and falls off in loose particles, it is sandy soil.

A simple squeeze of the soil though your fingers will reveal your soil's texture.

Once you recognize your soil type, you can plan your garden and select plants. You may want to grow vegetables, perennials, or a mix of landscape plants, but keep in mind that it's easier to work with the soil you have rather than to change it significantly. If your soil is one extreme or the other—either clay or sand—you can start improving the soil with organic matter, the most effective cure in either situation.

problem solver   THE FIRST SPRING CUTTING

The first lawn mowing of spring usually provides long, thick clippings, making it the one time it's worthwhile to rake the clippings rather than to let them decompose in place. Here are two good uses for an abundance of grass clippings: Spread them around the vegetables and flowers at least 2 inches thick as a short-term mulch. Or use them for quick-start compost. Alternate 4-inch layers of grass clippings with 4-inch layers of dry leaves or shredded newspaper. Your compost will be really cooking in a matter of days.

Bedsprings in the Spring Beds!

"My father always dragged bedsprings behind the small riding tractor to remove rocks from a clay tennis court, and it gave me this great idea for helping my garden dry faster in the spring," says Marge Vogel in Eden, New York.

"When the soil is drying in the spring but is too wet for walking or tilling, drag an old bedspring (child-size is easiest) over your raised beds. You don't need a tractor, but you do need two people. Each one walks on the paths on oppo-site sides of the garden beds, pulling the spring along by ropes. It breaks up the soil crust and stirs up any mulch you left on the garden, yet it's not so heavy as to damage soil structure. And one pass is all it takes. Of course, you can also rake the surface lightly to accomplish this, but that's a *lot* of work in a big garden!"

To use this technique, look for the old-fashioned open-coil bedsprings. You may find them at a curbside in the country, in dumps or junkyards, in basements or attics of old homes—or even under a mattress!

Put an old bedspring to work in the garden, where the wire coils can loosen the top crust of soil and drag out any rocks that have risen to the surface over the winter.

homegrown HINTS

OLD NEWSPAPERS, NEW BEDS

Joanne Tanner, a Master Gardener in Orchard Park, New York, says, "In late summer or early fall, I lay several sheets of newspaper right over the lawn where I want to make a new planting bed. On top of this, I put a couple of inches of compost (finished or not) topped with a few inches of shredded leaves. I finish it off with a covering of landscape fabric."

Sally Cunningham, author of *Great Garden Companions*, echoes this idea. "If your back is like mine, double-digging a new bed is out of the question." Sally suggests piling any organic matter you have on the newspaper, such as brush, manure, straw, leaves, or grass clippings. "Make each layer no thicker than 4 inches, and use the coarsest materials on the bottom." Sally says she's used this method to build beds anywhere from 8 inches to a few feet high. Sally finishes her layers off with compost for an early spring planting.

Build **Down**, Not Just *Up*

Peg Giermek, Master Gardener and owner of Nature Calls Landscaping in Erie County, New York, tries to convince her customers of the importance of building the soil before adding landscape plants. Not everybody wants to see a raised bed in the landscape, so she devised a method to build the soil while serving customer tastes.

"When installing a garden in an area of extremely poor soil, it's possible to do more than just raise the bed and amend. Dig a good 2 to 3 feet down into the soil and remove it. (Add the poor soil to a compost pile, where active microorganisms will bring it back to life.) Rebuild your garden by layering compost, peat moss, good-quality topsoil, and composted manure. Repeat the layering, making each layer a few inches thick. Continue layering until the garden has been raised above ground level as high as is practical in your situation."

The bed will sink a few inches in the first year, so take that into account as you layer.

Timely tip

With Peg's method of garden building, it's also very easy to incorporate small hills or berms into any size garden. Just start below ground, and keep building up on one side as desired.

Berms are a great asset for certain plantings. For example, plant tulips, daffodils, or other early-spring blooming bulbs on the far side of a hill or berm (from the viewing area), and plant irises in front of them. Tulips and daffodils will emerge first in the spring, followed by irises, which will hide the waning bulb foliage. Or, plant your bulbs on the north-facing side of your berm to delay their bloom a bit later than normal.

Yesterday's News

One of the great underused—but widely available—soil amendments is newspaper, according to Rochelle Smith, Master Gardener and owner of EarthCare, Inc., a landscape firm in Buffalo, New York. She encourages homeowners to work with an organic lawn and landscape program, and adding newspaper to the soil helps.

Rochelle uses at least six to eight sheets of newspaper under a layer of mulch. Newspaper blocks weeds, and earthworms love it. And earthworms provide valuable nitrogen, potassium, and phosphorus—three essential plant nutrients—all in a form that's readily available to your plants.

You put something free (the paper) into this processing plant (the worms), and out comes fertilizer! For faster action than the worms can provide, shred some newspaper into 1-inch strips and turn it into the soil, or spread it on the soil surface under mulch.

What *Becomes* of Peat?

A landscaper's daughter, Michele Diegelman of Buffalo learned from her dad that leftover peat moss does some great decomposing right in the bag. She put the bags in the basement in the fall and let them sit. In spring, after the peat had decomposed some more, she cut slits in the bags and added organic matter like grass clippings and compost. Then she planted spreading flowers in the bags. Voilà: instant container gardens!

homegrown HINTS

VOLUNTEER VINES

While she has never planted a pumpkin in compost on purpose, Nancy Smith, a compost teacher from East Aurora, New York, admits she does grow at least one pumpkin and a gourd or squash on the compost pile every summer. "Just watch for volunteers from the pumpkins you tossed in after Halloween, and pick the best plant!" Of course, you may not be sure exactly what is coming up, but that's part of the fun. And don't be surprised if the pumpkin grown in the compost turns out to be the biggest pumpkin in the garden.

Bury the *Rusty* Rake

Jean Seibert of East Aurora, New York, remembers the first composter she ever knew—her dad, Harry Harper. Jean says, "Dad would return home on trash day with the worst-looking rusty hoes and rakes."

Jean thought the find looked rather dubious. But he stuck the rusty tools upright in his compost, with the tool ends buried. When it came time to turn the pile, all he had to do was twist the tools up and out.

"And a second benefit," says Jean, "was the satisfaction that man took in never wasting anything!"

Wiggle-and-*Pull* Aeration

Most composting instructions tell you to put all the larger sticks and coarse brush on the bottom, but Sally Cunningham, author of *Great Garden Companions*, suggests saving the longest sticks for this use: As you build a compost pile, put long sticks (up to 2 inches in diameter) across the pile, every foot or so, with their ends sticking out. After you have a tall pile and the initial heat buildup slows down, you can wiggle the sticks to turn and aerate the compost. Or, use a wiggle-and-pull technique to remove the sticks and introduce some new air spaces.

Hiding Compost in the *Hedgerow*

OK, maybe you don't have an actual hedgerow, but even a cluster of shrubs will do. You can hide a compost pile behind or among trees or shrubs. Some people don't hide compost in these shady areas because they think that a pile needs sunlight—but it doesn't! The heat comes from *inside* the pile during decomposition, and shaded compost can be just as hot as that kept in full sun. Shaded compost can take longer to dry out, though, so keep a tarp handy to limit the rainfall on compost under the trees.

Don't Compost Those *Leaves*

Master Gardener Fran Evans, from Hamburg, New York, has found a better way to cope with fallen leaves. "Don't compost the leaves!" says Fran. "Instead, shred and bag them in the fall and hold them until summer. Then mulch the vegetable garden with them. Till them in the soil after the crops are harvested, and you'll create great humus for the following year."

Peas and Beans **Succeed**

Not only do climbing peas and beans grow beautifully up the sides of a compost pile, they also cover it for a long season with succession planting. Plant the peas as soon as you can poke a

Climbing peas and beans cover up compost with their flowering vines, and they also provide you with a summer's bounty of good eating.

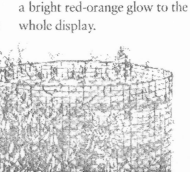

finger into cold soil. Later, beans replace them, and a fall crop of peas completes the cycle. Scarlet runner beans, planted every third plant, add a bright red-orange glow to the whole display.

Cover Compost with *Glory*

Morning glories are happy to climb up the sides of a chicken-wire compost bin, or one made of fencing or boards. If the sides aren't rough enough to provide places for the vines to cling, simply tie strings to the top of the bin, and attach them to the soil with pins to provide vertical trellises. Your pile will be a blaze of heavenly blue, white, red, purple, pink, or crimson from summer until frost makes its appearance.

Flower Boxes *on Top*

Some great gardening friends were traveling to a gardening conference, and one of the subjects of conversation was how to beautify a compost pile. Nobody remembers who thought it up first, but the gardeners, Marty, Mary, Sally, and Jean, now have the prettiest compost bins in New York State!

Try their creative idea: Make compost bins with the pallets laid sideways, so the closed end is up and the open ends are on the sides. Then use flower boxes on top, loaded

with trailing vines like licorice plants. They really beautify the business end of composting.

One gardener used wallpaper-soaking trays, which are just about the same length as a pallet, for the flower boxes. Plant trailing annuals like 'Pink Wave' petunias, and enjoy the view.

Flower boxes filled with trailing plants dress up a compost bin made from wooden shipping pallets.

Compost *Needs* a Chimney

Compost needs air to enable the microorganisms to do their job. You can always turn the pile, but that's hard work! Here are a few clever ways to get air into your compost pile with a minimum of labor.

PVC chimney: One way to get air into your compost pile is to provide a central "chimney," or a column of air that gets down into the center of the pile, to keep those microorganisms going. Poke a PVC or metal pipe with air holes right into the center of the compost pile.

Cinder-block chimney: Another method is to stack about four or five cinder blocks in the center of a 4-foot pile with the holes lined up vertically. When

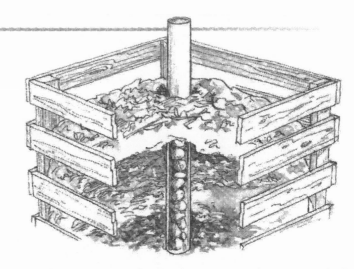

This cardboard compost chimney will decompose, leaving a stack of rocks—and air space—in the center of the pile, which is exactly what it needs. Best of all, there's no need to turn the pile.

you stack them, place some stones on top of each layer of cinder blocks to let air in from the sides.

Cardboard chimney: One gardener made a great chimney out of 4-inch cardboard tubing left over from a construction project. He then filled it with rocks. Yes, the cardboard decomposed in that hot compost heat—but by that time, the rocks were all lined up in a tall pile and provided lots of air space in the middle of the compost.

problem solver

FEED THE TOMATOES

In the great race for the neighborhood's first and largest tomato of the season, a compost pile can give you an edge. Just make a tall compost pile, at least 4 × 4 feet, and enclose it with the kind of wire mesh sold for tomato cages. ("Hog wire" will also do.) Plant tomatoes just outside the wire, and gently tie them right against the wire. Pluck off the lower leaves facing the pile. New roots will reach right into that rich compost where the leaves were plucked, and the tomatoes will be deliriously happy. And you don't have to wait until the compost pile is completed before planting the tomatoes. You can add to the pile all summer long, providing the tomatoes with a constant source of nutrition and helping them produce lots of fruit.

homegrown HINTS

THE HANDY COVER

Gardeners are the best scroungers, and smart ones see the potential for free tarps and covers from lots of sources. Possible free covers for the compost pile include: tarps that come with barbecue grills or lawn mowers, lawn furniture "overcoats," children's pool covers, painter's tarps, discarded shower curtains, and cast-off rugs, just for starters.

It is a good idea to have a tarp or cover that's 2 to 3 feet bigger than your compost pile so that the tarp can drape over the sides. Cover compost before a rain if the compost is already wet enough, or after a rain if you want to keep the moisture in. Adapt your cover-uncover routine, depending upon how much moisture you want to let in.

Strawberry Tower Compost

If you want a strawberry tower without paying the catalog price, make it with compost. As Sally Cunningham, author of *Great Garden Companions*, says, "You'll save the cost of fertilizer, too!"

1. First, make a chicken-wire cylinder, 4 to 5 feet high with at least a 2-foot diameter, and fill it with compost ingredients like yard waste, kitchen scraps, and manure—as raw and "hot" as you want. Finish with a 4-inch layer of soil, and then plant strawberries on top.

2. Enclose the cylinder with another circle of wire about 1 foot shorter and 9 inches larger in diameter than the center column. Fill that circle with more "raw" ingredients on the bottom and 4 inches of soil on the top. Plant another circle of strawberries.

3. Make as many outer circles as you want, each one about 1 foot lower than the previous one. But,

A chicken wire and compost strawberry tower can keep producing for years. Refresh it by adding soil or compost any time you replace an old strawberry plant with a young runner.

be sure you plan how to reach the center for picking later on! One suggestion is to break the circle, making the outer rings C-shaped rather than full circles. Use a footstool to reach the higher rings.

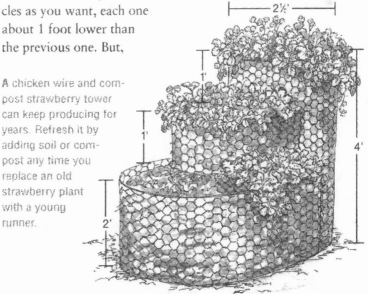

Surrounded by Sunflowers

A good place for building a compost pile is a back corner of the garden. It's convenient for adding in spent plants, leaves, and other garden debris, as well as for using the finished product.

To conceal active compost and still have it nearby, use tall plants like sunflowers. A double circle of sunflowers or hollyhocks or a combination of these with cosmos or tall nicotiana will hide the composting work in progress and provide a lovely focal point to enhance your garden's beauty.

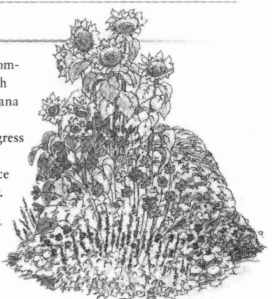

An arc of quick-growing, tall annual flowers is just the ticket for camouflaging an active compost pile.

Straw Planters Turned Compost

Nancy Ondra, nursery owner and garden writer, teaches this easy method for using straw bales as planters now and compost later. Place bales of straw wherever you'd like a raised bed or wherever you wish to grow vine crops but have soil that's too hard or nutrient-poor. Use a trowel or bulb planter to open up "pockets" on top of the bale, spacing them wherever you want to plant a vegetable or flower. Put compost into the pocket, and plant directly into it.

Poke holes in straw bales, fill them with compost, and plant vining flowers or vegetables. The bale makes a raised bed for a season, then decomposes to nourish next year's crops.

Nancy says, "You'll be surprised at how quickly the straw inside the bales begins to decompose, providing nutrients to the plant roots." She adds that this method is especially effective with vine crops like squash or melons. The vines will take up less space in your garden because they'll naturally trail down the sides of the bales. "They're also easy to water this way," she adds.

"By the end of the season, your straw will be nearly half composted. You can spread it in place and plant into it next season, or use it to activate a new compost pile. It will be full of hungry microorganisms and very valuable wherever you use it."

Compost Starters **for** **Cheap**—or *Free*

There's no need for you to buy compost starters to get those decomposing microorganisms going. Master composters know that manure, soil, and compost are loaded with them and will be happy to start a new batch for you! (For optimum production, just spread an inch or so of the material every 4 to 6 inches in your pile.)

Master Gardener John Holnbeck, from Colden, New York, says this, "If you are just starting out and the earthy elements are scarce, buy alfalfa meal from the feed store. It's cheaper than at the garden center, and it's the same stuff. It's high in nitrogen and gets things heated up quickly." Rabbit and horse feeds are made of alfalfa.

By the way, for city folks who don't have a feed store nearby, some cat box fillers are made of alfalfa meal. Won't the cat be surprised to see *clean* litter tossed out! (By the way, never put *used* cat litter on your compost pile, to avoid the possible spread of disease organisms.)

problem SOLVer   GET SOME LIFE IN YOUR CONTAINERS

Compost can add some much-needed life to container gardens, too—it's not just for traditional garden beds.

Some container-planting teachers tell you to use soilless mix (without synthetic fertilizers blended in) or potting soil in container plants because it is purer and you avoid soil "critters" that might cause problems in a contained situation. However, many potting soils are very light, and container plantings end up easily tipped over, or they dry out quickly. Also, organic gardeners tend to think that every soil should have some life in it, and soilless mixes surely need something.

Compost is the best answer. Use your choice of potting soil, but mix in compost (worms and all!). Compost improves the medium's texture and water-holding ability and delivers a gradual supply of nutrients, not to mention the valuable worm castings. Container plants with compost added literally spill over with beautiful flowers and lush foliage.

Give **Worms** What They **Want**

Penny McDowell, a Master Gardener and home landscaper in East Aurora, New York, says, "I find that worms are like kids. They like fruit better than vegetables. So I make sure that some fruit is mixed in with the kitchen scraps." And for even faster worm composting, run food scraps through your blender before feeding the worms. They'll turn blended scraps into rich compost in a mere three months!

Slow *May Be* Even Better

A study by Bob Kozlowski, of the Homes and Grounds Department at Cornell University, showed that compost made the slow way—without ever achieving real heat—was actually more nutrient-rich than compost that heated up and processed quickly. So, if you think your compost is a failure because it doesn't get hot, resist the temptation to heat it up. It may take longer, but in the end, it will be that much more valuable.

Creative Composting

Ingenious gardeners make compost bins out of many things, including snow fence, cinder block, pallets, window screens, and all kinds of fencing. Here are some of the more creative bin ideas.

Dog kennels: Some great compost bins resulted when one family took apart a series of dog boarding kennels. They were made of steel mesh framed in wood, and the doors (4 × 4 feet) and sides (4 × 6 feet) formed generous compost-bin rectangles, tied together with wire. Best of all, the front was already a door, complete with a hinge and a latch for easy access.

The last leaf collection: When it became too cold to build new compost piles, a gardener near Buffalo continued to build anyway. He simply gathered the late fall bags of leaves from the curbs around town and heaped them in a 4-foot circle around a low compost pile. The bags provided some heat, the contents decomposed slightly, and the center of the circle provided an unfrozen compost pile for accepting kitchen scraps all winter.

Double-duty pallets: Lots of gardeners make compost bins from pallets, but the pallets are usually positioned with the end boards horizontal and the open ends facing sideways. Instead, try placing them with the end boards in a vertical position and the open sides up. It's the perfect place to store garden stakes, long-handled tools, or row-cover hoops.

A compost bin can double as a storage site for tools or stakes. Add a wrought-iron shepherd's crook and brighten your bin with a hanging basket or two.

"Almost" Counts in Composting

A former Extension Agent and professional cut flower grower, Roxanne McCoy of Lilies of the Field in West Falls, New York, used to teach composting. She often joked with her class about the slides that show happy composters (neatly dressed, too) pushing fine, finished compost through a sieve.

"Fine compost, actually strained through a sieve!" said Roxanne. "Who can wait that long?"

In reality, most composting experts use their compost a lot sooner than the ready-to-strain stage. If there are still a few pieces of eggshell, grapefruit rind, or sticks showing, that's okay. Just use the finer parts and keep the big chunks to add to a new pile. These chunks are loaded with hungry microorganisms that will immediately go to work helping to break down the pile. If the chunks don't bother you, use the compost as is—chunks and all. Just turn the bigger pieces under a couple inches of soil, where they'll add important nutrients to your beds as they continue to decompose.

Build It Where **You** Want It

Many gardeners have reported variations on this idea—build the compost heap (or place the tumbler or portable bin) right where you want a new bed. If you do this in late summer or fall, and the compost is deep enough to become an active pile for a couple of months, you can use most of it in spring. Just dump or spread the compost around the former pile, and keep the unfinished material to move right along with the container for a new start somewhere else.

Kitchen-Door **Compost**

It can become a daunting task to lug food waste to the outer limits of your property—especially in bad weather. If you like to cook, consider keeping the compost right by the kitchen door near the garbage cans, where you're more likely to use it every day.

Keeping the compost near the kitchen door doesn't mean you'll have to look at the unsightly pile, however. Several types of commercial bins and tumblers are attractive and respectable looking. You can also mask your cans and compost with fencing, flowering vines such as clematis, moonvine, and morning glory, or perennials such as columbine, daylilies, and purple coneflower. Not only will you have a convenient compost pile, you'll have a pretty flowerbed, to boot!

Timely tip

Always keep some straw or leaves near the compost. Then, when you do make the trek to the compost bin with your food scraps, you can cover the food layers every time you add them.

problem SOLVER   FOOD SCRAPS ANONYMOUS

One deterrent to composting year-round is that people want the kitchen garbage out of sight as quickly as possible. But avid composters have devised all sorts of ways for holding food waste until it's time to take it out for composting. Here are just a few.

Containers on the counter: Cookie jars, decorative pots, large pitchers, an unused bread box, or a canister set all make great countertop containers for food scraps. If the container is airtight, it won't have a smell until you open it; but dump frequently since the anaerobic conditions make a powerful odor! If you poke holes in the containers for ventilation, you can simply dump them as needed.

Containers near the door: Some people camouflage the compost-in-waiting by putting it in bags or milk cartons and stashing these in wicker bins, decorated milk cans, large tins, or even an umbrella stand!

And outside, waiting for the final trip: Try stashing compostables in a pretty mailbox, an old milk box, or a window box or flower planter that is not in use during winter. Once the material is frozen, there is no odor and no hurry to bury it; just wait for some temperate days and add a whole compost layer at once. If you have really wet compost ingredients, add shredded newspaper with every addition to absorb some of the moisture.

How Much Compost?

Many gardening books recommend adding soil amendments in *pounds* per 100 square feet. Agricultural advisories even suggest *pounds or tons per acre!* Well, home gardeners don't usually have a scale around to measure pounds of compost (not to mention tons), so try the bushel basket rule of thumb. It's a lot more practical.

Try to make enough compost to spread 2 or 3 bushels per 100 square feet of your garden every year. (If you have a scale, that's about 1 to 1½ pounds per square foot.) Depending on your compost's texture, this amount should give you enough to spread compost an inch or more deep over the soil surface. Make sure to spread it before planting.

But just how much compost is in a pile, anyway? Here's another way to estimate how much compost you're creating. A 4 × 4 × 4-foot pile (64 cubic feet) should give you enough to spread over a 40 × 50-foot (or 2,000-square-foot) garden.

If all this math seems too complicated, don't worry. Just keep adding to that compost pile. After all, you can *never* have too much compost!

Start Compost on a **Tarp**

You don't need a fancy compost bin to start composting. You can start a compost pile on top of a tarp. Simply poke a few small drainage holes in it and start piling materials on! Some folks leave the compost for a few months, then pull out the tarp with a lot of the finished bottom layer on it. (You can also lift off the top two-thirds of the pile and pull out the bottom.)

Or, you can pull out the tarp earlier in the composting cycle, in about three weeks, to simulate a first turning. Just pull out the bottom stuff and put it back on top of the pile.

Start **Early** by Waiting *Longer*

Most gardeners know that you need people and machines kept off the soil so that soil texture, or *tilth,* isn't destroyed—especially when it is wet. But spring fever can make an eager gardener forget all that. To force yourself to put away the tiller or shovel for a while, remember this: If you really want an early start in the garden, *wait longer!*

Working wet soil—soil that still clumps in your hand when you squeeze it—causes it to form hard clods that do not dry out nearly as quickly as untouched soil. (The clay particles form a powder that combines with moisture and forms a rocklike texture.) The root hairs of transplants actually take longer to start growing in soil in this condition, compared to unpulverized soil. As a result, plants can take two to three weeks *longer* to start growing.

So what *can* you do when spring fever hits and it's too wet to work the soil? Fern Bradley, managing editor of Rodale Garden Books, recommends jumping in the car and visiting a nearby garden center. "Reward yourself for your self-control by buying one new exciting plant that you can plant when the soil is ready to till."

Portable **Pens** for **Manure** Makers

Many gardeners know the benefits of raising geese, chickens, and ducks for the organic fertilizer they produce. These barnyard fowl are also valuable as pest-control agents. But, admittedly, these animals don't always eat just what you'd like when you'd like it, and they need to be kept *out* of the garden when some plants are in the seedling or fruiting stage.

The solution? Make a lightweight, portable duck pen (about 4 × 5 feet) out of chicken wire and a ½ × ½-inch wood frame. Two people can easily move it whenever you want your helpers to patrol for pests or fertilize new territory.

Direct from the **Bunny**

Gathering compost materials tends to involve a lot of hauling. So plan ahead for ways to ease the burden. Marge Vogel, of Eden, New York, does. Marge keeps pet rabbits, which produce great fertilizer. The rabbit cages have floors that are half wood and half ½-inch mesh (large enough for rabbit droppings to fall through). On cage cleaning days, Marge sweeps the droppings from the solid sections right onto the open mesh to fall out. Underneath each cage she uses a child's wagon that is exactly the width of the cage.

For a great timesaving way to gather rabbit droppings for the compost, park a child's wagon beneath the pen.

After a cage cleaning, her child (the one who wanted the bunny) pulls the wagon to the compost pile.

homegrown HINTS

MULCH THAT MANURE

All kinds of manure make wonderful soil amendments and fertilizer, yet many gardeners are afraid to use it because it can be full of weed seeds (especially horse manure, which is the kind most readily available). The single answer from thousands of gardeners: If you use manure, plan on mulch! Generally a 3-inch mulch of leaves, grass clippings, straw, compost, or a combination will suffice to block weeds. In a landscape planting, wood chips also work well. The few weeds that do pop through will be weak and poorly attached to the soil, so they'll be easy to pull. And, since mulch is so good for plants—from trees to tomatoes—the garden will benefit twofold, from manure and mulch.

Old Tire *Worm* Bin

If you love the idea of *vermiculture*, but don't want a bin full of wriggly worms taking up residence in your house, try this creative idea from Brian Geary, Master Gardener in Erie County, New York, and owner of Northern Lights Landscape. He encourages homeowners to landscape with nature in the backyard as well as right by the kitchen door. Brian says, "Recycle rubber tires and make the perfect worm bin!"

To make your own steel-belted worm bin, stack the tires five or six deep, filling the rim of each with shredded newspaper. Then, in the bottom of the "bin," start layering shredded paper, kitchen scraps, and some starter worms (red wrigglers). Keep adding indoor and outdoor organic matter as you go, and the worms will just keep reproducing and making compost. Actually, worm castings are the *diamonds* in the "black gold" department!

Don't try making the worm compost bin without using the tires, though. They're much more than just a container. They also provide ideal insulation for cold climates. If the worms are cold, they move toward the center of the tires, and when it is warm, they climb higher and toward the outside. A filled-up tire bin should let red wrigglers survive through most winters, even the harsh ones Brian faces in Buffalo, New York.

Old tires offer perfect outdoor shelter for worms. They keep the worms warm in the winter so you don't have to house them under your kitchen sink!

problem solver   WHAT WOOD CHIPS STEAL, COMPOST RETURNS

Wood chip mulches are a great weed barrier, and they last a long time so you don't have to replace them often. But wood chips can tie up soil nitrogen. So what's a savvy gardener to do?

Compost solves the problem. It gives soil microbes a rich source of nutrients as they work on digesting the wood chips, so the microbes don't have to raid all the nitrogen that's present in your soil while they do their work. Just spread a layer of compost on the soil you want to mulch before you put down those nitrogen-stealing wood chips. In a landscape planting, this combo gives you and your plants the advantages of both mulch and compost.

Hooked on Caffeine

If you work in an office building, take advantage of something that usually gets dumped in the trash—coffee grounds. Find out where the coffeemakers are in your building, and leave a 3-pound covered tin marked "Used Grounds." Then make the rounds routinely and take home all that potential black gold. (You don't have to separate the coffee grounds from the paper filter. You can dump the grounds, filter and all, right into your compost pile, because the filter will decompose, too.)

Ellen Phillips, executive editor of Rodale Garden Books, collects the coffee grounds at her building every day. "I started collecting coffee grounds in the winter when I was adding lots of wood ashes to my compost pile," says Ellen. "Ashes are alkaline, and since coffee grounds are slightly acidic, I thought they would help neutralize the pile. Earthworms love coffee grounds, and of course they smell good, too. And I get a special bonus since I work at Rodale Press—our coffee grounds are organic!"

Pepper the Compost

Homeowners often worry that animals will be attracted to compost piles, especially in urban situations. As an extension educator, Sally Cunningham has learned to explain that if you bury food scraps at least 8 inches deep into the pile, there should be no odor or attraction for animals. And of course, use *no* meat scraps, bones, or fats!

However, a city dweller who refuses to give up composting in spite of neighborhood varmints recommends some extra insurance. Sprinkle pepper on the food layers every time you add them. The odor, taste, and sneeze-effect are all just too much—even for a rat!

Spring Fever? Turn Up the Heat!

Get a jump on spring planting by heating up your soil. It's easy if you have room for a raised bed and have access to fresh horse manure (other kinds work, too). Build a bed of manure and top it with 2 to 4 inches of soil or finished compost, then plant into the top and water normally. The composting manure will produce heat and get your plants growing even when air temperatures are low. Once you've harvested your crops, you can add the manure and soil into your permanent beds or return them to the compost pile. Next spring, repeat the process.

USE MANURE TO WARM SOIL SAFELY

To take advantage of the heat that fresh manure gives off as it composts, try this simple cardboard box trick.

Put the manure in cardboard boxes, and line them up or stack them around your raised beds. The heat may help the soil warm up in spring or fall, and when the manure matures and cools off, it is convenient for spreading. Even the cardboard boxes will be easy to open and lay flat to help block out weeds.

A *Home-Garden* Compost **Spreader**

Compost can be hard to spread evenly because it is heavy when damp, hard to dig with a shovel, and not very crumbly. This is especially true if you use it before it's fully decomposed. So why not steal an idea from farmers: Use a spreader.

With a little ingenuity—and an old wheelbarrow—you can build a garden-size spreader that helps you put an even layer of compost on your garden.

Here's how to make it:

1. Look for an old wheelbarrow at the local dump or at a garage sale. Or maybe you already own one.

2. Use a saw with a metal-cutting blade to carefully cut a window at the end of the wheelbarrow. Make the cuts right where the sides meet the bottom of the wheelbarrow. The opening should be 2½ to 3 inches wide and run from side to side at the front end of the wheelbarrow (the end over the wheel and opposite the handles).

3. Carefully bend the cut edges toward the outside of the wheelbarrow so that you don't cut yourself on them when you use the compost spreader.

Here's how to use it: This tool works best if you pull the wheelbarrow, rather than push it, and shake it from side to side as you go. The opening should be wide enough to drop clumps of compost or even amounts of manure or leaves as you pull it along. If your load is too clumpy to slide out easily, get a friend to act as the "spreader." Your friend can use a push broom or garden rake to shove the compost or manure out the opening as you move along.

Cut an opening in the front of an old wheelbarrow and it becomes a garden-size spreader. Just pull the wheelbarrow along your garden's rows, shaking it from side to side.

Never Renovate Without It!

If you are going to take on the work of renovating a perennial bed, don't do so without compost! Follow these basic steps for a renovated and rejuvenated bed.

1. Lift the plant.

2. Divide.

3. Work some compost into the planting hole.

4. Replant.

Once you've finished the digging and dividing, you may think you're finished, but you're not! You can also give a boost to the rest of the plants. Just dig a 6-inch-deep hole on either side of every plant, and fill them with compost.

Turn *a Slope* into a **Lush** Garden

If your property slopes, you don't have to give up on having a beautiful garden. Take a tip from Sally Cunningham, author of *Great Garden Companions*. She's successfully amended her soil on a long slope and has had wonderful results from her garden.

"I have a garden on a long sloping hill, and I've often wished I had started it higher up the hill for better drainage. So year by year I'm moving the garden up the hill and making better soil at the same time."

Every year during spring cleanup, Sally makes a new 3-foot-wide by 3-foot-deep compost pile along the length of her garden on the slope above it. She uses leaves, sticks, perennial debris, some manure, and the clippings she collects from the first few lawn mowings. "Some might just call it a raised bed, but I find some warm composting going on, too, when I use the manure or grass—enough to call it compost."

Sally leaves the compost—which is really the future bed—at the back of the garden all season, occasionally giving it a stir or working in some kitchen scraps. It is soon hidden by tall flowers or tomatoes. Meanwhile, if nutrients run out of it, they flow downward, into the garden. According to Sally, "It tends to settle all year so that by next spring I have 3 more feet of great garden to plant in. Over ten years I have moved that garden 30 feet up that hill!"

problem SOLVer

KEEP SIDE-DRESSING WHERE IT BELONGS

Most crops benefit from a side-dressing of compost about a month after planting. But compost is so valuable that it's a shame to see it run off into the garden path or away from the root zone if a spring rain comes just after you have spread it.

Prevent nutrient runoff by using a pointed hoe first. Drag the hoe beside the plants, about 4 inches from their centers, or far enough that you aren't hilling up soil on the plant stem, making a little trench along the row. Don't make the trenches more than 2 inches deep, and look to be sure you are not disturbing new roots. Then sprinkle your compost along the trench, and it will do its work where you want it—even if it pours that day.

creative

Garden Care

You've planted the garden, the seeds are sprouting, and the excitement is just beginning! To make caring for all of your beds, borders, and container gardens easier and more fun, here are dozens of ideas from creative gardeners just like you. From innovative ways for making garden walkways and inexpensive, clever ideas for supporting growing plants to new methods for winterizing delicate roses and the best watering techniques, taking care of the gardens you've so lovingly created has never been easier.

52

Passive-Aggressive **Stump** Removal

Getting rid of a tree stump doesn't have to be back-breaking work, claims Kay Lancaster of Hillsboro, Oregon. As Kay attests, using her method may take quite a while longer, but your back will love it!

"What I do is bore as many deep holes into the stump as I can," explains Kay. "Then I add a mixture of dilute fertilizer and ground-up rotting wood, preferably from the same species as the tree I've removed."

Next, Kay packs the mixture into the holes well and covers the stump with plastic or melted paraffin to hold moisture.

The result? In a couple of years, Kay can usually kick the stump apart and remove the pieces.

Kay adds, "If you have a really rotten piece of wood to inoculate the stump with and an old blender that you no longer use for food preparation, put the wood in the blender with plenty of water and mix it up. Then dribble the mixture into the holes."

Containing **Invasive** Plants

If you happen to love a plant that has a reputation for being invasive, you don't have to be afraid to grow it. You just need to take the appropriate precautions.

"To stop invasive plants—and here in Mexico we have many—plant them in a pot sunk in the ground," instructs Wendy Holdaway of Mexico City, Mexico. "The roots grow out the holes in the bottom, but they don't seem to send out suckers the way they do when planted directly in the ground."

For really big plants such as bamboo, Wendy suggests cutting the bottom out of a 4- or 5-gallon plastic container and burying it to surround the plant's roots. "It's not totally effective," she adds, "but it goes a long way toward controlling the spreading."

Terra-Cotta *Walkways*

"After I bought my house, I discovered a bunch of broken terra-cotta pots and tan cement drainpipes at the far end of the backyard," says garden writer Erin Hynes of Chapel Hill, North Carolina. "I broke them into chunks and laid them in the garden as short walkways.

"The smallest pieces I used are about 4 inches square, and some chunks are as big as 10 × 6 inches."

Make sure you turn all the pieces so that any sharp edges are safely embedded in the soil.

When you use recycled items, adding a pathway is quick, easy, and inexpensive. A mosaic path made from pieces of broken pots and drainage tiles lets you turn trash into treasure.

Bury Weeds *under* a Burlap Pathway

"We line our vegetable garden paths with burlap coffee bags salvaged from a local roaster. We fold the bags in half and slightly overlap the ends to form a continuous path of burlap," says Natalie McNair-Huff, an organic gardener in Tacoma, Washington.

Natalie says she pins the bags in place with homemade staples made from old wire hangers (see page 14).

"Now the weeds will have to make it through four layers of burlap. And because the bags decompose, we don't have to remove them."

Award-*Winning* Path

There are plenty of unusual items that can make great garden stepping stones, says Stephanie Ferguson of Indianapolis, Indiana. You just need to think creatively. "My husband plays racquetball pretty well and wins lots of award plaques. Since he doesn't care to hang them up, I'm going to make garden stepping stones out of them."

Broken Dishes Stepping Stones

"Use broken dishes and concrete to make really cool stepping stones," says Karen Macomber, a home gardener in Cohocton, New York.

For molds, she uses old clothes boxes because she can simply peel off the box and compost it after the stepping stones have hardened. She pours the concrete mix into the mold, lets it set a little, then presses pieces of broken pottery on top to simulate a stained-glass effect.

Karen adds that you can pour concrete into any shape container. "You can even use old pie tins or cake pans. Simply let the concrete set somewhat, then turn it out onto a flat surface and decorate. Or, you can make a form on the ground with sand and pour the concrete directly where you want it to go." The leftover sand around the edges simply washes away.

Create customized stepping stones when you press broken dishes into partially set concrete. You can use cardboard boxes, old cake pans, or other cast-off containers to shape the concrete.

Variation for a No-Dig Garden

Newspaper is the standard base for gardeners preparing their no-dig garden beds, but cardboard is the material of choice for Godfrey Pearlson, a home gardener in Baltimore, Maryland.

"My garden is big and I've had much better luck using flattened cardboard boxes—which you can easily get for free from grocery stores," Godfrey says. "Flattened cardboard boxes cover larger areas than newspaper, they last longer, and they don't blow away while you're laying out the garden."

Extra! Extra! Wet Paper Stays Put!

Here's the answer for anyone who has struggled to put down newspaper mulch on a breezy day. "When laying down newspaper for weed control, fill a bucket with water to dip the paper in before placing it on the ground," says Dominique Herman of Bound Brook, New Jersey.

The wet paper will stay in place as you spread straw, wood chips, or whatever you plan to put on top of the newspaper. Dominique adds, "I fill a 5-gallon bucket and dip in whole sections of the newspaper—probably 10 to 12 sheets, or roughly ½ inch—to cover each area of the garden."

Slow Strawberry Pot Evaporation

"Paint the inside of clay strawberry jars with pot paint (available at garden centers) to keep water evaporation to a minimum," recommends Pat Kolb of Phoenix. "Some strawberry jars already have this coating when you purchase them, but some don't."

Perennial **Swap**

You can get plenty of perennials without a trip to the garden center—and without the expense.

"My twice yearly event called the 'Perennial Swap' is my favorite ingenious gardening effort," says Mimi Luther of Portland, Oregon. "I inherited a well-maintained garden overflowing with beautiful perennials. But I wanted to put in some other plantings and simply had no space. So, I invited all my friends and neighbors to the first Perennial Swap.

"For this spring and autumn event, everyone digs up some of their plantings and brings them to trade and share." Mimi made room for some additions to her garden, shared some lovely old species, and saved a bundle.

If you host or attend a plant swap, remember these guidelines: Don't swap plants that have disease or insect problems or that come from beds that have serious weed problems. Also, if you're swapping something that's a rapid spreader or that self-sows prolifically, warn the recipient so she can plant it with due caution.

Tree-Slice Garden Path

"Tree slices cut from a log provide handy stepping stones for deep flowerbeds, and they're quite attractive," says home gardener Mary Leunissen of Guelph, Ontario. "You can cut them as thick as you want with a chain saw or a carpenter's saw. Mine are about 2 inches thick."

Don't worry about the wooden stepping stones decaying rapidly from moisture and mulch. Mary assures, "I cut my slices three years ago and they still look good, even though they get a fair amount of moisture dumped on them." Mary adds that her tree slices have saved more than one plant, too, since they are large enough to work from "without the usual balancing act and resultant squashed plants!"

Log slices make a sturdy path that lets you step lightly through your garden.

problem **solver**   SOD SOLUTION

When you dig out sod to make a new garden, you can compost it or use it to patch bare spots in your lawn. But if you have a lot, you can use it to build a living fence, like home gardener Tanya Huff of Ontario is doing.

"We're building a sod wall at the north end of our orchard," says Tanya. "It's about 20 feet long, 3 feet wide, and will, in time, be about 4 feet high. It's roughly based on a 17th century sod wall we saw at Culloden, Scotland."

To create the wall, Tanya lays the sod like haybales on a wagon—alternating lengthwise and crosswise pieces, and being careful to keep cut edges from aligning to prevent gaps. According to Tanya, "Grass needs very little encouragement to grow. I cut sod in spring and fall when the ground is moist and rain is frequent enough so the sod quickly roots into lower layers."

Winter Protection for Roses, **Part I**

Here's a quick way to get roses ready for the onset of cold weather. "I recycle 1-gallon (or larger) plastic pots that perennials are sold in, and use them as collars for my roses in the winter," explains home gardener Mary Leunissen of Guelph, Ontario.

"I use a utility knife to cut out the bottom and up one side so that they open up, like the letter C. I place two wrapped around each other and the rose bush, then fill them with mulched leaves and compost."

Snap a pair of modified large plastic pots around a rose bush, and you have a sturdy wall to hold insulating mulch or compost in place.

Leaf-Sucking Vacuum

Why rake when you can vacuum? "I take my trusty (and now rusty) shop vac outside and vacuum up the leaves," confesses Diana Pederson, editor of *The Enabling Gardener*, of Lansing, Michigan. "It's much faster than raking."

Although vacuuming is quick and easy, Diana offers a few cautions. "Watch that you don't vacuum up too big a wad of wet leaves—they stuff up the hose. Also, be sure to dry out the vacuum container afterward, or you'll wind up with a rusty one like I have!"

A **Big** Box of Leaves

You don't have to wrestle with stuffing raked leaves into garbage bags. Della Kapocius of Grand Forks, North Dakota, has an easier solution. "Rake your leaves into a large cardboard box laid on its side. It's much easier than using leaf bags, especially if you're trying to do the cleanup alone."

Della suggests asking your grocer for the large boxes that toiletpaper comes in. "They hold a lot of leaves, but even when they're full, they aren't too heavy to drag across the yard."

On-the-Fly Tree Protection

Young trees can be virtual magnets to rodents looking for something to eat, so they need to be protected.

"When you don't have a tree guard handy," says Ada Davis of West Fork, Arkansas, "wind small sections of bird or deer netting loosely around the bottom of young trees as a temporary mouse, vole, and rabbit barrier."

Try wrapping the tree with aluminum foil first, then follow up with the netting to ensure that no one can get his nose through the netting for a tasty tree-bark treat.

Winter Protection for Roses, **Part II**

Here's a method for protecting tender rose bushes and fertilizing them at the same time. "For winterizing, rose cones have drawbacks (such as moisture buildup inside), so I find that it's better to mound the bushes," explains home gardener Colette Tremblay of Québec.

"To hold the mounding material, instead of using the small, flimsy rose collars found in the stores, I make my own out of chicken wire." Colette recommends a 4 × 3-foot piece of wire, folded in half so it measures 48 × 18 inches. She ties the chicken wire into a circle with wire or twine to make a generous-sized collar—18 inches high and 15 inches in diameter—which can hold a lot of insulating material.

You can fill the collar with leaves, straw, or soil, but Colette prefers to use compost or well-rotted manure. "When added late in the fall when the ground is at least partially frozen, compost doesn't promote untimely growth, and next spring, when you remove the collars, you can rake the compost or manure over the bed and lightly work it in. *Voilà!* Most of the fertilizing is done for the season."

Colette adds, "When I use a fine-textured insulating material such as screened compost, I line the inside of the chicken wire with newspaper first, to prevent the compost from falling through the chicken-wire holes."

Photographic Memory

Don't trust your memory of what blooms when in your garden? "Take photographs of your flowerbeds every week or so while they are blooming," recommends Sharon Gordon of Ohio. "The photos make it easier to plan future plantings by showing what blooms at the same time."

To keep your photos organized, label them and put them in a photo album or garden journal, and keep them with your perennial and seed catalogs for easy winter browsing and planning.

problem solver   JUNK MAIL MULCH

At last, a use for all that junk mail. "For the past two years I have shredded my junk mail with a very inexpensive home paper shredder, saved it, and then used it as mulch on our garden," says horticulture specialist Jeanne Schwaller of Jefferson City, Missouri. "It works just great."

Jeanne puts an in-line drip system next to the plants, then adds about a 4- to 6-inch layer of shredded junk mail. Then she sets the timer on the drip system to keep the plants moist beneath the mulch. Jeanne recommends wetting the paper with a hose first to keep it from blowing away.

According to Jeanne, she's only had to spend about ten minutes a week pulling weeds since spreading the junk mail mulch on her garden. But, she adds, "The most therapeutic part of this is spreading the junk mail and knowing it actually did some good."

In the late fall, Jeanne tills the decomposed paper into the garden where, she reports, it has somewhat improved her clay soil.

homegrown HINTS

HOMEMADE WATERING CANS

If you don't want to go to the expense or bother of installing drip irrigation, try this simple "watering can" system from Dr. Jeanne Schwaller, a horticulture specialist in Jefferson City, Missouri.

Use a 6- or 8-penny nail to punch holes in the bottom of 5-pound coffee cans or institutional-size vegetable cans. "The bottom of the can will look similar to a sprinkler head, but with fewer holes," says Jeanne. Set one can by each plant, and fill the cans with water. This trick makes short work of watering and soaks the soil deeply and efficiently, like drip irrigation does, without washing the soil away from your plants' roots. Refill the cans as needed.

Slow Drip Fertilizer

"For deep watering and fertilization, I cut the top off a 2-liter bottle, drill small holes in the bottom, fill it three-quarters full with compost, and bury it between plants," says home gardener Kim Barwick, of Hoffman Estates, Illinois. "When I water, I fill the bottles with water, which releases a weak compost tea deep into the root zone."

Soda Pop Irrigation

"When I transplant my tomatoes, I also plant a plastic 2-liter bottle with the bottom cut off and a hole drilled in the cap. I stick the capped end in the soil where the roots will grow—about 4 to 6 inches deep—and put a bottle about 12 inches from each side of the plant," says Mike McLain of Leroy, Alabama. Then all Mike has to do is fill the soda bottles with water about twice a week, instead of watering the plants daily.

Mike says that the size of the hole you drill in the cap can vary for different loca-tions and conditions. "In my sandy loam soil, a 1/16-inch hole works fine, but you may need a larger hole if you have clay soil. I usually cut the bottoms off the bottles with my band saw, but I have also cut some with a utility knife. I find that soda bottles with a longer, V-shaped neck and bigger neck ring stay in place the best."

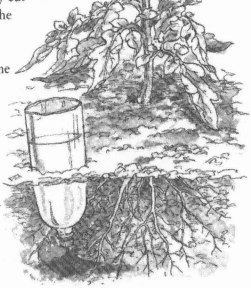

Take a break from daily watering with this practical soda bottle watering system. Your garden will enjoy the benefits of a steady supply of water while you tend to other garden tasks.

Boiled Eggs Aren't Just for Breakfast Anymore

"My grandmother taught me to use the water eggs are boiled in for watering plants, because it makes plants healthy and strong," says C. J. England of Hope, Idaho. "I've gotten in the habit of keeping all discarded eggshells in an odor-proof half-gallon container. When the container is about three-quarters full, I boil the eggshells and use the water on houseplants and in the garden. I've also had very good results using this water on seedlings. My grandmother used it to start plant cuttings, too."

Getting to the Roots

To encourage deep roots on sprawling or climbing vegetables—especially cucumbers, squash, and tomatoes—try this clever watering trick.

Yvonne Savio, Common Ground Gardening program manager for University of California Cooperative Extension in Los Angeles County, recommends burying a 5-gallon nursery container at the center of a planting hill, to within 3 inches of its rim, for a noncollapsible watering-and-fertilizing hole. "Plant seeds or seedlings in a slight depression just beyond the rim, and fill the depression with water to get the plants settled. Early in the season, each time you water the circle surrounding the container, also fill the container so water will seep out the bottom holes." By the time really hot weather comes, the plant roots will be deep enough that you can just fill the container when you water—you won't have to water from above. Your vegetable plants will appreciate the extra big drinks. And you'll love being able to just plunk the hose into the bucket.

For a midseason feeding, Yvonne recommends adding a shovelful of compost to the container. That way, you give your plants a dose of compost tea every time you fill the container with water.

Keep Moisture In

If you need to go out of town on business, you don't have to worry about your plants in clay pots drying out while you're away. According to Kathleen Weber of Upper Darby, Pennsylvania, you can simply wrap the clay pots with aluminum foil. "It keeps the clay pots damper for a longer period of time, so less watering is needed."

problem solver

RECYCLE YOUR COOKING WATER

Cooking dinner can use a surprising amount of water, and with a little advance planning, you can save that water and put it to good use. "Use the water from steaming vegetables, cooled down, of course, to water your potted plants," suggests Connie Gardner, assistant manager of Horsford's Nursery in Charlotte, Vermont. Just keep a plastic bucket on hand in your kitchen. Then when you're done steaming the veggies, pour the water into the bucket instead of down the drain. When dinner is done, the nutrient-filled water will be cool, and you can make the rounds of your houseplants or outdoor containers.

When to *Water*

Instead of guessing when it's time to water or using some fancy tool to check the moisture level of the soil, use a device that's always handy: your fingers. Stick them into the soil until they're completely covered, and feel for moisture. If they come up dry, it's time to turn on the sprinkler or get out the watering can.

PVC Pipeline *to the* Roots

While lots of gardeners have clever ways to water with soda bottles, you don't have to drink a lot of soda pop to create a watering system. Try this PVC pipeline tip from Natalie McNair-Huff, of Tacoma, Washington.

"Before you plant, bury all but the top of an 8- to 10-inch-long, 3-inch-diameter PVC pipe. Use one pipe for each plant. Then plant your tomatoes, peppers, or whatever beside the pipes. When the plants need deep watering, simply pour the water into the pipe."

You can use either perforated or regular PVC for this technique.

2-Liter **Irrigation** *Variation*

Here's another variation of the soda bottle watering system, from Laura Archbald of Clover, South Carolina.

Use a 2-liter soda bottle with the cap on, and punch about 8 to 12 holes in the top third of the empty bottle with a nail or awl. Turn the bottle upside down, and cut a hole about ½ inch from the bottom that is large enough for a garden hose to fit into. (Laura reports that she used to just cut off the bottom of the bottle, but she found that the water evaporated too quickly and the bottle would fill with debris, which would block the holes.)

Laura recommends burying about two-thirds of the bottle, capped end down, in the middle of a melon hill. "It also works great next to tomatoes. You can fill it with water once or twice a week, or use a watering can to fill it with a dilute fish-emulsion and seaweed combination," says Laura.

This twist on the soda bottle drip irrigation system leaves the bottom intact to reduce evaporation. Cut a hole that is just large enough for your hose to fit into, and you can make sure most of the water reaches your plants' roots.

Timely tip

Laura says that soda bottles last a few years. so here are her ideas for storing them between growing seasons. "The bottles clean up pretty well with the hose. Once they're clean and dry. you can hang them in the garage or basement and use them to store large seeds. bulbs. onion sets. and the like by stringing the bottles on a rope (tie the rope around the neck of each bottle). Or pull old panty hose or knee-high stockings over the bottles. knot them. and hang them by the knot.

Liquid *Life-Support* for Tomatoes

Kim Barwick, who gardens in Hoffman Estates, Illinois, shares her inexpensive method for making a funnel irrigation system for caged tomatoes. "This system encourages deep rooting," says Kim.

To make the funnel, drill a ¼-inch hole in the cap of an empty 2-liter soda bottle. Cut a 3-foot length of ¼-inch tubing, and push the end of the tubing into the hole, making sure it fits tightly.

Kim then cuts the bottom off the bottle and punches two small holes about 1 inch above the cut on opposite sides of the bottle. "Run a wire through the holes and use it to hang the inverted bottle on the tomato cage."

To complete the system, bury a 1- to 2-foot-long section of PVC pipe, at least 1¼ inches in diameter, at an angle about 1½ feet below the plant, so the end sticks out above the soil. Place the loose end of the ¼-inch tubing into the pipe. When you fill the bottle with water, it slowly drips into the PVC pipe, which channels the water directly to the roots.

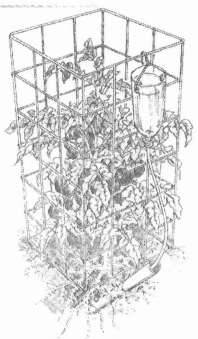

"Fill it and forget it" is all you have to do with this soda bottle watering system that sends a steady supply of water right to your tomato plant's roots. Water from the bottle "funnel" drips gradually into a pipe pushed into the soil, encouraging the plant to produce deep, healthy roots.

problem solver

PUT WATER EXACTLY WHERE YOU WANT IT

"There is no better watering tool than a battery filler," claims Pennsylvania garden writer Duane Campbell. "It looks like a turkey baster, but it is a bit bigger and sturdier. It's available for a few dollars from hardware or auto supply stores, and it puts exactly the amount of water exactly where you want it. No more mopping up water from the windowsills and floor when the spout overshoots."

With bushy plants, where the stream from a watering can spout runs off the leaves, you can slip the battery filler through the leaves and squirt the water right onto the soil. According to Duane, "The stream is gentle enough to water seedling flats, and you can control it to a drop at a time if you want. For very small pots, you can give them half an ounce at a time if needed. Best of all, one full squeeze gives you the same amount of water every time."

Duane adds, "When you go away for a few days and leave your houseplants' care to a brown-thumb neighbor, you can leave instructions to give this plant one squeeze, that one two, and so on."

homegrown HINTS

ICE YOUR HOUSEPLANTS

"I use ice cubes to water my houseplants because they don't run through the pot as fast as water does," says Gary Pierce, assistant agriculture extension agent in Smithville, North Carolina.

Gary recommends covering as much of the soil mix in the pot with ice as possible, being careful not to put the ice on the stem or leaves. "The ice doesn't freeze the roots, because the water has to be at least 33°F before it will flow into the soil. And, as the water makes contact with the soil particles, it gains heat. But if ice touches the stems or leaves, the plants can be damaged."

Since ice takes up more volume than water, Gary adds that overwatering is rarely a problem. As the ice cubes melt, they slowly release water. So there's plenty of time for the mix to absorb the water and become saturated, even if it's a mix that's rich in peat, which tends to shed water. Gary finds he only has to give his plants the ice treatment once or twice a week.

Weatherproof Rain Barrel

Toni Hawryluk of Seattle shares an idea for an inexpensive rain barrel that won't decay like the wooden ones.

"I found 45-gallon plastic drums at a discount store for just $15—and they live forever! I had a handyman attach a faucet near the bottom to control drainage, and then I put the drum on a rack under a downspout so my watering can fits under the faucet."

In addition to filling her watering can from her plastic rain barrel, Toni says, "I can also attach a garden hose to the faucet and dribble away."

$1 Rain Barrels

Grocery stores, bakeries, and restaurants are all good places to look for large plastic pails with handles and lids, which make perfect rain barrels in your garden. Food items such as flour and sugar are delivered in these pails, and you can often get them free—or at least cheap, in an array of sizes.

Gardener June Dean of Narragansett, Rhode Island, reports that she bought several of these pails for $1 each, and she uses them to both haul mulch and collect rainwater.

"They hold 40 pounds of mulch or 22 gallons of water. When not in use, these pails get tucked away out of sight. But when it rains, I take off their lids and capture the rainwater to pamper some of my plants that do better with rainwater than they do with chlorinated water from the tap."

Hanging Basket Oasis

Mary Yontz of Goshen, Indiana, shares this idea for preventing hanging baskets from drying out so quickly. "Put oasis or florist foam— the green stuff florists use in flower arrangements—into hanging baskets. It holds water longer so you don't have to water as often. I use about a 3-inch cube in the center of 8- to 10-inch pots, surrounded by potting soil."

Protecting Plants from Pets

Sometimes pets just don't respect garden boundaries. Here's a clever idea for a garden fence that looks nice while keeping dogs at bay.

"As I am owned by two Welsh Corgis who feel that they have a right to prowl through the garden at will, I have to work at keeping them off the newly emerging crowns of my perennials and herbs in the early spring," says Sue Murphy of Ogden, Utah. "What I came up with is cheap and easy."

Sue saves the prunings from a weeping mulberry and cuts them into 2½-foot sections. She uses the sections to edge her beds, pushing the ends into the soil and intertwining and overlapping them enough to eliminate Corgi-size holes.

Sue says, "This fence has worked very well and usually this looks so good that I leave it in for the growing season as a rustic edging to my walkways and borders. In the fall, I simply remove the twigs and then shred them."

In case you're wondering, Sue says no twig-ends have ever self-rooted.

If you don't happen to have a weeping mulberry, you can achieve the same effect in your garden using trimmings from trees such as weeping cherry, weeping willow, or any tree or shrub with flexible young branches, such as a forsythia.

Create a rustic fence or border for your garden with prunings of flexible branches. It's a great-looking solution for keeping dogs—and humans—on the path and out of the garden beds.

Temporary Bagging

If you receive bareroot perennials from a catalog before you have time to plant them, or if it's just too early to put them in the ground, here's a good solution for storing them until the time is right for planting.

Karen Helfert of Rockville, Maryland, reports that she stores bareroot hostas and peonies in freezer bags. "I put soil and the plants into plastic freezer bags, one plant per bag." To store them, put them in a plastic box and water them. Karen suggests leaving the bags open to prevent molding. You can store them inside, then move them to a porch as the weather warms, before finally transplanting them outside.

Timely tip

If you buy the freezer bags that have an area for labeling the contents, it's easy to record what type of plant is in each bag. And consider using the new ventilated zipper-top vegetable storage bags. That way you don't have to keep the bag open, and air can still circulate.

problem solver — MOLESKIN TO THE RESCUE

"When I'm going to do a lot of raking or heavy digging, I put a piece of adhesive-backed moleskin over the blister-prone area of my hand before putting on my gloves. Then I just peel it off when I'm done working," says Bambi Cantrell, of Jacksonville, North Carolina.

Bambi recommends using the moleskin on gardening tools, too, to cushion their handles.

Soothing Treatment *for* Gardener's Hands

Linda Pek of Vienna, Austria, swears by this healing hand treatment after a long day in the garden.

"After you come in from gardening all day with your hands all rough and red, scrub your hands to get rid of all the dirt, then slather them all over with lots of your favorite hand cream. Afterward, put on rubber gloves, and hand wash all the dirty dishes that your family deposited in the sink while you were outside. Be sure to use really hot water. There's something about doing it with very hot water that causes the hand cream to penetrate skin really well!"

Handy Drinks **Revive** Parched Gardeners

Freeze ahead for a supply of cold, refreshing drinking water to sip during those hot, tiring summer afternoons in the garden, suggests garden writer Barbara Ellis, author of *Taylor's Guide to Growing North America's Favorite Plants*.

Barbara saves 12- and 16-ounce plastic juice and water bottles, fills them three-quarters full of water, and freezes them. When she heads out to the garden, she tosses one in her garden cart.

"Just when I'm really starting to get hot, there's enough melted water in the bottle to quench my thirst," Barbara says.

Rice Remedy for Gardening **Aches** and **Pains**

Sometimes gardening is better for the soul than it is for the body. But there are ways to remedy aching muscles and other symptoms of garden over-indulgence.

Here's how Laura McKenzie of Springville, Alabama, handles gardening aches and pains. "I fill a bleached, clean sock—a thick sports sock—with rice, knot the top of it, and stick it in the freezer for treating garden-sore muscles. The rice conforms to the aching joint or limb better than ice or even a bag of frozen peas, and the soft sock is comfortable next to the skin," says Laura.

Timely tip

Laura says a sockful of rice is great for warm relief, too. "If you heat the sock in the microwave—with a cup of water next to it to be safe—it works as a heating pad. It even soothes bug bites." A word of caution with the microwave: Don't overheat the rice. Since you are heating it in a sock and not water, it can burn if it is cooked too long.

Easy Pruning Cleanup

"When you prune, first place a tarpaulin on the ground near your work space," recommends Peg Baseden, a Delaware Master Gardener. "Throw all the trimmings on it, and you can easily pull them to your compost pile."

Look for old bedspreads at yard sales to use as tarps. They're cheap and sturdy— and large enough to hold lots of trimmings.

Garden **Hose** Fencing

"You can make inexpensive fencing to define small garden plots, such as those in community gardens," says Peg Baseden, a Delaware Master Gardener. "If you're planning to discard a garden hose and old broom handles or similar wood, use the broom handles for posts and string the old hose between them."

Peg says to attach the hose near the top of the posts by tying it on with twine or tacking it on with nails. "It keeps people out of the plots and looks 'gardeny'."

Secure Tunnels

Tunnels covered with plastic sheeting are a great way to protect plants at the start and end of the growing season, but keeping the plastic from blowing off the arch supports can be a challenge. Stephanie Ferguson of Indianapolis has found a way that works for her raised box beds. "I have *finally* achieved success with tunnels!" she exclaims. Here's Stephanie's winning method.

Stephanie uses two sizes of PVC pipe to hold the plastic row covers in place over her arched tunnels—one about 2 inches in diameter and a second that is almost small enough to fit inside the 2-inch pipe. In addition to the PVC pipes, you'll need nuts and bolts for anchoring the plastic.

1. Cut each pipe in half lengthwise and nest the pipe with the smaller diameter inside the larger pipe, like two spoons nested together.

2. Drill holes along the length of each nesting pair of PVC pipes, about every 8 to 12 inches.

3. Separate the pipes, put the plastic between them, and nest them back together.

4. Secure the pipes together by putting bolts through the holes and fastening nuts on the bolts.

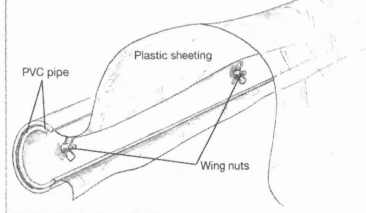

Hold plastic sheeting or floating row covers securely in place with nesting PVC pipe anchors. No more blowing away or tearing apart!

Anchoring Plastic Covers

"The nailing-strip edge of vinyl siding, which is quite strong because it is folded over a couple of times in manufacture, is commonly cut away around windows and doors in long strips during installation on a house," notes Terry Klokeid of Amblewood Farm on SaltSpring Island, British Columbia. "These long strips are great for attaching plastic over cold frames, rabbit hutches, and the like.

"The folded part gives the material some rigidity and holds the plastic sheeting down well, yet it's possible to attach the nailing strip to the wood frame of the structure with short screws. You don't need nails, which can pop out, or long screws, which make big holes and are hard to remove. Simply drill a small pilot hole through the vinyl, where it's one layer thick."

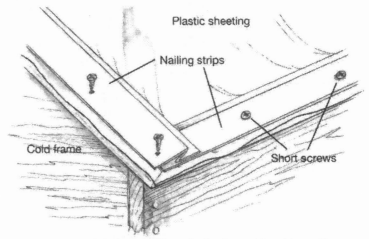

If you can get your hands on leftover vinyl siding nailing strips, either from your own home-improvement stash or a construction site in the neighborhood, they make a sturdy yet easy way to attach plastic sheeting to cold frames.

homegrown HINTS

EASY ANCHORS FOR TUNNEL HOOPS

Here's an easy way to anchor large plant tunnels. Find metal pipes narrower in diameter than the PVC you'll be using for the hoops. For example, use ½-inch-diameter metal piping for ¾-inch-diameter flexible PVC. "Cut the metal pipe into 2-foot lengths, and pound them about 1 foot into the ground, 18 to 24 inches apart within a row," explains Ginny Prins of Victoria, British Columbia.

Next, gather flexible PVC piping for the hoops. To frame your hoop house, "just slip your PVC over the metal pipes and you have the beginnings of a hoop greenhouse," Ginny says.

Snow Shovel Does Double Duty

"In the fall we wait until all the leaves are down, then my husband pushes them into a big pile with a plastic snow shovel," says Sue Blyth of Ottawa, Canada. "Because the snow shovel is plastic, the edge isn't sharp, so it just slides over the lawn or pavement and scoops everything in its path, including the acorns."

J-Channeling
Plastic Covers

Another type of vinyl-siding scrap can keep rigid plastic panels from blowing off cold frames and other structures, says Terry Klokeid of Amblewood Farm on SaltSpring Island, British Columbia.

"You can use scraps of J-channel from vinyl siding to support lightweight plastic or wood panels," says Terry. "If you use a rigid cover over a cold frame, then just a few bits of J-channel, strategically placed at the corners, will hold it firmly even in the wind."

Simply screw short lengths of the J-channel at the corners (or along the entire side if you prefer) on both of the sloping sides of the cold frame, and slide the cover in so it's sandwiched between the two Js.

The J-channel used to hold vinyl siding in place also works in the garden. Attached to a cold frame, it lets you slip a cover in or out.

Another piece of J-channel or a piece of scrap wood may be required on the lower edge of the frame to prevent the cover from sliding out.

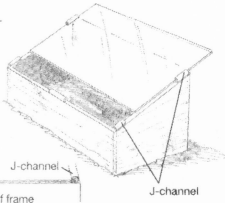

Top view — Plastic cover — J-channel — J-channel — Back edge of frame

Weighted
Row Covers

Here's an easy method for keeping row covers from blowing off of your garden. "If you need more weights than you have heavy rocks, fill some plastic gallon jugs nearly full with water," suggests Sharon Gordon, a bio-intensive gardener in Ohio. "Put the caps back on and use the jugs to weight the edge of the cover."

Save those plastic gallon jugs from milk, water, or juice, and fill them with water to use as weights to keep your row covers in place. When it's time to remove the row covers, you can use the weights to water your plants.

The *Light* Timing

Even if you don't have a timer for your indoor plant light setup, there's an easy way to make sure your seedlings consistently get 18 hours of strong light per day. Just make turning the lights on and off part of your daily routine, as Deborah Turton of Gaithersburg, Maryland, does. "I plug my lights in around dinnertime, leave them on all night, and unplug them around lunchtime," says Deborah. "This lets the seedlings have about 18 hours of intense light."

Get the *Upper Hand* on *Hanging Baskets*

Here's the answer if you've ever struggled to make a hanging basket where the plants hang out the sides and bottom. Instead of struggling to work with the basket on your potting bench, try hanging the basket at about chest height.

"When planting a hanging basket that will contain plants that will hang out of the bottom or sides, use a stepladder and broom or rake to create a convenient place to hang the basket," advises Della Kapocius of Grand Forks, North Dakota. "Open the stepladder and place the broom or rake handle across the roller-tray shelf and the opposite ladder rung. Hang your basket from the handle, and your basket will be positioned just right."

Planting the sides and bottom of a hanging basket can be tricky when it's resting on a table. Hang your basket from a broom handle slipped through the tray and top rung of a ladder, and plant all around your basket with ease.

problem solver

BUYING TIME FOR PERENNIALS

"When dividing perennials, I always pot up the divisions, using that pile of black gallon-size nursery containers I have carefully accumulated out in the garage," says gardener and garden writer Duane Campbell of Towanda, Pennsylvania.

Duane says that he gives some potted perennials to friends and sells others at his spring yard sale. Even those divisions he plans to replant in the garden get potted first. That gives Duane a few days to consider their new location rather than making a snap decision.

Duane also likes to keep at least one division in the pot for a season to see how it does. "Some of my best patio container plants are perennials that took well to container growing. Mums get divided every year and always produce more divisions than I can possibly use. But potted in gallon containers, they can grow strong and lush in an out-of-the-way spot (but near enough for the hose to reach them). Then in fall, when the annuals falter, I have dozens of mums ready to plop in their places and keep the garden looking great."

More Space for *Hanging* Plants

If you have a fenced-in yard, you can turn that fence into a display area for hanging baskets with the addition of some inexpensive garden lattice. Lyn Belisle, a home gardener from San Antonio, did just that.

"I nailed a 2-foot-wide strip of lattice horizontally onto the 2 × 2 that runs along the top of my fence like a cap board," says Lyn. (She let a little of the lattice board hang over the back of the fence for balance.) To hang baskets, lay a bamboo pole across the top of the lattice, then slip the hanging baskets up through the holes in the lattice and hook them over the bamboo.

"It's strong and sturdy, and I can move the plants around without any trouble just by repositioning the bamboo pole," says Lyn. And here's the real reason Lyn thought of this idea in the first place—she wanted to keep her cat from jumping over the fence. So if you know a curious cat that you'd like to keep in—or out—of your yard, try Lyn's hanging plant rack idea.

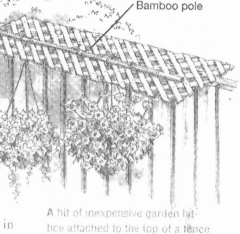

Bamboo pole

A bit of inexpensive garden lattice attached to the top of a fence can serve two purposes. It can give you a great place to display hanging baskets, which will brighten your garden. And it can keep your cat—or the neighbor's cat—from vaulting over the fence to areas where it doesn't belong.

homegrown HINTS

THE FINE ART OF SIFTING

If you have rocky soil or a supply of compost that needs to be sifted, Terry and Libby Klokeid of Amblewood Farm on SaltSpring Island, British Columbia, recommend sifting in two or more stages rather than just one, because it's easier. "We have had to sift rocks from all our garden soil, because our property has never been cultivated before."

Terry says they built a series of seven sifters, each measuring about 2 × 3 feet, with successively finer mesh, from chicken wire to window screen. Terry says, "We call the chicken wire sifter a 7 and the window screen a 1." Sift into a box, crate, or wheelbarrow, then repeat the process.

Terry adds, "We can customize what we do—for beds that will hold small-seeded plants such as carrots, the soil goes through a few siftings, using sifters 7, 5, and 3 or 2. Since crops like tomatoes don't mind a few sticks or rocks, we use larger sizes of mesh for sifting compost for those beds."

homegrown HINTS

PERFECT PEONY SUPPORT

Every gardener who loves the lush springtime blooms of peonies knows how tough it can be to keep them standing—especially after a spring shower. You can buy peony supports, but sometimes they are not enough to keep your peonies upright and beautiful.

"For beds of peony plants that are too big for those standard metal peony support rings," reports home gardener Edie Carlson of Saint Thomas, Ontario, "I use the 12-inch-tall lattice used for topping fences that you can buy at home-improvement or hardware centers. I simply construct a small fence that goes around the whole peony bed."

Lawn Edging Is **Child's** Play

For a tidy lawn edging that's easy enough for your kids to install, try this idea from Kathryn Marsh of County Dublin, Ireland.

"I keep a pile for all those irritating too-small-to-use stones that come up in the garden," says Kathryn. "Every so often the children have an entertaining hour or two arranging them in a 1-foot-wide band along a stretch of lawn edge, just below soil height. Then we sweep a mixture of sand and cement into the stones, and the kids go over it with the watering can."

The result of this "child's play" is a decorative lawn edging you can mow across, a good barrier to stop the grass from running into the borders, and happy kids. "And you will never need to neaten the lawn edge again."

Kathryn cautions that it is important to make the stone edging low enough so that the lawn mower blades won't hit it. One way to do this is to strip off the sod and put the layer of stones down on the soil underneath. Or you can simply have your helpers place the stones in a band on the soil at the existing edge between lawn and garden bed.

Stake Protection

"Cut a slice in old racquetballs or tennis balls that have lost their bounce, and slip the balls over the top of low stakes," recommends Susan Schoneweis, extension coordinator for Home/Environmental Horticulture at the University of Nebraska–Lincoln. That way, if someone trips and falls on a stake, they'll be less likely to injure themselves. If you don't have racquetballs or tennis balls, you can also use wads of old nylon hose and secure them with duct tape to the stakes, but it's a lot more work.

Be a **Cheap-Stakes** Winner

Don't find yourself short on stakes when plants flop. When freelance garden writer Veronica Lorson Fowler, of Ames, Iowa, did a remodeling project in her house, she saved pieces of quarter-round wooden molding that was used as trim along the floor. "The molding pieces make great plant stakes," Veronica says. "And whenever a tall tool, like a rake or broom, breaks, I always saw it off. Again, great staking material."

Wrap Up for Winter

"To help keep potted perennials from freezing, I line the insides of the pot with bubble wrap before planting," says home gardener Debra Schaefer, of Pittsboro, Indiana. "This allows me to leave marginally hardy plants outside and enables less-hardy ones to survive in the garage." But don't line the bottoms of pots, so water can still drain out of them.

Houseplant Insurance

"When you buy a new houseplant, always root a cutting as soon as possible and give it to a friend," quips garden writer Duane Campbell of Towanda, Pennsylvania. "That way, when yours dies, you'll know where to go to replace it."

Six-Pack Plant Supports

For staking perennials that die back each winter—specifically those with dense leaves at the top and stalky undergrowth, such as peonies—save the plastic six-pack rings from your soda or juice cans. Dawn Alleman, an extension agent from Norfolk, Virginia, says, "As the plants sprout in the spring, drop the intact plastic ring over the emerging shoots. As the shoots grow through the rings and raise them up, the rings support the plant so that it won't flop over with heavy buds and blooms."

Dawn suggests using several six-pack rings to support larger plants, and she reminds gardeners to be sure to put on the rings when the plants are just emerging. "As with any grow-through staking, if you wait too long, the stems will leaf out and you'll have to bend the plant into the holes."

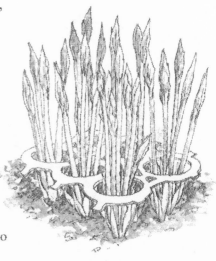

Instead of recycling the plastic rings from six-packs, reuse them as support for emerging peonies. As the foliage grows, the plastic holders won't be visible, and they'll help prevent the heavy blossoms from drooping.

Downspout Solution, **Part I**

"I planted Corsican mint (*Mentha requienii*) where my downspouts meet the grass," says home gardener Liz Bonfiglio of North Hills, Pennsylvania. "I don't use the weed wacker often, and the mint keeps the grass in check and adds a delightful mint scent when I mow the edges."

Liz adds that you can also use woolly thyme (*Thymus pseudolanuginosus*) instead of mint or grass, but only if your downspout area isn't consistently wet or soggy.

Downspout Solution, **Part II**

"I put pieces of broken clay pots under my downspouts to keep soil from washing into the yard or onto the sidewalk," says Candy Sheagley, an Advanced Master Gardener in Brookston, Indiana.

A *Means* of *Support*

Don't throw away that torn, bent, or broken umbrella. Take the cloth off the frame and use it to stake bush-type peas, which lean instead of climb.

"Stick the handle of a fully opened umbrella in the ground so that the spokes are about 5 to 6 inches above the ground," instructs Pat Lenzo of Boston, Georgia, editor and publisher of the *Home-steader's Connection*. "Plant peas below each spoke, and as they grow, the tendrils will grasp the spokes for support."

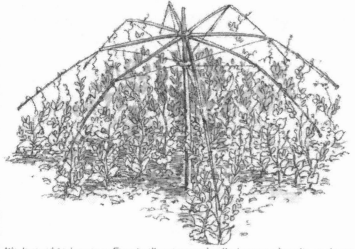

It's bound to happen. Eventually your umbrella tears or bends, and you need to replace it. But save the old one and remove the fabric. The metal frame is just the right size for supporting bush-style peas.

Clothespin Tension Line

"Tie twine through the springs of two clothespins, and clamp them to a stake on each side of a cucumber, pea, or other reluctant climbing vine to create a trellis," suggests Yvonne Savio, gardening education coordinator for the Los Angeles County Cooperative Extension Service. "The clothespins allow you to move or adjust the tension on the twine easily, without a lot of untying and retying knots that are hidden in the plant foliage."

Yvonne adds that you can use her twine and clothespin method in conjunction with trellis netting, too. She says that adding the twine over the trellis "helps tie in straggling and unruly growth that doesn't attach itself to the netting."

Poultry Netting to the **Rescue**

Poultry netting, also called chicken fencing or chicken wire, is easy to hang as a trellis support for lightweight vines. You can attach it to the side of a garden shed or to the edge of a porch roof with a staple gun or by hanging it on small nails.

"I use it to support morning glories and loofahs. I grow them where they provide shade for a west-facing window," explains home gardener Vera Smith of Rusk, Texas.

Timely tip

Vera has other ingenious uses for poultry netting. "I also use poultry netting as a type of bulletin board: I hang it on the shed wall and use clothespins to hang seed packages and garden plans. And I use it in a dark area to hang herbs to dry."

Low-Cost, *Flexible* Arbor

For an inexpensive arbor for climbing plants, consider a panel of cattle fencing. Gardener Vera Smith of Rusk, Texas, says she finds that it makes a great arbor.

"The panel is 16 feet long and 4½ feet high—and it's flexible. You can bend it into an arch and grow climbing plants on each side. The fencing bends to form an arch that is tall enough for adults to walk through."

Vera explains that to install her arbor, she simply bent the fencing and butted the ends next to the wooden sides of her raised garden beds to make an archway over the path area. She says that the tension of the wire keeps the flexed panel upright, and the raised beds anchor the arch at its base. "We like it because it provides a shady sitting spot out in the garden."

If you like Vera's arbor but don't have raised beds in the right position to hold it in place, anchor your fence-panel arbor with tent stakes instead. Make sure to wear gloves to protect your hands from rough edges or wire ends.

Updated **Bean-Pole** Teepee

Here's an improved version of the classic bean-pole teepee. "To make an hourglass bean teepee, pound three or more stakes into the ground several feet apart in a triangle or circle (so that they cross at their centers), and tie them together at the center," says Sharon Gordon of Ohio.

Sharon says that the beans will grow away from each other once they cross the center of the pole, making the beans easier to see and harvest.

"I use 6-foot stakes. Although 8-foot stakes would work well too, you'd need a ladder to stand on for pounding the stakes into the ground."

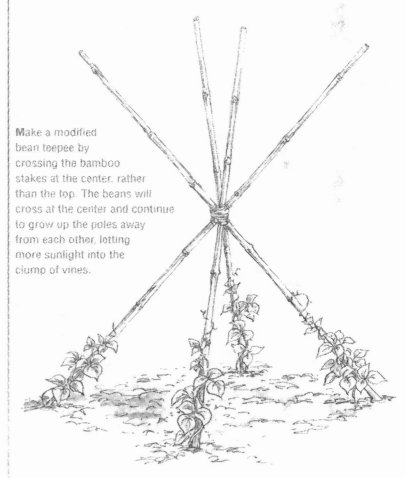

Make a modified bean teepee by crossing the bamboo stakes at the center, rather than the top. The beans will cross at the center and continue to grow up the poles away from each other, letting more sunlight into the clump of vines.

Bicycle Wheel Rims *Find New Life* as Plant Supports

If you have some old bicycle wheel rims laying about the garage or basement, give them new life as supports for climbing beans and peas. That's what Shona Lamoureaux of Christchurch, New Zealand, did. You need two rims for each unit you want to make, and according to Shona, each unit can support about 25 plants.

Just because your old bicycle is ready for the junkyard doesn't mean it's not good for something! Save the old wheel rims and use them to train climbing peas. All you need is some string and a wooden stake, and you can make this clever round trellis.

Here's Shona's technique:

1. Remove all the spokes from two rims.

2. Use a cross of wood or pipe to divide the center of one rim into four sections. You can nail the wood in place through the spoke holes.

3. Next, find a pole that's slightly taller than the height that your beans or peas will grow. (You'll push about

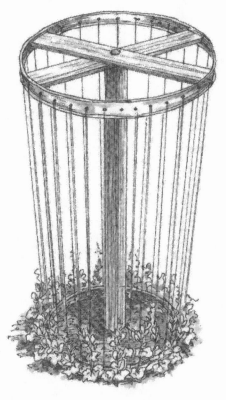

one-third of the pole into the ground to make it sturdy.) So if your peas grow to 6 feet tall, you'll need an 8-foot pole. Nail the pole to the center of the cross so that it's perpendicular to the plane of the rim. If you use a metal pole (which won't rot in the ground), you'll need to drill a hole to attach it to the wooden crosspieces.

4. Put one rim on the ground, and push the pole with the other rim attached to its top into the soil in the center of the rim on the ground. Connect the top and bottom rims by stringing twine through the spoke holes, then secure the bottom rim to the ground with tent pegs or ground staples. (See page 14 for information on making your own staples.)

5. You're ready to plant!

"Plant beans or peas around the bottom rim, and they will climb up the string," says Shona. "I usually plant a tomato plant or some sort of herb or flower in the center of the rings, too, to take advantage of the space."

snazzy

Season Stretchers

Few things gladden a gardener's heart as much as picking the first ripe tomato in the neighborhood or surprising friends with a garden-fresh dinner in midwinter. Finding methods for overcoming whatever adverse conditions come your way is what season extension is all about. Whether your garden goal is to gather the earliest harvest ever or to stretch your fall crops into winter and then into spring, you'll find lots of great tips to guide you and tools to help you. Get ideas from market gardeners and home gardeners who have figured out their own clever ways to outsmart the elements.

Mobile Gardens *Extend* the Seasons

"Container growing is the ultimate season extender, since the container can be placed wherever conditions are suitable," says Mac Cheever. Mac has to contend with subzero temperatures during much of the winter in his Zone 4 market garden in Milton, Wisconsin.

You can move potted garden plants anywhere when frost threatens—even into your house, Mac says. "Plants such as hot peppers generally survive winter in the house fairly well and take right off the next year like they never quit," he explains. "Both early and late production are enhanced, and you have the added benefit of red, ripe peppers outside the usual season."

Hanging baskets make nifty season stretchers, too. Many flowers and vegetables will grow quite nicely in them, and their hanging height can raise them above low spots where frost settles. "Hanging containers give you the option of concentrating them in an area that may be more easily covered during early frosts than a conventional garden is," adds Mac.

Four-Season Harvest Secrets

Eliot Coleman, author of *The New Organic Grower* and *Four-Season Harvest*, says there are basically just three secrets to his year-round garden production in Harborside, Maine:

1. Proper variety selection.

2. Carefully timed planting.

3. Simple season extenders.

Eliot plants only the most cold-hardy varieties. As the days grow shorter in fall, he makes successive plantings every few days inside his un-heated hoop houses. He then covers the beds with spun-bonded row covers.

Don't forget to water during the winter, Eliot advises. By keeping it moist, you can increase the minimum temperature by 4°F under the spunbonded covers.

Plant cold-hardy varieties in a hoop house, cover the beds with row cover, and you can enjoy fresh produce year-round.

problem solver

SUCCESS STARTS WITH SEED SELECTION

It's no surprise that Robert L. Johnston Jr. cites variety selection as the number one secret of success in extending the season. The founder and chairman of Johnny's Selected Seeds in Albion, Maine, knows that enjoying garden-fresh vegetables beyond the "normal" growing season starts with the seeds you sow.

"Grow really hardy varieties, and be sure to plant them so they mature at the right time of year," Rob says. "Then just leave them in the garden." As an example, he mentions one of his own favorite season-stretching vegetables, 'Roulette' cabbage.

"It's an English-type winter cabbage that may be harvested from the field all winter in New Jersey (Zone 6). It's like a big brussels sprout." Rob says the thin, slightly crinkled leaves of 'Roulette' are tops in taste for adding to salad or stir-fry, or for making coleslaw.

"In severe gardening climates, you can mulch 'Roulette' with leaves or straw to allow air circulation while protecting it from direct hits from frost," Rob explains. "It's too cold to do that in Maine," he adds, "but we have some in my root cellar here, and it stores well."

Don't *Fight* to Grow **Fussy** Crops

Instead of fighting to grow plants that are fussy about day length, temperature, or moisture, find substitutes that are more forgiving of the elements, recommends Milton, Wisconsin, market gardener Mac Cheever.

"I grow 'Stonehead' cabbage because the compact heads resist the splitting that can be caused by an early, hot summer following a cool, wet spring," says Mac. "Most cabbages keep quite well right in the ground. This year's 'Stonehead' cabbage was planted in April, and it still looked good before Christmas.

"Likewise, I substitute Swiss chard for lettuce and spinach," Mac adds. "It's incredibly cold-hardy in my Zone 4 garden, doesn't bolt, and makes it through the hot days of summer quite nicely when either one of the other two would fry. I also don't have to plant successive crops, which saves time and cultivation efforts, and helps to extend my enjoyment of the gardening season, as well as the length of the season itself."

homegrown HINTS

PICK THE RIGHT PLANTS

Engineer and inventor Buckminster Fuller's advice was, "Don't fight forces, use them." So Maine market gardener Eliot Coleman, author of *Four-Season Harvest*, asks himself which plants actually like cold. His list of favorites includes mache (corn salad), claytonia (miner's lettuce), and oriental greens such as mizuna and tatsoi.

"They not only like our growing conditions, but were designed to grow in them," says Eliot. "Sow tatsoi in September and, man, it is so happy in winter!"

But you'll get this enthusiastic response only if you plant early enough that your plants become established before the days get too short, Eliot cautions. "Where we are in coastal Maine we have less than ten hours of daylight from November 7 through February 7. Anything you plant during that time will just sit there."

Turn Up the Heat!

"The most ingenious thing we do to extend the season is live in the maritime Pacific Northwest," jokes Bob Gregson. Bob and his wife, Bonnie, are market gardeners who have little trouble raising most crops on Vashon Island in Puget Sound, Washington. But even in this mild climate, there are some crops that benefit from season extenders.

"Melons, tomatoes, and other heat-loving plants don't like the cool nights here, so we have to do everything we can to protect them," Bob says. "We harden off the plants well and try to get them out as early as we can."

The Gregsons transplant their sturdy seedlings into beds warmed by a layer of 6-mil clear plastic mulch and cover them with row cover.

The result is success: six kinds of canteloupes and three or four watermelon cultivars in a climate not meant for these heat lovers. Bob adds that he and Bonnie grow only small, short-season melon cultivars, like 'Earligold'.

Build a Big Box of *Extra-Early* Greens

If you have an unheated greenhouse and want to grow plants like lettuce that are only somewhat cold-hardy, take a tip from market gardener Elizabeth Henderson of Newark, New York.

"I built a wooden box cold frame in my greenhouse, and I transplant small lettuces into it in fall. They sit through winter, and in February they get going without my heating the greenhouse at all," says Elizabeth. Her planting box measures 5 × 10 feet. It's 2 feet deep and it's nearly filled with garden soil.

Elizabeth says she moves the lettuce into the cold frame in her double-poly hoop house (a hoop-shaped greenhouse covered with two layers of polyethylene) during the first week in October, when the plants are no more than 2 inches tall. She also transplants small collard plants (full-grown collards just go to seed), tatsoi, Chinese cabbage, and spinach into her homemade cold frame.

"The half-grown plants are the ones that really seem to overwinter well," she explains. "Then, in February, they really take off!"

Maintenance is a snap. "If it gets really, really cold, I just throw a tarp over the bed. Other than that, I don't do anything to protect the plants," Elizabeth says. "There is just one catch: In March, we start heat in the greenhouse for our newly planted seedlings. And as soon as they get heat, these overwintered plants get covered with aphids."

The solution to this problem is simple: Make sure to use up all your overwintered crops of greens before you turn up the heat in your greenhouse for starting seedlings.

A cold frame makes it easy to grow extra-early greens in an unheated hoop house.

A **Warm Spot** in *Early* Spring

To give his young plants a head start on Minnesota's short growing season, gardener Jim Tjepkema uses a heating cable to warm his 60 × 28-inch cold frame. The 33-foot-long cable is mounted on plywood and strung back and forth across the bottom of the frame beneath a layer of sand. A piece of hardware cloth on top of the sand provides a sturdy resting place for plants in pots or trays, Jim explains. He keeps the heating cable's thermostat set at 71°F.

"I take the cover off the frame on sunny days when I won't be at home to adjust the ventilation. I use a stick to hold it partway open on mild, sunny days if it gets too hot in the frame," Jim says. A thermometer in the frame lets him keep an eye on the temperature. "I close the frame at night, and on very cold nights, I cover it with old blankets. I have had good luck with a variety of plants for three years now."

Jim adds that it's important to follow the manufacturer's instructions when installing heating cables and similar items in a cold frame, to avoid the risk of fire and to make sure you keep your plants warm, but don't cook them.

Timely tip

If you're like Jim and can't always be around to uncover your heated cold frame on sunny days, consider putting a high-tech helper to work. A thermostatically controlled automatic vent opener, available from mail-order greenhouse- and garden-supply businesses, can be set to raise and lower the cover of your cold frame, depending on the temperature inside the frame.

problem solver
NEW PLASTICS SOFTEN THE SUN

West Point may not teach anything about organic gardening, but Michael Contratto says his West Point education in mechanical engineering has helped turn him into a better gardener.

When Mike began sharing a neighbor's greenhouse, it didn't take him long to figure out why it was overheating during the day. "We were getting too much light and cooking everything," says Mike, who gardens in Zone 5 in Chillicothe, Illinois. "I had to put up a shade cloth on the inside in order to keep the vegetables from cooking by late March and early April. It got up to 100°F in there!"

The shade cloth was only temporary. To make the greenhouse more manageable, Mike replaced its Plexiglas covering with double-pane, extruded plastic sheets. He says the new covering is very strong and flexible, and it diffuses sunlight much better than Plexiglas. The dead-air space between the two layers of plastic provides more heat-holding insulation at night and helps keep the temperature from soaring during the day. As a result, Mike says, "We harvest lettuce a month before anyone else can even think about it. It's so easy to walk out the back door and grab either a whole plant or just a couple of leaves."

Dig That *Crazy* Greenhouse!

All of the old gardening books advise digging pit greenhouses—it's a reliable and economical greenhouse design. So Keith Crotz decided to try it one summer in his Chillicothe, Illinois, garden. He and his neighbor Mike Contratto grabbed their spades and hand-dug a pit that measures 12 × 4 feet and extends a full 4 feet below ground. To make the greenhouse beds, they mounded 6 to 8 inches of topsoil on each side of the pit and added liberal amounts of compost to the beds themselves. Over the pit, they built a shallow A-shaped frame of 2 × 4s on a 2 × 12-inch foundation, and they covered it with ⅛-inch Plexiglas.

"As long as the outside temperature doesn't go below 10°F , nothing freezes in the

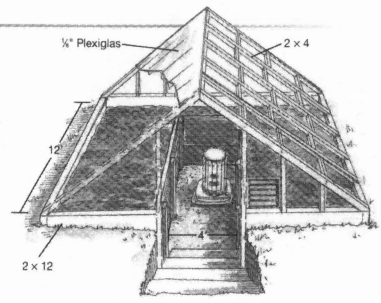

⅛" Plexiglas

2 × 4

12

2 × 12

4

With a kerosene heater to warm it on winter's coldest days, an easy-to-build pit greenhouse provides good growing space all year long.

pit," says Keith. "When it gets really cold, I put a kerosene heater on low inside, and everything is just fine."

Keith uses his greenhouse to get a jump-start on spring and to stretch the growing season. "I use the pit greenhouse to start all of my

flowers and vegetables," he says. "I start the peppers on a heat mat. Lettuce grows in there all winter in 6 to 8 inches of topsoil and compost on both sides of the pit.

"That's not all," Keith adds. "We overwinter Mike's bonsai collection in there!"

Fabric for a **Tougher** Tunnel

It's safe to say that a lot of gardening ingenuity has come from gardeners' desire for homegrown tomatoes. Binda Colebrook, author of *Winter Gardening in the Maritime*

Northwest, uses tunnels to coax yields from heat lovers such as tomatoes. Her success lies in the material she uses to cover her tunnels.

Instead of polyethylene, Binda uses Fabrene, a translucent spun greenhouse fabric

(see "Resources" on page 317 for product information).

"I use this for my summer tunnels, too," Binda says, "because with our cold, damp summer season, you just can't grow tomatoes and peppers without it."

Enjoy Your Garlic Twice

Nearly everyone who grows hardneck garlic cuts off the seedheads when they start emerging and coiling like snakes in June. Trimming off the flowerstalk down to where it emerges from between the leaves directs more of the plant's energy into the bulb and results in larger bulbs later in the summer. But what the heck do you do with all of those seed tops?

If you cut them early, before they have curled twice and become too hard and fibrous, you can eat them. "They're absolutely delicious!" says Emmaus, Pennsylvania, garlic grower George DeVault. "Our customers chop them up in salads and sauces or use them to add great garlic taste to stir-fry dishes. My favorite technique, though, is to pickle the tops in vinegar so that you can munch on garden-fresh garlic greens throughout the year."

Wear gloves when you cut the seedheads, notes George, because the seed stems contain the same aromatic juices as garlic bulbs. Store seedheads in a sealed plastic bag in your refrigerator, where they'll keep for about four weeks.

Storing *Heat*

To extend the growing season, "I spray 2-liter soda bottles with flat black paint and fill them with water," says Kim Barwick of Hoffman Estates, Illinois. "I use them in my cold frame in early spring, at the base of my tomato and pepper plants. They absorb heat during the day, then release it at night."

Gardening Undercover

"I'm a person who likes to bring fresh food into the house from the garden for just as long as I can," says Judy Dornstreich, a home gardener in Perkasie, Pennsylvania. To produce a continuous supply of zesty winter salads for her family of six, Judy depends on an unheated, plastic-covered hoop house.

"Select well-prepared ground that has had a lot of attention, compost, and manure. The site should be slightly raised so that there is good drainage," she advises. "We have made some slightly raised beds that are mulched with straw. That makes the hoop house extremely pleasant to work in." Judy waits until well into fall to cover the hoop-house framework with clear plastic. "If you cover it up after a rain, you probably won't have to water under the hoop house at all because the moisture doesn't evaporate that much."

Choose the crops for your undercover garden with care, Judy suggests. "Don't try to re-create summer," she warns. "Forget about tomatoes." Instead, try to extend spring and fall. "Plant cut-and-come-again lettuces, arugula, curly cress, mache—a variety of stuff—so you can cut a variety for your salads." Judy adds that Swiss chard, onion sets, lemon thyme, tarragon, sorrel, and even rosemary all overwinter nicely inside a hoop house. "They'll be ready for spring harvest a month earlier than normal."

Timely tip

While many herbs will thrive through the winter under the cover of an unheated hoop house, it's not for everything. "Don't try basil," Judy cautions. "It will just sit there and get white flies."

Straw, the Low-Tech Season *Extender*

All it takes is a good, thick layer of straw mulch over cold-hardy vegetables, and the soup's on well into winter in market gardener Melanie DeVault's Emmaus, Pennsylvania, kitchen.

Melanie recommends growing some good winter keepers in proximity to the house so that finding them under a cover of snow is easier and quicker. Her standard soup includes a mix of carrots, leeks, kale, turnips, parsley, and other herbs (and, of course, homegrown potatoes and onions taken from storage on the cool side of the basement).

"A quick trip to the garden and a little broth make a wonderful treat in January," Melanie says. "In half an hour you have a hearty, tasty meal."

Jill Jesiolowski Cebenko, senior editor at *Organic Gardening* magazine and fellow Pennsylvania gardener, agrees. "I have people over for dinner in winter and just go out to the garden to round up some parsnips and beets. Guests are both surprised and delighted," Jill says. "Using straw is a simple, low-tech season extender. You don't need a cold frame or anything."

Soup's on in no time when you grow an assortment of tasty winter vegetables.

Winter Mulch *without* Spring **Work**

Layers of heavy mulch can safely carry hardy plants through winter. But removing all that mulch can also create a lot of extra work in spring, when you already have too much to do in the garden. Here's a way to protect your plants without a lot of work.

"If you mulch perennial or biennial plants to protect them over winter, invert plastic flowerpots over them before dumping the mulch," says Bob Wildfong, a gardener in Kitchener, Ontario, who works with Seeds of Diversity Canada. "It makes it a lot easier to free them from the mulch in spring."

Keep a variety of different-size pots on hand. That way you'll be able to match the size of the pot to the size of the plant—and the pot won't end up crushing your plants.

Timely tip

Avoid using clay or terra-cotta pots for under-the-mulch protection, advises Bob. Both clay and terra-cotta absorb moisture, causing the pots to crack and break when they freeze.

Treasure in the Trash

"The best cold frame I have is made from a salvaged skylight. It's slanted and bubble-like, with two layers of Plexiglas," says Jill Jesiolowski Cebenko, a senior editor at *Organic Gardening* magazine. "All I had to do was build a rectangular wooden frame as the base to support the skylight. Now my lettuces, spinach, tatsoi, and mizuna stay cozy all winter. Keep an eye out for treasures in the trash pile!"

Avoiding the Crunch

Like many gardeners, John Boston of Tulsa, Oklahoma, uses clear 2-liter soda bottles with the bottoms cut off to protect seedlings early in the season. But his soda bottles also serve another purpose. "On very cold nights," John says, "I bury the entire bottle under a foot of straw to insulate the plants. The bottle then prevents the mulch from crushing the seedlings."

If you don't have straw on hand, try covering the plants with a blanket for insulation.

Custom Cart Cradles Clumsy Covers

Floating row covers, plastic row tunnels, and other crop protectors are great, but many come on such big rolls that they're nearly impossible for one person to handle. Andy Lee, Virginia gardener and author of *Backyard Market Gardening,* solved that problem by turning his home-made garden cart into a roll carrier. He bolted a 72-inch-long, 1-inch-square metal bar to the handlebars behind the cart box. He inserts a round rod of the same length into the cardboard tube holding the row cover and hangs it with wire from the support rod.

"All you have to do is move the cart into position at the end of the bed," Andy says. "Take the loose end of the material and walk to the other end of the bed. The roll of plastic or Reemay hanging down from the handlebars has plenty of clearance, yet it is low enough to the ground that a little breeze won't disrupt the laying procedure."

Timely tip

"Early morning and late afternoon are usually the calmest periods of the day," Andy notes. "Don't try to lay out protective covers if there is more than just a light wind—unless you want to go parasailing in the garden!"

An easy way to handle an awkward chore: Make a row-cover dispenser to attach to your garden cart.

homegrown HINTS

YOU'LL FALL FOR FALL PEAS

As a third-generation Pennsylvania Dutch farmer, Bob Hofstetter admits he can be a little set in his ways. Bob follows the tradition that says the best time to plant peas is around St. Patrick's Day (March 17). Never mind that gardening friends have been tempting him for years with fresh-picked peas in fall.

"Well, I finally tried late planting this year, and it worked beautifully!" exclaims Bob, who manages the Rodale family gardens at the original *Organic Gardening* Experimental Farm near Emmaus, Pennsylvania. "I planted 'Sugar Daddy' snap peas on July 28. The plants weren't quite as tall in fall as in spring, but I had good yields of crisp, sweet peas."

Roll Out
the Barrels

Not beer barrels, but the big blue plastic barrels that come packed with pickles, vinegar, and other food products make great temporary cloches, says Emmaus, Pennsylvania, market gardener George DeVault. "I buy them every time I see some for sale along the roadside or outside an institutional food purveyor. The biggest ones are almost the size of 55-gallon drums.

"Cut them in half lengthwise, and there is no end to the neat things you can do with them. I use them to keep frost off tender seedlings in spring and as a sort of cold frame to keep carrots and other root crops well into winter."

To split a barrel, you don't have to measure or mark anything. Take a saber saw and follow the seam all the way around. Just be careful not to saw off the handle on the top—it comes in handy when you're moving the barrel halves around.

Saw blue plastic food barrels in half and you'll have a handy holder/washtub for your harvest. The halves make quick cloches, too, when frost threatens.

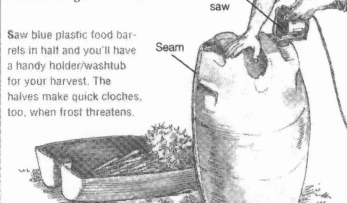

Saber saw

Seam

Timely tip

George's barrel halves also are handy at harvesttime. Each holds a couple of bushels of carrots, beets, or broccoli. Round bottoms make them easy to drag out of the garden by the handle. "Flop a garden hose inside, and they become instant hydro-coolers and great washtubs for freshly harvested vegetables," says George.

For Flowers Forever **Plant Early**—And *Late*

So many people call Lynn Byczynski the "Flower Farmer" that she used that nickname as the title of her book on raising and selling organic cut flowers. Here are two favorite season-extending tips from the Flower Farmer of Lawrence, Kansas:

1. "In fall, direct-seed anything that would normally self-sow in your garden, and the plants will be up and ready to go in spring just as soon as the temperature is right," Lynn says. Her fall-sowing list includes bachelor's button, larkspur, and agrostemma (corn cockle).

2. Start other flowers from seed, then grow transplants under hoops. "It's a little trickier because you never know just how cold it's going to get," Lynn warns. "If it's not much below 28°F under the row cover, you can safely use Reemay. It will warm up the plants during the day."

Lynn also lays down drip irrigation tape and black paper mulch at planting.

Drip tape extends under mulch

Paper mulch

Flower gardeners use vegetable-growing tools and techniques to get a big jump on the season. Lynn Byczynski's transplants flourish under covered hoops with paper mulch to block the weeds and drip tape to keep things moist.

Without the mulch, she says, weeds will grow faster than your flowers.

She recommends growing transplants of annual statice (*Limonium sinuatum*), pink poker (*Limonium suworowii*), snapdragons, bishop's weed (*Ammi majus*), lisianthus (*Eustoma grandiflorum*), and annual clary sage (*Salvia viridis*) under hoops. The plants need to be well rooted and hardened off thoroughly before you set them out.

To harden-off the plants, set them outside (in a protected area) for a little while each day for a week, gradually increasing their outdoor time.

Timely tip

Don't stop your season stretching with early plantings, Lynn adds. A lot of flowers can be planted up to the middle of summer. "You can plant cosmos, zinnias, and sunflowers as late as 50 days before the first hard frost of the season," Lynn says. "A mistake a lot of people make is thinking that they have to plant everything at once in spring, and then they're done."

Lynn's advice for successful season-long flower gardening is simple: "Plant before you're supposed to be able to and long past the time you're supposed to be finished." You'll be rewarded with a steady supply of color to enjoy both in your garden and as cut flowers.

Fall Blueberries— *Without the* Birds!

Frank Pollock tried everything to keep birds out of his blueberries. But nothing worked— not scare-eye balloons, not cheesecloth, not even shotgun-launched noise- makers. The birds just kept coming back for more of his early and midseason berries.

But by the time his late- season berries were ready to pick in September, it was a different story. There just weren't that many birds hanging around Frank's berry patch in Pennsylvania's Pocono Mountains.

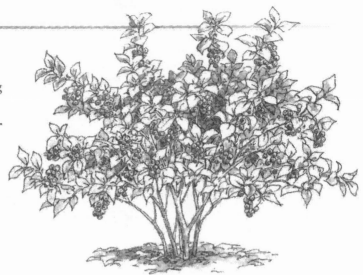

Plant late-season 'Elliott' blueberries for lots of fall fruit minus the birds.

"'Elliott' is the latest blooming and most prolific blueberry there is," Frank recommends. "It's the only one I plant now. That's the easiest and best way I know to extend the growing season for blueberries."

problem solver

SAVE SOME SPUDS FOR SUMMER PLANTING

David Ronniger offers some unusual varieties in his seed potato catalog (Ronniger's Seed and Potato Company). He also offers some unusual—and practical—season-extending advice for organic gardeners: Try summer potato planting. "Planting in the summer can be successful throughout the Mid-Atlantic, the southern Midwest, and into the Deep South—in fact, wherever fall is long and mild," David reports.

The best reason to plant this late (up to July 15) is to avoid the Colorado potato beetle. Reportedly, the beetle becomes less active by August, giving the plants (and the gardener) greater freedom from pests. Other advantages include easier soil preparation, quick emergence, ideal growing conditions, better keeping quality, and freshly dug new potatoes well into fall.

But just try to find seed potatoes in July. ("Potatoes?" laughed the clerk at a garden center in Pennsylvania. "Why, we've been sold out of seed potatoes since May 4!")

So include a few short-season (60-day) to midseason (80-day) varieties in your spring seed potato order, and keep them refrigerated until summer planting time rolls around. Or resist the temptation to eat all of your early spring potatoes. Save enough to plant a season-extending second crop in summer.

Pepper Protection— *By the Peck*

"I had 900 extra hot pepper plants and planted them close together everywhere, including between cucumber rows," says Milton, Wisconsin, market gardener Mac Cheever. "A surprising side effect of this surplus was a good deal of shelter later in the season. Although frost knocked the tops back, the bottoms were still fairly well protected by the cucumber leaves, and I harvested peppers for a few more weeks."

homegrown HINTS

DOUBLE COVERS KEEP GREENS GROWING

Sometimes, when fall nights start to turn chilly, an extra blanket on the bed is all it takes to keep you cozy without firing up the furnace. Likewise, using two layers of floating row cover instead of one is all Pennsylvania gardener Jill Jesiolowski Cebenko does to keep harvesting tasty greens such as spinach and lettuce well into the fall.

"A double layer of Reemay keeps my spinach and lettuce going much later in the fall," says Jill, a senior editor at *Organic Gardening* magazine. "It also keeps the plants in good shape through our milder winters for early spring harvest," she adds. "Using this method is very easy, too—just two layers of row cover lying right on top of the plants, anchored with rocks, boards, or what-have-you."

Put Row Covers in Their Place

Virginia gardener Andy Lee has found the perfect tool for firmly anchoring the edges of season extenders. His method works for both plastic mulch and floating row covers.

Using twine stretched between two stakes as a guide, Andy runs his wheel hoe—equipped with a furrower or moldboard—down each side of the bed. He keeps the vertical edge next to the bed, throwing soil to the right.

Next Andy unrolls the row cover and anchors the edges into the furrow by backfilling with soil he just turned over. Just be sure that the cover floats on the bed and is not too tight, he advises.

If you're applying row cover over a bed that already has plastic mulch, Andy recommends installing the cover at least 1 inch away from the plastic so that you don't pull up the plastic when you remove the cover in a few weeks.

A wheel hoe, available from farm-supply stores and mail-order tool companies, makes it easy to anchor row covers with a ridge of soil.

homegrown HINTS

OATS AID WINTER SPINACH

A carpet of oats helps organic market gardener Richard de Wilde get his spinach crop through the winter in Viroqua, Wisconsin. "The first week of September, we plant spinach just the way we plant it any other time of year," Richard says. The spinach comes up in about a week.

After the spinach is up, Richard broadcasts "a pretty heavy amount of oats" around the spinach, and then he cultivates it, so the cultivator covers up most of the oat seeds. "What I end up with going into winter is a growing carpet of oats all around the spinach," he explains. The oats winter-kill, providing a natural mulch that helps protect the spinach during winter.

"Most spinach varieties, especially some of the old savoyed ones, have consistently overwintered here for the past seven to eight years," Richard notes, adding that this spinach is the first crop he harvests in the spring. "The quality is far superior to anything planted in the spring or summer," he says. "It has a very thick leaf and is dark green and sweet. It's somewhat like spinach harvested late in the fall.

"The challenge," Richard adds, "is keeping the deer out of the spinach in the winter. They've been known to go through a foot of snow to get at it."

It's *in the* Bag

Plastic garbage bags can give your tomatoes an early boost. "I cut the end off a clear garbage bag to create a tube, and I slide the tube over my tomatoes cages in the early spring, securing the open top to the cage," says Kim Barwick of Hoffman Estates, Illinois. "It creates a warm, humid environment for young tomato and pepper plants—on a 50°F day, the temperature inside is about 80 to 85°F. With the top open, you don't have to worry about cooking your plants. On cold nights, you can slide a whole bag over the top."

A **Tomato** That *Waits* for You

Anyone who has ever gone on vacation for a week or two in August almost dreads returning to the garden—and all of those overripe tomatoes.

But what can you do? "Plant a tomato that will ripen on the plant—and then will just sit there for three to four weeks," recommends Robert L. Johnston Jr., chairman of Johnny's Selected Seeds in Albion, Maine.

There really is such a tomato, Rob explains. "It's not a so-called long-keeper, which contains a gene that actually prevents fruit from ripening on the plant. Rather, it's a tomato with a long shelf life—and good taste! And its name is 'Daniela'."

"If the fruit is allowed to get dead ripe on the plant, it is delicious," Rob says. "Before we put this variety in our catalog, we sampled it with gardeners throughout the country. I guarantee you it will keep for a good three weeks on the plant."

'Daniela' matures in 77 days and is resistant to verticillium and fusarium wilt and tobacco mosaic virus.

Nature's Freezer
Sweetens Spinach

"My husband, Bill Warner, and I grow spinach all winter without any heat in hoop houses—in southern Wisconsin (Zone 4)," says market gardener Judy Hageman. "We plant in September and harvest all winter."

The only real problem with this method, she says, is cold, cloudy days when the temperature outside stays right at 10°F. You can't harvest the spinach when it's frozen, but Judy doesn't let that hinder her.

To thaw the spinach before she picks it, Judy puts a small hoop-shaped plastic cover over the spinach inside the hoop house. This raises the temperature enough to let her gather unfrozen spinach. Judy says the freezing doesn't harm the crop—if anything, it improves it, because it increases the spinach's sugar level. "The spinach tastes just like candy after it freezes and thaws!"

This method not only lets Judy extend her spinach season, it also helps her beat the winter blues by allowing her to garden when the snow is flying and the temperature is dipping below 0°F.

Tunnel *Your Way* *to* Early Tomatoes

Warming the soil with black plastic mulch is the first step organic market gardener Richard de Wilde takes toward producing an early crop of tomatoes in Viroqua, Wisconsin. Then, once the plants are in place, he explains, "We put cages over them immediately. These 'cages' are really tunnels made from sections of the wire that is used to reinforce concrete. The tunnels serve as a support for the Reemay that we put over them." Richard cuts the reinforcing wire to form half-circles, 10 to 11 squares wide. He leaves 3-inch legs on each edge to poke into the ground to anchor the tunnels.

"We lay the tunnels almost end-to-end, leaving just space enough to walk through at the end of every other one," says Richard. He adds that he is relying more and more on low-cost, low-tech season extenders to stretch production in his market garden.

"We keep the tomatoes covered for three to four weeks, until it's 90°F in there or the tomatoes are bursting out of the tunnels." Later in the season, Richard plants tomatoes in bare ground. Then, as summer wears on, he stretches his tomato production in the other direction: "We actually mulch to cool the ground, to slow the tomatoes down so that we have a longer tomato harvesting season."

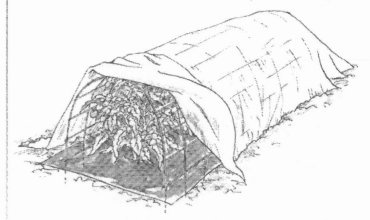

Combine simple season extenders like black plastic mulch and tunnels covered with floating row cover to enjoy extra-early tomatoes this summer, even in chilly northern regions.

Sleepover at Camp Kale

Whenever Arctic air breaks out of Canada and hurricane-force winds cause temperatures to plummet in the normally mild foothills of Washington's Cascade Mountains, Binda

Colebrook runs for her trusty old sleeping bag. A bunch of old sleeping bags, actually. She keeps them stashed in a shed near her garden.

"I throw them over the kale and spinach cold frames, then I cover the sleeping bags with

plastic so they don't get all wet," Binda explains. She takes advantage of the falling temperature to anchor everything in place: "I pour water over the plastic so that the water freezes and the covers won't blow off."

problem SOLVEr

SWEET POTATOES IN VERMONT!

Even in a mild winter, the temperature in central Vermont dips to -20°F for at least a few days. It gets so cold up there that winter weather kills an average of about half the blackberries every year—and blackberries are pretty tough.

But that doesn't stop Alan LePage. "We grow the marginal to the near-impossible," he says matter-of-factly. His favorite crop is sweet potatoes!

"We think we can grow almost any kind of sweet potato here," says Alan, who lives in Barre, Vermont. "We have never had a crop failure, and we've always had decent yields. We buy sweet potato plants (from Fred's Plant Farm in Tennessee)—we don't grow them. We want to receive them between May 15 and 20."

Alan tucks his sweet potato plants into raised beds that have been warmed for a few weeks with a covering of IRT (infrared transmitting) mulch, also called wave-

length selective mulch. IRT mulch warms the soil more quickly than black plastic by allowing near-infrared light to pass through while blocking the visible light that weed seeds need in order to sprout.

Frost protection is also critical. "There are threats of light frost into June," Alan says, "but we ignore those with row covers." To keep the frost off his tender sweet potatoes, Alan blankets them with Agrofabric Pro 17 row cover. This covering stays in place all season, until harvesting begins around September 1. In addition to keeping his sweet potatoes toasty, using row covers all season eliminates insect pests, Alan notes.

Alan says his favorite sweet potato variety is 'Vardaman'. "It doesn't need to be cured, and it resists splitting—a big problem in the North when we have periods of cold, rainy weather followed by hot spells," he explains.

sensational

Seed-Starting Secrets

What gardener doesn't live for the morning when that first seedling pops through the moist soil? And what gardener hasn't been disappointed by a seed that never sprouted? Use these ingenious tips for storing and organizing your seeds, germinating even the teeniest seeds, and taking care of those seedlings once they've sprouted. With foolproof ideas from the experts, you'll be presprouting, soil blocking, and transplanting before you can say, "Hand me a dibble."

Proper Seed Storage Saves $$$

Everyone wonders whether that forgotten packet of seeds from a couple of years ago is still worth planting. Bob Wildfong, who works with Seeds of Diversity Canada, in Ontario, says a little care with seed storage not only can give gardeners peace of mind but can also save them lots of money because they won't have to buy new seeds each year. The key, Bob says, is to store seeds in conditions opposite those needed for germination. Since seeds need warmth and moisture to germinate, cold and dryness are your tickets to successful storage. You can use the same package of seeds for several years if you store them correctly, he says.

To keep seeds cold and dry, store them in your refrigerator. Bob recommends placing seeds in paper envelopes inside a glass jar. (Add another envelope of silica gel or powdered milk to absorb moisture.) Seal the jar, then put it in the refrigerator. The seeds will remain viable for about twice as long as if they were stored at room temperature.

Try Coffee Filters for **Presprouting**

If you aren't sure whether your old seeds are still good, try presprouting to see if they will germinate. Every spring, *Organic Gardening* Senior Editor Jill Jesiolowski Cebenko presprouts larger seeds by moistening unbleached #2 coffee filters and evenly spacing the seeds in the moistened filters. "Place one or two coffee filters upright in an old yogurt container with a clear lid to hold the moisture in," she says. When (and if) the seeds germinate, Jill says you'll see a bulge in the coffee filter and you'll know the seeds are still viable.

Using the clear lid and the envelope-shaped filter makes it easy to check on the sprouting process, too. Check the seeds daily, and as soon as you see that a seed has sprouted, carefully remove the sprout with your fingers or tweezers, and plant it.

This presprouting method is a great space- and money-saver too. You don't waste space in a six-pack cell due to nongermination and you don't waste seed by oversowing directly into six-packs, Jill adds.

Presprout on *Top* of the Fridge

Bud Glendening says he presprouts most of his seeds on top of the refrigerator, placing the seed on damp paper towels in small plastic bags. "It's how I started sprouting seeds, and I really haven't found anything better," says Bud, the owner of Fox Hollow Seed Co. in McGrann, Pennsylvania. "I check them twice a day."

The top of the refrigerator provides just the right amount of warmth without getting too hot. Even pepper seeds like it. And it's a lot more cost-effective than using hot mats, Bud adds.

You need to keep a close eye on seeds you're presprouting, Bud says. You don't want to let them dry out from the warmth of the fridge or let them grow too long inside a plastic bag. As soon as seeds sprout, you need to get them out of the bag and into moist planting medium. Otherwise, their new roots may grow into the paper towel, making them likely to break off when you plant the seedlings.

Timely tip

Most seeds need a warm environment to germinate. But once they germinate, let them keep their cool, says Nancy Bubel, author of *The New Seed-Starter's Handbook.* "If you keep seedlings in a cool room, they won't lose as much moisture to transpiration."

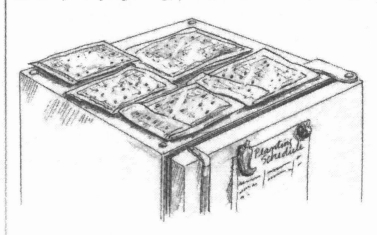

To presprout seeds, put them on top of the refrigerator. Put the seeds on damp paper towels inside plastic bags—that way they won't dry out too quickly.

Organize Packets by Planting Time

Market gardener Cass Peterson has devised a simple bag-and-tub system to keep her seeds separated and easy to find. Cass puts seed packets in sealable plastic bags that are labeled with the month of planting. She keeps the bags in lidded plastic tubs in the walk-in cooler so the right seeds are on hand when the greenhouse planting schedule shows that it's time to plant.

Cass says that she can't afford to forget a scheduled planting of arugula for her restaurant clients or sunflowers for the mixed bouquets that her farm, Flickerville Mountain Farm and Groundhog Ranch, in Warfordsburg, Pennsylvania, offers at farmer's markets. She needs to have seeds ready to go at a moment's notice. This system works so well for Cass that she suggests that home gardeners use the same system on a smaller scale.

The key is to organize your seed packets by putting vegetable and flower seeds in separate containers, labeling the containers by planting date, and keeping the sealed tub in the back of the refrigerator, a cool basement, or an unheated closet. When the calendar says it's planting day, just grab the right container and plant away!

If you're storing several kinds of seeds but no large quantities, you could even adapt Cass's system for use with a three-ring binder. Tuck your seed packets into the zippered plastic pockets that fit into a binder, then label and date each one with the proper planting time.

problem solver
SOAK STUBBORN SEEDS

When starting flowers from seed, keep in mind that some seeds (morning glories, asparagus fern, and lupines, for example) have a very hard seed coat and take days—or even weeks—to germinate. To help germination along, try soaking seeds in hot tap water for 12 to 24 hours before planting, says Bill Stockman, owner of Spider Web Gardens in Center Tuftonboro, New Hampshire.

Double Duo Aids Pea Germination

"You can cut pea seed germination time in half by taking two important measures," says *Organic Gardening* Senior Editor Jill Jesiolowski Cebenko. "Presoak all pea seeds and be faithful about inoculant," she says.

"These big seeds need a lot of moisture to puff up," Jill explains, and sometimes this can take a while in the garden. At the proper planting time, she wraps the seeds in a damp paper towel, sticks the towel in a plastic bag, and lets it sit for one to two days. "Then I pop them in a furrow in the garden with a sprinkling of inoculant," she says.

Legume inoculants, available through many seed catalogs and local garden centers, are dry, natural peat-based cultures of beneficial bacteria used to treat legume seed before planting. They're completely organic. The inoculant encourages formation of high-nitrogen nodules on plant roots for richer soil, bigger plants, and higher yields, explains the catalog from Johnny's Selected Seeds in Albion, Maine.

homegrown HINTS

FOOLING GLOBE ARTICHOKE SEED

If you ever want to grow globe artichokes and get them to set artichokes the first year, you can fool the seed, says Wanda Boop of Briar Patch Organic Farms in Mifflinburg, Pennsylvania. (Most globe varieties are biennial and produce artichokes in the second year if you can successfully overwinter them.)

"Fool the seed by placing it in the freezer in December and keeping it there until about February," says Wanda. This tricks the seed into "thinking" it's been through the cold season, and it will set flowers the first year, she says. Then, in February, soak the seed for 24 hours, and plant in trays. Set the seedlings outside when all danger of frost is past.

Tiny Helpers for Tiny Seeds

Planting seeds, especially those small seeds, can be a tricky business. So an expert gardener says she always keeps a good, old-fashioned pair of tweezers nearby for those times when she's planting teeny, tiny seeds. For thinning, she snips off extra seedlings with narrow-bladed scissors to avoid disturbing the roots of the seedlings she wants to keep.

Freeze Seeds for Better Germination

Some perennial and northern wildflower seeds need a period of deep cold before they'll germinate, but you can "fool" seeds like this by freezing them! The cold requirement is nature's way of telling the seeds when it's safe to sprout; winter freezing and spring thawing change the chemistry in the seeds, allowing them to sprout only in springtime. Gardener Bob Wildfong of Kitchener, Ontario, says you can simulate a winter freeze indoors by literally freezing your seeds.

"In the late fall or early winter, sow your perennial or wildflower seeds in a sealable plastic container, half full of vermiculite," he says. If the seeds are small, just sprinkle them on top of the vermiculite. Add enough water to saturate the vermiculite, and let the seeds soak for at least 24 hours. Once the seeds have absorbed some water, put the lid on the container and place the container in the freezer.

Leave the container in the freezer for at least two months (some seeds require up to three months of freezing). Once your simulated winter freeze is over, take the lid off the container and put it in a bright, warm place. You can cover the top of the container with plastic wrap to keep the vermiculite from drying out, Bob says. Some wildflowers germinate in a week, while others take up to four weeks. Be patient and keep the vermiculite damp, but don't soak it, he advises. You should soon see sprouts.

Timely tip

Nancy Bubel, author of *The New Seed-Starters Handbook*, says it's important to work with Mother Nature when starting plants outdoors. "Don't plant seeds outdoors after early September," she cautions. "Otherwise, they may not harden-off enough to endure harsh winter conditions."

Presprouting and **Plastic** Provide Early Corn

Getting corn to germinate in cold soil is an age-old problem, but Dan Tawczynski of Great Barrington, Massachusetts, has found a method that helps corn seed survive and thrive despite a chill. He presprouts early corn to get past that germination hurdle, and then plants the presprouted seed in beds prepared with black plastic mulch. The seed is set in holes in the black plastic at the proper planting intervals.

Dan germinates the seed by putting a little potting soil in a plastic flat (the kind that holds a half-dozen six-pack containers) to maintain moisture, and then filling the flat with corn. The trick is to plant seeds as soon as tiny white sprouts appear. It usually takes two days for the seeds to sprout. Three days can be too long.

"In Massachusetts, I've planted the presprouted seed on April 12, and it didn't freeze. We've had corn by the end of June," he says. The plastic protects the seed through most frosts. There can be danger of frost to the plant once it grows above the plastic; early corn is worth the risk.

Make a Simple **Seedling** Sprinkler

Remember the old sprinkler bottles that moms used to sprinkle clothes before ironing? Even though you can't buy them anymore, you can make a suitable substitute to water tender seedlings or seeds that haven't sprouted yet. "Take a good-size plastic bottle with a fair-size lid, like a big Cremora bottle, and poke about five holes in the lid with an awl," says Kris Johnson of Williston, Ohio. (A Cremora bottle is the size of a 1-quart bottle and has a wide-mouth lid that measures about 3 inches across.) She fills the bottle with water and compost tea or fish fertilizer and sprinkles her seed flats. "Presto! Watering seed flats is so much easier with a sprinkler bottle," she says.

Squirt Small Seeds

Instead of taking the time to plant tiny seeds individually, mix them in a gel solution, and squirt them down the plant row. "Mix one package of plain gelatin with 1 tablespoon of warm water, and stir until it's dissolved," instructs Pat Kolb of Phoenix. She adds water sparingly until the mixture is thick enough so that tiny seeds don't sink and thin enough so that the mixture flows evenly through a pull-top detergent bottle. Pat says you may need to experiment with the number of seeds in the solution in order to get a nice even flow of seeds when you "plant" your rows.

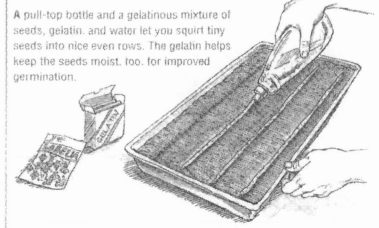

A pull-top bottle and a gelatinous mixture of seeds, gelatin, and water let you squirt tiny seeds into nice even rows. The gelatin helps keep the seeds moist, too, for improved germination.

problem solver

DOCTORED PLASTIC FORK IS TOPS

Take a plastic fork and remove the outer tines to make the best little seedling transplanting tool, says Kathy Moen, garden manager at Seed Savers Exchange, whose 170-acre headquarters in Decorah, Iowa, is a living museum of historic seed varieties.

The remaining prongs of the modified fork are close together so that you can dig under a seedling's tiny roots. Just lift up for easy transplanting.

Toothpick *Tricks*

Tiny flower and vegetable seeds can be real rascals when you try to plant them. Want an ingenious solution? Try using a plain old toothpick for planting tiny seeds, says Lawrence, Kansas, market gardener Lynn Byczynski, author of *The Flower Farmer*. Start by emptying the seed packet into a small bowl, then "just wet the end of a toothpick and use it to pick up a dry seed," Lynn explains. When you touch the seed to moist soil, it's attracted to the wetter soil surface and almost plants itself. And the process makes quick work of seed planting in the springtime. "You can get really fast with a toothpick!" says Lynn.

To quickly plant small seeds, wet the end of a toothpick, touch the toothpick to a seed, then deposit the seed onto moist soil.

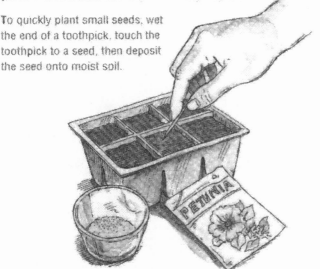

Grits Make Small Seeds *"Sow"* Easy

Sometimes seeds are so small that they're nearly impossible to sow evenly without spreading them too thickly. When Martha Daughdrill and her husband, Paul Benton, ran into trouble with using tiny seeds in a mechanical seeder at their Newburg Vegetable Farm in Maryland, Paul found a solution—in his breakfast cereal!

No matter how they set their seeder, the fine seeds came through the holes too fast. So Paul looked at the seeds and at the grits in the cupboard—and got an idea. He mixed dry grits with the seeds to thin them, and it worked beautifully. "He got a better stand with the small-seeded plants," Martha says, "and he almost never has to eat grits for breakfast!"

Timely tip

If you don't use a mechanical seeder, mix some grits with small seeds for hand sowing, too. The results will be the same (but you may have to eat more grits). Mixing small seeds with sand is another way to thin them out for more even sowing, and the sand makes it easy to see where you've sown.

Cut a *Yardstick* Down to Size

When sowing vegetable or flower seeds into seed flats, forget unpredictable broadcasting. Lay out tidy rows for the seed by using an old yardstick. Cut the yardstick into two pieces, one the length of the flat and the other the width of the flat, to mark rows in your flats in either direction, advises Cass Peterson of Flickerville Mountain Farm and Groundhog Ranch in Warfordsburg, Pennsylvania. The yardstick lengths make uniform, evenly spaced rows, and the seeding goes quickly.

Just spread moistened soil mix in a flat, and level it off. Take either of the yardstick lengths and use it to mark indentations about 1 inch apart, either across the width of the flat for short rows or down the length of the flat for longer rows. You can adjust the depth according to the seeds you're using, indenting rows slightly deeper for normal-size seeds or barely denting the surface for small seeds such as petunia that won't be covered with soil mix after planting. It's a quick and easy method for keeping seed rows neat.

Cut an old yardstick into pieces that match the dimensions of your seed flats to create a simple tool that speeds seed sowing.

Planting Boards **Save Time**

Kathy Moen, garden manager for Seed Savers Exchange in Decorah, Iowa, says one of her favorite tools is a planting board that marks planting holes for individual cell packs. A planting board is just a flat piece of wood cut to the size you need with a handle fastened on the back, and ½-inch-diameter dowels glued on the front. Wood or carpenter's glue is ideal for this project. You can cut the board to the size of a four-pack, for instance, and position four dowels so that they leave a shallow hole in the center of each cell in the pack. Or you can cut the board to the size of a larger container, such as a 32-cell, with 32 dowels glued to the board.

To use the board, turn the board dowel side down, line up the dowels with the center of the cell packs, and press the dowels into the soil to create planting holes.

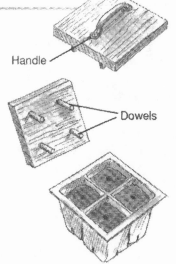

Handle

Dowels

Save time when planting into cell packs by making a planting board to mark planting holes.

Garlic Planting in *No Time*

Pennsylvania market gardener George DeVault uses a garden-size planting board when he plants garlic cloves outdoors. He cut old 1-inch square tomato stakes and screwed them together to create a rectangular frame. His planting board measures 8 × 30 inches. Instead of dowel dibbles, he spaced long drywall screws on the two 30-inch sides at 5-inch intervals, the ideal spacing for garlic. He says the idea was adapted from *Growing Great Garlic* by Ron L. Engelland.

To use the board, press the drywall screws into the soil to create planting holes. George says the system not only makes planting go extremely fast, but it also ensures planting at a constant depth. After dropping the garlic clove root end down into the hole, cover it with soil, and firmly press it down.

George says many market gardeners use similar planting-board devices when transplanting lettuce, fennel, and other crops outdoors in spring.

A homemade garlic planting board lets you plant garlic cloves precisely without fussing with stakes and string to measure and mark planting rows.

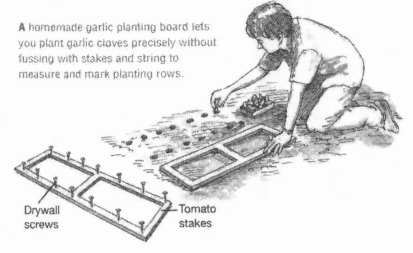

Drywall screws

Tomato stakes

problem SOLVER

MINIBLIND MARKERS

Cut old plastic, nonlead miniblinds into short lengths and use them as plant markers when starting seeds in six-packs or flats, advises Teena Bailey of Red Cat Farm, Germansville, Pennsylvania. "They're flexible, durable, and easily cleaned. They take pencil or markers perfectly," she says. And that's not all! As the seedlings grow into garden-ready transplants, she cuts the miniblinds into longer sections and uses them as markers right in the garden. (If you're unsure whether your miniblinds contain lead, you can buy an inexpensive lead testing kit at your local hardware store.)

Cass Peterson also uses old venetian blinds at her farm, Flickerville Mountain Farm and Groundhog Ranch, in Warfordsburg, Pennsylvania. She likes them because they're flexible and can be cut to lengths that are tall enough to spot in the field. Cass uses permanent markers to write plant names on the blinds. She's found that permanent marker ink doesn't fade on the blinds the way it does on wooden markers. At Flickerville Mountain Farm, they staple the blinds onto tomato stakes for extra durability. Cass says she reuses the plant markers by using liquid abrasive to take off the old plant names.

Just a *Little* Clip

Nancy Bubel of Wellsville, Pennsylvania, says there's nothing like an old pair of nail clippers for scarifying, or scratching, a seed coat to hasten germination. "They work really well to cut a hard seed like lupine," she says.

Take Note!

Market gardener George DeVault of Emmaus, Pennsylvania, is a firm believer in using a seeder. It makes planting for the home or market gardener go quickly and efficiently. But with all of the seed plates and seed sizes, sometimes it's hard to find just the right plate—especially when you're in a real rush to get seed planted.

For example, George's seeder has two pea plates—one for large peas and one for smaller. So what's what? George experiments the first year, then writes the cultivar name in permanent marker right on the plastic plate. Then he knows: 'Sugar Ann' snap peas take the small pea plate. Next year, when he's in a hurry to beat the weather, the information is right at hand.

homegrown HINTS

BE SURE TO SOAK YOUR SEED FLATS

"There's nothing like a good bottom soak for seed flats," says Bob Hofstetter, manager of the Rodale family gardens near Emmaus, Pennsylvania. Once you've filled the flat with moistened potting mix and planted the seed, just place the flat in tepid water about two-thirds the depth of the flat, he advises. This can be done in a sink or plastic-lined box or in any container that holds water. Make sure the soil is thoroughly wet before taking the flat out.

"There is no such thing as saying water every three days," he says. "The bottom line is never let it dry out. Normally in greenhouse conditions, the seeds will germinate while the soil is still moist from the first bottom soaking." However, Bob says he does resoak if the soil looks as if it's drying out. If just the top of the soil is dry, he'll mist the flat to replace any lost moisture. Bob says that bottom-watering is especially great for fine seed that can't cope with top-watering.

Bob says the key to success is to be sure that your potting mix is damp right at the start. He cautions that if the potting soil is very dry or if you're using a soilless mix, bottom-watering alone won't work, and you'll need to supplement with top-watering.

Go for the *Big* Roots

The trick to getting the best results from home-started seedlings is to choose the seedlings with the biggest root systems when you transplant. The length of the stem and size of the leaves isn't as important as hearty roots. "Throw out weak plants with few roots. They won't do well anyway," says Judy Dornstreich of Perkasie, Pennsylvania. Transplanting only those seedlings with strong root systems will be more time- and cost-efficient in the long run, because the plants will establish themselves more quickly and need less coddling.

Buffer the Heat

If you start seeds in flats on top of heating mats, you may need to raise the flat a bit to help diffuse the heat. Ellen Ogden, of The Cook's Garden in Londonderry, Vermont, raises her flats by putting a screen, a brick, or a plastic tray across the rack that extends over the mat. She says you need to take care not to let the plants get overheated.

Ellen uses commercial heating mats with temperature controls and usually keeps them at 68°F. "The home models are usually set at 72°F, and that's too hot for most plants," she says. Sometimes she stacks her flats so that the heat lovers get the most heat, but she makes sure all the flats get the warmth they need without being over-cooked. She loves heating mats because they "give germination an added boost." They're especially useful if you want to pretest the quality of old seed, Ellen says. The mats speed germination so you can quickly tell whether the seed is still viable.

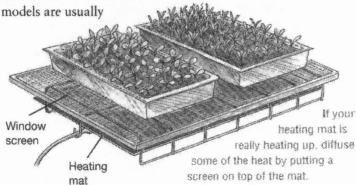

Window screen

Heating mat

If your heating mat is really heating up, diffuse some of the heat by putting a screen on top of the mat.

Self-Sowing Seeds

"I have kale and corn salad that sow themselves," says Binda Colebrook, a longtime organic gardener in Everson, Washington. She just lets a certain percentage of her Russian red and Siberian kale and corn salad plants go to seed before she uproots the plants. When the time comes to sow those crops, she clears a bed, rakes it, waters it, and the right species just pops up. If you're a sloppy harvester, she says, this process happens all by itself.

Seedlings *Love* Space Blankets

Commonly called a "space blanket," that shiny silver piece of Mylar found at camping stores is great for starting seedlings, says Bruce Butterfield, research director at the National Gardening Association in Burlington, Vermont. He spreads the Mylar blanket on the shelf under his plant lights and then sets seedling trays on it. He then pulls up each end of the blanket and tapes it to the outside cover of one of the fluorescent lights. "It not only concentrates the light," he attests, "but it also does a good job of holding in the heat."

Kitchen Utensils to the **Rescue**

If you find you have a lot of runoff when you water seedlings, try reaching into your kitchen drawer for a solution. "I use a turkey baster to direct the water right where I want it," says Esther Czekalski of Lancaster, Massachusetts. The seedlings get a steady water flow right where they need it—at the roots.

homegrown HINTS

COOL OFF YOUR HEAT MATS

If your heat mat tends to get too hot and doesn't have a temperature regulator, put the heat mat on a timer and set it so that it shuts off at night, says Bud Glendening of Fox Hollow Seed Company in McGrann, Pennsylvania. Or, he suggests, put it where it catches a draft—someplace where the air keeps moving so that it varies the heat level, like near a door that's opened frequently or near where you walk around and stir up air currents.

"The key is to mimic nature as much as possible," he says, "by creating 'daytime' heat and 'nighttime' cooling."

Do the *Seed Flat Switch*

If you rotate your flats under Gro-Lights but find that you're always crunched for space, follow Hal Seagraves's space-saving rotation system: Hal set up extra shelves with Gro-Lights across from the table, and once a day, he switches the seed flats under the lights with the seed flats on the shelves. He keeps the lights on all the time so the area stays warm and bright, and the plants love it. The arrangement works well for two reasons—the plants get both "rest time" on the shelf and bright, warm light for germination.

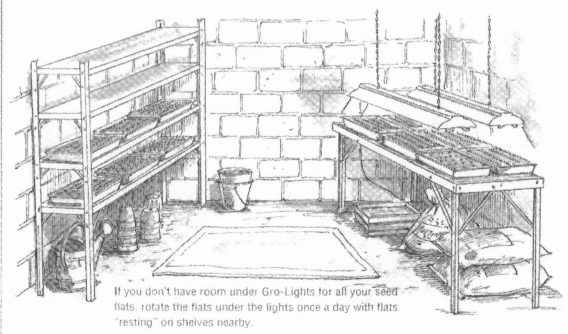

If you don't have room under Gro-Lights for all your seed flats, rotate the flats under the lights once a day with flats "resting" on shelves nearby.

Give Seedlings a **Bonemeal** Boost

Jill Jesiolowski Cebenko, *Organic Gardening* senior editor, says she noticed some of her tomato seedlings suffering from phosphorus deficiency (which gives the undersides of the leaves a telltale purplish tinge). Once she started adding a tablespoon of bonemeal to each gallon of the soil mix that she uses to pot up the transplants, the problem quickly disappeared.

"This is just enough bonemeal to solve the problem and give the plants a healthy green color," she says. "The little guys are in such a small space and the root system grows so fast, you have to give them a little something extra to ensure success."

Plastic Holds Up *for Years*

Many gardeners use paper cups or other makeshift containers to start seeds, but market gardener Lynn Byczynski of Lawrence, Kansas, thinks it makes more sense to invest in durable, easy-to-use plastic flats and inserts with clear plastic dome lids. "The plastic stuff holds up a long time—if you keep it out of the sunlight and take care of it," she says. "And that includes washing and disinfecting the trays after use."

Lynn, who's the author and editor of the *Growing for Market* newsletter, says she has had some of her trays for more than ten years and that they were well worth the investment.

Soak Parsley and Celery Seed

"Have trouble germinating parsley and celery seed?" asks Wanda Boop of Briar Patch Organic Farms in Mifflinburg, Pennsylvania. Soak the seeds for 24 hours before planting them in the garden or seed trays, she advises. "You will be amazed at the germination—almost 100 percent!"

Leeks **Love** Special Treatment

Broadcast leek seeds in a flat, cover with soil, and let them grow for a month so you can give them full protection during that delicate stage, says Pennsylvania gardener Judy Dornstreich. She says it takes leeks so long to germinate and grow that weeds would take over if you sowed the leeks outdoors. "We take the little leeks directly from the flat and plant them outside," she adds. Setting a larger leek in weed-free ground gives it a head start. The little leeks look like blades of grass, are easier to see at this size, and are less likely to be uprooted when you pull weeds, says Judy.

problem solver   SPHAGNUM STOPS DAMPING-OFF

Have a problem with damping-off? Cass Peterson of Flickerville Mountain Farm and Groundhog Ranch, in Warfordsburg, Pennsylvania, says that she sprinkles a fine layer of milled sphagnum moss over the top of a seed flat after seeding. "This helps keep the surface soil dry and keeps moisture away from the stems," she says. Cass recommends the moss for zinnias or any other seedlings that are susceptible to damping-off.

Fan Those Transplants

Use a small fan to circulate air around transplants that are under Gro-Lights, advises Bruce Butterfield, of the National Gardening Association. "It starts to harden them off and helps them fight danger by toughening them up a bit for when they're moved outside," he explains. It gives the transplants a taste of the outdoors and is good for both vegetable and flower seedlings, he adds. And the added air circulation helps prevent damping-off in the tender young transplants.

Fans can help preharden and toughen up transplants by giving them a taste of the outdoors—while they're still indoors.

Think Twice Before You Hill

Most seed packets offer the option of planting cucumbers, melons, squash, and pumpkins in "hills," but Bob Wildfong, of Seeds of Diversity Canada, Ontario, says most gardeners will have better results if they plant these crops directly into a garden bed. The theory behind the "hill is better" practice, says Bob, is that hilled soil warms up faster in the spring and causes the seeds to sprout earlier.

The down side is that the hill of soil also dries out faster in the summer, reducing fruit-set considerably, he explains. The method originated in Northern Europe, where spring is cooler and summers are wetter than in the United States. Settlers brought this trick with them, but in this part of the world, flatter is better.

Keep Watch for Slow-Start Seedlings

Pepper and leek seeds don't all germinate at once, so keep the seed-starting medium moist for a week or two after you've transplanted the seedlings that have already popped up, advises Kitchener, Ontario, gardener Bob Wildfong. "Keep watching because there are more on the way," he adds. Giving the seeds a little more time to germinate not only means more seedlings but also means less time spent germinating additional seeds.

Bob starts his pepper and leek seeds early by thickly sowing them in a small container of damp vermiculite. "When they sprout (two to three weeks for peppers, two to four weeks for the leeks), you should loosen the vermiculite with your fingers, gently pull the seedlings out, and transplant them into individual containers of potting soil," he explains. Even though you have to be quite careful transplanting most seedlings, peppers and leeks are tough enough to survive any beginner's fingers because they have very thick, sturdy roots, explains Bob.

Room to Grow

Mac Cheever of Milton, Wisconsin, starts seeds of warm-season vegetables in flats indoors early in the spring, then transplants them into 1-gallon nursery pots (you know, those black containers that almost everyone has left over from nursery plants). The larger pots afford the seedlings more room to grow if the outside weather isn't suitable for transplanting at the recommended time, Mac explains. When they're finally planted outdoors, the plants grow quickly because of their large, strong root systems.

In Wisconsin, Mac says he starts plants in early April and transplants them into the larger containers in early May, hoping to plant outdoors in late May or early June, depending on the weather. This works extremely well for tomatoes, peppers, cucumbers, pumpkins, squash, and gourds. "It gives you the added bonus of waiting for suitable weather without losing any growth," he says. "A well-established root system will take right off as soon as it is in the ground."

Or, Mac suggests that you may want to leave some of the plants in the large containers for the patio or porch. Remember to provide enough nutrition during the growing season for container plants, he says. You may want to use organic compost, liquid seaweed or kelp, or fish emulsion to promote healthy growth.

If you often play a waiting game with unpredictable spring weather, transplant seedlings into large, 1-gallon containers right from the flats. The bigger containers allow plants more room to grow if the weather is still too cold when the recommended planting time arrives.

Shade Saves Summer Lettuce

If you have trouble getting lettuce to germinate in hot summer soils, let your other garden plants lend a hand, recommends Wanda Boop of Briar Patch Organic Farms in Mifflinburg, Pennsylvania. "Sow your lettuce seed in the shade of taller plants, such as corn or peppers, and cover them with a quarter inch of soil and a board to keep them cool initially," she says. The secret to middle-of-the-summer lettuce is to keep the soil cool—the taller plants and the board work together to keep the soil from becoming too hot. As soon as the seeds germinate, remove the board, and water them generously. The shade of the taller plants will keep the lettuce roots cool and will help prevent the plants from bolting (setting seed).

Keep lettuce cool in hot summer soils by planting it in the shade of taller plants like corn or peppers.

Blocking Is **Best**

"I love soil blocks!" declares Eliot Coleman, author of *The New Organic Grower* and *Four-Season Harvest*. "I still think they are the simplest of all container systems because there is no container. There is no expense other than the soil," says the Harborside, Maine, market gardener. For those of you unfamiliar with soil blocks, they are simply blocks made out of lightly compressed potting soil, pressed out by a form (available in many seed catalogs). The block serves as both container and growing medium for a transplant seedling, Eliot explains. The only trick to successful soil blocking is finding the right soil block mix.

Eliot says that soil block mixes aren't available commercially in the United States (they're widely available in Europe, where soil blocking is more popular). So Eliot makes his own blocking mix using soil, compost, peat, and sand, along with smaller quantities of lime, bloodmeal, colloidal phosphate, and greensand.

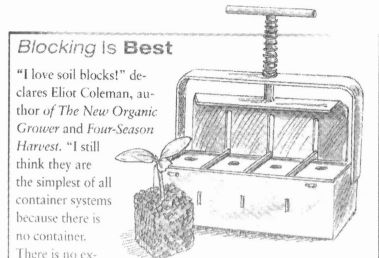

Stamped-out soil blocks make a perfect "containerless" container for starting seeds. They don't restrict root growth, so transplants take root as soon as they're planted in the garden.

Most importantly, he says, you need a very good quality peat—Eliot uses ProMix—that will give your soil block body.

Soil blocks have two important advantages over peat pots, says Eliot. For one thing, you don't have to worry about whether the transplant roots will grow through the peat pot once you've planted it in the garden. Also, there's no danger of moisture being wicked away from the roots, as there is when the edges of a peat pot stick up above soil level in the garden. Soil blocks don't restrict roots in any way, which means that transplants take root immediately, he says.

Soil Block Problems? **Lighten Up!**

The secret to successful soil blocking is in the soil used in the blocking mix, says Jerome Gust of Sparta, Wisconsin. Jerome makes his soil blocking mix of equal parts soil, compost, and peat moss, then adds dashes of greensand, bloodmeal, and lime.

"People try soil blocking and don't like it because they do not get good root growth," he says. "In most cases it's because they have a heavy clay soil that tends to pack, making it harder for roots to grow. Even when you're adding peat moss or sand, heavier soil still tends to pack," says Jerome, "so your best bet is to keep adding sand to loosen it up."

Hand-y Helpers

When making soil block mix, keep a box of latex gloves handy to protect your hands. The ingredients for soil block mix are often abrasive and can roughen up tender skin. And one of the staples of soil block mix—peat moss—may contain bacteria that can be harmful if you have cuts on your hands.

The *Right* Lights

A high-intensity sodium halide light is as much a part of raising transplants as the plants themselves for Michael Contratto. Once he transplants seedlings from trays into cell-type containers, Michael, who gardens in Chillicothe, Illinois, moves the trays under a 240-watt sodium halide light. "It provides better light and generates a lot of heat. I can put an awful lot more seedlings under one sodium halide light than I can under a fluorescent light because fluorescents have to be so close to the seeds," he says. Suspended 5 feet from the floor, his sodium halide light illuminates a 6 × 6-foot area—enough room for eight flats.

The two drawbacks to sodium halide lights are minor. First, the humidity in the area won't stay as high because of the heat that the bulb generates. Second, the initial investment for a sodium halide bulb is high. Each bulb costs about $70 and lasts about two years. In the long run, says Michael, it's actually cheaper to buy one sodium halide bulb than to replace all of those fluorescent tubes. The base unit for the sodium halide light also costs about $300, "a one-time investment," he says. Michael says he also gets his money's worth out of the sodium halide unit by using it to overwinter his collection of tropical bonsai.

Timely tip

Michael has a comprehensive system for seed starting before the sodium halide bulb even comes into play. "The last two years, I've started vegetable seeds in rows in trays and then transplanted into containers, rather than simply starting everything in containers. I have much better control," he says. He waters from underneath, keeping the moisture level up, and he hangs overhead fluorescent lights about 1 inch above the seeds, using eight 40-watt lights and alternating warm and cool white tubes.

Humidity Helper

A good way to increase humidity around potted seedlings is to set a couple of seedling pots in a larger pot of pebbles, says Nancy Bubel, author of *The New Seed-Starter's Handbook*. She stresses that the pebbles should be fingernail size and that there should be just a small amount of water in the pebble container—enough to create humid conditions, but not enough to touch the bottom of the pots. "You don't want potted seedlings in standing water all of the time because the roots will rot. I learned the hard way," she confesses.

Increase humidity around potted seedlings by setting the pots in a container of pebbles, then half submerging the pebbles in a little water.

Greenhouse *within* a Greenhouse

For proper germination, some seeds just like it *hot!* That's why Emmaus, Pennsylvania, market gardener Melanie DeVault built a miniature greenhouse inside her greenhouse. Melanie's miniature greenhouse measures 5 × 4 feet and is built around a wooden potting bench. Making your own miniature greenhouse is as easy as 1, 2, 3.

1. For uprights, cut two 2 × 4s into two 18-inch lengths each. Using screws or nails, attach one upright to each corner of a wooden potting bench.

2. Lay thermostatically controlled heating pads on the bench.

3. Drape a sheet of heavy clear plastic over the entire potting bench and uprights to form a tent over heat-loving seedlings. Do not attach the plastic permanently because you may want to raise the sides for ventilation. Just tuck the ends in here and there when you need to keep the heat in. On really sunny days, remove the plastic so the seedlings don't overheat.

You don't really need a greenhouse to make a mini-greenhouse. The same type of structure will work just fine on a table inside your house, barn, shed, or basement, providing you turn up the heat and place plant growth lights under the cover, says Melanie.

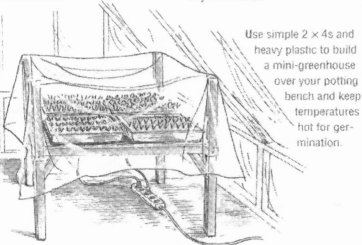

Use simple 2 × 4s and heavy plastic to build a mini-greenhouse over your potting bench and keep temperatures hot for germination.

Plant Nursery in a **Pot**

When rooting cuttings, Juanita Mitchell of Hunt, Texas, makes a clay pot nursery to keep the cuttings moist. She uses two clay pots, one twice the size of the other. She places a cork in the bottom hole of the smaller pot and fills the pot with water. She fills the bottom of the larger pot with potting soil, then places the water-filled smaller pot on top of the soil. Then Juanita adds soil to fill the space between the two pots, and places her cuttings in this loose soil. The water in the smaller pot provides moisture for the cuttings while they root, and the moist soil allows easy removal for transplanting.

Outdoor Solutions Work *Indoors*, Too

If you have trouble keeping seedling flats moist indoors, turn to an outdoor solution— floating row covers! These lightweight coverings let air circulate, admit light, and keep the humidity high for germination. Simply recycle a scrap of row covering from the garden, and lay it on top of the flat.

Mini-Greenhouse **Saves** on Heat

Heating an entire greenhouse can get awfully expensive. To keep costs manageable when germinating seeds, Tony Ricci, a market gardener in Pennsylvania, built a mini-greenhouse for seed starting right inside his larger greenhouse. He fashioned the miniature structure out of an existing greenhouse bench, metal conduit, conduit clamps, furring strips, and clear plastic, and you can do the same in your basement or shed. Just follow these steps.

1. Using a pipe bender (available at hardware stores or rental centers), bend two lengths of metal conduit into semicircular hoops. Fasten each end to the greenhouse bench with conduit clamps to create an arch.

2. Using conduit clamps, fasten a furring strip to the top of each arch to create supports for the plastic.

3. Drape the clear plastic over the furring strips, allowing enough length on each side to reach the top of the green-house bench. Using a staple gun, staple a furring strip to the cut edges of the plastic on two opposite sides of the bench; this allows you to roll up the plastic for ventilation.

4. To provide heat, place an electric space heater and thermostatically controlled germination mats inside the mini-greenhouse.

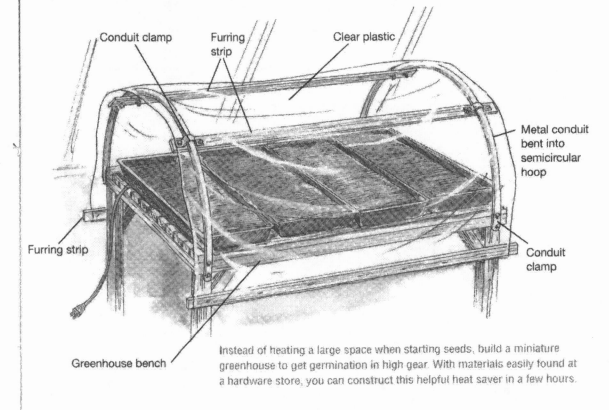

Instead of heating a large space when starting seeds, build a miniature greenhouse to get germination in high gear. With materials easily found at a hardware store, you can construct this helpful heat saver in a few hours.

smart

Solutions to Garden Problems

Most gardeners are nature lovers—except when "nature" gets the best of their garden! When it comes to controlling garden pests, diseases, and weeds, there isn't one best answer. But clever gardeners have devised all sorts of ways to discourage, trick, and repel animal pests, harmful insects, tenacious weeds, and plant diseases. From maintaining a natural habitat for wild animals to knowing which crops will keep pests away from your vegetables, you'll find dozens of solutions for keeping your plants healthy and your garden weed-free.

109

Know the Signs

Lots of animal-control methods work well—but only if they are directed at the right target! Save money, time, and frustration by correctly identifying the animal causing the problem. Nature centers, Co-operative Extensions, Soil and Water Conservation offices, and libraries are places that can teach you to identify animal tracks and signs. Here are two clues to get you started.

What ate the plants? Look at the place where the plant was nipped off. If the cut is smooth and slanted and just a few inches from the ground, it's probably a rabbit's work. (The distance above "ground" will vary if there is deep snow.) But if the tears are ragged—especially 3 to 4 feet above ground—they are most likely from grazing deer.

Who ripped up the lawn? Moles are one of nature's most maligned creatures, and often falsely accused! If you see open tunnels, you have meadow mice, or voles—not moles! The mole tunnels are under the soil surface—some are right under the surface and others are farther underground.

Who's Wearing the *Lamp Shade?*

Sometimes dogs, cats, or kids (or even chickens or wild animals) knock down your flowers. Wind is even worse about damaging delicate flower stems and can flatten a promising stand of annuals or perennials just when they begin to fill out nicely.

To prevent flowers from being flattened, "try using old lamp shades," says Penny McDowell, a Buffalo Master Gardener. Penny suggests looking for lamp shades at garage sales or at the curb in the trash. Then take off the fabric and place the shades over the plants that are at risk of being scratched at, laid on, walked on, or blown over.

"Once the flowers grow and fill out around the shade, you won't even know the frame is there," Penny points out. "Then they function as great plant supports!"

Prevent children, pets, and other critters from squashing your flowers. The bare frame of an old lamp shade will protect your plants from both two- and four-legged garden intruders.

Let **Dogs** Mark **Your** Territory

While the presence of dogs is generally a deterrent to wildlife in the yard, a more specific "product" helps to ward off rabbits, raccoons, squirrels, and other creatures. Get your dogs to mark their territory around the perimeter of your garden. Sally Cunningham, author of *Great Garden Companions*, has lots of wildlife around her country property, and lots of pets, too. Yet she has gardens that aren't eaten. According to Sally, the dogs and cats can help.

"Start a good habit by walking your dog on a leash right around your garden— outside the beds. If you take the dog straight from the house to that area, she is more likely to mark the territory with urine, and it will become a habit." (Be careful that the habit starts where you will continue to want dogs to go— maybe behind the garden or between the garden and the field or fence.)

Timely tip

Sally says that the routine walk around the garden has two other benefits, too. "First, dogs get the idea that this is their area to patrol, and they very likely will watch it more diligently during the growing season. So when the rabbits get interested, the dog is quicker to scare them away.

"Second, when you are training your dog using a choke collar, give a tug and say 'No, no!' in a firm voice that shows you mean business when she pulls to go *into* the garden. Even dogs can be trained to stay off the soil!"

homegrown HINTS

RED PEPPER PRODUCT BREAKTHROUGHS

While red pepper sprays have been used as home remedies to solve many garden pest problems, they do present
a problem of their own—they wash off easily. Try one of the
new products that combines ground-up hot red pepper
sauce with *wax*, and the essence of hot pepper will last
longer. Studies have shown that red pepper often discourages rabbits, chipmunks, and squirrels, and it's an effective insect repellent and miticide, too. You can use the
products on houseplants, where studies have shown they
are as effective as insecticidal soaps and better than traditional pesticides. Some of the hot pepper wax products,
such as Hot Pepper Wax, are labeled as safe for use on
vegetable plants, too. Call (888) NOPESTS for more information on this hot new option in gardening pest control.

Ferrets Are This Gardener's Best Friend

An unusual pet is the answer
to critter problems for Master
Gardener Penny McDowell of
Buffalo. Penny lives in the
country, where many crea-
tures could be attracted to her
vegetables, flowers, and
shrubs. She also tends the
flowerbeds for many land-
scape customers. Her answer
to pest control? Ferrets!

"If you have problems with
mice, moles, rabbits, or rats,"
says Penny, "get a ferret—or
make friends with the owner
of one." Why? Penny uses
wood shavings for her ferrets'
litter and then sprinkles their
used litter in the vegetable bed
and among the flowers.

Penny says that litter from
male ferrets works better than
litter from females. And she
adds, "If I plan to sprinkle
ferret litter on the lawn (especially to deter mice, who
know the smell of an
enemy!), I use clay litter. This
worked in the yards of 12 different customers, but I do
have some mole tunnels left
in a couple of beds. At the
very least, the litter and shavings add manure and make
great soil texture."

Red Pepper— Too **Hot** to **Handle** or Munch!

"I tried growing some really
hot chili peppers for my
family's favorite chili
sauce recipe," offers Sally
Cunningham, author and
extension educator, "but they
were too hot for the sauce and
way too hot to work with."
But because they grew prolifically, she had to think of
something to do with them.

Wearing gloves, Sally strung
her peppers on strings for dec-
oration. But she ended up
using them outdoors. "I put
the chili pepper strings around
the trunks of the crabapples. I
nailed one end of the string to
the ground and wound the
string like a candy cane right
up to the lowest branch. The
rabbits and mice didn't nibble
on the tender trunks as they
had in other years."

Timely tip

To keep the essence of pepper fresh
as the winter wears on, Sally suggests squeezing the peppers (remember to wear those gloves) occasionally after a rain or snowfall and,
later in the season, tying an extra
string of peppers that has been
stored inside around the tree.

homegrown HINTS

TAKE ADVANTAGE OF KITTY'S SENSES

When it comes to protecting their spring plantings from kitty's digging, some gardeners take advantage of cats' sensitive olfactory systems. Effective products for keeping cats away include onion sprays, a sprinkling of chopped onions or chives, and anything strongly perfumed, including the scented inserts from catalogs and magazines.

Cats and Chicken Wire Don't Mix

When you plant flower seeds or small plants in the spring, keep a roll of chicken wire handy, says Marge Vogel of Eden, New York.

"Cats don't like to step on anything coarse, so just unroll some chicken wire, and spread it out flat, at least around the outside of the beds," Marge suggests. "Cats won't walk over it to get to the inner areas. It's those soft, just-tilled beds they like to dig in, so once the plants get going or you mulch the beds, the cats will look elsewhere. Then you can take up the chicken wire."

Chicken wire is an easy solution to keeping cats—both the neighbor's and yours—off your flowerbeds, or even away from your birdbath. While garden plants and warm soil or mulch may be tempting to cats, they won't walk on the coarse wire to get to those delights.

Developing Good Personal Habits— *for the Cat!*

Cats are creatures of habit, and they're very fastidious, so appeal to their better natures when you set up your spring planting beds or vegetable garden. Here's one easy trick you can try. Put out some clean litter in a prepared section of soil that is removed from the garden. You might even put some droppings there to reinforce the hint. Show Kitty the area, and it most likely will become the "powder room."

Gutter Guard Bulb Protection

Planting bulbs under a flat layer of wire mesh or chicken wire is often recommended. The wire mesh protects the bulbs from hungry rodents, but it can also trap the young plants as they grow. Pulling up the wire can tear their young leaves and buds.

A better bulb-protecting solution is gutter guard. It's lightweight and has a more closely woven mesh so the emerging leaves of bulbs or small plants can push it up but won't get stuck in it.

Static-free Deer Repellent

If deer are a problem in your landscape, tie antistatic strips or strips of dryer sheets to your shrubs every few feet. These strongly perfumed white strips that go in the clothes dryer to prevent static and scent the clothes work just as well to repel deer, according to naturalists Beth and David Buckley of Ashford Hollow, New York. The Buckleys have studied a herd of deer for about 30 years, so they're aware of the landscape damage deer can do.

"We have rhododendrons, which are deer's absolute favorite, lining our driveway," says Beth. "And we have a herd of over 100 deer out there, but they won't touch the rhododendrons." An extra advantage with dryer sheets is that periodic rains revive the scent from the dryer strips, at least a few times, so that they only need replacing every couple of months.

No Corn without Roughage

Well-meaning folks often put out corn for hungry deer. While that's a good source of protein, deer also need *browse* material—roughage in the form of twigs and branches. If they can't get it in the field or woods, they'll get it from suburban landscapes. As David Buckley explains, "If you give them corn, they'll be drawn in toward your home and will want the *browse* material to go with it—your shrubs! So don't feed them unless you can provide the protein in the corn *and* the brush for browsing."

So how can you take care of the deer? The best thing you can do for deer is to leave some natural habitat, says this deer expert. The second best thing is to provide brush piles wherever you can. Walk your property in midwinter, and cut down scrub saplings and crowded young trees, sumac, or whatever you can spare. Make large piles with the coarsest logs on the bottom to provide shelter for pheasants, turkeys, and other small animals. The leaf buds and branch tips that would have been out of reach to deer now make great munching. Deer need this supplemental food most in late winter (February or March), when food is scarcest.

Instead of attracting deer to dine on your shrubbery by offering them corn and other food, give them a brush pile. The brush supplies what they need to nibble far away from your beloved azaleas.

homegrown HINTS

DEER ME

Bill Stockman, owner of Spider Web Gardens in Center Tuftonboro, New Hampshire, recommends draping aluminum foil spread with peanut butter over a single strand of electric fence in order to deter deer. He says, "Deer love peanut butter, and when they put their noses on the highly conductive foil—zap!—they aren't too happy about it."

Glads for Deer

Minnesota farmer Callie Frye says her neighbor gave her this idea for keeping deer out of the garden. Plant gladiolus in thick rows (about 1½ to 2 feet wide) along the edges of the garden, because deer don't like the tall stalks hitting them around the legs as they amble toward the beans. "It works in my neighbor's beautiful garden," Callie adds. "The blooms from the gladiolus also attract bees, and I have never seen tomatoes like his."

Plant a crop of gladiolus as a deer barrier. Deer won't eat them, and they don't like to walk through them to get to their favorite crops.

Deer *Won't Walk* on the Carpet

Master Gardener Flo Zack has no trouble with deer in her garden, even though she has gardened for several decades in Elma, New York, where a herd of deer live in the wild area right behind her house. Her secret? Carpets!

For years, Flo has picked up discarded carpet wherever she finds it—both used rugs placed along the curb for trash pickup and discarded remnants from new installations. She lays the carpet on the ground around the outside of her garden in a path 4 to 6 feet wide. And amazingly, deer won't put a foot on it. "They're suspicious of the texture," says Flo, "and won't take the chance of walking on it."

If you're concerned that when it snows in winter, the deer will just walk on the snow to get at the remaining perennials, shrubs, and fruit trees—don't worry. Flo explains, "By the time the snow is deep, the deer have developed their browsing and travel patterns, so they don't even walk on the snow that covers the carpets."

problem SOLver

BOARDS HELP KEEP DOGS ON THE PATH

In *Great Garden Companions*, author Sally Cunningham reports success with garden paths that keep foot traffic—including dogs—off the soil. "Most creatures take the path of least resistance," says Sally, "and dogs are smart enough to do that too. In fact, my older dogs would rather not get their feet damp or dirty. So I provide wide boards or even cardboard as garden paths. If the path points even partly in the direction they are going, the dogs will use the paths."

Sally's dogs will even stick with a path that curves! Sally explains that she made a mixed perennial/shrub border with a curving path that leads from deck to barn. "Even in a hurry, the dogs (or children) run on the path rather than through the planting, which is a really good thing!"

CDs Scare Birds and Stop Bugs

The out-of-date music or computer CDs your family no longer uses can find new life controlling pests in your garden or greenhouse.

"To discourage birds from pecking fruit before I can harvest it," explains Nancy Lewis of Saint Helens, Oregon, "I tie old CDs into the cherry and peach trees and string them above blueberry bushes and strawberries. They work as well as the bird-scare tape, but are 'free'."

Nancy uses CDs with yellow labels in the greenhouse to trap flying insects. "I spread a film of oil over the yellow

The shiny, reflective quality of CDs makes them scary objects to birds. Hang CDs with string from fruit tree branches to ward off would-be scavengers.

side and insert the CD into the slightly split end of a straight stick inserted upright in a pot."

Dogs Will Be *Dogs!*

When Sally Cunningham, author of *Great Garden Companions*, asked her dog trainer how to "break" dogs of digging in the garden, she learned that some dogs have the instinct to dig, and we should not try to fight it. Instead, the trainer suggested giving the young dogs an appropriate place to dig, and establishing the habit early of digging in that place only.

During the planting season, dig up a soft area by the garden, and play with your dog and his favorite chew toy or a scented rawhide bone. Then bury the toy in the soil while he's watching, and leave. He will delight in digging it up and bringing it to you. And next time he will be more likely to use that "best hiding place" rather than your recently tilled garden.

Timely tip

Just in case the dog you're trying to train is the independent type, lay out some chicken wire over new beds for a while, as added insurance against digging.

Baby Your Bulbs

When you find bulbs that have been dug up, it is usually squirrels who are guilty, although mice and chipmunks might have had a role in the mischief.

Sprinkle baby powder around bulb plantings to deter squirrels. They don't like the texture or odor. Plus, it lets you be a super sleuth—you'll know they were there from the footprints.

Season Your Bulbs with Onion

Many people report red pepper, black pepper, and onion juice (one of these or a combination) as their favorite repellent for keeping rodents away from their bulbs. You can sprinkle the bulbs well with these products before planting them, and follow up by sprinkling the soil surface liberally, as well.

Sally Cunningham, author of *Great Garden Companions*, says she keeps a cheese grater in the garden tool bucket to use to grind onion juice on any new planting. "I never throw away soft onions; I just put on a mask and grate them onto the plants!"

Bag Bulbs in Mesh

Nylon stockings or panty hose are too closely woven to let roots grow through, but when mesh stockings were "in," a stylish gardener reported a great use for her torn stockings. Make little bags for bulbs; the roots can grow down, the top can grow up, and the animals can't get at them. (Be sure the weave is open enough to let tops emerge.) You can even put several bulbs in a long stocking, tying a knot between bulbs to keep them separate.

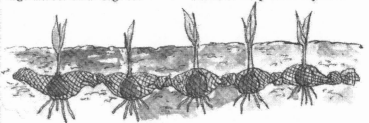

Look for mesh or fishnet stockings at your local thrift store. They provide protection for your bulbs from hungry squirrels, yet they still offer enough room for roots and plants to grow through.

Soda Bottle Transplant Collars

To discourage squirrels from digging up new transplants, Eleanor Rodini of Madison, Wisconsin, makes protective collars for her plants. She cuts soda bottles crosswise into 3-inch-wide rings. She places the rings around the stem of each new transplant, pushing the edge of the plastic into the ground just enough to hold it firmly in place. For a larger plant, she cuts the ring open to place it around the stem to prevent damaging the plant.

Eleanor says that squirrels sometimes scratch around the edges of the plastic rings, but they don't dig up the new transplants. "After a week or so, the squirrels lose interest in the site, and I remove the plastic ring and use it again."

Timely tip

Even if squirrels aren't a concern where you live, you may still find this soda bottle ring idea a valuable one. The rings also keep cutworms, slugs, and other undesirables from getting to plant stems.

homegrown HINTS

SOLID GROUNDCOVER BLOCKS SQUIRRELS

Some groundcovers are really tough to penetrate, so little animals may not bother fighting through them to dig up the bulbs. What to plant to protect your bulbs? Try sedums, creeping phlox, and sweet woodruff. Although squirrels find the groundcovers too dense to bother with, most spring bulbs can break through. As an added benefit, you can create many attractive groundcover and bulb combinations.

Squirrel-Proof Bird Feeder

Syl Wargo, a Master Gardener in Kenmore, New York, offers a unique design for a bird feeder that truly is squirrel-proof. After attending Master Gardener conferences all over the country, Syl found no other bird feeder quite like it: "It works 100 percent of the time," he says. And other gardeners he's talked to report a similar level of satisfaction.

To make your own squirrel-proof bird feeder, you'll need a 2-foot square of sheet metal, a 1¼-inch-wide galvanized pipe that is at least 8 feet long and threaded at one end, a large nail, and a drill. Make or buy a bird feeder, and attach it to the end of the galvanized pipe. Screw a thread-o-let to the threaded end of the

pole, then attach that to the bottom of the bird feeder.

Bury 2 feet of the pole in the ground, making sure that you place the feeder far away from the house and trees so that squirrels can't jump on top of the feeder from these outposts.

Drill a hole about halfway up the pole, and stick the nail through it. Cut a 2-foot diameter circle out of the sheet metal, as shown. Make a cut into the center of the circle, and cut away a smaller, center circle that will fit the pole loosely. Wrap the sheet metal circle around the pole so that it rests on the nail. The fit should be loose, so if a cunning squirrel should find some way to climb the pole or jump onto the shield, the metal cone will move and not support the squirrel's weight.

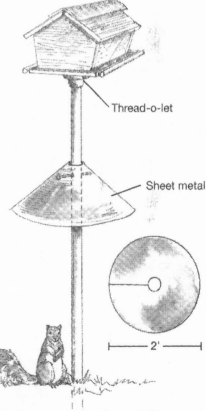

Thread-o-let

Sheet metal

⊢——— 2' ———⊣

Prevent squirrels from stealing your birdseed and encourage them to move to another neighborhood with this squirrel-proof bird feeder.

The *Hairy* Wreath

If a decorative grapevine wreath becomes too ragged for over the mantel or on the front door, you can recycle it in the garden to help keep away rabbits and other animals. The wreaths are perfect receptacles for holding dog hair. Just brush your dog and poke the tufts or clumps of hair into the spaces in the wreath. Hang the wreath so that its lowest point is about 9 inches above the ground. And don't worry about the weather. Whenever it rains, the wet-dog smell gets even stronger. In this case, the doggier it smells, the better!

The next time you need to brush Fido, don't dismay. The loose fur is a great rabbit repellent for your garden. Tuck the fur into a grapevine wreath and hang it near bunny's favorite snack food.

Braiding the Dog Hair

Here's another way to use dog hair to keep rodents out of the garden. Braid it with baling twine into a rope. Then drape the ropes around low garden fences. For added protection, drill holes through motel-type soap bars and dangle them on the dog hair braided ropes. Between the scent of the soap and the dog, critters will avoid your garden.

Twist dog hair into a twine rope to hang in the garden. Add a few bars of scented soap, and rodents won't want to dine in your vegetable garden.

Timely tip

Human hair works as an animal pest repellent, too! Just like dog hair, human hair says "Danger!" However, most human hair doesn't clump the way dog hair does. So gather the hair from your brush, local salon, beauty college, or barbershop, and put it in mesh bags or nylon stockings. Then hang your hair sachets anywhere around the border of the garden you want to protect. Hair is good in your compost pile, too, and it's also reported to have slug-repelling properties.

homegrown HINTS

IF YOU PLANT LETTUCE, THEY WILL COME

One smart Connecticut gardener reported "making a deal" with her garden-nibbling neighborhood rabbits. She took advantage of rabbits' timid natures—and their love of lettuce—and planted a lettuce border around the vegetable garden on the side where rabbits approach from the fields. Then she left a space between the lettuce and the larger garden and planted onions—not a rabbit favorite—in the first few feet of the main garden. Naturally, the rabbits ate what they found first, and they left the onions and everything else alone.

The Bean Alternative

Beans are a bunny favorite, but they're also a nitrogen-fixing, soil-improving cover crop. So improve your soil while you offer the bunnies something good to eat—which will keep them away from the rest of your crops.

Plant a 6-foot swath of beans on the side (or sides) of your garden toward the edge of your property. The rabbits will eat some of the plants, but most of them will survive just fine. And it's the roots you want for improving the soil, anyway. You may still get to pick a few beans, and you'll surely have your valuable bean plants to turn under and improve your soil.

Make the First Taste a Bad One

Fran Evans, a Master Gardener in Hamburg, New York, says that rabbits don't persist if their first bites of a crop are unnatural-tasting or bitter. He explains, "Rabbits generally begin eating at the end of a row of beans or peas. Dusting the first 2 to 3 feet with some bad-tasting dust or spray will discourage the little pests since one or two bites are enough to make them quit." In addition to red or black pepper and garlic/onion/chive sprays, try dusting your vegetables with talcum powder. Or flavor your garden with an organic commercial repellent mixture labeled for rabbits. (Be sure it's safe for use on edibles first.)

Flo's Bunny Prevention Trick

Master Gardener Flo Zack from Elma, New York, has used rotted hay for many years to keep rabbits from eating her beans, lettuce, strawberries, and other bunny favorites.

Flo buys the hay a year ahead of when she'll use it and leaves it outside to rot. The following year she mulches her vegetable garden with it.

Flow says that mulching one side of each row is enough. "Rabbits just don't like the smell of rotted hay. In fact, one time, I nearly stepped on a rabbit in the garden nibbling at some weeds, yet the strawberries with the rotted hay mulch weren't even touched."

Let Rabbits Eat Weeds!

Not everybody thinks rabbits are a problem. After all, as one study of Missouri cottontails reported, they do eat dandelions, knotweed, ragweed, crabgrass, and even poison ivy—often as a preference over garden vegetables. So leave the area around your garden unweeded to give rabbits the dietary weeds they love.

problem SOLVer

CREATE A MOLE HEAVEN

If you know you have a resident mole, you might try this trick, suggested by a real nature lover with a large yard. Give the mole a more appealing section of the yard, and it may just leave your preferred garden area intact. One way is to select a damp section of the yard and cover it with huge black plastic sheets or tarpaulins from late winter through spring. Mr. Mole will surely love the dark, moist soil that is so soft and easy to tunnel through. Of course, the covering will also kill the turf and weeds in that area, so it may also serve to prepare a place where you can plant wildflowers or wetland plants later in the season. And, if you patrol the rest of the yard and gardens with a cat and stamp down any unacceptable tunnels you spot, your mole "heaven" might keep Mr. Mole right where you want him.

Keep Them in Alfalfa

"I know farmers have real problems with woodchucks," admits Sally Cunningham, "but when I see one sitting complacently on his haunches, surveying his kingdom, I can't imagine that anybody would want to shoot one!"

Sally, the author of *Great Garden Companions,* tried this solution for woodchucks, with good results. She planted a 25 × 4-foot strip of alfalfa at the back of her mowed lawn area. She left about 150 feet between the alfalfa and the vegetable beds. Since woodchucks would rather not cross a large open area where dogs and other predators can find them, they stayed right around the alfalfa the whole season, where Sally says they looked fat and happy. "I think the alfalfa made the difference. Giving them what they want worked."

Woodchucks Sent *Packing*

To outsmart wily woodchucks, try using dried blood to drive them out of their homes. Woodchucks are one of the peskiest inhabitants of the garden and lawn. They'll steal your vegetables, nibble your flowers, and make holes in your lawn or garden. But there's one thing that woodchucks hate, according to Shelia Brackley, perennial production and sales assistant at Bigelow Nurseries, Inc., in Northboro, Massachusetts. "For easy woodchuck removal, dump ⅓ cup dried blood fertilizer in his hole, and he won't go home," Shelia says. With luck, he'll move right out of your yard. Dried blood is available at most garden centers.

Give a woodchuck its own alfalfa bed—away from your garden—and it just might leave your vegetables alone.

A Time to Sow, A Time to Weed

If you have problems with weeds (and what gardener doesn't?), remember that timing can make a difference. "It's best to pull weeds before they go to seed," says University of Georgia Extension weed scientist Greg Mac-Donald. "But if seedheads have already formed, weed *early* in the day. The moisture that's present in early morning can keep the seedheads from shattering and dropping seeds in the garden."

If you plan to weed during early morning when moisture is present, do it with care. Greg cautions, "My father always said never to walk in the garden very early in the morning or after a rain, because disease is easily transmitted by spreading dew or rain droplets from plant to plant."

Lettuce As a Spring Weed Blocker

Block spring weeds between your cabbage plants by sowing fast-growing leafy crops like lettuce between the cabbages. As soon as you transplant broccoli and other cabbage family crops into your spring garden (usually a few weeks before the last spring frost in your area), toss a thick sowing of seeds of lettuce, spinach, or other leafy greens around the transplants. Lettuce grows quickly, likes shade, and blocks most of the weeds. Don't let the lettuce

Prevent early weeds from taking hold while you wait for your broccoli or cabbages to grow. Instead of using traditional mulch, plant lettuce between the rows. It will block weeds and you can harvest it for crisp spring salads.

weed barrier go to waste. Thin the lettuce or greens as they grow, and use the thinnings for tender salads.

Have a Gardening Night Party!

You've heard of garden parties and gardening days, but a "gardening night party"?

According to some research studies, tilling at night prevents many weeds from germinating. Certain weeds need light in order to germinate, and just those few post-tilling hours of being exposed to air without light renders the seeds unproductive.

A gardener near Ithaca, New York, says his farming family declared a nighttime tilling and planting party in late spring, when the soil was warm enough to work. They rigged up dim lights on the tiller, walked ahead of it to pick up rocks, and—at least in theory—left a lot of disappointed and unfulfilled weed seeds turned up behind them.

The nighttime tilling scene was part magical and part comical, and best of all, one the family will never forget! While some weeds are sure to germinate even when the tilling is done in the dark of night, at least this family believes the weed count was way down. Plus, it's cooler working at night, and the party was certainly a lot of fun!

problem solver

TAP INTO SOIL NUTRIENTS

Dandelions, with their long, thick taproots, can capture nutrients from several feet below the surface of the soil. By composting dandelions, you can put those nutrients back into the soil surface. The trick is to let the rootstocks dry out before you compost your dandelions. Toss the pulled dandelions off to the side to dry in the sun for a couple of days. After they've dried and shriveled, you can toss them in the compost heap. Also, be sure to cut off the heads if they are even approaching the flower-to-seed stage!

Flame Weeder Recommendation

"We used a flame weeder last summer for the first time in our ¼-acre organic garden and found it to be worth its 30-pound weight," reports Amy LeBlanc, of Whitehill Farm in East Wilton, Maine. "I have a bad back, and it has been my savior."

While Amy found the flame weeder worked well on very small weeds, out of concern for insects and tiny animals that live on the soil surface, she used it mostly on weeds that had reached 2 to 4 inches tall. She found that regular flaming sets weeds back so they had far less impact on crops and never had the chance to flower and reseed. "The best thing about the flame weeder is that it is fast," Amy says.

"When you get the rhythm of your swing going, you can move right along and see the results only an hour or so later," she explains.

Amy recommends making another pass over the weeds a few days later to ensure you've gotten them all. She adds, "Our flame weeder has a special extra widget that is essentially a pilot light, which allows us to stop flaming for a moment then continue without having to completely stop and relight it. It's a great feature—and one that any serious gardener would appreciate!"

You can find flame weeders at some specialty garden centers and farm stores as well as through farm and garden catalogs.

Cardboard for Weed-Free Paths

Who has time to weed a path, when there are more important things to do in the garden? Whether your path is made of gravel, wood chips, flagstone, or sawdust, it is easy to prevent even the peskiest of weeds from working their way through. How? Use cardboard!

You can get cardboard free from the grocery store. A double thickness of cardboard box material will kill any weeds underneath it, and it lasts a long time.

One thickness of cardboard will work, but persistent weeds like quackgrass will find any cracks between the pieces. So "insure" the project by using a double layer of corrugated cardboard in your pathways.

Timely tip

Cardboard can be a little slippery as a walking surface, so use it as the bottom layer of the path. Start the path in a shallow trench, a couple of inches lower than the planting bed level. Put 2 to 3 inches of your chosen path material on top of the cardboard, and the sliding will be minimal.

homegrown HINTS

FIGHT WEEDS—AND WATER WOES—WITH WEEDS

"Broad-leaved weeds—and I mean *really* broad-leaved weeds—make a great midsummer mulch," reports Allentown, Pennsylvania, gardener Deb Martin.

"I had a couple of common burdock plants (*Arctium minus*) growing in my yard, and they were starting to bloom," Deb explains. "I wanted to get them out of there before they started spreading seeds everywhere." Deb used a pair of loppers to fell the 4-foot-tall weeds, then dragged them to the driveway to wilt in the sun.

"I cut the largest leaves off the burdock—they were easily a foot wide and 1 to 2 feet long—and laid them on the moist soil around some newly planted bee balm." The leaves covered the soil, then Deb dressed them up with about an inch of compost.

"I was away on vacation during a week when there was no rain, and my plants survived just fine," Deb says. "The burdock leaves really helped keep things moist. And they'll give my perennials a little nutrient boost as they decay."

Queen-Anne's-Lace—A Welcome Weed

Some gardeners select weeds for the garden on purpose! Sally Cunningham, author of *Great Garden Companions*, recommends allowing certain "weeds" such as Queen-Anne's-lace to volunteer around the garden.

"The trick," says Sally, "is to recognize these plants when they are tiny and to choose right then which ones you want in which location." Queen-Anne's-lace is desirable around the garden because of the many beneficial wasps and flies it attracts. Tachinids and several types of tiny parasitoid wasps flock to it because the nectar is so readily available. And it provides food for swallowtail butterfly caterpillars.

But, it's easy to weed the babies out along with ragweed and other unwelcome weed seedlings. And, Queen-Anne's-lace has a taproot, so it isn't easy to transplant. Sally

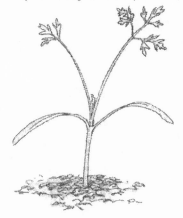

recommends getting to know this welcome weed by its seedlings and letting it stay in some parts of your garden.

But keep it away from the carrots, she cautions. Queen-Anne's-lace can carry aster yellows, a disease that affects carrots, asters, and mums. So keep this weed where beneficial insects can enjoy it, but make sure it benefits your garden—or pull it.

Learn to recognize seedlings of "beneficial" weeds such as Queen-Anne's-lace. As long as it's not growing in a bad spot, this is one weed that's pretty enough to keep, and it attracts and feeds beneficial insects, too.

Salad "Dressing" in the Flowerbeds

Most perennials start small in spring, and some arrive late—at least late enough to give weeds a good head start!

Try planting lettuce, spinach, or mesclun (mixed salad greens) all around the young perennials. They will block weeds, and you can pull them up and eat them by the time the perennials are ready to fill out the space.

Or, if you are planning to put tender annuals among the perennials, the lettuce will be done and ready to bolt (set seed) just about when the soil is warm enough to plant the annuals!

Desirable Weeds— Good for You and Your Garden

Some weeds are actually good for your garden. These desirable "weeds" are plants that attract beneficial insects. They include wild daisies, dandelions, dead nettle (stinging nettle), goldenrod, common sorrel, tansy, and even lamb's-quarters. If you let them share some of your garden space, they can help reduce insect problems on your "real" garden plants. And while you're at it, try harvesting edible weeds such as lamb's-quarters (*Chenopodium album*) and chickweed (*Stellaria media*). When young, they make a tasty salad.

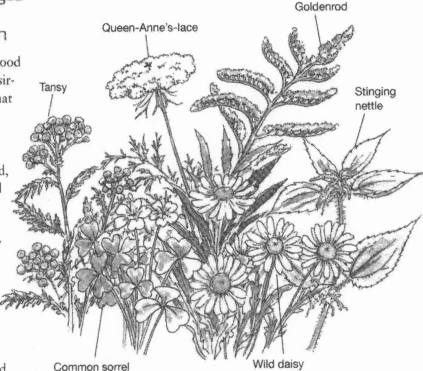

Some weeds get an undeserved bad rap. The weeds shown here all help your garden by providing food and shelter for beneficial insects that can help keep pest populations in check.

Tea and Botany

An elderly English gardener who had lived many years in a small town in New Jersey, commented, "I just don't understand why some Americans pay so much for those nasty herbicides just for weeds in the sidewalk! It's so easy to take care of them!"

Her solution? Every Sunday after church she prepared her tea and boiled a bit of extra water. While the tea steeped she took the boiling pot of water out to the sidewalk in front of the house and poured it along the cracks. "Once a week with boiling water is quite enough," she said.

Acid Test

Maintaining your brick or flagstone path doesn't need to be a time-consuming chore. A new, organic, acetic acid-based product from ECOVAL will destroy various common weeds in just hours.

Nature's Glory Fast Acting Weed and Grass Killer will kill the top growth of both annual and perennial weeds. Allentown, Pennsylvania, gardener Deb Martin decided to try it on the poison ivy in her yard. She reports that it burned the leaves but did not kill the plant. However, the spray also fell on some weedy violets nearby and took care of those invasive plants completely. Because the spray is nonselective, it's best to use it where it won't damage crops or ornamentals.

Deb says, "This product really does a number on weeds growing in driveway and sidewalk cracks. And I can use it without having to worry that it may harm my children if they play near where I spray."

For another equally effective and fast-acting weed killer, try dousing the offending plants with straight vinegar (use 3 percent acidity, if it's available). Vinegar has a drastic effect and can acidify the soil to the point where plants will not grow. Ordinary table salt, poured onto the soil and watered in, also will kill roots and make the soil uninhabitable. Be aware, however, that both vinegar and salt are more permanent methods, are nonselective, and can effectively sterilize the soil for months.

Save Beneficials by Mowing Just Half

Cover crops like rye, buckwheat, and clover build your soil and supply a place for beneficial insects to live and breed. But when you mow or turn under a crop, you kill or disrupt the beneficial insects. So how can you save the beneficials?

No matter what your "cover and mow" or "cover and turn" routine, do it in halves. Till or mow down the *right* side of every row the first time and down the *left* side two weeks later. Although you can't save every beneficial insect, this method lets you maintain a permanent habitat and some good hiding places for the population to grow in at every stage of the insects' development.

Timely tip

In the case of paths, one garden designer suggests that the main garden paths should be wide ones, planted in clover, which is an ideal draw for beneficial insects and bees. She recommends making the paths twice as wide as the lawn mower, which makes it easy to mow down half a path every two weeks.

A **New Use** for *The Wall Street Journal*

Rochelle Smith, a landscape designer and diagnostician in Grand Island, New York, is always looking for ways to provide customers with solutions to landscape problems at a reasonable cost. Rochelle writes, "I use the same weed barrier in all of my landscape installations—*The Wall Street Journal.*" While lots of landscapers use newspaper, Rochelle explains, "I prefer not to use the small inserts, since they take more time. My favorite is *The Wall Street Journal* because of its large, thick sections, and no inserts!

"Newspaper is especially useful in low-maintenance groundcover plantings where the plants need to be spaced for healthy development and where hand-weeding would increase the maintenance of the site." It works wonders—even on light slopes. To use newspaper in a landscape installation, Rochelle first prepares the soil thoroughly; then she installs the hardscape (paths, and so on) and plants the large trees and shrubs. Then it's time to put down the newspaper.

Rochelle says the goal is to have a cohesive layer of newspaper between the soil and the top mulch. To use her method, spread the newspaper in large open sections, six to eight sheets thick, with plenty of overlap between each section. Before planting, wet the paper with a light spray from the hose, and place a thin layer of mulch all over.

To complete the bed, punch through the paper with a trowel to plant small perennials, groundcover plants, and bulbs. (You do need to break the weed barrier for bulbs, because the paper does not let them push through.) Finish with 2 to 3 inches of mulch. The garden will look neat and tidy, while the mulch will both provide an effective insulator for plants and enhance the weed-controlling properties of the newspaper.

Timely tip

Rochelle and others have learned the hard way that laying newspaper can be difficult if you try to do too much at once—especially if the wind picks up! She suggests laying out small areas at a time—perhaps no more than 10 × 10-foot spaces, wetting the paper as you go.

Trip Up the Thrips

Many summer-flowering bulbs, such as freesia and gladiolas, are very susceptible to flower thrips, tiny insects that deform buds and ruin blooms. Bill Stockman, owner of Spider Web Gardens in Center Tuftonboro, New Hampshire, has discovered an easy way to protect these bulbs: Soak them in a dip of 1 gallon of warm water mixed with 2½ tablespoons of Lysol.

Bill says, "Let the bulbs sit at least 12 hours, then plant them straight from the dip. At bloom time later in the season, there will be no thrips!"

Tomato Hornworms Take Up ***Tobacco***!

Fran Evans is a Master Gardener who has eliminated tomato hornworms from his Hamburg, New York, garden. Fran says, "Plant one or two tobacco plants with the tomatoes. Hornworms prefer the tobacco plants and are easy to pick off the tobacco and destroy." Fran says this method can keep your garden hornworm-free for two to three years.

Insects—Are They *Pests* or *Friends*?

Insects are blamed for a lot of gardening disappointments, but most of the time the problem is really the growing conditions the gardener has provided. So before you kill an insect, make sure it's really the culprit you think it is. In many cases, the insect you see is a beneficial one, there to help you with the real pest. (Or at the very least, an innocent insect just passing by.)

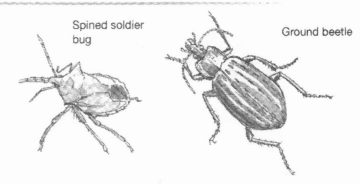

Spined soldier bug

Ground beetle

Get to know the good guys in your garden. Spined soldier bugs eat many kinds of caterpillars, plus Mexican bean beetle and Colorado potato beetle larvae. Ground beetles gobble up slugs, snails, cutworms, and many other pests.

Experts tell us that 95 to 99 percent of the insects in our yards and gardens are beneficial or harmless. So, make sure you've got a bad guy before you **squish**!

Use Growing-Degree Days to *Bypass* Pests

The time that certain insects or plants emerge is different from region to region. Nature doesn't use a calendar. Instead, insect and plant development are governed by signals from nature—especially the light and heat that have accumulated during the season.

So how can you plan for the onset of particular garden pests, such as Japanese beetles, forest tent caterpillars, and gypsy moth larvae? There is a formula, used to measure that accumulated heat, called growing-degree days (GDDs). This formula is the key to intelligent pest management. For instance, there is no point in taking any steps toward pest control if the pests aren't there yet. And they're only there when nature's signal tells them that it's time.

You can get charts of GDDs for insect and plant behaviors from your local Cooperative Extension or other educational sources, and the charts are good tools to have. Ask your local extension or weather station for the current GDDs, and then check the chart to anticipate insect emergence.

Slug Lite

"On night slug patrols, you usually need three hands—one to hold the flashlight, one to scoop up the slugs, and one to hold the slug container," notes Sharon Gordon of Ohio.

To make slug collection a two-handed operation, Sharon suggests buying a **headlight** from a camping or backpacking store. When you wear the headlight, the light will point wherever you look, leaving your hands free for scooping up slimy slugs and other pests that feed at night. A headlight will also help you gather greens after dark.

homegrown HINTS

TIME YOUR PLANTING AROUND INSECT LIFE CYCLES

Once you know when insect pests are likely to arrive (see the growing-degree days tip on page 127), make sure their favorite plants are not what you just planted! Here are some smart garden timing tips for better pest management.

Cabbage loopers: Plant cabbage early (about four to five weeks before the last frost), and harvest by late spring—before the cabbage loopers have emerged to begin chewing.

Corn borers: If you plant corn two weeks after the last frost date, you may just be able to avoid these pests.

Potato leafhoppers: These insects come on strong in July, so plant your potatoes as soon as possible in spring, and try to harvest them all by late July.

Carrot maggots: These pests are the worst when you plant early to get those first sweet carrots. Instead, wait until after June 1 in the North (or until early summer) to plant your carrots.

Of course, timing isn't everything, and there are other reasons to plant a crop early or late. But if a certain pest is your primary problem, look at the pest's timing to see if there are ways to avoid the problem.

Row Covers
Add a Few Ounces of Prevention

The old "ounce of prevention" adage is surely correct when it comes to using row covers (polyethylene fabric) to prevent many insect pests on crops. However, row covers often blow away in spring breezes, and they sometimes tear when you try to tack them down with boards, rocks, or pins.

Instead of leaving the fabric loose, try this idea from Sally Cunningham, author and organic gardener from East Aurora, New York. Staple the outside edges (on the long sides) to long ½ × ½-inch wooden strips, like the ones used for interior trim or moldings. "I find 6- or 8-foot lengths are the longest lengths that are still manageable," says Sally. "They give the tunnels structure, prevent blowing, and hug the ground."

If there are gaps or uneven ground, Sally recommends mounding a little soil over them. You can still use tunnel hoops if you want an elevated

Inexpensive molding stapled to the edges of row covers keeps the covers in place during prime insect time. When pests are no longer a problem, wrap up the covers and store them for next year.

tunnel. When it is time to remove the row covers, just wrap the cloth around your wood strips until next season.

Turn Torn Row Covers into *Plant Hoods*

If your row covers are torn repeatedly over a few years of use, cut the sections that are salvageable into squares, which you can fashion into little bags for individual plant covers. If you're handy with a sewing machine, fold the squares in half and sew down each side. Or, you can try the easy way—use clothespins!

Then you can place the individual bags, or hoods, over vulnerable plants in any part of the garden—from an eggplant hiding from the flea beetles to a newly planted hill of squash.

Salvage old, torn row covers by turning them into individual plant covers. You don't even have to sew! Simply pin the fabric edges together over the plants with pinch-type clothespins. Be sure to bury the bottom edges of the bags to prevent pests from finding their way into the bags.

Ants in Hot Water

Gerry Rising is a nature columnist for the *Buffalo Evening News* and a Master Gardener, as well. While ants aren't a serious problem in Buffalo, they surely are in other places.

Gerry says, "My mother-in-law lives in Alabama, where she has fire ant problems. She doesn't like to use harsh chemicals or gasoline on her lawn to rid herself of these terrible stingers, but she does want to get rid of them or at least partially control them. She boils a gallon of water and pours it down the center of the nest."

Birdcage Stand Makes a Great Garden Perch

You may find a discarded birdcage stand in the attic or at a yard sale. If it's not a valuable antique or suitable for an indoor cage, put it in the garden. (You may have to stake or tie it if it's in a windy location.) The stand can hold a hanging plant, and it will attract birds, who will perch on top of it. If you provide the home, the birds will patrol your garden for insects. Some birds will even make their nests in the plant. Perhaps the birds know the stand was designed to give them a place to hang out.

Invite birds to your garden to help in reducing the bug population. Birds need places to perch, and a hanging basket on an old birdcage stand will be irresistable to your feathered friends.

Post *a* Perch *for the* Birds

If you don't have the space for living perches, and your garden lacks bean poles or teepees, welcome insect-eating birds with a tall (8- to 10-foot) perch made from a pole topped by a wooden crosspiece of any length. You can use a ½-inch wooden strip, a piece of molding, or any small scrap of lumber for the cross-piece. However, a bird's little feet may feel best perching on a smooth piece of dowel.

Neighborhood birds will help to rid your garden of insect pests, as long as you give them a place to perch while they watch for bugs.

Tomato Cages **Help Birds** Hunt Insects

Birds eat insects—an important source of protein for them and their young—in summer, just when you and your garden need the help. Make their hunting easier by providing perches at high points around your garden. Tall tomato cages provide perches, but the birds will find your garden more attractive if there is at least one stake that is 1 to 2 feet higher than the tops of the cages. Put a short cross-piece atop each tall "perching" stake where birds can rest while they scan for insects.

"Plant" **Toads** *in the* **Peas**

Few things are as good for your garden as a resident toad—or two. You can't exactly *plant* a toad, but you can try to attract them to the pea patch. Toads love pea aphids and a lot of other pest insects; they even eat slugs. So offer toads shelter, such as an inverted clay pot with a "door" chipped out of the lip, and some water. A small sunken pool or even a shallow dish will do fine. Put these near the pea patch and the toads will come. And, when you find a toad around your yard, move him into your garden.

homegrown HINTS

SUPPORT BIRDS WITH SUNFLOWERS

A planting of sunflowers or any other tall annuals or perennials can help bring the birds to the garden, but the plants must be strong enough to offer a place to perch that doesn't collapse when the birds land there. If you have tall plants that are too wobbly to support even a bird's weight, try putting up a fence on the less visible side, or put up a wire cage around them. The flowers will add beauty to your garden while they attract birds and beneficial insects. And the birds and beneficial insects will help manage any pests that dare to venture into your garden. If you hope to save any sunflower seeds for yourself, cover one or two flowerheads with a piece of plastic mesh just as the seeds start to ripen.

Be Patient with Aphids

You can beat aphid attacks just by using a little patience. Aphids have so many predators that they rarely become a problem if you encourage predation and have a little patience. Something will come along to eat them—but only if you wait a little while and don't spray them!

If you do spray—organic, botanical, or otherwise—you'll probably kill off or discourage beneficial insects as they arrive. Or, you'll at least cut down the population of the attractive aphids just long enough so that the predators won't discover your garden. As a result, the aphids that survive the spraying (the strongest ones) will suddenly multiply, and there will be no army of predators ready to handle them. So you'll have to spray and spray again, and the problem continues.

If a particular crop or specific plants are seriously threatened by aphids while you're waiting for the beneficials to arrive, just spray them hard with a hose once a day until you see your insect allies arrive. You'll be glad you waited for reinforcements.

problem solver
APHIDS ARRIVE AFTER YOU PRUNE!

You can avoid a lot of aphids by pruning most of your trees and shrubs when they are dormant. The reason you find aphids on the tips of plants or on new leaves is that they are seeking nitrogen, which is concentrated in areas of new growth. Pruning your trees and shrubs, including roses, gives the plants a signal to produce nitrogen-rich new growth. So by trimming your plants while they're dormant, you'll make sure there is no nitrogen signal to attract aphids, and few, if any, aphids to attract anyway.

Note that some shrubs, such as lilacs, should be pruned during the growing season, after they finish flowering. But these shrubs seem to be less prone to aphid problems and have already produced their new leaves and flowers.

To keep aphid problems in check in your perennial beds, go light on nitrogen when you fertilize. It triggers the nitrogen-rich, aphid-attracting growth that follows summer pruning.

Trench Warfare Topples Armyworms

Armyworms sometimes march into the garden from neighboring fields and can do an impressive job of destroying beets, corn, and other vegetable crops. (This is especially true of the fall armyworm, which likes almost everything edible in its path.)

Armyworm problems are most severe in the southern and central United States, but these voracious pests sometimes work their way quite far north. Here's the trick to stopping these determined soldiers in their tracks.

If you have a big crop, dig a narrow (2-inch) trench along the sides of the garden, 6 to 8 inches deep. If you have a "ditch witch" or other trenching equipment—the equipment used when laying pipe or cable—available, the job is easy. Even if you have to dig the trenches manually, it's worth it. The worms will fall into the trenches before they can destroy your crops.

Keep a heavy pipe the width of the trench nearby. From time to time, drag it along the tunnel to squish the worms.

Garlic Is a Gardener's Friend

Planting garlic near cabbage or lettuce can help prevent pest problems, but it may be hard to grow enough garlic to do the job right.

Dave Swaciak, horticulture educator for Cornell Cooperative Extension of Cattaraugus County in New York, recommends, "If you grow hardneck garlic and use every clove for cooking or for planting next year's crop, then you can let one or two of the scapes mature." (Scapes are the flower stems that produce a bulblike part on top. The usual advice is to cut them off so they don't steal nutrients from the developing bulb.) Each scape holds a flower, which produces about a dozen tiny bulbs called bulbils. You can plant these bulbils throughout the garden and they will sprout the same year. Leave the bulbils in the ground over winter, remove them when you prepare your garden in the spring, and re-plant them after you have mixed in your soil amendments. Or leave them in the garden while you prepare your bed, and they will usually still find their way up! After a few years, they will even produce cloves that you can divide for further planting or cooking.

Don't let any of your garlic go to waste. Dave recommends that you chop any scapes that you do cut off for use in cooking—or use them as the basis of an insect-repelling spray.

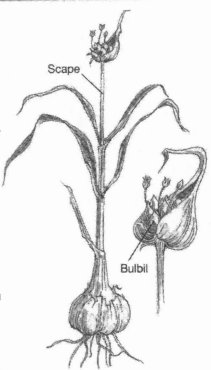

Scape

Bulbil

To get enough garlic to eat and to use for pest control, let a couple of scapes mature, and plant the resulting bulbils.

homegrown HINTS

CATCH CUCUMBER BEETLES WITH OLD SQUASH

Spotted cucumber beetles chew holes in all sorts of vine crops as well as in corn, potatoes, and some fruit crops. Even worse, they can spread serious diseases to your garden. But smart gardeners can put a stop to these troublesome pests early in the season.

If you have winter squash in storage, keep some until spring—even if they are getting soft. Scoop out a hole in each squash, and place it by the vulnerable crops soon after planting. Once these traps hold lots of cucumber beetles, toss squash and pests in the trash.

Battle **Birds** with *Fantastic Plastic* Bottle Baffle

If the birds are tasting your grapes before you are, try bottling them on the vine! "Bottling is easier than bagging," says Pennsylvania gardener Bill Dailey.

To guard your grapes from marauding birds, try Bill's simple technique. He cuts the neck off of a 1-liter plastic seltzer bottle, then makes a slit down the length of the bottle. To prevent condensation inside the bottle, Bill pokes a few holes in its bottom. Then he simply snaps the bottle over a developing fruit cluster. Bill adds that he always tries to slip the top of the slit bottle over a neighboring vine to help support the weight of the growing grape cluster.

"I put the bottles on when the grapes are about half-size, and I usually just do a few a night over a couple of weeks," he reports. Bill's reward is perfect, unpecked grapes at harvest time, with no disease or rotting.

Apple **Maggots** *in the* Bag

For years, organic gardeners have used red sticky balls, coated with Tanglefoot or another sticky substance, to simulate ripe apples so that they can catch the flies that lay apple maggot eggs. The problem is the sticky balls can be quite messy, and they need to be changed frequently. You have to hang two to eight traps per tree in the middle of June and leave them all summer. When the sticky traps become coated with flies or other debris, they are useless, and you have all the trouble and expense of changing them.

To avoid this end-of-summer mess, slip your new, clean balls into plastic sandwich bags, using twist ties to close the bags. (The twist ties can double as hangers, or you can use inexpensive red Christmas ornaments, complete with wire hangers.) Coat the bags with your sticky substance, and then hang them in the apple tree. When the sticky bags become too bug-encrusted to be effective, simply slip off the old bags and tie on new ones.

Lots of apple growers lure apple maggots to red sticky balls and away from ripening red apples. You can make the whole process less messy, however, by putting the balls in plastic sandwich bags first, and then coating the bags instead of the balls. Simply toss out used bags, and reuse the red balls.

homegrown HINTS

CABBAGEWORMS DON'T LIKE RED

Are cabbageworms ruthlessly butchering your cabbage? To save some for yourself, try planting red-leaved cabbage. Studies indicate that cabbageworms don't like them as well as they like green-leaved varieties. (And maybe the gardener can see the pest better and will hand-pick it more often!) It is also true that cabbages that have smoother leaves are attacked less frequently than crinkly leaved varieties.

To protect green cabbage varieties, try turning the leaves of broccoli, cauliflower, cabbage, and brussels sprouts white by dusting them with white flour. (It sticks best after a rain or on the morning dew.) Caterpillars eat the flour, get bloated, and die.

Sheer Protection from Cabbageworms

Row covers are a great way to protect members of the cabbage family, including broccoli and cauliflower, from imported cabbageworms and cabbage loopers. But row covers aren't practical if your garden is interplanted with flowers you would like to enjoy or if you don't plant in rows.

You can still protect your cabbage and broccoli, though, with their own personal covers made from your used nylon stockings or the legs of panty hose. Put the stockings right over each individual vegetable, and they will stretch as the cabbages or heads of broccoli

The sheer, stretchy fabric of nylon stockings offers perfect protection for growing vegetables. Air and light get through the fabric, but the snug fit keeps insects from eating your crops.

grow. However, if you threw the stockings out because of holes, the cabbage butterflies will find those same holes and lay eggs there! Avoid using the parts that are torn.

Spread the Sheets under the Pines

Conifer sawflies are a serious problem for pine and spruce trees in many parts of the country. To catch a lot of them in late spring, spread old bedsheets around the base of your evergreen trees. The conifer sawfly larvae will drop to the ground to pupate. You can gather them up and carry them to the trash or the bonfire before they have a chance to develop.

Timely tip

A brisk whack or shaking the tree a few times will encourage some of the conifer sawfly larvae to drop sooner than they expected!

Plant a *Winning Combination*

"This is not a new idea, but it's definitely underused," says Sally Cunningham, author of *Great Garden Companions*. "Everybody should plant rows of potatoes alternating with wide rows of bush beans."

Sally says this really works. Mexican bean beetles and Colorado potato beetles are both repelled by the mixed planting. "The pests just don't find their targets!"

Outsmart Mexican Bean Beetles

Master Gardener Fran Evans of Hamburg, New York, uses this timing trick to beat Mexican bean beetles.

The timing may differ in your zone, but the principle is the same. Plant snap beans as early as possible. Then pick the beans until the crop begins to dwindle. Pull up all the bean plants or mow them down and till them into the soil by the third or fourth week in July. "About 90 to 95 percent of the time, weather cooperating, you will be finished with the beans before the Mexican bean beetles can lay eggs and establish themselves," says Fran.

homegrown HINTS

SCOUT FOR CUTWORMS AFTER DARK

One old-timer who gardens in New York State suggests that after your first big planting day, when your body aches all over, sit for a while with a cool drink. But before you lie down, take one more walk out to the garden in the dark. Bend down and pick off those cutworms before they get going. Those last few bends and stretches won't kill you— but losing the crop by morning just might!

Nail Those Cutworms!

Stick a nail in the soil next to each seedling. Any size nail will do. Simply place it about ¼ inch away from the stem. The nail keeps cutworms from wrapping around a plant's stem, which is how they feed on—and sever—young plants.

Lure **Cutworms** with Clover

Cutworms like fresh-cut grass or clover, so make a few piles of it right in the garden near new seedlings. Look under it in a while for cutworms. If you find them, either discard the worms or pour boiling water over the whole pile, taking care not to get boiling water on your seedlings.

Old Forks Keep Cutworms at Bay

Keep some old forks stuck among your young plantings. Garden tools are too coarse and many are not handy to use around little seedlings. Instead, gently scrape and poke with a salad or dinner fork around the base of seedlings to dislodge the cutworms as they approach the tender stems of your transplants.

It's especially important to keep a careful eye on your transplants during the first few days after planting to keep cutworms away from your young plants. Keep old forks and other anticutworm equipment close at hand. Once the plants grow a bit older and tougher, cutworms will look elsewhere for tasty treats.

The **Bottle** Tree

One apple grower, Bill McKentley, stopped a lot of traffic with his "bottle trees." Before his apple trees were in bloom, he hung clear empty soda bottles from the branches, suspending them horizontally with ribbons tied at the neck and bottom. Why? He was catching codling moths in a mixture of vinegar and molasses, which he placed in every bottle. There are several methods for using vinegar and molasses combinations, but here's one easy method. Mix about 1 cup of molasses in ½ gallon of vinegar in the blender. Put just enough of the mixture into each bottle so you can lay the bottle sideways and the liquid won't spill out. (Bottles vary, but you'll need from 1 to 2 cups per bottle.)

Be sure to replace the bottle caps while you are hanging the bottles. Use twine or ribbon to attach the bottles to the tree. Tie one piece tight around the neck of each bottle with enough length to tie it to a branch. Use a second piece of twine in the form of a sling to suspend the lower half of the bottle so that it hangs parallel to the ground. If your area is windy, it helps to wind the twine once rather tightly around the bottle. Take the caps off, and you're ready to catch some moths.

Prevent codling moths from damaging your apple crop by capturing the moths—before your trees blossom—in homemade soda bottle traps.

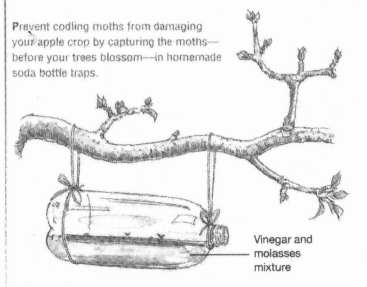

Vinegar and molasses mixture

Three Cheers for No More Caterpillars

Eastern tent caterpillars and fall webworms are destructive caterpillars that make white or gray webs or "tents" in trees.

While you can cut out the affected branches, here's a less invasive way to deal with the problem. A former cheerleader attached her old pompoms to a pole and poked them into the nests to pull out the offenders.

Dust Mop to *the Rescue*

Here's another clever way to rid your trees of tent caterpillars. One gardener recommends drenching a dust mop in *Bacillus thuringiensis* (BT) and shaking it over the nest to try to saturate the nest with the caterpillar poison. (BT is a biological stomach poison for leaf-eating caterpillars, but it does not harm birds or other creatures. It can kill the larvae of butterflies, however.) The long-handled dust mop makes it easier to get the BT through the webbing and onto the pest caterpillars inside.

Screwdriver Can *Prevent* Tents

Karen Soltys, garden book editor at Rodale Press, reports that she, too, had an annual problem with eastern tent caterpillars on her trees.

"Every year I'd have to cut out a branch or two from my weeping cherry tree when the tents appeared. Then I got smart and started looking for the caterpillars in my tree before they crafted their tents."

Karen now uses a screwdriver to lightly scrape the caterpillars out of the trees. She lets them fall onto paper on the ground below, then wraps up the paper and tosses the caterpillars out with the trash. There's nothing magical about the screwdriver. You can use any tool narrow enough to fit in branch crotches.

Flea Beetles Get Mixed Up

"My eggplants were the first plants to be riddled with flea beetle holes," reports Sally Cunningham, the author of *Great Garden Companions*. But Sally proposes a solution that relies on using the mixed plantings that are typical of her companion-style approach to gardening.

Sally says, "One year I planted eggplants all alone in one area, and in another place, I interspersed eggplants with marigolds and basil. Guess what? The 'solo' eggplants were full of holes, but the other ones were camouflaged enough that they squeaked through the season undiscovered! Flea beetles are easily confused."

Japanese Beetles *Drop & Disappear*

Every Japanese beetle you catch early is one that can't lay eggs to make more. So early in the season set your alarm clock early—before 7 A.M.—to get out there and get the beetles.

Spread a sheet under the plants the beetles prefer. Some say roses suffer the most, but there are hundreds of target plants—everything from grapevines to fruit trees. Then shake the plant or whack it with a broom and watch the beetles fall down and "play dead." Toss them into soapy water or put them in the trash.

problem SOLVer

CATCH FLEA BEETLES AS THEY JUMP

A Buffalo gardener had trouble with flea beetles in a community garden and risked some odd stares from fellow gardeners when she performed her clever jumping flea beetle ritual.

She coated a wide board with a homemade sticky substance (Tanglefoot would do) and brushed it along the top of the row,

just touching the plants. She enlisted the help of a friend, who used a ruler to jiggle the plants just enough so that the flea beetles all started jumping. They stuck to the board and were never heard from again!

Repeat this trick for three or four days in a row, and you'll have fewer flea beetles jumping about and feeding on your garden.

homegrown HINTS

THE FOUR-O'CLOCK CONNECTION

Companion gardener and author Sally Cunningham reports this tip, first offered by Clarence Mahan, an expert in Japanese iris with experience in Japan as well as America. Clarence has many gardeners planting drifts of four-o'-clocks (*Mirabilis jalapa*), a wonderful, fragrant, old-fashioned annual, slightly away from the garden. They are a favorite of Japanese beetles, and they work as a trap.

When you notice beetles attacking the four-o'clocks, hand-pick and squish them all in one place, or knock them off the flowers into a can of soapy water. In theory, you can even scoop up and discard your entire planting of four-o'-clocks, Japanese beetles and all—but upon seeing and smelling the flowers, who could?

Less Turf *Equals* Fewer Beetles!

According to nurseryman Skip Murray of Murray Brothers' Nursery in Orchard Park, New York, "Beetles like turf to lay their eggs." Skip explains, "In our nursery we have very few Japanese beetle problems—and it's not because we spray a lot of pesticides, because we don't.

"We're surrounded by fields, trees, and some groundcover. It's those massive suburban lawns—one after the other—that are perfect for breeding beetles!"

So, if you replace some of your lawn with more groundcover or garden areas, and keep the birds around with food, shelter, and water sources, Japanese beetles and other lawn grubs won't be as much of a problem.

Japanese Beetles *Like It Wet*

Female Japanese beetles only feed for about two days before laying their eggs. And many of the eggs that are laid in dry soil dry out and cannot mature. So, let your lawns and gardens dry out well between waterings. The adult females may seek other, damper, places to lay their eggs, which means they may even be drawn away to feed elsewhere while getting ready to start the new generation.

Spider Mites and the *Wet Blanket*

If spider mites are a problem on some of your landscape plantings (they especially like junipers), use the wet blanket trick. Spider mites dislike cold, wet conditions, so when you have a cold rain, make the most of the situation. Put a blanket over the shrub, and keep the blanket wet for a few days. (Don't deny your plant light for too long, of course.)

Or, if the blankets are too much trouble with a larger planting, just keep hosing the shrubs every day to simulate a cold, wet spring. Besides discouraging the problem mites, you will be helping beneficial predatory mites, which eat the "bad ones." Unlike problem mites, the beneficial mites happen to thrive in moisture, so you'll be skewing the odds in favor of the good guys!

Vaccinate the Vines

Gardener Craig Vogel of Eden, New York, takes care of squash borers with a hypodermic needle. He uses it to inject liquid *Bacillus thuringiensis* (BT), a stomach poison that only affects caterpillars, right into the stems of squash and pumpkin vines, wherever he suspects a squash borer may be lurking.

After the first discovery of a squash borer, Craig reports that he had no further problems with this pest. "An extra benefit," said Craig, "is that butterflies aren't affected. We have a butterfly garden, and I couldn't use BT where other caterpillars could get sick from it. But when the BT is right in the plant stems, only the vine borers get it."

Once you're sure you've eliminated borers from your squash vines, mound moistened soil over any damaged stems. Keep them well watered and they'll root and keep right on growing.

Instead of sprinkling BT crystals on squash plants, where any caterpillar can ingest them, try injecting the liquid variety directly into the squash vines, where it will affect only the squash vine borers.

High-Pressure Hosing for Squash Vine Borers

This tip is best performed in a bathing suit. Where you see yellow frass (insect excrement), which indicates a squash vine borer, make a small hole and a slit in the vine. Take your garden hose, and pump the water full force into the hole.

According to Craig Vogel of Eden, New York, the pressure knocks the "worm" right out or drowns it. Plus, your garden gets watered and you get quite a cooling shower in the process.

Squash Vine Borers Skewered Again

There are many ways to impale this pest, which can decimate a whole squash plant from the point where the stem meets the soil. Pennsylvania gardener Karen Soltys uses the jumbo-size paper clips to go after both squash vine borers and peach borers. "Paper clips are cheap, readily available, and easy to unbend and poke into the squash stem or tree bark to kill and remove damaging caterpillars," says Karen.

Skewer Your **Wireworm** Woes

A time-honored trick to trap wireworms is to bury pieces of potato where you plan to plant. Then dig up and discard the infested potatoes. However, sometimes people lose the potato pieces, resulting in even more well-fed wireworms!

To solve the missing potato pieces problem, some gardeners put the pieces on a stick. But that can lead to another problem—the sticks sometimes soften or rot in the spring rains.

Instead, use metal shish kebab skewers or fondue forks. (You can sometimes find these at bargain prices at yard sales.) Skewer the potatoes and bury them with half the handle showing above ground. Pull up the potato and the culprits to discard them, and bury another piece until the wireworms are gone. A few other equally good "skewers" include chopsticks, cocktail stirrers, plastic forks, and row-cover staples (U-shaped pins) that won't be in use until after planting, when the wireworm hunt is over.

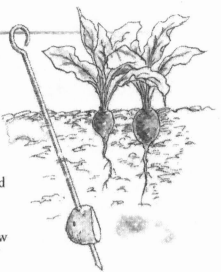

Raw potato wedges will attract wireworms away from your plants. Spear the potatoes on metal shish kebab skewers or fondue forks so that you can easily remove the bait once it has done the job.

Baking Soda *Is Still News*

Not only is baking soda the key ingredient in a well-respected home recipe for fungicide, but now it's legal! Many people have used the baking soda formula to control black spot on roses, rust on hollyhocks, and powdery mildew on many plants with considerable success.

But extension offices and those in the horticulture industry were careful about passing on the information to gardeners and farmers,

because baking soda had not been listed by the United States Department of Agriculture (USDA) for fungicide use.

Well, now it's official—baking soda has been approved by the USDA as a fungicide. If you have plants that are suceptible to rust or mildew, here's the formula:

Baking Soda Formula

1 teaspoon baking soda

1 tablespoon horticultural oil or light summer oil (acts as a sticking agent)

1 quart water

Mix together baking soda, horticultural oil, and water, and use it in any clean spray bottle. Spray on the vulnerable plants every seven to ten days. You'll need to reapply the spray after a heavy rain.

Timely tip

Although there are no reports of plant injuries caused by the baking soda treatment, it's always wise to test any treatment on a small portion of a plant and watch for a day to be sure that the cure is not worse than the problem.

Hosiery *to the* Rescue

If your row covers rip, you can patch them with pieces of discarded stockings or panty hose. The stretchy fabric is perfect for the job and the earth-tone colors are nearly invisible (unless you wear hot pink!). Simply cut the hosiery into patch-size pieces and whipstitch them in place with a few hand stitches.

Row Covers Stop *Diseases* and **Pests**

Row covers can prevent the spread of diseases by stopping insects that spread diseases. For example, "mosaic virus" is a name given to many strains of viruses that affect beans, tomatoes, and other crops. Leafhoppers and aphids spread mosaic virus. The damage these pests do is small compared to the damage caused by the diseases they spread. Use row covers to keep insects out and you'll block disease, too.

Timely tip

Buy extra-wide row cover fabric to make it extra easy to cover your crops. A 6- or 8-foot-wide cover can protect an entire raised bed or a couple of wide rows.

problem solver

BURY YOUR BROCCOLI FOR SAFER SOIL

To banish the deadly verticillium wilt from your soil, make sure it eats its broccoli. It doesn't matter which part of the vegetable you use, so go ahead and eat your favorite parts, and save stems, leaves, or whatever parts don't suit your fancy for the garden.

"It's true—decomposing a dose of broccoli or other cruciferous (cabbage-family) vegetables in soil creates a toxic gas that can reduce, if not completely rout, verticillium wilt and other soil-based fungi that afflict tomatoes, eggplant, and other garden yummies," says plant pathologist Themis Michailides of the University of California at Davis. One caution: Strawberries won't do very well in the treated soil, so try another solution for that crop.

For scientific measuring purposes, Dr. Michailides uses vegetation dry enough to be ground into a powder, but fresh works too, he says. Just keep in mind that much of the bulk of fresh vegetables is water, so use lots of veggies, chopped as finely as possible. Or, if you prefer, dehydrate the vegetables by cooking them in your oven, microwave, or dehydrator (time will vary according to the amount). Then, push the dried stuff through a fine-meshed sieve. Mix the vegetables thoroughly into the top 6 inches of soil. Dr. Michailides uses a 1 percent mixture, or 1 part cruciferous vegetables to 99 parts soil.

After mixing the vegetation into the soil, wet the soil completely for proper decomposition. Then cover the soil with a sheet of plastic to prevent the crucial gases from escaping. "How long it takes depends on the temperature. Warmer is better," Dr. Michailides says. Keep the soil covered for about a month, then wait a few more days after that before planting anything in the treated soil.

out in the Garden

EVEN AFTER YOUR GARDEN is up and growing, you can improve it and keep it at its very best by following some expert advice and homegrown good sense. From helpful hints for more vigorous vegetables to a wealth of ways to fine-tune your flower gardens, these chapters are packed with great ideas for the many different kinds of gardens you grow. Learn new ways to bring colorful butterflies and cheery songbirds to your yard. Produce a bumper crop of fresh fruit that's both delicious and care-free. You'll get more from every part of your garden with these smart ideas and clever techniques.

great Vegetable Gardens

Of all the things we do in the garden, growing vegetables delivers the most tangible rewards: luscious ripe tomatoes, bumper crops of beans, delicate asparagus spears, and so much more. And getting your vegetable garden to deliver bigger, earlier, better yields is what ingenious gardening is all about. Dig into this chapter and discover a treasure trove of unbeatable tips and techniques for clever crop combinations, super ways to solve everyday problems, and helpful how-to hints for humongous harvests.

From *Packaging* to **Pathways**

Clever gardeners across the country have discovered the many advantages of using layers of newspaper and mulch materials to turn sod or weedy areas into new garden beds. To create paths in and around new gardens, Master Gardener Margaret Ferry of Timonium, Maryland, recommends raiding your recycling for something a bit sturdier—cardboard boxes.

"Instead of newspaper, use cardboard cut to the size of the pathway you desire. Wet it down and cover it with 3 to 4 inches of wood chips," advises Margaret.

To make a pathway that's both free and built entirely from recycled materials, Margaret notes that it pays to be on the lookout for tree trimmers in your neighborhood. "They're usually glad to leave their wood chips at a nearby site, rather than haul them longer distances for disposal," she explains. "Just be sure you know the type of tree they're removing, and try to avoid getting a delivery of chips that include poison ivy or oak, sumac, black walnut, or thorny vines."

Garden Thrives *within* Bale Borders

There are a lot of advantages to having a few bales of straw around the vegetable garden, reports Master Gardener Teena Bailey of Germansville, Pennsylvania. Teena really means *around* the garden—she actually surrounds her entire garden with a border of straw bales each spring and finds that her garden really reaps multiple benefits.

"We place intact bales of clean straw around the edges of our garden to accomplish several things," Teena says.

"When my husband cuts the lawn around the garden, seed-heads from grass or weeds— yes, our lawn has weeds!— aren't blown into the garden, and the bales act as a bit of a barrier against the strong winds in our area."

The bales also reduce the amount of grass that creeps into the garden from the lawn, Teena adds. "When the bales begin to break down, we use them for mulch and replace them with fresh bales—any weed seeds or leftover grain they contain has probably sprouted by then and doesn't contaminate the garden."

Summer Plastic Beats Fall Weeds

The weed control you get from black plastic mulch lasts even after you remove the plastic, says farmer Jim Crawford of Hustontown, Pennsylvania. For example, when you're ready to replace a summer crop such as broccoli that's planted in black plastic with a winter crop like fall snap peas, Jim says it's time to take the plastic off. Removing the plastic reveals a completely weed-free planting bed for

your fall vegetables because the heat beneath the black plastic has killed the weed seeds.

"Or you can put down black plastic with the idea that you'll leave it on for three to four weeks, then pull off the plastic and save it to reuse elsewhere in the garden," Jim says. "When you remove the plastic, it has the same effect—the weed seeds are dead. You can even shallowly till the top 2 inches of the bed, and there is no viable weed seed," he adds.

Till **Soil** for Crops, *Not* for **Weeds**

Save time and effort this spring by tilling only where you plan to plant, says Sharon Thompson of Boone, Iowa. There's no need to till the paths between rows and beds in your garden, she explains. And by tilling only where you intend to plant, you avoid walking on and compacting tilled soil. Your feet stay on whatever weeds have dared to poke through the untilled parts of your garden, Sharon adds.

As a result, your boots stay cleaner, and your plants enjoy tilled soil while weeds languish in the uncultivated paths. Weeds grow more slowly in untilled soil, Sharon points out. "Hold off on any pathway tilling until it's needed—when the weeds grow enough for you to notice them or when they're large enough to compete with your vegetables."

Timely tip

Untilled paths also make a fine place to toss any weeds that you pull from your garden beds. There's little chance they'll root in the inhospitable pathway, and you can stay out of the mud as you tread on your fallen foes.

Wipe Out Weeds with Fall *Freezer Wrap*

To get a jump on spring planting and weed control, Dan Tawczynski, a farmer from Great Barrington, Massachusetts, prepares some of his planting beds in fall. Dan tills, adds organic fertilizer, and covers the beds with clear plastic. "We lay the clear plastic in October, then the weeds sprout and get frozen over winter. Come spring, we have no weeds under cover," he explains. Dan says this method works great for early spring transplants such as lettuce and broccoli.

Choose Chips for **Cheap**, *Natural* Weed-and-Feed

For good, cheap weed control and fertilizer, use wood chips, says gardener Eber Wright of Pierpont, Ohio. "It's better than sawdust, because it doesn't restrict water and oxygen like sawdust," he explains. Eber mixes wood chips and composted manure to make a combination mulch and fertilizer. "It gets the plants off to a good start, and it provides good weed control."

Tough on Weeds, **Easy on You**

For smart and simple cultivating, organic farmer Scott Case of Aaronsburg, Pennsylvania, says the best thing you can do is put aside that heavy, worn-out garden hoe and get one that's user-friendly.

Many older hoes are unnecessarily heavy and clunky and simply aren't productive tools for efficiently cutting out the weeds. Scott suggests novice gardeners check out the hoe descriptions in garden catalogs to see which features are most suited to their needs. He says he prefers a collinear hoe, like the one designed by Eliot Coleman and sold by Johnny's Selected Seeds of Albion, Maine. The 70-degree blade/handle angle lets you stand straight and use a comfortable thumbs-up grip while you easily remove the small, seedling-size weeds that can all too quickly overtake your vegetable seedlings.

Scott says he also appreciates the advantages of stirrup hoes, which come in various widths. These hoes feature an oscillating steel stirrup that cuts through weeds just below the soil surface.

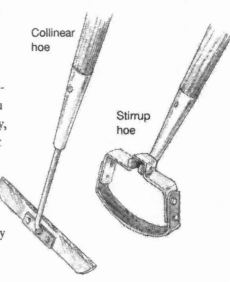

Collinear hoe

Stirrup hoe

A top-quality tool takes a lot of the hard work out of hoeing weeds. Choose a lightweight hoe that has a sharp blade to easily skim weeds off the surface of your garden.

Timely tip

Give weeds an early shot at your garden, then wipe them out before they know what happened, suggests Bruce Butterfield, research director at the National Gardening Association in Burlington, Vermont. Before you sow seeds, prepare the soil—work it up, rake, and tamp, then wait, Bruce says.

"As the weed seeds emerge, cultivate again, so you get rid of practically all the weeds," he says. Then you're ready to sow the crop that you want to grow there.

Flame Away
Weeds Around Slow-Rising Crops

Flame weeding is perfect for slow-emerging crops such as carrots, parsnips, dill, cilantro, and parsley, says Jim Crawford, a farmer in Hustontown, Pennsylvania. He explains that flaming lets you wipe out weeds at exactly the right time to give slow-to-germinate vegetables and herbs the advantage they need.

And flame weeders have become very affordable, Jim adds. The basic equipment, which is available from many mail-order garden suppliers, is a propane torch with a long wand and a portable propane tank.

Jim recommends these steps for flaming away weeds before your slow-emerging crops appear:

1. Prepare the soil, moisten it, and let it sit for two days.

2. Sow your crop seed.

3. Wait until the fifth or sixth day, then check the row for weed seedlings. When weeds start to appear, go over the rows with the flame weeder. "This kills the weeds and gets the crop off to a great start," Jim says.

Use a flame weeder to turn up the heat on weeds and give slow-starting crops like carrots and parsnips a fighting chance against their quicker competition.

Every Space Has a Use

Even the most efficiently planned garden will have the occasional unused or awkward spaces in it. And if you don't fill the empty spots in your garden, Mother Nature will quickly fill them for you—especially if the soil is completely bare. Instead of letting problems arise, with a little thought and advance planning, you can find clever, garden-enhancing uses for those empty or underused spots, says Darrell Frey of Sandy Lake, Pennsylvania.

At Three Sisters Farm, Darrell makes curved raised beds that follow the contour of the rolling land. But gardening on the contour means that some places are too wide and there is excess space where the vegetable beds don't fit.

"We make those places useful," Darrell says. "That's where we put our compost piles or manure tea buckets, or where we plant something like raspberries. Or, we let the area go naturally wild to attract beneficial insects. There's no reason to waste space, even if it's unused space."

homegrown HINTS

TIME PAPER PLACEMENT TO WIN OVER WEEDS

Newspaper mulch makes a great weed blocker around crops such as potatoes, says gardener Sharon Thompson of Boone, Iowa. But it's important to mulch at the right time to stop the weeds without slowing down your vegetables, she explains.

As potato plants grow, Sharon notes, their size makes it hard for the gardener to weed between the rows. Yet the weeds can still sneak in there with no trouble. To stop weed problems before they start, Sharon waits until her potatoes are growing and well established but not yet filling in the rows completely. Then she hoes between the plants one last time and lays down a two-sheet-thick layer of newspaper. "Toss a little soil on the edges to hold the paper down, or cover it with grass clippings or straw for cosmetic appeal," she says. The timing of this mulch gives the potatoes a boost and will save your back in weeks to come. Sharon's system works well for beans and other crops too, but she cautions against laying down a newspaper mulch too early in the season, noting that it's important to let the soil warm up first.

Use **Vine Crops** as Mulch

Many small seeds, including weed seeds, need light to germinate, and shade is your best weapon for preemergent weed control, says Mac Cheever, a market gardener from Milton, Wisconsin. "So use your vine crops as a mulch," he advises.

"Interplanting your taller plants with smaller vine crops won't affect either crop's yield much, but it will significantly reduce the need to cultivate," Mac says. "Flowers and vegetables mix nicely, too. Small-leaved cukes will do well under peppers or eggplants, for example, as well as around tall flowers like cleome and sunflowers."

Plant low-growing vines like cucumbers under taller crops like peppers to shade the soil and stop weed seeds from germinating.

Timely tip

Mac gets another season's use out of tall crops such as sunflowers—he turns them into next year's stakes! "Tough, old sunflower stalks may very well be next year's tomato stakes, or supports for the snap peas," he says.

Paper Your Way to *Problem-Free* Fencerows

Good fences make good neighbors, but they also make a refuge for weeds and other pests that can plague your garden. Diane Matthews-Gehringer of Kutztown, Pennsylvania, puts newspaper under the fence around her garden and puts a stop to its weed-harboring ways.

Diane's method is simple: She centers an open section of newspaper under the fence, then tops it with a little straw, and covers it with a layer of black plastic mulch, secured at the ends. "Make sure there's no gap where the fence meets the plastic," Diane warns, adding that her technique doesn't work with electric fencing. But around her garden, it keeps weeds at bay in this hard-to-maintain area, and it removes a favorite hiding place of garden-eaters like rabbits and voles.

Double-Cropping *Delivers* Multiple Benefits

Intelligent double-cropping can lead to higher yields, greater diversity, and more enjoyment of your garden. It can also help prevent pest problems and even give you mud-free paths, says Mac Cheever.

In his Milton, Wisconsin, market garden, Mac replaces early radishes with beans or peppers—which he starts in gallon containers to help them develop big root systems. He puts late broccoli where the peas were or plants late cabbage after the early lettuce.

"By double-cropping, you get two crops in the same space, and you have the opportunity to clear-cultivate once again (annual grasses are a plague in Wisconsin). You

Well-chosen crop combinations can cut down on weeds in the garden. Young tomatoes enjoy the company of maturing cabbages—the cabbages' large leaves make the shady soil beneath them an inhospitable place for weeds to grow.

also provide some simple rotation, which can alleviate pest buildup," he explains.

Mac plants cabbages between his rows of tomatoes. The broad leaves of the cabbage inhibit weeds. Sometimes he doesn't remove the large basal leaves after cutting the cabbage heads so that he can use the leaves as a natural, mud-free path to pick tomatoes. Otherwise, he removes the plants and lets the mature tomatoes fill the space after one more pass with the tiller.

Laugh at **Weeds** and **Mud** with *Living Mulch*

Chillicothe, Illinois, gardener Keith Crotz doesn't like walking in the mud. And he doesn't care much for weeds, either. "So we intercrop hairy vetch with our sweet corn," he says. The hairy vetch smothers the weeds, keeps the soil moist, and makes a living mulch that climbs up the corn stalks.

But that's not the limit of the benefits this mulch delivers: "If you inoculate it, the hairy vetch will pump about 50 pounds of nitrogen into the soil," says Keith, who also teaches college biology. Inoculation is a seed treatment that coats the vetch seed with beneficial bacteria that helps it "fix" or convert to a form plants can use—atmospheric nitrogen. You can order inoculants from most seed catalogs; applying an inoculant is usually a matter of moistening seeds slightly and then shaking the inoculant over them before you plant.

Keith says he plants his sweet corn on 36-inch centers to accommodate the width of his mower. "When the corn is about 1 foot tall, we broadcast the vetch seed. After a rain, the vetch comes up and within two weeks it's 8 to 10 inches tall." He warns against confusing benevolent hairy vetch (*Vicia villosa*) with its much more aggressive legume cousin crown vetch (*Coronilla varia*), which can easily take over your garden and everything around it.

When it's time to harvest the sweet corn, Keith uses a 26-inch mower to mow the hairy vetch between the rows. "We never have to worry about walking in mud because of the thick carpet of vetch," he adds.

Hairy vetch is a soil-building cover crop that makes an attractive, weed-smothering, moisture-conserving, plant-feeding, so-you-don't-have-to-walk-in-the-mud living mulch for a stand of sweet corn.

Weeds for Dinner Equals *Sweet Revenge*

Not only are many of the weeds that plague your garden edible, but they're also some of the best-tasting natural foods around, says Darrell Frey of Three Sisters Farm in Sandy Lake, Pennsylvania. That's why Darrell adds tender baby wild edibles to his gourmet salad mix, which is one of the most popular mixes he sells.

The wild edibles Darrell gathers for salad include chickweed, dandelion, lamb's-quarters (you can also cook the young shoots as you'd cook spinach), pigweed, purslane, and more. "Chickweed is a favorite of our customers," he adds.

"With the baby wild edibles, you get two crops in one space," he explains. "The wild edibles grow with the head lettuce, which takes four to five weeks to mature." Darrell harvests baby wild edibles both before and after the main crop of lettuce or other vegetables, then he tills the remaining "weeds" into the soil as a green manure.

If you gather wild salad greens from anyplace other than your own organic garden or lawn, make sure they haven't been sprayed. Better to have a boring salad than one dressed with herbicides or fertilizers!

Get even with weeds and stop them before they take over your garden: Call them "baby wild edibles" and eat them in a delicious dinner salad!

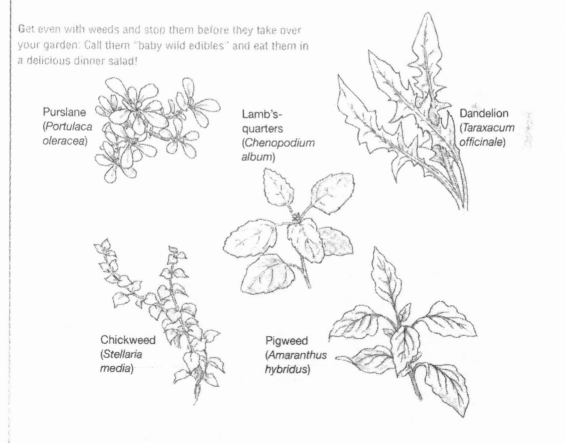

Purslane
(*Portulaca oleracea*)

Lamb's-quarters
(*Chenopodium album*)

Dandelion
(*Taraxacum officinale*)

Chickweed
(*Stellaria media*)

Pigweed
(*Amaranthus hybridus*)

Add *Cover Crop* at Last Cultivation

"On the last cultivation of my fall crops, especially broccoli and cabbage, I usually plant a cover crop like rye between the rows," says organic farmer Don Kretschmann of Rochester, Pennsylvania. "It takes a little while for the rye to get going, and this is a great time for it." The rye provides soil protection over the winter and helps keep any weeds from taking hold.

Here's how to use rye as a soil-building fall cover crop:

1. Cultivate around fall crops, sow the rye around them, then rake or hoe lightly to mix the seed into the soil.

2. The rye will sprout and grow to provide winter cover and prevent weed growth.

3. The following spring, at least two to three weeks before planting, mow the rye and till it into the soil.

Rye is a great soil builder, but it can suppress germination of other seeds when it's tilled in. Allow a couple of weeks between turning under the rye and planting spring crops.

Build Your **Soil** with a *Birdseed* Cover Crop

There are a lot of fancy plants that you can use for garden cover crops, says gardener Craig Cramer of Cortland, New York. Planting cover crops in the time between harvesting an early crop and planting a fall crop will help prevent erosion and keep weeds from invading, Craig points out. "But they're pretty pricey in small amounts, and you never seem to have them around when you need them," he says.

"So if it's hot, and you have an empty space in the garden, throw in some cheap birdseed mix. It's mostly millet and sorghum that will come up fast and give a quick summer cover you can dig into the soil before planting fall crops."

Timely tip

For an end-of-summer cover crop, Craig recommends cheap, cool-season covers such as annual ryegrass, rye, and wheat. Craig says annual ryegrass usually makes up the bulk of the "quick lawn" grass mixes, while rye is becoming more widely available in garden centers. You can also find cover crop seed in your grocery store's bulk food section—look for "wheat berries" if you want to sow a winter cover crop of wheat that you'd till under in the spring.

Leftover birdseed mix can be a handy source of seed for a summer cover crop.

A *New* Role for Rocks

If you have land that seems to grow rocks, turn them into a garden asset, says Master Gardener Teena Bailey of Germansville, Pennsylvania. After cold weather killed some of her grapevines during their first winter in the garden, Teena used rocks to give the replacement vines a fighting chance against the cold.

She filled clear plastic bags—the heavy-duty kind that sand is sold in—with rocks that "grew" in her garden. "We set partially filled bags on the windward side of the young vines," Teena explains. "The bags helped protect the grapevines from the strong wind, and the stones held enough solar heat to give the grapes the extra margin they needed until they got established."

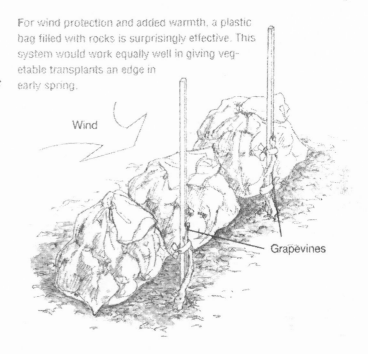

For wind protection and added warmth, a plastic bag filled with rocks is surprisingly effective. This system would work equally well in giving vegetable transplants an edge in early spring.

Wind

Grapevines

problem solver   SHADE CLOTH HELPS BLOCK THE BREEZE

Woven polyester—that stuff sold as shade cloth to help protect greenhouse crops from overexposure to the sun—is also a great garden protector, says Bruce Butterfield, research director at the National Gardening Association in Burlington, Vermont. When it's attached securely to fencing around your garden, shade cloth makes a terrific windscreen for your plants, Bruce explains.

He compares the way the screen works to a person seeking shelter outdoors from chilling winds, noting, "Plants like a little protection, too." The semipermeable fabric cuts the worst of the wind but still allows some air movement in the garden.

If you have wooden fence posts, Bruce recommends attaching the shade cloth with 1 × 2-inch strips of wood nailed to the post. If your fence posts are metal, you can fasten the cloth to them by sticking pieces of wire through the cloth and twisting the ends around the post.

In addition to shielding your plants from damaging winds, the shade cloth also warms things up a bit, Bruce adds, noting that a warm plant is a happy one.

Trellis Away Vine Troubles

If humidity hampers your vine crops in the summer, try this creative way to keep your plants happy and healthy, says Maryland Master Gardener Margaret Ferry. Margaret uses trendy—and unusual—trellises to keep the air moving around vining plants like cucumbers and melons as well as pole beans and morning glories.

Good air flow is important, she explains, because it helps keep diseases at bay when the humidity climbs in the summer months. But it's important to have some fun while you're fighting fungal problems, she

adds. "When it comes to trellises, you can use yard sale and flea market finds like ladders, old broom handles, bamboo fishing rods, and refrigerator shelves, especially from commercial units that are long and narrow."

Other innovative trellises might include the skeleton of a beach umbrella, with strings attached for a cascade of cucumbers and morning glories; an old hat rack transformed with scarlet runner beans (*Phaseolus coccineus*); or a vine scarecrow dressed in hyacinth beans (*Dolichos lablab*) and gourds.

Recycled trellises add panache to your garden and give vine crops a healthy boost. Heavy fruits like melons may need additional support—swing them in slings made from recycled nylon stockings.

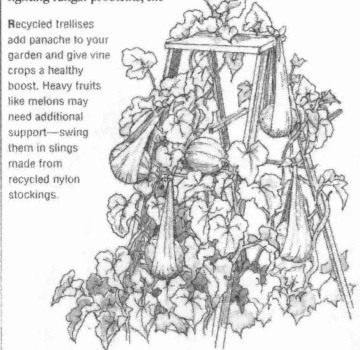

Timely tip

If cruising yard sales for trellising materials doesn't appeal to you, Margaret suggests looking around your own yard and neighborhood for woody materials to turn into simple twig trellises. "Bridal-wreath spirea (*Spiraea prunifolia*), willow, grapevines, wisteria, birch, redbud, and dogwood are easy to work into trellis shapes and will give you practice for bigger projects like arbors and even furniture," she says. And twig trellising is another way to recycle your pruning materials while lifting your vines up into the breeze!

Pipe Up Your Climbing Crops

Turn plumbing supplies into low-cost, custom-built supports for your garden's climbers, says Pennsylvania gardener Nancy Ondra. To make lightweight trellising for climbing vegetables, shape supports from long-lasting PVC pipes and connections. Or, do as Nancy does and use copper water piping and copper fittings to create attractive, durable supports for flowering vines. Nancy says she uses a tubing cutter to cut the pipes to the desired lengths and secures the joints with plumber's adhesive.

Crops **Cooperate** on Teeming Trellis

Combining climbing crops on one trellis makes smart use of space for gardener Sharon Carson of Delmar, Delaware, and the plants work to support one another. Sharon plants a trio of twining cucumbers, tomatoes, and beans together and enjoys good results. "The twining beans hold up the tomatoes, especially cherry types, quite well," she says. She grows small, pickling-type cucumbers, like lemon cucumbers.

Sharon uses sturdy wire mesh with 4-inch-square holes, fastened to rebar posts, to support her climbing crops. She says a strong trellis is important when you're counting on it to hold up three climbing crops. "But we get lots more food and save space with vertical planting."

New Life for Leftover **Drip Tape**

"We use leftover drip irrigation tape to secure the plastic on our hoop houses, instead of buying the usual stapling or greenhouse tape," says Martha Daughdrill of Newburg Vegetable Farm in Newburg, Maryland. The used drip tape holds the plastic well, Martha explains. "And it seems we have plenty of it left over each year, with no other use after its time in the field," she says.

To find a steady supply of used irrigation tape, check with an area nursery or market gardener. Or substitute a worn-out soaker hose. The tape is useful for attaching plastic to any wooden frame to keep the plastic from ripping.

problem solver — BE FIRM WITH SEEDS SOWN IN DRY SOIL

In 1874, Peter Henderson, known as "the great-grandfather of truck farming in America," did experiments showing that "trodding on" rows when the soil was dry increased germination and maturity of corn, beet, spinach, and turnip crops. More than 100 years later, Emmaus, Pennsylvania market gardener Melanie DeVault read of Peter Henderson's results and tried his method in her own garden.

In a year when Melanie's garden was in constant need of watering, she walked on rows of newly sown late turnips and spinach, and left other rows less firmed. "It really made a difference," she says. "Germination was consistent in the firmed rows, and the others were really spotty. I can still picture the difference.

"Peter Henderson found big differences in corn germination under dry conditions—4 days in firmed rows compared to 12 days in unfirmed ground. And in late spinach and turnips, firmed rows germinated well, while unfirmed rows germinated poorly." She adds that this method doesn't work in really wet weather.

"Firming the rows makes sense," Melanie says. "It's something so simple, and it has such a big payback. I've been walking on rows—and reading old gardening books—ever since trying Henderson's method."

Hide Your Heap with *Hungry Tomatoes*

If you circle your tomato plants around your compost pile, you'll enjoy several benefits, says California gardener Paul Barina. You'll have well-nourished tomatoes and a compost pile that's conveniently close for tossing garden waste into. And you'll save precious gardening and composting space while building your garden soil for future crops.

Here's Paul's method for creating a space-saving, soil-building, tomato-boosting compost garden:

1. Start by making a combination compost bin and tomato cage. Use a cylindrical cage about 6 feet in diameter, made of 48-inch-tall galvanized wire fencing with 2 × 4-inch mesh. Be sure it's galvanized, or it will rust badly.

2. Space six 6-foot metal fence posts evenly (about every 2 feet) around the cage, about 10 inches outside the fence.

3. Plant tomatoes halfway between each post.

4. Tie sisal twine from post to post, about 6 inches above the ground.

5. As the tomato plants grow, keep adding lines of twine about 6 inches above the previous one.

"As you accumulate compostable material—young weeds, grass clippings, leaves, spent annuals, kitchen waste—throw it into the compost and keep it moist," Paul says. "Don't worry about anything that falls through the mesh of the cage—it will serve as mulch." Watering the compost also helps keep the tomatoes watered, and nutrients wash into the soil to nourish the tomatoes. As the tomatoes grow, they shade the compost pile, helping to keep it more evenly moist.

Warm Those Transplants

Garden transplants really take kindly to soil that's been warmed up well before transplanting time, says farmer Dan Tawczynski of Great Barrington, Massachusetts. Dan says he has found that you can successfully transplant just about anything. He likes to get started earlier in the season to improve his odds of success by warming the soil with a layer of plastic mulch before he starts to plant.

But if you want to get your transplants in early, Dan says, you have to get your plastic down earlier. "The most common mistake people make is putting the plastic on too late," he says. So often, gardeners lay the poly mulch right before setting in their transplants. "To really benefit, the plastic has to be on a few days ahead of time to warm up the ground," he advises.

Timely tip

Putting down plastic mulch in early spring can be a bit tricky, Dan notes. He suggests waiting for a calm day to do this job, to avoid wrestling with sheets of plastic flapping in the breeze. To lay your mulch, use a hoe to make a trench down one side of the bed. Lay the plastic so that its edge is in the trench, then hoe along the edge of the trench to push the soil onto the plastic. Do the same along the other side of the bed, stretching the plastic across to make it taut, and bury the ends in the same way.

Good Use for Old Gallon Pots

Get that stack of gallon-size nursery pots out of your garage and into the garden, advises Jo Meller of Five Springs Farm in Bear Lake, Michigan. Jo turns empty plastic pots into useful watering tools for her vegetable garden.

"Bury a pot in the middle of a hill of summer squash or between four Swiss chard plants or two tomato plants," she says. "The pot should be most of the way in the ground—with 2 to 3 inches sticking out so that the holes of the pot are down by the roots. Then just fill the container two or three times when you water.

"It all goes to the roots, and the plants are so happy," Jo adds. "We even filled the pots half full of composted manure, so we made manure tea as we watered." It worked great, Jo says, "and it saved me a lot of anguish with our sandy soil."

Empty Pots Hold Rocks and *Don't Roll*

Don't toss out large, leftover nursery containers—use them in your garden, says Darrell Frey, owner of Three Sisters Farm in Sandy Lake, Pennsylvania. Darrell puts large plastic pots at the corners of his gardens, along the pathways—where the hose tends to whip over newly planted seedlings. Then, as rocks appear—as they always seem to—he pitches the rocks into the pots.

"The pots guide the hose through the garden, keeping the plants safe," Darrell says. But that's not the only benefit he gets from his pots full of rocks: "When you need rocks to hold row covers down, they're right there," he adds.

When It Rains, Don't Lose a Drop

Gardener Tom Gettings of Center Valley, Pennsylvania, captures treasure—liquid treasure—in a trash can. Tom has rigged up a simple water-collection system, using a plastic trash can, to create a convenient water source that's close to his garden.

He started by redirecting a downspout from his roof into a 30-gallon plastic trash can. "I put a spigot on the side near the bottom so that the height is just right for the watering can," Tom says. He cut a hole in the plastic trash can using a linoleum knife, and he made the hole just big enough to insert the spigot (available at any hardware store). He used plumber's glue around the faucet to prevent leaks, then set his new rain barrel under the downspout, right next to his garden. "Anytime I need water, I just turn on the spigot and fill the watering can," Tom says.

Meant for trash—but filled with treasure. The addition of a spigot turns a plastic trash can into a convenient water supply for your garden.

homegrown HINTS

STAKES YOU CAN HANDLE

Stakes aren't a high-cost item in Eber Wright's garden budget. The Pierpont, Ohio, gardener says you can get inexpensive wooden stakes for your garden from woodworking shops. And sawmills often have hardwood drying sticks that make fine stakes, he adds.

Emmaus, Pennsylvania market gardener George DeVault has a similar stake success story: He buys "reject" hoe handles from handle mills. "I was visiting my parents in Delaware, Ohio. Driving by the Union Fork and Hoe Co., I saw a sign out front: 'Tomato stakes 25¢.' I pulled right in and piled 100 of them into the back of my pickup.

"They were 5 feet long or longer. Some were a little thicker at one end than the other. Others had some minor cracks or extra grooves. That's why they ended up in the reject bin. The company had thousands of them!"

The handles George bought were white ash. "Despite the minor defects, they're nice and sturdy and will last years and years," he says. "One end is rounded, which makes them very easy to drive into the ground with a sledgehammer. The handles are also big enough to take staples for pea trellis or even light fencing." George adds that since they're unfinished, many of the handles are a bit rough. He recommends wearing gloves when carrying or handling them to avoid ending up with a handful of splinters from your discount stakes.

Holey Hose Does the Drip Trick

To provide efficient and inexpensive "drip irrigation" for his intensive plantings of peppers and tomatoes, Illinois gardener Michael Contratto simply took a nail and poked a bunch of small holes in an old length of regular garden hose. He capped one end of the hose and hooked the other end up to a faucet. "The water seeps out just as if you're using a soaker hose. Just don't turn the pressure up all the way or it comes out too fast," Michael cautions.

Still *Generous*, but *Thrifty*

"I'm always giving away plants," says Pennsylvania gardener Nancy Bubel. Her favorite low-cost container is a half-gallon milk carton. Nancy cuts the carton lengthwise down the center on one side, then across the ends. She folds the resulting flaps inside the carton and staples them to the sides, then pokes drainage holes in the bottom. "I don't have to worry about people returning pots," she says.

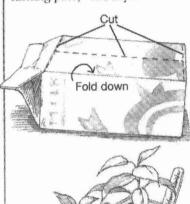

Modified milk cartons make it easy to share plants with friends without the expense of containers or the clutter of returned empty pots.

Buckwheat Keeps Gardens *Buzzing*

Planting buckwheat is a sure-fire way to bring bees into your garden, advises Bud Glendening of McGrann, Pennsylvania. And bees in the garden are a surefire way to improve pollination and yields, Bud explains.

"Buckwheat definitely works," he says, noting that its attractiveness to bees makes it a perfect addition to small gardens or orchards that bees otherwise might not find on their own.

Bud plants buckwheat wherever he has an extra square foot of space. As the owner of Fox Hollow Seed Co., his goal is to lure the bees *away* from his crops so he can gather uncrossed seeds.

If you plant buckwheat, bees will come. And while they're in your garden, they'll pollinate your vegetables and fruits, and you'll have a bigger harvest.

Flower Power— Nature's Pest Control

Permaculture advocates say you should provide plenty of habitat for beneficial insects around the edges of your garden. If that's good, reasons organic market gardener Steve Gilman, why not go one step further and put the habitat right in the middle of the garden? On his Ruckytucks Farm in upstate New York, Steve experimented by leaving 28-inch-wide grassy strips between his permanent raised beds.

"By allowing seasonal wildflowers to self-sow in the sod strips, we provide a pollen and nectar source that attracts honeybees, little wasps, and many other beneficials." Steve says the wildflowers range from dandelions and Queen-Anne's-lace to asters.

"After they produce pollen and nectar, but before the seed stage, we mow and blow them into the rows as a mulch because we don't want to create more problems," he says. Steve also sows Dutch white clover in the strips to ensure a steady supply of flowers for beneficials. "The grassy pathways also keep harvesters dry during the wet, muddy season," he adds.

Steve's system really works. "For the last four years," he says, "we have used no pest controls at all. We haven't noticed any ill effects, and we've seen a lot of good effects."

Battle *Slugs* with **Big** Leaves

Here's a simple way to get slugs out of your garden without hand-picking. All you need are some big-leaved veggies, such as cabbage, kale, or rhubarb, growing in your beds. Trim off a few leaves and lay them on top of the soil. The slugs will visit the leaves—and not your vegetables—for a meal, and they'll hide beneath the leaves when the sun comes up. Gather the leaves and dunk them in soapy water to get rid of the slugs. Or, lay the leaves—slug side up—where hungry birds can snatch up the slugs.

Toothpicks *Ward Off* Cutworm Troubles

To prevent cutworm damage, Wanda Boop of Briar Patch Organic Farms in Mifflinburg, Pennsylvania, places a toothpick next to each transplant's stem, with 1 inch stuck into the soil and 1 inch above the ground. Because of the toothpick, "the cutworm cannot completely circle the plant stem and cut it off at soil level," Wanda explains. "It works."

homegrown HINTS

STOP SLUGS WITH NIGHTTIME SNIPFEST

Don't get mad when slugs come after your young plants, and don't worry about having to touch the slimy pests to get rid of them. Gardener Nancy Bubel of Wellsville, Pennsylvania, doesn't do either of those things. She gets even with the voracious nighttime marauders—and she does it without hand-picking.

Nancy waits until well after dark when her unwelcome visitors are once again gorging themselves on tender young lettuce and other seedlings in the greenhouse. Then, with a pair of sharp scissors, "I go out there at night and snip the slugs in half." Don't worry, the half-slugs can't regenerate themselves the way earthworms can.

Comfrey Wrap Keeps **Cutworms** Away

Comfrey was the answer to the cutworm problem at Five Springs Farm in northwestern Michigan. Jo Meller and Jim Sluyter found relief from this persistent pest by wrapping their seedlings in comfrey leaves. The leaves seemed to protect young plants from cutworms, and "they also increased our production—we think from the calcium boost," say Jo and Jim.

If you grow your own comfrey, be careful: This plant can grow out of control and become a weed that spreads more quickly than mint.

Flea Beetles Can't Escape Simple Trap

There's nothing elaborate about the simple but effective trap recommended by Pennsylvania market gardener Cass Peterson to help reduce flea beetle populations in the garden. Cass suggests making a trap from a 6 × 6-inch piece of Styrofoam packing or a small Styrofoam plate.

"Attach it to a bamboo stick with some duct tape, coat it with Tangle-Trap, then put it out there in the garden like a little lollipop," she says.

Painting the trap yellow will attract the most beetles, but unpainted traps work, too.

Deer Detest Strongly *Scented* Soap

If deer are devastating your garden, give them a whiff of something that will send them hoofing, says Emmaus, Pennsylvania, market gardener George DeVault. "In our case, it's Irish Spring soap. But any really fragrant brand of soap will do," he says.

"Just cut a bar into several chunks and tie each piece in a recycled net bag or an old nylon stocking leg," George advises. "Tie the bags to fencing, fence posts, or stakes at intervals around your garden. And remember to re-place the soap with the fresh, whiffy stuff every few weeks or so, when you notice the scent fading."

Repel Deer with Runaway Mint

At last there's a use for the ex-cess of mint that almost in-evitably follows the planting of this fragrant herb. Maryland Master Gardener Margaret Ferry contains mint's runaway nature by planting it in recy-cled plastic pots that she sinks at intervals throughout her flowerbeds. She recommends planting containerized mints in areas of the garden where deer tend to browse, especially along the semishady edges of flowerbeds. "The potted mints planted in these beds will not invade the rest of the planting, and they will deter nibbling deer," she says.

Deer Netting Deters Birds, Too

Distressed by birds feeding on his strawberries, organic gar-dener Tom Gettings of Center Valley, Pennsylvania, set out to foil the robbers. He bought some inexpensive plastic mesh—the really wide kind that's sold for use as tall fencing to keep out deer. Then he cut some tomato stakes into 18-inch lengths.

Tom drove the stakes into the ground at 4-foot intervals around the outer edge of the bed and stapled the netting to the tops of the tomato stakes. He stuck taller green bamboo stakes in the middle of the bed to hold up the netting so that the patch was nicely tented.

"The sides flip up so you can pick easily, and you can take the netting apart at the end of the season and reuse it year after year," Tom explains. "Don't worry about pollina-tion—the bees can get through the netting just fine."

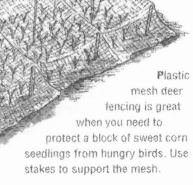

Plastic mesh deer fencing is great when you need to protect a block of sweet corn seedlings from hungry birds. Use stakes to support the mesh.

Avoid Fungal Disease Woes

Whether you're watering in a greenhouse or in the garden with a watering wand or sprayer nozzle, don't drop it on the ground, says Cass Peterson, of Flickerville Mountain Farm and Groundhog Ranch in Warfordsburg, Pennsylvania. "Put the wand on a bench or table, up off the floor. It'll pick up fungal spores from the ground," she warns. In the garden, hook your hose nozzle over the fence or on the handles of your cart.

homegrown HINTS

CALL HIM "CAPTAIN HOOK"

Keeping the watering wand or nozzle off the ground helps keep you from spreading soilborne disease organisms when you water. To help fight the spread of fungus, Emmaus, Pennsylvania, market gardener George DeVault put a few handy hooks around Pheasant Hill Farm. George put two plastic-coated screw-in hooks about a foot apart on the greenhouse potting bench to hold the watering wand. He added more hooks to a bench in the center of the greenhouse.

In the garden, single hooks placed here and there on wooden stakes make convenient hose nozzle holders. Not only do they help reduce the spread of disease spores, but they also save you from bending over so often to pick up the nozzle!

Pick Wisely to Avoid Spreading Disease

At Food Bank Farm, a community-supported agriculture operation in Hadley, Massachusetts, farmers Linda Hildebrand and Michael Docter make many successive plantings to ensure both consistent quantity and quality of produce. You can do the same thing, by starting more than one planting of your favorite crops, including lettuce, cucumbers, beans, tomatoes, and more. Just plant each crop at two- to three-week intervals to keep a steady harvest coming.

Linda and Michael explain that careful harvesting is the key to keeping all these slightly different stages of crops healthy and productive. When that second or third planting comes into production, they say, begin your harvesting in the newest section first and move from there into the older sections. That way you avoid spreading diseases such as anthracnose and powdery mildew that commonly appear on plants as they start to near maturity.

"On crops such as tomatoes, summer squash, peppers, and eggplant, which have a longer growing season, we always wait until the foliage has dried before we enter the field," Linda adds, explaining that this also helps prevent the spread of diseases like blight. Linda and Michael also remove diseased crops promptly. As soon as yields and quality start to decline, "we disk it in and plant a cover crop," Linda says. "Since we do not use sprays of any kind, this cultural practice is critical for disease management."

Early Fencing **Outfoxes** Groundhogs

You can create an inexpensive little fence in a short amount of time to outfox the nosiest—and hungriest—groundhogs and rabbits. The key is to start early enough, says organic farmer Don Kretschmann of Rochester, Pennsylvania.

"The important thing is to get the fence up *before* the groundhogs get used to feeding on anything in the garden," Don says. "They won't know what's on the other side."

Don pounds 2- to 3-foot-tall stakes—whatever you have on hand is fine—every 15 feet or so, then runs twine between the tops of the stakes. Then he takes pieces of used greenhouse plastic cut in strips about 3 feet wide and hangs the plastic from the twine with clothespins. He buries the bottom of the plastic in the soil. Don says his simple fence is a success at keeping the critters out of his garden, and it has the added benefit of preventing wind damage.

If you don't have used greenhouse plastic on hand, ask a local nursery owner or greenhouse grower. Most likely they'll have leftover plastic that they don't have a use for. Or you can purchase sheets of plastic at a hardware store or garden center.

Combine stakes, twine, clothespins, and used plastic greenhouse covering to make a simple, critter-stopping, wind-blocking fence for your garden.

Wood Ash *Works* on "Wascally **Wabbits"**

Melinda Ingalls of Copper Rose Farm in Howard, Ohio, had trouble with rabbits wreaking havoc on her tomato plants. Then she heard that wood ash would help keep the critters away.

"It really works!" she enthuses. Melinda has no trouble collecting enough wood ash—she heats her home with wood. "I just keep a big tub near the stove, and we save most of the ash. I sprinkle a little in a circle around the base of the plant as we put them out, and replenish it when I see that it's disappearing," she explains. She sprinkles the ashes 1 to 2 inches away from the base of each plant.

Melinda says she and her husband, Jim, also sprinkle wood ash on the leaves of bean plants when they're still damp with dew, replacing as necessary. The ash keeps the rabbits from eating the tender young plants.

"I don't know if it has anything to do with the wood ash, but I've even seen a decrease in tomato worms since I started sprinkling it," Melinda adds.

Proper Harvesting **Keeps** Produce *Pleasing*

Nothing keeps the zing in vegetables like proper harvesting, say Linda Hildebrand and Michael Docter. The farmers of Food Bank Farm in Hadley, Massachusetts, advise picking ripe tomatoes—for best flavor—into plastic buckets. Remove the stem from each fruit so that it doesn't pierce the other tomatoes. Fill your buckets only half to three-quarters full to avoid squashing th tomatoes on the bottom. Some heir loom varieties, suc as 'Brandywine', need more careful handling: Fill your bucket only one-third full. Once out of the garden, sort the tomatoes onto single-layer trays to reduce further bruising of thin-skinned varieties.

Save the rough stuff for overgrown zucchini, and harvest tomatoes gently. Remove their stems and use a smooth plastic bucket.

To Increase Vegetable Yields, **Pick Early!**

The best way to increase your garden's vegetable yield, says Bruce Butterfield, research director at the National Gardening Association in Burlington, Vermont, is to pick early. "A plant's purpose is to reproduce seed. Be diligent in picking, and the plant will always try to play catch-up," he explains.

The best example is broccoli, Bruce says. "Don't wait until a huge head has formed. I'll cut it at 3 to 4 inches across, and I get a lot more broccoli in the long run through sideshoots."

Beans and zucchini are other good examples. Keep picking them young, and they'll keep right on producing.

Keep tabs on plants so you know when to start picking. When flowers appear on your beans, you can plan to start picking within seven to ten days, Bruce says. For zucchini, the flower watch is particularly important. Once they start blooming, zucchini will appear—seemingly overnight—and grow to the size of baseball bats if you don't check daily from that point on.

Let's Hear It for Volunteers

"When I go out to till in spring, I always find interesting volunteers there," says Nancy Bubel, author of *The New Seed-Starter's Handbook*. Nancy says she saves these unexpected—but not unwelcome—volunteer seedlings. "I just pot them up and set them aside for another day. It helps me save a lot of perfectly good volunteers," she says, noting that her "free" seedlings have included spinach, two peach tree seedlings, and lots and lots of lettuce.

Interplant Asparagus *and* Cherry Tomatoes

New York State gardener Lois Morton interplants cherry tomatoes in her asparagus bed and enjoys two wonderful benefits: excellent weed control and reduced asparagus beetle infestations.

The weed control is most helpful around the beginning of July when the asparagus goes to seed, Lois says. The cherry tomatoes are leafy, vigorous growers that shade out weed seedlings, she explains. Lois adds that because cherry tomatoes self-sow readily, she only had to plant them once to have a steady supply of tomato seedlings amid the asparagus every year.

Let frost kill the tomato plants in the fall, Lois says. In early spring, lightly till the bed, and mulch as usual—Lois likes to use straw manure around her asparagus.

Tomatoes didn't eliminate her asparagus beetle problems, Lois says, "but when I compared rows where I interplanted tomato plants to a row in another portion of the garden, I didn't have as much defoliation of the asparagus."

Weeds can't compete with vigorous cherry tomatoes growing in your asparagus bed. The tomatoes seem to deter asparagus beetles, too.

Help Crops Keep Their Cool

"Pick lettuce and other fragile greens before the sun comes up—before they've accumulated any field heat," say Linda Hildebrand and Michael Docter of Food Bank Farm in Hadley, Massachusetts. Then immerse the greens in cold water as soon as possible. A plastic tub filled with cold well water works beautifully; you could also cool lettuce in a sinkful of cold water. Lettuce can soak for a half hour or so, but even a short dunk helps keep it crisp. After the cold bath, store your greens in a covered plastic container lined with dry paper towels, Linda adds.

"We wash most of our produce, with the exception of summer squash, spinach, basil, cilantro, and tomatoes," she says. For short-term storage, Linda and Michael cover the greens with wet burlap so that they will stay cool and crisp.

Timely tip

When it comes to crops in the cabbage family—kale, collards, broccoli, and others—Linda cites another benefit of a half-hour soak in cold water: "Not only does this reduce field heat to prolong life, but it also gets the cabbage loopers to the bottom of the barrel." she says.

ingenious
RECIPES

Too Many Beans?

"Never!" says Beth Seagraves of Westlake, Ohio. At least not since she started making good old-fashioned pickled beans. "I ask my husband to plant more," she laughs. Beth says she stumbled across a pickled bean recipe, tried different versions of it, and came up with her personal favorite. She started giving her preserved treats as gifts, and people started asking for more.

Just about every canning book has some basic recipes for pickled or "dilly" beans. Beth says the trick is to use a long, straight variety of bean, and to pick the beans on the same day that you preserve them. "You can adjust the flavor by adding different types of hot peppers," she says.

Beth's recipe is a secret, but she says the following instructions will get you started. To give the flavors enough time to blend, let the beans age for 12 weeks after canning before you eat them.

BASIC PICKLED BEANS

7½ cups water
5 cups vinegar
½ cup pickling salt
About 4 pounds green beans
8 heads of dill
8 slices onion *or* 8 cloves garlic
4 teaspoons mustard seed
8 hot peppers

Combine water, vinegar, and pickling salt, and bring to a boil. Wash beans and trim to fit pint jars. Use eight sterilized jars, and work while they're hot. Put a head of dill, a slice of onion or a clove of garlic, the mustard seed, and a hot pepper in the bottom of each jar, pack tightly with beans, and pour the boiling brine over them to fill jars, leaving ¼ inch of headspace. Wipe jar rims to ensure a good seal, then top with hot lids. Process 10 minutes in a boiling water bath or 5 minutes in a steam canner—Beth's favorite method. Yield: 8 pints

Beans and Peas Share Space, Save Time

To get double duty out of a single trellis, let your beans sort of run over your peas, says Steve Moore, of Wilson College's Center for Sustainable Living in Chambersburg, Pennsylvania. Plant your peas in early spring—when conditions are right in your area—Steve instructs. When the peas are producing well and around the time of your last frost date, plant pole beans 6 to 8 inches away from the peas so that the peas are between the beans and the trellis. Steve recommends scarlet runner beans or 'Fortex', an extra-long variety of pole bean, for this trellis-sharing technique, explaining that these climbers grow tall enough to bridge the distance over the peas to get to the trellis.

"When the beans are 1 to 2 feet tall and wanting to run, the peas are usually done and can be pulled out," Steve explains. Then, he says, apply a layer of mulch between the trellis and the beans to prevent weed problems. Put more mulch on the other side of the row of beans to push them gently toward the trellis.

Borage *Brings* in the *Bees*

To boost bean yields, plant borage, say Steve and Carol Moore, of the Center for Sustainable Living at Wilson College in Chambersburg, Pennsylvania. The borage attracts bees to your garden, and more bees means more beans, Steve explains.

You only need one borage plant for every 100-foot row of green beans in order to enjoy a bigger bean harvest, Steve says, adding that having borage nearby benefits smaller bean plantings as well. You can order borage seed through many catalogs, and it's easy to grow from seed, says Steve. "We let it self-seed, putting a little stake in to remind ourselves where the plants are."

Carol and Steve also enjoy the borage itself. "We pick the blossoms and toss them in salads. Carol absolutely loves them," Steve says.

Dainty borage flowers are just the thing to bring bees to your beans. The starry, edible blue blossoms make an attractive addition to salads, too.

Flea Beetles *Flee* Broccoli for Chinese Cabbage

If flea beetles are about to make you give up on late-summer broccoli, get some relief by interplanting with Chinese cabbage, recommends Pennsylvania market gardener Cass Peterson. "I plant Chinese cabbage among the broccoli and the cabbage to attract flea beetles," Cass says. And the flea beetles—which are a real problem for fall broccoli—like the Chinese cabbage better. "But Chinese cabbage is a rugged plant.

Enjoy pest-free broccoli in late summer, while the flea beetles dine on nearby Chinese cabbage. When cooler weather ends the flea beetles' feasting, you'll also get a nice crop of Chinese cabbage.

When autumn brings cooler temperatures, and the flea beetle population drops, the Chinese cabbage will bounce back and produce a crop," Cass explains.

Radishes *Help* Mark Carrot Rows

Hoeing to keep weeds away from a young carrot crop is risky because you can't always tell where your carrots are, explains organic farmer Scott Case of Aaronsburg, Pennsylvania. And crusty soil can make the growing tough for slender carrot seedlings.

To solve these carrot woes, the Patchwork Farm grower recommends radishes—not *instead* of carrots but *with* them. "I sow radish seeds right in with the carrot seed," Scott says. "The radishes are up in a couple of days, so they mark the rows, and they also help break the soil. And radish seed is cheap."

Save Your Old *Net Bags*

Beth Seagraves of Westlake, Ohio, says save those old potato, onion, or fruit bags—the ones made of netting with good air circulation. She uses them to store bulbs, hanging them from the ceiling in her basement. They're also good for keeping harvests of onions, shallots, or garlic from your garden well into winter.

Celeriac Offers Celery Flavor *All Winter*

Coaxing tall, leafy stalks of celery from the garden is more work than most gardeners want to invest in the quirky crop. But you can enjoy the flavor of celery without all the work by planting its relative, celeriac, also called celery root. Jim and Moie Crawford plant celeriac from transplants in April on their Hustontown, Pennsylvania, farm. "It's easier to grow than traditional celery," Jim says.

A type of celery grown for its big, white round root, celeriac has nearly fiberless flesh and pure celery flavor. On their New Morning Farm, the Crawfords harvest celeriac in November— "and it keeps until April," Jim says. "Just refrigerate it, keep it moist with some dirt on it, and you can use it all winter. It's good as a side dish with dinner, raw, or in hearty soups and stews," he says.

Most seed catalogs offer celeriac. Sow seeds 10 to 12 weeks before you want to transplant seedlings outdoors. Seedlings emerge in 2 to 3 weeks. When the seedlings have two true leaves, transplant them to cell packs, then transplant them outdoors when the weather is settled. You can harvest celeriac from late summer through fall when the roots reach 3 to 5 inches in diameter. To enhance celeriac's keeping qualities in storage, dunk the plants in cold water after harvesting to remove field heat before storing.

There's no need to struggle to get celery flavor from your garden when you plant easy-growing, long-keeping celeriac instead of the more tempermental celery.

Keep the Oomph in Cukes

Few things are more disappointing than cucumbers that vine everywhere but go nowhere. *Organic Gardening* contributing editor Jeff Cox of Kenwood, California, uses a two-pronged approach to ensure cucumber success: hand pollination and an anti-mildew spray.

"A lot of times the female cucumber blossom doesn't get pollinated," Jeff explains. "If you hand-pollinate, your cucumbers will set more fruit." Insects usually do the job of transferring pollen from the cucumber's male blossoms to its female flowers. You can do the same thing, using a small paintbrush, a cotton swab, or your fingertip.

To figure out who's who among the cucumber flowers, check the base of the blossom. If there's a small cucumber-shaped swelling at its base, the flower is female. Pick a male flower (one with no swelling) and rub the male flower's anthers (the yellow-tipped stems that protrude from the center of the blossom) on the central stigma of the female flower. Or brush pollen from the anthers with a small paint brush, then "paint" the pollen onto the female flower's stigma.

To prevent powdery mildew, Jeff mixes 1 tablespoon of baking soda in 1 gallon of water. He sprays this solution on his young vines every week and continues as they start to produce cucumbers.

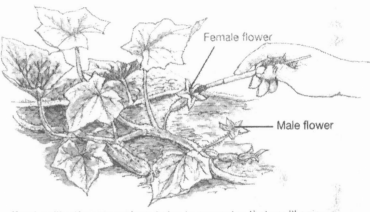

Female flower

Male flower

Hand-pollinating cucumbers helps to guarantee that you'll enjoy a healthy harvest of cukes. To make the most of your efforts, take a moment to be sure of the difference between female and male flowers before you begin.

problem solver

PLEASE DON'T SMOOSH THE FLOWERS

There's more to salad than grocery store croutons, bottled dressing, and hard-boiled eggs. Harborside, Maine, organic gardener Barbara Damrosch recommends edible flowers to give salads a boost in both flavor and color. Barbara, the author of *The Garden Primer*, says, "Sometimes I'll add a few Johnny-jump-ups or calendula. Sometimes nasturtiums—both flowers and leaves—and daylilies. They taste sweet."

But Barbara only adds flowers to a salad *after* it is fully dressed. "If you put the flowers in before you mix it all up, they all get smooshed."

Keep Crops Coming with *Careful* Cutting

When you harvest leafy crops like spinach, cut the leaves high enough to preserve the plant's growing tip, recommends Linda Hildebrand of Food Bank Farm in Hadley, Massachusetts. The plant will produce more leaves and you'll get more food from the plants.

This means leaving 1 to 2 inches at the base of the leaves for the plant to regrow from when clipping mature crops. Be sure to keep the base plants watered after harvesting. "We recut spinach, kale, broccoli rabe, mustards, and Swiss chard," says Linda.

Eggplant *Thrives* with **Mulch** and **Cover**

To achieve true success with your next crop of eggplant, try a special system that protects the young plants from flea beetle damage and gives them the warm soil they prefer. While working at the Rodale Institute Experimental Farm near Kutztown, Pennsylvania, Diane Matthews-Gehringer compared the effects of poly mulch (black plastic) and insect barrier (floating row cover) on eggplant production. She found that eggplant grown in poly mulch and covered with a floating row cover did much better than eggplant grown without either, and it also surpassed eggplant grown with just the poly mulch.

Today, Diane uses the winning system in her own garden at Gehringer Farm. She plants the eggplant in soil warmed by the poly mulch and covers the entire planting with a double width of floating row cover stapled together. She buries one side along the length of the 4-foot bed and rolls the other side, anchoring it with bricks, stones, or 2 × 4s to allow room for the plants. As the eggplant grows, she un-rolls the fabric a bit to give the plants more room.

"It's very important to watch for blossoms," Diane says. Once the plants begin to flower, she recommends opening the cover for a couple of hours in the morning if you're not getting fruit set, or if fungus mold develops on the blossoms. Eggplant flowers don't need insects for pollination, but air movement helps them, she explains. Or remove the cover when the plants start to bloom, since then they're big enough to withstand attacks from eggplant's number one enemy: flea beetles.

Fend off destructive flea beetles with a protective row cover over your eggplant. Black plastic mulch gives eggplants the warm soil they need for phenomenal growth and productivity.

Clip Kale for **Super** Crop

For a bumper crop of kale that is easier to harvest and is not riddled with flea beetle damage, Bud Glendening of McGrann, Pennsylvania, says the secret is all in the clipping. Bud, who plants 1,500 to 2,000 kale plants annually on his farm, says he harvests every leaf that's more than 8 inches long.

As the plants develop, he goes through the field and removes every leaf that has grown to more than 8 inches

You'll bend over less and enjoy more kale if you clip off all the longest leaves each time you harvest.

Trimming kale makes the plants grow taller, and it reduces flea beetle troubles, too.

in total length—and gets them out of the field. This has a shocking effect on the kale, encouraging the plants to grow really fast. He leaves the plants alone for two weeks, then returns to his kale planting for another harvest of all the leaves that are more than 7 to 8 inches long.

Bud says this method promotes rapid growth that seems to diminish the effects of any flea beetle feeding. As a result, the kale he harvests is nicer, with few holes in the leaves. At the same time, his method encourages the plants to grow tall and upright, making them easy to harvest with less bending.

Harvest Lettuce *All Summer*

Forget about lettuce that turns bitter and bolts in summer's heat. By planting heat-tolerant lettuce varieties and using a midday misting to help the crop keep its cool, you can grow lettuce all summer, says Jim Sluyter, of Five Springs Farm in Bear Lake, Michigan.

Jim says at Five Springs Farm they select "slow-to-bolt" or "heat-tolerant" varieties such as romaines, 'New Red Fire', and Batavian types (sometimes called summer crisp). All of these lettuces are unsurpassed in their tolerance for warm weather. "We grow them quickly in fertile soil with adequate moisture," Jim says.

"On hot days, we cool off the lettuce with a spray of water. We use misters from a drip irrigation supplier. Punched into a special hose at about 5-foot intervals, we run the misters for an hour or two each day when it's hot. This changes the microclimate around the lettuce plants without overwatering them," Jim says. Misters and other irrigation tools are available from local or mail-order irrigation equipment suppliers.

homegrown HINTS

SUMMER COOLING SOWS LETTUCE SUCCESS

To keep leftover lettuce seed in peak condition for late-season planting (or even for next year's garden), store it in your refrigerator for the summer. Steve and Carol Moore, of the Center for Sustainable Living at Wilson College in Chambersburg, Pennsylvania, say that lettuce seed stored in the refrigerator during the summer germinates better than lettuce seed that's not kept cool in warm weather.

Carol says they keep their lettuce seed in the refrigerator during June, July, and August, because they notice improved germination rates in seed that's kept cool. They simply put the extra seed back in the packet, put the packet in a plastic bag, then close the bag with a twist tie. The bag can go anywhere in the fridge, says Carol. During the rest of the year, they store their lettuce seed on a shelf. Many market gardeners routinely store their seeds in a cooler or refrigerator year-round, since cool temperatures do tend to prolong seed life.

Baby Your Lettuce

Cass Peterson of Flickerville Mountain Farm and Groundhog Ranch in Warfordsburg, Pennsylvania, says one of the best ways to use garden space wisely is to grow baby lettuce. It matures more quickly than standard-size lettuce so that you can harvest more greens from the same space. You can plant baby lettuce as close as 6 inches apart, and it only takes five to six weeks to mature from transplants. Cass says her favorite is 'Diamond Gem' baby romaine; 'Red Lollo' is another popular baby lettuce.

Or if you grow some French crisphead and Batavian varieties that form a rosette of small leaves at the "baby" stage, you can plant them closer than normal and harvest every other plant as baby lettuce, leaving the remaining plants to grow to standard size. Good varieties for this treatment are 'Sierra' and 'Nevada'.

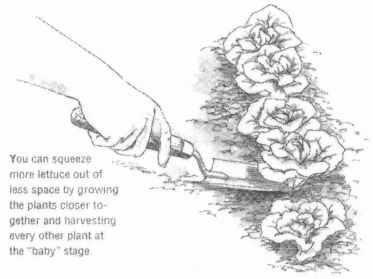

You can squeeze more lettuce out of less space by growing the plants closer together and harvesting every other plant at the "baby" stage.

Lettuce and Glads Go *Great Together*

At her Common Ground Farm in Spring Mills, Pennsylvania, Leslie Zuck mixes up an unlikely planting combination that's both eye-catching and smart: head lettuce and gladiolus. Using staggered rows of head lettuce with glads planted in between, Leslie gets two crops from the same space while enjoying a pretty-as-a-picture planting.

"We'll plant a row of lettuce, two trowel-blade-lengths apart in each direction," Leslie says, explaining, "when you're in the field, that's an easy way to measure." Leslie grows her lettuce-and-glad combo in raised beds that hold three rows of lettuce.

The second row of lettuce is staggered from the first, then the third row is planted so it's even with the first row. "The glad bulbs go in between the lettuce. They come up at the same time, and you waste no space!" she enthuses.

An application of compost gives the plants what they need to get a good start, and a thick hay mulch keeps the weeds down before the lettuce takes off. The lettuce eventually fills in the space between the glads to provide further weed control. Once the flowers bloom—they're used for cut flowers—"it looks so pretty," says Leslie, "especially with green and red lettuce." She adds that this "glad" combination works well with leaf lettuce, too.

Kohlrabi Is a **Keeper!**

It may look like an alien vegetable, but kohlrabi will be very much at home in your garden. And the best thing about kohlrabi, say Jim and Moie Crawford, farmers in Hustontown, Pennsylvania, is its staying power. "We direct-seed in early August, harvest in November, and can keep it until March in plastic bags in the fridge," says Jim.

Kohlrabi is great sliced raw in salads or for dips, or cooked like potatoes and turnips and used in casseroles, stews, soups, or omelets. Peel the globes before cooking. The leaves are edible too, and can be cooked like cabbage.

Tell the kids that aliens have taken over the garden, but don't be turned off by kohlrabi's appearance—its crunchy texture and mild flavor make it a super low-cal snack.

problem solver   ROW COVERS GIVE GREENS THE GO-AHEAD

At Food Bank Farm in Hadley, Massachusetts, all greens are covered with row covers to keep flea beetles off and improve the texture, says Linda Hildebrand. If you've ever tried to start kale in mid- to late summer for a fall crop, you know what flea beetles can do—enough damage to give you nothing more than unappealing leaves filled with holes, Linda explains. The row covers keep the flea beetles away from the young plants and create conditions for healthy growth that give the greens a wonderful texture.

homegrown HINTS

LIMAS GIVE BRUSSELS SPROUTS A BOOST

Eber Wright of Pierpont, Ohio, interplants lima beans and brussels sprouts and gets a generous crop from both. How does he do it? His system uses a four-pole teepee to support pole-type lima beans, and he plants four brussels sprout plants under the teepee. The lima beans shade the brussels sprouts—giving the sprouts the cool conditions they prefer, keeping weeds to a minimum, and ensuring that Eber enjoys an ample harvest of limas and brussels sprouts.

Plastic *Keeps* Wandering Melons **Weed-Free**

Melons grow great in soil covered by plastic mulch. But limiting the mulch to just a 3- to 4-foot-wide strip—and limiting your melons to that same space—may be reducing the benefits you get from this method. Bonnie Wilson of Doylesburg, Pennsylvania, traded row-size strips of plastic for larger block-shaped sheets and says she and her melon crop will never go back to the narrower stuff.

"We planted watermelon and cantaloupe on row plastic for years," Bonnie says. "And it just did not work." The melons would wander off the plastic into the weeds, and the sun could not reach them.

Now Bonnie uses a system her father tried. "He took a 40 × 100-foot sheet of plastic from an old greenhouse, laid it on a patch, and planted into that." The plastic suppressed weeds around the melons and kept the soil warm and moist for the melons.

Bonnie explains that the larger mulched area has another benefit for her and for the melons—there's no "rearranging" the melon vines to put them back onto a narrow strip of plastic. That makes less work for her, and it's less disturbance for the plants. The planting holes in the plastic allow enough water to reach the melon roots, and they do fine with overhead watering. Bonnie adds that you can eliminate puddles of water on top of

the plastic by puncturing low spots with the tines of a pitchfork.

To get a low-cost sheet of plastic for your melon block, ask local farmers or greenhouse growers for old plastic they'd like to get rid of. Or you can create bigger blocks of plastic mulch by overlapping the edges of row-size plastic sheets, making sure there are no gaps where weeds can pop up.

Timely tip

Plastic isn't the only thing that will keep your melon patch weed-free; cardboard works well, too. Cut up large cardboard boxes—like those appliances come in—and overlap the pieces on top of your patch. Then cut small holes out of the cardboard and plant your seeds through the holes.

Grafting Melons

Grafting melons is a practical technique that Chinese gardeners use to overcome serious problems with nematodes and soilborne diseases. "In southern China and Taiwan, virtually all melons are grafted onto a hardy gourd rootstock," says Missouri market gardener Steve Salt.

"It is extremely easy to graft," adds Steve. "It's cleft grafting, which is ridiculously easy at the two-leaf stage."

To try your hand at melon grafting, follow the steps described below. To make the cuts, you'll need a sharp razor blade. It's easier to graft in a greenhouse or on a potting bench than in your garden.

Grafting a melon onto a hardy gourd rootstock involves cutting a cleft into the rootstock and shaping a point on the melon seedling. Cover the grafted plant and keep it out of direct sunlight while the graft heals.

1. Make sure that the rootstock (the plant that will be used for its roots) and the scion (the plant you want to produce fruits) are well watered.

2. Start with young rootstock that has two true leaves. The true leaves look like the actual leaves of the plant; they are not the seed leaves, or cotyledons, that first appear when the seed sprouts. The stem diameter of the rootstock and the scion should be about the same.

3. "You essentially decapitate the rootstock. Take off the leaves down to the cotyledon," Steve explains. Cut a V-shaped cleft into the top of the rootstock stem.

4. Cut the root end off the seedling that you want to graft onto the rootstock: Just above the cotyledon, cut a pointed end on that scion piece, and fit it into the V on the rootstock.

5. Wrap the completed graft with paraffin sheets or tape to keep the graft moist. Cover the plant with a plastic bag or plastic sheeting for two to three days to hold in moisture until the tissue knits itself together. Keep the plant out of direct sunlight. For larger plants, Steve recommends staking the graft with a popsicle stick and a twist tie.

You may lose some plants in the beginning, Steve says, but with practice, "nine times out of ten, the graft will take." He adds that this technique is very similar to one used for fruit trees, but the success rate is generally higher. Grafting vegetables is easier than grafting fruitwood, Steve says, but "it's just not what most people do." But he stresses the disease-preventing advantages of grafting melons and cucumbers onto hardy gourd and watermelon rootstocks over the technique's novelty.

Try Luffas Two Ways

Don't limit your thoughts of luffa gourds (*Luffa aegyptiaca*, also called sponge gourds) to the scrubby sponges you can make from their insides, says gardener Steve Salt of Kirksville, Missouri. "They're great in a stir-fry!" Steve exclaims. "I really like luffas!

"They're also called Chinese okra in some seed catalogs," Steve adds, noting that the gourds are not related to okra. "Just pick them when they're young. They're very crisp and tasty."

Steve says he usually harvests luffas for eating when they're only 5 to 6 inches long. When in doubt, he says, scrape the skin with your thumbnail. If the skin tears easily, the luffas are just fine for fresh eating. And if they're too mature, let them keep growing and harvest them for sponges later in the season.

Unlike zucchini, when luffa gourds outgrow their young, edible stage, they're still useful for the natural sponges you can harvest from their insides.

problem SOLVER

MULCH-BED GARDENING PLEASES PEAS

Gene Logsdon, author of *The Contrary Farmer's Invitation to Gardening* and a farmer in Upper Sandusky, Ohio, is a big fan of mulch-bed gardening, and he says the technique works especially well for peas.

Mulch-bed gardening, he explains in his book, is mimicking nature in the forest or on the prairie. You cover the soil surface with more organic matter each year. Leaves work beautifully, but anything that will rot into humus can be used. The plants or seeds go directly into these beds of rotting organic matter, and you keep right on mulching, Gene says.

"We plant peas into a mulch bed in spring," Gene says. He sets up two lengths of rabbit fence about a foot apart, and sprinkles pea seed into the mulch bed between the fencing. Rabbit fence is welded wire fence, available at garden centers, with narrower holes at the bottom and gradually larger openings near the top. He uses his foot to press the seed down into the mulch. "As the peas come up, I dribble compost on; I use finely chopped leaves with the compost," Gene explains. "The peas come up without the worry of weeds and cultivation. They grow up on the trellises, and best of all—for this part of Ohio, anyway—the trellis keeps the rabbits out!"

Gene says the mulch-bed system works well for various vegetables and lasts from year to year. He recommends giving your mulch beds a break every five to ten years and cultivating them for a year to put a stop to any weed problems that might be cropping up.

Peas and Gourds Make a Perfect Match

When you're planting a tall variety of pea, whether it's a sugar snap, a snow pea, or a shelling variety, Leslie Zuck of Common Ground Farm in Spring Mills, Pennsylvania, says it's just as easy to plan ahead for another crop at the same time. She plants a few gourd seeds right along with the pea seed. The gourd seeds can be planted early but require a long growing season—125 days for birdhouse or bottle gourds—so the double-teaming works well.

Here's how she does it: Leslie plants the peas in double rows—two rows parallel to one another, about 4 to 6 inches apart. She pounds in 4-foot high posts or stakes, spaced about 6 feet apart, and plants two gourd seeds at each of these posts. When the peas are about 6 inches high, she cultivates around them and puts up pea trellis between the posts. (Trellis is available at most garden centers).

Leslie uses a mulch of straw or grass clippings to keep the weeds down between the double rows of peas and in the 4- to 6-foot pathways between trellised plantings. The Executive Director of Pennsylvania Certified Organic, Leslie says she likes planting birdhouse gourds with her peas because the gourds have beautiful flowers, few insect problems, and are really prolific. But just about any vining gourd or melon crop will do. "The peas fix nitrogen, so they don't take away from the gourds," Leslie adds. "When the pea vine dies, the longer-season gourds continue to grow."

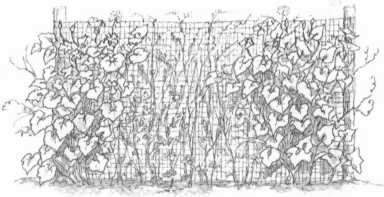

Sow long-season gourds with quick-growing peas to get two crops on one trellis. Birdhouse gourds look especially pretty as peas start to fade.

Transplanting Gives Peas a Snappy Start

Transplant sugar snap peas for a fast, dependable, earlier start, says Steve Moore of Wilson College's Center for Sustainable Living in Chambersburg, Pennsylvania. Plant peas (presoaked for 24 hours) into 3-inch-deep flats, using mature, sifted compost or a 1:1 mixture of compost and your best garden soil. Steve grows the pea seedlings in the flats for 10 to 15 days. "You shouldn't let them get above 6 to 8 inches," he says. "Plant the transplants on 1½- to 2-inch centers in offset row spacings." In just a few weeks you'll enjoy the pleasures of a successful and early harvest of sugar snap peas.

Check Out Fresh Peanut Flavor

Did you ever eat what Alan LaPage of Barre, Vermont, calls a *real* peanut? That is, a peanut picked fresh from the garden?

"They're called *peanuts* for a reason," Alan says. "They're as sweet as a pea. The flavor is just phenomenal. It is a delight in cooking."

Garden-fresh peanuts are the magic ingredient in curries, peanut sauces, and other Indian dishes. Peanuts from the grocery store don't taste as sweet because their sugars long ago turned to starch. "But as a fresh vegetable, it is quite unique and really worth the effort," says Alan. He grows peanuts in central Vermont under floating row covers that stay on the whole season.

Many seed and garden supply catalogs, including Park Seed and Shumway, offer peanuts. Alan says he favors 'Virginia Jumbos'. "The smaller Spanish peanuts are much earlier, but they really suffer in a poor year," he adds.

Peanuts can be planted, either hulled or in their shells, as early as mid-April in Massachusetts. They grow best in humus-rich soil. For quick germination, plant the seeds 1½ inches deep in the North. In the South, plant peanuts at least 4 inches deep. In cool, cloudy weather, germination may take several weeks. Cultivate when the plants are 6 inches tall. Hill the rows as you would potatoes when they are a foot high, then mulch heavily between the rows. Peanuts are ready for harvest when the leaves yellow and the veins in the pods turn dark, often around the time of the first frost in your area.

But don't eat every peanut you harvest, Alan cautions. Save the very best ones for seed. "Gradually, you will end up with a peanut that is well-suited to your local conditions," he explains.

You don't have to live in the South to enjoy fresh peanut flavor. This intriguing crop is fascinating to watch as its flowers "peg" into the soil and form the peanuts below ground.

Spice Up Your Cooking

Enjoy a winter's worth of fresh-from-the-garden flavor with this simple mixture from gardener Beth Seagraves of Westlake, Ohio. All it takes are some hot-to-your-taste peppers, garlic, and butter.

"Bring a stick of butter to room temperature, mince one or two peppers, and crush garlic, to taste. Add a little lime juice, and mix it all up," Beth explains. She freezes the mix in "stick-size" quantities and keeps them in small plastic bags in the freezer.

Then when she's cooking, Beth slices off a bit of seasoned butter, and fresh garden flavor is at hand. It's great for sauteeing chicken, stir-frys, and vegetables, she says.

ingenious RECIPES

Salsa Kit Delivers Garden Fun and Flavor

Brighten a friend's day with this new twist on gifts from the garden: Give him a make-your-own-salsa kit, complete with home-grown ingredients and your favorite recipe. Emmaus, Pennsylvania, market gardener Melanie DeVault says she had a great response from recipients of the salsa kits she created for subscribers to Pheasant Hill Farm's produce delivery program. Melanie packed fresh-picked tomatoes, onion, garlic, hot and sweet peppers, and cilantro in a 2-quart box topped with a piece of mesh to hold everything in. Then she attached her recipe for Salsa Cruda to each kit with a raffia bow.

"Our customers really liked it," she says. "They were so happy to have everything they needed to make their own fresh salsa. And the kit was a fun, easy thing for us to assemble—we grew everything that was in it." Here's Melanie's salsa recipe:

SALSA CRUDA

1 cup seeded, diced tomatoes

2 tablespoons diced onion

1 or 2 garlic cloves, minced

½ teaspoon sugar

Salt, to taste

1 seeded, minced jalapeno or serrano pepper

1 seeded, minced sweet yellow pepper

Chopped cilantro, to taste

Combine tomatoes, onion, garlic, sugar, salt, jalapeno and yellow peppers, and cilantro, and mix well. Let salsa stand for 30 minutes before serving.

Staggered Picking Spurs Pepper Success

Get the most out of your bell pepper plants by picking some fruit in the green, immature stage, then leaving the rest of it on the plant to color up and mature. Here are three good reasons to stagger your picking, according to market gardener Cass Peterson of Flickerville Mountain Farm and Groundhog Ranch in Warfordsburg, Pennsylvania.

➤ Peppers commonly form their first fruits in a center cluster. If you leave all of these fruits to ripen, they may rot from moisture trapped between them.

➤ Leaving the first flush of fruit untouched will discourage the plant from setting a second flush of fruit.

➤ Picking the first fruits is a bonus for green pepper lovers, since they're larger than later ones.

Timely tip

Pick peppers when they're slightly underripe, says Cass. This reduces the likelihood of rot and saves your colorful crop from being eaten by pests, she explains. "When we let peppers color up completely on the plant, we lose up to 75 percent of them to rot or to insect, bird, or rodent damage. If we pick when they're 50 to 75 percent colored, we lose almost none."

Store the peppers in a cool, dark area of your house, and they'll finish ripening naturally in a couple of days.

homegrown HINTS

PATIENCE PAYS IN POTATO PLANTING

Bonnie Wilson admits to having been skeptical when she first heard about planting potatoes at the end of June in central Pennsylvania. "But it worked for us," she says. Now, the motto at Highland Acres in Doylesburg, Pennsylvania, is "just be patient."

Bonnie says that by being patient and waiting to plant potatoes, "you miss the insect cycle. Those potatoes planted earlier come up just as the insects come out." Bonnie adds that potatoes planted earlier don't emerge until the soil is warm enough anyway.

"My dad put his in early in a cold, wet year, and they rotted," she says. But when she planted fingerlings and other potatoes at the end of June, there was no problem with rotting; the potatoes took off and grew well in the warm soil. Bonnie notes that the only concern with the delayed planting schedule is that the potatoes will need irrigation to grow during the summer in a really dry year.

Trick Those Spuds!

If you want more spuds per square foot, Steve and Carol Moore, of the Center for Sustainable Living, Wilson College, Chambersburg, Pennsylvania, say to plant potatoes in a 4- to 5-foot-wide raised bed. "Then put stakes and string around to keep the plants up, tricking them to continue to grow and make more spuds per square foot," Steve says.

He explains that the staked potato plants tend to grow for a longer period of time than unstaked potatoes. It's a hormonal phenomenon—normally, when the plants' tops fall over, the plants begin to wind down. Staking the potatoes so that they can't flop over as they normally would tricks them into continuing to grow, and they keep getting larger.

Staking also makes weeding easier, Steve adds. Having the potato tops growing up instead of sprawling all over the ground will leave weeds uncovered—and vulnerable to your waiting hands.

Jungle Warfare Dooms Potato Beetles

With clean cultivation between rows and crops planted in solid blocks, serious garden pests such as the dreaded Colorado potato beetle can ravage an entire vegetable planting like wind-whipped wildfire. But put a few roadblocks in their way, then fortify those defenses with legions of soldier bugs and other beneficial insects, and the beetles are "nowhere, man," says Steve Gilman of Stillwater, New York.

Steve plants all of his crops in 52-inch-wide permanent raised beds. Only occasionally does he mow the sod strips between beds. "Leaving the strips unmowed keeps pests isolated and turns the grass into a jungle, creating an ideal habitat for the predators that live there full-time," he says.

As if that's not enough, Steve plants potatoes four or five beds apart. When those nasty potato beetles go in search of food, they run into a fatal ambush of hungry soldier bugs in his homegrown jungle between the beds.

A *No-Dig* Potato Patch

Want to grow plenty of pest- and disease-free potatoes without digging a trench or making hills? All you need is some leaf mulch, wood chips, and wheat straw, says Minneapolis organic gardener Shar Feldheim.

Shar layers 6 inches of leaf mulch over 4 inches of wood chips on his 8 × 10-foot plot. He tops the leaf mulch with a sprinkling of dry, composted cow manure and a handful of bonemeal, then nestles his seed potatoes in the leaves. The leaf mulch helps to create the acidic growing conditions potatoes prefer. Shar covers the potatoes with wheat straw and lets them grow. Without any additional work over the course of the growing season, Shar says he harvests a satisfying amount— more than 20 pounds—of clean, scab-free potatoes from his potato patch. And he never has to lift a shovel to do it.

Free Fall **Radishes**!

By giving up a few of the radishes from her spring harvest, Sharon Thompson of Boone, Iowa, reaps a free fall crop of the crunchy roots. Sharon recommends letting one radish plant go to seed every 5 to 6 inches. "When the seed pods dry, till through the row of plants you left, and hope for fall rains," she says. Or you can water to help ensure that the seeds will sprout. "Later, you'll have a carpet of fall radishes—mild and crisp and free."

Don't despair if your radishes have bloomed and set seed pods. Although the roots are no longer worth bothering with, the young seed pods are crunchy and mildly spicy while they're still tender. Once they dry, you can till the pods into the soil and water them to get a free crop of fall radishes.

Santa Spuds?

While many gardeners strive mightily to get their early potatoes planted by April Fool's Day, Steve and Carol Moore, of the Center for Sustainable Living, Wilson College, Chambersburg, Pennsylvania, are already eating freshly dug new potatoes by then. One year, on the day after Christmas, Steve and Carol planted 'Red Gold' potatoes 8 to 9 inches deep in the double-dug beds inside their greenhouse.

The greenhouse is unheated, so it's like a big cold frame, Steve explains. For extra protection, they covered the potato beds with a layer of heavy plastic stretched over plastic bows.

Through winter, the growth was phenomenal. "We had to tie the plants back a bit so they wouldn't flop out into the walkway," Steve says. Then on March 20, they dug the first of their extra-early potatoes.

"We've grown bigger potatoes, but this was some of the best eating ever," Steve says. If you don't have a greenhouse for a winter potato crop, cover a raised bed with a sheet of plastic under a second plastic layer supported by hoops.

Grow Your Own "Great Pumpkin"

Ever wonder how those growers of large pumpkins at the fair manage to get them so big? Wanda Boop of Briar Patch Organic Farms in Mifflinburg, Pennsylvania, knows the secret. Here are her instructions for growing a megapumpkin of your own: "Sow 'Atlantic Giant' pumpkins indoors in pots approximately three weeks before your last frost," says Wanda.

"Meanwhile, incorporate lots of compost into your garden soil and put down black plastic to warm the soil for two weeks."

When the pumpkin seedling is approximately two weeks old and properly hardened off, transplant it into the warmed ground in the plastic, she explains. "Place a toothpick in the soil right next to the stem to deter cutworms, and spray the transplant with fish emul-sion to help relieve transplant shock. Water the plant with fish emulsion every week. As fruit forms, choose the sturdiest-looking pumpkins and cut off the weaker fruits. Make sure the plants are always well watered."

As the plant gets larger, hill up the soil at the base of the plant to deter vine borers. "Then find a forklift," Wanda jokes. "You'll need one to get your pumpkin out of the garden!"

homegrown HINTS

EARLY SPRING SPINACH TAKES A 'BOUGH'

Jo Meller, of Five Springs Farm in northern Michigan, plants spinach seeds in late August for an extra-early spring harvest. "Cover the seedlings loosely with ever-green boughs to prevent compaction of snow; we use hemlock or juniper boughs," Jo says. You can protect the young plants before the first hard frost arrives in your area, she explains. "Uncover the plants in the spring, and let them continue to grow."

Use evergreen branches to keep snow from pressing down on a fall-sown crop of spinach. Insulated through the winter by their covering of snow and branches, the plants will really take off when spring arrives.

Bye-Bye Beer Nuts, Hello *Soybeans!*

Looking for a tasty and different snack food? Take a tip from the Japanese, who enjoy the buttery, crunchy flavor of *edamame*—fresh, green soybeans. "In Japan, they are certainly standard summer fare," explains Rick Davis, a long-time organic gardener who lives in rural Ashigawa, Japan. "They are eaten everywhere— in homes, restaurants, bars, and beer gardens."

But you don't have to go all the way to Japan to enjoy *edamame*. You can grow green soybeans in your garden. "They're easy to grow, have no pest problems, and are much faster than ordinary soybeans," says Rick. These beans grow anywhere that farmers grow regular soybeans. In fact, they are better adapted to northern growing conditions than lima beans, which they resemble somewhat in taste.

"We grow them here!" declares Robert L. Johnston Jr., president of Johnny's Selected Seeds in Albion, Maine. The two varieties in his catalog are 'Envy', a 75-day bean, and the 90-day 'Butterbean'.

"Most of the pods ripen at the same time," Rob explains. To harvest your green soybeans, clip the plants near the base when the soybeans are plump in their pods and just as the pods begin to lose their bright green color.

Strip the pods from the plants, rinse, and boil in salted water for ten minutes. Flush with cold water to cool the pods and enjoy by popping beans out of the pod. (You can also package the shelled soybeans for freezing at this point.)

"They go great with a cold

Fresh green soybeans look a lot like their field-grown relatives, but their flavor earns them the nickname "butterbeans."

beer at the end of the day!" exclaims Rick, who grows as many green soybeans as he can. "I can get only one crop of ordinary soybeans in a year, but can harvest *edamame* very often by staggering the plantings," adds Rick. He typically gathers his final harvest around the beginning of September.

problem solver   TRAP SQUASH TROUBLES BEFORE THEY START

To keep that age-old pest—the squash vine borer—under control, Sharon Carson of Delmar, Delaware, recommends setting out a little preventive medicine. "Take a gallon plastic milk jug and cut a big hole in the top of the side. Then put about a quart of water, 3 to 4 tablespoons of molasses, and a little vinegar in the bottom. Set your jugs out here and there when the squash are in bloom. It traps the moths that lay the eggs that grow into squash borers," she says.

homegrown HINTS

GIVE SQUASH AND MELONS A SUPER START

Start seeds of winter squash and melons inside in mid-May, recommends Jim Sluyter, of Five Springs Farm in Bear Lake, Michigan. Jim uses the molded brown cardboard containers sold in garden centers and garden supply catalogs. This lets him tear away the containers at transplanting time to avoid disturbing the young plants' roots.

When you start the seeds, also begin preparing the ground for your crops. "Make your hills by digging down 1 foot and filling the hill with composted manure. Then cover the hill with garden soil," he says. This warms the soil nicely and gets the melons and winter squash off to a good start, Jim explains, noting that it also makes the use of black plastic unnecessary.

Jim gives his squash and melon crops one last advantage to ensure success: "We also surround melons and winter and summer squash with hairy vetch," he says. "Any low-growing cover crop works well." He sows the hairy vetch when he transplants squash and melons, or shortly afterward. The vetch controls weeds throughout the growing season, and Jim tills it under in the fall to enrich the soil for future crops.

Choose *Wisely* for *Surefire* Sweet Potatoes

Although traditionally considered a southern crop, sweet potatoes can be grown just about all over the United States—if you pick the right variety. "A short-season variety such as 'Georgia Jet' works just fine in northern gardens," says Dr. Booker T. Whatley, a retired sweet potato breeder from Tuskegee University in Alabama.

"When I was an adjunct professor at Cornell University in Ithaca, New York, there was a professor there who was successfully raising sweet potatoes all the way up north in Ithaca! He was using 'Georgia Jet', a 90-day variety, and getting good yields.

"Besides the proper variety, you need well-drained soil, and a soil test to make sure your potassium level is relatively high. Other than that," Dr. Whatley says, "there is just not much to it."

Don't rule out sweet potatoes if you live in the North. By choosing short-season varieties, you can enjoy these nutritious orange vegetables no matter where you garden.

To Enjoy Sweet Potatoes, Store Them Right

Few things are more frustrating than harvesting a bumper crop from your garden only to have it quickly deteriorate in storage. Unfortunately, that happens all too often with sweet potatoes. That's because there is no place in the average American home that has the proper conditions for storing sweet potatoes, says Dr. Booker T. Whatley, who developed the popular 'Carver' variety of sweet potato at Tuskegee University in Alabama.

"The only safe place to store sweet potatoes for any length of time is in your freezer. Coat each root with vegetable oil and bake in a conventional oven—not a microwave—at 375°F for 90 minutes. Once the roots have cooled, wrap each one in aluminum foil and put them in your freezer," advises Dr. Whatley.

"Any sweet potato recipe should be started with baked sweet potatoes," Dr. Whatley declares. "Dr. George Washington Carver recommended baking sweet potatoes over all other methods of preparing them almost 100 years ago. The only time you should use your microwave oven for sweet potatoes is to warm them up after they come out of your freezer."

Young Tomatoes Like It Cool

A big mistake gardeners tend to make with tomatoes is keeping them too warm at the seedling stage. Young tomatoes need to keep their cool during the day if they're in a hoop house, greenhouse, or even a bright window situation. They also like cool nights—50°F is perfect, says Michael Brownback, a certified organic commercial grower in Loysville, Pennsylvania. "Cool conditions keep seedlings fairly short. If they get too warm, they get leggy, and you want stocky, sturdy plants so they can withstand wind," explains Michael.

Tomatoes— A Month Early

If you're after those early tomatoes, try this method from Wanda Boop of Briar Patch Organic Farms in Mifflinburg, Pennsylvania. Wanda recommends starting a few short-season tomatoes in the greenhouse or under growing lights at the end of January. "Around March 20, set Wall O' Water plant protectors in the garden, fill them with water, and let them warm up the soil for approximately two weeks.

"Meanwhile, on really sunny days, start to harden off your seedlings a bit outdoors—only a couple of hours at a time," she says. Then, around April 1st, transplant the tomatoes with plenty of compost into your Wall O' Waters, making sure they close completely at the top.

As the weather warms and all danger of frost has passed, pull open the Wall O' Waters. Allowing more air and sun in begins preparing the plants for the outside temperature. After a few days, it's safe to remove the Wall O' Waters entirely. "The plants look a bit straggly but will perk up in a week or so," Wanda notes. "Stake the plants well. And enjoy those early tomatoes!"

Tomato Cages That Last *"Forever"*

He's tried all types of systems for staking tomatoes, but organic grower Scott Case of Aaronsburg, Pennsylvania, says he is sold on wire cages made of the heavy-duty mesh used for reinforcing concrete. "They're cheap to make, and they last forever," he says.

Scott buys 5-foot-tall wire mesh in a 150-foot roll. Then he just cuts off 6-foot sections with wire cutters and fastens them together into a circular cage. "We plant the tomatoes, and about a week later go through and cage them," he explains. "These cages hold up great and don't rust."

To make fewer cages, have your building supply center cut off only as much wire as you

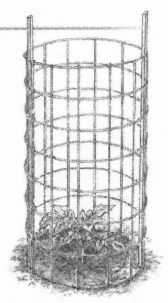

The heavy wire mesh used to reinforce concrete also makes strong, long-lasting tomato cages.

need, or split a whole roll with a gardening friend. You can also use the sturdy mesh to protect young fruit trees or as a trellis for peas, pole beans, or other climbing crops.

Pamper Tomatoes with *Pruning*

James Weaver of Kutztown, Pennsylvania, started pampering heirloom tomatoes well before heirlooms became the rage they are today. And he found that one of the best ways to pamper the tasty gems—to pamper all of his field-grown tomatoes, in fact—is to prune them.

James and his son prune the suckers—sprouts that form in the angles where a branch emerges from a main stem—off the plants up to the first flower cluster. The pruning improves air flow and keeps the fruit up off the ground. "You get less fruit this way, but what you get is earlier, by a week or so, and it's much nicer and bigger," Jim explains.

Tomatoes *Need* Calcium

"Calcium is very important to tomatoes," says organic grower Michael Brownback of Loysville, Pennsylvania. In fact, he says ensuring that the plant has enough calcium and watering evenly are two critical factors if you want incredible tomatoes.

"Blossom-end rot can be aggravated if there is too little water and if there isn't enough calcium in the plant," he says.

The best way to know if your garden soil has enough calcium is to do a soil test. Specific recommendations are included in the test results. (Check with your local exten-

sion office for information on soil testing, or look in the "Resources" section, starting on page 317.) Too busy to test the soil for your tomato plants? Stir a handful of gypsum (available in small bags at most garden centers) into the soil at the beginning of the planting season to give your tomatoes a little boost.

Boost Tomato *Yields* in a Short Season

It may take a little more care, but Jo Meller, of Five Springs Farm in Bear Lake, Michigan, says it's possible to get big yields of great tomatoes even in short-summer areas. Jo recommends the following method: "Pick off blossoms, if any, before you plant each tomato plant in the garden, and bury the plant up to the top leaves," she says. Snip off the remaining leaves. "All of the stem that is under ground turns into roots."

Trellis the plants, keep them thinned to one or two stems, and trim off all suckers, she adds. "In late July, when there are five fruit/blossom clusters per plant, cut the top off and re-move any additional flowers as they form. This speeds the ripening time of the fruit, al-lowing much higher yields in a short growing season," Jo explains. At Five Springs Farm, the last frost is around the end of May and their first frost arrives in mid-October, so they've gotten used to hur-rying the tomatoes in order to produce a timely crop.

problem SOLVER   DON'T SQUEEZE YOUNG TOMATOES

"The number one tip I can offer for growing tomatoes," says Michael Brownback of Loysville, Pennsylvania, is give them plenty of room at the seedling stage. Michael should know. He specializes in tomatoes at his 200-acre Spiral Path Farm.

Michael says his staff starts tomatoes by scattering seed in an open flat and covering lightly. When the seedlings develop their first true leaves—those that look like the leaves of a mature tomato plant—they transplant the seedlings into 4-inch or larger pots. Transplanting at this point gives the roots room to grow, and it also allows the tops of the plants to spread out. That way you get good buds and good tomatoes, without stress. "You have a balanced plant from the beginning," he says.

The system they use at Spiral Path Farm works equally well on a smaller scale. Simply sow tomato seeds indoors five to six weeks before your last frost date. If you sow more than one variety of tomato in a seed flat, sprinkle the seeds in rows and label them to avoid confusion later on. At the true-leaf stage, transplant the healthiest plants to 4-inch or larger pots. You'll be surprised at how much difference a little growing room makes.

Snatch Tomatoes from the **Jaws of Death**

Have you ever picked a gorgeous, perfectly ripe 'Brandywine' tomato only to find that one of your four-footed adversaries has already gnawed a big hole in it? Fight back by picking early, says Michael Brownback, a Loysville, Pennsylvania, or-ganic farmer. "Once a tomato has started to ripen, it doesn't need light. Pick it, and take it inside to finish," he says. "You'll have a perfect, firmer tomato." Once you have them indoors and out of harm's way, put your tomatoes in a cool spot to finish ripening. A base-ment shelf is great for this, but they'll ripen on the kitchen counter, too. Just keep toma-toes out of the refrigerator where too-cold temperatures will retard ripening and ruin their home-grown flavor.

Delay Effects
of Late Blight

It's a little bit of extra work, but Bud Glendening of Fox Hollow Seed Co. in McGrann, Pennsylvania, says he finds the preventive work well worth the effort in delaying late blight on his tomatoes. "It'll get you eventually," he says, "but I find spraying with hydrogen peroxide really delays the effects of the disease."

Bud says you can use pharmacy-strength, 3 percent hydrogen peroxide solution, straight, to fend off late blight, which causes irregular, black, water-soaked patches on tomato leaves along with dark-colored spots on the fruits. Bud sprays the mild preventive on his tomato plants each evening starting in late August or early September. "It tends to perk up pepper plants, too," he says.

Fend off late blight with a simple hydrogen peroxide spray. Late blight usually appears during humid weather with cool nights (below 60°F) and warm days (70 to 85°F).

Hoops *Are a Must* for Undercover Tomatoes

"When we put our tomatoes out, we like to put row covers over them—with wire hoop support," says Michael Brownback. The Pennsylvania commercial grower explains that it's important to use hoops because plants like tomatoes can't take fabric row covers without support. Their stems aren't strong enough to hold up a "blanket" and be whipped around by wind. (In addition to the supported row covers, plastic mulch underneath gives the quickest heating of the soil, he adds.)

Michael uses 60-inch hoops, which leave about 18 inches of head room for the tomato plants underneath the cover. That gives his young plants plenty of unrestricted growing room, unlike the tight confines found beneath milk-jug covers and similar makeshift protectors. The ends of the rows are covered also, and the edges of the cover are firmly tucked in the soil to prevent the wind from getting under it and carrying it to Oz. Leave the row cover on until it begins to push against the tomatoes' tops or until their blossoms start to open.

Timely tip

Be careful with row covers on tomatoes, Michael cautions. "When the temperature is over 90 degrees, the pollen is affected. It can hurt a bud, and the bud won't be able to set fruit," he explains. So keep an eye on the weather, and be ready to ventilate or remove covers from tomatoes when temperatures start to climb.

A **New Twist** on Tomato Stakes

If you've yet to discover your "perfect tomato stake," take a look at the curvy creation called Spira-stake. Designed by gardener and artist Jim Jeansonne, Spira-stake provides both aesthetically pleasing support and a way to supply fertilizer directly to the roots. As the tomato plant grows, you simply guide it up the curves of the spiral-shaped support, eliminating the need for all those ties.

Made of UV-stabilized recycled plastic, Spira-stake is hollow, and the part that goes into the ground is perforated. This lets you pour water and liquid fertilizers down through the hollow plant holder to emerge at the root zone. Late in the season, when the tomato plants in Jim's Louisiana garden are heavily laden with fruit, he uses horizontal connector rods between the stakes to provide additional support. The result is an uncluttered garden look, a productive root system, and unique, durable stakes that last for many years. (See "Resources," on page 317, for information on where to find this product.)

The twists in Spira-stakes offer no-tie support for your tomatoes. The hollow stakes also make it easy to put water and fertilizer right where they're needed.

Give Zucchini Some **Manure**

Coaxing earlier, more prolific production out of zucchini and other squash family members is as easy as starting with a shovelful of manure, says Wade Bitner, Utah State University extension horticulturist for Salt Lake County in Salt Lake City, Utah. When growing zucchini and other squash crops, Wade recommends this system: Dig a hole in your garden a shovel's depth and a shovel's width in diameter, and replace the soil with horse manure. Then cover it with the soil you removed from the hole. This makes a 4- to 6-inch mound of soil.

Make a 2-inch-deep trench around the mound to hold water, then plant the zucchini seed (one is usually enough unless you are willing to thin) on the top of the mound. When it gets moist, the decomposing manure warms up the soil to create the conditions squash thrive in. "And when the roots hit the manure, the plants practically shoot out of the ground!"

helpful
Herb Gardening Hints

Herbs are some of the most versatile plants

you can add to the garden or landscape.

Whether you want to harvest herbs for

their medicinal value and culinary bene-

fits or simply use them to enhance the

beauty of your ornamental beds, herbs are

the hottest thing going. Herbs have other

uses, too—aromatherapy, craft projects,

beauty aids, and more. In this chapter,

you'll find tips and ideas to make your

herb growing—and using—successful,

from seed germination to the final harvest

and beyond.

190

Save *Lavender* from **Winterkill**

In areas without reliable snow cover, lavender commonly suffers from winterkill. Typically, you can prevent winterkill with a thick layer of mulch, which acts as an insulating blanket over tender plants.

However, heavy mulches can inflict lavender with fatal "wet feet." What's a lavender-lover to do?

"Here's my solution," advises Barbara Steele, co-owner of Alloway Gardens and Herb Farm, located in Littlestown, Pennsylvania. "After Christmas, I cut the boughs off the holiday tree and stuff small branches around the base of the lavender plants. This loose mulch insulates against winter winds that can dry out the roots of the plants, without creating a wet spot."

Barbara doesn't worry about the acidic effect that the evergreen needles can have on the soil. To neutralize the extra acidity, Barbara says, "I remove the branches once the weather settles out and then sprinkle wood ashes around the plants."

Grow *Gorgeous* Lavender in **Mounds**

Lavender plants need full sun and good drainage to grow their best. Dr. Arthur O. Tucker, a renowned herb researcher and cocurator of the Claude E. Phillips Herbarium in the Department of Agriculture and Natural Resources at Delaware State University, recommends planting lavender in mounds in areas with less-than-perfect drainage.

"Preparing a mound for lavender plantings is well worth the extra effort," claims Dr. Tucker. "The plants look spectacular and have a much longer life span."

Dr. Tucker says it's ideal to prepare mounds in the fall before spring planting to allow time to solve any settling problems. However, unless you live in a bog, success is all but guaranteed, even without this advance planning. Here is Dr. Tucker's technique.

Mark the edges of the bed. Work in an area about 1½ to 2 feet wide and allow about 2 feet between plants. Loosen the existing soil with a spading fork.

Create a well-drained site for lavender by forming mounds of soil, sand, compost, and gravel.

Make a soil mix consisting of 1 part native soil, 1 part sand, and 1 part compost in a wheelbarrow. Mix in a third as much pea gravel, or mixed rock of about ½ inch in diameter, and about 1 cup of lime. You may use more or less, depending upon how big your mounds will be and whether your soil is acidic or alkaline.

Pour this mix onto the site and shape it into a mound from 8 to 18 inches high, using higher mounds in wetter areas. Taper the edges of the mound to meet the soil level. (Within a year, the mound will settle to about half its original height.)

To plant the lavender in the prepared mounds, make a cone of the soil mix (try to use mostly soil around the roots, brushing any gravel away), and spread the roots of the plant over the cone. Cover the roots with mix, and water thoroughly.

Place a bareroot lavender plant on each mound. Then cover with the soil, sand, compost, and gravel mixture.

Topdressing for Lavender

"Top-dress lavender plants with 1 inch of white sand," suggests herb researcher Dr. Arthur O. Tucker. "The reflectivity increases the light available to the inner leaves of the plants. In my research, plants mulched with sand grew more quickly and also achieved better form."

Dr. Tucker adds that sand isn't the only mulch you can use. Light-colored mulches such as gravel, marble chips, or oyster shells would also work, but he warns against wood chips and peat moss.

Surefire *Lavender* Cuttings

Timid about taking lavender cuttings? There's no need to fuss with bottom heat, perlite, and rooting hormone powder. When new growth starts in the spring, trim and shape plants, removing up to a third of each plant. Look through the trimmings for sturdy stalks with vigorous sideshoots. Rip sideshoots off the stem, leaving a piece of the stem, or heel, attached to each "cutting." Shove cuttings into soil under the existing lavender plant, and water well. Cuttings will be rooted in three to four weeks.

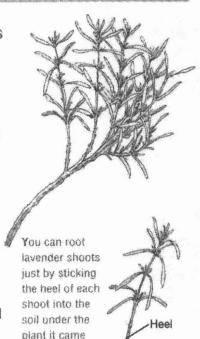

You can root lavender shoots just by sticking the heel of each shoot into the soil under the plant it came from.

Heel

problem solver   FRAGRANT HERBAL PATHWAYS

Drooling over photographs of garden pathways festooned with thyme and chamomile, but worried that they're too much work to achieve? "It's not that difficult," claims Nancy McDonald, cofounder and managing editor of the quarterly *The American Cottage Gardener,* and whose own garden in Grand Marais, Michigan, houses the northern test garden of the American Dianthus Society.

Nancy laid cement pavers for a pathway, spread fine sand in between them, and then sowed seed of English thyme between the pavers Nancy kept the area well watered, and by summer's end, she had a well-established herbal carpet. Talk about low maintenance—an annual mowing keeps it trimmed!

Nancy also recommends putting a weed barrier down before laying the pavers. She used cardboard; other potential weed-proofing materials include thick layers of newspaper, old carpets, and commercial weed barrier fabric. She cautions, "Don't put a weed barrier where you plant the thyme. Too much mulch will make it difficult for the thyme roots to reach the soil below." Instead, Nancy used a layer of straw to block weeds until the thyme grew in and covered the area.

homegrown HINTS

FRENCH LAVENDER GROWS LARGER AND LIVES LONGER

Most herb gardeners love growing lavender, but *Lavandula angustifolia* and its cultivars, also known as true lavender, don't grow nearly as tall or live as long as French lavender, or lavandin. To boost lavender production in your garden, plant lavandin cultivars, instead of true lavender.

"Most of the lavender grown in France for the perfume industry is derived from lavandin (*Lavandula × intermedia*), hybrids that can only be grown from cuttings," explains Dr. Arthur O. Tucker, cocurator of the Claude E. Phillips Herbarium in the Department of Agriculture and Natural Resources at Delaware State University.

According to Dr. Tucker, lavandin will eventually usurp lavender's popularity in the home garden. In his research done in Delaware (Zone 7), lavandin is hardier than lavender and rarely succumbs to root rot, a fungus disease that plagues lavenders in humid climates. This disease resistance contributes to lavandin's longer life span of up to ten years, whereas a well-tended lavender plant rarely survives for longer than five years.

Lavandins are gradually making their way into garden centers but the term lavandin is rarely used. Look for such cultivar names as 'Dutch', 'Grosso', and 'Seal'.

Presto—You Have an Herb Garden!

If you want to plant herbs but you're deterred by the labor of preparing a garden site, take heart. There is an easier way. "Here's the easiest way to get growing," suggests Tina James, an herbalist and teacher in Reisterstown, Maryland.

Determine the dimensions of the garden. Mow the turf as low as possible. Cover it with newspaper—at least six pages thick—and drench the newspaper with water. Cover the wet paper with at least 2 inches of mulch. (Tina likes to use a mixture of green grass clippings and shredded leaves.) Wait at least three weeks for the sod underneath to begin decomposing—then dig holes right through the mulch and newspaper to set the transplants into the soil. Adjust the newspaper to make sure it's covering the sod. Add more mulch if needed around planted herbs. And you're done!

Tina says you can plant immediately where there is no sod or where the soil is loose. "My sister has a virtual sandlot for a backyard, so we were able to put the plants in the same day we made the garden. If you have sod or very hard soil, it will be a lot harder to plant, but herbs are tough!"

Timely tip

Tina adds that this bed preparation method is ideal to try in the fall, because there will be more time for the sod to break down. "To make things really mellow for spring planting, strip the sod and lay it back down with the roots face up before spreading the newspaper."

Bag-Dry Herbs in the **Fridge**

Some leafy green herbs, such as parsley, dill, and basil, are slow to air-dry and generally lose their bright color during the process. Here's a better way to dry them. Stuff herb stalks loosely in paper lunch bags, then label the bags and close them with clothespins. Place the herb bags in a frost-less refrigerator. In a few days, the herbs will be perfectly dried, thanks to the refrigerator's dehumidifying action. You can leave the dried herbs in the fridge indefinitely. Tape the bags to the side of the refrigerator with masking tape to save space— or transfer the herbs to air-tight containers and store them in a cool, dark place.

You can dry herbs and keep them green when you put them in a paper bag in a frost-free refrigerator.

Fall Sowing Saves Time in *Spring*

"Some herbs naturally lend themselves to fall planting," suggests Janika Eckert, manager of the herb seed program at Johnny's Selected Seeds in Albion, Maine. "I plant perennials like anise hyssop, angelica (a biennial), catnip, dandelion, horehound, Joe-Pye weed, lemon balm, lovage, ginseng, goldenseal, mullein, St.-John's-wort, marsh mallow, motherwort, mugwort, and valerian in late summer to early fall. Many of these herbs germinate better after a cold period. Annual weeds, often a problem in direct seedings, will winter-kill with this fall method of planting. Plus, this method saves time in the spring." Janika recommends sowing seeds in a protected area and then transplanting them after they germinate the following spring and have grown big enough to handle.

Janika has also found that many herbs self-sow, including catnip, calendula, yarrow, anise hyssop, holy basil (*Ocimum sanctum*)—the only basil that reliably self-sows—angelica, caraway, chamomile, chives, fennel, evening primrose, vervain, motherwort, mugwort, valerian, and echinacea (purple coneflower). Self-sowing is only a problem if you don't want the particular herb in your garden next year, but the "volunteer" seedlings can be weeded out easily.

Timely tip

If you're particular about where you want volunteer herb plants to pop up, harvest seeds from self-sowing herbs when they start to shatter, and plant them right away. After all, Mother Nature knows the best time for them to germinate!

homegrown HINTS

MAKE LEMON VERBENA LAST

Hate to lose your lemon verbena (*Aloysia triphylla*) over the winter? You don't have to, with this tip from Jim Long, author of *Herbs, Just for Fun—A Beginner's Guide to Growing and Using Herbs* and owner of Long Creek Herbs in Oak Creek, Arkansas. "Lemon verbena is actually a tropical shrub and will produce leaves almost year-round if well cared for," claims Jim.

Jim grows his lemon verbena in the herb garden throughout the summer. In the fall, he cuts the plant back to about 15 inches, digs it up, and trims back some of the roots before placing it in a clay pot. "Once you bring the plant indoors, it will drop all its leaves, but don't give up on it," insists Jim. "Keep the soil moist and place the pot near a sunny window or under a grow light where temperatures remain above 60°F. Within about ten days, the plant will sprout new leaves. In just a few weeks, you'll be able to harvest the tasty leaves again."

Jim replants his lemon verbena in the ground once the weather warms up the following spring and all danger of frost has passed. "Don't plant lemon verbena in the ground in a pot," he cautions. "This constrains the roots too much. Lemon verbena really likes to grow. Mine reaches 3 to 4 feet in one season."

Rejuvenate Muddled Mints

Here's a tip for keeping a bed of mint looking good and producing well. "Unless it is divided occasionally, a stand of mint becomes a dense mat, which literally chokes itself out after a few years," acknowledges Jim Long, the owner of Long Creek Herb Farm and author of *Herbs, Just for Fun—A Beginner's Guide to Growing and Using Herbs*.

Jim's solution is to rototill the mint bed every two years. He covers the bed with a bit of compost and then tills the area well.

The last step is to pull out and dispose of two-thirds of the roots. "Don't worry," Jim assures. "Within several weeks, the chopped-up roots will sprout and produce plenty of robust and flavorful mint all over again."

Timely tip

Here's another mint tip. Don't plant more than one variety of mint in the same area. Crossbreeding will blur distinctive flavors and aromas.

Divide All Your Potted Mints, Too

If you grow your mint in sunken pots rather than directly in the garden soil to prevent unwanted spreading, you can still spruce up your mint bed.

Every few years, you may need to unearth the pots, divide off several portions of the plant, and repot one section per pot back in the garden.

Use the leftover portions to give to friends, donate to a local plant sale, or make into refreshing mint tea.

homegrown HINTS

HERB WINDOW BOXES FOR ANY EXPOSURE

Different herbs thrive under different light conditions. When you plan a window-box herb garden, be sure to consider the sun exposure it will receive.

Jane Kuitems, owner of Jane's Herb Farm in Webster, New York, plants stunning containers for her demonstration gardens. "Over the years, I've found several combinations that are absolutely ideal," says Jane.

For a spectacular pot for a sunny southern spot, Jane uses bronze fennel in the center flanked with a mixture of yellow miniroses, golden feverfew, golden lemon thyme, and 'Woodcote' sage. "I use a shallow container that is 24 inches wide and 8 inches deep for this planting," says Jane. "The bronze, yellow, and chartreuse color combination is really breathtaking."

For a western exposure, Jane plants an oblong wooden cradle with purple sage, common thyme, chives, 'Kent Beauty' oregano, prostrate rosemary, violas, and sweet marjoram. Jane says, "This spring-planted container thrives throughout the summer in a wave of mauve and green. The perennials in this planter have lasted for three years now, so I don't have to replace the whole container every season."

For a shadier eastern or northern exposure, Jane uses perilla (a purple-leafed herb known as shisho in Japan), curly parsley, and trailing helichrysum (a downy, gray-leafed beauty sometimes called licorice plant, although it's actually a type of strawflower), and then adds a few flowers likes pansies, impatiens, and torenia. "For northern exposures, this planting works best if placed up against the wall of a building," says Jane. "The reflected light is enough to keep these plants thriving even though sunlight is limited."

To give your window-box herbs something to sink their roots into, fill your containers with a quick-draining planting mix. Stir in a couple of trowelfuls of compost for light nourishment and so they don't dry out too quickly.

Lovely Lovage Subs for *Celery*

Lovage (*Levisticum officinale*) is a beautiful perennial herb with a distinct celery flavor, but it's much easier to grow than celery. You can either start from seed or buy transplants. Plant lovage in sun or partial shade in moist soil.

One or two plants will yield a continuous supply of leaves and stalks to mince in salads or stews. A little lovage goes a long way—use it in the same proportion as most other culinary herbs for seasoning.

And here's another bonus—the hollow stalks make tasty straws for Bloody Marys!

Lovage (*Levisticum officinale*) is an easy-to-grow herb that substitutes for celery in your recipes.

problem SOLVer

LOTS OF LEMON BASIL

Lemon basil is ideal for fish and chicken dishes, and it makes a delectable pesto, as well. The trouble is, the common variety generally bolts as soon as transplants take hold. For better results, sow lemon basil seeds directly in the garden once the soil has completely warmed rather than setting in transplants.

"For even more productive plants, try growing the heirloom 'Mrs. Burns' Famous Lemon Basil'," advises Maryland herbalist Tina James. "This unique variety is much taller—up to 3 feet—and very slow to flower, so yields are much greater. The flavor is distinctly lemon with an undertone of spice—it's great for seasoning seafood as well as for making tea and potpourri."

Great Herb Gardens-to-Go

Most culinary herbs make great container plants. Basil, savory, calendula, chives, tarragon, marjoram, thyme, rosemary, and oregano meet two important criteria for container growing: compact growth and drought resistance. The bigger challenge is finding enough large, inexpensive containers in which to plant.

"Bushel baskets are my solution," says garden writer Tina James. "They don't overheat the soil like plastic containers do, and they're large enough to save me from constant watering." Tina says she lines each basket with a trash bag, punches a few holes in the bag to ensure good drainage, and then fills the basket with her regular soil mix, consisting of 1 part sand, 1 part compost, and 1 part potting soil. To extend the life span of the basket, Tina places it on a slate or on a couple of bricks so that it's not sitting directly on the ground or on the deck.

"Bushel basket containers cost next to nothing and last for at least two seasons," claims Tina. "And here's another bonus. Bushel baskets have handles, so it's easy to take one as a gift—even up in the elevator to the 40th floor, as I did!"

Herbs Solve Wet Landscape Challenges, Too

While many herbs flourish in dry conditions, you can also turn to herbs when you have a wet site to landscape. Sweet woodruff, a May-flowering herb used in Germany to flavor May wine, will spread easily to form a low-maintenance carpet in a shaded spot.

Other choices for a low groundcover are pennyroyal and corsican mint. Both are noninvasive members of the mint family. Chervil, an annual with a delicate part-parsley, part-anise flavor, will form an attractive patch if sown from seed in the fall. It bolts quickly in the heat but will readily self-sow in a moist, partly shaded location.

Taller plants that thrive in moist locations include the perennials valerian, meadowsweet, bee balm, and lemon balm. Keep in mind, however, that these are not refined garden plants, and they will reseed and spread happily if you give them the right conditions. If you have a damp area to fill and an informal garden fits in your plans, these attractive plants will be good choices for you.

Herbs Suited to Shade

While lots of herbs prefer full sun and well-drained soil, you can grow herbs in the shade—especially medicinal herbs. "It's true—most culinary herbs perform best in full sun," says Maryland herbalist Tina James. "But I live in the woods, so I've chosen a different tack. Many native medicinal plants need shade, so I decided to give them a try."

Tina says that many woodland plants are difficult to start from seed. To find transplants, check local nurseries that specialize in growing herbs and wildflowers, or order plants from a reputable mail-order source (see "Resources" on page 317). To learn how to use woodland medicinals, consult one of the references listed in "Recommended Reading" on page 327, or take a course with a knowledgeable herbalist.

Although Tina grows many different medicinal herbs, here are the six that she likes the best—and that she says are easiest to grow:

- Black cohosh (*Cimicifuga racemosa*)

- Bloodroot (*Sanguinaria canadensis*)

- Bowman's root or Indian physic (*Gillenia trifoliata*)

- Wintergreen (*Gaultheria procumbens*)

- Solomon's seal (*Polygonatum biflorum*)

- Twin leaf (*Jeffersonia diphylla*)

homegrown HINTS

HERBAL GROUNDCOVERS FOR SLOPES

Some groundcovers such as oregano, sweet fern, lamb's-ears, and wormwood can tolerate sloped terrain, while providing you with aromatic herbs for cuisine or crafts. In addition, you might consider planting mints, comfrey, or tansy along your slopes. But don't make your decision quickly. Because all three of these herbs spread by rhizomes, they are tough plants to get rid of once established, so choose their locations carefully.

Herb Forecast: Hot, *Dry*, and *Sunny*

If you have an extremely hot, dry, sunny site that seems just impossible to landscape, think herbs! Many herbs are as tough as weeds and can tolerate even the worst conditions. Not only that, you can harvest herbs for use in cooking, crafting, or healing.

Try planting some of the many varieties of thyme or oregano along walkways. Both are very useful groundcovers with attractive flowers. An added benefit is the scent that is released as you brush or step on the foliage.

Another useful, scented plant to use on a larger scale is sweet fern (*Comptonia peregrina*), which is not a fern at all but a deciduous member of the bayberry family that tolerates hot, dry sandy soils. Even in exposed, infertile sites, sweet fern will spread slowly to make a 4-foot-high, flat-topped colony with a fernlike appearance and a spicy fragrance.

Also, consider silver- or gray-leafed plants, such as lavender, santolina, lamb's-ears, and wormwood, which thrive in sunny, dry locations.

Almost Instant Knot Garden

A knot garden, with its formal, mazelike design, can create a stunning focal point for the herb garden.

The trouble is, herbs such as germander, box, myrtle, and lavender—the traditional knot garden choices—grow very slowly and are often difficult to establish in some regions.

"Why not knot with lettuce?" suggests Tina James, an herbalist and teacher who gardens in central Maryland. "Select five to seven different colors and shapes of leaf lettuce. Start the seeds in a seedbed or buy transplants. Then lay out the knot design with lettuce plants!"

Tina adds that using lettuce gives you a chance to see the shape in three dimen-

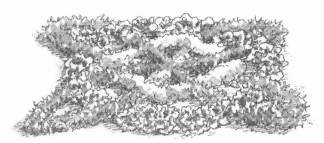

This typical sixteenth-century knot garden design is very formal.

A contemporary knot garden design can be a bit more whimsical.

sions and make sure you like it before you invest in costlier herb plants. As an added bonus, you can eat the results in a salad!

"This year," says Tina, "I think I'll replant my knot garden, using different types of basil when the lettuce goes to seed."

problem solver   QUICK-DRY HERBS

Want to dry herbs without the bother of hanging them up and waiting for them to dry? Here's a quick tip. On a warm sunny day, spread newspaper on the seats and floors of your car. Spread the herbs on the newspaper and then cover with another layer of newspaper. Leave the car windows just slightly cracked.

By the end of the day, most herbs will be crackly dry and ready to store in airtight containers. (Some herbs with thicker leaves, like sage, may take a few more sunny days to dry.) Handle the dried herb leaves with as little crumbling as possible to preserve their essential oils. The time to crumble the leaves is when you use them in cooking.

Stay Healthy
with Juicy Herbs

Fruit and vegetable juices are refreshing on their own, but when you add herbs, they provide even more pleasure and health benefits. Maggie Oster, author of *The Herbal Palate Cookbook*, recommends adding 1 teaspoon of fresh herbs for every 1 cup of juice. If you're using an electric juice extractor, add fresh herbs as the juice is being made. For store-bought juices, allow minced herbs to stand in juice at least 30 minutes, then strain before serving. There's no need to strain juice made using a juice extractor.

FRUIT/VEGETABLE/HERB	HEALTH BENEFITS
Apple with sage or thyme	good for sore throats
Berry juice with mint	stimulates digestion
Carrot juice with marjoram or burnet	soothing
Celery juice with lovage, parsley or chives	mineral-rich
Cherry juice with lavender	eases headache
Cranberry juice with gingerroot or rosemary	relieves nausea
Grape juice with thyme	good for sore throats
Grapefruit juice with angelica or sweet cicely	calming
Papaya juice with marjoram	soothing
Peach or nectarine juice with coriander seeds	good digestive
Raspberry juice with rose geranium	soothing
Tomato juice with basil	eases headache

Spicy
Nigella Seeds

Here's a spicy alternative to plain old black pepper. The seeds of *Nigella sativa*, sometimes called black cumin or black caraway, have a slightly peppery, nutty taste and have been used since biblical times to flavor breads, stews, salads, and condiments. In fact, nigella seeds dotted the first New York bagels.

You can easily grow this annual, which produces decorative parchment-colored seed pods that dry naturally on the plant and self-sow readily once established. The only hard part may be finding a seed source. Seeds of *Nigella damascena*, also known as love-in-a-mist, are readily available but have little flavor.

To use nigella seeds, leave them whole to season breads or flavor chutneys. Grind nigella seeds in a peppermill or crush them with a rolling pin to use them as a substitute for pepper on vegetables or mixed into soft cheese.

Black cumin (*Nigella sativa*) seeds are a flavorful substitute for black pepper.

Summer Cilantro for *Sizzling* Salsas

Cilantro (*Coriandrum sativum*) is a necessity for summer salsas, but it bolts readily in hot summers. Shade cloth prolongs the season for a week or two, but sooner or later, the plants poop out.

For hard-core salsa addicts, who want their summer and cilantro, too, Maryland herbalist Tina James suggests trying some of the cilantro "mimics," herbs that are reputed to have cilantro-like flavor but can take the heat.

"I've tried Vietnamese coriander (*Polygonum odoratum*), but to my taste, you might as well use the common smartweed," says Tina. "So I switched to papalo (*Porophyllum ruderale* subsp. *macrocephalum*), a Mexican herb that grows to 8 feet, and quillquina (*Porophyllum ruderale*), a shorter plant (4 to 5 feet) from Bolivia. I wouldn't say that either plant tastes exactly like cilantro, but they're spicy-sweet and good in salsa."

Tina says these plants don't taste alike, but are similar. Her husband, who doesn't care for cilantro, is fond of these substitutes. Tina says, "I've used both these herbs to garnish all kinds of salsas—tomato or fruit, sweet or spicy—they're all good!"

While Tina has enjoyed both of these plants, she cautions that planting one of each is more than plenty. Quillquina is tall and bushy with thinner leaves, while papalo has larger, more rounded leaves and is bushier than quillquina, according to Tina's results. Tina recommends growing either of these plants by planting seeds in a seedbed after danger of frost, then transplanting them to the garden. Since both of these cilantro stand-ins grow quickly, there's no need to start them indoors.

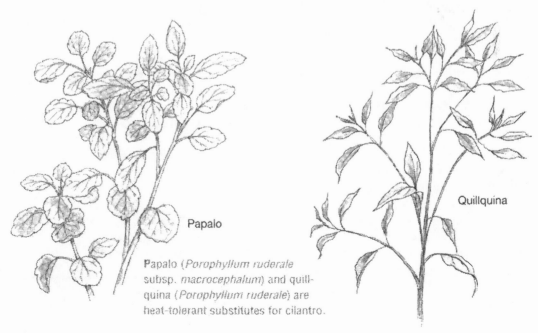

Papalo

Quillquina

Papalo (*Porophyllum ruderale* subsp. *macrocephalum*) and quillquina (*Porophyllum ruderale*) are heat-tolerant substitutes for cilantro.

Sweet Success with *Lemongrass*

Lemongrass (*Cymbopogon citratus*) is a tender perennial native to southern India and Sri Lanka that gives an indispensable, unique flavor to teas, syrups, fish stews, poached or steamed seafood, and other delights associated with Asian cuisine. Given rich soil and full sun, a purchased plant or root cutting will form a billowy clump of lime-green blades by midsummer. So, asks the bewildered gourmet, how do you cook with this stuff?

To harvest lemongrass for cooking, choose outside stems that are about ½ inch thick. (Proceed carefully—those grassy blades are

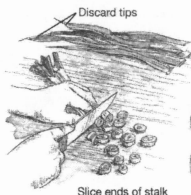

Discard tips

Slice ends of stalk

Lemongrass (*Cymbopogon citratus*) adds a wonderful flavor to Asian dishes.

sharp!) Use scissors to cut each stem at the base. Cut off and discard the leafy upper section. You can cut the stems into 2- to 3-inch lengths, or chop them. Unless very finely minced, the stems are removed from a cooked dish before serving because they're quite tough.

Lemongrass is usually treated as an annual. The stalks lose most of their flavor if dried, but they freeze well. Wrap single stems in aluminum foil, label, date, and freeze.

ingenious RECIPES

Lemonade with a Rosemary Twist

Here's a refreshing twist on a summer standby from herb lover Sandra Seymour from Solihull, England. To extract the greatest amount of juice, Sandra uses lemons at room temperature and rolls them on a hard surface for a minute or two before cutting and squeezing. Sandra also freezes her lemon verbena leaves in ice cubes for added flavor and fun.

ROSEMARY LEMONADE

1 heaping tablespoon fresh rosemary leaves
1 cup sugar
4 cups water
4 lemons

In a covered saucepan, simmer the rosemary leaves and sugar in 1 cup of the water for 5 minutes. Add the remaining 3 cups water and the juice from the lemons. Serve ice-cold.

Yield: about 4 servings

ingenious RECIPES

Tender Tricks with Lemon Verbena

Lemon verbena has lovely fragrance and flavor, but the leaves remain tough even after cooking. Carol Costenbader, author of the *Well-Stocked Pantry* series as well as *The Big Book of Preserving the Harvest*, has a solution. "If you grind the dried leaves, the pieces will be small enough to use as seasoning even without cooking," Carol suggests. "The blender or a small food processor works great. But since ground herbs lose their punch quickly, make small batches."

Here's one of Carol's favorite spice mixes. "This blend has a complex Thai flavor that's great on rice as well as stir-fried vegetables."

ASIAN SEASONING MIX

4 tablespoons dried mint leaves

2 tablespoons dried lemon zest

3 teaspoons ground white pepper

2 teaspoons dried lemon verbena leaves

½ teaspoon ground cayenne powder

¼ teaspoon cumin

Combine all ingredients and mix well. In a blender or a clean coffee grinder, grind to a fine consistency only the amount you will use right away (to prevent flavor loss). Sprinkle over cooked rice or add to a stir-fry. Store the remaining mix in an airtight container in a cool, dark place until needed.

Yield: about ½ cup

Nasturtium Capers

Pickled nasturtium flower buds and unripened seedpods make great stand-ins for capers. Harvest the buds while they're still tight, and harvest seedpods before they harden.

Place buds and seedpods in a clean glass bottle, and cover with vinegar. They'll be ready to eat in three days, and they'll keep well for at least a year. And, there's no need to refrigerate.

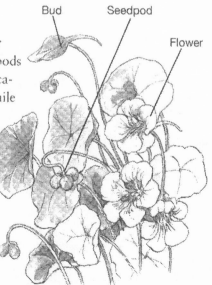

Bud   Seedpod   Flower

Make your own capers from the seedpods and buds of nasturtium (*Tropaeolum majus*).

Use Wood Sorrel for Lemon Juice

Out of lemons? Pluck a few sprigs of wood sorrel (*Oxalis acetosella*), a common weed also called shamrock or sourgrass, which appears in late spring. Minced fine, the sour leaves give tuna, pasta, and chicken salads a lemony twist.

Wood sorrel (*Oxalis acetosella*) can give your recipes a lemony tang.

ingenious RECIPES

5-Minute Kitchen Wreath

Here's a "recipe" for a completely edible herb wreath that you can twist together in five minutes from Jim Long, author of *Classic Herb Blends*. Jim has created many unique herbal crafts during his years at Long Creek Farm in Oak Grove, Arkansas.

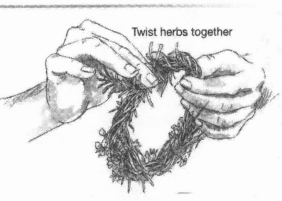

Twist herbs together

EDIBLE WREATH

Gather the following fresh herbs:

Several leaves or flower stems of garlic or onion chives

2 or 3 sprigs of rosemary, 8 to 12 inches long

2 or 3 sprigs marjoram, 5 to 6 inches long

2 or 3 parsley leaves with long stems

1. To make the wreath, lay the chives together unevenly so that the ends do not meet.

Chive stems

2. Twist the chives together like a rope, then make a circle about 5 inches in diameter, pinch ends together, and hold with one hand to keep from unraveling.

3. Twist the first sprig of rosemary into the chives, then keep twisting as you add the remaining sprigs. Keep twisting to incorporate the remaining herbs, tucking the end of each herb under part of the previous herb.

4. Continue around the circle until you have a small wreath.

5. With a little practice, you can twist the wreath together and tuck the ends in and under so it will hold together by itself, but feel free to bind it together with string if it seems too loose. When finished, add a decorative ribbon.

6. Hang the cooking wreath in the kitchen, or use it to decorate a bottle of herbal vinegar. To use, remove the ribbon (as well as any string) and toss the wreath into soup or stew during the last half hour of cooking.

Finished wreath

ingenious RECIPES

Gourmet Preserves with Herbs

Fresh herbs add a gourmet touch to home-made jams, jellies, conserves, chutneys, and other pantry treats. Simply place one or two fresh herb sprigs in sterilized jars before pouring in the hot preserves. The flavor and fragrance are subtle, providing an intriguing memory of summer flavors and fragrances.

Another idea is to place a pretty leaf like a rose-scented geranium on top of the fruit before sealing, using a sterilized spoon to submerge the leaf. It's more for looks than flavor, but it will make a sweet reminder of summer when you open the jar in January!

DELECTABLE PRESERVE-HERB COMBINATIONS:

Apple jelly with rose-scented geranium, cinnamon basil, or sage

Peach preserves with bronze fennel or holy basil

Grape jelly with thyme

Tomato jam with rosemary

Plum jam with anise hyssop or lemongrass

Pear butter with nutmeg-scented geranium or bronze fennel

Strawberry jam with lemon verbena, lemon basil, or lemon balm

ingenious RECIPES

Pesto— Not Just for Basil!

Traditionally, pesto is made from fresh basil—lots of it—ground with fruity olive oil, garlic, Parmesan cheese, and pine nuts and is served hot or cold over linguine. But you don't have to wait for summer and a stand of fresh basil to make pesto. Try making pesto with watercress, spinach, parsley, mint, dill, cilantro, or chives—you can even try a combination of these herbs.

BASIC PESTO SAUCE

2 cups fresh greens or herbs (tough stems removed), coarsely chopped

2 cloves garlic, minced or chopped (more to taste)

¼ cup Parmesan cheese

2 tablespoons toasted nuts or seeds, such as pine nuts, walnuts, pistachios, sunflower seeds, or pumpkin seeds

½ cup extra-virgin olive oil

1 pound linguine, cooked

Salt and pepper (to taste)

Place fresh herbs or greens, garlic, cheese, and nuts or seeds in a blender or food processor. Add olive oil in a steady stream until you have a smooth puree. Toss pesto with linguini. Add salt and pepper, then garnish with more cheese and nuts, if desired.

Yield: about 1 cup of pesto sauce

ingenious RECIPES

Skinny Veggie-Herb Sauces

Looking for skinny sauces to dress up your favorite dishes? Vegetable juice sauces seasoned with fresh herbs are the perfect solution, and the technique is simple. Juice a few vegetables, simmer, add a little thickener such as arrowroot powder, then remove from the heat and whisk in some herbs.

Root vegetables like carrots and beets are good candidates for sauces and produce brightly colored, clear sauces that keep for up to two weeks in the refrigerator. Use these sauces with fish or meats—they also make good dips for raw or roasted vegetables.

Vegetable herb sauces are fat-free unless you add a small amount of browned butter to give the sauce a silkier texture. To brown butter, sauté unsalted butter in a small saucepan until it turns golden.

Here's one versatile gourmet herb-veggie sauce to add to your low-fat repertoire.

CARROT DILL SAUCE

2 large carrots, juiced in a juice extractor

1 teaspoon arrowroot powder dissolved in 2 tablespoons water

1 teaspoon rice vinegar or lemon juice

1 teaspoon fresh dill, finely chopped

1 teaspoon fresh chives, finely chopped

½ teaspoon browned butter (optional)

Whisk carrot juice in a small pan over medium heat until it begins to bubble. Add arrowroot mixture and simmer until sauce thickens. Whisk in vinegar or lemon juice. Remove from heat. Add dill and chives, and blend gently. Stir in browned butter. Serve sauce warm or cold. Try with grilled chicken, poached salmon, or baked potatoes.

ingenious RECIPES

Low-Fat Herb Mayonnaise

Here's an herbal spread that stands up to mayonnaise, without the fat or cholesterol. Use it on sandwiches as well as to dress leftover meats or poached fish. It doesn't keep long, so make small batches as needed.

HERB MAYONNAISE

2 tablespoons rice vinegar (or herbal vinegar such as tarragon)

2 tablespoons Dijon mustard

2 tablespoons minced capers or pickled nasturtiums

½ cup mixed fresh herbs and greens, such as sorrel, parsley, arugula, watercress, chervil, mint, and tarragon, stems removed, coarsely chopped

6 tablespoons extra-virgin olive oil

Salt to taste

Place vinegar, mustard, capers, herbs and greens, olive oil, and salt in a food processor or blender. Process until well blended. Serve immediately. Store any remaining sauce in the refrigerator, where it will keep for two to three days.

Yield: about ½ cup

Prevent the Itch of *Poison Ivy*

Instead of rubbing jewelweed plants on your skin to ease the itch of poison ivy, try drinking jewelweed tea to *prevent* the rash.

Mary Ann Burke, of Smallwood, New York, says, "In summer, I make jewelweed tea and freeze it. I drink the tea before poison ivy season starts—one cup in March, and another cup in April. That's all it takes." Mary Ann is highly allergic to poison ivy, but she hasn't had more than a few spots since using this tea.

To make jewelweed tea, Mary Ann simmers "a good handful" of the leaves in 2 cups of water for five minutes. Cool, strain, and freeze the liquid until spring.

Use jewelweed (*Impatiens capensis*) to make a tea that prevents poison ivy.

Help from Honey-Herb Mixtures

Preserving herbs in honey captures all of the plant's goodness—and the results are easy to swallow. "Honey has been used as a preservative since ancient times," explains herbalist Chanchal Cabrera, owner of Gaia Garden Herbal Dispensary in Vancouver, British Columbia. "In fact, honey is both sterile and an excellent solvent."

To make herb honeys, it's important to use only dried herbs because the moisture in fresh herbs may dilute the honey, enabling bacteria such as botulism to grow. Sterilize a glass jar: wash it, dry it, then fill it with boiling water and let it stand for five minutes. Let it air-dry completely. Fill the jar with the dried herb—chop or grind tough root parts or hard ingredients like rose hips first. Then cover the herbs with unpasteurized honey.

You should note that honey sold in grocery stores is usually pasteurized. Unless the label says otherwise, assume the honey is pasteurized. Gourmet shops and health food stores usually carry unpasteurized honey, or for a real adventure, search out a local beekeeper and buy your honey direct from the source.

Chanchal says she typically uses dried marsh mallow root, slippery elm bark, thyme, sage, or hyssop, all of which are used to soothe coughs and sore throats.

After preparing them, let your honey-herb mixtures steep in a cool, dark place for two weeks, then strain and rebottle them. To use herb honeys, take by the teaspoonful or dissolve a teaspoonful into a soothing cup of herbal tea.

Timely tip

Chanchal adds that local honey is beneficial even without herbs, so buy it whenever possible. "Exposure to the pollen gathered in the honey-making process helps build up natural immunity to potential allergens. One of the best remedies for hay fever is to take 1 to 2 teaspoons of local, raw, unpasteurized honey every day." (The heat of pasteurization can denature some active compounds.)

"For this method to work, it's important to get a head start. Begin taking local honey in the fall to prevent or alleviate spring allergy attacks," Chanchal recommends.

Grow Your Own **Echinacea**

Echinacea, widely known for its immune-stimulant properties, is now the top-selling herbal product in the United States. But at $13 an ounce, it makes sense to grow your own supply of echinacea by planting easy-to-grow purple coneflowers (*Echinacea purpurea*). And contrary to what you might have read or heard, you don't need to destroy the beautiful plants by harvesting the roots.

"Every part of *Echinacea purpurea* has active healing properties," claims Rosemary Gladstar, a well-known herbalist and author of *Herbal Healing for Women*, who makes her home in East Barre, Vermont. "You don't need to use any roots to make an effective echinacea tincture that helps ward off a cold or boosts your immunity after an illness. I harvest the flowering tops—the stalk, leaves, and unopened flower buds from new growth—throughout the season. The plant will keep growing and you can harvest again in a few weeks."

Purple coneflower roots were used in traditional Native American remedies when the plants were very abundant. "That doesn't mean that the other parts of the plant are useless—they just weren't studied," Rosemary says. "And because echinacea is now so popular, it's been overharvested from the wild by poachers eager to make a quick buck."

To help preserve the remaining stands of native coneflowers, which were once widespread in America's heartland, Rosemary urges everyone to grow their own echinacea for tincture or buy products that clearly state that they've been made from organic cultivated plantings of purple coneflower.

"*Echinacea purpurea* is the easiest variety to grow and makes an excellent tincture," Rosemary says. "It will grow almost anywhere in full sun to part shade. Two or three plants will spread into a generous clump in several years. You can begin making your own tincture from the flowering tops during the first year of growth," she says.

Homemade Tinctures

To make your own tincture from fresh herbs (which will be a lot less expensive than the store-bought variety), loosely fill a clean glass jar with the plant material. Cover with vodka, minimum 60 proof. (The ratio should be about 2:1, alcohol to plant.) Cap the jar tightly, label, and date it. Let the tincture steep for two to three weeks at room temperature, then strain it. Pour some tincture into an eye-drop bottle for daily use (again label and date it), and store the remainder in a glass jar in a cool, dark place. The tincture will keep for up to five years. Refill the eye-drop bottle as needed.

You can use the stalks, leaves, and buds of purple coneflowers—not just the roots—to make medicinal tinctures.

homegrown HINTS

HERBS FOR MEDICINE MAKERS

Pay attention to what you plant if you're interested in growing medicinal herbs to make homemade remedies such as teas, tinctures, and herb-infused oils (use only dried herbs for these). Look for strains of herbs developed for higher concentrations of essential oils and other chemicals responsible for the healing action of the plant when you're planning your herb garden.

Janika Eckert, manager of the herb seed program at Johnny's Selected Seeds in Albion, Maine, says they now offer strains of many medicinal herbs, including St.-John's-wort, calendula, valerian, marsh mallow, lemon balm, chamomile, marjoram, agrimony, caraway, dill, sage,

summer savory, and yarrow, that contain significantly more essential oil in their leaves.

"Many of these cultivars have been developed in Germany, where extensive research has been done on the effectiveness of medicinal herbs," advises Janika. Some of the powerhouse herbs that you may want to try include 'Erfurter Orangefarbige' calendula, 'Bona' and 'Bodegold' chamomile (two varieties of German chamomile), 'Topas' St.-John's-wort, 'Aromata' summer savory, and 'Proa' yarrow.

Southern Exposure Seeds in Earlysville, Virginia, and Richter's in Canada also offer a selection of herb varieties specifically developed for medicinal uses.

Sage Cools "Power Surges"

"Sage (*Salvia officinalis*) is a great help for women in their menopausal years," says herbalist Susun Weed, author of *Menopausal Years—The Wise Woman Way*. Susun reports that there is no other herb as effective as sage for drying up sweats that accompany some women's hot flashes. "One dose can provide relief within two hours, and the effects can last for up to two days."

Susun finds that with regular use, the nutrients in sage (notably calcium, potassium, zinc, and thiamine) can ease nerves, headaches, dizziness, trembling, and emotional swings. Sage also has antiseptic and antioxidant qualities. As if that's not enough, using the tea as a hair rinse darkens graying hair!

If you use sage as a remedy, Susun cautions to not go overboard, as it will cause dry mouth. She recommends 1 to 2 tablespoons of very strong

tea one to eight times daily (that's one cup of tea sipped throughout the day) or 15 to 40 drops of the tincture one to three times a week. Also, do not use sagebrush (*Seriphidium tridentatum*), which is also known as *Artemisia tridentata*, internally—that's a completely different plant.

To make the sage tea, use 1 ounce of dried sage or 2 ounces of fresh sage to 4 cups of boiling water; brew for at least one hour.

Herbal Calcium **Boosters**

Looking for an ingenious way to boost your daily dose of calcium? Try herbs!

Sage, nettles, yellow dock, chickweed, red clover flowers, oat straw (the stems of oats that are harvested when the oats are green rather than dried), parsley, raspberry leaves, plantain leaves and seeds, borage, and dandelion leaves are all excellent sources of dietary calcium and are easily absorbed by the body. Make some tea with these leaves, singly or mixed, and drink 2 cups daily. This tea will provide approximately 250 to 300 milligrams of calcium.

In addition, if you use a juice extractor, chickweed, dandelion, and parsley are excellent when juiced along with vegetables and fruits. Try them with a blend of carrot, apple, and celery.

Timely tip

As you're working to build your calcium intake, remember that certain foods, most notably soft drinks, coffee, sugar, salt, and alcohol, deplete calcium from the body.

Garden **Soother** for *Bee Stings*

For quick relief, look for plantains (*Plantago* spp.), a common weed that grows just about everywhere. Rub the leaf vigorously between your thumbs (or chew the leaf) to extract some juice, and press the juice on the sting. Whew! Repeat as needed until the pain is gone. Both the broad-leaved and the narrow-leaved plantain work, although the broad-leaved form is juicier.

Another way to take advantage of the healing power of plantain is to grow ornamental cultivars. Here are two varieties recommended by free-lance garden writer and nursery owner Nancy Ondra, of Emmaus, Pennsylvania: purple-leaved plantain (*Plantago major* 'Rubrifolia'), which has purple foliage, and rose plantain (*Plantago major* 'Rosularis'), which has the well-known green leaves, but in place of the common flower spike, grows green bracts that look like tiny green roses.

Nancy says that both of these plants are fun to grow in the garden as ornamentals. But they will self-sow. To prevent that, simply pinch off the flower heads before they set seed. "Actually, there's no need to let the purple-leaved plantain flower spikes even bloom. The beauty of the plant is the foliage. For the rose plantain, simply pinch off the green roses as they start to fade."

Timely tip

If you happen to be in your garden when a bee stings, there are two garden flowers you can turn to for relief. Bee balm leaves (*Monarda didyma*) and calendula flowers (*Calendula officinalis*) also take away the sting. Use them just as you would a plantain leaf.

Broad-leaved plantain (*Plantago major*), *left*, and Narrow-leaved plantain (*Plantago lanceolata*), *right*, can be used to soothe bee stings and insect bites.

Magic Mint Mask

"Summer heat and sweat can cause even the nicest skin to get a little ragged," admits Stephanie Tourles, licensed aesthetician and author of *The Herbal Body Book* and *Natural Foot Care*. "For just pennies, this refreshing mask sloughs off dead skin cells, absorbs excess oil, and refines your pores."

To make the mask, you'll need ten large peppermint leaves, ⅓ cup water, and 1 tablespoon white clay (available at health food stores or through mail order sources). Put the peppermint and water in the blender, and puree until green and frothy. Strain out the solids.

Place the clay in a small bowl. Add enough mint liquid to make a spreadable paste. Spread paste onto your clean face, keeping it away from your eyes. Lie down and relax until the paste is dry. ("If the doorbell rings, don't answer it!" says Stephanie.)

Rinse your face with tepid water, then blot gently to dry. Look in the mirror and admire the beautiful results.

Homemade Herbal *Aftershave* Splash

Most cosmetic recipes are formulated for women, but here's an easy recipe for men from Rita C. Karydas, owner of Lunar Farms, who makes and sells her own line of herbal body care products in Gilmer, Texas.

This recipe focuses on homegrown herbs and pantry staples, with the exception of the optional addition of benzoin, a resin extracted from a tropical tree. "Benzoin is super for aftershave as it soothes dry cracked skin and helps retain skin elasticity," says Rita. "It also has fixative qualities, which enhance the fragrance of other ingredi-

ents." (To purchase benzoin, check your local health food store or order from an herbal supplier. For this recipe, look for liquid resin benzoin, rather than solid benzoin, because it will mix easily.)

"This recipe is just to get you started," adds Rita. "Experiment with herbs and spices that appeal to you. Vanilla beans are one of my favorites."

Herbal Aftershave

2 cups witch hazel

Handful of fresh rosemary and mint leaves, bruised

2 medium-sized fresh comfrey leaves, chopped

2 cinnamon sticks

10 whole cloves

2 to 4 strips each, orange and lemon peel

10 drops benzoin resin (optional)

1 sprig rosemary or mint

Place witch hazel, rosemary, mint, and comfrey in a large jar. Steep in a cool dark place for four to six weeks, or longer if you want a stronger fragrance. Strain liquid into a measuring cup to make it easy to pour into another clean bottle. Add cinnamon sticks, cloves, orange and lemon peels, and benzoin, as well as a decorative sprig of rosemary or mint. Label and date. Aftershave will keep for up to a year, or longer if stored in a cool place.

Yield: about 2 cups of aftershave

Easy-to-Make Herb Stamps

Have a favorite herb you'd like to use as a personal logo? There's no need to buy a rubber stamp when you have the real thing growing right there in your garden.

New Jersey artist Laura Donnelly Bethmann, author of *Nature Printing with Herbs, Fruits and Flowers*, offers an easy technique for leaf stamping. "The only materials required are a stamp pad and a leaf," says Laura, "but it's good to have waxed paper and tweezers on hand, too."

You can use Laura's technique to personalize recipe cards, labels for homemade goodies, stationery and gift wrap, or even an herb diary. "Stamp-pad ink adheres especially well with herbs that have downy, textured, or curiously shaped leaves, like lamb's ears, sage, wormwood, geranium, lady's mantle, or sprigs of oregano and rue," Laura suggests. "I've also had good results with feathery leaves like yarrow and chamomile. You may want to practice on bond or newsprint paper a few times until you get a feel for how much ink is needed and how much pressure to apply."

1. Lay the leaf underside down onto the stamp pad. (The leaf veins are usually more pronounced on the underside.) Sponge-type stamp pads sold for stamping projects work best.

2. Cover the leaf with a small piece of wax paper. Press all around, feeling through the paper. Make sure the ink adheres to the leaf, but don't ink it completely, or the texture will be lost.

3. Remove the leaf from the stamp pad with tweezers.

4. Lay the leaf on the project paper. Cover it with a small piece of newsprint paper, and press with the heel of your hand. If the leaf is large, hold it in place with the thumb of one hand, and press all around with the other hand. Remove the newsprint, and lift the leaf with the tweezers. If the print lacks detail, there's too much or too little ink. To remove excess ink, press the leaf onto the practice paper a few times. If the image doesn't improve, try a fresh leaf. The ink should dry within 15 minutes; then your project is ready to use.

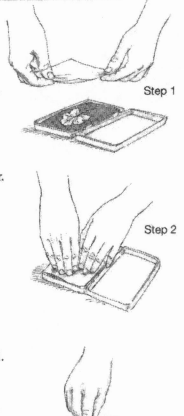

Step 1

Step 2

Step 3

Step 4

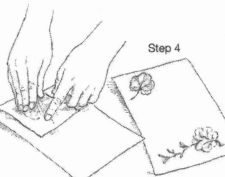

Use leaves from your garden and a stamp pad to create beautiful customized stationery.

Herb-Dyed
Easter Eggs

"Coloring Easter eggs with natural plant dyes is an organic and wonderful way to introduce children to herbs," says Rhonda Hart, author of *Easter Eggs by the Dozen*, who has created and tested dozens of egg-decorating projects with her family in Chattaroy, Washington. "Eggs symbolize new life, hope, and joy. What better way to celebrate spring?"

Rhonda says the process couldn't be easier. Gather the plant materials, simmer them for an hour, and then add the eggs. "The mistake most people make is that they don't use enough plant material. It takes a whole pot of herbs to create good color. And don't expect the neon colors that artificial dyes render. Natural dyes reflect their source—beautiful earthy tones."

Use hard-boiled or raw eggs for this project. Raw eggs may be blown out after dyeing. Since a small amount of dye leaches into the egg through the porous shell, be aware that not all herb-based dyes are safe to eat. Also, never eat eggs that are unrefrigerated for more than two hours.

Loosely fill a 2-quart stainless steel or enamel stockpot with the chosen herb, and cover with water. Bring the water to a boil. Cover the pot and simmer for one hour. Let water cool to room temperature. Add hard-boiled or raw eggs to the pot of herbs, making sure to cover with water. Leave eggs in dye bath until they reach the desired shade—which may mean overnight. Remove eggs from dye bath, and blot dry.

Herb Dyes

Stinging nettle greens *(Urtica dioica)* yield khaki green

Sage leaves yield a soft greenish gray

Fresh dandelion flower heads yield bright yellow

Marigolds yield a deeper yellow or orange

Larkspur blossoms yield blue

Red onion peels yield red

Hops yield brown

Note: Here's an extra tip for harvesting stinging nettle. Wear heavy gloves, long sleeves, and let only your scissors touch the plant. Use tongs to handle the stalks once indoors.

Fresh Face
Herb Toner

"My recipe for an inexpensive facial toner is gentle enough to use on a baby's skin," says Katherine Glynn, owner of The Fragrant Garden in Port Perry, Ontario. "The lactose in the milk provides cleansing action while the butterfat softens the skin."

Note: Use fresh herbs, not dried.

Herbal Face Toner

1 cup buttermilk

2 tablespoons peppermint leaves, finely chopped

1 tablespoon rosemary leaves, finely chopped

1 tablespoon lavender flowers

Place buttermilk in a small glass or ceramic bowl. Stir in the peppermint, rosemary, and lavender. Cover the mixture with plastic wrap and let steep overnight in the refrigerator. Strain.

To use, dip a cotton ball in the infusion and gently wipe your face and throat. Rinse your face with tepid water and blot dry. Store any remaining toner in the refrigerator. Use leftovers within 3 days or freeze into ice cubes; thaw as needed.

Sweet Dreams
with Herb-Stuffed Pillows

"Selecting herbs for dreams is a form of aromatherapy," explains Jim Long, owner of Long Creek Herbs in Oak Grove, Arkansas, and author of *Profits with Dream Pillows*. "Certain flowers and herbs have been found to evoke various kinds of dreams. In fact, 'comfort pillows,' as they were once called, were used in hospitals and sickrooms to ease the nightmares that the odors in those places can trigger."

Jim points out that dream blends are different from potpourri. "The fragrance is subtle and should only be slightly noticeable. During sleep, your head rolls around on the pillow, which lightly crushes the herbs to release their aromas."

He adds that you should begin to notice a change in the kind of dreams you have within a night or two. "For best results, use the dream pillow for seven to ten days, then remove it and sleep without it for that same length of time."

Jim also cautions against using any kind of essential oil in dream blends. Essential oils are so potent that the effects can be overwhelming after many hours of exposure.

Most people respond very well to dream pillows, but you may have allergies. The cure is simple—if you start sneezing, stop using your pillow.

Here's Jim Long's herbal blend recipe, formulated to stimulate quiet, peaceful dreams:

Peaceful Dreams Herb Blend

½ cup dried rose petals

½ cup dried mugwort

⅛ cup dried rosemary

¼ cup dried lavender flowers

1 tablespoon dried sweet marjoram

Combine rose petals, mugwort, rosemary, lavender, and marjoram. Seal them in a plastic bag to allow fragrances to blend for about 2 days.

To use, remove ¼ cup of the dream blend and place it in a little cloth bag, such as a 3 × 5-inch cotton drawstring bag—it's easy to make one yourself. Tie the bag closed and place it in your pillowcase. You'll have enough mix to make a pillow for a friend.

Make a Versatile Herbal Body Rinse

"Herbal body rinses are a snap to make and have multitudes of cosmetic uses," claims Stephanie Tourles, owner of September's Sun Herbal Soap Company in West Hyannisport, Massachusetts, and author of *The Herbal Body Book*. "I use this recipe as a body and hair rinse after showering to soften and restore the natural pH. It also makes a soothing and deodorizing soak for smelly feet."

Stephanie recommends fresh sage leaves for brunettes and chamomile flowers for blondes and redheads.

Multipurpose Herbal Rinse

½ cup chopped sage leaves or whole chamomile flowers, tightly packed

1 teaspoon borax (check the laundry aisle in the grocery store)

6 cups boiling water

½ cup apple cider vinegar

Place borax and sage or chamomile in a large saucepan or bowl. Pour in boiling water. Steep for 15 minutes. Stir in vinegar. Strain. Use liberally as a rinse for hair and body, or pour into a pan and soak feet. Refrigerate any leftovers for up to 10 days.

Fragrant Potpourri *Bookmarks*

Crafting an herbal bookmark like the one shown below is a fun way to use your home-made potpourri, and it makes a thoughtful gift—but be sure to make an extra one for yourself. You'll need to buy ½ yard of 2-inch-wide decorative ribbon. Stamped lace ribbon looks especially pretty.

Cut a length of ribbon into two equal-length pieces. Lay the pieces on top of each other with wrong sides together. Whipstitch the edges together, leaving an opening at one end to insert the potpourri.

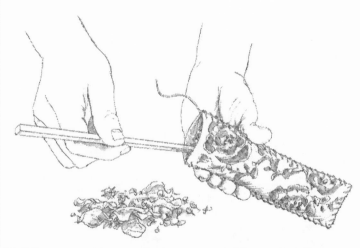

Stuff the potpourri between the two layers of ribbon so that it's no more than ¼ inch thick, using a chopstick to push in the dried herbs.

Stitch the opening closed to complete the bookmark.

Quick and *Easy* Herb Soap for Gardeners

What gardener doesn't suffer from grubby hands and fingernails?

"Here's a fragrant way to scrub your skin clean without resorting to harsh soaps," says Katherine Glynn, owner of The Fragrant Garden, a Canadian mail-order company featuring imported potpourri, essential oils, and other scented delights. "The little bits of rosemary in my herb soap lift off dirt without scraping your skin."

Here's Katherine's method: Chop 1 tablespoon dried rosemary leaves. Place the leaves in a small saucepan. Pour ¼ cup boiling water over herbs and steep 15 minutes.

Meanwhile, grate 2 cups castille or glycerin soap. Place in mixing bowl. Reheat the herbs and water to boiling. Pour the mixture over the shredded soap and let it stand 15 minutes. Add five or six drops of rosemary essential oil, if desired, to increase the fragrance. Mold soap into balls or bars, and allow them to harden, which takes up to three or four days.

fun
with Fruits & Berries

From jugs of doom to blankets of straw, garden experts from around the country offer the benefits of their years of experience for making fruit growing fun and flavorful. With these ingenious tips, you'll discover how to keep your fruit and berry crops pest-free, and how to make tree and plant maintenance a snap. Planting the right variety or cultivar can also make a difference at harvesttime, so read on for advice on choosing the most scrumptious fruits and berries for your garden.

Early Ripening Means *Fewer* Bugs

"Organic growers have it tough when it comes to apples," asserts Michael McConkey, owner of Edible Landscaping in Afton, Virginia. The fruit takes so long to ripen that it's an inviting banquet for all kinds of insect pests throughout the growing season. But Michael has a simple yet ingenious solution. "If you plant a crop of early ripening apples, you can reduce that dangerous time and create a small window in which you have a great chance of getting good fruit."

"While I was growing up, the only really early apple was 'Lodi', which made good sauce but wasn't a dessert apple," says Michael. Now there are 'Williams Pride' and 'Pristine', which ripen near the end of June, the same time as 'Lodi', but which offer big, red, tasty eating apples. They're disease-resistant, too, notes Michael. Because 'Williams Pride' and 'Pristine' ripen much faster than other apple cultivars, your chances of getting bugged by bugs are minimized.

A Snip in Time

"Thinning my apples used to make my fingers sore," says Marie Bedics, a home gardener from Whitehall, Pennsylvania. "I can't believe it took me so long to wise up and switch to scissors!" Marie uses a pair of regular all-purpose scissors to snip off the extra apples from her trees so that she'll get bigger fruit from those apples remaining on the tree.

After the natural fruit drop (when the tree sheds lots of extras on its own), Marie steps in to thin the rest so that there's just one or two of the best remaining in each cluster. She says she used to pinch the fruit off, followed by an attempt at using pruners, but all that squeezing made her wrists sore. "Scissors are much faster and easier," she says. "They slice right through the stems."

Marie has another tip for new snippers—use orange-handled scissors. There's so much going on outside, she says, that she gets distracted and lays the scissors down to watch a bird or look at the flowers. Orange handles are easy to find, laughs Marie.

problem SOLVer

HENS: SUPER ORCHARD HELPERS

Squawk! Awk! Put a landscape crew to work in your orchard from dawn to dusk every day—for pennies! Even a small orchard will support a few chickens, and you'll have plenty to show for it besides eggs. Hens will gobble up pests, weeds, weed seeds, and disease-harboring dropped fruit. They'll provide your trees with nitrogen-rich organic fertilizer for super crops. And their loony carryings-on will brighten each and every gardening day. Just make sure your orchard is predator-proofed with a good fence before sending your "crew" to the site.

Fruitful Vines Produce Privacy Fast

Privacy is a problem for many of us, as more and more houses are built on smaller and smaller lots in planned communities. All the fencing solutions seem to have drawbacks—a solid wood or masonry fence is expensive, wire fences are unsightly, and hedges take forever to grow. What can you do? Solve your privacy problems with prolific fruiting vines!

Hardy kiwi vines are legendary for fast, luxuriant growth, with glossy dark green leaves and fragrant white flowers. And recent research shows that gram for gram, kiwis are the most nutritious fruits of all. Hardy kiwis are smaller and smoother than their fuzzy cousins, but they'll take winter lows of -20 to -25°F, making them hardy from Zones 5 to 9. Plant them 8 feet apart on a sturdy wire fence or a wood-and-wire trellis for beauty and bounty. Plant a male kiwi vine for every two or three females for good pollination.

Grapevines, with their beautiful foliage and delicious fruit, are also great for privacy and productivity. Choose a variety that's trouble-free in your area—for example, 'Concord', 'Niagara', and 'Canadice' are three of the best for the northeastern United States. Or try maypop (*Passiflora incarnata*), a cold-hardy species of passionfruit. This perennial vine has roots that are hardy from Zones 5 to 10, and it climbs readily on a fence or trellis.

homegrown HINTS

A NEW ERA IN APPLES

The introduction of disease resistance is the most important advance in apples, says Jim Cummins, retired fruit breeder at Cornell University's Geneva research station. A consortium (known as P.R.I.) of scientists from Purdue University, Rutgers University, and the University of Illinois have introduced more than 50 scab-resistant varieties. These low-spray varieties are certain to find a place in the home garden and in the specialty farmstand.

The most successful introduction from Cornell's program so far is 'Liberty'. There are three new varieties from the P.R.I. cooperative (often identified by the letters "pri" somewhere in their names): 'Pristine,' Enterprise,' and 'GoldRush'. 'Pristine' is an early-maturing variety, while 'Enterprise' and 'GoldRush' mature late and are designed for long-term storage. Even fruit fanciers in the Deep South may soon be able to grow apples without fungicides because a Brazilian offshoot of the P.R.I. program has developed a scab-immune apple called 'Primicia' that requires little winter chilling, says Jim.

Orchard Bees for Fruitful Trees

Haven't seen too many honeybees buzzing around your fruit trees lately? The low numbers may be due to the mite epidemic that's wreaking havoc on our beloved honeybees. While scientists search for a safe, effective remedy, you can do something right now to ensure that your crops are pollinated: Order a box of orchard mason bees to hang in your trees. These peaceful native bees are great pollinators, visiting thousands of blossoms every day, and they're immune to the mites. Raintree Nursery, in Morton, Washington, sells a starter pack of orchard mason bees and a "bee condo" to house them, as well as a book on mason bees and a video, too. With these nonaggressive bees in your orchard, you won't get honey, but you *will* get heavy fruit crops.

Best of the New Breed

If you hunger for the crunch of a fresh apple in December, look for an apple variety that's a "long keeper." Long-keeping apples retain their texture and flavor for months after picking in your refrigerator crisper drawer.

'GoldRush', a disease-resistant cultivar that's perfect for the backyard fruit grower, gets Jill Vorbeck's vote as the best of the new bunch of trouble-free apples. Jill tastes all kinds of apples every year as owner of Applesource, a company that ships samplers of popular and unusual varieties for taste-testing. With built-in resistance to such apple plagues as scab, 'GoldRush' bears bountiful crops and boasts great flavor. "This is the first new long-keeper we think has top quality," she says. It's a green apple with an old-fashioned look because it lacks the polished skin of modern favorites. But it's definitely a *keeper*, in both the figurative and most literal senses of the word, says Jill: "It keeps for as long as nine months in the refrigerator," she marvels.

Add *Living* Art with **Espalier**

Espalier, the technique of training fruit trees along wires in ways nature never intended, is much easier than it looks and can be a great way to add a work of art to a strictly functional garden, says Mark Trela, manager of Fragrant Farms in New Harmony, Indiana.

"The hardest part is deciding what shape you want the tree to grow into. Once you have that decided and have the wires in place, it's easy," he says.

If the tree will be against a wall or fence, Mark trains it with a straight vertical trunk and straight horizontal branches, but if it will be a free-standing tree, he angles the trunk on a diagonal to make it more interesting to the eye. "The tree looks great any time of year," he says, "because you've created a living work of art in the garden. I don't know which season I like best: spring, when it blooms; summer, when the branches get softened by leaves; fall, when it's dotted with apples; or winter, when you can appreciate the abstract form."

Here's Mark's technique for espaliered fruit trees:

1. Set two 4 × 4 × 10 posts into the ground about 8 feet apart with the young, flexible-trunked tree (dwarf fruit trees are the best candidates) halfway between the posts.

2. Stretch four parallel rows of wires between the posts, placing a wire about every 12 inches up the height of the posts, starting about 12 inches above ground level.

3. Coax the lowest branches into position by loosely tying them with rag strips to the lowest wires. Work up to the top branches in the same manner. Generally, Mark aims for four branches extending out from each side of the trunk. "Think in 2-D instead of 3-D," says Mark. "The espalier will appear almost flat when you look at it from the side."

4. As the tree and branches grow, cut off any shoots or branches that don't fit your plan. Snip back any side branches that sprout from the main limbs, leaving only short fruiting spurs attached. The spring is the best time to do any major pruning, but since the tree is growing constantly, you may need to do minor pruning throughout the growing season.

5. Add more ties to each branch as it gets longer.

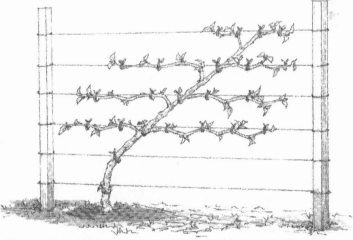

Use espalier techniques to train young, flexible trees to grow along wires. You benefit in two ways: First, you can fit an espalier tree into a small area, and second, you add a work of art to your garden.

homegrown HINTS

BATS BEAT BAD FRUIT BUGS

Codling moths and other night-flying pests can turn your dream fruit crop into a holey nightmare. But help is at hand. Bats can eat up to 600 pests an *hour*, and they will take up residence in a special bat house you can build or buy.

Hang the house in your trees, and soon little brown bats (or another helpful species) will be on pest patrol for you every night. You can buy bat houses and easy-to-assemble kits at wild-bird specialty stores and through many mail-order catalogs that offer gardening supplies. When you hang one up, bear in mind that the bats will be resting in it during the day, so site it where it's shaded by branches and far enough off the ground to avoid predators.

Taste Test
Before You Plant

Catalogs are full of mouth-watering descriptions of apple varieties, but how can you tell how sweet "sweet" is, or how tart "tart" is, let alone understand esoteric descriptions like "complex flavor?" The best way is to sample the real thing, and Applesource, owned by Tom and Jill Vorbeck of Chapin, Illinois, lets you do just that.

Applesource will send you a listing of about 100 varieties so you can custom-make your own mix, or they will send a selection of one each of 12 varieties of their choice. Recent samplers have included such delectable beauties as 'Melrose' and 'Mutsu', and antiques such as 'Ashmead's Kernel', a connoisseur variety, which Jill says belies its intense flavor with a russet skin that makes it look like an Idaho potato. 'Esopus Spitzenberg' is another outstanding apple that was supposedly Thomas Jefferson's personal favorite, according to Jill.

Applesource features a wide selection of antique varieties that they get from specialty growers. "Antiques tend to have intense flavor," notes Jill. They're wonderful for cooking too. Applesource will ship apples from late October through early January. Once you have found your favorite apple, you'll know which cultivar to ask for at your local nursery in the spring.

Fruiting for
Small Spaces

Don't let a lack of garden space keep you from growing your favorite fruit. Many fruit varieties are self-fertile, so you only need one plant to produce fruit. But if your favorite apple, pear, or you-name-it fruit needs another variety to act as pollinator and you only have room for one tree, don't give up in despair.

If you have fruit-growing friends or neighbors or there's an orchard near you, just ask them for a flowering branch of a compatible variety, and tie it among your tree's branches. The bees will do the rest! Remember: Both of the varieties must be in bloom at the same time for this solution to work.

Foil "Curcs" with *Plastic Bags*

The dastardly plum curculio, or "curc," is an insect pest that plagues apple growers. Its larvae tunnel through the fruit's flesh, causing many of the apples to fall from the tree. Organic remedies don't offer total protection, but Michael McConkey, owner of Edible Landscaping in Afton, Virginia, has found a fool-proof way to outwit the pest—he bags his young fruits to keep bugs out.

At thinning time, Michael removes all but the "prettiest" marble-sized apple in each cluster of fruits. Then he slips a plastic bag over the little apple and staples it in place, close to the stem on both sides. The bag is closed loosely enough to allow some air to enter the bag and prevent moisture buildup, but it will discourage pests by hiding the fruit. "You might think it's a chore," he says, "but it's more work to spray the tree three or four times." Bagging the apples on a dwarf tree takes about an hour and a half, he estimates. To be successful, Michael adds, choose only blemish-free fruits to bag. "There's no use bagging a fruit that's already been damaged.

"The Japanese have bagged fruits for thousands of years," Michael notes. "Today they use different-size bags for different fruits."

Staple small plastic bags over apples to protect them from dreaded pests like plum curculio.

problem SOLVer

CHANCE ENCOUNTERS OF THE BEST KIND

After a chance encounter with a 'Golden Delicious' apple tree, Debbe Burdick of Mt. Vernon, Indiana, says she learned you can reap rewards by starting with the right variety. Leaning over a fence in the neglected backyard of a derelict downtown house was a venerable 'Golden Delicious' apple tree, its branches bending under the load of fruit.

Debbe was inspired by that long-forgotten tree, so she bought a young one and planted it in her yard. Her tree is 15 years old now, and it has never felt the touch of pruners, let alone sprays or fertilizer. But she gets enough almost-perfect apples from it that she has to give some away—and she feels like a successful fruit grower. "I'm the ultimate lazy gardener," laughs Debbe. "Plant it, forget it, and pick it—that's my motto."

Debbe says that the stout-hearted 'Golden Delicious' tree shrugs off the pesky problems that can affect specimens of less stalwart constitutions. It's a great choice for gardeners who'd rather spend their time on something other than pruning and spraying fruit trees.

Neatness Counts with Netting

Cherries seem to have a built-in homing device for attracting birds, and tried-and-true mesh netting is still the best antibird bargain around, says Mark Trela, manager of the all-organic Fragrant Farms in New Harmony, Indiana. He stores his netting from season to season on large cardboard tubes—the kind you'd find at carpet stores. He cuts the long rugged tubes into easy-to-manage lengths, then rolls the flattened netting onto the tubes. To protect the netting during winter storage, just cover the tubes with plastic.

Getting the netting on the tree isn't always an easy job, but Mark says he just swoops it over the tree top, then uses sticks or brooms to maneuver it into place. The swooping technique takes a little practice and a little patience, so don't despair. If wind is a problem in your area, Mark suggests using 2-liter soda bottles partially filled with water or small weights tied to the netting to keep it from lifting up or blowing away.

homegrown HINTS

FRIGHT IN THE TREETOPS

"Scare-eyes balloons really work," asserts fruit grower Bill Hall, owner of Country Heritage Nurseries and Seed in Hartford, Michigan, who recommends the devices to protect fruit crops of any kind. He not only sells a lot of them, but also uses them himself. To get the very best results with the balloons, Bill recommends hanging them from a tall pole, about 12 feet high, that has some give—like a cane fishing pole. Then the balloons can wiggle around a lot and scare off flying fruit thieves.

The 18-inch balloons are made of tough plastic, with vivid scary eyes on four sides, so there's always a new frightful face coming into view. The devices aren't totally foolproof, admits Bill. They don't keep robins away, he says, but in most cases they do make a difference.

Time to *Avoid* Avian Temptation

Sweet and sour cherries and blueberries are so appealing to birds that many a gardener despairs of ever getting more than a taste of the crop. Netting or caging the plants with wire screening is one way to outwit the feathered fiends, but Michael McConkey, owner of Edible Landscaping in Afton, Virginia, has learned another trick. "An Amish friend from the Lancaster, Pennsylvania, area tells me that 'Ulster' cherry is one of the best cherries a backyard gardener can grow. It ripens late, so the birds eat local wild cherries first when they're hungriest, during nesting time, instead of bothering your cherries." By the time 'Ulster' ripens, says Michael, the birds have apparently lost interest and moved on to a new menu.

Michael's own trials with blueberries have illustrated the same principle. His rabbiteye and hybrid berries, including 'Tifblue', 'Misty Blue', 'Powder Blue', and 'Climax', ripen late in the season. By the time the crop is ready in August, says Michael, there's not a berry-eating wood thrush around!

Making *Pawpaws Feel at Home*

Large, lush leaves and rich, tropical-tasting fruit have made the native American pawpaw tree a *cause célèbre*, as pawpaw fans extol the plant to an ever-growing audience. But a gardener's burst of enthusiasm is often tempered by the cautions about pawpaws being difficult to transplant and slow to establish. Hector Black, founder of Hidden Springs Nursery, in Cookeville, Tennessee, has grown hundreds of pawpaws over the years and has found a simple way to establish the plants successfully. "If you have access to a pawpaw patch, take a handful of its soil and put it in the hole when you plant a pawpaw tree," he urges.

Hector surmises that soil from a pawpaw patch may contain beneficial mycorrhizal fungi that help generate better root growth (each type of plant responds best to particular fungi).

Hector says that bareroot trees establish themselves as well as container-grown specimens do. The trees grow slowly, so don't be discouraged, says Annie Black, Hector's daughter and co-owner of the nursery. During the first few years, most of a pawpaw's growth takes place underground because it's developing a long taproot, she says. Pawpaws require well-drained, fertile loam soil, but otherwise you'll need to do very little maintenance in the proper conditions.

Add a handful of soil from an existing pawpaw tree when you're digging a hole for a new pawpaw to generate better root growth.

Try **Pest-Free** Asian Pears

If you're looking for a fruit tree that produces sweet fruit and has virtually no pest woes, try an Asian pear tree. "It's not bothered by 90 percent of the pests that commonly bother other fruits," says Ed Fackler, president of North American Fruit Explorers and a commercial orchardist. And compared to other fruits, it's easy to grow.

Prune Asian pear trees as you would an apple to keep the tree's branches open and to keep the fruit in easy reach, Ed says. Asian pears are so productive that the fruits must be severely thinned to just one per cluster as soon as you see them developing. The heavy, yellow fruits are "crisp and sweet," he says, but flavor quality varies among the varieties. Ed grows some 70 varieties of Asian pears, but has two top favorites. "'Korean Giant' and 'Chojuro' have excellent flavor, almost a butterscotch nuance," he says. With a mouthwatering recommendation like that, who could resist adding an Asian flavor to the garden?

homegrown HINTS

MEET FELLOW FRUIT FANCIERS

In the good old days, folks could gather around the potbellied stove in the general store or chat at the post office about their gardens and crops. But unless you show up at the local diner to have breakfast with the farmers, you probably don't have much chance of swapping tales and learning lessons from others who share your gardening fancies. Enter the North American Fruit Explorers (NAFEX), a modern-day alternative to the cracker-barrel conversation. "It's the best $10 you can spend!" says president Ed Fackler, who doubles up his executive duties with ownership of Rocky Meadow Orchard and Nursery in New Salisbury, Indiana. "It's great for networking with people who share your interests."

Some of the 2,700-plus members dabble in exotic fruits like kiwis, persimmons, and pawpaws, while other members grow classic tree fruits, brambles, grapes, and other goodies. Most members are "backyard people," says Ed, although commercial growers also belong. Membership includes: a quarterly journal, with articles that members write about growing their fruits; a lending library that includes videos; and an annual meeting, often at a research university. And the group is as close as your computer. Many members are online, so advice is just keystrokes away. Visit NAFEX online at www.nafex.org, or obtain membership information from NAFEX at 1716 Apples Road, Chapin, IL 62628.

Painting Peaches

Wet or chilly spring weather can cause a dramatic decrease in your crop of peaches, because pollinating insects stay home instead of visiting the flowers. You can cross your fingers when weather like this persists while peaches are at peak bloom, or you can pull out a paintbrush and give the insects an assist, suggests home gardener Marie Bedics of Whitehall, Pennsylvania.

Using a soft watercolor paintbrush, swipe the brush against the anthers of a blossom to pick up pollen, then wipe the pollen against the stigma of a different flower. It goes a lot faster than you'd think, says Marie, who learned the trick from an elderly gardener from Europe. Marie's trees reach about 10 feet tall, so she can't reach all the blossoms. "You can tell the difference between the branches I 'painted' and ones I didn't get to," she says, "because that's where the peaches are!"

When pollinators are scarce, use a paintbrush to pollinate your peach tree. Swipe the anthers of a blossom to pick up pollen, then brush the pollen onto another flower.

Mulberries *without* the Mess

"Mulberries are just as good as blueberries in a muffin," declares Michael McConkey, owner of Edible Landscaping in Afton, Virginia. But the notorious purple stains from the fruit, spread far and wide by birds, are an unwelcome side effect of growing mulberries. So it's white mulberries to the rescue! As Michael says, the fruits are white (or pale lavender), and they lack the problematic purple juice.

His favorite is 'Beautiful Day', a cultivar that can reach 30 feet, but which grows slowly—it can be kept bushy by pruning during the summer months. The mulberries are 1 inch long and about ⅜ inch in diameter, the perfect size for popping in your mouth. Or cut them in half and drop them into muffin batter.

Weeping mulberries, dwarf or regular size, are another option, says Michael. The berries drop within the narrower branch line of the tree instead of all over the place, so you're less likely to track the staining fruit into the house. (But birds may still make unwanted "deposits" elsewhere.) And while you're waiting for berries, the privacy within the drooping branches of the tree "makes a great playhouse for kids," notes Michael.

Weeping mulberries produce delicious fruit in the late summer and create the coolest natural playhouse for kids.

Mulberries Lure Birds from *More Luscious* Fruits

Most of the year, gardeners love to have birds in our backyards. But when our homegrown fruits start ripening, our formerly welcome guests can become unwanted pests.

To keep birds from plundering your cherries and digging into your other tree fruits, plant a mulberry nearby. Birds prefer mulberries to all other fruits— they'll ignore *your* favorites while they feast on the mulberries. Gardener Pam Ruch of Macungie, Pennsylvania, even protects her blueberries by using a mulberry tree as a decoy.

There are several varieties of mulberry that have been bred specifically for flavorful berries, including 'Illinois Everbearing', 'Wellington', and 'Oscar', so you may find yourself munching on a handful as well—if the birds leave any.

But remember: Never plant a mulberry tree near a path, sidewalk, or parking space—mulberry-colored bird droppings will get all over everything.

Get Your Fill of Fresh Berries

If sun-warmed raspberries are ambrosia to your palate, make the berry-picking season last by planting cultivars that bear in succession. A couple of bushes of each variety will give you plenty of berries for your breakfast cereal and your after-dinner ice cream, so you can fit a season's worth of fruit into a single strip of berry plants.

Michael McConkey, a confirmed berry lover and owner of Edible Landscaping in Afton, Virginia, suggests starting with early summer bearers. "Blackcaps are the earliest ripeners," he says,

"followed by red raspberries like 'Latham' and 'Citadel'." Planting early, midseason, and late varieties of red raspberries will give you many weeks' worth of berries. In late summer, fall-bearing raspberries come into their own, with cultivars like 'Autumn Bliss', 'Heritage', and 'Golden

Harvest' extending the berry season until frost. Make your berry-picking easy by planting the bushes in the order they ripen, with early bearers at one end of the row, midseason in the middle, and latecomers at the far end.

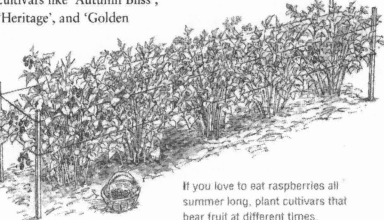

If you love to eat raspberries all summer long, plant cultivars that bear fruit at different times.

Make the Most of Strawberry Flavor

Many newer strawberry cultivars produce firm, long-lasting fruit that holds up better during shipping, but lacks flavor.

Strawberry lovers should steer away from the varieties grown for the supermarket, says Bill Hall, owner of Country Heritage Nurseries and Seed, Inc., in Hartford,

Michigan, and look for older varieties that have both flavor and some disease resistance.

- 'Sparkle'—ripens late; Zones 4 to 7.
- 'Honeoye'—ripens midseason; Zones 4 to 6.
- 'Jewel'—ripens midseason; Zones 4 to 6.
- 'Allstar'—ripens midseason; Zones 5 to 7.

To maximize the flavor potential of your berries, plant them in full sun, in a warm, protected site, says Bill. Loam and clay soils, which must be well drained, add to the taste, too. Sandy soils may make berries less flavorful. Avoid planting strawberries in an area that was used for peppers, tomatoes, melons, or raspberries. These crops may leave behind diseases that affect strawberries.

homegrown HINTS

STRAWBERRY FIELDS FOREVER

If you'd rather not replant your strawberry bed every year, try this: Treat your strawberries like perennials. Create a rich, well-drained bed for them; keep them mulched, watered, and fed during the growing season; and remove energy-draining runners. Your plants should get bigger and more productive every year. If the day dawns that the plants start losing steam and aren't producing a lot of fruit, just let them form runners that year, remove the mother plants, and start over.

Mix Up a Jug of Doom

Like many gardeners, Jeanette Manske, of Stoddard, Wisconsin, learned the basics at her mother's knee. One trick that Jeanette uses has cut down dramatically on the insect pests around her fruit and berry plants. To use her trick, you'll need a plastic milk jug or deep plastic container (like an ice-cream bucket) with a lid. The liquid in the container will tempt insects to enter the container, and they'll fall to their watery doom.

Just mix up the recipe and set the jugs or buckets among your raspberries, strawberries, apple trees, or other garden plants. One batch will usually last through the summer, but you may need to renew the recipe if the liquid in the container evaporates to less than 4 inches deep. You may also want to leave the jug in the garden until after cold weather comes so that it won't smell so bad when you discard it. The mixture has become a regional favorite, passed on from one gardening friend to another.

Mix up a jug of doom to lure insects away from your fruit crop. The pests will head for the enticing liquid, then fall to their watery grave inside the container.

Liquid Doom

1 gallon-size plastic milk jug or similar-volume plastic container with lid
1 cup sugar
1 cup white vinegar
Water
2 banana peels

Pour sugar and vinegar into the container. Fill with water to a couple of inches from top. Fasten on lid. Shake well. Open lid and push in banana peels. If you're using a milk jug, keep the lid off and set the jug in the garden. If you're using a wide-mouth container, cut a few 1-inch triangular flaps in the lid and bend them back so bugs can get in.

What to Do When the **Icemen** Cometh

Mulch and a garden hose are two weapons strawberry-loving gardener Jeanette Manske of Stoddard, Wisconsin, has learned to rely on to protect her early blooming berry plants from the tough Wisconsin weather.

"Sometimes in May, the 'Icemen' come," she cautions, explaining that this is her name for the unexpected and heavy late spring frosts that can nip the tender strawberry flowers or young fruit. To ward off the Icemen, Jeanette keeps her strawberries mulched with a generous scattering of straw from fall until after berry season. The soil doesn't soak up the early spring warmth and so stays cooler longer, slowing down bloom time. And if a nip of unusual cold does come along, she's ready with her garden hose, out before the sun to wash the frost from the plants before it can damage the buds or berries.

"I have way too much garden," laughs 74-year-old Jeanette, a lifelong gardener. Through the years, she's discovered ingenious ways to deal with garden problems.

A *Groundcover* Good Enough *to Eat*

Biodynamic gardener Mark Trela of New Harmony, Indiana, uses strawberries as a groundcover for a slightly sloping hillside on his property. "I used to spend a lot of time keeping my strawberries under control," says Mark. One summer, he tried a new approach and planted pinched-off runners on the slope where he planned to use a groundcover. The strawberries filled in quickly, sending runners to cover every bit of open space.

To plant runners, Mark merely pushes the crowns of the plantlets, many of which are already rooted, into the moist, loose soil with his thumb, making firm plant-to-soil contact but being careful not to cover the point where the leaves emerge. The berries are much smaller than those of the coddled plants in his garden, he says, "but they taste just as good." Mark also uses strawberries, and the hybrid pink-flowered 'Pink Panda' to edge sidewalks. He likes to plant them along curbs and walls, where they can sprawl over the edges, and he says, the leaves and white flowers are very pretty. Some of his gardens are along public sidewalks, and Mark says he especially enjoys seeing tourists who come to visit his historic hometown stop to snitch a berry.

Strawberries make great groundcovers! Just pinch off excess runners from your plants, then push the roots of the runners into the soil, tamping the soil with your hands.

Double Your Pleasure with *Edible Landscaping*

Why plant the usual boring shade trees and hedge plants that everyone else does when you can fill your yard with flavorful fruit *and* beauty at the same time? If your soil is acidic, plant a beautiful blueberry hedge, and enjoy its gorgeous red fall foliage as well as a bumper crop of luscious berries.

If your soil is neutral or more alkaline, rugosa roses with their purple, pink, or white blooms make a gorgeous hedge complete with deeply crinkled foliage and huge, vitamin C–rich hips. Or try cranberry bush, gooseberries, or currants. If you need a groundcover, strawberries are a delicious choice. Choose grapes or hardy kiwis rather than roses on trellises. And you'd be surprised at how many trees bear fruit or nuts while providing shade.

For nuts, think walnuts, pecans, butternuts, hickory nuts, and tree filberts. Fruits include apples and crabapples—'Centennial' is an apple-crabapple cross with bright red, sweet fruits for fresh eating—persimmons, pears, cherries, and Juneberries. For an exotic look, try pawpaws in the North and citrus in the Deep South and Southwest.

A Blanket of Insurance for Blackberries

Myron Nixon of Chesterfield, Illinois, a pioneer in selecting his own cultivars of thornless blackberries (though, as he says, other breeders' introductions "beat him to it"), is a big fan of the fruits. But he knows that some of the thornless commercial cultivars are less hardy than their prickly cousins. His Zone 5 winters can be rigorous, so he tucks in his bushes for the season by slipping straw bales under the arching canes for support and burying the branches in a layer of loose straw "until you can't see them."

If the canes freeze back, the new growth won't bear until the following year, causing you to lose out on a summer of delicious berries. To protect his berries, Myron covers his plants during the last week of

November and uncovers them the last week of March. You can use the method for any bramble fruits that are of questionable hardiness for your area. "Whether to bother with this kind of insurance," laughs Myron, "depends on whether you like berries or leaves."

A little blanket of straw goes a long way toward protecting brambles from cold weather. Slip bales of straw under the canes to support them, then bury the entire bush in loose straw.

Easy Access with Slip-Through Wires

Maintaining a row of trellised brambles means maneuvering over, under, and between the wires you use to hold up the canes. Myron Nixon, a blackberry grower from Chesterfield, Illinois, uses a system of slip-through wires to make maintenance a snap. He attaches the wires, one down each side of the row to turn-buckles on the supports he uses at either end of his row. The supports are hand-me-down telephone pole crossarms he received as castoffs when the local phone company switched to using underground cable.

His support wires are also freebies from the phone company—they're the wires that used run along the roadways. But whether your wire comes from Ma Bell or your local home supply store, you can adapt his method. At the end of the season, Myron unhooks the wire from the turnbuckle and pulls it right through the row, coiling it up. Then he performs any needed maintenance on the patch with

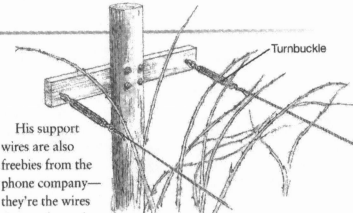

Turnbuckle

A wire trellis makes bramble maintenance a snap. Just unhook the wire from the turnbuckle, pull the wire through the row, and coil it up. Now you have access to the canes without reaching through the support wires.

free access. Replacing the wires is easy because you've pruned the long canes.

problem solver   MAKE ROOM FOR WINEBERRIES

Raspberries and blackberries are well known, but one of their relatives has escaped notice by most gardeners, even though it's a favorite among many berry connoisseurs. "Wineberries are wonderful!" exclaims Michael McConkey of Afton, Virginia, because of their complex mix of sweetness and tartness. As owner of Edible Landscaping, Michael grows a lot of different berries, but he ranks the flavorful, jewel-like wineberry number one.

For an unusual and ornamental planting with berries, try planting an arching bush of wineberries between stalwart, upright ornamental grasses, like pampas grass (*Cortaderia selloana*) or maiden grass (*Miscanthus sinensis*), says Michael. These grasses mellow to tan in winter, providing a beautiful backdrop to the fuzzy red canes of the wineberry. Wineberries naturalize like black raspberries—the canes will arch and root from their tips. The canes are hardier if they go through the winter with their tips in the ground; they produce berries on second-year wood. It may be necessary for you to prune the canes to control their steady spread, especially if they're planted between ornamental grasses.

ingenious
RECIPES

Better Than Blueberries

"I like Juneberries best in a pie," says fruit fancier Hector Black of Cookeville, Tennessee. "They're better than blueberries. And if you know me, you know that's saying a lot!" Juneberries (also known as service-berries) are delectable, and they're pretty plants too, with early blooming white flowers. Unlike most fruiting plants, Juneberries don't need pruning to bear a good crop. They aren't fussy about soil pH, and they have few pest problems.

Hector's favorite is 'Regent' Juneberry (*Amelanchier alnifolia* 'Regent')—only 3 to 4 feet tall and shrubby. It's not invasive and it's very productive. The flowers are ornamental, and the leaves turn red and yellow in fall. Hector likes everything about Juneberries, even the seeds, which are tiny, like those of blueberries. The seeds have a delicious almond flavor that comes out when you bake them, he says. And garden writer Sally Roth's recipe for Easy Juneberry Crisp will have your mouth watering in no time.

EASY JUNEBERRY CRISP

Topping

1 cup unsifted all-purpose flour

½ cup rolled oats

1 cup light brown sugar, packed

½ cup butter or margarine, melted

Filling

4 cups Juneberries, or 2 cups Juneberries and 2 cups sliced fresh peaches

½ cup sugar

¼ cup unsifted all-purpose flour

⅛ teaspoon ground nutmeg

½ cup water

Heat oven to 375°F. Combine flour, rolled oats, and brown sugar; stir in butter with a fork to make a crumbly mixture. Set aside. Grease an 8 × 8 × 2-inch baking dish. Combine Juneberries, sugar, flour, and nutmeg in a dish; stir in water. Sprinkle topping over filling. Bake about half an hour until the crumbs are golden. Let stand for 10 minutes while juice thickens. Serve warm with vanilla frozen yogurt.

Let the Sun Do It

Open your fruit trees to good health by letting the sun shine in. Longtime fruit grower Ed Fackler of New Salisbury, Indiana, says "early morning dryout is one basic thing that really helps." He prunes so that the sun can reach into the interior branches of the tree, encouraging flower bud development and successful fruit ripening. "You want to be able to see clear through the tree with no obstructions."

When branches are dense, the drying rays of the sun can't evaporate the moisture and remove the humidity that bring insect and disease problems. Dwarf trees are very easy to prune, notes Ed, and they're easy to fit into even the smallest yard. With fewer branches and less vigorous growth to contend with, you can hone your pruning techniques in a hurry, leading to bountiful crops of good fruit on a healthy, sunlit tree.

fabulous

Flower Gardens

Add a sense of adventure to your flower

garden. Experiment with some wonderful

new annuals and perennials or some

unusual ways to use your tried-and-true

favorites. Try some clever tricks to make

maintenance easier and more fun. Learn

about the latest plant introductions and

creative combinations, then discover

great ideas for soil preparation and

propagation. These hands-on projects

and ingenious tips will brighten your

landscape and keep you in blooms all

season long.

No-Fuss Zinnias

When the weather turns cool and humid, zinnia foliage often turns ugly with powdery mildew. To avoid the mildew mess, try hybrids like 'Profusion Cherry' and 'Profusion Orange'. These mildew-tolerant charmers grow about 1 foot tall and bear single 2-inch-wide flowers.

"They combine the good looks of garden zinnia (*Zinnia elegans*) with the durability of narrow-leaf zinnia (*Z. angustifolia*)," says Nona Wolfram-Koivula, executive director of All-America Selections and the National Garden Bureau.

After the Tourists Leave

When summer comes to Florida, impatiens and geraniums fizzle. But there are heat-loving annuals that provide much-needed color when the temperature turns torrid. "The best annual for heat and drought is the French marigold (*Tagetes patula*)," says Marina Blomberg, garden columnist for *The Gainesville Sun*. "Salvias, verbenas, and moss rose (*Portulaca* spp.) also do well during the summer here."

Scattering the Cosmos

There's no need to start annual flowers indoors, says Pam Ruch, a Pennsylvania garden designer. She has learned from experience that the most reliable way to establish reseeding annuals is to sow seeds directly into the garden and go easy on the mulch. "The time to sow is when the plants are dropping their seeds, anytime from midsummer on, depending on the flower," she says.

Pam carries a supply of envelopes to collect seeds when she visits gardening friends. When she gets home, she empties the seeds into her garden. By the following June, her seedlings are usually well established. Some annuals to start this way include:

- Rocket larkspur (*Consolida ambigua*). Upright spikes of blue, pink, or white flowers.

- Love-in-a-mist (*Nigella damascena*). Feathery foliage; low-growing blue or white flowers. Decorative seedpods follow the flowers.

- Jewels of Opar (*Talinum paniculatum*). Chartreuse green foliage; delicate sprays of tiny, red jewel-like flowers.

- Cleome (*Cleome hassleriana*). Showy, bushy, rosy pink to white flowers.

- Cosmos (*Cosmos bipinnatus, C. sulphureus*). Robust plants with abundant daisylike blossoms in a variety of colors.

Pinwheel Plant Labels

For colorful flower pinwheel labels, Tennessee gardener Dawn Flagg gets the neighborhood kids busy with crayons. Dawn asks them to draw pictures of the flowers she plans to plant. Then she traces the flower outlines on squares of medium-weight cardboard that are marked as shown in the illustration at right. She has the children color both sides of the cardboard with crayons, and then she cuts along the diagonal lines on the cardboard to separate the pinwheel "petals." She also pokes a hole at each corner of the cardboard square, and one in the middle.

To make a pinwheel, Dawn bends two opposite petals backward and the other two petals forward, so that all four corner holes align with the center hole, as shown below.

She pushes a straight pin through the aligned holes to hold the petals in place. Then she pokes the pin through a plastic straw, bends the sharp end of the pin down and tapes it against the straw.

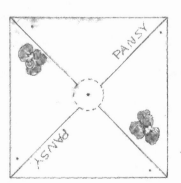

For fun flower labels that twirl in the breeze, decorate cardboard squares and shape them into pinwheels. Attach each pinwheel to a plastic straw "stem," and it's ready for the garden.

Great Blooming Groundcovers

Use annuals as bright ground-covers! It's easy to give your garden a whole new look from year to year just by changing the color scheme of the flowers you select. Try spreading colorful annuals around other flowers in a sunny border, using them to brighten the base of shrubs and trees, or cascading them out of containers. Any of these terrific annual groundcovers will fit the bill:

➢ 'Purple Wave' petunia is a favorite of garden writer Susan McClure. 'Purple Wave' will spread about 4 feet across on long-blooming stems. In addition to 'Purple Wave', you can find newer varieties such as 'Pink Wave', 'Rose Wave', and 'Misty Lilac Wave'.

➢ Tapien verbena hybrids include 'Blue-Violet', 'Lavender', 'Pink', 'Powder Blue', and 'Soft Pink'. They feature lacy foliage and long-blooming flower clusters on 3- to 4-foot-long creeping stems. These heat-loving, mildew-resistant plants are bred for use in hanging baskets or planters. They also grow well in rock gardens or along retaining walls. Ron Ferguson, horticulturist for Bear Creek Gardens in Oregon, likes to plant Tapien hybrids 18 to 20 inches apart to create a carpet of color.

➢ Temari verbena hybrids include 'Bright Pink', 'Bright Red', and 'Violet'. They have large leaves and dramatic baseball-size flower clusters on 3- to 4-foot-long stems.

homegrown HINTS

TROPICALS AS ANNUALS

If you're tired of the same old annuals, look into the increasing array of tropical flowers you can substitute for them. Debbie Lonnee, horticulturist for wholesalers Bailey Nursery in St. Paul, Minnesota, says, "There are many new plants that offer the same long-season interest as plain old geraniums, but these plants have a different look." Try one or all of the following tropicals during the frost-free growing season for a change of pace:

• Mandevilla (*Mandevilla* X *amabilis*): Pink, trumpet-shaped flowers with golden throats emerge all season on large-leaved, drought-tolerant vines. Debbie allows this vine to grow up the handrail at her back step. Plant in full sun.

• Egyptian star cluster (*Pentas lanceolata*): Large clusters of star-shaped pink, lavender, or red flowers on plants that can grow 10 inches high and wide, making an interesting geranium replacement in a container or patio garden. Plant in full sun.

• Candle plant (*Plectranthus forsteri* 'Marginatus'): This trailing plant with white-edged scalloped leaves makes an interesting alternative to periwinkles (*Vinca* spp.) as a groundcover or filler. Plant in sun or shade.

Coax Kids With a *Floral Clubhouse*

An age-old way of fostering a love of gardening in kids is to provide their own garden space. For an ingenious new twist, let them build an easy teepee frame and cover it with annual vines, suggests Dawn Flagg, the youth gardening chairman for the Tennessee Federation of Garden Clubs, Inc. "My kids love their teepee. They take books out there and read for hours," Dawn says.

Start with a dozen 7-foot-long bamboo poles. Space the poles evenly in a 3-foot-wide circle, then insert one end of each pole about 6 inches into the ground at an angle. Tie the tops together with wire or twine to pull the poles into a teepee shape.

Have the children plant some quick-growing vines, such as scarlet runner beans or morning glories (remember to soak the seeds overnight to crack their shells and ensure quick germination). Dawn says, "Annuals are better than perennials because annuals give kids a chance to replant every year."

Create a garden space for kids by building a teepee frame, then help them plant quick-growing annual vines around its base.

problem solver
UPLIFT YOUR ANNUALS WITH BAMBOO

If your potted flowers droop, use bamboo loop supports to keep the stems up. Bamboo, a staple in Japanese gardens, is commonly used in its upright form for tomato staking. To support annual flowers, look for bamboo that has been molded into arches or more upright loops. The arches and loops are perfect for supporting floppy plants like cosmos, which have a tendency to lean.

They also make great supports for vines like periwinkles (*Vinca* spp.) and nasturtiums that like to grow up and over nearby plants. Bamboo is stronger, more flexible, and much more attractive than metal of the same thickness, plus it's lighter and less expensive, says Phil Hallam, bamboo apprentice with Eastern Star Trading Company in Libertyville, Illinois.

Mini-Petunia Equals *Maxi*-Bloom

For more flowers than you can imagine, plant Million Bells *Calibrachoa* hybrids. This hybridized wild Brazilian relative of the petunia has hundreds of tiny, bell-shaped flowers, each one no larger than a quarter, and it blooms for an exceptionally long time, says Jim Sims of Bear Creek Gardens in Oregon. It also tolerates drought more readily than many petunias.

problem solver

SURFINIA PETUNIAS LOVE SUMMER HEAT

For more color and lavish growth than you can imagine from a hanging basket, treat yourself to Surfinia petunias. These tender perennials grow and flower nonstop through the heat of summer, reaching 3 to 4 feet in length. Their extra-vigorous nature stems from their parentage—a large-flowering, creeping, tropical Brazilian petunia that relishes heat. "Fertilize Surfinias each time you water them. They need to be well fed to display their superior vigor," says Charlene Harwood of Bear Creek Gardens in Oregon. Use compost tea or liquid kelp for best results.

Victorian Annuals for Modern Gardens

Look to the past to fill your garden with fragrant flowers. During the opulent Victorian era, every annual garden wafted floral perfumes, reports garden historian Doris Bickford-Swarthout. Here are three easy-to-find annuals that were mainstays in many Victorian gardens:

- Sweet peas (*Lathyrus odoratus*): Sweet peas, fragrant-flower vines that thrive in spring, were a Victorian standard. Beloved favorites still available today are 'Blanche Ferry' (with crimson, pink, and white flowers), 'Butterfly' (with white and mauve flowers), and 'Painted Lady' (with white and rose-pink flowers that climb from 4 to 6 feet high).

- Flowering tobacco (*Nicotiana alata*): Another favorite was flowering tobacco, with long white, pink, or red floral trumpets and a height of 2 to 3 feet. White flowers were popular in Victorian white-night gardens.

- Common heliotrope (*Heliotropium arborescens*): Bearing blue flowers in tight slightly domed clusters, this 2-foot-high beauty was coveted. This annual was originally called by the name cherry pie, despite its vanilla scent.

Fuchsias That Scoff at Heat

If you have trouble with fuchsias that falter in the summer heat, try two new Angel Earrings fuchsia cultivars (*Fuchsia* Angel Earrings hybrids). They continue to thrive after most other fuchsias have given up the ghost.

Bred from wild fuchsias found in hot, tropical Brazil, these great garden annuals revel in heat as long as the soil is kept moist, but not wet. 'Dainty' is compact, growing 9 inches high and 24 inches across. It has small fuchsia-pink petals and purple bells, and its upright habit makes it an ideal bedding plant. 'Cascading' can grow to 4 feet wide and has pink petals and purple bells.

"These fuchsias are really revolutionary. While others collapse in heat, these stay nice and lush," says Ron Ferguson, horticulturist for Bear Creek Gardens in Oregon. He recommends fertilizing Angel Earrings fuchsias three times during the growing season with Epsom salts in addition to using a balanced organic fertilizer like compost tea regularly.

Cherry Tomato Basket **Protects** Bulbs

You can keep burrowing herbivores from chewing on a prized lily, amaryllis, or tulip bulb without paying a cent for protective gear. All you have to do is remember to save plastic mesh baskets from the grocery store, and to place one bulb in each basket when planting. The mesh forms a barrier on the bottom and sides and limits access for hungry critters.

Deep Planting Frustrates Voles

Plant tulip bulbs 10 to 12 inches deep in the soil instead of the usually recommended depth of 6 to 8 inches, and you might escape the destructive tunnels and voracious appetites of voles, says Master Gardener Jan Adams. Voles tend to dig shallow tunnels, so they won't find deep-planted bulbs. Planting extra-deep may also help tulips perform better for a longer time, since it discourages bulbs from multiplying.

Color Fun with **Tulips**

Add a touch of drama to an early spring garden by planting a tulip that changes color as the days go by. 'Georgette', a favorite of Master Gardener Jan Adams, produces a cluster of flowers on each flowering stalk and provides a color-filled show in the garden. "The flowers open a light cream color and then deepen to yellow with a red edge," Jan says. The color changes will provide daily interest.

Bold Foliage *with Bananas*

Bananas aren't just for slicing on cereal and yogurt anymore. Their huge, oblong leaves make them outstanding foliage plants. Dan Benarcik, a horticulturist for Chanticleer Foundation, a public garden in Wayne, Pennsylvania, often uses bananas as a garden high point, surrounding them with other annuals and perennials. Here's a sampling of his favorite plant combinations:

- Blood banana (*Musa zebrina*, also known as *M. sumatrana*) is a burgundy-leaved variety that looks wonderful with 'Inky Fingers' coleus or the red stems of vining Malabar spinach (*Basella alba*). It can grow to 6 feet tall.

- Pink banana (*Musa velutina*) has pale pink flowers that complement purple-leaved 'Chameleon' spurge (*Euphorbia dulcis* 'Chameleon'). The banana plant may grow to 5 feet.

The huge, burgundy leaves of the blood banana make an eye-catching combo with 'Inky Fingers' coleus.

Submerged Pots Stop Vole Damage

One of the main threats to spring-flowering bulbs are voles, which may burrow in tunnels 6 to 8 inches deep, feasting on crocus, hyacinth, and tulip bulbs. Voles may also travel through mole runs to reach your bulbs. One easy way to stop their predations, says Maryland Master Gardener Jan Adams, is to plant susceptible bulbs in plastic pots with drainage holes, setting the pot rim at the soil surface.

"Voles won't go through the plastic, nor will they

come up to the surface to get to the bulbs through the top of the pot," Jan explains.

Protect your spring-flowering bulbs from hungry voles by planting the bulbs in plastic pots with drainage holes.

Circling the Wagons for Tulip Safety

Growing elegant, rainbow-colored tulips is a risky proposition if you have hungry, bulb-eating rodents around who sweep through a planting, eating every bulb. You can defend your tulips, however, by hiding a cluster of tulip bulbs within a circle of daffodils. The daffodils contain bad-tasting, poisonous alkaloids that these pesky herbivores detest.

As host of the Saturday morning radio talk show

Planting for Pleasure with Jan, in Salisbury, Maryland, Master Gardener Jan Adams has offered this antirodent advice many times to her callers.

"I call this the covered wagon method, and in my experience, it seems to work," says Jan. She says to dig a large, flat-bottomed hole 6 to 8 inches deep. Set a cluster of 5, 7, or more tulips of a single cultivar in the center, spacing them 1 to 2 inches apart. Surround them with 11, 13, or more bulbs of a single cultivar of daffodils, also spaced 1 to 2 inches apart. Refill the hole with soil, and rest easy, says Jan.

Foil bulb-eating rodents by planting tulip bulbs within a cluster of daffodil bulbs. The bad-tasting daffodils help deter rodents before they reach your tasty tulips.

problem solver

PLEASING TRANSITIONS

Interplant your beds with daffodils, verbena (*Verbena* spp.), and liriopes (*Liriope* spp.) so that you have flowers in bloom throughout the growing season and great foliage cover to boot, says Maryland Master Gardener Jan Adams.

Jan likes to set daffodils such as 'King Alfred', 'Mt. Hood', and 'Salome' behind 'Silvery Sunproof' liriope (*Liriope exiliflora* 'Silvery Sunproof') and 'Sissinghurst' verbena. The daffodil flowers shine as the cream and green liriope leaves emerge. When the daffodils are fading, the verbena fills in to hide their yellowing leaves. From July to September, liriope sends up dense spikes of purple flowers to finish out the season of color.

Interplanting Bulbs for Dazzling Color Blends

Just as you might underplant a tree with ivy or a rose with violets, you can get double the flower power in your bulb bed by interplanting bulbs of varying heights that bloom at the same time. The resulting two-tiered flower display has more dramatic contrasts in color and texture than ordinary single-species clumps.

In autumn, plant large bulbs deeply, and put a more shallow layer of small bulbs above and around them. In spring, you'll find lower-growing bulbs carpeting the earth beneath taller bulbs. You can also mingle early tulips with later daffodils for a lighthearted blend of colors.

Combining flowers with different textures, colors, and heights creates unique multi-level displays, says Tim Schipper, a third-generation Dutch bulb merchant.

Here are three surefire pairings Tim suggests:

- 'Princeps' tulip and 'White Splendour' Grecian wind-flower (*Anemone blanda* 'White Splendour')

- 'Thalia' daffodil (Triandrus Division) with Armenian grape hyacinths (*Muscari armeniacum*)

- 'Red Emperor' tulip with 'Ice Follies' daffodil

Bulb Storage Success

Wilt-Pruf, an antitranspirant used on evergreens to reduce windburn in winter, also will help tender bulbs overwinter indoors without shriveling. Apply it in the fall, just after you dig up tender bulbs such as cannas, glads, and dahlias. Rinse or shake off any clinging soil and allow the bulbs to dry. Mix a solution of Wilt-Pruf (make a 1:10 dilution with water) and use it to coat the bulbs. Let them dry outdoors in the daylight. Wilt-Pruf will bond into a film that acts as a protective coating to hold in moisture. Store the treated bulbs in boxes of peat moss in a cool basement.

Wilt-Pruf was invented after World War II when people resumed landscaping in the middle of the summer. It was so hot that Dr. Luther Baumgartner came up with the idea of making an anti-transpirant that would reduce wilting problems in newly planted landscapes. Brad Nichols of Wilt-Pruf says that the product is derived from a pine oil resin and can be used to coat foliage, bulbs, or dormant plants.

homegrown HINTS

FUN WITH TULIP FOLIAGE

Instead of expecting the show to be over when tulip flowers fade, try planting a large mass—20, 40, or 60 bulbs of a tulip—with handsome mottled foliage. Tim Schipper, third-generation Dutch bulb merchant, recommends both 'Amazon' and 'Red Riding Hood' for their flowers and foliage. The planting will look great from the moment the leaves appear in spring until they begin to fade weeks later.

Sparkling Complementary Colors

While traditional gardens celebrate spring with massed plantings of identical bulbs, go a step farther by mingling equal parts of two compatibly colored, simultaneously blooming cultivars. "Integrate, don't segregate," says Tim Schipper, third-generation flower bulb merchant.

Start with two tulip cultivars that will flower at the same time in spring and that will look handsome together. Gently toss a large quantity of bulbs over a prepared planting bed, letting them mingle naturally. Plant them where they fall, and adjust the spacing of the bulbs if necessary so that they are no more than 4 inches apart.

"The mix of colors looks great together, even when a few bulbs of the same color end up in a bunch. Like fireworks or a snowflake, no two displays are alike," Tim says. Any of these tulip combinations will provide exciting color next spring:

- 'Orange Emperor' with a deep purple tulip from the Triumph Group

- Red 'Oxford' with white 'Purissima' (also known as 'White Emperor')

- Maroon 'Queen of Night' with yellow 'West Point'

- Pink and white 'Meissner Porzellan' with red 'Kingsblood'

- 'China Pink' and 'White Triumphator'

Forget Flowers, Focus on Foliage

Instead of growing a canna for its flowers, think of its tropical leaves as the star of the show. The brilliant 'Tropicanna' (also known as 'Phasion') has exceptionally vivid foliage and is striped with burgundy, red, pink, yellow, gold, or green.

Judy Glattstein, instructor for the New York Botanical Garden, says, "As foliage plants, cannas are really coming along and can produce the look of the tropics wherever they are planted. I much prefer the leaves to the flowers on modern hybrids and most usually just snip the flowers off."

Judy grows 'Tropicanna' in a large, 22-inch-wide pot beside a half whiskey barrel bearing an apricot-flower angel's trumpet (*Brugmansia* 'Charles Grimaldi') and a black-leaf sweet potato (*Ipomoea batatas* 'Blackie'). 'Tropicanna' is perennial in Zone 7 and south and can grow to 6 feet tall. Further north, dig the rhizome in the fall after the leaves die back, and store it in a cool, dry place until the danger of frost passes in spring.

How to Plant **100 Bulbs** in a Half Hour

Tim Schipper, third-generation bulb merchant, has been planting bulbs the fast-and-easy way for years. His method takes a little muscle, but is extremely efficient and successful.

1. Strip sod from a 5 × 5-foot area of your yard. Remove the soil to a depth of 7 inches, and place it on a large sheet of plywood or on a tarp.

2. Spread 100 tulip or daffodil bulbs across the bulb bed, setting them with their pointed ends up and root ends down. Don't worry if a few tip slightly to the side; they can naturally align themselves for proper growth. Try to avoid planting upside down because this may cause premature bulb failure.

3. Slide the soil off the plywood or tarp and over the bulbs, leveling it with a rake. Firm up the soil with the back of a shovel. When spring arrives, this planting will reward your efforts with a spectacular display of flowers that will outshine an equal number of individually planted bulbs.

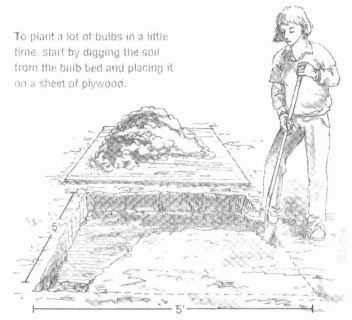

To plant a lot of bulbs in a little time, start by digging the soil from the bulb bed and placing it on a sheet of plywood.

Next, spread the bulbs across the bed with their pointed ends up. Once the bulbs are in place, slide the soil from the plywood back over them.

The **Stars** Are Out in Summer

Make your summer extra-spectacular with big-blossomed summer bulbs and color-coordinated summer perennials. Try these combinations from Viki Ferreniea, horticulturist for Breck's:

- Leichtlin camass (*Camassia leichtlinii*), 'Wargrave Pink' Endress cranesbill (*Geranium endressii* 'Wargrave Pink'), and 'Mrs. Franklin D. Roosevelt' peony. If partial shade is available, add 'Peach Blossom' astilbe and common bleeding heart (*Dicentra spectabilis*)

- Ornamental onion (*Allium ostrowskianum*), 'Silver Brocade' beach wormwood (*Artemisia stelleriana* 'Silver Brocade'), and Chilean shamrock (*Oxalis adenophylla*)

- Star of Persia (*Allium christophii*), 'Royal Purple' purple smoke tree (*Cotinus coggygria* 'Royal Purple'), and white rose campion (*Lychnis coronaria* 'Alba'). Cut the smoke tree branches to the ground each fall to control its size.

A *New Direction* in Climbing Roses

Instead of training climbing roses upright, pin them to the ground, says Judith McKeon, chief horticulturist and rosarian for Morris Arboretum in Philadelphia. The horizontal habit can make roses produce more flowers than ever before. When you use wire "staples" to pin floppy-stemmed roses to the ground, they'll root along the stems and produce strong, upright shoots that bloom heavily—that's why they make great groundcovers. You can try this technique with many of the older roses that have floppy habits like Bourbon and damask, as well as cultivars like 'Louise Odier' and 'Reine des Violettes'.

Turn climbing roses into a beautiful groundcover by pinning each cane to the ground.

Crabby Climbing Roses

Instead of building a trellis for a climbing or rambling rose, use a bare crabapple trunk to support its lovely, lanky stems. In northern climates, try this with super-hardy, disease-resistant Explorer roses, including the unbeatable 'William Baffin'.

Plant a young rose 3 feet from the tree, positioning the rose so that the stems lean toward the trunk. Build a framework of bamboo stakes to support and direct the rose stems up the bottom of the trunk. When the rose canes reach the first tree branch, they will be able to climb on their own.

"I've enjoyed this so much that I used up every crabapple I could find and now am on a quest to find other trees for rambling roses," says Judith McKeon, chief horticulturist and rosarian for Morris Arboretum in Philadephia.

homegrown HINTS

IMPROVING THE BOTTOM LINE OF SHRUB ROSES

Camouflage the barren and prickly bases of mature shrub roses with pretty perennials that offer a beautiful veil of foliage and flowers. Mixing old-fashioned and species roses with other garden plants maximizes their best assets—their height, their bright and fragrant flowers, and their colorful hips—and it minimizes their limitations, including a single season of bloom and occasional naked knees, says Judith McKeon, chief horticulturist and rosarian for Morris Arboretum in Philadelphia. Judith says there are a number of ingenious ideas for dressing up the area around shrub roses.

Remove lower limbs from large rose bushes. Prune just enough to let in sun, and leave space for the spontaneous growth of self-sowing foxgloves (*Digitalis* spp.), larkspurs (*Consolida* spp.), and annual poppies. The colorful annuals will arise around, under, and through the thorny stems.

Underplant with perennials that bloom at the same time. Judith suggests blending yellow-flowered golden rose of China (*Rosa xanthina f. hugonis*) with the petite blue blossoms of Siberian bugloss (*Brunnera macrophylla*). Since complementary, or opposite colors, are so pleasing, you may want to try 'Harison's Yellow' rose (*Rosa × harisonii* 'Harison's Yellow') with 'Purple Sensation' Persian onion (*Allium aflatunense* 'Purple Sensation') or 'Johnson's Blue' geranium (*Geranium* 'Johnson's Blue'). Another good combination is wine-colored French roses (*Rosa gallica* hybrids such as 'Tuscany') with orange-red campions (*Lychnis coronaria*) or yellow-flowered 'Happy Returns' daylily.

Feature a foliage plant at the knees. Underplant lower-growing roses with silver-leaf 'Powis Castle' artemisia. The base of the rosebush will be clothed in a veil of silver with just the bright flowers and hips of the rose emerging through. Silvery lamb's-ears (*Stachys byzantina*) also make handsome partners for low-growing roses. Choose a nonflowering cultivar such as 'Silver Carpet'.

Lobster Traps Lend **Roses** *Lasting* Support

Finding sturdy, weatherproof supports for climbing roses can be difficult, but The Roseraie at Bayfields has discovered that lobster trap metal can be molded into pillars and pyramids and is durable enough to last for years in outdoor conditions. The supports are made from vinyl-coated heavy-gauge wire—the same durable wire that has been used to make deep-sea lobster traps for years. "If it survives in the ocean, you can imagine how well it holds up in the garden," says Lloyd Brace, owner of the mail-order rose nursery.

Instead of being woven into lobster traps, however, the weather-friendly wire mesh has been formed into decoratively shaped supports to hold climbing roses. Lloyd says the support practically disappears from sight as the roses climb and fill out. The three-legged tripod design and four-legged pyramidal shapes should be planted with a rose beside each leg for best coverage. Or one or two legs of the shapes can be planted with clematis for foliage and texture variations.

Moving Made Easy

In an ideal world, you could plant a rose and let it live its entire life in that location—growing bigger and better with age. But in the real world, encroaching shade, a house sale, or a change in your plans for your yard may mean your roses need to move to a new spot. Lloyd Brace, owner of The Roseraie at Bayfields, has a no-fail method for moving roses. "Skeptics who have tried this have had fabulous results. For such a simple thing, it works so well," he says. Here are Lloyd's step-by-step directions for successfully transplanting rose bushes:

1. Scrape out a shallow basin of soil above the rose roots.

2. Attach a spray nozzle to your hose, set it for a hard stream, and turn the water on full blast. Push the nozzle into the soil all around the basin, transforming the entire area into a mud pie.

3. When the earth becomes liquid, you can tease the rose out without losing roots, especially the delicate feeder roots responsible for liquid intake.

4. Transplant the rose immediately, replanting at the same depth it grew at before and watering it well.

Making mud makes it easier to move a rose bush while keeping most of its roots intact.

A Lover's Salad

Toss a little love into your next salad with cabbage rose petals. The old-fashioned cabbage rose (*Rosa × centifolia*) is as edible as it is beautiful, says Barry Dimock, lecturer and writer. "Roses have been a symbol of love for centuries," he says. But he cautions that you should use only organically grown roses from your own garden—never those from a florist.

To use cabbage rose petals, snip off the bitter white base of the petals first, then toss the velvety petals with the rest of your salad ingredients.

For a very special picnic, try dainty rose petal sandwiches (made with homemade bread, butter or cream cheese, and lots of petals).

7-Up for Cut Flowers

Extend the vase life of edible flowers like tulips, roses, pansies, pot marigolds (*Calendula officinalis*), and chives—and keep them edible—by adding a little 7-Up to the water. Mix one part 7-Up with two parts water in a vase before adding the fresh-cut flowers. Don't use florist's preservatives on flowers you might eat.

Fabulous Foliage and Flowers, Too

Instead of growing a rose for flowers alone, try growing one with spectacular leaves. Red-leaf rose (*Rosa glauca*) has tall, arching red canes with eye-catching purple leaves. The single, petite pink flowers play second fiddle to the interesting foliage. "I love this rose for the foliage," says Susan Beard, garden designer and lecturer in Oakbrook, Illinois. Susan also says that wonderful rose hips follow the unassuming flowers. The hips turn orange first, then orange-pink, red-orange, and finally red, she says. And they brighten the garden all winter.

Susan's choices for perennials and shrubs that look stunning next to the beautiful purple foliage of the redleaf rose include:

- White and pink peonies.
- 'Louise Odier' rose, with gray-green leaves and pink flowers.
- 'Purpurea' ground clematis (*Clematis recta* 'Purpurea'), a bush clematis with purple leaves and white flowers.
- 'Roseum' European cranberrybush viburnum (*Viburnum opulus* 'Roseum'), with simultaneously blooming white flowers.
- 'Purple Sensation' Persian onion (*Allium aflatunense* 'Purple Sensation'), with deep purple flower globes.
- Pink Asiatic hybrid lilies and early-blooming lilies in many colors.
- Fall-blooming asters, with mounds of daisylike blooms in rich colors.

Two-for-One Trellises

Get double-duty from your trellises by having them bear an early-summer blooming climbing rose and a later-blooming clematis. Train an old-fashioned climbing rose such as 'Honorine de Brabany' on a trellis or pillar for flowers in early summer. Once the blooms are past, the rose provides quiet greenery through fall. To keep the color coming later in the season, plant a summer- or fall-blooming clematis on the same trellis, suggests Judith McKeon, chief horticulturist and rosarian for Morris Arboretum in Philadelphia. Judith says the clematis will twine up, over, and around the rose and provide a second floral show for late summer.

problem solver — FIBERGLASS PLANTERS IMPROVE WITH TIME

If you like the classic look of planting in big metal urns but can't bear to haul their heavy bulk around, consider using a lightweight fiberglass alternative. New fiberglass planters from Claycraft (available from Smith and Hawken, Gardener's Supply, and Plow and Hearth) have actual metallic finishes fused onto fiberglass resins, which gives the pot an authentic look. The bronze finish develops a verdigris patina as it ages, and the cast iron finish turns a rust color.

"These containers improve with age, like fine furniture does. When their newness wears off, they blend better than ever into the landscape," says Martin Gottlieb, horticulturist. A large pot usually sells for over $100.

homegrown HINTS

IRRIGATION-LESS CONTAINER GARDENS

If you're a city dweller and have a container garden on a rooftop, balcony, or windowsill, you have to make the most of intensely sunny and arid conditions. Instead of running unsightly hoses or irrigation tubing through these "every-inch-counts" gardens, consider the easiest solution: Plant drought-tolerant plants from the aster family (Asteraceae), which includes plants such as marigolds, zinnias, sunflowers, and black-eyed Susans.

Although they will still need water, even daily during hot dry weather, these plants are more likely to survive occasional shortages than impatiens, hostas, and other plants from moisture-loving plant families. Add extra compost to the planting mix, then mulch with cocoa or buckwheat hulls to help retain moisture and further reduce your container garden's water needs.

"These plants evolved in many of the world's hottest and driest geographic locations—Africa, Central and South America, and the Great Plains of North America, for example. They luxuriate in summer's heat and tolerate incredibly lean soils," says Scott D. Appell, urban garden designer, lecturer, and director of education for the Horticultural Society of New York in New York City. Here are Scott's top plant selections for sunny urban container gardens that don't have to be shackled to a tangle of irrigation tubing:

- Mexican sunflower (*Tithonia rotundifolia*), a Mexican annual growing to 7 feet tall and bearing bright orange-red flowers.

Attracts hummingbirds and butterflies even to urban rooftops.

- Common sunflower (*Helianthus annuus*), especially some of the newer, shorter, and less top-heavy cultivars such as 'Pastiche' (a yellow, red, and buff mixture) and 'Italian White' (crisp off-white flowers 4 inches across). Adds height to container plantings and provides a steady supply of cut flowers.

- Narrow-leaf zinnia (*Zinnia angustifolia*), a dainty little plant glowing with orange flowers.

- Signet marigold (*Tagetes tenuifolia*), a diminutive Central American species featuring cultivars such as 'Golden Gem' and 'Lemon Gem'. Has lacy foliage, small blossoms, and some have a citrus odor. A similar species, Irish lace marigold (*Tagetes filifolia*), has finely cut foliage and tiny yellow-green flowers.

- Black-foot daisy (*Melampodium paludosum*), a 12-inch-tall plant covered from early spring to frost with metallic yellow blossoms.

- 'Moonbeam' threadleaf coreopsis (*Coreopsis verticillata* 'Moonbeam'), a hardy and long-blooming perennial for summer and fall. Has creamy yellow flowers and fine feathery leaves.

- 'Magnus' purple coneflower (*Echinacea purpurea* 'Magnus'), produces crimson red coneflowers for about six weeks in summer. Leave the spiky central cones for winter interest and food for goldfinches.

Light Mulching Pleases *Peonies*

To be sure your peonies give you the best bloom, go easy on mulch. "Don't mulch peonies between their stems, and you may not want to mulch them at all," warns Shelia Brackley, perennial production and sales assistant at Bigelow Nurseries, Inc., in Northboro, Massachusetts. Too much mulch around peonies can have the same effect as planting too deeply: They won't bloom. So plant bareroot peonies in early fall, covering the buds, or "eyes," with about 2 inches of soil. Firm the soil from the sides, not the top, so you don't break off any buds.

Fill a Space with *Fragrance*

If you've removed a dying shrub and need to fill a 3-foot-square space, plant the perennial 'Blue Fortune' giant hyssop (*Agastache* 'Blue Fortune'). The leaves have a licorice scent while the steel blue flower spikes attract butterflies and bees, says Mary Ann McGourty, co-owner of Hillside Gardens, Norfolk, Connecticut.

Double-Decker *Decorating*

If you need to liven up a patio or yard for a special occasion, use two-tiered topiaries for quick, yet dramatic, floral displays. The two-tiered topiary system was patented by Mike Ruibal, a garden center owner in Texas, and features a moss- or coco-lined basket supported on a pole that rises from a clay pot bottom.

"I generally use this system when I decorate golf courses for professional tournaments," says Jim Kerwin of Terrona Farms in Peotone, Illinois. Jim plants a showy blend of flowers and interesting foliage to create the "really big show" that he needs for the event. The two-tiered system is also perfect for ivy and seasonal annuals.

The topiary system is available from Ruibal's Topiary Systems, The Horchow Collection, and Alsto's Handy Helpers catalogs; see "Resources" on page 317.

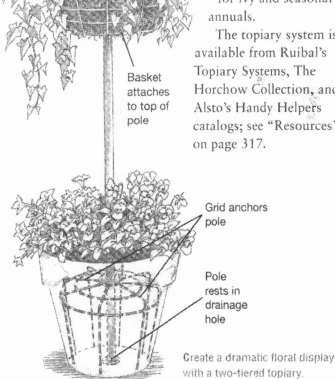

Basket attaches to top of pole

Grid anchors pole

Pole rests in drainage hole

Create a dramatic floral display with a two-tiered topiary.

problem solver

NEW BEE BALM NEEDS NOTHING EXTRA

Bee balm, which has an enticing fragrance and attracts hummingbirds and butterflies, also can get leggy and have mildew problems. These disadvantages disappear with new 'Petite Delight' bee balm (*Monarda didyma* 'Petite Delight'). "It has tight internodes (the sections of stem between sets of leaves), making it half the size of other bee balm cultivars," says Debbie Lonnee, horticulturist for Bailey Nursery in Minnesota. "You can bring it to the front of the border and enjoy its nice foliage and pleasant clump shape." 'Petite Delight' bears clusters of rose-lavender flowers on 12- to 15-inch-high plants.

To care for 'Petite Delight', provide organic-rich, well-drained soil in full sun. Fertilize lightly in spring, remove faded flowers in summer, and cut back the old foliage in fall.

Topsy Turvy No More!

If you like to grow tall bananas, large upright flowers, and other plants that can catch the wind and cause a pot to tip over in a gust or storm, fill the bottom half of the pot with compost. Moist compost, which is heavier than peat-based mix, will help stabilize the pot, says Dan Benarcik, a horticulturist for the Chanticleer Foundation.

Plants for *Doting* Urban *Gardeners*

If you grow potted flowers on a shady balcony or courtyard in a city setting, and you like to water and pamper your plants, try growing calla lilies (*Zantedeschia* spp.) and jack-in-the-pulpits (*Arisaema* spp.). Members of the arum family (Araceae), these plants love compost-laden, manure-rich, moisture-retentive soil, says Scott D. Appell, urban garden designer in New York City. They also thrive in deep shade.

If you're a hands-on, likes-to-fuss gardener, try these plants in the arum family for container gardens in moist, shady locations:

- Italian arum hybrids (*Arum italicum* hybrids), have striking winter foliage in silver, white, lemon-lime, and purple. Cream-color flowers arrive in spring and are followed by clusters of orange berries.

- Caladiums (*Caladium bicolor*, also known as *C. hortulanum*) have large, flamboyantly colored leaves. 'Miss Muffet' has creamy chartreuse foliage flecked with raspberry, and 'Pink Gem' has straplike leaves that range from apricot to raspberry to deep green.

- Mouse plant (*Arisarum proboscideum*) is a little charmer with flowers that resemble mice running with their tails up.

- 'Black Magic' taro (*Colocasia* 'Black Magic') has powdery purple-black leaves that grow to 3 feet long.

- Giant taro (*Alocasia macrorrhiza*) has enormous shield-shaped leaves. 'Hilo Beauty' has smaller, apple green leaves with cream and white variegation. Tolerates full sun if kept moist.

- Imperial taro (*Colocasia esculenta* 'Illustris') has broad, emerald green foliage with black markings. Tolerates full sun if soil is kept moist.

There's Nothing *Cooler* Than Cocobaskets

Make an easy-care flowering basket by using a woven, long coconut fiber (also know as coir) liner in a wire basket frame. Called cocobaskets, these containers have a pleasant earthy color and natural texture. "As growers, we like cocobaskets because they keep plant roots cool. White plastic pots heat up so severely in summer that they can cook the roots," says Fiona Brinks of Bordine Nursery in Detroit, Michigan.

You don't have to water cocobaskets quite as frequently, Fiona says, because the baskets are extra large and hold more soil. Plant roots can even grow into the coconut fiber. If emptied in fall and stored in a dry place during winter, some liners can be reused for three to five years, she adds.

Fiona likes to plant baskets with a combination of yellow, pink, red, and blue flowers and often includes geraniums, Swan River daisies (*Brachycome iberidifolia*), English ivy, marigolds, and impatiens for an interesting, colorful display.

Peat Takes a Back Seat

Replace ordinary potting soil and peat-based planting mixes with coir planting mixes for great performance from potted plants. Coir planting mixes, made of coconut husk fibers and available in some garden centers, hold both nutrients and moisture similarly to composted bark and aren't hard to rewet, like peat-based mixes. They're also naturally richer in phosphorus and potassium. "Although coconut fiber mix is more expensive than peat, plants seem to grow better in it," says Jim Kerwin of Terrona Farms in Peotone, Illinois.

homegrown HINTS

THRIFTY PLANTING MIX DOES SUMMER MAGIC

If you're spending more than you'd like on peat-based potting mix, you can cut your expenses in half and get great performance, to boot. Dan Benarcik, horticulturist for the Chanticleer Foundation in Wayne, Pennsylvania, says compost is the perfect substitute for potting mix.

Dan fills the bottom half of his pots with well-rotted compost—worms and all. Then he tops the pot with peat-based growing mix. "Young plants root fast in the peat mix. By the summer, they have tapped into the moist, rich, and cool compost, which helps them keep growing even when the weather is hot," Dan says.

Enhance plant performance by filling the bottom half of a pot with compost and topping it off with peat-based growing mix.

Making Hosta **Bonsai**

Oriental bonsai, specially trained dwarfed trees or shrubs grown in small trays, is no longer limited to woody plants. Miniature herbaceous perennials and grasses are now accepted in bonsai with a style and grace all their own. Harry Abel Jr., a bonsai enthusiast who's been experimenting with hosta bonsai for 23 years, has an easy, step-by-step procedure for gardeners who want to try their hand at creating hosta bonsai.

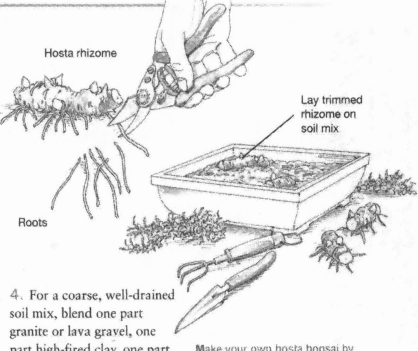

Hosta rhizome

Roots

Lay trimmed rhizome on soil mix

Make your own hosta bonsai by trimming off the thin, white roots of a dormant plant to one inch below the thicker rhizomes. Fill a bonsai bowl with a well-drained soil mix, and lay the rhizome on top of the mix.

1. Dig up a dormant hosta plant before the leaves emerge in spring. Wash the soil off the roots. (If the soil is dry enough, shake it off first, then wash the roots.) Cut off the thin, white roots 1 inch below the thick rhizome.

2. Cut the rhizome to any desired length, but be certain it has at least one growth bud—the tiny white bumps at the base of last year's growth.

3. Select a bonsai bowl that is 1½, 3, or 6 inches deep. Cover the drainage holes with a piece of mesh screen to keep the soil in place.

4. For a coarse, well-drained soil mix, blend one part granite or lava gravel, one part high-fired clay, one part ground pine or fir bark, and one part compost. Add 1 pound of organic fertilizer to each wheelbarrow load of planting mix. Harry doesn't recommend making substitutions because the soil mix's particle size is important to its success. This soil mix will need regular watering.

5. Set the rhizome pieces horizontally on or just beneath the soil surface. You can cover the soil surface with low-growing mosses or little club mosses (*Selaginella* spp.) to hold the soil in place and decorate the surface.

6. Once the leaves emerge, place the pot in as much sun as possible without burning the leaves. The leaf size of the hostas will be reduced proportionately to the container size, but flowers will remain large. Remove any oversize leaves that look awkward. You may want to clip off flower and seed-bearing stems after they're done blooming.

Hosta Ideal for Bonsai

These are Harry Abel Jr.'s favorite hosta cultivars for bonsai.

Small Hosta
'Blue Cadet'
'Butter Rim'
'Chartreuse Wiggles'
'Ginko Craig'
'Ground Master'
'Kabitan'
'Vera Verde'

Large Hosta
'August Moon'
'Halcyon'
'Love Pat'
'Patriot'
'Sum and Substance'
'Wide Brim'

Banana Peels for Roses

Roses love potassium, so Lynne Kosobucki, a home gardener from Philadelphia, uses banana peels as a source of organic potassium. "I'm pretty low-tech with the peels. I just lay them on the ground at the base of the rosebush about 2 to 4 inches away from the stem. I've never had a problem with insects being attracted to the peels," she says.

Match Foliage to Flowers

Mix startling shades of foliage with vivid flowers to create a memorable hanging basket. Judy Glattstein, instructor at the New York Botanical Garden, recommends combining a yellow-and-purple coleus with orange-flowered lantana and purple-leaf 'Purpurea' spiderwort (*Tradescantia pallida* 'Purpurea', also known as *Setcreasea pallida* 'Purple Heart'). "I clearly like to mix it up," Judy says.

Self-Watering Pots for Busy Folks

Container gardening, although it can be easy, fast, and floriferous, requires regular attention to watering. An easy solution to this time-consuming task is a self-watering pot. "It's a relief to know if I go out of town for a weekend, my self-watering potted plants will still look good when I return," says Susan McClure, garden writer.

The Bemis pot, available at nationwide retailers Target and Home Base, uses a perforated platform to keep plant roots above a water reservoir. Feeder roots grow through slots in the bottom of the pot into the moisture below. An opening in the base of the pot lets you refill the reservoir and lets fresh air reach the roots.

problem solver   A TRUE ROCK GARDEN

Instead of growing flowers in plastic or terra-cotta pots, grow them in purchased pumice boulders. These lightweight gray volcanic rocks come drilled with 4- to 6-inch-wide openings—perfect for slipping a pot or plant inside. There's even a drainage hole in the bottom to prevent waterlogged soil. "I like to put bushy plants like mums and ferns in my rock planters on the patio," says Linda Gillespie of Far West Forest. "The natural color of the stone looks good with any kind of flower."

Garden-Lite rock planters, available from Frank's Nursery and Crafts, Gardener's Supply, and Whatever Works catalogs, come in 12- to 18-inch and 18- to 24-inch sizes.

Overwintering Bananas Indoors

If you like big, languid banana leaves in your garden but tire of treating them like annuals and buying pricey new plants every year, try overwintering existing plants indoors. "You don't need a greenhouse—any basement will do," says Dan Benarcik, horticulturist for Chanticleer Foundation in Wayne, Pennsylvania. Leave the banana plant outdoors until just before the first fall frost. Cool weather will slow growth and prepare it for complete dormancy indoors.

Here is Dan's step-by-step process for overwintering bananas indoors.

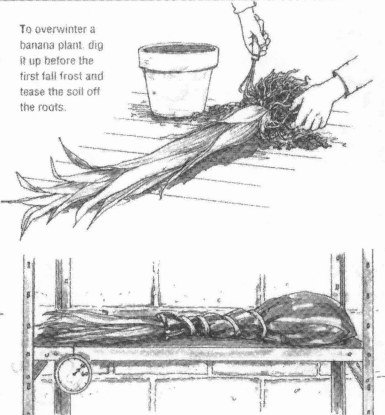

To overwinter a banana plant, dig it up before the first fall frost and tease the soil off the roots.

Wrap the base of the plant in a garbage bag before placing it in a cool, dark basement until spring.

1. Dig up the plant, leaving a 12-inch-wide rootball for a plant with a 6-inch-diameter trunk or an 18-inch-wide rootball for a multi-stemmed clump.

2. Tease most of the soil off the roots with a garden fork.

3. Wrap the base of the plant (up to about 3 feet high) in a heavy-duty, black plastic garbage bag. Tie the top snugly, but not tightly, around the trunk to hold in moisture.

4. Move the banana plant to a dark basement with a temperature of 50 to 70 degrees. It will go dormant and need no further attention until spring.

5. In mid-April, repot the banana plant and move it to a sunny location in the house. Resume watering and fertilizing the plant as you did during the growing season.

6. As the last spring frost date approaches, harden off the plant by moving it outdoors into increasing sunshine for gradually longer periods. Once it is acclimated and the weather is frost-free, the banana plant can stay outdoors in a pot or you can transplant it into a garden bed to grow in the ground until next fall.

problem solver

PERENNIAL MEADOW FOR WHEELCHAIR USERS

Wheelchair users can also be gardeners with their own easily tended colorful pocket meadow. Even the smallest meadows, just a few square yards in size, can bring great joy, says Steven Davis, former executive director of the American Horticultural Therapy Association. Choose easy-care perennials that don't need lots of hugs and kisses from the gardener, such as spike gayfeather (*Liatris spicata*), Ozark sundrops (*Oenothera missouriensis*), black-eyed Susan (*Rudbeckia hirta*), and purple coneflower (*Echinacea purpurea*). These perennials need only simple care—dead-heading, watering, weeding, and winter cleanup.

Start the meadow by broadcasting seed, a task that can be done from a wheelchair. You'll need to thin the seedlings to avoid overcrowding—this can be accomplished fairly easily if the gardener has a lightweight, long-handled hoe. Use the corner of the hoe to uproot individual or small clumps of unwanted seedlings when they are only several inches high. "The key is to involve gardeners with disabilities in the gardening tasks and have them benefit physically as well as mentally from working the garden," Steven says.

Sense-Stimulating Perennials for Seniors

"Flowers are a great way to reach out to older adults, especially those who once counted gardening as their favorite pastime," says Steven Davis, former executive director of the American Horticultural Therapy Association. If you plant flowers and grasses that stimulate the senses of smell, touch, sound, and sight, your garden will appeal even to older people who may have weakened senses.

Plant scented geraniums or heirloom roses (especially fragrant cultivated varieties more familiar to older adults) and furry lamb's-ears (*Stachys* spp.) that will provide tactile pleasures. Long-leaf ornamental grasses will add sound to the garden as their leaves rustle in the breeze, and butterfly-attracting plants like butterfly bushes (*Buddleia* spp.) will delight the eyes.

Pulmonarias for *Foliage* and *Flowers* in Shade

When planting a shade garden, look to the new pulmonarias for stunning silver leaves and attractive flowers. These silvery *Pulmonaria* hybrids make great groundcovers and look terrific with purple-leaf heucheras (*Heuchera* spp.) and silver-variegated Japanese painted fern (*Athyrium niponicum* 'Pictum'), says hybridizer Dan Heims of Terra Nova Nurseries in Oregon. He's also excited about the flowers on these cultivars. "The flowers are borne on compact stems instead of the old ungainly stalks that flop or break in the wind. They were selected for their rosette shape and shortened petioles, so they don't flop in the wind," Dan says.

Dan's pulmonaria hybrids have exciting features like ruffle-edged silver leaves, undulating silver foliage complemented by raspberry-pink flowers, and silver leaves edged in green. Ask your local garden center to order some of Dan's plants, or order them by writing to one of Terra Nova Nurseries' vendors (see "Resources" on page 317).

problem SOLVer

NEW KID ON THE BLOCK

Move over hostas, there's a new foliage plant for the shade garden, says Tony Avent, hybridizer at Plant Delights Nursery in Raleigh, North Carolina. It's the sacred lily of Japan (*Rohdea japonica*), a treasure seldom seen in America. Sacred lilies grow easily in dry, shady soil in Zones 6 through 10. In Zone 5, they die back during winter and take longer to reach full size.

The species has 1-foot-long and 2-inch-wide straplike leaves and grows into a vase-shaped clump about 2 feet wide. In the fall, the plants display clusters of red berries that harmonize with the surrounding autumn colors.

Fancy-leaf forms include 'Asian Valley', which has wavy green leaves bordered with a narrow edge of creamy white. 'Mure Suzume', a miniature, makes small rosettes of white-streaked leaves. 'Suncrest' has black-green leaves with a white dragon crest running down the center of each.

A Collection for Small Spaces

If you like to experiment with a variety of new perennials, devote a special part of your yard to making a collector's garden. Ruth Rogers Clausen, perennial collector and horticulture editor for *Country Living Gardener* magazine, suggests starting in a small space and focusing on just a few plants. For example, put a few alpines in a stone trough, or devote an area to just one genus like *Dianthus* (pinks). "When you focus on specific plants, you'll have an opportunity to dig into their folklore, uses, and other interesting details that make the garden so much richer," Ruth says.

She also says to forget about elaborate garden designs and concentrate on giving your plants the best growing conditions you can. Ruth tries to duplicate the plants' original habitat, soil makeup, and moisture needs. She often grows the same plant in several different parts of the garden, then compares results before finding a permanent location for that special plant in her collection.

No-Spray Garden Phlox

While many forms of garden phlox (*Phlox paniculata*) suffer from powdery mildew unless sprayed regularly with fungicides, one cultivar stands alone for exceptional disease resistance. 'David', a beautiful white phlox, is not quite mildew-proof, but it does come close, says Mary Ann McGourty. 'David' is fragrant, grows to about 4 feet high, and bears large flower trusses from July to September.

This Astilbe Will Be *Big*

A perfect perennial for milder areas, the monstrously large, purple-leaf giant astilbe (*Astilbe grandis*) has a 5-foot-wide basal rosette and a 5-foot-high flower spike. Growing from seed to flowering size in just 1½ years, this new discovery was found in Asia, where plant collector Tony Avent of Plant Delights Nursery travels in search of promising perennials. This astilbe will make an exciting conversation piece for your garden, says Tony.

Save Time with Hedge Shears

Use handheld hedge shears for fast and easy trims of bushy plants like asters, mums, and boltonias (*Boltonia* spp.), says Tracy DiSabato-Aust, author of *The Well-Tended Perennial Garden*. The long blades can do the job in 1 or 2 cuts instead of the 10 to 20 required by shorter pruning shears. Most perennials benefit from pinching, shearing, or cutting back to keep the rest of the plant looking nice during spring, summer, and fall, says Tracy. She uses hedge shears for the following jobs:

Shearing back the tips of mums, asters, and sedums in spring to encourage bushier, self-supporting plants.

Cutting off old flowers on pinks (*Dianthus* spp.), thrifts (*Armeria* spp.), rock cresses (*Arabis* spp.), and others after they bloom.

Removing old foliage of ornamental grasses and coneflowers (*Echinacea* spp,) in spring, or old leaves of peonies and other perennials in fall.

Make quick work of removing old foliage from ornamental grasses by simply trimming them with handheld hedge shears.

A *Tidy* Drink of *Water*

Allentown, Pennsylvania gardener Deb Martin has found an easy way to water the plants on her office windowsill without making a mess. She fills a sport-top water bottle with water, then directs the water stream at the plants' roots. The plants get the moisture they need, and Deb's windowsill stays moisture-free.

homegrown HINTS

BONSAI SCISSORS FOR TIGHT SPACES

Have you noticed that the new buds emerging on long-blooming perennials like bellflowers (*Campanula* spp.) and balloon flowers (*Platycodon* spp.) are commonly right next to the fading flowers you're trying to deadhead? If your handheld pruning shears tend to damage future flowers, use slim and sharp bonsai or never-dull scissors to slip into the smallest spaces and remove dead flowers.

"Bonsai scissors allow for careful deadheading and are the right size for small hands, too," says Tracy DiSabato-Aust, author of *The Well-Tended Perennial Garden*. Look for bonsai scissors at well-stocked garden centers, or order from mail-order garden and specialty suppliers.

homegrown HINTS

UMBRELLAS FOR VINES

When Richard Szalasny found a discarded table-size umbrella, he put it to good use in his garden: He removed the fabric cover and inserted the pole into a pipe that he'd driven into the ground. He planted morning glories and let them spill over the skeleton of the umbrella. "With the right vine, all the spokes can be covered," says Dick, a Master Gardener from Eden, New York. You could also create a smaller version by using a regular hand-held umbrella.

Wintering Mums under Plastic Pots

If your chrysanthemums seldom survive winter, they may be perishing due to intense cold or soggy soils. You can avoid both problems by wintering your chrysanthemums in a double-deck set of pots in your garage. "I saved six plants using this method last year. They came through like real troupers and awed me with flowers from late July through September," says David Glasier, Ohio experimental amateur gardener and television critic. Here is David's step-by-step method:

1. Cut down mum shoots to 1 inch as soon as the plant has finished blooming.

2. Dig up the rootball and gently knock away excess clods of soil. Put about 2 inches of fresh potting soil in the bottom of a pot. Place the rootball in the pot, then cover the rootball with potting soil.

3. Water the soil enough to make the roots moist. Let the pot sit outside for a day to drain well.

4. Cover the pot with a slightly larger, inverted plastic pot that fits snugly rim to rim. The top pot must have drainage holes for air circulation.

5. Store the double-deck pots in a protected but unheated place, like a garage or shed.

6. Several weeks before the last frost date, remove the top pot. The plants will have sent up yellow-green sprouts. Water and lightly fertilize. Gradually move the mums into brighter light until the leaves green up.

7. Plant the mums out in the garden after the danger of spring frost passes.

Holes for air circulation

Save your chrysanthemums from winter's elements by cutting them back, digging them up, and keeping them in a pair of pots in your garage.

Reliable, **Easy**, and a **New** Look to Boot

Even though some gardeners consider the bell-shaped flowers of Jacob's ladder (*Polemonium caeruleum*) the stars of the show, the foliage on a new variety, 'Brise d'Anjou', will give the pretty flowers a run for their money. 'Brise d'Anjou' flaunts creamy-edged, fernlike foliage that looks like the rungs of a ladder.

Gary Doerr, owner of wholesale Peppergrove Nursery in Lapeer, Michigan, says 'Brise d'Anjou' grows in Zones 4 to 8 and should be planted in light to full shade and moist, rich, well-drained soil. It combines nicely with goat's beards (*Aruncus* spp.) and can be massed with astilbes, bergenias (*Bergenia* spp.), hostas, Lenten rose (*Helleborus orientalis*), and sweet woodruff (*Galium odoratum*).

problem solver

INSECT-EATING PERENNIALS IN A POT

Put perennials to work eating unwanted flies, mosquitoes, and other pests by planting insectivorous pitcher plants in a containerized bog garden. Karen Colini, landscape horticulturist with Sweet Bay Gardens in Ohio, says the bog garden is beautiful, easy to maintain, and fascinating to watch in action.

Pitcher plants, which naturally grow in sterile, acidic bogs, use insects as fertilizer. Their tube-shaped leaves contain insect-attracting nectar. Flies and other creatures slip down into the tube and are held there by a barrier of downward-pointing hairs. The insects break down into nitrogen and other necessary elements for pitcher plant growth.

Karen grows pitcher plants with sphagnum moss, bog cranberry (*Vaccinium macrocarpon*), and bog rosemary (*Andromeda polifolia*) in a black plastic cement mixing tub filled with water. She uses hardy species of pitcher plants that can stay outside during winter without any problem. "All I do to take care of them is fill the tub with water when it begins to get dry," says Karen.

For pitcher plant sources, see "Resources" on page 317.

The *Glories* of the *Gazing Ball*

Don't be an outsider in your own garden! "Gazing balls allow you to see yourself in the garden, rather than just being a passive admirer," says C. Colston Burrell, garden writer and lecturer. Bask in the glory of all that growing by adding a gazing ball—a mirrored globe of blue, purple, gold, green, or another color—to your flowerbeds.

Cole has five gazing balls in his garden. He says that gazing balls are an important color element, and he coordinates them with the colors of nearby flowers. He uses bright yellow and blue gazing balls in his shady garden, and purple gazing balls beside yellow and purple perennials in his sunny garden.

Timely tip

Instead of placing gazing balls on the ground where they might be hidden by surrounding foliage, make them seem even more magical by raising them up on nearly invisible supports. Cole suggests elevating a gazing ball on the bottom of a metal tomato cage or tall votive candle holder, which can raise a gazing ball 1 to 3 feet high.

The More, the Merrier

Double your perennial garden pleasure by planting two perennials in a single space, says Illinois garden designer Harriet Kelly. Dual plantings provide the extra color and support that make a perennial garden beautiful, right from the start.

"If you only put a single plant in each space, perennials like 'Johnson's Blue' geranium (*Geranium* 'Johnson's Blue') will flop until a couple years down the road when the garden gets crowded enough to hold the plants together," Kelly says. Plant 'Johnson's Blue' close beside purple coneflowers (*Echinacea* spp.) or 'Zagreb' threadleaf coreopsis (*Coreopsis verticillata* 'Zagreb') because they provide support and a summer season of bloom, she says. Here are other effective interplanting ideas:

- 'Mrs. Kendall Clark' meadow cranesbill (*Geranium pratense* 'Mrs. Kendall Clark') with cardinal flower (*Lobelia cardinalis*).

- Bigroot cranesbill (*Geranium macrorrhizum*) with daylilies.

- Armenian cranesbill (*Geranium psilostemon*) with betony (*Stachys macrantha*).

- Drumstick chives (*Allium sphaerocephalum*) with bluebeard (*Caryopteris* × *clandonensis*).

Peonies That Won't Flop

Peonies, which have one short, glorious bout of bloom in spring, can be knocked flat by a drenching downpour. You can eliminate that problem by selecting plants carefully, says Harriet Kelly, landscape designer for Kelly Gardens. "People in the Chicago area complain a lot about flopping peonies," Harriet says. "That's why I try not to plant big, full-headed peonies, and I stick with smaller-flower Japanese singles, instead. The singles don't get heavy and waterlogged, nor do they fade and look like old tissues."

Selecting peonies based on flower type alone is not enough, though. Harriet inspects the bottom of the stem of a nursery plant, checking the distance between the leaf nodes. A shorter internode, the space between leaves, means a stockier stem and a self-supporting plant. 'Dawn Pink', a single pink-flower peony, 'Heritage', a semi-double red-flower peony, and 'Doreen' garden peony, a single pink, have passed Harriet's internode test for self-supporting peonies.

Internodes

When selecting peonies, check the distance between the leaf nodes. Short internodes mean stockier stems and self-supporting plants.

Dry Summer? Try a Durable Daisy Tree

Most gardeners recognize a daisy flower, but there aren't many people who have seen a daisy tree. This drought-tolerant plant comes from South Africa and is perfect for a large pot on your patio. "The daisy tree (*Euryops pectinatus* 'Viridis') blooms all summer, even when I forget to water it," says Julie Andracki, an Indianapolis-based member of the staff of Monrovia Nurseries. "It doesn't mind drying out be- cause it's a desert plant. If it wilts, it pops back up as soon as it gets water."

The so-called daisy tree, which is actually a shrub known as the golden shrub daisy, features finely cut, bright green leaves and 2-inch-wide golden daisylike flowers. Provide full sun with a little afternoon shade in the heat of the day for best results. Because the golden shrub daisy is hardy only to Zone 8, Julie discards it in fall. In warm climates, she says, you can enjoy its flowers for years.

homegrown HINTS

THIS FALSE SUNFLOWER IS TRULY UNIQUE

Consider planting a mass of brilliant new 'Loraine Sunshine' sunflower heliopsis (*Heliopsis helianthoides* 'Loraine Sunshine') for the unusual variegated foliage as well as its golden flowers, says Brent Hanson, plant introducer from Rhinelander Floral Company in Wisconsin. The remarkable foliage is white with green veins and is the only variegated false sunflower known in the world, says Brent. The plant was named in memory of Rhinelander employee Loraine Mark, who discovered it growing in her garden.

The sunflower heliopsis will grow in a wide range of conditions, but it does best in full sun and average soil that doesn't dry out. The plant will reach 30 inches tall, grows in Zones 3 to 9, and blooms from July until frost.

Pretty as a Picture

Make your perennial garden look beautiful the first year by adding unusual annuals and tender perennials to fill out the spaces between the young perennials, says C. Colston Burrell, garden writer and lecturer. He likes to use fast-growing flowers that have a natural look. Cole says moss verbena (*Verbena tenuisecta*) is a good choice because it weaves nicely between the smaller perennial plants.

Cole also recommends Texas sage hybrids (*Salvia coccinea* hybrids), nicotianas (*Nicotiana langsdorffii, N. sylvestris*), tall hybrids of flowering tobacco (*Nicotiana alata*), and Brazilian vervain (*Verbena bonariensis*).

Timely tip

For a quick-maturing perennial garden that's full of just perennials, plant cranesbills (*Geranium* spp.), coreopsis (*Coreopsis* spp.), bee balms (*Monarda* spp.), ajuga (*Ajuga* spp.), creeping phlox (*Phlox stolonifera*), gold-and-silver chrysanthemum (*Chrysanthemum pacificum*), and Japanese anemone (*Anemone tomentosa* 'Robustissima'), suggests Cole.

Getting into the Swim with Cannas

Instead of growing cannas in soil, slip a few into a bog, water garden, or pond for a colorful garden scene that won't need weeding or watering. Cannas love a lot of water and are swamp plants in the wild, says Judy Glattstein, instructor for the New York Botanical Garden. She says to pot the rhizomes and set the pot in a shallow pan of water. After several days, increase the depth of the water. Keep increasing the depth of the water every few days until water covers the top of the roots—this will gradually acclimate the root system. Try this with 'Tropicanna', 'Taney', and 'Erebus' cannas.

Purple-Leaf Cannas Shine in Good Company

For a spectacular display of color in a garden of green foliage, combine purple-leaf cannas with blossoms of clear red, green, or purple, says Judy Glattstein, instructor at the New York Botanical Garden. Or use maroon-highlighted flowers for a more subtle color mix.

Start by planting 'Black Knight', 'Red King Humbert', or 'TyTy Red' cannas, then add any of the following: gladiolus (*Gladiolus callianthus*), clear red zinnias, green-flower 'Envy' zinnia, nicotiana (*Nicotiana langsdorffii*), or purple-flower Brazilian verbena (*Verbena bonariensis*).

Hot Daylilies for Warm Climates

If you want to grow daylilies in hot climates, says Florida garden writer Marina Blomberg, choose heat-tolerant evergreen cultivars with light-colored flowers, such as the following (most are available through mail order from Daylily Discounters; see "Resources" on page 317):

- 'Apple Tart', red with a green throat.
- 'Becky Lynn', rose with a white midrib.
- 'Cosmic Hummingbird', pink-peach with honey yellow.
- 'Green Glitter', yellow with a green throat.
- 'Irish Elf', lemon-chartreuse.

More Daylilies for Your Money

While conscientious deadheading keeps daylilies looking neat, it eliminates a propagation possibility. On some daylily cultivars, the old flower stems produce proliferations (minature plants that emerge on the stem below a faded flower). Dr. Winston Dunwell, associate professor of horticulture at the University of Kentucky, says, "If you can use the profilerations to multiply a $100 plant into two plants, you will come out ahead."

Watch for proliferations in late summer. They arise from a bud that grows into a little cluster of leaves and, by August and September, also sprouts tiny roots. Cut them free, roots and all, and move them to a separate pot. Or plant them beside the mother plant for easy identification, suggests Dr. Dunwell.

Some of the daylily cultivars that may sprout proliferations include: 'Coral Crab', 'Fairy Tale Pink', 'Lullaby Baby', 'Prairie Blue Eyes', and 'Siloam Red Toy'.

Have Your *Daylily* and *Eat It Too*

Don't limit yourself to a visual feast when your daylilies are in bloom. Use their flowers and buds as unique vegetables. Barry Dimock, plant consultant, lecturer, and writer, says fresh daylily flowers, minus their pistils and stamens, are a great addition to a salad. You can use the chopped petals, whole flowers, or about-to-open buds. "Lightly sauteed buds (in unsalted butter, of course) make a delightful vegetable offering to many dishes," says Barry. "And people who have a good collection of these enduring perennials in their garden can enjoy dining on the varieties as they bloom in sequence."

Even **Watering** Top to Bottom

If the water runs out of the holes in your strawberry pot when you try to water your

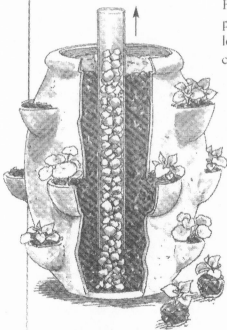

To create a watering channel in a strawberry pot, add planting mix around a cardboard tube filled with pebbles. After planting, slide the tube out.

plants, Pennsylvania landscape architect Joan Meschter has a solution that helps the bottommost plants in the jar get the crucial water they need. First, hold a cardboard wrapping paper tube (at least as long as the pot is tall) vertically in the center of the pot and fill it with pebbles, perlite, or sand. Then add soil mix and plants around it, working up from the bottom holes. Wrap each seedling in sheet sphagnum moss to protect the roots from drying out.

When the pot is fully planted and is filled with planting mix, gently slide the tube out, allowing the draining medium to settle into place. Plant the top, leaving the center open for watering. Now when you water, even the bottom plants will get their share.

Prevent Winterkill with *Summer Water*

To prevent winter losses among your roses, be more conscientious about summer watering, says Lloyd Brace, owner of The Roseraie at Bayfields. In August, roses produce fewer flowers and begin to store energy for the spring in their roots. Even though it doesn't look like the roses are growing, it's vital that they have enough water during this time in order for the roots to support new spring growth. A typical rose plant needs 2 to 3 gallons of water every five to seven days.

Plan to water your roses during the whole growing season, right up until the ground freezes, says Lloyd. If you can't be home, he recommends hiring a neighborhood kid or installing an automatic watering system.

Put a **Pomegranate** on *Your* Patio

The pomegranate (*Punica granatum*), a tropical shrub hardy in Zones 8 to 10, is well known for its juicy red fruit. But you don't have to live in warm southern climates to enjoy the pomegranate's delightful foliage and flowers. "I leave my tree out through a light frost or two until it drops its leaves and goes dormant. Then I slide it over to my attached, unheated garage and leave it there until spring," says Julie Andracki, an Indianapolis gardener and staff member of Monrovia Nursery.

Pomegranate stems arch like a fountain, reaching about 4 feet high when grown in a 12- to 18-inch patio pot. The glossy foliage is blushed with red when it emerges and matures into handsome dark green. The tree should be watered generously until it's growing strong, then it can tolerate some drought.

Try fancy-flower pomegranate cultivars like 'California Sunset' (coral red flowers with light stripes on the petals), 'Nochi Shibari' (double-flower and dark red), 'Toyosho' (double-flower, pale apricot, and shaped like a tree peony flower). Annuals that make bright combinations with pomegranates include red-leaved amaranth, 'Strawberry Fields' globe amaranth, and red- or orange-flowered New Guinea impatiens.

homegrown HINTS

BANANAS BEYOND THE TROPICS

Even if you live in a cool climate, you can enjoy the tropical lushness of growing banana plants without hauling tender plants in for the winter. Try Japanese banana (*Musa basjoo*), which is hardy to Zone 7 and even persists in protected areas in Zone 6. "It can be a real pleasure to grow a banana that provides repeat performances in moderately cold climates," says Dan Benarcik, a horticulturist for Chanticleer Foundation, Wayne, Pennsylvania.

Peanuts for Cannas

If peanuts used for packing drive you nuts, use them to help canna roots overwinter, says Erie County, New York, Master Gardener Tom Smith. Pack your canna roots in recycled packing peanuts and sprinkle lightly with water for winter storage. "The past two years I've placed canna roots in the peanuts inside both cardboard boxes and empty dog food bags and stored them in a cool corner of my basement. They've weathered the winter quite well," says Tom.

Squat Pots *Minimize* Watering

If you'd like to water your potted plants less often, plant your container garden in squat pots. Squat pots are large-diameter pots, about half the height of standard upright pots but twice as wide. Because of the squat pot's shape, less water drains out of it, giving you double the moisture reserves of standard pots. And the more moisture that stays in the soil, the less you have to water.

problem solver

CAPTURE 'NEARLY WILD' ROSES

For untamed color with minimal effort, plant large clusters of 'Nearly Wild' rose (*Rosa* 'Nearly Wild') in your sunny flower and shrub gardens. 'Nearly Wild' has five-petaled pink flowers and blooms vigorously from late spring through the middle of fall. It grows into handsome rounded bushes 3 to 4 feet high and is one of the most durable roses, resisting most diseases.

'Nearly Wild' looks particularly good when mass-planted and paired with anything containing blue or gray, like Russian sage (*Perovskia atriplicifolia*) or 'Longwood Blue' bluebeard (*Caryopteris* × *clandonensis* 'Longwood Blue'), says Tim Wood, horticulturist for wholesale Spring Meadow Nursery in Grand Haven, Michigan.

Mycorrhizae Give Roses a Healthy Start

Help your newly planted bareroot roses regain the beneficial mycorrhizal fungi that were lost when the plant was prepped for selling and shipping. Use mycorrhizal mycelium, a vegetative fungal growth that has been dried and chopped until it looks like cornmeal, as a soil amendment or fertilizer supplement. Mycorrhizal fungi are important because they help roses, flowers, trees, and other plants gather phosphorus when the soil is lacking in nutrients. The mycelium is available from The Roseraie at Bayfields; see "Resources" on page 317.

Roses that are sold bareroot are subject to all kinds of fungal invasions when they're stored and shipped, says Lloyd Brace, owner of The Roseraie. "We do all we can to keep the roots clean, including sterilizing them with a diluted bleach solution. This, unfortunately, kills any natural mycorrhizal fungi as well as disease organisms." Lloyd believes it's important to return rose roots to their natural balance, putting back the mycorrhizal fungi that were washed off. He says it's particularly helpful in new or nutrient-poor gardens where the mycorrhizae make conditions better for rose growth.

Quick Color from Coleus Cuttings

When a pot of annuals faded into obscurity at midsummer, Deb Martin, an Allentown, Pennsylvania, organic gardener, wanted something to fill the gap in her container garden. Spotting some coleus that needed to be pinched back, she nipped off the tops from a few of her favorites and stuck them into the moist potting soil of the empty pot.

"I was really pleased when they rooted and started growing," Deb says. "All it took was careful attention to keeping the cuttings well-watered for a couple of weeks, and I ended up with a free pot of coleus."

Timely tip

Location is everything when it comes to container plant survival, Deb says. "I've killed many potted plants over the years by putting them in spots where I didn't see them very often." This year, Deb created a large container garden along the sidewalk leading to her front door. "I walk past those plants at least twice a day—so they always get water when they need it."

lively

Landscaping Techniques

When you look around your yard, the view

should make you sigh with contentment.

After all, your landscape is a reflection of

your own style and taste. In this chapter,

we'll help start you down the path to a

landscape you'll love—or help you make

a good one even better—by offering tips

on plant selection, problem solving,

maintenance, design, and more. We've

chosen ideas that are ingenious, yet rel-

atively simple to execute. That way, you'll

still have time to sit back and enjoy the

fruits of your labor at the end of the day.

264

Uniting Soil and Water

When designing a water garden, you might want to forgo rocks piled around the edges. They can be overbearing and unnatural-looking, especially in small settings, says Edd Harris, who has been a pond gardener in Pueblo, Colorado, for 16 years. Instead, consider preserving the lawn as close to the edge of the water as possible and using a concrete and gravel slope or edge as a buffer between the water and the soil.

A concrete and gravel edge that extends about 6 inches into the lawn and about 2 feet into the pond water has a much more natural look, Edd says. Plus, this type of edge works well for hiding the pond liner. It's also sturdier than a rock edge, which may cave in if you step on it.

This type of edge allows for easy mowing around the pond, too. Remember to run the mower so that the grass clippings are blown into the yard instead of into the pond. You may want to catch the clippings in your mower bag or rake them up afterward to keep them out of the water.

Stone Substitution

If you use heavy stones to hold down a water garden liner, they may cause the sides of the pool to collapse, especially if the water overflows during a heavy rain, warns Doug Akers, Purdue Cooperative Extension Educator for Boone County, Indiana. To avoid a collapse, edge your water garden with thin stone, such as Pennsylvania flagstone. Thin stone has another advantage, Doug points out. It's lighter, so it's easier to handle.

Wise Ways with Wheelbarrows

A wheelbarrow is essential for many landscaping projects, but simply lifting and pushing a wheelbarrow can be enough to land you in the examining room. To avoid injuring your back, the secret is to balance your load properly. Always put the load or the heaviest part of the load to the *front* of the wheelbarrow, advises Andrea Morgante, co-owner of Siteworks in Hinesburg, Vermont. "Keep your knees and elbows bent as you lift the load, then straighten them out when you're on your way."

problem SOLVeR WATER GARDEN HARDWARE

Looking for inexpensive water garden containers? Take a walk around your local hardware store, suggests Brian Greary, owner of Northern Lights Landscape in Williamsville, New York. Barrel inserts are readily available and work well for 2½- to 3-foot-deep water plantings. For plants that prefer shallow water, such as cardinal flower (*Lobelia cardinalis*) and chameleon plant (*Houttuynia cordata*), 8-inch deep plastic cement mixer trays are ideal.

Keeping Corners Square

Here's how to maintain a square corner when installing a fence manufactured in 4-foot sections. Tie a string to the post at the corner and measure out 3 feet toward where you want the next post to turn the corner. Temporarily mark your place by tying the string around a stake. Measure with the other end of the string 5 feet back to the next-to-last post from the end, and tie the string to the post. Adjust the stake until the string is taut. You can use multiples of these ratios, such as 6, 8, and 10 feet, if your fence sections come in 8-foot lengths.

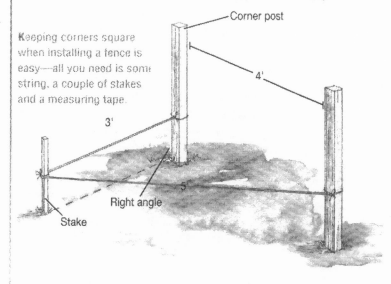

Keeping corners square when installing a fence is easy—all you need is some string, a couple of stakes and a measuring tape.

Corner post

4'

3'

5'

Right angle

Stake

No More Chain Links

If you need a fence to keep critters out and pets in, but you don't care for the look of chain links, try this setup. Install cedar post-and-rail fencing, and staple green vinyl-coated wire mesh to the posts and rails. Plant your favorite vine next to the fence, and soon you'll hardly see the mesh. Plus, the cedar posts will resist rotting and will weather naturally without requiring paint.

Fence *Face-Lift*

You can dress up an ugly stockade fence with lattice. Simply buy ready-made lattice at a home improvement store or construct your own. Once attached, the lattice becomes a support for climbing vines such as clematis, honeysuckle, or trumpet vine. Or be more creative and use it to support specially pruned trees and shrubs, such as espalier.

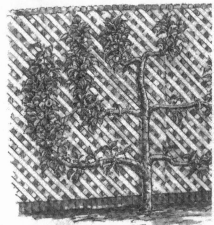

Prefabricated lattice turns an unsightly stockade fence into a trellis for vines or espalier.

Keeping Posts *Plumb*

Installing fencing can be tricky, especially on a slope. The key is to keep the posts plumb. Here's how: As you set each pole in place, hold a carpenter's level against the side of the post, and adjust the post until the level is plumb. Then carefully backfill the hole, making sure you don't push the post out of position as you work. When you install the fencing, follow the slope, twisting the sections a little to climb the slope as you go (there's always some give in the framework). Or, step the sections up the slope as shown in the illustration below.

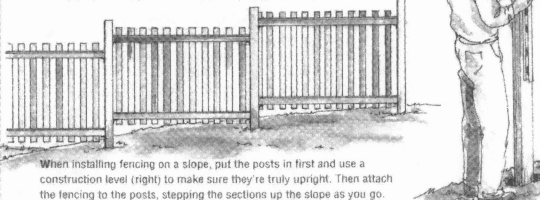

When installing fencing on a slope, put the posts in first and use a construction level (right) to make sure they're truly upright. Then attach the fencing to the posts, stepping the sections up the slope as you go.

problem solver

THYME-LY ADVICE

A bit of borax can help keep a thyme groundcover growing strong when the heat is on. Low-growing thyme is one of the best groundcovers to plant between stepping stones, because it can withstand being stepped on—it even gives off a pleasant herbal scent when crushed underfoot. But in the middle of summer, when rainfall is scarce and the hot summer sun beats relentlessly down on surrounding paving stones, the heat can burn thyme foliage. So before your thyme dries out in hot weather, water it with a mixture of 1 tablespoon borax to 1 gallon water. "Water with this mixture only once a year, and it will prevent the burning," says Shelia Brackley, perennial production and sales assistant at Bigelow Nurseries, Inc., in Northboro, Massachusetts.

Three Cheers for Perennials

To get three extra benefits from your perennials, wait until early spring to cut them back, recommends Connie Gardner, assistant manager at Horsford's Nursery in Charlotte, Vermont. First, the yellowed, dried foliage and stems will add color and interest to your garden during the winter. Second, birds and wildlife will visit to eat seeds from dried seedheads and probe the stems for overwintering insects. And third, the stems will trap snow, which insulates roots and bulbs from severe cold.

Wisteria Boost

Even though you've pruned, watered, and coddled your wisteria, it still isn't blooming with the bravado you expect. "What it's missing," says Shelia Brackley, perennial production and sales assistant at Bigelow Nurseries, Inc., in Northboro, Massachusetts, "is Epsom salts!" To encourage wisteria to bloom, Shelia suggests watering once in the fall with a solution of 1 tablespoon Epsom salts to 1 gallon of water. Dose the plants with the Epsom salts solution again in April, and in late spring, you should see a wealth of wisteria flowers.

Paint-Free Fencing

You won't have to spend valuable gardening time painting fence posts if you install PVC post-and-rail fencing—it never needs painting! The fencing is available from Saratoga Rail Fence and Supply, Inc., in two- or three-rail sections as well as in ornamental pickets. For more information see "Resources" on page 317.

Fencing Sense

When installing yards of fencing, save yourself time and aggravation by digging the holes for one section and then installing the posts and rails *before* moving on to the next section. Digging all of the holes first leaves room for error—if one hole is off by a few inches, it quickly becomes a 6-inch problem. And who wants to redig all those holes?

Timely tip

If you install fencing, be sure the posts are set securely in the ground. A good rule of thumb is to bury them 6 inches deep for every 12 inches of post exposed above the ground.

Dogwood Signals Drought

How do you know when your plants are getting drought stressed—*before* it's too late? Keep your eye on your flowering dogwood, one of the first landscape plants to show symptoms of drought. "The first sign that your dogwood is suffering is wilting leaves in the heat of day," says University of Georgia Extension Service horticulturist Jim Midcap. "That's your signal to set out a soaker hose early the next morning." (Early morning is the best time to water because the water soaks into the ground before the day's heat can evaporate it—and because any water on plant leaves dries before evening, reducing the spread of disease.) And what happens if you don't quench your dogwood's thirst?

"The cells on the outside of the leaves begin to die, subsequently turning the leaf edges brown," Jim explains. Other plants may not be so obvious about their stress level, however, so watch your dogwood carefully for the signal to water your other trees and shrubs, too.

problem solver   PLANTS LIKE GRAY WATER

When summers are dry, do you worry about restrictions on garden watering? End your worries by tapping some of the waste water from your everyday household activity. "You can use alternative watering sources, such as the gray water from your washing machine and showers, provided you use biodegradable soap," says Charlie Plonski, garden center manager of Horsford's Nursery in Charlotte, Vermont. Check local ordinances to be sure your community allows a separate gray water pipe. You may need the services of a plumber to set up a system to divert and store gray water for your garden.

Be Safe, Not Sorry

Working smart when you're cutting down a tree can be a life-or-death matter. If you need to cut down a small or midsize tree in your yard, whizzing through the trunk with a chain saw may seem like a fast and easy approach. But for safety's sake, don't cut to the point of letting the tree fall. Instead, stop your cut short and use wedges to force the tree over. "This affords much more control and eliminates having to worry about a running chain saw in the event of an emergency," says Steve Tworig, president of North Branch Landscape Co., Inc., in Stamford, Vermont. When the tree is notched and ready for the last cut, shut off the saw and insert one or more plastic wedges into the notch. Use a maul to hammer the wedge in, and watch out for the falling timber.

A smart way to cut down a tree is to stop your cut short, insert plastic wedges into the notch, and use the wedges to force the tree over.

homegrown HINTS

TARPS SAVE CLEANUP TIME

Take a small tarp along when you prune or plant for quick and easy cleanup. Peter Baecher of Davis Landscape Company in Lisbon, Maine, suggests spreading a tarp where it will catch most of the trimmings when you prune a shrub or tree. Then it's a quick and easy job to haul the trimmings to a brush pile or load them into a vehicle to take to your neighborhood composting site.

Landscape designer and author Jane von Trapp finds her tarp handy at planting time. She recommends spreading the tarp beside the planting site and piling the soil on the tarp. Once the plant is positioned in the hole, spread a few shovelfuls of soil around the roots, and then simply pour the rest of the soil off the tarp and into the hole. Planting goes quickly, and there's no soil to rake off the lawn when you're finished with the job.

Rope Up a Brush Pile

Here's a trick of the trade that landscapers use when they have a lot of brush to haul across a yard or in a pickup truck. Lay a thick rope in a straight line on the ground in the area where you'll be piling the brush. Stack the brush on top of the rope, laying it perpendicular to the rope, with all cut ends facing the same direction. Then wrap the rope around the pile and tie it securely on top. When you pull on the rope, the whole load will come with you, making the hauling seem like a piece of cake.

Andrea Morgante, co-owner of Siteworks in Hinesburg, Vermont, advises pulling the load with the cut ends of the brush facing toward you. "This method works great in the back of a pickup truck, too," Andrea says. "Lay the rope across the back end of the bed of the truck, pile the brush on top, and tie. When you want to dump the load, just pull on the rope, and it all comes out at once!"

Soil Sample for *Measuring* Moisture

Deep watering encourages your lawn to send roots farther into the soil, so your lawn can last longer between rains or watering without becoming stressed. But how can you tell whether you're watering deeply enough? The answer is underground. Start by giving your lawn at least 1 inch of water. After the water soaks in, use a spade to cut 3 to 5 inches into the soil. Then make a second cut about 1 inch away, and lift the sample of soil out of the ground. You should be able to feel the point where water penetration stopped. If it's less than 3 inches below the soil surface, you didn't water long enough.

Timely tip

You can also help your lawn survive with less watering by mowing high. "In hot summer months," says Clayton Johnson of New England Turf, Inc., in West Kingston, Rhode Island, and president of the New England Nursery and Landscape Association, "raise your mowing height from 1½ to 2½ inches, which will help conserve the moisture in the ground."

problem solver

A CYCLONE SPREADER SAVES TIME

Make the most of your time when spreading grass seed or organic fertilizer on your lawn by using the right tool for the job. In this case, that means a broadcast spreader. A broadcast spreader works better than a drop spreader because it sprays, rather than drops, the material from the canister, allowing you to cover a larger area of lawn in less time. It also ensures that you'll get a pretty even distribution of seed or fertilizer over your lawn. (Adjust the baffle inside the spreader to avoid spraying seed on walkways, in swimming pools, and so on.) Cover your lawn in straight rows going one direction, then walk with the spreader perpendicular to those rows to ensure that you don't miss any spots.

Control Cattails with a Snip

Here's an easy way to control cattails that have gotten out of control in your water garden, says Fiona Wood of Baltimore, Ontario. In late fall, cut all the leaves off the plant to below the water level. Once the pond freezes, the cattails will drown because they can't breathe. Although this method isn't foolproof, it will prevent cattails from taking over the pond.

Smart Dos are Don'ts

Sometimes the smartest things you do in your landscape are the things you *don't* do. Here are some landscaping tasks that are better left alone:

- Don't waste water by spraying it high into the air with a hose or sprinkler. Instead, use a soaker hose or drip irrigation to put water right where it's needed.

- Don't fertilize landscape plants after midsummer. The resulting late-season growth is tender and easily injured by fall frosts.

- Don't prune heavily after midsummer—unless you want to promote growth. Pruning during the second half of summer stimulates new growth that doesn't have time to harden before cold weather arrives.

- Don't pile mulch directly around the trunks of trees and shrubs. While mulching conserves moisture, it also provides ideal conditions for fungal diseases if the mulch is piled directly against woody plants.

- Don't plant a tree without doing a little research. The tree will probably outlive you. Take the time to check its mature size and habit, ideal growing conditions, and potential disease and insect problems. You can find this information at your university cooperative extension office.

- Don't top-prune your trees. And if your tree service suggests topping your trees, get a second opinion. Topping trees makes them more prone to disease and encourages a flush of unsightly, witches'-broom regrowth.

- Don't forget that your landscape is for your pleasure more than for that of passersby. Check out the views from your windows; sit on your back porch; walk your pathways—and only then decide where and what to plant.

No More *Scarred* Trunks

Prevent scarring on trunks by annually pruning one lower branch off each of your young shade trees, says Charlie Proutt, landscape architect and owner of Horsford's Nursery in Charlotte, Vermont. Pruning shade trees while they're young instead of waiting until they're mature helps them heal quickly and completely. And removin[g] only one branch per yea[r] also helps the tree keep i[ts] natural look. Allow abo[ut] 7 feet between the lowes[t] limb on the tree and the ground if the tree is next to a walkway or patio.

Remove only one low branch at a time to maintain a shade tree's natural appearance while clearing a path for walking or mowing under it.

Removable Latticework

You can grow vines on a fence or on the side of your house and still easily maintain and paint the fence or siding behind them. The trick is to attach a lattice to the house or fence with hinges at the bottom and hooks and eyes at the top. Make sure you fasten spacers (1-inch-thick blocks of wood or porcelain electric fence insulators) at various intervals between the lattice and the other surface. (All fastening hardware should be galvanized to prevent rust stains.) Grow the vines on the lattice. When painting time comes, simply unhook the hooks and carefully lay the lattice down on the ground with the vines still attached. Be gentle as you bend the lattice and vine outward. If the vine is woody, rest the lattice against the top of a stepladder instead of folding it clear to the ground. Not only are you able to paint behind the plants, but you've created an air space that minimizes the risks of rot and mildew on house and fence surfaces.

Create a removable lattice by attaching the lattice to the side of your house using hinges, hooks and eyes, and spacers. When it's time to paint your house, simply unhook the lattice and lay it down on the ground.

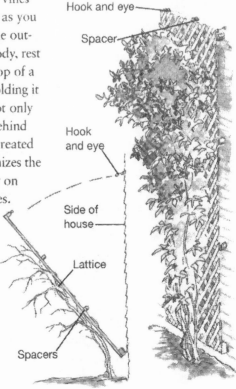

Hook and eye

Spacer

Hook and eye

Side of house

Lattice

Spacers

Dressing Up Concrete

Concrete wall systems are reasonably priced and weekend-warrior friendly when it comes to construction. The wall blocks fit together easily, and it's only a matter of putting a good base of gravel (from 6 to 12 inches, depending on how deep the ground freezes in your region) under the wall and leveling the first set of blocks. But concrete is concrete, and if you don't like the man-made look, you're stuck. Or are you?

For a little more money, you can cap (add a finishing layer) the wall and steps with a nat-ural material like bluestone. Use 1½-inch-thick pieces cut at the quarry to the desired width and length. Bond the bluestone or slate to the last layer of blocks with a wet concrete slurry so that it doesn't move. The gray-blue color of bluestone blends well with the color of the concrete. If you use stone that is slightly wider than the concrete blocks and project it over the edge of the blocks, you'll have your guests thinking the concrete is as natural as the bluestone! Concrete wall systems are available from Keystone Retaining Walls, Risi Stone Systems, and Ideal Concrete Block Co. (See "Resources" on page 317.)

Give a natural look to a concrete wall system by using bluestone to finish off the wall. Or, you can use stone that's slightly wider than the concrete and project it over the blocks to achieve the same effect.

Frozen Drinks for Thirsty Plants

A midwinter thaw can mean death to your plants. That's because a thaw triggers plants to grow, and if the roots can't find water, the plants will dry out and die. To keep your plants alive, water them until the ground freezes. Then when a thaw strikes, the water frozen in the ground will be readily available for those thirsty plants.

Although all plants, even established ones, will benefit from such watering, newly planted evergreens really reap the rewards. Pam Tworig, treasurer of North Branch Landscape Co., Inc., in Stamford, Vermont, recommends *heavily* watering newly planted evergreens right before a freeze. She says it doesn't matter what time of day you water; just make sure to concentrate your efforts on the base of the tree—watering the foliage won't do the tree any good. Pam also notes that you can give newly planted evergreens supplemental watering during any deep thaws that occur throughout winter.

Slow Drip **Saves** Time

Drip irrigation can save you lots of time and effort on watering plants in containers, and with a homemade system, you can have the convenience of drip irrigation with little cost. Your container plants dry out fast in hot weather, and they may need watering once—or more—every day.

Timer

Old garden hose

To make your own drip irrigation system for container gardens, punch some holes in an old garden hose. Plug one end of the hose, attach a timer to the other end, and hook it up to an outdoor faucet.

To provide your plants with the water they need, simply attach a timer and an old garden hose to an outdoor faucet near your containers. Punch holes in the hose, string it through the containers, and plug the end. Test the pressure to make sure the water will drip out slowly, then set the timer to turn on the water several times a day. Your plants will never be thirsty again.

Simple *Silt* Barrier

A layer of fabric is the secret to keeping silt from seeping through a retaining wall. Simply place a layer of woven landscape fabric up against the back of the newly built wall before you add backfill material behind the wall. Leave a flap of the fabric exposed at the top of the wall. Once you've put the backfill stone in place, spread the flap over the stone. Then spread soil on top of the fabric. This prevents the soil from being washed down into the backfill stone, so you can plant right up to the edge of your wall.

Place woven landscape fabric against the back of a new retaining wall before you fill in behind it. Fold a flap of the fabric back over your backfill and top it off with soil to create a garden area right to the edge of the wall.

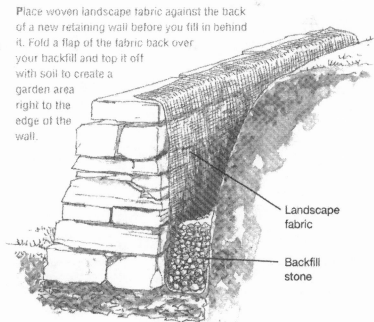

Landscape fabric

Backfill stone

Checking *the Pitch*

With a few simple props you can check whether the soil around your foundation is graded to allow water to flow away from it. (Water that flows toward your foundation can run underneath it, eventually cracking it.)

Cut two wooden stakes, each about 4 feet long, and drive one of them about a foot into the ground right next to the foundation. Walk at least 8 feet away (more is better) perpendicular to the house and drive the other stake into the ground. Tie a string between them and attach a line level to make sure the string is level from stake to stake. Use a measuring tape to measure the distance from the ground to the string at various intervals, beginning at the house and moving out to the other stake. If your measurement increases as you move to the outer stake, you have positive grade and the water will flow correctly. You need only 1 inch of pitch (slope) in 8 feet of length. If you don't have enough pitch, you can easily shave off the top inch or so of soil at the problem area so that the water flows in the right direction.

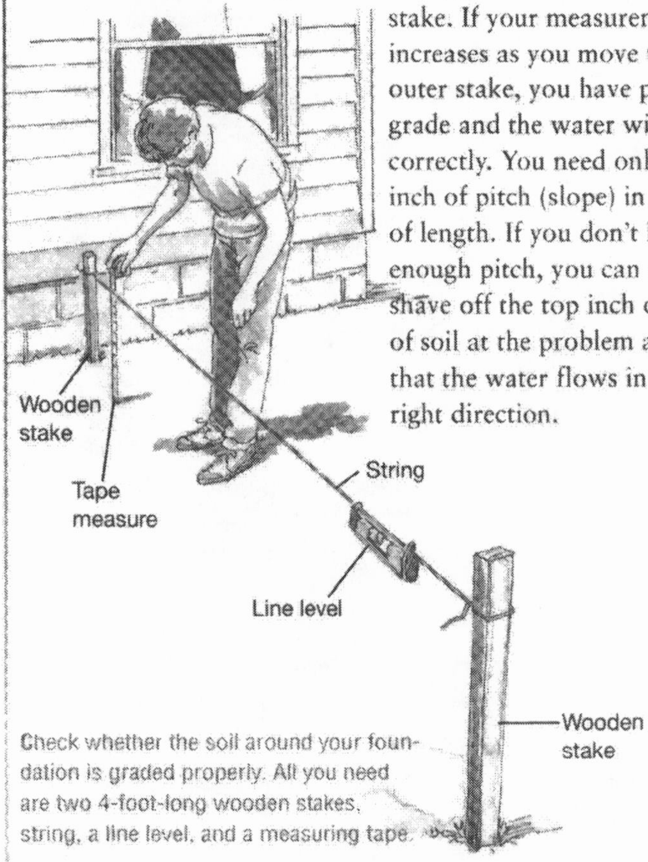

Wooden stake

Tape measure

String

Line level

Wooden stake

Check whether the soil around your foundation is graded properly. All you need are two 4-foot-long wooden stakes, string, a line level, and a measuring tape.

Share and Save

"It's much cheaper to rent a tool for a day or two than to own it for a lifetime," says Roger Cook, landscape contractor on television's *This Old House* and *The Victory Garden*. So if you need a large, elaborate tool for a landscape project, check the cost of renting it. The price may be more affordable than you think, especially if you share the rental with a neighbor who has a similar project going in his yard.

A sod stripper is a good candidate for a rental share. Or, if you're doing grading work, rent a skid-steer loader for excavation and moving boulders and soil. It's fairly easy to run and speeds up those tedious, backbreaking jobs. If you want to create a big bed on soil that's never been turned before, a large-size, rear-tine tiller (8 horse-power or more) is another good piece of equipment to rent. You take the machine for the morning; your neighbor has it for the after-noon, and the day's rental is minimal for both of you. Sure beats a wheelbarrow!

homegrown HINTS

SPRUCE UP THAT STOOP

You can dress up an old concrete stoop and steps as long as they don't have large cracks in them or pieces of concrete missing. Here's how you do it. First, thoroughly clean the concrete with muriatic acid to remove any old oil or grime that have built up over time. Repair small cracks with mortar. Then coat half-brick pavers or bluestone with a slurry of powdered cement and water. Brush the mixture onto the stoop too, then cover the stoop with the pavers or stones, keeping the joints as tight as possible. (If you cover the vertical portions of the stoop as well as the horizontal ones, you'll need to prop up the pavers with shims until the slurry has dried.) Let the stone dry for a day, then mix up a batch of grouting material in a wheelbarrow. Use about ten shovelfuls of sand, one-half bag of powdered cement, and a little water to make a mixture the consistency of thick, dry peanut butter. With a jointer, fill in all of the joints with this grouting mixture. Let the grout dry for a day before using the stoop. Now your stoop wears a coat of a different color—and for just a little bit of work!

Give an old concrete stoop a face-lift by attaching half-brick pavers with a slurry of powdered cement and water.

Screened Coverage for **Potted Plants**

Use a piece of window screening instead of pebbles to cover the drainage hole in the bottom of a clay pot. Screening "keeps stuff like roots and soil in, while keeping out slugs, which you wouldn't want to bring into the house when you over-winter your plants," explains Ray Rogers, award-winning flower show entrant and senior garden editor at DK Publishing, Inc., in New York City.

Wrought-Iron *Alternative*

Like the look of wrought-iron fencing but not the expense or maintenance? Aluminum is a great alternative. It doesn't cost as much, and you don't have to scrape and paint it regularly. Sections come in 4-foot lengths. With a post-hole digger and concrete, you can give your landscape a Victorian look. Aluminum picket-style fencing is available from Delgard Aluminum Ornamental Fencing and Jerith Manufacturing Co. (See "Resources" on page 317 for details.)

Containers on the Cheap

Container gardening is the hottest craze, but you needn't spend hundreds on pots for the garden and patio. Instead, use your imagination and you'll keep those dollars in your wallet. Punch a few holes in the bottom of an old plastic kiddie pool and fill it with a few

Turn terra-cotta flue tiles into creative containers for plants, including succulents like hens and chicks.

tomato plants bordered by pest-repelling marigolds. An old watering can or a galvanized trash barrel can add a dash of creativity to an otherwise boring deck. A salvaged animal trough can take on new life when planted with annuals such as impatiens. And terra-cotta flue tiles have a pleasing rectangular shape and raise an arrangement of succulents such as hens and chicks to new heights.

Natural Trellises

Instead of buying a trellis, why not make your own with supplies from your backyard? The supple wood from willows, apple trees, and grapevines makes natural, attractive trellises. It's best to make your trellises in spring, when the new growth is green and flexible. Figure out how high you want your trellis to be, double that number, then allow for the width of the arch. (For example, for a 4-foot trellis, cut 10-foot sections of branch.) Bend some of the branches into an arch. Twist other branches around the arch and weave or twist the branches to form a structure. When the branches dry, they'll hold their shape. You can insert small trellises in containers to support climbing ivy and other vines, and use larger trellises right in the garden as props for drooping delphinium, peonies, and other lazy perennials.

Turn supple wood from your own backyard into a beautiful, natural trellis.

Flood Relief for Your *Lawn*

Heavy rains can lead to temporary flooding around your yard from surface runoff. When the water subsides, don't be too concerned if there's a layer of flood-deposited soil on the grass: It may actually do your lawn some good if you know what to do with it. And that might be nothing, says extension educator Sally Cunningham of Erie County, New York.

"If your lawn has an inch or so of soil over it, don't walk on it or do anything at all until the soil dries," suggests Sally. Walking on the wet lawn and compacting the soil even more is the worst thing you can do to the already-stressed turf.

"In most cases," Sally says, "the silt and muck will gradually filter down through the grass and disappear, and can actually improve your lawn by acting as a mild fertilizer." After the muck settles, Sally recommends testing your soil's pH, just in case the runoff included some highly alkaline or acidic substance. Give your lawn plenty of time to recover, and don't let it suffer from drought later in the growing season, she says.

Sally adds that trying to wash excess soil off your lawn with a power hose only makes things worse: "It compacts the soil and adds even more water—the last thing the drowning roots need. You'll be surprised at how many lawns will grow right past this problem, and will do better if you do less!"

Timely tip

When flooding deposits a thick layer—2 inches or more—of soil on your lawn, you may want to lift or slice off some of the excess, says Sally. She suggests you try using a broad, flat snow shovel to scoop off the soil, and standing on boards to distribute your weight more evenly and to keep from sinking into the mire. "The goal is to avoid further damage to the lawn from compaction," Sally notes.

problem solver   A SECOND LIFE FOR SOD

Construction in your yard means a muddy mess, but if you're working in a small area, there's an easy way to solve the mud situation: Reuse the grass. If you remove the grass carefully and store it properly, it will take hold again (this technique works best when the construction project will take only a couple of days). Using a spade, cut through the grass in straight strips about 4 feet long, 18 inches wide, and 2 inches deep. Roll the sod up and store it in the shade until it's needed. Then regrade and rake the soil in the construction area, unroll the sod on top, tamp it down firmly, and water well until the grass reroots (you'll know the grass has rerooted once you see topgrowth).

If the construction is long-term, lay the strips grass-side-up on an empty bed. Keep them watered, and they'll root in. When it's time to replace the sod, dig under it in the same way that you did originally, leaving at least 2 inches of roots. Immediately re-lay it on the raked and graded area, tamp it down, and water well.

homegrown HINTS

TAMING YOUR WILD MEADOW

Creating a natural area in your yard is great for wildlife—and it can cut your maintenance work in a big way, too. But if you just stop mowing a part of your yard, the transition from lawn to wild meadow may look awkward. To set off the wild area nicely, try defining the boundary with a fence. Decide how much of your yard you want to keep under control, and install a fence around that part. Even a see-through post-and-rail fence is often enough to set off the wild areas.

Give *Your* Garden the **Hose Test**

A garden hose is a great prop to use when laying out garden beds, and you can also use it to test whether your bed layout will work with the way you use your yard. "The flexibility of a hose lends itself to smooth curves,"

says Peter Baecher of Davis Landscape Company in Lisbon, Maine. "Leave the hose in place for 48 hours and live with the shapes you've chosen before you cut out the beds," adds Roger Cook, owner of K&R Tree and Landscape Co. in Burlington, Massachusetts, and landscaper-in-residence on television's *The Victory Garden* and *This Old House.* You may discover that your bed layout is awkward to walk around or that it intrudes into a play area. If so, you can adjust the hose until you have exactly the right shape for your bed. Then just cut the sod right along the line of the hose, says Peter.

To test a proposed site for a garden bed, use a garden hose to outline the bed, and leave it in place for a few days. A stake or shovel stuck in your chosen spot can help you decide whether planting a tree there is a good idea.

Timely tip

Roger also has a clever method for testing whether he's chosen the best site for planting a tree. He "plants" stakes or a shovel in the ground at the proposed spot and lives with the surrogate "tree" for a few days before digging the planting hole.

Screen with a Natural Scene

To give your yard privacy and the feeling of a natural forest at the same time, don't just plant a wall of trees. "If you want to create a natural screen between you and your neighbors, mix up the sizes and varieties of the plants you use," says Andrew Brodtman, landscape designer at Twombly Nursery in Monroe, Connecticut. "How often do you see all the same size trees in a pine forest?"

To create a beautiful, forest-like screen, start at the edge of your property. Plant a back- drop of some stiff-needle trees like spruce with soft-needle trees, using a mix of 8- to 14-foot trees at staggered intervals. Add a few small, flow- ering trees, such as crabapples and dogwoods, in front of them. As a final touch, plant small flowering shrubs and perennials in the foreground.

To get the most from a planting to add privacy, use a mix of trees, shrubs, and perennials of different heights.

Spilled Milk Garden Design

When dreaming up the shape for an island bed, "picture a glass of spilled milk," suggests Holly Weir, co-owner of Rocky Dale Gardens in Bristol, Vermont. Then mow around the shape and let the grass grow within it, suggests Bill Pollard, Holly's husband and co-owner of Rocky Dale Gardens. Seeing the relief will help you decide if you like the shape. Then you can cut and remove the sod and build your dream bed.

problem solver

THE RULE OF FOUR

When you plan a new garden bed, you need to make sure you have plenty of space for everything you want to put in it. A good rule of thumb is to allow 4 square feet per plant, says Holly Weir, co-owner of Rocky Dale Gardens in Bristol, Vermont. Divide your total square footage by four, and you'll know how many plants will fit in the bed. "An empty bed looks huge, and most people don't make their planting beds large enough," Holly remarks. "They cram too many plants into the space, and it quickly becomes overgrown and un- sightly." Of course, when you actually plant, you'll space some plants closer and others farther apart. Small mounding perennials like columbines may need only 1 square foot. Pe- onies and strong spreaders like yarrow require more than 4 square feet of growing room, and so do clethra, hy- drangeas, boxwood, and other shrubs.

Work Some Winter Wonder

Berries, branches, and bark can change a garden from dull to dramatic in the winter. "Winter can be an exciting time in the garden," says Andrew Brodtman, landscape designer at Twombly Nursery in Monroe, Connecticut. To create winter interest in the garden, think beyond flowers, he suggests. Plant some trees and shrubs such as crabapples, viburnums, and winterberry (*Ilex verticillata*), which hang onto their berries into winter and will add color to a stark landscape. Try Harry Lauder's walking stick (*Corylus avellana* 'Contorta') and other shrubs with twisting branches—they become garden sculptures once their leaves drop. The peeling bark of birches and cherries, the red and yellow barks of certain dogwoods, and the green-and-white striped branches of striped maple (*Acer pensylvanicum*) add appeal to a humdrum landscape, too. And winter flowers aren't out of the question, Andrew notes. Just plant Chinese witch hazel (*Hamamelis mollis*) for flowers in February.

Evergreen shrubs are the mainstay of winter landscapes, but to really make your yard something special in winter, add shrubs with beautiful bark or unusual branches to the scene.

Pathway to *Paradise*

To add a sense of romance and interest to a flat site, make a sunken garden like the one created by Bill Pollard, co-owner of Rocky Dale Gardens in Bristol, Vermont.

"I had a wooded plot to make into a new garden," Bill says. "My lot was flat and I felt it needed some topography, so I dug the pathways to about 18 inches deep and threw the soil to each side into the garden to build the garden up as I went. Since the plot was a woodland, I planted it with groundcovers, ferns, fast-spreading campanulas, and lots of other woodland wildflowers. The result is a sort of tunnel-like pathway system through a woodland garden. The feeling is cool and magical."

Pathways need not be reserved just for flat sites, however. Bill notes that he always likes to start with the pathways when he develops a new area of his landscape. That way the garden areas are completely accessible both for maintenance and for enjoyment.

It's Just a Landscape Phase

Creating a master plan for your yard is a smart idea. Planting it in phases is even smarter. Of course, planting in phases is easier on the budget than undertaking a whole-yard makeover at one time, but there are other solid reasons to implement your changes in phases, as well. When you work in phases, "there's more chance of having many small successes instead of one big failure," says Dale Pierson, owner of Pierson Nurseries, Inc., in Biddeford, Maine.

Here's the best order in which to tackle a master landscape plan:

1. Plant trees and other large plants that are sited relatively far from your house. These are the biggest chore to plant, so it's best to tackle them right away, when you're the most enthusiastic. Large trees and shrubs also take the longest time to grow, so get them started right away.

2. Plant foundation shrubs and large plants near the house. As you do this, "make a large project into a series of smaller ones," suggests Roger Cook, landscape contractor on television's *This Old House*. "It's very easy to lose interest after spending several weekends trying to complete a large project."

3. Plant small border plants like groundcovers and perennials last. These ornamentals are the icing on the cake, and they are also the easiest to plant when you are running out of steam.

Timely tip

When you create a master plan for your yard, leave the door open for future changes. For example, you may decide to put in a swing set next year, or even to put an addition on your house. "Don't place barriers to change that are costly to overcome," warns Dale. So try to dream ahead, and don't plant a beautiful shade tree on the site where you may eventually want to build a sunroom or install a swimming pool.

problem solver

FILL YOUR FOUNDATION WITH COLOR

If you want a foundation bed that's colorful from spring through fall, break the annuals habit and choose a mix of bulbs and perennials instead, recommends Andrew Brodtman, landscape designer at Twombly Nursery in Monroe, Connecticut. A mix of spring-, summer-, and fall-blooming perennials will provide season-long color. Plant a layer of tulips, daffodils, and alliums at the front of the bed, and overplant them with perennials. That way you'll have early spring color, but the perennials will bloom in time to hide the bulb foliage as it dies back. Creeping phlox (*Phlox stolonifera*), irises, and hardy cranesbills (*Geranium* spp.) are all reliable early bloomers that you can plant and then forget about until they fill the spring garden with vibrant color next year.

"People will drive past your place and wonder why their house doesn't look as good as yours!" Andrew says.

Helpful *Hint* for **Picking** Plants

Visit a botanical garden or a yard with mature plantings to help you decide what will look good in *your* yard. By seeing the plants in the landscape—rather than in pots at a garden center—you'll gain clues about how they'll behave in your garden. For example, you may decide you want a narrower-growing plant, or one that's wider at the base. Plus, you'll be able to see the plants at their mature size. Stick to the garden center for checking flower color or leaf texture.

Take the **Long View** on Landscapers

Landscape designers like to advertise their work by putting signs on their newly installed landscapes. You've probably seen some in your neighborhood, and the yard looked fresh and fancy. But don't be fooled by initial appearances. The smart way to judge landscape designers is by visiting their mature designs—those installed five years ago or more. That way, you'll be able to see if the design still looks good and if the plants are holding up well. Ask friends or staff at your local garden center for names of landscapers they'd recommend. Then make your final decision by looking at time-tested results.

Timely tip

Having a landscape installed professionally can be a hefty expense, but you can keep costs in line by hiring a firm that both designs and builds the landscape. Such firms usually have a higher profit margin built into the construction phase of the project, so the design plan is greatly discounted or even free.

A **Rock-Solid** Idea

It's fun to include large boulders in your landscape, but to make them look like they really belong there, "plant" them the way Mother Nature might have, recommends Roger Cook, chief landscaper on television's *This Old House* and *The Victory Garden*. Big rocks work well as backdrops for tall and short perennials and shrubs, but not if they're just plopped down on the soil. For the most natural effect, decide which part of the rock looks best, and be sure that side will face forward. Then dig a hole large enough so that one-third to one-half of the rock will be below ground level. Use a crowbar to move and turn the rock until you manipulate it into the hole. Slide the end of the crowbar under the large boulder, and then place a small rock up against the crowbar. The small rock will give you extra leverage when you push on the bar.

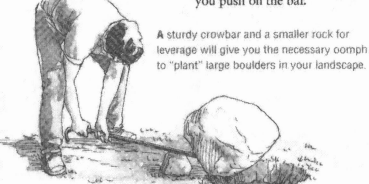

A sturdy crowbar and a smaller rock for leverage will give you the necessary oomph to "plant" large boulders in your landscape.

Brighten Up Bracing

Gazebos, arbors, and trellises can add interest to any landscape, but the extra bracing these structures need to keep them sturdy may be less than appealing. One clever way to hide shear braces is by hanging plants on brackets attached to the braces. Good choices for hanging plants include geraniums, petunias, and tuberous begonias. If hiding the braces isn't an option, you can purchase old orna-

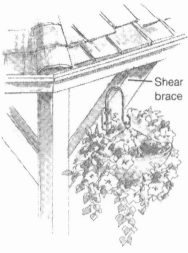

— Shear brace

Hide less-than-attractive shear braces on gazebos, arbors, and trellises with hanging plants. Simply attach brackets to the braces to hold the plants.

Fence Defense

No one wants to argue with the neighbor over painting fences or pruning hedges that run along the property line. To maintain harmony with the folks next door, position all property dividers, live or otherwise, a few feet in from your property line. You'll lose a little bit of your yard, but you'll avoid potential hassles. Plus, you'll have a buffer zone that's legally yours to work in when you need to paint or prune.

Shady Way to a Prettier Deck

Pep up a wooden deck roof with open slats and add shade at the same time by planting fast-growing vines like morning glories or scarlet runner beans at the base of the deck posts. You can also plant vines in large pots next to the posts. (You may need to help the vines start climbing by gently tying them to the posts with twine or old panty hose.) The plants will climb and cover the posts and roof, adding visual interest while protecting you from the summer sun's rays.

homegrown HINTS

WHITE HOT IN THE SHADE

Want dazzle in your shady nook? White flowers can be just as hot in the shade as any pink flower is in sunlight. Lots of white-flowering, shade-loving plants are available to electrify the darker areas of your yard. Try shrubs like clethra (*Clethra ainifolia*) and viburnums, perennials like striped violet (*Viola striata*) and double-flowered dropwort (*Filipendula vulgaris* 'Flore Pleno'), and annuals like impatiens. And don't forget about plants with variegated and silvery leaves. Hosta, pulmonarias, and 'White Nancy' spotted lamium, which shines like tinfoil, are just a few of the possibilities. Make sure you mix up your plantings so you have lots of different sizes, shapes, and textures to add interest.

Landscaping 101

Ever wonder how to get that professional look for your landscape without calling in the professionals? The key is to establish one theme and stick to it throughout the design. In other words, if the planting beds are curved, use the same curved lines in the walkway or patio. If you use brick for the walkway, use similar material throughout the landscape. Try to build with stone that's found naturally in your area or with materials that complement the architecture and materials used in your house. The best designs are simple and subtle—not like a Hollywood movie set!

Cool Colors for Depth

Create the illusion of depth in a narrow flowerbed by using two tricks that professional garden designers use. First, simply plant layers of cool-colored flowers amid bright, hot colors. Cool colors, such as blues, whites, and greens, recede from your eye. Second, vary plant height. For example, plant tall, spikey delphiniums behind clumps of midsize flat flowers like scabiosa. By combining these two techniques, you'll make your garden appear bigger without having to put in the work required to increase its actual size.

Mixing It Up with Annuals

Have some vegetable beds that need a little oomph—especially as the veggies wax and wane? You can easily brighten things up by adding annuals to the mix. "Try tucking marigolds, petunias, or other annuals in at the ends of rows, at the corners of raised beds, or along edges of pathways," says James Lawrence, publisher at Microcosm, Ltd., a company that produces books on ponds and water gardens, in Shelburne, Vermont. You'll find that your garden will be more colorful and interesting with little extra work on your part. Cosmos, zinnias, or other tall annuals that grow quickly and flower to frost can also effectively frame an otherwise ordinary vegetable garden, James notes.

Timely tip

When brightening up vegetable beds with annuals, you can gain an added benefit by planting annuals that attract beneficial insects to your vegetable garden. Some good choices include calendulas, cosmos, sunflowers, sweet alyssum, zinnias, and marigolds.

Tie It Up with Ribbon Grass

Don't let your water garden stick out like a sore thumb from the rest of your landscape. Instead, use ribbon grass (*Phalaris arundicancea var. picta*) as an accent plant to tie your water feature to its surroundings. Ribbon grass, with its green-and-white striped foliage, adds a nice contrast to the dark greens of aquatic plants, says Janice LaCorte of Stone Ridge, New York. Plant the grass in a bare spot of soil next to your water garden, and watch as its green-and-white spikes and tall seedheads blend the land and water garden together. Be aware, however, that ribbon grass can spread rapidly. If you'd like to plant something that's not as invasive, try Japanese sedge (*Carex hachioensis*) instead.

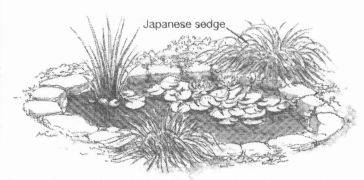
Japanese sedge

Use a moisture-loving grass like Japanese sedge to tie your water garden to the rest of your landscape.

problem solver   QUICK COLOR FILLER

Do you have a little more empty space between the wall of your house and that line of trees or hedgerow than you'd like? A quick-and-easy solution is to install a prefabricated trellis between the trees and the house walls. Plant quick-growing annual vines like sweet peas and morning glories near the trellises each season, and they'll scramble up in no time, filling the void with color.

Swimming Pool **Shade**

You *can* have shade trees around your swimming pool—without the hassle of skimming leaves off the water. Just plant oak trees near the pool. The leaves on oaks hang on the branches well into winter, long after you cover the pool.

Make Way for **Moss**

Want the well-used, cool, and classic garden look of moss growing on your brick walkways and terra-cotta pots? Spray the area with sour milk and in a couple of weeks, your pot will be covered with moss, says Bill Stockman, owner of Spider Web Gardens in Center Tuftonboro, New Hampshire.

Clematis Cover

Clematis is not only a great climber, it's also a great spreader. Train it to grow horizontally, and you'll have a unusual flowering groundcover. To make a truly special combination, train the clematis over an evergreen shrub.

homegrown HINTS

DIVERSITY FOR DURABILITY

Protect your landscape from pest and disease disasters by mixing up your plant selections. A large group of the same kind of plant, like hostas, is susceptible to the same disease and insect problems. So a serious infection or infestation can wipe out the entire planting. Choose several different kinds of trees, shrubs, and perennials instead of fixating on one or two favorite species of each. The result will be more interesting, more natural looking, and also more pest-resistant.

Shady Solution

Is there an area in your yard where the sun doesn't shine and the lawn doesn't grow? Plant shade-loving groundcovers in the space and watch those bare spots disappear. Groundcovers like pachysandra and periwinkle take a few years to fill in, but once established, they will continue to spread and will take quite a bit of abuse. Other shade-loving groundcovers to try include ajugas, lily-of-the-valley, hostas, and lamium.

Turn a Shrub into a Trellis

Plant a clematis vine near a small ornamental shrub like a viburnum or spirea, and you'll have an instant trellis for the vine—and waves of flowers, too. Just train the vine on a short stake at the base of the shrub, and the clematis will grow up into the shrub. This pairing works best with a hybrid clematis that won't get big and that you can cut back to a couple of bud sets each year in early spring before growth begins. A good choice is 'Comtesse de Bouchard'. Ray Rogers, garden editor at DK Publishing, Inc., in New York City, likes sweet autumn clematis (*Clematis paniculata*) planted with American holly (*Ilex opaca*). The white-flowered clematis complements the holly's green foliage.

Quick Fence Fix

A smart way to get a living fence going is to plant quick-growing trees and shrubs, such as Lombardy poplar (*Populus nigra* 'Italica') and Russian olive (*Eleagnus angustifolia*). But the quick growth of these plants means they're weak-wooded and short-lived—not the ideal for a living fence.

To plan for their eventual demise, plant long-lived, sturdy evergreens and shrubs, such as fir (*Abies* spp.) or hemlock (*Tsuga* spp.) in the same area as the quick-growers. Evergreens and shrubs grow more slowly but will be ready to take the place of the faster-growing plants when they're removed so that your living fence remains intact.

Timely tip

If you're using your living fence as a windbreak, make sure you plant trees that can take the breeze. 'Austriaca' Austrian pine (*Pinus nigra* 'Austriaca') and Scotch pine (*Pinus sylvestris*) are two types that grow well in windy spaces. Avoid trees like white pine and hemlock that burn easily in the wind.

Balanced Entryway

Mirror-image plantings of sculpted evergreens are a popular choice for foundation plantings, but for something more exciting, try a design that breaks the traditional mold. You don't need exact symmetry for a successful entrance planting—you just need a feeling of balance in your design. You can achieve balance by placing one large plant on one side of your entryway and three smaller plants on the other side. For example, try a flowering shrub such as a lilac against barberry. Or balance one bed with two smaller beds. Without a mirror image, you'll create a more casual-looking design.

Forgo symmetry in your entryway planting and still achieve a balanced look by planting two smaller beds opposite a larger bed.

A Whole "**New**" Walkway

Dress up a boring walkway that's still in good shape (and that you don't want to remove) by installing precast concrete pavers on either side. It's easiest to install a double row of brick-shaped pavers because you don't have to cut the pavers. On each side of the existing walkway, dig a trench about 8 inches wide and 6 to 12 inches deep. The depth depends on how deep the ground freezes in your region—the colder it is, the deeper the trench should be. Fill the trench with ¾-inch plant mix (a gravel with mixed sizes ranging from stone dust to ¾-inch stone) to make a base for the pavers, leaving room for the thickness of the pavers and 1 inch of coarse bedding sand. Compact the gravel by tamping it down with your hand. Top the gravel with a 1-inch-deep layer of coarse sand. Bed the pavers in the sand and arrange them in a staggered running bond pattern, as shown at left, so that the joints don't overlap.

Pavers

You can give a boring walkway a face-lift by installing concrete pavers along the sides.

Gravel topped with coarse sand

problem SOLver

GREEN DISGUISE FOR EYESORES

Hide ugly electric meters, junction boxes, wellheads, basement hatch doors, and propane tanks with flowers, shrubs, and trees. Plant in layers with large evergreen plants near the object and smaller shrubs and flowers in front of the evergreen backdrop. This layered approach looks less contrived than if you just plant a ring of shrubs around the object you want to hide. What you end up with is a bed or island forming an attractive focal point, disguising the eyesore behind it. Just remember to leave access for the person who services the monstrosity or he may drip oil on or trample your hard work. A few stepping stones will show him exactly where to step.

Emphasizing the Right Entrance

If you have two doors on one side of your house, do guests know which is the main entrance? You can minimize confusion by installing a low picket fence outside the door you don't want guests to use and planting an island bed filled with perennials next to the fence. Both the fence and the bed will separate the door from the main walkway and will help guide visitors to the preferred entrance.

Help emphasize the right entryway into your home by installing a low picket fence and an island bed to shield a secondary entrance.

Create an Edible Landscape

Gardener Angie Eckert of Belleville, Illinois, uses vegetables as ornamentals and gets double the benefit. "Some vegetables offer uniquely beautiful attributes," she says. "Celery, rhubarb, cabbage, and asparagus are excellent candidates for use in flowerbeds."

Asparagus, with its tall but soft lacy fronds, is perfect for anchoring the background of a perennial garden, yet it can be harvested early in the season for eating, says Angie.

"The large, coarse leaves and brilliant red stems of rhubarb add color and texture to the garden," she adds. "Deep purple leaves of red cabbage can be used to fill gaps in the perennial garden. Cabbage adds color interest to the garden in the early spring. It can be replaced with flowering annuals as the weather starts to warm."

So if a vegetable garden sounds like too much work for you, Angie says, "Simply tuck veggies into your ornamental beds for an attractive, edible landscape!"

homegrown HINTS

WET-SITE WONDERS

Do you have a wet area in the yard where grass won't grow? Make a planting bed and fill it with plants that love wet feet. Many shrubs and trees enjoy the moisture, and you can make a layered planting that includes moisture-loving perennials, too. Try corkscrew willow (*Salix matsudana* 'Tortuosa') with twisted twigs and branches, or dwarf purple osier (*S. purpurea* 'Nana') with blue-green foliage and purple branches. Red-osier dogwood (*Cornus stolonifera*) and yellow-twig dogwoods (*C. stolonifera* 'Flaviramea') love wet feet, as do swamp azalea (*Rhododendron viscosum*) and blueberries. For the foreground, many irises, marsh marigolds (*Caltha* spp.), and primroses are quite at home in a wet site.

Delight the Kids (*and Yourself!*)

Everyone likes surprises, so for a great treat, tuck everbearing strawberries everywhere: under the foundation plantings, in the flowerbeds, in a pot on the back porch, by the side yard walkway, and at the lawn's edge, suggests Jeff Cox, an *Organic Gardening* contributing editor. "Then enjoy sweet little morsels throughout summer everywhere you walk on your property!"

Garden Books Aren't the Gospel

"Don't always take what you read as gospel," warns Jeff O'Donal, president of O'Donal's Nursery, Inc., in Gorham, Maine. Many garden books and catalogs cite zones where a plant is hardy, but it's smart to double-check that information with local certified nursery and landscape experts at your garden center, extension service, or garden clubs.

"Many references, including major nursery suppliers, will cheat a zone, listing a plant as hardy in a zone where it's only margin-ally hardy. This results in more plants sold, but it sets people up to fail," cautions Jeff. Also, a book's advice that a plant will grow in a certain zone doesn't mean the plant will survive or thrive anywhere in your yard.

When you call an expert, be prepared to tell her about wind conditions, outbuildings, and exposure in your yard. "There are many places within a hardiness zone where plants will not survive because of frost pockets or exposure," Jeff says. For example, your property at the bottom of a slope may be more prone to frost than other nearby sites.

Small Plants Are a *Smart* Buy

"Bigger isn't always better," says Jeff O'Donal, president of O'Donal's Nursery, Inc., in Gorham, Maine. "Research has shown that younger plants recover faster than older plants after transplanting." So when you go to the garden center, choose small, vigorous plants over bigger, more mature ones. You can buy more plants for your money, you're less likely to have to replace them, and they'll catch up to older, larger plants in no time because of their youth and increased vigor.

Light Up the Night

Add a new twist to landscaping that's been in place for years by installing outdoor lighting. Low-voltage lighting is a good choice because the fixtures are subtle, but the light can be powerful and plentiful, depending on bulb wattage. And you can achieve lots of interesting effects while still providing enough illumination to light your way. Use downlighting when you want light to spill down from a branch of a tree to the ground for interest and lighting tasks. Uplighting shows the nooks and crannies on the bark of trees and shrubs, and it shines like a beacon to guide you down a dark path. Place backlighting behind an object, like a trellis or plant, to project its shadow onto a wall.

Uplighting

Timely tip

Low-voltage lighting can be more effective at deterring burglars than traditional spotlights. When you hang low-voltage lights in trees or install them at ground level, the lighting directs light toward your house, which is best for discouraging would-be intruders. Spotlights attached to the upper corners of your house walls shine light out, leaving shadows and darkness near the windows and doors of your home, and inviting burglars in.

Downlighting

Backlighting

Uplighting works well for illuminating a dark path and for showcasing bark on trees; use downlighting when you want to light small trees or shrubs from above; generate interesting silhouettes with backlighting.

Buy in *Full Bloom*

"You get what you pay for," goes the old adage. Maybe so, warns Leonard Perry, extension ornamental horticulturist at the University of Vermont. "When buying plants, always try to buy flowering shrubs and perennials in full bloom, not because you need to know what the flowers look like, but because the plants may be mislabeled." This is especially important when buying for a certain color, such as a purple versus a white lilac. There is really no way to tell what color the flowers will be if the plants are the same species. Leonard has found mix-ups stemming from everything from handling problems at the grower's nursery to well-meaning customers who removed a tag to read it and then put it back on the wrong plant.

If you can't buy when the plants are in bloom and you end up with a mislabeled plant, take it back to the nursery where you bought it and ask them to replace it for you. Nurseries that grow their own plants have less potential for offering mislabeled plants.

Best Plants for **Living Fences**

If you're creating a living fence along the edge of your yard, you'll want as much privacy as you can get. The best plants to use are those that have branches down to the ground, such as firs (*Abies* spp.), red pine (*Pinus resinosa*), and Austrian pine (*P. nigra*). Beware that several types of evergreens lose their lower branches with age, which may defeat the purpose of the planting. In particular, avoid spruces (*Picea* spp.), because they defrock themselves over time. If you have a living fence that's lost its lower branches, try planting a layer of shrubs in front to screen the opening.

Dwarf Species for *Tight* Places

Don't miss out on wonderful plants such as spirea, lilacs, or crabapples simply because you think they'll get too big for your landscape. Plant dwarf species and cultivars, instead. 'Snowmound' Nippon spirea (*Spiraea nipponica* 'Snowmound') has the familiar white flowers in spring but only grows to 5 feet tall and wide. Dwarf Korean lilac (*Syringa meyeri* 'Palibin') has lavender flowers and grows only 6 feet tall. Sargent crabapple (*Malus sargentii*) is a slow-growing 8-footer with white flowers and excellent disease resistance. Check garden centers for small varieties of your favorites.

problem solver

FAST-GROWING POND PLANT

Need some fast-growing plants for your water garden? Do as Judy Bechtel of Merced, California, does and hop over to your nearest grocery store to pick up a bunch of watercress. Place the watercress (still tied together) in your pond, close to moving water, such as a fountain or waterfall, if you have one. In a mere two days the watercress will start to root, and in another three it will start to spread, giving you a lush green plant—and sandwich filler, too. (Keep in mind that watercress will remain green year-round in tropical or moderate temperatures, but will die in cold weather.)

Under the *Walnut*

If you're having trouble keeping rhododendrons and birch trees alive near your majestic old black walnut trees (*Juglans nigra*), you're not alone. Those are just a few of the plants damaged by juglone, a chemical substance released into the soil by black walnut roots, buds, and nut hulls.

Juglone can be present even beyond the canopies of the walnut trees and can remain in the soil for years after trees are removed. But this doesn't mean that the ground under your walnut tree has to remain bare.

You can resolve the problem by building a raised bed. The walnut roots won't penetrate it, and you can toss a sheet of ½-inch black plastic mesh over the bed to keep it free from leaves and nut hulls. Be sure to empty the mesh (which is barely visible) often to keep it from being weighed down by nuts or wet leaves. (Don't compost the nuts or leaves.) In addition to making raised beds, you can also plant juglone-tolerant plants, listed at right, near walnut trees.

Good Neighbors *for Problem Walnuts*

Because walnut trees produce a substance called juglone that harms many types of plants, the easiest way to garden near walnut trees is to stick with plants that can tolerate exposure to the toxin. Below are some good juglone-tolerant flower, shrub, and tree choices:

Perennials
Ajuga (*Ajuga reptans*)
Astilbes (*Astilbe* spp.)
Chrysanthemums (*Dendranthema* spp., also called *Chrysanthemum* spp.)
Cinnamon fern (*Osmunda cinnamomea*)
Tawny daylily (*Hemerocallis fulva*)
Hostas (*Hosta* spp.)
Siberian iris (*Iris sibirica*)
Garden phlox (*Phlox paniculata*)
Pulmonarias (*Pulmonaria* spp.)
Showy stonecrop (*Sedum spectabile*)
Lamb's-ears (*Stachys byzantina*)

Annuals
Fibrous and 'Non Stop' tuberous begonias (*Begonia* spp.)
Morning glory (*Ipomoea tricolor*)
Pansy (*Viola* × *wittrockiana*)
Horned violet (*Viola cornuta*)

Bulbs
Crocuses (*Crocus* spp.)
Daffodils (*Narcissus* spp.)
Common grape hyacinth (*Muscari botryoides*)
Darwin Hybrid, Greigii, and Parrot Group tulips (*Tulipa* spp.)

Trees
Canada hemlock (*Tsuga canadensis*)
Japanese maple (*Acer palmatum*)

Vines and Shrubs
Knap Hill-Exbury hybrid azaleas (*Rhododendron* Knap Hill-Exbury hybrids)
Late, large-flowered clematis cultivars, such as 'Rouge Cardinal' clematis (*Clematis* spp.)
February daphne (*Daphne mezereum*)
Weeping forsythia (*Forsythia suspensa*)
Tatarian honeysuckle (*Lonicera tatarica*)
Rose-of-Sharon (*Hibiscus syriacus*)

problem solver

PLANT HIGH IN HEAVY CLAY

Heavy clay soils drain slowly, which can restrict the root growth of newly planted trees and shrubs. But there's a way to help plants cope: "If the soil is heavy clay, plant trees nearly on top of the ground," suggests Connie Gardner, assistant manager at Horsford's Nursery in Charlotte, Vermont. Dig a shallow hole to accommodate just the base or lower half of the rootball. Make the hole twice as wide as the rootball. Amend the soil removed from the hole with equal parts of sand and peat moss to lighten it. Then set the plant in place, and mound the amended soil around the rootball. "The new roots will have the benefit of the lighter mix to get established, and they'll adapt much more easily than if they're smothered in thick, wet clay," Connie says.

Bag the Burlap Wrap

If you plant your broadleaf and needle evergreens wisely, you won't need to use ugly burlap to protect them from winter sun and wind—elements that can harm evergreens beyond repair. Simply give these plants a northern or eastern exposure near house or garage walls, which will give them some protection from sun or wind damage.

Treat *New Trees* to Drip

When watering newly transplanted trees, a little goes a long way, says Todd Kennedy, past president of the National Landscape Association. He advocates using a drip irrigation system rather than handwatering with a hose.

According to Todd, "Three days of drip is better than three hours of standing with a hose." The result? Transplanted trees establish themselves more quickly, and you'll have fewer casualties.

If you don't have a drip irrigation system, you can improvise one by attaching a filter with a pressure regulator to the end of your garden hose and then attaching a small emitter hose to the pressure regulator (you can find these items at most garden centers). Position the emitter hose so the emitters will release water to the root zone of the new trees.

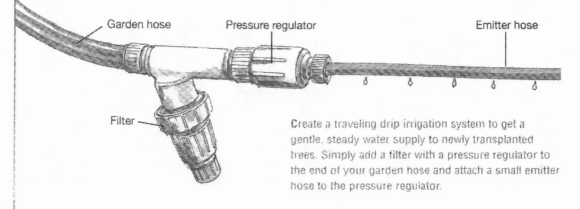

Garden hose   Pressure regulator   Emitter hose

Filter

Create a traveling drip irrigation system to get a gentle, steady water supply to newly transplanted trees. Simply add a filter with a pressure regulator to the end of your garden hose and attach a small emitter hose to the pressure regulator.

problem solver

TRY A PERENNIAL TRANSPLANTING TRICK

When you plant a perennial bed, it's best to leave plenty of space between plants so that they have room to grow to their mature height and spread. That means your bed will have lots of gaps for the first few years after you plant it. You can plant colorful annuals in the gaps, but you'll have to buy new plants each year. Instead, with a little extra planning, you can plant "filler" perennials that you'll eventually transplant elsewhere, explains Mike Guidosh of Klyn Nurseries in Perry, Ohio. "Careful planning is time well-spent on the front end of any planting project," Mike says. Just select some other spots in your yard where you'll eventually want perennials. Plant your new bed densely with perennials, and then transplant them as the bed becomes crowded. You'll save money and beautify other planting beds year after year!

Creating a Lush Lawn

To get the most out of seeding a new lawn, keep the top inch of soil moist after you sow. You can keep the soil moist by setting up an oscillating sprinkler on a timer early in the morning (about 5 A.M.) and letting it run for two hours. (Avoid watering at night because the cool, wet conditions can promote fungal disease.) Keep using the sprinkler system as needed until you've mowed your new lawn twice.

Speedy Bulb Planting

Here's how to plant lots of bulbs fast, while still getting that natural look, according to Charlie Proutt, a landscape architect and the owner of Horsford's Nursery in Charlotte, Vermont.

1. Dig a 24-inch round hole to the proper depth for the bulbs you're planting (cut right through the sod if you're planting in the lawn). Place the sod next to the hole, then put the dirt in a wheelbarrow and place the desired number of bulbs in the hole.

2. Take one giant step (about 2 to 3 feet) and dig another 24-inch hole, putting the sod aside. As you dig, throw the soil into the first hole to cover the bulbs. Then place more bulbs in the hole you just dug.

3. Repeat Step 2 until you have planted all of your bulbs. Use the soil that you put in the wheelbarrow to backfill the final hole. Then gently replace the sod on top of each hole.

2-3'

Take giant steps—between planting holes, that is—to quickly achieve a natural look with bulbs.

Success with *Sod*

If you spring for sod when you plant your lawn, you'll want to do everything possible to make sure it succeeds. Try these tips to give your new grass a chance to shine:

- Order only the amount of sod you can lay in one day (better to order less than more) because sod has no shelf life.

- When the sod arrives, store the pallets in dense shade or make a tent over the pallets to shade them. Don't lay plastic sheeting directly on the pallets of sod because they'll heat up and burn.

- Don't soak the sod as it lays in rolls because sodden sod is too muddy to handle. Instead, sprinkle lightly to keep the rolls from drying out.

- Stagger the joints when laying sod strips side by side. No two pieces should be lined up (staggering helps the joints knit together).

- Use a roller after the job is finished to ensure that the roots are in full contact with the soil. Any air pockets will result in dead sod.

- Protect any sod that adjoins a garden, walkway, or driveway from drying out on the edges by covering the sod with soil or mulch.

Once your sod is laid, make sure to water it well to help establish a healthy root system. And keep people (and pets) from walking on it until the roots have taken hold.

When laying sod, make sure to stagger the joints, instead of lining them up. And keep a hose nearby to lightly sprinkle the sod rolls so that they don't dry out.

Rock That Rootball

When you plant a tree, it's important that the top of the rootball be even with the soil surface. But what do you do if you dig the hole, slide the tree into place, and it's at the wrong height? Don't panic; you don't need to remove the tree to make adjustments. Just pull on the trunk a little to rock the still-intact rootball onto an angle. If the tree is set too low, add some soil under the rootball. If it's too high, remove some soil. Then rock the tree back in the other direction, and add or remove soil under the other side of the rootball.

Stomp Away *Air Pockets*

Boot out deadly pockets of air, which dry out the root systems of woody trees and shrubs. After digging the hole and placing the plant in, begin to backfill in layers. Shovel about one-third of the soil into the hole and then literally stomp the soil with the heel of your boot around the circumference of the rootball. Repeat twice more, and add extra soil if needed after the final stomping.

Rough Up the Roots

"Gardeners are too nice to their plants," says Amy Rose-White, perennial grower at Rocky Dale Gardens in Bristol, Vermont. Instead of handling container plants delicately, rough them up a little so that you don't end up with potbound plants whose roots continue to bind themselves after they're in the ground. Fred Dabney, owner of Quansett Nurseries in South Dartmouth, Massachusetts, suggests slicing the roots of a container plant vertically to

Give potbound plants some extra help in getting established by slicing the rootball before transplanting. Using a knife, make a slice 1 inch deep every 3 to 4 inches around the circumference of the rootball.

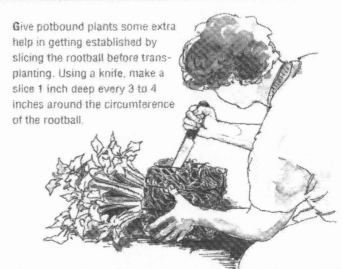

eliminate any possibility of girdling roots and to help stimulate new root growth. Turn the rootball in your hand

and use a knife to carefully make a slice approximately 1 inch deep every 3 to 4 inches around its circumference.

Beware of the Flare

Confused about how deep to plant? "Proper planting depth is best determined by the location of the 'trunk flare,'"

says Tom Vanicek, production manager at Quansett Nurseries in South Dartmouth, Massachusetts. Trunk flare is the area where the base of the trunk widens at

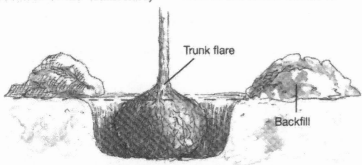

Trunk flare

Backfill

Locate the trunk flare—where the base of the trunk widens at ground level—and use that as a planting depth guide.

ground level. Tom warns that after transporting and handling, the plant settles into the soil of the rootball and the flare is often covered up. So peel the burlap off of the rootball to properly locate the flare. Tom also recommends making sure the top of the ball sticks up 1 to 3 inches above what will be your finished grade around the plant. You'll know you have the trunk flare where it's supposed to be if you can see a slight arc from the rootball to ground level, says Tom.

homegrown HINTS

RHODODENDRON SUCCESS SECRETS

You *can* have lush rhododenrons without having to tinker with soil pH—you just have to start afresh and plant them differently. Here are some secrets to getting rhododendrons to flourish from Pam Tworig, treasurer of North Branch Landscape Co., Inc., in Stamford, Vermont. Choose a shady site and amend the soil with rich, composted bark mulch (preferably softwood) and composted leaves. Rhododendrons don't like soggy feet, so raise them a little higher in the planting hole if you need to improve drainage. And never let the soil completely dry out.

Transplanting
Trees in Full Leaf

Want to defy Mother Nature and transplant a young, established tree in full leaf in July? Here's a suggestion from Steve Tworig, president of North Branch Landscape Co., Inc., in Stamford, Vermont, and a director of the New England Nursery and Landscape Association. He has had excellent success with up to 1½-inch-thick sugar maples (*Acer saccharum*).

1. Thoroughly water the tree.

2. Strip off all leaves (you may want to remove the petioles, too, because they will look less than attractive if left on). Use a stepladder to reach the leaves near the top of the tree.

3. Wait a day or two, then dig up the tree and transplant it, making sure you water the tree thoroughly when it's settled in its new site.

4. Water the tree every other day during hot weather, and about three times a week throughout the fall.

By removing the leaves, you reduce moisture loss through them, which means there is more moisture available to help the tree establish itself in its new home. A second set of leaves will grow back before the end of the season.

New Use for Old News

Reuse your daily newspaper and help your plants in the process. Soak your paper in water, then line planting holes with pieces of the wet paper before you put in the plants. Tom Strangfeld, director of sales and marketing at Weston Nurseries, Inc., in Hopkinton, Massachusetts, says he and other gardeners did just that at the Public Gardens in Boston. They were following the advice of avid gardener Polly Wakefield, who says the papers slow the loss of moisture from the newly planted rootballs.

Easy Plant I.D.

Here are a couple of easy ways to remember what you planted, from Leonard Perry, extension ornamental horticulturist at the University of Vermont. To start, make permanent labels as soon as you get home from the nursery with new plants. Use plastic tabs (less expensive than metal labels) and write the name on the tab with a #2 pencil. Also, keep a log of the plant and its location in your landscape.

brilliant

Bird & Butterfly Gardens

Discover wonderful ways to bring more color and life into your gardens (and a little creature company, too!). From far-out feeders to flower favorites, find out how to entice your favorite birds to your backyard and provide food, water, and cover for your feathered friends. You'll discover that the right selection of plants is the easiest way to attract an interesting array of birds. To lure eye-catching butterflies to your flower garden, follow these gardener-tested tips and techniques that will bring flutters of brilliant color all season long.

Compass Plants Have Impact

"Birds love the seeds of the compass plant," says Jim Becker, who gardens with birds in Oregon. The compass plant looks something like a giant yellow hollyhock from a distance, with a spire of golden daisy flowers that can grow to reach 8 feet tall. An imposing clump makes a grand statement beside a garden gate— but make sure it's in easy view of an indoor window so that you can enjoy the parade of finches, juncos, sparrows, downy woodpeckers, and other seed-eaters who will be stopping by all fall and winter. Compass plant (*Silphium laciniatum*) grows best in moist, well-drained, humus-rich soil in full sun.

Christmas *Celebrations*

Winter birds love a Christmas feast even after the holiday. Set your Christmas tree outside where it's sheltered from the wind, then gather leftovers from holiday baking to make garlands of raisins, nuts, and dried fruit slices. Fill citrus rinds with peanut butter and fruit for ornaments.

Birds *Love* Love-Lies-Bleeding

Let things go to seed in your garden and you'll be surprised at the birds you attract, says Jim Becker, co-owner of Goodwin Creek Gardens in Williams, Oregon. "We grow amaranth and a decorative millet and sell the seeds, and we have to cover the plants when the seeds are ripe to fight off sparrows and juncos. But the birds love the seeds so much that we always leave some for them when we're done harvesting," says Jim.

Jim and his wife, Dottie, grow love-lies-bleeding (*Amaranthus caudatus*), an annual with long strands of deep pink flowers that look like thick, soft yarn, and 'Hopi Dye' amaranth, an upright, plumey type. "Both amaranths are great for dried flowers as well as for birdseed," Jim says.

Sow seeds outdoors after all danger of frost has passed and the soil is warm. Amaranth will ripen most of its grain 90 days after sowing.

Native sparrows, like this song sparrow, love the tasty, tiny seeds of love-lies-bleeding (*Amaranthus caudatus*), an old-fashioned garden annual.

problem solver
WITH BIRD FEEDERS, BIGGER IS BETTER

When you're hosting a lot of backyard birds, a feeder can empty quickly as hungry beaks snatch up sunflower seeds and other morsels. Save time refilling feeders by choosing large-capacity feeders that hold more seed. One ingenious option is hopper feeders that refill themselves as the seed level drops. Hopper feeders prevent waste, too, because windy, rainy weather doesn't soak the whole buffet, only the portion that's in the tray of the feeder.

Betsy Colwell, president of Droll Yankees, a company that's been making high-quality bird feeders for decades, says her favorite feeder is a large hopper model called the Jagunda. "I'm busy all week," she says, "so I can fill it up at the beginning of the week and not have to refill it until the weekend." When birds are depending on your banquet, a big feeder means they won't go away hungry when supplies run out and you're not home.

An A-**maize**-ing Hedge for Birds

Pauline Hoehn Gerard of Henderson, Kentucky, wanted to keep alive her memories of her childhood farm, so she planted

Blue jay

Cardinal

Woodpecker

a triple row of corn along her property line. "I planned to pick the ears for decorations, but the birds beat me to it. We had cardinals galore, blue jays, blackbirds, even woodpeckers feasting on our corn hedge," she says.

Pauline says she loves watching corn grow, and she needed a quick-growing hedge for privacy at her new home. Her corn grew quickly to towering heights, giving her home a farmlike feel, along with protection from prying eyes, and brought with it the added bonus of fun-to-watch birds at harvesttime.

Plant a unique bird-attracting hedge by spacing sweet corn or field corn seeds 2 inches apart, in three staggered rows 6 inches apart, for maximum privacy.

Back-to-**Back** for Bluebirds

Bluebirds often face very stiff competition for birdhouses, especially from tree swallows. Since bluebirds aren't aggressive, the swallows usually end up with possession of the houses, but David H. Drake, president of Coveside Conservation Products, a birdhouse manufacturing company, says the solution is simple.

"Mount two bluebird houses back to back or very close together, and tree swallows and bluebirds will live happily as neighbors."

The key to this idea's success is knowing that birds of the same species, like two families of tree swallows, won't nest in adjoining apartments, even though they will nest as nearby neighbors. By putting the houses back to back, you play on the tree swallows' natural instinct not to share space. Birds of different species, however, will coexist contentedly even if their homes are very close together.

If tree swallows have been usurping your bluebird houses, mount a pair of nest boxes back to back. Swallows get one house, bluebirds get the other, and you get to enjoy two species of birds instead of just one.

problem solver

FEATURE THE FOOD CHAIN

Prairie wildflowers, like coneflowers (*Echinacea* and *Ratibida* spp.), Joe-Pye weed (*Eupatorium* spp.), and many others, not only produce edible seeds for birds but are also unparalleled at attracting insects—the foundation of the food chain, notes Neil Diboll, chairman of Prairie Nursery, Inc., in Westfield, Wisconsin.

"Insects are the number one food for baby birds, so plant the prairie plants, attract the bugs, and feed the birds!" says Neil. When you plant perennial wildflowers that attract insects, you're bound to attract the birds that dine on them. If you buy large plants, you'll get flowers the first year you plant. After the flowers are finished, sparrows, finches, and other songbirds will enjoy the seeds from fall right through winter.

Slip-Sliding Away

"I love squirrels," says Heidi Doss, "but sometimes they get into my birdhouses and destroy the nests." So Heidi made simple baffles for her birdhouse posts out of 30-inch lengths of PVC pipe. She slips the pipe over the post and lets it slide to the ground, then she mounts the house on top of the pipe. The squirrels can't get a climbing grip on the slippery plastic barrier.

"My wrens are much more relaxed," says Heidi, a teaching naturalist at Wesselman Woods Nature Preserve. "It's as if they know the squirrels won't be able to reach their eggs or babies."

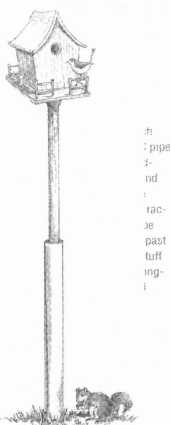

Benefits of *Bayberries*

Bird lovers should try planting bayberry (*Myrica pensylvanica*), recommends Mike Hradel, owner of Coldstream Farm in Michigan. This easy-to-grow shrub not only offers evergreen shelter year-round, providing what Mike calls a "visual shield" to keep birds safe, but it also provides a winter banquet for birds. "It's unusual to find food and cover on the same bush in winter," he says.

Bayberry is tops with just about every bird that's around in winter. "More than 20 kinds of birds eat the berries," Mike notes, including pheasants, wild turkeys, flickers, downy woodpeckers, chickadees, Carolina wrens, and yellow-rumped warblers. "The one I could hardly believe is the tree swallow," he says. "I thought they ate only insects. But they love bayberries!"

The native shrub thrives in many soil conditions, including acid soils and poor, sterile, sandy soils, and is salt tolerant. Plant bayberry shrubs in full sun to partial shade in Zones 2 to 7.

The Cupboard *Gourmet*

Cleaning out the cupboards used to yield nothing more than a trash can full of stale food, so birdwatcher Deborah Burdick of Mount Vernon, Indiana, decided to make a special recipe for her backyard birds. "I emptied the last inch or two of all the cereal boxes, added some raisins that were hard as rocks, and mushed in the leftover oatmeal from breakfast," she relates. "Then I spooned out dabs of the stuff right onto the ground." Sparrows arrived before she even got back in the house, and they were soon joined by the local mockingbird and a bunch of noisy blue jays.

Now she crumbles stale crackers by hand so the pieces are smaller, and sometimes she treats her birds to a dollop of peanut butter for a tastier mix. Deborah says that natural cereals (without a lot of added sugar or preservatives) are best for the birds because they supply healthy calories that provide longer-lasting energy. Cereals with nuts or berries in the mix are always surefire favorites, too.

A MIX OF MILLETS SUITS SPARROWS

Small seed-eaters like sparrows, juncos, buntings, and finches love the tiny, round seeds of millets, a group of annual grasses. Any type of millet is perfect for feeding birds from summer through winter because the birds pick every seed clean, says David A. Kester, owner of Kester's Wild Game Food Nurseries. Some millets shed their seeds and provide a banquet for sparrows and other ground-feeding birds. Other millets keep their seedheads intact on the plants, making sturdy landing pads for the finches who feed on the seeds.

David's company sells a millet mix that includes the familiar birdseed proso millet (*Panicum miliaceum*), which has an arching, branching seedhead that ripens in only 65 to 70 days. Siberian millet (*Setaria italica*), also called German millet, is another member of the mix. *S. berian* millet has interesting solid seedheads that "droop like a long finger," according to David. Seedheads like cattail pokers are the trademark of pearl millet (*Pennisetum glaucum*), another good bird plant. Japanese millet (*Echinochloa crusgalli*), with seedheads shaped like a turkey's foot, and several other types, round out the menu.

Plant a *Food Patch* for Birds

Tempt pheasants, quail, bobwhites, doves, and dozens of smaller birds with a patch of food plants just for them. David A. Kester, owner of Kester's Wild Game Food Nurseries in Omro, Wisconsin, encourages bird lovers to plant a special bird garden that includes both perennials and annuals. He recommends clovers, including bird's-foot trefoil (*Lotus corniculatus*), which sports clusters of sunny yellow blossoms, and bush clovers (*Lespedeza* spp.), which have small pink or purple pealike flowers. For fast payoff, include annuals like sorghum, buckwheat, and small-seeded soybeans and peas. Prepare a small planting bed, mix together a handful of seeds, and sow the seeds over the bed. Water generously until the seeds germinate, then take the low-maintenance approach—just wait for the bird visitors to arrive.

problem solver

SOME LIKE THEIR GARDENS WILD

Find a discreet part of your garden and let it go wild, and you'll get all kinds of pleasant bird surprises, says Jim Becker, co-owner of Goodwin Creek Gardens in Williams, Oregon. Birds love weed seeds even better than birdseed. "Let some weeds stand, and you'll have birds visiting until every seed is gone," he says, pointing to chicory and wild lettuce as two favorites of feathered friends. Goldfinches are particularly fond of both plants, he adds.

Lamb's-quarters, dock, and ragweed (if you don't have allergies) are top-notch, too. Jim says that even a small patch of weeds (about 3 × 3 feet), will provide plenty of great edibles for feathered friends. If you have room, let an even larger patch go wild, and you'll be on your way to creating a natural bird habitat. Be sure to keep your wild patch well away from your vegetable garden, though, so that stray seeds don't sow a crop of heavy labor for next season.

Warm Water in Winter

Second-story condo resident and bird lover Elizabeth Castaldi of Washington, D.C., says supplying fresh water in the winter to birds is a challenge. On cold days, she fills a clay saucer with warm water in early morning. "The birds have learned my schedule," she says. "They're already in line for baths when I bring the water outside." When she heads to work, she brings the saucer indoors until the next morning's birdie bath time.

Plant a Birdseed Garden

When bird-feeder traffic drops off in late spring, Heidi Doss of Evansville, Indiana, has an ingenious solution for getting rid of the last few inches of birdseed. "I know whatever's left won't last until fall, when feeding season picks up again, so I use it to plant a garden for my birds." Heidi prepares a bed just as she would for planting annuals, then she scatters the leftover seed and covers it lightly with soil.

Plant mixed seed so that you can learn what kind of plants grow from birdseed. "Buckwheat really surprised me—I had no idea it was so pretty," says Heidi. Let the birdseed plants mature in place so that the birds can enjoy the seeds just as they grow. Birds will come and go in the patch all winter long, says Heidi.

Plant birdseed mix just as you would annual flowers for a true surprise garden. Many birdseed plants, like the buckwheat shown here, are as pretty as ornamentals.

Appreciating the Ordinary

Starlings, pigeons, and English sparrows were just "city birds" to Gretchen Harrison of Boston, but that changed when her two-year-old daughter, Erica, discovered the "birdies." Looking at the city bird life through fresh eyes, Gretchen found these birds as fascinating as any songbirds.

She and Erica feed their little troupe of feathered friends just what cosmopolitan birds like most—slices of sourdough bread, leftover French pastries, scraps of cream-cheese Danish, and the remnants of corned beef sandwiches. As the birds linger over the feast, Gretchen and her daughter learn their habits and personalities, and now they bird-watch daily on their sojourns through the city.

Once you change your outlook on city birds, you'll find they can be very interesting to watch. "Now I see how tender the pigeons are with their mates, and I love to watch the feathers on the starlings change colors in the sun, and listen to them sing," Gretchen says. "Even the English sparrows are pretty darn cute—especially if they're all you have!"

Wreath of Welcome

As soon as bird enthusiast Janice Ostock of Bethlehem, Pennsylvania, moved into her new home, she hung a grapevine wreath beside her front door. "I was still unpacking boxes when I noticed a house finch bringing sticks to the porch, and when I checked, I found a pair of them were making a nest in my wreath!" she exclaims.

Since finches, robins, and other songbirds often nest near human haunts, wreaths and hanging baskets located near the doorway all make great nest sites.

Janice's birds built their deep cup-shaped nest on the bottom of the wreath. "It looked just like the wreaths you see in the shops," she says, "except instead of an artificial nest, mine was real—and had birds in it."

Create an instant nest site for house finches or robins by hanging a decorative grapevine wreath near your front door. These friendly birds will let you enjoy a close-up look at how they raise a family.

problem solver

BIRDS AREN'T BREAD SNOBS

If you're baking and things don't turn out quite right, put the "failures" out for the birds. Like Janice Ostock of Bethlehem, Pennsylvania, you may find that you end up baking just for the birds. When Janice experimented with her new electric bread maker, the first loaves were rejects, so she tossed them outside for the birds. "When I finally gave up on baking, I saw the birds were still coming for the leftovers—except there weren't any. I couldn't let them down, so I still bake—just for them! They aren't fussy at all about how the bread turns out," she says.

A loaf of her dense, chewy bread, chock-full of nuts and raisins, probably costs more than the day-old bread she could buy at a bakery outlet, but Janice says she doesn't mind. She likes baking for an appreciative audience who relishes even the mistakes.

View Vines As Opportunity

With their tangle of stems and often luxuriant leaves, vines are favorite hiding places and homesites for many song-birds. Learn to look in vines and you'll discover lots of bird nests, says Marie Bedics, whose Pennsylvania farm-house has a wall covered with Boston ivy (*Parthenocissus tricuspidata*). The ivy shelters neighborhood wrens, spar-rows, and robins at night, and its thick growth also provides a home for a catbird that has lived in her yard for well over a decade.

Other vines favored by birds include: Virginia creeper (*Parthenocissus quinquefolia*), English ivy (*Hedera helix*), autumn clematis (*Clematis terniflora*), anemone clematis (*Clematis montana*), and grapevines. All are excellent bird homes and hideouts.

Marie says the best part of the ivy-covered nests is that you never know there are any birds there. "But at night, just before dark, I can hear them twittering as they settle down to sleep," she says. "And I watch the catbirds coming and going with food for their babies."

Keep the Neighbors Happy

Natural-looking gardens make birds and butterflies happy, but they may stir up trouble in a neighborhood of tradition-ally groomed lawns. Jean Hadley, whose natural land-scape covers acres in Solitude, Indiana, suggests a couple of simple tricks to keep neighbors content. "That feeling of the yard being out of control seems to be what bothers neighbors most," she says. "If you're making the transition from grass to plants in your yard, make sure you have nice, neat, wide paths going through it. That gives it a planned look that signals the plantings are intentional and not just noxious weeds left to roam."

Jean says that a fence helps, too—not to hide the gardens, but just to give them a civi-lized feel. A jumble of plants along a split-rail fence looks a lot better to most people than a so-called weed patch, she says. Even though you could have the same plants with either scenario, adding the fence can make a huge difference in how the garden is perceived.

homegrown HINTS

WINTER FRUIT FOR WILD BIRDS

Most trees drop their fruit in fall, says Mike Hradel, owner of Coldstream Farm in Free Soil, Michigan, when there's more than the birds can eat. But in winter, when they really need it, there's little available. Good bird plants for wintertime, he suggests, are dogwoods and crabapples; he also recommends small-fruited crabapples like 'Sargent' and 'Zumi', which bear perfectly bite-size fruit for avian visitors.

Paint *Is for* People

"Birds would much rather be in a birdhouse that's made as inconspicuous as it could be," says David H. Drake, president of Coveside Conservation Products in Maine. "Otherwise it's easier for predators to find them." He recommends leaving nesting boxes *au naturel*, with no paint or decorations, so that they blend in with the landscape as easily as tree bark.

A coat of paint won't deter birds, but David adds, "Paint is for people—the birds don't care!" Sometimes paint can be a good thing, he says. If your spring weather swings from warm to cold, a dark-painted birdhouse will soak up heat and keep it cozy. If you put a birdhouse in full sun, a coat of white paint will keep it cooler inside by reflecting those warming rays.

Best Bets for Nest Building

Indian hemp (*Apocynum cannabinum*) and the very similar-looking dogbane (*A. androsaemifolium*) supply perfect nest-building materials for orioles and vireos, says Jean Hadley of Solitude, Indiana. Colonies of these plants grow at the wood's edge and in the meadow on Jean's property. All winter long, the stems of the plants weather in the rain and snow to become bird magnets by late spring. That's when Baltimore orioles, vireos, and the occasional yellow warbler descend to pull apart the old stems, stripping off thin, soft strings that are as tough as dental floss—just the thing for weaving nests. Plant dogbane and Indian hemp where the plants have room to spread naturally into a colony.

Get Wild with "Wild Ones"

If joining together with other nature lovers for seed exchanges, chats with kindred spirits, nature hikes, field trips, excursions, and tours of backyard wildlife gardens sounds like your cup of tea, get in touch with Wild Ones—Natural Landscapers, Ltd., a nonprofit group dedicated to educating and sharing information among "regular people" who love to learn about wildlife.

Members share information about gardening with native plants, attracting birds to their gardens and flowerbeds, and generally creating wildlife-friendly, ecologically sound backyards. For more information, write to Wild Ones—Natural Landscapers, Ltd., P.O. Box 23576, Milwaukee, WI 23576.

Keep the Peanut Eaters Happy

Peanuts are a big draw for woodpeckers, blue jays, chickadees, titmice, and nuthatches, but the nuts disappear fast when you offer them in an open feeder. The perfect solution is a tube feeder of stainless steel wire mesh with ¼-inch holes, says Betsy Colwell, president of Droll Yankees. The mesh holes are too small to let birds grab whole peanuts, but plenty big for woodpeckers and others to hammer through and get pieces.

The big draw for the peanut feeder is the woodpeckers, says Betsy. "They love peanuts! They'll bang away, just like they do on trees." Squirrels don't bother the feeder, she says, because they can't chew through the mesh.

If you're the handy type, you can make a homemade peanut feeder by replacing the plastic tube of an existing tube feeder. Here's how:

1. Measure the circumference and height of the tube of the existing feeder. (For example, some tubes measure 11 inches around and 12 inches high.) Buy a piece of stainless steel, ¼-inch wire mesh to correspond to the measurements you took. If you can't find stainless steel mesh, use hardware cloth.

2. Roll the wire mesh into a tube shape to fit the feeder's top and bottom, then bend the mesh over itself to anchor the edges together.

3. Fasten the feeder top and bottom to the mesh. Usually, the bottom of the feeder will hold tight when inserted into the mesh, and the top is held in place with the wire hooks at the ends of the handle.

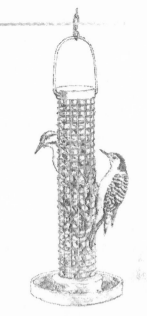

Replace the plastic tube of a thistle feeder with ¼-inch wire mesh to make a whole-peanut feeder for woodpeckers, blue jays, and other nut lovers.

4. Insert the bottommost perch of the feeder.

5. Fill with shelled whole peanuts, and hang the feeder in a spot where you can watch the visiting birds.

Faking It

Many gardeners use red flowers to lure hummingbirds to their garden, where they'll stay to sample flowers of other colors, too, but natural-garden lover Jean Hadley of Solitude, Indiana, had trouble fitting fire-engine red into her romantic pastel color scheme. So she turned to subterfuge—a quick trip to the local discount store gave her an armload of red silk flowers that she wired to nearly everything in the garden. "It worked like a charm!" laughs Jean.

Now she has hummingbirds every summer, returnees who remember her garden of nectar-filled flowers, even though the red silk deception is long gone.

Shape Is What Matters

If you love hummingbirds, plant a garden specifically for them. Jim Becker, co-owner of Goodwin Creek Gardens, says flower shape, not color, is what matters most when planning a hummingbird garden. Tubular flowers, whether they're tiny mint flowers or 8-inch datura blossoms, are what hummingbirds seek. Their long, skinny beaks are exactly right for reaching the nectaries at the base of these flowers. "Red gets their attention, but they really like deep purples and blues, too," he notes.

Hummingbirds will go to just about any flower, Jim says. If it proves to be a good nectar source, they'll return to it over and over. One of Jim's favorite hummingbird flowers is a white-flowered selection of normally bright red cardinal flower (*Lobelia cardinalis*), which he selected from a batch of seed-grown plants.

Buying new annuals or perennials for your garden? Check the flower shape—if it's tubular, it will attract hummingbirds, no matter what size or color the flowers are. The penstemon, salvia, and bee balm shown here are three examples of the many tubular flowers you can use.

Natural Nectar

Hummingbirds are hungry after migratory flights, so treat them to nectar-rich early bloomers. Jim Becker, co-owner of Goodwin Creek Gardens in Oregon, suggests planting red flowering currant (*Ribes sanguineum*), a graceful shrub or small tree native to the Pacific Northwest that's also at home in Zones 6 through 8. A buffet table in a bush, dangling clusters of red-to-pink fragrant flowers decorate the branches very early in spring.

High-Rise Hummingbirds

Hummingbirds have such an eye for red that they'll go to great lengths—or heights—to investigate, says Elizabeth Castaldi of Washington, D.C. Trying to brighten her small second-story balcony, she added a pot of bright red zonal geraniums (*Pelargonium* spp.) that could take the all-day sun and heat. Within days, she noticed a male ruby-throated hummingbird at the flowers. When migration time came in early fall, she had a constant stream of tiny winged visitors humming with delight at her bright container garden.

problem SOLVER

BRING ON THE HUMMERS

"Hummingbirds return from migration in early spring, when there's not a lot blooming in the garden," says Jim Becker, who co-owns Goodwin Creek Gardens with his wife, Dottie. Luckily, the long-spurred, nectar-filled blooms of native American columbines are just hitting full stride when the zippy little birds return to the scene. Jim and Dottie grow both the eastern and western wild columbine (*Aquilegia canadensis, A. formosa*). Both are great garden plants as well as hummingbird plants. Columbines bloom for weeks, sustaining the birds until other plants come into flower.

Advantages of Agastaches

Their Latin name may be a mouthful, but perennials from the genus *Agastache* are sure-fire hummingbird attractors. Most plants have foliage with a delicious licorice scent, which has given more than one species the nickname licorice plant, or anise hyssop. But it's the whorled spikes of small tubular flowers that are the prime attraction for hummingbirds.

Many gardeners are familiar with anise hyssop (*Agastache foeniculum*), but there are many more to be discovered, says Jim Becker, co-owner of Goodwin Creek Gardens in Oregon. Native mostly to the American Southwest and Mexico, agas-

taches include many plants of surprising cold hardiness, usually to Zone 6.

Agastache species and hybrids offer a variety of flower color, including blue-purple, salmon, rosy orange, pink, and pale blue. Hummingbirds love all of them. Jim recommends 'Apricot Sunrise', whose beautiful orangey apricot flowers light up perennial gardens. 'Firebird' is a vivid orange-salmon flowered hybrid that creates a full, branching plant.

Richly fragrant rock anise hyssop (*Agastache rupestris*) has gray-green foliage and rich, rosy orange flowers; hardy to Zone 5, it blooms for almost two months straight. Plant in lean, well-drained soil in full sun.

Perch-Free Means *Predator*-Free

Perches on birdhouses are so common that it doesn't occur to most people that perches allow predators access to baby birds. If you're building new birdhouses, eliminate the predator threat by skipping the perches, or saw off the perches from an existing birdhouse, says David H. Drake, president of Coveside Conservation Products.

If you think about it, natural nesting cavities don't come with perches—nearby twigs and branches serve as landing platforms for arriving bird parents. Birdhouse perches offer raccoons or cats a balancing spot and allow them to reach an exploring paw inside the nest box, which often proves fatal to young nestlings.

Help **Birds** *Get a Grip*

Rough-sawed boards are cheaper than finished lumber and better for birdhouses, says David H. Drake, owner of Coveside Conservation Products. Rough-sawed boards make it easy for little bird feet to get a grip on the roof, sides, or front of the house.

Handy
Hinges Make
Cleaning *Easy*

Cleaning out a birdhouse is easy if the house has a hinged side or front, says David H. Drake, president of Coveside Conservation Products. On birdhouses with hinged openings, you'll need to undo the fastener, open the side, and make one swipe with your rubber-gloved hand to neaten things for the next resident. If you decide to clean out old nesting materials, it may be best to wait until the beginning of the breeding season to allow time for beneficial wasps to emerge from hibernation in the old nest. Wasps help control parasitic blowfly populations that can lower the survival rate of nestlings.

Hinged sides on a birdhouse make it easy to clean out old nesting materials.

Squirrel-
Proofing Your
Birdhouses

You may have visions of happy bird families when you mount that new birdhouse, but your neighborhood squirrels have other plans. Rambunctious squirrels often gnaw the entrance holes to enlarge them so the squirrels can move in instead of the birds. You can squirrel-proof nest boxes with a slate or metal barrier to keep out the varmints, says David H. Drake, president of Coveside Conservation Products, makers of high-quality wooden birdhouses fitted with antisquirrel devices. The guards are easy to cut and install, although you may find it easier to have a masonry or metal shop make them.

A metal or slate squirrel guard will keep bushytails from using their teeth to enlarge the entrance hole to suit their own furry bodies.

You will need a square of slate or sheet metal twice the size of the birdhouse's entrance hole. For example, if the entrance hole measures 2¼ inches in diameter, the slate or metal should be 4½ inches square. Drill a hole the same size as the entrance hole in the center of the slate or metal square, using a masonry drill bit if drilling through slate. Place the guard flush with the front of the birdhouse, aligning the holes. Drill into the wood along the outer edges of the guard, then attach it to the birdhouse, using the heads of the screws to anchor the guard in place.

Let the *Sun Shine* In

The latest bird-behavior research shows that house sparrows prefer a dark home to a light-filled one, so you can discourage them from monopolizing your birdhouses by retrofitting your existing houses to allow light in through the roof, says David H. Drake, president of Coveside Conservation Products.

You can test the theory in your own backyard by making a few quick changes to your existing bird boxes, but be sure to use this method only on boxes that are placed in shaded areas so that the interior temperatures of the boxes don't soar when the sun pours in.

To discourage house sparrows, there are two methods that allow the sun to shine in, yet keep predators out. The first method (Steps 1–3) uses heavy-duty wire mesh and is the easiest to install, but it doesn't offer the birds any protection from the rain. The second method (the "Timely Tip" that follows) uses Plexiglas, requires a saw and an electric drill, and provides shelter from the rain if the birdhouse is in an open area.

Both methods work for flat-roof and sloped-roof houses.

1. Remove the roof from the existing house.

2. Using wire cutters, cut a piece of ¼-inch or ½-inch wire mesh (as heavy-duty as possible) 1 inch wider than the inside diameter of the top of your birdhouse.

3. Bend the sides of the mesh up so that the mesh fits snugly within the width of the birdhouse. Using a staple gun and staples, staple the mesh securely to the inside of the house about 2 inches from the top edge. The mesh will let in sunlight but keep out predators.

You can easily discourage house sparrows from usurping your bluebird houses by retrofitting the houses with a Plexiglas or wire mesh roof. The added light will keep house sparrows away since they prefer to nest in darkness.

Timely tip

To keep nesting birds protected from the rain *and* discourage house sparrows in the process, David says that you can also substitute a Plexiglas roof for the existing roof on your birdhouse. Using a coping saw or an electric saber saw and the existing birdhouse roof as a pattern, cut Plexiglas to fit the birdhouse. Using an electric drill, drill holes for screws to attach the Plexiglas roof to the birdhouse. Screw the new roof to the top of the birdhouse.

The **Magic** of Running Water

"I've read that birds are attracted to the sound of running water," says Heidi Doss of Evansville, Indiana, "but I'm a long way from the closest creek." So when Heidi found a small, battery-operated submersible pump for $20 at her local home-supply store, she set it right in her birdbath amongst the river stones. "I get to see all kinds of birds coming to drink—orioles, tanagers, warblers, vireos, plus the usual robins and catbirds—and I get to soak up that wonderful soothing sound," she says. She keeps her pump on the lowest setting so there's only a gentle gurgle through the outlet pipe, just enough to make the sound of water music.

Add a small submersible pump and stones to a pottery birdbath to create the sound of water music.

Poke Your *Perspective*

Pokeberries aren't people-friendly—they're poisonous—but birds devour them with great enjoyment. Mockingbirds, robins, thrashers, waxwings, thrushes, downy woodpeckers, flickers, and many others flock to pokeberries. "A lot of people think of poke as a weedy thing," says Jim Becker, co-owner of Goodwin Creek Gardens, but when a photograph of pokeweed (*Phytolacca americana*) and artemisias in a garden setting appeared in a national magazine, he noted that interest in the plant surged. "In the right setting it can be very pretty—those big, tall, arching, reddish purple stems and the purple fruits in fall."

Sometimes more unusual bird visitors show up. Jim notes he got a good look at a pileated woodpecker on his poke plant. The almost crow-size bird was hanging upside down to eat the fruit.

Don't pull every pokeweed seedling you see. Even though it's considered a common weed by some, bird watchers will be thrilled to see the visitors, like this mockingbird, that it attracts.

Pokeweed seedling

Mockingbird

Grasses for *Bird Safety*

Thick-growing prairie grasses or other ornamental grasses planted here and there in the landscape provide a safe haven for birds that need to make a quick dash to safety. They grow fast, too, making them useful from the first season they're in the soil. And most stay useful over winter, offering birds a tangle of sheltering stems, not to mention a bounty of nutritious seeds and nesting material in the spring. Neil Diboll, chairman of Prairie Nursery, Inc., in Westfield, Wisconsin, says that prairie grasses can play a starring role in a wildlife-friendly garden. "The plants of the prairie have the unique ability to combine both habitat and beauty," he says. Try these easy-to-grow prairie grasses: big bluestem (*Andropogon gerardii*), switchgrass (*Panicum virgatum*), and Indian grass (*Sorghastrum nutans*).

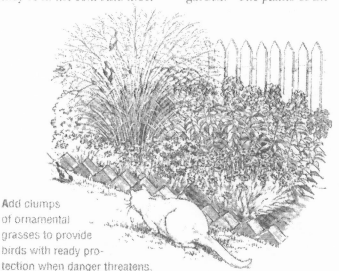

Add clumps of ornamental grasses to provide birds with ready protection when danger threatens. Many cultivars, like this striking switchgrass (*Panicum virgatum* 'Heavy Metal'). combine beautifully with pinks and garden phlox.

Timely tip

Because meadow flowers and field flowers are so good as nectar plants, people tend to forget the role that grasses play with butterflies, Neil says. "Many butterfly and moth caterpillars use grasses and sedges for food sources. Grasses also serve as resting areas for adult butterflies—when it's a really windy day, they go down into the grasses for protection," he adds.

Grasses serve as host plants for many species of skippers; sedges also attract skippers, in addition to satyrs. Native prairie grasses like little bluestem (*Schizachyrium scoparium*), switchgrass (*Panicum virgatum*), and others add beauty into a naturalistic or prairie garden.

Butterflies Zip for Zinnias

Marie Bedics of Whitehall, Pennsylvania, used to grow zinnias every year, but one spring she planted pricier perennials instead. "The difference was amazing," she says. "I was used to having lots of butterflies, and all of a sudden I had hardly any. They liked my cheap zinnias better than any of the five-dollar perennials I'd replaced them with!"

Now a patch of zinnias is always a standard part of her garden. "If you sit on my porch," says Marie, "you can watch the butterflies come across the field into my yard and head straight for the zinnias. Once they're here, they'll visit the other flowers, but they always hit the zinnias first."

Fruit Feeder Attracts *Butterflies*

Ripened fruit attracts many species of butterflies, says David Roth-Mark of New Harmony, Indiana. He offers butterflies all kinds of fruit buffets, and has discovered that they seem to like pears and bananas the best, "especially when the fruit is really soft and brown."

David surmises that the butterflies are more easily able to pierce the flesh of the fruit with their proboscis when it's overripe. He peels the bananas and slices the pears in half lengthwise before putting them on his feeder. "One pear can last for a week," he says, "so it doesn't cost much to keep them happy."

Instead of tossing overripe fruit into the compost pile, invite a few fluttery friends to dine on your past-prime leftovers.

Watermelon Magnet for Monarchs

Watermelon on the patio is a regular part of summer life—a slice of summer that butterflies, especially monarchs, enjoy, too, says nature lover Pauline Hoehn Gerard of Henderson, Kentucky. "I keep a chunk of watermelon on the deck rail just for butterflies," says Pauline. "In late summer, there might be a dozen butterflies eating at the same time." She adds that the butterflies seem to enjoy the watermelon most when it's overripe.

Swallowtails Think Purple

Many backyard butterfly enthusiasts have noticed that big swallowtails seem to prefer the color purple, and Jim Becker, co-owner of Goodwin Creek Gardens, agrees. "It seems that purple and swallowtails go together," he says. "Brazilian vervain (*Verbena bonariensis*) is absolutely excellent for attracting butterflies."

This tall, bare-stemmed perennial offers its clusters of tiny, soft purple flowers for months, until frosts stop it for

The Mutt and Jeff of the verbena clan—tall, skinny Brazilian vervain and low, sprawling 'Homestead Purple' vervain—are irresistible to swallowtail butterflies.

the season. It's easy to plant anywhere in the garden, but be sure to keep some near the front of the bed, where you can watch the butterflies that come to visit. Jim also recommends another verbena, a sprawling hybrid called 'Homestead Purple' that grows so fast you can use it as a groundcover.

Nature Versus Nurture

Sometimes Mother Nature's haphazard plantings teach the most useful lessons about gardening. "I planted all the flowers the books said in order to attract butterflies," says Pauline Hoehn Gerard of Henderson, Kentucky, "but I still didn't have many." Then she remembered how many butterflies she saw fluttering over the milkweed (*Asclepias* spp.), ironweed (*Vernonia noveboracensis*), and asters along the dirt lane to her house when she was a girl. She brought home some of these "weeds" from her mother's land, and she quickly found that butterfly visitations increased dramatically. It turns out that Pauline's old "weed" favorites are all-American natives that bloom from the middle of summer on, when butterfly populations are at their peak.

Barbara Trick, office manager for Aullwood Audubon Center and Farm, uses native trees to attract butterflies. Tulip trees, hackberries, maples, oaks, and white ash are nurseries for swallowtails, giant silk moths, and other winged beauties.

'Beefsteak' for Butterflies

When her 'Beefsteak' tomato crop swelled and cracked one year in the heat, Deborah Burdick of Mt. Vernon, Indiana, discovered that the cracked, leaking fruits turned out to be butterfly attractors. "I was walking out for my mail when I saw motion at the tomato plants. There were a bunch of butterflies—beautiful golden ones that I learned were hackberry butterflies, and some beautiful black and blue red-spotted purples! Now I leave some of my cracked tomatoes on the vine just for the butterflies."

All Around the Butterfly Bush

The single butterfly bush (*Buddleia davidii*) in the back of Janice Ostock's garden in Bethlehem, Pennsylvania, drew a steady stream of butterflies, but it was hard to get a glimpse of the butterfly visitors close up. So she created her own butterfly visitors' center by adding a path that circled the bush. The butterflies often retreat to the back of the bush when an observer comes near, says Janice, but the new walkway puts the nectar sippers in full view.

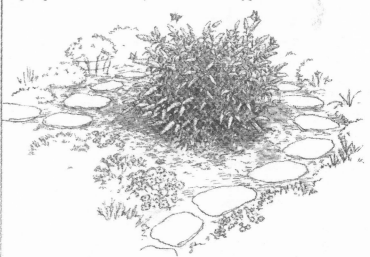

Give garden visitors a great view of visiting butterflies by making paths all the way around a butterfly bush.

Early Bloomers for *Early* Butterflies

When a few days of unseasonably warm weather late in winter coax early butterflies from their sheltered niches beneath bark, not many flowers are waiting to greet them. Nature lover Pauline Hoehn Gerard of Henderson, Kentucky, felt sorry for the early butterflies because there was no nectar to sip, so she planted early-blooming autumn-flowering cherry (*Prunus subhirtella* 'Autumnalis'), which she notes blooms not only in fall but also in late winter, whenever the weather turns mild for just two or three days.

Pauline also recommends winter-flowering witch hazel (*Hamamelis* × *intermedia* 'Arnold Promise'), whose ribbony-petaled flowers offer sustenance until real spring arrives. Pussy willow is another great food source for butterflies. When early butterflies such as the tiny blue spring azures and the elegant, understated mourning cloaks emerge from winter slumber, there's a banquet of rich nectar waiting for them.

Butterflies Think *Lavender Is Lovely*

Barbara Trick, office manager for Aullwood Audubon Center and Farm in Ohio, loves her patch of lavender. When the sweet blue-purple flowers bloom, "it's absolutely covered with butterflies and bumblebees," she says. "There are so many honeybees and bumblebees at it that the plants practically vibrate." Jim Becker, co-owner of Goodwin Creek Gardens in Oregon, concurs with Barbara about lavender. "Lavender has proven to be an excellent butterfly flower for us," he says, noting that his visitors include masses of skippers and western swallowtails.

Spritz the Bricks for *Butterflies*

As David Roth-Mark of New Harmony, Indiana, was watering the potted plants on the family deck one July, he noticed that butterflies were attracted to the wet spots on the bricks. So a couple of times a day, he wets down the bricks with the hose to give butterflies a drink. Many butterflies are puddle-sippers and seek out hospitable wet spots to congregate and drink. If you don't have bricks to wet with the hose, you can keep a spot of gravel wet or make a butterfly drinking station out of an old cookie sheet or big clay saucer lined with gravel or river stones.

Spray your brick walk or patio with the hose whenever you're out in the garden, and colorful, thirsty butterflies will soon become regulars.

Resources

To help you find great plants, garden supplies, and even more ingenious gardening ideas, we've compiled the following list of plant associations, gardening organizations, mail-order nurseries, garden suppliers, and product manufacturers. When you contact associations or specialty nurseries by mail, please enclose a self-addressed, stamped envelope with your inquiry. Notes in italics indicate particular products, plants, or services offered.

ASSOCIATIONS AND ORGANIZATIONS

American Dianthus Society
Rand B. Lee
P.O. Box 22232
Santa Fe, NM 87502-2232

American Horticultural
Therapy Assn.
909 York St.
Denver, CO 80206-3799
Phone: (301) 948-3010
E-mail: ahta@ahta.org
Web site: www.ahta.org

American Iris Society
Marilyn Harlow, Dept. E
P.O. Box 55
Freedom, CA 95019
Web site: www.iso
media.com/home/AIS

American Rose Society
P.O. Box 30000
Shreveport, LA 71130-0030
Phone: (318) 938-5402
Fax: (318) 938-5405
E-mail: ars@ars-hq.org
Web site: www.ars.org

Backyard Wildlife
Habitat Program
National Wildlife Federation
8925 Leesburg Pike
Vienna, VA 22184-0001
Web site: http://nwf.org/nwf
/habitats

Bio-Dynamic Farming
& Gardening Assn.
Bldg. 1002B
Thoreau Center
The Presidio
P.O. Box 29135
San Francisco, CA 94129-0135
Phone: (800) 516-7797
Fax: (415) 561-7796
Web site: www.bio
dynamics.com

California Certified
Organic Farmers
1115 Mission St.
Santa Cruz, CA 95060
Phone: (831) 423-2263
Fax: (831) 423-4528

The Lady Bird Johnson
Wildflower Center
4801 La Crosse Ave.
Austin, TX 78739
Phone: (512) 292-4100
E-mail: nwrc@onr.com
Web site: www.wildflower.org

The Maine Organic Farmers
& Gardeners Assn.
P.O. Box 2176
Augusta, ME 04338
Phone: (207) 622-3118
Fax: (207) 622-3119
Web site: www.mofga.org

National Gardening Assn.
180 Flynn Ave.
Burlington, VT 05401
Phone: (802) 863-1308
Fax: (802) 863-5962
Web site: www2.garden.org
/ngA

North American
Butterfly Assn. (NABA)
4 Delaware Rd.
Morristown, NJ 07960
Phone: (973) 285-0907
Fax: (973) 285-0936
E-mail: naba@naba.org
Web site: www.naba.org

North American Fruit
Explorers (NAFEX)
1716 Apples Rd.
Chapin, IL 62628
Web site: www.nafex.org

Northeast Organic
Farming Assn. (NOFA)
Web site: www.nofa.org
/index.html
*An affiliation of seven state
chapters—CT, MA, NH, NJ,
RI, VT. Check Web site for
state contacts.*

Rodale Institute
Experimental Farm
611 Siegfriedale Rd.
Kutztown, PA 19530
Phone: (610) 683-1400
Fax: (610) 683-8548

Seed Savers Exchange
3076 N. Winn Rd.
Decorah, Iowa 52101
Phone: (319) 382-5990

Seeds of Diversity Canada
P.O. Box 36
Station Q
Toronto, Ontario
M4T 2L7 Canada
Phone: (905) 623-0353
E-mail: sodc@interlog.com
Web site: www.interlog.com
/~sodc

Wild Ones–Natural
Landscapers, Ltd.
P.O. Box 23576
Milwaukee, WI 23576
*Nonprofit group dedicated to
educating and sharing infor-
mation among those who love
wildlife.*

BENEFICIAL INSECTS

Bountiful Gardens
18001 Shafer Ranch Rd.
Willits, CA 95490-9626
Phone/fax: (707) 459-6410

Gardens Alive!
5100 Schenley Pl.
Lawrenceburg, IN 47025
Phone: (812) 537-8650
Fax: (812) 537-5108

Gurney's Seed & Nursery Co.
110 Capital St.
Yankton, SD 57079
Phone: (605) 665-1930
Fax: (605) 665-9718

Harmony Farm
Supply & Nursery
P.O. Box 460
Graton, CA 95444
Phone: (707) 823-9125
Fax: (707) 823-1734
E-mail: info@harmony
farm.com
Web site: www.harmony
farm.com

The Natural Gardening Co.
217 San Anselmo Ave.
San Anselmo, CA 94960
Phone: (707) 766-9303
Fax: (707) 766-9747
E-mail: info@natural
gardening.com
Web site: www.natural
gardening.com

Peaceful Valley Farm Supply
P.O. Box 2209
Grass Valley, CA 95945
Phone: (530) 272-4769
Fax: (530) 272-4794
Web site: www.grow
organic.com

Territorial Seed Co.
P.O. Box 157
Cottage Grove, OR
97424-0061
Phone: (541) 942-9547
Fax: (888) 657-3131
E-mail: tertrl@srv1.vsite.com
Web site: www.territorial
seed.com

BIRD AND BUTTERFLY SUPPLIES

The Audubon Workshop
5200 Schenley Pl.
Lawrenceburg, IN 47025
Phone: (812) 537-3583

Coveside Conservation
Products
202 U.S. Route One
Box 374
Falmouth, ME 04105
Phone: (207) 774-7606
Fax: (207) 774-7613
E-mail: coveside@maine.com
Web site: www.maine.com
/coveside
Manufacturer of birdhouses

Down to Earth
4 Highland Circle
Lucas, TX 75002
Phone: (800) 865-1996
Fax: (972) 442-2816
E-mail: sales@downto
earth.com
Web site: www.downto
earth.com

Droll Yankees Inc.
27 Mill Rd.
Foster, RI 02825
Phone: (800) 352-9164
Fax: (401) 647-7620
E-mail: custserv@droll
yankees.com
Web site: http://droll
yankees.com
Manufacturer of bird feeders

Duncraft
102 Fisherville Rd.
Concord, NH 03303-9020
Phone: (800) 763-7878
Fax: (603) 226-3735
E-mail: info@duncraft.com
Web site: www.duncraft.com

Kester's Wild Game
Food Nurseries, Inc.
P.O. Box 516
Omro, WI 54963
Phone: (920) 685-2929
Fax: (920) 685-6727
E-mail: pkester@vbe.com
Web site: www.vbe.com
/~pkester

Wild Bird Centers
of America, Inc.
Phone: (800) 945-3247
Web site: www.wildbird
center.com

Wild Birds Unlimited
Phone: (800) 326-4928
Web site: www.wbu.com

Wildlife Nurseries, Inc.
P.O. Box 2724
Oshkosh, WI 54903-2724
Phone: (920) 231-3780
Fax: (920) 231-3554

BULBS

Breck's
6523 North Galena Rd.
Peoria, IL 61632
Phone: (309) 689-3850
Web site: www.springhill
nursery.com/brecks.html

Brent & Becky's Bulbs
7463 Heath Trail
Gloucester, VA 23061
Phone: (804) 693-3966
Fax: (804) 693-9436
E-mail: BBHeath@aol.com
Web site: www.brentand
beckysbulbs.com

Dutch Gardens
P.O. Box 200
Adelphia, NJ 07710-0200
Phone: (800) 775-2852
Fax: (732) 780-7720
E-mail: cs@dutchgardens.nl
Web site: www.dutchgardens.nl

McClure & Zimmerman
P.O. Box 368
108 W. Winnebago
Friesland, WI 53935-0368
Phone: (920) 326-4220
Fax: (800) 692-5864
Web site: www.mzbulb.com

Van Bourgondien Bros.
P.O. Box 1000
Babylon, NY 11702-9004
Phone: (800) 622-9959
Fax: (516) 669-1228
E-mail: blooms@dutch
   bulbs.com
Web site: www.dutchbulbs.com

FLOWERS AND ORNAMENTAL GRASSES

Abundant Life Seed Foundation
P.O. Box 772
Port Townsend, WA 98368
Phone: (360) 385-5660
Fax: (360) 385-7455
E-mail: abundant@olypen.com
Web site: http://csf.Colorado
   .edu/perma/abundant

Kurt Bluemel, Inc.
2740 Greene Lane
Baldwin, MD 21013-9523
Phone: (410) 557-7229
Fax: (410) 557-9785
E-mail: kbi@bluemel.com
Web site: www.blue
   mel.com/kbi

Bountiful Gardens
18001 Shafer Ranch Rd.
Willits, CA 95490-9626
Phone/fax: (707) 459-6410

Burns Water Gardens
R.R. #2
Baltimore, Ontario
K0K 1C0 Canada
Phone: (905) 372-2737
Fax: (905) 372-8625
E-mail: wtrgdn@eagle.ca
Web site: www.eagle.ca
   /~wtrgdn

W. Atlee Burpee & Co.
300 Park Ave.
Warminster, PA 18991-0001
Phone: (800) 888-1447
Fax: (800) 487-5530
Web site: www.burpee.com

Busse Gardens
5873 Oliver Ave., SW
Cokato, MN 55321-4229
Phone: (800) 544-3192
Fax: (320) 286-6601
E-mail: bussegardens@
   cmgate.com

California Carnivores
7020 Trenton-Healdsburg Rd.
Forestville, CA 95436
Phone: (707) 838-1630
Fax: (707) 838-9899
E-mail: califcarn@aol.com
Web site: www.california
   carnivores.com
*Commercially propagated
   pitcher plants (Sarracenia)*

Carroll Gardens
444 E. Main St.
Westminster, MD 21157
Phone: (800) 638-6334
Fax: (410) 857-4112

Collector's Nursery
16804 N.E. 102nd Ave.
Battle Ground, WA 98604
Phone: (360) 574-3832
Fax: (360) 571-8540
E-mail: dianar@collectors
   nursery.com
Web site: www.collectors
   nursery.com
*Pulmonarias by Terra Nova
   Nurseries*

Daydreamer Aquatic
& Perennial Gardens
Route 1, Box 438
Belpre, OH 45714
Phone: (800) 741-3867
Fax: (740) 423-4355
E-mail: trishatdpg@aol.com
Web site: www.daydreamer
   gardens.com

Daylily Discounters
1 Daylily Plaza
Alachua, FL 32615
Phone: (904) 462-1539
Fax: (904) 462-5111
E-mail: daylily@earthlink.com
Web site: www.daylily
   discounters.com

Ferry-Morse Seed Co.
P.O. Box 488
Fulton, KY 42041-0488
Phone: (800) 283-3400
Fax: (800) 283-2700
Web site: www.gardennet.com/
   FerryMorse

Forestfarm
990 Tetherow Rd.
Williams, OR 97544-9599
Phone: (541) 846-7269
Fax: (541) 846-6963
E-mail: forestfarm@aone
   pro.net
Web site: www.forestfarm.com

Fragrant Farms, Inc.
413 Woods Lane
New Harmony, IN 47631
Phone: (888) 814-4665
Fax: (812) 682-4577
E-mail: mark@fragrant
   farms.com
Peony plants and cut flowers

The Fragrant Path
P.O. Box 328
Fort Calhoun, NE 68023
*Seeds of fragrant, old-
   fashioned, and rare plants*

Goodness Grows, Inc.
Highway 77 N
P.O. Box 311
Lexington, GA 30648
Phone: (706) 743-5055
Fax: (706) 743-5112

Goodwin Creek Gardens
P.O. Box 83
Williams, OR 97544
Phone: (541) 846-7357

Greer Gardens
1280 Goodpasture Island Rd.
Eugene, OR 97401-1794
Phone: (541) 686-8266
Fax: (541) 686-0910

Heronswood Nursery
7530 N.E. 288th St.
Kingston, WA 98346
Phone: (360) 297-4172
Fax: (360) 297-8321
Web site: www.herons
   wood.com
*Pulmonarias by Terra Nova
Nurseries*

Jackson & Perkins
P.O. Box 1028
Medford, OR 97501
Phone: (800) 292-4769
Fax: (800) 242-0329
Web site: www.jacksonand
   perkins.com

Johnny's Selected Seeds
Foss Hill Rd.
Albion, ME 04910-9731
Phone: (207) 437-4357
Fax: (800) 437-4290
E-mail: customerservice@
   johnnyseeds.com
Web site: www.johnny
   seeds.com

J. W. Jung Seed Co.
335 S. High St.
Randolph, WI 53957-0001
Phone: (800) 297-3123
Fax: (800) 692-5864

Limerock Ornamental
Grasses, Inc.
70 Sawmill Rd.
Port Matilda, PA 16870
Phone: (814) 692-2272
Fax: (814) 692-9848

Logee's Greenhouses, Ltd.
141 North St.
Danielson, CT 06239-1939
Phone: (860) 774-8038
Fax: (888) 774-9932
E-mail: logee-info@logees.com
Web site: http://logees.com/www

Louisiana Nursery
5833 Highway 182
Opelousas, LA 70570
Phone: (318) 948-3696
Fax: (318) 942-6404

Dan Majeski Nurseries
P.O. Box 674
117 French Rd.
West Seneca, NY 14224-0674
Phone: (716) 825-6410
Fax: (716) 827-8537
E-mail: danjr@majeski
   nursery.com
Web site: www.majeski
   nursery.com
*Pulmonarias by Terra Nova
Nurseries*

Milaeger's Gardens
4838 Douglas Ave.
Racine, WI 53402-2498
Phone: (800) 669-9956
Fax: (414) 639-1855

The Natural Garden
38W443 Highway 64
St. Charles, IL 60175
Phone: (630) 584-0150
Fax: (630) 584-0185

Niche Gardens
1111 Dawson Rd.
Chapel Hill, NC 27516
Phone: (919) 967-0078
Fax: (919) 967-4026
E-mail: orders@nichegdn.com
Web site: www.nichegdn.com

Nichols Garden Nursery
1190 N. Pacific Highway
Albany, OR 97321-4580
Phone: (541) 928-9280
Fax: (541) 967-8406
E-mail: info@gardennursery.com
Web site: www.garden
   nursery.com

Park Seed
1 Parkton Ave.
Greenwood, SC 29647-0001
Phone: (800) 845-3369
Fax: (800) 275-9941
E-mail: orders@parkseed.com
Web site: http://parkseed.com

Pinetree Garden Seeds
Box 300
616A Lewiston Rd.
New Gloucester, ME 04260
Phone: (207) 926-3400
Fax: (888) 527-3337
E-mail: superseeds@world
   net.att.net
Web site: www.superseeds.com

Plant Delights Nursery, Inc.
9241 Sauls Rd.
Raleigh, NC 27603
Phone: (919) 772-4794
Fax: (919) 662-0370
E-mail: office@plantdel.com
Web site: www.plantdel.com
*Nursery propagated pitcher
plants (Sarracenia)*

Prairie Moon Nursery
Route 3, Box 163
Winona, MN 55987
Phone: (507) 452-1362
Fax: (507) 454-5238

Prairie Nursery
P.O. Box 306
Westfield, WI 53964
Phone: (608) 296-3679
Fax: (608) 296-2741
Web site: www.prairie
   nursery.com

Roslyn Nursery
211 Burrs Lane
Dix Hills, NY 11746
Phone: (516) 643-9347
Fax: (516) 427-0894
E-mail: roslyn@concentric.net
Web site: www.cris.com/
~Roslyn
*Pulmonarias by Terra Nova
Nurseries*

Seeds Blüm
HC 33, Box 2057
Boise, ID 83706
Phone: (800) 742-1423
Fax: (208) 338-5658
E-mail: 103374.167@compu
serve.com
Web site: www.seedsblum.com

Seeds of Change
P.O. Box 15700
Sante Fe, NM 87506-5700
Phone: (888) 762-7333
Fax: (888) 329-4762
E-mail: service@seedsof
change.com
Web site: www.seedsof
change.com

Shepherd's Garden Seeds
30 Irene St.
Torrington, CT 06790-6658
Phone: (860) 482-3638
Web site: www.shepherd
seeds.com

Southern Perennials & Herbs
98 Bridges Rd.
Tylertown, MS 39667-9338
Phone: (800) 774-0079
Fax: (601) 684-3729
E-mail: sph@neosoft.com
Web site: www.s-p-h.com

Stokes Seeds Inc.
P.O. Box 548
Buffalo, NY 14240-0548
Phone: (716) 695-6980
Fax: (888) 834-3334
E-mail: Stokes@stokeseeds.com
Web site: www.stokeseeds.com

Territorial Seed Co.
P.O. Box 157
Cottage Grove, OR 97424-0061
Phone: (541) 942-9547
Fax: (888) 657-3131
E-mail: tertrl@srv1.vsite.com
Web site: www.territorial
-seed.com

Thompson & Morgan, Inc.
P.O. Box 1308
Jackson, NJ 08527-0308
Phone: (800) 274-7333
Fax: (888) 466-4769
E-mail: c-svcs@thompson
-morgan.com
Web site: http://thompson
-morgan.com

Van Ness Water Gardens
2460 North Euclid Ave.
Upland, CA 91784-1199
Phone: (909) 982-2425
Fax: (909) 949-7217
E-mail: vnwg@vnwg.com
Web site: www.vnwg.com

Wayside Gardens
1 Garden Lane
Hodges, SC 29695-0001
Phone: (800) 845-1124
Fax: (800) 457-9712
E-mail: orders@wayside
gardens.com
Web site: www.wayside
gardens.com

We-Du Nurseries
Route 5, Box 724
Marion, NC 28752
Phone: (704) 738-8300
Fax: (704) 738-8131

White Flower Farm
P.O. Box 50
Litchfield, CT 06759-0050
Phone: (800) 411-6159
Fax: (860) 496-1418
Web site: www.whiteflower
farm.com

Wildseed Farms
P.O. Box 3000
425 Wildflower Hills
Fredericksburg, TX 78624-3000
Phone: (800) 848-0078
Fax: (830) 990-8090
Web site: www.wildseed
farms.com

Woodlanders, Inc.
1128 Colleton Ave.
Aiken, SC 29801
Phone/fax: (803) 648-7522

FRUITS AND BERRIES

Adams County Nursery, Inc.
26 Nursery Rd.
P.O. Box 108
Aspers, PA 17304
Phone: (717) 677-8105
Fax: (717) 677-4124
E-mail: acn@cvn.net
Web site: www.acnursery.com

Applesource
1716 Apples Rd.
Chapin, IL 62628
Phone: (800) 588-3854
Fax: (217) 245-7844
E-mail: vorbeck@csj.net
Web site: www.apple
source.com
Apples only, not apple trees

Bear Creek Nursery
P.O. Box 411
Northport, WA 99157
Phone: (509) 732-6219
Fax: (509) 732-4417
E-mail: BearCreek@plix.com
Web site: http://BearCreek
Nursery.com

Country Carriage
Nurseries & Seed, Inc.
P.O. Box 548
Hartford, MI 49057
Phone: (616) 621-2491

Cummins Nursery
18 Glass Factory Bay Rd.
Geneva, NY 14456
Phone: (315) 789-7083
E-mail: jmc1@epix.net
Web site: www.dabney.com/
cumminsnursery

Edible Landscaping
361 Spirit Ridge Lane
P.O. Box 77
Afton, VA 22920-0077
Phone: (804) 361-9134
Fax: (804) 361-1916
E-mail: el@cstone.net
Web site: www.eat-it.com

Hidden Springs Nursery
170 Hidden Springs Lane
Cookeville, TN 38501
Phone: (931) 268-2592
Grafted bareroot fruit trees

Indiana Berry & Plant Co.
5218 West 500 South
Huntingburg, IN 47542
Phone: (812) 683-3055
Fax: (812) 683-2004
E-mail: inberry@psci.net

Raintree Nursery
391 Butts Rd.
Morton, WA 98356
Phone: (360) 496-6400
Fax: (888) 770-8358
E-mail: leonard@rain
treenursery.com
Web site: www.rain
treenursery.com

Rocky Meadow
Orchard & Nursery
360 Rocky Meadow Rd. NW
New Salisbury, IN 47161
Phone: (812) 347-2213
Fax: (812) 347-2488
E-mail: rockymdw@net
pointe.com

St. Lawrence Nurseries
325 S. H. 345
Potsdam, NY 13676
Phone: (315) 265-6739
E-mail: trees@sln.pots
dam.ny.us
Web site: www.sln.pots
dam.ny.us

Southmeadow Fruit Gardens
P.O. Box 211
10603 Cleveland Ave.
Baroda, MI 49101
Phone: (616) 422-2411
Fax: (616) 422-1464
E-mail: smfruit@aol.com

Stark Bro's Nurseries
& Orchards Co.
P.O. Box 10
Louisiana, MO 63353
Phone: (800) 478-2759
Fax: (573) 754-5290
E-mail: service@starkbros.com
Web site: www.starkbros.com

GARDENING SUPPLIES AND TOOLS

Alsto's Handy Helpers
Route 150 East
P.O. Box 1267
Galesburg, IL 61402-1267
Phone: (800) 447-0048
Fax: (800) 522-5786

Bountiful Gardens
18001 Shafer Ranch Rd.
Willits, CA 95490-9626
Phone/fax: (707) 459-6410

W. Atlee Burpee & Co.
300 Park Ave.
Warminster, PA 18991-0001
Phone: (800) 888-1447
Fax: (800) 487-5530
Web site: www.burpee.com

Delgard Aluminum
Ornamental Fencing
Delair Group, Inc.
8600 River Rd.
Delair, NJ 08110
Phone: (800) 235-0185
Fax: (609) 663-1297
Web site: www.delair
group.com/delgard
*Manufacturers of decorative
fencing, including aluminum
picket-style fencing*

Dripworks
231 E. San Francisco St.
Willits, CA 95490
Phone: (800) 616-8321
Fax: (707) 459-9645
E-mail: dripwrks@pacific.net
Web site: www.dripworks
usa.com
Drip irrigation products

Gardener's Supply Co.
128 Intervale Rd.
Burlington, VT 05401-2850
Phone: (800) 863-1700
Fax: (800) 551-6712
E-mail: info@gardeners.com
Web site: www.gardeners.com

Gardens Alive!
5100 Schenley Pl.
Lawrenceburg, IN 47025
Phone: (812) 537-8650
Fax: (812) 537-5108

Harmony Farm
Supply & Nursery
P.O. Box 460
Graton, CA 95444
Phone: (707) 823-9125
Fax: (707) 823-1734
E-mail: info@harmonyfarm.com
Web site: www.harmony
farm.com

The Horchow Collection
P.O. Box 620048
Dallas, TX 75262-0048
Phone: (800) 456-7000
Web site: www.nmdirect.com
/hc.html
Two-tiered topiary system

Ideal Concrete Block Co.
55 Power Rd.
Westford, MA 01886
Phone: (978) 692-3076
Fax: (978) 692-0817
Concrete wall systems

Jim Jeansonne
Baton Enterprises
8867 Highland Rd.
Suite 160
Baton Rouge, LA 70806
Phone: (225) 766-1268
Fax: (225) 757-8161
E-mail: info@spira-stake.com
Web site: www.spira-stake.com
Spira-stake

Jerith Manufacturing Co., Inc.
3901 G St.
Philadelphia, PA 19124
Phone: (800) 344-2242
Fax: (215) 739-4844
E-mail: sales@jerith.com
Web site: www.jerith.com
*Manufacturers of decorative
fencing, including aluminum
picket-style fencing*

Johnny's Selected Seeds
Foss Hill Rd.
Albion, ME 04910-9731
Phone: (207) 437-4357
Fax: (800) 437-4290
E-mail: customerservice@
johnnyseeds.com
Web site: www.johnny
seeds.com

Keystone Retaining Walls, Inc.
4444 W. 78th St.
Bloomington, MN 55435
Phone: (800) 747-8971
Fax: (612) 897-3858
Web site: http://psld.ipr.com
/keystone
Concrete wall systems

Kinsman Co., Inc.
P.O. Box 357
River Rd.
Point Pleasant, PA 18950
Phone: (800) 733-4146
Fax: (215) 297-0450
E-mail: contact@kinsman
garden.com
Web site: www.kinsman
garden.com

A. M. Leonard, Inc.
241 Fox Drive
Piqua, OH 45356
Phone: (800) 543-8955
Fax: (800) 433-0633
E-mail: info@amleo.com
Web site: www.amleo.com

The Natural Gardening Co.
217 San Anselmo Ave.
San Anselmo, CA 94960
Phone: (707) 766-9303
Fax: (707) 766-9747
E-mail: info@natural
gardening.com
Web site: www.natural
gardening.com

Ohio Earth Food, Inc.
5488 Swamp St., NE
Hartville, OH 44632
Phone: (330) 877-9356
Fax: (330) 877-4237

Peaceful Valley Farm Supply
P.O. Box 2209
Grass Valley, CA 95945
Phone: (530) 272-4769
Fax: (530) 272-4794
Web site: www.grow
organic.com

Pinetree Garden Seeds
Box 300
616A Lewiston Rd.
New Gloucester, ME 04260
Phone: (207) 926-3400
Fax: (888) 527-3337
E-mail: superseeds@world
net.att.net
Web site: www.superseeds.com

Plow & Hearth
P.O. Box 5000
Madison, VA 22727-1500
Phone: (800) 627-1712
Fax: (800) 843-2509

Risi Stone Systems
Le Parc Office Tower
8500 Leslie St., Suite 390
Thornhill, Ontario
L3T 7P1 Canada
Phone: (905) 882-5898 *or*
(800) 626-WALL
Fax: (905) 882-4556
E-mail: info@risistone.com
Web site: www.risistone.com
Concrete wall systems

Ruibal's Topiary Systems
1118 S. Central Expressway
Dallas, TX 75201
Phone: (214) 744-3434
Two-tiered topiary system

Saratoga Rail Fence & Supply Co.
P.O. Box 13864
Albany, NY 12212-9600
Phone: (800) 869-8703
Fax: (518) 869-8755
PVC post and rail fencing

Seeds of Change
P.O. Box 15700
Sante Fe, NM 87506-5700
Phone: (888) 762-7333
Fax: (888) 329-4762
E-mail: service@seedsof
change.com
Web site: www.seedsof
change.com

Smith & Hawken
Two Arbor Lane
Box 6900
Florence, KY 41022-6900
Phone: (800) 981-9888 *catalog
requests only*
Fax: (606) 727-1166
Web site: www.smith
-hawken.com

Sto-Cote Products, Inc.
P.O. Box 310
Richmond, IL, 60071
Phone: (800) 435-2621
Fabrene

Territorial Seed Co.
P.O. Box 157
Cottage Grove, OR 97424-0061
Phone: (541) 942-9547
Fax: (888) 657-3131
E-mail: tertrl@srv1.vsite.com
Web site: www.territorial
-seed.com

Unilock New York, Inc.
51 International Blvd.
Brewster, NY 10509
Phone: (914) 278-6700
Fax: (914) 278-6788
E-mail: newyork@unilock.com
Web site: www.unilock.com
Paving stones, retaining walls, and curbing

Whatever Works
Earth Science Bldg.
74 20th St.
Brooklyn, NY 11232
Phone: (800) 499-6757
Fax: (718) 499-1005
Web site: www.whatever
works.com
Garden-Lite rock planters

Worm's Way
7850 N. Highway 37
Bloomington, IN 47404
Phone: (800) 274-9676
Fax: (800) 316-1264
e-mail: info@wormsway.com
Web site: http://wormsway.com

HERBS

Fox Hollow Seed Co.
P.O. Box 148
McGrann, PA 16236
Phone: (412) 548-7333
Fax: (412) 543-5751

The Fragrant Garden
Katherine Glynn
P.O. Box 281
Port Perry, Ontario
L9L 1A3 Canada
Phone: (905) 985-0079
Fax: (905) 985-4788
E-mail: kglynn@sprint.ca
Potpourri, essentials oils, and other fragrance products

Gaia Garden Herbal
Dispensary
Chanchal Cabrera
2672 West Broadway
Vancouver, B.C.
V6K 2G3 Canada
Phone: (604) 734-4372
Fax: (604) 734-4376
E-mail: GAIA
GARDEN@bc.sympatico.ca
Classically trained English herbalist who teaches internationally

Goodwin Creek Gardens
P.O. Box 83
Williams, OR 97544
Phone: (541) 846-7357

Horizon Herbs
P.O. Box 69
Williams, OR 97544
Phone: (541) 846-6704
E-mail: herbseed@chatlink.com
Web site: www.budget.net
/~herbseed
Seed, rootstock, and live plants of medicinal herbs

Johnny's Selected Seeds
Foss Hill Rd.
Albion, ME 04910-9731
Phone: (207) 437-4357
Fax: (800) 437-4290
E-mail: customerservice@
johnnyseeds.com
Web site: www.johnny
seeds.com

Long Creek Herbs
Route 4, Box 730
Oak Grove, AR 72660
Phone: (417) 779-5450
Fax: (417) 779-5450
E-mail: LCHerbs@tri-lakes.net
Web site: www.longcreek
herbs.com
Herb products and books; demonstration gardens open to public

Lunar Farms Herbals
3 Highland-Greenhills
Gilmer, TX 75644
Phone: (800) 687-1052
E-mail: spritsong1@aol.com
Web site: www.herbworld.com
/lunarfarms
Herbal salves, oils, and personal care products

Nichols Garden Nursery
1190 N. Pacific Highway
Albany, OR 97321-4580
Phone: (541) 928-9280
Fax: (541) 967-8406
E-mail: info@garden
nursery.com
Web site: www.garden
nursery.com

Richters Herb Catalogue
357 Hwy. 47
Goodwood, Ontario
L0C 1A0 Canada
Phone: (905) 640-6677
Fax: (905) 640-6641
E-mail: inquiry@richters.com
Web site: www.richters.com

Sage Mountain Herbs
Rosemary Gladstar
P.O. Box 420
E. Barre, VT 05649
Phone: (802) 479-9825
Fax: (802) 476-3722
Ongoing classes, apprenticeship program, and correspondence course

The Sandy Mush Herb Nursery
316 Surrett Cove Rd.
Leicester, NC 28748
Phone: (704) 683-2014

Shepherd's Garden Seeds
30 Irene St.
Torrington, CT 06790-6658
Phone: (860) 482-3638
Web site: www.shepherd
seeds.com

Well-Sweep Herb Farm
205 Mt. Bethel Rd.
Port Murray, NJ 07865
Phone: (908) 852-5390

SOIL TESTING

Cook's Consulting
R.D. 2, Box 13
Lowville, NY 13367
Phone: (315) 376-3002
*Organic recommendations,
free soil testing kit*

Peaceful Valley Farm Supply
P.O. Box 2209
Grass Valley, CA 95945
Phone: (530) 272-4769
Fax: (530) 272-4794
Web site: www.grow
organic.com
*Basic soil test as well as one for
micronutrients; organic
recommendations provided*

Timberleaf Soil Testing Services
39648 Old Spring Rd.
Murrieta, CA 92563
Phone: (909) 677-7510
*Basic and trace mineral soil
tests; organic recommendations provided*

Wallace Laboratories
365 Coral Circle
El Segundo, CA 90245
Phone: (310) 615-0116
Fax: (310) 640-6863
*Analyses for essential nutrients
along with nonessential potentially toxic heavy metals;
analyses of water, plant tissues,
composts, fertilizers, and
building materials; recommendations provided*

Woods End Research Laboratory
P.O. Box 297
Mt. Vernon, ME 04352
Phone: (207) 293-2457
Fax: (207) 293-2488
*Soil testing for homeowners
and soil life testing; compost
testing kit*

TREES, SHRUBS, AND VINES

Carroll Gardens
444 E. Main St.
Westminster, MD 21157
Phone: (800) 638-6334
Fax: (410) 857-4112

Forestfarm
990 Tetherow Rd.
Williams, OR 97544-9599
Phone: (541) 846-7269
Fax: (541) 846-6963
E-mail: forestfarm@aonepro.net
Web site: www.forestfarm.com

Greer Gardens
1280 Goodpasture Island Rd.
Eugene, OR 97401-1794
Phone: (541) 686-8266
Fax: (541) 686-0910

Gurney's Seed & Nursery Co.
110 Capital St.
Yankton, SD 57079
Phone: (605) 665-1930
Fax: (605) 665-9718

Pickering Nurseries, Inc.
670 Kingston Rd.
Pickering, Ontario
L1V 1A6 Canada
Phone: (905) 839-2111
Fax: (905) 839-4807
Roses

The Roseraie at Bayfields
P.O. Box R
Waldoboro, ME 04572-0919
Phone: (207) 832-6330
Fax: (800) 933-4508
E-mail: zapus@roseraie.com
Web site: www.roseraie.com
*Roses and lobster-trap metal
climbing rose supports*

Roslyn Nursery
211 Burrs Lane
Dix Hills, NY 11746
Phone: (516) 643-9347
Fax: (516) 427-0894
E-mail: roslyn@concentric.net
Web site: www.cris.com
/~Roslyn

Wayside Gardens
1 Garden Lane
Hodges, SC 29695-0001
Phone: (800) 845-1124
Fax: (800) 457-9712
E-mail: orders@wayside
gardens.com
Web site: www.wayside
gardens.com

White Flower Farm
P.O. Box 50
Litchfield, CT 06759-0050
Phone: (800) 411-6159
Fax: (860) 496-1418
Web site: www.whiteflower
farm.com

Woodlanders, Inc.
1128 Colleton Ave.
Aiken, SC 29801
Phone/fax: (803) 648-7522

VEGETABLES

Abundant Life Seed Foundation
P.O. Box 772
Port Townsend, WA 98368
Phone: (360) 385-5660
Fax: (360) 385-7455
E-mail: abundant@olypen.com
Web site: http://csf.Colorado
.edu/perma/abundant

W. Atlee Burpee & Co.
300 Park Ave.
Warminster, PA 18991-0001
Phone: (800) 888-1447
Fax: (800) 487-5530
Web site: www.burpee.com

The Cook's Garden
P.O. Box 535
Londonderry, VT 05148
Phone: (800) 457-9703
Fax: (800) 457-9705
Web site: www.cooks
garden.com

Johnny's Selected Seeds
Foss Hill Rd.
Albion, ME 04910-9731
Phone: (207) 437-4357
Fax: (800) 437-4290
E-mail: customerservice@
johnnyseeds.com
Web site: www.johnny
seeds.com

Ferry-Morse Seed Co.
P.O. Box 488
Fulton, KY 42041-0488
Phone: (800) 283-3400
Fax: (800) 283-2700
Web site: www.gardennet.com
/FerryMorse

Fox Hollow Seed Co.
P.O. Box 148
McGrann, PA 16236
Phone: (412) 548-7333
Fax: (412) 543-5751

Gurney's Seed & Nursery Co.
110 Capital St.
Yankton, SD 57079
Phone: (605) 665-1930
Fax: (605) 665-9718

Native Seeds/Search
2509 N. Campbell Ave., #325
Tucson, AZ 85719
Phone: (520) 327-9123
  no orders
Fax: (520) 327-5821
  orders welcome
Web site: http://desert.net/seeds

Park Seed
1 Parkton Ave.
Greenwood, SC 29647-0001
Phone: (800) 845-3369
Fax: (800) 275-9941
E-mail: orders@parkseed.com
Web site: http://parkseed.com

Pinetree Garden Seeds
Box 300
616A Lewiston Rd.
New Gloucester, ME 04260
Phone: (207) 926-3400
Fax: (888) 527-3337
E-mail: superseeds@world
net.att.net
Web site: www.superseeds.com

Ronniger's Seed & Potato Co.
P.O. Box 307
Ellensburg, WA 98926
Phone: (800) 846-6178

Seeds Blüm
HC 33, Box 2057
Boise, ID 83706
Phone: (800) 742-1423
Fax: (208) 338-5658
E-mail: 103374.167@compu
serve.com
Web site: www.seedsblum.com

Seeds of Change
P.O. Box 15700
Sante Fe, NM 87506-5700
Phone: (888) 762-7333
Fax: (888) 329-4762
E-mail: service@seedsof
change.com
Web site: www.seedsof
change.com

Shepherd's Garden Seeds
30 Irene St.
Torrington, CT 06790-6658
Phone: (860) 482-3638
Web site: www.shepherd
seeds.com

R. H. Shumway, Seedsman
P.O. Box 1
Graniteville, SC 29829-0001
Phone: (803) 663-9771
Fax: (803) 663-9772

Southern Exposure
Seed Exchange
P.O. Box 170
Earlysville, VA 22936
Phone: (804) 973-4703
Fax: (804) 973-8717
E-mail: gardens@southern
exposure.com
Web site: www.southern
exposure.com

WILDFLOWERS

Abundant Life Seed Foundation
P.O. Box 772
Port Townsend, WA 98368
Phone: (360) 385-5660
Fax: (360) 385-7455
E-mail: abundant@olypen.com
Web site: http://csf.Colorado
.edu/perma/abundant

Clyde Robin Seed Co.
P.O. Box 2366
Castro Valley, CA 94546
Phone: (510) 785-0425
Fax: (510) 785-6463
Web site: www.clyderobin.com

Native Seeds/Search
2509 N. Campbell Ave., #325
Tucson, AZ 85719
Phone: (520) 327-9123
  no orders
Fax: (520) 327-5821
  orders welcome
Web site: http://desert.net/seeds

The Natural Garden
38W443 Highway 64
St. Charles, IL 60175
Phone: (630) 584-0150
Fax: (630) 584-0185

Plants of the Southwest
Agua Fria Rd.
Route 6, Box 11A
Santa Fe, NM 87501
Phone: (505) 471-2212
Fax: (505) 438-8800
E-mail: contact@plantsofthe
southwest.com
Web site: www.plantsofthe
southwest.com

Prairie Moon Nursery
Route 3, Box 163
Winona, MN 55987
Phone: (507) 452-1362
Fax: (507) 454-5238

Prairie Nursery
P.O. Box 306
Westfield, WI 53964
Phone: (608) 296-3679
Fax: (608) 296-2741
Web site: www.prairie
nursery.com

Wildseed Farms
P.O. Box 3000
425 Wildflower Hills
Fredericksburg, TX
  78624-3000
Phone: (800) 848-0078
Fax: (830) 990-8090
Web site: www.wildseed
farms.com

Recommended Reading

BIRD AND BUTTERFLY GARDENS

Adams, George. *Birdscaping Your Garden.* Emmaus, PA: Rodale Press, 1994.

Roth, Sally. *Attracting Birds to Your Backyard.* Emmaus, PA: Rodale Press, 1998.

————. *Natural Landscaping.* Emmaus, PA: Rodale Press, 1997.

Schneck, Marcus. *Butterflies.* Emmaus, PA: Rodale Press, 1990.

————. *Your Backyard Wildlife Year.* Emmaus, PA: Rodale Press, 1996.

COMPOSTING AND SOIL

Appelhof, Mary. *Worms Eat My Garbage.* Kalamazoo, MI: Flower Press, 1982.

Greshuny, Grace. *Start with the Soil.* Emmaus, PA: Rodale Press, 1993.

Hynes, Erin. *Rodale's Successful Organic Gardening: Improving the Soil.* Emmaus, PA: Rodale Press, 1994.

Martin, Deborah, and Grace Gershuny, eds. *The Rodale Book of Composting.* Emmaus, PA: Rodale Press, 1992.

GENERAL GARDENING

Benjamin, Joan, ed. *Great Garden Shortcuts.* Emmaus, PA: Rodale Press, 1996.

Bradley, Fern Marshall, and Barbara Ellis, eds. *Rodale's All-New Encyclopedia of Organic Gardening.* Emmaus, PA: Rodale Press, 1992.

Coleman, Eliot. *The New Organic Grower.* White River Junction, VT: Chelsea Green Publishing Co., 1995.

Costenbader, Carol W. *The Big Book of Preserving the Harvest.* Pownal, VT: Storey Communications, 1997.

Cunningham, Sally Jean. *Great Garden Companions.* Emmaus, PA: Rodale Press, 1998.

Lanza, Patricia. *Lasagna Gardening.* Emmaus, PA: Rodale Press, 1998.

Logsdon, Gene. *The Contrary Farmer's Invitation to Gardening.* White River Junction, VT: Chelsea Green Publishing Co., 1997.

Stone, Pat. *Easy Gardening 101.* Pownal, VT: Storey Communications, 1998.

Swain, Roger. *The Practical Gardener.* Boston: Little, Brown and Company, 1989. Reprint, New York: Galahad Books, 1998.

FRUITS AND BERRIES

McClure, Susan. *Rodale's Successful Organic Gardening: Fruits and Berries.* Emmaus, PA: Rodale Press, 1996.

Nick, Jean, and Fern Marshall Bradley. *Growing Fruits and Vegetables Organically.* Emmaus, PA: Rodale Press, 1994.

Reich, Lee. *Uncommon Fruits Worthy of Attention.* Reading, MA: Addison-Wesley Publishing Co., 1991.

HERBS AND CRAFTS

Bethman, Laura Donnelly. *Nature Printing with Herbs, Fruits, and Flowers.* Pownal, VT: Storey Communications, 1996.

Duke, James A. *The Green Pharmacy.* Emmaus, PA: Rodale Press, 1997.

Gladstar, Rosemary. *Herbal Healing for Women.* New York: Simon & Schuster, 1993.

Hart, Rhonda. *Easter Eggs—By the Dozens!: Fun and Creative Egg Decorating Projects for All Ages!* Pownal, VT: Storey Communications, 1993.

James, Tina. *The Salad Bar in Your Own Backyard.* Reisterstown, MD: Gardening from the Heart, 1996.

Kowalchik, Claire, and William H. Hylton. *Rodale's Illustrated Encyclopedia of Herbs.* Emmaus, PA: Rodale Press, 1987.

Long, Jim. *Herbs, Just For Fun: A Beginner's Guide to Starting an Herb Garden.* Oak Grove, AR: Long Creek Herbs, 1996.

———. *Classic Herb Blends.* Oak Grove, AR: Long Creek Herbs, 1996.

McClure, Susan. *The Herb Gardener: A Guide for All Seasons.* Pownal, VT: Storey Communication, 1995.

Oster, Maggie. *Herbal Vinegar.* Pownal, VT: Storey Communication, 1994.

Oster, Maggie, and Sal Gilbertie. *The Herbal Palate Cookbook.* Pownal, VT: Storey Communications, 1996.

Smith, Miranda. *Your Backyard Herb Garden.* Emmaus, PA: Rodale Press, 1997.

Sombke, Laurence. *Beautiful Easy Herbs.* Emmaus, PA: Rodale Press, 1997.

Tourles, Stephanie. *The Herbal Body Book.* Pownal, VT: Storey Communications, 1994.

———. *Natural Foot Care.* Pownal, VT: Storey Communications, 1998.

Weed, Susun. *Healing Wise.* Woodstock, NY: Ash Tree Publishing, 1989.

———. *Menopausal Years: The Wise Woman Way.* Woodstock, NY: Ash Tree Publishing, 1992.

LANDSCAPE AND FLOWER GARDENING

Bender, Steve, and Felder Rushing. *Passalong Plants.* Chapel Hill, NC: The University of North Carolina Press, 1993.

Bradley, Fern Marshall, ed. *Gardening with Perennials.* Emmaus, PA: Rodale Press, 1996.

Byczynski, Lynn. *The Flower Farmer: An Organic Grower's Guide to Raising and Selling Cut Flowers.* White River Junction, VT: Chelsea Green Publishing Co., 1997.

Cox, Jeff. *Perennial All-Stars: The 150 Best Perennials for Great-Looking, Trouble-Free Gardens.* Emmaus, PA: Rodale Press, 1998.

D'Amato, Peter. *The Savage Garden: Cultivating Carnivorous Plants.* Berkeley, CA: Ten Speed Press, 1998.

DiSabato-Aust, Tracy. *The Well-Tended Perennial Garden: Planting and Pruning Techniques.* Portland, OR: Timber Press, 1998.

Ellis, Barbara. *Taylor's Guide to Growing North America's Favorite Plants.* Boston: Houghton Mifflin, 1998.

Harper, Pamela, and Frederick McGourty. *Perennials: How to Select, Grow and Enjoy.* Los Angeles: Price Stern Sloan, Inc., 1985.

McKeon, Judy. *The Encyclopedia of Roses.* Emmaus, PA: Rodale Press, 1995.

Phillips, Ellen, and C. Colston Burrell. *Rodale's Illustrated Encyclopedia of Perennials.* Emmaus, PA: Rodale Press, 1993.

Sombke, Laurence. *Beautiful Easy Flower Gardens.* Emmaus, PA: Rodale Press, 1995.

Taylor, Norman. *Taylor's Guide to Annuals.* Rev. ed. Boston: Houghton Mifflin Co., 1986.

PEST MANAGEMENT

Ellis, Barbara W., and Fern Marshall Bradley. *The Organic Gardener's Handbook of Natural Insect and Disease Control.* Emmaus, PA: Rodale Press, 1992.

Gilkeson, Linda, et al. *Rodale's Pest and Disease Problem Solver.* Emmaus, PA: Rodale Press, 1996.

Hart, Rhonda. *Bugs, Slugs, and Other Thugs.* Pownal, VT: Storey Communications, 1991.

SEASON EXTENSION

Colebrook, Binda. *Winter Gardening in the Maritime Northwest.* Seattle, WA: Sasquatch Books, 1989.

Coleman, Eliot. *Four-Season Harvest: How to Harvest Fresh, Organic Vegetables from Your Home Garden All Year Long.* White River Junction, VT: Chelsea Green Publishing Co., 1992.

SEED STARTING

Bubel, Nancy. *The New Seed-Starter's Handbook.* Emmaus, PA: Rodale Press, 1988.

Ondra, Nancy, and Barbara Ellis. *Easy Plant Propagation.* (Taylor's Weekend Gardening Guides.) Boston: Houghton Mifflin Co., 1998.

Powell, Eileen. *From Seed to Bloom.* Pownal, VT: Storey Communications, 1995.

WEEDS

Hynes, Erin. *Rodale's Successful Organic Gardening: Controlling Weeds.* Emmaus, PA: Rodale Press, 1995.

Pleasant, Barbara. *The Gardener's Weed Book.* Pownal, VT: Storey Communications, 1996.

MAGAZINES AND NEWSLETTERS

Avant Gardener, The, P.O. Box 489, New York, NY 10028

Common Sense Pest Control Quarterly, Bio-Integral Resource Center (BIRC), P.O. Box 7414, Berkeley, CA 94707-0414

Country Living Gardener, 224 W. 57th St., New York, NY 10019

Growing for Market, P.O. Box 3747, Lawrence, KS 66046

Homesteader's Connection, P.O. Box 5186, Cookeville, TN 38505

HortIdeas, 750 Black Lick Road, Gravel Switch, KY 40328

Organic Gardening, Rodale Press Inc., 33 E. Minor St., Emmaus, PA 18098

330

Index

Note: Page references in **boldface** indicate illustrations.

T

U

V

Vegetables. *See also* Recipes
  growing near compost piles, 38, 39, **39**
  mixing annuals with, 284
  as ornamentals, 288
  supports for vining (*see* Plant supports for vegetables)
Velcro, 17, 29
Verbena bonariensis, 314, **314**
Verbena hybrids, 234
Vermiculture, 48
Verticillium wilt, 141
Vicia villosa, 150, **150**
Vines
  and compost bins, 38, 39, **39**, 40, 45
  as privacy screens, 217
  supports for ornamental, 235, 245, 266, **266**, 276, **276**, 286
  supports for vegetable (*see* Plant supports for vegetables)
  using annual, 42, 235, **235**, 283
Voles
  protecting bulbs from, 237, 238, **238**
  tunnels of, 109

W

Walkways. *See* Paths
Wall O' Water, 185
Walls
  concrete systems, 272, **272**
  sod, 55
Watercress, 291

Water gardens
  accenting with grasses, 285, **285**
  cattail control in, 270
  containers for plants in, 265
  designing, 264
  edging of, 264
  plants for, 291
  stone and, 265
Watering, 59, 60, 268, 270
  of container plants, 62, 251, 255, 262, 273, **273**
  devices for gardens, 6, **6**, 22, 58, **58**, 59, 60, **60**, 61, **61**, 157
  and disease prevention, 162
  drip irrigation systems, 158, 273, **273**, 293, **293**
  under hoops, 85
  of lawns, 269, 294
  of seed flats, 99
  and seedlings, 12, 95, 100
  of trees, 6, **6**, 22, 293, **293**
  in winter, 272
Weeding, 121
  flame weeders, 122, 147, **147**
  gloves for, 10, 11
  tools for, 23, 30, **30**, 146, **146**
Weeds
  beneficial aspects of, 123, 124, **124**, 159
  cover crops and, 121, 150, **150**, 152
  edible, 151, **151**
  as food for rabbits, 119
  hens and, 217
  interplanting and, 148, **148**, 150 **150**
  mulches and, 85, **85**, 123,

126, 145, 146, 148, 149, 174
  preventing in paths, 122, 125, 192
Wet sites, plants for, 260, 289
Wheelbarrows
  adding wheels to, 24
  as compost spreaders, 50, **50**
  lifting, 265
  padding handles of, 20
Wheel hoe, 87, **87**
Wildlife, brush piles for, 159
Wild Ones—Natural Landscapers, Ltd., 306
Wilt-Pruf, 239
Wind, preventing damage from, 110, **110**, 153, **153**
Windbreaks, trees for, 286
Wineberries, 230
Wireworms, 140, **140**
Wisteria, 267
Woodchucks, 120, **120**
Wood sorrel, 203, **203**
Worm bin, 48, **48**
Worm composting, 43
Wormwood, 198

Y

Yarrow, spacing for, 279

Z

Zantedeschia, 248
Zinnia, narrow-leaf, 246
Zinnia 'Profusion Cherry', 232
Zinnia 'Profusion Orange', 232
Zinnia angustifolia, 246
Zinnias, powdery mildew resistant, 232
Zucchini, 164, 189

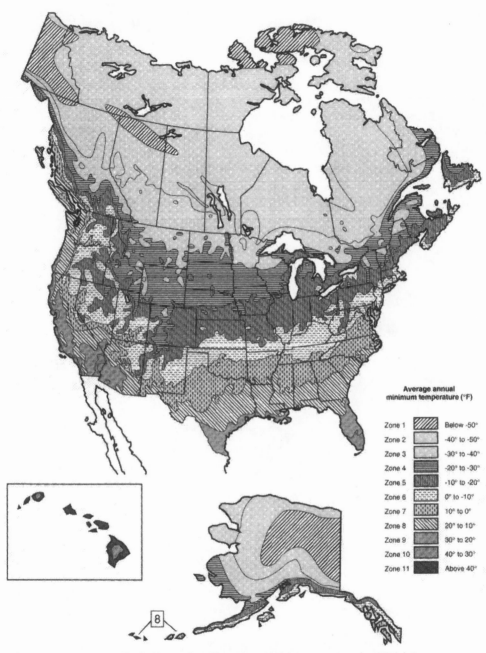

Average annual
minimum temperature (°F)

Zone 1		Below -50°
Zone 2		-40° to -50°
Zone 3		-30° to -40°
Zone 4		-20° to -30°
Zone 5		-10° to -20°
Zone 6		0° to -10°
Zone 7		10° to 0°
Zone 8		20° to 10°
Zone 9		30° to 20°
Zone 10		40° to 30°
Zone 11		Above 40°

This map was revised in 1990 to reflect the original USDA map, done in 1965. It is now recognized as the best indicator of minimum temperatures available. Look at the map to find your area, then match its pattern to the key at the right. When you've found your pattern, the key will tell you what hardiness zone you live in. Remember that the map is a general guide; your particular conditions may vary.